D0974617

German
Dictionary

German ▸ English English ▸ German

Collins Gem

An Imprint of HarperCollinsPublishers

first published in this edition 1978
sixth edition 2000

© William Collins Sons & Co. Ltd. 1978, 1988
© HarperCollins Publishers 1993, 1997, 1999, 2000

ISBN 0-00-711004-9

Collins Gem® and Bank of English® are registered
trademarks of HarperCollins Publishers Limited

The Collins Gem website address is
www.collins-gem.com

_____

contributors
Christine Bahr, Susie Beattie, Anne Dickinson
Helga Holtkamp, Horst Kopleck
Joyce Littlejohn, Val McNulty
John Podbielski, Beate Wengel

based on the first edition by
Ute Nicol, Veronika Schnorr,
Peter Terrell, John Whitlam

_____

All rights reserved

A catalogue record for this book
is available from the British Library

Typeset by Morton Word Processing Ltd, Scarborough

Printed and bound in Great Britain by
Omnia Books Ltd, Glasgow, G64

INHALT		CONTENTS

EINLEITUNG

Wir freuen uns, dass Sie sich zum Kauf dieses Collins Gem German Wörterbuchs entschlossen haben und hoffen, dass es Ihnen in der Schule, zu Hause, im Urlaub oder im Büro nützlich ist und Freude macht.

Diese Einleitung enthält Tips, wie Sie das Beste aus ihrem Wörterbuch herausholen können — nicht nur aus der umfangreichen Wortliste, sondern auch aus den Informationen, die in jedem Artikel stehen. Das wird Ihnen dabei helfen, modernes Englisch zu lesen und zu verstehen und sich auf Englisch auszudrücken und zu verständigen.

Vorn in diesem Wörterbuch steht eine Liste der im Text verwendeten Abkürzungen und eine Erläuterung der Symbole der Lautschrift. Hinten finden Sie deutsche Verbtabellen und englische unregelmäßige Verben und abschließend einen Abschnitt über Zahlen und Uhrzeit.

ZUM GEBRAUCH IHRES COLLINS GEM WÖRTERBUCHS

Das Wörterbuch enthält eine Fülle von Informationen, die mithilfe von unterschiedlichen Schriften und Schriftgrößen, Symbolen, Abkürzungen und Klammern vermittelt werden. Die dabei verwendeten Regeln und Symbole werden in den folgenden Abschnitten erklärt.

iii

Stichwörter

Die Wörter, die Sie im Wörterbuch nachschlagen — „Stichwörter" — sind alphabetisch geordnet. Sie sind **fett** gedruckt, damit man sie schnell erkennt. Die beiden Stichwörter oben auf jeder Seite geben das erste und letzte Wort an, das auf der betreffenden Seite behandelt wird.

Informationen zur Verwendung oder zur Form bestimmter Stichwörter stehen in Klammern hinter der Lautschrift. Sie erscheinen meist in abgekürzter Form und sind kursiv gedruckt (z. B. *(fam, (COMM)*.

Wo es angebracht ist, werden mit dem Stichwort verwandte Wörter im selben Artikel behandelt (z. B. **accept, acceptance**). Sie sind wie das Stichwort fett, aber etwas kleiner gedruckt.
Häufig verwendete Ausdrücke, in denen das Stichwort vorkommt (z. B. **to be cold**), sind in einer anderen Schrift halbfett gedruckt.

Lautschrift

Die Lautschrift für jedes Stichwort (zur Angabe seiner Aussprache) steht in eckigen Klammern direkt hinter dem Stichwort (z. B. **Quark** [kvark], **knead** [niːd]). Die Symbole der Lautschrift sind auf Seite xii erklärt.

Übersetzungen

Die Übersetzungen des Stichworts sind normal gedruckt. Wenn es mehr als eine Bedeutung oder Verwendung des Stichworts gibt, sind diese durch ein Semikolon voneinander getrennt. Vor den Übersetzungen stehen oft andere, kursiv gedruckte Wörter in Klammern. Sie geben an, in welchem Zusammenhang das Stichwort erscheinen könnte (z. B. **rough** *(voice)* oder *(weather)*, oder sie sind Synonyme (z. B. **rough** *(violent)*).

Schlüsselwörter

Besonders behandelt werden bestimmte deutsche und englische Wörter, die man als „Schlüsselwörter" der jeweiligen Sprache betrachten kann. Diese Wörter kommen beispielsweise sehr häufig vor oder werden unterschiedlich verwendet (z. B. **sein, auch; get, that**). Mithilfe von Rauten und Ziffern können Sie die verschiedenen Wortarten und Verwendungen unterscheiden. Weitere nützliche Hinweise finden Sie kursiv und in Klammern in der jeweiligen Sprache des Benutzers.

Grammatische Informationen

Wortarten stehen in abgekürzter Form kursiv gedruckt hinter der Aussprache des Stichworts (z. B. **vt, adv, conj**).

Die unregelmäßigen Formen englischer Substantive und Verben stehen in Klammern vor der Wortart (z. B. **man** (*pl* **men**) *n*, **give** (*pt* **gave**, *pp* **given**) *vt*).

Die deutsche Rechtschreibreform

Dieses Wörterbuch folgt durchweg der reformierten deutschen Rechtschreibung. Alle Stichwörter auf der deutsch-englischen Seite, die von der Rechtschreibreform betroffen sind, sind mit ▲ gekennzeichnet. Alte Schreibungen, die sich wesentlich von der neuen Schreibung unterscheiden und an einem anderen alphabetischen Ort erscheinen, sind jedoch weiterhin aufgeführt und werden zur neuen Schreibung verwiesen. Diese alten Schreibungen sind mit △ gekennzeichnet.

INTRODUCTION

We are delighted you have decided to buy the Collins Gem German Dictionary and hope you will enjoy and benefit from using it at school, at home, on holiday or at work.

This introduction gives you a few tips on how to get the most out of your dictionary — not simply from its comprehensive wordlist but also from the information provided in each entry. This will help you to read and understand modern German, as well as communicate and express yourself in the language.

The Collins Gem German Dictionary begins by listing the abbreviations used in the text and illustrating the sounds shown by the phonetic symbols. You will find German verb tables and English irregular verbs at the back, followed by a final section on numbers and time expressions.

USING YOUR COLLINS GEM DICTIONARY

A wealth of information is presented in the dictionary, using various typefaces, sizes of type, symbols, abbreviations and brackets. The conventions and symbols used are explained in the following sections.

Headwords

The words you look up in a dictionary — "headwords" — are listed alphabetically. They are printed in **bold type** for rapid identification. The two headwords appearing at the top of each page indicate the first and last word dealt with on the page in question.

Information about the usage or form of certain headwords is given in brackets after the phonetic spelling. This usually appears in abbreviated form and in italics (e.g. (*umg*), (*COMM*)).

Where appropriate, words related to headwords are grouped in the same entry (**Glück, glücken**) in a slightly smaller bold type than the headword.
Common expressions in which the headword appears are shown in a different bold roman type (e.g. **Glück haben**).

Phonetic spellings

The phonetic spelling of each headword (indicating its pronunciation) is given in square brackets immediately after the headword (e.g. **Quark** [kvark]). A list of these symbols is given on page xii.

Meanings

Headword translations are given in ordinary type and, where more than one meaning or usage exists, these are separated by a semi-colon. You will often find other words in italics in brackets before the translations. These offer suggested contexts in which the headword might appear (e.g. **eng** (*Kleidung*) or (*Freundschaft*)) or provide synonyms (e.g. **eng** (*fig: Horizont*)).

"Key" words

Special status is given to certain German and English words which are considered as "key" words in each language. They may, for example, occur very frequently or have several types of usage (e.g. **sein, auch; get, that**). A combination of lozenges and numbers helps you to distinguish different parts of speech and different meanings. Further helpful information is provided in brackets and in italics in the relevant language for the user.

Grammatical information

Parts of speech are given in abbreviated form in italics after the phonetic spellings of headwords (e.g. *vt, adv, konj*).

Genders of German nouns are indicated as follows: m for a masculine and f for a feminine and nt for a neuter noun. The genitive and plural forms of regular nouns are shown on the table on page xi. Nouns which do not follow these rules have the genitive and plural in brackets immediately preceding the gender (e.g. **Spaß**, (-es, ¨-e), *m*).

Adjectives are normally shown in their basic form (e.g. **groß** *adj*), but where they are only used attributively (i.e. before a noun) feminine and neuter endings follow in brackets (hohe (r, s) *adj attrib*).

The German spelling reform

The German spelling reform has been fully implemented in this dictionary. All headwords on the Kenn-English side which are affected by the spelling changes are marked ▲. Old spellings which are significantly different from the new ones and have a different alphabetical position are still listed and are cross-referenced to the new spellings. The old spellings are marked △.

Warenzeichen

Wörter, die unseres Wissens eingetragene Warenzeichen darstellen, sind als solche gekennzeichnet. Es ist jedoch zu beachten, daß weder das Vorhandensein noch das Fehlen derartiger Kennzeichnungen die Rechtslage hinsichtlich eingetragener Warenzeichen berührt.

Note on trademarks

Words which we have reason to believe constitute trademarks have been designated as such. However, neither the presence nor the absence of such designation should be regarded as affecting the legal status of any trademark.

ABKÜRZUNGEN

ABBREVIATIONS

Abkürzung	**abk, abbr**	abbreviation
Adjektiv	**adj**	adjective
Akkusativ	**acc**	accusative
Adverb	**adv**	adverb
Landwirtschaft	**AGR**	agriculture
Akkusativ	**akk**	accusative
Anatomie	**ANAT**	anatomy
Architektur	**ARCHIT**	architecture
Astrologie	**ASTROL**	astrology
Astronomie	**ASTRON**	astronomy
attributiv	**attrib**	attributive
Kraftfahrzeuge	**AUT**	automobiles
Hilfsverb	**aux**	auxiliary
Luftfahrt	**AVIAT**	aviation
besonders	**bes**	especially
Biologie	**BIOL**	biology
Botanik	**BOT**	botany
britisch	**BRIT**	British
Chemie	**CHEM**	chemistry
Film	**CINE**	cinema
Konjunktion	**conj**	conjunction
Handel	**COMM**	commerce
Komparativ	**compar**	comparative
Computer	**COMPUT**	computing
Kochen und Backen	**COOK**	cooking
zusammengesetztes Wort	**cpd**	compound
Dativ	**dat**	dative
bestimmter Artikel	**def art**	definite article
dekliniert	**dekl**	decline
Diminutiv	**dimin**	diminutive
kirchlich	**ECCL**	ecclesiastical
Eisenbahn	**EISENB**	railways
Elektrizität	**ELEK, ELEC**	electricity
besonders	**esp**	especially
und so weiter	**etc**	et cetera
etwas	**etw**	something
Euphemismus, Hüllwort	**euph**	euphemism
Interjektion, Ausruf	**excl**	exclamation
Femininum	**f**	feminine
übertragen	**fig**	figurative
Finanzwesen	**FIN**	finance
nicht getrennt gebraucht	**fus**	(phrasal verb) inseparable
Genitiv	**gen**	genitive
Geografie	**GEOG**	geography
Geologie	**GEOL**	geology
gewöhnlich	**gew**	usually

ABKÜRZUNGEN

ABBREVIATIONS

Grammatik	GRAM	grammar
Geschichte	HIST	history
unpersönlich	impers	impersonal
unbestimmter Artikel	indef art	indefinite article
umgangssprachlich	inf(!)	informal (! particularly
(! vulgär)		offensive)
Infinitiv, Grundform	infin	infinitive
nicht getrennt gebraucht	insep	inseparable
unveränderlich	inv	invariable
unregelmäßig	irreg	irregular
jemand	jd	somebody
jemandem	jdm	(to) somebody
jemanden	jdn	somebody
jemandes	jds	somebody's
Rechtswesen	JUR	law
Kochen und Backen	KOCH	cooking
Komparativ	kompar	comparative
Konjunktion	konj	conjunction
Sprachwissenschaft	LING	linguistics
Literatur	LITER	of literature
Maskulinum	m	masculine
Mathematik	MATH	mathematics
Medizin	MED	medicine
Meteorologie	MET	meteorology
Militär	MIL	military
Bergbau	MIN	mining
Musik	MUS	music
Substantiv, Hauptwort	n	noun
nautisch, Seefahrt	NAUT	nautical, naval
Nominativ	nom	nominative
Neutrum	nt	neuter
Zahlwort	num	numeral
Objekt	obj	object
oder	od	or
sich	o.s.	oneself
Parlament	PARL	parliamentary
abschätzig	pej	pejorative
Fotografie	PHOT	photography
Physik	PHYS	physics
Plural	pl	plural
Politik	POL	politics
Präfix, Vorsilbe	pp	prefix
Präposition	präp, prep	preposition
Typografie	PRINT	printing
Pronomen, Fürwort	pron	pronoun
Psychologie	PSYCH	psychology

ABKÜRZUNGEN

ABBREVIATIONS

1. Vergangenheit, Imperfekt	pt	past tense
Partizip Perfekt	pp	past participle
Radio	RAD	radio
Eisenbahn	RAIL	railways
Religion	REL	religion
jemand(-en, -em)	sb	someone, somebody
Schulwesen	SCH	school
Naturwissenschaft	SCI	science
Singular, Einzahl	sg	singular
etwas	sth	something
Konjunktiv	sub	subjunctive
Subjekt	subj	(grammatical) subject
Superlativ	superl	superlative
Technik	TECH	technology
Nachrichtentechnik	TEL	telecommunications
Theater	THEAT	theatre
Fernsehen	TV	television
Typografie	TYP	printing
umgangssprachlich (! vulgär)	umg(!)	colloquial (! particularly) offensive)
Hochschulwesen	UNIV	university
unpersönlich	unpers	impersonal
unregelmäßig	unreg	irregular
(nord)amerikanisch	US	(North) America
gewöhnlich	usu	usually
Verb	vb	verb
intransitives Verb	vi	intransitive verb
reflexives Verb	vr	reflexive verb
transitives Verb	vt	transitive verb
Zoologie	ZOOL	zoology
zusammengesetztes Wort	zW	compound
zwischen zwei Sprechern	—	change of speaker
ungefähre Entsprechung	≅	cultural equivalent
eingetragenes Warenzeichen	®	registered trademark

REGULAR GERMAN NOUN ENDINGS

nom		gen	pl
-ant	m	-anten	-anten
-anz	f	-anz	-anzen
-ar	m	-ar(e)s	-are
-chen	nt	-chens	-chen
-e	f	-	-n
-ei	f	-ei	-eien
-elle	f	-elle	-ellen
-ent	m	-enten	-enten
-enz	f	-enz	-enzen
-ette	f	-ette	-etten
-eur	m	-eurs	-eure
-euse	f	-euse	-eusen
-heit	f	-heit	-heiten
-ie	f	-ie	-ien
-ik	f	-ik	-iken
-in	f	-in	-innen
-ine	f	-ine	-inen
-ion	f	-ion	-ionen
-ist	m	-isten	-isten
-ium	nt	-iums	-ien
-ius	m	-ius	-iusse
-ive	f	-ive	-iven
-keit	f	-keit	-keiten
-lein	nt	-leins	-lein
-ling	m	-lings	-linge
-ment	nt	-ments	-mente
-mus	m	-mus	-men
-schaft	f	-schaft	-schaften
-tät	f	-tät	-täten
-tor	m	-tors	-toren
-ung	f	-ung	-ungen
-ur	f	-ur	-uren

PHONETIC SYMBOLS / LAUTSCHRIFT

[:] *length mark* *Längezeichen* ['] *stress mark* *Betonung*
[|] *glottal stop* *Knacklaut*

all vowel sounds are approximate only
alle Vokallaute sind nur ungefähre Entsprechungen

bet	[b]	Ball		[e]	Metall
dim	[d]	dann		[e:]	geben
face	[f]	Fass	set	[ɛ]	hässlich
go	[g]	Gast		[ɛ̃:]	Cousin
hit	[h]	Herr	pity	[ɪ]	Bischof
you	[j]	ja		[i]	vital
čat	[k]	kalt	green	[i:]	viel
lick	[l]	Last	rot	[ɔ]	Post
must	[m]	Mast	board	[ɔ:]	Moral
nut	[n]	Nuss		[o:]	oben
bang	[ŋ]	lang		[õ]	Champignon
pepper	[p]	Pakt		[ø]	ökonomisch
red	[r]	Regen		[œ]	gönnen
sit	[s]	Rasse	full	[u]	kulant
shame	[ʃ]	Schal	root	[u:]	Hut
tell	[t]	Tal	come	[ʌ]	
chat	[tʃ]	tschüs		[ʊ]	Pult
vine	[v]	was		[y]	physisch
wine	[w]			[y:]	für
loch	[x]	Bach		[ʏ]	Müll
	[ç]	ich	above	[ə]	bitte
zero	[z]	Hase	girl	[ə:]	
leisure	[ʒ]	Genie			
join	[dʒ]		lie	[aɪ]	weit
thin	[θ]		now	[aʊ]	
this	[ð]			[aʊ]	Haut
			day	[eɪ]	
hat	[a]	Hast	fair	[ɛə]	
	[æ]		beer	[ɪə]	
farm	[ɑ:]	Bahn	toy	[ɔɪ]	
	[a:]			[ɔʏ]	Heu
	[ã:]	Ensemble	pure	[ʊə]	
fiancé	[ɑ̃:]				

['] r can be pronounced before a vowel;
Bindungs-R

xii

ZAHLEN		NUMBERS
ein(s)	1	one
zwei	2	two
drei	3	three
vier	4	four
fünf	5	five
sechs	6	six
sieben	7	seven
acht	8	eight
neun	9	nine
zehn	10	ten
elf	11	eleven
zwölf	12	twelve
dreizehn	13	thirteen
vierzehn	14	fourteen
fünfzehn	15	fifteen
sechzehn	16	sixteen
siebzehn	17	seventeen
achtzehn	18	eighteen
neunzehn	19	nineteen
zwanzig	20	twenty
einundzwanzig	21	twenty-one
zweiundzwanzig	22	twenty-two
dreißig	30	thirty
vierzig	40	forty
fünfzig	50	fifty
sechzig	60	sixty
siebzig	70	seventy
achtzig	80	eighty
neunzig	90	ninety
hundert	100	a hundred
hunderteins	101	a hundred and one
zweihundert	200	two hundred
zweihunderteins	201	two hundred and one
dreihundert	300	three hundred
dreihunderteins	301	three hundred and one
tausend	1000	a thousand
tausend(und)eins	1001	a thousand and one
fünftausend	5000	five thousand
eine Million	1000000	a million

erste(r, s)	1.	first	1st
zweite(r, s)	2.	second	2nd
dritte(r, s)	3.	third	3rd
vierte(r, s)	4.	fourth	4th
fünfte(r, s)	5.	fifth	5th
sechste(r, s)	6.	sixth	6th
siebte(r, s)	7.	seventh	7th
achte(r, s)	8.	eighth	8th
neunte(r, s)	9.	ninth	9th
zehnte(r, s)	10.	tenth	10th
elfte(r, s)	11.	eleventh	11th
zwölfte(r, s)	12.	twelfth	12th
dreizehnte(r, s)	13.	thirteenth	13th
vierzehnte(r, s)	14.	fourteenth	14th
fünfzehnte(r, s)	15.	fifteenth	15th
sechzehnte(r, s)	16.	sixteenth	16th
siebzehnte(r, s)	17.	seventeenth	17th
achtzehnte(r, s)	18.	eighteenth	18th
neunzehnte(r, s)	19.	nineteenth	19th
zwanzigste(r, s)	20.	twentieth	20th
einundzwanzigste(r, s)	21.	twenty-first	21st
dreißigste(r, s)	30.	thirtieth	30th
hundertste(r, s)	100.	hundredth	100th
hunderterste(r, s)	101.	hundred-and-first	101st
tausendste(r, s)	1000.	thousandth	1000th

Brüche usw.

Fractions etc.

ein Halb	$\frac{1}{2}$	a half	
ein Drittel	$\frac{1}{3}$	a third	
ein Viertel	$\frac{1}{4}$	a quarter	
ein Fünftel	$\frac{1}{5}$	a fifth	
null Komma fünf	0,5	(nought) point five	0.5
drei Komma vier	3,4	three point four	3.4
sechs Komma acht neun	6,89	six point eight nine	6.89
zehn Prozent	10%	ten per cent	
hundert Prozent	100%	a hundred per cent	

Beispiele

Examples

er wohnt in Nummer 10	he lives at number 10
es steht in Kapitel 7	it's in chapter 7
auf Seite 7	on page 7
er wohnt im 7. Stock	he lives on the 7th floor
er wurde 7.	he came in 7th
Maßstab eins zu zwanzigtausend	scale one to twenty thousand

UHRZEIT	THE TIME

wie viel Uhr ist es?, wie spät ist es?

what time is it?

es ist ...

it's ...

Mitternacht, zwölf Uhr nachts	midnight, twelve p.m.
ein Uhr (morgens *or* früh)	one o'clock (in the morning), one (a.m.)
fünf nach eins, ein Uhr fünf	five past one
zehn nach eins, ein Uhr zehn	ten past one
Viertel nach eins, ein Uhr fünfzehn	a quarter past one, one fifteen
fünf vor halb zwei, ein Uhr fünfundzwanzig	twenty-five past one, one twenty-five
halb zwei, ein Uhr dreißig	half past one, one thirty
fünf nach halb zwei, ein Uhr fünfunddreißig	twenty-five to two, one thirty-five
zwanzig vor zwei, ein Uhr vierzig	twenty to two, one forty
Viertel vor zwei, ein Uhr fünfundvierzig	a quarter to two, one forty-five
zehn vor zwei, ein Uhr fünfzig	ten to two, one fifty
zwölf Uhr (mittags), Mittag	twelve o'clock, midday, noon
halb eins (mittags *or* nachmittags), zwölf Uhr dreißig	half past twelve, twelve thirty (p.m.)
zwei Uhr (nachmittags)	two o'clock (in the afternoon), two (p.m.)
halb acht (abends)	half past seven (in the evening), seven thirty (p.m.)

um wie viel Uhr?

at what time?

um Mitternacht	at midnight
um sieben Uhr	at seven o'clock
in zwanzig Minuten	in twenty minutes
vor fünfzehn Minuten	fifteen minutes ago

A, a

Aal [a:l] (-(e)s, -e) *m* eel
Aas [a:s] (-es, -e *od* **Äser**) *nt* carrion

SCHLÜSSELWORT

---

ab [ap] *präp +dat* from; **Kinder ab 12 Jahren** children from the age of 12; **ab morgen** from tomorrow; **ab sofort** as of now
♦ *adv* **1** off; **links ab** to the left; **der Knopf ist ab** the button has come off; **ab nach Hause!** off you go home
2 (*zeitlich*): **von da ab** from then on; **von heute ab** from today, as of today
3 (*auf Fahrplänen*): **München ab 12.20** leaving Munich 12.20
4: **ab und zu** *od* **an** now and then *od* again

Abänderung [ˈapˌɛndəruŋ] *f* alteration
Abbau [ˈapbau] (-(e)s) *m* (*+gen*) dismantling; (*Verminderung*) reduction (in); (*Verfall*) decline (in); (*MIN*) mining, quarrying; (*CHEM*) decomposition; **a~en** *vt* to dismantle; (*MIN*) to mine; to quarry; (*verringern*) to reduce; (*CHEM*) to break down
abbeißen [ˈapbaisən] (*unreg*) *vt* to bite off
abbekommen [ˈapbəkɔmən] (*unreg*) *vt* (*Deckel, Schraube, Band*) to loosen; **etwas ~** (*beschädigt werden*) to get damaged; (*: Person*) to get injured
abbestellen [ˈapbəʃtɛlən] *vt* to cancel
abbezahlen [ˈapbətsaːlən] *vt* to pay off
abbiegen [ˈapbiːgən] (*unreg*) *vi* to turn off; (*Straße*) to bend ♦ *vt* to bend; (*verhindern*) to ward off

abbilden [ˈapbɪldən] *vt* to portray; **Abbildung** *f* illustration
abblenden [ˈapblɛndən] *vt, vi* (*AUT*) to dip (*BRIT*), to dim (*US*)
Abblendlicht [ˈapblɛndlɪçt] *nt* dipped (*BRIT*) *od* dimmed (*US*) headlights *pl*
abbrechen [ˈapbrɛçən] (*unreg*) *vt, vi* to break off; (*Gebäude*) to pull down; (*Zelt*) to take down; (*aufhören*) to stop; (*COMPUT*) to abort
abbrennen [ˈapbrɛnən] (*unreg*) *vt* to burn off; (*Feuerwerk*) to let off ♦ *vi* (*aux sein*) to burn down
abbringen [ˈapbrɪŋən] (*unreg*) *vt*: **jdn von etw ~** to dissuade sb from sth; **jdn vom Weg ~** to divert sb
abbröckeln [ˈapbrœkəln] *vt, vi* to crumble off *od* away
Abbruch [ˈapbrʊx] *m* (*von Verhandlungen etc*) breaking off; (*von Haus*) demolition; **jdm/etw ~ tun** to harm sb/sth; **a~reif** *adj* only fit for demolition
abbrühen [ˈapbryːən] *vt* to scald; **abgebrüht** (*umg*) hard-boiled
abbuchen [ˈapbuːxən] *vt* to debit
abdanken [ˈapdaŋkən] *vi* to resign; (*König*) to abdicate; **Abdankung** *f* resignation; abdication
abdecken [ˈapdɛkən] *vt* (*Loch*) to cover; (*Tisch*) to clear; (*Plane*) to uncover
abdichten [ˈapdɪçtən] *vt* to seal; (*NAUT*) to caulk
abdrehen [ˈapdreːən] *vt* (*Gas*) to turn off; (*Licht*) to switch off; (*Film*) to shoot ♦ *vi* (*Schiff*) to change course
Abdruck [ˈapdrʊk] *m* (*Nachdrucken*) reprinting; (*Gedrucktes*) reprint; (*Gipsabdruck, Wachsabdruck*) impression;

(*Fingerabdruck*) print; **a~en** vt to print, to publish

abdrücken ['apdrʏkən] vt (*Waffe*) to fire; (*Person*) to hug, to squeeze

Abend ['a:bənt] (-s, -e) m evening; **guten ~** good evening; **zu ~ essen** to have dinner od supper; **heute ~** this evening; **~brot** nt supper; **~essen** nt supper; **~garderobe** f evening dress; **~kasse** f box office; **~kleid** nt evening dress; **~kurs** m evening classes pl; **~land** nt (*Europa*) West; **a~lich** adj evening; **~mahl** nt Holy Communion; **~rot** nt sunset; **a~s** adv in the evening

Abenteuer ['a:bəntɔyər] (-s, -) nt adventure; **a~lich** adj adventurous; **~urlaub** m adventure holiday

Abenteurer (-s, -) m adventurer; **~in** f adventuress

aber ['a:bər] konj but; (*jedoch*) however ♦ adv: **das ist ~ schön** that's really nice; **nun ist ~ Schluss!** now that's enough!; **vielen Dank - ~ bitte!** thanks a lot - you're welcome; **A~glaube** m superstition; **~gläubisch** adj superstitious

aberkennen ['ap|ɛrkɛnən] (unreg) vt (*JUR*): **jdm etw ~** to deprive sb of sth, to take sth (away) from sb

abermals ['a:bərmals] adv once again

abertausend, Abertausend ['a:bər-tauzənt] indef pron: **tausend und ~** thousands upon thousands

Abf. abk (= *Abfahrt*) dep.

abfahren ['apfa:rən] (unreg) vi to leave, to depart ♦ vt to take od cart away; (*Strecke*) to drive; (*Reifen*) to wear; (*Fahrkarte*) to use

Abfahrt ['apfa:rt] f (*SKI*) descent; (*Piste*) run; **~szeit** f departure time

Abfall ['apfal] m waste; (*von Speisen etc*) rubbish (*BRIT*), garbage (*US*); (*Neigung*) slope; (*Verschlechterung*) decline; **~eimer** m rubbish bin (*BRIT*), garbage can (*US*); **a~en** (unreg) vi (*auch fig*) to

fall od drop off; (*sich neigen*) to fall or drop away

abfällig ['apfɛlɪç] adj disparaging, deprecatory

abfangen ['apfaŋən] (unreg) vt to intercept; (*Person*) to catch; (*unter Kontrolle bringen*) to check

abfärben ['apfɛrbən] vi to lose its colour; (*Wäsche*) to run; (*fig*) to rub off

abfassen ['apfasən] vt to write, to draft

abfertigen ['apfɛrtɪgən] vt to prepare for dispatch, to process; (*an der Grenze*) to clear; (*Kundschaft*) to attend to

Abfertigungsschalter m (*Flughafen*) check-in desk

abfeuern ['apfɔyərn] vt to fire

abfinden ['apfɪndən] (unreg) vt to pay off ♦ vr to come to terms; **sich mit jdm/~nicht ~** to put up with/not get on with sb

Abfindung f (*von Gläubigern*) payment; (*Geld*) sum in settlement

abflauen ['apflaʊən] vi (*Wind, Erregung*) to die away, to subside; (*Nachfrage, Geschäft*) to fall od drop off

abfliegen ['apfli:gən] (unreg) vi (*Flugzeug*) to take off; (*Passagier auch*) to fly ♦ vt (*Gebiet*) to fly over

abfließen ['apfli:sən] (unreg) vi to drain away

Abflug ['apflu:k] m departure; (*Start*) take-off; **~halle** f departure lounge; **~zeit** f departure time

Abfluss ▲ ['apflʊs] m draining away; (*Öffnung*) outlet; **~rohr** ▲ nt drain pipe; (*von sanitären Anlagen auch*) waste pipe

abfragen ['apfra:gən] vt (*bes SCH*) to test orally (on)

Abfuhr ['apfu:r] (-, -en) f removal; (*fig*) snub, rebuff

abführen ['apfy:rən] vt to lead away; (*Gelder, Steuern*) to pay ♦ vi (*MED*) to have a laxative effect

Abführmittel ['apfy:rmɪtəl] nt laxative, purgative

abfüllen ['apfʏlən] *vt* to draw off; (*in Flaschen*) to bottle

Abgabe ['apgaːbə] *f* handing in; (*von Ball*) pass; (*Steuer*) tax; (*eines Amtes*) giving up; (*einer Erklärung*) giving

Abgang ['apgaŋ] *m* (*von Schule*) leaving; (*THEAT*) exit; (*Abfahrt*) departure; (*der Post, von Waren*) dispatch

Abgas ['apgaːs] *nt* waste gas; (*AUT*) exhaust

abgeben ['apgeːbən] (*unreg*) *vt* (*Gegenstand*) to hand *od* give in; (*Ball*) to pass; (*Wärme*) to give off; (*Amt*) to hand over; (*Erklärung*) to give; (*darstellen, sein*) to make ♦ *vr*: **sich mit jdm/etw ~** to associate with sb/bother with sth; **jdm etw ~** (*überlassen*) to let sb have sth

abgebrüht ['apgəbryːt] (*umg*) *adj* (*skrupellos*) hard-boiled

abgehen ['apgeːən] (*unreg*) *vi* to go away, to leave; (*THEAT*) to exit; (*Knopf etc*) to come off; (*Straße*) to branch off ♦ *vt* (*Strecke*) to go *od* walk along; **etw geht jdm ab** (*fehlt*) sb lacks sth

abgelegen ['apgəleːgən] *adj* remote

abgemacht ['apgəmaxt] *adj* fixed; **~!** done!

abgeneigt ['apgənaikt] *adj* disinclined

abgenutzt ['apgənʊtst] *adj* worn

Abgeordnete(r) ['apgəʔɔrdnətə(r)] *f(m)* member of parliament; elected representative

abgeschlossen ['apgəʃlɔsən] *adj attrib* (*Wohnung*) self-contained

abgeschmackt ['apgəʃmakt] *adj* tasteless

abgesehen ['apgəzeːən] *adj*: **es auf jdn/etw ~ haben** to be after sb/sth; **~ von** ... apart from ...

abgespannt ['apgəʃpant] *adj* tired *od* exhausted

abgestanden ['apgəʃtandən] *adj* stale; (*Bier auch*) flat

abgestorben ['apgəʃtɔrbən] *adj* numb; (*BIOL, MED*) dead

abgetragen ['apgətraːgən] *adj* shabby, worn out

abgewinnen ['apgəvɪnən] (*unreg*) *vt*: **einer Sache etw/Geschmack ~** to get sth/pleasure from sth

abgewöhnen ['apgəvøːnən] *vt*: **jdm/ sich etw ~** to cure sb of sth/give sth up

Abgrund ['apgrʊnt] *m* (*auch fig*) abyss

abhacken ['aphakən] *vt* to chop off

abhaken ['aphaːkən] *vt* (*auf Papier*) to tick off

abhalten ['aphaltən] (*unreg*) *vt* (*Versammlung*) to hold; **jdn von etw ~** (*fern halten*) to keep sb away from sth; (*hindern*) to keep sb from sth

abhanden [apˈhandən] *adj*: **~ kommen** to get lost

Abhandlung [apˈhandlʊŋ] *f* treatise, discourse

Abhang ['aphaŋ] *m* slope

abhängen ['aphɛŋən] *vt* (*Bild*) to take down; (*Anhänger*) to uncouple; (*Verfolger*) to shake off ♦ *vi* (*unreg: Fleisch*) to hang; **von jdm/etw ~** to depend on sb/sth

abhängig ['aphɛŋɪç] *adj*: **~ (von)** dependent (on); **A~keit** *f* **A~keit (von)** dependence (on)

abhärten ['aphɛrtən] *vt, vr* to toughen (o.s.) up; **sich gegen etw ~** to inure o.s. to sth

abhauen ['aphauən] (*unreg*) *vt* to cut off; (*Baum*) to cut down ♦ *vi* (*umg*) to clear off *od* out

abheben ['apheːbən] (*unreg*) *vt* to lift (up); (*Karten*) to cut; (*Geld*) to withdraw, to take out ♦ *vi* (*Flugzeug*) to take off; (*Rakete*) to lift off ♦ *vr* to stand out

abheften ['apheftən] *vt* (*Rechnungen etc*) to file away

abhetzen 4 ablesen

abhetzen ['aphɛtsən] *vt* to wear *od* tire o.s. out

Abhilfe ['aphɪlfə] *f* remedy; **~ schaffen** to put things right

abholen ['aphoːlən] *vt* (*Gegenstand*) to fetch, to collect; (*Person*) to call for; (*am Bahnhof etc*) to pick up, to meet

abholzen ['aphɔltsən] *vt* (*Wald*) to clear

abhorchen ['aphɔrçən] *vt* (*MED*) to listen to a patient's chest

abhören ['aphøːrən] *vt* (*Vokabeln*) to test; (*Telefongespräch*) to tap; (*Tonband etc*) to listen to

Abhörgerät *nt* bug

Abitur [abi'tuːr] (**-s, -e**) *nt* German school-leaving examination; **~i'ent(in**) *m(f)* candidate for school-leaving certificate

---
Abitur

The **Abitur** is the German school-leaving examination taken in four subjects by pupils at a **Gymnasium** at the age of 18 or 19. It is necessary for entry to university.

Abk. *abk* (= *Abkürzung*) abbr.

abkapseln ['apkapsəln] *vr* to shut *od* cut o.s. off

abkaufen ['apkaufən] *vt*: **jdm etw ~** (*auch fig*) to buy sth from sb

abkehren ['apkeːrən] *vt* (*Blick*) to avert, to turn away ♦ *vr* to turn away

abklingen ['apklɪŋən] (*unreg*) *vi* to die away; (*Radio*) to fade out

abknöpfen ['apknœpfən] *vt* to unbutton; **jdm etw ~** (*umg*) to get sth off sb

abkochen ['apkɔxən] *vt* to boil

abkommen ['apkɔmən] (*unreg*) *vi* to get away; **von der Straße/von einem Plan ~** to leave the road/give up a plan; **A~ (-s, -)** *nt* agreement

abkömmlich ['apkœmlɪç] *adj* available, free

abkratzen ['apkratsən] *vt* to scrape off

♦ *vi* (*umg*) to kick the bucket

abkühlen ['apkyːlən] *vt* to cool down ♦ *vr* (*Mensch*) to cool down *od* off; (*Wetter*) to get cool; (*Zuneigung*) to cool

abkürzen ['apkvrtsən] *vt* to shorten; (*Wort auch*) to abbreviate; **den Weg ~** to take a short cut

Abkürzung *f* (*Wort*) abbreviation; (*Weg*) short cut

abladen ['aplaːdən] (*unreg*) *vt* to unload

Ablage ['aplaːgə] *f* (*für Akten*) tray; (*für Kleider*) cloakroom

ablassen ['aplasən] (*unreg*) *vt* (*Wasser, Dampf*) to let off; (*vom Preis*) to knock off ♦ *vi*: **von etw ~** to give sth up, to abandon sth

Ablauf ['aplauf] *m* (*Abfluss*) drain; (*von Ereignissen*) course; (*einer Frist, Zeit*) expiry (*BRIT*), expiration (*US*); **a~en** (*unreg*) *vi* (*abfließen*) to drain away; (*Ereignisse*) to happen; (*Frist, Zeit, Pass*) to expire ♦ *vt* (*Sohlen*) to wear (down *od* out)

ablegen ['apleːgən] *vt* to put *od* lay down; (*Kleider*) to take off; (*Gewohnheit*) to get rid of; (*Prüfung*) to take, to sit; (*Zeugnis*) to give

Ableger (-s, -) *m* layer; (*fig*) branch, offshoot

ablehnen ['apleːnən] *vt* to reject; (*Einladung*) to decline, to refuse ♦ *vi* to decline, to refuse

ablehnend *adj* (*Haltung, Antwort*) negative; (*Geste*) disapproving; **ein ~er Bescheid** a rejection

Ablehnung *f* rejection; refusal

ableiten ['aplaitən] *vt* (*Wasser*) to divert; (*deduzieren*) to deduce; (*Wort*) to derive; **Ableitung** *f* diversion; deduction; derivation; (*Wort*) derivative

ablenken ['aplɛŋkən] *vt* to turn away, to deflect; (*zerstreuen*) to distract ♦ *vi* to change the subject; **Ablenkung** *f* distraction

ablesen ['apleːzən] (*unreg*) *vt* to read out; (*Messgeräte*) to read

ablichten ['aplıçtən] vt to photocopy

abliefern ['apliːfərn] vt to deliver; **etw bei jdm ~** to hand sth over to sb

Ablieferung f delivery

ablösen ['apløːzən] vt (abtrennen) to take off, to remove; (in Amt) to take over from; (Wache) to relieve

Ablösung f removal; relieving

abmachen ['apmaxən] vt to take off; (vereinbaren) to agree; **Abmachung** f agreement

abmagern ['apmaːgərn] vi to get thinner

Abmagerungskur f diet; **eine ~ machen** to go on a diet

abmarschieren ['apmarʃiːrən] vi to march off

abmelden ['apmɛldən] vt (Zeitungen) to cancel; (Auto) to take off the road ♦ vr to give notice of one's departure; (im Hotel) to check out; **jdn bei der Polizei ~** to register sb's departure with the police

abmessen ['apmɛsən] (unreg) vt to measure; **Abmessung** f measurement

abmontieren ['apmɔntiːrən] vt to take off

abmühen ['apmyːən] vr to wear o.s. out

Abnahme ['apnaːmə] f (+gen) removal; (COMM) buying; (Verringerung) decrease (in)

abnehmen ['apneːmən] (unreg) vt to take off, to remove; (Führerschein) to take away; (Prüfung) to hold; (Maschen) to decrease ♦ vi to decrease; (schlanker werden) to lose weight; **(jdm) etw ~** (Geld) to get sth (out of sb); (kaufen, umg: glauben) to buy sth (from sb); **jdm Arbeit ~** to take work off sb's shoulders

Abnehmer (-s, -) m purchaser, customer

Abneigung ['apnaɪɡʊŋ] f aversion, dislike

abnorm [ap'nɔrm] adj abnormal

abnutzen ['apnʊtsən] vt to wear out; **Abnutzung** f wear (and tear)

Abo ['abo] (umg) nt abk = **Abonnement**

Abonnement [abɔn(ə)'maː] (-s, -s) nt subscription; **Abonnent(in)** [abɔ'nɛnt(ɪn)] m(f) subscriber; **abonnieren** [abɔ'niːrən] vt to subscribe to

Abordnung ['apɔrdnʊŋ] f delegation

abpacken ['appakən] vt to pack

abpassen ['appasən] vt (Person, Gelegenheit) to wait for

Abpfiff ['appfɪf] m final whistle

abplagen ['applaːgən] vr to work o.s. out

abprallen ['appralən] vi to bounce off; to ricochet

abraten ['apraːtən] (unreg) vi: **jdm von etw ~** to advise or warn sb against sth

abräumen ['aprɔʏmən] vt to clear up od away

abreagieren ['apreagiːrən] vt: **seinen Zorn (an jdm/etw) ~** to work one's anger off (on sb/sth) ♦ vr to calm down

abrechnen ['apreçnən] vt to deduct, to take off ♦ vi to settle up; (fig) to get even

Abrechnung f settlement; (Rechnung) bill

Abrede ['apreːdə] f: **etw in ~ stellen** to deny od dispute sth

Abreise ['apraɪzə] f departure; **a~n** vi to leave, to set off

abreißen ['apraɪsən] (unreg) vt (Haus) to tear down; (Blatt) to tear off

abrichten ['apriçtən] vt to train

abriegeln ['apriːgəln] vt (Straße, Gebiet) to seal off

Abruf ['apruːf] m: **auf ~** on call; **a~en** (unreg) vt (Mensch) to call away; (COMM: Ware) to request delivery of

abrunden ['aprʊndən] vt to round off

abrupt [a'brʊpt] adj abrupt

abrüsten ['aprystən] vi to disarm; **Abrüstung** f disarmament

abrutschen ['aprʊtʃən] vi to slip; (AVIAT) to sideslip

Abs. abk (= Absender) sender, from

Absage ['apza:gə] f refusal; **a~n** vt to cancel, to call off; (Einladung) to turn down ♦ vi to cry off; (ablehnen) to decline

absahnen ['apza:nən] vt to skim ♦ vi (fig) to rake in

Absatz ['apzats] m (COMM) sales pl; (Bodensatz) deposit; (neuer Abschnitt) paragraph; (Treppenabsatz) landing; (Schuhabsatz) heel; **~gebiet** nt (COMM) market

abschaffen ['apʃafən] vt to abolish, to do away with; **Abschaffung** f abolition

abschalten ['apʃaltən] vt, vi (auch umg) to switch off

abschätzen ['apʃɛtsən] vt to estimate; (Lage) to assess; (Person) to size up

abschätzig ['apʃɛtsɪç] adj disparaging, derogatory

Abschaum ['apʃaʊm] (-(e)s) m scum

Abscheu ['apʃɔy] (-(e)s) m loathing, repugnance; **~ erregend** repulsive, loathsome; **a~lich** [ap'ʃɔylɪç] adj abominable

abschicken ['apʃɪkən] vt to send off

abschieben ['apʃi:bən] (unreg) vt to push away; (Person) to pack off; (: POL) to deport

Abschied ['apʃi:t] (-(e)s, -e) m parting; (von Armee) discharge; **(von jdm) ~ nehmen** to say goodbye (to sb), to take one's leave (of sb); **seinen ~ nehmen** (MIL) to apply for discharge; **~sbrief** m farewell letter; **~sfeier** f farewell party

abschießen ['apʃi:sən] (unreg) vt (Flugzeug) to shoot down; (Geschoss) to fire

abschirmen ['apʃɪrmən] vt to screen

abschlagen ['apʃla:gən] (unreg) vt (abhacken, COMM) to knock off; (ablehnen) to refuse; (MIL) to repel

abschlägig ['apʃlɛ:gɪç] adj negative

Abschlagszahlung f interim payment

Abschlepp- ['apʃlɛp] zW: **~dienst** m (AUT) breakdown service (BRIT), towing company (US); **a~en** vt (to take in) tow; **~seil** nt towrope

abschließen ['apʃli:sən] (unreg) vt (Tür) to lock; (beenden) to conclude, to finish; (Vertrag, Handel) to conclude ♦ vr (sich isolieren) to cut o.s. off; **~d** adj concluding

Abschluss ▲ ['apʃlʊs] m (Beendigung) close, conclusion; (COMM: Bilanz) balancing; (von Vertrag, Handel) conclusion; **zum ~** in conclusion; **~feier** f (SCH) end of term party; **~prüfung** f final exam

abschneiden ['apʃnaɪdən] (unreg) vt to cut off ♦ vi to do, to come off

Abschnitt ['apʃnɪt] m section; (MIL) sector; (Kontrollabschnitt) counterfoil; (MATH) segment; (Zeitabschnitt) period

abschrauben ['apʃraʊbən] vt to unscrew

abschrecken ['apʃrɛkən] vt to deter, to put off; (mit kaltem Wasser) to plunge in cold water; **~d** adj deterrent; **~des Beispiel** warning

abschreiben ['apʃraɪbən] (unreg) vt to copy; (verloren geben) to write off; (COMM) to deduct

Abschrift ['apʃrɪft] f copy

Abschuss ▲ ['apʃʊs] m (eines Geschützes) firing; (Herunterschießen) shooting down; (Tötung) shooting

abschüssig ['apʃʏsɪç] adj steep

abschwächen ['apʃvɛçən] vt to lessen; (Behauptung, Kritik) to tone down ♦ vr to lessen

abschweifen ['apʃvaɪfən] vi to digress

abschwellen ['apʃvɛlən] (unreg) vi (Geschwulst) to go down; (Lärm) to die down

abschwören ['apʃvø:rən] vi (+dat) to renounce

absehbar ['apze:ba:r] adj foreseeable; **in ~er Zeit** in the foreseeable future;

das Ende ist ~ the end is in sight

absehen ['apzeːən] (unreg) vt (Ende, Folgen) to foresee ♦ vi: **von etw ~** to refrain from sth; (nicht berücksichtigen) to leave sth out of consideration

abseilen ['apzailən] vr (Bergsteiger) to abseil (down)

abseits ['apzaits] adv out of the way ♦ präp +gen away from; **A~** nt (SPORT) offside

absenden ['apzɛndən] (unreg) vt to send off, to dispatch **Absender (-s, -)** m sender

absetzen ['apzɛtsən] vt (niederstellen, aussteigen lassen) to put down; (abnehmen) to take off; (COMM: verkaufen) to sell; (FIN: abziehen) to deduct; (entlassen) to dismiss; (König) to depose; (streichen) to drop; (hervorheben) to pick out ♦ vr (sich entfernen) to clear off; (sich ablagern) to be deposited **Absetzung** f (FIN: Abzug) deduction; (Entlassung) dismissal; (von König) deposing

absichern ['apzɪçɐn] vt to make safe; (schützen) to safeguard ♦ vr to protect o.s.

Absicht ['apzɪçt] f intention; **mit ~** on purpose; **a~lich** adj intentional, deliberate

absinken ['apzɪŋkən] (unreg) vi to sink; (Temperatur, Geschwindigkeit) to decrease

absitzen ['apzɪtsən] (unreg) vi to dismount ♦ vt (Strafe) to serve

absolut [apzoˈluːt] adj absolute; **A~ismus** m absolutism

absolvieren [apzɔlˈviːrən] vt (SCH) to complete

absonder- ['apzɔndɐ] zW: **~lich** adj odd, strange; **~n** vt to separate; (ausscheiden) to give off, to secrete ♦ vr to cut o.s. off; **A~ung** f separation; (MED) secretion

abspalten ['apʃpaltən] vt to split off

abspannen ['apʃpanən] vt (Pferde) to unhitch; (Wagen) to uncouple

abspeisen ['apʃpaizən] vt (fig) to fob off

abspenstig ['apʃpɛnstɪç] adj: **(jdm) ~ machen** to lure away (from sb)

absperren ['apʃpɛran] vt to block od close off; (Tür) to lock; **Absperrung** f (Vorgang) blocking od closing off; (Sperre) barricade

abspielen ['apʃpiːlən] vt (Platte, Tonband) to play; (SPORT: Ball) to pass ♦ vr to happen

Absprache ['apʃpraːxə] f arrangement

absprechen ['apʃpreçən] (unreg) vt (vereinbaren) to arrange; **jdm etw ~** to deny sb sth

abspringen ['apʃprɪŋən] (unreg) vi to jump down/off; (Farbe, Lack) to flake off; (AVIAT) to bale out; (sich distanzieren) to back out

Absprung ['apʃprʊŋ] m jump

abspülen ['apʃpyːlən] vt to rinse; (Geschirr) to wash up

abstammen ['apʃtamən] vi to be descended; (Wort) to be derived; **Abstammung** f descent; derivation

Abstand ['apʃtant] m distance; (zeitlich) interval; **davon ~ nehmen, etw zu tun** to refrain from doing sth; **mit ~ der Beste** by far the best

abstatten ['apʃtatən] vt (Dank) to give; (Besuch) to pay

abstauben ['apʃtaubən] vt, vi to dust; (umg: stehlen) to pinch; (: schnorren) to scrounge

Abstecher ['apʃtɛçɐ] (-s, -) m detour

abstehen ['apʃteːən] (unreg) vi (Ohren, Haare) to stick out; (entfernt sein) to stand away

absteigen ['apʃtaigən] (unreg) vi (vom Rad etc) to get off, to dismount; (in die zweite Liga) ~ to be relegated (to the second division)

abstellen ['apʃtɛlən] vt (niederstellen)

---

to put down; (*entfernt stellen*) to pull
out; (*hinstellen: Auto*) to park;
(*ausschalten*) to turn od switch off;
(*Missstand, Unsitte*) to stop

Abstellraum m storage room

abstempeln ['apʃtɛmpəln] vt to stamp

absterben ['apʃtɛrbən] (*unreg*) vi to
die; (*Körperteil*) to go numb

Abstieg ['apʃtiːk] (-(e)s, -e) m descent;
(*SPORT*) relegation; (*fig*) decline

abstimmen ['apʃtɪmən] vi to vote ♦ vt:
~ **(auf** +akk) (*Instrument*) to tune (to);
(*Interessen*) to match (with); (*Termine,
Ziele*) to fit in (with) ♦ vr to agree

Abstimmung f vote

Abstinenz [apsti'nɛnts] f abstinence;
teetotalism; **~ler(in)** (-s, -) m(f) teetotaller

abstoßen ['apʃtoːsən] (*unreg*) vt to
push off od away; (*verkaufen*) to unload; (*anekeln*) to repel, to repulse; **~d**
adj repulsive

abstrakt [ap'ʃtrakt] adj abstract ♦ adv
abstractly, in the abstract

abstreiten ['apʃtraitən] (*unreg*) vt to
deny

Abstrich ['apʃtrɪç] m (*Abzug*) cut; (*MED*)
smear; **~e machen** to lower one's
sights

abstufen ['apʃtuːfən] vt (*Hang*) to terrace; (*Farben*) to shade; (*Gehälter*) to
grade

Absturz ['apʃtʊrts] m fall; (*AVIAT*) crash

abstürzen ['apʃtʏrtsən] vi to fall;
(*AVIAT*) to crash

absuchen ['apzuːxən] vt to scour, to
search

absurd [ap'zʊrt] adj absurd

Abszess ▲ [aps'tsɛs] (-es, -e) m abscess

Abt [apt] (-(e)s, ⁼e) m abbot

Abt. abk (= *Abteilung*) dept.

abtasten ['aptastən] vt to feel, to
probe

abtauen ['aptauən] vt, vi to thaw

Abtei [ap'tai] (-, -en) f abbey

Abteil [ap'tail] (-(e)s, -e) nt compart-

ment; **'a~n** vt to divide up; (*abtrennen*)
to divide off; **~ung** f (*in Firma, Kaufhaus*) department; (*in Krankenhaus*)
section; (*MIL*) unit

abtippen ['aptɪpən] vt (*Text*) to type
up

abtransportieren ['aptransporti:rən]
vt to take away, to remove

abtreiben ['aptraibən] (*unreg*) vt (*Boot,
Flugzeug*) to drive off course; (*Kind*) to
abort ♦ vi to be driven off course; to
abort

Abtreibung f abortion

abtrennen ['aptrɛnən] vt (*lostrennen*)
to detach; (*entfernen*) to take off; (*ab-
teilen*) to separate off

abtreten ['aptreːtən] (*unreg*) vt to wear
out; (*überlassen*) to hand over, to cede
♦ vi to go off; (*zurücktreten*) to step
down

Abtritt ['aptrɪt] m resignation

abtrocknen ['aptrɔknən] vt, vi to dry

abtun ['aptuːn] (*unreg*) vt (*fig*) to dismiss

abwägen [apvɛːɡən] (*unreg*) vt to
weigh up

abwälzen ['apvɛltsən] vt (*Schuld, Verantwortung*): ~ **(auf** +akk) to shift
(onto)

abwandeln ['apvandəln] vt to adapt

abwandern ['apvandərn] vi to move
away; (*FIN*) to be transferred

abwarten ['apvartən] vt to wait for
♦ vi to wait

abwärts ['apvɛrts] adv down

Abwasch ['apvaʃ] (-(e)s, e) m washing-
up; **a~en** vt (*Schmutz*) to wash
off; (*Geschirr*) to wash (up)

Abwasser ['apvasər] (-s, -wässer) nt
sewage

abwechseln ['apvɛksəln] vi, vr to alternate; (*Personen*) to take turns; **~d**
alternate; **Abwechslung** f change;
abwechslungsreich adj varied

abwegig ['apveːɡɪç] adj wrong

Abwehr ['apveːr] (-) f defence;
(*Schutz*) protection; (~*dienst*) counter-

intelligence (service); **a~en** vt to ward off; (Tier) to skin; (Bett) to strip; (Truppen) to withdraw; (subtrahieren) to take away, to subtract; (kopieren) to run off ♦ vi to go away; (Truppen) to withdraw

abweichen ['apvaiçən] (unreg) vi to deviate; (Meinung) to differ

abweisen ['apvaizən] (unreg) vt to turn away; (Antrag) to turn down; **~d** adj (Haltung) cold

abwenden ['apvɛndən] (unreg) vt to avert ♦ vr to turn away

abwerfen ['apvɛrfən] (unreg) vt to throw off; (Profit) to yield; (aus Flugzeug) to drop; (Spielkarte) to discard

abwerten ['apvertən] (FIN) to devalue

abwertend adj (Worte, Sinn) pejorative

Abwertung f (von Währung) devaluation

abwesend ['apvezənt] adj absent

Abwesenheit ['apvezənhait] f absence

abwickeln ['apvikəln] vt to unwind; (Geschäft) to wind up

abwimmeln ['apvimɛln] (umg) vt (Menschen) to get shot of

abwischen ['apvɪʃən] vt to wipe off od away; (putzen) to wipe

Abwurf ['apvʊrf] m throwing off; (von Bomben etc) dropping; (von Reiter, SPORT) throw

abwürgen ['apvYrgən] (umg) vt to scotch; (Motor) to stall

abzahlen ['aptsa:lən] vt to pay off

abzählen ['aptsɛ:lən] vt, vi to count (up)

Abzahlung f repayment; **auf ~ kaufen** to buy on hire purchase

abzapfen ['aptsapfən] vt to draw off; **jdm Blut ~** to take blood from sb

abzäunen ['aptsɔynən] vt to fence off

Abzeichen ['aptsaiçən] nt badge; (Orden) decoration

abzeichnen ['aptsaiçnən] vt to draw, to copy; (Dokument) to initial ♦ vr to stand out; (fig: bevorstehen) to loom

abziehen ['aptsi:ən] (unreg) vt to take

off; (Tier) to skin; (Bett) to strip; (Truppen) to withdraw; (subtrahieren) to take away, to subtract; (kopieren) to run off ♦ vi to go away; (Truppen) to withdraw

abzielen ['aptsi:lən] vi: **~ auf** +akk to be aimed at

Abzug ['aptso:k] m departure; (von Truppen) withdrawal; (Kopie) copy; (Subtraktion) subtraction; (Betrag) deduction; (Rauchabzug) flue; (von Waffen) trigger

abzüglich ['aptsy:klɪç] präp +gen less

abzweigen ['aptsvaigən] vi to branch off ♦ vt to set aside

Abzweigung f junction

ach [ax] excl oh; **~ ja!** (oh) yes; **~ so!** I see; **mit A~ und Krach** by the skin of one's teeth

Achse ['aksə] f axis; (AUT) axle

Achsel ['aksəl] (-, -n) f shoulder; **~höhle** f armpit

acht¹ [axt] num eight; **~ Tage** a week; **A~** (-, -en) f eight; (beim Eislaufen etc) figure eight

Acht² (-, -en) f: **~ geben (auf** +akk) to pay attention (to); **sich in ~ nehmen (vor** +dat) to be careful (of), to watch out (for); **etw außer ~ lassen** to disregard sth; **a~bar** adj worthy

acht- zW: **~e(r, s)** adj eighth; **A~el** num eighth; **~en** vt to respect ♦ vi: **~en (auf** +akk) to pay attention (to); **~en, dass ...** to be careful that ...

ächten ['ɛçtən] vt to outlaw, to ban

Achterbahn ['axtər-] f roller coaster

acht- zW: **~fach** adj eightfold; **~geben** △ (unreg) vi siehe **Acht²**; **~hundert** num eight hundred; **~los** adj careless; **~mal** adv eight times; **~sam** adj attentive

Achtung ['axtʊŋ] f attention; (Ehrfurcht) respect ♦ excl look out!; (MIL) attention!; **alle ~!** good for you/him etc

achtzehn num eighteen

achtzig *num* eighty

ächzen ['ɛçtsən] *vi* to groan

Acker ['akər] **(-s, ∼)** *m* field; **a∼n** *vt, vi* to plough; (*umg*) to slog away

ADAC [a:de:'a:tse:] *abk* (= *Allgemeiner Deutscher Automobil-Club*) ≈ AA, RAC

Adapter [a'daptər] **∼** *m* adapter

addieren [a'di:rən] *vt* to add (up); **Addition** [aditsi'o:n] *f* addition

Adel ['a:dəl] **(-s)** *m* nobility; **a∼ig** *adj* noble; **a∼n** *vt* to raise to the peerage

Ader ['a:dər] **(-, -n)** *f* vein

Adjektiv ['atjɛkti:f] **(-s, -e)** *nt* adjective

Adler ['a:dlər] **(-s, -)** *m* eagle

adlig *adj* noble

Adopt- *zW:* **a∼ieren** [adɔp'ti:rən] *vt* to adopt; **∼ion** [adɔptsi'o:n] *f* adoption; **∼iveltern** *pl* adoptive parents; **∼ivkind** *nt* adopted child

Adressbuch ▲ *nt* directory; (*privat*) address book

Adress- *zW:* **∼e** [a'drɛsə] *f* address; **a∼ieren** [adrɛ'si:rən] *vt:* **a∼ieren** (*an +akk*) to address (to)

Adria ['a:dria] **(-)** *f* Adriatic

Advent [at'vɛnt] **(-(e)s, -e)** *m* Advent; **∼skalender** *m* Advent calendar; **∼skranz** *m* Advent wreath

Adverb [at'vɛrp] *nt* adverb

Aerobic [a'fe:ra] *f* aerobics *sg*

Affäre [a'fɛ:rə] *f* affair

Affe ['afə] **(-n, -n)** *m* monkey

Affekt [a'fɛkt] **(-(e)s, -e)** *m:* **im ∼ handeln** to act in the heat of the moment; **a∼iert** [afɛk'ti:rt] *adj* affected

Affen- *zW:* **a∼artig** *adj* like a monkey; **mit a∼artiger Geschwindigkeit** like a flash; **∼hitze** (*umg*) *f* incredible heat

affig ['afɪç] *adj* affected

Afrika ['a:frika] **(-s)** *nt* Africa; **∼ner(in)** [-'ka:nər(ɪn)] **(-s, -)** *m(f)* African; **a∼nisch** *adj* African

AG [a:'ge:] *abk* (= *Aktiengesellschaft*) ≈ plc (*BRIT*), ≈ Inc. (*US*)

Agent [a'gɛnt] *m* agent; **∼ur** *f* agency

Aggregat [agre'ga:t] **(-(e)s, -e)** *nt* aggregate; (*TECH*) unit

Aggress- *zW:* **∼ion** [agrɛsi'o:n] *f* aggression; **a∼iv** [agrɛ'si:f] *adj* aggressive; **∼ivität** [agrɛsivi'tɛ:t] *f* aggressiveness

Agrarpolitik [a'gra:r-] *f* agricultural policy

Ägypten [ɛ'gʏptən] **(-s)** *nt* Egypt; **ägyptisch** *adj* Egyptian

aha [a'ha:] *excl* aha

ähneln ['ɛ:nəln] *vi +dat* to be like, to resemble **∤** *vr* to be alike *od* similar

ahnen ['a:nən] *vt* to suspect; (*Tod, Gefahr*) to have a presentiment of

ähnlich ['ɛ:nlɪç] *adj (+dat)* similar (to); **Ä∼keit** *f* similarity

Ahnung ['a:nʊŋ] *f* idea, suspicion; presentiment; **a∼slos** *adj* unsuspecting

Ahorn ['a:hɔrn] **(-s, -e)** *m* maple

Ähre ['ɛ:rə] *f* ear

Aids [e:dz] *nt* AIDS *sg*

Airbag ['ɛ:abɛk] **(-s)** *m* airbag

Akademie [akade'mi:] *f* academy; **Aka∼demiker(in)** **(-s, -)** *m(f)* university graduate; **akademisch** *adj* academic

akklimatisieren [aklimati'zi:rən] *vr* to become acclimatized

Akkord [a'kɔrt] **(-(e)s, -e)** *m* (*MUS*) chord; **im ∼ arbeiten** to do piecework

Akkordeon [a'kɔrdeɔn] **(-s, -s)** *nt* accordion

Akku ['aku] **(-s, -s)** *m* rechargeable battery

Akkusativ ['akuzati:f] **(-s, -e)** *m* accusative

Akne ['aknə] *f* acne

Akrobat(in) [akro'ba:t(ɪn)] **(-en, -en)** *m(f)* acrobat

Akt [akt] **(-(e)s, -e)** *m* act; (*KUNST*) nude

Akte ['aktə] *f* file

Akten- *zW:* **∼koffer** *m* attaché case; **a∼kundig** *adj* on the files; **∼schrank** *m* filing cabinet; **∼tasche** *f* briefcase

Aktie ['aktsiə] *f* share

Aktien- *zW:* **∼gesellschaft** *f* public limited company; **∼index** **(-(e)s, -e** *od* **-indices)** *m* share index; **∼kurs** *m* share price

Aktion 11 allerhand

Aktion [aktsi'o:n] f campaign; (*Polizeiaktion, Suchaktion*) action

Aktionär [aktsio'nɛ:r] (**-s, -e**) m shareholder

aktiv [ak'ti:f] adj active; (*MIL*) regular; **~ieren** [-'vi:rən] vt to activate; **A~i'tät** f activity

Aktualität [aktuali'tɛ:t] f topicality; (*einer Mode*) up-to-dateness

aktuell [aktu'ɛl] adj topical; up-to-date

Akupunktur [akupuŋk'tu:ər] f acupuncture

Akustik [a'kʊstɪk] f acoustics pl

akut [a'ku:t] adj acute

Akzent [ak'tsɛnt] m accent; (*Betonung*) stress

akzeptabel [aktsɛp'ta:bl] adj acceptable

akzeptieren [aktsɛp'ti:rən] vt to accept

Alarm [a'larm] (**-(e)s, -e**) m alarm; **a~bereit** adj standing by; **a~bereitschaft** f stand-by; **a~ieren** [-'mi:rən] vt to alarm

Albanien [al'ba:niən] (**-s**) nt Albania

albanisch adj Albanian

albern ['albərn] adj silly

Albtraum ▲ ['alptraʊm] m nightmare

Album ['albʊm] (**-s, Alben**) nt album

Alge ['algə] f algae

Algebra ['algebra] (**-**) f algebra

Algerier(in) [al'ge:riər] (**-s, -**) m(f) Algerian

algerisch adj Algerian

alias ['a:lias] adv alias

Alibi [a'li:bi] (**-s, -s**) nt alibi

Alimente [ali'mɛntə] pl alimony sg

Alkohol ['alkohɔl] (**-s, -e**) m alcohol; **a~frei** adj non-alcoholic; **~iker(in)** [alko'ho:likər(ɪn)] (**-s, -**) m(f) alcoholic; **a~isch** adj alcoholic; **~verbot** nt ban on alcohol

All [al] (**-s**) nt universe

all'abendlich adj every evening

'allbekannt adj universally known

SCHLÜSSELWORT

alle(r, s) ['alə(r,s)] adj **1** (*sämtliche*) all; **wir alle** all of us; **alle Kinder waren da** all the children were there; **alle Kinder mögen** ... all children like ...; **alle** both of us/them; **sie kamen alle** they all came; **alles Gute** all the best; **alles in allem** all in all

2 (*mit Zeit- oder Maßangaben*) every; **alle vier Jahre** every four years; **alle fünf Meter** every five metres

♦ pron everything; **alles was er sagt** everything he says, all that he says

♦ adv (*zu Ende, aufgebraucht*) finished; **die Milch ist alle** the milk's all gone, there's no milk left; **etw alle machen** to finish sth up

Allee [a'le:] f avenue

allein [a'laɪn] adv alone; (*ohne Hilfe*) on one's own, by oneself ♦ konj but, only; **nicht ~** (*nicht nur*) not only; **~ stehend** single; **A~erziehende(r)** f(m) single parent; **A~gang** m: **im A~gang** on one's own

allemal ['alə'ma:l] adv (*jedes Mal*) always; (*ohne weiteres*) with no bother; *siehe* Mal

allenfalls ['alən'fals] adv at all events; (*höchstens*) at most

aller- ['alər] zW: **~beste(r, s)** adj very best; **~dings** adv (*zwar*) admittedly; (*gewiss*) certainly

Allergie [alɛr'gi:] f allergy; **al'lergisch** adj allergic

aller- zW: **~hand** (*umg*) adj inv all sorts of; **das ist doch ~hand!** that's a bit much; **~hand!** (*lobend*) good show!; **A~heiligen** nt All Saints' Day

Allerheiligen

Allerheiligen (*All Saints' Day*) is celebrated on November 1st and is a public holiday in some parts of Ger-

---

many and in Austria. **Allerseelen** *(All Souls' Day) is celebrated on November 2nd in the Roman Catholic Church. It is customary to visit cemeteries and place lighted candles on the graves of relatives and friends.*

aller- *zW:* **~höchstens** *adv* at the very most; **~lei** *adj inv* all sorts of; **~letzte(r, s)** *adj* very last; **A~seelen (-s)** *nt* All Souls' Day; **~seits** *adv* on all sides; **prost ~seits!** cheers everyone!

Allerwelts- *in zW (Durchschnitts-)* common; *(nichts sagend)* commonplace

alles *pron* everything; ~ **in allem** all in all; ~ **Gute!** all the best!

Alleskleber (-s, -) *m* multi-purpose glue

allgemein [ˈalgəmaɪn] *adj* general; **im A~en** in general; ~ **gültig** generally accepted; **A~wissen** *nt* general knowledge

Alliierte(r) [aliˈiːrtə(r)] *m* ally

all- *zW:* **~jährlich** *adj* annual; **~mächtig** *adj* almighty; **~mählich** *adj* gradual; **A~tag** *m* everyday life; **~täglich** *adj, adv* daily; *(gewöhnlich)* commonplace; **~tags** *adv* on weekdays; **~wissend** *adj* omniscient; **~zu** *adv* all too; ~ **oft** all too often; ~ **viel** too much

Allzweck- [ˈaltsvɛk-] *in zW* multipurpose

Alm [alm] **(-, -en)** *f* alpine pasture

Almosen [ˈalmoːzən] **(-s, -)** *nt* alms *pl*

Alpen [ˈalpən] *pl* Alps; **~vorland** *nt* foothills *pl* of the Alps

Alphabet [alfaˈbeːt] **(-(e)s, -e)** *nt* alphabet; **a~isch** *adj* alphabetical

Alptraum [ˈalptraʊm] = **Albtraum**

als [als] *konj* **1** *(zeitlich)* when; *(gleichzeitig)* as; **damals, als ...** (in the days) when ...; **gerade, als ...** just as ...

2 *(in der Eigenschaft)* than; **als Antwort** as an answer; **als Kind** as a

child

3 *(bei Vergleichen)* than; **ich kam später als er** I came later than he (did) *od* later than him; **lieber ... als ...** rather ... than ...; **nichts als Ärger** nothing but trouble

4: **als ob/wenn** as if

also [ˈalzoː] *konj* so; *(folglich)* therefore; ~ **gut** *od* **schön!** okay then!; ~, **so was!** well really!; **na ~!** there you are then!

Alsterwasser [ˈalstɐ-] *nt* shandy *(BRIT)*, beer and lemonade

Alt [alt] **(-s, -e)** *m (MUS)* alto

alt *adj* old; **alles beim A~en lassen** to leave everything as it was

Altar [alˈtaːr] **(-(e)s, -äre)** *m* altar

Alt- *zW:* **~bau** *m* old building; **a~bekannt** *adj* long-known; **~bier** *nt* top-fermented German dark beer; **a~eisen** *nt* scrap iron

Alten(wohn)heim *nt* old people's home

Alter [ˈaltɐ] **(-s, -)** *nt* age; *(hohes)* old age; **im ~ von** at the age of; **a~n** *vi* to grow old, to age

Alternativ- [alternaˈtiːf-] *in zW* alternative; **~e** *f* alternative

Alters- *zW:* **~grenze** *f* age limit; **~heim** *nt* old people's home; **~rente** *f* old age pension; **a~schwach** *adj (Mensch)* frail; **~versorgung** *f* old age pension

Altertum [ˈaltɐtuːm] *nt* antiquity

Alt- *zW:* **A~glas** *nt* glass for recycling; **A~glascontainer** *m* bottle bank; **~klug** *adj* precocious; **a~modisch** *adj* old-fashioned; **A~papier** *nt* waste paper; **A~stadt** *f* old town

Alufolie [ˈaluˌfoːliə] *f* aluminium foil

Aluminium [aluˈmiːnium] **(-s)** *nt* aluminium, aluminum *(US)*

Alzheimerkrankheit [ˈaltshaɪmɐˌkraŋkhaɪt] *f* Alzheimer's (disease)

am [am] = **an dem**; ~ **Schlafen** *(umg)*

sleeping; ~ **15. März** on March 15th; ~ **besten/schönsten** best/most beautiful

Amateur [ama'tø:ɐ̯] *m* amateur

Amboss ▲ ['ambɔs] (-es, -e) *m* anvil

ambulant [ambu'lant] *adj* outpatient; **Ambulanz** *f* outpatients *sg*

Ameise ['a:maɪzə] *f* ant

Ameisenhaufen *m* ant hill

Amerika [a'me:rika] (-s) *nt* America; ~**ner(in)** [-'ka:nɐr(ɪn)] (-s, -) *m(f)* American; **a~nisch** [-'ka:nɪʃ] *adj* American

Amnestie [amnɛs'ti:] *f* amnesty

Ampel ['ampəl] (-, -n) *f* traffic lights *pl*

amputieren [ampu'ti:rən] *vt* to amputate

Amsel ['amzəl] (-, -n) *f* blackbird

Amt [amt] (-(e)s, ≈er) *nt* office; (*Pflicht*) duty; (*TEL*) exchange; **a~ieren** [am'ti:rən] *vi* to hold office; **a~lich** *adj* official

Amts- *zW:* ~**richter** *m* district judge; ~**stunden** *pl* office hours; ~**zeichen** *nt* dialling tone; ~**zeit** *f* period of office

amüsant [amy'zant] *adj* amusing

amüsieren [amy'zi:rən] *vt* to amuse ♦ *vr* to enjoy o.s.

Amüsierviertel *nt* nightclub district

an [an] *präp +dat* 1 (*räumlich: wo?*) at; (*auf, bei*) on; (*nahe bei*) near; **an diesem Ort** at this place; **an der Wand** on the wall; **zu nahe an etw** too near to sth; **unten am Fluss** down by the river; **Köln liegt am Rhein** Cologne is on the Rhine

2 (*zeitlich: wann?*) on; **an diesem Tag** on this day; **an Ostern** at Easter

3: **arm an Fett** low in fat; **an etw sterben** to die of sth; **an (und für) sich** actually

♦ *präp +akk* 1 (*räumlich: wohin?*) to; **er ging ans Fenster** he went (over) to

the window; **etw an die Wand hängen/schreiben** to hang/write sth on the wall

2 (*zeitlich: woran?*): **an etw denken** to think of sth

3 (*gerichtet an*) to; **ein Gruß/eine Frage an dich** greetings/a question to you

♦ *adv* 1 (*ungefähr*) about; **an die hundert** about a hundred

2 (*auf Fahrplänen*): **Frankfurt an 18.30** arriving Frankfurt 18.30

3 (*ab*): **von dort/heute an** from there/today onwards

4 (*angeschaltet, angezogen*) on; **das Licht ist an** the light is on; **ohne etwas an** with nothing on; *siehe auch* **am**

analog [ana'lo:k] *adj* analogous; **A~ie** [-'gi:] *f* analogy

Analphabet(in) [an|alfa'be:t(ɪn)] (-en, -en) *m(f)* illiterate (person)

Analyse [ana'ly:zə] *f* analysis

analysieren [analy'zi:rən] *vt* to analyse

Ananas ['ananas] (-, - *od* -se) *f* pineapple

Anarchie [anar'çi:] *f* anarchy

Anatomie [anato'mi:] *f* anatomy

anbahnen ['anba:nən] *vt, vr* to open up

Anbau ['anbaʊ] *m* (*AGR*) cultivation; (*Gebäude*) extension; **a~en** *vt* (*AGR*) to cultivate; (*Gebäudeteil*) to build on

anbehalten ['anbəhaltən] (*unreg*) *vt* to keep on

anbei [an'baɪ] *adv* enclosed

anbeißen ['anbaɪsən] (*unreg*) *vt* to bite into ♦ *vi* to bite; (*fig*) to swallow the bait; **zum A~** (*umg*) good enough to eat

anbelangen ['anbəlaŋən] *vt* to concern; **was mich anbelangt** as far as I am concerned

anbeten ['anbe:tən] vt to worship

Anbetracht ['anbətraxt] m: **in ~** +gen in view of

anbieten ['anbi:tən] (unreg) vt to offer ♦ vr to volunteer

anbinden ['anbɪndən] (unreg) vt to tie up; **kurz angebunden** (fig) curt

Anblick ['anblɪk] m sight; **a~en** vt to look at

anbraten ['anbra:tən] vt to brown

anbrechen ['anbrɛçən] (unreg) vt to start; (Vorräte) to break into ♦ vi to start; (Tag) to break; (Nacht) to fall

anbrennen ['anbrɛnən] (unreg) vt to catch fire; (KOCH) to burn

anbringen ['anbrɪŋən] (unreg) vt to bring; (Ware) to sell; (festmachen) to fasten

Anbruch ['anbrʊx] m beginning; **~ des Tages/der Nacht** dawn/nightfall

anbrüllen ['anbrʏlən] vt to roar at

Andacht ['andaxt] (-, -en) f devotion; (Gottesdienst) prayers pl; **andächtig** adj ['andɛçtɪç] devout

andauern ['andauərn] vi to last, to go on; **~d** adj continual

Anden ['andən] pl Andes

Andenken ['andɛŋkən] (-s, -) nt memory; souvenir

andere(r, s) ['andərə(r, z)] adj other; (verschieden) different; **ein ~s Mal** another time; **kein ~** nobody else; **von etw ~m sprechen** to talk about something else; **~rseits** adv on the other hand

andermal adv: **ein ~** some other time

ändern ['endərn] vt to alter, to change ♦ vr to change

andernfalls ['andərnfals] adv otherwise

anders ['andərs] adv: **~ (als)** differently (from); **wer ~?** who else?; **jd/ irgendwo ~** sb/somewhere else; **~ aussehen/klingen** to look/sound different; **~artig** adj different; **~herum** adv the other way round; **~wo** adv somewhere else; **~woher** adv from

somewhere else

anderthalb ['andərt'halp] adj one and a half

Änderung ['endərʊŋ] f alteration, change

Änderungsschneiderei f tailor (who does alterations)

anderweitig ['andərvaitɪç] adj other ♦ adv otherwise; (anderswo) elsewhere

andeuten ['andɔytən] vt to indicate; (Wink geben) to hint at; **Andeutung** f indication; hint

Andrang ['andraŋ] m crush

andrehen ['andre:ən] vt to turn od switch on; **jdm etw ~** (umg) to unload sth onto sb

androhen ['andro:ən] vt: **jdm etw ~** to threaten sb with sth

aneignen ['anaignən] vt: **sich** dat **etw ~** to acquire sth; (widerrechtlich) to appropriate sth

aneinander ['anai'nandər] adv at/on/ to etc one another od each other; **~ geraten** to clash

Anekdote [anɛk'do:tə] f anecdote

anekeln ['anʔe:kəln] vt to disgust

anerkannt ['anʔerkant] adj recognized, acknowledged

anerkennen ['anʔerkɛnən] (unreg) vt to recognize, to acknowledge; (würdigen) to appreciate; **~d** adj appreciative

Anerkennung f recognition, acknowledgement; appreciation

anfachen ['anfaxən] vt to fan into flame; (fig) to kindle

anfahren ['anfa:rən] (unreg) vt to deliver; (fahren gegen) to hit; (Hafen) to put into; (fig) to bawl out ♦ vi to drive up; (losfahren) to drive off

Anfahrt ['anfa:rt] f (~sweg, ~szeit) journey

Anfall ['anfal] m (MED) attack; **a~en** (unreg) vt to attack; (fig) to overcome ♦ vi (Arbeit) to come up; (Produkt) to be obtained

anfällig ['anfɛlɪç] adj delicate; **~ für etw** prone to sth

Anfang ['anfaŋ] (-(e)s, -fänge) *m* beginning, start; **von ~ an** right from the beginning; **zu ~** at the beginning; **~ Mai** at the beginning of May; **a~en** (*unreg*) *vt, vi* to begin, to start; (*machen*) to do

Anfänger(in) ['anfɛŋər(ɪn)] (-s, -) *m(f)* beginner

anfänglich ['anfɛŋlɪç] *adj* initial

anfangs *adv* at first; **A~buchstabe** *m* initial *od* first letter; **A~gehalt** *nt* starting salary

anfassen ['anfasən] *vt* to handle; (*berühren*) to touch ♦ *vi* to lend a hand ♦ *vr* to feel

anfechten ['anfɛçtən] (*unreg*) *vt* to dispute

anfertigen ['anfɛrtɪgən] *vt* to make

anfeuern ['anfɔyərn] *vt* (*fig*) to spur on

anflehen ['anfleːən] *vt* to implore

anfliegen ['anfliːgən] (*unreg*) *vt* to fly to

Anflug ['anfluːk] *m* (AVIAT) approach; (*Spur*) trace

anfordern ['anfɔrdərn] *vt* to demand; (COMM) to requisition

Anforderung *f* (+gen) demand (for)

Anfrage ['anfraːgə] *f* inquiry; **a~n** *vi* to inquire

anfreunden ['anfrɔyndən] *vr* to make friends

anfügen ['anfyːgən] *vt* to add; (*beifügen*) to enclose

anfühlen ['anfyːlən] *vt, vr* to feel

anführen ['anfyːrən] *vt* to lead; (*zitieren*) to quote; (*umg: betrügen*) to lead up the garden path

Anführer *m* leader

Anführungszeichen *pl* quotation marks, inverted commas

Angabe ['angaːbə] *f* statement; (TECH) specification; (*umg: Prahlerei*) boasting; (SPORT) service

angeben ['angeːbən] (*unreg*) *vt* to give; (*anzeigen*) to inform on; (*bestimmen*)

to set ♦ *vi* (*umg*) to boast; (SPORT) to serve

Angeber (-s, -) (*umg*) *m* show-off; **Angebe'rei** (*umg*) *f* showing-off

angeblich ['angeːplɪç] *adj* alleged

angeboren ['angəboːrən] *adj* inborn, innate

Angebot ['angəboːt] *nt* offer; **~ (an** +*dat*) (COMM) supply (of)

angebracht ['angəbraxt] *adj* appropriate, in order

angegriffen ['angəgrɪfən] *adj* exhausted

angeheitert ['angəhaɪtərt] *adj* tipsy

angehen ['angeːən] (*unreg*) *vt* to concern; (*angreifen*) to attack; (*bitten*): **jdn ~ (um)** to approach sb (for) ♦ *vi* (*Feuer*) to light; (*umg: beginnen*) to begin; **~d** *adj* prospective

angehören ['angəhøːrən] *vi* (+ *dat*) to belong to; (*Partei*) to be a member of

Angehörige(r) *f(m)* relative

Angeklagte(r) ['angəklaːktə(r)] *f(m)* accused

Angel ['aŋəl] (-, -n) *f* fishing rod; (*Türangel*) hinge

Angelegenheit ['angəleːgənhaɪt] *f* affair, matter

Angel- *zW:* **~haken** *m* fish hook; **a~n** *vt* to catch ♦ *vi* to fish; **~n** (-s) *nt* angling, fishing; **~rute** *f* fishing rod; **~schein** *m* fishing permit

angemessen ['angəmɛsən] *adj* appropriate, suitable

angenehm ['angəneːm] *adj* pleasant; **~!** (*bei Vorstellung*) pleased to meet you

angeregt [angəreːkt] *adj* animated, lively

angesehen ['angəzeːən] *adj* respected

angesichts ['angəzɪçts] *präp* +*gen* in view of, considering

angespannt ['angəʃpant] *adj* (*Aufmerksamkeit*) close; (*Arbeit*) hard

Angestellte(r) ['angəʃtɛltə(r)] *f(m)* employee

angestrengt ['angəʃtrɛŋt] *adv* as hard as one can

angetan ['angəta:n] *adj*: **von jdm/etw ~ sein** to be impressed by sb/sth; **es jdm ~ haben** to appeal to sb

angetrunken ['angətrʊŋkən] *adj* tipsy

angewiesen ['angəvi:zən] *adj*: **auf jdn/etw ~ sein** to be dependent on sb/sth

angewöhnen ['angəvø:nən] *vt*: **jdm/sich etw ~** to get sb/become accustomed to sth

Angewohnheit ['angəvo:nhaɪt] *f* habit

angleichen ['anglaɪçən] (*unreg*) *vt, vr* to adjust

Angler ['aŋlər] (**-s, -**) *m* angler

angreifen ['angraɪfən] (*unreg*) *vt* to attack; (*beschädigen*) to damage

Angreifer (**-s, -**) *m* attacker

Angriff ['angrɪf] *m* attack; **etw in ~ nehmen** to make a start on sth

Angst (**-, ⁼e**) *f* fear; **jdm ist a~** sb is afraid od scared; **~ haben** (**vor** +dat) to be afraid od scared (of); **~ haben um jdn/etw** to be worried about sb/sth; **jdm ~ machen** to scare sb; **~hase** (*umg*) *m* chicken, scaredy-cat

ängst- ['ɛŋst] *zW*: **~igen** *vt* to frighten ♦ *vr*: **sich ~igen** (**vor** +dat od **um**) to worry (o.s.) (about); **~lich** *adj* nervous; (*besorgt*) worried; **A~lichkeit** *f* nervousness

anhaben ['anha:bən] (*unreg*) *vt* to have on; **er kann mir nichts ~** he can't hurt me

anhalt- ['anhalt] *zW*: **~en** (*unreg*) *vt* to stop ♦ *vi* to stop; (*andauern*) to persist; **(jdm) etw ~en** to hold sth up (against sb); **jdn zur Arbeit/Höflichkeit ~en** to make sb work/be polite; **~end** *adj* persistent; **A~er(in)** (**-s, -**) *m(f)* hitchhiker; **per A~er fahren** to hitch-hike; **A~spunkt** *m* clue

anhand [an'hant] *präp* +gen with

Anhang ['anhaŋ] *m* appendix; (*Leute*)

family; supporters *pl*

anhäng- ['anhɛŋ] *zW*: **~en** (*unreg*) *vt* to hang up; (*Wagen*) to couple up; (*Zusatz*) to add (on); **A~er** (**-s, -**) *m* supporter; (*AUT*) trailer; (*am Koffer*) tag; (*Schmuck*) pendant; **A~erschaft** *f* supporters *pl*; **~lich** *adj* devoted; **A~lichkeit** *f* devotion; **A~sel** (**-s, -**) *nt* appendage

Anhäufung ['anhɔyfʊŋ] *f* accumulation

anheben ['anhe:bən] (*unreg*) *vt* to lift up; (*Preise*) to raise

anheizen ['anhaɪtsən] *vt* (*Stimmung*) to lift; (*Moral*) to boost

Anhieb ['anhi:b] *m*: **auf ~** at the very first go; (*kurz entschlossen*) on the spur of the moment

Anhöhe ['anhø:ə] *f* hill

anhören ['anhø:rən] *vt* to listen to; (*anmerken*) to hear ♦ *vr* to sound

animieren [ani'mi:rən] *vt* to encourage, to urge on

Anis [a'ni:s] (**-es, -e**) *m* aniseed

Ankauf ['ankaʊf] *m* (*von Wertpapieren, Devisen, Waren*) purchase; **a~en** *vt* to purchase, to buy

Anker ['ankər] (**-s, -**) *m* anchor; **vor ~ gehen** to drop anchor

Anklage ['ankla:gə] *f* accusation; (*JUR*) charge; **~bank** *f* dock; **a~n** *vt* to accuse; **jdn (eines Verbrechens) a~n** (*JUR*) to charge sb (with a crime)

Ankläger ['anklɛ:gər] *m* accuser

Anklang ['anklaŋ] *m*: **bei jdm ~ finden** to meet with sb's approval

Ankleidekabine *f* changing cubicle

ankleiden ['anklaɪdən] *vt, vr* to dress

anklopfen ['anklɔpfən] *vi* to knock

anknüpfen ['anknʏpfən] *vt* to fasten od tie on; (*fig*) to start ♦ *vi* (*anschließen*): **~ an** +akk to refer to

ankommen ['ankɔmən] (*unreg*) *vi* to arrive; (*näher kommen*) to approach; (*Anklang finden*): **bei jdm (gut) ~** to go down well with sb; **es kommt da-**

rauf an it depends; (*wichtig sein*) that (is what) matters; **es darauf ~ lassen** to let things take their course; **gegen jdn/etw ~** to cope with sb/sth/etw; **bei jdm schlecht ~** to go down badly with sb

ankreuzen ['ankrɔytsən] *vt* to mark with a cross; (*hervorheben*) to highlight

ankündigen ['ankʏndɪgən] *vt* to announce; **Ankündigung** *f* announcement

Ankunft ['ankʊnft] (-, **-künfte**) *f* arrival; **~szeit** *f* time of arrival

ankurbeln ['ankʊrbəln] *vt* (*fig*) to boost

Anlage ['anla:gə] *f* disposition; (*Begabung*) talent; (*Park*) gardens *pl*; (*Beilage*) enclosure; (*TECH*) plant; (*FIN*) investment; (*Entwurf*) layout

Anlass ▲ ['anlas] (-es, **-lässe**) *m*: **~ (zu)** cause (for); (*Ereignis*) occasion; **aus** +*gen* on the occasion of; **~ zu etw geben** to give rise to sth; **etw zum ~ nehmen** to take the opportunity of sth

anlassen (*unreg*) *vt* to leave on; (*Motor*) to start ♦ *vr* (*umg*) to start off

Anlasser (-s, -) *m* (*AUT*) starter

anlässlich ▲ ['anlɛslɪç] *präp* +*gen* on the occasion of

Anlauf ['anlaʊf] *m* run-up; **a~en** (*unreg*) *vi* to begin; (*neuer Film*) to show; (*SPORT*) to run up; (*Fenster*) to mist up; (*Metall*) to tarnish ♦ *vt* to call at; **rot a~en** to blush; **angelaufen kommen** to come running up

anlegen ['anle:gən] *vt* to put; (*anziehen*) to put on; (*gestalten*) to lay out; (*Geld*) to invest ♦ *vt* to dock; **etw an etw** *akk* **~** to put sth against od on sth; **ein Gewehr ~ (auf** +*akk***)** to aim a weapon (at); **es auf etw** *akk* **~** to be out for sth/to do sth; **sich mit jdm ~** (*umg*) to quarrel with sb

Anlegestelle *f* landing place

anlehnen ['anle:nən] *vt* to lean; (*Tür*) to leave ajar; (*sich*) **an etw** *akk* **~** to lean on/against sth

Anleihe ['anlaɪə] *f* (*FIN*) loan

anleiten ['anlaɪtən] *vt* to instruct; **Anleitung** *f* instructions *pl*

anliegen ['anli:gən] (*unreg*) *vi* (*Kleidung*) to cling; **A~** (-s, -) *nt* matter; (*Wunsch*) wish; **~d** *adj* adjacent; (*beigefügt*) enclosed

Anlieger (-s, -) *m* resident; **„~ frei"** "residents only"

anmachen ['anmaxən] *vt* to attach; (*Elektrisches*) to put on; (*Zigarette*) to light; (*Salat*) to dress

anmaßen ['anma:sən] *vt*: **sich** *dat* **etw ~** (*Recht*) to lay claim to sth; **~d** *adj* arrogant

Anmaßung *f* presumption

anmelden ['anmɛldən] *vt* to announce ♦ *vr* (*sich ankündigen*) to make an appointment; (*polizeilich, für Kurs etc*) to register

Anmeldung *f* announcement; appointment; registration

anmerken ['anmɛrkən] *vt* to observe; (*anstreichen*) to mark; **sich** *dat* **nichts ~ lassen** to not give anything away

Anmerkung *f* note

anmieten ['anmi:tən] *vt* to rent; (*auch Auto*) to hire

Anmut ['anmu:t] (-) *f* grace; **a~en** *vt* to give a feeling; **a~ig** *adj* charming

annähen ['annɛ:ən] *vt* to sew on

annähern ['annɛ:ərn] *vt* to get closer; **~d** *adj* approximate

Annäherung *f* approach

Annäherungsversuch *m* advances *pl*

Annahme ['anna:mə] *f* acceptance; (*Vermutung*) assumption

annehm- ['annɛm] *zW*: **~bar** *adj* acceptable; **~en** (*unreg*) *vt* to accept; (*Namen*) to take; (*Kind*) to adopt; (*vermuten*) to suppose, to assume ♦ *vr* (+*gen*) to take care (of); **A~lichkeit** *f* comfort

Annonce [a'nõ:sə] f advertisement

annoncieren [anõ'si:rən] vt, vi to advertise

annullieren [anu'li:rən] vt to annul

anonym [ano'ny:m] adj anonymous

Anorak ['anorak] (-s, -s) m anorak

anordnen ['an|ɔrdnən] vt to arrange; (befehlen) to order

Anordnung f arrangement; order

anorganisch ['an|ɔrga:nɪʃ] adj inorganic

anpacken ['anpakən] vt to grasp; (fig) to tackle; **mit ~** to lend a hand

anpassen ['anpasən] vt: (jdm) ~ to fit (on sb); (fig) to adapt ♦ vr to adapt

anpassungsfähig adj adaptable

Anpfiff ['anpfif] m (SPORT) (starting) whistle; kick-off; (umg) rocket

anprallen ['anpralən] vi: ~ (gegen od an +akk) to collide (with)

anprangern ['anpraŋərn] vt to denounce

anpreisen ['anpraizən] (unreg) vt to extol

Anprobe ['anpro:bə] f trying on

anprobieren ['anprobi:rən] vt to try on

anrechnen ['anrɛçnən] vt to charge; (fig) to count; **jdm etw hoch ~** to think highly of sb for sth

Anrecht ['anrɛçt] nt: ~ (auf +akk) right (to)

Anrede ['anre:də] f form of address; **a~n** vt to address; (belästigen) to accost

anregen ['anre:gən] vt to stimulate; **angeregte Unterhaltung** lively discussion; **~d** adj stimulating

Anregung f stimulation; (Vorschlag) suggestion

anreichern ['anraiçərn] vt to enrich

Anreise ['anraizə] f journey; **a~n** vi to arrive

Anreiz ['anraits] m incentive

Anrichte ['anrɪçtə] f sideboard; **a~n** vt to serve up; **Unheil a~n** to make mis-

chief

anrüchig ['anryçiç] adj dubious

anrücken ['anrykən] vi to approach; (MIL) to advance

Anruf ['anru:f] m call; **~beantworter** [-bə'|antvortər] (-s, -) m answering machine; **a~en** (unreg) vt to call on; (bitten) to call on; (TEL) to ring up, to phone, to call

ans [ans] = an das

Ansage ['anza:gə] f announcement; **a~n** vt to announce ♦ vr to say one will come; **~r(in)** (-s, -) m(f) announcer

ansammeln ['anzaməln] vt (Reichtümer) to amass ♦ vr (Menschen) to gather, to assemble; (Wasser) to collect; **Ansammlung** f collection; (Leute) crowd

ansässig ['anzɛsɪç] adj resident

Ansatz ['anzats] m start; (Haaransatz) hairline; (Halsansatz) base; (Verlängerungsstück) extension; (Veranschlagung) estimate; **~punkt** m starting point

anschaffen ['anʃafən] vt to buy, to purchase; **Anschaffung** f purchase

anschalten ['anʃaltən] vt to switch on

anschau- ['anʃau] zW: **~en** vt to look at; **~lich** adj illustrative; **A~ung** f (Meinung) view; **aus eigener A~ung** from one's own experience

Anschein ['anʃain] m appearance; **allem ~ nach** to all appearances; **den ~ haben** to seem, to appear; **a~end** adj apparent

anschieben ['anʃi:bən] vt to push

Anschlag ['anʃla:k] m notice; (Attentat) attack; (COMM) estimate; (auf Klavier) touch; (Schreibmaschine) character; **a~en** ['anʃla:gən] (unreg) vt to put up; (beschädigen) to chip; (Akkord) to strike; (Kosten) to estimate ♦ vi to hit; (wirken) to have an effect; (Glocke) to ring; **an etw** akk **a~en** to hit against sth

anschließen ['anʃli:sən] (unreg) vt to connect up; (Sender) to link up ♦ vi:

an etw akk ~ to adjoin sth; (zeitlich) to follow sth ♦ vr: **sich jdm/etw ~** to join sb/sth; (beipflichten) to agree with sb/sth; **sich an etw** akk ~ to adjoin sth; **~d** adj adjacent; (zeitlich) subsequent ♦ adv afterwards

Anschluss ▲ ['anʃlʊs] m (ELEK, EISENB) connection; (von Wasser etc) supply; **im ~ an** +akk following; **~ finden** to make friends; **~flug** m connecting flight

anschmiegsam ['anʃmiːkzaːm] adj affectionate

anschnallen ['anʃnalən] vt to buckle on ♦ vr to fasten one's seat belt

anschneiden ['anʃnaidən] (unreg) vt to cut into; (Thema) to introduce

anschreiben ['anʃraibən] (unreg) vt to write (up); (COMM) to charge up; (benachrichtigen) to write to

anschreien ['anʃraiən] (unreg) vt to shout at

Anschrift ['anʃrɪft] f address

Anschuldigung ['anʃʊldɪgʊŋ] f accusation

anschwellen ['anʃvelən] (unreg) vi to swell (up)

anschwindeln ['anʃvindəln] vt to lie to

ansehen ['anzeːən] (unreg) vt to look at; **jdm etw ~** to see sth from sb's face; **jdn/etw als etw ~** to look on sb/sth as sth; **~ für** to consider; **A~** (-s) nt respect; (Ruf) reputation

ansehnlich ['anzeːnlɪç] adj fine-looking; (beträchtlich) considerable

ansetzen ['anzɛtsən] vt (festlegen) to fix; (entwickeln) to develop; (Fett) to put on; (Blätter) to grow; (zubereiten) to prepare ♦ vi (anfangen) to start, to begin; (Entwicklung) to set in; (dick werden) to put on weight ♦ vr (Rost etc) to start to develop; **~ an** +akk (anfügen) to fix on to; (anlegen, an Mund etc) to put to

Ansicht ['anzɪçt] f (Anblick) sight; (Meinung) view, opinion; **zur ~** on approval; **meiner ~ nach** in my opinion; **~skarte** f picture postcard; **~ssache** f matter of opinion

ansonsten [an'zɔnstən] adv otherwise

anspannen ['anʃpanən] vt to harness; (Muskel) to strain; **Anspannung** f strain

anspielen ['anʃpiːlən] vi (SPORT) to start play; **auf etw** akk ~ to refer od allude to sth

Anspielung f: **~ (auf** +akk) reference (to), allusion (to)

Anspitzer ['anʃpɪtsər] (-s, -) m pencil sharpener

Ansporn ['anʃpɔrn] (-(e)s) m incentive

Ansprache ['anʃpraːxə] f address

ansprechen ['anʃprɛçən] (unreg) vt to speak to; (bitten, gefallen) to appeal to ♦ vi: **(auf etw** akk) ~ to react to sth); **jdn auf etw** akk (hin) ~ to ask sb about sth; **~d** adj attractive

anspringen ['anʃprɪŋən] (unreg) vi (AUT) to start ♦ vt to jump at

Anspruch ['anʃprʊx] m (Recht): **~ (auf** +akk) claim (to); **hohe Ansprüche stellen/haben** to demand/expect a lot; **jdn/etw in ~ nehmen** to occupy sb/take up sth; **a~slos** adj undemanding; **a~svoll** adj demanding

anstacheln ['anʃtaxəln] vt to spur on

Anstalt ['anʃtalt] f (-, -en) f institution; **~en machen, etw zu tun** to prepare to do sth

Anstand ['anʃtant] m decency

anständig ['anʃtendɪç] adj decent; (umg) proper; (groß) considerable

anstandslos adv without any ado

anstarren ['anʃtarən] vt to stare at

anstatt [an'ʃtat] präp +gen instead of ♦ konj: **~ etw zu tun** instead of doing sth

Ansteck- ['anʃtek] zW: **a~en** vt to pin on; (MED) to infect; (Pfeife) to light;

(*Haus*) to set fire to ♦ *vr:* **ich habe mich bei ihm angesteckt** I caught it from him ♦ *vi* (*fig*) to be infectious; **a~end** *adj* infectious; **~ung** *f* infection

anstehen [ˈanʃteːən] (*unreg*) *vi* to queue (up) (*BRIT*), to line up (*US*)

ansteigen [ˈanʃtaɪɡən] *vt* (*Straße*) to climb; (*Gelände, Temperatur, Preise*) to rise

anstelle, an Stelle [anˈʃtɛlə] *präp +gen* in place of; **~n** [ˈanˌ-] *vt* (*einschalten*) to turn on; (*Arbeit geben*) to employ; (*machen*) to do ♦ *vr* to queue (up) (*BRIT*), to line up (*US*); (*umg*) to act

Anstellung *f* employment; (*Posten*) post, position

Anstieg [ˈanʃtiːk] (*-(e)s, -e*) *m* (*+gen*) climb; (*fig: von Preisen etc*) increase (in)

anstiften [ˈanʃtɪftən] *vt* (*Unglück*) to cause; **jdn zu etw ~** to put sb up to sth

anstimmen [ˈanʃtɪmən] *vt* (*Lied*) to strike up with; (*Geschrei*) to set up

Anstoß [ˈanʃtoːs] *m* impetus; (*Ärgernis*) offence; (*SPORT*) kick-off; **der erste ~** the initiative; **~ nehmen an** +*dat* to take offence at; **a~en** (*unreg*) *vt* to push; (*mit Fuß*) to kick ♦ *vi* to knock, to bump; (*mit der Zunge*) to lisp; (*mit Gläsern*): **a~en (auf** +*akk*) to drink (to), to drink a toast (to)

anstößig [ˈanʃtøːsɪç] *adj* offensive, indecent

anstreichen [ˈanʃtraɪçən] (*unreg*) *vt* to paint

anstrengen [ˈanʃtrɛŋən] *vt* to strain; (*JUR*) to bring ♦ *vr* to make an effort; **~d** *adj* tiring

Anstrengung *f* effort

Anstrich [ˈanʃtrɪç] *m* coat of paint

Ansturm [ˈanʃturm] *m* rush; (*MIL*) attack

Antarktis [antˈʔarktɪs] (*-*) *f* Antarctic

antasten [ˈantastən] *vt* to touch; (*Recht*) to infringe upon; (*Ehre*) to question

Anteil [ˈantaɪl] (*-s, -e*) *m* share; (*Mitge-*

fühl) sympathy; **~ nehmen (an** +*dat*) to share (in); (*sich interessieren*) to take an interest (in); **~nahme** (*-*) *f* sympathy

Antenne [anˈtɛnə] *f* aerial

Anti- [ˈanti] *in zW* anti; **~alko'holiker** *m* teetotaller; **a~autori'tär** *adj* antiauthoritarian; **~babypille** *f* contraceptive pill; **~biotikum** [antibiˈoːtikum] (*-s, -ka*) *nt* antibiotic

antik [anˈtiːk] *adj* antique; **A~e** *f* (*Zeitalter*) ancient world

Antiquariat [antikvariˈaːt] (*-(e)s, -e*) *nt* secondhand bookshop

Antiquitäten [antikviˈtɛːtən] *pl* antiques; **~händler** *m* antique dealer

Antrag [ˈantraːk] (*-(e)s, -träge*) *m* proposal; (*PARL*) motion; (*Gesuch*) application; **~steller(in)** (*-s, -*) *m(f)* claimant; (*für Kredit*) applicant

antreffen [ˈantrɛfən] (*unreg*) *vt* to meet

antreiben [ˈantraɪbən] (*unreg*) *vt* to drive on; (*Motor*) to drive

antreten [ˈantreːtən] (*unreg*) *vt* (*Amt*) to take up; (*Erbschaft*) to come into; (*Beweis*) to offer; (*Reise*) to start, to begin ♦ *vi* (*MIL*) to fall in; (*SPORT*) to line up; **gegen jdn ~** to play/fight (against) sb

Antrieb [ˈantriːp] *m* (*auch fig*) drive; **aus eigenem ~** of one's own accord

antrinken [ˈantrɪŋkən] (*unreg*) *vt* (*Flasche, Glas*) to start to drink from; **sich dat Mut/einen Rausch ~** to give o.s. Dutch courage/get drunk; **angetrunken sein** to be tipsy

Antritt [ˈantrɪt] *m* beginning, commencement; (*eines Amts*) taking up

antun [ˈantuːn] (*unreg*) *vt*: **jdm etw ~** to do sth to sb; **sich dat Zwang ~** to force o.s.; **sich dat etwas ~** to (try to) take one's own life

Antwort [ˈantvɔrt] (*-, -en*) *f* answer, reply; **a~en** *vi* to answer, to reply

anvertrauen [ˈanfɛrtraʊən] *vt*: **jdm etw ~** to entrust sb with sth; **sich jdm ~** to confide in sb

anwachsen [ˈanvaksən] (*unreg*) *vi* to grow; (*Pflanze*) to take root

Anwalt ['anvalt] (-(e)s, -wälte) m solicitor; lawyer; (fig) champion

Anwältin ['anvɛltɪn] f siehe **Anwalt**

Anwärter ['anvɛrtər] m candidate

anweisen ['anvaɪzən] (unreg) vt to instruct; (zuteilen) to assign

Anweisung f instruction; (COMM) remittance; (Postanweisung, Zahlungsanweisung) money order

anwend- ['anvɛnd] zW: **~bar** ['anvɛnt-] adj practicable, applicable; **~en** (unreg) vt to use, to employ; (Gesetz, Regel) to apply; **A~ung** f use; application

anwesend ['anveːzənt] adj present; **die A~en** those present

Anwesenheit f presence

anwidern ['anviːdərn] vt to disgust

Anwohner(in) ['anvoːnər(ɪn)] (-s, -) m(f) neighbour

Anzahl ['antsaːl] f: **~ (an** +dat) number (of); **a~en** vt to pay on account; **~ung** f deposit, payment on account

Anzeichen ['antsaɪçən] nt sign, indication

Anzeige ['antsaɪgə] f (Zeitungsanzeige) announcement; (Werbung) advertisement; (bei Polizei) report; **~ erstatten gegen jdn** to report sb (to the police); **a~n** vt (zu erkennen geben) to show; (bekannt geben) to announce; (bei Polizei) to report

anziehen ['antsiːən] (unreg) vt to attract; (Kleidung) to put on; (Mensch) to dress; (Seil) to pull tight; (Schraube) to tighten; (Knie) to draw up ♦ vr to get dressed; **~d** adj attractive

Anziehung f (Reiz) attraction; **~skraft** f power of attraction; (PHYS) force of gravitation

Anzug ['antsuːk] m suit; (Herankommen): **im ~ sein** to be approaching

anzüglich ['antsyːklɪç] adj (anstößig) offensive; **A~keit** f offensiveness; (Bemerkung) personal remark

anzünden ['antsʏndən] vt to light

anzweifeln ['antsvaɪfəln] vt to doubt

apathisch [a'paːtɪʃ] adj apathetic

Apfel ['apfəl] (-s, ⸚) m apple; **~saft** m apple juice; **~sine** [-'ziːnə] f orange; **~wein** m cider

Apostel [a'pɔstəl] (-s, -) m apostle

Apotheke [apo'teːkə] f chemist's (shop), drugstore (US); **a~npflichtig** [-pflɪçtɪç] adj available only at a chemist's shop (BRIT) or pharmacy; **~r(in)** (-s, -) m(f) chemist, druggist (US)

> **Apotheke**
>
> The **Apotheke** is a pharmacy selling medicines available only on prescription and toiletries. The pharmacist is qualified to give advice on medicines and treatments.

Apparat [apa'raːt] (-(e)s, -e) m piece of apparatus; camera; telephone; (RADIO, TV) set; **am ~!** speaking!; **~ur** [-'tuːr] f apparatus

Appartement [apart(ə)'maː] (-s, -s) nt flat

appellieren [ape'liːrən] vi: **~ (an** +akk) to appeal (to)

Appetit [ape'tiːt] (-(e)s, -e) m appetite; **guten ~!** enjoy your meal; **a~lich** adj appetizing; **~losigkeit** f lack of appetite

Applaus [a'plaus] (-es, -e) m applause

Aprikose [apri'koːzə] f apricot

April [a'prɪl] (-(s), -e) m April

Aquarell [akva'rɛl] (-s, -e) nt watercolour

Äquator [ɛ'kvaːtor] (-s, -en) m equator

Arab- ['arap] zW: **~er(in)** (-s, -) m(f) Arab; **~ien** [a'raːbiən] (-s) nt Arabia; **a~isch** [a'raːbɪʃ] adj Arabian

Arbeit ['arbaɪt] (-, -en) f work no art; (Stelle) job; (Erzeugnis) piece of work; (wissenschaftliche) dissertation; (Klassenarbeit) test; **das war eine ~** that was a hard job; **a~en** vi to work ♦ vt to work, to make; **~er(in)** (-s, -) m(f) worker; (ungelernt) labourer; **~erschaft** f workers pl, labour force; **~geber** (-s, -) m employer; **~nehmer** (-s, -) m employee

Arbeits- in zW labour; **a~am** adj industrious; **~amt** nt employment exchange; **~erlaubnis** f work permit; **a~fähig** adj fit for work, able-bodied; **~gang** m operation; **~kräfte** pl (Mitarbeiter) workforce; **a~los** adj unemployed, out-of-work; **~lose(r)** f(m) unemployed person; **~losigkeit** f unemployment; **~markt** m job market; **~platz** m job; place of work; **a~scheu** adj workshy; **~tag** m work(ing) day; **a~unfähig** adj unfit for work; **~zeit** f working hours pl; **~zimmer** nt study

Archäologe [arçeo'lo:gə] (-n, -n) m archaeologist

Architekt(in) [arçi'tɛkt] (-en, -en) m(f) architect; **~ur** [-'tu:r] f architecture

Archiv [ar'çi:f] (-s, -e) nt archive

arg [ark] adj bad, awful ♦ adv awfully, very

Argentinien [argɛn'ti:niən] (-s) nt Argentina, the Argentine

argentinisch adj Argentinian

Ärger ['ɛrgər] (-s) m (Wut) anger; (Unannehmlichkeit) trouble; **ä~lich** adj (zornig) angry; (lästig) annoying, aggravating; **ä~n** vt to annoy ♦ vr to get annoyed

arg- zW: **~listig** adj cunning, insidious; **~los** adj guileless, innocent

Argument [argu'mɛnt] nt argument

argwöhnisch adj suspicious

Arie ['a:riə] f aria

Aristokrat [aristo'kra:t] (-en, -en) m aristocrat; **~ie** [-'ti:] f aristocracy

Arktis ['arktis] (-) f Arctic

Arm [arm] (-(e)s, -e) m arm; (Flussarm) branch

arm adj poor

Armatur [arma'tu:r] f (ELEK) armature;

~enbrett nt instrument panel; (AUT) dashboard

Armband nt bracelet; **~uhr** f (wrist) watch

Arme(r) f(m) poor man (woman); **die ~n** the poor

Armee [ar'me:] f army

Ärmel ['ɛrmǝl] (-s, -) m sleeve; **etw aus dem ~ schütteln** (fig) to produce sth just like that; **~kanal** m English Channel

ärmlich ['ɛrmlıç] adj poor

armselig adj wretched, miserable

Armut ['armu:t] (-) f poverty

Aroma [a'ro:ma] (-s, Aromen) nt aroma; **~therapie** f aromatherapy; **a~tisch** [aro'ma:tıʃ] adj aromatic

arrangieren [arã'ʒi:rən] vt to arrange ♦ vr to come to an arrangement

Arrest [a'rɛst] (-(e)s, -e) m detention

arrogant [aro'gant] adj arrogant

Arsch [arʃ] (-es, ²e) (umg!) m arse (BRIT), ass (US!)

Art [a:rt] (-, -en) f (Weise) way; (Sorte) kind, sort; (BIOL) species; **eine ~ (von)** Frucht a kind of fruit; **Häuser aller ~** houses of all kinds; **es ist nicht seine ~, das zu tun** it's not like him to do that; **ich mache das auf meine ~** I do that my (own) way

Arterie [ar'te:riə] f artery; **~nverkalkung** f arteriosclerosis

artig ['a:rtıç] adj good, well-behaved

Artikel [ar'ti:kəl] (-s, -) m article

Artillerie [artılə'ri:] f artillery

Artischocke [artı'ʃɔkə] f artichoke

Artist(in) [ar'tıst(ın)] (-en, -en) m(f) (circus/variety) artiste or performer

Arznei [a:rts'nai] f medicine; **~mittel** nt medicine, medicament

Arzt [a:rtst] (-es, ²e) m doctor; **~helferin** f (doctor's) receptionist

Ärztin [ɛ:rtstın] f woman doctor

ärztlich ['ɛ:rtstlıç] adj medical

As △ [as] (-ses, -se) nt = **Ass**

Asche ['aʃə] f (-, -n) ash, cinder

Aschen- zW: **~bahn** f cinder track;

~**becher** m ashtray
Aschermittwoch m Ash Wednesday
Äser [ˈɛːzər] pl von **Aas**
Asiat(in) [aziˈaːt(ɪn)] (-en, -en) m(f) Asian; **asiatisch** [-ˈaːtɪʃ] adj Asian
Asien [ˈaːziən] (-s) nt Asia
asozial [ˈazotsiaːl] adj antisocial; (Familien) asocial
Aspekt [asˈpɛkt] (-(e)s, -e) m aspect
Asphalt [asˈfalt] (-(e)s, -e) m asphalt; **a~ieren** vt to asphalt
Ass ▲ (-es, -e) nt ace
aß etc [aːs] vb siehe **essen**
Assistent(in) [asɪsˈtɛnt(ɪn)] m(f) assistant
Assoziation [asotsiatsiˈoːn] f association
Ast [ast] (-(e)s, ̈-e) m bough, branch
ästhetisch [ɛsˈteːtɪʃ] adj aesthetic
Asthma [ˈastma] (-s) nt asthma; **~tiker(in)** (-s, -) m(f) asthmatic
Astro- [astro] zW: ~**'loge** (-n, -n) m astrologer; ~**lo'gie** f astrology; ~**'naut** (-en, -en) m astronaut; ~**'nom** (-en, -en) m astronomer; ~**no'mie** f astronomy
Asyl [aˈzyːl] (-s, -e) nt asylum; (Heim) home; (Obdachlosenasyl) shelter; ~**ant(in)** [azyˈlant(ɪn)] (-en, -en) m(f) asylum-seeker
Atelier [ateliˈeː] (-s, -s) nt studio
Atem [ˈaːtəm] (-s) m breath; **den ~ anhalten** to hold one's breath; **außer ~** out of breath; **a~beraubend** adj breathtaking; **a~los** adj breathless; ~**not** f difficulty in breathing; ~**pause** f breather; ~**zug** m breath
Atheismus [ateˈɪsmus] m atheism
Atheist m atheist; **a~isch** adj atheistic
Athen [aˈteːn] (-s) nt Athens
Äthiopien [ɛtiˈoːpiən] (-s) nt Ethiopia
Athlet [atˈleːt] (-en, -en) m athlete
Atlantik [atˈlantɪk] (-s) nt Atlantic (Ocean)
Atlas [ˈatlas] (- od -ses, -se od Atlan-

ten) m atlas
atmen [ˈaːtmən] vt, vi to breathe
Atmosphäre [atmoˈsfɛːrə] f atmosphere; **atmosphärisch** adj atmospheric
Atmung [ˈaːtmʊŋ] f respiration
Atom [aˈtoːm] (-s, -e) nt atom; **a~ar** adj atomic; ~**bombe** f atom bomb; ~**energie** f atomic od nuclear energy; ~**kern** m atomic nucleus; ~**kraftwerk** nt nuclear power station; ~**krieg** m nuclear od atomic war; ~**müll** m atomic waste; ~**strom** m (electricity generated by) nuclear power; ~**versuch** m atomic test; ~**waffen** pl atomic weapons; **a~waffenfrei** adj nuclear-free; ~**zeitalter** nt atomic age
Attentat [atɛnˈtaːt] (-(e)s, -e) nt: ~ **(auf** +akk) (attempted) assassination (of)
Attentäter [atɛnˈtɛːtər] m (would-be) assassin
Attest [aˈtɛst] (-(e)s, -e) nt certificate
Attraktion [atraktsiˈoːn] f (Tourismus, Zirkus) attraction
attraktiv [atrakˈtiːf] adj attractive
Attrappe [aˈtrapə] f dummy
Attribut [atriˈbuːt] (-(e)s, -e) nt (GRAM) attribute
ätzen [ˈɛtsən] vi to be caustic; ~**d** adj (Säure) corrosive; (fig: Spott) cutting
au [au] excl ouch!; ~ **ja!** oh yes!
Aubergine [obɛrˈʒiːnə] f aubergine, eggplant

SCHLÜSSELWORT

auch [aux] adv 1 (ebenfalls) also, too, as well; **das ist auch schön** that's nice too od as well; **er kommt - ich auch** he's coming - so am I, me too; **auch nicht** not ... either; **ich auch nicht** nor I, me neither; **oder auch** or; **auch das noch!** that as well too!

2 (selbst, sogar) even; **auch wenn das Wetter schlecht ist** even if the

weather is bad; **ohne auch nur zu fragen** without even asking

3 (*wirklich*) really; **du siehst müde aus - bin ich auch** you look tired - **so** I am; **so sieht es auch aus** it looks like it too

4 (*auch immer*): **wer auch** whoever; **was auch** whatever; **wie dem auch sei** be that as it may; **wie sehr er sich auch bemühte** however much he tried

---

SCHLÜSSELWORT

---

auf [auf] *präp +dat (wo?)* on; **auf dem Tisch** on the table; **auf der Reise** on the way; **auf der Post/dem Fest** at the post office/party; **auf der Straße** on the road; **auf dem Land/der ganzen Welt** in the country/the whole world

♦ *präp +akk* 1 (*wohin?*) on(to); **auf den Tisch** on(to) the table; **auf die Post gehen** go to the post office; **auf das Land** into the country; **etw auf einen Zettel schreiben** to write sth on a piece of paper

2: **auf Deutsch** in German; **auf Lebenszeit** for my/his lifetime; **bis auf ihn** except for him; **auf einmal** at once; **auf seinen Vorschlag (hin)** at his suggestion

♦ *adv* 1 (*offen*) open; **auf sein** (*umg*) (*Tür, Geschäft*) to be open; **das Fenster ist auf** the window is open

2 (*hinauf*) up; **auf und ab** up and down; **auf und davon** up and away; **auf!** (*los!*) come on!

3 (*aufgestanden*) up; **auf sein** to be up; **ist er schon auf?** is he up yet?

♦ *konj*: **auf dass** (old) that

aufatmen ['aufʔaːtmən] *vi* to heave a sigh of relief

aufbahren ['aufbaːrən] *vt* to lay out

Aufbau ['aufbau] *m* (*Bauen*) building, construction; (*Struktur*) structure; (*aufgebautes Teil*) superstructure; **a~en** *vt* to erect, to build (up); (*Existenz*) to make; (*gestalten*) to construct; **a~en (auf** +*dat*) (*gründen*) to found *od* base (on)

aufbauschen ['aufbauʃən] *vt* to puff out; (*fig*) to exaggerate

aufbekommen ['aufbəkɔmən] (*unreg*) *vt* (*öffnen*) to get open; (*Hausaufgaben*) to be given

aufbessern ['aufbɛsərn] *vt* (*Gehalt*) to increase

aufbewahren ['aufbəvaːrən] *vt* to keep; (*Gepäck*) to put in the left-luggage office (*BRIT*) *od* baggage check (*US*)

Aufbewahrung f (*safe*)keeping; (*Gepäckaufbewahrung*) left-luggage office (*BRIT*), baggage check (*US*)

aufbieten ['aufbiːtən] (*unreg*) *vt* (*Kraft*) to summon (up); (*Armee, Polizei*) to mobilize

aufblasen ['aufblaːzən] (*unreg*) *vt* to blow up, to inflate ♦ *vr* (*umg*) to become bigheaded

aufbleiben ['aufblaibən] (*unreg*) *vi* (*Laden*) to remain open; (*Person*) to stay up

aufblenden ['aufblɛndən] *vt* (*Scheinwerfer*) to switch on full beam ♦ *vi* (*Fahrer*) to have the lights on full beam; (*AUT: Scheinwerfer*) to be on full beam

aufblicken ['aufblikən] *vi* to look up; **~ zu** to look up at; (*fig*) to look up to

aufblühen ['aufblyːən] *vi* to blossom, to flourish

aufbrauchen ['aufbrauxən] *vt* to use up

aufbrausen ['aufbrauzən] *vi* (*fig*) to flare up; **~d** *adj* hot-tempered

aufbrechen ['aufbrɛçən] (*unreg*) *vt* to break *od* prise (*BRIT*) open ♦ *vi* to burst open; (*gehen*) to start, to set off

aufbringen ['aufbriŋən] (*unreg*) *vt* (*öffnen*) to open; (*in Mode*) to bring into fashion; (*beschaffen*) to procure;

(FIN) to raise; (ärgern) to irritate; **Verständnis für etw ~** to be able to understand sth

Aufbruch ['aʊfbrʊx] *m* departure

aufbrühen ['aʊfbryːən] *vt* (Tee) to make

aufbürden ['aʊfbʏrdən] *vt*: **jdm etw ~** to burden sb with sth

aufdecken ['aʊfdɛkən] *vt* to uncover

aufdrängen ['aʊfdrɛŋən] *vt*: **jdm etw ~** to force sth on sb ♦ *vi* (Mensch): **sich jdm ~** to intrude on sb

aufdrehen ['aʊfdreːən] *vt* (Wasserhahn etc) to turn on; (Ventil) to open up

aufdringlich ['aʊfdrɪŋlɪç] *adj* pushy

aufeinander [aʊfɛlaɪˈnandɐ] *adv* on top of each other; (schießen) at each other; (vertrauen) each other; **~ folgen** to follow one another; **~ folgend** consecutive; **~ prallen** to hit one another

Aufenthalt ['aʊfɛnthalt] *m* stay; (Verzögerung) delay; (EISENB: Halten) stop; (Ort) haunt

Aufenthaltserlaubnis *f* residence permit

auferlegen ['aʊfɛɐleːgən] *vt*: **(jdm) ~** to impose (upon sb)

Auferstehung ['aʊfɛɐˈʃteːʊŋ] *f* resurrection

aufessen ['aʊfɛsən] (*unreg*) *vt* to eat up

auffahr- ['aʊffaːɐ] *zW*: **~en** (*unreg*) *vi* (herankommen) to draw up; (hochfahren) to jump up; (wütend werden) to flare up; (in den Himmel) to ascend ♦ *vt* (Kanonen, Geschütz) to bring up; **~en auf** +*akk* (Auto) to run up or crash into; **~end** *adj* hot-tempered; **A~t** *f* (Hausauffahrt) drive; (Autobahnauffahrt) slip road (BRIT), (freeway) entrance (US); **A~unfall** *m* pile-up

auffallen ['aʊffalən] (*unreg*) *vi* to be noticeable; **jdm ~** to strike sb

auffällig ['aʊffɛlɪç] *adj* conspicuous, striking

auffangen ['aʊffaŋən] (*unreg*) *vt* to catch; (Funkspruch) to intercept; (Preise) to peg

auffassen ['aʊffasən] *vt* to understand, to comprehend; (auslegen) to see, to view

Auffassung *f* (Meinung) opinion; (Auslegung) view, concept; (auch: **~sgabe**) grasp

auffindbar ['aʊffɪntbaːɐ] *adj* to be found

auffordern ['aʊffɔrdərn] *vt* (befehlen) to call upon, to order; (bitten) to ask

Aufforderung *f* (Befehl) order; (Einladung) invitation

auffrischen ['aʊffrɪʃən] *vt* to freshen up; (Kenntnisse) to brush up; (Erinnerungen) to reawaken ♦ *vi* (Wind) to freshen

aufführen ['aʊffyːrən] *vt* (THEAT) to perform; (in einem Verzeichnis) to list, to specify ♦ *vr* (sich benehmen) to behave

Aufführung *f* (THEAT) performance; (Liste) specification

Aufgabe ['aʊfgaːbə] *f* task; (SCH) exercise; (Hausaufgabe) homework; (Verzicht) giving up; (von Gepäck) registration; (von Post) posting; (von Inserat) insertion

Aufgang ['aʊfgaŋ] *m* ascent; (Sonnenaufgang) rise; (Treppe) staircase

aufgeben ['aʊfgeːbən] (*unreg*) *vt* (verzichten) to give up; (Paket) to send, to post; (Gepäck) to register; (Bestellung) to give; (Inserat) to insert; (Rätsel, Problem) to set ♦ *vi* to give up

Aufgebot ['aʊfgəboːt] *nt* supply; (Eheaufgebot) banns *pl*

aufgedunsen ['aʊfgədʊnzən] *adj* swollen, puffed up

aufgehen ['aʊfgeːən] (*unreg*) *vi* (Sonne, Teig) to rise; (sich öffnen) to open; (klar werden) to become clear; (MATH) to come out exactly; **~ (in** +*dat*) (sich widmen) to be absorbed (in); **in Rauch/**

Flammen ~ to go up in smoke/flames

aufgelegt ['aufgəleːkt] adj: **gut/ schlecht** ~ **sein** to be in a good/bad mood; **zu etw** ~ **sein** to be in the mood for sth

aufgeregt ['aufgəreːkt] adj excited

aufgeschlossen ['aufgəʃlɔsən] adj open, open-minded

aufgeweckt ['aufgəvɛkt] adj bright, intelligent

aufgießen ['aufgiːsən] (unreg) vt (Wasser) to pour over; (Tee) to infuse

aufgreifen ['aufgraifən] (unreg) vt (Thema) to take up; (Verdächtige) to pick up, to seize

aufgrund, auf Grund [auf'grunt] präp +gen on the basis of; (wegen) because of

aufhaben ['aufhaːbən] (unreg) vt to have on; (Arbeit) to have to do

aufhalsen ['aufhalzən] (umg) vt: **jdm etw** ~ to saddle od lumber sb with sth

aufhalten ['aufhaltən] (unreg) vt (Person) to detain; (Entwicklung) to check; (Tür, Hand) to hold open; (Augen) to keep open ♦ vr (wohnen) to live; (bleiben) to stay; **sich mit etw** ~ to waste time over sth

aufhängen ['aufhɛŋən] (unreg) vt (Wäsche) to hang up; (Menschen) to hang ♦ vr to hang o.s.

Aufhänger (-s, -) m (am Mantel) loop; (fig) peg

aufheben ['aufheːbən] (unreg) vt (hochheben) to raise, to lift; (Sitzung) to wind up; (Urteil) to annul; (Gesetz) to repeal, to abolish; (aufbewahren) to keep ♦ vr to cancel itself out; **bei jdm gut aufgehoben sein** to be well looked after at sb's; **viel A~(s) machen (von)** to make a fuss (about)

aufheitern ['aufhaitərn] vt, vr (Himmel, Miene) to brighten; (Mensch) to cheer up

aufhellen ['aufhɛlən] vt, vr to clear up; (Farbe, Haare) to lighten

aufhetzen ['aufhɛtsən] vt to stir up

aufholen ['aufhoːlən] vt to make up ♦ vi to catch up

aufhorchen ['aufhɔrçən] vi to prick up one's ears

aufhören ['aufhøːrən] vi to stop; ~, **etw zu tun** to stop doing sth

aufklappen ['aufklapən] vt to open

aufklären ['aufklɛːrən] vt (Geheimnis etc) to clear up; (Person) to enlighten; (sexuell) to tell the facts of life to; (MIL) to reconnoitre ♦ vr to clear up

Aufklärung f (von Geheimnis) clearing up; (Unterrichtung, Zeitalter) enlightenment; (sexuelle) sex education; (MIL, AVIAT) reconnaissance

aufkleben ['aufkleːbən] vt to stick on; **Aufkleber (-s, -)** m sticker

aufknöpfen ['aufknœpfən] vt to unbutton

aufkommen ['aufkɔmən] (unreg) vi (Wind) to come up; (Zweifel, Gefühl) to arise; (Mode) to start; **für jdn/etw** ~ to be liable od responsible for sb/sth

aufladen ['auflaːdən] (unreg) vt to load

Auflage ['auflaːgə] f edition; (Zeitung) circulation; (Bedingung) condition

auflassen ['auflasən] (unreg) vt (offen) to leave open; (aufgesetzt) to leave on

auflauern ['auflauərn] vi: **jdm** ~ to lie in wait for sb

Auflauf ['auflauf] m (KOCH) pudding; (Menschenauflauf) crowd

aufleben ['aufleːbən] vi (Mensch, Gespräch) to liven up; (Interesse) to revive

auflegen ['aufleːgən] vt to put on; (Telefon) to hang up; (TYP) to print

auflehnen ['aufleːnən] vt to lean on ♦ vr to rebel

Auflehnung f rebellion

auflesen ['aufleːzən] (unreg) vt to pick up

aufleuchten ['auflɔyçtən] vi to light up

auflisten ['auflistən] vt to list

auflockern ['auflɔkərn] vt to loosen; (fig: Eintönigkeit etc) to liven up

auflösen ['aufløːzən] vt to dissolve;

(*Haare etc*) to loosen; (*Missverständnis*) to sort out ♦ *vr* to dissolve; to come undone; to be resolved; (**in Tränen**) **aufgelöst sein** to be in tears

Auflösung *f* dissolving; (*fig*) solution

aufmachen ['aufmaxən] *vt* to open; (*Kleidung*) to undo; (*zurechtmachen*) to do up ♦ *vr* to set out

Aufmachung *f* (*Kleidung*) outfit, get-up; (*Gestaltung*) format

aufmerksam ['aufmɛrkza:m] *adj* attentive; **jdn auf etw** *akk* ~ **machen** to point sth out to sb; **A~keit** *f* attention, attentiveness

aufmuntern ['aufmʊntərn] *vt* (*ermutigen*) to encourage; (*erheitern*) to cheer up

Aufnahme ['aufna:mə] *f* reception; (*Beginn*) beginning; (*in Verein etc*) admission; (*in Liste etc*) inclusion; (*Notieren*) taking down; (*PHOT*) shot; (*auf Tonband etc*) recording; **a~fähig** *adj* receptive; **~prüfung** *f* entrance test

aufnehmen ['aufne:mən] (*unreg*) *vt* to receive; (*hochheben*) to pick up; (*beginnen*) to take up; (*in Verein etc*) to admit; (*in Liste etc*) to include; (*fassen*) to hold; (*notieren*) to take down; (*fotografieren*) to photograph; (*auf Tonband, Platte*) to record; (*FIN: leihen*) to take out; **es mit jdm** ~ **können** to be able to compete with sb

aufopfern ['aufɔpfərn] *vt, vr* to sacrifice; **~d** *adj* selfless

aufpassen ['aufpasən] *vi* (*aufmerksam sein*) to pay attention; (*auf jdn/etw* ~ to look after or watch sb/sth; **aufgepasst!** look out!

Aufprall ['aufpral] (-**s**, -**e**) *m* impact; **a~en** *vi* to hit, to strike

Aufpreis ['aufprais] *m* extra charge

aufpumpen ['aufpʊmpən] *vt* to pump up

aufräumen ['aufrɔʏmən] *vt, vi* (*Dinge*) to clear away; (*Zimmer*) to tidy up

aufrecht ['aufrɛçt] *adj* (*auch fig*) upright; **~erhalten** (*unreg*) *vt* to maintain

aufreg- ['aufre:g] *zW*: **~en** *vt* to excite ♦ *vr* to get excited; **~end** *adj* exciting; **A~ung** *f* excitement

aufreibend ['aufraibənd] *adj* strenuous

aufreißen ['aufraisən] (*unreg*) *vt* (*Umschlag*) to tear open; (*Augen*) to open wide; (*Tür*) to throw open; (*Straße*) to take up

aufreizen ['aufraitsən] *vt* to incite, to stir up; **~d** *adj* exciting, stimulating

aufrichten ['aufrɪçtən] *vt* to put up, to erect; (*moralisch*) to console ♦ *vr* to rise; (*moralisch*): **sich** ~ (**an** +*dat*) to take heart (from)

aufrichtig ['aufrɪçtɪç] *adj* sincere, honest; **A~keit** *f* sincerity

aufrücken ['aufrʏkən] *vi* to move up; (*beruflich*) to be promoted

Aufruf ['aufru:f] *m* summons; (*zur Hilfe*) call; (*des Namens*) calling out; **a~en** (*unreg*) *vt* (*Namen*) to call out; (*auffordern*): **jdn a~en** (**zu**) to call upon sb (for)

Aufruhr ['aufru:r] (-(**e**)**s**, -**e**) *m* uprising, revolt

aufrührerisch ['aufry:rərɪʃ] *adj* rebellious

aufrunden ['aufrʊndən] *vt* (*Summe*) to round up

Aufrüstung ['aufrʏstʊŋ] *f* rearmament

aufrütteln ['aufrʏtəln] *vt* (*auch fig*) to shake up

aufs [aufs] = **auf das**

aufsagen ['aufza:gən] *vt* (*Gedicht*) to recite

aufsässig ['aufzɛsɪç] *adj* rebellious

Aufsatz ['aufzats] *m* (*Geschriebenes*) essay; (*auf Schrank etc*) top

aufsaugen ['aufzaugən] (*unreg*) *vt* to soak up

aufschauen ['aufʃauən] *vi* to look up

aufscheuchen ['aufʃɔʏçən] *vt* to scare *od* frighten away

Spelling Reform: ▲ *new spelling* △ *old spelling* (*to be phased out*)

aufschieben ['aʊfʃiːbən] (unreg) vt to push over; (verzögern) to put off, to postpone

Aufschlag ['aʊfʃlaːk] m (Ärmelaufschlag) cuff; (Jackenaufschlag) lapel; (Hosenaufschlag) turn-up; (Aufprall) impact; (Preisaufschlag) surcharge; (Tennis) service; **a~en** [-gən] (unreg) vt (öffnen) to open; (verwunden) to cut; (hochschlagen) to turn up; (aufbauen: Zelt, Lager) to erect; (Wohnsitz) to take up ♦ vi (aufprallen) to hit; (teurer werden) to go up; (Tennis) to serve

aufschließen ['aʊfʃliːsən] (unreg) vt to open up, to unlock ♦ vi (aufrücken) to close up

aufschlussreich ▲ adj informative, illuminating

aufschnappen ['aʊfʃnapən] vt (umg) to pick up ♦ vi to fly open

aufschneiden ['aʊfʃnaɪdən] (unreg) vt (Brot) to cut up; (MED) to lance ♦ vi to brag

Aufschneider (-s, -) m boaster, braggart

Aufschnitt ['aʊfʃnɪt] m (slices of) cold meat

aufschrauben ['aʊfʃraʊbən] vt (festschrauben) to screw on; (lösen) to unscrew

aufschrecken ['aʊfʃrɛkən] vt to startle ♦ vi (unreg) to start up

aufschreiben ['aʊfʃraɪbən] (unreg) vt to write down

aufschreien ['aʊfʃraɪən] (unreg) vi to cry out

Aufschrift ['aʊfʃrɪft] f (Inschrift) inscription; (auf Etikett) label

Aufschub ['aʊfʃuːp] (-(e)s, -schübe) m delay, postponement

Aufschwung ['aʊfʃvʊŋ] m (Elan) boost; (wirtschaftlich) upturn, boom; (SPORT) circle

aufsehen ['aʊfzeːən] (unreg) vi to look up; ~ **zu** to look up at; (fig) to look up to; **A~** (-s) nt sensation, stir; ~ **erre-**

gend sensational

Aufseher(in) (-s, -) m(f) guard; (im Betrieb) supervisor; (Museumsaufseher) attendant; (Parkaufseher) keeper

auf sein siehe **auf**

aufsetzen ['aʊfzɛtsən] vt to put on; (Dokument) to draw up ♦ vr to sit up(right) ♦ vi (Flugzeug) to touch down

Aufsicht ['aʊfzɪçt] f supervision; **die ~ haben** to be in charge

Aufsichtsrat m (supervisory) board

aufsitzen ['aʊfzɪtsən] (unreg) vi (aufrecht hinsitzen) to sit up; (aufs Pferd, Motorrad) to mount, to get on; (Schiff) to run aground; **jdm ~** (umg) to be taken in by sb

aufsparen ['aʊfʃpaːrən] vt to save (up)

aufsperren ['aʊfʃpɛrən] vt to unlock; (Mund) to open wide

aufspielen ['aʊfʃpiːlən] vr to show off

aufspießen ['aʊfʃpiːsən] vt to spear

aufspringen ['aʊfʃprɪŋən] (unreg) vi (hochspringen) to jump up; (sich öffnen) to spring open; (Hände, Lippen) to become chapped; **auf etw** akk ~ to jump onto sth

aufspüren ['aʊfʃpyːrən] vt to track down, to trace

aufstacheln ['aʊfʃtaxəln] vt to incite

Aufstand ['aʊfʃtant] m insurrection, rebellion; **aufständisch** ['aʊfʃtɛndɪʃ] adj rebellious, mutinous

aufstehen ['aʊfʃteːən] (unreg) vi to get up; (Tür) to be open

aufsteigen ['aʊfʃtaɪgən] (unreg) vi (hochsteigen) to climb; (Rauch) to rise; **auf etw** akk ~ to get onto sth

aufstellen ['aʊfʃtɛlən] vt (aufrecht stellen) to put up; (aufreihen) to line up; (nominieren) to nominate; (formulieren: Programm etc) to draw up; (leisten: Rekord) to set up

Aufstellung f (SPORT) line-up; (Liste) list

Aufstieg ['aʊfʃtiːk] (-(e)s, -e) m (auf Berg) ascent; (Fortschritt) rise; (beruflich, SPORT) promotion

aufstocken ['aʊfʃtɔkən] vt (Kapital) to increase

aufstoßen ['aʊfʃtoːsən] (unreg) vt to push open ♦ vi to belch

aufstützen ['aʊfʃtʏtsən] vt (Körperteil) to prop, to lean; (Person) to prop up ♦ vr: **sich auf etw** akk ~ to lean on sth

aufsuchen ['aʊfzuːxən] vt (besuchen) to visit; (konsultieren) to consult

Auftakt ['aʊftakt] m (MUS) upbeat; (fig) prelude

auftanken ['aʊftaŋkən] vi to get petrol (BRIT) od gas (US) ♦ vt to refuel

auftauchen ['aʊftaʊxən] vi to appear; (aus Wasser etc) to emerge; (U-Boot) to surface; (Zweifel) to arise

auftauen ['aʊftaʊən] vt to thaw ♦ vi to thaw; (fig) to relax

aufteilen ['aʊftaɪlən] vt to divide up; (Raum) to partition; **Aufteilung** f division; partition

Auftrag ['aʊftraːk] (-(e)s, -träge) m order; (Anweisung) commission; (Aufgabe) mission; **im ~ von** on behalf of; **a~en** [-gən] (unreg) vt (Essen) to serve; (Farbe) to put on; (Kleidung) to wear out; **jdm etw a~en** to tell sb sth; **dick a~en** (fig) to exaggerate; **~geber** (-s, -) m (COMM) purchaser, customer

auftreiben ['aʊftraɪbən] (unreg) vt (umg: beschaffen) to raise

auftreten ['aʊftreːtən] (unreg) vt to kick open ♦ vi to appear; (mit Füßen) to tread; (sich verhalten) to behave; **A~** (-s) nt (Vorkommen) appearance; (Benehmen) behaviour

Auftrieb ['aʊftriːp] m (PHYS) buoyancy, lift; (fig) impetus

Auftritt ['aʊftrɪt] m (des Schauspielers) entrance; (Szene: auch fig) scene

aufwachen ['aʊfvaxən] vi to wake up

aufwachsen ['aʊfvaksən] (unreg) vi to grow up

Aufwand ['aʊfvant] (-(e)s) m expenditure; (Kosten auch) expense; (Luxus)

aufwändig ▲ ['aʊfvɛndɪç] adj costly

aufwärmen ['aʊfvɛrmən] vt to warm up; (alte Geschichten) to rake up

aufwärts ['aʊfvɛrts] adv upwards; **A~entwicklung** f upward trend

Aufwasch ['aʊfvaʃ] m washing-up

aufwecken ['aʊfvɛkən] vt to wake up, to waken up

aufweisen ['aʊfvaɪzən] (unreg) vt to show

aufwenden ['aʊfvɛndən] (unreg) vt to expend; (Geld) to spend; (Sorgfalt) to devote

aufwendig adj siehe **aufwändig**

aufwerfen ['aʊfvɛrfən] (unreg) vt (Fenster etc) to throw open; (Probleme) to throw up, to raise

aufwerten ['aʊfvɛrtən] vt (FIN) to revalue; (fig) to raise in value

aufwickeln ['aʊfvɪkəln] vt (aufrollen) to roll up; (umg: Haar) to put in curlers

aufwiegen ['aʊfviːgən] (unreg) vt to make up for

Aufwind ['aʊfvɪnt] m up-current

aufwirbeln ['aʊfvɪrbəln] vt to whirl up; **Staub ~** (fig) to create a stir

aufwischen ['aʊfvɪʃən] vt to wipe up

aufzählen ['aʊftsɛːlən] vt to list

aufzeichnen ['aʊftsaɪçnən] vt to sketch; (schriftlich) to jot down; (auf Band) to record

Aufzeichnung f (schriftlich) note; (Tonbandaufzeichnung) recording; (Filmaufzeichnung) record

aufzeigen ['aʊftsaɪgən] vt to show, to demonstrate

aufziehen ['aʊftsiːən] (unreg) vt (hochziehen) to raise, to draw up; (öffnen) to pull open; (Uhr) to wind; (umg: necken) to tease; (großziehen: Kinder) to raise, to bring up; (Tiere) to rear

Aufzug ['aʊftsuːk] m (Fahrstuhl) lift, elevator; (Aufmarsch) procession, parade; (Kleidung) get-up; (THEAT) act

---

Spelling Reform: ▲ *new spelling* △ *old spelling (to be phased out)*

aufzwingen ['aʊftsvɪŋən] (unreg) vt: **jdm etw ~** to force sth upon sb

Augapfel ['aʊkʔapfəl] m eyeball; (fig) apple of one's eye

Auge ['aʊgə] (-s, -n) nt eye; (Fettauge) globule of fat; **unter vier ~n** in private

Augen- zW: **~blick** m moment; **im ~blick** at the moment; **a~blicklich** adj (sofort) instantaneous; (gegenwärtig) present; **~braue** f eyebrow; **~optiker(in)** m(f) optician; **~weide** f sight for sore eyes; **~zeuge** m eye witness

August [aʊ'gʊst] (-(e)s od -, -e) m August

Auktion [aʊktsi'oːn] f auction

Aula ['aʊla] (-, Aulen od -s) f assembly hall

SCHLÜSSELWORT

aus [aʊs] präp +dat **1** (räumlich) out of; (von … her) from; **er ist aus Berlin** he's from Berlin; **aus dem Fenster** out of the window

2 (gemacht/hergestellt aus) made of; **ein Herz aus Stein** a heart of stone

3 (auf Ursache deutend) out of; **aus Mitleid** out of sympathy; **aus Erfahrung** from experience; **aus Spaß** for fun

4: aus ihr wird nie etwas she'll never get anywhere

♦ adv **1** (zu Ende) finished, over; **aus sein** to be over; **aus und vorbei** over and done with

2 (ausgeschaltet, ausgezogen) out; (Aufschrift an Geräten) off; **aus sein** (nicht brennen) to be out; (abgeschaltet sein: Radio, Herd) to be off; **Licht aus!** lights out!

3 (nicht zu Hause): **aus sein** to be out

4 (in Verbindung mit von): **von Rom aus** from Rome; **vom Fenster aus** out of the window; **von sich aus** (selbstständig) of one's own accord; **von ihm aus** as far as he's concerned

ausarbeiten ['aʊsʔarbaɪtən] vt to work

ausarten ['aʊsʔartən] vi to degenerate

ausatmen ['aʊsʔaːtmən] vi to breathe out

ausbaden ['aʊsbaːdən] (umg) vt: **etw ~ müssen** to carry the can for sth

Ausbau ['aʊsbaʊ] m extension, expansion; removal; **a~en** vt to extend, to expand; (herausnehmen) to take out, to remove; **a~fähig** adj (fig) worth developing

ausbessern ['aʊsbɛsərn] vt to mend, to repair

ausbeulen ['aʊsbɔʏlən] vt to beat out

Ausbeute ['aʊsbɔʏtə] f yield; (Fische) catch; **a~n** vt to exploit; (MIN) to work

ausbild- ['aʊsbɪld] zW: **~en** vt to educate; (Lehrling, Soldat) to instruct, to train; (Fähigkeiten) to develop; (Geschmack) to cultivate; **A~er** (-s, -) m instructor; **A~ung** f education; training, instruction; development; cultivation

ausbleiben ['aʊsblaɪbən] (unreg) vi (Personen) to stay away, not to come; (Ereignisse) to fail to happen, not to happen

Ausblick ['aʊsblɪk] m (auch fig) prospect, outlook, view

ausbrechen ['aʊsbrɛçən] (unreg) vi to break out ♦ vt to break off; **in Tränen/Gelächter ~** to burst into tears/out laughing

ausbreiten ['aʊsbraɪtən] vt to spread (out); (Arme) to stretch out ♦ vr to spread; **sich über ein Thema ~** to expand od enlarge on a topic

ausbrennen ['aʊsbrɛnən] (unreg) vt to scorch; (Wunde) to cauterize ♦ vi to burn out

Ausbruch ['aʊsbrʊx] m outbreak; (von Vulkan) eruption; (Gefühlsausbruch) outburst; (von Gefangenen) escape

ausbrüten ['aʊsbryːtən] vt (auch fig) to hatch

Ausdauer ['aʊsdaʊər] f perseverance, stamina; **a~nd** adj persevering

ausdehnen ['aʊsdeːnən] vt, vr

(räumlich) to expand; *(zeitlich, auch Gummi)* to stretch; *(Nebel, fig: Macht)* to extend

ausdenken ['aʊsdɛŋkən] *unreg* vt: **sich** *dat* **etw ~** to think sth up

Ausdruck ['aʊsdrʊk] *m* expression, phrase; *(Kundgabe, Gesichtsausdruck)* expression; *(COMPUT)* print-out, hard copy; **a~en** vt *(COMPUT)* to print out

ausdrücken ['aʊsdrʏkən] vt *(auch vr: formulieren, zeigen)* to express; *(Zigarette)* to put out; *(Zitrone)* to squeeze

ausdrücklich *adj* express, explicit

ausdrucks- *zW:* **~los** *adj* expressionless, blank; **~voll** *adj* expressive; **A~weise** *f* mode of expression

auseinander [aʊsʔaɪ'nandər] *adv (getrennt)* apart; **~ schreiben** to write as separate words; **~ bringen** to separate; **~ fallen** to fall apart; **~ gehen** *(Menschen)* to separate; *(Meinungen)* to differ; *(Gegenstand)* to fall apart; **~ halten** to tell apart; **~ nehmen** to take to pieces, to dismantle; **~ setzen** *(erklären)* to set forth, to explain; **sich ~ setzen** *(sich verständigen)* to come to terms, to settle; *(sich befassen)* to concern o.s.; **A~setzung** *f* argument

ausfahren ['aʊsfaːrən] *unreg* vt *(spazieren fahren: im Auto)* to take for a drive; *(: im Kinderwagen)* to take for a walk; *(liefern)* to deliver

Ausfahrt *f (des Zuges etc)* leaving, departure; *(Autobahnausfahrt)* exit; *(Garagenausfahrt)* exit, way out; *(Spazierfahrt)* drive, excursion

Ausfall ['aʊsfal] *m* loss; *(Nichtstattfinden)* cancellation; *(MIL)* sortie; *(radioaktiv)* fall-out; **a~en** *unreg vi (Zähne, Haare)* to fall out; *(nicht stattfinden)* to be cancelled; *(wegbleiben)* to be omitted; *(Person)* to drop out; *(Lohn)* to be stopped; *(nicht funktionieren)* to break down; *(Resultat haben)* to turn out; **~straße** *f* arterial

road

ausfertigen ['aʊsfɛrtɪgən] vt *(förmlich: Urkunde, Pass)* to draw up; *(Rechnung)* to make out

Ausfertigung ['aʊsfɛrtɪgʊŋ] *f* drawing up; making out; *(Exemplar)* copy

ausfindig ['aʊsfɪndɪç] *adj:* **~ machen** to discover

ausfließen ['aʊsfliːsən] *(unreg)* vt *(her-):* **~ (aus)** to flow out (of); *(auslaufen: Öl etc):* **~ (aus)** to leak (out of)

Ausflucht ['aʊsflʊxt] *(-, -flüchte)* *f* excuse

Ausflug ['aʊsfluːk] *m* excursion, outing; **Ausflügler** ['aʊsflyːklər] *(-s, -) m* tripper

Ausflugslokal *nt* tourist café

Ausfluss ▲ ['aʊsflʊs] *m* outlet; *(MED)* discharge

ausfragen ['aʊsfraːgən] vt to interrogate, to question

ausfressen ['aʊsfrɛsən] *(unreg)* vt to eat up; *(aushöhlen)* to corrode; *(umg: anstellen)* to be up to

Ausfuhr ['aʊsfuːr] *(-, -en)* *f* export, exportation ♦ *in zW* export

ausführ- ['aʊsfyːr-] *zW:* **~en** vt *(verwirklichen)* to carry out; *(Person)* to take out; *(Hund)* to take for a walk; *(COMM)* to export; *(erklären)* to give details of; **~lich** *adj* detailed ♦ *adv* in detail; **A~lichkeit** *f* detail; **A~ung** *f* execution, performance; *(Durchführung)* completion; *(Herstellungsart)* version; *(Erklärung)* explanation

ausfüllen ['aʊsfʏlən] vt to fill up; *(Fragebogen etc)* to fill in; *(Beruf)* to be fulfilling for

Ausgabe ['aʊsgaːbə] *f (Geld)* expenditure, outlay; *(Aushändigung)* giving out; *(Gepäckausgabe)* left-luggage office; *(Buch)* edition; *(Nummer)* issue; *(COMPUT)* output

Ausgang ['aʊsgaŋ] *m* way out, exit; *(Ende)* end; *(~spunkt)* starting point;

(*Ergebnis*) result; (*Ausgehtag*) free time, time off; **kein ~** no exit

Ausgangs- zW: **~punkt** m starting point; **~sperre** f curfew

ausgeben ['aʊsgeːbən] (*unreg*) vt (*Geld*) to spend; (*austeilen*) to issue, to distribute ♦ vr: **sich für etw/jdn ~** to pass o.s. off as sth/sb

ausgebucht ['aʊsgəbuːxt] adj (*Vorstellung, Flug, Maschine*) fully booked

ausgedient ['aʊsgədiːnt] adj (*Soldat*) discharged; (*verbraucht*) no longer in use; **~ haben** to have done good service

ausgefallen ['aʊsgəfalən] adj (*ungewöhnlich*) exceptional

ausgeglichen ['aʊsgəglɪçən] adj (*well-*)balanced; (*Mensch*) even-tempered; **A~heit** f balance; (*von Mensch*) even-temperedness

ausgehen ['aʊsgeːən] (*unreg*) vi to go out; (*zu Ende gehen*) to come to an end; (*Benzin*) to run out; (*Haare, Zähne*) to fall out come out; (*Feuer, Ofen, Licht*) to go out; (*Strom*) to go off; (*Resultat haben*) to turn out; **mir ging das Benzin aus** I ran out of petrol (BRIT) od gas (US); **von etw ~** (*wegführen*) to lead away from sth; (*herrühren*) to come from sth; (*zugrunde legen*) to proceed from sth; **wir können davon ~, dass ...** we can take as our starting point that ...; **leer ~** to get nothing

ausgelassen ['aʊsgəlasən] adj boisterous, high-spirited

ausgelastet ['aʊsgəlastət] adj fully occupied

ausgelernt ['aʊsgəlɛrnt] adj trained, qualified

ausgemacht ['aʊsgəmaxt] adj settled; (*umg: Dummkopf etc*) out-and-out, downright; **es war eine ~e Sache, dass ...** it was a foregone conclusion that ...

ausgenommen ['aʊsgənɔmən] präp +*gen* except ♦ *konj* except; **Anwesende sind ~** present company excepted

ausgeprägt ['aʊsgəprɛːkt] adj distinct

ausgerechnet ['aʊsgərɛçnət] adv just, precisely; **~ du/heute** you of all people/today of all days

ausgeschlossen ['aʊsgəʃlɔsən] adj (*unmöglich*) impossible, out of the question

ausgeschnitten ['aʊsgəʃnɪtən] adj (*Kleid*) low-necked

ausgesprochen ['aʊsgəʃprɔxən] adj (*Faulheit, Lügner*) out-and-out; (*unverkennbar*) marked ♦ adv decidedly

ausgezeichnet ['aʊsgətsaɪçnət] adj excellent

ausgiebig ['aʊsgiːbɪç] adj (*Gebrauch*) thorough, good; (*Essen*) generous, lavish; **~ schlafen** to have a good sleep

ausgießen ['aʊsgiːsən] vt to empty (*Behälter*); to empty

Ausgleich ['aʊsglaɪç] (-(e)s, -e) m balance; (*Vermittlung*) reconciliation; (SPORT) equalization; **zum ~ einer Sache** gen in order to offset sth; **a~en** (*unreg*) vt to balance (out); to reconcile; (*Höhe*) to even up ♦ vi (SPORT) to equalize

ausgraben ['aʊsgraːbən] (*unreg*) vt to dig up; (*Leichen*) to exhume; (*fig*) to unearth

Ausgrabung f excavation; (*Ausgraben auch*) digging up

Ausguss ▲ ['aʊsgʊs] m (*Spüle*) sink; (*Abfluss*) outlet; (*Tülle*) spout

aushalten ['aʊshaltən] (*unreg*) vt to bear, to stand; (*Geliebte*) to keep ♦ vi to hold out; **das ist nicht zum A~** that is unbearable

aushandeln ['aʊshandəln] vt to negotiate

aushändigen ['aʊshɛndɪgən] vt: **jdm etw ~** to hand sth over to sb

Aushang ['aʊshaŋ] m notice

aushängen ['aʊshɛŋən] (*unreg*) vt (*Meldung*) to put up; (*Fenster*) to take off its hinges ♦ vi to be displayed

ausharren ['aʊsharən] vi to hold out

ausheben ['aʊsheːbən] (*unreg*) vt (*Erde*)

to lift out; (*Grube*) to hollow out; (*Tür*) to take off its hinges; (*Diebesnest*) to clear out; (*MIL*) to enlist

aushecken ['aushɛkən] (*umg*) *vt* to cook up

aushelfen ['aushɛlfən] (*unreg*) *vi: jdm ~* to help sb out

Aushilfe ['aushilfə] *f* help, assistance; (*Person*) (temporary) worker

Aushilfs- *zW:* **~kraft** *f* temporary worker; **a~weise** *adv* temporarily, as a stopgap

ausholen ['aushoːlən] *vi* to swing one's arm back; (*zur Ohrfeige*) to raise one's hand; (*beim Gehen*) to take long strides

aushorchen ['aushɔrçən] *vt* to sound out, to pump

auskennen ['auskɛnən] (*unreg*) *vr* to know a lot; (*an einem Ort*) to know one's way about; (*in Fragen etc*) to be knowledgeable

Ausklang ['ausklaŋ] *m* end

auskleiden ['ausklaɪdən] *vr* to undress ♦ *vt* (*Wand*) to line

ausklingen ['ausklɪŋən] (*unreg*) *vi* (*Ton, Lied*) to die away; (*Fest*) to peter out

ausklopfen ['ausklɔpfən] *vt* (*Teppich*) to beat; (*Pfeife*) to knock out

auskochen ['auskɔxən] *vt* to boil; (*MED*) to sterilize; **ausgekocht** (*fig*) out-and-out

Auskommen (-s) *nt: sein A~ haben* to have a regular income; **a~** (*umg*) *vi: mit jdm a~* to get on with sb; **mit etw a~** to get by with sth

auskosten ['auskɔstən] *vt* to enjoy to the full

auskundschaften ['auskʊntʃaftən] *vt* to spy out; (*Gebiet*) to reconnoitre

Auskunft ['auskʊnft] (-, **-künfte**) *f* information; (*nähere*) details *pl*, particulars *pl*; (*Stelle*) information office; (*TEL*) directory inquiries *sg*

auslachen ['auslaxən] *vt* to laugh at,

to mock

ausladen ['auslaːdən] (*unreg*) *vt* to unload; (*umg: Gäste*) to cancel an invitation to

Auslage ['auslaːgə] *f* shop window (display); *~n pl* (*Ausgabe*) outlay *sg*

Ausland ['auslant] *nt* foreign countries *pl*; *im ~* abroad; *ins ~* abroad

Ausländer(in) ['auslɛndər(ɪn)] (-s, -) *m(f)* foreigner

ausländisch *adj* foreign

Auslands- *zW:* **~gespräch** *nt* international call; **~reise** *f* trip abroad; **~schutzbrief** *m* international travel cover

auslassen ['auslasən] (*unreg*) *vt* to leave out; (*Wort etc auch*) to omit; (*Fett*) to melt; (*Kleidungsstück*) to let out ♦ *vr: sich über etw akk ~* to speak one's mind about sth; **seine Wut etc an jdm ~** to vent one's rage *etc* on sb

Auslassung *f* omission

Auslauf ['auslauf] *m* (*für Tiere*) run; (*Ausfluss*) outflow, outlet; **a~en** (*unreg*) *vi* to run out; (*Behälter*) to leak; (*NAUT*) to put out (to sea); (*langsam aufhören*) to run down

Ausläufer ['auslɔyfər] *m* (*von Gebirge*) spur; (*Pflanze*) runner; (*MET: von Hoch*) ridge; (*: von Tief*) trough

ausleeren ['ausleːrən] *vt* to empty

auslegen ['ausleːgən] *vt* (*Waren*) to lay out; (*Köder*) to put down; (*Geld*) to lend; (*bedecken*) to cover; (*Text etc*) to interpret

Auslegung *f* interpretation

ausleiern ['auslaɪərn] *vt* (*Gummi*) to wear out

Ausleihe ['auslaɪə] *f* issuing; (*Stelle*) issue desk; **a~n** (*unreg*) *vt* (*verleihen*) to lend; **sich dat etw a~n** to borrow sth

Auslese ['ausleːzə] *f* selection; (*Elite*) elite; (*Wein*) choice wine; **a~n** (*unreg*) *vt* to select; (*umg: zu Ende lesen*) to finish

---

Spelling Reform: ▲ *new spelling* △ *old spelling (to be phased out)*

ausliefern ['auˈsliːfərn] vt to deliver (up), to hand over; (COMM) to deliver; **jdm/etw ausgeliefert sein** to be at the mercy of sb/sth

auslöschen ['auslœʃən] vt to extinguish; (fig) to wipe out, to obliterate

auslosen ['auslɔːzən] vt to draw lots for

auslösen ['auslœːzən] vt (Explosion, Schuss) to set off; (hervorrufen) to cause, to produce; (Gefangene) to ransom; (Pfand) to redeem

ausmachen ['ausmaxən] vt (Licht, Radio) to turn off; (Feuer) to put out; (entdecken) to make out; (vereinbaren) to agree; (beilegen) to settle; (Anteil darstellen, betragen) to represent; (bedeuten) to matter; **macht es Ihnen etwas aus, wenn ...?** would you mind if ...?

ausmalen ['ausmaːlən] vt to paint; (fig) to describe; **sich** dat **etw ~** to imagine sth

Ausmaß ['ausmaːs] nt dimension; (fig auch) scale

ausmessen ['ausmɛsən] (unreg) vt to measure

Ausnahme ['ausnaːmə] f exception; **~fall** m exceptional case; **~zustand** m state of emergency

ausnahms- zW: **~los** adv without exception; **~weise** adv by way of exception, for once

ausnehmen ['ausneːmən] (unreg) vt to take out, to remove; (Tier) to gut; (Nest) to rob; (umg: Geld abnehmen) to clean out; (ausschließen) to make an exception of ♦ vr to look, to appear; **~d** adj exceptional

ausnützen ['ausnʏtsən] vt (Zeit, Gelegenheit) to use, to turn to good account; (Einfluss) to use; (Mensch, Gutmütigkeit) to exploit

auspacken ['auspakən] vt to unpack

auspfeifen ['auspfaifən] (unreg) vt to hiss/boo at

ausplaudern ['ausplaudərn] vt (Ge-

heimnis) to blab

ausprobieren ['ausprobiːrən] vt to try (out)

Auspuff ['auspuf] (-(e)s, -e) m (TECH) exhaust; **~rohr** nt exhaust (pipe)

ausradieren ['ausradiːrən] vt to erase, to rub out; (fig) to annihilate

ausrangieren ['ausrãʒiːrən] (umg) vt to chuck out

ausrauben ['ausraubən] vt to rob

ausräumen ['ausrɔymən] vt (Dinge) to clear away; (Schrank, Zimmer) to empty; (Bedenken) to dispel

ausrechnen ['ausrɛçnən] vt to calculate, to reckon

Ausrede ['ausreːdə] f excuse; **a~n** vi to have one's say ♦ vt: **jdm etw a~n** to talk sb out of sth

ausreichen ['ausraiçən] vi to suffice, to be enough; **~d** adj sufficient, adequate; (SCH) adequate

Ausreise ['ausraizə] f departure; **bei der ~** when leaving the country; **~erlaubnis** f exit visa; **a~n** vi to leave the country

ausreißen ['ausraisən] (unreg) vt to tear od pull out ♦ vi (Riss bekommen) to tear; (umg) to make off, to scram

ausrenken ['ausrɛŋkən] vt to dislocate

ausrichten ['ausrɪçtən] vt (Botschaft) to deliver; (Gruß) to pass on; (Hochzeit etc) to arrange; (in gerade Linie bringen) to get in a straight line; (angleichen) to bring into line; (TYP) to justify; **ich werde es ihm ~** I'll tell him; **etwas/nichts bei jdm ~** to get somewhere/nowhere with sb

ausrotten ['ausrɔtən] vt to stamp out, to exterminate

Ausruf ['ausruːf] m (Schrei) cry, exclamation; (Bekanntmachung) proclamation; **a~en** (unreg) vt to cry out, to exclaim; to call out; **~ezeichen** nt exclamation mark

ausruhen ['ausruːən] vt, vi to rest

ausrüsten ['ausrʏstən] vt to equip, to fit out

Ausrüstung f equipment

ausrutschen ['ausrʊtʃən] vi to slip

Aussage ['auszaːgə] f (JUR) statement; **a~n** vt to say, to state ♦ vi (JUR) to give evidence

ausschalten ['ausʃaltən] vt to switch off; (fig) to eliminate

Ausschank ['ausʃaŋk] (-(e)s, -schänke) m dispensing, giving out; (COMM) selling; (Theke) bar

Ausschau ['ausʃau] f: ~ halten (nach) to look out (for), to watch (for); **a~en** vi: ~en (nach) to look out (for), to be on the look-out (for)

ausscheiden ['ausʃaidən] (unreg) vt to take out; (MED) to secrete ♦ vi: ~ (aus) to leave; (SPORT) to be eliminated (from) od knocked out (of)

Ausscheidung f separation; secretion; elimination; (aus Amt) retirement

ausschenken ['ausʃeŋkən] vt (Alkohol, Kaffee) to pour out; (COMM) to sell

ausschildern ['ausʃɪldərn] vt to signpost

ausschimpfen ['ausʃɪmpfən] vt to scold, to tell off

ausschlafen ['ausʃlaːfən] (unreg) vi, vr to have a good sleep ♦ vt to sleep off; **ich bin nicht ausgeschlafen** I didn't have od get enough sleep

Ausschlag ['ausʃlaːk] m (MED) rash; (Pendelausschlag) swing; (Nadelausschlag) deflection; **den ~ geben** (fig) to tip the balance; **a~en** [-gən] (unreg) vt to knock out; (auskleiden) to deck out; (verweigern) to decline ♦ vi (Pferd) to kick out; (BOT) to sprout; **a~gebend** adj decisive

ausschließen ['ausʃliːsən] (unreg) vt to shut od lock out; (fig) to exclude

ausschließlich adj exclusive ♦ adv exclusively ♦ präp +gen exclusive of, excluding

Ausschluss ▲ ['ausʃlʊs] m exclusion

ausschmücken ['ausʃmʏkən] vt to

decorate; (fig) to embellish

ausschneiden ['ausʃnaidən] (unreg) vt to cut out; (Büsche) to trim

Ausschnitt ['ausʃnɪt] m (Teil) section; (von Kleid) neckline; (Zeitungsausschnitt) cutting; (aus Film etc) excerpt

ausschreiben ['ausʃraibən] (unreg) vt (ganz schreiben) to write out (in full); (ausstellen) to write (out); (Stelle, Wettbewerb etc) to announce, to advertise

Ausschreitung ['ausʃraitʊŋ] f (usu pl) riot

Ausschuss ▲ ['ausʃʊs] m committee, board; (Abfall) waste, scraps pl; (COMM: auch: ~ware) reject

ausschütten ['ausʃʏtən] vt to pour out; (Eimer) to empty; (Geld) to pay ♦ vr to shake (with laughter)

ausschweifend ['ausʃvaifənt] adj (Leben) dissipated, debauched; (Fantasie) extravagant

aussehen ['auszeːən] (unreg) vi to look; **es sieht nach Regen aus** it looks like rain; **es sieht schlecht aus** things look bad; **A~** (-s) nt appearance

aus sein ▲ siehe aus

außen ['ausən] adv outside; (nach ~) outwards; **~ ist es rot** it's red (on the) outside

Außen- zW: **~dienst** m: **im ~dienst sein** to work outside the office; **~handel** m foreign trade; **~minister** m foreign minister; **~ministerium** nt foreign office; **~politik** f foreign policy; **a~politisch** adj (Entwicklung, Lage) foreign; **~seite** f outside; **~seiter (-s, -)** m outsider; **~stände** pl outstanding debts; **~stehende(r)** f(m) outsider; **~welt** f outside world

außer ['ausər] präp +dat (räumlich) out of; (abgesehen von) except ♦ konj (ausgenommen) except; **~ Gefahr** out of danger; **~ Zweifel** beyond any doubt; **~ Betrieb** out of order; **~ Dienst** retired; **~ Landes** abroad; **~ sich** ad

sein to be beside o.s.; **~ sich** akk **geraten** to go wild; **~ wenn** unless; **~ dass** except; **~dem** konj besides, in addition

äußere(r, s) ['ɔʏsərə(r,s)] adj outer, external

außergewöhnlich adj unusual

außerhalb präp +gen outside ♦ adv outside

äußerlich adj external

äußern vt to utter, to express; (zeigen) to show ♦ vr to give one's opinion; (Krankheit etc) to show itself

außerordentlich adj extraordinary

außerplanmäßig adj unscheduled

äußerst ['ɔʏsərst] adv extremely, most; **~e(r, s)** adj utmost; (räumlich) farthest; (Termin) last possible; (Preis) highest

Äußerung f remark, comment

aussetzen ['auszɛtsən] vt (Kind, Tier) to abandon; (Boote) to lower; (Belohnung) to offer; (Urteil, Verfahren) to postpone ♦ vi (aufhören) to stop; (Pause machen) to have a break; **jdm/etw ausgesetzt sein** to be exposed to sth/sb; **an jdm/etw etwas ~** to find fault with sb/sth

Aussicht ['auszɪçt] f view; (in Zukunft) prospect; **etw in ~ haben** to have sth in view

Aussichts- zW: **a~los** adj hopeless; **~punkt** m viewpoint; **a~reich** adj promising; **~turm** m observation tower

aussöhnen ['auszø:nən] vt to reconcile ♦ vr to reconcile o.s., to become reconciled

aussondern ['auszɔndərn] vt to separate, to select

aussortieren ['auszɔrti:rən] vt to sort out

ausspannen ['ausʃpanən] vt to spread od stretch out; (Pferd) to unharness; (umg: Mädchen): **(jdm) jdn ~** to steal sb (from sb) ♦ vi to relax

aussperren ['ausʃpɛrən] vt to lock out

ausspielen ['ausʃpi:lən] vt (Karte) to lead; (Geldprämie) to offer as a prize ♦ vi (KARTEN) to lead; **jdn gegen jdn ~**

to play sb off against sb; **ausgespielt haben** to be finished

Aussprache ['ausʃpra:xə] f pronunciation; (Unterredung) (frank) discussion

aussprechen ['ausʃprɛçən] (unreg) vt to pronounce; (äußern) to say, to express ♦ vr (sich äußern): **sich ~ (über +akk)** to speak (about); (sich anvertrauen) to unburden o.s. (über od an); (diskutieren) to discuss ♦ vi (zu Ende sprechen) to finish speaking

Ausspruch ['ausʃprɔx] m saying, remark

ausspülen ['ausʃpy:lən] vt to wash out; (Mund) to rinse

Ausstand ['ausʃtant] m strike; **in den ~ treten** to go on strike

ausstatten ['ausʃtatən] vt (Zimmer etc) to furnish; (Person) to equip, to kit out

Ausstattung ['ausʃtatʊŋ] f (Ausstatten) provision; (Kleidung) outfit; (Aufmachung) make-up; (Einrichtung) furnishing

ausstechen ['ausʃtɛçən] (unreg) vt (Augen, Rasen, Graben) to dig out; (Kekse) to cut out; (übertreffen) to outshine

ausstehen ['ausʃte:ən] (unreg) vt to stand, to endure ♦ vi (noch nicht da sein) to be outstanding

aussteigen ['ausʃtaɪgən] (unreg) vi to get out, to alight

ausstellen ['ausʃtɛlən] vt to exhibit, to display; (umg: ausschalten) to switch off; (Rechnung etc) to make out; (Pass, Zeugnis) to issue

Ausstellung f exhibition; (FIN) drawing up; (einer Rechnung) making out; (eines Passes etc) issuing

aussterben ['ausʃtɛrbən] (unreg) vi to die out

Aussteuer ['ausʃtɔʏər] f dowry

Ausstieg ['ausʃti:k] (-(e)s, -e) m exit

ausstopfen ['ausʃtɔpfən] vt to stuff

ausstoßen ['ausʃto:sən] (unreg) vt (Luft, Rauch) to give off, to emit; (aus Verein etc) to expel, to exclude; (Auge) to poke out

ausstrahlen ['ausʃtra:lən] vt, vi to radiate; (RADIO) to broadcast

Ausstrahlung f radiation; (fig) charisma

ausstrecken ['aʊsʃtrɛkən] vt, vr to stretch out

ausstreichen ['aʊsʃtraɪçən] (unreg) vt to cross out; (glätten) to smooth (out)

ausströmen ['aʊsʃtrø:mən] vi (Gas) to pour out, to escape ♦ vt to give off; (fig) to radiate

aussuchen ['aʊszu:xən] vt to select, to pick out

Austausch ['aʊstaʊʃ] m exchange; a~bar adj exchangeable; a~en vt to exchange, to swap

austeilen ['aʊstaɪlən] vt to distribute, to give out

Auster ['aʊstər] (-, -n) f oyster

austoben ['aʊsto:bən] vr (Kind) to run wild; (Erwachsene) to sow one's wild oats

austragen ['aʊstra:gən] (unreg) vt (Post) to deliver; (Streit etc) to decide; (Wettkämpfe) to hold

Australien [aʊs'tra:liən] (-s) nt Australia; **Australier(in)** (-s, -) m(f) Australian; **australisch** adj Australian

austreiben ['aʊstraɪbən] (unreg) vt to drive out, to expel; (Geister) to exorcize

austreten ['aʊstre:tən] (unreg) vt (zur Toilette) to be excused ♦ vt (Feuer) to tread out, to trample; (Schuhe) to wear out; (Treppe) to wear down; **aus etw ~** to leave sth

austrinken ['aʊstrɪŋkən] (unreg) vt (Glas) to drain; (Getränk) to drink up ♦ vi to finish one's drink, to drink up

Austritt ['aʊstrɪt] m emission; (aus Verein, Partei etc) retirement, withdrawal

austrocknen ['aʊstrɔknən] vt, vi to dry up

ausüben ['aʊsʔy:bən] vt (Beruf) to practise, to carry out; (Funktion) to perform; (Einfluss) to exert; **einen Reiz**

auf jdn ~ to hold an attraction for sb; **eine Wirkung auf jdn ~** to have an effect on sb

Ausverkauf ['aʊsfɛrkaʊf] m sale; **a~en** vt to sell out; (Geschäft) to sell up; **a~t** adj (Karten, Artikel) sold out; (THEAT: Haus) full

Auswahl ['aʊsva:l] f: **eine ~ (an +dat)** a selection (of), a choice (of)

auswählen ['aʊsvɛ:lən] vt to select, to choose

Auswander- ['aʊsvandər] zW: **~er** m emigrant; **a~n** vi to emigrate; **~ung** f emigration

auswärtig ['aʊsvɛrtɪç] adj (nicht am/vom Ort) out-of-town; (ausländisch) foreign

auswärts ['aʊsvɛrts] adv outside; (nach außen) outwards; **~ essen** to eat out; **A~spiel** ['aʊsvɛrtsʃpi:l] nt away game

auswechseln ['aʊsvɛksəln] vt to change, to substitute

Ausweg ['aʊsve:k] m way out; **a~los** adj hopeless

ausweichen ['aʊsvaɪçən] (unreg) vi: **jdm/etw ~** to move aside or make way for sb/sth; (fig) to side-step sb/sth; **~d** adj evasive

ausweinen ['aʊsvaɪnən] vr to have a (good) cry

Ausweis ['aʊsvaɪs] (-es, -e) m identity card; passport; (Mitgliedsausweis, Bibliotheksausweis etc) card; **a~en** [-zən] (unreg) vt to expel, to banish ♦ vr to prove one's identity; **~kontrolle** f identity check; **~papiere** pl identity papers; **~ung** f expulsion

ausweiten ['aʊsvaɪtən] vt to stretch

auswendig ['aʊsvɛndɪç] adv by heart

auswerten ['aʊsvɛrtən] vt to evaluate; **Auswertung** f evaluation, analysis; (Nutzung) utilization

auswirken ['aʊsvɪrkən] vr to have an effect; **Auswirkung** f effect

auswischen ['aʊsvɪʃən] vt to wipe out;

jdm eins ~ (umg) to put one over on sb

Auswuchs ['aʊsvuːks] m (out)growth; (fig) product

auszahlen ['aʊstsaːlən] vt (Lohn, Summe) to pay out; (Arbeiter) to pay off; (Miterbe) to buy out ♦ vr (sich lohnen) to pay

auszählen ['aʊstsɛːlən] vt (Stimmen) to count

auszeichnen ['aʊstsaɪçnən] vt to honour; (MIL) to decorate; (COMM) to price ♦ vr to distinguish o.s.

Auszeichnung f distinction, (COMM) pricing; (Ehrung) awarding of decoration; (Ehre) honour; (Orden) decoration; **mit ~** with distinction

ausziehen ['aʊstsiːən] (unreg) vt (Kleidung) to take off; (Haare, Zähne, Tisch etc) to pull out; (nachmalen) to trace ♦ vr to undress ♦ vi (aufbrechen) to leave; (aus Wohnung) to move out

Auszubildende(r) ['aʊstsʊbɪldəndə(r)] f(m) trainee

Auszug ['aʊstsuːk] m (aus Wohnung) removal; (aus Buch etc) extract; (Kontoauszug) statement; (Ausmarsch) departure

Auto ['aʊto] (-s, -s) nt (motor)car; **~ fahren** to drive; **~atlas** m road atlas; **~bahn** f motorway; **~bahndreieck** nt motorway junction; **~bahngebühr** f toll; **~bahnkreuz** nt motorway intersection; **~bus** m bus; **~fähre** f car ferry; **~fahrer(in)** m(f) motorist, driver; **~fahrt** f drive; **a~gen** [-'geːn] adj autogenous; **~'gramm** nt autograph

Auto- zW: **~'mat** (-en, -en) m machine; **~matik** [aʊto'maːtɪk] f (AUT) automatic; **a~'matisch** adj automatic; **a~nom** ['noːm] adj autonomous

Autor(in) ['aʊtɔr(ɪn)] (-s, -en) m(f) author

Auto- zW: **~radio** nt car radio; **~reifen** m car tyre; **~reisezug** m motorail train; **~rennen** nt motor racing

autoritär [aʊtori'tɛːr] adj authoritarian

Autorität f authority

Auto- zW: **~telefon** nt car phone; **~unfall** m car od motor accident; **~vermietung** f car hire (BRIT) od rental; **~waschanlage** f car wash

Axt [akst] (-, ¨e) f axe

B, b

Baby ['beːbi] (-s, -s) nt baby; **~nahrung** f baby food; **~sitter** (-s, -) m baby-sitter

Bach [bax] (-(e)s, ¨e) m stream, brook

Backbord (-(e)s, -e) nt (NAUT) port

Backe ['bakə] f cheek

backen ['bakən] (unreg) vt, vi to bake

Backenzahn m molar

Bäcker(in) ['bɛkər(ɪn)] (-s, -) m baker; **~ei** f bakery; (~eiladen) baker's (shop)

Back- zW: **~form** f baking tin; **~obst** nt dried fruit; **~ofen** m oven; **~pflaume** f prune; **~pulver** nt baking powder; **~stein** m brick

Bad [baːt] (-(e)s, ¨er) nt bath; (Schwimmen) bathe; (Ort) spa

Bade- ['baːdə] zW: **~anstalt** f (swimming) baths pl; **~anzug** m bathing suit; **~hose** f bathing od swimming trunks pl; **~kappe** f bathing cap; **~mantel** m bath(ing) robe; **~meister** m baths attendant; **b~n** vi to bathe, to have a bath ♦ vt to bath; **~ort** m spa; **~tuch** nt bath towel; **~wanne** f bath (tub); **~zimmer** nt bathroom

Bagatelle [baga'tɛlǝ] f trifle

Bagger ['bagɐ] (-s, -) m excavator; (NAUT) dredger; **b~n** vt, vi to excavate; to dredge

Bahn [baːn] (-, -en) f railway, railroad (US); (Weg) road, way; (Spur) lane; (Rennbahn) track; (ASTRON) orbit; (Stoffbahn) length; **b~brechend** adj pioneering; **~Card** ['baːnkaːrd] (-, -s) ® f ≈ railcard; **~damm** m railway embankment; **b~en** vt: sich/jdm einen Weg **b~en** to clear a way/a way for sb; **~fahrt** f railway journey; **~fracht** f rail freight; **~hof** (-, -s) m station; auf dem **~hof** at the station; **~hofshalle** f station concourse; **~linie** f (railway) line; **~steig** m platform; **~übergang** m level crossing, grade crossing (US)

Bahre ['baːrǝ] f stretcher

Bakterien [bak'teːriǝn] pl bacteria pl

Balance [ba'lãːsǝ] f balance, equilibrium

balan'cieren vt, vi to balance

bald [balt] adv (zeitlich) soon; (beinahe) almost; **~ig** ['baldɪç] adj early, speedy

Baldrian ['baldriaːn] (-s, -e) m valerian

Balkan ['balkaːn] (-s) m: der ~ the Balkans pl

Balken ['balkǝn] (-s, -) m beam; (Tragbalken) girder; (Stützbalken) prop

Balkon [bal'kõː] (-s, -s od -e) m balcony; (THEAT) (dress) circle

Ball [bal] (-(e)s, *e) m ball; (Tanz) dance, ball

Ballast ['balast] (-(e)s, -e) m ballast; (fig) weight, burden

Ballen ['balǝn] (-s, -) m bale; (ANAT) ball; **b~** vt (formen) to make into a ball; (Faust) to clench ♦ vr (Wolken etc) to build up; (Menschen) to gather

Ballett [ba'lɛt] (-(e)s, -e) nt ballet

Ballkleid nt evening dress

Ballon [ba'lõː] (-s, -s od -e) m balloon

Ballspiel nt ball game

Ballungsgebiet ['balʊŋsgǝbiːt] nt conurbation

Baltikum ['baltikʊm] (-s) nt: das ~ the Baltic States

Banane [ba'naːnǝ] f banana

Band¹ [bant] (-(e)s, *e) m (Buchband) volume

Band² (-(e)s, *er) nt (Stoffband) ribbon, tape; (Fließband) production line; (Tonband) tape; (ANAT) ligament; etw auf ~ aufnehmen to tape sth; am laufenden ~ (umg) non-stop

Band³ (-(e)s, -e) nt (Freundschaftsband) bond

Band⁴ [bɛnt] (-, -s) f band, group

band etc vb siehe binden

Bandage [ban'daːʒǝ] f bandage

banda'gieren vt to bandage

Bande ['bandǝ] f band; (Straßenbande) gang

bändigen ['bɛndɪgǝn] vt (Tier) to tame; (Trieb, Leidenschaft) to control, to restrain

Bandit [ban'diːt] (-en, -en) m bandit

Band- zW: **~nudel** f (KOCH: gew pl) ribbon noodles pl; **~scheibe** f (ANAT) disc; **~wurm** m tapeworm

bange ['baŋǝ] adj scared; (besorgt) anxious; **jdm wird es ~** sb is becoming scared; **jdm B~ machen** to scare sb; **~n** vi: um **jdn/etw ~n** to be anxious od worried about sb/sth

Bank¹ [baŋk] (-, *e) f (Sitz~) bench; (Sand~ etc) (sand)bank, (sand)bar

Bank² [baŋk] (-, -en) f (Geldbank) bank; **~anweisung** f banker's order; **~einzug** m direct debit

Bankett [baŋ'kɛt] (-(e)s, -e) nt (Essen) banquet; (Straßenrand) verge (BRIT), shoulder (US)

Bankier [baŋki'eː] (-s, -s) m banker

Bank- zW: **~konto** m bank account; **~leitzahl** f bank sort code number;

~note f banknote; **~raub** m bank robbery

Bankrott [baŋ'krɔt] (-(e)s, -e) m bankruptcy; **~ machen** to go bankrupt; **b~** adj bankrupt

Bankverbindung f banking arrangements pl; **geben Sie bitte Ihre ~ an** please give your account details

Bann [ban] (-(e)s, -e) m (HIST) ban; (Kirchenbann) excommunication; (fig: Zauber) spell; **b~en** vt (Geister) to exorcize; (Gefahr) to avert; (bezaubern) to enchant; (HIST) to banish

Banner (-s, -) nt banner, flag

Bar (-, -s) f bar

bar [baːr] adj (+gen) (unbedeckt) bare; (frei von) lacking (in); (offenkundig) utter, sheer; **~e(s) Geld** cash; **etw (in) ~ bezahlen** to pay sth (in) cash; **etw für ~e Münze nehmen** (fig) to take sth at its face value

Bär [bɛːr] (-en, -en) m bear

Baracke [ba'raka] f hut

barbarisch [bar'baːrɪʃ] adj barbaric, barbarous

Bar- zW: **b~fuß** adj barefoot; **~geld** nt cash, ready money; **b~geldlos** adj non-cash

Barkauf m cash purchase

Barkeeper ['baːrkiːpər] (-s, -) m barman, bartender

barmherzig [barm'hɛrtsɪç] adj merciful, compassionate

Baron [ba'roːn] (-s, -e) m baron; **~in** f baroness

Barren ['barən] (-s, -) m parallel bars pl; (Goldbarren) ingot

Barriere [bari'ɛːrə] f barrier

Barrikade [bari'kaːdə] f barricade

Barsch [barʃ] (-(e)s, -e) m perch

barsch [barʃ] adj brusque, gruff

Bar- zW: **~schaft** f ready money; **~scheck** m open od uncrossed cheque (BRIT), open check (US)

Bart [baːrt] (-(e)s, ²e) m beard; (Schlüsselbart) bit; **bärtig** ['bɛːrtɪç] adj bearded

Barzahlung f cash payment

Base ['baːzə] f (CHEM) base; (Kusine) cousin

Basel ['baːzəl] nt Basle

Basen pl von Base; Basis

basieren [ba'ziːrən] vt to base ♦ vi to be based

Basis ['baːzɪs] (-, Basen) f basis

Bass ▲ [bas] (-es, -e) m bass

Bassin [ba'sɛ̃ː] (-s, -s) nt pool

basteln ['bastəln] vt to make ♦ vi to do handicrafts

bat etc [baːt] vb siehe bitten

Bataillon [batal'joːn] (-s, -e) nt battalion

Batik ['baːtɪk] f (Verfahren) batik

Batterie [bata'riː] f battery

Bau [bau] (-(e)s) m (~en) building, construction; (Aufbau) structure; (Körperbau) frame; (~stelle) building site; (pl -e: Tierbau) hole, burrow; (: MIN) working(s); (pl ~ten: Gebäude) building; **sich im ~ befinden** to be under construction; **~arbeiten** pl building od construction work sg; **~arbeiter** m building worker

Bauch [baux] (-(e)s, Bäuche) m belly; (ANAT auch) stomach, abdomen; **~fell** nt peritoneum; **b~ig** adj bulbous; **~nabel** m navel; **~redner** m ventriloquist; **~schmerzen** pl stomachache; **~weh** nt stomachache

Baudenkmal nt historical monument

bauen ['bauən] vt, vi to build; (TECH) to construct; **auf jdn/etw ~** to depend od count upon sb/sth

Bauer¹ ['bauər] (-n od -s, -n) m farmer; (Schach) pawn

Bauer² ['bauər] (-s, -) nt od m (bird)cage

Bäuerin ['bɔyərɪn] f farmer; (Frau des Bauers) farmer's wife

bäuerlich adj rustic

Bauern- zW: **~haus** nt farmhouse; **~hof** m farm(yard)

Bau- zW: **b~fällig** adj dilapidated; **~gelände** f building site; **~genehmigung**

f building permit; **~gerüst** *nt* scaffolding; **~herr** *m* purchaser; **~kasten** *m* box of bricks; **~land** *nt* building land; **b~lich** *adj* structural

Baum [baʊm] **(-(e)s, Bäume)** *m* tree

baumeln ['baʊməln] *vi* to dangle

bäumen ['bɔymən] *vr* to rear (up)

Baum- *zW:* **~schule** *f* nursery; **~stamm** *m* tree trunk; **~stumpf** *m* tree stump; **~wolle** *f* cotton

Bau- *zW:* **~plan** *m* architect's plan; **~platz** *m* building site

bauspar- *zW:* **~en** *vi* to save with a building society; **B~kasse** *f* building society; **B~vertrag** *m* building society savings agreement

Bau- *zW:* **~stein** *m* building stone, freestone; **~stelle** *f* building site; **~teil** *nt* prefabricated part (of building); **~ten** *pl von* **Bau**; **~unternehmer** *m* building contractor; **~weise** *f* (method of) construction; **~werk** *nt* building; **~zaun** *m* hoarding

Bayern ['baɪərn] *nt* Bavaria

bayrisch ['baɪrɪʃ] *adj* Bavarian

Bazillus [ba'tsɪlʊs] **(-, Bazillen)** *m* bacillus

beabsichtigen [bə'apzɪçtɪgən] *vt* to intend

beacht- [bə'axt] *zW:* **~en** *vt* to take note of; (*Vorschrift*) to obey; (*Vorfahrt*) to observe; **~lich** *adj* considerable; **B~ung** *f* notice, attention, observation

Beamte(r) [bə'amtə(r)] **(-n, -n)** *m* official; (*Staatsbeamte*) civil servant; (*Bankbeamte etc*) employee

Beamtin *f siehe* **Beamte(r)**

beängstigend [bə'ɛŋstɪgənt] *adj* alarming

beanspruchen [bə'anʃprʊxən] *vt* to claim; (*Zeit, Platz*) to take up, to occupy; **jdn ~** to take up sb's time

beanstanden [bə'anʃtandən] *vt* to complain about, to object to

beantragen [bə'antragən] *vt* to apply for, to ask for

beantworten [bə'antvɔrtən] *vt* to answer; **Beantwortung** *f* (+*gen*) reply (to)

bearbeiten [bə'arbaɪtən] *vt* to work; (*Material*) to process; (*Thema*) to deal with; (*Land*) to cultivate; (*CHEM*) to treat; (*Buch*) to revise; (*umg: beeinflussen wollen*) to work on

Bearbeitung *f* processing; cultivation; treatment; revision

Bearbeitungsgebühr *f* handling charge

Beatmung [bə'a:tmʊŋ] *f* respiration

beaufsichtigen [bə'aʊfzɪçtɪgən] *vt* to supervise; **Beaufsichtigung** *f* supervision

beauftragen [bə'aʊftra:gən] *vt* to instruct; **jdn mit etw ~** to entrust sb with sth

Beauftragte(r) *f(m)* representative

bebauen [bə'baʊən] *vt* to build on; (*AGR*) to cultivate

beben ['be:bən] *vi* to tremble, to shake; **B~ (-s, -)** *nt* earthquake

Becher ['bɛçər] **(-s, -)** *m* mug; (*ohne Henkel*) tumbler

Becken ['bɛkən] **(-s, -)** *nt* basin; (*MUS*) cymbal; (*ANAT*) pelvis

bedacht [bə'daxt] *adj* thoughtful, careful; **auf etw** *akk* **~ sein** to be concerned about sth

bedächtig [bə'dɛçtɪç] *adj* (*umsichtig*) thoughtful, reflective; (*langsam*) slow, deliberate

bedanken [bə'daŋkən] *vr:* **sich (bei jdm) ~** to say thank you (to sb)

Bedarf [bə'darf] **(-(e)s)** *m* need, requirement; (*COMM*) demand; **je nach ~** according to demand; **bei ~** if necessary; **~ an etw** *dat* **haben** to be in need of sth

Bedarfs- *zW:* **~fall** *m* case of need; **~haltestelle** *f* request stop

---

bedauerlich [bə'dau̯ərlɪç] *adj* regrettable

bedauern [bə'dau̯ərn] *vt* to be sorry for; (*bemitleiden*) to pity; **B~ (-s)** *nt* regret; **~swert** *adj* (*Zustände*) regrettable; (*Mensch*) pitiable, unfortunate

bedecken [bə'dɛkən] *vt* to cover

bedeckt *adj* covered; (*Himmel*) overcast

bedenken [bə'dɛŋkən] (*unreg*) *vt* to think over, to consider

Bedenken (-s, -) *nt* (*Überlegen*) consideration; (*Zweifel*) doubt; (*Skrupel*) scruple

bedenklich *adj* doubtful; (*bedrohlich*) dangerous, risky

Bedenkzeit *f* time to think

bedeuten [bə'dɔytən] *vt* to mean; to signify; (*wichtig sein*) to be of importance; **~d** *adj* important; (*beträchtlich*) considerable

bedeutsam *adj* (*wichtig*) significant

Bedeutung *f* meaning; significance; (*Wichtigkeit*) importance; **b~slos** *adj* insignificant, unimportant; **b~svoll** *adj* momentous, significant

bedienen [bə'di:nən] *vt* to serve; (*Maschine*) to work, to operate ♦ *vr* (*beim Essen*) to help o.s.; **sich jds/ einer Sache ~** to make use of sb/sth

Bedienung *f* service; (*Kellnerin*) waitress; (*Verkäuferin*) shop assistant; (*Zuschlag*) service (charge)

Bedienungsanleitung *f* operating instructions *pl*

bedingen [bə'dɪŋən] *vt* (*verursachen*) to cause

bedingt *adj* (*Richtigkeit*, *Tauglichkeit*) limited; (*Zusage*, *Annahme*) conditional

Bedingung *f* condition; (*Voraussetzung*) stipulation; **b~slos** *adj* unconditional

bedrängen [bə'drɛŋən] *vt* to pester, to harass

bedrohen [bə'dro:ən] *vt* to threaten; **Bedrohung** *f* threat, menace

bedrücken [bə'drʏkən] *vt* to oppress, to trouble

bedürf- [bə'dʏrf] *zW*: **~en** (*unreg*) *vi* +*gen* to need, to require; **B~nis (-ses, -se)** *nt* need; **~tig** *adj* in need, poor, needy

beeilen [bə'aɪlən] *vr* to hurry

beeindrucken [bə'aɪndrʊkən] *vt* to impress, to make an impression on

beeinflussen [bə'aɪnflʊsən] *vt* to influence

beeinträchtigen [bə'aɪntrɛçtɪgən] *vt* to affect adversely; (*Freiheit*) to infringe upon

beend(ig)en [bə'ɛnd(ɪg)ən] *vt* to end, to finish, to terminate

beengen [bə'ɛŋən] *vt* to cramp; (*fig*) to hamper, to oppress

beerben [bə'ɛrbən] *vt*: **jdn ~** to inherit from sb

beerdigen [bə'eːrdɪgən] *vt* to bury; **Beerdigung** *f* funeral, burial

Beere ['beːrə] *f* berry; (*Traubenbeere*) grape

Beet [beːt] *(-(e)s, -e)* *nt* bed

befähigen [bə'fɛːɪgən] *vt* to enable

befähigt *adj* (*begabt*) talented; **~ (für)** (*fähig*) capable (of)

Befähigung *f* capability; (*Begabung*) talent, aptitude

befahrbar [bə'faːrbaːr] *adj* passable; (*NAUT*) navigable

befahren [bə'faːrən] (*unreg*) *vt* to use, to drive over; (*NAUT*) to navigate ♦ *adj* used

befallen [bə'falən] (*unreg*) *vt* to come over

befangen [bə'faŋən] *adj* (*schüchtern*) shy, self-conscious; (*voreingenommen*) biased

befassen [bə'fasən] *vr* to concern o.s.

Befehl [bə'feːl] *(-(e)s, -e)* *m* command, order; **b~en** (*unreg*) *vt* to order ♦ *vi* to give orders; **jdm etw b~en** to order sb to do sth; **~sverweigerung** *f* insubordination

befestigen [bə'fɛstɪgən] *vt* to fasten; (*stärken*) to strengthen; (*MIL*) to fortify; **~ an** +*dat* to fasten to

Befestigung f fastening; strengthening; (MIL) fortification

befeuchten [bəˈfɔʏçtən] vt to damp(en), to moisten

befinden [bəˈfɪndən] (unreg) vr to be; (sich fühlen) to feel ♦ vt: **jdn/etw für od als etw** ~ to deem sb/sth to be sth ♦ vi: ~ (**über** +akk) to decide (on), to adjudicate (on); **B**~ (**-s**) nt health, condition; (Meinung) view, opinion

befolgen [bəˈfɔlgən] vt to comply with, to follow

befördern [bəˈfœrdərn] vt (senden) to transport, to send; (beruflich) to promote; **Beförderung** f transport; promotion

befragen [bəˈfraːgən] vt to question

befreien [bəˈfraɪən] vt to set free; (erlassen) to exempt; **Befreiung** f liberation, release; (Erlassen) exemption

befreunden [bəˈfrɔʏndən] vr to make friends; (mit Idee etc) to acquaint o.s.

befreundet adj friendly

befriedigen [bəˈfriːdɪgən] vt to satisfy; **~d** adj satisfactory

Befriedigung f satisfaction, gratification

befristet [bəˈfrɪstət] adj limited

befruchten [bəˈfrʊxtən] vt to fertilize; (fig) to stimulate

Befruchtung f: **künstliche** ~ artificial insemination

Befugnis [bəˈfuːknɪs] (**-**, **-se**) f authorization, powers pl

befugt adj authorized, entitled

Befund [bəˈfʊnt] (**-(e)s**, **-e**) m findings pl; (MED) diagnosis

befürchten [bəˈfʏrçtən] vt to fear; **Befürchtung** f fear, apprehension

befürworten [bəˈfyːrvɔrtən] vt to support, to speak in favour of; **Befürworter** (**-s**, **-**) m supporter, advocate

begabt [bəˈgaːpt] adj gifted

Begabung [bəˈgaːbʊŋ] f talent, gift

begann etc [bəˈgan] vb siehe **beginnen**

begeben [bəˈgeːbən] (unreg) vr (gehen) to betake o.s.; (geschehen) to occur; **sich** ~ **nach od zu** to proceed to(wards); **B**~**heit** f occurrence

begegnen [bəˈgeːgnən] vi: **jdm** ~ to meet sb; (behandeln) to treat sb; **einer Sache** dat ~ to meet with sth

Begegnung f meeting

begehen [bəˈgeːən] (unreg) vt (Straftat) to commit; (abschreiten) to cover; (Straße etc) to use, to negotiate; (Feier) to celebrate

begehren [bəˈgeːrən] vt to desire

begehrt adj in demand; (Junggeselle) eligible

begeistern [bəˈgaɪstərn] vt to fill with enthusiasm, to inspire ♦ vr: **sich für etw** ~ to get enthusiastic about sth

begeistert adj enthusiastic

Begierde [bəˈgiːrdə] f desire, passion

begierig [bəˈgiːrɪç] adj eager, keen

begießen [bəˈgiːsən] (unreg) vt to water; (mit Alkohol) to drink to

Beginn [bəˈgɪn] (**-(e)s**) m beginning; **zu** ~ at the beginning; **b**~**en** (unreg) vt, vi to start, to begin

beglaubigen [bəˈglaʊbɪgən] vt to countersign; **Beglaubigung** f countersignature

begleichen [bəˈglaɪçən] (unreg) vt to settle, to pay

Begleit- [bəˈglaɪt] zW: **b**~**en** vt to accompany; (MIL) to escort; **~er** (**-s**, **-**) m companion; (Freund) escort; (MUS) accompanist; **~schreiben** nt covering letter; **~umstände** pl concomitant circumstances; **~ung** f company; (MIL) escort; (MUS) accompaniment

beglücken [bəˈglʏkən] vt to make happy, to delight

beglückwünschen [bəˈglʏkvʏnʃən] vt: ~ (**zu**) to congratulate (on)

begnadigen [bəˈgnaːdɪgən] vt to pardon; **Begnadigung** f pardon, amnesty

begnügen [bə'gny:gən] *vr* to be satisfied, to content o.s.

begonnen *etc* [bə'gɔnən] *vb siehe* **beginnen**

begraben [bə'gra:bən] (*unreg*) *vt* to bury; **Begräbnis** (-ses, -se) [bə'grɛ:pnɪs] *nt* burial, funeral

begreifen [bə'graıfən] (*unreg*) *vt* to understand, to comprehend

begreiflich [bə'graıflıç] *adj* understandable

begrenzen [bə'grɛntsən] *vt* (*beschränken*) to limit

Begrenztheit [bə'grɛntsthaıt] *f* limitation, restriction; (*fig*) narrowness

Begriff [bə'grɪf] (-(e)s, -e) *m* concept, idea; **im ~ sein, etw zu tun** to be about to do sth; **schwer von ~** (*umg*) slow, dense

begriffsstutzig *adj* slow, dense

begründ- [bə'grʏnd] *zW*: **~en** *vt* (*Gründe geben*) to justify; **~et** *adj* well-founded, justified; **B~ung** *f* justification, reason

begrüßen [bə'gry:sən] *vt* to greet, to welcome; **Begrüßung** *f* greeting, welcome

begünstigen [bə'gʏnstıgən] *vt* (*Person*) to favour; (*Sache*) to further, to promote

begutachten [bə'gu:t|axtən] *vt* to assess

begütert [bə'gy:tərt] *adj* wealthy, well-to-do

behaart [bə'ha:rt] *adj* hairy

behagen [bə'ha:gən] *vi*: **das behagt ihm nicht** he does not like it

behaglich [bə'ha:klıç] *adj* comfortable, cosy; **B~keit** *f* comfort, cosiness

behalten [bə'haltən] (*unreg*) *vt* to keep, to retain; (*im Gedächtnis*) to remember

Behälter [bə'hɛltər] (-s, -) *m* container, receptacle

behandeln [bə'handəln] *vt* to treat; (*Thema*) to deal with; (*Maschine*) to handle

Behandlung *f* treatment; (*von Maschine*) handling

beharren [bə'harən] *vi*: **auf etw** *dat* ~ to stick *od* keep to sth

beharrlich [bə'harlıç] *adj* (*ausdauernd*) steadfast, unwavering; (*hartnäckig*) tenacious, dogged; **B~keit** *f* steadfastness; tenacity

behaupten [bə'hauptən] *vt* to claim, to assert, to maintain; (*sein Recht*) to defend ♦ *vr* to assert o.s.

Behauptung *f* claim, assertion

beheben [bə'he:bən] (*unreg*) *vt* to remove

behelfen [bə'hɛlfən] (*unreg*) *vr*: **sich mit etw ~** to make do with sth

behelfsmäßig *adj* improvised, makeshift; (*vorübergehend*) temporary

behelligen [bə'hɛlıgən] *vt* to trouble, to bother

beherbergen [bə'hɛrbergən] *vt* to put up, to house

beherrsch- [bə'hɛrʃ] *zW*: **~en** *vt* (*Volk*) to rule, to govern; (*Situation*) to control; (*Sprache, Gefühle*) to master ♦ *vr* to control o.s.; **~t** *adj* controlled; **B~ung** *f* rule; control; mastery

beherzigen [bə'hɛrtsıgən] *vt* to take to heart

beherzt *adj* courageous, brave

behilflich [bə'hılflıç] *adj* helpful; **jdm ~ sein (bei)** to help sb (with)

behindern [bə'hındərn] *vt* to hinder, to impede

Behinderte(r) *f(m)* disabled person

Behinderung *f* hindrance; (*Körperbehinderung*) handicap

Behörde [bə'hø:rdə] *f* (*auch pl*) authorities *pl*

behördlich [bə'hø:rtlıç] *adj* official

behüten [bə'hy:tən] *vt* to guard; **jdn vor etw** *dat* ~ to preserve sb from sth

behutsam [bə'hu:tza:m] *adj* cautious, careful; **B~keit** *f* caution, carefulness

---

SCHLÜSSELWORT

---

bei [baı] *präp* +*dat* **1** (*nahe bei*) near;

(zum Aufenthalt) at, with; (unter, zwischen) among; **bei München** near Munich; **bei uns** at our place; **beim Friseur** at the hairdresser's; **bei seinen Eltern wohnen** to live with one's parents; **bei einer Firma arbeiten** to work for a firm; **etw bei sich haben** to have sth on one; **jdn bei sich haben** to have sb with one; **bei Goethe** in Goethe; **beim Militär** in the army **2** (zeitlich) at; on; (während) during; (Zustand, Umstand) in; **bei Nacht** at night; **bei Nebel** in fog; **bei Regen** if it rains; **bei solcher Hitze** in such heat; **bei meiner Ankuft** on my arrival; **bei der Arbeit** when I'm etc working; **beim Fahren** while driving

beibehalten ['baɪbəhaltən] (unreg) vt to keep, to retain

beibringen ['baɪbrɪŋən] (unreg) vt (Beweis, Zeugen) to bring forward; (Gründe) to adduce; **jdm etw ~** (lehren) to teach sb sth; (zu verstehen geben) to make sb understand sth; (zufügen) to inflict sth on sb

Beichte ['baɪçtə] f confession; **b~n** vt to confess ♦ vi to go to confession

beide(s) ['baɪdə(s)] pron, adj both; **meine ~n Brüder** my two brothers, both my brothers; **die ersten ~n** the first two; **wir ~** we two; **einer von ~n** one of the two; **alles ~s** both of them

beider- ['baɪdər] zW: **~lei** adj inv of both; **~seitig** adj mutual, reciprocal; **~seits** adv mutually ♦ präp +gen on both sides of

beieinander [baɪaɪ'nandər] adv together

Beifahrer ['baɪfaːrər] m passenger

Beifall ['baɪfal] (-(e)s) m applause; (Zustimmung) approval

beifügen ['baɪfyːgən] vt to enclose

beige ['beːʒ] adj beige, fawn

beigeben ['baɪgeːbən] (unreg) vt (zufügen) to add; (mitgeben) to give ♦ vi (nachgeben) to give in

Beihilfe ['baɪhɪlfə] f aid, assistance; (Studienbeihilfe) grant; (JUR) aiding and abetting

beikommen ['baɪkɔmən] (unreg) vi +dat to get at; (einem Problem) to deal with

Beil [baɪl] (-(e)s, -e) nt axe, hatchet

Beilage ['baɪlaːgə] f (Buchbeilage etc) supplement; (KOCH) vegetables and potatoes pl

beiläufig ['baɪlɔyfɪç] adj casual, incidental ♦ adv casually, by the way

beilegen ['baɪleːgən] vt (hinzufügen) to enclose, to add; (beimessen) to attribute, to ascribe; (Streit) to settle

Beileid ['baɪlaɪt] nt condolence, sympathy; **herzliches ~** deepest sympathy

beiliegend ['baɪliːgənt] adj (COMM) enclosed

beim [baɪm] = **bei dem**

beimessen ['baɪmɛsən] (unreg) vt (+dat) to attribute (to), to ascribe (to)

Bein [baɪn] (-(e)s, -e) nt leg

beinah(e) ['baɪnaː(ə)] adv almost, nearly

Beinbruch m fracture of the leg

beinhalten [bə'ʔɪnhaltən] vt to contain

Beipackzettel ['baɪpaktsetəl] m instruction leaflet

beipflichten ['baɪpflɪçtən] vi: **jdm/etw ~** to agree with sb/sth

beisammen [baɪ'zamən] adv together; **B~sein** (-s) nt get-together

Beischlaf ['baɪʃlaːf] m sexual intercourse

Beisein ['baɪzaɪn] (-s) nt presence

beiseite [baɪ'zaɪtə] adv to one side, aside; (stehen) on one side, aside; **etw ~ legen** (sparen) to put sth by

beisetzen ['baɪzɛtsən] vt to bury; **Beisetzung** f funeral

Beisitzer ['baɪzɪtsər] (-s, -) m (bei

Prüfung) assessor

Beispiel ['baiʃpiːl] (-(e)s, -e) nt example; **sich** +dat **an** jdm ein ~ **nehmen** to take sb as an example; **zum ~** for example; **b~haft** adj exemplary; **b~los** adj unprecedented; **b~sweise** adv for instance od example

beißen ['baisən] (unreg) vt, vi to bite; *(stechen: Rauch, Säure)* to burn ♦ vr *(Farben)* to clash; **~d** adj biting, caustic; *(fig auch)* sarcastic

Beistand ['baiʃtant] (-(e)s, ²e) m support, help; *(JUR)* adviser

beistehen ['baiʃteːən] (unreg) vi: **jdm ~** to stand by sb

beisteuern ['baiʃtɔyərn] vt to contribute

Beitrag ['baitraːk] (-(e)s, ²e) m contribution; *(Zahlung)* fee, subscription; *(Versicherungsbeitrag)* premium; **b~en** ['baitraːgən] (unreg) vt, vi: **b~en (zu)** to contribute (to); *(mithelfen)* to help (with)

beitreten ['baitreːtən] (unreg) vi +dat to join

Beitritt ['baitrɪt] m joining, membership

Beiwagen ['baivaːgən] m *(Motorradbeiwagen)* sidecar

beizeiten [bai'tsaitən] adv in time

bejahen [bə'jaːən] vt *(Frage)* to say yes to, to answer in the affirmative; *(gutheißen)* to agree with

bekämpfen [bə'kɛmpfən] vt *(Gegner)* to fight; *(Seuche)* to combat ♦ vr to fight; **Bekämpfung** f fight, struggle

bekannt [bə'kant] adj (well-)known; *(nicht fremd)* familiar; ~ **sein** to announce publicly; **mit** jdm ~ **sein** to know sb; ~ **machen** to announce; jdn **mit** jdm ~ **machen** to introduce sb to sb; **das ist mir** ~ I know that; **es/sie kommt mir** ~ **vor** it/she seems familiar; **B~e(r)** f(m) acquaintance; friend; **B~enkreis** m circle of friends; **~lich** adv as is well known, as you know; **B~machung** f publication; announce-

ment; **B~schaft** f acquaintance

bekehren [bə'keːrən] vt to convert ♦ vr to be od become converted

bekennen [bə'kɛnən] (unreg) vt to confess; *(Glauben)* to profess; **Farbe ~** *(umg)* to show where one stands

Bekenntnis [bə'kɛntnɪs] (-ses, -se) nt admission, confession; *(Religion)* confession, denomination

beklagen [bə'klaːgən] vt to deplore, to lament ♦ vr to complain

bekleiden [bə'klaidən] vt to clothe; *(Amt)* to occupy, to fill

Bekleidung f clothing

beklemmen [bə'klɛmən] vt to oppress

beklommen [bə'klɔmən] adj anxious, uneasy

bekommen [bə'kɔmən] (unreg) vt to get, to receive; *(Kind)* to have; *(Zug)* to catch, to get ♦ vi: **jdm ~** to agree with sb

bekömmlich [bə'kœmlɪç] adj easily digestible

bekräftigen [bə'krɛftɪgən] vt to confirm, to corroborate

bekreuzigen [bə'krɔytsɪgən] vr to cross o.s.

bekunden [bə'kundən] vt *(sagen)* to state; *(zeigen)* to show

belächeln [bə'lɛçəln] vt to laugh at

beladen [bə'laːdən] (unreg) vt to load

Belag [bə'laːk] (-(e)s, ²e) m covering, coating; *(Brotbelag)* spread; *(Zahnbelag)* tartar; *(auf Zunge)* fur; *(Bremsbelag)* lining

belagern [bə'laːgərn] vt to besiege; **Belagerung** f siege

Belang [bə'laŋ] (-(e)s) m importance; **~e** pl *(Interessen)* interests, concerns; **b~los** adj trivial, unimportant

belassen [bə'lasən] (unreg) vt *(in Zustand, Glauben)* to leave; *(in Stellung)* to retain

belasten [bə'lastən] vt to burden; *(fig: bedrücken)* to trouble, to worry; *(COMM: Konto)* to debit; *(JUR)* to incriminate ♦ vr to weigh o.s. down;

(JUR) to incriminate o.s.; **~d** *adj* *(JUR)* incriminating

belästigen [bəˈlɛstɪgən] *vt* to annoy, to pester; **Belästigung** *f* annoyance, pestering

Belastung [bəˈlastʊŋ] *f* load; *(fig: Sorge etc)* weight; *(COMM)* charge, debit(ing); *(JUR)* incriminatory evidence

belaufen [bəˈlaʊfən] *(unreg)* *vr*: **sich ~ auf** *+akk* to amount to

beleben [bəˈleːbən] *vt (anregen)* to liven up; *(Konjunktur, jds Hoffnungen)* to stimulate ♦ *vr (Augen)* to light up; *(Stadt)* to come to life

belebt [bəˈleːpt] *adj (Straße)* busy

Beleg [bəˈleːk] **(-(e)s, -e)** *m (COMM)* receipt; *(Beweis)* documentary evidence, proof; *(Beispiel)* example; **b~en** *vt* to cover; *(Kuchen, Brot)* to spread; *(Platz)* to reserve, to book; *(Kurs, Vorlesung)* to register for; *(beweisen)* to verify, to prove; *(MIL: mit Bomben)* to bomb; **~schaft** *f* personnel, staff; **b~t** *adj*: **b~tes Brot** open sandwich

belehren [bəˈleːrən] *vt* to instruct, to teach; **Belehrung** *f* instruction

beleibt [bəˈlaɪpt] *adj* stout, corpulent

beleidigen [bəˈlaɪdɪgən] *vt* to insult, to offend; **Beleidigung** *f* insult; *(JUR)* slander, libel

beleuchten [bəˈlɔʏçtən] *vt* to light, to illuminate; *(fig)* to throw light on

Beleuchtung *f* lighting, illumination

Belgien [ˈbɛlgiən] *nt* Belgium; **Belgier(in)** *m(f)* Belgian; **belgisch** *adj* Belgian

belichten [bəˈlɪçtən] *vt* to expose

Belichtung *f* exposure; **~smesser** *m* exposure meter

Belieben [bəˈliːbən] *nt*: **(ganz) nach ~** (just) as you wish

beliebig [bəˈliːbɪç] *adj* any you like ♦ *adv* as you like; **ein ~es Thema** any subject you like *od* want; **~ viel/viele** as much/many as you like

beliebt [bəˈliːpt] *adj* popular; **sich bei jdm ~ machen** to make o.s. popular with sb; **B~heit** *f* popularity

beliefern [bəˈliːfərn] *vt* to supply

bellen [ˈbɛlən] *vi* to bark

belohnen [bəˈloːnən] *vt* to reward; **Belohnung** *f* reward

Belüftung [bəˈlʏftʊŋ] *f* ventilation

belügen [bəˈlyːgən] *(unreg)* *vt* to lie to, to deceive

belustigen [bəˈlʊstɪgən] *vt* to amuse; **Belustigung** *f* amusement

bemalen [bəˈmaːlən] *vt* to paint

bemängeln [bəˈmɛŋəln] *vt* to criticize

bemerk- [bəˈmɛrk] *zW:* **~bar** *adj* perceptible, noticeable; **sich ~bar machen** *(Person)* to make *od* get o.s. noticed; *(Unruhe)* to become noticeable; **~en** *vt (wahrnehmen)* to notice, to observe; *(sagen)* to say, to mention; **~enswert** *adj* remarkable, noteworthy; **B~ung** *f* remark; *(schriftlich auch)* note

bemitleiden [bəˈmɪtlaɪdən] *vt* to pity

bemühen [bəˈmyːən] *vr* to take trouble *od* pains; **Bemühung** *f* trouble, pains *pl*, effort

benachbart [bəˈnaxbaːrt] *adj* neighbouring

benachrichtigen [bəˈnaːxrɪçtɪgən] *vt* to inform; **Benachrichtigung** *f* notification, information

benachteiligen [bəˈnaːxtaɪlɪgən] *vt* to put at a disadvantage; to victimize

benehmen [bəˈneːmən] *(unreg)* *vr* to behave; **B~** **(-s)** *nt* behaviour

beneiden [bəˈnaɪdən] *vt* to envy; **~swert** *adj* enviable

benennen [bəˈnɛnən] *(unreg)* *vt* to name

Bengel [ˈbɛŋəl] **(-s, -)** *m* (little) rascal *od* rogue

benommen [bəˈnɔmən] *adj* dazed

benoten [bəˈnoːtən] *vt* to mark

benötigen [bəˈnøːtɪgən] *vt* to need

benutzen [bəˈnʊtsən] vt to use

Benutzer (-s, -) m user

Benutzung f utilization, use

Benzin [bɛntˈsiːn] (-s, -e) nt petrol (BRIT), gas(oline) (US); **~kanister** m petrol (BRIT) od gas (US) can; **~tank** m petrol tank (BRIT), gas tank (US); **~uhr** f petrol (BRIT) od gas (US) gauge

beobachten [bəˈloːbaxtən] vt to observe; **Beobachter** (-s, -) m observer; (eines Unfalls) witness; (PRESSE, TV) correspondent; **Beobachtung** f observation

bepacken [bəˈpakən] vt to load, to pack

bequem [bəˈkveːm] adj comfortable; (Ausrede) convenient; (Person) lazy, indolent; **~en** vr: **sich ~en(, etw zu tun)** to condescend (to do sth); **B~lichkeit** [-ˈlɪçkaɪt] f convenience, comfort; (Faulheit) laziness, indolence

beraten [bəˈraːtən] (unreg) vt to advise; (besprechen) to discuss, to debate ♦ vr to consult; **gut/schlecht ~ sein** to be well/ill advised; **sich ~ lassen** to get advice

Berater (-s, -) m adviser

Beratung f advice; (Besprechung) consultation; **~stelle** f advice centre

berauben [bəˈraʊbən] vt to rob

berechenbar [bəˈrɛçənbaːr] adj calculable

berechnen [bəˈrɛçnən] vt to calculate; (COMM: anrechnen) to charge; **~d** adj (Mensch) calculating, scheming

Berechnung f calculation; (COMM) charge

berechtigen [bəˈrɛçtɪgən] vt to entitle; to authorize; (fig) to justify

berechtigt [bəˈrɛçtɪçt] adj justifiable, justified

Berechtigung f authorization; (fig) justification

bereden [bəˈreːdən] vt (besprechen) to discuss; (überreden) to persuade ♦ vr to discuss

Bereich [bəˈraɪç] (-(e)s, -e) m (Bezirk) area; (PHYS) range; (Ressort, Gebiet) sphere

bereichern [bəˈraɪçərn] vt to enrich ♦ vr to get rich

bereinigen [bəˈraɪnɪgən] vt to settle

bereisen [bəˈraɪzən] vt (Land) to travel through

bereit [bəˈraɪt] adj ready, prepared; **zu etw ~ sein** to be ready for sth; **sich ~erklären** to declare o.s. willing; **~en** vt to prepare, to make ready; (Kummer, Freude) to cause; **~halten** (unreg) vt to keep in readiness; **~legen** vt to lay out; **~machen** vt, vr to prepare, to get ready; **~s** adv already; **B~schaft** f readiness; (Polizei) alert; **B~schaftsdienst** m emergency service; **~stehen** (unreg) vi (Person) to be prepared; (Ding) to be ready; **~stellen** vt (Kisten, Pakete etc) to put ready; (Geld etc) to make available; (Truppen, Maschinen) to put at the ready; **~willig** adj willing, ready; **B~willigkeit** f willingness, readiness

bereuen [bəˈrɔʏən] vt to regret

Berg [bɛrk] (-(e)s, -e) m mountain; hill; **b~ab** adv downhill; **~arbeiter** m miner; **b~auf** adv uphill; **~bahn** f mountain railway; **~bau** m mining

bergen [ˈbɛrgən] (unreg) vt (retten) to rescue; (Ladung) to salvage; (enthalten) to contain

Berg- zW: **~führer** m mountain guide; **~gipfel** m peak, summit; **b~ig** [ˈbɛrgɪç] adj mountainous; hilly; **~kette** f mountain range; **~mann** (-leute) m miner; **~rettungsdienst** m mountain rescue team; **~rutsch** m landslide; **~steigen** nt mountaineering; **~steiger(in)** (-s, -) m(f) mountaineer, climber; **~tour** f mountain climb

Bergung [ˈbɛrgʊŋ] f (von Menschen) rescue; (von Material) recovery; (NAUT) salvage

Berg- zW: **~wacht** f mountain rescue service; **~wanderung** f hike in the mountains; **~werk** nt mine

Bericht [bəˈrɪçt] (-(e)s, -e) *m* report, account; **b~en** *vt, vi* to report; **~erstatter** (-s, -) *m* reporter; (newspaper) correspondent

berichtigen [bəˈrɪçtɪgən] *vt* to correct; **Berichtigung** *f* correction

Bernstein [ˈbɛrnʃtain] *m* amber

bersten [ˈbɛrstən] (*unreg*) *vi* to burst, to split

berüchtigt [bəˈrʏçtɪçt] *adj* notorious, infamous

berücksichtigen [bəˈrʏkzɪçtɪgən] *vt* to consider, to bear in mind; **Berücksichtigung** *f* consideration

Beruf [bəˈruːf] (-(e)s, -e) *m* occupation, profession; (*Gewerbe*) trade; **b~en** (*unreg*) *vt*: **b~en zu** to appoint to ♦ *vr*: **sich auf jdn/etw b~en** to refer ad appeal to sb/sth ♦ *adj* competent, qualified; **b~lich** *adj* professional

Berufs- *zW*: **~ausbildung** *f* job training; **~berater** *m* careers adviser; **~beratung** *f* vocational guidance; **~geheimnis** *nt* professional secret; **~leben** *nt* professional life; **~schule** *f* vocational *od* trade school; **~sportler** [-ʃpɔrtlər] *m* professional (sportsman); **b~tätig** *adj* employed; **b~unfähig** *adj* unfit for work; **~verkehr** *m* rush-hour traffic

Berufung *f* vocation, calling; (*Ernennung*) appointment; (*JUR*) appeal; **~ einlegen** to appeal

beruhen [bəˈruːən] *vi*: **auf etw** *dat* **~** to be based on sth; **etw auf sich ~ lassen** to leave sth at that

beruhigen [bəˈruːɪgən] *vt* to calm, to pacify, to soothe ♦ *vr* (*Mensch*) to calm (o.s.) down; (*Situation*) to calm down

Beruhigung *f* soothing; (*der Nerven*) calming; **zu jds ~** (in order) to reassure sb; **b~smittel** *nt* sedative

berühmt [bəˈryːmt] *adj* famous; **B~heit** *f* (*Ruf*) fame; (*Mensch*) celebrity

berühren [bəˈryːrən] *vt* to touch; (*ge-*

fühlsmäßig bewegen) to affect; (*flüchtig erwähnen*) to mention, to touch on ♦ *vr* to meet, to touch

Berührung *f* contact

besagen [bəˈzaːgən] *vt* to mean

besänftigen [bəˈzɛnftɪgən] *vt* to soothe, to calm

Besatz [bəˈzats] (-es, ⁼e) *m* trimming, edging

Besatzung *f* garrison; (*NAUT, AVIAT*) crew

Besatzungsmacht *f* occupying power

beschädigen [bəˈʃɛːdɪgən] *vt* to damage; **Beschädigung** *f* damage; (*Stelle*) damaged spot

beschaffen [bəˈʃafən] *vt* to get, to acquire ♦ *adj*: **das ist so ~, dass** that is such that; **B~heit** *f* (*von Mensch*) constitution, nature

Beschaffung *f* acquisition

beschäftigen [bəˈʃɛftɪgən] *vt* to occupy; (*beruflich*) to employ ♦ *vr* to occupy *od* concern o.s.

beschäftigt *adj* busy, occupied

Beschäftigung *f* (*Beruf*) employment; (*Tätigkeit*) occupation; (*Befassen*) concern

beschämen [bəˈʃɛːmən] *vt* to put to shame; **~d** *adj* shameful; (*Hilfsbereitschaft*) shaming

beschämt *adj* ashamed

Bescheid [bəˈʃait] (-(e)s, -e) *m* information; (*Weisung*) directions *pl*; **~ wissen** (**über +akk**) to be well-informed (about); **ich weiß ~** I know; **jdm ~ geben** *od* **sagen** to let sb know

bescheiden [bəˈʃaidən] (*unreg*) *vr* to content o.s. ♦ *adj* modest; **B~heit** *f* modesty

bescheinen [bəˈʃainən] (*unreg*) *vt* to shine on

bescheinigen [bəˈʃainɪgən] *vt* to certify; (*bestätigen*) to acknowledge

Bescheinigung *f* certificate; (*Quittung*)

receipt

beschenken [bə'ʃɛŋkən] *vt*: jdn mit etw ~ to give sb sth as a present

bescheren [bə'ʃeːrən] *vt*: jdm etw ~ to give sb sth as a Christmas present; jdn ~ to give Christmas presents to sb

Bescherung *f* giving of Christmas presents; (*umg*) mess

beschildern [bə'ʃildərn] *vt* to put signs/a sign on

beschimpfen [bə'ʃimpfən] *vt* to abuse; **Beschimpfung** *f* abuse; insult

Beschlag [bə'ʃlaːk] (-(e)s, ᵉe) *m* (*Metallband*) fitting; (*auf Fenster*) condensation; (*auf Metall*) tarnish; finish; (*Hufeisen*) horseshoe; jdn/etw in ~ nehmen *od* mit ~ belegen to monopolize sb/sth; **b~en** [bə'ʃlaːgən] (*unreg*) *vt* to cover; (*Pferd*) to shoe ♦ *vi*, *vr* (*Fenster etc*) to mist over; **b~en sein** (in *od* auf +*dat*) to be well versed (in); **b~nahmen** *vt* to seize, to confiscate; to requisition; **~nahmung** *f* confiscation (to)

beschleunigen [bə'ʃlɔynigən] *vt* to accelerate, to speed up ♦ *vi* (*AUT*) to accelerate; **Beschleunigung** *f* acceleration

beschließen [bə'ʃliːsən] (*unreg*) *vt* to decide on; (*beenden*) to end, to close

Beschluss ▲ [bə'ʃlus] (-es, ᵉe) *m* decision, conclusion; (*Ende*) conclusion, end

beschmutzen [bə'ʃmutsən] *vt* to dirty, to soil

beschönigen [bə'ʃøːnigən] *vt* to gloss over

beschränken [bə'ʃrɛŋkən] *vt*, *vr*: (sich) ~ (auf +*akk*) to limit *od* restrict (o.s.) (to)

beschränk- *zW*: **~t** *adj* confined, restricted; (*Mensch*) limited, narrow-minded; **B~ung** *f* limitation

beschreiben [bə'ʃraibən] (*unreg*) *vt* to describe; (*Papier*) to write on

Beschreibung *f* description

beschriften [bə'ʃriftən] *vt* to mark, to label; **Beschriftung** *f* lettering

beschuldigen [bə'ʃuldigən] *vt* to accuse; **Beschuldigung** *f* accusation

Beschuss ▲ [bə'ʃus] *m*: jdn/etw unter ~ nehmen (*MIL*) to open fire on sb/sth

beschützen [bə'ʃʏtsən] *vt*: ~ (vor +*dat*) to protect (from); **Beschützer** (-s, -) *m* protector

Beschwerde [bə'ʃveːrdə] *f* complaint; (*Mühe*) hardship; **~n** *pl* (*Leiden*) trouble

beschweren [bə'ʃveːrən] *vt* to weight down; (*fig*) to burden ♦ *vr* to complain

beschwerlich *adj* tiring, exhausting

beschwichtigen [bə'ʃviçtigən] *vt* to soothe, to pacify

beschwindeln [bə'ʃvindəln] *vt* (*betrügen*) to cheat; (*belügen*) to fib to

beschwingt [bə'ʃviŋt] *adj* in high spirits

beschwipst [bə'ʃvipst] (*umg*) *adj* tipsy

beschwören [bə'ʃvøːrən] (*unreg*) *vt* (*Aussage*) to swear to; (*anflehen*) to implore; (*Geister*) to conjure up

beseitigen [bə'zaitigən] *vt* to remove; **Beseitigung** *f* removal

Besen ['beːzən] (-s, -) *m* broom; **~stiel** *m* broomstick

besessen [bə'zɛsən] *adj* possessed

besetz- [bə'zɛts] *zW*: **~en** *vt* (*Haus, Land*) to occupy; (*Platz*) to take, to fill; (*Posten*) to fill; (*Rolle*) to cast; (*mit Edelsteinen*) to set; **~t** *adj* full; (*TEL*) engaged, busy; (*Platz*) taken; (*WC*) engaged; **B~tzeichen** *nt* engaged tone; **B~ung** *f* occupation; filling; (*von Rolle*) casting; (*die Schauspieler*) cast

besichtigen [bə'ziçtigən] *vt* to visit, to have a look at; **Besichtigung** *f* visit

besiegen [bə'ziːgən] *vt* to defeat, to overcome

besinn- [bə'zin] *zW*: **~en** (*unreg*) *vi* (*nachdenken*) to think, to reflect; (*erinnern*) to remember; **sich anders ~** to change one's mind; **B~ung** *f* consciousness; **zur B~ung kommen** to recover consciousness; (fig) to come to one's senses; **~ungslos** adj unconscious

Besitz [bə'zɪts] (-es) m possession; (Eigentum) property; **b~en** (unreg) vt to possess, to own; (Eigenschaft) to have; **~er(in)** (-s, -) m(f) owner, proprietor; **~ergreifung** f occupation, seizure

besoffen [bə'zɔfən] (umg) adj drunk, stoned

besohlen [bə'zo:lən] vt to sole

Besoldung [bə'zɔldʊŋ] f salary, pay

besondere(r, s) [bə'zɔndərə(r, s)] adj special; (eigen) particular; (gesondert) separate; (eigentümlich) peculiar

Besonderheit [bə'zɔndərhaɪt] f peculiarity

besonders [bə'zɔndərs] adv especially, particularly; (getrennt) separately

besonnen [bə'zɔnən] adj sensible, level-headed

besorg- [bə'zɔrg] zW: **~en** vt (beschaffen) to acquire; (kaufen auch) to purchase; (erledigen: Geschäfte) to deal with; (sich kümmern um) to take care of; **B~nis** (-, -se) f anxiety, concern; **~t** [bə'zɔrçt] adj anxious, worried; **B~ung** f acquisition; (Kauf) purchase

bespielen [bə'spi:lən] vt to record

bespitzeln [bə'spɪtsəln] vt to spy on

besprechen [bə'spreçən] (unreg) vt to discuss; (Tonband etc) to record, to speak onto; (Buch) to review ♦ vr to discuss, to consult; **Besprechung** f meeting, discussion; (von Buch) review

besser ['bɛsər] adj better; **es geht ihm ~** he is feeling better; **~n** vt to make better, to improve ♦ vr to improve; (Menschen) to reform; **B~ung** f improvement; **gute B~ung!** get well soon!; **B~wisser (-s, -)** m know-all

Bestand [bə'ʃtant] (-(e)s, ¨e) m (Fortbestehen) duration, stability; (Kassenbestand) amount, balance; (Vorrat) stock; **~ haben, von ~ sein** to last long, to

endure

beständig [bə'ʃtɛndɪç] adj (ausdauernd: auch fig) constant; (Wetter) settled; (Stoffe) resistant; (Klagen etc) continual

Bestandsaufnahme [bə'ʃtantsaʊfna:mə] f stocktaking

Bestandteil m part, component; (Zutat) ingredient

bestärken [bə'ʃtɛrkən] vt: **jdn in etw** dat **~** to strengthen od confirm sb in sth

bestätigen [bə'ʃtɛ:tɪgən] vt to confirm; (anerkennen, COMM) to acknowledge; **Bestätigung** f confirmation; acknowledgement

bestatten [bə'ʃtatən] vt to bury

Bestattung f funeral

Bestattungsinstitut nt funeral director's

bestaunen [bə'ʃtaʊnən] vt to marvel at, gaze at in wonder

beste(r, s) [bə'stə(r, s)] adj best; **so ist es am ~n** it's best that way; **am ~n gehst du gleich** you'd better go at once; **jdn zum B~n haben** to pull sb's leg; **einen Witz etc zum B~n geben** to tell a joke etc; **aufs B~** od ~ in the best possible way; **zu jds B~n** for the benefit of sb

bestechen [bə'ʃteçən] (unreg) vt to bribe; **bestechlich** adj corruptible; **Bestechung** f bribery, corruption

Besteck [bə'ʃtɛk] (-(e)s, -e) nt knife, fork and spoon, cutlery; (MED) set of instruments

bestehen [bə'ʃte:ən] (unreg) vi to be; to exist; (andauern) to last ♦ vt (Kampf, Probe, Prüfung) to pass; **~ auf** +dat to insist on; **~ aus** to consist of

bestehlen [bə'ʃte:lən] (unreg) vt: **jdn (um etw) ~** to rob sb (of sth)

besteigen [bə'ʃtaɪgən] (unreg) vt to climb, to ascend; (Pferd) to mount; (Thron) to ascend

Bestell- [bə'ʃtɛl] zW: **~buch** nt order

book; **b~en** vt to order; (kommen lassen) to arrange to see; (nominieren) to name; (Acker) to cultivate; (Grüße, Auftrag) to pass on; **~formular** nt order form; **~nummer** f order code; **~ung** f (COMM) order; (~en) ordering

bestenfalls ['bestan'fals] adv at best

bestens ['bestans] adv very well

besteuern [bə'ʃtɔyərn] vt (jdn, Waren) to tax

Bestie ['bestiə] f (auch fig) beast

bestimm- [bə'ʃtɪm] zW: **~en** vt (Regeln) to lay down; (Tag, Ort) to fix; (beherrschen) to characterize; (vorsehen) to mean; (ernennen) to appoint; (definieren) to define; (veranlassen) to induce; **~t** adj (entschlossen) firm; (gewiss) certain, definite; (Artikel) definite ♦ adv (gewiss) definitely, for sure; **suchen Sie etwas B~tes?** are you looking for something in particular?; **B~theit** f firmness; certainty; **B~ung** f (Verordnung) regulation; (Festsetzen) determining; (Verwendungszweck) purpose; (Schicksal) fate; (Definition) definition; **B~ungsland** nt (country of) destination; **B~ungsort** m (place of) destination

Bestleistung f best performance

bestmöglich adj best possible

bestrafen [bə'ʃtra:fən] vt to punish; **Bestrafung** f punishment

bestrahlen [bə'ʃtra:lən] vt to shine on; (MED) to treat with X-rays

Bestrahlung f (MED) X-ray treatment, radiotherapy

Bestreben [bə'ʃtre:bən] (-s) nt endeavour, effort

bestreiten [bə'ʃtraitən] (unreg) vt (abstreiten) to dispute; (finanzieren) to pay for, to finance

bestreuen [bə'ʃtrɔyən] vt to sprinkle, to dust; (Straße) to grit

bestürmen [bə'ʃtʏrmən] vt (mit Fragen, Bitten etc) to overwhelm, to swamp

bestürzend [bə'ʃtʏrtsənd] adj (Nachrichten) disturbing

bestürzt [bə'ʃtʏrtst] adj dismayed

Bestürzung f consternation

Besuch [bə'zu:x] (-(e)s, -e) m visit; (Person) visitor; **einen ~ machen bei jdm** to pay sb a visit od call; **~ haben** to have visitors; **jdn auf od zu ~ sein** to be visiting sb; **b~en** vt to visit; (SCH etc) to attend; **gut b~t** well-attended; **~er(in)** (-s, -) m(f) visitor, guest; **~szeit** f visiting hours pl

betätigen [bə'tɛ:tɪgən] vt (bedienen) to work, to operate ♦ vr to involve o.s.; **sich als etw ~** to work as sth

Betätigung f activity; (beruflich) occupation; (TECH) operation

betäuben [bə'tɔybən] vt to stun; (fig: Gewissen) to still; (MED) to anaesthetize

Betäubung f (Narkose): **örtliche ~** local anaesthetic

Betäubungsmittel nt anaesthetic

Bete ['be:tə] f: **Rote ~** beetroot (BRIT), beet (US)

beteilig- [bə'tailig] zW: **~en** vr: **sich ~en** (an +dat) to take part (in), to participate (in), to share (in); (an Geschäft: finanziell) to have a share (in) ♦ vt: **jdn ~en** (an +dat) to give sb a share of interest (in); **B~te(r)** f(m) (Mitwirkender) partner; (finanziell) shareholder; **B~ung** f participation; (Anteil) share, interest; (Besucherzahl) attendance

beten ['be:tən] vt, vi to pray

beteuern [bə'tɔyərn] vt to assert; (Unschuld) to protest

Beton [be'tɔ:] (-s, -s) m concrete

betonen [bə'to:nən] vt to stress

betonieren [beto'ni:rən] vt to concrete

Betonung f stress, emphasis

betr. abk (= betrifft) re

Betracht [bə'traxt] m: **in ~ kommen** to be considered od relevant; **etw in ~ ziehen** to take sth into consideration; **außer ~ bleiben** not to be considered; **b~en** vt to look at; (fig) to look at, to consider; **~er(in)** (-s, -) m(f) observer

beträchtlich [bə'trɛçtlıç] *adj* considerable

Betrachtung *f* (*Ansehen*) examination; (*Erwägung*) consideration

Betrag [bə'tra:k] (-(e)s, ⸗e) *m* amount; **b~en** (*unreg*) *vt* to amount to ♦ *vr* to behave; **~en** (-s) *nt* behaviour

Betreff *m*: ~ **Ihr Schreiben vom ...** re your letter of ...

betreffen [bə'trɛfən] (*unreg*) *vt* to concern, to affect; **was mich betrifft** as for me; **~d** *adj* relevant, in question

betreffs [bə'trɛfs] *präp* +*gen* concerning, regarding, (*COMM*)

betreiben [bə'traıbən] (*unreg*) *vt* (*ausüben*) to practise; (*Politik*) to follow; (*Studien*) to pursue; (*vorantreiben*) to push ahead; (*TECH: antreiben*) to drive

betreten [bə'tre:tən] (*unreg*) *vt* to enter; (*Bühne etc*) to step onto ♦ *adj* embarrassed; **B~ verboten** keep off/out

Betreuer(in) [bə'trɔʏər(ın)] *m(f)* (*einer Person*) minder; (*eines Gebäudes, Arbeitsgebiets*) caretaker; (*SPORT*) coach

Betreuung *f* care

Betrieb [bə'tri:p] (-(e)s, -e) *m* (*Firma*) firm, concern; (*Anlage*) plant; (*Tätigkeit*) operation; (*Treiben*) traffic; **außer ~ sein** to be out of order; **in ~ sein** to be in operation

Betriebs- *zW*: **~ausflug** *m* works outing; **b~bereit** *adj* operational; **b~fähig** *adj* in working order; **~ferien** *pl* company holidays (*BRIT*), company vacation *sg* (*US*); **~klima** *nt* (working) atmosphere; **~kosten** *pl* running costs; **~rat** *m* workers' council; **b~sicher** *adj* safe (to operate); **~störung** *f* breakdown; **~system** *nt* (*COMPUT*) operating system; **~unfall** *m* industrial accident; **~wirtschaft** *f* economics

betrinken [bə'trıŋkən] (*unreg*) *vr* to get drunk

betroffen [bə'trɔfən] *adj* (*bestürzt*) full

of consternation; **von etw ~ werden** *od* **sein** to be affected by sth

betrüben [bə'try:bən] *vt* to grieve

betrübt [bə'try:pt] *adj* sorrowful, grieved

Betrug [bə'tru:k] (-(e)s) *m* deception; (*JUR*) fraud

betrügen [bə'try:gən] (*unreg*) *vt* to cheat; (*JUR*) to defraud; (*Ehepartner*) to be unfaithful to ♦ *vr* to deceive o.s.

Betrüger (-s, -) *m* cheat, deceiver; **b~isch** *adj* deceitful; (*JUR*) fraudulent

betrunken [bə'trʊŋkən] *adj* drunk

Bett [bɛt] (-(e)s, -en) *nt* bed; **ins** *od* **zu ~ gehen** to go to bed; **~bezug** *m* duvet cover; **~decke** *f* blanket; (*Daunenbett*) quilt; (*Überwurf*) bedspread

Bettel- ['bɛtəl] *zW*: **b~arm** *adj* very poor, destitute; **~ei** [bɛtə'laı] *f* begging; **b~n** *vi* to beg

bettlägerig ['bɛtlɛ:gərıç] *adj* bedridden

Bettlaken *nt* sheet

Bettler(in) ['bɛtlər(ın)] (-s, -) *m(f)* beggar

Bett- *zW*: **~tuch** ▲ *nt* sheet; **~vorleger** *m* bedside rug; **~wäsche** *f* bed linen; **~zeug** *nt* bed linen *pl*

beugen ['bɔʏgən] *vt* to bend; (*GRAM*) to inflect ♦ *vr* (*sich fügen*) to bow

Beule ['bɔʏlə] *f* bump, swelling

beunruhigen [bə'ʊnru:ıgən] *vt* to disturb, to alarm ♦ *vr* to become worried

Beunruhigung *f* worry, alarm

beurlauben [bə'u:rlaʊbən] *vt* to give leave *od* a holiday to (*BRIT*), to grant vacation time to (*US*)

beurteilen [bə'ʊrtaılən] *vt* to judge; (*Buch etc*) to review

Beurteilung *f* judgement; review; (*Note*) mark

Beute ['bɔʏtə] (-) *f* booty, loot

Beutel (-s, -) *m* bag; (*Geldbeutel*) purse; (*Tabakbeutel*) pouch

Bevölkerung [bə'fœlkərʊŋ] *f* population

Spelling Reform: ▲ *new spelling* △ *old spelling (to be phased out)*

bevollmächtigen [bəˈfɔlmɛçtɪɡən] vt to authorize

Bevollmächtigte(r) f(m) authorized agent

bevor [bəˈfoːr] konj before; **~munden** vt insep to treat like a child; **~stehen** (unreg) vi: (jdm) **~stehen** to be in store (for sb); **~stehend** adj imminent, approaching; **~zugen** vt insep to prefer

bewachen [bəˈvaxən] vt to watch, to guard

Bewachung f (Bewachen) guarding; (Leute) guard, watch

bewaffnen [bəˈvafnən] vt to arm

Bewaffnung f (Vorgang) arming; (Ausrüstung) armament, arms pl

bewahren [bəˈvaːrən] vt to keep; jdn vor jdm/etw ~ to save sb from sth/sb

bewähren [bəˈvɛːrən] vr to prove o.s.; (Maschine) to prove its worth

bewahrheiten [bəˈvaːrhaɪtən] vr to come true

bewährt adj reliable

Bewährung f (Jur) probation

bewältigen [bəˈvɛltɪɡən] vt to overcome; (Arbeit) to finish; (Portion) to manage

bewandert [bəˈvandərt] adj expert, knowledgeable

bewässern [bəˈvɛsərn] vt to irrigate

Bewässerung f irrigation

bewegen [bəˈveːɡən] vt, vr to move; jdn zu etw ~ to induce sb to do sth; **~d** adj touching, moving

Beweg- [bəˈveːk] zW: **~grund** m motive; **b~lich** adj movable; (flink) quick; **b~t** adj (Leben) eventful; (Meer) rough; (ergriffen) touched

Bewegung f movement, motion; (innere) emotion; (körperlich) exercise; **~sfreiheit** f freedom of movement; (fig) freedom of action; **b~ungslos** adj motionless

Beweis [bəˈvaɪs] (-es, -e) m proof; (Zeichen) sign; **b~en** (-zen) (unreg) vt to prove; (zeigen) to show; **~mittel** nt evidence

Bewerb- [bəˈvɛrb] zW: **b~en** (unreg) vr to apply (for); **~er(in)** (-s, -) m(f) applicant; **~ung** f application

bewerkstelligen [bəˈvɛrkʃtɛlɪɡən] vt to manage, to accomplish

bewerten [bəˈvɛrtən] vt to assess

bewilligen [bəˈvɪlɪɡən] vt to grant, to allow

Bewilligung f granting

bewirken [bəˈvɪrkən] vt to cause, to bring about

bewirten [bəˈvɪrtən] vt to feed, to entertain (to a meal)

bewirtschaften [bəˈvɪrtʃaftən] vt to manage

Bewirtung f hospitality

bewog etc [bəˈvoːk] vb siehe bewegen

bewohn- [bəˈvoːn] zW: **~bar** adj habitable; **~en** vt to inhabit, to live in; **B~er(in)** (-s, -) m(f) inhabitant; (von Haus) resident

bewölkt [bəˈvœlkt] adj cloudy, overcast

Bewölkung f clouds pl

Bewunder- [bəˈvondər] zW: **~er** (-s, -) m admirer; **b~n** vt to admire; **b~nswert** adj admirable, wonderful; **~ung** f admiration

bewusst ▲ [bəˈvʊst] adj conscious; (absichtlich) deliberate; sich dat einer Sache gen ~ sein to be aware of sth; **~los** adj unconscious; **B~losigkeit** f unconsciousness; **B~sein** nt consciousness; bei B~sein conscious

bezahlen [bəˈtsaːlən] vt to pay for

Bezahlung f payment

bezaubern [bəˈtsaubərn] vt to enchant, to charm

bezeichnen [bəˈtsaɪçnən] vt (kennzeichnen) to mark; (nennen) to call; (beschreiben) to describe; (zeigen) to show, to indicate; **~d** adj: **~d (für)** characteristic (of), typical (of)

Bezeichnung f (Zeichen) mark, sign; (Beschreibung) description

bezeugen [bəˈtsɔʏɡən] vt to testify to

Bezichtigung [bəˈtsɪçtɪɡʊŋ] f accusation

beziehen [bə'tsi:ən] (unreg) vt (mit Überzug) to cover; (Bett) to make; (Haus, Position) to move into; (Standpunkt) to take up; (erhalten) to receive; (Zeitung) to subscribe to, to take ♦ vr (Himmel) to cloud over; **etw auf jdn/ etw ~** to relate sth to sb/sth; **sich ~ auf** +akk to refer to

Beziehung f (Verbindung) connection; (Zusammenhang) relation; (Verhältnis) relationship; (Hinsicht) respect; **~en haben** (vorteilhaft) to have connections od contacts; **b~sweise** adv or; (genauer gesagt auch) that is, or rather

Bezirk [bə'tsɪrk] (-(e)s, -e) m district

Bezug [bə'tsu:k] (-(e)s, ⁻e) m (Hülle) covering; (COMM) ordering; (Gehalt) income, salary; (Beziehung): **~ (zu)** relation(ship) (to); **in ~ auf** +akk with reference to; **~ nehmen auf** +akk to refer to

bezüglich [bə'tsy:klɪç] präp +gen concerning, referring to ♦ adj (GRAM) relative; **auf etw** akk **~** relating to sth

bezwecken [bə'tsvɛkən] vt to aim at

bezweifeln [bə'tsvaɪfəln] vt to doubt, to query

BH m abk von Büstenhalter

Bhf. abk (= Bahnhof) station

Bibel ['bi:bəl] (-, -n) f Bible

Biber ['bi:bər] (-s, -) m beaver

Biblio- [bi:blio] zW: **~grafie** ▲ [-gra'fi:] f bibliography; **~thek** [-'te:k] (-, -en) f library; **~thekar(in)** [-te'ka:r(ɪn)] (-s, -e) m(f) librarian

biblisch ['bi:blɪʃ] adj biblical

bieder ['bi:dər] adj upright, worthy; (Kleid etc) plain

bieg- ['bi:g] zW: **~en** (unreg) vt, vr to bend ♦ vi to turn; **~sam** ['bi:k-] adj flexible; **B~ung** f bend, curve

Biene ['bi:nə] f bee

Bienenhonig m honey

Bienenwachs nt beeswax

Bier [bi:r] (-(e)s, -e) nt beer; **~deckel** m beer mat; **~garten** m beer garden; **~krug** m beer mug; **~zelt** nt beer tent

Biest [bi:st] (-s, -er) (umg: pej) nt (Tier) beast, creature; (Mensch) beast

bieten ['bi:tən] (unreg) vt to offer; (bei Versteigerung) to bid ♦ vr (Gelegenheit): **sich jdm ~** to present itself to sb; **sich auf etw ~ lassen** to put up with sth

Bikini [bi'ki:ni] (-s, -s) m bikini

Bilanz [bi'lants] f balance; (fig) outcome; **~ ziehen (aus)** to take stock (of)

Bild [bɪlt] (-(e)s, -er) nt (auch fig) picture; photo; (Spiegelbild) reflection; **~bericht** m photographic report

bilden ['bɪldən] vt to form; (erziehen) to educate; (ausmachen) to constitute ♦ vr to arise; (erziehen) to educate o.s.

Bilderbuch nt picture book

Bilderrahmen m picture frame

Bild- zW: **~fläche** f screen; (fig) scene; **~hauer** (-s, -) m sculptor; **b~hübsch** adj lovely, pretty as a picture; **b~lich** adj figurative; pictorial; **~schirm** m television screen; (COMPUT) monitor; **~schirmschoner** m (COMPUT) screen saver; **b~schön** adj lovely

Bildung [bɪldʊŋ] f formation; (Wissen, Benehmen) education

Billard ['bɪljart] (-s, -e) nt billiards sg; **~kugel** f billiard ball

billig ['bɪlɪç] adj cheap; (gerecht) fair, reasonable; **~en** ['bɪlɪgən] vt to approve of

Binde ['bɪndə] f bandage; (Armbinde) band; (MED) sanitary towel; **~gewebe** nt connective tissue; **~glied** nt connecting link; **~hautentzündung** f conjunctivitis; **b~n** (unreg) vt to bind, to tie; **~strich** m hyphen

Bindfaden ['bɪnt-] m string

Bindung f bond, tie; (Skibindung) bind-

binnen ['bɪnən] *präp* (+*dat od gen*) within; **B~hafen** *m* river port; **B~handel** *m* internal trade

Bio- [bio-] *in zW* bio-; **~chemie** *f* biochemistry; **~grafie** ▲ [-gra'fiː] *f* biography; **~laden** *m* wholefood shop; **~loge** [-'loːgə] (-n, -n) *m* biologist; **~logie** [-lo'giː] *f* biology; **b~logisch** [-'loːgɪʃ] *adj* biological; **~top** *m od nt* biotope

---
Bioladen

A **Bioladen** is a shop specializing in environmentally-friendly products such as phosphate-free washing powders, recycled paper and organically-grown vegetables.

Birke ['bɪrkə] *f* birch
Birne ['bɪrnə] *f* pear; (*ELEK*) (light) bulb

SCHLÜSSELWORT

bis [bɪs] *präp* +*akk*, *adv* **1** (*zeitlich*) till, until; (*bis spätestens*) by; **Sie haben bis Dienstag Zeit** you have until *od* till Tuesday; **bis Dienstag muss es fertig sein** it must be ready by Tuesday; **bis auf weiteres** until further notice; **bis in die Nacht** into the night; **bis bald/gleich** see you later/soon

2 (*räumlich*) (up) to; **ich fahre bis Köln** I'm going to *od* I'm going as far as Cologne; **bis an unser Grundstück** (right *od* up) to our plot; **bis hierher** this far

3 (*bei Zahlen*) up to; **bis zu** up to

4: **bis auf etw** *akk* (*außer*) except sth; (*einschließlich*) including sth
♦ *konj* **1** (*mit Zahlen*) to; **10 bis 20** 10 to 20

2 (*zeitlich*) till, until; **bis es dunkel wird** till *od* until it gets dark; **von ... bis ...** from ... to ...

Bischof ['bɪʃɔf] (-s, ⁼e) *m* bishop; **bischöflich** ['bɪʃøːflɪç] *adj* episcopal
bisher [bɪs'heːr] *adv* till now, hitherto

~ig *adj* till now
Biskuit [bɪs'kviːt] (-(e)s, -s *od* -e) *m od nt* (fatless) sponge
Biss ▲ [bɪs] (-es, -e) *m* bite
biss ▲ *etc vb siehe* **beißen**
bisschen ▲ ['bɪsçən] *adj, adv* bit
Bissen ['bɪsən] (-s, -) *m* bite, morsel
bissig ['bɪsɪç] *adj* (*Hund*) snappy; (*Bemerkung*) cutting, biting
bist [bɪst] *vb siehe* **sein**
bisweilen [bɪs'vailən] *adv* at times, occasionally
Bitte ['bɪtə] *f* request; **b~** *excl* please; (*wie b~?*) (I beg your) pardon? ♦ *interj* (*als Antwort auf Dank*) you're welcome; **darf ich? – aber b~!** may I? – please do; **b~ schön!** it was a pleasure; **b~n** (*unreg*) *vt, vi*: **b~n** (*um*) to ask (for); **b~nd** *adj* pleading, imploring
bitter ['bɪtər] *adj* bitter; **~böse** *adj* very angry; **B~keit** *f* bitterness; **~lich** *adj* bitter
Blähungen ['blɛːʊŋən] *pl* (*MED*) wind *sg*
blamabel [bla'maːbəl] *adj* disgraceful
Blamage [bla'maːʒə] *f* disgrace
blamieren [bla'miːrən] *vr* to make a fool of o.s., to disgrace o.s. ♦ *vt* to let down, to disgrace
blank [blaŋk] *adj* bright; (*unbedeckt*) bare; (*sauber*) clean, polished; (*umg: ohne Geld*) broke; (*offensichtlich*) blatant
blanko ['blaŋko] *adv* blank; **B~scheck** *m* blank cheque
Blase ['blaːzə] *f* bubble; (*MED*) blister; (*ANAT*) bladder; **~balg** (-(e)s, -bälge) *m* bellows *pl*; **b~n** (*unreg*) *vt, vi* to blow; **~nentzündung** *f* cystitis
Blas- ['blaːs] *zW*: **~instrument** *nt* wind instrument; **~kapelle** *f* brass band
blass ▲ [blas] *adj* pale
Blässe ['blɛsə] (-) *f* paleness, pallor
Blatt [blat] (-(e)s, ⁼er) *nt* leaf; (*von Papier*) sheet; (*Zeitung*) newspaper; (*KARTEN*) hand
blättern ['blɛtərn] *vi*: **in etw** *dat* ~ to

Blätterteig   57   Blut

leaf through sth

Blätterteig m flaky od puff pastry

blau [blau] adj blue; (umg) drunk, stoned; (KOCH) boiled; (Auge) black; **~er Fleck** bruise; **Fahrt ins B~e** mystery tour; **~äugig** adj blue-eyed

Blech [blɛç] (-(e)s, -e) nt tin, sheet metal; (Backblech) baking tray; **~büchse** f tin, can; **~dose** f tin, can; **b~en** vt, vi to fork out; **~schaden** m (AUT) damage to bodywork

Blei [blaɪ] (-(e)s, -e) nt lead

Bleibe [blaɪbə] f roof over one's head; **b~n** (unreg) vi to stay, to remain; **~ lassen** to leave alone; **b~nd** adj (Erinnerung) lasting; (Schaden) permanent

bleich [blaɪç] adj faded, pale; **~en** vt to bleach

Blei- zW: **b~frei** adj leaden; **b~frei** (Benzin) lead-free; **~stift** m pencil

Blende [blɛndə] f (PHOT) aperture; **b~n** vt to blind, to dazzle; (fig) to hoodwink; **b~nd** (umg) adj grand; **b~nd aussehen** to look smashing

Blick [blɪk] (-(e)s, -e) m (kurz) glance, glimpse; (Anschauen) look; (Aussicht) view; **b~en** vi to look; **sich b~en lassen** to put in an appearance; **~fang** m eye-catcher

blieb etc [bliːp] vb siehe **bleiben**

blind [blɪnt] adj blind; (Glas etc) dull; **~er Passagier** stowaway; **B~darm** m appendix; **B~darmentzündung** f appendicitis; **B~enschrift** [blɪndən-] f Braille; **B~heit** f blindness; **~lings** adv blindly

blink- [blɪŋk] zW: **~en** vi to twinkle, to sparkle; (Licht) to flash, to signal; (AUT) to indicate ♦ vt to flash, to signal; **B~er** (-s, -) m (AUT) indicator; **~licht** nt (AUT) indicator; (an Bahnübergängen usw) flashing light

blinzeln [blɪntsəln] vi to blink, to wink

Blitz [blɪts] (-es, -e) m (flash of) lightning; **~ableiter** m lightning conduc-

tor; **b~en** vi (aufleuchten) to flash, to sparkle; **es b~t** (MET) there's a flash of lightning; **~licht** nt flashlight; **b~schnell** adj lightning ♦ adv (as) quick as a flash

Block [blɔk] (-(e)s, ⁻e) m block; (von Papier) pad; **~ade** [blɔˈkaːdə] f blockade; **~flöte** f recorder; **b~frei** adj (POL) unaligned; **~haus** nt log cabin; **b~ieren** [blɔˈkiːrən] vt to block ♦ vi (Räder) to jam; **~schrift** f block letters pl

blöd [bløːt] adj silly, stupid; **~eln** [bløːdəln] (umg) vi to act the goat (fam), to fool around; **B~sinn** m nonsense; **~sinnig** adj silly, idiotic

blond [blɔnt] adj blond, fair-haired

SCHLÜSSELWORT

bloß [bloːs] adj 1 (unbedeckt) bare; (nackt) naked; **mit der bloßen Hand** with one's bare hand; **mit bloßem Auge** with the naked eye

2 (alleinig, nur) mere; **der bloße Gedanke** the very thought; **bloßer Neid** sheer envy

♦ adv only, merely; **lass das bloß!** just don't do that!; **wie ist das bloß passiert?** how on earth did that happen?

Blöße [bløːsə] f bareness; nakedness; (fig) weakness

bloßstellen vt to show up

blühen [blyːən] vi to bloom (lit), to be in bloom; (fig) to flourish; **~d** adj (Pflanze) blooming; (Aussehen) blooming, radiant; (Handel) thriving, booming

Blume [bluːmə] f flower; (von Wein) bouquet

Blumen- zW: **~kohl** m cauliflower; **~topf** m flowerpot; **~zwiebel** f bulb

Bluse [bluːzə] f blouse

Blut [bluːt] (-(e)s) nt blood; **b~arm** adj anaemic; (fig) penniless; **b~befleckt**

Spelling Reform: ▲ new spelling △ old spelling (to be phased in)

adj bloodstained; **~bild** *nt* blood count; **~druck** *m* blood pressure

Blüte ['blyːtə] *f* blossom; *(fig)* prime

Blut- *zW:* **b~en** *vi* to bleed; **~er** *m* *(MED)* haemophiliac; **~erguss ▲** *m* haemorrhage; *(auf Haut)* bruise

Blütezeit *f* flowering period; *(fig)* prime

Blut- *zW:* **~gruppe** *f* blood group; **b~ig** *adj* bloody; **b~jung** *adj* very young; **~probe** *f* blood test; **~spender** *m* blood donor; **~transfusion** *f* *(MED)* blood transfusion; **~ung** *f* bleeding, haemorrhage; **~vergiftung** *f* blood poisoning; **~wurst** *f* black pudding

Bö [bøː] *f* (-, -en) *f* squall

Bock [bɔk] *f* (-(e)s, ≃e) *m* buck, ram; *(Gestell)* trestle, support; *(SPORT)* buck; **~wurst** *f* type of pork sausage

Boden ['boːdən] *m* (-s, ≃) *m* ground; *(Fußboden)* floor; *(Meeresboden, Fassboden)* bottom; *(Speicher)* attic; **b~los** *adj* bottomless; *(umg)* incredible; **~nebel** *m* ground mist; **~personal** *nt* *(AVIAT)* ground staff; **~schätze** *pl* mineral resources; **~see** *m*: **der ~see** Lake Constance; **~turnen** *nt* floor exercises *pl*

Böe ['bøːə] *f* squall

Bogen ['boːgən] *m* (-s, -) *m* *(Biegung)* curve; *(ARCHIT)* arch; *(Waffe, MUS)* bow; *(Papier)* sheet

Bohne ['boːnə] *f* bean

bohnern *vt* to wax, to polish

Bohnerwachs *nt* floor polish

Bohr- ['boːr] *zW:* **b~en** *vt* to bore; **~er** (-s, -) *m* drill; **~insel** *f* oil rig; **~maschine** *f* drill; **~turm** *m* derrick

Boiler ['bɔylər] (-s, -) *m* (hot-water) tank

Boje ['boːjə] *f* buoy

Bolzen ['bɔltsən] (-s, -) *m* bolt

bombardieren [bɔmbar'diːrən] *vt* to bombard; *(aus der Luft)* to bomb

Bombe ['bɔmbə] *f* bomb

Bombenangriff *m* bombing raid

Bombenerfolg *(umg)* *m* smash hit

Bon [bɔŋ] (-s, -s) *m* voucher, chit

Bonbon [bɔŋ'bõː] (-s, -s) *nt od* sweet

Boot [boːt] (-(e)s, -e) *nt* boat

Bord [bɔrt] (-(e)s, -e) *m* *(AVIAT, NAUT)* board ♦ *nt* *(Brett)* shelf; **an ~** on board

Bordell [bɔr'dɛl] (-s, -e) *nt* brothel

Bordstein *m* kerb(stone)

borgen ['bɔrgən] *vt* to borrow; **jdm etw ~** to lend sb sth

borniert [bɔr'niːrt] *adj* narrow-minded

Börse ['bœrzə] *f* stock exchange; *(Geldbörse)* purse; **~nmakler** *m* stockbroker

Borte ['bɔrtə] *f* edging; *(Band)* trimming

bös [bøːs] *adj* = **böse**

bösartig ['bøːz-] *adj* malicious

Böschung ['bœʃʊŋ] *f* slope; *(Uferböschung etc)* embankment

böse ['bøːzə] *adj* bad, evil; *(zornig)* angry

boshaft ['boːshaft] *adj* malicious, spiteful

Bosheit *f* malice, spite

Bosnien ['bɔsniən] (-s) *nt* Bosnia; **~ und Herzegowina** [-hɛrtsə'goːvina] *nt* Bosnia (and) Herzegowina

böswillig ['bøːsvɪlɪç] *adj* malicious

bot *etc* [boːt] *vb siehe* **bieten**

Botanik [bo'taːnɪk] *f* botany; **botanisch** *adj* botanical

Bot- ['boːt] *zW:* **~e** (-n, -n) *m* messenger; **~schaft** *f* message, news; *(POL)* embassy; **~schafter** (-s, -) *m* ambassador

Bottich ['bɔtɪç] (-(e)s, -e) *m* vat, tub

Bouillon [bʊl'jõː] (-, -s) *f* consommé

Bowle ['boːlə] *f* punch

Box- ['bɔks] *zW:* **b~en** *vi* to box; **~er** (-s, -) *m* boxer; **~kampf** *m* boxing match

boykottieren [bɔykɔ'tiːrən] *vt* to boycott

brach *etc* [braːx] *vb siehe* **brechen**

brachte *etc* ['braxtə] *vb siehe* **bringen**

Branche ['brãːʒə] *f* line of business

Branchenverzeichnis *nt* Yellow Pages

® pl

Brand [brant] (-(e)s, ᵉe) m fire; (MED) gangrene; **b~en** ['brandən] vi to surge; (Meer) to break; (fig) to brand; (fig) to stigmatize; **~salbe** f ointment for burns; **~stifter** [-ʃtiftər] m arsonist, fire raiser; **~stiftung** f arson; **~ung** f surf

Branntwein ['brantvain] m brandy

Brasilien [bra'ziːliən] nt Brazil

Brat- ['braːt] zW: **~apfel** m baked apple; **b~en** (unreg) vt to roast; to fry; **~en** (-s, -) m roast, joint; **~hähnchen** nt roast chicken; **~huhn** nt roast chicken; **~kartoffeln** pl fried od roast potatoes; **~pfanne** f frying pan

Bratsche ['braːtʃə] f viola

Bratspieß m spit

Bratwurst f grilled/fried sausage

Brauch [braux] (-(e)s, Bräuche) m custom; **b~bar** adj usable, serviceable; (Person) capable; **b~en** vt (bedürfen) to need; (müssen) to have to; (umg: verwenden) to use

Braue ['braʊə] f brow

brauen ['braʊən] vt to brew

Braue'rei f brewery

braun [braun] adj brown; (von Sonne auch) tanned; **~ gebrannt** tanned

Bräune ['brɔʏnə] f brownness; (Sonnenbräune) tan; **b~n** vt to make brown; (Sonne) to tan

Brause ['braʊzə] f shower bath; (von Gießkanne) rose; (Getränk) lemonade; **b~n** vi to roar; (auch vr: duschen) to take a shower

Braut [braut] (-, Bräute) f bride; (Verlobte) fiancée

Bräutigam ['brɔʏtɪɡam] (-s, -e) m bridegroom; fiancé

Brautpaar nt bride and (bride)groom, bridal pair

brav [braːf] adj (artig) good; (ehrenhaft) worthy, honest

bravo ['braːvo] excl well done

BRD ['beːˈɛrˈdeː] (-) f abk = **Bundesrepublik Deutschland**

Brech- ['brɛç] zW: **~eisen** nt crowbar; **b~en** (unreg) vt, vi to break; (Licht) to refract; (fig: Mensch) to crush; (speien) to vomit; **~reiz** m nausea, retching

Brei [brai] (-(e)s, -e) m (Masse) pulp; (KOCH) gruel; (Haferbrei) porridge

breit [brait] adj wide, broad; **sich ~ machen** to spread o.s. out; **B~e** f width; (bes bei Maßangaben) breadth; (GEOG) latitude; **~en** vt: etw über etw akk **~en** to spread sth over sth; **B~engrad** m degree of latitude; **~treten** (unreg) (umg) vt to go on about

Brems- [brɛms] zW: **~belag** m brake lining; **~e** [-zə] f brake; (ZOOL) horsefly; **b~en** [-zən] vi vt to brake ♦ vt (Auto) to brake; (fig) to slow down; **~flüssigkeit** f brake fluid; **~licht** nt brake light; **~pedal** nt brake pedal; **~spur** f skid mark(s pl); **~weg** m braking distance

Brenn- ['brɛn] zW: **b~bar** adj inflammable; **b~en** (unreg) vi to burn, to be on fire; (Licht, Kerze etc) to burn ♦ vt (Holz etc) to burn; (Ziegel, Ton) to fire; (Kaffee) to roast; **darauf b~en, etw zu tun** to be dying to do sth; **~nessel** ▲ f stinging nettle; **~punkt** m (PHYS) focal point; (Mittelpunkt) focus; **~stoff** m fuel

brenzlig ['brɛntslɪç] adj (fig) precarious

Bretagne [brə'tanjə] f: **die ~** Brittany

Brett [brɛt] (-(e)s, -er) nt board, plank; (Bord) shelf; (Spielbrett) board; **~er** pl (SKI) skis; (THEAT) boards; **schwarzes ~** notice board; **~erzaun** m wooden fence; **~spiel** nt board game

Brezel ['breːtsəl] (-, -n) f pretzel

brichst etc [brɪçst] vb siehe **brechen**

Brief [briːf] (-(e)s, -e) m letter; **~freund** m penfriend; **~kasten** m letterbox; **b~lich** adj, adv by letter; **~marke** f (postage) stamp; **~papier** nt notepaper; **~tasche** f wallet; **~träger** m postman; **~umschlag** m envelope; **~waage** f letter scales; **~wechsel** m correspondence

briet etc [briːt] vb siehe **braten**

Brikett [bri'kɛt] (-s, -s) nt briquette

brillant [brɪl'jant] adj (fig) brilliant; **B~** (-en, -en) m brilliant, diamond

Brille ['brɪlə] f spectacles pl; (Schutzbrille) goggles pl; (Toilettenbrille) (toilet) seat; **~ngestell** nt (spectacle) frames

bringen ['brɪŋən] (unreg) vt to bring; (mitnehmen, begleiten) to take; (einbringen: Profit) to bring in; (veröffentlichen) to publish; (THEAT, CINE) to show; (RADIO, TV) to broadcast; (in einen Zustand versetzen) to get; (umg: tun können) to manage; **jdn dazu ~, etw zu tun** to make sb do sth; **jdn nach Hause ~** to take sb home; **jdn um etw ~** to make sb lose sth; **jdn auf eine Idee ~** to give sb an idea

Brise ['briːzə] f breeze

Brit- [brɪt] zW: **~e** m Briton; **~in** f Briton; **b~isch** adj British

bröckelig ['brœkəlɪç] adj crumbly

Brocken ['brɔkən] (-s, -) m piece, bit; (Felsbrocken) lump of rock

brodeln ['broːdəln] vi to bubble

Brokkoli ['brɔkoli] pl (BOT) broccoli

Brombeere ['brɔmbeːrə] f blackberry, bramble (BRIT)

Bronchien ['brɔnçiən] pl bronchia(l tubes) pl

Bronchitis [brɔn'çiːtɪs] (-) f bronchitis

Bronze ['brõːsə] f bronze

Brosche ['brɔʃə] f brooch

Broschüre [brɔ'ʃyːrə] f pamphlet

Brot [broːt] (-(e)s, -e) nt bread; (Laib) loaf

Brötchen ['brøːtçən] nt roll

Bruch [brʊx] (-(e)s, **ⁿe**) m breakage; (zerbrochene Stelle) break; (fig) split, breach; (MED: Eingeweidebruch) rupture, hernia; (Beinbruch etc) fracture; (MATH) fraction

brüchig ['brʏçɪç] adj brittle, fragile; (Haus) dilapidated

Bruch- zW: **~landung** f crash landing; **~strich** m (MATH) line; **~stück** nt fragment; **~teil** m fraction; **~zahl** [brʊxtsaːl] f (MATH) fraction

Brücke ['brʏkə] f bridge; (Teppich) rug

Bruder ['bruːdər] (-s, **ⁿ**) m brother; **brüderlich** adj brotherly

Brühe ['bryːə] f broth, stock; (pej) muck

brüllen ['brʏlən] vi to bellow, to roar

brummen ['brʊmən] vi (Bär, Mensch etc) to growl; (Insekt) to buzz; (Motoren) to roar; (murren) to grumble

brünett [brʏ'nɛt] adj brunette, dark-haired

Brunnen ['brʊnən] (-s, -) m fountain; (tief) well; (natürlich) spring

Brust [brʊst] (-, **ⁿe**) f breast; (Männerbrust) chest

brüsten ['brʏstən] vr to boast

Brust- zW: **~kasten** m chest; **~schwimmen** nt breast-stroke

Brüstung ['brʏstʊŋ] f parapet

Brut [bruːt] (-, -en) f brood; (Brüten) hatching

brutal [bru'taːl] adj brutal; **B~i'tät** f brutality

brüten ['bryːtən] vi (auch fig) to brood

Brutkasten m incubator

brutto ['brʊto] adv gross; **B~einkommen** nt gross salary; **B~gehalt** nt gross salary; **B~gewicht** nt gross weight; **B~lohn** m gross wages pl; **B~sozialprodukt** nt gross national product

BSE f abk (= Bovine Spongiforme Enze-
phalopathie) BSE
Bube ['buːbə] (-n, -n) m (Schurke)
rogue; (KARTEN) jack
Buch [buːx] (-(e)s, ⸚er) nt book; (COMM)
account book; **~binder** m bookbinder;
~drucker m printer
Buche f beech tree
buchen vt to book; (Betrag) to enter
Bücher- ['byːçər] zW: **~brett** nt book-
shelf; **~ei** [-'raɪ] f library; **~regal** nt
bookshelves pl, bookcase; **~schrank**
m bookcase
Buch- zW: **~führung** f book-keeping,
accounting; **~halter(in)** (-s, -) m(f)
book-keeper; **~handel** m book trade;
~händler(in) m(f) bookseller; **~hand-
lung** f bookshop
Büchse ['byksə] f tin, can; (Holzbüchse)
box; (Gewehr) rifle; **~nfleisch** nt
tinned meat; **~nmilch** f (KOCH) evapo-
rated milk, tinned milk; **~nöffner** m
tin od can opener
Buch- zW: **~stabe** (-ns, -n) m letter (of
the alphabet; **b~stabieren**
[buːxʃtaˈbiːrən] vt to spell; **b~stäblich**
['buːxʃtɛːplɪç] adj literal
Bucht ['bʊxt] (-, -en) f bay
Buchung ['buːxʊŋ] f booking; (COMM)
entry
Buckel ['bʊkəl] (-s, -) m hump
bücken ['bʏkən] vr to bend
Bude ['buːdə] f booth, stall; (umg) digs
pl (BRIT)
Büfett [by'fet] (-s, -s) nt (Anrichte) sideboard; (Geschirrschrank) dresser; **kaltes
~** cold buffet
Büffel ['bʏfəl] (-s, -) m buffalo
Bug [buːk] (-(e)s, -e) m (NAUT) bow;
(AVIAT) nose
Bügel ['byːgəl] (-s, -) m (Kleider-)
hanger; (Steig-) stirrup; (Brillen-) arm;
~brett nt ironing board; **~eisen** nt
iron; **~falte** f crease; **b~frei** adj
crease-resistant, noniron; **b~n** vt, vi to

iron
Bühne ['byːnə] f stage; **~nbild** nt set,
scenery
Buhruf ['buːruːf] m boo
buk etc [buːk] vb siehe backen
Bulgarien [bul'gaːriən] nt Bulgaria
Bull- ['bʊl] zW: **~auge** nt (NAUT) porthole; **~dogge** f bulldog; **~dozer**
['bʊldoːzər] (-s, -) m bulldozer; **~e** (-n,
-n) m bull
Bumerang ['buːməraŋ] (-s, -e) m
boomerang
Bummel ['bʊməl] (-s, -) m stroll;
(Schaufensterbummel) window-shop-
ping; **~ant** [-'lant] m slowcoach; **~ei**
[-'laɪ] f wandering; dawdling; skiving;
b~n vi to wander, to stroll; (trödeln) to
dawdle; (faulenzen) to skive, to loaf
around; **~streik** ['bʊməlʃtraɪk] m go-
slow
Bund¹ [bʊnt] (-(e)s, ⸚e) m
(Freundschaftsbund etc) bond; (Organisation) union; (POL) confederacy; (Ho-
senbund, Rockbund) waistband
Bund² [bʊnt] (-(e)s, -e) nt bunch; (Strohbund)
bundle
Bündel ['bʏndəl] (-s, -) nt bundle,
bale; **b~n** vt to bundle
Bundes- ['bʊndəs] in zW Federal;
~bürger m German citizen; **~haupt-
stadt** f Federal capital; **~kanzler** m
Federal Chancellor; **~land** nt Land;
~liga f football league; **~präsident** m
Federal President; **~rat** m upper house
of German Parliament; **~regierung** f
Federal government; **~republik** f Federal Republic (of Germany); **~staat** m
Federal state; **~straße** f Federal road;
~tag m German Parliament; **~wehr** f
German Armed Forces pl; **b~weit** adj
nationwide

Bundespräsident

The **Bundespräsident** is the head of
state of the Federal Republic of Ger-

---

many. He is elected every 5 years - no-one can be elected more than twice - by the members of the Bundesversammlung, a body formed especially for this purpose. His role is to represent Germany at home and abroad. In Switzerland the Bundespräsident is the head of the government, known as the Bundesrat.

The Bundesrat is the Upper House of the German Parliament whose 68 members are nominated by the parliaments of the Länder. Its most important function is to approve federal laws concerned with the jurisdiction of the Länder, it can raise objections to other laws, but can be outvoted by the Bundestag. In Austria the Länder are also represented in the Bundesrat.

Bundestag

The Bundestag is the Lower House of the German Parliament and is elected by the people by proportional representation. There are 672 MPs, half of them elected directly from the first vote (Erststimme), and half from the regional list of parliamentary candidates resulting from the second vote (Zweitstimme). The Bundestag exercises parliamentary control over the government.

Bündnis ['byntnɪs] (**-ses, -se**) *nt* alliance

bunt [bʊnt] *adj* coloured; (*gemischt*) mixed; **jdm wird es zu ~** it's getting too much for sb; **B~stift** *m* coloured pencil, crayon

Burg [bʊrk] (**-, -en**) *f* castle, fort

Bürge ['byrgə] (**-n, -n**) *m* guarantor; **b~n** *vi* **b~n für** to vouch for

Bürger(in) ['byrgər(ɪn)] (**-s, -**) *m(f)* citizen; member of the middle class; **~krieg** *m* civil war; **b~lich** *adj* (*Rechte*) civil; (*Klasse*) middle-class; (*pej*) bour-

geois; **~meister** *m* mayor; **~recht** *nt* civil rights *pl*; **~schaft** *f* (*Vertretung*) City Parliament; **~steig** *m* pavement

Bürgschaft *f* surety; **~ leisten** to give security

Büro [by'roː] (**-s, -s**) *nt* office; **~angestellte(r)** *f(m)* office worker; **~klammer** *f* paper clip; **~kra'tie** *f* bureaucracy; **b~'kratisch** *adj* bureaucratic; **~schluss ▲** *m* office closing time

Bursche ['bʊrʃə] (**-n, -n**) *m* lad, fellow; (*Diener*) servant

Bürste ['byrstə] *f* brush; **b~n** *vt* to brush

Bus [bʊs] (**-ses, -se**) *m* bus; **~bahnhof** *m* bus/coach (*BRIT*) station

Busch [bʊʃ] (**-(e)s, ⁼e**) *m* bush, shrub

Büschel ['byʃəl] (**-s, -**) *nt* tuft

buschig *adj* bushy

Busen ['buːzən] (**-s, -**) *m* bosom; (*Meerbusen*) inlet, bay

Bushaltestelle *f* bus stop

Buße ['buːsə] *f* atonement, penance; (*Geld*) fine

büßen ['byːsən] *vi* to do penance, to atone ♦ *vt* to do penance for, to atone for

Bußgeld ['buːsgɛlt] *nt* fine; **~bescheid** *m* notice of payment due (*for traffic offence etc*)

Büste ['byːstə] *f* bust; **~nhalter** *m* bra

Butter ['bʊtər] (**-**) *f* butter; **~blume** *f* buttercup; **~brot** *nt* (piece of) bread and butter; (*umg*) sandwich; **~brotpapier** *nt* greaseproof paper; **~dose** *f* butter dish; **~milch** *f* buttermilk; **b~weich** ['bʊtərvaɪç] *adj* soft as butter; (*fig, umg*) soft

b. w. *abk* (= *bitte wenden*) p.t.o.

bzgl. *abk* (= *bezüglich*) re

bzw. *abk* = **beziehungsweise**

C, c

ca. [ka] *abk* (= *circa*) approx.

Café [ka'fe:] (-s, -s) *nt* café

Cafeteria [kafete'ri:a] (-, -s) *f* cafeteria

Camcorder *m* camcorder

Camp- ['kɛmp] *zW:* **c~en** *vi* to camp; **~er** (-s, -) *m* camper; **~ing** (-s) *nt* camping; **~ingführer** *m* camping guide (book); **~ingkocher** *m* camping stove; **~ingplatz** *m* camp(ing) site

CD-Spieler *m* CD (player)

Cello ['tʃɛlo] (-s, -s *od* **Celli**) *nt* cello

Celsius ['tsɛlzɪʊs] (-) *nt* centigrade

Champagner [ʃam'panjər] (-s, -) *m* champagne

Champignon ['ʃampɪnjõ] (-s, -s) *m* button mushroom

Chance ['ʃãːs(ə)] *f* chance, opportunity

Chaos ['ka:ɔs] (-, -) *nt* chaos; **chaotisch** [ka'o:tiʃ] *adj* chaotic

Charakter [ka'raktar, *pl* karak'te:rə] (-s, -e) *m* character; **c~fest** *adj* of firm character, strong; **c~isieren** [karakte'ri:zn] *vt* to characterize; **c~istisch** [karakte'rɪstɪʃ] *adj:* **c~istisch (für)** characteristic (of), typical (of); **c~los** *adj* unprincipled; **~losigkeit** *f* lack of principle; **~schwäche** *f* weakness of character; **~stärke** *f* strength of character; **~zug** *m* characteristic, trait

charmant [ʃar'mant] *adj* charming

Charme [ʃarm] (-s) *m* charm

Charterflug ['tʃartərfluːk] *m* charter flight

Chauffeur [ʃɔ'føːr] *m* chauffeur

Chauvinist [ʃovi'nɪst] *m* chauvinist, jingoist

Chef [ʃɛf] (-s, -s) *m* head; (*umg*) boss; **~arzt** *m* senior consultant; **~in** (*umg*) *f* boss

Chemie [çe'mi:] (-) *f* chemistry; **~faser** *f* man-made fibre

Chemikalie [çemi'ka:liə] *f* chemical

Chemiker ['çe:mikər] (-s, -) *m* (industrial) chemist

chemisch ['çe:mɪʃ] *adj* chemical; **~e Reinigung** dry cleaning

Chicorée ['ʃikore:] (-s) *m od* chicory

Chiffre ['ʃɪfrə] *f* (*Geheimzeichen*) cipher; (*in Zeitung*) box number

Chile ['tʃi:le] *nt* Chile

Chin- ['çi:n] *zW:* **~a** *nt* China; **~akohl** *m* Chinese leaves; **~ese** [-'ne:zə] *m* Chinese; **~esin** *f* Chinese; **c~esisch** *adj* Chinese

Chip [tʃɪp] (-s, -s) *m* (*Kartoffelchips*) crisp (*BRIT*), chip (*US*); (*COMPUT*) chip; **~karte** *f* smart card

Chirurg [çi'rʊrg] (-en, -en) *m* surgeon; **~ie** [-'gi:] *f* surgery; **c~isch** *adj* surgical

Chlor [klo:r] (-s) *nt* chlorine; **~o'form** (-s) *nt* chloroform

cholerisch [ko'le:rɪʃ] *adj* choleric

Chor [ko:r] (-(e)s, ⸚e) *m* choir; (*Musikstück, THEAT*) chorus; **~al** [ko'ra:l] (-s, ⸚äle) *m* chorale

Choreograf ▲ [koreo'gra:f] (-en, -en) *m* choreographer

Christ [krɪst] (-en, -en) *m* Christian; **~baum** *m* Christmas tree; **~entum** *nt* Christianity; **~in** *f* Christian; **~kind** *nt* ≈ Father Christmas; (*Jesus*) baby Jesus; **c~lich** *adj* Christian; **~us** (-) *m* Christ

Chrom [kro:m] (-s) *nt* (*CHEM*) chromium; chrome

Chron- ['kro:n] *zW:* **~ik** *f* chronicle; **c~isch** *adj* chronic; **c~ologisch** [-o'lo:gɪʃ] *adj* chronological

circa ['tsɪrka] *adv* about, approximately

Clown [klaʊn] (-s, -s) *m* clown

Cocktail ['kɔkteːl] (-s, -s) *m* cocktail

Cola ['ko:la] (-, -s) *f* Coke ®

Computer [kɔm'pju:tər] (-s, -) *m* computer; **~spiel** *nt* computer game

Cord [kɔrt] (-s) *m* cord, corduroy

Couch [kaʊtʃ] (-, -es *od* -en) *f* couch

Coupon [ku'põ:] (-s, -s) *m* = **Kupon**

Cousin

Cousin [ku'zɛː] (-s, -s) m cousin; **~e** [ku'ziːnə] f cousin

Creme [kreːm] (-, -s) f cream; (*Schuhcreme*) polish; (*Zahncreme*) paste; (*KOCH*) mousse; **c~farben** adj cream(-coloured)

cremig ['kreːmɪç] adj creamy

Curry ['kari] (-s) m od nt curry powder; **~pulver** nt curry powder; **~wurst** f curried sausage

D, d

SCHLÜSSELWORT

da [daː] adv **1** (*örtlich*) there; (*hier*) here; **da draußen** out there; **da sein** to be there; **da bin ich** here I am; **da, wo** where; **ist noch Milch da?** is there any milk left?

2 (*zeitlich*) then; (*folglich*) so

3: da haben wir Glück gehabt we were lucky there; **da kann man nichts machen** nothing can be done about it ♦ konj (*weil*) as, since

dabehalten (*unreg*) vt to keep

dabei [da'baɪ] adv (*räumlich*) close to it; (*noch dazu*) besides; (*zusammen mit*) with them; (*zeitlich*) during this; (*obwohl doch*) but, however; **was ist schon ~?** what of it?; **es ist doch nichts ~, wenn ...** it doesn't matter if ...; **bleiben wir ~** let's leave it at that; **es bleibt ~** that's settled; **das Dumme/Schwierige ~** the stupid/difficult part of it; **er war gerade ~ zu gehen** he was just leaving; **~ sein** (*anwesend*) to be present; (*beteiligt*) to be involved; **~stehen** (*unreg*) vi to stand around

Dach [dax] (-(e)s, -er) nt roof; **~boden** m attic, loft; **~decker** (-s, -) m slater, tiler; **~fenster** nt skylight; **~gepäckträger** m roof rack; **~luke** f sky-

light; **~pappe** f roofing felt; **~rinne** f gutter

Dachs [daks] (-es, -e) m badger

dachte [ˈdaxtə] vb siehe **denken**

Dackel [ˈdakəl] (-s, -) m dachshund

dadurch [daˈdʊrç] adv (*räumlich*) through it; (*durch diesen Umstand*) thereby, in that way; (*deshalb*) because of that, for that reason ♦ konj: **~, dass** because

dafür [daˈfyːr] adv for it; (*anstatt*) instead; **er kann nichts ~** he can't help it; **er ist bekannt ~** he is well-known for that; **was bekomme ich ~?** what will I get for it?

dagegen [daˈgeːgən] adv against it; (*im Vergleich damit*) in comparison with it; (*bei Tausch*) for it/them ♦ konj however; **ich habe nichts ~** I don't mind; **ich war ~** I was against it; **~ kann man nichts tun** one can't do anything about it; **~halten** (*unreg*) vt (*vergleichen*) to compare with it; (*entgegnen*) to object to it; **~sprechen** vi: **es spricht nichts ~** there's no reason why not

daheim [daˈhaɪm] adv at home; **D~** (-s) nt home

daher [daˈheːr] adv (*räumlich*) from there; (*Ursache*) from that ♦ konj (*deshalb*) that's why

dahin [daˈhɪn] adv (*räumlich*) there; (*zeitlich*) then; (*vergangen*) gone; **~ gehend** on this matter; **~'gegen** konj on the other hand; **~gestellt** adv: **~gestellt bleiben** to remain to be seen; **~gestellt sein lassen** to leave open od undecided

dahinten [daˈhɪntən] adv over there

dahinter [daˈhɪntər] adv behind it; **~ kommen** to get to the bottom of it

dalli [ˈdali] (*umg*) adv chop chop

damalig [ˈdaːmaːlɪç] adj of that time, then

damals [ˈdaːmaːls] adv at that time, then

Dame [ˈdaːmə] f lady; (*SCHACH, KARTEN*)

queen; (Spiel) draughts sg; **~nbinde** f sanitary towel od napkin (US); **d~nhaft** adj ladylike; **~ntoilette** f ladies' toilet od restroom (US); **~nwahl** f ladies' excuse-me

damit [da'mɪt] adv with it; (be-gründend) by that ♦ konj in order that, in order to; **was meint er ~?** what does he mean by that?; **genug ~!** that's enough!

dämlich ['dɛ:mlɪç] (umg) adj silly, stupid

Damm [dam] (-(e)s, -e) m dyke; (Stau-damm) dam; (Hafendamm) mole; (Bahndamm, Straßendamm) embankment

dämmen ['dɛmən] vt (Wasser) to dam up; (Schmerzen) to keep back

dämmer- zW: **~ig** adj dim, faint; **~n** vi (Tag) to dawn; (Abend) to fall; **D~ung** f twilight; (Morgendämmerung) dawn; (Abenddämmerung) dusk

Dampf [dampf] (-(e)s, -e) m steam; (Dunst) vapour; **d~en** vi to steam

dämpfen ['dɛmpfən] vt (KOCH) to steam; (bügeln) to iron with a damp cloth; (fig) to dampen, to subdue

Dampf- zW: **~schiff** nt steamship; **~walze** f steamroller

danach [da'na:x] adv after that; (zeit-lich) after that, afterwards; (gemäß) accordingly; according to which, according to that; **er sieht ~ aus** he looks it

Däne ['dɛ:nə] (-n, -n) m Dane

daneben [da'ne:bən] adv beside it; (im Vergleich) in comparison; **~benehmen** (unreg) vr to misbehave; **~gehen** (un-reg) vi to miss; (Plan) to fail

Dänemark ['dɛ:nəmark] nt Denmark; **Dänin** f Dane; **dänisch** adj Danish

Dank [daŋk] (-(e)s) m thanks pl; **vielen** od **schönen ~** many thanks; **jdm ~ sa-gen** to thank sb; **d~** präp (+dat od gen) thanks to; **d~bar** adj grateful; (Auf-

gabe) rewarding; **~barkeit** f gratitude; **d~e** excl thank you, thanks; **d~en** vi +dat to thank; **d~enswert** adj (Arbeit) worthwhile; rewarding; (Bemühung) kind; **d~sagen** vi to express one's thanks

dann [dan] adv then; **~ und wann** now and then

daran [da'ran] adv on it; (stoßen) against it; **es liegt ~, dass ...** the cause of it is that ...; **gut/schlecht ~ sein** to be well-/badly off; **das Beste/ Dümmste ~** the best/stupidest thing about it; **ich war nahe ~ zu ...** I was on the point of ...; **er ist ~ gestorben** he died from it od of it; **~gehen** (un-reg) vi to start; **~setzen** vt to stake

darauf [da'rauf] adv (räumlich) on it; (zielgerichtet) towards it; (danach) afterwards; **es kommt ganz ~ an, ob ...** it depends whether ...; **die Tage ~** the days following od thereafter; **am Tag ~** the next day; **~folgend** (Tag, Jahr) next, following; **~ legen** to lay od put on top

daraus [da'raus] adv from it; **was ist ~ geworden?** what became of it?; **~ geht hervor, dass ...** this means that ...

Darbietung ['da:rbi:tuŋ] f perfor-mance

darf etc [darf] vb siehe **dürfen**

darin [da'rin] adv in (there), in it

darlegen ['da:rle:gən] vt to explain, to expound, to set forth; **Darlegung** f explanation

Darleh(e)n (-s, -) nt loan

Darm [darm] (-(e)s, -e) m intestine; (Wurstdarm) skin; **~grippe** f (MED) gastric influenza od flu

darstell- ['da:rʃtɛl] zW: **~en** vt (abbil-den, bedeuten) to represent; (THEAT) to act; (beschreiben) to describe ♦ vr to appear to be; **D~er(in)** (-s, -) m(f) ac-tor (actress); **D~ung** f portrayal, depiction

darüber [da'ry:bər] *adv* (*räumlich*) over it, above it; (*fahren*) over it; (*mehr*) more; (*währenddessen*) meanwhile; (*sprechen, streiten*) about it; **~ geht nichts** there's nothing like it

darum [da'rʊm] *adv* (*räumlich*) round it ♦ *konj* that's why; **er bittet ~** he is pleading for it; **es geht ~, dass ...** the thing is that ...; **er würde viel ~ geben, wenn ...** he would give a lot to ...; **ich tue es ~, weil ...** I am doing it because ...

darunter [da'rʊntər] *adv* (*räumlich*) under it; (*weniger*) less; **ein Stockwerk ~** one floor below (it); **was verstehen Sie ~?** what do you understand by that?

das [das] *def art the* ♦ *pron that*

Dasein ['da:zain] (*-s*) *nt* (*Leben*) life; (*Anwesenheit*) presence; (*Bestehen*) existence

da sein ▲ *siehe* **da**

dass ▲ [das] *konj* that

dasselbe [das'zɛlbə] *art, pron* the same

dastehen ['da:ʃte:ən] (*unreg*) *vi* to stand there

Datei [da'tai] *f* file

Daten- ['da:tən] *zW:* **~bank** *f* data base; **~schutz** *m* data protection; **~verarbeitung** *f* data processing

datieren [da'ti:rən] *vt* to date

Dativ ['da:ti:f] (*-s, -e*) *m* dative (case)

Dattel ['datəl] (*-, -n*) *f* date

Datum ['da:tʊm] (*-s, Daten*) *nt* date;
Daten *pl* (*Angaben*) data *pl*

Dauer ['dauər] (*-, -n*) *f* duration; (*gewisse Zeitspanne*) length; (*Bestand, Fortbestehen*) permanence; **es war nur von kurzer ~** it didn't last long; **auf die ~** in the long run; (*auf längere Zeit*) indefinitely; **~auftrag** *m* standing order; **d~haft** *adj* lasting, durable; **~karte** *f* season ticket; **~lauf** *m* jog(ging); **d~n** *vi* to last; **es hat sehr lang gedauert, bis er ...** it took him a long time to ...; **d~nd** *adj* constant;

~parkplatz *m* long-stay car park; **~welle** *f* perm, permanent wave; **~wurst** *f* German salami; **~zustand** *m* permanent condition

Daumen ['dauman] (*-s, -*) *m* thumb

Daune ['daunə] *f* down; **~ndecke** *f* down duvet, down quilt

davon [da'fɔn] *adv* of it; (*räumlich*) away; (*weg von*) from it; (*Grund*) because of it; **das kommt ~!** that's what you get; **~ abgesehen** apart from that; **~ sprechen/wissen** to talk/know of *od* about it; **was habe ich ~?** what's the point?; **~kommen** (*unreg*) *vi* to escape; **~laufen** (*unreg*) *vi* to run away

davor [da'fo:r] *adv* (*räumlich*) in front of it; (*zeitlich*) before (that); **~warnen** to warn about it

dazu [da'tsu:] *adv* (*legen, stellen*) by it; (*essen, singen*) with it; **und ~ noch** in addition; **ein Beispiel/seine Gedanken ~** one example for/his thoughts on this; **wie komme ich denn ~?** why should I?; **~ fähig sein** to be capable of it; **sich ~ äußern** to say something on it; **~gehören** *vi* to belong to it; **~kommen** (*unreg*) *vi* (*Ereignisse*) to happen too; (*an einen Ort*) to come along

dazwischen [da'tsvɪʃən] *adv* in between; (*räumlich auch*) between (them); (*zusammen mit*) among them; **~kommen** (*unreg*) *vi* (*hineingeraten*) to get caught in it; **es ist etwas ~gekommen** something cropped up; **~reden** *vi* (*unterbrechen*) to interrupt; (*sich einmischen*) to interfere; **~treten** (*unreg*) *vi* to intervene

---

DDR

The DDR (*Deutsche Demokratische Republik*) was the name by which the former Communist German Democratic Republic was known. It was founded in 1949 from the Soviet-occupied zone. After the Berlin Wall was built in 1961 it was virtually sealed off from the West. Mass demonstrations and demands for reform forced the opening of the borders in 1989 and the DDR merged in 1990 with the BRD.

Debatte [de'batə] *f* debate

Deck [dɛk] (-(e)s, -s *od* -e) *nt* deck; **an ~ gehen** to go on deck

Decke *f* cover; (*Bettdecke*) blanket; (*Tischdecke*) tablecloth; (*Zimmerdecke*) ceiling; **unter einer ~ stecken** to be hand in glove; **~l** (-s, -) *m* lid; **d~n** *vt* to cover ♦ *vi* to coincide

Deckung *f* (*Schützen*) covering; (*Schutz*) cover; (*SPORT*) defence; (*Übereinstimmen*) agreement

Defekt [de'fɛkt] (-(e)s, -e) *m* fault, defect; **d~** *adj* faulty

defensiv [defɛn'siːf] *adj* defensive

definieren [defi'niːrən] *vt* to define; **Definition** [definitsi'oːn] *f* definition

Defizit ['deːfitsɪt] (-s, -e) *nt* deficit

deftig ['dɛftɪç] *adj* (*Essen*) large; (*Witz*) coarse

Degen ['deːgən] (-s, -) *m* sword

degenerieren [degene'riːrən] *vi* to degenerate

dehnbar ['deːnbaːr] *adj* elastic; (*fig: Begriff*) loose

dehnen *vt* to stretch

Deich [daɪç] (-(e)s, -e) *m* dyke, dike

deichseln (*umg*) *vt* (*fig*) to wangle

dein(e) [daɪn(ə)] *adj* your; **~e(r, s)** yours; **~er** (*gen von du*) *pron* of you; **~erseits** *adv* on your part; **~esgleichen** *pron* people like you; **~etwegen** *adv* (*für dich*) for your sake; (*wegen dir*) on your account; **~etwillen** *adv*: **um ~etwillen** = deinetwegen; **~ige** *pron*: **der/die/das ~ige** *od* **D~ige** yours

Deklination [deklinatsi'oːn] *f* declension

deklinieren [dekli'niːrən] *vt* to decline

Dekolleté, Dekolletee ▲ [dekɔl'teː]

(-s, -s) *nt* low neckline

Deko- [deko] *zW*: **~rateur** [-ra'tøːr] *m* window dresser; **~ration** [-ratsi'oːn] *f* decoration; (*in Laden*) window dressing; **d~rativ** [-ra'tiːf] *adj* decorative; **d~rieren** [-'riːrən] *vt* to decorate; (*Schaufenster*) to dress

Delegation [delegatsi'oːn] *f* delegation

delegieren [dele'giːrən] *vt*: **~ an** +*akk* (*Aufgaben*) to delegate to

Delfin ▲ [dɛl'fiːn] (-s, -e) *m* dolphin

delikat [deli'kaːt] *adj* (*zart, heikel*) delicate; (*köstlich*) delicious

Delikatesse [delika'tɛsə] *f* delicacy; **~n** *pl* (*Feinkost*) delicatessen food; **~ngeschäft** *nt* delicatessen

Delikt [de'lɪkt] (-(e)s, -e) *nt* (*JUR*) offence

Delle ['dɛlə] (*umg*) *f* dent

Delphin △ [dɛl'fiːn] (-s, -e) *m* = **Delfin**

dem [de(:)m] *art dat von* **der**

Demagoge [dema'goːgə] (-n, -n) *m* demagogue

dementieren [demɛn'tiːrən] *vt* to deny

dem- *zW*: **~gemäß** *adv* accordingly; **~nach** *adv* accordingly; **~nächst** *adv* shortly

Demokrat [demo'kraːt] (-en, -en) *m* democrat; **~ie** [-'tiː] *f* democracy; **d~isch** *adj* democratic; **d~isieren** [-i'ziːrən] *vt* to democratize

demolieren [demo'liːrən] *vt* to demolish

Demon- [demɔn] *zW*: **~strant(in)** [-'strant(ɪn)] *m(f)* demonstrator; **~stration** [stratsi'oːn] *f* demonstration; **d~strativ** [-stra'tiːf] *adj* demonstrative; (*Protest*) pointed; **d~strieren** [-'striːrən] *vt, vi* to demonstrate

Demoskopie [demosko'piː] *f* public opinion research

Demut ['deːmuːt] (-) *f* humility

demütig ['deːmyːtɪç] *adj* humble; **~en**

Spelling Reform: ▲ new spelling △ old spelling (to be phased out)

['de:my:tɪgən] vt to humiliate; **D~ung** f humiliation

demzufolge ['de:mtsu'fɔlgə] adv accordingly

den [de(:)n] art akk von **der**;

denen ['de:nən] pron dat pl von **der**; **die**; **das**

Denk- [dɛŋk] zW: **d~bar** adj conceivable; **~en** (-s) nt thinking; **d~en** (unreg) vt, vi to think; **d~faul** adj lazy; **~fehler** m logical error; **~mal** (-s) nt monument; **~malschutz** m protection of historical monuments; **unter ~malschutz stehen** to be classified as a historical monument; **d~würdig** adj memorable; **~zettel** m: **jdm einen ~zettel verpassen** to teach sb a lesson

denn [dɛn] konj for ♦ adv then; (nach Komparativ) than; **warum ~?** why?

dennoch ['dɛnnɔx] konj nevertheless

Denunziant [denʊntsi'ant(n)] m informer

Deodorant [de|odo'rant] (-s, -s od -e) nt deodorant

Deponie [depo'ni:] f dump

deponieren [depo'ni:rən] vt (COMM) to deposit

Depot [de'po:] (-s, -s) nt warehouse; (Busdepot, EISENB) depot; (Bankdepot) strongroom, safe (US)

Depression [depresi'o:n] f depression; **depres'siv** adj depressive

deprimieren [depri'mi:rən] vt to depress

―――――――――――――――――
SCHLÜSSELWORT
―――――――――――――――――

der [de(:)r] (f **die**, nt **das**, gen **des**, **der**, **des**, dat **dem**, **der**, **dem**, akk **den**, **die**, **das**, pl **die**) def art the; **der Rhein** the Rhine; **der Klaus** (umg) Klaus; **die Frau** (im Allgemeinen) women; **der Tod/das Leben** death/life; **der Fuß des Berges** the foot of the hill; **gib es der Frau** give it to the woman; **er hat sich die Hand verletzt** he has hurt his hand

♦ relativ pron (bei Menschen) who, that; (bei Tieren, Sachen) which, that; **der Mann, den ich gesehen habe** the man who od whom od that I saw

♦ demonstrativ pron he/she/it; (jener, dieser) that; (pl) those; **der/die war es** it was him/her; **der mit der Brille** the one with glasses; **ich will den (da)** I want that one

derart ['de:r|a:rt] adv so; (solcher Art) such; **~ig** adj such, this sort of

derb [dɛrp] adj sturdy; (Kost) solid; (grob) coarse

der- zW: **'~'gleichen** pron such; **'~'jenige** pron he; she; it; the one (who); that (which); **'~'maßen** adv to such an extent, so; **~'selbe** art, pron the same; **'~'weil(en)** adv in the meantime; **'~'zeitig** adj present, current; (damalig) then

des [dɛs] art gen von **der**

desertieren [dezɛr'ti:rən] vi to desert

desgleichen ['dɛs'glaɪçən] adv likewise, also

deshalb ['dɛs'halp] adv therefore, that's why

Desinfektion [dɛzɪnfɛktsi'o:n] f disinfection; **~smittel** nt disinfectant

desinfizieren [dɛzɪnfi'tsi:rən] vt to disinfect

dessen ['dɛsən] pron gen von **der**; **das**; **~ ungeachtet** nevertheless, regardless

Dessert [dɛ'se:r] (-s, -s) nt dessert

destillieren [dɛstɪ'li:rən] vt to distil

desto ['dɛsto] adv all the, so much the; **~ besser** all the better

deswegen ['dɛs've:gən] konj therefore, hence

Detail [de'taɪ] (-s, -s) nt detail

Detektiv [detɛk'ti:f] (-s, -e) m detective

deut- ['dɔyt] zW: **~en** vt to interpret, to explain ♦ vi: **~en** (auf +akk) to point (to od at); **~lich** adj clear; (Unterschied) distinct; **D~lichkeit** f clarity; distinctness

Deutsch

diesjährig

Deutsch [dɔytʃ] nt German

deutsch adj German; **auf D~** in German; **D~e Demokratische Republik** (HIST) German Democratic Republic, East Germany; **~es Beefsteak** ≃ hamburger; **D~e(r)** mf German; **ich bin D~er** I am German; **D~land** nt Germany

Devise [de'viːzə] f motto, device; **~n** pl (FIN) foreign currency, foreign exchange

Dezember [de'tsɛmbər] (-s, -) m December

dezent [de'tsɛnt] adj discreet

dezimal [detsi'maːl] adj decimal; **D~system** nt decimal system

d. h. abk (= das heißt) i.e.

Dia ['diːa] (-s, -s) nt (PHOT) slide, transparency

Diabetes [dia'beːtes] (-, -) m (MED) diabetes

Diagnose [dia'gnoːzə] f diagnosis

diagonal [diago'naːl] adj diagonal

Dialekt [dia'lɛkt] (-(e)s, -e) m dialect; **d~isch** adj dialectal; (Logik) dialectical

Dialog [dia'loːk] (-(e)s, -e) m dialogue

Diamant [dia'mant] m diamond

Diaprojektor ['diːaprojɛktɔr] m slide projector

Diät [di'ɛːt] (-, -en) f diet

dich [dɪç] (akk von du) pron you; yourself

dicht [dɪçt] adj dense; (Nebel) thick; (Gewebe) close; (undurchlässig) (water)tight; (fig) concise ♦ adv: **~ an/bei** close to; **~ bevölkert** densely od heavily populated; **D~e** f density; thickness; closeness; (water)tightness; (fig) conciseness

dichten vt (dicht machen) to make watertight, to seal; (NAUT) to caulk; (LITER) to compose ♦ vi to compose, to write

Dichter(in) (-s, -) m(f) poet; (Autor) writer; **d~isch** adj poetical

dichthalten (unreg) (umg) vi to keep one's mouth shut

Dichtung f (TECH) washer; (AUT) gasket; (Gedichte) poetry; (Prosa) (piece of) writing

dick [dɪk] adj thick; (fett) fat; **durch~ und dünn** through thick and thin; **D~darm** m (ANAT) colon; **D~e** f thickness; fatness; **~flüssig** adj viscous; **D~icht** (-s, -e) nt thicket; **D~kopf** m mule; **D~milch** f soured milk

die [diː] def art siehe der

Dieb(in) [diːp, 'diːbɪn] (-(e)s, -e) m(f) thief; **d~isch** adj thieving; (umg) immense; **~stahl** (-(e)s, ♦e) m theft; **~stahlversicherung** f insurance against theft

Diele ['diːlə] f (Brett) board; (Flur) hall, lobby

dienen ['diːnən] vi: **(jdm) ~** to serve (sb)

Diener (-s, -) m servant; **~in** f (maid)servant; **~schaft** f servants pl

Dienst [diːnst] (-(e)s, -e) m service; **außer ~** retired; **~ haben** to be on duty; **~ habend** (Arzt) on duty

Dienstag ['diːnstaːk] m Tuesday; **d~s** adv on Tuesdays

Dienst- zW: **~bote** m servant; **~geheimnis** nt official secret; **~gespräch** nt business call; **~leistung** f service; **d~lich** adj official; **~mädchen** nt (house)maid; **~reise** f business trip; **~stelle** f office; **~vorschrift** f official regulations pl; **~weg** m official channels pl; **~zeit** f working hours pl; (MIL) period of service

dies [diːs] pron (demonstrativ: sg) this; (: pl) these; **~bezüglich** adj (Frage) on this matter; **~e(r, s)** ['diːzə(r, s)] pron this (one)

Diesel ['diːzəl] m (Kraftstoff) diesel

dieselbe [diː'zɛlbə] pron, art the same

Dieselmotor m diesel engine

diesig ['diːzɪç] adj drizzly

dies- zW: **~jährig** adj this year's; **~mal**

Spelling Reform: ▲ new spelling △ old spelling (to be phased out)

adv this time; **~seits** *präp +gen* on this side; **D~seits** (-) *nt* this life

Dietrich ['diːtrɪç] (-s, -e) *m* picklock

diffamieren [dɪfa'miːrən] (*pej*) *vt* to defame

Differenz [dɪfe'rɛnts] (-, -en) *f* (*Unterschied*) difference; **~en** *pl* (*Meinungsverschiedenheit*) difference (of opinion); **d~ieren** *vt* to make distinctions in; **d~iert** *adj* (*Mensch etc*) complex

differenzial ▲ [dɪferɛntsia:l] *adj* differential; **D~rechnung** ▲ *f* differential calculus

digital [digi'ta:l] *adj* digital; **D~fernsehen** *f* digital TV

Dikt- [dɪkt] *zW:* **~afon, ~aphon** [-a'foːn] *nt* dictaphone; **~at** [-'taːt] (-(e)s, -e) *nt* dictation; **~ator** [-'taːtɔr] *m* dictator; **d~atorisch** [-a'toːrɪʃ] *adj* dictatorial; **~atur** [-a'tuːr] *f* dictatorship; **d~ieren** [-'tiːrən] *vt* to dictate

Dilemma [di'lema] (-s, -s *od* -ta) *nt* dilemma

Dilettant [dile'tant] *m* dilettante, amateur; **d~isch** *adj* amateurish, dilettante

Dimension [dimɛnzi'oːn] *f* dimension

DIN *f abk* (= *Deutsche Industrie-Norm*) German Industrial Standard

Ding [dɪŋ] (-(e)s, -e) *nt* thing, object; **d~lich** *adj* real, concrete; **~s(bums)** ['dɪŋks(bums)] (-) (*umg*) *nt* thingummybob

Diplom [di'ploːm] (-(e)s, -e) *nt* diploma, certificate; **~at** [-'maːt] (-en, -en) *m* diplomat; **~atie** [-a'tiː] *f* diplomacy; **d~atisch** [-'maːtɪʃ] *adj* diplomatic; **~ingenieur** *m* qualified engineer

dir [diːr] (*dat von du*) *pron* (*to*) you

direkt [di'rɛkt] *adj* direct; **D~flug** *m* direct flight; **D~or** *m* director; (*SCH*) principal, headmaster; **D~übertragung** *f* live broadcast

Dirigent [diri'gɛnt(ɪn)] *m* conductor

dirigieren [diri'giːrən] *vt* to direct; (*MUS*) to conduct

Diskette [dɪs'kɛta] *f* diskette, floppy disk

Diskont [dɪs'kɔnt] (-s, -e) *m* discount; **~satz** *m* rate of discount

Diskothek [dɪsko'teːk] (-, -en) *f* disco(theque)

diskret [dɪs'kreːt] *adj* discreet; **D~ion** *f* discretion

diskriminieren [dɪskrimi'niːrən] *vt* to discriminate against

Diskussion [dɪskusi'oːn] *f* discussion; debate; **zur ~ stehen** to be under discussion

diskutieren [dɪsku'tiːrən] *vt, vi* to discuss; to debate

Distanz [dɪs'tants] *f* distance; **distan'zieren** *vr*: **sich von jdm/etw d~ieren** to distance o.s. from sb/sth

Distel ['dɪstal] (-, -n) *f* thistle

Disziplin [dɪstsi'pliːn] *f* discipline

Dividende [divi'dɛnda] *f* dividend

dividieren [divi'diːrən] *vt*: (**durch etw**) **~** to divide (by sth)

DM [deː'ɛm] *abk* (= *Deutsche Mark*) German Mark

D-Mark ['deːmark] *f* D Mark, German Mark

SCHLÜSSELWORT

doch [dɔx] *adv* **1** (*dennoch*) after all; (*sowieso*) anyway; **er kam doch noch** he came after all; **du weißt es ja doch besser** you know better than I do anyway; **und doch ...** and yet ...

2 (*als bejahende Antwort*) yes I do/it does *etc*; **das ist nicht wahr - doch!** that's not true - yes it is!

3 (*auffordernd*): **komm doch** do come; **lass ihn doch** just leave him; **nicht doch!** oh no!

4: **sie ist doch noch so jung** but she's still so young; **Sie wissen doch, wie das ist** you know how it is(, don't you?); **wenn doch** if only

♦ *konj* (*aber*) but; (*trotzdem*) all the same; **und doch hat er es getan** but still he did it

---

Docht [dɔxt] (-(e)s, -e) *m* wick

Dock [dɔk] (-s, -s od -e) nt dock

Dogge ['dɔgə] f bulldog

Dogma ['dɔgma] (-s, -men) nt dogma; **d~tisch** adj dogmatic

Doktor ['dɔktɔr, pl -'toːrən] (-s, -en) m doctor

Dokument [doku'mɛnt] nt document

Dokumentar- [dokumɛn'taːr] zW: **~bericht** m documentary; **~film** m documentary (film); **d~isch** adj documentary

Dolch [dɔlç] (-(e)s, -e) m dagger

dolmetschen ['dɔlmɛtʃən] vt, vi to interpret; **Dolmetscher(in)** (-s, -) m(f) interpreter

Dom [doːm] (-(e)s, -e) m cathedral

dominieren [domi'niːrən] vt to dominate ♦ vi to predominate

Donau ['doːnau] f Danube

Donner ['dɔnər] (-s, -) m thunder; **d~n** vi unpers to thunder

Donnerstag ['dɔnərstaːk] m Thursday

doof [doːf] (umg) adj daft, stupid

Doppel ['dɔpəl] (-s, -) nt duplicate (SPORT) doubles; **~bett** nt double bed; **d~deutig** adj ambiguous; **~fenster** nt double glazing; **~gänger** (-s, -) m double; **~punkt** m colon; **~stecker** m two-way adapter; **d~t** adj double; in **d~ter Ausführung** in duplicate; **~verdiener** m person with two incomes; (pl: Paar) two-income family; **~zentner** m 100 kilograms; **~zimmer** nt double room

Dorf [dɔrf] (-(e)s, -̈er) nt village; **~bewohner** m villager

Dorn [dɔrn] (-(e)s, -en) m (BOT) thorn; **d~ig** adj thorny

Dörrobst ['dœrɔpst] nt dried fruit

Dorsch [dɔrʃ] (-(e)s, -e) m cod

dort [dɔrt] adv there; **~ drüben** over there; **~her** adv from there; **~hin** adv (to) there; **~ig** adj of that place; in that town

Dose ['doːzə] f box; (Blechdose) tin, can

Dosen pl von **Dose; Dosis**

Dosenöffner m tin od can opener

Dosis ['doːzɪs] (-, **Dosen**) f dose

Dotter ['dɔtər] (-s, -) m (egg) yolk

Drache ['draxə] (-n, -n) m (Tier) dragon

Drachen (-s, -) m kite; **~fliegen** (-s) nt hang-gliding

Draht [draːt] (-(e)s, -̈e) m wire; **auf ~ sein** to be on the ball; **d~ig** adj (Mann) wiry; **~seil** nt cable; **~seilbahn** f cable railway, funicular

Drama ['draːma] (-s, **Dramen**) nt drama, play; **~tiker** [-'maːtikər] (-s, -) m dramatist; **d~tisch** [-'maːtɪʃ] adj dramatic

dran [dran] (umg) adv: **jetzt bin ich ~!** it's my turn now; siehe **daran**

Drang [draŋ] (-(e)s, -̈e) m (Trieb): **~ (nach)** impulse (for), urge (for), desire (for); (Druck) pressure

drängeln ['drɛŋəln] vt, vi to push, to jostle

drängen ['drɛŋən] vt (schieben) to push, to press; (antreiben) to urge ♦ vi (eilig sein) to be urgent; (Zeit) to press; **auf etw akk ~** to press for sth

drastisch ['drastɪʃ] adj drastic

drauf [drauf] (umg) adv = **darauf**; **D~gänger** (-s, -) m daredevil

draußen ['drausən] adv outside, out-of-doors

Dreck [drɛk] (-(e)s, -e) m mud, dirt; **d~ig** adj dirty, filthy

Dreh- ['dreː] zW: **~arbeiten** pl (CINE) shooting sg; **~bank** f lathe; **~buch** nt (CINE) script; **d~en** vt to turn, to rotate; (Zigaretten) to roll; (Film) to shoot ♦ vi to turn, to rotate ♦ vt to turn; (handeln von): **es d~t sich um ...** it's about ...; **~orgel** f barrel organ; **~tür** f revolving door; **~ung** f (Rotation) rotation; (Umdrehung, Wendung) turn; **~zahl** f rate of revolutions; **~zahlmesser** m rev(olution) counter

drei [draɪ] *num* three; **~viertel** three quarters; **D~eck** *nt* triangle; **~eckig** *adj* triangular; **~einhalb** *num* three and a half; **~erlei** *adj inv* of three kinds; **~fach** *adj* triple, treble ♦ *adv* three times; **~hundert** *num* three hundred; **D~königsfest** *nt* Epiphany; **~mal** *adv* three times; **~malig** *adj* three times

dreinreden ['draɪnre:dən] *vi*: **jdm ~** (*dazwischenreden*) to interrupt sb; (*sich einmischen*) to interfere with sb

Dreirad *nt* tricycle

dreißig ['draɪsɪç] *num* thirty

dreist [draɪst] *adj* bold, audacious

drei- *zW*: **~viertel** △ *num siehe* **drei**; **D~viertelstunde** *f* three-quarters of an hour; **~zehn** *num* thirteen

dreschen ['drɛʃən] (*unreg*) *vt* (*Getreide*) to thresh; (*umg: verprügeln*) to beat up

dressieren [drɛ'si:rən] *vt* to train

drillen ['drɪlən] *vt* (*bohren*) to drill, to bore; (*MIL*) to drill; (*fig*) to train

Drilling *m* triplet

drin [drɪn] (*umg*) *adv* = **darin**

dringen ['drɪŋən] (*unreg*) *vi* (*Wasser, Licht, Kälte*): **~ (durch/in +akk)** to penetrate (through/into); **auf etw akk ~** to insist on sth

dringend ['drɪŋənt] *adj* urgent

Dringlichkeit *f* urgency

drinnen ['drɪnən] *adv* inside, indoors

dritte(r, s) ['drɪtə(r, s)] *adj* third; **D~ Welt** Third World; **D~s Reich** Third Reich; **D~l** (**-s, -**) *nt* third; **~ns** *adv* thirdly

DRK [de:ɛr'ka:] *nt abk* (= *Deutsches Rotes Kreuz*) German Red Cross

droben ['dro:bən] *adv* above, up there

Droge ['dro:gə] *f* drug

drogen *zW*: **~abhängig** *adj* addicted to drugs; **D~händler** *m* drug pedlar, pusher

Drogerie [drogə'ri:] *f* chemist's shop

Drogerie

The **Drogerie** *as opposed to the* **Apotheke** *sells medicines not requir-*

ing a prescription. It tends to be cheaper and also sells cosmetics, perfume and toiletries.

Drogist [dro'gɪst] *m* pharmacist, chemist

drohen ['dro:ən] *vi*: (**jdm**) **~** to threaten (sb)

dröhnen ['drø:nən] *vi* (*Motor*) to roar; (*Stimme, Musik*) to ring, to resound

Drohung ['dro:ʊŋ] *f* threat

drollig ['drɔlɪç] *adj* droll

Drossel ['drɔsəl] (**-, -n**) *f* thrush

drüben ['dry:bən] *adv* over there, on the other side

drüber ['dry:bər] (*umg*) *adv* = **darüber**

Druck [drʊk] (**-(e)s, -e**) *m* (*PHYS: Zwang*) pressure; (*TYP: Vorgang*) printing; (*: Produkt*) print; (*fig: Belastung*) burden, weight; **~buchstabe** *m* block letter

drücken ['drykən] *vt* (*Knopf, Hand*) to press; (*zu eng sein*) to pinch; (*fig: Preise*) to keep down; (*: belasten*) to oppress, to weigh down ♦ *vi* to press; to pinch ♦ *vr*: **sich vor etw** *dat* **~** to get out of (doing) sth; **~d** *adj* oppressive

Drucker (**-s, -**) *m* printer

Drücker (**-s, -**) *m* button; (*Türdrücker*) handle; (*Gewehrdrücker*) trigger

Druck- *zW*: **~erei** *f* printing works, press; **~erschwärze** *f* printer's ink; **~fehler** *m* misprint; **~knopf** *m* press stud, snap fastener; **~sache** *f* printed matter; **~schrift** *f* block *od* printed letters *pl*

drum [drʊm] (*umg*) *adv* = **darum**

drunten ['drʊntən] *adv* below, down there

Drüse ['dry:zə] *f* gland

Dschungel ['dʒʊŋəl] (**-s, -**) *m* jungle

du [du:] (*nom*) *pron* you; **~ sagen** = **duzen**

Dübel ['dy:bəl] (**-s, -**) *m* Rawlplug ®

ducken ['dʊkən] *vt* (*Kopf, Person*) to duck; (*fig*) to take down a peg or two ♦ *vr* to duck

Duckmäuser ['dʊkmɔʏzər] (**-s, -**) *m*

yes man

Dudelsack ['du:dəlzak] m bagpipes pl

Duell [du'ɛl] (-s, -e) nt duel

Duft [dʊft] (-(e)s, ᵉe) m scent, odour; **d~en** vi to smell, to be fragrant; **d~ig** adj (Stoff, Kleid) delicate, diaphanous

dulden ['dʊldən] vt to suffer; (zulassen) to tolerate ♦ vi to suffer

dumm [dʊm] adj stupid; (ärgerlich) annoying; **der D~e sein** to be the loser; **~erweise** adv stupidly; **D~heit** f stupidity; (Tat) blunder, stupid mistake; **D~kopf** m blockhead

dumpf [dʊmpf] adj (Ton) hollow, dull; (Luft) musty; (Erinnerung, Schmerz) vague

Düne ['dy:nə] f dune

düngen ['dyŋən] vt to manure

Dünger (-s, -) m dung, manure; (künstlich) fertilizer

dunkel ['dʊŋkəl] adj dark; (Stimme) deep; (Ahnung) vague; (rätselhaft) obscure; (verdächtig) dubious, shady; **im D~n tappen** (fig) to grope in the dark

Dunkel- zW: **~heit** f darkness; (fig) obscurity; **~kammer** f (PHOT) darkroom; **d~n** vi unpers to grow dark; **~ziffer** f estimated number of unreported cases

dünn [dyn] adj thin; **~flüssig** adj watery, thin

Dunst [dʊnst] (-es, ᵉe) m vapour; (Wetter) haze

dünsten ['dʏnstən] vt to steam

dunstig ['dʊnstɪç] adj vaporous; (Wetter) hazy, misty

Duplikat [dupli'ka:t] (-(e)s, -e) nt duplicate

Dur [du:r] (-, -) nt (MUS) major

SCHLÜSSELWORT

durch [dʊrç] präp +akk **1** (hindurch) through; **durch den Urwald** through the jungle; **durch die ganze Welt reisen** to travel all over the world

2 (mittels) through, by (means of);

(aufgrund) due to, owing to; **Tod durch Herzschlag/den Strang** death from a heart attack/by hanging; **durch die Post** by post; **durch seine Bemühungen** through his efforts

♦ adv **1** (hindurch) through; **die ganze Nacht durch** all through the night; **den Sommer durch** during the summer; **8 Uhr durch** past 8 o'clock; **durch und durch** completely

2 (durchgebraten etc): **(gut) durch** well-done

---

durch- zW: **~arbeiten** vt, vi to work through ♦ vr to work one's way through; **~'aus** adv completely; (unbedingt) definitely; **~aus nicht** absolutely not

Durchblick ['dʊrçblɪk] m view; (fig) comprehension; **d~en** vi to look through; (umg: verstehen): **(bei etw) d~en** to understand (sth); **etw d~en lassen** (fig) to hint at sth

durchbrechen ['dʊrçbrɛçən] (unreg) vt, vi to break

durch'brechen [dʊrç'brɛçən] (unreg) vt insep (Schranken) to break through; (Schallmauer) to break; (Gewohnheit) to break free from

durchbrennen ['dʊrçbrɛnən] (unreg) vi (Draht, Sicherung) to burn through; (umg) to run away

durchbringen (unreg) vt (Kranken) to pull through; (umg: Familie) to support; (durchsetzen: Antrag, Kandidat) to get through; (vergeuden: Geld) to get through, to squander

Durchbruch ['dʊrçbrʊx] m (Öffnung) opening; (MIL) breach; (von Gefühlen etc) eruption; (der Zähne) cutting; (fig) breakthrough; **zum ~ kommen** to break through

durch- zW: **~dacht** [-'daxt] adj well thought-out; **~'denken** (unreg) vt to think out; **~drehen** vt (Fleisch) to

---

mince ♦ vi (umg) to crack up

durcheinander [dʊrçlaɪˈnandər] adv in a mess, in confusion; (umg: verwirrt) confused; ~ **bringen** to mess up; (verwirren) to confuse; ~ **reden** to talk at the same time; **D~** (-s) nt (Verwirrung) confusion; (Unordnung) mess

durch- zW: ~**fahren** (unreg) vi (~ Tunnel usw) to drive through; (ohne Unterbrechung) to drive straight through; (ohne anzuhalten): **der Zug fährt bis Hamburg** ~ the train runs direct to Hamburg; (ohne Umsteigen): **können wir ~fahren?** can we go direct?, can we go non-stop?; **D~fahrt** f transit; (Verkehr) thoroughfare; **D~fall** m (MED) diarrhoea; ~**fallen** (unreg) vi to fall through; (in Prüfung) to fail; ~**finden** (unreg) vr to find one's way through; ~**fragen** ~ to find one's way by asking

durchführ- [ˈdʊrçfyːr] zW: ~**bar** adj feasible, practicable; ~**en** vt to carry out; **D~ung** f execution, performance

Durchgang [ˈdʊrçgaŋ] m passage(-way); (bei Produktion, Versuch) run; (SPORT) round; (bei Wahl) ballot; „~ **verboten**" "no thoroughfare"

Durchgangsverkehr m through traffic

durchgefroren [ˈdʊrçgəfroːrən] adj (Mensch) frozen stiff

durchgehen [ˈdʊrçgeːən] (unreg) vt (behandeln) to go over ♦ vi to go through; (ausreißen: Pferd) to break loose; (Mensch) to run away; **mein Temperament ging mit mir durch** my temper got the better of me; **jdm etw ~ lassen** to let sb get away with sth; ~**d** adj (Zug) through; (Öffnungszeiten) continuous

durch- zW: ~**greifen** (unreg) vi to take strong action; ~**halten** (unreg) vi to last out ♦ vt to keep up; ~**kommen** (unreg) vi to get through; (überleben) to pull through; ~**kreuzen** vt insep to thwart, to frustrate; ~**lassen** (unreg) vt

(Person) to let through; (Wasser) to let in; ~**lesen** (unreg) vt to read through; ~**leuchten** vt insep to X-ray; ~**machen** vt to go through; **die Nacht** ~**machen** to make a night of it

Durchmesser (-s, -) m diameter

durch- zW: ~**nässen** vt insep to soak (through); ~**nehmen** (unreg) vt to go over; ~**nummerieren** ▲ vt to number consecutively; ~**queren** [dʊrçˈkveːrən] vt insep to cross; **D~reise** f transit; **auf der D~reise** passing through; (Güter) in transit; ~**ringen** (unreg) vr to reach a decision after a long struggle

durchs [dʊrçs] = **durch das**

Durchsage [ˈdʊrçzaːgə] f intercom od radio announcement

durchschauen [ˈdʊrçʃaʊən] vi to look od see through; (Person, Lüge) to see through

durchscheinen [ˈdʊrçʃaɪnən] (unreg) vi to shine through; ~**d** adj translucent

Durchschlag [ˈdʊrçʃlaːk] m (Doppel) carbon copy; (Sieb) strainer; **d~en** [-gən] (unreg) vt (entzweischlagen) to split (in two); (sieben) to sieve ♦ vi (zum Vorschein kommen) to emerge, to come out ♦ vr to get by

durchschlagend adj resounding

durchschneiden [ˈdʊrçʃnaɪdən] (unreg) vt to cut through

Durchschnitt [ˈdʊrçʃnɪt] m (Mittelwert) average; **über/unter dem** ~ above/below average; **im** ~ on average; **d~lich** adj average ♦ adv on average

Durchschnittswert m average

durch- zW: **D~schrift** f copy; ~**sehen** (unreg) vt to look through; ~**setzen** vt to enforce ♦ vr (Erfolg haben) to succeed; (sich behaupten) to get one's way; **seinen Kopf ~setzen** to get one's way; ~**setzen** vt insep to mix

Durchsicht [ˈdʊrçzɪçt] f looking through, checking; **d~ig** adj transparent

durch- zW: ~**sprechen** (unreg) vt to talk over; ~**stehen** (unreg) vt to live through; **~stellen** vt (an Telefon) to put through; **~stöbern** (auch untr) vt (Kisten) to rummage through, to rifle through; (Haus, Wohnung) to ransack; **'~streichen** (unreg) vt to cross out; **~'suchen** vt insep to search; **D~'suchung** f search; **~'wachsen** adj (Speck) streaky; (fig: mittelmäßig) so-so; **D~wahl** f (TEL) direct dialling; **~weg** adv throughout, completely; **~ziehen** (unreg) vt (Faden) to draw through ♦ vi to pass through; **D~zug** m (Luft) draught; (von Truppen, Vögeln) passage

---

SCHLÜSSELWORT

dürfen ['dyrfən] (unreg) vi **1** (Erlaubnis haben) to be allowed to; **ich darf das** I'm allowed to (do that); **darf ich?** may I?; **darf ich ins Kino?** can od may I go to the cinema?; **es darf geraucht werden** you may smoke
2 (in Verneinungen): **er darf das nicht** he's not allowed to (do that); **das darf nicht geschehen** that must not happen; **da darf sie sich nicht wundern** that shouldn't surprise her
3 (in Höflichkeitsformeln): **darf ich Sie bitten, das zu tun?** may od could I ask you to do that?; **was darf es sein?** what can I do for you?
4 (können): **das dürfen Sie mir glauben** you can believe me
5 (Möglichkeit): **das dürfte genug sein** that should be enough; **es dürfte Ihnen bekannt sein, dass ...** as you would probably know ...

---

dürftig ['dyrftıç] adj (ärmlich) needy, poor; (unzulänglich) inadequate
dürr [dyr] adj dried-up; (Land) arid; (mager) skinny, gaunt; **D~e** f aridity; (Zeit) drought; (Magerkeit) skinniness
Durst [dʊrst] (-(e)s) m thirst; **~ haben** to be thirsty; **d~ig** adj thirsty
Dusche ['dʊʃə] f shower; **d~en** vi, vr to have a shower
Düse ['dy:zə] f nozzle; (Flugzeugdüse) jet
Düsen- zW: **~antrieb** m jet propulsion; **~flugzeug** nt jet (plane); **~jäger** m jet fighter
Dussel ['dʊsəl] (-s, -) (umg) m twit
düster ['dy:stər] adj dark; (Gedanken, Zukunft) gloomy
Dutzend ['dotsənt] (-s, -e) nt dozen; **~(e) od d~(e) Mal(e)** a dozen times
duzen ['du:tsən] vt: **(jdn) ~** to use the familiar form of address "du" (to od with sb)

---

duzen

There are two different forms of address in Germany: du and Sie. **Duzen** means addressing someone as 'du' - used with children, family and close friends - and **siezen** means addressing someone as 'Sie' - used for all grown-ups and older teenagers. Students almost always use 'du' to each other.

Dynamik [dy'na:mik] f (PHYS) dynamics sg; (fig: Schwung) momentum; (von Mensch) dynamism; **dynamisch** adj (auch fig) dynamic
Dynamit [dyna'mi:t] (-s) nt dynamite
Dynamo [dy'na:mo] (-s, -s) m dynamo
DZ nt abk = **Doppelzimmer**
D-Zug ['de:tsu:k] m through train

E, e

Ebbe ['ɛbə] f low tide
eben ['e:bən] adj level, flat; (glatt) smooth ♦ adv just; (bestätigend) exactly; **~ deswegen** just because of that; **~bürtig** adj: **jdm ~bürtig sein** to be sb's equal; **E~e** f plain; (fig) level; **~falls** adv likewise; **~so** adv just as

---

Eber ['e:bər] (-s, -) m boar

ebnen ['e:bnən] vt to level

Echo ['ɛço] (-s, -s) nt echo

echt [ɛçt] adj genuine; (typisch) typical; **E~heit** f genuineness

Eck- ['ɛk] zW: **~ball** m corner (kick); **~e** f corner; (MATH) angle; **e~ig** adj angular; **~zahn** m eye tooth

ECU ['e:ky:] (-, -s) m (FIN) ECU

edel ['e:dəl] adj noble; **E~metall** nt rare metal; **E~stahl** m high-grade steel; **E~stein** m precious stone

EDV [e:de:'faʊ] (-) f abk (= elektronische Datenverarbeitung) electronic data processing

Efeu ['e:fɔy] (-s) m ivy

Effekt [ɛ'fɛkt] (-s, -e) m effect

Effekten [ɛ'fɛktən] pl stocks

effektiv [ɛfɛk'ti:f] adj effective, actual

EG ['e:'ge:] f abk (= Europäische Gemeinschaft) EC

egal [e'ga:l] adj all the same

Ego- [e:go] zW: **~ismus** [-'ɪsmʊs] m selfishness, egoism; **~ist** [-'ɪst] m egoist; **e~istisch** adj selfish, egoistic

Ehe ['e:ə] f marriage

ehe konj before

Ehe- zW: **~beratung** f marriage guidance (counselling); **~bruch** m adultery; **~frau** f married woman; wife; **~leute** pl married people; **e~lich** adj matrimonial; (Kind) legitimate

ehemalig adj former

ehemals adv formerly

Ehe- zW: **~mann** m married man; husband; **~paar** nt married couple

eher ['e:ər] adv (früher) sooner; (lieber) rather, sooner; (mehr) more

Ehe- zW: **~ring** m wedding ring; **~schließung** f marriage ceremony

eheste(r, s) ['e:əstə(r, s)] adj (früheste) first, earliest; **am ~n** (liebsten) soonest; (meist) most; (wahrscheinlichst) most probably

Ehr- ['e:r] zW: **e~bar** adj honourable, respectable; **E~** f honour; **e~en** vt to honour

Ehren- ['e:rən] zW: **e~amtlich** adj honorary; **~gast** m guest of honour; **e~haft** adj honourable; **~platz** m place of honour or (US) honor; **~runde** f lap of honour; **~sache** f point of honour; **e~voll** adj honourable; **~wort** nt word of honour

Ehr- zW: **~furcht** f awe, deep respect; **e~fürchtig** adj reverent; **~gefühl** nt sense of honour; **~geiz** m ambition; **e~geizig** adj ambitious; **e~lich** adj honest; **~lichkeit** f honesty; **e~los** adj dishonourable; **~ung** f honour(ing); **e~würdig** adj venerable

Ei [aɪ] (-(e)s, -er) nt egg

Eich- zW: **e~** ['aɪçə] f oak (tree); **~el** (-, -n) f acorn; **~hörnchen** nt squirrel

Eichmaß nt standard

Eid [aɪt] (-(e)s, -e) m oath

Eidechse ['aɪdɛksə] f lizard

eidesstattlich adj: **~e Erklärung** affidavit

Eidgenosse m Swiss

Eier- zW: **~becher** m eggcup; **~kuchen** m omelette; pancake; **~likör** m advocaat; **~schale** f eggshell; **~stock** m ovary; **~uhr** f egg timer

Eifer ['aɪfər] (-s) m zeal, enthusiasm; **~sucht** f jealousy; **e~süchtig** adj: **e~süchtig (auf** +akk) jealous (of)

eifrig ['aɪfrɪç] adj zealous, enthusiastic

Eigelb ['aɪgɛlp] (-(e)s, -) nt egg yolk

eigen ['aɪgən] adj own; (~artig) peculiar; **mit der/dem ihm ~en ...** with that ... peculiar to him; **sich** dat **etw zu E~ machen** to make sth one's own; **E~art** f peculiarity; characteristic; **e~artig** adj peculiar; **E~bedarf** m: **zum E~bedarf** for (one's own) personal use/domestic requirements; **der Vermieter machte E~bedarf geltend** the landlord showed he needed the house/flat for himself; **~händig** adj with one's own hand; **E~heim** nt owner-occupied house; **E~heit** f peculiarity; **e~mächtig** adj high-handed; **E~name** m proper name; **~s** adv expressly, on purpose; **E~schaft** f quality, property, attribute; **E~sinn** m obstinacy; **~sinnig** adj obstinate; **~tlich** adj actual, real ♦ adv actually, really; **E~tor** nt own goal; **E~tum** nt property; **E~tümer(in)** (-s, -) m(f) owner, proprietor; **~tümlich** adj peculiar; **E~tümlichkeit** f peculiarity; **E~tumswohnung** f freehold flat

eignen ['aignan] vr to be suited; **Eignung** f suitability

Eil- ['ail] zW: **~bote** m courier; **~brief** m express letter; **~e** f haste; **es hat keine ~e** there's no hurry; **e~en** vi (Mensch) to hurry; (dringend sein) to be urgent; **e~ends** adv hastily; **~gut** nt express goods pl, fast freight (US); **e~ig** adj hasty, hurried; (dringlich) urgent; **es e~ig haben** to be in a hurry; **~zug** m semi-fast train, limited stop train

Eimer ['aimar] (-s, -) m bucket, pail

ein ['ain] adv: **nicht ~ noch aus wissen** not to know what to do

ein(e) ['ain(ə)] num one ♦ indef art a, an

einander [ai'nandər] pron one another, each other

einarbeiten ['ain|arbaitən] vt to train ♦ vr: **sich in etw akk ~** to familiarize o.s. with sth

einatmen ['ain|a:tmən] vt, vi to inhale, to breathe in

Einbahnstraße ['ainba:nʃtra:sə] f one-way street

Einband ['ainbant] m binding, cover

einbauen ['ainbauən] vt to build in; (Motor) to install, to fit

Einbaumöbel pl built-in furniture sg

einbegriffen ['ainbəɡrifən] adj included

einberufen ['ainbəru:fən] (unreg) vt to convene; (MIL) to call up

Einbettzimmer nt single room

einbeziehen ['ainbətsi:ən] (unreg) vt to include

einbiegen ['ainbi:ɡən] (unreg) vi to turn

einbilden ['ainbildən] vt: **sich dat etw ~** to imagine sth

Einbildung f imagination; (Dünkel) conceit; **~skraft** f imagination

Einblick ['ainblik] m insight

einbrechen ['ainbreçən] (unreg) vi (in Haus) to break in; (Nacht) to fall; (Winter) to set in; (durchbrechen) to break; **~ in** +akk (MIL) to invade

Einbrecher (-s, -) m burglar

einbringen ['ainbriŋən] (unreg) vt to bring in; (Geld, Vorteil) to yield; (mitbringen) to contribute

Einbruch ['ainbrʊx] m (Hauseinbruch) break-in, burglary; (Eindringen) invasion; (des Winters) onset; (Durchbrechen) break; (MET) approach; (MIL) penetration; **(bei/vor) ~ der Nacht** at/before nightfall; **e~sicher** adj burglar-proof

einbürgern ['ainbyrɡərn] vt to naturalize ♦ vr to become adopted

einbüßen ['ainby:sən] vt to lose, to forfeit

einchecken ['aintʃekən] vt, vi to check in

eincremen ['ainkre:mən] vt to put cream on

eindecken ['aindekən] vr: **sich (mit etw) ~** to lay in stocks (of sth); to stock up (with sth)

eindeutig ['aindɔytiç] adj unequivocal

eindringen ['aindriŋən] (unreg) vi: **~ (in +akk)** to force one's way in(to); (in Haus) to break in(to); (in Land) to invade; (Gas, Wasser) to penetrate; **(auf jdn) ~** (mit Bitten) to pester (sb)

eindringlich adj forcible, urgent

Eindringling m intruder

Eindruck ['aindrʊk] m impression

eindrücken ['aindrykən] vt to press in

eindrucksvoll adj impressive

eine(r, s) pron one; (jemand) someone

eineiig ['aɪn|aɪç] adj (Zwillinge) identical

eineinhalb ['aɪn|aɪn'halp] num one and a half

einengen ['aɪn|ɛŋən] vt to confine, to restrict

einer- ['aɪnər] zW: **'E~lei (-s)** nt sameness; '**~'lei** adj (gleichartig) the same kind of; **es ist mir ~lei** it is all the same to me; **~seits** adv on the one hand

einfach ['aɪnfax] adj simple; (nicht mehrfach) single ♦ adv simply; **E~heit** f simplicity

einfädeln ['aɪnfɛːdəln] vt (Nadel, Faden) to thread; (fig) to contrive

einfahren ['aɪnfaːrən] (unreg) vt to bring in; (Barriere) to knock down; (Auto) to run in ♦ vi to drive in; (Zug) to pull in; (MIN) to go down

Einfahrt f (Vorgang) driving in; pulling in; (MIN) descent; (Ort) entrance

Einfall ['aɪnfal] m (Idee) idea, notion; (Lichteinfall) incidence; (MIL) raid; **e~en** (unreg) vi (Licht) to fall; (MIL) to raid; (einstürzen) to fall in, to collapse; (einstimmen): **(in etw akk) e~en** to join in (with sth); **etw fällt jdm ein** etw occurs to sb; **das fällt mir gar nicht ein** I wouldn't dream of it; **sich dat etw e~en lassen** to have a good idea

einfältig ['aɪnfɛltɪç] adj simple(-minded)

Einfamilienhaus [aɪnfa'miːliənhaʊs] nt detached house

einfarbig ['aɪnfarbɪç] adj all one colour; (Stoff etc) self-coloured

einfetten ['aɪnfɛtən] vt to grease

einfließen ['aɪnfliːsən] (unreg) vi to flow in

einflößen ['aɪnfløːsən] vt: **jdm etw ~** to give sb sth; (fig) to instil sth in sb

Einfluss ▲ ['aɪnflʊs] m influence; **~bereich** m sphere of influence

einförmig ['aɪnfœrmɪç] adj uniform; **E~keit** f uniformity

einfrieren ['aɪnfriːrən] (unreg) vi to

freeze (up) ♦ vt to freeze

Einfuhr ['aɪnfuːr] (-) f import; **~be-schränkung** f import restrictions pl; **~bestimmungen** pl import regulations

einführen ['aɪnfyːrən] vt to bring in; (Mensch, Sitten) to introduce; (Ware) to import

Einführung f introduction

Eingabe ['aɪngaːbə] f petition; (COMPUT) input

Eingang ['aɪngaŋ] m entrance; (COMM: Ankunft) arrival; (Erhalt) receipt

eingeben ['aɪngeːbən] (unreg) vt (Arznei) to give; (Daten etc) to enter

eingebildet ['aɪngəbɪldət] adj imaginary; (eitel) conceited

Eingeborene(r) ['aɪngəboːrənə(r)] f(m) native

Eingebung f inspiration

eingefleischt ['aɪngəflaɪʃt] adj (Gewohnheit, Vorurteile) deep-rooted

eingehen ['aɪngeːən] (unreg) vi (Aufnahme finden) to come in; (Sendung, Geld) to be received; (Tier, Pflanze) to die; (Firma) to fold; (schrumpfen) to shrink ♦ vt to enter into; (Wette) to make; **auf etw akk ~** to go into sth; **auf jdn ~** to respond to sb; **jdm ~** (verständlich sein) to be comprehensible to sb; **~d** adj exhaustive, thorough

Eingemachte(s) ['aɪngəmaxtə(s)] nt preserves pl

eingenommen ['aɪngənɔmən] adj: **~ (von)** fond (of), partial (to); **~ (gegen)** prejudiced (against)

eingeschrieben ['aɪngəʃriːbən] adj registered

eingespielt ['aɪngəʃpiːlt] adj: **aufeinander ~ sein** to be in tune with each other

Eingeständnis ['aɪngəʃtɛntnɪs] (-ses, -se) nt admission, confession

eingestehen ['aɪngəʃteːən] (unreg) vt to confess

eingestellt ['aɪngəʃtɛlt] adj: **auf etw ▲**

sein to be prepared for sth

eingetragen ['aɪngətraːgən] adj
(COMM) registered

Eingeweide ['aɪngəvaɪdə] (-s, -) nt innards pl, intestines pl

Eingeweihte(r) ['aɪngəvaɪtə(r)] f(m)
initiate

eingewöhnen ['aɪngəvøːnən] vr: sich
~ in +akk to settle (down) in

eingleisig ['aɪnglaɪzɪç] adj single-track

eingreifen ['aɪngraɪfən] (unreg) vi to
intervene, to interfere; (Zahnrad) to
mesh

Eingriff ['aɪngrɪf] m intervention, interference; (Operation) operation

einhaken ['aɪnhaːkən] vt to hook in
♦ vr: sich bei jdm ~ to link arms with
sb ♦ vi (sich einmischen) to intervene

Einhalt ['aɪnhalt] m: ~ gebieten +dat
to put a stop to; e~en (unreg) vt (Regel) to keep ♦ vi to stop

einhändigen ['aɪnhɛndɪgən] vt to hand in

einhängen ['aɪnhɛŋən] vt to hang;
(Telefon) to hang up ♦ vi (TEL) to hang up; sich bei jdm ~ to link arms with sb

einheimisch ['aɪnhaɪmɪʃ] adj native;
E~e(r) f(m) local

Einheit ['aɪnhaɪt] f unity; (Maß, MIL)
unit; e~lich adj uniform; ~spreis m standard price

einholen ['aɪnhoːlən] vt (Tau) to haul
in; (Fahne, Segel) to lower; (Vorsprung
aufholen) to catch up with; (Verspätung) to make up; (Rat, Erlaubnis) to
ask ♦ vi (einkaufen) to shop

einhüllen ['aɪnhʏlən] vt to wrap up

einhundert ['aɪn'hʊndɐt] num one
hundred, a hundred

einig ['aɪnɪç] adj (vereint) united; ~ gehen to agree; sich dat ~ sein to be in
agreement; ~ werden to agree

einige(r, s) ['aɪnɪgə(r, s)] adj, pron some
♦ pl some; (mehrere) several; ~ Mal a

few times

einigen vt to unite ♦ vr: sich ~ (auf
+akk) to agree (on)

einigermaßen adv somewhat; (leidlich)
reasonably

einig- zW: **E~keit** f unity; (Übereinstimmung) agreement; **E~ung** f agreement; (Vereinigung) unification

einkalkulieren ['aɪnkalkuliːrən] vt to
take into account, to allow for

Einkauf ['aɪnkaʊf] m purchase; **e~en** vt
to buy ♦ vi to shop; **e~en gehen** to go
shopping

Einkaufs- zW: **~bummel** m shopping
spree; **~korb** m shopping basket;
~wagen m shopping trolley; **~zentrum** nt shopping centre

einklammern ['aɪnklamɐn] vt to put
in brackets, to bracket

Einklang ['aɪnklaŋ] m harmony

einklemmen ['aɪnklɛmən] vt to jam

einkochen ['aɪnkɔxən] vt to boil
down; (Obst) to preserve, to bottle

Einkommen ['aɪnkɔmən] (-s, -) nt income; **~(s)steuer** f income tax

Einkünfte ['aɪnkʏnftə] pl income sg,
revenue sg

einladen ['aɪnlaːdən] (unreg) vt (Person)
to invite; (Gegenstände) to load; jdn
ins Kino ~ to take sb to the cinema

Einladung f invitation

Einlage ['aɪnlaːgə] f (Programmeinlage)
interlude; (Spareinlage) deposit; (Schuheinlage) insole; (Fußstütze) support;
(Zahneinlage) temporary filling; (KOCH)
noodles pl, vegetables pl etc in soup

einlagern ['aɪnlaːgɐn] vt to store

Einlass ▲ ['aɪnlas] (-es, -e) m (Zutritt)
admission

einlassen ['aɪnlasən] (unreg) vt to let
in; (einsetzen) to set in ♦ vr: sich mit
jdm/auf etw akk ~ to get involved
with sb/sth

Einlauf ['aɪnlaʊf] m arrival; (von Pferden) finish; (MED) enema; **e~en** (unreg)

Spelling Reform: ▲ new spelling △ old spelling (to be phased out)

vi to arrive, to come in; (*in Hafen*) to enter; (*SPORT*) to finish; (*Wasser*) to run in; (*Stoff*) to shrink ♦ *vr* (*Schuhe*) to break in ♦ *vr* (*SPORT*) to warm up; (*Motor, Maschine*) to run in; **jdm das Haus e~en** to invade sb's house

einleben ['aɪnle:bən] *vr* to settle down

einlegen ['aɪnle:gən] *vt* (*einfügen: Blatt, Sohle*) to insert; (*KOCH*) to pickle; (*Pause*) to have; (*Protest*) to make; (*Veto*) to use; (*Berufung*) to lodge; (*AUT: Gang*) to engage

einleiten ['aɪnlaɪtən] *vt* to introduce, to start; (*Geburt*) to induce; **Einleitung** *f* introduction; induction

einleuchten ['aɪnlɔʏçtən] *vi*: (**jdm**) ~ to be clear *od* evident (to sb); **~d** *adj* clear

einliefern ['aɪnli:fərn] *vt*: ~ (**in** +*akk*) to take (into)

Einlieferungsschein *m* certificate of posting

Einliegerwohnung ['aɪnli:gərvo:nʊŋ] *f* self-contained flat; (*für Eltern, Großeltern*) granny flat

einlösen ['aɪnlø:zən] *vt* (*Scheck*) to cash; (*Schuldschein, Pfand*) to redeem; (*Versprechen*) to keep

einmachen ['aɪnmaxən] *vt* to preserve

einmal ['aɪnma:l] *adv* once; (*erstens*) first; (*zukünftig*) sometime; **nehmen wir ~ an** just let's suppose; **noch ~** once more; **nicht ~** not even; **auf ~** all at once; **es war ~** once upon a time there was/were; **E~'eins** *nt* multiplication tables *pl*; **~ig** *adj* unique; (*nur einmal erforderlich*) single; (*prima*) fantastic

Einmarsch ['aɪnmarʃ] *m* entry; (*MIL*) invasion; **e~ieren** *vi* to march in

einmischen ['aɪnmɪʃən] *vr*: **sich ~ (in** +*akk*) to interfere (with)

einmütig ['aɪnmy:tɪç] *adj* unanimous

Einnahme ['aɪnna:mə] *f* (*von Medizin*) taking; (*MIL*) capture, taking; **~n** *pl* (*Geld*) takings, revenue *sg*; **~quelle** *f* source of income

einnehmen ['aɪnne:mən] (*unreg*) *vt* to take; (*Stellung, Raum*) to take up; **~ für/gegen** to persuade in favour of/ against; **~d** *adj* charming

einordnen ['aɪnɔrdnən] *vt* to arrange, to fit in ♦ *vr* to adapt; (*AUT*) to get into lane

einpacken ['aɪnpakən] *vt* to pack (up)

einparken ['aɪnparkən] *vt* to park

einpendeln ['aɪnpɛndəln] *vr* to even out

einpflanzen ['aɪnpflantsən] *vt* to plant; (*MED*) to implant

einplanen ['aɪnpla:nən] *vt* to plan for

einprägen ['aɪnprɛ:gən] *vt* to impress, to imprint; (*beibringen*): (**jdm**) ~ to impress (on sb); **sich** *dat* **etw ~** to memorize sth

einrahmen ['aɪnra:mən] *vt* to frame

einräumen ['aɪnrɔʏmən] *vt* (*ordnend*) to put away; (*überlassen: Platz*) to give up; (*zugestehen*) to admit, to concede

einreden ['aɪnre:dən] *vt*: **jdm/sich etw ~** to talk sb/o.s. into believing sth

einreiben ['aɪnraɪbən] (*unreg*) *vt* to rub in

einreichen ['aɪnraɪçən] *vt* to hand in; (*Antrag*) to submit

Einreise ['aɪnraɪzə] *f* entry; **~bestimmungen** *pl* entry regulations; **~erlaubnis** *f* entry permit; **~genehmigung** *f* entry permit; **e~n** *vi*: (**in ein Land**) **e~n** to enter (a country)

einrichten ['aɪnrɪçtən] *vt* (*Haus*) to furnish; (*schaffen*) to establish, to set up; (*arrangieren*) to arrange; (*möglich machen*) to manage ♦ *vr* (*in Haus*) to furnish one's house; **sich ~ (auf** +*akk*) (*sich vorbereiten*) to prepare o.s. (for); (*sich anpassen*) to adapt (to)

Einrichtung *f* (*Wohnungseinrichtung*) furnishings *pl*; (*öffentliche Anstalt*) organization; (*Dienste*) service

einrosten ['aɪnrɔstən] *vi* to get rusty

einrücken ['aɪnrʏkən] *vi* (*MIL: in Land*) to move in

Eins [aɪns] (-, -en) f one; **e~** num one; **es ist mir alles e~** it's all one to me

einsam ['aɪnzaːm] adj lonely, solitary; **E~keit** f loneliness, solitude

einsammeln ['aɪnzamln] vt to collect

Einsatz ['aɪnzats] m (Teil) inset; (an Kleid) insertion; (Verwendung) use, employment; (Spieleinsatz) stake; (Risiko) risk; (MIL) operation; (MUS) entry; **im ~** in action; **e~bereit** adj ready for action

einschalten ['aɪnʃaltn] vt (einfügen) to insert; (Pause) to make; (ELEK) to switch on; (Anwalt) to bring in ♦ vr (dazwischentreten) to intervene

einschärfen ['aɪnʃɛrfn] vt: **jdm etw ~** to impress sth (up)on sb

einschätzen ['aɪnʃɛtsn] vt to estimate, to assess ♦ vr to rate o.s.

einschenken ['aɪnʃɛŋkn] vt to pour out

einschicken ['aɪnʃɪkn] vt to send in

einschl. abk (= einschließlich) incl.

einschlafen ['aɪnʃlaːfn] (unreg) vi to fall asleep, to go to sleep

einschläfernd ['aɪnʃlɛːfərnt] adj (MED) soporific; (langweilig) boring; (Stimme) lulling

Einschlag ['aɪnʃlaːk] m impact; (fig: Beimischung) touch, hint; **e~en** [-gən] (unreg) vt to knock in; (Fenster) to smash, to break; (Zähne, Schädel) to smash in; (AUT: Räder) to turn; (kürzer machen) to take up; (Ware) to pack, to wrap up; (Weg, Richtung) to take ♦ vi to hit; (sich einigen) to agree; (Anklang finden) to work, to succeed; **in etw akk/auf jdn e~en** to hit sth/sb

einschlägig ['aɪnʃlɛːgɪç] adj relevant

einschließen ['aɪnʃliːsn] (unreg) vt (Kind) to lock in; (Häftling) to lock up; (Gegenstand) to lock away; (Bergleute) to cut off; (umgeben) to surround; (MIL) to encircle; (fig) to include, to comprise ♦ vr to lock o.s. in

einschließlich adv inclusive ♦ präp +gen inclusive of, including

einschmeicheln ['aɪnʃmaɪçln] vr: **sich ~ (bei)** to ingratiate o.s. (with)

einschnappen ['aɪnʃnapn] vi (Tür) to click to; (fig) to be touchy; **eingeschnappt sein** to be in a huff

einschneidend ['aɪnʃnaɪdənt] adj drastic

Einschnitt ['aɪnʃnɪt] m cutting; (MED) incision; (Ereignis) decisive point

einschränken ['aɪnʃrɛŋkn] vt to limit, to restrict; (Kosten) to cut down, to reduce ♦ vr to cut down on expenditure; **Einschränkung** f restriction, limitation; reduction; (von Behauptung) qualification

Einschreib- ['aɪnʃraɪb] zW: **~(e)brief** m recorded delivery letter; **e~en** (unreg) vr to write in; (Post) to send recorded delivery ♦ vr to register; (UNIV) to enrol; **~en** nt recorded delivery letter

einschreiten ['aɪnʃraɪtn] (unreg) vi to step in, to intervene; **~ gegen** to take action against

einschüchtern ['aɪnʃʏçtɐn] vt to intimidate

einschulen ['aɪnʃuːlən] vt: **eingeschult werden** (Kind) to start school

einsehen ['aɪnzeːən] (unreg) vt (hineinsehen in) to realize; (Akten) to have a look at; (verstehen) to see; **E~ (-s)** nt understanding; **ein E~ haben** to show understanding

einseitig ['aɪnzaɪtɪç] adj one-sided

Einsend- ['aɪnzɛnd] zW: **e~en** (unreg) vt to send in; **~er (-s, -)** m sender, contributor; **~ung** f sending in

einsetzen ['aɪnzɛtsn] vt to put (in); (in Amt) to appoint, to install; (Geld) to stake; (verwenden) to use; (MIL) to employ ♦ vi (beginnen) to set in; (MUS) to enter, to come in ♦ vr to work hard; **sich für jdn/etw ~** to support sb/sth

Einsicht ['aɪnzɪçt] f insight; (in Akten) look, inspection; **zu der ~ kommen, dass ...** to come to the conclusion that ...; **e~ig** adj (Mensch) judicious; **e~slos** adj unreasonable; **e~svoll** adj understanding

einsilbig ['aɪnzɪlbɪç] adj (auch fig) monosyllabic; (Mensch) uncommunicative

einspannen ['aɪnʃpanən] vt (Papier) to insert; (Pferde) to harness; (umg: Person) to rope in

Einsparung ['aɪnʃpaːrʊŋ] f economy, saving

einsperren ['aɪnʃpɛran] vt to lock up

einspielen ['aɪnʃpiːlən] vr (SPORT) to warm up ♦ vt (Film: Geld) to bring in; (Instrument) to play in; **sich aufeinander ~** to become attuned to each other; **gut eingespielt** running smoothly

einsprachig ['aɪnʃpraːxɪç] adj monolingual

einspringen ['aɪnʃprɪŋən] vi (unreg) (aushelfen) to help out, to step into the breach

Einspruch ['aɪnʃprʊx] m protest, objection; **~srecht** nt veto

einspurig ['aɪnʃpuːrɪç] adj (EISENB) single-track; (AUT) single-lane

einst [aɪnst] adv once; (zukünftig) one day, some day

einstecken ['aɪnʃtɛkən] vt to stick in, to insert; (Brief) to post; (ELEK: Stecker) to plug in; (Geld) to pocket; (mitnehmen) to take; (überlegen sein) to put in the shade; (hinnehmen) to swallow

einstehen ['aɪnʃteːən] vi (unreg) vi: **für jdn/etw ~** to guarantee sb/sth; (verantworten): **für etw ~** to answer for sth

einsteigen ['aɪnʃtaɪgən] vi (unreg) vi to get in od on; (in Schiff) to go on board; (sich beteiligen) to come in; (hineinklettern) to climb in

einstellen ['aɪnʃtɛlən] vt (aufhören) to stop; (Geräte) to adjust; (Kamera etc)

to focus; (Sender, Radio) to tune in; (unterstellen) to put; (in Firma) to employ, to take on ♦ vi (Firma) to take on staff/workers ♦ vr (anfangen) to set in; (kommen) to arrive; **sich auf jdn ~** to adapt to sb; **sich auf etw akk ~** to prepare o.s. with

Einstellung f (Aufhören) suspension; adjustment; focusing; (von Arbeiter etc) appointment; (Haltung) attitude

Einstieg ['aɪnʃtiːk] (-(e)s, -e) m entry; (fig) approach

einstig ['aɪnstɪç] adj former

einstimmig ['aɪnʃtɪmɪç] adj unanimous; (MUS) for one voice

einstmals adv once, formerly

einstöckig ['aɪnʃtœkɪç] adj two-storeyed

Einsturz ['aɪnʃtʊrts] m collapse

einstürzen ['aɪnʃtʏrtsən] vi to fall in, to collapse

einst- zW: **~weilen** adv meanwhile; (vorläufig) temporarily, for the time being; **~weilig** adj temporary

eintägig ['aɪntɛːgɪç] adj one-day

eintauschen ['aɪntauʃən] vt: **~ (gegen** od **für)** to exchange (for)

eintausend ['aɪntaozənt] num one thousand

einteilen ['aɪntaɪlən] vt (in Teile) to divide (up); (Menschen) to assign

einteilig ['aɪntaɪlɪç] adj one-piece

eintönig ['aɪntøːnɪç] adj monotonous

Eintopf ['aɪntɔpf] m stew

Eintracht ['aɪntraxt] (-) f concord, harmony; **einträchtig** ['aɪntrɛçtɪç] adj harmonious

Eintrag ['aɪntraːk] (-(e)s, -e) m entry; **amtlicher ~** entry in the register; **e~en** [-gən] (unreg) vt (in Buch) to enter; (Profit) to yield ♦ vr to put one's name down

einträglich ['aɪntrɛːklɪç] adj profitable

eintreffen ['aɪntrɛfən] vi (unreg) vi to happen; (ankommen) to arrive

eintreten ['aɪntreːtən] vi (unreg) vi to occur; (sich einsetzen) to intercede ♦ vt

(Tür) to kick open; **~ in** *+akk* to enter; *(in Klub, Partei)* to join

Eintritt ['aıntrıt] *m (Betreten)* entrance; *(Anfang)* commencement; *(in Klub etc)* joining

Eintritts- *zW:* **~geld** *nt* admission charge; **~karte** *f* (admission) ticket; **~preis** *m* admission charge

einüben ['aınjy:bən] *vt* to practise

Einvernehmen ['aınfernejmən] *(-s, -)* *nt* agreement, harmony

einverstanden ['aınferʃtandən] *excl* agreed, very well ♦ *adj:* **~ sein** to agree, to be agreed

Einverständnis ['aınferʃtentnıs] *nt (gleiche Meinung)* understanding; *(gleiche Meinung)* agreement

Einwand ['aınvant] *(-(e)s, =e)* *m* objection

Einwand- *zW:* **~erer** ['aınvandərər] *m* immigrant; **e~ern** *vi* to immigrate; **~erung** *f* immigration

einwandfrei *adj* perfect ♦ *adv* absolutely

Einweg- ['aınve:g-] *zW:* **~flasche** *f* no-deposit bottle; **~spritze** *f* disposable syringe

einweichen ['aınvaıçən] *vt* to soak

einweihen ['aınvaıən] *vt (Kirche)* to consecrate; *(Brücke)* to open; *(Gebäude)* to inaugurate; **~ in** *+akk (Person)* to initiate (in); **Einweihung** *f* consecration; opening; inauguration; initiation

einweisen ['aınvaızən] *(unreg)* *vt (in Amt)* to install; *(in Arbeit)* to introduce; *(in Anstalt)* to send

einwenden ['aınvendən] *(unreg)* *vt:* **etwas ~ gegen** to object to, to oppose

einwerfen ['aınverfən] *(unreg)* *vt* to throw in; *(Brief)* to post; *(Geld)* to put in, to insert; *(Fenster)* to smash; *(äußern)* to interpose

einwickeln ['aınvıkəln] *vt* to wrap up; *(fig: umg)* to outsmart

einwilligen ['aınvılıgən] *vi:* **~ (in** *+akk)* to consent (to), to agree (to); **Einwilligung** *f* consent

einwirken ['aınvırkən] *vi:* **auf jdn/etw ~** to influence sb/sth

Einwohner(in) ['aınvo:nər] *(-s, -)* *m* inhabitant; **~meldeamt** *nt* registration office; **~schaft** *f* population, inhabitants *pl*

Einwurf ['aınvurf] *m (Öffnung)* slot; *(von Münze)* insertion; *(von Brief)* posting; *(Einwand)* objection; *(SPORT)* throw-in

Einzahl ['aıntsa:l] *f* singular; **e~en** *vt* to pay in; **~ung** *f* paying in; **~ungsschein** *m* paying-in slip, deposit slip

einzäunen ['aıntsɔynən] *vt* to fence in

Einzel ['aıntsəl] *(-s, -)* *nt (TENNIS)* singles; **~fahrschein** *m* one-way ticket; **~fall** *m* single instance, individual case; **~handel** *m* retail trade; **~handelspreis** *m* retail price; **~heit** *f* particular, detail; **~kind** *nt* only child; **e~n** *adj* single; *(vereinzelt)* the odd ♦ *adv* singly; **e~n angeben** to specify; **der/die E~ne** the individual; **das E~ne** the particular; **ins E~ne gehen** to go into detail(s); **~teil** *nt* component (part); **~zimmer** *nt* single room; **~zimmerzuschlag** *m* single room supplement

einziehen ['aıntsi:ən] *(unreg)* *vt* to draw in, to take in; *(Kopf)* to duck; *(Fühler, Antenne, Fahrgestell)* to retract; *(Steuern, Erkundigungen)* to collect; *(MIL)* to draft, to call up; *(aus dem Verkehr ziehen)* to withdraw; *(konfiszieren)* to confiscate ♦ *vi* to move in; *(Friede, Ruhe)* to come; *(Flüssigkeit)* to penetrate

einzig ['aıntsıç] *adj* only; *(ohnegleichen)* unique; **das E~e** the only thing; **der/die E~e** the only one; **~artig** *adj* unique

Einzug ['aıntsu:k] *m* entry, moving in

Eis [aɪs] (-es, -) nt ice; (Speiseeis) ice cream; **~bahn** f ice od skating rink; **~bär** m polar bear; **~becher** m sundae; **~bein** nt pig's trotters pl; **~berg** m iceberg; **~café** nt ice-cream parlour (BRIT) od parlor (US); **~decke** f sheet of ice; **~diele** f ice-cream parlour

Eisen ['aɪzən] (-s, -) nt iron

Eisenbahn f railway, railroad (US); **~er** (-s, -) m railwayman, railway employee, railroader (US); **~schaffner** m railway guard; **~wagen** m railway carriage

Eisenerz nt iron ore

eisern ['aɪzərn] adj iron; (Gesundheit) robust; (Energie) unrelenting; (Reserve) emergency

Eis- zW: **e~frei** adj clear of ice; **~hockey** nt ice hockey; **e~ig** ['aɪzɪç] adj icy; **e~kalt** adj icy cold; **~kunstlauf** m figure skating; **~laufen** nt ice skating; **~pickel** m ice axe; **~schrank** m fridge, icebox (US); **~würfel** m ice cube; **~zapfen** m icicle; **~zeit** f ice age

eitel ['aɪtəl] adj vain; **E~keit** f vanity

Eiter ['aɪtər] (-s) m pus; **e~ig** adj suppurating; **e~n** vi to suppurate

Eiweiß (-es, -e) nt white of an egg; (CHEM) protein

Ekel¹ ['eːkəl] (-s, -) m (umg: Mensch) nauseating person

Ekel² ['eːkəl] (-s) m nausea, disgust; **~ erregend** nauseating, disgusting; **e~haft** adj nauseating, disgusting; **e~ig** adj nauseating, disgusting; **e~n** vt to disgust ♦ vr: **sich e~n (vor** +dat) to loathe, to be disgusted (at); be es~t jdn od jdm sb is disgusted; **eklig** adj nauseating, disgusting

Ekstase [ek'staːzə] f ecstasy

Ekzem [ɛk'tseːm] (-s, -e) nt (MED) eczema

Elan [e'lã:] (-s) m elan

elastisch [e'lastɪʃ] adj elastic

Elastizität [elastitsi'tɛːt] f elasticity

Elch [ɛlç] (-(e)s, -e) m elk

Elefant [ele'fant] m elephant

elegant [ele'gant] adj elegant

Eleganz [ele'gants] f elegance

Elek- [e'lɛk] zW: **~triker** [-trikər] (-s, -) m electrician; **e~trisch** [-trɪʃ] adj electric; **e~trisieren** [-tri'ziːrən] vt (auch fig) to electrify; (Mensch) to give an electric shock to ♦ vr to get an electric shock; **~trizität** [tritsi'tɛːt] f electricity; **~trizitätswerk** nt power station; (Gesellschaft) electric power company

Elektro- [e'lɛktro] zW: **~de** [-'troːdə] f electrode; **~gerät** nt electrical appliance; **~herd** m electric cooker; **~n** (-s, -en) nt electron; **~nenrechner** [elɛk'troːnən-] m computer; **~nik** f electronics sg, e~nisch adj electronic; **~rasierer** m electric razor; **~technik** f electrical engineering

Element [ele'mɛnt] (-s, -e) nt element; (ELEK) cell, battery; **e~ar** [-'taːr] adj elementary; (naturhaft) elemental

Elend ['eːlɛnt] (-s) nt misery; **e~** adj miserable; **~sviertel** nt slum

elf [ɛlf] num eleven; **E~** (-, -en) f (SPORT) eleven

Elfe f elf

Elfenbein nt ivory

Elfmeter m (SPORT) penalty (kick)

Elite [e'liːtə] f elite

Ell- zW: **~bogen** m elbow; **~e** ['ɛlə] f ell; (Maß) yard; **~enbogen** m elbow; **~(en)bogenfreiheit** f (fig) elbow room

Elsass ▲ ['ɛlzas] (- od -es) nt: **das ~** Alsace

Elster ['ɛlstər] (-, -n) f magpie

Eltern ['ɛltərn] pl parents; **~beirat** m (SCH) ≈ PTA (BRIT), parents' council; **~haus** nt home; **e~los** adj parentless

E-Mail ['iːmeːl] (-, -s) f E-mail

Emaille [e'maljə] (-s, -s) f enamel

emaillieren [ema'jiːrən] vt to enamel

Emanzipation [emantsipatsi'oːn] f emancipation

emanzipieren vt to emancipate

Embryo ['ɛmbryo] (-s, -s od Embryonen) m embryo

Emigrant 85 Ensemble

Emi- zW: **~'grant(in)** m(f) emigrant; **~gration** f emigration; **e~grieren** vi to emigrate

Emissionen [emɪsiˈoːnən] fpl emissions

Empfang [ɛmˈpfaŋ] (**-(e)s**, **⸗e**) m reception; (*Erhalten*) receipt; **in ~ nehmen** to receive; **e~en** (*unreg*) vt to receive ♦ vi (*schwanger werden*) to conceive

Empfäng- [ɛmˈpfɛŋ] zW: **~er** (**-s**, **-**) m receiver; (*COMM*) addressee, consignee; **~erabschnitt** m receipt slip; **e~lich** adj receptive, susceptible; **~nis** (**-**, **-se**) f conception; **~nisverhütung** f contraception

Empfangs- zW: **~bestätigung** f acknowledgement; **~dame** f receptionist; **~schein** m receipt; **~zimmer** nt reception room

empfehlen [ɛmˈpfeːlən] (*unreg*) vt to recommend ♦ vr to take one's leave; **~swert** adj recommendable

Empfehlung f recommendation

empfiehlst etc [ɛmˈpfiːlst] vb siehe **empfehlen**

empfind- [ɛmˈpfɪnt] zW: **e~en** [-dən] (*unreg*) vt to feel; **~lich** adj sensitive; (*Stelle*) sore; (*reizbar*) touchy; **~sam** adj sentimental; **E~ung** [-dʊŋ] f feeling, sentiment

empfohlen etc [ɛmˈpfoːlən] vb siehe **empfehlen**

empor [ɛmˈpoːr] adv up, upwards

empören [ɛmˈpøːrən] vt to make indignant; to shock ♦ vr to become indignant; **~d** adj outrageous

Emporkömmling [ɛmˈpoːrkœmlɪŋ] m upstart, parvenu

Empörung f indignation

emsig [ˈɛmzɪç] adj diligent, busy

End- [ˈɛnd] in zW final; **~e** (**-s**, **-n**) nt end; **am ~e** at the end; (*schließlich*) in the end; **am ~e sein** to be at the end of one's tether; **~e Dezember** at the

end of December; **zu ~e sein** to be finished; **e~en** vi to end; **e~gültig** [ˈɛnt-] adj final, definite

Endivie [ɛnˈdiːviə] f endive

End- zW: **e~lich** adj final; (*MATH*) finite ♦ adv finally; **e~lich!** at last!; **komm e~lich!** come on!; **e~los** adj endless, infinite; **~spiel** nt final(s); **~spurt** m (*SPORT*) final spurt; **~station** f terminus; **~ung** f ending

Energie [enɛrˈɡiː] f energy; **~bedarf** m energy requirement; **e~los** adj lacking in energy, weak; **~verbrauch** m energy consumption; **~versorgung** f supply of energy; **~wirtschaft** f energy industry

energisch [eˈnɛrɡɪʃ] adj energetic

eng [ɛŋ] adj narrow; (*Kleidung*) tight; (*fig: Horizont*) narrow, limited; (*Freundschaft, Verhältnis*) close; **~ an etw** dat close to sth

Engagement [ãɡaʒəˈmãː] (**-s**, **-s**) nt engagement; (*Verpflichtung*) commitment

engagieren [ãɡaˈʒiːrən] vt to engage ♦ vr to commit o.s.

Enge [ˈɛŋə] f (*auch fig*) narrowness; (*Landenge*) defile; (*Meerenge*) straits pl; **jdn in die ~ treiben** to drive sb into a corner

Engel [ˈɛŋəl] (**-s**, **-**) m angel; **e~haft** adj angelic

England [ˈɛŋlant] nt England; **Engländer(in)** m(f) Englishman(-woman); **englisch** adj English

Engpass ▲ m defile, pass; (*fig, Verkehr*) bottleneck

en gros [ã'ɡro] adv wholesale

engstirnig [ˈɛŋʃtɪrnɪç] adj narrow-minded

Enkel [ˈɛŋkəl] (**-s**, **-**) m grandson; **~in** f granddaughter; **~kind** nt grandchild

enorm [eˈnɔrm] adj enormous

Ensemble [ãˈsãbəl] (**-s**, **-s**) nt company, ensemble

Spelling Reform: ▲ *new spelling* △ *old spelling (to be phased out)*

entbehr- [ent'be:r-] zW: **~en** vt to do without, to dispense with; **~lich** adj superfluous; **E~ung** f deprivation

entbinden [ent'bɪndən] (unreg) vt (+gen) to release (from); (MED) to deliver ♦ vi (MED) to give birth; **Entbindung** f release; (MED) confinement; **Entbindungsheim** nt maternity hospital

entdeck- [ent'dek] zW: **~en** vt to discover; **E~er** (-s, -) m discoverer; **E~ung** f discovery

Ente ['entə] f duck; (fig) canard, false report

enteignen [ent'aɪgnən] vt to expropriate; (Besitzer) to dispossess

enterben [ent'erbən] vt to disinherit

entfallen [ent'falən] (unreg) vi to drop, to fall; (wegfallen) to be dropped; **jdm ~** (vergessen) to slip sb's memory; **auf jdn ~** to be allotted to sb

entfalten [ent'faltən] vt to unfold; (Talente) to develop ♦ vr to open; (Mensch) to develop one's potential; **Entfaltung** f unfolding; (von Talenten) development

entfern- [ent'fern] zW: **~en** vt to remove; (hinauswerfen) to expel ♦ vr to go away, to withdraw; **~t** adj distant; **weit davon ~t sein, etw zu tun** to be far from doing sth; **E~ung** f distance; (Wegschaffen) removal

entfremden [ent'fremdən] vt to estrange, to alienate; **Entfremdung** f alienation, estrangement

entfrosten [ent'frɔstən] vt to defrost

Entfroster (-s, -) m (AUT) defroster

entführ- [ent'fy:r] zW: **~en** vt to carry off, to abduct; to kidnap; **E~er** m kidnapper; **E~ung** f abduction; kidnapping

entgegen [ent'ge:gən] präp +dat contrary to, against ♦ adv towards; **~bringen** (unreg) vt to bring; **jdm etw ~bringen** (fig) to show sb sth; **~gehen** (unreg) vi +dat to go to meet, to go towards; **~gesetzt** adj opposite; (widersprechend) opposed; **~halten**

(unreg) vt (fig) to object; **E~kommen** nt obligingness; **~kommen** (unreg) vi +dat to approach; to meet; (fig) to accommodate; **~kommend** adj obliging; **~nehmen** (unreg) vt to receive, to accept; **~sehen** (unreg) vi +dat to await; **~setzen** vr to oppose; **~treten** (unreg) vi +dat to step up to; (fig) to oppose, to counter; **~wirken** vi +dat to counteract

entgegnen [ent'ge:gnən] vt to reply, to retort

entgehen [ent'ge:ən] (unreg) vi (fig): **jdm ~** to escape sb's notice; **sich** dat **etw ~ lassen** to miss sth

Entgelt [ent'gelt] (-(e)s, -e) nt compensation, remuneration

entgleisen [ent'glaɪzən] vi (EISENB) to be derailed; (fig: Person) to misbehave; **~ lassen** to derail

entgräten [ent'grɛ:tən] vt to fillet, to bone

Enthaarungscreme [ent'ha:ruŋs-] f hair-removing cream

enthalten [ent'haltən] (unreg) vt to contain ♦ vr: **sich (von etw) ~** to abstain (from sth), to refrain (from sth)

enthaltsam [ent'haltza:m] adj abstinent, abstemious

enthemmen [ent'hemən] vt: **jdn ~** to free sb from his inhibitions

enthüllen [ent'hylən] vt to reveal, to unveil

Enthusiasmus [entuzi'asmos] m enthusiasm

entkommen [ent'kɔmən] (unreg) vi: **~ (aus** od +dat**)** to get away (from), to escape (from)

entkräften [ent'kreftən] vt to weaken, to exhaust; (Argument) to refute

entladen [ent'la:dən] (unreg) vt to unload; (ELEK) to discharge ♦ vr (ELEK: Gewehr) to discharge; (Ärger etc) to vent itself

entlang [ent'laŋ] adv along; **~ dem Fluss, den Fluss ~** along the river; **~gehen** (unreg) vi to walk along

entlarven [ɛntˈlarfən] vt to unmask, to expose

entlassen [ɛntˈlasən] (unreg) vt to discharge; (Arbeiter) to dismiss; **Entlassung** f discharge; dismissal

entlasten [ɛntˈlastən] vt to relieve; (Achse) to relieve the load on; (Angeklagten) to exonerate; (Konto) to clear

Entlastung f relief; (COMM) crediting

Entlastungszug m relief train

entlegen [ɛntˈleːgən] adj remote

entlocken [ɛntˈlɔkən] vt: (jdm etw) ~ to elicit (sth from sb)

entmutigen [ɛntˈmuːtɪgən] vt to discourage

entnehmen [ɛntˈneːmən] (unreg) vt (+dat) to take out (of), to take (from); (folgern) to infer (from)

entreißen [ɛntˈraɪsən] (unreg) vt: jdm etw ~ to snatch sth (away) from sb

entrichten [ɛntˈrɪçtən] vt to pay

entrosten [ɛntˈrɔstən] vt to remove rust from

entrümpeln [ɛntˈrʏmpəln] vt to clear out

entrüst- [ɛntˈrʏst] zW: **~en** vt to incense, to outrage ♦ vr to be filled with indignation; **~et** adj indignant, outraged; **E~ung** f indignation

entschädigen [ɛntˈʃɛːdɪgən] vt to compensate; **Entschädigung** f compensation

entschärfen [ɛntˈʃɛrfən] vt to defuse; (Kritik) to tone down

Entscheid [ɛntˈʃaɪt] (-(e)s, -e) m decision; **e~en** [-dən] (unreg) vt, vi, vr to decide; **e~end** adj decisive; (Stimme) casting; **~ung** f decision

entschieden [ɛntˈʃiːdən] adj decided; (entschlossen) resolute; **E~heit** f firmness, determination

entschließen [ɛntˈʃliːsən] (unreg) vr to decide

entschlossen [ɛntˈʃlɔsən] adj determined, resolute; **E~heit** f determina-tion

Entschluss ▲ [ɛntˈʃlɔs] m decision; **e~freudig** adj decisive; **~kraft** f determination, decisiveness

entschuldigen [ɛntˈʃʊldɪgən] vt to excuse ♦ vr to apologize

Entschuldigung f apology; (Grund) excuse; **jdn um ~ bitten** to apologize to sb; **~! excuse me; (Verzeihung) sorry

entsetz- [ɛntˈzɛts] zW: **~en** vt to horrify; (MIL) to relieve ♦ vr to be horrified od appalled; **E~en (-s)** nt horror, dismay; **~lich** adj dreadful, appalling; **~t** adj horrified

Entsorgung [ɛntˈzɔrgʊŋ] f (von Kraftwerken, Chemikalien) (waste) disposal

entspannen [ɛntˈʃpanən] vt, vr (Körper) to relax; (POL: Lage) to ease

Entspannung f relaxation, rest; (POL) détente; **~spolitik** f policy of détente

entsprechen [ɛntˈʃprɛçən] (unreg) vi +dat to correspond to; (Anforderungen, Wünschen) to meet, to comply with; **~d** adj appropriate ♦ adv accordingly

entspringen [ɛntˈʃprɪŋən] (unreg) vi (+dat) to spring (from)

entstehen [ɛntˈʃteːən] (unreg) vi: ~ (aus od durch) to arise (from), to result (from)

Entstehung f genesis, origin

entstellen [ɛntˈʃtɛlən] vt to disfigure; (Wahrheit) to distort

entstören [ɛntˈʃtøːrən] vt (RADIO) to eliminate interference from

enttäuschen [ɛntˈtɔʏʃən] vt to disappoint; **Enttäuschung** f disappointment

entwaffnen [ɛntˈvafnən] vt (lit, fig) to disarm

entwässern [ɛntˈvɛsərn] vt to drain; **Entwässerung** f drainage

entweder [ɛntˈveːdər] konj either

entwenden [ɛntˈvɛndən] (unreg) vt to purloin, to steal

entwerfen [ɛntˈvɛrfən] (unreg) vt

(*Zeichnung*) to sketch; (*Modell*) to design; (*Vortrag, Gesetz etc*) to draft

entwerten [ɛntˈveːrtən] *vt* to devalue; (*stempeln*) to cancel

Entwerter (-s, -) *m* ticket punching machine

entwickeln [ɛntˈvɪkəln] *vt, vr* (*auch* PHOT) to develop; (*Mut, Energie*) to show (o.s.), to display (o.s.)

Entwicklung [ɛntˈvɪklʊŋ] *f* development; (*PHOT*) developing

Entwicklungs- *zW:* **~hilfe** *f* aid for developing countries; **~land** *nt* developing country

entwöhnen [ɛntˈvøːnən] *vt* to wean; (*Süchtige*) to cure; (*einer Sache od von etw*) ~ to cure (of sth)

Entwöhnung *f* weaning; cure, curing

entwürdigend [ɛntˈvʏrdɪgənt] *adj* degrading

Entwurf [ɛntˈvʊrf] *m* outline, design; (*Vertragsentwurf, Konzept*) draft

entziehen [ɛntˈtsiːən] (*unreg*) *vt* (+*dat*) to withdraw (from), to take away (from); (*Flüssigkeit*) to draw (from), to extract (from) ♦ *vr* (+*dat*) to escape (from); (*jds Kenntnis*) to be outside *od* beyond; (*der Pflicht*) to shirk (from)

Entziehung *f* withdrawal; **~sanstalt** *f* drug addiction/alcoholism treatment centre; **~skur** *f* treatment for drug addiction/alcoholism

entziffern [ɛntˈtsɪfərn] *vt* to decipher; to decode

entzücken [ɛntˈtsʏkən] *vt* to delight; **E~** (-s) *nt* delight; **~d** *adj* delightful, charming

entzünden [ɛntˈtsʏndən] *vt* to light, to set light to; (*fig, MED*) to inflame; (*Streit*) to spark off ♦ *vr* (*auch fig*) to catch fire; (*Streit*) to start; (*MED*) to become inflamed

Entzündung *f* (*MED*) inflammation

entzwei [ɛntˈtsvai] *adv* broken; in two; **~brechen** (*unreg*) *vt, vi* to break in two; **~en** *vt* to set at odds ♦ *vr* to fall out; **~gehen** (*unreg*) *vi* to break (in two)

Enzian [ˈɛntsiaːn] (-s, -e) *m* gentian

Epidemie [epideˈmiː] *f* epidemic

Epilepsie [epilɛpˈsiː] *f* epilepsy

Episode [epiˈzoːdə] *f* episode

Epoche [eˈpɔxə] *f* epoch; ~ **machend** epoch-making

Epos [ˈeːpɔs] (-s, Epen) *nt* epic (poem)

er [eːr] (*nom*) *pron* he; it

erarbeiten [ɛrˈʔarbaitən] *vt* to work for, to acquire; (*Theorie*) to work out

erbarmen [ɛrˈbarmən] *vr* (+*gen*) to have pity *od* mercy (on); **E~** (-s) *nt* pity

erbärmlich [ɛrˈbɛrmlɪç] *adj* wretched, pitiful; **E~keit** *f* wretchedness

erbarmungslos [ɛrˈbarmʊŋsloːs] *adj* pitiless, merciless

erbau- [ɛrˈbau] *zW:* ~**en** *vt* to build, to erect; (*fig*) to edify; **E~er** (-s, -) *m* builder; **~lich** *adj* edifying

Erbe¹ [ˈɛrbə] (-n, -n) *m* heir

Erbe² [ˈɛrbə] *nt* inheritance; (*fig*) heritage

erben *vt* to inherit

erbeuten [ɛrˈbɔytən] *vt* to carry off; (*MIL*) to capture

Erb- [ɛrb] *zW:* ~**faktor** *m* gene; ~**folge** *f* (line of) succession; ~**in** *f* heiress

erbittern [ɛrˈbɪtərn] *vt* to embitter; (*erzürnen*) to incense

erbittert [ɛrˈbɪtərt] *adj* (*Kampf*) fierce, bitter

erblassen [ɛrˈblasən] *vi* to (turn) pale

erblich [ˈɛrplɪç] *adj* hereditary

erblinden [ɛrˈblɪndən] *vi* to go blind

erbrechen [ɛrˈbrɛçən] (*unreg*) *vt, vr* to vomit

Erbschaft *f* inheritance, legacy

Erbse [ˈɛrpsə] *f* pea

Erbstück *nt* heirloom

Erd- [eːrd] *zW:* ~**achse** *f* earth's axis; ~**atmosphäre** *f* earth's atmosphere; ~**beben** *nt* earthquake; ~**beere** *f* strawberry; ~**boden** *m* ground; ~**e** *f* earth; *zu ebener* ~**e** at ground level; **e~en** *vt* (*ELEK*) to earth

erdenklich [ɛrˈdɛŋklɪç] *adj* conceivable

Erd- zW: **~gas** nt natural gas; **~geschoss** ▲ nt ground floor; **~kunde** f geography; **~nuss** ▲ f peanut; **~öl** nt (mineral) oil

erdrosseln [ɛrˈdrɔsəln] vt to strangle, to throttle

erdrücken [ɛrˈdrʏkən] vt to crush

Erd- zW: **~rutsch** m landslide; **~teil** m continent

erdulden [ɛrˈdʊldən] vt to endure, to suffer

ereignen [ɛrˈaɪɡnən] vr to happen

Ereignis [ɛrˈaɪɡnɪs] (**-ses, -se**) nt event; **e~los** adj uneventful; **e~reich** adj eventful

ererbt [ɛrˈɛrpt] adj (Haus) inherited; (Krankheit) hereditary

erfahren [ɛrˈfaːrən] (unreg) vt to learn, to find out; (erleben) to experience ♦ adj experienced

Erfahrung f experience; **e~sgemäß** adv according to experience

erfassen [ɛrˈfasən] vt to seize; (fig: einbeziehen) to include, to register; (verstehen) to grasp

erfind- [ɛrˈfɪnt] zW: **~en** (unreg) vt to invent; **E~er** (**-s, -**) m inventor; **~erisch** adj inventive; **E~ung** f invention

Erfolg [ɛrˈfɔlk] (**-(e)s, -e**) m success; (Folge) result; **e~en** [-gən] vi to follow; (sich ergeben) to result; (stattfinden) to take place; (Zahlung) to be effected; **e~los** adj unsuccessful; **~losigkeit** f lack of success; **e~reich** adj successful

erforderlich adj requisite, necessary

erfordern [ɛrˈfɔrdərn] vt to require, to demand

erforschen [ɛrˈfɔrʃən] vt (Land) to explore; (Problem) to investigate; (Gewissen) to search; **Erforschung** f exploration; investigation; searching

erfreuen [ɛrˈfrɔʏən] vr: **sich ~ an** +dat to enjoy ♦ vt to delight; **sich einer Sache** gen **~** to enjoy sth

erfreulich [ɛrˈfrɔʏlɪç] adj pleasing, gratifying; **~erweise** adv happily, luckily

erfrieren [ɛrˈfriːrən] (unreg) vi to freeze (to death); (Glieder) to get frostbitten; (Pflanzen) to be killed by frost

erfrischen [ɛrˈfrɪʃən] vt to refresh; **Erfrischung** f refreshment

Erfrischungs- zW: **~getränk** nt (liquid) refreshment; **~raum** m snack bar, cafeteria

erfüllen [ɛrˈfʏlən] vt (Raum etc) to fill; (fig: Bitte etc) to fulfil ♦ vr to come true

ergänzen [ɛrˈɡɛntsən] vt to supplement, to complete ♦ vr to complement one another; **Ergänzung** f completion; (Zusatz) supplement

ergeben [ɛrˈɡeːbən] (unreg) vt to yield, to produce ♦ vr to surrender; (folgen) to result ♦ adj devoted, humble

Ergebnis [ɛrˈɡeːpnɪs] (**-ses, -se**) nt result; **e~los** adj without result, fruitless

ergehen [ɛrˈɡeːən] (unreg) vi to be issued, to go out ♦ vi unpers: **es ergeht ihm gut/schlecht** he's faring ok/ getting on well/badly ♦ vr: **sich in etw** dat **~** to indulge in sth; **etw über sich ~ lassen** to put up with sth

ergiebig [ɛrˈɡiːbɪç] adj productive

Ergonomie [ɛrɡonoˈmiː] f ergonomics sg

Ergonomik [ɛrɡoˈnoːmɪk] f = **Ergonomie**

ergreifen [ɛrˈɡraɪfən] (unreg) vt (auch fig) to seize; (Beruf) to take up; (Maßnahmen) to resort to; (rühren) to move; **~d** adj moving, touching

ergriffen [ɛrˈɡrɪfən] adj deeply moved

Erguss ▲ [ɛrˈɡʊs] m discharge; (fig) outpouring, effusion

erhaben [ɛrˈhaːbən] adj raised, embossed; (fig) exalted, lofty; **über etw** akk **~ sein** to be above sth

erhalten [ɛrˈhaltən] (unreg) vt to receive; (bewahren) to preserve, to main-

tain; **gut ~** in good condition
erhältlich [ɛr'hɛltlɪç] *adj* obtainable, available
Erhaltung *f* maintenance, preservation
erhärten [ɛr'hɛrtən] *vt* to harden; (*These*) to substantiate, to corroborate
erheben [ɛr'he:bən] (*unreg*) *vt* to raise; (*Protest, Forderungen*) to make; (*Fakten*) to ascertain, to establish ♦ *vr* to rise (up)
erheblich [ɛr'he:plɪç] *adj* considerable
erheitern [ɛr'haitərn] *vt* to amuse, to cheer (up)
Erheiterung *f* exhilaration; **zur allgemeinen ~** to everybody's amusement
erhitzen [ɛr'hitsən] *vt* to heat ♦ *vr* to heat up; (*fig*) to become heated
erhoffen [ɛr'hɔfən] *vt* to hope for
erhöhen [ɛr'hø:ən] *vt* to raise; (*verstärken*) to increase
erhol- [ɛr'ho:l] *zW:* **~en** *vr* to recover; (*entspannen*) to have a rest; **~sam** *adj* restful; **E~ung** *f* recovery; relaxation, rest; **~ungsbedürftig** *adj* in need of a rest, run-down; **E~ungsgebiet** *nt* ≈ holiday area; **E~ungsheim** *nt* convalescent home
erhören [ɛr'hø:rən] *vt* (*Gebet etc*) to hear; (*Bitte etc*) to yield to
erinnern [ɛr'ɪnərn] *vt:* **~ (an** +*akk*) to remind (of) ♦ *vr:* **sich (an** *akk* **etw) ~** to remember (sth)
Erinnerung *f* memory; (*Andenken*) reminder
erkältet [ɛr'kɛltət] *adj* with a cold; **~ sein** to have a cold
Erkältung *f* cold
erkennbar *adj* recognizable
erkennen [ɛr'kɛnən] (*unreg*) *vt* to recognize; (*sehen, verstehen*) to see
erkennt- *zW:* **~lich** *adj:* **sich ~lich zeigen** to show one's appreciation; **E~lichkeit** *f* gratitude; (*Geschenk*) token of one's gratitude; **E~nis** (-, **-se**) *f* knowledge; (*das Erkennen*) recognition; (*Einsicht*) insight; **zur E~nis kommen** to realize

Erkennung *f* recognition
Erkennungszeichen *nt* identification
Erker ['ɛrkər] (**-s, -**) *m* bay
erklär- [ɛr'klɛːr] *zW:* **~bar** *adj* explicable; **~en** *vt* to explain; **~lich** *adj* explicable; (*verständlich*) understandable; **E~ung** *f* explanation; (*Aussage*) declaration
erkranken [ɛr'kraŋkən] *vi* to fall ill; **Erkrankung** *f* illness
erkund- [ɛr'kʊnd] *zW:* **~en** *vt* to find out, to ascertain; (*bes MIL*) to reconnoitre, to scout; **~igen** *vr:* **sich ~igen (nach)** to inquire (about); **E~igung** *f* inquiry; **E~ung** *f* reconnaissance, scouting
erlahmen [ɛr'la:mən] *vi* to tire; (*nachlassen*) to flag, to wane
erlangen [ɛr'laŋən] *vt* to attain, to achieve
Erlass ▲ [ɛr'las] (**-es, ⁻e**) *m* decree; (*Aufhebung*) remission
erlassen (*unreg*) *vt* (*Verfügung*) to issue; (*Gesetz*) to enact; (*Strafe*) to remit; **jdm etw ~** to release sb from sth
erlauben [ɛr'lauban] *vt:* **(jdm etw) ~** to allow o.d permit (sb to do sth) ♦ *vr* to permit o.s., to venture
Erlaubnis [ɛr'laupnɪs] (-, **-se**) *f* permission; (*Schriftstück*) permit
erläutern [ɛr'bʏtərn] *vt* to explain; **Erläuterung** *f* explanation
erleben [ɛr'le:bən] *vt* to experience; (*Zeit*) to live through; (*miterleben*) to witness; (*noch miterleben*) to live to see
Erlebnis [ɛr'le:pnɪs] (**-ses, -se**) *nt* experience
erledigen [ɛr'le:dɪgən] *vt* to take care of, to deal with; (*Antrag etc*) to process; (*umg: erschöpfen*) to wear out; (: *ruinieren*) to finish; (: *umbringen*) to do in
erleichtern [ɛr'laiçtərn] *vt* to make easier; (*fig: Last*) to lighten; (*lindern, beruhigen*) to relieve; **Erleichterung** *f* facilitation; lightening; relief
erleiden [ɛr'laidən] (*unreg*) *vt* to suffer,

to endure

erlernen [ɛrˈlɛrnən] vt to learn, to acquire

erlesen [ɛrˈleːzən] adj select, choice

erleuchten [ɛrˈlɔyçtən] vt to illuminate; (fig) to inspire

Erleuchtung f (Einfall) inspiration

Erlös [ɛrˈløːs] (-es, -e) m proceeds pl

erlösen [ɛrˈløːzən] vt to redeem, to save; **Erlösung** f release; (REL) redemption

ermächtigen [ɛrˈmɛçtɪɡən] vt to authorize, to empower; **Ermächtigung** f authorization; authority

ermahnen [ɛrˈmaːnən] vt to exhort, to admonish; **Ermahnung** f admonition, exhortation

ermäßigen [ɛrˈmɛːsɪɡən] vt to reduce; **Ermäßigung** f reduction

ermessen [ɛrˈmɛsən] (unreg) vt to estimate, to gauge; **E~** (-s) nt estimation; discretion; **in jds E~ liegen** to lie within sb's discretion

ermitteln [ɛrˈmɪtəln] vt to determine; (Täter) to trace ♦ vi: **gegen jdn ~** to investigate sb

Ermittlung f determination; (Polizeiermittlung) investigation

ermöglichen [ɛrˈmøːklɪçən] vt (+dat) to make possible (for)

ermorden [ɛrˈmɔrdən] vt to murder

ermüden [ɛrˈmyːdən] vt, vi to tire; (TECH) to fatigue; **~d** adj tiring; (fig) wearisome

Ermüdung f fatigue

ermutigen [ɛrˈmuːtɪɡən] vt to encourage

ernähr- [ɛrˈnɛːr] zW: **~en** vt to feed, to nourish; (Familie) to support ♦ vr to support o.s., to earn a living; **sich ~en von** to live on; **E~er** (-s, -) m breadwinner; **E~ung** f nourishment; nutrition; (Unterhalt) maintenance

ernennen [ɛrˈnɛnən] (unreg) vt to appoint; **Ernennung** f appointment

erneu- [ɛrˈnɔy] zW: **~ern** vt to renew; to restore; to renovate; **E~erung** f renewal; restoration; renovation; **~t** adj renewed, fresh ♦ adv once more

ernst [ɛrnst] adj serious; **~ gemeint** meant in earnest, serious; **E~** (-es) m seriousness; **das ist mein E~** I'm quite serious; **im E~** in earnest; **E~ machen mit etw** to put sth into practice; **E~fall** m emergency; **~haft** adj serious; **E~haftigkeit** f seriousness; **~lich** adj serious

Ernte [ˈɛrntə] f harvest; **e~n** vt to harvest; (Lob etc) to earn

ernüchtern [ɛrˈnʏçtərn] vt to sober up; (fig) to bring down to earth

Erober- [ɛrˈoːbər] zW: **~er** (-s, -) m conqueror; **e~n** vt to conquer; **~ung** f conquest

eröffnen [ɛrˈœfnən] vt to open ♦ vr to present itself; **jdm etw ~** to disclose sth to sb

Eröffnung f opening

erörtern [ɛrˈœrtərn] vt to discuss

Erotik [eˈroːtɪk] f eroticism; **erotisch** adj erotic

erpress- [ɛrˈprɛs] zW: **~en** vt (Geld etc) to extort; (Mensch) to blackmail; **E~er** (-s, -) m blackmailer; **E~ung** f extortion; blackmail

erprobt [ɛrˈproːpt] adj (Gerät, Medikamente) proven, tested

erraten [ɛrˈraːtən] (unreg) vt to guess

erreg- [ɛrˈreːɡ] zW: **~en** vt to excite; (ärgern) to infuriate; (hervorrufen) to arouse, to provoke ♦ vr to get excited od worked up; **E~er** (-s, -) m causative agent; **E~ung** f excitement

erreichbar adj accessible, within reach

erreichen [ɛrˈraɪçən] vt to reach; (Zweck) to achieve; (Zug) to catch

errichten [ɛrˈrɪçtən] vt to erect, to put up; (gründen) to establish, to set up

erringen [ɛrˈrɪŋən] (unreg) vt to gain,

to win

erröten [ɛrˈrøːtən] vi to blush, to flush

Errungenschaft [ɛrˈrʊŋənʃaft] f achievement; (umg: Anschaffung) acquisition

Ersatz [ɛrˈzats] (-es) m substitute; replacement; (Schadenersatz) compensation; (MIL) reinforcements pl; **~dienst** m (MIL) alternative service; **~reifen** m (AUT) spare tyre; **~teil** nt spare (part)

erschaffen [ɛrˈʃafən] (unreg) vt to create

erscheinen [ɛrˈʃaɪnən] (unreg) vi to appear; **Erscheinung** f appearance; (Geist) apparition; (Gegebenheit) phenomenon; (Gestalt) figure

erschießen [ɛrˈʃiːsən] (unreg) vt to shoot (dead)

erschlagen [ɛrˈʃlaːgən] (unreg) vt to strike dead

erschöpf- [ɛrˈʃœpf] zW: **~en** vt to exhaust; **~end** adj exhaustive, thorough; **E~ung** f exhaustion

erschrecken [ɛrˈʃrɛkən] vt to startle, to frighten ♦ vi to be frightened od startled; **~d** adj alarming, frightening

erschrocken [ɛrˈʃrɔkən] adj frightened, startled

erschüttern [ɛrˈʃʏtərn] vt to shake; (fig) to move deeply; **Erschütterung** f shaking; shock

erschweren [ɛrˈʃveːrən] vt to complicate

erschwinglich adj within one's means

ersetzen [ɛrˈzɛtsən] vt to replace; **jdm Unkosten** etc **~** to pay sb's expenses etc

ersichtlich [ɛrˈzɪçtlɪç] adj evident, obvious

ersparen [ɛrˈʃpaːrən] vt (Ärger etc) to spare; (Geld) to save

Ersparnis (-, -se) f saving

SCHLÜSSELWORT

erst [eːrst] adv 1 first; **mach erst mal die Arbeit fertig** first finish your work; **wenn du das erst mal hinter dir hast** once you've got that behind you

2 (nicht früher als, nur) only; (nicht bis) not till; **erst gestern** only yesterday; **erst morgen** not until tomorrow; **erst als** only when, not until; **wir fahren erst später** we're not going until later; **er ist (gerade) erst angekommen** he's only just arrived

3: **wäre er doch erst zurück!** if only he were back!

---

erstatten [ɛrˈʃtatən] vt (Kosten) to (re)pay; **Anzeige** etc **gegen jdn ~** to report sb; **Bericht ~** to make a report

Erstattung f (von Kosten) refund

Erstaufführung [ˈeːrst|aʊffyːrʊŋ] f first performance

erstaunen [ɛrˈʃtaʊnən] vt to astonish ♦ vi to be astonished; **E~** (-s) nt astonishment

erstaunlich adj astonishing

erst- [ˈeːrst] zW: **E~ausgabe** f first edition; **~beste(r, s)** adj first that comes along; **~e(r, s)** adj first

erstechen [ɛrˈʃtɛçən] (unreg) vt to stab (to death)

erstehen [ɛrˈʃteːən] (unreg) vt to buy ♦ vi to (a)rise

erstens [ˈeːrstəns] adv firstly, in the first place

ersticken [ɛrˈʃtɪkən] vt (auch fig) to stifle; (Mensch) to suffocate; (Flammen) to smother ♦ vi (Mensch) to suffocate; (Feuer) to be smothered; **in Arbeit ~** to be snowed under with work

erst- zW: **~klassig** adj first-class; **~malig** adj first; **~mals** adv for the first time

erstrebenswert [ɛrˈʃtreːbənsveːrt] adj desirable, worthwhile

erstrecken [ɛrˈʃtrɛkən] vr to extend, to stretch

ersuchen [ɛrˈzuːxən] vt to request

ertappen [ɛrˈtapən] vt to catch, to detect

erteilen [ɛrˈtaɪlən] vt to give

Ertrag [ɛrˈtraːk] (-(e)s, ⁼e) m yield; (Gewinn) proceeds pl

ertragen [ɛr'traːgən] (*unreg*) *vt* to bear, to stand

erträglich [ɛr'trɛːklɪç] *adj* tolerable, bearable

ertrinken [ɛr'trɪŋkən] (*unreg*) *vi* to drown; **E~** (-s) *nt* drowning

erübrigen [ɛr'lyːbrɪgən] *vt* to spare ♦ *vr* to be unnecessary

erwachen [ɛr'vaxən] *vi* to awake

erwachsen [ɛr'vaksən] *adj* grown-up; **E~e(r)** *f(m)* adult; **E~enbildung** *f* adult education

erwägen [ɛr'vɛːgən] *vt* to consider; **Erwägung** *f* consideration

erwähn- [ɛr'vɛːn] *zW*: **~en** *vt* to mention; **~enswert** *adj* worth mentioning; **E~ung** *f* mention

erwärmen [ɛr'vɛrmən] *vt* to warm, to heat ♦ *vr* to get warm, to warm up; **sich ~ für** to warm to

Erwarten *nt*: **über meinen/unseren** *usw* **~** beyond my/our *etc* expectations; **wider ~** contrary to expectations

erwarten [ɛr'vartən] *vt* to expect; (*warten auf*) to wait for; **etw kaum ~ können** to be hardly able to wait for sth

Erwartung *f* expectation

erwartungsgemäß *adv* as expected

erwartungsvoll *adj* expectant

erwecken [ɛr'vɛkən] *vt* to rouse, to awake; **den Anschein ~** to give the impression

Erweis [ɛr'vaɪs] (-es, -e) *m* proof; **e~en** (*unreg*) *vt* to prove ♦ *vr* sich **e~en** (**als**) to prove (to be); **jdm einen Gefallen/Dienst e~en** to do sb a favour/service

Erwerb [ɛr'vɛrp] (-(e)s, -e) *m* acquisition; (*Beruf*) trade; **e~en** [-bən] (*unreg*) *vt* to acquire

erwerbs- *zW*: **~los** *adj* unemployed; **E~quelle** *f* source of income; **~tätig** *adj* (gainfully) employed

erwidern [ɛr'viːdərn] *vt* to reply; (*vergelten*) to return

erwischen [ɛr'vɪʃən] (*umg*) *vt* to catch, to get

erwünscht [ɛr'vʏnʃt] *adj* desired

erwürgen [ɛr'vʏrgən] *vt* to strangle

Erz [eːrts] (-es, -e) *nt* ore

erzähl- [ɛr'tsɛːl] *zW*: **~en** *vt* to tell ♦ *vi*: **sie kann gut ~en** she's a good storyteller; **E~er** (-s, -) *m* narrator; **E~ung** *f* story, tale

Erzbischof *m* archbishop

erzeug- [ɛr'tsɔʏg] *zW*: **~en** *vt* to produce; (*Strom*) to generate; **E~nis** (-ses, -se) *nt* product, produce; **E~ung** *f* production; generation

erziehen [ɛr'tsiːən] (*unreg*) *vt* to bring up; (*bilden*) to educate, to train; **Erzieher(in)** (-s, -) *m(f)* (*Berufsbezeichnung*) teacher; **Erziehung** *f* bringing up; (*Bildung*) education; **Erziehungsbeihilfe** *f* educational grant; **Erziehungsberechtigte(r)** *f(m)* parent; guardian

erzielen [ɛr'tsiːlən] *vt* to achieve, to obtain; (*Tor*) to score

erzwingen [ɛr'tsvɪŋən] (*unreg*) *vt* to force, to obtain by force

es [ɛs] (*nom, akk*) *pron* it

Esel ['eːzəl] (-s, -) *m* donkey, ass

Eskalation [ɛskalatsi'oːn] *f* escalation

ess- ▲ ['ɛs] *zW*: **~bar** ['ɛsbaːr] *adj* eatable, edible; **E~besteck** *nt* knife, fork and spoon; **E~ecke** *f* dining area

essen ['ɛsən] (*unreg*) *vt, vi* to eat; **E~** (-s, -) *nt* meal; food

Essig ['ɛsɪç] (-s, -e) *m* vinegar

Ess- ▲ *zW*: **~kastanie** *f* sweet chestnut; **~löffel** *m* tablespoon; **~tisch** *m* dining table; **~waren** *pl* foodstuffs, provisions; **~zimmer** *nt* dining room

etablieren [eta'bliːrən] *vr* to become established; to set up in business

Etage [e'taːʒə] *f* floor, storey; **~nbetten** *pl* bunk beds; **~nwohnung** *f* flat

---

Spelling Reform: ▲ new spelling △ old spelling (to be phased out)

Etappe [e'tapə] f stage

Etat [e'ta:] (-s, -s) m budget

etc abk (= et cetera) etc

Ethik ['e:tɪk] f ethics sg; **ethisch** adj ethical

Etikett [eti'kɛt] (-(e)s, -e) nt label; tag; **~e** f etiquette, manners pl

etliche ['ɛtlɪçə] pron pl some, quite a few; **~s** pron a thing or two

Etui [ɛt'vi:] (-s, -s) nt case

etwa ['ɛtva] adv (ungefähr) about; (vielleicht) perhaps; (beispielsweise) for instance; **nicht ~** by no means; **~ig** ['ɛtvaɪç] adj possible

etwas pron something; anything; (ein wenig) a little ♦ adv a little

euch [ɔʏç] pron (akk von ihr) you; yourselves; (dat von ihr) (to) you

euer ['ɔʏər] pron (gen von ihr) of you ♦ adj your

Eule ['ɔʏlə] f owl

eure ['ɔʏrə] adj f siehe euer

eure(r, s) ['ɔʏrɐ(r, s)] pron yours; **~rseits** adv on your part; **~s** adj nt siehe euer; **~sgleichen** pron people like you; **~twegen** adv (für euch) for your sakes; (wegen euch) on your account; **~twillen** adv: **um ~twillen =** euretwegen

eurige ['ɔʏrɪgə] pron: **der/die/das ~** od **E~** yours

Euro ['ɔʏro:] (-, -s) m (FIN) euro

Euro- zW: **~pa** [ɔʏ'ro:pa] nt Europe; **~päer(in)** [ɔʏro'pɛ:ər(ɪn)] m(f) European; **e~päisch** adj European; **~pameister** [ɔʏ'ro:pa-] m European champion; **~paparlament** nt European Parliament; **~scheck** m (FIN) eurocheque

Euter ['ɔʏtər] (-s, -) nt udder

ev. abk = evangelisch

evakuieren [evaku'i:rən] vt to evacuate

evangelisch [evaŋ'ge:lɪʃ] adj Protestant

Evangelium [evaŋ'ge:liʊm] nt gospel

eventuell [eventu'ɛl] adj possible ♦ adv

possibly, perhaps

evtl. abk = **eventuell**

EWG [e:ve:'ge:] (-) f abk (= Europäische Wirtschaftsgemeinschaft) EEC, Common Market

ewig ['e:vɪç] adj eternal; **E~keit** f eternity

EWU [e:ve:'u:] f abk (= Europäische Währungsunion) EMU

exakt [ɛ'ksakt] adj exact

Examen [ɛ'ksa:mən] (-s, - od **Examina**) nt examination

Exemplar [ɛksɛm'pla:r] (-s, -e) nt specimen; (Bücher~) copy; **e~isch** adj exemplary

Exil [ɛ'ksi:l] (-s, -e) nt exile

Existenz [ɛksɪs'tɛnts] f existence; (Unterhalt) livelihood, living; (pej: Mensch) character; **~minimum** (-s) nt subsistence level

existieren [ɛksɪs'ti:rən] vi to exist

exklusiv [ɛksklu'zi:f] adj exclusive; **~e** adv exclusive of, not including ♦ präp +gen exclusive of, not including

exotisch [ɛ'kso:tɪʃ] adj exotic

Expedition [ɛkspeditsi'o:n] f expedition

Experiment [ɛksperi'mɛnt] nt experiment; **e~ell** [-'tɛl] adj experimental; **e~ieren** [-'ti:rən] vi to experiment

Experte [ɛks'pɛrtə] (-n, -n) m expert, specialist

Expertin f expert, specialist

explo- [ɛksplo] zW: **~dieren** [-'di:rən] vi to explode; **E~sion** [-zi'o:n] f explosion; **~siv** [-'zi:f] adj explosive

Export [ɛks'pɔrt] (-(e)s, -e) m export; **~eur** [-'ø:r] m exporter; **~handel** m export trade; **e~ieren** [-'ti:rən] vt to export; **~land** nt exporting country

Express- ▲ [ɛks'prɛs] zW: **~gut** nt express goods pl, express freight; **~zug** m express (train)

extra ['ɛkstra] adj inv (umg: gesondert) separate; (besondere) extra ♦ adv (gesondert) separately; (speziell) specially; (absichtlich) on purpose; (vor Adjekti-

ven, zusätzlich) extra; **E~** **(-s, -s)** *nt* extra; **E~ausgabe** *f* special edition; **E~blatt** *nt* special edition

Extrakt [ɛks'trakt] **(-(e)s, -e)** *m* extract

extravagant [ɛkstrava'gant] *adj* extravagant

extrem [ɛks'tre:m] *adj* extreme; **~istisch** [-'mɪstɪʃ] *adj* (POL) extremist; **E~itäten** [-mi'tɛ:tən] *pl* extremities

exzentrisch [ɛks'tsɛntrɪʃ] *adj* eccentric

EZ *nt abk* = Einzelzimmer

EZB *f abk* (= Europäische Zentralbank) ECB

F, f

Fa. *abk* (= Firma) firm; (*in Briefen*) Messrs

Fabel ['fa:bəl] **(-, -n)** *f* fable; **f~haft** *adj* fabulous, marvellous

Fabrik [fa'bri:k] *f* factory; **~ant** [-'kant] *m* (*Hersteller*) manufacturer; (*Besitzer*) industrialist; **~arbeiter** *m* factory worker; **~at** [-'ka:t] **(-(e)s, -e)** *nt* manufacture, product; **~gelände** *nt* factory site

Fach [fax] **(-(e)s, ¨er)** *nt* compartment; (*Sachgebiet*) subject; **ein Mann vom ~** an expert; **~arbeiter** *m* skilled worker; **~arzt** *m* (medical) specialist; **~ausdruck** *m* technical term

Fächer ['fɛçər] **(-s, -)** *m* fan

Fach- *zW*: **~geschäft** *nt* specialist shop; **~hochschule** *f* technical college; **~kraft** *f* skilled worker, trained employee; **f~kundig** *adj* expert, specialist; **f~lich** *adj* professional; expert; **~mann** *m* (*pl* **-leute**) *m* specialist; **f~männisch** *adj* professional; **~schule** *f* technical college; **~simpeln** *vi* to talk shop; **~werk** *nt* timber frame

Fackel ['fakəl] **(-, -n)** *f* torch

fad(e) [fa:t, 'fa:də] *adj* insipid; (*langweilig*) dull

Faden ['fa:dən] **(-s, ¨)** *m* thread; **f~scheinig** *adj* (*auch fig*) threadbare

fähig ['fɛ:ɪç] *adj*: **~ (zu** *od* **+gen)** capable

(of); able (to); **F~keit** *f* ability

fahnden ['fa:ndən] *vi*: **~ nach** to search for; **Fahndung** *f* search

Fahndungsliste *f* list of wanted criminals, wanted list

Fahne ['fa:nə] *f* flag, standard; **eine ~ haben** (*umg*) to smell of drink; **~nflucht** *f* desertion

Fahr- *zW*: **~ausweis** *m* ticket; **~bahn** *f* carriageway (*BRIT*), roadway

Fähre ['fɛ:rə] *f* ferry

fahren ['fa:rən] (*unreg*) *vt* to drive; (*Rad*) to ride; (*befördern*) to drive, to take; (*Rennen*) to drive in ♦ *vi* (*sich bewegen*) to go; (*Schiff*) to sail; (*abfahren*) to leave; **mit dem Auto/Zug ~** to go *od* travel by car/train; **mit der Hand ~ über** *+akk* to pass one's hand over

Fahr- *zW*: **~er(in)** **(-s, -)** *m(f)* driver; **~erflucht** *f* hit-and-run; **~gast** *m* passenger; **~geld** *nt* fare; **~karte** *f* ticket; **~kartenausgabe** *f* ticket office; **~kartenautomat** *m* ticket machine; **~kartenschalter** *m* ticket office; **f~lässig** *adj* negligent; **f~lässige Tötung** manslaughter; **~lehrer** *m* driving instructor; **~plan** *m* timetable; **f~planmäßig** *adj* scheduled; **~preis** *m* fare; **~prüfung** *f* driving test; **~rad** *nt* bicycle; **~radweg** *m* cycle lane; **~schein** *m* ticket; **~scheinentwerter** *m* (automatic) ticket stamping machine

Fährschiff ['fɛ:rʃɪf] *nt* ferry(boat)

Fahr- *zW*: **~schule** *f* driving school; **~spur** *f* lane; **~stuhl** *m* lift (*BRIT*), elevator (*US*)

Fahrt [fa:rt] **(-, -en)** *f* journey; (*kurz*) trip; (*AUT*) drive; (*Geschwindigkeit*) speed; **gute ~!** I have a good journey

Fährte ['fɛ:rtə] *f* track, trail

Fahrt- *zW*: **~kosten** *pl* travelling expenses; **~richtung** *f* course, direction

Fahrzeit *f* time for the journey

Fahrzeug *nt* vehicle; **~brief** *m* log

fair book; **~papiere** pl vehicle documents

fair [fɛːr] adj fair

Fakt [fakt] (-(e)s, -en) m fact

Faktor [ˈfaktor] m factor

Fakultät [fakulˈtɛːt] f faculty

Falke [ˈfalkə] (-n, -n) m falcon

Fall [fal] (-(e)s, ∸e) m (Sturz) fall; (Sachverhalt, JUR, GRAM) case; **auf jeden ~, auf alle Fälle** in any case; (bestimmt) definitely; **auf keinen ~!** no way!

Falle f trap

fallen (unreg) vi to fall; **etw ~ lassen** to drop sth; (Bemerkung) to make sth; (Plan) to abandon sth, to drop sth

fällen [ˈfɛlən] vt (Baum) to fell; (Urteil) to pass

fällig [ˈfɛlɪç] adj due

falls [fals] adv in case, if

Fallschirm m parachute; **~springer** m parachutist

falsch [falʃ] adj false; (unrichtig) wrong

fälschen [ˈfɛlʃən] vt to forge

fälsch- zW: **~lich** adj false; **~licherweise** adv mistakenly; **F~ung** f forgery

Falte [ˈfaltə] f (Knick) fold, crease; (Hautfalte) wrinkle; (Rockfalte) pleat; **f~n** vt to fold; (Stirn) to wrinkle

faltig [ˈfaltɪç] adj (Hände, Haut) wrinkled; (zerknittert: Rock) creased

familiär [familiˈɛːr] adj familiar

Familie [faˈmiːliə] f family

Familien- zW: **~betrieb** m family business; **~kreis** m family circle; **~mitglied** nt member of the family; **~name** m surname; **~stand** m marital status

Fanatiker [faˈnaːtikər] (-s, -) m fanatic; **fanatisch** adj fanatical

fand etc [fant] vb siehe **finden**

Fang [faŋ] (-(e)s, ∸e) m catch; (Jagen) hunting; (Kralle) talon, claw; **f~en** (unreg) vt to catch ♦ vr to get caught; (Flugzeug) to level out; (Mensch: nicht fallen) to steady o.s.; (fig) to get back on form

Fantasie ▲ [fantaˈziː] f imagination;

f~los adj unimaginative; **f~ren** vi to fantasize; **f~voll** adj imaginative

fantastisch ▲ [fanˈtastɪʃ] adj fantastic

Farb- [farb] zW: **~abzug** m colour print; **~aufnahme** f colour photograph; **~band** nt typewriter ribbon; **~e** f colour; (zum Malen etc) paint; (Stoffarbe) dye; **f~echt** adj colourfast

färben [ˈfɛrbən] vt to colour; (Stoff, Haar) to dye

farben- [ˈfarbən] zW: **~blind** adj colour-blind; **~freudig** adj colourful; **~froh** adj colourful, gay

Farb- zW: **~fernsehen** nt colour television; **~film** m colour film; **~foto** nt colour photograph; **f~ig** adj coloured; **~ige(r)** f(m) coloured (person); **~kasten** m paintbox; **f~lich** adj colour; **f~los** adj colourless; **~stift** m coloured pencil; **~stoff** m dye; **~ton** m hue, tone

Färbung [ˈfɛrbuŋ] f colouring; (Tendenz) bias

Farn [farn] (-(e)s, -e) m fern; bracken

Fasan [faˈzaːn] (-(e)s, -e(n)) m pheasant

Fasching [ˈfaʃɪŋ] (-s, -e od -s) m carnival

Faschismus [faˈʃɪsmʊs] m fascism

Faschist m fascist

Faser [ˈfaːzər] (-, -n) f fibre; **f~n** vi to fray

Fass ▲ [fas] (-es, ∸er) nt vat, barrel; (für Öl) drum; **Bier vom ~** draught beer

Fassade [faˈsaːdə] f façade

fassen [ˈfasən] vt (ergreifen) to grasp, to take; (inhaltlich) to hold; (Entschluss etc) to take; (verstehen) to understand; (Ring etc) to set; (formulieren) to formulate, to phrase ♦ vr to calm down; **nicht zu ~** unbelievable

Fassung [ˈfasuŋ] f (Umrahmung) mounting; (Lampenfassung) socket; (Wortlaut) version; (Beherrschung) composure; **jdn aus der ~ bringen** to upset sb; **f~slos** adj speechless

fast [fast] *adv* almost, nearly

fasten ['fastən] *vi* to fast; **F~zeit** *f* Lent

Fastnacht *f* Shrove Tuesday; carnival

faszinieren [fastsi'ni:rən] *vt* to fascinate

fatal [fa'ta:l] *adj* fatal; (*peinlich*) embarrassing

faul [faʊl] *adj* rotten; (*Person*) lazy; (*Ausreden*) lame; **daran ist etwas ~** there's something fishy about it; **~en** *vi* to rot; **~enzen** *vi* to laze; **F~enzer** (-s, -) *m* idler, loafer; **F~heit** *f* laziness; **~ig** *adj* putrid

Faust [faʊst] (-, **Fäuste**) *f* fist; **auf eigene ~** off one's own bat; **~handschuh** *m* mitten

Favorit [favo'ri:t] (-en, -en) *m* favourite

Fax [faks] (-, -(e)) *nt* fax

faxen ['faksən] *vt* to fax; **jdm etw ~** to fax sth to sb

FCKW *m abk* (= *Fluorchlorkohlenwasserstoff*) CFC

Februar ['fe:brua:r] (-(s), -e) *m* February

fechten ['fɛçtən] (*unreg*) *vi* to fence

Feder ['fe:dər] (-, -n) *f* feather; (*Schreibfeder*) pen nib; (*TECH*) spring; **~ball** *m* shuttlecock; **~bett** *nt* continental quilt; **~halter** *m* penholder, pen; **f~leicht** *adj* light as a feather; **f~n** *vi* (*nachgeben*) to be springy; (*sich bewegen*) to bounce ♦ *vt* to spring; **~ung** *f* (*AUT*) suspension

Fee [fe:] (-, -n) *f* fairy

fegen ['fe:gən] *vt* to sweep

fehl [fe:l] *adj:* **~ am Platz** *od* **Ort** out of place; **F~betrag** *m* deficit; **~en** *vi* to be wanting *od* missing; (*abwesend sein*) to be absent; **etw ~t jdm** sb lacks sth; **du ~st mir** I miss you; **was ~t ihm?** what's wrong with him?; **F~er** (-s, -) *m* mistake, error; (*Mangel, Schwäche*) fault; **~erfrei** *adj* faultless; without any mistakes; **~erhaft** *adj* incorrect; faulty;

~erlos *adj* flawless, perfect; **F~geburt** *f* miscarriage; (*unreg*) *vi* to go astray; **F~griff** *m* blunder; **F~konstruktion** *f* badly designed thing; **~schlagen** (*unreg*) *vi* to fail; **F~start** *m* (*SPORT*) false start; **F~zündung** *f* (*AUT*) misfire, backfire

Feier ['faɪər] (-, -n) *f* celebration; **~abend** *m* time to stop work; **~abend machen** to stop, to knock off; **jetzt ist ~abend!** that's enough!; **f~lich** *adj* solemn; **~lichkeit** *f* solemnity; **~lichkeiten** *pl* (*Veranstaltungen*) festivities; **f~n** *vt, vi* to celebrate; **~tag** *m* holiday

feig(e) [faɪk, 'faɪgə] *adj* cowardly

Feige ['faɪgə] *f* fig

Feigheit *f* cowardice

Feigling *m* coward

Feile ['faɪlə] *f* file

feilschen ['faɪlʃən] *vi* to haggle

fein [faɪn] *adj* fine; (*vornehm*) refined; (*Gehör etc*) keen; **~! great!**

Feind [faɪnt] (-(e)s, -e) *m* enemy; **f~lich** *adj* hostile; **~schaft** *f* enmity; **f~selig** *adj* hostile

Fein- *zW:* **f~fühlig** *adj* sensitive; **~gefühl** *nt* delicacy, tact; **~heit** *f* fineness; refinement; keenness; **~kostgeschäft** *nt* delicatessen (shop); **~schmecker** (-s, -) *m* gourmet; **~wäsche** *f* delicate clothing (*when washing*); **~waschmittel** *m* mild detergent

Feld [fɛlt] (-(e)s, -er) *nt* field; (*SCHACH*) square; (*SPORT*) pitch; **~herr** *m* commander; **~stecher** (-s, -) *m* binoculars *pl*; **~weg** *m* path; **~zug** *m* (*fig*) campaign

Felge ['fɛlgə] *f* (*wheel*) rim

Fell [fɛl] (-(e)s, -e) *nt* fur; coat; (*von Schaf*) fleece; (*von toten Tieren*) skin

Fels [fɛls] (-en, -en) *m* rock; (*Klippe*) cliff

Felsen ['fɛlzən] (-s, -) *m* = **Fels**; **f~fest** *adj* firm

feminin [femi'ni:n] *adj* feminine

Fenster ['fɛnstər] (-s, -) nt window; **~bank** f windowsill; **~laden** m shutter; **~leder** nt chamois (leather); **~scheibe** f windowpane

Ferien ['feːriən] pl holidays, vacation sg (US); **~ haben** to be on holiday; **~bungalow** [-bʊŋgalo] (-s, -s) m holiday bungalow; **~haus** nt holiday home; **~kurs** m holiday course; **~lager** nt holiday camp; **~reise** f holiday; **~wohnung** f holiday apartment

Ferkel ['fɛrkəl] (-s, -) nt piglet

fern [fɛrn] adj, adv far-off, distant; **~ von hier** a long way (away) from here; **der F~e Osten** the Far East; **~halten** to keep away; **F~bedienung** f remote control; **F~e** f distance; **~er** adj further ♦ adv further; (weiterhin) in future; **F~gespräch** nt trunk call; **F~glas** nt binoculars pl; **F~licht** nt (AUT) full beam; **F~rohr** nt telescope; **F~ruf** m (förmlich) telephone number; **F~schreiben** nt telex; **F~sehapparat** m television set; **F~sehen** (-s) nt television; **im F~sehen** on television; **~sehen** (unreg) vi to watch television; **F~seher** m television; **F~sehturm** m television tower; **F~sprecher** m telephone; **F~steuerung** f remote control; **F~straße** f ≈ 'A' road (BRIT), highway (US); **F~verkehr** m long-distance traffic

Ferse ['fɛrzə] f heel

fertig ['fɛrtɪç] adj (bereit) ready; (beendet) finished; (gebrauchsfertig) ready-made; **~ bringen** (fähig sein) to be capable of; **~ machen** (beenden) to finish; (umg: Person) to finish; (: körperlich) to exhaust; (: moralisch) to get down; **sich ~ machen** to get ready; **~ stellen** to complete; **F~gericht** nt precooked meal; **F~haus** nt kit house, prefab; **F~keit** f skill

Fessel ['fɛsəl] (-, -n) f fetter; **f~n** vt to bind; (mit ~n) to fetter; (fig) to spellbind; **f~nd** adj fascinating, captivating

Fest (-(e)s, -e) nt party; festival; **frohes ~!** Happy Christmas!

fest [fɛst] adj firm; (Nahrung) solid; (Gehalt) regular; **~e Kosten** fixed cost ♦ adv (schlafen) soundly; **~ angestellt** permanently employed; **~binden** (unreg) vt to tie, to fasten; **~bleiben** (unreg) vi to stand firm; **F~essen** nt banquet; **~halten** (unreg) vt to seize, to hold fast; (Ereignis) to record ♦ vr: **sich ~halten** (an +dat) to hold on (to); **~igen** vt to strengthen; **F~igkeit** f strength; **F~ival** ['fɛstival] (-s, -s) nt festival; **F~land** nt mainland; **~legen** vt to fix ♦ vr to commit o.s.; **~lich** adj festive; **~liegen** (unreg) vi (~stehen: Termin) to be confirmed, be fixed; **~machen** vt to fasten; (Termin etc) to fix; **F~nahme** f arrest; **~nehmen** (unreg) vt to arrest; **F~preis** m (COMM) fixed price; **~setzen** vt to fix, to settle; **F~spiele** pl (Veranstaltung) festival sg; **~stehen** (unreg) vi to be certain; **~stellen** vt to establish; (sagen) to remark; **F~tag** m feast day, holiday; **F~ung** f fortress; **F~wochen** pl festival sg

Fett [fɛt] (-(e)s, -e) nt fat, grease

fett adj fat; (Essen etc) greasy; (TYP) bold; **~arm** adj low fat; **~en** vt to grease; **F~fleck** m grease stain; **~ig** adj greasy, fatty

Fetzen ['fɛtsən] (-s, -) m scrap

feucht [fɔɪçt] adj damp; (Luft) humid; **F~igkeit** f dampness; humidity; **F~igkeitscreme** f moisturizing cream

Feuer ['fɔɪər] (-s, -) nt fire; (zum Rauchen) a light; (fig: Schwung) spirit; **~alarm** m fire alarm; **f~fest** adj fireproof; **~gefahr** f danger of fire; **f~gefährlich** adj inflammable; **~leiter** f fire escape ladder; **~löscher** (-s, -) m fire extinguisher; **~melder** (-s, -) m fire alarm; **f~n** vt, vi (auch fig) to fire; **~stein** m flint; **~treppe** f fire escape; **~wehr** (-, -en) f fire brigade; **~wehrauto** nt fire engine; **~wehrmann** m fireman; **~werk** nt fireworks pl; **~zeug** nt (cigarette) lighter

Fichte ['fɪçtə] f spruce, pine

Fieber ['fiːbər] (-s, -) nt fever, temperature; **f~haft** adj feverish; **~thermometer** nt thermometer; **fiebrig** adj (Erkältung) feverish

fiel etc [fiːl] vb siehe **fallen**

fies [fiːs] (umg) adj nasty

Figur [fi'guːr] (-, -en) f figure; (Schachfigur) chessman, chess piece

Filet [fi'leː] (-s, -s) nt (KOCH) fillet

Filiale [fili'aːlə] (-, -n) f (COMM) branch

Film [fɪlm] (-(e)s, -e) m film; **~aufnahme** f shooting; **f~en** vt, vi to film; **~kamera** f cine camera

Filter ['fɪltər] (-s, -) m filter; **f~n** vt to filter; **~papier** nt filter paper; **~zigarette** f tipped cigarette

Filz [fɪlts] (-es, -e) m felt; **f~en** vt (umg) to frisk ♦ vi (Wolle) to mat; **~stift** m felt-tip pen

Finale [fi'naːlə] (-s, -(s)) nt finale; (SPORT) final(s)

Finanz [fi'nants] f finance; **~amt** nt Inland Revenue office; **~beamte(r)** m revenue officer; **f~iell** [-tsi'el] adj financial; **f~ieren** [-'tsiːrən] vt to finance; **f~kräftig** adj financially strong; **~minister** m Chancellor of the Exchequer (BRIT), Minister of Finance

Find- ['fɪnd] zW: **f~en** (unreg) vt to find; (meinen) to think ♦ vr to be (found); (sich fassen) to compose o.s.; ich f~e nichts dabei, wenn ... I don't see what's wrong if ...; das wird sich f~en things will work out; **~er** (-s, -) m finder; **~erlohn** m reward (for sb who finds sth); **f~ig** adj resourceful

fing etc [fɪŋ] vb siehe **fangen**

Finger ['fɪŋər] (-s, -) m finger; **~abdruck** m fingerprint; **~nagel** m fingernail; **~spitze** f fingertip

fingiert adj made-up, fictitious

Fink ['fɪŋk] (-en, -en) m finch

Finn- [fɪn] zW: **~e (-n, -n)** m Finn; **~in** f Finn; **f~isch** adj Finnish; **~land** nt Finland

finster ['fɪnstər] adj dark, gloomy; (verdächtig) dubious; (verdrossen) grim; (Gedanke) dark; **F~nis** (-) f darkness, gloom

Firma ['fɪrma] (-, -men) f firm

Firmen- ['fɪrmən] zW: **~inhaber** m owner of firm; **~schild** nt (shop) sign; **~wagen** m company car; **~zeichen** nt trademark

Fisch [fɪʃ] (-(e)s, -e) m fish; **~e** pl (ASTROL) Pisces sg; **f~en** vt, vi to fish; **~er** (-s, -) m fisherman; **~e'rei** f fishing, fishery; **~fang** m fishing; **~geschäft** nt fishmonger's (shop); **~gräte** f fishbone; **~stäbchen** [-ʃtɛːpçən] nt fish finger (BRIT), fish stick (US)

fit [fɪt] adj fit; **'F~ness ▲** (-, -) f (physical) fitness

fix [fɪks] adj fixed; (Person) alert, smart; **~ und fertig** finished; (erschöpft) done in; **F~er(in)** m(f) (umg) junkie; **F~erstube** f (umg) junkies' centre; **~ieren** [fɪ'ksiːrən] vt to fix; (anstarren) to stare at

flach [flax] adj flat; (Gefäß) shallow

Fläche ['flɛçə] f area; (Oberfläche) surface

Flachland nt lowland

flackern ['flakərn] vi to flare, to flicker

Flagge ['flagə] f flag; **f~n** vi to fly a flag

flämisch ['flɛːmɪʃ] adj (LING) Flemish

Flamme ['flamə] f flame

Flandern ['flandərn] nt Flanders

Flanke ['flaŋkə] f flank; (SPORT: Seite) wing

Flasche ['flaʃə] f bottle; (umg: Versager) wash-out

Flaschen- zW: **~bier** nt bottled beer; **~öffner** m bottle opener; **~zug** m pulley

flatterhaft adj flighty, fickle

flattern ['flatərn] vi to flutter

flau [flaʊ] *adj* weak, listless; (*Nachfrage*) slack; **jdm ist ~** sb feels queasy

Flaum [flaʊm] (*-(e)s*) *m* (*Feder*) down; (*Haare*) fluff

flauschig ['flaʊʃɪç] *adj* fluffy

Flaute ['flaʊtə] *f* calm; (*COMM*) recession

Flechte ['flɛçtə] *f* plait; (*MED*) dry scab; (*BOT*) lichen; (*unreg*) *vt* to plait; (*Kranz*) to twine

Fleck [flɛk] (*-(e)s, -e*) *m* spot; (*Schmutzfleck*) stain; (*Stofffleck*) patch; (*Makel*) blemish; **nicht vom ~ kommen** (*auch fig*) not to get any further; **vom ~ weg** straight away

Flecken (*-s, -*) *m* = **Fleck**; **f~los** *adj* spotless; **~mittel** *nt* stain remover; **~wasser** *nt* stain remover

fleckig *adj* spotted; stained

Fledermaus ['fleːdərmaʊs] *f* bat

Flegel ['fleːgəl] (*-s, -*) *m* (*Mensch*) lout; **f~haft** *adj* loutish, unmannerly; **~jahre** *pl* adolescence *sg*

flehen ['fleːən] *vi* to implore; **~tlich** *adj* imploring

Fleisch ['flaɪʃ] (*-(e)s*) *nt* flesh; (*Essen*) meat; **~brühe** *f* beef tea, meat stock; **~er** (*-s, -*) *m* butcher; **~erei** *f* butcher's (shop); **f~ig** *adj* fleshy; **f~los** *adj* meatless, vegetarian

Fleiß [flaɪs] (*-es*) *m* diligence, industry; **f~ig** *adj* diligent, industrious

fletschen ['flɛtʃən] *vt* (*Zähne*) to show

flexibel [flɛksiːbəl] *adj* flexible

Flicken ['flɪkən] (*-s, -*) *m* patch; **f~** *vt* to mend

Flieder ['fliːdər] (*-s, -*) *m* lilac

Fliege ['fliːgə] *f* fly; (*Kleidung*) bow tie; **f~n** (*unreg*) *vt, vi* to fly; **auf jdn/etw f~n** (*umg*) to be mad about sb/sth; **~npilz** *m* toadstool; **~r** (*-s, -*) *m* flier, airman

fliehen ['fliːən] (*unreg*) *vi* to flee

Fliese ['fliːzə] *f* tile

Fließ- [fliːs] *zW*: **~band** *nt* production *od* assembly line; **f~en** (*unreg*) *vi* to flow; **f~end** *adj* flowing; (*Rede,*

Deutsch) fluent; (*Übergänge*) smooth

flimmern ['flɪmərn] *vi* to glimmer

flink [flɪŋk] *adj* nimble, lively

Flinte ['flɪntə] *f* rifle; shotgun

Flitterwochen *pl* honeymoon *sg*

flitzen ['flɪtsən] *vi* to flit

flog *etc* [floːk] *vb siehe* **fliegen**

Floh [floː] (*-(e)s, -e*) *m* flea; **~markt** *m* flea market

florieren [floˈriːrən] *vi* to flourish

Floskel ['flɔskəl] (*-, -n*) *f* set phrase

floss [flɔs] (*-es, -e*) *nt* raft, float

f~artig *adj* hasty

Flosse ['flɔsə] *f* fin

Flöte ['fløːtə] *f* flute; (*Blockflöte*) recorder

flott [flɔt] *adj* lively; (*elegant*) smart; (*NAUT*) afloat; **F~e** *f* fleet, navy

Fluch [fluːx] (*-(e)s, -e*) *m* curse; **f~en** *vi* to curse, to swear

Flucht [fluxt] (*-, -en*) *f* flight; (*Fensterflucht*) row; (*Zimmerflucht*) suite; **f~artig** *adj* hasty

flücht- ['flʏçt] *zW*: **~en** *vi, vr* to flee, to escape; **~ig** *adj* fugitive; (*vergänglich*) transitory; (*oberflächlich*) superficial; (*eilig*) fleeting; **F~igkeitsfehler** *m* careless slip; **F~ling** *m* fugitive, refugee

Flug [fluːk] (*-(e)s, -e*) *m* flight; **~blatt** *nt* pamphlet

Flügel ['flyːgəl] (*-s, -*) *m* wing; (*MUS*) grand piano

Fluggast *m* airline passenger

Flug- *zW*: **~gesellschaft** *f* airline (company); **~hafen** *m* airport; **~lärm** *m* aircraft noise; **~linie** *f* airline; **~plan** *m* flight schedule; **~platz** *m* airport; (*klein*) airfield; **~reise** *f* flight; **~schein** *m* (*Ticket*) plane ticket; (*Pilotenschein*) pilot's licence; **~steig** *-staik] (*-(e)s, -e*) *m* gate; **~verbindung** *f* air connection; **~verkehr** *m* air traffic; **~zeug** *nt* (*aero*)plane, airplane (*US*); **~zeugentführung** *f* hijacking of a plane; **~zeughalle** *f* hangar; **~zeugträger** *m* aircraft carrier

Flunder ['flʊndər] (-, -n) f flounder

flunkern ['flʊŋkərn] vi to fib, to tell stories

Fluor ['fluːɔr] (-s) nt fluorine

Flur [fluːr] (-(e)s, -e) m hall; (Treppenflur) staircase

Fluss ▲ [flʊs] (-es, ⸚e) m river; (Fließen) flow

flüssig ['flʏsɪç] adj liquid; ~ machen (Geld) to make available; **F~keit** f liquid; (Zustand) liquidity

flüstern ['flʏstərn] vt, vi to whisper

Flut [fluːt] (-, -en) f (auch fig) flood; (Gezeiten) high tide; **f~en** vi to flood; **~licht** nt floodlight

Fohlen ['foːlən] (-s, -) nt foal

Föhn¹ ['føːn] (-(e)s, -e) m (warmer Fallwind) föhn

Föhn² (-(e)s, -e) ▲ (Haartrockner) hair-dryer; **f~en** ▲ vt to (blow) dry; **~frisur** ▲ f blow-dry hairstyle

Folge ['fɔlgə] f series, sequence; (Fortsetzung) instalment; (Auswirkung) result; **in rascher ~** in quick succession; **etw zur ~ haben** to result in sth; **~n haben** to have consequences; **einer Sache** dat **~ leisten** to comply with sth; **f~n** vi +dat to follow; (gehorchen) to obey; **jdm f~n können** (fig) to follow od understand sb; **f~nd** adj following; **f~ndermaßen** adv as follows, in the following way; **f~rn** vt; **f~rn** (aus) to conclude (from); **~rung** f conclusion

folglich ['fɔlklɪç] adv consequently

folgsam ['fɔlkzaːm] adj obedient

Folie ['foːliə] f foil

Folklore ['fɔlkloːər] f folklore

Folter ['fɔltər] (-, -n) f torture; (Gerät) rack; **f~n** vt to torture

Fön [føːn] (-(e)s, -e) ® m hair dryer

Fondue [fõdy:] (-s, -s od -, -s) nt od f (KOCH) fondue

fönen ▲ vt siehe **föhnen**

Fönfrisur △ f siehe **Föhnfrisur**

Fontäne [fɔn'tɛːnə] f fountain

Förder- ['fœrdər] zW: **~band** nt conveyor belt; **~korb** m pit cage; **f~lich** adj beneficial

fordern ['fɔrdərn] vt to demand

fördern ['fœrdərn] vt to promote; (unterstützen) to help; (Kohle) to extract

Forderung ['fɔrdərʊŋ] f demand

Förderung ['fœrdərʊŋ] f promotion; help; extraction

Forelle [fo'rɛlə] f trout

Form [fɔrm] (-, -en) f shape; (Gestaltung) form; (Guss~) mould; (Back~) baking tin; **in ~ sein** to be in good form od shape; **in ~ von** in the shape of

Formalität f formality

Format [fɔr'maːt] (-(e)s, -e) nt format; (fig) distinction

formbar adj malleable

Formblatt nt form

Formel (-, -n) f formula

formell [fɔr'mɛl] adj formal

formen vt to form, to shape

Formfehler m faux pas, gaffe; (JUR) irregularity

formieren [fɔr'miːrən] vt to form ♦ vr to form up

förmlich ['fœrmlɪç] adj formal; (umg) real; **F~keit** f formality

formlos adj shapeless; (Benehmen etc) informal

Formular [fɔrmu'laːr] (-s, -e) nt form

formulieren [fɔrmu'liːrən] vt to formulate

forsch [fɔrʃ] adj energetic, vigorous

forsch- zW: **~en** vi: **~en (nach)** to search (for); (wissenschaftlich) to (do) research; **~end** adj searching; **F~er** (-s, -) m research scientist; (Naturforscher) explorer; **F~ung** f research

Forst [fɔrst] (-(e)s, -e) m forest

Förster ['fœrstər] (-s, -) m forester; (für Wild) gamekeeper

fort [fɔrt] adv away; (verschwunden)

gone; (*vorwärts*) on; **und so ~** and so on; **in einem ~** on and on; **~beste-hen** (*unreg*) *vi* to survive; **~bewegen** *vt, vr* to move away; **F~dauer** *f* continuance; **~fahren** (*unreg*) *vi* to depart; (*~setzen*) to go on, to continue; **~führen** *vt* to continue, to carry on; **~gehen** (*unreg*) *vi* to go away; **~geschritten** *adj* advanced; **~pflanzen** *vr* to reproduce; **F~pflanzung** *f* reproduction

fort- *zW:* **~schaffen** *vt* to remove; **~schreiten** (*unreg*) *vi* to advance

Fortschritt ['fɔrtʃrɪt] *m* advance; **~e machen** to make progress; **f~lich** *adj* progressive

fort- *zW:* **~setzen** *vt* to continue; **F~setzung** *f* continuation; (*folgender Teil*) instalment; **F~setzung folgt** to be continued; **~während** *adj* incessant, continual

Foto ['foːto] (**-s, -s**) *nt* photo(graph); **~apparat** *m* camera; **~'graf** *m* photographer; **~gra'fie** *f* photography; (*Bild*) photograph; **f~gra'fieren** *vt* to photograph ♦ *vi* to take photographs; **~kopie** *f* photocopy

Fr. *abk* (= *Frau*) Mrs, Ms

Fracht [fraxt] (**-, -en**) *f* freight; (*NAUT*) cargo; (*Preis*) carriage; **~ zahlt Empfänger** (*COMM*) carriage forward; **~er** (**-s, -**) *m* freighter, cargo boat; **~gut** *nt* freight

Frack [frak] (**-(e)s, ⁼e**) *m* tails *pl*

Frage ['fraːgə] (**-, -n**) *f* question; **jdm eine ~ stellen** to ask sb a question, to put a question to sb; *siehe* **infrage**; **~bogen** *m* questionnaire; **f~n** *vt, vi* to ask; **~zeichen** *nt* question mark

fraglich *adj* questionable, doubtful

fraglos *adv* unquestionably

Fragment [fra'gment] *nt* fragment

fragwürdig ['fraːkvʏrdɪç] *adj* questionable, dubious

Fraktion [fraktsi'oːn] *f* parliamentary party

frankieren [fraŋ'kiːrən] *vt* to stamp, to frank

franko ['fraŋko] *adv* post-paid; carriage paid

Frankreich ['fraŋkraɪç] (**-s**) *nt* France

Franzose [fran'tsoːzə] *m* Frenchman; **Französin** [fran'tsœːzɪn] *f* Frenchwoman; **französisch** *adj* French

fraß *etc* [fraːs] *vb siehe* **fressen**

Fratze ['fratsə] *f* grimace

Frau [frau] (**-, -en**) *f* woman; (*Ehefrau*) wife; (*Anrede*) Mrs, Ms; **~ Doktor** Doctor

Frauen- *zW:* **~arzt** *m* gynaecologist; **~bewegung** *f* feminist movement; **~haus** *nt* women's refuge; **~zimmer** *nt* female, broad (*US*)

Fräulein ['frɔɪlaɪn] *nt* young lady; (*Anrede*) Miss, Ms

fraulich ['frauliç] *adj* womanly

frech [freç] *adj* cheeky, impudent; **F~heit** *f* cheek, impudence

frei [fraɪ] *adj* free; (*Stelle, Sitzplatz*) free, vacant; (*Mitarbeiter*) freelance; (*unbekleidet*) bare; **von etw ~ sein** to be free of sth; **im F~en** in the open air; **~ sprechen** to talk without notes; **~ Haus** (*COMM*) carriage paid; **~er Wettbewerb** (*COMM*) fair/open competition; **F~bad** *nt* open-air swimming pool; **~bekommen** (*unreg*) *vt:* **einen Tag ~bekommen** to get a day off; **~beruflich** *adj* self-employed; **~gebig** *adj* generous; **~halten** (*unreg*) *vt* to keep free; **~händig** *adv* (*fahren*) with no hands; **F~heit** *f* freedom; **~heitlich** *adj* liberal; **F~heitsstrafe** *f* prison sentence; **F~karte** *f* free ticket; **~lassen** (*unreg*) *vt* to (set) free; **~legen** *vt* to expose; **~lich** *adv* certainly, admittedly; **ja ~lich** yes of course; **F~lichtbühne** *f* open-air theatre; **F~lichtmuseum** *nt* open-air museum; **~machen** *vt* (*Post*) to frank ♦ *vr* to arrange to be free; (*entkleiden*) to undress; **Tage ~machen** to take days off,

~**nehmen** ▲ (unreg) vt: **sich** dat einen Tag ~**nehmen** to take a day off; ~**sprechen** (unreg) vt: ~**sprechen (von)** to acquit (of); **F~spruch** m acquittal; ~**stehen** (unreg) vi: **es steht dir ~, das zu tun** you're free to do that; (leer stehen: Wohnung, Haus) to lie/stand empty; ~**stellen** vr: **jdm etw ~stellen** to leave sth (up) to sb; **F~stoß** m free kick

Freitag m Friday; **f~s** adv on Fridays **frei-** zW: ~**willig** adj voluntary; **F~zeit** f spare od free time; **F~zeitpark** m amusement park; **F~zeitzentrum** nt leisure centre; ~**zügig** adj liberal, broad-minded; (mit Geld) generous

fremd [frɛmt] adj (unvertraut) strange; (ausländisch) foreign; (nicht eigen) someone else's; **etw ist jdm ~** sth is foreign to sb; ~**artig** adj strange; **F~enführer** [-'frɛmdən-] m (tourist) guide; **F~enverkehr** m tourism; **F~enverkehrsamt** nt tourist board; **F~enzimmer** nt guest room; **F~körper** m foreign body; ~**ländisch** adj foreign; **F~sprache** f foreign language; **F~wort** nt foreign word

Frequenz [fre'kvɛnts] f (RADIO) frequency

fressen ['frɛsən] (unreg) vt, vi to eat **Freude** ['frɔydə] f joy, delight **freudig** adj joyful, happy

freuen ['frɔyən] vt unpers to make happy od pleased ♦ vr to be glad od happy; **freut mich!** pleased to meet you; **sich auf etw** akk ~ to look forward to sth; **sich über etw** akk ~ to be pleased about sth

Freund ['frɔynt] (-(e)s, -e) m friend; boyfriend; ~**in** [-dɪn] f friend; girlfriend; **f~lich** adj kind, friendly; **f~licherweise** adv kindly; **~lichkeit** f friendliness, kindness; **~schaft** f friendship; **f~schaftlich** adj friendly

Frieden ['fri:dən] (-s, -) m peace; **im ~**

in peacetime

Friedens- zW: ~**schluss** ▲ m peace agreement; ~**vertrag** m peace treaty; **~zeit** f peacetime

fried- ['fri:t] zW: ~**fertig** adj peaceable; **F~hof** m cemetery; ~**lich** adj peaceful

frieren ['fri:rən] (unreg) vt, vi to freeze; **ich friere, es friert mich** I'm freezing, I'm cold

Frikadelle [frika'dɛlə] f rissole **Frikassee** [frika'se:] (-s, -s) nt (KOCH) fricassee

frisch [frɪʃ] adj fresh; (lebhaft) lively; ~**gestrichen!** wet paint!; **sich ~ machen** to freshen (o.s.) up; **F~e** f freshness; liveliness; **F~haltefolie** f cling film

Friseur [fri'zø:r] m hairdresser **Friseuse** [fri'zø:zə] f hairdresser **frisieren** [fri'zi:rən] vt to do (one's hair); (fig: Abrechnung) to fiddle, to doctor ♦ vr to do one's hair **Frisiersalon** m hairdressing salon **frisst** ▲ [frɪst] vb siehe **fressen**

Frist [frɪst] (-, -en) f period; (Termin) deadline; **f~gerecht** adj within the stipulated time od period; **f~los** adj (Entlassung) instant

Frisur [fri'zu:r] f hairdo, hairstyle **frivol** [fri'vo:l] adj frivolous **froh** [fro:] adj happy, cheerful; **ich bin ~, dass ...** I'm glad that ...

fröhlich ['frø:lɪç] adj merry, happy; **F~keit** f merriness, gaiety

fromm [frɔm] adj pious, good; (Wunsch) idle; **Frömmigkeit** ['frœmɪçkaɪt] f piety

Fronleichnam [fro:n'laɪçna:m] (-(e)s) m Corpus Christi

Front [frɔnt] (-, -en) f front; **f~al** [frɔn'ta:l] adj frontal

fror etc [fro:r] vb siehe **frieren**

Frosch [frɔʃ] (-(e)s, ⁼e) m frog; (Feuerwerk) squib; ~**mann** m frogman; ~**schenkel** m frog's leg

Frost [frɔst] (-(e)s, ⸚e) m frost; **~beule** f chilblain

frösteln ['frœstəln] vi to shiver

frostig adj frosty

Frostschutzmittel nt antifreeze

Frottier(hand)tuch [frɔ'tiːr(hant)tuːx] nt towel

Frucht [fruxt] (-, ⸚e) f fruit; (Getreide) corn; **f~bar** adj fruitful, fertile; **~barkeit** f fertility; **f~ig** adj (Geschmack) fruity; **f~los** adj fruitless; **~saft** m fruit juice

früh [fry:] adj, adv early; **heute ~** this morning; **F~aufsteher** (-s, -) m early riser; **F~e** f early morning; **f~er** adj earlier; (ehemalig) former ♦ adv formerly; **~er war das anders** that used to be different; **~estens** adv at the earliest; **F~jahr** nt, **F~ling** m spring; **~reif** adj precocious; **F~stück** nt breakfast; **f~stücken** vi to (have) breakfast; **F~stücksbüfett** nt breakfast buffet; **~zeitig** adj early; (pej) untimely

frustrieren [frʊs'triːrən] vt to frustrate

Fuchs [fʊks] (-es, ⸚e) m fox; **f~en** (umg) vt to rile, to annoy; **f~teufelswild** adj hopping mad

Fuge ['fuːgə] f joint; (MUS) fugue

fügen ['fyːgən] vt to place, to join ♦ vr: **sich ~ (in** +akk) to be obedient (to); (anpassen) to adapt oneself (to) ♦ vr unpers to happen

fühl- zW: ~ **bar** adj perceptible, noticeable; **~en** vt, vi, vr to feel; **F~er** (-s, -) m feeler

fuhr etc [fu:r] vb siehe **fahren**

führen ['fyːrən] vt to lead; (Geschäft) to run; (Name) to bear; (Buch) to keep ♦ vi to lead ♦ vr to behave

Führer ['fyːrər] (-s, -) m leader; (Fremdenführer) guide; **~schein** m driving licence

Führung ['fyːrʊŋ] f leadership; (eines Unternehmens) management; (MIL) command; (Benehmen) conduct; (Museumsführung) conducted tour; **~szeugnis** nt certificate of good conduct

Fülle ['fʏlə] f wealth, abundance; **f~n** vt to fill; (KOCH) to stuff ♦ vr to fill (up)

Füll- zW: **~er** (-s, -) m fountain pen; **~federhalter** m fountain pen; **~ung** f filling; (Holzfüllung) panel

fummeln ['fʊməln] (umg) vi to fumble

Fund [fʊnt] (-(e)s, -e) m find

Fundament [fʊnda'mɛnt] nt foundation; **fundamen'tal** adj fundamental

Fund- zW: **~büro** nt lost property office, lost and found (US); **~grube** f (fig) treasure trove

fünf [fʏnf] num five; **~hundert** num five hundred; **~te(r, s)** adj fifth; **F~tel** (-s, -) nt fifth; **~zehn** num fifteen; **~zig** num fifty

Funk [fʊŋk] (-s) m radio, wireless; **~e** (-ns, -n) m (auch fig) spark; **f~eln** vi to sparkle; **~en** (-s, -) m (auch fig) spark; **f~en** vi (durch Funk) to signal, to radio; (umg: richtig funktionieren) to work ♦ vt (Funken sprühen) to shower with sparks; **~er** (-s, -) m radio operator; **~gerät** nt radio set; **~rufempfänger** m pager, paging device; **~streife** f police radio patrol; **~telefon** nt cellphone

Funktion [fʊŋktsi'oːn] f function; **f~ieren** [-'niːrən] vi to work, to function

für [fy:r] präp +akk for; **was ~** what kind of sort of; **das F~ und Wider** the pros and cons pl; **Schritt ~ Schritt** step by step

Furche ['fʊrçə] f furrow

Furcht [fʊrçt] (-) f fear; **f~bar** adj terrible, frightful

fürchten ['fʏrçtən] vt to be afraid of, to fear ♦ vr: **sich ~ (vor** +dat) to be afraid (of)

fürchterlich adj awful

furchtlos adj fearless

füreinander [fy:rai'nandər] adv for each other

Furnier [fʊr'niːr] (-s, -e) nt veneer

fürs [fy:rs] = **für das**

Fürsorge ['fy:rzɔrgə] f care; (Sozial-fürsorge) welfare; **~r(in)** (-s, -) m(f) welfare worker; **~unterstützung** f social security, welfare benefit (US); **fürsorglich** adj attentive, caring

Fürsprache f recommendation; (um Gnade) intercession

Fürsprecher m advocate

Fürst [fʏrst] m (-en, -en) prince; **~entum** nt principality; **~in** f princess; **f~lich** adj princely

Fuß [fu:s] m (-es, :e) m foot; (von Glas, Säule etc) base; (von Möbel) leg; **zu ~** on foot; **~ball** m football; **~ballplatz** m football pitch; **~ballspiel** nt football match; **~ballspieler** m footballer; **~boden** m floor; **~bremse** f (AUT) footbrake; **~ende** nt foot; **~gänger(in)** (-s, -) m(f) pedestrian; **~gängerzone** f pedestrian precinct; **~nagel** m toenail; **~note** f footnote; **~spur** f footprint; **~tritt** m kick; (Spur) footstep; **~weg** m footpath

Futter ['fʊtər] (-s, -) nt fodder, feed; (Stoff) lining; **~al** [-'ra:l] (-s, -e) nt case

füttern ['fʏtərn] vt to feed; (Kleidung) to line

Futur [fu'tu:r] (-s, -e) nt future

G, g

g abk = Gramm

gab etc [ga:p] vb siehe **geben**

Gabe ['ga:bə] f gift

Gabel ['ga:bəl] (-, -n) f fork; **~ung** f fork

gackern ['gakərn] vi to cackle

gaffen ['gafən] vi to gape

Gage ['ga:ʒə] f fee; salary

gähnen ['gɛ:nən] vi to yawn

Galerie [galə'ri:] f gallery

Galgen ['galgən] (-s, -) m gallows sg; **~frist** f respite; **~humor** m macabre humour

Galle ['galə] f gall; (Organ) gall bladder; **~nstein** m gallstone

gammeln ['gaməln] (umg) vi to bum around; **Gammler(in)** (-s, -) (pej) m(f) layabout, loafer (inf)

Gämse ▲ ['gɛmzə] f chamois

Gang [gaŋ] m (-(e)s, :e) m walk; (Boten-gang) errand; (~art) gait; (Abschnitt eines Vorgangs) operation; (Essengang, Ablauf) course; (Flur etc) corridor; (Durchgang) passage; (TECH) gear; **in ~ bringen** to start up; (fig) to get off the ground; **in ~ sein** to be in operation; (fig) to be under way

gang adj: **~ und gäbe** usual, normal

gängig ['gɛŋɪç] adj common, current; (Ware) in demand, selling well

Gangschaltung f gears pl

Ganove [ga'no:və] (-n, -n) (umg) m crook

Gans [gans] (-, :e) f goose

Gänse- ['gɛnzə] zW: **~blümchen** nt daisy; **~füßchen** (umg) pl (An-führungszeichen) inverted commas; **~haut** f goose pimples pl; **~marsch** m: **im ~marsch** in single file; **~rich** (-s, -e) m gander

ganz [gants] adj whole; (vollständig) complete ♦ adv quite; (völlig) completely; **~ Europa** all Europe; **sein ~es Geld** all his money; **~ und gar nicht** not at all; **es sieht ~ so aus** it really looks like it; **aufs G~e gehen** to go for the lot

gänzlich ['gɛntslɪç] adj complete, entire ♦ adv completely, entirely

Ganztagsschule f all-day school

gar [ga:r] adj cooked, done ♦ adv quite; **~ nicht/nichts/keiner** not/nothing/nobody at all; **~ nicht schlecht** not bad at all

Garage [ga'ra:ʒə] f garage

Garantie [garan'ti:] f guarantee; **g~ren** vt to guarantee; **er kommt g~rt** he's guaranteed to come

---

Spelling Reform: ▲ *new spelling* △ *old spelling (to be phased out)*

Garbe ['garbə] f sheaf

Garde ['gardə] f guard

Garderobe [gardə'ro:bə] f wardrobe; (Abgabe) cloakroom; **~nfrau** f cloakroom attendant

Gardine [gar'di:nə] f curtain

garen ['ga:rən] vt, vi to cook

gären ['gɛ:rən] (unreg) vi to ferment

Garn [garn] (-(e)s, -e) nt thread; yarn (auch fig)

Garnele [gar'ne:lə] f shrimp, prawn

garnieren [gar'ni:rən] vt to decorate; (Speisen, fig) to garnish

Garnison [garni'zo:n] (-, -en) f garrison

Garnitur [garni'tu:r] f (Satz) set; (Unterwäsche) set of (matching) underwear; **erste ~** (fig) top rank; **zweite ~** (fig) second rate

garstig ['garstiç] adj nasty, horrid

Garten ['gartən] (-s, ⁻) m garden; **~arbeit** f gardening; **~gerät** nt gardening tool; **~lokal** nt beer garden; **~tür** f garden gate

Gärtner(in) ['gɛrtnər(in)] (-s, -) m(f) gardener; **~ei** [-'rai] f nursery; (Gemüsegärtnerei) market garden (BRIT), truck farm (US)

Gärung ['gɛ:ruŋ] f fermentation

Gas [ga:s] (-es, -e) nt gas; **~ geben** (AUT) to accelerate, to step on the gas; **~hahn** m gas tap; **~herd** m gas cooker; **~kocher** m gas cooker; **~leitung** f gas pipe; **~pedal** nt accelerator, gas pedal

Gasse ['gasə] f lane, alley

Gast [gast] (-es, ⁻e) m guest; (in Lokal) patron; **bei jdm zu ~ sein** to be sb's guest; **~arbeiter(in)** m(f) foreign worker

Gäste- ['gɛstə] zW: **~buch** nt visitors' book, guest book; **~zimmer** nt guest od spare room

Gast- zW: **g~freundlich** adj hospitable; **g~geber** (-s, -) m host; **~geberin** f hostess; **~haus** nt hotel, inn; **~hof** m hotel, inn; **g~ieren** [-'ti:rən] vi (THEAT)

to (appear as a) guest; **g~lich** adj hospitable; **~rolle** f guest role; **~spiel** nt (THEAT) guest performance; **~stätte** f restaurant; pub; **~wirt** m innkeeper; **~wirtschaft** f hotel, inn

Gaswerk nt gasworks sg

Gaszähler m gas meter

Gatte ['gatə] (-n, -n) m husband, spouse

Gattin f wife, spouse

Gattung ['gatuŋ] f genus; kind

Gaudi ['gaudi] (umg: SÜDD, ÖSTERR) nt od f fun

Gaul [gaul] (-(e)s, Gäule) m horse; nag

Gaumen ['gaumən] (-s, -) m palate

Gauner ['gaunər] (-s, -) m rogue; **~ei** [-'rai] f swindle

geb. abk = **geboren**

Gebäck [gə'bɛk] (-(e)s, -e) nt pastry

gebacken [gə'bakən] adj baked; (gebraten) fried

Gebälk [gə'bɛlk] (-(e)s) nt timberwork

Gebärde [gə'bɛ:rdə] f gesture; **g~n** vr to behave

gebären [gə'bɛ:rən] (unreg) vt to give birth to, to bear

Gebärmutter f uterus, womb

Gebäude [gə'bɔydə] (-s, -) nt building; **~komplex** m (building) complex

geben ['ge:bən] (unreg) vt, vi to give; (Karten) to deal ♦ vb unpers: **es gibt** there is/are; there will be ♦ vr (sich verhalten) to behave; to act; (aufhören) to abate; **jdm etw ~** to give sb sth od sth to sb; **was gibts?** what's up?; **was gibt es im Kino?** what's on at the cinema?; **sich geschlagen ~** to admit defeat; **das wird sich schon ~** that'll soon sort itself out

Gebet [gə'be:t] (-(e)s, -e) nt prayer

gebeten [gə'be:tən] vb siehe **bitten**

Gebiet [gə'bi:t] (-(e)s, -e) nt area; (Hoheitsgebiet) territory; (fig) field; **g~en** (unreg) vt to command, to demand; **g~erisch** adj imperious

Gebilde [gə'bildə] (-s, -) nt object

gebildet adj cultured, educated

Gebirge [gə'bɪrgə] (-s, -) nt mountain chain

Gebiss [gə'bɪs] (-es, -e) nt teeth pl; (künstlich) dentures pl

gebissen vb siehe **beißen**

geblieben [gə'bli:bn] vb siehe **bleiben**

geblümt [gə'bly:mt] adj (Kleid, Stoff, Tapete) floral

geboren [gə'bo:rən] adj born; (Frau) née

geborgen [gə'bɔrgən] adj secure, safe

Gebot [gə'bo:t] (-(e)s, -e) nt command; (REL) commandment; (bei Auktion) bid

geboten [gə'bo:tən] vb siehe **bieten**

Gebr. abk (= Gebrüder) Bros.

gebracht [gə'braxt] vb siehe **bringen**

gebraten [gə'bra:tən] adj fried

Gebrauch [gə'braox] (-(e)s, Gebräuche) m use; (Sitte) custom; **g~en** vt to use

gebräuchlich [gə'brɔyçlɪç] adj usual, customary

Gebrauchs- zW: **~anweisung** f directions pl for use; **g~fertig** adj ready for use; **~gegenstand** m commodity

gebraucht [gə'braoxt] adj used; **G~wagen** m secondhand od used car

gebrechlich [gə'brɛçlɪç] adj frail

Gebrüder [gə'bry:dər] pl brothers

Gebrüll [gə'brʏl] (-(e)s) nt roaring

Gebühr [gə'by:r] (-, -en) f charge, fee; **nach ~** fittingly; **über ~** unduly; **g~en** vi: **jdm g~en** to be sb's due od due to sb ♦ vr to be fitting; **g~end** adj fitting, appropriate ♦ adv fittingly, appropriately

Gebühren- zW: **~einheit** f (TEL) unit; **~erlass** ▲ m remission of fees; **~ermäßigung** f reduction of fees; **g~frei** adj free of charge; **~ordnung** f scale of charges, tariff; **g~pflichtig** adj subject to a charge

gebunden [gə'bʊndən] vb siehe **binden**

Geburt [gə'bu:rt] (-, -en) f birth

Geburtenkontrolle f birth control

Geburtenregelung f birth control

gebürtig [gə'bʏrtɪç] adj born in, native of; **~e Schweizerin** native of Switzerland

Geburts- zW: **~anzeige** f birth notice; **~datum** nt date of birth; **~jahr** nt year of birth; **~ort** m birthplace; **~tag** m birthday; **~urkunde** f birth certificate

Gebüsch [gə'bʏʃ] (-(e)s, -e) nt bushes pl

gedacht [gə'daxt] vb siehe **denken**

Gedächtnis [gə'dɛçtnɪs] (-ses, -se) nt memory; **~feier** f commemoration

Gedanke [gə'daŋkə] (-ns, -n) m thought; **sich über etw** akk **~n machen** to think about sth

Gedanken- zW: **~austausch** m exchange of ideas; **g~los** adj thoughtless; **~strich** m dash; **~übertragung** f thought transference, telepathy

Gedeck [gə'dɛk] (-(e)s, -e) nt cover(ing); (Speisenfolge) menu; **ein ~ auflegen** to lay a place

gedeihen [gə'daiən] (unreg) vi to thrive, to prosper

Gedenken nt: **zum ~ an jdn** in memory of sb

gedenken [gə'dɛŋkən] (unreg) vi +gen (beabsichtigen) to intend; (sich erinnern) to remember

Gedenk- zW: **~feier** f commemoration; **~minute** f minute's silence; **~stätte** f memorial; **~tag** m remembrance day

Gedicht [gə'dɪçt] (-(e)s, -e) nt poem

gediegen [gə'di:gən] adj (good) quality; (Mensch) reliable, honest

Gedränge [gə'drɛŋə] (-s) nt crush, crowd

gedrängt adj compressed; **~ voll** packed

gedrückt [gə'drʏkt] adj (deprimiert) low, depressed

Spelling Reform: ▲ *new spelling* △ *old spelling (to be phased out)*

gedrungen [gə'droŋən] *adj* thickset, stocky

Geduld [gə'dolt] *f* patience; **g~en** [gə'doldən] *vt* to be patient; **g~ig** *adj* patient, forbearing; **~sprobe** *f* trial of (one's) patience

gedurft [gə'dorft] *vb siehe* **dürfen**

geehrt [gə'e:rt] *adj:* **Sehr ~e Frau X!** Dear Mrs X

geeignet [gə'aıgnət] *adj* suitable

Gefahr [gə'fa:r] *f* (-, **-en**) *f* danger; **~ laufen, etw zu tun** to run the risk of doing sth; **auf eigene ~** at one's own risk

gefährden [gə'fɛ:rdən] *vt* to endanger

Gefahren- *zW:* **~quelle** *f* source of danger; **~zulage** *f* danger money

gefährlich [gə'fɛ:rlɪç] *adj* dangerous

Gefährte [gə'fɛ:rtə] (**-n, -n**) *m* companion; (*Lebenspartner*) partner

Gefährtin [gə'fɛ:rtɪn] *f* (female) companion; (*Lebenspartner*) (female) partner

Gefälle [gə'fɛlə] (**-s, -**) *nt* gradient, incline

Gefallen¹ [gə'falən] (**-s, -**) *m* favour

Gefallen² [gə'falən] (**-s**) *nt* pleasure; **an etw** *dat* **~ finden** to derive pleasure from sth

gefallen *pp von* **fallen** ♦ *vi:* **jdm ~** to please sb; **er/es gefällt mir** I like him/it; **das gefällt mir an ihm** that's one thing I like about him; **sich** *dat* **etw ~ lassen** to put up with sth

gefällig [gə'fɛlɪç] *adj* (*hilfsbereit*) obliging; (*erfreulich*) pleasant; **G~keit** *f* favour; helpfulness; **etw aus G~keit tun** to do sth out of the goodness of one's heart

gefangen [gə'faŋən] *adj* captured; (*fig*) captivated; **~ halten** to keep prisoner; **~ nehmen** to take prisoner; **G~e(r)** *f(m)* prisoner, captive; **G~nahme** *f* capture; **G~schaft** *f* captivity

Gefängnis [gə'fɛŋnɪs] (**-ses, -se**) *nt* prison; **~strafe** *f* prison sentence; **~wärter** *m* prison warder; **~zelle** *f*

prison cell

Gefäß [gə'fɛ:s] (**-es, -e**) *nt* vessel; (*auch* ANAT) container

gefasst ▲ [gə'fast] *adj* composed, calm; **auf etw** *akk* **~ sein** to be prepared *od* ready for sth

Gefecht [gə'fɛçt] (**-(e)s, -e**) *nt* fight; (MIL) engagement

Gefieder [gə'fi:dər] (**-s, -**) *nt* plumage, feathers *pl*

gefleckt [gə'flɛkt] *adj* spotted, mottled

geflogen [gə'flo:gən] *vb siehe* **fliegen**

geflossen [gə'flɔsən] *vb siehe* **fließen**

Geflügel [gə'fly:gəl] (**-s**) *nt* poultry

Gefolgschaft [gə'fɔlkʃaft] *f* following

gefragt [gə'fra:kt] *adj* in demand

gefräßig [gə'frɛ:sɪç] *adj* voracious

Gefreite(r) [gə'fraıtə(r)] *m* lance corporal; (NAUT) able seaman; (AVIAT) aircraftman

Gefrierbeutel *m* freezer bag

gefrieren [gə'fri:rən] (*unreg*) *vi* to freeze

Gefrier- *zW:* **~fach** *nt* icebox; **~fleisch** *nt* frozen meat; **g~getrocknet** [-gətrɔknət] *adj* freeze-dried; **~punkt** *m* freezing point; **~schutzmittel** *nt* antifreeze; **~truhe** *f* deep-freeze

gefroren [gə'fro:rən] *vb siehe* **frieren**

Gefühl [gə'fy:l] (**-(e)s, -e**) *nt* feeling; **etw im ~ haben** to have a feel for sth; **g~los** *adj* unfeeling

gefühls- *zW:* **~betont** *adj* emotional; **G~duselei** [-du:zə'laı] *f* oversentimentality; **~mäßig** *adj* instinctive

gefüllt [gə'fʏlt] *adj* (KOCH) stuffed

gefunden [gə'fondən] *vb siehe* **finden**

gegangen [gə'gaŋən] *vb siehe* **gehen**

gegeben [gə'ge:bən] *vb siehe* **geben** ♦ *adj* given; **zu ~er Zeit** in good time

gegebenenfalls [gə'ge:bənənfals] *adv* if need be

SCHLÜSSELWORT

gegen ['ge:gən] *präp +akk* **1** against; **nichts gegen jdn haben** to have nothing against sb; **X gegen Y** (SPORT,

jur) X versus Y; **ein Mittel gegen
Schnupfen** something for colds
2 (_in Richtung auf_) towards; **gegen
Osten** to(wards) the east; **gegen
Abend** towards evening; **gegen einen
Baum fahren** to drive into a tree
3 (_ungefähr_) round about; **gegen 3
Uhr** around 3 o'clock
4 (_gegenüber_) towards; (_ungefähr_)
around; **gerecht gegen alle** fair to all
5 (_im Austausch für_) for; **gegen bar** for
cash; **gegen Quittung** against a receipt
6 (_verglichen mit_) compared with

Gegenangriff m counter-attack
Gegenbeweis m counter-evidence
Gegend ['ge:gənt] (-, -en) f area, district
Gegen- zW: **g~ei'nander** adv against
one another; **~fahrbahn** f oncoming
carriageway; **~frage** f counter-
question; **~gewicht** nt counterbal-
ance; **~gift** nt antidote; **~leistung** f
service in return; **~maßnahme** f
countermeasure; **~mittel** nt antidote,
cure; **~satz** m contrast; **~sätze
überbrücken** to overcome differences;
g~sätzlich adj contrary, opposite;
(_widersprüchlich_) contradictory;
g~seitig adj mutual, reciprocal; **sich
g~seitig helfen** to help each other;
~spieler m opponent; **~sprechanla-
ge** f (two-way) intercom; **~stand** m
object; **~stimme** f vote against;
~stoß m counterblow; **~stück** nt
counterpart; **~teil** nt opposite; **im
~teil** on the contrary; **g~teilig** adj opposite, contrary

gegenüber [ge:gən'|y:bər] präp +dat
opposite; (_zu_) to(wards); (_angesichts_)
in the face of ♦ adv opposite; **G~** (-s,
-) nt person opposite; **~liegen** (_unreg_)
vr to face each other; **~stehen** (_unreg_)
vr to be opposed (to each other);

~stellen vt to confront; (_fig_) to contrast; **G~stellung** f confrontation; (_fig_)
contrast; **~treten** (_unreg_) vi +dat to face
Gegen- zW: **~verkehr** m oncoming
traffic; **~vorschlag** m counterpro-
posal; **~wart** f present; **g~wärtig** adj
present ♦ adv at present; **das ist mir
nicht mehr g~wärtig** that has slipped
my mind; **~wert** m equivalent; **~wind**
m headwind; **g~zeichnen** vt, vi to
countersign

gegessen [gə'gɛsən] vb siehe **essen**
Gegner ['ge:gnər] (-s, -) m opponent;
g~isch adj opposing
gegr. abk (= gegründet) est.
gegrillt [gə'grɪlt] adj grilled
Gehackte(s) [gə'haktə(s)] nt mince(d
meat)
Gehalt¹ [gə'halt] (-(e)s, -e) m content
Gehalt² [gə'halt] (-(e)s, -er) nt salary
Gehalts- zW: **~empfänger** m salary
earner; **~erhöhung** f salary increase;
~zulage f salary increment
gehaltvoll [gə'haltfɔl] adj (_nahrhaft_)
nutritious
gehässig [gə'hɛsɪç] adj spiteful, nasty
Gehäuse [gə'hɔyzə] (-s, -) nt case; casing; (_von Apfel etc_) core
Gehege [gə'he:gə] (-s, -) nt reserve;
(_im Zoo_) enclosure
geheim [gə'haɪm] adj secret; **~ halten**
to keep secret; **G~dienst** m secret service, intelligence service; **G~nis** (-ses,
-se) nt secret; mystery; **g~nisvoll** adj
mysterious; **G~polizei** f secret police
gehemmt [gə'hɛmt] adj inhibited,
self-conscious
gehen [ge:ən] (_unreg_) vt, vi to go; (_zu
Fuß ~_) to walk ♦ vb unpers: **wie geht es
(dir)?** how are you of things?; **~ nach**
(_Fenster_) to face; **mir/ihm geht es gut**
I'm/he's (doing) fine; **geht das?** is
that possible?; **gehts noch?** can you
manage?; **es geht** not too bad, O.K.;
das geht nicht that's not on; **es geht**

um etw it has to do with sth, it's about sth; **sich ~ lassen** (unbeherrscht sein) to lose control (of o.s.); **jdn ~ lassen** to leave sb alone; **lass mich ~!** leave me alone!

geheuer [gə'hɔyər] adj: **nicht ~** eerie; (fragwürdig) dubious

Gehilfe [gə'hɪlfə] (-n, -n) m assistant; **Gehilfin** f assistant

Gehirn [gə'hɪrn] (-(e)s, -e) nt brain; **~erschütterung** f concussion; **~hautentzündung** f meningitis

gehoben [gə'ho:bən] pp von **heben** ♦ adj (Position) elevated; high

geholfen [gə'hɔlfən] vb siehe **helfen**

Gehör [gə'hø:r] (-(e)s) nt hearing; **musikalisches ~** ear; **~ finden** to gain a hearing; **jdm ~ schenken** to give sb a hearing

gehorchen [gə'hɔrçən] vi +dat to obey

gehören [gə'hø:rən] vi to belong ♦ vr unpers to be right od proper

gehörig adj proper; **~ zu** od +dat belonging to; part of

gehörlos adj deaf

gehorsam [gə'ho:rza:m] adj obedient; **G~** (-s) m obedience

Geh- ['ge:-] zW: **~steig** m pavement, sidewalk (US); **~weg** m pavement, sidewalk (US)

Geier ['gaiər] (-s, -) m vulture

Geige ['gaigə] f violin; **~r** (-s, -) m violinist

geil [gail] adj randy (BRIT), horny (US)

Geisel ['gaizəl] (-, -n) f hostage

Geist [gaist] (-(e)s, -er) m spirit; (Verstand) mind

geisterhaft adj ghostly

Geistes- zW: **g~abwesend** adj absent-minded; **~blitz** m brainwave; **~gegenwart** f presence of mind; **g~krank** adj mentally ill; **~kranke(r)** f(m) mentally ill person; **~krankheit** f mental illness; **~wissenschaften** pl the arts; **~zustand** m state of mind

geist- zW: **~ig** adj intellectual; mental; (Getränke) alcoholic; **~ig behindert**

mentally handicapped; **~lich** adj spiritual, religious; clerical; **G~liche(r)** m clergyman; **G~lichkeit** f clergy; **~los** adj uninspired, dull; **~reich** adj clever; witty; **~voll** adj intellectual; (weise) wise

Geiz [gaits] (-es) m miserliness, meanness; **g~en** vi to be miserly; **~hals** m miser; **g~ig** adj miserly, mean; **~kragen** m miser

gekannt [gə'kant] vb siehe **kennen**

gekonnt [gə'kɔnt] adj skilful ♦ vb siehe **können**

gekünstelt [ge'kʏnstəlt] adj artificial, affected

Gel [ge:l] (-s, -e) nt gel

Gelächter [gə'lɛçtər] (-s, -) nt laughter

geladen [gə'la:dən] adj loaded; (ELEK) live; (fig) furious

gelähmt [gə'le:mt] adj paralysed

Gelände [gə'lɛndə] (-s, -) nt land, terrain; (von Fabrik, Sportgelände) grounds pl; (Baugelände) site; **~lauf** m cross-country race

Geländer [gə'lɛndər] (-s, -) nt railing; (Treppengeländer) banister(s)

gelangen [gə'laŋən] vi: **~ (an +akk od zu)** to reach; (erwerben) to attain; **in jds Besitz** akk **~** to come into sb's possession

gelangweilt [gə'laŋvailt] adj bored

gelassen [gə'lasən] adj calm, composed; **G~heit** f calmness, composure

Gelatine [ʒela'ti:nə] f gelatine

geläufig [gə'lɔyfiç] adj (üblich) common; **das ist mir nicht ~** I'm not familiar with that

gelaunt [gə'launt] adj: **schlecht/gut ~** in a bad/good mood; **wie ist er ~?** what sort of mood is he in?

gelb [gɛlp] adj yellow; (Ampellicht) amber; **~lich** adj yellowish; **G~sucht** f jaundice

Geld [gɛlt] (-(e)s, -er) nt money; **etw zu ~ machen** to sell sth off; **~anlage** f investment; **~automat** m cash dispenser; **~beutel** m purse; **~börse** f purse; **~geber** (-s, -) *m* financial backer; **g~gierig** *adj* avaricious; **~schein** *m* banknote; **~schrank** *m* safe, strongbox; **~strafe** *f* fine; **~stück** *nt* coin; **~wechsel** *m* exchange (of money)

Gelee [ʒe'le:] (-s, -s) *nt od m* jelly

gelegen [gə'le:gən] *adj* situated; (*passend*) convenient, opportune ♦ *vb siehe* **liegen; etw kommt jdm ~** sth is convenient for sb

Gelegenheit [gə'le:gənhart] *f* opportunity; (*Anlaß*) occasion; **bei jeder ~** at every opportunity; **~sarbeit** *f* casual work; **~skauf** *m* bargain

gelegentlich [gə'le:gəntlıç] *adj* occasional ♦ *adv* occasionally; (*bei Gelegenheit*) some time (or other) ♦ *präp +gen* on the occasion of

gelehrt [gə'le:rt] *adj* learned; **G~e(r)** *f(m)* scholar; **G~heit** *f* scholarliness

Geleise [gə'laızə] (-s, -) *nt* = **Gleis**

Geleit [gə'laıt] (-(e)s, -e) *nt* escort; **g~en** *vt* to escort

Gelenk [gə'leŋk] (-(e)s, -e) *nt* joint; **g~ig** *adj* supple

gelernt [gə'lernt] *adj* skilled

Geliebte(r) [gə'li:ptə(r)] *f(m)* sweetheart, beloved

geliehen [gə'li:ən] *vb siehe* **leihen**

gelind(e) [gə'lınd(ə)] *adj* mild, light; (*fig: Wut*) fierce; **~ gesagt** to put it mildly

gelingen [gə'lıŋən] (*unreg*) *vi* to succeed; **es ist mir gelungen, etw zu tun** I succeeded in doing sth

geloben [gə'lo:bən] *vt, vi* to vow, to swear

gelten ['gɛltən] (*unreg*) *vt* (*wert sein*) to be worth ♦ *vi* (*gültig sein*) to be valid; (*erlaubt sein*) to be allowed ♦ *vb unpers*: **es gilt, etw zu tun** it is necessary to do sth; **jdm viel/wenig ~** to mean a lot/not to mean much to sb; **was gilt die Wette?** what do you bet?; **etw ~ lassen** to accept sth; **als od für etw ~**

to be considered to be sth; **jdm od für jdn ~** (*betreffen*) to apply to od for sb; **~d** *adj* prevailing; **etw ~d machen** to assert sth; **sich ~d machen** to make itself/o.s. felt

Geltung ['gɛltʊŋ] *f*: **~ haben** to have validity; **sich/etw** *dat* **~ verschaffen** to establish one's position/the position of sth; **etw zur ~ bringen** to show sth to its best advantage; **zur ~ kommen** to be seen/heard etc to its best advantage

Geltungsbedürfnis *nt* desire for admiration

Gelübde [gə'lYpdə] (-s, -) *nt* vow

gelungen [gə'lʊŋən] *adj* successful

gemächlich [gə'mɛːçlıç] *adj* leisurely

Gemahl [gə'ma:l] (-(e)s, -e) *m* husband; **~in** *f* wife

Gemälde [gə'mɛ:ldə] (-s, -) *nt* picture, painting

gemäß [gə'mɛːs] *präp +dat* in accordance with ♦ *adj* (+*dat*) appropriate (to)

gemäßigt *adj* moderate; (*Klima*) temperate

gemein [gə'maın] *adj* common; (*niederträchtig*) mean; **etw ~ haben (mit)** to have sth in common with/have

Gemeinde [gə'maındə] *f* district, community; (*Pfarrgemeinde*) parish; (*Kirchengemeinde*) congregation; **~steuer** *f* local rates *pl*; **~verwaltung** *f* local administration; **~wahl** *f* local election

Gemein- *zW*: **g~gefährlich** *adj* dangerous to the public; **~heit** *f* commonness; mean thing to do/to say; **g~nützig** *adj* charitable; **g~nütziger Verein** non-profit-making organization; **g~sam** *adj* joint, common (*AUCH MATH*) ♦ *adv* together, jointly; **g~same Sache mit jdm machen** to be in cahoots with sb; **etw g~sam haben** to have sth in common; **~samkeit** *f*

---

community, having in common; **~schaft** f community; **in ~schaft mit** jointly od together with; **g~schaftlich** adj = gemeinsam; **~schaftsarbeit** f teamwork; team effort; **~sinn** m public spirit

Gemenge [gə'mɛŋə] (-s, -) nt mixture; (*Handgemenge*) scuffle

gemessen [gə'mɛsən] adj measured

Gemetzel [gə'mɛtsəl] (-s, -) nt slaughter, carnage, butchery

Gemisch [gə'mɪʃ] (-es, -e) nt mixture; **g~t** adj mixed

gemocht [gə'mɔxt] vb siehe **mögen**

Gemse △ ['gɛmzə] f siehe **Gämse**

Gemurmel [gə'mʊrməl] (-s) nt murmur(ing)

Gemüse [gə'my:zə] (-s, -) nt vegetables pl; **~garten** m vegetable garden; **~händler** m greengrocer

gemusst ▲ [gə'mʊst] vb siehe **müssen**

gemustert [gə'mʊstərt] adj patterned

Gemüt [gə'my:t] (-(e)s, -er) nt disposition, nature; person; **sich** dat **etw zu ~e führen** (*umg*) to indulge in sth; **die ~er erregen** to arouse strong feelings; **g~lich** adj comfortable, cosy; (*Person*) good-natured; **~lichkeit** f comfortableness, cosiness; amiability

Gemüts- zW: **~mensch** m sentimental person; **~ruhe** f composure; **~zustand** m state of mind

Gen [ge:n] (-s, -e) nt gene

genannt [gə'nant] vb siehe **nennen**

genau [gə'nau] adj exact, precise ♦ adv exactly, precisely; **etw ~ nehmen** to take sth seriously; **~ genommen** strictly speaking; **G~igkeit** f exactness, accuracy; **~so** adv just the same; **~so gut** just as good

genehm [gə'ne:m] adj agreeable, acceptable; **~igen** vt to approve, to authorize; **sich** dat **etw ~igen** to indulge in sth; **G~igung** f approval, authorization; (*Schriftstück*) permit

General [genə'ra:l] (-s, -e od -¨e) m general; **~direktor** m director general;

~konsulat nt consulate general; **~probe** f dress rehearsal; **~streik** m general strike; **g~überholen** vt to overhaul thoroughly; **~versammlung** f general meeting

Generation [generatsi'o:n] f generation

Generator [genə'ra:tɔr] m generator, dynamo

generell [genə'rɛl] adj general

genesen [gə'ne:zən] (*unreg*) vi to convalesce, to recover; **Genesung** f recovery, convalescence

genetisch [ge'ne:tɪʃ] adj genetic

Genf ['gɛnf] nt Geneva; **der ~er See** Lake Geneva

genial [geni'a:l] adj brilliant

Genick [gə'nɪk] (-(e)s, -e) nt (back of the) neck

Genie [ʒe'ni:] (-s, -s) nt genius

genieren [ʒe'ni:rən] vt to bother ♦ vr to feel awkward od self-conscious

genieß- zW: **~bar** adj edible; drinkable; **~en** [gə'ni:sən] (*unreg*) vt to enjoy; to eat; to drink; **G~er** (-s, -) m epicure; pleasure lover; **~erisch** adj appreciative ♦ adv with relish

genmanipuliert ['ge:nmanipuli:rt] adj genetically modified

genommen [gə'nɔmən] vb siehe **nehmen**

Genosse [gə'nɔsə] (-n, -n) m (*bes POL*) comrade, companion; **~nschaft** f cooperative (association)

Genossin f (*bes POL*) comrade, companion

Gentechnik ['ge:ntɛçnɪk] f genetic engineering

genug [gə'nu:k] adv enough

Genüge [gə'ny:gə] f: **jdm/etw ~ tun** od **leisten** to satisfy sb/sth; **g~n** vi (+dat) to be enough (for); **g~nd** adj sufficient

genügsam [gə'ny:kza:m] adj modest, easily satisfied; **G~keit** f moderation

Genugtuung [gə'nu:ktu:ʊŋ] f satisfaction

Genuss ▲ [gə'nʊs] (-es, ᵉe) m pleasure; (Zusichnehmen) consumption; **in den ~ von etw kommen** to receive the benefit of sth; **genüsslich** ▲ [gə'nʏslɪç] adv with relish

Genussmittel ▲ pl (semi-)luxury items

geöffnet [gə'œfnət] adj open

Geograf ▲ [geo'graːf] (-en, -en) m geographer; **Geografie** ▲ f geography; **g~isch** adj geographical

Geologe [geo'loːgə] (-n, -n) m geologist; **Geolo'gie** f geology

Geometrie [geome'triː] f geometry

Gepäck [gə'pɛk] (-(e)s) nt luggage, baggage; **~abfertigung** f luggage office; **~annahme** f luggage office; **~aufbewahrung** f left-luggage office (BRIT), baggage check (US); **~aufgabe** f luggage office; (AVIAT) luggage reclaim; **~netz** nt luggage rack; **~träger** m porter; (Fahrrad) carrier; **~versicherung** f luggage insurance; **~wagen** m luggage van (BRIT), baggage car (US)

gepflegt [gə'pfleːkt] adj well-groomed; (Park etc) well looked after

Gerade [gə'raːdə] f straight line; **g~aus** adv straight ahead; **g~he'raus** adv straight out, bluntly; **g~stehen** (unreg) vi: **für jdn/etw g~stehen** to be answerable for sb('s actions)/sth; **g~wegs** adv direct, straight; **g~zu** adv (beinahe) virtually, almost

───────────────
SCHLÜSSELWORT
───────────────

gerade [gə'raːdə] adj straight; (aufrecht) upright; **eine gerade Zahl** an even number

♦ adv 1 (genau) just, exactly; (speziell) especially; **gerade deshalb** that's just od exactly why; **das ist es ja gerade!** that's just it!; **gerade du** you especially; **warum gerade ich?** why me (of all people)?; **jetzt gerade nicht!** not

now!; **gerade neben** right next to 2 (eben, soeben) just; **er wollte gerade aufstehen** he was just about to get up; **gerade erst** only just; **gerade noch** (only) just

gerannt [gə'rant] vb siehe **rennen**

Gerät ▲ [gə'rɛːt] (-(e)s, -e) nt device; (Werkzeug) tool; (SPORT) apparatus; (Zubehör) equipment no pl

geraten [gə'raːtn] (unreg) vi (gedeihen) to thrive; (gelingen): **(jdm) ~** to turn out well (for sb); **gut/schlecht ~** to turn out well/badly; **an jdn ~** to come across sb; **in etw** akk **~** to get into sth; **nach jdm ~** to take after sb

Geratewohl [gəraːtə'voːl] nt: **aufs ~** on the off chance; (bei Wahl) at random

geräuchert [gə'rɔʏçɐt] adj smoked

geräumig [gə'rɔʏmɪç] adj roomy

Geräusch [gə'rɔʏʃ] (-(e)s, -e) nt sound, noise; **g~los** adj silent

gerben ['gɛrbn] vt to tan

gerecht [gə'rɛçt] adj just, fair; **jdm/etw ~ werden** to do justice to sb/sth; **G~igkeit** f justice, fairness

Gerede [gə'reːdə] (-s) nt talk, gossip

geregelt [gə'reːgəlt] adj (Arbeit) steady, regular; (Mahlzeiten) regular, set

gereizt [gə'raɪtst] adj irritable; **G~heit** f irritation

Gericht [gə'rɪçt] (-(e)s, -e) nt court; (Essen) dish; **mit jdm ins ~ gehen** (fig) to judge sb harshly; **das Jüngste ~** the Last Judgement; **g~lich** adj judicial, legal ♦ adv judicially, legally

Gerichts- zW: **~barkeit** f jurisdiction; **~hof** m court of law; **~kosten** pl (legal) costs; **~medizin** f forensic medicine; **~saal** m courtroom; **~verfahren** nt legal proceedings pl; **~verhandlung** f trial; **~vollzieher** m bailiff

gerieben [gə'riːbən] adj grated; (umg: schlau) smart, wily ♦ vb siehe **reiben**

gering [gə'rɪŋ] *adj* slight, small; *(niedrig)* low; *(Zeit)* short; **~fügig** *adj* slight, trivial; **~schätzig** *adj* disparaging

geringste(r, s) *adj* slightest, least; **~nfalls** *adv* at the very least

gerinnen [gə'rɪnən] *(unreg) vi* to congeal; *(Blut)* to clot; *(Milch)* to curdle

Gerippe [gə'rɪpə] *(-s, -) nt* skeleton

gerissen [gə'rɪsən] *adj* wily, smart

geritten [gə'rɪtən] *vb siehe* **reiten**

gern(e) ['gɛrn(ə)] *adv* willingly, gladly; **~ haben, ~ mögen** to like; **etwas ~ tun** to like doing something; **ich möchte ~ ...** I'd like ...; **ja, ~** yes, please; yes, I'd like to; **~ geschehen** it's a pleasure

gerochen [gə'rɔxən] *vb siehe* **riechen**

Geröll [gə'rœl] *(-(e)s, -e) nt* scree

Gerste ['gɛrstə] *f* barley; **~nkorn** *nt (im Auge)* stye

Geruch [gə'rʊx] *(-(e)s, =e) m* smell, odour; **g~los** *adj* odourless

Gerücht [gə'rʏçt] *(-(e)s, -e) nt* rumour

geruhsam [gə'ru:zam] *adj (Leben)* peaceful; *(Nacht, Zeit)* peaceful, restful; *(langsam: Arbeitsweise, Spaziergang)* leisurely

Gerümpel [gə'rʏmpəl] *(-s) nt* junk

Gerüst [gə'rʏst] *(-(e)s, -e) nt (Baugerüst)* scaffold(ing); frame

gesalzen [gə'zaltsən] *pp von* **salzen** ♦ *adj (umg: Preis, Rechnung)* steep

gesamt [gə'zamt] *adj* whole, entire; *(Kosten)* total; *(Werke)* complete; **im G~en** all in all; **~deutsch** *adj* all-German; **G~eindruck** *m* general impression; **G~heit** *f* totality, whole; **G~schule** *f* ≈ comprehensive school

---

Gesamtschule

The **Gesamtschule** is a comprehensive school for pupils of different abilities. Traditionally pupils go to either a *Gymnasium*, *Realschule* or *Hauptschule*, depending on ability. The **Gesamtschule** seeks to avoid the elitism of many *Gymnasium*. However, these schools are still very controversial, with many parents still preferring the traditional education system.

---

gesandt [gə'zant] *vb siehe* **senden**

Gesandte(r) [gə'zantə(r)] *m* envoy

Gesandtschaft [gə'zantʃaft] *f* legation

Gesang [gə'zaŋ] *(-(e)s, -e) m* song; *(Singen)* singing; **~buch** *nt (REL)* hymn book

Gesäß [gə'zɛːs] *(-es, -e) nt* seat, bottom

Geschäft [gə'ʃɛft] *(-(e)s, -e) nt* business; *(Laden)* shop; *(~sabschluß)* deal; **g~ig** *adj* active, busy; *(pej)* officious; **g~lich** *adj* commercial ♦ *adv* on business

Geschäfts- *zW:* **~bedingungen** *pl* terms *pl* of business; **~bericht** *m* financial report; **~frau** *f* businesswoman; **~führer** *m* manager; *(Klub)* secretary; **~geheimnis** *nt* trade secret; **~jahr** *nt* financial year; **~lage** *f* business conditions *pl*; **~mann** *m* businessman; **g~mäßig** *adj* businesslike; **~partner** *m* business partner; **~reise** *f* business trip; **~schluss** ⚠ *m* closing time; **~stelle** *f* office, place of business; **g~tüchtig** *adj* business-minded; **~viertel** *nt* business quarter; shopping centre; **~wagen** *m* company car; **~zeit** *f* business hours *pl*

geschehen [gə'ʃeːən] *(unreg) vi* to happen; **es war um ihn ~** that was the end of him

gescheit [gə'ʃait] *adj* clever

Geschenk [gə'ʃɛŋk] *(-(e)s, -e) nt* present, gift

Geschichte [gə'ʃɪçtə] *f* story; *(Sache)* affair; *(Historie)* history

geschichtlich *adj* historical

Geschick [gə'ʃɪk] *(-(e)s, -e) nt* aptitude; *(Schicksal)* fate; **~lichkeit** *f* skill, dexterity; **g~t** *adj* skilful

geschieden [gə'ʃiːdən] *adj* divorced

geschienen [gə'ʃiːnən] *vb siehe* **schei-**

nen

Geschirr [gə'ʃɪr] (-(e)s, -e) nt crockery; pots and pans pl; (Pferdegeschirr) harness; **~spülmaschine** f dishwasher; **~spülmittel** nt washing-up liquid; **~tuch** nt dish cloth

Geschlecht [gə'ʃlɛçt] (-(e)s, -er) nt sex; (GRAM) gender; (Gattung) race; family; **g~lich** adj sexual

Geschlechts- zW: **~krankheit** f venereal disease; **~teil** nt genitals pl; **~verkehr** m sexual intercourse

geschlossen [gə'ʃlɔsən] adj shut ♦ vb siehe **schließen**

Geschmack [gə'ʃmak] (-(e)s, =e) m taste; **nach jds ~** to sb's taste; **~ finden an etw** akt to (come to) like sth; **g~los** adj tasteless; (fig) in bad taste; **~ssinn** m sense of taste; **g~voll** adj tasteful

geschmeidig [gə'ʃmaɪdɪç] adj supple; (formbar) malleable

Geschnetzelte(s) [gə'ʃnɛtsəltə(s)] nt (KOCH) strips of meat stewed to produce a thick sauce

geschnitten [gə'ʃnɪtən] vb siehe **schneiden**

Geschöpf [gə'ʃœpf] (-(e)s, -e) nt creature

Geschoss ▲ [gə'ʃɔs] (-es, -e) nt (MIL) projectile, missile; (Stockwerk) floor

geschossen [gə'ʃɔsən] vb siehe **schießen**

geschraubt [gə'ʃraopt] adj stilted, artificial

Geschrei [gə'ʃraɪ] (-s) nt cries pl, shouting; (fig: Aufheben) noise, fuss

geschrieben [gə'ʃriːbən] vb siehe **schreiben**

Geschütz [gə'ʃʏts] (-es, -e) nt gun, cannon; **ein schweres ~ auffahren** (fig) to bring out the big guns

geschützt adj protected

Geschw. abk siehe **Geschwister**

Geschwätz [gə'ʃvɛts] (-es) nt chatter,

gossip; **g~ig** adj talkative

geschweige [gə'ʃvaɪgə] adv: **~ (denn)** let alone, not to mention

geschwind [gə'ʃvɪnt] adj quick, swift; **G~igkeit** [-dɪçkaɪt] f speed, velocity; **G~igkeitsbeschränkung** f speed limit; **G~igkeitsüberschreitung** f exceeding the speed limit

Geschwister [gə'ʃvɪstɐ] pl brothers and sisters

geschwommen [gə'ʃvɔmən] vb siehe **schwimmen**

Geschworene(r) [gə'ʃvoːrənə(r)] f(m) juror; **~n** pl jury

Geschwulst [gə'ʃvʊlst] (-, =e) f swelling; growth, tumour

geschwungen [gə'ʃvʊŋən] pp von **schwingen** ♦ adj curved, arched

Geschwür [gə'ʃvyːr] (-(e)s, -e) nt ulcer

Gesell- [gə'zɛl] zW: **~e (-n, -n)** m fellow; (Handwerkgeselle) journeyman; **g~ig** adj sociable; **~igkeit** f sociability; **~schaft** f society; (Begleitung, COMM) company; (Abendgesellschaft etc) party; **g~schaftlich** adj social; **~schaftsordnung** f social structure; **~schaftsschicht** f social stratum

gesessen [gə'zɛsən] vb siehe **sitzen**

Gesetz [gə'zɛts] (-es, -e) nt law; **~buch** nt statute book; **~entwurf** m (draft) bill; **~gebung** f legislation; **g~lich** adj legal, lawful; **g~licher Feiertag** statutory holiday; **g~los** adj lawless; **g~mäßig** adj lawful; **g~t** adj (Mensch) sedate; **g~widrig** adj illegal, unlawful

Gesicht [gə'zɪçt] (-(e)s, -er) nt face; **das zweite ~** second sight; **das ist mir nie zu ~ gekommen** I've never laid eyes on that

Gesichts- zW: **~ausdruck** m (facial) expression; **~creme** f face cream; **~farbe** f complexion; **~punkt** m point of view; **~wasser** nt face lotion; **~züge** pl features

---

Spelling Reform: ▲ *new spelling* △ *old spelling (to be phased out)*

Gesindel [gəˈzɪndəl] (-s) nt rabble

gesinnt [gəˈzɪnt] adj disposed, minded

Gesinnung [gəˈzɪnʊŋ] f disposition; (Ansicht) views pl

gesittet [gəˈzɪtət] adj well-mannered

Gespann [gəˈʃpan] (-(e)s, -e) nt team; (umg) couple

gespannt adj tense, strained; (begierig) eager; **ich bin ~, ob** I wonder if od whether; **auf etw/jdn ~ sein** to look forward to sth/meeting sb

Gespenst [gəˈʃpɛnst] (-(e)s, -er) nt ghost, spectre

gesperrt [gəˈʃpɛrt] adj closed off

Gespött [gəˈʃpœt] (-(e)s) nt mockery; **zum ~ werden** to become a laughing stock

Gespräch [gəˈʃprɛːç] (-(e)s, -e) nt conversation; discussion(s); (Anruf) call; **g~ig** adj talkative

gesprochen [gəˈʃprɔxən] vb siehe **sprechen**

gesprungen [gəˈʃprʊŋən] vb siehe **springen**

Gespür [gəˈʃpyːr] (-s) nt feeling

Gestalt [gəˈʃtalt] (-, -en) f form, shape; (Person) figure; **in ~ von** in the form of; **~ annehmen** to take shape; **g~en** vt (formen) to shape, to form; (organisieren) to arrange, to organize ♦ vr: **sich g~en (zu)** to turn out (to be); **~ung** f formation; organization

gestanden [gəʃtandən] vb siehe **stehen**

Geständnis [gəˈʃtɛntnɪs] (-ses, -se) nt confession

Gestank [gəˈʃtaŋk] (-(e)s) m stench

gestatten [gəˈʃtatən] vt to permit, to allow; **~ Sie?** may I?; **sich** dat **~, etw zu tun** to take the liberty of doing sth

Geste [ˈgɛstə] f gesture

gestehen [gəˈʃteːən] (unreg) vt to confess

Gestein [gəˈʃtaın] (-(e)s, -e) nt rock

Gestell [gəˈʃtɛl] (-(e)s, -e) nt frame; (Regal) rack, stand

gestern [ˈgɛstərn] adv yesterday; **~**

Abend/Morgen yesterday evening/ morning

Gestirn [gəˈʃtɪrn] (-(e)s, -e) nt star; (Sternbild) constellation

gestohlen [gəˈʃtoːlən] vb siehe **stehlen**

gestorben [gəˈʃtɔrbən] vb siehe **sterben**

gestört [gəˈʃtœːrt] adj disturbed

gestreift [gəˈʃtraıft] adj striped

gestrichen [gəˈʃtrıçən] adj cancelled

gestrig [ˈgɛstrıç] adj yesterday's

Gestrüpp [gəˈʃtrʏp] (-(e)s, -e) nt undergrowth

Gestüt [gəˈʃtyːt] (-(e)s, -e) nt stud farm

Gesuch [gəˈzuːx] (-(e)s, -e) nt petition; (Antrag) application; **g~t** adj (COMM) in demand; wanted; (fig) contrived

gesund [gəˈzʊnt] adj healthy; **wieder ~ werden** to get better; **G~heit** f health(iness); **G~heit!** bless you!; **~heitlich** adj health attrib, physical ♦ adv: **wie geht es Ihnen ~heitlich?** how's your health?; **~heitsschädlich** adj unhealthy; **G~heitswesen** nt health service; **G~heitszustand** m state of health

gesungen [gəˈzʊŋən] vb siehe **singen**

getan [gəˈtaːn] vb siehe **tun**

Getöse [gəˈtøːzə] (-s) nt din, racket

Getränk [gəˈtrɛŋk] (-(e)s, -e) nt drink; **~ekarte** f wine list

getrauen [gəˈtrauən] vr to dare, to venture

Getreide [gəˈtraıdə] (-s, -) nt cereals pl, grain; **~speicher** m granary

getrennt [gəˈtrɛnt] adj separate

Getriebe [gəˈtriːbə] (-s, -) nt (Leute) bustle; (AUT) gearbox

getrieben vb siehe **treiben**

getroffen [gəˈtrɔfən] vb siehe **treffen**

getrost [gəˈtroːst] adv without any bother

getrunken [gəˈtrʊŋkən] vb siehe **trinken**

Getue [gəˈtuːə] (-s) nt fuss

geübt [gəˈʔyːpt] adj experienced

Gewächs [gəˈvɛks] (-es, -e) nt growth;

(Pflanze) plant

gewachsen [gəˈvaksən] *adj*: **jdm/etw ~ sein** to be sb's equal/equal to sth

Gewächshaus [gəˈvɛks-] *nt* greenhouse

gewagt [gəˈvaːkt] *adj* daring, risky

gewählt [gəˈvɛːlt] *adj (Sprache)* refined, elegant

Gewähr [gəˈvɛːr] *(-)* f guarantee; **keine ~ übernehmen für** to accept no responsibility for; **g~en** *vt* to grant; *(ge-ben)* to provide; **g~leisten** *vt* to guarantee

Gewahrsam [gəˈvaːrzaːm] *(-s, -e)* m safekeeping; *(Polizeigewahrsam)* custody

Gewalt [gəˈvalt] *(-, -en)* f power; *(große Kraft)* force; *(~taten)* violence; **mit aller ~** with all one's might; **~an-wendung** f use of force; **g~ig** *adj* tremendous; *(Irrtum)* huge; **~marsch** m forced march; **g~sam** *adj* forcible; **g~tätig** *adj* violent

Gewand [gəˈvant] *(-(e)s, ˝er)* nt gown, robe

gewandt [gəˈvant] *adj* deft, skilful; *(er-fahren)* experienced; **G~heit** f dexterity, skill

gewann *etc* [gəˈvan] *vb siehe* **gewin-nen**

Gewässer [gəˈvɛsər] *(-s, -)* nt waters pl

Gewebe [gəˈveːbə] *(-s, -)* nt *(Stoff)* fabric; *(BIOL)* tissue

Gewehr [gəˈveːr] *(-(e)s, -e)* nt gun; rifle; **~lauf** m rifle barrel

Geweih [gəˈvai] *(-(e)s, -e)* nt antlers pl

Gewerb- [gəˈverb] *zW:* **~e** *(-s, -)* nt trade, occupation; **Handel und ~** trade and industry; **~eschule** f technical school; **~ezweig** m line of trade

Gewerkschaft [gəˈverkʃaft] f trade union; **~ler** *(-s, -)* m trade unionist; **~sbund** m trade unions federation

gewesen [gəˈveːzən] *pp von* **sein**

Gewicht [gəˈvɪçt] *(-(e)s, -e)* nt weight; *(fig)* importance

gewieft [gəˈviːft] *adj* shrewd, cunning

gewillt [gəˈvɪlt] *adj* willing, prepared

Gewimmel [gəˈvɪməl] *(-s)* nt swarm

Gewinde [gəˈvɪndə] *(-s, -)* nt *(Kranz)* wreath; *(von Schraube)* thread

Gewinn [gəˈvɪn] *(-(e)s, -e)* m profit; *(bei Spiel)* winnings pl; **~ bringend** profitable; **etw mit ~ verkaufen** to sell sth at a profit; **~- und Verlust-rechnung** *(COMM)* profit and loss account; **~beteiligung** f profit-sharing; **g~en** *(unreg)* vt to win; *(erwerben)* to gain; *(Kohle, Öl)* to extract ♦ vi to win; *(profitieren)* to gain; **an etw** *dat* **g~en** to gain (in) sth; **g~end** *adj (Lächeln, Aussehen)* winning, charming; **~er(in)** *(-s, -)* m(f) winner; **~spanne** f profit margin; **~ung** f winning; gaining; *(von Kohle etc)* extraction

Gewirr [gəˈvɪr] *(-(e)s, -e)* nt tangle; *(von Straßen)* maze

gewiss ▲ [gəˈvɪs] *adj* certain ♦ *adv* certainly

Gewissen [gəˈvɪsən] *(-s, -)* nt conscience; **g~haft** *adj* conscientious; **g~los** *adj* unscrupulous

Gewissens- *zW:* **~bisse** pl pangs of conscience, qualms; **~frage** f matter of conscience; **~konflikt** m moral conflict

gewissermaßen [gəvɪsərˈmaːsən] *adv* more or less, in a way

Gewissheit ▲ [gəˈvɪshait] f certainty

Gewitter [gəˈvɪtər] *(-s, -)* nt thunder-storm; **g~n** *vi unpers*: **es g~t** there's a thunderstorm

gewitzt [gəˈvɪtst] *adj* shrewd, cunning

gewogen [gəˈvoːgən] *adj (+dat)* well-disposed (towards)

gewöhnen [gəˈvøːnən] *vt*: **jdn an etw** *akk* **~** to accustom sb to sth; *(erziehen zu)* to teach sb sth ♦ *vr*: **sich an etw** *akk* **~** to get used od accustomed to sth

Gewohnheit [gəˈvoːnhait] f habit;

(*Brauch*) custom; **aus ~** from habit; **zur ~ werden** to become a habit

Gewohnheits- zW: **~mensch** m creature of habit; **~recht** nt common law

gewöhnlich [gə'vø:nlɪç] adj usual; ordinary; (*pej*) common; **wie ~** as usual

gewohnt [gə'vo:nt] adj usual; **etw ~ sein** to be used to sth

Gewöhnung f: **~ (an +akk)** getting accustomed (to)

Gewölbe [gə'vœlbə] (-s, -) nt vault

gewollt [gə'vɔlt] adj affected, artificial

gewonnen [gə'vɔnən] vb siehe **gewinnen**

geworden [gə'vɔrdən] vb siehe **werden**

geworfen [gə'vɔrfən] vb siehe **werfen**

Gewühl [gə'vy:l] (-(e)s) nt throng

Gewürz [gə'vʏrts] (-es, -e) nt spice, seasoning; **g~t** adj spiced

gewusst ▲ [gə'vʊst] vb siehe **wissen**

Gezeiten [gə'tsaɪtən] pl tides

gezielt [gə'tsiːlt] adj with a particular aim in mind, purposeful; (*Kritik*) pointed

gezogen [gə'tsoːgən] vb siehe **ziehen**

Gezwitscher [gə'tsvɪtʃər] (-s) nt twitter(ing), chirping

gezwungen [gə'tsvʊŋən] adj forced; **~ermaßen** adv of necessity

ggf. abk von **gegebenenfalls**

gibst etc [giːpst] vb siehe **geben**

Gicht [gɪçt] (-) f gout

Giebel ['giːbəl] (-s, -) m gable; **~dach** nt gable(d) roof; **~fenster** nt gable window

Gier [giːr] (-) f greed; **g~ig** adj greedy

gießen ['giːsən] (unreg) vt to pour; (*Blumen*) to water; (*Metall*) to cast; (*Wachs*) to mould

Gießkanne f watering can

Gift [gɪft] (-(e)s, -e) nt poison; **g~ig** adj poisonous; (*fig: boshaft*) venomous; **~müll** m toxic waste; **~stoff** m toxic substance; **~zahn** m fang

ging etc [gɪŋ] vb siehe **gehen**

Gipfel ['gɪpfəl] (-s, -) m summit, peak; (*fig: Höhepunkt*) height; **g~n** vi to cul-

minate; **~treffen** nt summit meeting

Gips [gɪps] (-es, -e) m plaster; (*MED*) plaster (of Paris); **~abdruck** m plaster cast; **g~en** vt to plaster; **~verband** m plaster (cast)

Giraffe [gi'rafə] f giraffe

Girlande [gɪr'landə] f garland

Giro ['ʒiːro] (-s, -s) nt giro; **~konto** nt current account

Gitarre [gi'tarə] f guitar

Gitter ['gɪtər] (-s, -) nt grating, bars pl; (*für Pflanzen*) trellis; (*Zaun*) railing(s); **~bett** nt cot; **~fenster** nt barred window; **~zaun** m railing(s)

Glanz [glants] (-es) m shine, lustre; (*fig*) splendour

glänzen ['glɛntsən] vi to shine (*also fig*), to gleam ♦ vt to polish; **~d** adj shining; (*fig*) brilliant

Glanz- zW: **~leistung** f brilliant achievement; **g~los** adj dull; **~zeit** f heyday

Glas [glaːs] (-es, ⁻er) nt glass; **~er** (-s, -) m glazier; **~faser** f fibreglass; **g~ieren** [gla'ziːrən] vt to glaze; **g~ig** adj glassy; **~scheibe** f pane; **~ur** [gla'zuːr] f glaze; (*KOCH*) icing

glatt [glat] adj smooth; (*rutschig*) slippery; (*Absage*) flat; (*Lüge*) downright; **~gehen** (unreg) vi to go smoothly

Glätte f smoothness; slipperiness

Glatteis nt (black) ice; **jdn aufs ~ führen** (*fig*) to take sb for a ride

glätten vt to smooth out

Glatze ['glatsə] f bald head; **eine ~ bekommen** to go bald

Glaube ['glaubə] (-ns, -n) m: **~ (an +akk)** faith (in); belief (in); **g~n** vt, vi to believe; to think; **jdm g~n** to believe sb; **an etw akk g~n** to believe in sth; **daran g~n müssen** (umg) to be for it

glaubhaft ['glaubhaft] adj credible

gläubig ['glɔybɪç] adj (*REL*) devout; (*vertrauensvoll*) trustful; **G~e(r)** f(m) believer; **die G~en** the faithful; **G~er** (-s, -) m creditor

glaubwürdig ['glaubvʏrdɪç] adj credible; (*Mensch*) trustworthy; **G~keit** f credibility; trustworthiness

gleich [glaɪç] adj equal; (identisch) (the) same, identical ♦ adv equally; (sofort) straight away; (bald) in a minute; ~ **es ist mir** ~ it's all the same to me; ~ **bleibend** constant; ~ **gesinnt** likeminded; **2 mal 2 ~ 4** 2 times 2 is od equals 4; ~ **groß** the same size; ~ **nach/an** right after/at; ~**altrig** adj of the same age; ~**artig** adj similar; ~**bedeutend** adj synonymous; **G~berechtigung** f equal rights pl; ~**en** (unreg) vi: **jdm/etw** ~**en** to be like sb/sth ♦ vr to be alike; ~**falls** adv likewise; **danke** ~**falls!** the same to you; **G~förmigkeit** f uniformity; **G~gewicht** nt equilibrium, balance; ~**gültig** adj indifferent; (unbedeutend) unimportant; **G~gültigkeit** f indifference; **G~heit** f equality; ~**kommen** (unreg) vi +dat to be equal to; ~**mäßig** adj even, equal; ~**sam** adv as it were; **G~schritt** m: **im G~schritt gehen** to walk in step; ~**stellen** vt (rechtlich etc) to treat as (an) equal; **G~strom** m (ELEK) direct current; ~**tun** (unreg) vi: **es jdm** ~**tun** to match sb; **G~ung** f equation; ~**viel** adv no matter; ~**wertig** adj (Geld) of the same value; (Gegner) evenly matched; ~**zeitig** adj simultaneous

Gleis [glaɪs] (-es, -e) nt track, rails pl; (Bahnsteig) platform

gleiten ['glaɪtən] (unreg) vi to glide; (rutschen) to slide

Gleitzeit f flex(i)time

Gletscher ['glɛtʃər] (-s, -) m glacier; ~**spalte** f crevasse

Glied [gliːt] (-(e)s, -er) nt member; (Arm, Bein) limb; (von Kette) link; (MIL) rank(s); **g~ern** [-dərn] vt to organize, to structure; ~**erung** f structure, organization

glimmen ['glɪmən] (unreg) vi to glow, to gleam

glimpflich ['glɪmpflɪç] adj mild, lenient; ~ **davonkommen** to get off lightly

glitschig ['glɪtʃɪç] adj (Fisch, Weg) slippery

glitzern ['glɪtsərn] vi to glitter; to twinkle

global [glo'baːl] adj global

Globus ['gloːbʊs] (- od -ses, Globen od -se) m globe

Glocke ['glɔkə] f bell; **etw an die große** ~ **hängen** (fig) to shout sth from the rooftops

Glocken- zW: ~**blume** f bellflower; ~**geläut** nt peal of bells; ~**spiel** nt chime(s) (MUS) glockenspiel; ~**turm** m bell tower

Glosse ['glɔsə] f comment

glotzen ['glɔtsən] (umg) vi to stare

Glück [glyk] (-(e)s) nt luck, fortune; (Freude) happiness; ~ **haben** to be lucky; **viel** ~! good luck!; **zum** ~ fortunately; **g~en** vi to succeed; **es g~te ihm, es zu bekommen** he succeeded in getting it

gluckern ['glʊkərn] vi to glug

glück- zW: ~**lich** adj fortunate; (froh) happy; ~**licherweise** adv fortunately; ~'**selig** adj blissful

Glücks- zW: ~**fall** m stroke of luck; ~**kind** nt lucky person; ~**sache** f matter of luck; ~**spiel** nt game of chance

Glückwunsch m congratulations pl, best wishes pl

Glüh- ['glyː] zW: ~**birne** f light bulb; **g~en** vi to glow; ~**wein** m mulled wine; ~**würmchen** nt glow-worm

Glut [gluːt] (-, -en) f (Röte) glow; (Feuersglut) fire; (Hitze) heat; (fig) ardour

GmbH [geːˈʔɛmbeːˈhaː] f abk (= Gesellschaft mit beschränkter Haftung) limited company, Ltd

Gnade ['gnaːdə] f (Gunst) favour; (Erbarmen) mercy; (Milde) clemency

Gnaden- zW: **~frist** f reprieve, respite; **g~los** adj merciless; **~stoß** m coup de grâce

gnädig ['gnɛːdɪç] adj gracious; (voll Erbarmen) merciful

Gold [gɔlt] (-(e)s) nt gold; **g~en** adj golden; **~fisch** m goldfish; **~grube** f goldmine; **g~ig** ['gɔldɪç] (umg) adj (fig: allerliebst) sweet, adorable; **~regen** m laburnum; **~schmied** m goldsmith

Golf¹ [gɔlf] (-(e)s, -e) m gulf

Golf² [gɔlf] (-s) nt golf; **~platz** m golf course; **~schläger** m golf club

Golfstrom m Gulf Stream

Gondel ['gɔndəl] (-, -n) f gondola; (Seilbahn) cable car

gönnen ['gœnən] vt: jdm etw ~ not to begrudge sb sth; **sich** dat etw ~ to allow o.s. sth

Gönner (-s, -) m patron; **g~haft** adj patronizing

Gosse ['gɔsə] f gutter

Gott [gɔt] (-es, -er) m god; **mein ~!** for heaven's sake!; **um ~es willen!** for heaven's sake!; **grüß ~!** hello; ** weiß Dank!** thank God!; **~heit** f deity

Göttin ['gœtɪn] f goddess

göttlich adj divine

gottlos adj godless

Götze ['gœtsə] (-n, -n) m idol

Grab [graːp] (-(e)s, -er) nt grave; **g~en** ['graːbən] (unreg) vt to dig; **~en** (-s, -) m ditch; (MIL) trench; **~stein** m gravestone

Grad [graːt] (-(e)s, -e) m degree

Graf [graːf] (-en, -en) m count, earl

Grafiker(in) ▲ ['graːfɪkər(ɪn)] (-s, -) m(f) graphic designer

grafisch ▲ ['graːfɪʃ] adj graphic

Gram [graːm] (-(e)s) m grief, sorrow

grämen ['grɛːmən] vr to grieve

Gramm [gram] (-s, -e) nt gram(me)

Grammatik [gra'matɪk] f grammar

Granat [gra'naːt] (-(e)s, -e) m (Stein) garnet

Granate f (MIL) shell; (Handgranate) grenade

Granit [gra'niːt] (-s, -e) m granite

Gras [graːs] (-es, -er) nt grass; **g~en** ['graːzən] vi to graze; **~halm** m blade of grass

grassieren [gra'siːrən] vi to be rampant, to rage

grässlich ▲ ['grɛslɪç] adj horrible

Grat [graːt] (-(e)s, -e) m ridge

Gräte ['grɛːtə] f fishbone

gratis ['graːtɪs] adj, adv free (of charge); **G~probe** f free sample

Gratulation [gratulatsi'oːn] f congratulation(s)

gratulieren [gratu'liːrən] vi: jdm ~ (zu etw) to congratulate sb (on sth); **(ich) gratuliere!** congratulations!

grau [grau] adj grey

Gräuel ▲ ['grɔʏəl] (-s, -) m horror, revulsion; **etw ist jdm ein ~** sb loathes sth

Grauen (-s) nt horror; **g~** vi unpers: **es graut jdm vor etw** sb dreads sth, sb is afraid of sth ♦ vr: **sich g~ vor** to dread, to have a horror of; **g~haft** adj horrible

grauhaarig adj grey-haired

gräulich ▲ ['grɔʏlɪç] adj horrible

grausam ['grauzaːm] adj cruel; **G~keit** f cruelty

Grausen ['grauzən] (-s) nt horror; **g~** vb = grauen

gravieren [gra'viːrən] vt to engrave; **~d** adj grave

graziös [gratsi'øːs] adj graceful

greifbar adj tangible, concrete; **in ~er Nähe** within reach

greifen ['graɪfən] (unreg) vt to seize; to grip; **nach etw ~** to reach for sth; **um sich ~** (fig) to spread; **zu etw ~** (fig) to turn to sth

Greis [graɪs] (-es, -e) m old man; **g~enhaft** adj senile; **~in** f old woman

grell [grɛl] adj harsh

Grenz- ['grɛnts] zW: **~beamte(r)** m frontier official; **~e** f boundary; (Staatsgrenze) frontier; (Schranke) limit; **g~en** vi: **g~en (an** +akk) to border (on);

g~enlos adj boundless; **~fall** m borderline case; **~kontrolle** f border control; **~übergang** m frontier crossing

Greuel △ ['grɔyəl] (-s, -) m siehe **Gräuel**

greulich △ siehe **gräulich**

Griech- ['griːç] zW: **~e** (-n, -n) m Greek; **~enland** nt Greece; **~in** f Greek; **g~isch** adj Greek

griesgrämig ['griːsgrɛːmɪç] adj grumpy

Grieß [griːs] (-es, -e) m (KOCH) semolina

Griff [grɪf] (-(e)s, -e) m grip; (Vorrichtung) handle; **g~bereit** adj handy

Grill [grɪl] m grill; **~e** f cricket; **g~en** vt to grill; **~fest** nt barbecue party

Grimasse [grɪ'masə] f grimace

grimmig ['grɪmɪç] adj furious; (heftig) fierce, severe

grinsen ['grɪnzən] vi to grin

Grippe ['grɪpə] f influenza, flu

grob [groːp] adj coarse, gross; (Fehler, Verstoß) gross; **G~heit** f coarseness; coarse expression

grölen ['grøːlən] (pej) vt to bawl, to bellow

Groll [grɔl] (-(e)s) m resentment; **g~en** vi (Donner) to rumble; **g~en** (mit od +dat) to bear ill will (towards)

groß [groːs] adj big, large; (hoch) tall; (fig) great ♦ adv greatly; **im G~en und Ganzen** on the whole; **bei jdm ~geschrieben werden** to be high on sb's list of priorities; **~artig** adj great, splendid; **G~aufnahme** f (CINE) close-up; **G~britannien** nt Great Britain

Größe ['grøːsə] f size; (Höhe) height; (fig) greatness

Groß- zW: **~einkauf** m bulk purchase; **~eltern** pl grandparents; **g~enteils** adv mostly; **~format** nt large size; **~handel** m wholesale trade; **~händler** m wholesaler; **~macht** f great power; **~mutter** f grandmother; **~rechner** m

mainframe (computer); **g~schreiben** (unreg) vt (Wort) to write in block capitals; siehe **groß**; **g~spurig** adj pompous; **~stadt** f city, large town

größte(r, s) [grøːstə(r, s)] adj superl von groß; **~nteils** adv for the most part

Groß- zW: **g~tun** (unreg) vi to boast; **~vater** m grandfather; **g~ziehen** (unreg) vt to raise; **g~zügig** adj generous; (Planung) on a large scale

grotesk [gro'tɛsk] adj grotesque

Grotte ['grɔtə] f grotto

Grübchen ['gryːpçən] nt dimple

Grube ['gruːbə] f pit; mine

grübeln ['gryːbəln] vi to brood

Gruft [gruft] (-, "e) f tomb, vault

grün [gryːn] adj green; **der ~e Punkt** green spot symbol on recyclable packaging

---

grüner Punkt

The grüner Punkt is a green spot which appears on packaging that should be kept separate from normal household refuse to be recycled through the recycling company, DSD (Duales System Deutschland). The recycling is financed by licences bought by the packaging manufacturer from DSD. These costs are often passed on to the consumer.

Grünanlage f park

Grund [grʊnt] (-(e)s, "e) m ground; (von See, Gefäß) bottom; (fig) reason; **im ~e genommen** basically; siehe **aufgrund**; **~ausbildung** f basic training; **~besitz** m land(ed property), real estate; **~buch** nt land register

gründen ['gryndən] vt to found ♦ vr: **sich ~ auf** (+dat) to be based (on); vr: **auf +akk** to base on

Gründer (-s, -) m founder

Grund- zW: **~gebühr** f basic charge; **~gesetz** nt constitution; **~lage** f foun-

---

dation; **g~legend** adj fundamental
gründlich adj thorough
Grund- zW: **g~los** adj groundless; **~regel** f basic rule; **~riss** ▲ m plan; (fig) outline; **~satz** m principle; **g~sätzlich** adj fundamental; (Frage) of principle ♦ adv fundamentally; (prinzipiell) on principle; **~schule** f elementary school; **~stein** m foundation stone; **~stück** nt estate; plot
Grundwasser nt ground water

Grundschule

The Grundschule is a primary school which children attend for 4 years from the age of 6 to 10. There are no formal examinations in the Grundschule but parents receive a report on their child's progress twice a year. Many children attend a Kindergarten from 3-6 years before going to the Grundschule, though no formal instruction takes place in the Kindergarten.

Grünstreifen m central reservation
grunzen ['grʊntsən] vi to grunt
Gruppe ['grʊpə] f group; **~nermäßigung** f group reduction; **g~nweise** adv in groups
gruppieren [grʊ'piːrən] vt, vr to group
gruselig adj creepy
gruseln ['gruːzəln] vi unpers: **es gruselt jdm vor etw** sth gives sb the creeps ♦ vr to have the creeps
Gruß [gruːs] (**-es**, **⁀e**) m greeting; (MIL) salute; **viele Grüße** best wishes; **mit freundlichen Grüßen** yours sincerely; **Grüße an** +akk regards to
grüßen ['gryːsən] vt to greet; (MIL) to salute; **jdn von jdm ~** to give sb sb's regards; **jdn ~ lassen** to send sb one's regards
gucken ['gʊkən] vi to look
gültig ['gʏltɪç] adj valid; **G~keit** f validity
Gummi ['gʊmi] (**-s**, **-s**) nt od m rubber;

(~harze) gum; **~band** nt rubber od elastic band; (Hosenband) elastic; **~bärchen** nt ≈ jelly baby (BRIT); **~baum** m rubber plant; **g~eren** [gu'miːrən] vt to gum; **~stiefel** m rubber boot
günstig ['gʏnstɪç] adj convenient; (Gelegenheit) favourable; **das habe ich ~ bekommen** it was a bargain
Gurgel ['gʊrgəl] (**-**, **-n**) f throat; **g~n** vi to gurgle; (im Mund) to gargle
Gurke ['gʊrkə] f cucumber; **saure ~** pickled cucumber, gherkin
Gurt [gʊrt] (**-(e)s**, **-e**) m belt
Gürtel ['gʏrtəl] (**-s**, **-**) m belt; (GEOG) zone; **~reifen** m radial tyre
GUS f abk (= Gemeinschaft unabhängiger Staaten) CIS
Guss ▲ [gʊs] (**-es**, **⁀e**) m casting; (Regenguss) downpour; (KOCH) glazing; **~eisen** nt cast iron

---

gut adj good; **alles Gute** all the best; **also gut** all right then
♦ adv well; **gut gehen** to work, to come off; **es geht jdm gut** sb's doing fine; **gut gemeint** well meant; **gut schmecken** to taste good; **jdm gut tun** to do sb good; **gut, aber ...** OK, but ...; (na) **gut, ich komme** all right, I'll come; **gut drei Stunden** a good three hours; **das kann gut sein** that may well be; **lass es gut sein** that'll do

---

Gut [guːt] (**-(e)s**, **⁀er**) nt (Besitz) possession; **Güter** pl (Waren) goods; **~achten** (**-s**, **-**) nt (expert) opinion; **~achter** (**-s**, **-**) m expert; **g~artig** adj good-natured; (MED) benign; **g~bürgerlich** adj (Küche) (good) plain; **~dünken** nt: **nach ~dünken** at one's discretion
Güte ['gyːtə] f goodness, kindness; (Qualität) quality
Güter- zW: **~abfertigung** f (EISENB)

goods office; **~bahnhof** m goods station; **~wagen** m goods waggon (BRIT), freight car (US); **~zug** m goods train (BRIT), freight train (US)

Gütezeichen nt quality mark; ≃ kite mark

gut- zW: **~gehen** △ (unreg) vi unpers siehe gut; **~gemeint** △ adj siehe gut; **~gläubig** adj trusting; **G~haben** (-s) nt credit; **~heißen** (unreg) vt to approve (of)

gütig ['gy:tɪç] adj kind

Gut- zW: **g~mütig** adj good-natured; **~schein** m voucher; **g~schreiben** (unreg) vt to credit; **~schrift** f (Betrag) credit; **g~tun** △ (unreg) vi siehe gut; **g~willig** adj willing

Gymnasium [gʏm'na:ziʊm] nt grammar school (BRIT), high school (US)

Gymnasium

The Gymnasium is a selective secondary school. After nine years of study pupils sit the Abitur so they can go on to higher education. Pupils who successfully complete six years at a Gymnasium automatically gain the mittlere Reife.

Gymnastik [gʏm'nastɪk] f exercises pl, keep fit

H, h

Haag [ha:k] m: **Den ~** the Hague

Haar [ha:r] (-(e)s, -e) nt hair; **um ein ~** nearly; **an den ~en herbeigezogen** (umg: Vergleich) very far-fetched; **~bürste** f hairbrush; **h~en** vi, vr to lose hair; **~esbreite** f: **um ~esbreite** by a hair's-breadth; **~festiger** (-s, -) m (hair) setting lotion; **h~genau** adv precisely; **h~ig** adj hairy; **h~klammer** f hairgrip; **~nadel** f hair-

pin; **h~scharf** adv (beobachten) very sharply; (daneben) by a hair's breadth; **~schnitt** m haircut; **~spange** f hair slide; **h~sträubend** adj hair-raising; **~teil** nt hairpiece; **~waschmittel** nt shampoo

Habe ['ha:bə] (-) f property

haben ['ha:bən] (unreg) vt, vb aux to have; **Hunger/Angst ~** to be hungry/afraid; **woher hast du das?** where did you get that from?; **was hast du denn?** what's the matter (with you)?; **du hast zu schweigen** you're to be quiet; **ich hätte gern I** would like; **H~** (-s, -) nt credit

Habgier f avarice; **h~ig** adj avaricious

Habicht ['ha:bɪçt] (-s, -e) m hawk

Habseligkeiten ['ha:psze:lɪçkaɪtən] pl belongings

Hachse ['haksə] f (KOCH) knuckle

Hacke ['hakə] f hoe; (Ferse) heel; **h~n** vt to hack, to chop; (Erde) to hoe

Hackfleisch nt mince, minced meat

Hafen ['ha:fən] (-s, ᵂ) m harbour, port; **~arbeiter** m docker; **~rundfahrt** f boat trip round the harbour; **~stadt** f port

Hafer ['ha:fər] (-s, -) m oats pl; **~flocken** pl rolled oats; **~schleim** m gruel

Haft [haft] (-) f custody; **h~bar** adj liable, responsible; **~befehl** m warrant (for arrest); **h~en** vi to stick, to cling; **h~en für** to be liable of responsible for; **h~en bleiben** (+dat) to stick (to); **~häftling** m prisoner; **~pflicht** f liability; **~pflichtversicherung** f (AUT) third party insurance; **~schalen** pl contact lenses; **~ung** f liability; **~ungsbeschränkung** f limitation of liability

Hagebutte ['ha:gəbʊtə] f rose hip

Hagel ['ha:gəl] (-s) m hail; **h~n** vi unpers to hail

hager ['ha:gər] adj gaunt

Hahn [ha:n] (-(e)s, ᵂe) m cock; (Wasser-

hahn) tap, faucet (*US*)

Hähnchen ['hɛːnçən] *nt* cockerel; (*KOCH*) chicken

Hai(fisch) ['hai(fɪʃ)] (-(e)s, -e) *m* shark

häkeln ['hɛːkəln] *vt* to crochet

Haken ['haːkən] (-s, -) *m* hook; (*fig*) catch; **~kreuz** *nt* swastika; **~nase** *f* hooked nose

halb [halp] *adj* half; **~ eins** half past twelve; **~ offen** half-open; **ein ~es Dutzend** half a dozen; **H~dunkel** *nt* semi-darkness

halber ['halbər] *präp +gen (wegen)* on account of; *(für)* for the sake of

Halb- *zW:* **~heit** *f* half-measure; **h~ieren** *vt* to halve; **~insel** *f* peninsula; **~jahr** *nt* six months; (*auch: COMM*) half-year; **h~jährlich** *adj* half-yearly; **~kreis** *m* semicircle; **~leiter** *m* semiconductor; **~mond** *m* half-moon; (*fig*) crescent; **~pension** *f* half-board; **~rechte(r)** *mf* (*SPORT*) inside right; **~schuh** *m* shoe; **h~tags** *adv:* **h~tags arbeiten** to work part-time, to work mornings/afternoons; **h~wegs** *adv* halfway; **h~wegs besser** more or less better; **~zeit** *f* (*SPORT*) half; (*Pause*) half-time

Halde ['haldə] *f* (*Kohlen*) heap

half [half] *vb siehe* **helfen**

Hälfte ['hɛlftə] *f* half

Halfter ['halftər] (-s, -) *m od nt* (*für Tiere*) halter

Halle ['halə] *f* hall; (*AVIAT*) hangar; **h~n** *vi* to echo, to resound; **~nbad** *nt* indoor swimming pool

hallo [ha'loː] *excl* hello

Halluzination [halutsinatsi'oːn] *f* hallucination

Halm ['halm] (-(e)s, -e) *m* blade; stalk

Halogenlampe [halo'geːnlampə] *f* halogen lamp

Hals [hals] (-es, ⁼e) *m* neck; (*Kehle*) throat; **~ über Kopf** in a rush; **~band** *nt* (*von Hund*) collar; **~kette** *f* necklace; **~-Nasen-Ohren-Arzt** *m* ear, nose and throat specialist; **~schmerzen** *pl*

sore throat *sg*; **~tuch** *nt* scarf

Halt [halt] (-(e)s, -e) *m* stop; (*fester ~*) hold; (*innerer ~*) stability; **~ od h~!** stop!, halt!; **~ machen** to stop; **h~bar** *adj* durable; (*Lebensmittel*) non-perishable; (*MIL, fig*) tenable; **~barkeit** *f* durability; (non-)perishability

halten ['haltən] (*unreg*) *vt* to keep; (*festhalten*) to hold ♦ *vi* to hold; (*frisch bleiben*) to keep; (*stoppen*) to stop ♦ *vr* (*frisch bleiben*) to keep; (*sich behaupten*) to hold out; **~ für** to regard as; **~ von** to think of; **an sich ~** to restrain o.s.; **sich rechts/links ~** to keep to the right/left

Halte- *zW:* **~stelle** *f* stop; **~verbot** *nt:* **hier ist ~verbot** there's no waiting here

Halt- *zW:* **~los** *adj* unstable; **h~machen** △ *vi siehe* **Halt**; **~ung** *f* posture; (*fig*) attitude; (*Selbstbeherrschung*) composure

Halunke [ha'luŋkə] (-n, -n) *m* rascal

hämisch ['hɛːmɪʃ] *adj* malicious

Hammel ['haməl] (-s, ⁼ *od* -s) *m* wether; **~fleisch** *nt* mutton

Hammer ['hamər] (-s, ⁼) *m* hammer

hämmern ['hɛmərn] *vt, vi* to hammer

Hämorr(ho)iden [hɛmɔro'iːdən, hɛmɔ'riːdən] *pl* haemorrhoids

Hamster ['hamstər] (-s, -) *m* hamster; **~ei** [-'rai] *f* hoarding; **h~n** *vi* to hoard

Hand [hant] (-, ⁼e) *f* hand; **~arbeit** *f* manual work; (*Nadelarbeit*) needlework; **~ball** *m* (*SPORT*) handball; **~bremse** *f* handbrake; **~buch** *nt* handbook, manual

Händedruck ['hɛndədrʊk] *m* handshake

Handel ['handəl] (-s) *m* trade; (*Geschäft*) transaction

Handeln ['handəln] (-s) *nt* action

handeln ['handəln] *vi* to trade; (*agieren*) to act ♦ *vr unpers:* **sich ~ um** to be a question of, to be about; **~ von** to be about

Handels- *zW:* **~bilanz** *f* balance of

trade; **~kammer** f chamber of commerce; **~reisende(r)** m commercial traveller; **~schule** f business school; **h~üblich** adj customary; (Preis) going attrib; **~vertreter** m sales representative

Hand- zW: **~feger** (-s, -) m hand brush; **h~fest** adj hefty; **h~gearbeitet** adj handmade; **~gelenk** nt wrist; **~gemenge** nt scuffle; **~gepäck** nt hand luggage; **h~geschrieben** adj handwritten; **h~greiflich** adj palpable; **h~greiflich werden** to become violent; **~griff** m flick of the wrist; **h~haben** vt insep to handle

Händler ['hɛndlər] (-s, -) m trader, dealer

handlich ['hantlɪç] adj handy

Handlung ['handlʊŋ] f act(ion); (in Buch) plot; (Geschäft) shop

Hand- zW: **~schelle** f handcuff; **~schrift** f handwriting; (Text) manuscript; **~schuh** m glove; **~stand** m (SPORT) handstand; **~tasche** f handbag; **~tuch** nt towel; **~umdrehen** nt: **im ~umdrehen** in the twinkling of an eye; **~werk** nt trade, craft; **~werker** (-s, -) m craftsman, artisan; **~werkzeug** nt tools pl

Handy ['hɛndi] (-s, -s) nt mobile (telephone)

Hanf [hanf] (-(e)s) m hemp

Hang [haŋ] (-(e)s, ⁼e) m inclination; (Abhang) slope

Hänge- ['hɛŋə] in zW hanging; **~brücke** f suspension bridge; **~matte** f hammock

hängen ['hɛŋən] (unreg) vi to hang ♦ vt: etw (an etw akk) ~ to hang sth (on sth); ~ an +dat (fig) to be attached to; **sich ~ an** +akk to hang on to, to cling to; ~ **bleiben** to be caught, to stick; ~ **bleiben an** +dat to catch od get caught on; ~ **lassen** (vergessen) to leave; **den Kopf ~ lassen** to get downhearted

hänseln ['hɛnzəln] vt to tease

Hansestadt ['hanzəʃtat] f Hanse town

hantieren [han'tiːrən] vi to work, to be busy; **mit etw ~** to handle sth

hapern ['haːpərn] vi unpers: **es hapert an etw** dat there is a lack of sth

Happen ['hapən] (-s, -) m mouthful

Harfe ['harfə] f harp

Harke ['harkə] f rake; **h~n** vt, vi to rake

harmlos ['harmloːs] adj harmless; **H~igkeit** f harmlessness

Harmonie [harmo'niː] f harmony; **h~ren** vi to harmonize

harmonisch [har'moːnɪʃ] adj harmonious

Harn [harn] (-(e)s, -e) m urine; **~blase** f bladder

Harpune [har'puːnə] f harpoon

harren ['harən] vi: ~ (**auf** +akk) to wait (for)

hart [hart] adj hard; (fig) harsh; ~ **gekocht** hard-boiled

Härte ['hɛrtə] f hardness; (fig) harshness

hart- zW: **~herzig** adj hard-hearted; **~näckig** adj stubborn

Harz [haːrts] (-es, -e) nt resin

Haschee [ha'ʃeː] (-s, -s) nt hash

Haschisch ['haʃɪʃ] (-) nt hashish

Hase ['haːzə] (-n, -n) m hare

Haselnuss ▲ ['haːzəlnʊs] f hazelnut

Hasenscharte f harelip

Hass ▲ [has] (-es) m hate, hatred

hassen ['hasən] vt to hate

hässlich ▲ ['hɛslɪç] adj ugly; (gemein) nasty; **H~keit** f ugliness; nastiness

Hast [hast] f haste

hast vb siehe **haben**

hasten vi to rush

hastig adj hasty

hat [hat] vb siehe **haben**

hatte etc ['hatə] vb siehe **haben**

Haube ['haubə] f hood; (Mütze) cap;

Spelling Reform: ▲ new spelling △ old spelling (to be phased out)

(AUT) bonnet, hood (US)

Hauch [haʊx] (-(e)s, -e) m breath; (Lufthauch) breeze; (fig) trace; **h~dünn** adj extremely thin

Haue ['haʊə] f hoe, pick; (umg) hiding; **h~n** (unreg) vt to hew, to cut; (umg) to thrash

Haufen ['haʊfən] (-s, -) m heap; (Leute) crowd; **ein ~ (x)** (umg) loads od a lot (of x); **auf einem ~** in one heap

häufen ['hɔʏfən] vt to pile up ♦ vr to accumulate

haufenweise adv in heaps; in droves; **etw ~ haben** to have piles of sth

häufig ['hɔʏfɪç] adj frequent ♦ adv frequently; **H~keit** f frequency

Haupt [haʊpt] (-(e)s, Häupter) nt head; (Oberhaupt) chief ♦ in zW main; **~bahnhof** m central station; **h~beruflich** adv as one's main occupation; **~darsteller(in)** m(f) leading actor (actress); **~fach** nt (SCH, UNIV) main subject, major (US); **~gericht** nt (KOCH) main course

Häuptling ['hɔʏptlɪŋ] m chief(tain)

Haupt- zW: **~mann** (pl -leute) m (MIL) captain; **~person** f central figure; **~quartier** nt headquarters pl; **~rolle** f leading part; **~sache** f main thing; **h~sächlich** adj chief ♦ adv chiefly; **~saison** f high season, peak season; **~schule** f ≃ secondary school; **~stadt** f capital; **~straße** f main street; **~verkehrszeit** f rush-hour, peak traffic hours pl

---

Hauptschule

The Hauptschule is a non-selective school which pupils may attend after the Grundschule. They complete five years of study and most go on to do some vocational training.

Haus [haʊs] (-es, Häuser) nt house; **h~halten** (sparen) to economize; **nach ~e** home; **zu ~e** at home; **~apotheke** f medicine cabinet; **~arbeit** f house-

work; (SCH) homework; **~arzt** m family doctor; **~aufgabe** f (SCH) homework; **~besitzer(in)** m(f) house owner; **~besuch** m (von Arzt) house call; **~durchsuchung** f police raid; **h~eigen** adj belonging to a/the hotel/firm

Häuser- ['hɔʏzər] zW: **~block** m block (of houses); **~makler** m estate agent (BRIT), real estate agent (US)

Haus- zW: **~flur** m hallway; **~frau** f housewife; **h~gemacht** adj homemade; **~halt** m household; (POL) budget; **h~halten** (unreg) vi △ siehe **Haus**; **~hälterin** f housekeeper; **~haltsgeld** nt housekeeping (money); **~haltsgerät** nt domestic appliance; **~herr** m host; (Vermieter) landlord; **h~hoch** adv: **h~hoch verlieren** to lose by a mile

hausieren [haʊˈziːrən] vi to peddle

Hausierer (-s, -) m pedlar (BRIT), peddler (US)

häuslich ['hɔʏslɪç] adj domestic

Haus- zW: **~meister** m caretaker, janitor; **~nummer** f street number; **~ordnung** f house rules pl; **~putz** m house cleaning; **~schlüssel** m front door key; **~schuh** m slipper; **~tier** nt pet; **~tür** f front door; **~wirt** m landlord; **~wirtschaft** f domestic science; **~zelt** nt frame tent

Haut [haʊt] (-, Häute) f skin; (Tierhaut) hide; **~creme** f skin cream; **h~eng** adj skin-tight; **~farbe** f complexion; **~krebs** m skin cancer

Haxe ['haksə] f = **Hachse**

Hbf. abk = **Hauptbahnhof**

Hebamme ['heːpʔamə] f midwife

Hebel ['heːbəl] (-s, -) m lever

heben ['heːbən] (unreg) vt to raise, to lift

Hecht [hɛçt] (-(e)s, -e) m pike

Heck [hɛk] (-(e)s, -e) nt stern; (von Auto) rear

Hecke ['hɛkə] f hedge

Heckenschütze m sniper

Heckscheibe f rear window

Heer [heːɐ] (-(e)s, -e) *nt* army

Hefe ['heːfə] *f* yeast

Heft ['hɛft] (-(e)s, -e) *nt* exercise book; (Zeitschrift) number; (von Messer) haft; **h~en** *vt*: **h~en (an** +akk) to fasten (to); (nähen) to tack ((on) to); **etw an etw** akk **h~en** to fasten sth to sth; **~er** (-s, -) *m* folder

heftig *adj* fierce, violent; **H~keit** *f* fierceness, violence

Heft- zW: **~klammer** *f* paper clip; **~pflaster** *nt* sticking plaster; **~zwecke** *f* drawing pin

hegen ['heːgən] *vt* (Wild, Bäume) to care for, to tend; (fig, geh: empfinden: Wunsch) to cherish; (: Misstrauen) to feel

Hehl [heːl] *m od nt*: **kein(en) ~ aus etw machen** to make no secret of sth; **~er** (-s, -) *m* receiver (of stolen goods), fence

Heide[1] ['haɪdə] (-n, -n) *m* heathen, pagan

Heide[2] ['haɪdə] *f* heath, moor; **~kraut** *nt* heather

Heidelbeere *f* bilberry

Heidentum *nt* paganism

Heidin *f* heathen, pagan

heikel ['haɪkəl] *adj* awkward, thorny

Heil [haɪl] (-(e)s) *nt* well-being; (Seelenheil) salvation; **h~** *adj* in one piece, intact; **~and** (-(e)s, -e) *m* saviour; **h~bar** *adj* curable; **h~en** *vt* to cure ♦ *vi* to heal; **h~froh** *adj* very relieved

heilig ['haɪlɪç] *adj* holy; **~ sprechen** to canonize; **H~abend** *m* Christmas Eve; **H~e(r)** f(m) saint; **~en** *vt* to sanctify, to hallow; **H~enschein** *m* halo; **H~keit** *f* holiness; **H~tum** *nt* shrine; (Gegenstand) relic

Heil- zW: **h~los** *adj* unholy; (fig) hopeless; **~mittel** *nt* remedy; **~praktiker(in)** m(f) non-medical practitioner; **h~sam** *adj* (fig) salutary; **~sarmee** *f* Salvation Army; **~ung** *f* cure

Heim [haɪm] (-(e)s, -e) *nt* home; **h~** *adv* home

Heimat ['haɪmaːt] (-, -en) *f* home (town/country etc); **~land** *nt* homeland; **h~lich** *adj* native, home attrib; (Gefühle) nostalgic; **h~los** *adj* homeless; **~ort** *m* home town/area

Heim- zW: **~computer** *m* home computer; **h~fahren** (unreg) *vi* to drive home; **~fahrt** *f* journey home; **h~gehen** (unreg) *vi* to go home; (sterben) to pass away; **h~isch** *adj* (gebürtig) native; **sich h~isch fühlen** to feel at home; **~kehr** (-, -en) *f* homecoming; **h~kehren** *vi* to return home; **h~lich** *adj* secret; **~lichkeit** *f* secrecy; **~reise** *f* journey home; **~spiel** *nt* (SPORT) home game; **h~suchen** *vt* to afflict; (Geist) to haunt; **~trainer** *m* exercise bike; **h~tückisch** *adj* malicious; **~weg** *m* way home; **~weh** *nt* homesickness; **~werker** (-s, -) *m* handyman; **h~zahlen** *vt*: **jdm etw h~zahlen** to pay sb back for sth

Heirat ['haɪraːt] (-, -en) *f* marriage; **h~en** *vt* to marry ♦ *vi* to marry, to get married ♦ *vi* to get married; **~santrag** *m* proposal

heiser ['haɪzɐ] *adj* hoarse; **H~keit** *f* hoarseness

heiß [haɪs] *adj* hot; **~e(s) Eisen** (umg) hot potato; **~blütig** *adj* hot-blooded

heißen ['haɪsən] (unreg) *vi* to be called; (bedeuten) to mean ♦ *vt* to command; (nennen) to name ♦ *vi unpers*: **es heißt** it says; it is said; **das heißt** that is (to say)

Heiß- zW: **~hunger** *m* ravenous hunger; **h~laufen** (unreg) *vi, vr* to overheat

heiter ['haɪtɐ] *adj* cheerful; (Wetter) bright; **H~keit** *f* cheerfulness; (Belustigung) amusement

Heiz- ['haɪts] zW: **h~bar** *adj* heated; (Raum) with heating; **h~en** *vt* to heat; **~körper** *m* radiator; **~öl** *nt* fuel oil;

Spelling Reform: ▲ *new spelling* △ *old spelling (to be phased out)*

~sonne f electric fire; **~ung** f heating
hektisch ['hɛktɪʃ] adj hectic
Held [hɛlt] (-en, -en) m hero;
h~enhaft adj heroic; **~in** f heroine
helfen ['hɛlfən] (unreg) vi to help;
(nützen) to be of use ♦ vb unpers: es
hilft nichts, du musst ... it's no use,
you'll have to ...; **jdm (bei etw)** ~ to
help sb (with sth); **sich** dat **zu** ~ **wissen** to be resourceful
Helfer (-s, -) m helper, assistant;
~shelfer m accomplice
hell [hɛl] adj clear, bright; (Farbe, Bier)
light; **~blau** adj light blue; **~blond** adj
ash blond; **H~e (-)** f clearness, bright-
ness; **~hörig** adj (Wand) paper-thin;
~hörig werden (fig) to prick up one's
ears; **H~seher** m clairvoyant; **~wach**
adj wide-awake
Helm [hɛlm] (-(e)s, -e) m helmet
Hemd [hɛmt] (-(e)s, -en) nt shirt; (Unterhemd) vest; **~bluse** f blouse
hemmen ['hɛmən] vt to check, to
hold up; **gehemmt sein** to be inhibited; **Hemmung** f check; (PSYCH) inhi-
bition; **hemmungslos** adj unre-
strained, without restraint
Hengst [hɛŋst] (-es, -e) m stallion
Henkel ['hɛŋkəl] (-s, -) m handle
Henker (-s, -) m hangman
Henne ['hɛnə] f hen

SCHLÜSSELWORT
---

her [heːr] adv 1 (Richtung): **komm her
zu mir** come here (to me); **von England her** from England; **von weit her**
from a long way away; **her damit!**
hand it over!; **wo hat er das her?**
where did he get that from?
2 (Blickpunkt): **von der Form her** as far
as the form is concerned
3 (zeitlich): **das ist 5 Jahre her** that
was 5 years ago; **wo bist du her?**
where do you come from?; **ich kenne
ihn von früher her** I know him from
before

herab [hɛˈrap] adv down(ward(s));
~hängen (unreg) vi to hang down;
~lassen (unreg) vt to let down ♦ vr to
condescend; **~lassend** adj condescending; **~setzen** vt to lower, to reduce; (fig) to belittle, to disparage
heran [hɛˈran] adv: **näher** ~! come up
closer!; ~ **zu mir!** come up to me!;
~bringen (unreg) vt: **~bringen (an**
+akk) to bring up (to); **~fahren** (unreg)
vi: **~fahren (an** +akk) to drive up (to);
~kommen (unreg) vi: **~kommen (an
+akk/jdn/etw)** to approach (sb/sth), to
come near (to sb/sth); **~machen** vr:
sich an jdn ~machen to make up to
sb; **~treten** (unreg) vi: **mit etw an jdn
~treten** to approach sb with sth;
~wachsen (unreg) vi to grow up;
~ziehen (unreg) vt to pull nearer; (aufziehen) to raise; (ausbilden) to train;
jdn zu etw ~ziehen to call upon sb to
help in sth

herauf [hɛˈrauf] adv up(ward(s)), up
here; **~beschwören** (unreg) vt to conjure up, to evoke; **~bringen** (unreg) vt
to bring up; **~setzen** vt (Preise, Miete)
to raise, put up

heraus [hɛˈraus] adv out; **~bekom-
men** (unreg) vt to get out; (fig) to find
od figure out; **~bringen** (unreg) vt to
bring out; (Geheimnis) to elicit;
~finden (unreg) vt to find out; **~for-
dern** vt to challenge; **H~forderung** f
challenge; provocation; **~geben** (unreg) vt to hand over, to surrender; (zurückgeben) to give back; (Buch) to edit;
(veröffentlichen) to publish; **H~geber
(-s, -)** m editor; (Verleger) publisher;
~gehen (unreg) vi: **aus sich ~gehen** to
come out of one's shell; **~halten** (unreg) vr: **sich aus etw ~halten** to keep
out of sth; **~hängen¹** vt to hang out;
~hängen² vi to hang out;
~holen vt: **~holen (aus)** to get out
(of); **~kommen** (unreg) vi to come
out; **dabei kommt nichts ~** nothing

will come of it; **~nehmen** (unreg) vt to remove (from), take out (of); **sich** dat etw **~nehmen** to take liberties; **~rei-ßen** (unreg) vt to tear out; to pull out; **~rücken** vt (Geld) to fork out, to hand over; **mit** etw **~rücken** (fig) to come out with sth; **~stellen** vr: **sich ~stellen (als)** to turn out (to be); **~suchen** vt: **sich** dat jdn/etw **~suchen** to pick sb/sth out; **~ziehen** (unreg) vt to pull out, to extract

herb [hɛrp] adj (slightly) bitter, acid; (Wein) dry; (fig: schmerzlich) bitter

herbei [hɛr'baı] adv (over) here; **~führen** vt to bring about; **~schaffen** vt to procure

herbemühen ['hɛrbəmy:ən] vr to take the trouble to come

Herberge ['hɛrbɛrgə] f shelter; hostel, inn

Herbergsmutter f warden

Herbergsvater m warden

herbitten (unreg) vt to ask to come (here)

Herbst [hɛrpst] (-(e)s, -e) m autumn, fall (US); **h~lich** adj autumnal

Herd [he:rt] (-(e)s, -e) m cooker; (fig, MED) focus, centre

Herde ['he:rdə] f herd; (Schafherde) flock

herein [hɛr'aın] adv in here, here; **~!** come in!; **~bitten** (unreg) vt to ask in; **~brechen** (unreg) vi to set in; **~brin-gen** (unreg) vt to bring in; **~fallen** (un-reg) vi to be caught, to be taken in; **~fallen auf** +akk to fall for; **~kommen** (unreg) vi to come in; **~lassen** (unreg) vt to admit; **~legen** vt: **jdn ~legen** to take sb in; **~platzen** (umg) vi to burst in

Her- zW: **~fahrt** f journey here; **h~fallen** (unreg) vi: **h~fallen über** +akk to fall upon; **~gang** m course of events; **h~geben** (unreg) vt to give, to hand (over); **sich zu etw h~geben** to

lend one's name to sth; **h~gehen** (un-reg) vi: **hinter jdm h~gehen** to follow sb; **es geht hoch h~** there are a lot of goings-on; **h~halten** (unreg) vt to hold out; **h~halten müssen** (umg) to have to suffer; **h~hören** vi to listen

Hering ['he:rıŋ] (-s, -e) m herring

her- [her] zW: **~kommen** (unreg) vi to come; **komm mal ~!** come here!; **~kömmlich** adj traditional; **H~kunft** (-, -künfte) f origin; **H~kunftsland** nt country of origin; **H~kunftsort** m place of origin; **~laufen** (unreg) vi: **~laufen hinter** +dat to run after

hermetisch [hɛr'me:tıʃ] adj hermetic ♦ adv hermetically

her'nach adv afterwards

Heroin [hero'i:n] (-s) nt heroin

Herr [her] (-(e)n, -en) m master; (Mann) gentleman; (REL) Lord; (vor Namen) Mr.; **mein ~!** sir!; **meine ~en!** gentlemen!

Herren- zW: **~haus** nt mansion; **~kon-fektion** f menswear; **h~los** adj owner-less; **~toilette** f men's toilet od rest-room (US)

herrichten ['hɛrrıçtn] vt to prepare

Herr- zW: **~in** f mistress; **h~isch** adj domineering; **h~lich** adj marvellous, splendid; **~lichkeit** f splendour, mag-nificence; **~schaft** f power, rule; (~ und ~in) master and mistress; **meine ~schaften!** ladies and gentlemen!

herrschen ['hɛrʃn] vi to rule; (beste-hen) to prevail, to be

Herrscher(in) (-s, -) m(f) ruler

her- zW: **~rühren** vi to arise, to origi-nate; **~sagen** vt to recite; **~stellen** vt to make, to manufacture; **H~steller** (-s, -) m manufacturer; **H~stellung** f manufacture

herüber [he'ry:bɐ] adv over (here), across

herum [he'rʊm] adv about, (a)round; **um** etw **~** around sth; **~führen** vt to show around; **~gehen** (unreg) vi to walk about; **um etw ~gehen** to walk od go round sth; **~kommen** (unreg) vi (um Kurve etc) to come round, to turn (round); **~kriegen** (umg) vt to bring od talk about; **~lungern** (umg) vi to hang about od around; **~sprechen** (unreg) vt to get around, to be spread; **~treiben** vi, vt to drift about; **~ziehen** vi, vt to wander about

herunter [hɛˈrʊntɐ] adv downward(s), down (there); **~gekommen** adj rundown; **~kommen** (unreg) vi to come down; (fig) to come down in the world; **~machen** vt to take down; (schimpfen) to have a go at

hervor [hɛrˈfoːɐ] adv out, forth; **~bringen** (unreg) vt to produce; (Wort) to utter; **~gehen** (unreg) vi to emerge, to result; (als Kontrast) to set off; **~ragend** adj (fig) excellent; **~rufen** (unreg) vt to cause, to give rise to; **~treten** (unreg) vi to come out (from behind/between/ below); (Adern) to stand out

Herz [hɛrts] (-ens, -en) nt heart; (KARTEN) hearts pl; **~anfall** m heart attack; **~fehler** m heart defect; **h~haft** adj hearty

herziehen [ˈhɛrtsiːən] (unreg) vi: **über jdn/etw ~** (umg: auch fig) to pull sb/ sth to pieces (inf)

Herz- zW: **~infarkt** m heart attack; **~klopfen** nt palpitation; **h~lich** adj cordial; **h~lichen Glückwunsch** m congratulations pl; **h~liche Grüße** best wishes; **h~los** adj heartless

Herzog [ˈhɛrtsoːk] (-(e)s, ⸚e) m duke; **~tum** nt duchy

Herz- zW: **~schlag** m heartbeat; **~stillstand** m cardiac arrest; **h~zerreißend** adj heartrending

Hessen [ˈhɛsən] (-s) nt Hesse

hessisch adj Hessian

Hetze [ˈhɛtsə] f (Eile) rush; **h~n** vt to hunt; (verfolgen) to chase ♦ vi (eilen) to rush; **jdn/etw auf jdn/etw h~n** to set

sb/sth on sb/sth; **h~n gegen** to stir up feeling against; **h~n zu** to agitate for

Heu [hɔy] (-(e)s) nt hay; **Geld wie ~** stacks of money

Heuch- [ˈhɔyç] zW: **~elei** [-əˈlai] f hypocrisy; **h~eln** vt to pretend, to feign ♦ vi to be hypocritical; **~ler(in)** (-s, -) m(f) hypocrite; **h~lerisch** adj hypocritical

heulen [ˈhɔylən] vi to howl; to cry

Heurige(r) [ˈhɔyrɪɡə(r)] m new wine

Heu- zW: **~schnupfen** m hay fever; **~schrecke** [-ˈʃrɛkə] f grasshopper; locust

heute [ˈhɔytə] adv today; **~ Abend/ früh** this evening/morning

heutig [ˈhɔytɪç] adj today's

heutzutage [ˈhɔytsuːtaːɡə] adv nowadays

Hexe [ˈhɛksə] f witch; **h~n** vi to practise witchcraft; **ich kann doch nicht h~n** I can't work miracles; **~nschuss** ▲ m lumbago; **~'rei** f witchcraft

Hieb [hiːp] (-(e)s, -e) m blow; (Wunde) cut, gash; (Stichelei) cutting remark; **~e bekommen** to get a thrashing

hielt etc [hiːlt] vb siehe **halten**

hier [hiːr] adv here; **~ behalten** to keep here; **~ bleiben** to stay here; **~ lassen** to leave here; **~auf** adv thereupon; (danach) after that; **~bei** adv herewith, enclosed; **~durch** adv by this means; (örtlich) through here; **~her** adv this way, here; **~hin** adv here; **~mit** adv hereby; **~nach** adv hereafter; **~von** adv about this, hereof; **~zulande, ~ zu Lande** adv in this country

hiesig [ˈhiːzɪç] adj of this place, local

hieß etc [hiːs] vb siehe **heißen**

Hilfe [ˈhɪlfə] f help; aid; **erste ~** first aid; **~!** help!

Hilf- zW: **h~los** adj helpless; **~losigkeit** f helplessness; **h~reich** adj helpful

Hilfs- zW: **~arbeiter** m labourer; **h~bedürftig** adj needy; **h~bereit** adj ready to help; **~kraft** f assistant, helper

hilfst [hɪlfst] vb siehe **helfen**

Himbeere 131 hinter

Himbeere ['hɪmbeːrə] *f* raspberry

Himmel ['hɪməl] (-s, -) *m* sky; (REL, *auch fig*) heaven; **~bett** *nt* four-poster bed; **h~blau** *adj* sky-blue; **~fahrt** *f* Ascension; **~srichtung** *f* direction

himmlisch ['hɪmlɪʃ] *adj* heavenly

SCHLÜSSELWORT

hin [hɪn] *adv* **1** (*Richtung*): **hin und zurück** there and back; **hin und her** to and fro; **bis zur Mauer hin** up to the wall; **wo ist er hin?** where has he gone?; **Geld hin, Geld her** money or no money

2 (*auf ... hin*): **auf meine Bitte hin** at my request; **auf seinen Rat hin** on the basis of his advice

3: **mein Glück ist hin** my happiness has gone

---

hinab [hɪ'nap] *adv* down; **~gehen** (*unreg*) *vi* to go down; **~sehen** (*unreg*) *vi* to look down

hinauf [hɪ'nauf] *adv* up; **~arbeiten** *vr* to work one's way up; **~steigen** (*unreg*) *vi* to climb

hinaus [hɪ'naus] *adv* out; **~gehen** (*unreg*) *vi* to go out; **~gehen über** +*akk* to exceed; **~laufen** (*unreg*) *vi* to run out; **~laufen auf** +*akk* to come to, to amount to; **~schieben** (*unreg*) *vt* to put off, to postpone; **~werfen** (*unreg*) *vt* (*Gegenstand, Person*) to throw out; **~wollen** *vi* to want to go out; **~wollen auf** +*akk* to drive at, to get at

Hinblick ['hɪnblɪk] *m*: **in o im ~ auf** +*akk* in view of

hinder- ['hɪndər-] **~lich** *adj*: **~lich sein** to be a hindrance *od* nuisance; **~n** *vt* to hinder, to hamper; **jdn an etw** *dat* **~n** to prevent sb from doing sth; **H~nis** (**-ses, -se**) *nt* obstacle; **H~nisrennen** *nt* steeplechase

hindeuten ['hɪndɔʏtən] *vi*: **~ auf** +*akk* to point to

hindurch [hɪn'dʊrç] *adv* through; across; (*zeitlich*) through(out)

hinein [hɪ'naɪn] *adv* in; **~fallen** (*unreg*) *vi* to fall in; **~fallen in** +*akk* to fall into; **~gehen** (*unreg*) *vi* to go in; **~gehen in** +*akk* to go into, to enter; **~geraten** (*unreg*) *vi*: **~geraten in** +*akk* to get into; **~passen** *vi* to fit in; **~passen in** +*akk* to fit into; (*fig*) to fit in with; **~steigern** *vr* to get worked up; **~versetzen** *vr*: **sich ~versetzen in** +*akk* to put o.s. in the position of sb; **~ziehen** (*unreg*) *vt* to pull in ♦ *vi* to go in

hin- ['hɪn] *zW*: **~fahren** (*unreg*) *vi* to go; to drive ♦ *vt* to take; to drive; **H~fahrt** *f* journey there; **~fallen** (*unreg*) *vi* to fall down; **~fällig** *adj* (*fig: ungültig*) invalid; **H~flug** *m* outward flight; **H~gabe** *f* devotion; **~geben** (*unreg*) *vt* +*dat* to give o.s. up to, to devote o.s. to; **~gehen** (*unreg*) *vi* to go; (*Zeit*) to pass; **~halten** (*unreg*) *vt* to hold out; (*warten lassen*) to put off, to stall

hinken ['hɪŋkən] *vi* to limp; (*Vergleich*) to be unconvincing

hinkommen (*unreg*) *vi* (*an Ort*) to arrive

hin- ['hɪn] *zW*: **~legen** *vt* to put down ♦ *vr* to lie down; **~nehmen** (*unreg*) *vt* (*fig*) to put up with, to take; **H~reise** *f* journey out; **~reißen** (*unreg*) *vt* to carry away, to enrapture; **sich ~reißen lassen, etw zu tun** to get carried away and do sth; **~richten** *vt* to execute; **H~richtung** *f* execution; **~setzen** *vt* to put down ♦ *vr* to sit down; **~sichtlich** *präp* +*gen* with regard to; **~stellen** *vt* to put (down) ♦ *vr* to place o.s.

hinten ['hɪntən] *adv* at the back; behind; **~herum** *adv* round the back; (*fig*) secretly

hinter ['hɪntər] *präp* (+*dat od akk*) behind; (: *nach*) after; **~ jdm her sein** to

---

be after sb; **H~achse** f rear axle;
H~bliebene(r) f(m) surviving relative;
~e(r, s) adj rear, back; **~einander** adv
one after the other; **H~gedanke** m ulterior motive; **~gehen** (unreg) vi to deceive; **H~grund** m background;
H~halt m ambush; **H~hältig** adj under-
hand, sneaky; **~her** adv afterwards,
after; **H~hof** m backyard; **H~kopf** m
back of one's head; **~lassen** (unreg) vt
to leave; **~legen** vt to deposit; **H~list**
f cunning, trickery; (Handlung) trick,
dodge; **~listig** adj cunning, crafty;
H~mann m person behind; **H~rad** nt
back wheel; **H~radantrieb** m (AUT)
rear wheel drive; **~rücks** adv from behind; **H~tür** f back door; (fig: Ausweg)
loophole; **~ziehen** vr (Steuern)
to evade

hinüber [hɪˈnyːbər] adv across, over;
~gehen (unreg) vi to go over od across

hinunter [hɪˈnʊntər] adv down; **bringen** (unreg) vt to take down; **~schlu-
cken** vt (auch fig) to swallow; **~stei-
gen** (unreg) vi to descend

Hinweg [ˈhɪnveːk] m journey out
hinweghelfen [hɪnˈvɛk-] (unreg) vi:
jdm über etw akk ~ to help sb to get
over sth
hinwegsetzen [hɪnˈvɛk-] vr: sich ~
über +akk to disregard

hin- [ˈhɪn] zW: **H~weis** (-es, -e) m (Andeutung) hint; (Anweisung) instruction;
(Verweis) reference; **~weisen** (unreg)
vi: **~weisen auf** +akk (anzeigen) to
point to; (sagen) to point out, to refer
to; **~werfen** (unreg) vt to throw down;
~ziehen (unreg) vr (fig) to drag on

hinzu [hɪnˈtsuː] adv in addition;
~fügen vt to add; **~kommen** (unreg)
vi (Mensch) to arrive, to turn up; (Umstand) to ensue

Hirn [hɪrn] (-(e)s, -e) nt brain(s); **~ge-
spinst** (-(e)s, -e) nt fantasy
Hirsch [hɪrʃ] (-(e)s, -e) m stag
Hirt [hɪrt] (-en, -en) m herdsman;
(Schafhirt, fig) shepherd

hissen [ˈhɪsən] vt to hoist
Historiker [hɪsˈtoːrikər] (-s, -) m historian
historisch [hɪsˈtoːrɪʃ] adj historical
Hitze [ˈhɪtsə] (-) f heat; **h~beständig**
adj heat-resistant; **h~frei** adj: **h~frei
haben** to have time off school because
of excessively hot weather; **~welle** f
heat wave
hitzig [ˈhɪtsɪç] adj hot-tempered; (Debatte) heated
Hitzkopf m hothead
Hitzschlag m heatstroke
hl. abk von heilig
H-Milch [ˈhaːmɪlç] f long-life milk
Hobby [ˈhɔbi] (-s, -s) nt hobby
Hobel [ˈhoːbəl] (-s, -) m plane; **~bank**
f carpenter's bench; **h~n** vt, vi to
plane; **~späne** pl wood shavings
Hoch [hoːx] (-s, -s) nt (Ruf) cheer; (MET) anti-
cyclone
hoch [hoːx] (attrib **hohe(r, s)**) adj high;
♦ adv: **~ achten** to respect; **~ begabt**
extremely gifted; **~ dotiert** highly
paid; **H~achtung** f respect, esteem;
~achtungsvoll adv yours faithfully;
H~amt nt high mass; **~arbeiten** vr to
work one's way up; **H~betrieb** m intense activity; (COMM) peak time;
H~burg f stronghold; **H~deutsch** nt
High German; **H~druck** m high pressure; **H~ebene** f plateau; **H~form** f
top form; **H~gebirge** nt high mountains pl; **H~glanz** m (PHOT) high gloss
print; **etw auf H~glanz bringen** to
make sth sparkle like new; **~halten**
(unreg) vt to hold up; (fig) to uphold,
to cherish; **H~haus** nt multi-storey
building; **~heben** (unreg) vt to lift (up);
H~konjunktur f boom; **H~land** nt
highlands pl; **~leben** vi: **jdn ~leben
lassen** to give sb three cheers;
H~mut m pride; **~mütig** adj proud,
haughty; **~näsig** adj stuck-up, snooty;
H~ofen m blast furnace; **~prozentig**
adj (Alkohol) strong; **H~rechnung** f
projection; **H~saison** f high season;

H~schule f college; university;
H~sommer m middle of summer;
H~spannung f high tension;
H~sprung m high jump
höchst [høːçst] adv highly, extremely
Hochstapler ['hoːxstaːplər] (-s, -) m
swindler
höchste(r, s) adj highest; (äußerste)
extreme
Höchst- zW: **h~ens** adv at the most;
~geschwindigkeit f maximum
speed; **h~persönlich** adv in person;
~preis m maximum price;
h~wahrscheinlich adv most probably
Hoch- zW: **~verrat** m high treason;
~wasser nt high water; (Überschwemmung) floods pl
Hochzeit ['hɔxtsaɪt] (-, -en) f wedding;
~sreise f honeymoon
hocken ['hɔkən] vi, vr to squat, to
crouch
Hocker (-s, -) m stool
Höcker ['hœkər] (-s, -) m hump
Hoden ['hoːdən] (-s, -) m testicle
Hof [hoːf] (-(e)s, ⁻e) m (Hinterhof) yard;
(Bauernhof) farm; (Königshof) court
hoff- ['hɔf] zW: **~en** vi: **~en (auf** +akk)
to hope (for); **~entlich** adv I hope,
hopefully; **H~nung** f hope
Hoffnungs- zW: **h~los** hopeless;
~losigkeit f hopelessness; **h~voll** adj
hopeful
höflich ['høːflɪç] adj polite, courteous;
H~keit f courtesy, politeness
hohe(r, s) ['hoːə(r, s)] adj attrib siehe
hoch
Höhe ['høːə] f height; (Anhöhe) hill
Hoheit ['hoːhaɪt] (-, -en) f (POL) sovereignty;
(Titel) Highness
Hoheits- zW: **~gebiet** nt sovereign
territory; **~gewässer** nt territorial waters pl
Höhen- ['høːən] zW: **~luft** f mountain
air; **~messer** (-s, -) m altimeter;
~sonne f sun lamp; **~unterschied** m

difference in altitude
Höhepunkt m climax
höher adj, adv higher
hohl [hoːl] adj hollow
Höhle ['høːlə] f cave, hole; (Mund-
höhle) cavity; (fig, ZOOL) den
Hohlmaß nt measure of volume
Hohn [hoːn] (-(e)s) m scorn
höhnisch adj scornful, taunting
holen ['hoːlən] vt to get, to fetch;
(Atem) to take; **jdn/etw ~ lassen** to
send for sb/sth
Holland ['hɔlant] nt Holland; **Holländer** ['hɔlɛndər] m Dutchman; **holländisch** adj Dutch
Hölle ['hœlə] f hell
höllisch ['hœlɪʃ] adj hellish, infernal
holperig ['hɔlpərɪç] adj rough, bumpy
Holunder [ho'lundər] (-s, -) m elder
Holz [hɔlts] (-es, ⁻er) nt wood
hölzern ['hœltsərn] adj (auch fig)
wooden
Holz- zW: **~fäller** (-s, -) m lumberjack,
woodcutter; **h~ig** adj woody; **~kohle**
f charcoal; **~schuh** m clog; **~weg** m
(fig) wrong track; **~wolle** f fine wood
shavings pl
Homöopathie [homøopa'tiː] f
homeopathy
homosexuell [homozɛksu'ɛl] adj
homosexual
Honig ['hoːnɪç] (-s, -e) m honey; **~me-
lone** f (BOT, KOCH) honeydew melon;
~wabe f honeycomb
Honorar [hono'raːr] (-s, -e) nt fee
Hopfen ['hɔpfən] (-s, -) m hops pl
hopsen ['hɔpsən] vi to hop
Hörapparat m hearing aid
hörbar adj audible
horchen ['hɔrçən] vi to listen; (pej) to
eavesdrop
Horde ['hɔrdə] f horde
hör- ['høːr] zW: **~en** vt, vi to hear;
Musik/Radio: to listen to music/
the radio; **H~er** (-s, -) m hearer;

(RADIO) listener; (UNIV) student; (Telefonhörer) receiver; **H~funk** (-s) nt radio; **~geschädigt** [-gəʃeːdɪçt] adj hearing-impaired

Horizont [hori'tsɔnt] (-(e)s, -e) m horizon; **h~al** [-'taːl] adj horizontal

Hormon [hɔr'moːn] (-s, -e) nt hormone

Hörmuschel f (TEL) earpiece

Horn [hɔrn] (-(e)s, =er) nt horn; **~haut** f horny skin

Hornisse [hɔr'nɪsə] f hornet

Horoskop [horo'skoːp] (-s, -e) nt horoscope

Hörspiel nt radio play

Hort [hɔrt] (-(e)s, -e) m (SCH) day centre for schoolchildren whose parents are at work

horten ['hɔrtən] vt to hoard

Hose ['hoːzə] f trousers pl, pants pl (US)

Hosen- zW: **~anzug** m trouser suit; **~rock** m culottes pl; **~tasche** f (trouser) pocket; **~träger** m braces pl (BRIT), suspenders pl (US)

Hostie ['hɔstiə] f (REL) host

Hotel [ho'tɛl] (-s, -s) nt hotel; **~ier** (-s, -s) [hoteli'eː] m hotelkeeper, hotelier; **~verzeichnis** nt hotel register

Hubraum ['huːp-] m (AUT) cubic capacity

hübsch [hypʃ] adj pretty, nice

Hubschrauber ['huːpʃraubər] (-s, -) m helicopter

Huf ['huːf] (-(e)s, -e) m hoof; **~eisen** nt horseshoe

Hüft- [hyft] zW: **~e** f hip; **~gürtel** m girdle; **~halter** (-s, -) m girdle

Hügel ['hyːgəl] (-s, -) m hill; **h~ig** adj hilly

Huhn [huːn] (-(e)s, =er) nt hen; (KOCH) chicken

Hühner- ['hyːnər] zW: **~auge** nt corn; **~brühe** f chicken broth

Hülle ['hylə] f cover(ing); wrapping; in **~ und Fülle** galore; **h~n** vt: **h~n** (in +akk) to cover (with); to wrap (in)

Hülse ['hylzə] f husk, shell; **~nfrucht** f pulse

human [hu'maːn] adj humane; **~i'tär** adj humanitarian; **H~i'tät** f humanity

Hummel ['homəl] (-, -n) f bumblebee

Hummer ['homər] (-s, -) m lobster

Humor [hu'moːr] (-s, -e) m humour; **~ haben** to have a sense of humour; **~ist** [-'rɪst] m humorist; **h~voll** adj humorous

humpeln ['hompəln] vi to hobble

Humpen ['hompən] (-s, -) m tankard

Hund [hont] (-(e)s, -e) m dog

Hunde- ['hondə] zW: **~hütte** f (dog) kennel; **h~müde** (umg) adj dog-tired

hundert ['hondərt] num hundred; **H~jahrfeier** f centenary; **~prozentig** adj, adv one hundred per cent

Hundesteuer f dog licence fee

Hündin ['hyndɪn] f bitch

Hunger ['hoŋər] (-s) m hunger; **~ haben** to be hungry; **h~n** vi to starve; **~snot** f famine

hungrig ['hoŋrɪç] adj hungry

Hupe ['huːpə] f horn; **h~n** vi to hoot, to sound one's horn

hüpfen ['hypfən] vi to hop; to jump

Hürde ['hyrdə] f hurdle; (für Schafe) pen; **~nlauf** m hurdling

Hure ['huːrə] f whore

hurtig ['hortɪç] adj brisk, quick ♦ adv briskly, quickly

huschen ['hoʃən] vi to flit; to scurry

Husten ['huːstən] (-s) m cough; **h~** vi to cough; **~anfall** m coughing fit; **~bonbon** m od nt cough drop; **~saft** m cough mixture

Hut¹ [huːt] (-(e)s, =e) m hat

Hut² [huːt] (-) f guard; **auf der ~ sein** to be on one's guard

hüten ['hyːtən] vt to guard ♦ vr to watch out; **sich ~, zu** to take care not to; **sich ~ (vor)** to beware (of), to be on one's guard (against)

Hütte ['hytə] f hut; cottage; (Eisenhütte) forge

Hütten- zW: **~käse** m (KOCH) cottage cheese; **~schuh** m slipper sock

Hydrant [hy'drant] m hydrant

hydraulisch [hy'drao̯lıʃ] adj hydraulic

Hygiene [hygi'e:nə] (-) f hygiene

hygienisch [hygi'e:nıʃ] adj hygienic

Hymne ['hʏmnə] f hymn; anthem

Hypno- [hʏp'no:] zW: **~se** f hypnosis; **h~tisch** adj hypnotic; **~tiseur** [-ti'zø:r] m hypnotist; **h~tisieren** vt to hypnotize

Hypothek [hypo'te:k] (-, -en) f mortgage

Hypothese [hypo'te:zə] f hypothesis

Hysterie [hʏste'ri:] f hysteria

hysterisch [hʏs'te:rıʃ] adj hysterical

I, i

ICE [i:tse:'ʔe:] m abk = **Intercity-Expresszug**

Ich (-(s), -(s)) nt self; (PSYCH) ego

ich [ıç] pron I; **~ bins!** it's me!

Ideal [ide'a:l] (-s, -e) nt ideal; **ideal** adj ideal; **idealistisch** [-'lıstıʃ] adj idealistic

Idee [i'de:] (, pl i'de:ən) f idea

identifizieren [identifi'tsi:rən] vt to identify

identisch [i'dentıʃ] adj identical

Identität [identi'tɛ:t] f identity

Ideo- [ideo] zW: **~loge** [-'lo:gə] (-n, -n) m ideologist; **~logie** [-lo'gi:] f ideology; **ideologisch** [-'lo:gıʃ] adj ideological

Idiot [idi'o:t] (-en, -en) m idiot; **idiotisch** adj idiotic

idyllisch [i'dʏlıʃ] adj idyllic

Igel ['i:gəl] (-s, -) m hedgehog

ignorieren [ıgno'ri:rən] vt to ignore

ihm [i:m] (dat von er, es) pron (to) him; (to) it

ihn [i:n] (akk von er, es) pron (to) him; **~en** (dat von sie pl) pron (to) them; **Ihnen** (dat von Sie pl) pron (to) you

ihr [i:r] pron 1 (nom pl) you; **ihr seid es** it's you

2 (dat von sie) to her; **gib es ihr** give it to her; **er steht neben ihr** he is standing beside her

♦ possessiv pron 1 (sg) her, its; (: bei Tieren, Dingen) its; **ihr Mann** her husband

2 (pl) their; **die Bäume und ihre Blätter** the trees and their leaves

ihr(e) [i:r] adj (sg) her, its; (pl) their; **Ihr(e)** adj your

ihre(r, s) pron (sg) hers, its; (pl) theirs; **Ihre(r, s)** pron yours; **~r** (gen von sie sg/pl) pron of her/them; **Ihrer** (gen von Sie) pron of you; **~rseits** adv for her/their part; **~sgleichen** pron people like her/them; (von Dingen) others like it; **~twegen** adv (für sie) for her/its/their sake; (wegen ihr) on her/its/their account; **~twillen** adv: **um ~twillen** = **ihretwegen**

ihrige ['i:rıgə] pron: **der/die/das ~** od **I~** hers; its; theirs

illegal ['ılega:l] adj illegal

Illusion [ıluzi'o:n] f illusion

illusorisch [ılu'zo:rıʃ] adj illusory

illustrieren [ılʊs'tri:rən] vt to illustrate

Illustrierte f magazine

im [ım] = **in dem**

Imbiss ▲ ['ımbıs] (-es, -e) m snack; **~stube** f snack bar

imitieren [ımi'ti:rən] vt to imitate

Imker ['ımkər] (-s, -) m beekeeper

immatrikulieren [ımatriku'li:rən] vi, vr to register

immer ['ımər] adv always; **~ wieder** again and again; **~ noch** still; **~ noch nicht** still not; **für ~** forever; **~ wenn ich ...** every time I ...; **~ schöner/trauriger** more and more beautiful/sadder and sadder; **was/wer (auch) ~** whatever/whoever; **~hin** adv al the same; **~zu** adv all the time

Immobilien [ɪmo'biːliən] pl real estate sg; **~makler** m estate agent (BRIT), realtor (US)

immun [ɪ'muːn] adj immune; **Immunität** [-i'tɛːt] f immunity; **Immunsystem** nt immune system

Imperfekt ['ɪmpɛrfɛkt] (-s, -e) nt imperfect (tense)

Impf- ['ɪmpf] zW: **impfen** vt to vaccinate; **~stoff** m vaccine, serum; **~ung** f vaccination

imponieren [ɪmpo'niːrən] vi +dat to impress

Import [ɪm'pɔrt] (-(e)s, -e) m import; **~eur** m importer; **importieren** vt to import

imposant [ɪmpo'zant] adj imposing

impotent ['ɪmpotɛnt] adj impotent

imprägnieren [ɪmprɛ'gniːrən] vt to (water)proof

improvisieren [ɪmprovi'ziːrən] vt, vi to improvise

Impuls [ɪm'pʊls] (-es, -e) m impulse; **impulsiv** [-'ziːf] adj impulsive

imstande, **im Stande** [ɪm'ʃtandə] adj: **~ sein** to be in a position; (fähig) to be able

─────────────────────────
SCHLÜSSELWORT
─────────────────────────

in [ɪn] präp +akk **1** (räumlich: wohin?) in, into; **in die Stadt** into town; **in die Schule gehen** to go to school
2 (zeitlich): **bis ins 20. Jahrhundert** into up to the 20th century
♦ präp +dat **1** (räumlich: wo) in; **in der Stadt** in town; **in der Schule sein** to be at school
2 (zeitlich: wann): **in diesem Jahr** this year; (in jenem Jahr) in that year; **heute in zwei Wochen** two weeks today

Inanspruchnahme [ɪn'anʃpruxnaːmə] f (+gen) demands pl (on)

Inbegriff ['ɪnbəɡrɪf] m embodiment, personification; **inbegriffen** adv included

indem [ɪn'deːm] konj while; **~ man etw macht** (dadurch) by doing sth

Inder(in) ['ɪndər(ɪn)] m(f) Indian

indes(sen) [ɪn'dɛs(ən)] adv however; (inzwischen) meanwhile ♦ konj while

Indianer(in) [ɪndi'aːnər(ɪn)] (-s, -) m(f) American Indian, native American; **indianisch** adj Red Indian

Indien ['ɪndiən] nt India

indirekt ['ɪndirɛkt] adj indirect

indisch ['ɪndɪʃ] adj Indian

indiskret ['ɪndɪskreːt] adj indiscreet

indiskutabel ['ɪndɪskutaːbəl] adj out of the question

individuell [ɪndividu'ɛl] adj individual

Individuum [ɪndi'viːduɔm] (-s, -en) nt individual

Indiz [ɪn'diːts] (-es, -ien) nt (JUR) clue; **~ (für)** sign (of)

industrialisieren [ɪndustriali'ziːrən] vt to industrialize

Industrie [ɪndus'triː] f industry ♦ in zW industrial; **~gebiet** nt industrial area; **~ und Handelskammer** f chamber of commerce; **~zweig** m branch of industry

ineinander [ɪn|ar'nandər] adv in(to) one another od each other

Infarkt [ɪn'farkt] (-(e)s, -e) m coronary (thrombosis)

Infektion [ɪnfɛktsi'oːn] f infection; **~skrankheit** f infectious disease

Infinitiv ['ɪnfinitiːf] (-s, -e) m infinitive

infizieren [ɪnfi'tsiːrən] vt to infect ♦ vr: **sich (bei jdm) ~** to be infected (by sb)

Inflation [ɪnflatsi'oːn] f inflation

inflationär [ɪnflatsio'nɛːr] adj inflationary

infolge [ɪn'fɔlɡə] präp +gen as a result of, owing to; **~dessen** [-'dɛsən] adv consequently

Informatik [ɪnfɔr'maːtɪk] f information studies pl

Information [ɪnfɔrmatsi'oːn] f information no pl

informieren [ɪnfɔr'miːrən] vt to inform ♦ vr: **sich ~** (**über** +akk) to find out (about)

infrage [ɪn'fraːgə] adv: **~ stellen** to question sth; **nicht ~ kommen** to be out of the question

Ingenieur [ɪnʒeni'øːr] m engineer; **~schule** f school of engineering

Ingwer ['ɪŋvɐ] (**-s**) m ginger

Inh. abk (= Inhaber) prop.; (= Inhalt) contents

Inhaber(in) ['ɪnhaːbər(ɪn)] (**-s, -**) m(f) owner; (Hausinhaber) occupier; (Lizenzinhaber) licensee, holder; (FIN) bearer

inhaftieren [ɪnhaf'tiːrən] vt to take into custody

inhalieren [ɪnha'liːrən] vt, vi to inhale

Inhalt ['ɪnhalt] (**-(e)s, -e**) m contents pl; (eines Buchs etc) content; (MATH) area; volume; **inhaltlich** adj as regards content

Inhalts- zW: **~angabe** f summary; **~verzeichnis** nt table of contents

inhuman ['ɪnhumaːn] adj inhuman

Initiative [initsia'tiːvə] f initiative

inklusive [ɪnklu'ziːvə] präp +gen inclusive of ♦ adv inclusive

In-Kraft-Treten [ɪn'kraftˌtreːtən] (**-s**) nt coming into force

Inland ['ɪnlant] (**-(e)s**) nt (GEOG) inland; (POL, COMM) home (country); **~flug** m domestic flight

inmitten [ɪn'mɪtən] präp +gen in the middle of; **~ von** amongst

innehaben ['ɪnəhaːbən] (unreg) vt to hold

innen ['ɪnən] adv inside; **Innenarchitekt** m interior designer; **Inneneinrichtung** f (interior) furnishings pl; **Innenhof** m inner courtyard; **Innenminister** m minister of the interior, Home Secretary (BRIT); **Innenpolitik** f domestic policy; **~politisch** adj (Entwicklung, Lage) internal, domestic; **Innenstadt** f town/city centre

inner- ['ɪnər] zW: **~e(r, s)** adj inner; (im Körper, inländisch) internal; **Innere(s)** nt inside; (Mitte) centre; (fig) heart; **Innereien** [-'raɪən] pl innards; **~halb** adv within; (räumlich) inside ♦ präp +gen within; inside; **~lich** adj internal; (geistig) inward; **~ste(r, s)** adj innermost; **Innerste(s)** nt heart

innig ['ɪnɪç] adj (Freundschaft) close

inoffiziell ['ɪnʔofitsiɛl] adj unofficial

ins [ɪns] = **in das**

Insasse ['ɪnzasə] (**-n, -n**) m (Anstalt) inmate; (AUT) passenger

Insassenversicherung f passenger insurance

insbesondere [ɪnsbə'zɔndərə] adv (e)specially

Inschrift ['ɪnʃrɪft] f inscription

Insekt [ɪn'zɛkt] (**-(e)s, -en**) nt insect

Insektenschutzmittel nt insect repellent

Insel ['ɪnzəl] (**-, -n**) f island

Inser- zW: **~at** [ɪnze'raːt] (**-(e)s, -e**) nt advertisement; **~ent** [ɪnze'rɛnt] m advertiser; **inserieren** [ɪnze'riːrən] vt, vi to advertise

insgeheim [ɪnsgə'haɪm] adv secretly

insgesamt [ɪnsgə'zamt] adv altogether, all in all

insofern [ɪnzo'fɛrn] adv in this respect ♦ konj if; (deshalb) (and) so; **~ als** in so far as

insoweit [ɪnzo'vaɪt] = **insofern**

Installateur [ɪnstala'tøːr] m electrician; plumber

Instandhaltung [ɪn'ʃtanthaltʊŋ] f maintenance

inständig [ɪn'ʃtɛndɪç] adj urgent

Instandsetzung [ɪn'ʃtantˌzɛtsʊŋ] f overhaul; (eines Gebäudes) restoration

Instanz [ɪn'stants] f authority; (JUR) court

Instinkt [ɪn'stɪŋkt] (**-(e)s, -e**) m instinct; **instinktiv** [-'tiːf] adj instinctive

Institut [ɪnsti'tuːt] (**-(e)s, -e**) nt insti-

tute
Instrument [ɪnstru'mɛnt] *nt* instrument
Intell- [ɪntɛl] *zW:* **intellektuell** [-ɛk-tu'ɛl] *adj* intellectual; **intelligent** [-i'gɛnt] *adj* intelligent; **~igenz** [-i'gɛnts] *f* intelligence; (*Leute*) intelligentsia *pl*
Intendant [ɪntɛn'dant] *m* director
intensiv [ɪntɛn'ziːf] *adj* intensive; **Intensivstation** *f* intensive care unit
Intercity [ɪntər'sɪti] *zW:* **~-Expresszug** ▲ *m* high-speed train; **~-Zug** *m* intercity (train); **~-Zuschlag** *m* intercity supplement
Interess- *zW:* **interessant** [ɪntɛre'sant] *adj* interesting; **interessanterweise** *adv* interestingly enough; **~e** [ɪntɛ'rɛsə] (-s, -n) *nt* interest; **~e haben an** +*dat* to be interested in; **~ent** [ɪntɛre'sɛnt] *m* interested party; **interessieren** [ɪntɛre'siːrən] *vt* to interest ♦ *vr*: **sich interessieren für** to be interested in
intern [ɪn'tɛrn] *adj* (*Angelegenheiten, Regelung*) internal; (*Besprechung*) private
Internat [ɪntɛr'naːt] (-(e)s, -e) *nt* boarding school
inter- [ɪntɛr] *zW:* **~national** [-natsio-'naːl] *adj* international; **I~net** ['ɪntarnɛt] (-s) *nt*: **das I~net** the Internet; **I~net-Café** *nt* Internet café; **~pretieren** [-pre'tiːrən] *vt* to interpret; **Intervall** [-'val] (-s, -e) *nt* interval; **In-terview** [-'vjuː] (-s, -s) *nt* interview; **~viewen** [-'vjuːən] *vt* to interview
intim [ɪn'tiːm] *adj* intimate; **Intimität** *f* intimacy
intolerant ['ɪntolerant] *adj* intolerant
Intrige [ɪn'triːgə] *f* intrigue, plot
Invasion [ɪnvazi'oːn] *f* invasion
Inventar [ɪnvɛn'taːr] (-s, -e) *nt* inventory
Inventur [ɪnvɛn'tuːr] *f* stocktaking; **~ machen** to stocktake
investieren [ɪnvɛs'tiːrən] *vt* to invest
inwie- [ɪnvi'] *zW:* **~fern** *adv* how far, to what extent; **~weit** *adv* how far, to

what extent
inzwischen [ɪn'tsvɪʃən] *adv* meanwhile
Irak [i'raːk] (-s) *m*: **der ~** Iraq; **irakisch** *adj* Iraqi
Iran [i'raːn] (-s) *m*: **der ~** Iran; **iranisch** *adj* Iranian
irdisch ['ɪrdɪʃ] *adj* earthly
Ire ['iːrə] (-n, -n) *m* Irishman
irgend ['ɪrgɛnt] *adv* at all; **wann/was/wer ~** whenever/whatever/whoever; **~etwas** *pron* something/anything; **~jemand** *pron* somebody/anybody; **~ein(e, s)** *adj* some, any; **~einmal** *adv* sometime or other; (*fragend*) ever; **~wann** *adv* sometime; **~wie** *adv* somehow; **~wo** *adv* somewhere; anywhere; **~wohin** *adv* somewhere; anywhere
Irin ['iːrɪn] *f* Irishwoman
Irland ['ɪrlant] (-s) *nt* Ireland
Ironie [iro'niː] *f* irony; **ironisch** [i'roːnɪʃ] *adj* ironic(al)
irre ['ɪrə] *adj* crazy, mad; **Irre(r)** *f(m)* lunatic; **~führen** *vt* to mislead; **~machen** *vt* to confuse; **~n** *vi* to be mistaken; (*umherirren*) to wander, to stray ♦ *vr* to be mistaken; **Irrenanstalt** *f* lunatic asylum
Irr- ['ɪr] *zW:* **~garten** *m* maze; **i~ig** ['ɪrɪç] *adj* incorrect, wrong; **i~itieren** [ɪri'tiːrən] *vt* (*verwirren*) to confuse; (*ärgern*) to irritate; (*stören*) to annoy; **irrsinnig** *adj* mad, crazy; (*umg*) terrific; **~tum** (-s, -tümer) *m* mistake, error; **irrtümlich** *adj* mistaken
Island ['iːslant] (-s) *nt* Iceland
Isolation [izolatsi'oːn] *f* isolation; (*ELEK*) insulation
Isolier- [izo'liːr] *zW:* **~band** *nt* insulating tape; **isolieren** *vt* to insulate; (*ELEK*) to insulate; **~station** *f* (*MED*) isolation ward; **~ung** *f* isolation; (*ELEK*) insulation
Israel ['ɪsraeːl] (-s) *nt* Israel; **~i** (-s, -s) [-'eːli] *m* Israeli; **israelisch** *adj* Israeli
isst ▲ [ɪst] *vb siehe* **essen**
ist [ɪst] *vb siehe* **sein**

Italien [i'ta:liən] (-s) nt Italy; **~er(in)** (-s) m(f) Italian; **italienisch** adj Italian

i. V. abk = **in Vertretung**

J, j

---

ja [ja:] adv **1** yes; **haben Sie das gesehen? - ja** did you see it? - yes(, I did); **ich glaube ja** (yes) I think so

2 (fragend) really?; **ich habe gekündigt - ja?** I've quit - have you?; **du kommst, ja?** you're coming, aren't you?

3: sei ja vorsichtig do be careful; **Sie wissen ja, dass ...** as you know, ...; **tu das ja nicht!** don't do that!; **ich habe es ja gewusst** I just knew it; **ja, also** ... well you see ...

Jacht [jaxt] (-, -en) f yacht

Jacke ['jakə] f jacket; (Wolljacke) cardigan

Jackett [ʒa'kɛt] (-s, -s od -e) nt jacket

Jagd [ja:kt] (-, -en) f hunt; (Jagen) hunting; **~beute** f kill; (Jagen) fighter; **~hund** m hunting dog

jagen ['ja:gən] vi to hunt; (eilen) to race ♦ vt to hunt; (wegjagen) to drive (off); (verfolgen) to chase

Jäger ['jɛ:gɐ] (-s, -) m hunter; **~schnitzel** nt (KOCH) pork in a spicy sauce with mushrooms

jäh [jɛ:] adj sudden, abrupt; (steil) steep, precipitous

Jahr [ja:ɐ] (-(e)s, -e) nt year; **j~elang** adv for years

Jahres- zW: **~abonnement** nt annual subscription; **~abschluss** ▲ m end of the year; (COMM) annual statement of account; **~beitrag** m annual subscription; **~karte** f yearly season ticket;

~tag m anniversary; **~wechsel** m turn of the year; **~zahl** f date; year; **~zeit** f season

Jahr- zW: **~gang** m age group; (von Wein) vintage; **~'hundert** (-s, -e) nt century; **jährlich** [jɛ:ɐlɪç] adj, adv yearly; **~markt** m fair; **~tausend** nt millennium; **~'zehnt** nt decade

Jähzorn ['jɛ:tsɔrn] m sudden anger; hot temper; **j~ig** adj hot-tempered

Jalousie [ʒalu'zi:] f venetian blind

Jammer ['jamɐ] (-s) m misery; **es ist ein ~, dass ...** it is a crying shame that ...

jämmerlich ['jɛmɐlɪç] adj wretched, pathetic

jammern vi to wail ♦ vt unpers: **es jammert jdn** it makes sb feel sorry

Januar ['janua:ɐ] (-(s), -e) m January

Japan ['ja:pan] (-s) nt Japan; **~er(in)** [-'pa:nɐr(ɪn)] (-s, -s) m(f) Japanese; **j~isch** adj Japanese

jäten ['jɛ:tən] vt: **Unkraut ~** to weed

jauchzen ['jauxtsən] vi to rejoice

jaulen ['jaulən] vi to howl

jawohl [ja'vo:l] adv yes (of course)

Jawort ['ja:vɔrt] nt consent

Jazz [dʒæz] (-) m Jazz

---

je [je:] adv **1** (jemals) ever; **hast du so was je gesehen?** did you ever see anything like it?

2 (jeweils) every, each; **sie zahlten je 3 Mark** they paid 3 marks each

♦ konj **1: je nachdem** depending on; **je nachdem, ob ...** depending on whether ...

2: je eher, desto od **umso besser** the sooner the better

Jeans [dʒi:nz] pl jeans

jede(r, s) ['je:də(r, s)] adj every, each ♦ pron everybody; (~ Einzelne) each; **~s Mal** every time, each time; **ohne ~ x**

---

without any x

jedenfalls adv in any case

jedermann pron everyone

jederzeit adv at any time

jedoch [je'dɔx] adv however

jeher ['je:he:r] adv: **von/seit ~** always

jemals ['je:ma:ls] adv ever

jemand ['je:mant] pron somebody; anybody

jene(r, s) ['je:nɐ(r, s)] adj that ♦ pron that one

jenseits ['je:nzaits] adv on the other side ♦ präp +gen on the other side of, beyond

Jenseits nt: **das ~** the hereafter, the beyond

jetzig ['jɛtsɪç] adj present

jetzt [jɛtst] adv now

jeweilig adj respective

jeweils adv: **~ zwei zusammen** two at a time; **zu ~ 5 DM** at 5 marks each; **~ das Erste** the first each time

Jh. abk = **Jahrhundert**

Job [dʒɔp] (-s, -s) m (umg) job; **j~ben** ['dʒɔbən] vi (umg) to work

Jockei ['dʒɔke] (-s, -s) m jockey

Jod [jo:t] (-(e)s) nt iodine

jodeln ['jo:dəln] vi to yodel

joggen ['dʒɔgən] vi to jog

Jog(h)urt ['jo:gʊrt] (-s, -s) m od nt yogurt

Johannisbeere [jo'hanɪsbe:rə] f redcurrant; **schwarze ~** blackcurrant

johlen ['jo:lən] vi to yell

jonglieren [ʒõ'gli:rən] vi to juggle

Journal [ʒʊr'na:l] zW: **~ismus** [-'lɪsmʊs] m journalism; **~ist(in)** [-'lɪst(ɪn)] m(f) journalist; **journa'listisch** adj journalistic

Jubel ['ju:bəl] (-s) m rejoicing; **j~n** vi to rejoice

Jubiläum [jubi'lɛ:ʊm] (-s, **Jubiläen**) nt anniversary; jubilee

jucken ['jʊkən] vi to itch; vt: **es juckt mich am Arm** my arm is itching

Juckreiz ['jʊkraits] m itch

Jude ['ju:də] (-n, -n) m Jew

Juden- zW: **~tum** (-) nt Judaism; Jewry; **~verfolgung** f persecution of the Jews

Jüdin ['jy:dɪn] f Jewess

jüdisch ['jy:dɪʃ] adj Jewish

Jugend ['ju:gənt] (-) f youth; **j~frei** (CINE) U (BRIT), G (US), suitable for children; **~herberge** f youth hostel; **~herbergsausweis** m youth hostelling card; **j~lich** adj youthful; **~liche(r)** f(m) teenager, young person

Jugoslaw- [jugo'sla:v] zW: **~ien** (-s) nt Yugoslavia; **j~isch** adj Yugoslavian

Juli ['ju:li] (-(s), -s) m July

jun. abk (= junior) jr.

jung [jʊŋ] adj young; **J~e** (-n, -n) m boy, lad ♦ nt young animal; **J~en** pl (von Tier) young pl

Jünger ['jyŋɐr] (-s, -) m disciple

jünger adj younger

Jung- zW: **~frau** f virgin; (ASTROL) Virgo; **~geselle** m bachelor; **~gesellin** f unmarried woman

jüngst [jyŋst] adv lately, recently; **~e(r, s)** adj youngest; (neueste) latest

Juni ['ju:ni] (-(s), -s) m June

Junior ['ju:niɔr] (-s, -en) m junior

Jurist [ju'rɪst] m jurist, lawyer; **j~isch** adj legal

Justiz [jʊs'ti:ts] (-) f justice; **~beamte(r)** m judicial officer; **~irrtum** m miscarriage of justice; **~minister** m ≈ Lord (High) Chancellor (BRIT), ≈ Attorney General (US)

Juwel [ju'veːl] (-s, -en) nt od m jewel

Juwelier [juve'li:r] (-s, -e) m jeweller; **~geschäft** nt jeweller's (shop)

Jux [jʊks] (-es, -e) m joke, lark

K, k

Kabarett [kaba'rɛt] (-s, -e od -s) nt cabaret; **~ist** [-'tɪst] m cabaret artiste

Kabel ['ka:bəl] (-s, -) nt (ELEK) wire; (stark) cable; **~fernsehen** nt cable television

Kabeljau ['kaːbəljaʊ] (-s, -e od -s) m cod

Kabine [ka'biːnə] f cabin; (Zelle) cubicle

Kabinenbahn f cable railway

Kabinett [kabi'nɛt] (-s, -e) nt (POL) cabinet

Kachel ['kaxəl] (-, -n) f tile; k~n vt to tile; ~ofen m tiled stove

Käfer ['kɛːfər] (-s, -) m beetle

Kaffee ['kafe] (-s, -s) m coffee; ~haus nt café; ~kanne f coffeepot; ~löffel m coffee spoon

Käfig ['kɛːfɪç] (-s, -e) m cage

kahl [kaːl] adj bald; ~ geschoren shaven, shorn; ~köpfig adj bald-headed

Kahn [kaːn] (-(e)s, ̈e) m boat, barge

Kai [kaɪ] (-s, -e od -s) m quay

Kaiser ['kaɪzər] (-s, -) m emperor; ~in f empress; k~lich adj imperial; ~reich nt empire; ~schnitt m (MED) Caesarian (section)

Kakao [ka'kaːo] (-s, -s) m cocoa

Kaktee [kak'teː(ə)] (-, -n) f cactus

Kaktus ['kaktʊs] (-, -teen) m cactus

Kalb [kalp] (-(e)s, ̈er) nt calf; k~en ['kalbən] vi to calve; ~fleisch nt veal; ~sleder nt calf(skin)

Kalender [ka'lɛndər] (-s, -) m calendar; (Taschenkalender) diary

Kaliber [ka'liːbər] (-s, -) nt (auch fig) calibre

Kalk [kalk] (-(e)s, -e) m lime; (BIOL) calcium; ~stein m limestone

kalkulieren [kalku'liːrən] vt to calculate

Kalorie [kalo'riː] f calorie

kalt [kalt] adj cold; mir ist (es) ~ I am cold; ~ bleiben (fig) to remain unmoved; ~ stellen to chill; ~blütig adj cold-blooded; (ruhig) cool

Kälte ['kɛltə] (-) f cold; coldness; ~grad m degree of frost od below zero; ~welle f cold spell

kalt- zW: ~herzig adj cold-hearted;

~schnäuzig adj cold, unfeeling; ~stellen vt (fig) to leave out in the cold

kam etc [kaːm] vb siehe kommen

Kamel [ka'meːl] (-(e)s, -e) nt camel

Kamera ['kaməra] (-, -s) f camera

Kamerad [kamə'raːt] (-en, -en) m comrade, friend; ~schaft f comradeship; k~schaftlich adj comradely

Kameramann (-(e)s, -männer) m cameraman

Kamille [ka'mɪlə] f camomile; ~ntee m camomile tea

Kamin [ka'miːn] (-s, -e) m (außen) chimney; (innen) fireside, fireplace; ~kehrer (-s, -) m chimney sweep

Kamm [kam] (-(e)s, ̈e) m comb; (Berg-kamm) ridge; (Hahnenkamm) crest

kämmen ['kɛmən] vt to comb ♦ vr to comb one's hair

Kammer ['kamər] (-, -n) f chamber; small bedroom; ~diener m valet

Kampagne [kam'panjə] f campaign

Kampf [kampf] (-(e)s, ̈e) m fight, battle; (Wettbewerb) contest; (fig: Anstrengung) struggle; k~bereit adj ready for action

kämpfen ['kɛmpfən] vi to fight

Kämpfer (-s, -) m fighter, combatant

Kampf- zW: ~handlung f action; k~los adj without a fight; ~richter m (SPORT) referee; (TENNIS) umpire; ~stoff m: chemischer/biologischer ~stoff chemical/biological weapon

Kanada ['kanada] (-s) nt Canada; **Kanadier(in)** [ka'naːdiər(ɪn)] m(f) Canadian; **ka'nadisch** adj Canadian

Kanal [ka'naːl] (-s, Kanäle) m (Fluss) canal; (Rinne, Armelkanal) channel; (für Abfluss) drain; ~inseln pl Channel Islands; ~isation [-izatsi'oːn] f sewage system; ~tunnel m: der ~tunnel the Channel Tunnel

Kanarienvogel [ka'naːriənfoːgəl] m canary

Spelling Reform: ▲ *new spelling* △ *old spelling (to be phased out)*

kanarisch [ka'na:rɪʃ] adj: **K~e Inseln** Canary Islands, Canaries

Kandi- [kandi] zW: **~dat** [-'da:t] (-en, -en) m candidate; **~datur** [-da'tu:r] f candidature, candidacy; **k~dieren** [-'di:rən] vi to stand, to run

Kandis(zucker) ['kandɪs(tsʊkar)] (-) m candy

Känguru ▲ ['kɛnɡuru] (-s, -s) nt kangaroo

Kaninchen [ka'ni:nçən] nt rabbit

Kanister [ka'nɪstər] (-s, -) m can, canister

Kännchen ['kɛnçən] nt pot

Kanne ['kanə] f (Krug) jug; (Kaffeekanne) pot; (Milchkanne) churn; (Gießkanne) can

kannst etc [kanst] vb siehe **können**

Kanone [ka'no:nə] f gun; (HIST) cannon; (fig: Mensch) ace

Kante ['kantə] f edge

Kantine [kan'ti:nə] f canteen

Kanton [kan'to:n] (-s, -e) m canton

Kanton is the term for a state or region of Switzerland. Under the Swiss constitution the Kantone enjoy considerable autonomy. The Swiss Kantone are Aargau, Appenzell, Basel, Bern, Fribourg, Geneva, Glarus, Graubünden, Luzern, Neuchâtel, St. Gallen, Schaffhausen, Schwyz, Solothurn, Ticino, Thurgau, Unterwalden, Uri, Valais, Vaud, Zug and Zürich.

Kanu ['ka:nu] (-s, -s) nt canoe

Kanzel ['kantsəl] (-, -n) f pulpit

Kanzler ['kantslər] (-s, -) m chancellor

Kap [kap] (-s, -e) nt cape (GEOG)

Kapazität [kapatsi'tɛ:t] f capacity; (Fachmann) authority

Kapelle [ka'pɛlə] f (Gebäude) chapel; (MUS) band

kapieren [ka'pi:rən] (umg) vt, vi to get, to understand

Kapital [kapi'ta:l] (-s, -e od -ien) nt capital; **~anlage** f investment; **~ismus** [-'lɪsmʊs] m capitalism; **~ist** [-'lɪst] m capitalist; **k~istisch** adj capitalist

Kapitän [kapi'tɛ:n] (-s, -e) m captain

Kapitel [ka'pɪtəl] (-s, -) nt chapter

Kapitulation [kapitulatsi'o:n] f capitulation

kapitulieren [kapitu'li:rən] vi to capitulate

Kappe ['kapə] f cap; (Kapuze) hood

kappen vt to cut

Kapsel ['kapsəl] (-, -n) f capsule

kaputt [ka'pʊt] (umg) adj kaput, broken; (Person) exhausted, finished; **am Auto ist etwas ~** there's something wrong with the car; **~gehen** (unreg) vi to break; (Schuhe) to fall apart; (Firma) to go bust; (Stoff) to wear out; (sterben) to cop it (umg); **~machen** vt to break; (Mensch) to exhaust, to wear out

Kapuze [ka'pu:tsə] f hood

Karamell ▲ [kara'mɛl] (-s) m caramel; **~bonbon** m od nt toffee

Karate [ka'ra:tə] (-s) nt karate

Karawane [kara'va:nə] f caravan

Kardinal [kardi'na:l] (-s, **Kardinäle**) m cardinal; **~zahl** f cardinal number

Karfreitag [ka:r'fraita:k] m Good Friday

karg [kark] adj (Landschaft, Boden) barren; (Lohn) meagre

kärglich ['kɛrklɪç] adj poor, scanty

Karibik [ka'ri:bɪk] (-) f: **die ~** the Caribbean

karibisch [ka'ri:bɪʃ] adj: **K~e Inseln** Caribbean Islands

kariert [ka'ri:rt] adj (Stoff) checked; (Papier) squared

Karies [ka:riɛs] (-) f caries

Karikatur [karika'tu:r] f caricature; **~ist** [-'rɪst] m cartoonist

Karneval ['karnəval] (-s, -e od -s) m carnival

Karneval is the time immediately be-

fore Lent when people gather to eat, drink and generally have fun before the fasting begins. **Rosenmontag,** the day before Shrove Tuesday, is the most important day of **Karneval** on the Rhine. Most firms take a day's holiday on that day to enjoy the celebrations. *In South Germany and Austria* **Karneval** *is called* **Fasching.**

Karo ['ka:ro] (-s, -s) *nt* square; (KARTEN) diamonds

Karosserie [karɔsə'ri:] *f* (AUT) body(work)

Karotte [ka'rɔtə] *f* carrot

Karpfen ['karpfən] (-s, -) *m* carp

Karre ['karə] *f* cart, barrow

Karren (-s, -) *m* cart, barrow

Karriere [kari'e:rə] *f* career; ~ **machen** to get on, to get to the top; ~**macher** (-s, -) *m* careerist

Karte ['kartə] *f* card; (Landkarte) map; (Speisekarte) menu; (Eintrittskarte, Fahrkarte) ticket; **alles auf eine ~ setzen** to put all one's eggs in one basket

Kartei [kar'taɪ] *f* card index; ~**karte** *f* index card

Kartell [kar'tɛl] (-s, -e) *nt* cartel

Karten- *zW:* ~**spiel** *nt* card game; pack of cards; ~**telefon** *nt* cardphone; ~**vorverkauf** *m* advance booking office

Kartoffel [kar'tɔfəl] (-, -n) *f* potato; ~**brei** *m* mashed potatoes *pl;* ~**mus** *nt* mashed potatoes *pl;* ~**püree** *nt* mashed potatoes *pl;* ~**salat** *m* potato salad

Karton [kar'tõ:] (-s, -s) *m* cardboard; (Schachtel) cardboard box; **k~iert** [karto'ni:rt] *adj* hardback

Karussell [karo'sɛl] (-s, -s) *nt* roundabout (BRIT), merry-go-round

Karwoche ['ka:rvɔxə] *f* Holy Week

Käse ['kɛ:zə] (-s, -) *m* cheese; ~**glocke**

f cheese (plate) cover; ~**kuchen** *m* cheesecake

Kaserne [ka'zɛrnə] *f* barracks *pl;* ~**nhof** *m* parade ground

Kasino [ka'zi:no] (-s, -s) *nt* club; (MIL) officers' mess; (Spielkasino) casino

Kaskoversicherung ['kasko-] *f* (Teilkasko) ≈ third party, fire and theft insurance; (Vollkasko) ≈ fully comprehensive insurance

Kasse ['kasə] *f* (Geldkasten) cashbox; (in Geschäft) till, cash register; cash desk, checkout; (Kinokasse, Theaterkasse etc) box office; ticket office; (Krankenkasse) health insurance; (Sparkasse) savings bank; ~ **machen** to count the money; **getrennte ~ führen** to pay separately; **an der ~** (in Geschäft) at the desk; **gut bei ~ sein** to be in the money

Kassen- *zW:* ~**arzt** *m* panel doctor (BRIT); ~**bestand** *m* cash balance; ~**patient** *m* panel patient (BRIT); ~**prüfung** *f* audit; ~**sturz** *m:* ~**sturz machen** to check one's money; ~**zettel** *m* receipt

Kassette [ka'sɛtə] *f* small box; (Tonband, PHOT) cassette; (Bücherkassette) case

Kassettenrekorder (-s, -) *m* cassette recorder

kassieren [ka'si:rən] *vt* to take ♦ *vi:* **darf ich ~?** would you like to pay now?

Kassierer [ka'si:rər] (-s, -) *m* cashier; (von Klub) treasurer

Kastanie [kas'ta:niə] *f* chestnut; (Baum) chestnut tree

Kasten ['kastən] (-s, ⁀) *m* (auch SPORT) box; case; (Truhe) chest

kastrieren [kas'tri:rən] *vt* to castrate

Katalog [kata'lo:k] (-(e)s, -e) *m* catalogue

Katalysator [kataly'za:tɔr] *m* catalyst; (AUT) catalytic converter

katastrophal [katastro'fa:l] *adj* catastrophic

Katastrophe [kata'stro:fə] f catastrophe, disaster

Kat-Auto ['kat|auto] nt car fitted with a catalytic converter

Kategorie [katego'ri:] f category

kategorisch [kate'go:rɪʃ] adj categorical

Kater ['ka:tər] (-s, -) m tomcat; (umg) hangover

kath. abk (= katholisch) Cath.

Kathedrale [kate'dra:lə] f cathedral

Katholik [kato'li:k] (-en, -en) m Catholic

katholisch [ka'to:lɪʃ] adj Catholic

Kätzchen ['kɛtsçən] nt kitten

Katze ['katsə] f cat; **für die Katz** (umg) in vain, for nothing

Katzen- zW: **~auge** nt cat's eye; (Fahrrad) rear light; **~sprung** (umg) m stone's throw; short journey

Kauderwelsch ['kaudərvɛlʃ] (-(s)) nt jargon; (umg) double Dutch

kauen ['kauən] vt, vi to chew

kauern ['kauərn] vi to crouch down; (furchtsam) to cower

Kauf [kauf] (-(e)s, Käufe) m purchase, buy; (~en) buying; **ein guter ~** a bargain; **etw in ~ nehmen** to put up with sth; **k~en** vt to buy

Käufer(in) ['kɔyfər(ɪn)] (-s, -) m(f) buyer

Kauf- zW: **~frau** f businesswoman; **~haus** nt department store; **~kraft** f purchasing power

käuflich ['kɔyflɪç] adj purchasable, for sale; (pej) venal ♦ adv: **~ erwerben** to purchase

Kauf- zW: **k~lustig** adj interested in buying; **~mann** (pl -leute) m businessman; shopkeeper; **k~männisch** adj commercial; **k~männische Angestellter** office worker; **~preis** m purchase price; **~vertrag** m bill of sale

Kaugummi ['kaugʊmi] m chewing gum

Kaulquappe ['kaulkvapə] f tadpole

kaum [kaum] adv hardly, scarcely

Kaution [kautsi'o:n] f deposit; (JUR) bail

Kauz [kauts] (-es, Käuze) m owl; (fig) queer fellow

Kavalier [kava'li:r] (-s, -e) m gentleman, cavalier; **~sdelikt** nt peccadillo

Kaviar ['ka:viar] m caviar

keck [kɛk] adj daring, bold

Kegel ['ke:gəl] (-s, -) m skittle; (MATH) cone; **~bahn** f skittle alley; bowling alley; **k~n** vi to play skittles

Kehle ['ke:lə] f throat

Kehlkopf m larynx

Kehre ['ke:rə] f turn(ing), bend; **k~n** vt, vi (wenden) to turn; (mit Besen) to sweep; **sich an etw** dat **nicht k~n** not to heed sth

Kehricht ['ke:rɪçt] (-s) m sweepings pl

Kehrseite f reverse, other side; wrong side; bad side

kehrtmachen vi to turn about, to about-turn

keifen ['kaifən] vi to scold, to nag

Keil [kail] (-(e)s, -e) m wedge; (MIL) arrowhead; **~riemen** m (AUT) fan belt

Keim [kaim] (-(e)s, -e) m bud; (MED, fig) germ; **k~en** vi to germinate; **k~frei** adj sterile; **~zelle** f (fig) nucleus

kein [kain] adj not ... any; **~e(r, s)** pron no one, nobody; none; **~erlei** adj attrib no ... whatsoever

keinesfalls adv on no account

keineswegs adv by no means

keinmal adv not once

Keks [ke:ks] (-es, -e) m od nt biscuit

Kelch [kɛlç] (-(e)s, -e) m cup, goblet, chalice

Kelle ['kɛlə] f (Suppenkelle) ladle; (Maurerkelle) trowel

Keller ['kɛlər] (-s, -) m cellar

Kellner(in) ['kɛlnər(ɪn)] (-s, -) m(f) waiter(-tress)

keltern ['kɛltərn] vt to press

kennen ['kɛnən] (unreg) vt to know; **~ lernen** to get to know; **sich ~ lernen** to get to know each other; (zum ersten

Mal) to meet

Kenner (-s, -) *m* connoisseur

kenntlich *adj* distinguishable, discernible; **etw ~ machen** to mark sth

Kenntnis (-, -se) *f* knowledge *no pl;* **etw zur ~ nehmen** to note sth; **von etw ~ nehmen** to take notice of sth; **jdn in ~ setzen** to inform sb

Kenn- *zW:* **~zeichen** *nt* mark, characteristic; **k~zeichnen** *vt insep* to characterize; **~ziffer** *f* reference number

kentern ['kɛntərn] *vi* to capsize

Keramik [ke'raːmɪk] (-, -en) *f* ceramics *pl,* pottery

Kerbe ['kɛrbə] *f* notch, groove

Kerker ['kɛrkər] (-s, -) *m* prison

Kerl [kɛrl] (-s, -e) *m* chap, bloke *(BRIT),* guy

Kern [kɛrn] (-(e)s, -e) *m (Obstkern)* pip, stone; *(Nusskern)* kernel; *(Atomkern)* nucleus; *(fig)* heart, core; **~energie** *f* nuclear energy; **~forschung** *f* nuclear research; **~frage** *f* central issue; **k~gesund** *adj* thoroughly healthy, fit as a fiddle; **k~ig** *adj (kraftvoll)* robust; *(Ausspruch)* pithy; **~kraftwerk** *nt* nuclear power station; **k~los** *adj* seedless, without pips; **~physik** *f* nuclear physics *sg;* **~spaltung** *f* nuclear fission; **~waffen** *pl* nuclear weapons

Kerze ['kɛrtsə] *f* candle; *(Zündkerze)* plug; **k~ngerade** *adj* straight as a die; **~nständer** *m* candle holder

kess ▲ [kɛs] *adj* saucy

Kessel ['kɛsəl] (-s, -) *m* kettle; *(von Lokomotive etc)* boiler; *(GEOG)* depression; *(MIL)* encirclement

Kette ['kɛtə] *f* chain; **k~n** *vt* to chain; **~nrauchen** (-s) *nt* chain smoking; **~nreaktion** *f* chain reaction

Ketzer ['kɛtsər] (-s, -) *m* heretic

keuchen ['kɔʏçən] *vi* to pant, to gasp

Keuchhusten *m* whooping cough

Keule ['kɔʏlə] *f* club; *(KOCH)* leg

keusch [kɔʏʃ] *adj* chaste; **K~heit** *f* chastity

kfm. *abk* = **kaufmännisch**

Kfz [kaːˈɛfˈtsɛt] *nt abk* = **Kraftfahrzeug**

KG [kaːˈgeː] (-, -s) *f abk* (= *Kommanditgesellschaft*) limited partnership

kg *abk* = **Kilogramm**

kichern ['kɪçərn] *vi* to giggle

kidnappen ['kɪtnɛpən] *vt* to kidnap

Kiefer¹ ['kiːfər] (-s, -) *m* jaw

Kiefer² ['kiːfər] (-, -n) *f* pine; **~nzapfen** *m* pine cone

Kiel [kiːl] (-(e)s, -e) *m (Federkiel)* quill; *(NAUT)* keel

Kieme ['kiːmə] *f* gill

Kies [kiːs] (-es, -e) *m* gravel

Kilo ['kiːlo] *nt* kilo; **~gramm** [kiloˈgram] *nt* kilogram; **~meter** [kiloˈmeːtər] *m* kilometre; **~meterzähler** *m* milometer

Kind [kɪnt] (-(e)s, -er) *nt* child; **von ~ auf** from childhood

Kinder- ['kɪndər] *zW:* **~betreuung** *f* crèche; **~ei** [ˈraɪ] *f* childishness; **~garten** *m* nursery school, playgroup; **~gärtnerin** *f* nursery school teacher; **~geld** *nt* child benefit *(BRIT);* **~heim** *nt* children's home; **~krippe** *f* crèche; **~lähmung** *f* poliomyelitis; **k~leicht** *adj* childishly easy; **k~los** *adj* childless; **~mädchen** *nt* nursemaid; **k~reich** *adj* with a lot of children; **~sendung** *f (RADIO, TV)* children's programme; **~sicherung** *f (AUT)* childproof safety catch; **~spiel** *nt (fig)* child's play; **~tagesstätte** *f* day nursery; **~wagen** *m* pram, baby carriage *(US);* **~zimmer** *nt (für ~)* children's room; *(für Säugling)* nursery

---

Kindergarten

A **Kindergarten** *is a nursery school for children aged between 3 and 6 years. The children sing and play but do not receive any formal instruction. Most Kindergärten are financed by the*

---

town or the church with parents paying a monthly contribution towards
the cost.

Kind- *zW:* **~heit** *f* childhood; **k~isch**
adj childish; **k~lich** *adj* childlike

Kinn [kɪn] (-(e)s, -e) *nt* chin; **~haken**
m (BOXEN) uppercut

Kino ['kiːno] (-s, -s) *nt* cinema; **~besu-
cher** *m* cinema-goer; **~programm** *nt*
film programme

Kiosk [ki'ɔsk] (-(e)s, -e) *m* kiosk

Kippe ['kɪpə] *f* cigarette end; (umg)
fag; **auf der ~ stehen** (fig) to be touch
and go

kippen *vi* to topple over, to overturn
♦ *vt* to tilt

Kirch- ['kɪrç] *zW:* **~e** *f* church; **~enlied**
nt hymn; **~ensteuer** *f* church tax;
~gänger (-s, -) *m* churchgoer; **~hof**
m churchyard; **k~lich** *adj* ecclesiastical

Kirmes ['kɪrmɛs] (-, -sen) *f* fair

Kirsche ['kɪrʃə] *f* cherry

Kissen ['kɪsən] (-s, -) *nt* cushion; (Kopf-
kissen) pillow; **~bezug** *m* pillowslip

Kiste ['kɪstə] *f* box; chest

Kitsch [kɪtʃ] (-(e)s, -e) *m* kitsch; **k~ig** *adj*
kitschy

Kitt [kɪt] (-(e)s, -e) *m* putty

Kittel (-s, -) *m* overall, smock

kitten *vt* to putty; (fig: Ehe etc) to cement

kitzelig ['kɪtsəlɪç] *adj* (auch fig) ticklish

kitzeln *vt/i* to tickle

Kiwi ['kiːvi] (-, -s) *f* (BOT, KOCH) kiwi fruit

KKW [kaːkaː'veː] *nt abk* = **Kernkraftwerk**

Klage ['klaːgə] *f* complaint; (JUR) action; **k~n** *vi* (wehklagen) to lament, to
wail; (sich beschweren) to complain;
(JUR) to take legal action

Kläger(in) ['klɛːgər(ɪn)] (-s, -) *m(f)*
plaintiff

kläglich ['klɛːklɪç] *adj* wretched

klamm [klam] *adj* (Finger) numb;
(feucht) damp

Klammer ['klamər] (-, -n) *f* clamp; (in

Text) bracket; (Büroklammer) clip;
(Wäscheklammer) peg; (Zahnklammer)
brace; **k~n** *vr:* **sich k~n an** +akk to
cling to

Klang [klaŋ] (-(e)s, ⁺e) *m* sound;
k~voll *adj* sonorous

Klappe ['klapə] *f* valve; (Ofenklappe)
damper; (umg: Mund) trap; **k~n** *vi*
(Geräusch) to click; (Sitz etc) to tip ♦ *vt*
to tip ♦ *vb unpers* to work

Klapper ['klapər] (-, -n) *f* rattle; **k~ig**
adj run-down, worn-out; **k~n** *vi* to
clatter, to rattle; **~schlange** *f* rattle-
snake; **~storch** *m* stork

Klapp- *zW:* **~messer** *nt* jackknife; **~rad**
nt collapsible bicycle; **~stuhl** *m* folding
chair; **~tisch** *m* folding table

Klaps [klaps] (-es, -e) *m* slap

klar [klaːr] *adj* clear; (NAUT) ready for
sea; (MIL) ready for action; **sich dat**
(über etw akk) ~ **werden** to get (sth)
clear in one's mind; **sich dat im K~en
sein über** +akk to be clear about; **ins
K~e kommen** to get clear; (na) ~! of
course!; ~ **sehen** to see clearly

Kläranlage *f* purification plant

klären ['klɛːrən] *vt* (Flüssigkeit) to purify; (Probleme) to clarify ♦ *vt* to clear (itself) up

Klarheit *f* clarity

Klarinette [klari'nɛtə] *f* clarinet

klar- *zW:* **~legen** *vt* to clear up, to explain; **~machen** *vt* (Schiff) to get
ready for sea; **jdm etw ~machen** to
make sth clear to sb; **~sehen** △ (un-
reg) *vi siehe* **klar**; **K~sichtfolie** *f* transparent film; **~stellen** *vt* to clarify

Klärung ['klɛːrʊŋ] *f* (von Flüssigkeit)
purification; (von Probleme) clarification

klarwerden △ (unreg) *vi siehe* **klar**

Klasse ['klasə] *f* class; (SCH) class, form

klasse *adj* (umg) smashing

Klassen- *zW:* **~arbeit** *f* test; **~gesell-
schaft** *f* class society; **~lehrer** *m* form
master; **k~los** *adj* classless; **~spre-
cher(in)** *m(f)* form prefect; **~zimmer**

nt classroom

klassifizieren [klasifiˈtsiːrən] *vt* to classify

Klassik [ˈklasɪk] *f* (*Zeit*) classical period; (*Stil*) classicism; **~er** (-s, -) *m* classic

klassisch *adj* (*auch fig*) classical

Klatsch [klatʃ] (-(e)s, -e) *m* smack, crack; (*Gerede*) gossip; **~base** *f* gossip, scandalmonger; **~e** (*umg*) *f* crib; **k~en** *vi* (*Geräusch*) to clash; (*reden*) to gossip; (*applaudieren*) to applaud, to clap ♦ *vt*: **jdm Beifall k~en** to applaud sb; **~mohn** *m* (corn) poppy; **k~nass ▲**, **~naß** *adj* soaking wet

Klaue [ˈklauə] *f* claw; (*umg*: *Schrift*) scrawl; **k~n** (*umg*) *vt* to pinch

Klausel [ˈklauzəl] (-, -n) *f* clause

Klausur [klauˈzuːr] *f* seclusion; **~arbeit** *f* examination paper

Klavier [klaˈviːr] (-s, -e) *nt* piano

Kleb- [ˈkleːb] *zW*: **k~en** [ˈkleːbən] *vt, vi*: **k~en** (**an** +*akk*) to stick (to); **k~rig** *adj* sticky; **~stoff** *m* glue; **~streifen** *m* adhesive tape

kleckern [ˈklɛkərn] *vi* to make a mess ♦ *vt* to spill

Klecks [klɛks] (-es, -e) *m* blot, stain

Klee [kleː] (-s) *m* clover; **~blatt** *nt* cloverleaf; (*fig*) trio

Kleid [klait] (-(e)s, -er) *nt* garment; (*Frauenkleid*) dress; **~er** *pl* (~*ung*) clothes; **k~en** [ˈklaidən] *vt* to clothe, to dress; to suit ♦ *vr* to dress

Kleider- [ˈklaidər] *zW*: **~bügel** *m* coat hanger; **~bürste** *f* clothes brush; **~schrank** *m* wardrobe

Kleid- *zW*: **k~sam** *adj* flattering; **~ung** *f* clothing; **~ungsstück** *nt* garment

klein [klain] *adj* little, small; **~ hacken** to chop, to mince; **~ schneiden** to chop up; **K~e(r, s)** *mf* little one; **K~format** *nt* small size; **im K~format** small-scale; **K~geld** *nt* small change; **K~igkeit** *f* trifle; **K~kind** *nt* infant; **K~kram** *m* details *pl*; **~laut** *adj* de-

jected, quiet; **~lich** *adj* petty, paltry; **K~od** [ˈklainoːt] (-s, -odien) *nt* gem, jewel; treasure; **K~stadt** *f* small town; **~städtisch** *adj* provincial; **~stmöglich** *adj* smallest possible

Kleister [ˈklaistər] (-s, -) *m* paste

Klemme [ˈklɛmə] *f* clip; (*MED*) clamp; (*fig*) jam; **k~n** *vt* (*festhalten*) to jam; (*quetschen*) to pinch, to nip ♦ *vr* to catch o.s.; (*sich hineinzwängen*) to squeeze o.s. ♦ *vi* (*Tür*) to stick, to jam; **sich hinter jdn/etw k~n** to get on to sb/down to sth

Klempner [ˈklɛmpnər] (-s, -) *m* plumber

Klerus [ˈkleːrʊs] (-) *m* clergy

Klette [ˈklɛtə] *f* burr

Kletter- [ˈklɛtər] *zW*: **~er** (-s, -) *m* climber; **k~n** *vi* to climb; **~pflanze** *f* creeper

Klient(in) [kliˈɛnt(ɪn)] *m(f)* client

Klima [ˈkliːma] (-s, -s *od* -te) *nt* climate; **~anlage** *f* air conditioning; **~wechsel** *m* change of air

klimpern [ˈklɪmpərn] (*umg*) *vi* (*mit Münzen, Schlüsseln*) to jingle; (*auf Klavier*) to plonk (away)

Klinge [ˈklɪŋə] *f* blade; sword

Klingel [ˈklɪŋəl] (-, -n) *f* bell; **~beutel** *m* collection bag; **k~n** *vi* to ring

klingen [ˈklɪŋən] (*unreg*) *vi* to sound; (*Gläser*) to clink

Klinik [ˈkliːnɪk] *f* hospital, clinic

Klinke [ˈklɪŋkə] *f* handle

Klippe [ˈklɪpə] *f* cliff; (*im Meer*) reef; (*fig*) hurdle

klipp und klar [ˈklɪpʊntklaːr] *adj* clear and concise

klirren [ˈklɪrən] *vi* to clank, to jangle; (*Gläser*) to clink; **~de Kälte** biting cold

Klischee [kliˈʃeː] (-s, -s) *nt* (*Druckplatte*) plate, block; (*fig*) cliché; **~vorstellung** *f* stereotyped idea

Klo [kloː] (-s, -s) (*umg*) *nt* loo (*BRIT*); john (*US*)

Spelling Reform: ▲ *new spelling* △ *old spelling (to be phased out)*

Kloake ['kloːˌaːkə] f sewer

klobig ['kloːbɪç] adj clumsy

Klopapier (umg) nt loo paper (BRIT)

klopfen ['klɔpfən] vi to knock; (Herz) to thump ♦ vt to beat; **es klopft** somebody's knocking; **jdm auf die Schulter ~** to tap sb on the shoulder

Klopfer (-s, -) m (Teppichklopfer) beater; (Türklopfer) knocker

Klops [klɔps] (-es, -e) m meatball

Klosett [klo'zɛt] (-s, -e od -s) nt lavatory, toilet; **~papier** nt toilet paper

Kloß [kloːs] (-es, -e) m (im Hals) lump; (KOCH) dumpling

Kloster ['kloːstər] (-s, -) nt (Männerkloster) monastery; (Frauenkloster) convent; **klösterlich** [klø:stərlıç] adj monastic; convent cpd

Klotz [klɔts] (-es, -e) m log; (Hackklotz) block; **ein ~ am Bein** (fig) a drag, a millstone round (sb's) neck

Klub [klup] (-s, -s) m club; **~sessel** m easy chair

Kluft [klʊft] (-, -e) f cleft, gap; (GEOG) gorge, chasm

klug [kluːk] adj clever, intelligent; **K~heit** f cleverness, intelligence

Klumpen ['klʊmpən] (-s, -) m (Erdklumpen) clod; (Blutklumpen) clot; (Goldklumpen) nugget; (KOCH) lump

km abk = Kilometer

knabbern ['knabərn] vt, vi to nibble

Knabe ['knaːbə] (-n, -n) m boy

Knäckebrot ['knɛkəbroːt] nt crispbread

knacken ['knakən] vt, vi (auch fig) to crack

Knacks [knaks] (-es, -e) m crack; (fig) defect

Knall [knal] (-(e)s, -e) m bang; (Peitschenknall) crack; **~ und Fall** (umg) unexpectedly; **~bonbon** nt cracker; **k~en** vi to bang; to crack; **k~rot** adj bright red

knapp [knap] adj tight; (Geld) scarce; (Sprache) concise; **eine ~e Stunde** just under an hour; **~ unter/neben** just under/by; **K~heit** f tightness; scarcity; conciseness

knarren ['knarən] vi to creak

Knast [knast] (-(e)s) (umg) m (Haftstrafe) porridge (inf), time (inf); (Gefängnis) slammer (inf), clink (inf)

knattern ['knatərn] vi to rattle; (Maschinengewehr) to chatter

Knäuel ['knɔʏəl] (-s, -) m od nt (Wollknäuel) ball; (Menschenknäuel) knot

Knauf [knauf] (-(e)s, Knäufe) m knob; (Schwertknauf) pommel

Knebel ['kneːbəl] (-s, -) m gag

kneifen ['knaɪfən] (unreg) vt to pinch; vi to pinch; (sich drücken) to back out; **vor etw ~** to dodge sth

Kneipe ['knaɪpə] (umg) f pub

kneten ['kneːtən] vt to knead; (Wachs) to mould

Knick [knɪk] (-(e)s, -e) m (Sprung) crack; (Kurve) bend; (Falte) fold; **k~en** vt, vi (springen) to crack; (brechen) to break; (Papier) to fold; **geknickt sein** to be downcast

Knicks [knɪks] (-es, -e) m curtsey

Knie [kniː] (-s, -) nt knee; **~beuge** f knee bend; **~bundhose** m knee breeches; **~gelenk** nt knee joint; **~kehle** f back of the knee; **~n** vi to kneel; **~scheibe** f kneecap; **~strumpf** m knee-length sock

Kniff [knɪf] (-(e)s, -e) m (fig) trick, knack; **k~elig** adj tricky

knipsen ['knɪpsən] vt (Fahrkarte) to punch; (PHOT) to take a snap of, to snap ♦ vi to take a snap od snaps

Knirps [knɪrps] (-es, -e) m little chap; (® Schirm) telescopic umbrella

knirschen ['knɪrʃən] vi to crunch; **mit den Zähnen ~** to grind one's teeth

knistern ['knɪstərn] vi to crackle

Knitter- ['knɪtər] zW: **~falte** f crease; **k~frei** adj non-crease; **k~n** vi to crease

Knoblauch ['knoːplaux] (-(e)s) m garlic; **~zehe** f (KOCH) clove of garlic

Knöchel ['knœçəl] (-s, -) m knuckle;

(Fußknöchel) ankle

Knochen ['knɔxən] (-s, -) *m* bone; **~bruch** *m* fracture; **~gerüst** *nt* skeleton; **~mark** *nt* bone marrow

knöchern ['knœçərn] *adj* bone

knochig ['knɔxɪç] *adj* bony

Knödel ['knøːdəl] (-s, -) *m* dumpling

Knolle ['knɔlə] *f* tuber

Knopf [knɔpf] (-(e)s, ⍩e) *m* button; (Kragenknopf) stud

knöpfen ['knœpfən] *vt* to button

Knopfloch *nt* buttonhole

Knorpel ['knɔrpəl] (-s, -) *m* cartilage, gristle; **k~ig** *adj* gristly

Knospe ['knɔspə] *f* bud

Knoten ['knoːtən] (-s, -) *m* knot; (BOT) node; (MED) lump; **k~** *vt* to knot; **~punkt** *m* junction

Knüller ['knʏlər] (-s, -) (umg) *m* hit; (Reportage) scoop

knüpfen ['knʏpfən] *vt* to tie; (Teppich) to knot; (Freundschaft) to form

Knüppel ['knʏpəl] (-s, -) *m* cudgel; (Polizeiknüppel) baton, truncheon; (AVIAT) (joy)stick

knurren ['knʊrən] *vi* (Hund) to snarl, to growl; (Magen) to rumble; (Mensch) to mutter

knusperig ['knʊspərɪç] *adj* crisp; (Keks) crunchy

k. o. [kaːˈoː] *adj* knocked out; (fig) done in

Koalition [koalitsiˈoːn] *f* coalition

Kobold ['koːbɔlt] (-(e)s, -e) *m* goblin, imp

Koch [kɔx] (-(e)s, ⍩e) *m* cook; **~buch** *nt* cook(ery) book; **k~en** *vt*, *vi* to cook; (Wasser) to boil; **~er** (-s, -) *m* stove, cooker; **~gelegenheit** *f* cooking facilities *pl*

Köchin ['kœçɪn] *f* cook

Koch- zW: **~löffel** *m* kitchen spoon; **~nische** *f* kitchenette; **~platte** *f* hotplate; **~salz** *nt* cooking salt; **~topf** *m* saucepan, pot

Köder ['køːdər] (-s, -) *m* bait, lure

ködern *vt* (Tier) to trap with bait; (Person) to entice, to tempt

Koexistenz [koɛksɪsˈtɛnts] *f* coexistence

Koffein [kɔfeˈiːn] (-s) *nt* caffeine; **k~frei** *adj* decaffeinated

Koffer ['kɔfər] (-s, -) *m* suitcase; (Schrankkoffer) trunk; **~kuli** *m* (luggage) trolley; **~radio** *nt* portable radio; **~raum** *m* (AUT) boot (BRIT), trunk (US)

Kognak ['kɔnjak] (-s, -s) *m* brandy, cognac

Kohl [koːl] (-(e)s, -e) *m* cabbage

Kohle ['koːlə] *f* coal; (Holzkohle) charcoal; (CHEM) carbon; **~hydrat** (-(e)s, -e) *nt* carbohydrate

Kohlen- zW: **~dioxid** (-s) *nt* carbon dioxide; **~händler** *m* coal merchant, coalman; **~säure** *f* carbon dioxide; **~stoff** *m* carbon

Kohlepapier *nt* carbon paper

Koje ['koːjə] *f* cabin; (Bett) bunk

Kokain [kokaˈiːn] (-s) *nt* cocaine

kokett [koˈkɛt] *adj* coquettish, flirtatious

Kokosnuss ▲ ['koːkɔsnʊs] *f* coconut

Koks [koːks] (-es, -e) *m* coke

Kolben ['kɔlbən] (-s, -) *m* (Gewehrkolben) rifle butt; (Keule) club; (CHEM) flask; (TECH) piston; (Maiskolben) cob

Kolik ['koːlɪk] *f* colic, the gripes *pl*

Kollaps [kɔˈlaps] (-es, -e) *m* collapse

Kolleg [kɔˈleːk] (-s, -s) *nt* lecture course; **~e** [kɔˈleːgə] (-n, -n) *m* colleague; **~in** *f* colleague; **~ium** *nt* working party; (SCH) staff

Kollekte [kɔˈlɛktə] *f* (REL) collection

kollektiv [kɔlɛkˈtiːf] *adj* collective

Köln [kœln] (-s) *nt* Cologne

Kolonie [koloˈniː] *f* colony

kolonisieren [koloniˈziːrən] *vt* to colonize

Kolonne [koˈlɔnə] *f* column; (von Fahr-

Spelling Reform: ▲ *new spelling* △ *old spelling (to be phased out)*

zeugen) convoy

Koloss ▲ [kɔ'lɔs] (**-es, -e**) m colossus; **kolos'sal** adj colossal

Kölsch [kœlʃ] (**-(-)**, **-**) nt (Bier) ≃ (strong) lager

Kombi- ['kɔmbi] zW: **~nation** [-natsi'o:n] f combination; (Vermutung) conjecture; (Hemdhose) combinations pl; **k~nieren** [-'ni:rən] vt to combine ♦ vi to deduce, to work out; (vermuten) to guess; **~wagen** m station wagon; **~zange** f (pair of) pliers pl

Komet [ko'me:t] (**-en, -en**) m comet

Komfort [kɔm'fo:r] (**-s**) m luxury

Komik ['ko:mik] f humour, comedy; **~er** (**-s, -**) m comedian

komisch ['ko:mɪʃ] adj funny

Komitee [komi'te:] (**-s, -s**) nt committee

Komma ['kɔma] (**-s, -s** od **-ta**) nt comma; **2 ~ 3** 2 point 3

Kommand- [kɔ'mand] zW: **~ant** [-'dant] m commander, commanding officer; **k~ieren** [-'di:rən] vt, vi to command; **~o** (**-s, -s**) nt command, order; (Truppe) detachment, squad; **auf ~o** to order

kommen ['kɔmən] (unreg) vi to come; (näher kommen) to approach; (passieren) to happen; (gelangen, geraten) to get; (Blumen, Zähne, Tränen etc) to appear; (in die Schule, das Zuchthaus etc) to go; **~ lassen** to send for; **das kommt in den Schrank** that goes in the cupboard; **zu sich ~** to come round od to; **zu etw ~** to acquire sth; **um etw ~** to lose sth; **nichts auf jdn/etw ~ lassen** to have nothing said against sb/sth; **jdm frech ~** to get cheeky with sb; **auf jeden vierten kommt ein Platz** there's one place for every fourth person; **wer kommt zuerst?** who's first?; **unter ein Auto ~** to be run over by a car; **wie hoch kommt das?** what does that cost?; **komm gut nach Hause!** safe journey (home); **~den Sonntag** next Sunday;

K~ (**-s**) nt coming

Kommentar [kɔmɛn'ta:r] m commentary; **kein ~** no comment; **k~los** adj without comment

Kommentator [kɔmɛn'ta:tɔr] m (TV) commentator

kommentieren [kɔmɛn'ti:rən] vt to comment on

kommerziell [kɔmɛrtsi'ɛl] adj commercial

Kommilitone [kɔmili'to:nə] (**-n, -n**) m fellow student

Kommissar [kɔmɪ'sa:r] m police inspector

Kommission [kɔmɪsi'o:n] f (COMM) commission; (Ausschuss) committee

Kommode [kɔ'mo:də] f (chest of) drawers

kommunal [kɔmu'na:l] adj local; (von Stadt auch) municipal

Kommune [kɔ'mu:nə] f commune

Kommunikation [kɔmunikatsi'o:n] f communication

Kommunion [kɔmuni'o:n] f communion

Kommuniqué, Kommunikee ▲ [kɔmyni'ke:] (**-s, -s**) nt communiqué

Kommunismus [kɔmu'nɪsmʊs] m communism

Kommunist(in) [kɔmu'nɪst(ɪn)] m(f) communist; **k~isch** adj communist

kommunizieren [kɔmuni'tsi:rən] vi to communicate

Komödie [ko'mø:diə] f comedy

Kompagnon [kɔmpan'jõ:] (**-s, -s**) m (COMM) partner

kompakt [kɔm'pakt] adj compact

Kompanie [kɔmpa'ni:] f company

Kompass ▲ [kɔmpas] (**-es, -e**) m compass

kompatibel [kɔmpa'ti:bəl] adj compatible

kompetent [kɔmpe'tɛnt] adj competent

Kompetenz f competence, authority

komplett [kɔm'plɛt] adj complete

Komplex [kɔm'plɛks] (**-es, -e**) m (Ge-

bäudekomplex) complex

Komplikation [komplikatsi'o:n] *f* complication

Kompliment [kompli'mɛnt] *nt* compliment

Komplize [kɔm'pli:tsə] (**-n, -n**) *m* accomplice

kompliziert [kompli'tsi:rt] *adj* complicated

komponieren [kompo'ni:rən] *vt* to compose

Komponist [kompo'nɪst(ɪn)] *m* composer

Komposition [kompozitsi'o:n] *f* composition

Kompost [kɔm'pɔst] (**-(e)s, -e**) *m* compost

Kompott [kɔm'pɔt] (**-(e)s, -e**) *nt* stewed fruit

Kompromiss ▲ [kompro'mɪs] (**-es, -e**) *m* compromise; **k~bereit** *adj* willing to compromise

Kondens- [kɔn'dɛns] *zW:* **~ation** [kɔndɛnzatsi'o:n] *f* condensation; **k~ieren** [kɔndɛn'zi:rən] *vt* to condense; **~milch** *f* condensed milk

Kondition [kɔnditsi'o:n] *f* (COMM, FIN) condition; *(Durchhaltevermögen)* stamina; *(körperliche Verfassung)* physical condition, state of health

Konditionstraining [kɔnditsi'o:nstre:nɪŋ] *nt* fitness training

Konditor [kɔn'di:tɔr] *m* pastry cook; **~ei** [-'rai] *f* café; cake shop

Kondom [kɔn'do:m] (**-s, -e**) *nt* condom

Konferenz [kɔnfe'rɛnts] *f* conference, meeting

Konfession [kɔnfɛsi'o:n] *f* (religious) denomination; **k~ell** [-'nɛl] *adj* denominational; **k~slos** *adj* non-denominational

Konfirmand [kɔnfɪr'mant] *m* candidate for confirmation

Konfirmation [kɔnfɪrmatsi'o:n] *f* (REL) confirmation

konfirmieren [kɔnfɪr'mi:rən] *vt* to confirm

konfiszieren [kɔnfɪs'tsi:rən] *vt* to confiscate

Konfitüre [kɔnfi'ty:rə] *f* jam

Konflikt [kɔn'flɪkt] (**-(e)s, -e**) *m* conflict

konfrontieren [kɔnfrɔn'ti:rən] *vt* to confront

konfus [kɔn'fu:s] *adj* confused

Kongress ▲ [kɔn'grɛs] (**-es, -e**) *m* congress; **~zentrum** *nt* conference centre

Kongruenz [kɔŋgru'ɛnts] *f* agreement, congruence

König ['kø:nɪç] (**-(e)s, -e**) *m* king; **~in** ['kø:nɪɡɪn] *f* queen; **k~lich** *adj* royal; **~reich** *nt* kingdom

Konjugation [kɔnjugatsi'o:n] *f* conjugation

konjugieren [kɔnju'gi:rən] *vt* to conjugate

Konjunktion [kɔnjuŋktsi'o:n] *f* conjunction

Konjunktiv ['kɔnjʊŋkti:f] (**-s, -e**) *m* subjunctive

Konjunktur [kɔnjʊŋk'tu:r] *f* economic situation; *(Hochkonjunktur)* boom

konkret [kɔn'kre:t] *adj* concrete

Konkurrent(in) [kɔŋkʊ'rɛnt(ɪn)] *m(f)* competitor

Konkurrenz [kɔŋkʊ'rɛnts] *f* competition; **k~fähig** *adj* competitive; **~kampf** *m* competition; rivalry, competitive situation

konkurrieren [kɔŋkʊ'ri:rən] *vi* to compete

Konkurs [kɔn'kʊrs] (**-es, -e**) *m* bankruptcy

Können (**-s**) *nt* ability

SCHLÜSSELWORT

können ['kœnən] (*pt* **konnte**, *pp* **gekonnt** *od* (*als Hilfsverb*) **können**) *vt, vi*

---

1 to be able to; **ich kann es machen** I can do it, I am able to do it; **ich kann es nicht machen** I can't do it, I'm not able to do it; **ich kann nicht ...** I can't ..., I cannot ...; **ich kann nicht mehr** I can't go on
2 (*wissen, beherrschen*) to know; **können Sie Deutsch?** can you speak German?; **er kann gut Englisch** he speaks English well; **sie kann keine Mathematik** she can't do mathematics
3 (*dürfen*) to be allowed to; **kann ich gehen?** can I go?; **könnte ich ...?** could I ...?; **kann ich mit?** (*umg*) can I come with you?
4 (*möglich sein*): **Sie könnten Recht haben** you may be right; **das kann sein** that's possible; **kann sein** maybe

Könner *m* expert
konnte *etc* ['kɔntə] *vb siehe* **können**
konsequent [kɔnze'kvɛnt] *adj* consistent
Konsequenz [kɔnze'kvɛnts] *f* consistency; (*Folgerung*) conclusion
Konserv- *zW*: **k~ativ** [-a'tiːf] *adj* conservative; **~ative(r)** [-a'tiːvə(r)] *f(m)* (*POL*) conservative; **~e** *f* tinned food; **~enbüchse** *f* tin, can; **k~ieren** [-'viːrən] *vt* to preserve; **~ierung** *f* preservation; **~ierungsstoff** *m* preservatives
Konsonant [kɔnzo'nant] *m* consonant
konstant [kɔn'stant] *adj* constant
konstru- *zW*: **~ieren** [kɔnstru'iːrən] *vt* to construct; **k~kteur** [kɔnstruk'tøːr] *m* designer; **K~ktion** [kɔnstruktsi'oːn] *f* construction; **k~ktiv** [kɔnstruk'tiːf] *adj* constructive
Konsul ['kɔnzul] (**-s, -n**) *m* consul; **~at** [-'laːt] *nt* consulate
konsultieren [kɔnzul'tiːrən] *vt* to consult
Konsum [kɔn'zuːm] (**-s**) *m* consumption; **~artikel** *m* consumer article; **~ent** [-'mɛnt] *m* consumer; **k~ieren**

[-'miːrən] *vt* to consume

Kontakt [kɔn'takt] (**-(e)s, -e**) *m* contact; **k~arm** *adj* unsociable; **k~freudig** *adj* sociable; **~linsen** *pl* contact lenses
kontern ['kɔntərn] *vt, vi* to counter
Kontinent [kɔnti'nɛnt] *m* continent
Kontingent [kɔntɪŋ'gɛnt] (**-(e)s, -e**) *nt* quota; (*Truppenkontingent*) contingent
kontinuierlich [kɔntinu'iːrlɪç] *adj* continuous
Konto ['kɔnto] (**-s, Konten**) *nt* account; **~auszug** *m* statement (of account); **~inhaber(in)** *m(f)* account holder; **~stand** *m* balance
Kontra ['kɔntra] (**-s, -s**) *nt* (*KARTEN*) double; **jdm ~ geben** (*fig*) to contradict sb; **~bass ▲** *m* double bass; **~hent** *m* (*COMM*) contracting party; **~punkt** *m* counterpoint
Kontrast [kɔn'trast] (**-(e)s, -e**) *m* contrast
Kontroll- [kɔn'trɔl] *zW*: **~e** *f* control, supervision; (*Passkontrolle*) passport control; **~eur** [-'løːr] *m* inspector; **k~ieren** [-'liːrən] *vt* to control, to supervise; (*nachprüfen*) to check
Konvention [kɔnvɛntsi'oːn] *f* convention; **k~ell** [-'nɛl] *adj* conventional
Konversation [kɔnvɛrzatsi'oːn] *f* conversation; **~slexikon** *nt* encyclop(a)edia
Konvoi ['kɔnvɔy] (**-s, -s**) *m* convoy
Konzentration [kɔntsɛntratsi'oːn] *f* concentration
Konzentrationslager *nt* concentration camp
konzentrieren [kɔntsɛn'triːrən] *vt, vr* to concentrate
konzentriert *adj* concentrated ♦ *adv* (*zuhören, arbeiten*) intently
Konzern [kɔn'tsɛrn] (**-s, -e**) *m* combine
Konzert [kɔn'tsɛrt] (**-(e)s, -e**) *nt* concert; (*Stück*) concerto; **~saal** *m* concert hall
Konzession [kɔntsɛsi'oːn] *f* licence; (*Zugeständnis*) concession

Konzil [kɔn'tsiːl] (-s, -e od -ien) nt council

kooperativ [ko|opera'tiːf] adj cooperative

koordinieren [ko|ɔrdi'niːrən] vt to co-ordinate

Kopf [kɔpf] (-(e)s, ⁼e) m head; **~haut** f scalp; **~hörer** m headphones pl; **~kissen** nt pillow; **k~los** adj panic-stricken; **k~rechnen** vi to do mental arithmetic; **~salat** m lettuce; **~schmerzen** pl headache sg; **~sprung** m header, dive; **~stand** m headstand; **~stütze** f (in Auto etc) headrest, head restraint; **~tuch** nt headscarf; **~weh** nt headache; **~zerbrechen** nt: jdm **~zerbrechen machen** to be a headache for sb

Kopie [ko'piː] f copy; **k~ren** vt to copy

Kopiergerät nt photocopier

Koppel¹ ['kɔpəl] (-, -n) f (Weide) enclosure

Koppel² ['kɔpəl] (-s, -) nt (Gürtel) belt

koppeln vt to couple

Koppelung f coupling

Koralle [ko'ralə] f coral

Korb [kɔrp] (-(e)s, ⁼e) m basket; jdm **einen ~ geben** (fig) to turn sb down; **~ball** m basketball; **~stuhl** m wicker chair

Kord [kɔrt] (-(e)s, -e) m cord, corduroy

Kordel ['kɔrdəl] (-, -n) f cord, string

Kork [kɔrk] (-(e)s, -e) m cork; **~en** (-s, -) m stopper, cork; **~enzieher** (-s, -) m corkscrew

Korn [kɔrn] (-(e)s, ⁼er) nt corn, grain; (Gewehr) sight

Körper ['kœrpər] (-s, -) m body; **~bau** m build; **k~behindert** adj disabled; **~geruch** m body odour; **~gewicht** nt weight; **~größe** f height; **k~lich** adj physical; **~pflege** f personal hygiene; **~schaft** f corporation; **~schaftssteuer** f corporation tax; **~teil** m part of the body; **~verletzung** f bodily od physical injury

korpulent [kɔrpu'lɛnt] adj corpulent

korrekt [kɔ'rɛkt] adj correct; **K~ur** [-'tuːr] f (eines Textes) proofreading; (Text) proof; (SCH) marking, correction

Korrespond- [kɔrɛspɔnd] zW: **~ent(in)** [-'dɛnt(in)]m(f) correspondent; **~enz** [-'dɛnts] f correspondence; **k~ieren** vi to correspond

Korridor ['kɔridɔːr] (-s, -e) m corridor

korrigieren [kɔri'giːrən] vt to correct

Korruption [kɔrʊptsi'oːn] f corruption

Kose- ['koːzə] zW: **~form** f pet form; **~name** m pet name; **~wort** nt term of endearment

Kosmetik [kɔs'meːtik] f cosmetics pl; **~erin** f beautician

kosmetisch adj cosmetic; (Chirurgie) plastic

kosmisch ['kɔsmiʃ] adj cosmic

Kosmo- [kɔsmo] zW: **~naut** [-'naut] (-en, -en) m cosmonaut; **k~politisch** adj cosmopolitan; **~s** (-) m cosmos

Kost [kɔst] (-) f (Nahrung) food; (Verpflegung) board; **k~bar** adj precious; (teuer) costly, expensive; **~barkeit** f preciousness; costliness, expensiveness; (Wertstück) valuable

Kosten pl cost(s); (Ausgaben) expenses; **auf ~ von** at the expense of; **k~** vt to cost; (versuchen) to taste ♦ vi to taste; **was kostet ...?** what does ... cost, how much is ...?; **~anschlag** m estimate; **k~los** adj free (of charge)

köstlich ['kœstliç] adj precious; (Einfall) delightful; (Essen) delicious; **sich ~ amüsieren** to have a marvellous time

Kostprobe f taste; (fig) sample

kostspielig adj expensive

Kostüm [kɔs'tyːm] (-s, -e) nt costume; (Damenkostüm) suit; **~fest** nt fancy-dress party; **k~ieren** [kɔsty'miːrən] vt, vr to dress up; **~verleih** m costume agency

Kot [koːt] (-(e)s) m excrement

Kotelett [kotə'lɛt] (-(e)s, -e od -s) nt

Spelling Reform: ▲ new spelling △ old spelling (to be phased out)

cutlet, chop; **~en** pl (Bart) sideboards

Köter ['kø:tər] (-s, -) m cur

Kotflügel m (AUT) wing

kotzen ['kɔtsən] (umg!) vi to puke (umg), to throw up (umg)

Krabbe ['krabə] f shrimp; **k~ln** vi to crawl

Krach [krax] (-(e)s, -s od -e) m crash; (andauernd) noise; (umg: Streit) quarrel, argument; **k~en** vi to crash; (beim Brechen) to crack ♦ vr (umg) to argue, to quarrel

krächzen ['krɛçtsən] vi to croak

Kraft [kraft] (-, ¨e) f strength; power; force; (Arbeitskraft) worker; **in ~ treten** to come into force; **k~** präp +gen by virtue of; **~fahrer** m (motor) driver; **~fahrzeug** nt motor vehicle; **~fahrzeugbrief** m logbook; **~fahrzeugsteuer** f ≈ road tax; **~fahrzeugversicherung** f car insurance

kräftig ['krɛftɪç] adj strong; **~en** vt to strengthen

Kraft- zW: **k~los** adj weak; powerless; (JUR) invalid; **~probe** f trial of strength; **~stoff** m fuel; **k~voll** adj vigorous; **~werk** nt power station

Kragen ['kra:gən] (-s, -) m collar; **~weite** f collar size

Krähe ['krɛ:ə] f crow; **k~n** vi to crow

Kralle ['kralə] f claw; (Vogelkralle) talon; **k~n** vt to clutch; (krampfhaft) to claw

Kram [kra:m] (-(e)s) m stuff, rubbish; **k~en** vi to rummage; **~laden** (pej) m small shop

Krampf [krampf] (-(e)s, ¨e) m cramp; (zuckend) spasm; **~ader** f varicose vein; **k~haft** adj convulsive; (fig: Versuche) desperate

Kran [kra:n] (-(e)s, ¨e) m crane; (Wasserkran) tap, faucet (US)

krank [kraŋk] adj ill, sick; **K~e(r)** f(m) sick person, invalid; patient; **k~en** vi: **an etw** dat **~en** (fig) to suffer from sth

kränken ['krɛŋkən] vt to hurt

Kranken- zW: **~geld** nt sick pay; **~gymnastik** f physiotherapy; **~haus**

nt hospital; **~kasse** f health insurance; **~pfleger** m nursing orderly; **~schein** m health insurance card; **~schwester** f nurse; **~versicherung** f health insurance; **~wagen** m ambulance

Krank- zW: **k~haft** adj diseased; (Angst etc) morbid; **~heit** f illness; disease; **~heitserreger** m disease-causing agent

kränklich ['krɛŋklɪç] adj sickly

Kränkung f insult, offence

Kranz [krants] (-es, ¨e) m wreath, garland

krass ▲ [kras] adj crass

Krater ['kra:tər] (-s, -) m crater

Kratz- ['krats] zW: **~bürste** f (fig) crosspatch; **k~en** vt, vi to scratch; **~er** (-s, -) m scratch; (Werkzeug) scraper

Kraul [kraʊl] (-s) nt crawl; **~ schwimmen** to do the crawl; **k~en** vi (schwimmen) to do the crawl ♦ vt (streicheln) to fondle

kraus [kraʊs] adj crinkly; (Haar) frizzy; (Stirn) wrinkled

Kraut [kraʊt] (-(e)s, Kräuter) nt plant; (Gewürz) herb; (Gemüse) cabbage

Krawall [kra'val] (-s, -e) m row, uproar

Krawatte [kra'vatə] f tie

kreativ [krea'ti:f] adj creative

Krebs [kre:ps] (-es, -e) m crab; (MED, ASTROL) cancer; **k~krank** adj suffering from cancer

Kredit [kre'di:t] (-(e)s, -e) m credit; **~institut** nt bank; **~karte** f credit card

Kreide ['kraɪdə] f chalk; **k~bleich** adj as white as a sheet

Kreis [kraɪs] (-es, -e) m circle; (Stadtkreis etc) district; **im ~ gehen** (auch fig) to go round in circles

kreischen ['kraɪʃən] vi to shriek, to screech

Kreis- zW: **~el** ['kraɪzəl] (-s, -) m top; (~verkehr) roundabout (BRIT), traffic circle (US); **k~en** ['kraɪzən] vi to spin; **~lauf** m (MED) circulation; (fig: der Natur etc) cycle; **~säge** f circular saw; **~stadt** f county town; **~verkehr** m roundabout traffic

Krematorium [krema'to:riom] *nt* crematorium

Kreml ['kre:ml] (-s) *m* Kremlin

krepieren [kre'pi:rən] (*umg*) *vi* (*sterben*) to die, to kick the bucket

Krepp [krep] (-s, -s *od* -e) *m* crepe; **~papier** ▲ *nt* crepe paper

Kresse ['kresə] *f* cress

Kreta ['kre:ta] (-s) *nt* Crete

Kreuz [krɔyts] (-es, -e) *nt* cross; (*ANAT*) small of the back; (*KARTEN*) clubs; **k~en** *vt, vr* to cross ♦ *vi* (*NAUT*) to cruise; **~er** (-s, -) *m* (*Schiff*) cruiser; **~fahrt** *f* cruise; **~feuer** *nt* (*fig*): **ins ~feuer geraten** to be under fire from all sides; **~gang** *m* cloisters *pl*; **k~igen** *vt* to crucify; **~igung** *f* crucifixion; **~ung** *f* (*Verkehrskreuzung*) crossing, junction; (*Züchten*) cross; **~verhör** *nt* cross-examination; **~weg** *m* crossroads; (*REL*) Way of the Cross; **~worträtsel** *nt* crossword puzzle; **~zug** *m* crusade

Kriech- ['kri:ç] *zW* **k~en** (*unreg*) *vi* to crawl, to creep; (*pej*) to grovel, to crawl; **~er** (-s, -) *m* crawler; **~spur** *f* crawler lane; **~tier** *nt* reptile

Krieg [kri:k] (-(e)s, -e) *m* war

kriegen ['kri:gən] (*umg*) *vt* to get

Kriegs- *zW* **~erklärung** *f* declaration of war; **~fuß** *m*: **mit jdm/etw auf ~fuß stehen** to be at loggerheads with sb/to have difficulties with sth; **~gefangene(r)** *m* prisoner of war; **~gefangenschaft** *f* captivity; **~gericht** *nt* court-martial; **~schiff** *nt* warship; **~verbrecher** *m* war criminal; **~versehrte(r)** *m* person disabled in the war; **~zustand** *m* state of war

Krim [krɪm] (-) *f* Crimea

Krimi ['kri:mi] (-s) (*umg*) *m* thriller

Kriminal- [krimi'na:l] *zW* **~beamte(r)** *m* detective; **~i'tät** *f* criminality; **~'polizei** *f* ≈ Criminal Investigation Department (*BRIT*), Federal Bureau of

Investigation (*US*); **~ro'man** *m* detective story

kriminell [krimi'nel] *adj* criminal; **K~e(r)** *m* criminal

Krippe ['krɪpə] *f* crib; (*Kinderkrippe*) crèche

Krise ['kri:zə] *f* crisis; **k~ln** *vi*: **es k~lt** there's a crisis

Kristall [krɪs'tal] (-s, -e) *m* crystal ♦ *nt* (*Glas*) crystal

Kriterium [kri'te:riom] *nt* criterion

Kritik [kri'ti:k] *f* criticism; (*Zeitungskritik*) review, write-up; **~er** ['kri:tikər] (-s, -) *m* critic; **k~los** *adj* uncritical

kritisch ['kri:tɪʃ] *adj* critical

kritisieren [kriti'zi:rən] *vt, vi* to criticize

kritzeln ['krɪtsəln] *vt, vi* to scribble, to scrawl

Kroatien [kro'a:tsiən] *nt* Croatia

Krokodil [kroko'di:l] (-s, -e) *nt* crocodile

Krokus ['kro:kus] (-, -*od* -se) *m* crocus

Krone ['kro:nə] *f* crown; (*Baumkrone*) top

krönen ['krø:nən] *vt* to crown

Kron- *zW* **~korken** *m* bottle top; **~leuchter** *m* chandelier; **~prinz** *m* crown prince

Krönung ['krø:nʊŋ] *f* coronation

Kropf [krɔpf] (-(e)s, -e) *m* (*MED*) goitre; (*von Vogel*) crop

Kröte ['krø:tə] *f* toad

Krücke ['krykə] *f* crutch

Krug [kru:k] (-(e)s, -e) *m* jug; (*Bierkrug*) mug

Krümel ['kry:məl] (-s, -) *m* crumb; **k~n** *vt, vi* to crumble

krumm [krɔm] *adj* (*auch fig*) crooked; (*kurvig*) curved; **jdm etw ~ nehmen** to take sth amiss; **k~beinig** *adj* bandy-legged; **~lachen** (*umg*) *vr* to laugh o.s. silly

Krümmung ['krymʊŋ] *f* bend, curve

Krüppel ['krypəl] (-s, -) *m* cripple

Spelling Reform: ▲ *new spelling* △ *old spelling (to be phased out)*

Kruste ['krʊstə] f crust

Kruzifix [krutsi'fɪks] (-es, -e) nt crucifix

Kübel ['kyːbəl] (-s, -) m tub; (*Eimer*) pail

Kubikmeter [ku'biːkmeːtər] m cubic metre

Küche ['kʏçə] f kitchen; (*Kochen*) cooking, cuisine

Kuchen ['kuːxən] (-s, -) m cake; ~**form** f baking tin; ~**gabel** f pastry fork

Küchen- zW: ~**herd** m cooker, stove; ~**schabe** f cockroach; ~**schrank** m kitchen cabinet

Kuckuck ['kʊkʊk] (-s, -e) m cuckoo; ~**suhr** f cuckoo clock

Kugel ['kuːgəl] (-, -n) f ball; (MATH) sphere; (MIL) bullet; (*Erdkugel*) globe; (SPORT) shot; **k~förmig** adj spherical; ~**lager** nt ball bearing; **k~rund** adj (*Gegenstand*) round; (umg: *Person*) tubby; ~**schreiber** m ball-point (pen), Biro ®; **k~sicher** adj bulletproof; ~**stoßen** (-s) nt shot put

Kuh [kuː] (-, -̈e) f cow

kühl [kyːl] adj (*auch fig*) cool; **K~anlage** f refrigeration plant; **K~e** (-) f coolness; ~**en** vt to cool; **K~er** (-s, -) m (AUT) radiator; **K~erhaube** f (AUT) bonnet (BRIT), hood (US); **K~raum** m cold storage chamber; **K~schrank** m refrigerator; **K~truhe** f freezer; **K~ung** f cooling; **K~wasser** nt radiator water

kühn [kyːn] adj bold, daring; **K~heit** f boldness

Kuhstall m byre, cattle shed

Küken ['kyːkən] (-s, -) nt chicken

kulant [ku'lant] adj obliging

Kuli ['kuːli] (-s, -s) m coolie; (umg: *Kugelschreiber*) Biro ®

Kulisse [ku'lɪsə] f scenery

kullern ['kʊlərn] vi to roll

Kult [kʊlt] (-(e)s, -e) m worship, cult; **mit etw einen ~ treiben** to make a cult out of sth

kultivieren [kʊlti'viːrən] vt to cultivate

kultiviert adj cultivated, refined

Kultur [kʊl'tuːr] f culture; civilization;

(*des Bodens*) cultivation; ~**banause** (umg) m philistine, low-brow; ~**beutel** m toilet bag; **k~ell** [-u'rɛl] adj cultural; ~**ministerium** nt ministry of education and the arts

Kümmel ['kʏməl] (-s, -) m caraway seed; (*Branntwein*) kümmel

Kummer ['kʊmər] (-s) m grief, sorrow

kümmerlich ['kʏmərlɪç] adj miserable, wretched

kümmern ['kʏmərn] vt to concern ♦ vr: **sich um jdn ~** to look after sb; **das kümmert mich nicht** that doesn't worry me; **sich um etw ~** to see to sth

Kumpel ['kʊmpəl] (-s, -) (umg) m mate

kündbar ['kʏntbaːr] adj redeemable, recallable; (*Vertrag*) terminable

Kunde[1] ['kʊndə] (-n, -n) m customer

Kunde[2] ['kʊndə] f (*Botschaft*) news

Kunden- zW: ~**dienst** m after-sales service; ~**konto** nt charge account; ~**nummer** f customer number

Kund- zW: **k~geben** (unreg) vt to announce; ~**gebung** f announcement; (*Versammlung*) rally

Künd- ['kʏnd] zW: **k~igen** vi to give in one's notice ♦ vt to cancel; **jdm k~igen** to give sb his notice; **die Stellung/Wohnung k~igen** to give notice that one is leaving one's job/house; **jdm die Stellung/Wohnung k~igen** to give sb notice to leave his/her job/house; ~**igung** f notice; ~**igungsfrist** f period of notice; ~**igungsschutz** m protection against wrongful dismissal

Kundin f customer

Kundschaft f customers pl, clientele

künftig ['kʏnftɪç] adj future ♦ adv in future

Kunst [kʊnst] (-, -̈e) f art; (*Können*) skill; **das ist doch keine ~** it's easy; ~**dünger** m artificial manure; ~**faser** f synthetic fibre; ~**fertigkeit** f skilfulness; ~**gegenstand** m art object; ~**gerecht** adj skilful; ~**geschichte**

history of art; **~gewerbe** nt arts and crafts pl; **~griff** m trick, knack; **~händler** m art dealer

Künstler(in) ['kʏnstlər(ɪn)] (-s, -) m(f) artist; **k~isch** adj artistic; **~name** m pseudonym

künstlich ['kʏnstlɪç] adj artificial

Kunst- zW: **~sammler** (-s, -) m art collector; **~seide** f artificial silk; **~stoff** m synthetic material; **~stück** nt trick; **~turnen** nt gymnastics sg; **k~voll** adj artistic; **~werk** nt work of art

kunterbunt ['kʊntərbʊnt] adj higgledy-piggledy

Kupee ▲ [ku'peː] (-s, -s) nt coupé

Kupfer ['kʊpfər] (-s) nt copper; **k~n** adj copper

Kupon [ku'põː; ku'pɔŋ] (-s, -s) m coupon; (Stoff~) length of cloth

Kuppe ['kʊpə] f (Bergkuppe) top; (Fingerkuppe) tip

Kuppel (-, -n) f dome; **k~n** vi (JUR) to procure; (AUT) to declutch ♦ vt to join

Kupplung f coupling; (AUT) clutch

Kur [kuːr] (-, -en) f cure, treatment

Kür [kyːr] (-, -en) f (SPORT) free exercises pl

Kurbel ['kʊrbəl] (-, -n) f crank, winder; **~welle** f crankshaft

Kürbis ['kʏrbɪs] (-ses, -se) m pumpkin; (exotisch) gourd

Kurgast m visitor (to a health resort)

kurieren [ku'riːrən] vt to cure

kurios [kuri'oːs] adj curious, odd; **K~i'tät** f curiosity

Kurort m health resort

Kurs [kʊrs] (-es, -e) m course; (FIN) rate; **~buch** nt timetable; **k~ieren** [kʊr'ziːrən] vi to circulate; **k~iv** [kʊr'ziːf] adv in italics; **~us** ['kʊrzʊs] (-, Kurse) m course; **~wagen** m (EISENB) through carriage

Kurtaxe f -taksə] (-, -n) f visitors' tax (at health resort or spa)

Kurve ['kʊrvə] f curve; (Straßenkurve) curve, bend; **kurvig** adj (Straße) bendy

kurz [kʊrts] adj short; **~ gesagt** in short; **~ halten** to keep short; **zu ~ kommen** to come off badly; **den Kürzeren ziehen** to get the worst of it; **K~arbeit** f short-time work; **~ärm(e)lig** adj short-sleeved

Kürze ['kʏrtsə] f shortness, brevity; **k~n** vt to cut short; (in der Länge) to shorten; (Gehalt) to reduce

kurz- zW: **~erhand** adv on the spot; **~fristig** adj short-term; **K~geschichte** f short story; **~halten** △ (unreg) vt siehe **kurz**; **~lebig** adj short-lived

kürzlich ['kʏrtslɪç] adv lately, recently

Kurz- zW: **~schluss** △ m (ELEK) short circuit; **k~sichtig** adj short-sighted

Kürzung f (eines Textes) abridgement; (eines Theaterstück, des Gehalts) cut

Kurzwelle f short wave

kuscheln ['kʊʃəln] vr to snuggle up

Kusine [ku'ziːnə] f cousin

Kuss △ [kʊs] (-es, -e) m kiss

küssen ['kʏsən] vt, vr to kiss

Küste ['kʏstə] f coast, shore

Küstenwache f coastguard

Küster ['kʏstər] (-s, -) m sexton, verger

Kutsche ['kʊtʃə] f coach, carriage; **~r** (-s, -) m coachman

Kutte ['kʊtə] f habit

Kuvert [ku'vɛrt] (-s, -e od -s) nt envelope; cover

KZ nt abk von Konzentrationslager

L, l

l. abk = Liter

labil [la'biːl] adj (MED: Konstitution) delicate

Labor [la'boːr] (-s, -e od -s) nt lab; **~ant(in)** m(f) lab(oratory) assistant

Labyrinth [laby'rɪnt] (-s, -e) nt labyrinth

Lache ['laxə] f (Flüssigkeit) puddle; (von Blut, Benzin etc) pool

lächeln ['lɛçəln] vi to smile; **L~** (-s) nt smile

lachen ['laxən] vi to laugh

lächerlich ['lɛçərlıç] adj ridiculous

Lachgas nt laughing gas

lachhaft adj laughable

Lachs [laks] (-es, -e) m salmon

Lack [lak] (-(e)s, -e) m lacquer, varnish; (von Auto) paint; **l~ieren** [la'ki:rən] vt to varnish; (Auto) to spray; **~ierer** [la'ki:rər] (-s, -) m varnisher

Laden ['la:dən] (-s, -) m shop; (Fensterladen) shutter

laden ['la:dən] (unreg) vt (Lasten) to load; (JUR) to summon; (einladen) to invite

Laden- zW: **~dieb** m shoplifter; **~diebstahl** m shoplifting; **~schluss** ▲ m closing time; **~tisch** m counter

Laderaum m freight space; (AVIAT, NAUT) hold

Ladung ['la:dʊŋ] f (Last) cargo, load; (Beladen) loading; (JUR) summons; (Einladung) invitation; (Sprengladung) charge

Lage ['la:gə] f position, situation; (Schicht) layer; **in der ~ sein** to be in a position

Lageplan m ground plan

Lager ['la:gər] (-s, -) nt camp; (COMM) warehouse; (Schlaflager) bed; (von Tier) lair; (TECH) bearing; **~bestand** m stocks pl; **~feuer** nt campfire; **~haus** nt warehouse, store

lagern ['la:gərn] vi (Dinge) to be stored; (Menschen) to camp ♦ vt to store; (betten) to lay down; (Maschine) to bed

Lagune [la'gu:nə] f lagoon

lahm [la:m] adj lame; **~ legen** to paralyse

lahmen vi to be lame

Lähmung f paralysis

Laib [laip] (-s, -e) m loaf

Laie ['laiə] (-n, -n) m layman; **l~nhaft** adj amateurish

Laken ['la:kən] (-s, -) nt sheet

Lakritze [la'krıtsə] f liquorice

lallen ['lalən] vt, vi to slur; (Baby) to babble

Lamelle [la'mɛlə] f lamella; (ELEK) lamina; (TECH) plate

Lametta [la'mɛta] (-s) nt tinsel

Lamm [lam] (-(e)s, ¨er) nt lamb

Lampe ['lampə] f lamp

Lampen- zW: **~fieber** nt stage fright; **~schirm** m lampshade

Lampion [lampi'õ:] (-s, -s) m Chinese lantern

Land [lant] (-(e)s, ¨er) nt land; (Nation, nicht Stadt) country; (Bundesland) state; **auf dem ~(e)** in the country; siehe **hierzulande**; **~besitz** m landed property; **~ebahn** f runway; **l~en** ['landən] vt, vi to land

> **Land**
>
> A *Land* (plural *Länder*) is a member state of the BRD and of Austria. There are 16 *Länder* in Germany, namely Baden-Württemberg, Bayern, Berlin, Brandenburg, Bremen, Hamburg, Hessen, Mecklenburg-Vorpommern, Niedersachsen, Nordrhein-Westfalen, Rheinland-Pfalz, Saarland, Sachsen, Sachsen-Anhalt, Schleswig-Holstein and Thüringen. Each *Land* has its own parliament and constitution. The 9 *Länder* of Austria are Vorarlberg, Tirol, Salzburg, Oberösterreich, Niederösterreich, Kärnten, Steiermark, Burgenland and Wien.

Landes- ['landəs] zW: **~farben** pl national colours; **~innere(s)** nt inland region; **~sprache** f national language; **l~üblich** adj customary; **~verrat** m high treason; **~währung** f national currency; **l~weit** adj nationwide

Land- zW: **~haus** nt country house; **~karte** f map; **~kreis** m administrative region; **l~läufig** adj customary

ländlich ['lɛntlɪç] adj rural

Land- zW: **~schaft** f countryside; (KUNST) landscape; **~schaftsschutzgebiet** nt nature reserve; **~sitz** m country seat; **~straße** f country road; **~streicher** (-s, -) m tramp; **~strich** m region

Landung ['landʊŋ] f landing; **~sbrücke** f jetty, pier

Land- zW: **~weg** m: **etw auf dem ~weg befördern** to transport sth by land; **~wirt** m farmer; **~wirtschaft** f agriculture; **~zunge** f spit

lang [laŋ] adj (Mensch) tall; **~atmig** adj long-winded; **~e** adv (or a long time); (dauern, brauchen) a long time

Länge ['lɛŋə] f length; (GEOG) longitude

langen ['laŋən] vi (ausreichen) to do, to suffice; (fassen): **~ (nach)** to reach (for) ♦ vt: **jdm etw ~** to hand od pass sb sth; **es langt mir** I've had enough

Längengrad m longitude

Längenmaß nt linear measure

lang- zW: **L~eweile** f boredom; **~fristig** adj long-term; **~jährig** adj (Freundschaft, Gewohnheit) longstanding; **L~lauf** m (SKI) cross-country skiing

länglich adj longish

längs [lɛŋs] präp (+gen od dat) along ♦ adv lengthwise

lang- zW: **~sam** adj slow; **L~samkeit** f slowness; **L~schläfer(in)** m(f) late riser

längst [lɛŋst] adv: **das ist ~ fertig** that was finished a long time ago, that has been finished for a long time; **~e(r, s)** adj longest

lang- zW: **~weilen** vt to bore ♦ vr to be bored; **~weilig** adj boring, tedious; **L~welle** f long wave; **~wierig** adj lengthy, long-drawn-out

Lanze ['lantsə] f lance

Lappalie [la'pa:liə] f trifle

Lappen ['lapən] (-s, -) m cloth, rag; (ANAT) lobe

läppisch ['lɛpɪʃ] adj foolish

Lapsus ['lapsʊs] (-, -) m slip

Laptop ['lɛptɔp] (-s, -s) m laptop (computer)

Lärche ['lɛrçə] f larch

Lärm [lɛrm] (-(e)s) m noise; **l~en** vi to be noisy, to make a noise

Larve ['larfə] f (BIOL) larva

lasch [laʃ] adj slack

Laser ['le:zər] (-s, -) m laser

SCHLÜSSELWORT

lassen ['lasən] (pt **ließ**, pp **gelassen** od (als Hilfsverb) **lassen**) vt **1** (unterlassen) to stop; (momentan) to leave; **das (sein!)** don't (do it)!; (hör auf) stop it!; **lass mich!** leave me alone; **lassen wir das!** let's leave it; **er kann die Trinken nicht lassen** he can't stop drinking

2 (zurücklassen) to leave; **etw lassen, wie es ist** to leave sth (just) as it is

3 (überlassen): **jdn ins Haus lassen** to let sb into the house

♦ vi: **lass mal, ich mache das schon** leave it, I'll do it

♦ Hilfsverb **1** (veranlassen): **etw machen lassen** to have od get sth done; **sich dat etw schicken lassen** to have sth sent (to one)

2 (zulassen): **jdn etw wissen lassen** to let sb know sth; **das Licht brennen lassen** to leave the light on; **jdn warten lassen** to keep sb waiting; **das lässt sich machen** that can be done

3: lass uns gehen let's go

lässig ['lɛsɪç] adj casual; **L~keit** f casualness

Last [last] (-, -en) f load, burden; (NAUT, AVIAT) cargo; (meist pl: Gebühr) charge; **jdm zur ~ fallen** to be a burden to sb;

~auto nt lorry, truck; **l~en** vi: **l~en auf** +dat to weigh on; **~enauzug** m goods lift od elevator (US)

Laster ['lastər] (-s, -) nt vice

lästern ['lɛstərn] vt, vi (Gott) to blaspheme; (schlecht sprechen) to mock

Lästerung f/ibe; (Gotteslästerung) blasphemy

lästig ['lɛstɪç] adj troublesome, tiresome

Last- zW: **~kahn** m barge; **~kraftwagen** m heavy goods vehicle; **~schrift** f debit; **~wagen** m lorry, truck; **~zug** m articulated lorry

Latein [la'taɪn] (-s) nt Latin; **~amerika** nt Latin America

latent [la'tɛnt] adj latent

Laterne [la'tɛrnə] f lantern; (Straßenlaterne) lamp, light; **~npfahl** m lamppost

latschen ['laːtʃən] (umg) vi (gehen) to wander, to go; (lässig) to slouch

Latte ['latə] f lath; (SPORT) goalpost; (quer) crossbar

Latzhose ['latsho:zə] f dungarees pl

lau [lao] adj (Nacht) balmy; (Wasser) lukewarm

Laub [laop] (-(e)s) nt foliage; **~baum** m deciduous tree; **~frosch** m tree frog; **~säge** f fretsaw

Lauch [laox] (-(e)s, -e) m leek

Lauer ['laoər] f: auf der ~ sein od liegen to lie in wait; **l~n** vi to lie in wait; (Gefahr) to lurk

Lauf [laof] (-(e)s, Läufe) m run; (Wettlauf) race; (Entwicklung, ASTRON) course; (Gewehrlauf) barrel; einer Sache dat ihren ~ lassen to let sth take its course; **~bahn** f career

laufen ['laofən] (unreg) vt, vi to run; (umg: gehen) to walk; **~d** adj running; (Monat, Ausgaben) current; auf dem **~den sein/halten** to be/keep up to date; am **~den Band** (fig) continuously

Läufer ['lɔyfər] (-s, -) m (Teppich, SPORT) runner; (Fußball) half-back; (Schach)

bishop

Lauf- zW: **~masche** f run, ladder (BRIT); **~pass** ▲ m: jdm den **~pass geben** (umg) to send sb packing (inf); **~stall** m playpen; **~steg** m catwalk; **~werk** nt (COMPUT) disk drive

Lauge ['laogə] f soapy water; (CHEM) alkaline solution

Laune ['laonə] f mood, humour; (Einfall) caprice; (schlechte) temper; **l~nhaft** adj capricious, changeable

launisch adj moody; bad-tempered

Laus [laos] (-, Läuse) f louse

lauschen ['laoʃən] vi to eavesdrop, to listen in

lauschig ['laoʃɪç] adj snug

lausig ['laozɪç] (umg: pej) adj measly; (Kälte) perishing

laut [laot] adj loud ♦ adv loudly; (lesen) aloud ♦ präp (+gen od dat) according to; **L~** (-(e)s, -e) m sound

Laute ['laotə] f lute

lauten ['laotən] vi to say; (Urteil) to be

läuten ['lɔytən] vt, vi to ring, to sound

lauter ['laotər] adj (Wasser) clear, pure; (Wahrheit, Charakter) honest ♦ adj inv (Freude, Dummheit etc) sheer ♦ adv nothing but, only

laut- zW: **~hals** adv at the top of one's voice; **~los** adj noiseless, silent; **L~schrift** f phonetics pl; **L~sprecher** m loudspeaker; **~stark** adj vociferous; **L~stärke** f (RADIO) volume

lauwarm ['laovarm] adj (auch fig) lukewarm

Lavendel [la'vɛndəl] (-s, -) m lavender

Lawine [la'vi:nə] f avalanche; **~ngefahr** f danger of avalanches

lax [laks] adj lax

Lazarett [latsa'rɛt] (-(e)s, -e) nt (MIL) hospital, infirmary

leasen ['li:zən] vt to lease

Leben (-s, -) nt life

leben ['le:bən] vt, vi to live; **~d** adj living; **~dig** [le'bɛndɪç] adj living, alive; (lebhaft) lively; **L~digkeit** f liveliness

Lebens- zW: **~art** f way of life; **~er-**

wartung *f* life expectancy; **l~fähig** *adj* able to live; **~freude** *f* zest for life; **~gefahr** *f*: **~gefahr!** danger!; **in ~gefahr** dangerously ill; **l~gefährlich** *adj* dangerous; (*Verletzung*) critical; **~haltungskosten** *pl* cost of living *sg*; **~jahr** *nt* year of life; **l~länglich** *adj* (*Strafe*) for life; **~lauf** *m* curriculum vitae; **~mittel** *nt* food *sg*; **~mittelgeschäft** *nt* grocer's (shop); **~mittelvergiftung** *f* (MED) food poisoning; **l~müde** *adj* tired of life; **~retter** *m* lifesaver; **~standard** *m* standard of living; **~unterhalt** *m* livelihood; **~versicherung** *f* life insurance; **~wandel** *m* way of life; **~weise** *f* lifestyle, way of life; **l~wichtig** *adj* vital, essential; **~zeichen** *nt* sign of life

Leber ['le:bər] (-, -n) *f* liver; **~fleck** *m* mole; **~tran** *m* cod-liver oil; **~wurst** *f* liver sausage

Lebewesen *nt* creature

leb- ['le:p] *zW*: **~haft** *adj* lively, vivacious; **L~kuchen** *m* gingerbread; **~los** *adj* lifeless

Leck [lɛk] (-(e)s, -e) *nt* leak; **l~** *adj* leaky, leaking; **l~en** *vi* (*Loch haben*) to leak; (*schlecken*) to lick ♦ *vt* to lick

lecker ['lɛkər] *adj* delicious, tasty; **L~bissen** *m* dainty morsel

Leder ['le:dər] (-s, -) *nt* leather; **~hose** *f* lederhosen; **l~n** *adj* leather; **~waren** *pl* leather goods

ledig ['le:dɪç] *adj* single; **einer Sache** *gen* **~ sein** to be free of sth; **~lich** *adv* merely, solely

leer [le:r] *adj* empty; vacant; **~ machen** to empty; **~ stehend** empty; **L~e** (-) *f* emptiness; **~en** *vt, vr* to empty; **L~gewicht** *nt* weight when empty; **L~gut** *nt* empties *pl*; **L~lauf** *m* neutral; **L~ung** *f* emptying; (*Post*) collection

legal [le'ga:l] *adj* legal, lawful; **l~i'sieren** *vt* to legalize

legen ['le:gən] *vt* to lay, to put, to

place; (*Ei*) to lay ♦ *vr* to lie down; (*fig*) to subside

Legende [le'gɛndə] *f* legend

leger [le'ʒe:r] *adj* casual

Legierung [le'gi:rʊŋ] *f* alloy

Legislative [legɪsla'ti:və] *f* legislature

legitim [legi'ti:m] *adj* legitimate

legitimieren [legiti'mi:rən] *vt* to legitimate ♦ *vr* to prove one's identity

Lehm [le:m] (-(e)s, -e) *m* loam; **l~ig** *adj* loamy

Lehne ['le:nə] *f* arm; back; **l~n** *vt, vr* to lean

Lehnstuhl *m* armchair

Lehr- *zW*: **~amt** *nt* teaching profession; **~buch** *nt* textbook

Lehre ['le:rə] *f* teaching, doctrine; (*beruflich*) apprenticeship; (*moralisch*) lesson; (*TECH*) gauge; **l~n** *vt* to teach

Lehrer(in) (-s, -) *m(f)* teacher; **~zimmer** *nt* staff room

Lehr- *zW*: **~gang** *m* course; **~jahre** *pl* apprenticeship *sg*; **~kraft** *f* (*förmlich*) teacher; **~ling** *m* apprentice; **~plan** *m* syllabus; **l~reich** *adj* instructive; **~stelle** *f* apprenticeship; **~zeit** *f* apprenticeship

Leib [laɪp] (-(e)s, -er) *m* body; **halt ihn mir vom ~!** keep him away from me!; **l~haftig** *adj* personified; (*Teufel*) incarnate; **l~lich** *adj* bodily; (*Vater etc*) own; **~schmerzen** *pl* stomach pains; **~wache** *f* bodyguard

Leiche ['laɪçə] *f* corpse; **~nhalle** *f* mortuary; **~nwagen** *m* hearse

Leichnam ['laɪçna:m] (-(e)s, -e) *m* corpse

leicht [laɪçt] *adj* light; (*einfach*) easy; **jdm ~ fallen** to be easy for sb; **es sich** *dat* **~ machen** to make things easy for o.s.; **L~athletik** *f* athletics *sg*; **~fertig** *adj* frivolous; **~gläubig** *adj* gullible, credulous; **~hin** *adv* lightly; **L~igkeit** *f* easiness; **mit L~igkeit** with ease; **L~sinn** *m* carelessness; **~sinnig** *adj* careless

Leid [laɪt] (-(e)s) nt grief, sorrow; **es tut mir/ihm ~** I am/he is sorry; **er/ das tut mir ~** I am sorry for him/it; **l~** adj: **etw l~ haben** od **sein** to be tired of sth; **l~en** (unreg) vt to suffer; (erlauben) to permit ♦ vi to suffer; **jdn/etw nicht l~en können** not to be able to stand sb/sth; **~en** [laɪdən] (-s, -) nt suffering; (Krankheit) complaint; **~enschaft** f passion; **l~enschaftlich** adj passionate

leider ['laɪdər] adv unfortunately; **ja, ~** yes, I'm afraid so; **~ nicht** I'm afraid not

leidig ['laɪdɪç] adj worrying, troublesome

leidlich [laɪtlɪç] adj tolerable ♦ adv tolerably

Leid- zW: **~tragende(r)** f(m) bereaved; (Benachteiligter) one who suffers; **~wesen** nt: **zu jds ~wesen** to sb's disappointment

Leier ['laɪər] (-s, -) f lyre; (fig) old story; **~kasten** m barrel organ

Leihbibliothek f lending library

Leihbücherei f lending library

leihen ['laɪən] (unreg) vt to lend; **sich** dat **etw ~** to borrow sth

Leih- zW: **~gebühr** f hire charge; **~haus** nt pawnshop; **~wagen** m hired car

Leim [laɪm] (-(e)s, -e) m glue; **l~en** vt to glue

Leine ['laɪnə] f line, cord; (Hundeleine) leash, lead

Leinen nt linen; **l~** adj linen

Leinwand f (KUNST) canvas; (CINE) screen

leise ['laɪzə] adj quiet; (sanft) soft, gentle

Leiste ['laɪstə] f ledge; (Zierleiste) strip; (ANAT) groin

leisten ['laɪstən] vt (Arbeit) to do; (Gesellschaft) to keep; (Ersatz) to supply; (vollbringen) to achieve; **sich** dat **etw ~ können** to be able to afford sth

Leistung f performance; (gute) achievement; **l~sdruck** m pressure; **l~sfähig** adj efficient

Leitartikel m leading article

Leitbild nt model

leiten ['laɪtən] vt to lead; (Firma) to manage; (in eine Richtung) to direct; (ELEK) to conduct

Leiter¹ ['laɪtər] (-s, -) m leader, head; (ELEK) conductor

Leiter² ['laɪtər] (-, -n) f ladder

Leitfaden m guide

Leitplanke f crash barrier

Leitung f (Führung) direction; (CINE, THEAT etc) production; (von Firma) management; directors pl; (Wasserleitung) pipe; (Kabel) cable; **eine lange ~ haben** to be slow on the uptake

Leitungs- zW: **~draht** m wire; **~rohr** nt pipe; **~wasser** nt tap water

Lektion [lɛktsi'oːn] f lesson

Lektüre [lɛk'tyːrə] f (das Lesen) reading; (Lesestoff) reading matter

Lende ['lɛndə] f loin; **~nstück** nt fillet

lenk- ['lɛŋk] zW: **~bar** adj (Fahrzeug) steerable; (Kind) manageable; **~en** vt to steer; (Kind) to guide; (Blick, Aufmerksamkeit): **~en (auf** +akk) to direct (at); **~rad** nt steering wheel; **L~radschloss** ▲ nt steering (wheel) lock; **L~stange** f handlebars pl; **L~ung** f steering

Lepra ['leːpra] (-) f leprosy

Lerche ['lɛrçə] f lark

lernbegierig adj eager to learn

lernen ['lɛrnən] vt to learn

lesbar ['leːsbaːr] adj legible

Lesbierin ['lɛsbiərɪn] f lesbian

lesbisch ['lɛsbɪʃ] adj lesbian

Lese ['leːzə] f (Wein) harvest

Lesebrille f reading glasses

Lesebuch nt reading book, reader

lesen (unreg) vt, vi to read; (ernten) to gather, to pick

Leser(in) (-s, -) m(f) reader; **~brief** m reader's letter; **l~lich** adj legible

Lesezeichen nt bookmark

Lesung ['le:zʊŋ] f (PARL) reading

letzte(r, s) ['lɛtstə(r, s)] adj last; (neueste) latest; **zum ~n Mal** for the last time; **~ns** adv lately; **~re(r, s)** latter

Leuchte ['lɔʏçtə] f lamp, light; **l~n** vi to shine, to gleam; **~r (-s, -)** m candlestick

Leucht- zW: **~farbe** f fluorescent colour; **~rakete** f flare; **~reklame** f neon sign; **~röhre** f strip light; **~turm** m lighthouse

leugnen ['lɔʏgnən] vt to deny

Leukämie [lɔʏkɛ'mi:] f leukaemia

Leukoplast [lɔʏko'plast] ® (R), -(e)s, -e) nt Elastoplast ®

Leumund ['lɔʏmʊnt] (-(e)s, -e) m reputation

Leumundszeugnis nt character reference

Leute ['lɔʏtə] pl people pl

Leutnant ['lɔʏtnant] (-s, -s od -e) m lieutenant

leutselig ['lɔʏtze:lɪç] adj amiable

Lexikon ['lɛksikɔn] (-s, Lexiken od Lexika) nt encyclop(a)edia

Libelle [li'bɛlə] f dragonfly; (TECH) spirit level

liberal [libe'ra:l] adj liberal; **L~e(r)** f(m) liberal

Licht [lɪçt] (-(e)s, -er) nt light; ~bild nt photograph; (Dia) slide; **~blick** m cheering prospect; **l~empfindlich** adj sensitive to light; **l~en** vt to clear; (Anker) to weigh ♦ vr to clear up; (Haar) to thin; **l~erloh** adv: **l~erloh brennen** to be ablaze; **~hupe** f flashing of headlights; **~jahr** nt light year; **~maschine** f dynamo; **~schalter** m light switch; **~schutzfaktor** m protection factor

Lichtung f clearing, glade

Lid [li:t] (-(e)s, -er) nt eyelid; **~schatten** m eyeshadow

lieb [li:p] adj dear; **das ist ~ von dir**

that's kind of you; **~ gewinnen** to get fond of; **~ haben** to be fond of; **~äugeln** ['li:bɔʏgəln] vi insep: **mit etw ~äugeln** to have one's eye on sth; **mit dem Gedanken ~äugeln, etw zu tun** to toy with the idea of doing sth

Liebe ['li:bə] f love; **l~bedürftig** adj: **l~bedürftig sein** to need love; **l~n** vt to love; to like

liebens- zW: **~wert** adj loveable; **~würdig** adj kind; **~würdigerweise** adv kindly; **L~würdigkeit** f kindness

lieber ['li:bər] adv rather, preferably; **ich gehe ~ nicht** I'd rather not go; siehe auch **gern**; **lieb**

Liebes- zW: **~brief** m love letter; **~kummer** m: **~kummer haben** to be lovesick; **~paar** nt courting couple, lovers pl

liebevoll adj loving

lieb- [li:p] zW: **~gewinnen** △ (unreg) vt siehe **lieb**; **~haben** △ (unreg) vt siehe **lieb**; **L~haber (-s, -)** m lover; **L~haberei** f hobby; **~kosen** [li:pko:zən] vt insep to caress; **~lich** adj lovely, charming; **L~ling** m darling; **L~lings-** in zW favourite; **~los** adj unloving; **L~schaft** f love affair

Lied [li:t] (-(e)s, -er) nt song; (REL) hymn; **~erbuch** ['li:dər-] nt songbook; hymn book

liederlich ['li:dərlɪç] adj slovenly; (Lebenswandel) loose, immoral; **L~keit** f slovenliness; immorality

lief etc [li:f] vb siehe **laufen**

Lieferant [li:fə'rant] m supplier

Lieferbedingungen pl terms of delivery

liefern ['li:fərn] vt to deliver; (versorgen mit) to supply; (Beweis) to produce

Liefer- zW: **~schein** m delivery note; **~termin** m delivery date; **~ung** f delivery; supply; **~wagen** m van; **~zeit** f delivery period

Liege ['li:gə] f bed

liegen ['li:gən] (*unreg*) vi to lie; (*sich befinden*) to be; **mir liegt nichts/viel daran** it doesn't matter to me/it matters a lot to me; **es liegt bei Ihnen, ob ...** it's up to you whether ...; **Sprachen ~ mir nicht** languages are not my line; **woran liegt es?** what's the cause?; **~ bleiben** (*im Bett*) to stay in bed; (*nicht aufstehen*) to stay lying down; (*vergessen werden*) to be left (behind); **~ lassen** (*vergessen*) to leave behind

Liege- *zW*: **~sitz** m (*AUT*) reclining seat; **~stuhl** m deck chair; **~wagen** m (*EISENB*) couchette

Lift [lɪft] (-(e)s, -e *od* -s) m lift

Likör [li'kø:r] (-s, -e) m liqueur

lila ['li:la] *adj inv* purple, lilac; **L~** (-s, -s) *nt* (*Farbe*) purple, lilac

Lilie ['li:liə] f lily

Limonade [limo'na:də] f lemonade

Limone [li'mo:nə] f lime

Linde ['lɪndə] f lime tree, linden

lindern ['lɪndərn] vt to alleviate, to soothe; **Linderung** f alleviation

Lineal [line'a:l] (-s, -e) *nt* ruler

Linie ['li:niə] f line

Linien- *zW*: **~blatt** *nt* ruled sheet; **~flug** m scheduled flight; **~richter** m linesman

linieren [li'ni:rən] vt to line

Linke ['lɪŋkə] f left side; left hand; (*POL*) left

linkisch *adj* awkward, gauche

links [lɪŋks] *adv* left; to *od* on the left; **~ von mir** *od* to my left; **L~händer(in)** (-s, -) m(f) left-handed person; **L~kurve** f left-hand bend; **L~verkehr** m driving on the left

Linoleum [li'no:leum] (-s) *nt* lino(leum)

Linse ['lɪnzə] f lentil; (*optisch*) lens sg

Lippe ['lɪpə] f lip; **~nstift** m lipstick

lispeln ['lɪspəln] vi to lisp

Lissabon ['lɪsabɔn] (-s) *nt* Lisbon

List [lɪst] (-, -en) f cunning; trick, ruse

Liste ['lɪstə] f list

listig ['lɪstɪç] *adj* cunning, sly

Liter ['li:tər] (-s, -) *nt od* m litre

literarisch [lite'ra:rɪʃ] *adj* literary

Literatur [litera'tu:r] f literature

Litfaßsäule ['lɪtfaszɔylə] f advertising pillar

Liturgie [litur'gi:] f liturgy

liturgisch [li'torgɪʃ] *adj* liturgical

Litze ['lɪtsə] f braid; (*ELEK*) flex

Lizenz [li'tsɛnts] f licence

Lkw [ɛlka:'ve:] (-(s), -(s)) m abk = **Lastkraftwagen**

Lob [lo:p] (-(e)s) *nt* praise

loben ['lo:bən] vt to praise; **~swert** *adj* praiseworthy

löblich ['lø:plɪç] *adj* praiseworthy, laudable

Loch [lɔx] (-(e)s, ⁻er) *nt* hole; **l~en** vt to punch holes in; **~er** (-s, -) m punch

löcherig ['lœçərɪç] *adj* full of holes

Lochkarte f punch card

Lochstreifen m punch tape

Locke ['lɔkə] f lock, curl; **l~n** vt to entice; (*Haare*) to curl; **~nwickler** (-s, -) m curler

locker ['lɔkər] *adj* loose; **~lassen** (*unreg*) vi: **nicht ~lassen** not to let up; **~n** vt to loosen

lockig ['lɔkɪç] *adj* curly

lodern ['lo:dərn] vi to blaze

Löffel ['lœfəl] (-s, -) m spoon

löffeln vt to spoon

Loge ['lo:ʒə] f (*THEAT*) box; (*Freimaurer*) (masonic) lodge; (*Pförtnerloge*) office

Logik ['lo:gɪk] f logic

logisch ['lo:gɪʃ] *adj* logical

Logopäde [logo'pɛ:də] (-n, -n) m speech therapist

Lohn [lo:n] (-(e)s, ⁻e) m reward; (*Arbeitslohn*) pay, wages pl; **~büro** *nt* wages office; **~empfänger** m wage earner

lohnen ['lo:nən] vr unpers to be worth it ♦ vt: (jdm etw)~ to reward (sb for sth); **~d** *adj* worthwhile

Lohn- *zW*: **~erhöhung** f pay rise;

~steuer f income tax; **~steuerkarte** f (income) tax card; **~streifen** m pay slip; **~tüte** f pay packet

Lokal [loˈkaːl] (-(e)s, -e) nt pub(lic house)

lokal adj local; **~isieren** vt to localize

Lokomotive [lokomoˈtiːvə] f locomotive

Lokomotivführer m engine driver

Lorbeer [ˈlɔrbeːr] (-s, -en) m auch (fig) laurel; **~blatt** nt (KOCH) bay leaf

Los [loːs] (-es, -e) nt (Schicksal) lot, fate; (Lotterielos) lottery ticket

los [loːs] adj (locker) loose; **~! go on!**; etw **~ sein** to be rid of sth; **was ist ~?** what's the matter?; **dort ist nichts/viel ~** there's nothing/a lot going on there; **~binden** (unreg) vt to untie

Löschblatt [ˈlœʃblat] nt sheet of blotting paper

löschen [ˈlœʃən] vt (Feuer, Licht) to put out, to extinguish; (Durst) to quench; (COMM) to cancel; (COMPUT) to delete; (Tonband) to erase; (Fracht) to unload ♦ vi (Feuerwehr) to put out a fire; (Tinte) to blot

Lösch- zW: **~fahrzeug** nt fire engine; fire boat; **~gerät** nt fire extinguisher; **~papier** nt blotting paper

lose [ˈloːzə] adj loose

Lösegeld nt ransom

losen [ˈloːzən] vi to draw lots

lösen [ˈløːzən] vt to loosen; (Rätsel etc) to solve; (Verlobung) to call off; (CHEM) to dissolve; (Partnerschaft) to break up; (Fahrkarte) to buy ♦ vr (aufgehen) to come loose; (Zucker etc) to dissolve; (Problem, Schwierigkeit) to (re)solve itself

los- zW: **~fahren** (unreg) vi to leave; **~gehen** (unreg) vi to set out; (anfangen) to start; (Bombe) to go off; **auf jdn ~gehen** to go for sb; **~kaufen** vt (Gefangene, Geißeln) to pay ransom for; **~kommen** (unreg) vi: **von etw**

~kommen to get away from sth; **~lassen** (unreg) vt (Seil) to let go of; (Schimpfe) to let loose; **~laufen** (unreg) vi to run off

löslich [ˈløːslɪç] adj soluble; **L~keit** f solubility

los- zW: **~lösen** vt: **(sich) ~lösen** to free (o.s.); **~machen** to loosen; (Boot) to unmoor vr to get away; **~schrauben** vt to unscrew

Losung [ˈloːzʊŋ] f watchword, slogan

Lösung [ˈløːzʊŋ] f (Lockermachen) loosening; (eines Rätsels, CHEM) solution; **~smittel** nt solvent

los- zW: **~werden** (unreg) vt to get rid of; **~ziehen** (unreg) (umg) vi (sich aufmachen) to set off

Lot [loːt] (-(e)s, -e) nt plumbline; **im ~** vertical; (fig) on an even keel

löten [ˈløːtən] vt to solder

Lothringen [ˈloːtrɪŋən] (-s) nt Lorraine

Lotse [ˈloːtsə] (-n, -n) m pilot; (AVIAT) air traffic controller; **l~n** vt to pilot; (umg) to lure

Lotterie [lɔtəˈriː] f lottery

Lotto [ˈlɔto] (-s, -s) nt national lottery; **~zahlen** pl winning lottery numbers

Löwe [ˈløːvə] (-n, -n) m lion; (ASTROL) Leo; **~nanteil** m lion's share; **~nzahn** m dandelion

loyal [loaˈjaːl] adj loyal; **L~ität** f loyalty

Luchs [lʊks] (-es, -e) m lynx

Lücke [ˈlʏkə] f gap

Lücken- zW: **~büßer** (-s, -) m stopgap; **l~haft** adj full of gaps; (Versorgung, Vorräte etc) inadequate; **l~los** adj complete

Luft [lʊft] (-, -e) f air; (Atem) breath; **in der ~ liegen** to be in the air; **jdn wie ~ behandeln** to ignore sb; **~angriff** m air raid; **~ballon** m balloon; **~blase** f air bubble; **l~dicht** adj airtight; **~druck** m atmospheric pressure

lüften [ˈlʏftən] vt to air; (Hut) to lift, to raise ♦ vi to let some air in

Luft- _zW:_ ~**fahrt** _f_ aviation; ~**fracht** _f_ air freight; **l~gekühlt** _adj_ air-cooled; ~**gewehr** _nt_ air rifle, airgun; **l~ig** _adj_ (_Ort_) breezy; (_Raum_) airy; (_Kleider_) summery; ~**kissenfahrzeug** _nt_ hovercraft; ~**kurort** _m_ health resort; **l~leer** _adj:_ **l~leerer Raum** vacuum; ~**linie** _f:_ **in der ~linie** as the crow flies; ~**loch** _nt_ air hole; (_AVIAT_) air pocket; ~**matratze** _f_ Lilo ® (_BRIT_), air mattress; ~**pirat** _m_ hijacker; ~**post** _f_ airmail; ~**pumpe** _f_ air pump; ~**röhre** _f_ (_ANAT_) windpipe; ~**schlange** _f_ streamer; ~**schutzkeller** _m_ air-raid shelter; ~**verkehr** _m_ air traffic; ~**verschmutzung** _f_ air pollution; ~**waffe** _f_ air force; ~**zug** _m_ draught

Lüge ['ly:gə] _f_ lie; **jdn/etw ~n strafen** to give the lie to sb/sth; **l~n** (_unreg_) _vi_ to lie

Lügner(in) (**-s, -**) _m(f)_ liar

Luke ['lu:kə] _f_ dormer window; hatch

Lump [lʊmp] (**-en, -en**) _m_ scamp, rascal

Lumpen ['lʊmpən] (**-s, -**) _m_ rag

lumpen ['lʊmpən] _vi:_ **sich nicht ~ lassen** not to be mean

lumpig ['lʊmpɪç] _adj_ shabby

Lupe ['lu:pə] _f_ magnifying glass; **unter die ~ nehmen** (_fig_) to scrutinize

Lust [lʊst] (**-, ~e**) _f_ joy, delight; (_Neigung_) desire; **~ haben** _zu od_ **auf etw** _akk_**/etw zu tun** to feel like sth/doing sth

lüstern ['lʏstərn] _adj_ lustful, lecherous

lustig ['lʊstɪç] _adj_ (_komisch_) amusing, funny; (_fröhlich_) cheerful

Lust- _zW:_ **l~los** _adj_ unenthusiastic; ~**mord** _m_ sex(ual) murder; ~**spiel** _nt_ comedy

lutschen ['lʊtʃən] _vt, vi_ to suck; **am Daumen ~** to suck one's thumb

Lutscher (**-s, -**) _m_ lollipop

luxuriös [lʊksuri'øːs] _adj_ luxurious

Luxus ['lʊksʊs] (**-**) _m_ luxury; ~**artikel** _pl_ luxury goods; ~**hotel** _nt_ luxury hotel

Luzern [lu'tsɛrn] (**-s**) _nt_ Lucerne

Lymphe ['lʏmfə] _f_ lymph

lynchen ['lʏnçən] _vt_ to lynch

Lyrik ['ly:rɪk] _f_ lyric poetry; ~**er** (**-s, -**) _m_ lyric poet

lyrisch ['ly:rɪʃ] _adj_ lyrical

M, m

m _abk_ = **Meter**

Machart _f_ make

machbar _adj_ feasible

machen ['maxən] _vt_ **1** to do; (_herstellen, zubereiten_) to make; **was machst du da?** what are you doing (there)?; **das ist nicht zu machen** that can't be done; **das Radio leiser machen** to turn the radio down; **aus Holz gemacht** made of wood

2 (_verursachen, bewirken_) to make; **jdm Angst machen** to make sb afraid; **das macht die Kälte** it's the cold that does that

3 (_ausmachen_) to matter; **das macht nichts** that doesn't matter; **die Kälte macht mir nichts** I don't mind the cold

4 (_kosten, ergeben_) to be; **3 und 5 macht 8** 3 and 5 are 8; **was od wie viel macht das?** how much does that make?

5: **was macht die Arbeit?** how's the work going?; **was macht dein Bruder?** how is your brother doing?; **das Auto machen lassen** to have the car done; **machs gut!** take care!; (_viel Glück_) good luck!

♦ _vi:_ **mach schnell!** hurry up!; **Schluss machen** to finish (off); **mach schon!** come on!; **das macht müde** it makes you tired; **in etw** _dat_ **machen** to be _od_ deal in sth

♦ _vr_ (_sich anstellen_) **sich an etw** _akk_ **machen** to set about sth; **sich verständlich machen** to make o.s.

understood; **sich** dat **viel aus jdm/ etw machen** to like sb/sth

Macht [maxt] (-, ⁻e) f power; **~haber** (-s, -) m ruler

mächtig ['mɛçtɪç] adj powerful, mighty; (umg: ungeheuer) enormous

Macht- zW: **m~los** adj powerless; **~probe** f trial of strength; **~wort** nt: **ein ~wort sprechen** to exercise one's authority

Mädchen ['mɛːtçən] nt girl; **m~haft** adj girlish; **~name** m maiden name

Made ['maːdə] f maggot

madig ['maːdɪç] adj maggoty; **jdm etw ~ machen** to spoil sth for sb

mag etc [maːk] vb siehe **mögen**

Magazin [maga'tsiːn] (-s, -e) nt magazine

Magen ['maːgən] (-s, - od ⁻) m stomach; **~geschwür** nt (MED) stomach ulcer; **~schmerzen** pl stomachache sg

mager ['maːgər] adj lean; (dünn) thin; **M~keit** f leanness; thinness

Magie [ma'giː] f magic

magisch ['maːgɪʃ] adj magic

Magnet [ma'gneːt] (-s od -en, -en) m magnet; **m~isch** adj magnetic; **~nadel** f magnetic needle

mähen ['mɛːən] vt, vi to mow

Mahl [maːl] (-(e)s, -e) nt meal; **m~en** (unreg) vt to grind; **~zeit** f meal ♦ excl enjoy your meal

Mahnbrief m reminder

Mähne ['mɛːnə] f mane

mahn- ['maːn] zW: **~en** vt to remind; (warnend) to warn; (wegen Schuld) to demand payment from; **M~mal** nt memorial; **M~ung** f reminder; admonition, warning

Mai [maɪ] (-(e)s, -e) m May; **~glöckchen** nt lily of the valley

Mailand ['maɪlant] nt Milan

mailändisch adj Milanese

Mais [maɪs] (-es, -e) m maize, corn

(US); **~kolben** m corncob; **~mehl** nt (KOCH) corn meal

Majestät [majɛs'tɛːt] f majesty; **m~isch** adj majestic

Majonäse ▲ [majo'nɛːzə] f mayonnaise

Major [ma'joːr] (-s, -e) m (MIL) major; (AVIAT) squadron leader

Majoran [majo'raːn] (-s, -e) m marjoram

makaber [ma'kaːbər] adj macabre

Makel [maːkəl] (-s, -) m blemish; (moralisch) stain; **m~los** adj immaculate, spotless

mäkeln ['mɛːkəln] vi to find fault

Makler(in) ['maːklər(ɪn)] (-s, -) m(f) broker

Makrele [ma'kreːlə] f mackerel

Mal [maːl] (-(e)s, -e) nt mark, sign; (Zeitpunkt) time; **ein für alle ~** once and for all; **m~** adv times; (umg) siehe **einmal** ♦ suffix: **-m~** -times

malen vt, vi to paint

Maler [-ər] m painter; **Male'rei** f painting; **m~isch** adj picturesque

Malkasten m paintbox

Mallorca [ma'jɔrka, ma'lɔrka] (-s) nt Majorca

malnehmen (unreg) vt, vi to multiply

Malz [malts] (-es) nt malt; **~bier** nt (KOCH) malt beer; **~bonbon** m cough drop; **~kaffee** m malt coffee

Mama ['mama:] (-, -s) (umg) f mum(my) (BRIT), mom(my) (US)

Mami ['mami] (-, -s) = **Mama**

Mammut ['mamot] (-s, -e od -s) nt mammoth

man [man] pron one, you; **~ sagt, ...** they od people say ...; **wie schreibt ~ das?** how do you write it?, how is it written?

Manager(in) ['mɛnɪdʒər(ɪn)] (-s, -) m(f) manager

manch [manç] (unver) pron many a

manche(r, s) ['mançə(r, s)] adj many

a; (*pl: einige*) a number of ♦ *pron* some

mancherlei [manʃər'laɪ] *adj inv* various ♦ *pron inv* a variety of things

manchmal *adv* sometimes

Mandant(in) [man'dant(ɪn)] *m(f)* (JUR) client

Mandarine [manda'ri:nə] *f* mandarin, tangerine

Mandat [man'da:t] (-(e)s, -e) *nt* mandate

Mandel ['mandəl] (-, -n) *f* almond; (ANAT) tonsil; **~entzündung** *f* (MED) tonsillitis

Manege [ma'ne:ʒə] *f* ring, arena

Mangel ['maŋəl] (-s, ²) *m* lack; (*Knappheit*) shortage; (*Fehler*) defect, fault; **~ an** +*dat* shortage of; **~erscheinung** *f* deficiency symptom; **m~haft** *adj* poor; (*fehlerhaft*) defective, faulty; **m~n** *vi unpers*: **es m~t jdm an etw** *dat* sb lacks sth ♦ *vt* (*Wäsche*) to mangle

mangels *präp* +*gen* for lack of

Manie [ma'ni:] *f* mania

Manier [ma'ni:r] (-) *f* manner; style; (*pej*) mannerism; **~en** *pl* (*Umgangsformen*) manners; **m~lich** *adj* well-mannered

Manifest [mani'fɛst] (-es, -e) *nt* manifesto

Maniküre [mani'ky:rə] *f* manicure

manipulieren [manipu'li:rən] *vt* to manipulate

Manko ['maŋko] (-s, -s) *nt* deficiency; (COMM) deficit

Mann [man] (-(e)s, ²er) *m* man; (*Ehemann*) husband; (NAUT) hand; **seinen ~ stehen** to hold one's own

Männchen ['mɛnçən] *nt* little man; (*Tier*) male

Mannequin ['manəkɛ:] (-s, -s) *nt* fashion model

männlich ['mɛnlɪç] *adj* (BIOL) male; (*fig*, GRAM) masculine

Mannschaft *f* (SPORT, *fig*) team; (AVIAT, NAUT) crew; (MIL) other ranks *pl*

Manöver [ma'nø:vər] (-s, -) *nt* manoeuvre

manövrieren [manø'vri:rən] *vt*, *vi* to manoeuvre

Mansarde [man'zardə] *f* attic

Manschette [man'ʃɛtə] *f* cuff; (TECH) collar; sleeve; **~nknopf** *m* cufflink

Mantel ['mantəl] (-s, ²) *m* coat; (TECH) casing, jacket

Manuskript [manu'skrɪpt] (-(e)s, -e) *nt* manuscript

Mappe ['mapə] *f* briefcase; (*Aktenmappe*) folder

Märchen ['mɛːrçən] *nt* fairy tale; **m~haft** *adj* fabulous; **~prinz** *m* Prince Charming

Margarine [marga'ri:nə] *f* margarine

Margerite [margə'ri:tə] *f* (BOT) marguerite

Marienkäfer [ma'ri:ənkɛːfər] *m* ladybird

Marine [ma'ri:nə] *f* navy; **m~blau** *adj* navy blue

marinieren [mari'ni:rən] *vt* to marinate

Marionette [mario'nɛtə] *f* puppet

Mark[1] [mark] (-, -) *f* (*Münze*) mark

Mark[2] [mark] (-(e)s) *nt* (*Knochenmark*) marrow; **jdm durch ~ und Bein gehen** to go right through sb

markant [mar'kant] *adj* striking

Marke ['markə] *f* mark; (*Warensorte*) brand; (*Fabrikat*) make; (*Rabattmarke*, *Briefmarke*) stamp; (*Essenmarke*) ticket; (*aus Metall etc*) token, disc

Markenartikel *m* proprietary article

markieren [mar'ki:rən] *vt* to mark; (*umg*) to act ♦ *vi* (*umg*) to act it

Markierung *f* marking

Markise [mar'ki:zə] *f* awning

Markstück *nt* one-mark piece

Markt [markt] (-(e)s, ²e) *m* market; **~forschung** *f* market research; **~lücke** *f* (COMM) opening, gap in the market; **~platz** *m* market place; **m~üblich** *adj* (*Preise*, *Mieten*) standard, usual; **~wert** *m* (COMM) market value; **~wirtschaft** *f* market economy

Marmelade [marmə'la:də] *f* jam

Marmor [ˈmarmɔr] (-s, -e) m marble; **m~ieren** [-ˈriːrən] vt to marble

Marokko [maˈrɔko] (-s) nt Morocco

Marone [maˈroːnə] (-, -n od **Maroni** f) f chestnut

Marotte [maˈrɔtə] f fad, quirk

Marsch¹ [marʃ] (-, -en) f marsh

Marsch² [marʃ] (-(e)s, -e) m march ♦ excl march!; **~befehl** m marching orders pl; **m~bereit** adj ready to move; **m~ieren** [marˈʃiːrən] vi to march

Märtyrer(in) [ˈmɛrtyrər(ɪn)] (-s, -) m(f) martyr

März [mɛrts] (-(es), -e) m March

Marzipan [martsiˈpaːn] (-s, -e) nt Marzipan

Masche [ˈmaʃə] f mesh; (Strickmasche) stitch; **das ist die neueste** – that's the latest thing; **~ndraht** m wire mesh; **m~nfest** adj run-resistant

Maschine [maˈʃiːnə] f machine; (Motor) engine; (Schreibmaschine) typewriter; **~ schreiben** to type; **m~ll** [maʃiˈnɛl] adj machine(-); mechanical

Maschinen- zW: **~bauer** m mechanical engineer; **~gewehr** nt machine gun; **~pistole** f submachine gun; **~schaden** m mechanical fault; **~schlosser** m fitter; **~schrift** f typescript

Maschinist [maʃiˈnɪst] m engineer

Maser [ˈmaːzər] (-, -n) f (von Holz) grain; **~n** pl (MED) measles sg

Maske [ˈmaskə] f mask; **~nball** m fancy-dress ball

maskieren [masˈkiːrən] vt to mask; (verkleiden) to dress up ♦ vr to disguise o.s.; to dress up

Maskottchen [masˈkɔtçən] nt (lucky) mascot

Maß¹ [maːs] (-es, -e) nt measure; (Mäßigung) moderation; (Grad) degree, extent; **~ halten** to exercise moderation

Maß² [maːs] (-, -(e)) f litre of beer

Massage [maˈsaːʒə] f massage

Maßanzug m made-to-measure suit

Maßarbeit f (fig) neat piece of work

Masse [ˈmasə] f mass

Maßeinheit f unit of measurement

Massen- zW: **~artikel** m mass-produced article; **~grab** nt mass grave; **m~haft** adj loads of; **~medien** pl mass media pl; **~veranstaltung** f mass meeting; **m~weise** adv on a large scale

Masseur [maˈsøːr] m masseur; **~in** f masseuse

maßgebend adj authoritative

maßhalten △ (unreg) vi siehe **Maß¹**

massieren [maˈsiːrən] vt to massage; (MIL) to mass

massig [ˈmasɪç] adj massive; (umg) massive amount of

mäßig [ˈmɛːsɪç] adj moderate; **~en** [ˈmɛːsɪgən] vt to restrain, to moderate; **M~keit** f moderation

Massiv (-s, -e) nt massif

massiv [maˈsiːf] adj solid; (fig) heavy, rough

Maß- zW: **~krug** m tankard; **m~los** adj extreme; **~nahme** f measure, step; **~stab** m rule, measure; (fig) standard; (GEOG) scale; **m~voll** adj moderate

Mast [mast] (-(e)s, -e(n)) m mast; (ELEK) pylon

mästen [ˈmɛstən] vt to fatten

Material [mateˈriaːl] (-s, -ien) nt material(s); **~fehler** m material defect; **~ismus** [-ˈlɪsmʊs] m materialism; **m~istisch** [-ˈlɪstɪʃ] adj materialistic

Materie [maˈteːriə] f matter, substance

materiell [materiˈɛl] adj material

Mathematik [matemaˈtiːk] f mathematics sg; **~er(in)** [mateˈmaːtikər(ɪn)] (-s, -) m(f) mathematician

mathematisch [mateˈmaːtɪʃ] adj mathematical

Matjeshering [ˈmatjəsheːrɪŋ] m (KOCH) young herring

Spelling Reform: ▲ *new spelling* △ *old spelling (to be phased out)*

Matratze [ma'tratsə] f mattress

Matrixdrucker ['ma:trɪks-] m dot-matrix printer

Matrose [ma'tro:zə] (-n, -n) m sailor

Matsch [matʃ] (-(e)s) m mud; (*Schneematsch*) slush; **m~ig** adj muddy; slushy

matt [mat] adj weak; (*glanzlos*) dull; (*PHOT*) matt; (*SCHACH*) mate

Matte ['matə] f mat

Mattscheibe f (*TV*) screen

Mauer ['mauər] (-, -n) f wall; **m~n** vi to build; to lay bricks ♦ vt to build

Maul [maul] (-(e)s, Mäuler) nt mouth; **m~en** (umg) vi to grumble; **~esel** m mule; **~korb** m muzzle; **~sperre** f lockjaw; **~tasche** f (*KOCH*) pasta envelopes stuffed and used in soup; **~tier** nt mule; **~wurf** m mole

Maurer ['maurər] (-s, -) m bricklayer

Maus [maus] (-, Mäuse) f (auch *COMPUT*) mouse

Mause- ['mauzə] zW: **~falle** f mousetrap; **m~n** vi to catch mice ♦ vt (umg) to pinch; **m~tot** adj stone dead

Maut- ['maut] zW: **~gebühr** f toll (charge); **~straße** f toll road

maximal [maksi'ma:l] adj maximum ♦ adv at most

Mayonnaise [majɔ'nɛːzə] f mayonnaise

Mechan- [me'çaːn] zW: **~ik** f mechanics sg; (*Getriebe*) mechanics pl; **~iker** (-s, -) m mechanic, engineer; **m~isch** adj mechanical; **~ismus** m mechanism

meckern ['mɛkərn] vi to bleat; (umg) to moan

Medaille [me'daljə] f medal

Medaillon [medal'jõː] (-s, -s) nt (*Schmuck*) locket

Medikament [medika'mɛnt] nt medicine

Meditation [meditatsi'oːn] f meditation

meditieren [medi'tiːrən] vi to meditate

Medizin [medi'tsiːn] (-, -en) f medicine; **m~isch** adj medical

Meer [meːr] (-(e)s, -e) nt sea; **~enge** f straits pl; **~esfrüchte** pl seafood sg; **~esspiegel** m sea level; **~rettich** m horseradish; **~schweinchen** nt guinea-pig

Mehl [meːl] (-(e)s, -e) nt flour; **m~ig** adj floury; **~schwitze** f (*KOCH*) roux; **~speise** f (*KOCH*) flummery

mehr [meːr] adj, adv more; **~deutig** adj ambiguous; **~ere** adj several; **~eres** pron several things; **~fach** adj multiple; (*wiederholt*) repeated; **M~fahrtenkarte** f multi-journey ticket; **M~heit** f majority; **m~malig** adj repeated; **~mals** adv repeatedly; **~stimmig** adj for several voices; **~stimmig singen** to harmonize; **M~wertsteuer** f value added tax; **M~zahl** f majority; (*GRAM*) plural

Mehrzweck- in zW multipurpose

meiden ['maidən] (unreg) vt to avoid

Meile ['mailə] f mile; **~nstein** m milestone; **m~nweit** adj for miles

mein(e) [main] adj my; **~e(r, s)** pron mine

Meineid ['mainait] m perjury

meinen ['mainən] vi to think ♦ vt to think; (*sagen*) to say; (*sagen wollen*) to mean; **das will ich ~** I should think so

mein- zW: **~erseits** adv for my part; **~etwegen** adv (*für mich*) for my sake; (*wegen mir*) on my account; (*von mir aus*) as far as I'm concerned; I don't care or mind; **~etwillen** adv: **um ~etwillen** for my sake, on my account

Meinung ['mainuŋ] f opinion; **ganz meine ~** I quite agree; **jdm die ~ sagen** to give sb a piece of one's mind

Meinungs- zW: **~austausch** m exchange of views; **~umfrage** f opinion poll; **~verschiedenheit** f difference of opinion

Meise ['maizə] f tit(mouse)

Meißel ['maisəl] (-s, -) m chisel

meist [maist] adj most ♦ adv mostly; **am ~en** the most; **~ens** adv generally, usually

Meister ['maɪstər] (-s, -) m master; (SPORT) champion; **m~haft** adj masterly; **m~n** vt (Schwierigkeiten etc) to overcome, conquer; **~schaft** f mastery; (SPORT) championship; **~stück** nt masterpiece; **~werk** nt masterpiece

Melancholie [melaŋko'li:] f melancholy; **melancholisch** [melaŋ'ko:lɪʃ] adj melancholy

Melde- ['meldə] zW: **~frist** f registration period; **m~n** vt to report ♦ vr to report; (SCH) to put one's hand up; (freiwillig) to volunteer; (auf etw, am Telefon) to answer; **sich m~n bei** to report to; to register with; **sich zu Wort m~n** to ask to speak; **~pflicht** f obligation to register with the police; **~schluss** ▲ m closing date; **~stelle** f registration office

Meldung ['meldʊŋ] f announcement; (Bericht) report

meliert [me'li:rt] adj (Haar) greying; (Wolle) flecked

melken ['mɛlkən] (unreg) vt to milk

Melodie [melo'di:] f melody, tune

melodisch [me'lo:dɪʃ] adj melodious, tuneful

Melone [me'lo:nə] f melon; (Hut) bowler (hat)

Membran [mɛm'bra:n] (-, -en) f (TECH) diaphragm

Memoiren [memo'a:rən] pl memoirs

Menge ['mɛŋə] f quantity; (Menschenmenge) crowd; (große Anzahl) lot (of); **m~n** vt to mix ♦ vr: **sich m~n in** +akk to meddle with; **~nlehre** f (MATH) set theory; **~nrabatt** m bulk discount

Mensch [mɛnʃ] (-en, -en) m human being, man; person ♦ excl hey!; **kein ~** nobody

Menschen- zW: **~affe** m (ZOOL) ape; **m~freundlich** adj philanthropical; **~kenner** m judge of human nature; **m~leer** adj deserted; **m~möglich** adj

humanly possible; **~rechte** pl human rights; **m~unwürdig** adj beneath human dignity; **~verstand** m: **gesunder ~verstand** common sense

Mensch- zW: **~heit** f humanity, mankind; **m~lich** adj (auch: (human)) humane; **~lichkeit** f humanity

Menstruation [menstruatsi'o:n] f menstruation

Mentalität [mentali'tɛ:t] f mentality

Menü [me'ny:] (-s, -s) nt (auch COMPUT) menu

Merk- ['mɛrk] zW: **~blatt** nt instruction sheet od leaflet; **m~en** vt to notice; **sich dat etw m~en** to remember sth; **m~lich** adj noticeable; **~mal** nt sign, characteristic; **m~würdig** adj odd

messbar ▲ ['mɛsba:r] adj measurable

Messbecher ▲ m measuring jug

Messe ['mɛsə] f fair; (ECCL) mass; **~gelände** nt exhibition centre; **~halle** f pavilion at a fair

messen (unreg) vt to measure ♦ vr to compete

Messer (-s, -) nt knife; **~spitze** f knife point; (in Rezept) pinch

Messestand m stall at a fair

Messgerät ▲ nt measuring device, gauge

Messing ['mɛsɪŋ] (-s) nt brass

Metall [me'tal] (-s, -e) nt metal; **m~isch** adj metallic

Meter ['me:tər] (-s, -) nt od m metre; **~maß** nt tape measure

Methode [me'to:də] f method; **methodisch** adj methodical

Metropole [metro'po:lə] f metropolis

Metzger ['mɛtsgər] (-s, -) m butcher; **~ei** [-'raɪ] f butcher's (shop)

Meute ['mɔytə] f pack; **~rei** f mutiny; **m~rn** vi to mutiny

miauen [mi'aʊən] vi to miaow

mich [mɪç] (akk von ich) pron me; myself

Miene ['mi:nə] f look, expression

Spelling Reform: ▲ new spelling △ old spelling (to be phased out)

mies [miːs] *(umg) adj* lousy

Miet- ['miːt] *zW:* **~auto** *nt* hired car; **~e** *f* rent; **zur ~e wohnen** to live in rented accommodation; **m~en** *vt* to rent; *(Auto)* to hire; **~er(in)** *(-s, -) m(f)* tenant; **~shaus** *nt* tenement, block of (rented) flats; **~vertrag** *m* lease

Migräne [mi'grɛːnə] *f* migraine

Mikro- ['mikro] *zW:* **~fon**, **~phon** [-'foːn] *(-s, -e) nt* microphone; **~skop** [-'skoːp] *(-s, -e) nt* microscope; **m~skopisch** *adj* microscopic; **~wellenherd** *m* microwave (oven)

Milch [mɪlç] *(-) f* milk; **~glas** *nt* frosted glass; **m~ig** *adj* milky; **~kaffee** *m* white coffee; **~mann** *(pl -männer) m* milkman; **~mixgetränk** *nt (KOCH)* milkshake; **~pulver** *nt* powdered milk; **~straße** *f* Milky Way; **~zahn** *m* milk tooth

mild [mɪlt] *adj* mild; *(Richter)* lenient; *(freundlich)* kind, charitable; **M~e** *f* mildness; leniency; **~ern** *vt* to mitigate, to soften; *(Schmerz)* to alleviate; **~ernde Umstände** extenuating circumstances

Milieu [mili'øː] *(-s, -s) nt* background, environment; **m~geschädigt** *adj* maladjusted

Mili- [mili] *zW:* **m~tant** [-'tant] *adj* militant; **~tär** [-'tɛːr] *(-s) nt* military, army; **~'tärgericht** *nt* military court; **m~'tärisch** *adj* military

Milli- [mɪli] *zW:* **~ardär** [-ar'dɛːr] *m* multimillionaire; **~arde** [-'ardə] *f* milliard; billion *(BRIT)*; **~meter** *m* millimetre; **~meterpapier** *nt* graph paper

Million [mil'joːn] *(-, -en) f* million; **~är** [-o'nɛːr] *m* millionaire

Milz [mɪlts] *(-, -en) f* spleen

Mimik ['miːmik] *f* mime

Mimose [mi'moːzə] *f* mimosa; *(fig)* sensitive person

minder ['mɪndər] *adj* inferior ♦ *adv* less; **M~heit** *f* minority; **m~jährig** *adj* minor; **M~jährige(r)** *f(m)* minor; **~n** *vt, vr* to decrease, to diminish; **M~ung** *f* de-

crease; **~wertig** *adj* inferior; **M~wertigkeitskomplex** *m* inferiority complex

Mindest- ['mɪndəst] *zW:* **~alter** *nt* minimum age; **~betrag** *m* minimum amount; **m~e(r, s)** *adj* least; **zum ~en** *od* **m~en** at least; **m~ens** *adv* at least; **~haltbarkeitsdatum** *nt* best-before date; **~lohn** *m* minimum wage; **~maß** *nt* minimum

Mine ['miːnə] *f* mine; *(Bleistiftmine)* lead; *(Kugelschreibermine)* refill

Mineral [mine'raːl] *(-s, -e od -ien) nt* mineral; **m~isch** *adj* mineral; **~wasser** *nt* mineral water

Miniatur [minia'tuːr] *f* miniature

Mini- [mini] *zW:* **~golf** ['miːngɔlf] *m* miniature golf, crazy golf; **m~mal** [mini'maːl] *adj* minimal; **~mum** ['miːnimɔm] *nt* minimum; **~rock** *m* miniskirt

Minister [mi'nɪstər] *(-s, -) m* minister; **m~iell** *adj* ministerial; **~ium** *nt* ministry; **~präsident** *m* prime minister

Minus ['miːnus] *(-) nt* deficit

minus *adv* minus; **M~zeichen** *nt* minus sign

Minute [mi'nuːtə] *f* minute

Minze ['mɪntsə] *f* mint

mir [miːr] *(dat von* **ich***) pron* (to) me; **~ nichts, dir nichts** just like that

Misch- [mɪʃ] *zW:* **~brot** *nt* bread made from more than one kind of flour; **~ehe** *f* mixed marriage; **m~en** *vt* to mix; **~ling** *m* half-caste; **~ung** *f* mixture

miserabel [mizə'raːbəl] *(umg) adj (Essen, Film)* dreadful

Miss- ▲ ['mɪs] *zW:* **~behagen** *nt* discomfort, uneasiness; **~bildung** *f* deformity; **m~billigen** *vt insep* to disapprove of; **~brauch** *m* abuse; *(falscher Gebrauch)* misuse; **m~'brauchen** *vt insep* to abuse; **jdn zu od für etw m~brauchen** to use sb for od to do sth; **~erfolg** *m* failure; **~fallen** *(-s) nt* displeasure; **m~'fallen** *(unreg) vi insep:*

jdm m~fallen to displease sb; **~geschick** nt misfortune; **m~glücken** [mɪsˈglʏkən] vi insep to fail; **jdm m~glückt etw** sb does not succeed with sth; **~griff** m mistake; **~gunst** f envy; **m~günstig** adj envious; **m~handeln** vt insep to ill-treat; **~'handlung** f ill-treatment

Mission [mɪsiˈoːn] f mission; **~ar(in)** m(f) missionary

Miss- ▲ zW: **~klang** m discord; **~kredit** m discredit; **m~lingen** [mɪsˈlɪŋən] (unreg) vi insep to fail; **~mut** m sullenness; **m~mutig** adj sullen; **m~'raten** (unreg) vi insep to turn out badly ♦ adj ill-bred; **~stand** m bad state of affairs; abuse; **m~trauen** vi insep to mistrust; **~trauen (-s)** nt distrust, suspicion; **~trauensantrag** m (POL) motion of no confidence; **m~trauisch** adj distrustful, suspicious; **~verhältnis** nt disproportion; **~verständnis** nt misunderstanding; **m~verstehen** (unreg) vt insep to misunderstand; **~wirtschaft** f mismanagement

Mist [mɪst] (-(e)s) m dung; dirt; (umg) rubbish

Mistel (-, -n) f mistletoe

Misthaufen m dungheap

mit [mɪt] präp +dat with; **(~tels)** by ♦ adv along, too; **~ der Bahn** by train; **~10 Jahren** at the age of 10; **wollen Sie ~?** do you want to come along?

Mitarbeit [ˈmɪtʔarbaɪt] f cooperation; **m~en** vi to cooperate, to collaborate; **~er(in)** m(f) collaborator; co-worker ♦ pl (Personal) staff

Mit- zW: **~bestimmung** f participation in decision-making; **m~bringen** (unreg) vt to bring along

miteinander [mɪtʔaɪˈnandər] adv together, with one another

miterleben vt to see; to witness

Mitesser [ˈmɪtʔɛsər] (**-s, -**) m blackhead

mitfahr- zW: **~en** vi to accompany;

(auf Reise auch) to travel with; **m~gelegenheit** f lift; **M~zentrale** f agency for arranging lifts

mitfühlend adj sympathetic, compassionate

Mit- zW: **m~geben** (unreg) vt to give; **~gefühl** nt sympathy; **m~gehen** (unreg) vi to go/come along; **m~genommen** adj done in, in a bad way; **~gift** f dowry

Mitglied [ˈmɪtgliːt] nt member; **~sbeitrag** m membership fee; **~schaft** f membership

Mit- zW: **m~halten** (unreg) vi to keep up; **m~helfen** (unreg) vi to help; **~hilfe** f help, assistance; **m~hören** vt to listen in to; **m~kommen** (unreg) vi to come along; (verstehen) to keep up, to follow; **~läufer** m hanger-on; (POL) fellow traveller

Mitleid nt sympathy; (Erbarmen) compassion; **m~ig** adj sympathetic; **m~slos** adj pitiless, merciless

Mit- zW: **m~machen** vt to join in, to take part in; **~mensch** m fellow man; **m~nehmen** (unreg) vt to take along/away; (anstrengen) to wear out, to exhaust; **zum ~nehmen** to take away; **m~reden** vi: **bei etw m~reden** to have a say in sth; **m~reißen** (unreg) vt to carry away/along; (fig) to thrill, captivate

mitsamt [mɪtˈzamt] präp +dat together with

Mitschuld f complicity; **m~ig** adj: **m~ig (an** +dat) implicated (in); (an Unfall) partly responsible (for)

Mit- zW: **~schüler(in)** m(f) schoolmate; **m~spielen** vi to join in, to take part; **~spieler(in)** m(f) partner

Mittag [ˈmɪtaːk] (**-(e)s, -e**) m midday, lunchtime; **(zu) ~ essen** to have lunch; **heute/morgen ~** today/tomorrow at lunchtime od noon; **~essen** nt lunch, dinner

---

Spelling Reform: ▲ *new spelling* △ *old spelling (to be phased out)*

mittags adv at lunchtime od noon; **M~pause** f lunch break; **M~schlaf** m early afternoon nap, siesta

Mittäter(in) ['mɪttɛːtər(ɪn)] m(f) accomplice

Mitte ['mɪtə] f middle; (POL) centre; **aus unserer ~** from our midst

mitteilen ['mɪttaɪlən] vt: **jdm etw ~** to inform sb of sth, to communicate sth to sb

Mitteilung f communication

Mittel ['mɪtəl] (-s -) nt means; method; (MATH) average; (MED) medicine; ein ~ **zum Zweck** a means to an end; **~alter** nt Middle Ages pl; **m~alterlich** adj mediaeval; **~ding** nt cross; **~europa** nt Central Europe; **~gebirge** nt low mountain range; **m~mäßig** adj mediocre, middling; **~mäßigkeit** f mediocrity; **~meer** nt Mediterranean; **~ohrentzündung** f inflammation of the middle ear; **~punkt** m centre; **~stand** m middle class; **~streifen** m central reservation; **~stürmer** m centreforward; **~weg** m middle course; **~welle** f (RADIO) medium wave

mitten ['mɪtən] adv in the middle; ~ **auf der Straße/in der Nacht** in the middle of the street/night

Mitternacht ['mɪtərnaxt] f midnight

mittlere(r, s) ['mɪtlərə(r, s)] adj middle; (durchschnittlich) medium, average; ~ **Reife** ≈ O-levels

---

mittlere Reife

*The **mittlere Reife** is the standard certificate gained at a Realschule or Gymnasium on successful completion of 6 years' education there. If a pupil at a Realschule attains good results in several subjects he is allowed to enter the 11th class of a Gymnasium to study for the Abitur.*

---

mittlerweile ['mɪtlər'vaɪlə] adv meanwhile

Mittwoch ['mɪtvɔx] m (-(e)s, -e) m Wednesday; **m~s** adv on Wednesdays

mitunter [mɪt'ʊntər] adv occasionally, sometimes

Mit- zW: **m~verantwortlich** adj jointly responsible; **m~wirken** vi: **m~wirken (bei)** to contribute (to); (THEAT) to take part (in); **~wirkung** f contribution; participation

Mobbing ['mɔbɪŋ] (-s) nt workplace bullying

Möbel ['møːbəl] pl furniture sg; **~wagen** m furniture od removal van

Mit- zW: **m~verantwortlich** adj jointly

mobil [mo'biːl] adj mobile; (MIL) mobilized; **M~iar** [mobili'aːr] (-s, -e) nt furnishings pl; **M~machung** f mobilization; **M~telefon** nt mobile phone

möblieren [mø'bliːrən] vt to furnish; **möbliert wohnen** to live in furnished accommodation

möchte etc ['mœçtə] vb siehe **mögen**

Mode ['moːdə] f fashion

Modell [mo'dɛl] (-s, -e) nt model; **m~ieren** [-'liːrən] vt to model

Modenschau f fashion show

moderig ['moːdərɪç] adj (Keller) musty; (Luft) stale

modern [mo'dɛrn] adj modern; (modisch) fashionable; **~i'sieren** vt to modernize

Mode- zW: **~schau** f fashion show; **~schmuck** m fashion jewellery; **~schöpfer(in)** m(f) fashion designer; **~wort** nt fashionable word, buzz word

modisch ['moːdɪʃ] adj fashionable

Mofa ['moːfa] (-s, -s) nt small moped

mogeln ['moːgəln] (umg) vi to cheat

SCHLÜSSELWORT

mögen ['møːgən] (pt mochte, pp gemocht od (als Hilfsverb) **mögen**) vt, vi to like; **magst du/mögen Sie ihn?** do you like him?; **ich möchte ...** I would like ..., I'd like ...; **er möchte in die Stadt** he'd like to go into town; **ich möchte nicht, dass du ...** I wouldn't like you to ...; **ich mag nicht mehr**

I've had enough
♦ *Hilfsverb* to like to; (*wollen*) to want; **möchtest du etwas essen?** would you like something to eat?; **sie mag nicht bleiben** she doesn't want to stay; **das mag wohl sein** that may well be; **was mag das heißen?** what might that mean?; **Sie möchten zu Hause anrufen** could you please call home?

möglich ['møːklɪç] *adj* possible; **~erweise** *adv* possibly; **M~keit** *f* possibility; **nach M~keit** if possible; **~st** *adv* as ... as possible

Mohn [moːn] (-(e)s, -e) *m* (~*blume*) poppy; (~*samen*) poppy seed

Möhre ['møːrə] *f* carrot

Mohrrübe ['moːrryːbə] *f* carrot

mokieren [moˈkiːrən] *vr*: **sich ~ über** +*akk* to make fun of

Mole ['moːlə] *f* (*harbour*) mole

Molekül [moleˈkyːl] (-s, -e) *nt* molecule

Molkerei [mɔlkəˈraɪ] *f* dairy

Moll [mɔl] (-, -) *nt* (MUS) minor (key)

mollig *adj* cosy; (*dicklich*) plump

Moment [moˈmɛnt] (-(e)s, -e) *m* moment ♦ *nt* factor; **im ~** at the moment; **~ (mal)!** just a moment; **m~an** [-'taːn] *adj* momentary ♦ *adv* at the moment

Monarch [moˈnarç] (-en, -en) *m* monarch; **~ie** [monarˈçiː] *f* monarchy

Monat ['moːnat] (-(e)s, -e) *m* month; **m~elang** *adv* for months; **m~lich** *adj* monthly

Monats- *zW*: **~gehalt** *nt*: **das dreizehnte ~gehalt** Christmas bonus (*of one month's salary*); **~karte** *f* monthly ticket

Mönch [mœnç] (-(e)s, -e) *m* monk

Mond [moːnt] (-(e)s, -e) *m* moon; **~finsternis** *f* eclipse of the moon; **m~hell** *adj* moonlit; **~landung** *f*

moon landing; **~schein** *m* moonlight

Mono- [mono] *in zW* mono; **~log** [-'loːk] (-s, -e) *m* monologue; **~pol** [-'poːl] (-s, -e) *nt* monopoly; **m~polisieren** [-poliˈziːrən] *vt* to monopolize; **m~ton** [-'toːn] *adj* monotonous; **~tonie** [-toːˈniː] *f* monotony

Montag ['moːntaːk] (-(e)s, -e) *m* Monday

Montage [mɔnˈtaːʒə] *f* (PHOT *etc*) montage; (TECH) assembly; (*Einbauen*) fitting

Monteur [mɔnˈtøːr] *m* fitter

montieren [mɔnˈtiːrən] *vt* to assemble

Monument [monuˈmɛnt] *nt* monument; **m~al** [-'taːl] *adj* monumental

Moor [moːr] (-(e)s, -e) *nt* moor

Moos [moːs] (-es, -e) *nt* moss

Moped [ˈmoːpɛt] (-s, -s) *nt* moped

Moral [moˈraːl] (-, -en) *f* morality; (*einer Geschichte*) moral; **m~isch** *adj* moral

Morast [moˈrast] (-(e)s, -e) *m* morass, mire; **m~ig** *adj* boggy

Mord [mɔrt] (-(e)s, -e) *m* murder; **~anschlag** *m* murder attempt

Mörder(in) ['mœrdər(ɪn)] (-s, -) *m(f)* murderer (murderess)

mörderisch *adj* (*fig: schrecklich*) terrible, dreadful ♦ *adv* (*umg: entsetzlich*) terribly, dreadfully

Mord- *zW*: **~kommission** *f* murder squad; **~sglück** (*umg*) *nt* amazing luck; **m~smäßig** (*umg*) *adj* terrific, enormous; **~verdacht** *m* suspicion of murder; **~waffe** *f* murder weapon

morgen [ˈmɔrgən] *adv* tomorrow; **~früh** tomorrow morning; **M~** (-s, -) *m* morning; **M~mantel** *m* dressing gown; **M~rock** *m* dressing gown; **M~röte** *f* dawn; **~s** *adv* in the morning

morgig ['mɔrgɪç] *adj* tomorrow's; **der ~e Tag** tomorrow

Morphium ['mɔrfiʊm] *nt* morphine

morsch [mɔrʃ] *adj* rotten

Morsealphabet ['mɔrzəʔalfabeːt] *nt* Morse code

morsen *vi* to send a message by Morse code

Mörtel ['mœrtəl] (-s, -) *m* mortar

Mosaik [moza'iːk] (-s, -en *od* -e) *nt* mosaic

Moschee [mɔ'ʃeː] (-, -n) *f* mosque

Moskito [mɔs'kiːto] (-s, -s) *m* mosquito

Most [mɔst] (-(e)s, -e) *m* (unfermented) fruit juice; (*Apfelwein*) cider

Motel [mo'tɛl] (-s, -s) *nt* motel

Motiv [mo'tiːf] (-s, -e) *nt* motive; (*MUS*) theme; ~**ation** [-vatsi'oːn] *f* motivation; **m~ieren** [moti'viːrən] *vt* to motivate

Motor ['moːtɔr, *pl* mo'toːrən] (-s, -en) *m* engine; (*bes ELEK*) motor; ~**boot** *nt* motorboat; ~**haube** *f* (*von Auto*) bonnet (*BRIT*), hood (*US*); **m~isieren** *vt* to motorize; ~**öl** *nt* engine oil; ~**rad** *nt* motorcycle; ~**roller** *m* (motor) scooter; ~**schaden** *m* engine trouble *od* failure

Motte ['mɔtə] *f* moth; ~**nkugel** *f* mothball(s)

Motto ['mɔto] (-s, -s) *nt* motto

Möwe ['møːvə] *f* seagull

Mücke ['mʏkə] *f* midge, gnat; ~**nstich** *m* midge *od* gnat bite

müde ['myːdə] *adj* tired

Müdigkeit ['myːdɪçkaɪt] *f* tiredness

Muffel (-s, -) *m* (*umg*) killjoy, sourpuss

muffig *adj* (*Luft*) musty

Mühe ['myːə] *f* trouble, pains *pl*; **mit Müh und Not** with great difficulty; **sich** *dat* ~ **geben** to go to a lot of trouble; **m~los** *adj* without trouble, easy; **m~voll** *adj* laborious, arduous

Mühle ['myːlə] *f* mill; (*Kaffeemühle*) grinder

Müh- *zW:* ~**sal** (-, -e) *f* tribulation; **m~sam** *adj* arduous, troublesome; **m~selig** *adj* arduous, laborious

Mulde ['mʊldə] *f* hollow, depression

Mull [mʊl] (-(e)s, -e) *m* thin muslin

Müll [mʏl] (-(e)s) *m* refuse; ~**abfuhr** *f* rubbish disposal; (*Leute*) dustmen *pl*; ~**abladeplatz** *m* rubbish dump; ~**eimer** *m* dustbin, garbage can (*US*); ~**haufen** *m* rubbish heap; ~**schlucker** (-s, -) *m* garbage disposal unit; ~**tonne** *f* dustbin; ~**verbrennungsanlage** *f* incinerator

mulmig ['mʊlmɪç] *adj* rotten; (*umg*) dodgy; **jdm ist** ~ sb feels funny

multiplizieren [mʊltipli'tsiːrən] *vt* to multiply

Mumie ['muːmiə] *f* mummy

Mumm [mʊm] (-s) (*umg*) *m* gumption, nerve

Mumps [mʊmps] (-) *m od f* (*MED*) mumps

München ['mʏnçən] (-s) *nt* Munich

Mund [mʊnt] (-(e)s, *pl* "er) *m*; ~**art** *f* dialect

münden ['mʏndən] *vi*: ~ **in** +*akk* to flow into

Mund- *zW:* **m~faul** *adj* taciturn; ~**geruch** *m* bad breath; ~**harmonika** *f* mouth organ

mündig ['mʏndɪç] *adj* of age; **M~keit** *f* majority

mündlich ['mʏntlɪç] *adj* oral

Mundstück *nt* mouthpiece; (*Zigarettenmundstück*) tip

Mündung ['mʏndʊŋ] *f* (*von Fluss*) mouth; (*Gewehr*) muzzle

Mund- *zW:* ~**wasser** *nt* mouthwash; ~**werk** *nt*: **ein großes ~werk haben** to have a big mouth; ~**winkel** *m* corner of the mouth

Munition [munitsi'oːn] *f* ammunition; ~**slager** *nt* ammunition dump

munkeln ['mʊŋkəln] *vi* to whisper, to mutter

Münster ['mʏnstər] (-s, -) *nt* minster

munter ['mʊntər] *adj* lively

Münze ['mʏntsə] *f* coin; **m~n** *vt* to coin, to mint; **auf jdn gemünzt sein**

to be aimed at sb

Münzfernsprecher ['mʏntsfɛrnʃprɛçər] m callbox (BRIT), pay phone

mürb(e) ['mʏrb(ə)] adj (Gestein) crumbly; (Holz) rotten; (Gebäck) crisp; **jdn ~ machen** to wear sb down; **M~eteig** ['mʏrbataɪç] m shortcrust pastry

murmeln ['mʊrməln] vt, vi to murmur, to mutter

murren ['mʊrən] vi to grumble, to grouse

mürrisch ['mʏrɪʃ] adj sullen

Mus [muːs] (-es, -e) nt purée

Muschel ['mʊʃəl] (-, -n) f mussel; (~schale) shell; (Telefonmuschel) receiver

Muse ['muːzə] f muse

Museum [mu'zeːʊm] (-s, Museen) nt museum

Musik [mu'ziːk] f music; (Kapelle) band; **m~alisch** [-'kaːlɪʃ] adj musical; **~ant(in)** [-'kant(ɪn)] (-en, -en) m(f) musician; **~box** f jukebox; **~er** [-] m musician; **~hochschule** f college of music; **~instrument** nt musical instrument

musisch ['muːzɪʃ] adj (Mensch) artistic

musizieren [muzi'tsiːrən] vi to make music

Muskat [mʊs'kaːt] (-(e)s, -e) m nutmeg

Muskel ['mʊskəl] (-s, -n) m muscle; **~kater** m: **~kater haben** to be stiff

Muskulatur [mʊskula'tuːr] f muscular system

muskulös [mʊsku'løːs] adj muscular

Müsli ['myːsli] (-s, -) nt (KOCH) muesli

Muss ▲ [mʊs] (-) nt necessity, must

Muße ['muːsə] (-) f leisure

müssen ['mʏsən] (pt musste, pp gemusst od als Hilfsverb) müssen) vi

1 (Zwang) must (nur im Präsens), to have to; **ich muss es tun** I must do it, I have to do it; **ich musste es tun** I had to do it; **er muss es nicht tun** he doesn't have to do it; **muss ich?** must I?, do I have to?; **wann müsst ihr zur Schule?** when do you have to go to school?; **er hat gehen müssen** he (has) had to go; **muss das sein?** is that really necessary?; **ich muss mal** (umg) I need the toilet

2 (sollen): **das musst du nicht tun!** you ought'n't to od shouldn't do that; **Sie hätten ihn fragen müssen** you should have asked him

3: **es muss geregnet haben** it must have rained; **es muss nicht wahr sein** it needn't be true

müßig ['myːsɪç] adj idle

Muster ['mʊstər] (-s, -) nt model; (Dessin) pattern; (Probe) sample; **m~gültig** adj exemplary; **m~n** vt (Tapete) to pattern; (fig, MIL) to examine; (Truppen) to inspect; **~ung** f (von Stoff) pattern; (MIL) inspection

Mut [muːt] m courage; **nur ~!** cheer up!; **jdm ~ machen** to encourage sb; **m~ig** adj courageous; **m~los** adj discouraged, despondent

mutmaßlich ['muːtmaːslɪç] adj presumed ♦ adv probably

Mutprobe f test od trial of courage

Mutter¹ ['mʊtər] (-, ¨) f mother

Mutter² ['mʊtər] (-, -n) f (Schraubenmutter) nut

mütterlich ['mʏtərlɪç] adj motherly; **~erseits** adv on the mother's side

Mutter- zW: **~liebe** f motherly love; **~mal** nt birthmark; **~milch** f mother's milk; **~schaft** f motherhood, maternity; **~schutz** m maternity regulations; **'~'seelena∣llein** adj all alone; **~sprache** f native language; **~tag** m Mother's Day

---

Spelling Reform: ▲ new spelling △ old spelling (to be phased out)

Mutti ['mʊti] (-, -s) f mum(my) (BRIT), mom(my) (US)

mutwillig ['muːtvɪlɪç] adj malicious, deliberate

Mütze ['mʏtsə] f cap

MwSt abk (= Mehrwertsteuer) VAT

mysteriös [mʏsteri'øːs] adj mysterious

Mythos ['myːtɔs] (-, **Mythen**) m myth

N, n

na [na] excl well; **~ gut** okay then

Nabel ['naːbəl] (-s, -) m navel; **~schnur** f umbilical cord

SCHLÜSSELWORT

nach [naːx] präp +dat **1** (örtlich) to; **nach Berlin** to Berlin; **nach links/rechts** (to the) left/right; **nach oben/hinten** up/back

2 (zeitlich) after; **einer nach dem anderen** one after the other; **nach Ihnen!** after you!; **zehn (Minuten) nach drei** ten (minutes) past three

3 (gemäß) according to; **nach dem Gesetz** according to the law; **dem Namen nach** judging by his/her name; **nach allem, was ich weiß** as far as I know

♦ adv: **ihm nach!** after him!; **nach und nach** gradually, little by little; **nach wie vor** still

nachahmen ['naːxaːmən] vt to imitate

Nachbar(in) ['naːxbaːr(ɪn)] (-s, -n) m(f) neighbour; **~haus** nt: **im ~haus** next door; **~lich** adj neighbourly; **~schaft** f neighbourhood; **~staat** m neighbouring state

nach- zW: **~bestellen** vt: **50 Stück ~bestellen** to order another 50; **N~bestellung** f (COMM) repeat order; **N~bildung** f imitation, copy; **~blicken** vi to gaze after; **~datieren** vt to postdate

nachdem [naːx'deːm] konj after; (weil) since; **je ~ (ob)** it depends (whether)

nachdenken (unreg) vi: **~ über** +akk to think about; **N~** (-s) nt reflection, meditation

nachdenklich adj thoughtful, pensive

Nachdruck ['naːxdrʊk] m emphasis; (TYP) reprint, reproduction

nachdrücklich ['naːxdrʏklɪç] adj emphatic

nacheinander [naːx|aɪ'nandər] adv one after the other

nachempfinden ['naːx|ɛmpfɪndən] (unreg) vt: **jdm etw ~** to feel sth with sb

Nacherzählung ['naːx|ɛrtseːluŋ] f reproduction (of a story)

Nachfahr ['naːxfaːr] (-s, -en) m descendant

Nachfolge ['naːxfɔlgə] f succession; **n~n** vi +dat to follow; **~r(in)** (-s, -) m(f) successor

nachforschen vt, vi to investigate

Nachforschung f investigation

Nachfrage ['naːxfraːgə] f inquiry; (COMM) demand; **n~n** vi to inquire

nach- zW: **~füllen** vt to refill; **~geben** (unreg) vi to give way, to yield; **N~gebühr** f (POST) excess postage

nachgehen ['naːxgeːən] (unreg) vi (+dat) to follow; (erforschen) to inquire (into); (Uhr) to be slow

Nachgeschmack ['naːxgəʃmak] m aftertaste

nachgiebig ['naːxgiːbɪç] adj soft, accommodating; **N~keit** f softness

nachhaltig ['naːxhaltɪç] adj lasting; (Widerstand) persistent

nachhause adv (österreichisch, schweizerisch) home

nachhelfen ['naːxhɛlfən] (unreg) vi +dat to assist, to help

nachher [naːx'heːr] adv afterwards

Nachhilfeunterricht ['naːxhɪlfəʊntərɪçt] m extra tuition

nachholen ['naːxhoːlən] vt to catch up with; (Versäumtes) to make up for

Nachkomme ['naːxkɔmə] (-, -n) *m* descendant

nachkommen (*unreg*) *vi* to follow; (*einer Verpflichtung*) to fulfil; **N~schaft** *f* descendants *pl*

Nachkriegszeit *f* postwar period

Nach- *zW:* **~lass** ▲ (-es, -lässe) *m* (COMM) discount, rebate; (*Erbe*) estate; **n~lassen** (*unreg*) *vt* (*Strafe*) to remit; (*Summe*) to take off; (*Schulden*) to cancel ♦ *vi* to decrease, to ease off; (*Sturm*) to die down, to ease off; (*schlechter werden*) to deteriorate; **er hat n~gelassen** he has got worse; **n~lässig** *adj* negligent, careless

nachlaufen ['naːxlaʊfən] (*unreg*) *vi* +*dat* to run after, to chase

nachlösen ['naːxløːzən] *vi* (*Zuschlag*) to pay on the train, pay at the other end; (*zur Weiterfahrt*) to pay the supplement

nachmachen ['naːxmaxən] *vt* to imitate, to copy; (*fälschen*) to counterfeit

Nachmittag ['naːxmɪtaːk] *m* afternoon; **am ~** in the afternoon; **n~s** *adv* in the afternoon

Nach- *zW:* **~nahme** *f* cash on delivery; **per ~nahme** C.O.D.; **~name** *m* surname; **~porto** *nt* excess postage

nachprüfen ['naːxpryːfən] *vt* to check, to verify

nachrechnen ['naːxrɛçnən] *vt* to check

nachreichen ['naːxraɪçən] *vt* (*Unterlagen*) to hand in later

Nachricht ['naːxrɪçt] (-, -en) *f* (*piece of*) news; (*Mitteilung*) message; **~en** *pl* (*Neuigkeiten*) news

Nachrichten- *zW:* **~agentur** *f* news agency; **~dienst** *m* (MIL) intelligence service; **~sprecher(in)** *m(f)* newsreader; **~technik** *f* telecommunications *sg*

Nachruf ['naːxruːf] *m* obituary

nachsagen ['naːxzaːgən] *vt* to repeat;

jdm etw ~ to say sth of sb

Nachsaison ['naːxzɛzɔ̃] *f* off-season

nachschicken ['naːxʃɪkən] *vt* to forward

nachschlagen ['naːxʃlaːgən] (*unreg*) *vt* to look up

Nachschlagewerk *nt* reference book

Nachschlüssel *m* duplicate key

Nachschub ['naːxʃuːp] *m* supplies *pl*; (*Truppen*) reinforcements *pl*

nachsehen ['naːxzeːən] (*unreg*) *vt* (*prüfen*) to check ♦ *vi* (*erforschen*) to look and see; **jdm etw ~** to forgive sb sth; **das N~ haben** to come off worst

Nachsendeantrag *m* application to have one's mail forwarded

nachsenden ['naːxzɛndən] (*unreg*) *vt* to send on, to forward

nachsichtig *adj* indulgent, lenient

nachsitzen ['naːxzɪtsən] (*unreg*) *vi:* **(müssen)** (SCH) to be kept in

Nachspeise ['naːxʃpaɪzə] *f* dessert, sweet, pudding

Nachspiel ['naːxʃpiːl] *nt* epilogue; (*fig*) sequel

nachsprechen ['naːxʃprɛçən] (*unreg*) *vt:* **(jdm) ~** to repeat (after sb)

nächst [nɛːçst] *präp +dat* (*räumlich*) next to; (*außer*) apart from; **~beste(r, s)** *adj* first that comes along; (*zweitbeste*) next best; **N~e(r)** *f(m)* neighbour; **~e(r, s)** *adj* next; (*~gelegen*) nearest

nachstellen ['naːxʃtɛlən] *vt* (TECH: *neu einstellen*) to adjust

nächst *zW:* **N~enliebe** *f* love for one's fellow men; **~ens** *adv* shortly, soon; **~liegend** *adj* nearest; (*fig*) obvious; **~möglich** *adj* next possible

Nacht [naxt] (-, ⁻e) *f* night; **~dienst** *m* night shift

Nachteil ['naːxtaɪl] *m* disadvantage; **n~ig** *adj* disadvantageous

Nachthemd *nt* (*Herrennachthemd*) nightshirt; (*Damennachthemd*) nightdress

---

Spelling Reform: ▲ *new spelling* △ *old spelling (to be phased out)*

Nachtigall ['naxtɪgal] (-, -en) f nightingale

Nachtisch ['naːxtɪʃ] m = **Nachspeise**

Nachtklub m night club

Nachtleben nt nightlife

nächtlich ['nɛçtlɪç] adj nightly

Nachtlokal nt night club

Nach- zW: **~trag** (-(e)s, -träge) m supplement; **n~tragen** (unreg) vt to carry; (zufügen) to add; **jdm etw n~tragen** to hold sth against sb; **n~träglich** adj later, subsequent; additional ♦ adv later, subsequently; additionally; **n~trauern** vi: **jdm/etw n~trauern** to mourn the loss of sb/sth

Nacht- zW: **n~s** adv at od by night; **~schicht** f nightshift; **~schwester** f night nurse; **~tarif** m off-peak tariff; **~tisch** m bedside table; **~wächter** m night watchman

Nach- zW: **~untersuchung** f checkup; **n~wachsen** (unreg) vi to grow again; **~wahl** f (POL) ≃ by-election

Nachweis ['naːxvaɪs] (-es, -e) m proof; **n~bar** adj provable, demonstrable; **n~en** (unreg) vt to prove; **jdm etw n~en** to point sth out to sb; **n~lich** adj evident, demonstrable

nach- zW: **~wirken** vi to have aftereffects; **N~wirkung** f aftereffect; **N~wort** nt epilogue; **N~wuchs** m offspring; (berufliche etc) new recruits pl; **~zahlen** vt, vi to pay extra; **N~zahlung** f additional payment; (zurückdatiert) back pay; **~ziehen** (unreg) vt (hinter sich herziehen: Bein) to drag; **N~zügler** (-s, -) m straggler

Nacken ['nakən] (-s, -) m nape of the neck

nackt [nakt] adj naked; (Tatsachen) plain, bare; **N~badestrand** m nudist beach; **N~heit** f nakedness

Nadel ['naːdəl] (-, -n) f needle; (Steck-nadel) pin; **~öhr** nt eye of a needle; **~wald** m coniferous forest

Nagel ['naːgəl] (-s, =) m nail; **~bürste** f nailbrush; **~feile** f nailfile; **~lack** m nail

varnish od polish (BRIT); **n~n** vt, vi to nail; **n~neu** adj brand-new; **~schere** f nail scissors pl

nagen ['naːgən] vt, vi to gnaw

Nagetier ['naːgətiːr] nt rodent

nah(e) ['naː(ə)] adj (räumlich) near(by); (Verwandte) near; (Freunde) close; (zeitlich) near, close ♦ adv near(by); near, close; (verwandt) closely ♦ präp (+dat) near (to), close to; **der Nahe Osten** the Near East; **~ gehen** (+dat) to grieve; **~ kommen** (+dat) to get close (to); **jdm etw ~ legen** to suggest sth to sb; **~ liegen** to be obvious; **~ liegend** obvious; **~ stehen** (+dat) to be close (to); **einer Sache ~ stehen** to sympathize with sth; **~ stehend** close; **jdm (zu) ~ treten** to offend sb

Nahaufnahme f close-up

Nähe ['nɛːə] (-) f nearness, proximity; (Umgebung) vicinity; **in der ~** close by; at hand; **aus der ~** from close to

nah(e)bei adv nearby

nahen vi, vr to approach, to draw near

nähen ['nɛːən] vt, vi to sew

näher adj, adv nearer; (Erklärung, Erkundigung) more detailed; **(sich) ~ kommen** to get closer; **N~e(s)** nt details pl, particulars pl

Naherholungsgebiet nt recreational area (close to a town)

nähern vr to approach

nahezu adv nearly

Nähgarn nt thread

Nahkampf m hand-to-hand fighting

Nähkasten m sewing basket, workbox

nahm etc [naːm] vb siehe **nehmen**

Nähmaschine f sewing machine

Nähnadel f needle

nähren ['nɛːrən] vt to feed ♦ vr (Person) to feed o.s.; (Tier) to feed

nahrhaft ['naːrhaft] adj nourishing, nutritious

Nahrung ['naːrʊŋ] f food; (fig auch) sustenance

Nahrungs- zW: **~mittel** nt foodstuffs pl; **~mittelindustrie** f food industry;

~suche f search for food

Nährwert m nutritional value

Naht [naːt] (-, ⸚e) f seam; (MED) suture; (TECH) join; **n~los** adj seamless; **n~los ineinander übergehen** to follow without a gap

Nah- zW: **~verkehr** m local traffic; **~verkehrszug** m local train; **~ziel** nt immediate objective

Name ['naːmə] (-ns, -n) m name; **im ~n von** on behalf of; **n~ns** adv by the name of; **~nstag** m name day, saint's day; **n~ntlich** adj by name ♦ adv particularly, especially

---

Namenstag

In Catholic areas of Germany the Namenstag is often a more important celebration than a birthday. This is the day dedicated to the saint after whom a person is called, and on that day the person receives presents and invites relatives and friends round to celebrate.

---

namhaft ['naːmhaft] adj (berühmt) famed, renowned; (beträchtlich) considerable; **~ machen** to name

nämlich ['nɛːmlɪç] adv that is to say, namely; (denn) since

nannte etc ['nantə] vb siehe **nennen**

Napf [napf] (-(e)s, ⸚e) m bowl, dish

Narbe ['narbə] f scar; **narbig** adj scarred

Narkose [nar'koːzə] f anaesthetic

Narr [nar] (-en, -en) m fool; **n~en** vt to fool; **Närrin** ['nɛrɪn] f fool; **närrisch** adj foolish, crazy

Narzisse [nar'tsɪsə] f narcissus; daffodil

naschen ['naʃən] vt, vi to nibble; (heimlich kosten) to pinch a bit

naschhaft adj sweet-toothed

Nase ['naːzə] f nose

Nasen- zW: **~bluten** (-s) nt nosebleed; **~loch** nt nostril; **~tropfen** pl nose drops

naseweis adj pert, cheeky; (neugierig) nosey

Nashorn ['naːshɔrn] nt rhinoceros

nass ▲ [nas] adj wet

Nässe ['nɛsə] (-) f wetness; **n~n** vt to wet

nasskalt ▲ adj wet and cold

Nassrasur ▲ f wet shave

Nation [natsi'oːn] f nation

national [natsio'naːl] adj national; **N~feiertag** m national holiday; **N~hymne** f national anthem; **~isieren** [-i'ziːrən] vt to nationalize; **N~ismus** ['-lɪsmʊs] m nationalism; **~istisch** ['-lɪstɪʃ] adj nationalistic; **N~ität** [-i'tɛːt] f nationality; **N~mannschaft** f national team; **N~sozialismus** m national socialism

Natron ['naːtrɔn] (-s) nt soda

Natter ['natər] (-, -n) f adder

Natur [na'tuːr] f nature; (körperlich) constitution; **~ell** (-es, -e) nt disposition; **~erscheinung** f natural phenomenon od event; **n~farben** adj natural coloured; **n~gemäß** adj natural; **~gesetz** nt law of nature; **n~getreu** adj true to life; **~katastrophe** f natural disaster

natürlich [na'tyːrlɪç] adj natural ♦ adv naturally; **ja, ~!** yes, of course; **N~keit** f naturalness

Natur- zW: **~park** m ≈ national park; **~produkt** nt natural product; **n~rein** adj natural, pure; **~schutz** m nature conservation; **unter ~schutz stehen** to be legally protected; **~schutzgebiet** nt nature reserve; **~wissenschaft** f natural science; **~wissenschaftler(in)** m(f) scientist

nautisch ['nautɪʃ] adj nautical

Nazi ['naːtsi] (-s, -s) m Nazi

NB abk (= nota bene) nb

n. Chr. abk (= nach Christus) A.D.

Nebel ['neːbəl] (-s, -) m fog, mist; **n~ig** adj

---

adj foggy, misty; **~scheinwerfer** *m* fog lamp

neben ['ne:bən] *präp* (+akk od dat) next to; (+dat: außer) apart from, besides; **~an** [ne:ban'an] *adv* next door; **N~anschluss** ▲ *m* (TEL) extension; **N~ausgang** *m* side exit; **~bei** [ne:ban'bai] *adv* at the same time; (außerdem) additionally; (beiläufig) incidentally; **N~beruf** *m* second job; **N~beschäftigung** *f* second job; **N~buhler(in)** (-s, -) *m(f)* rival; **~einander** [ne:ban'ai'nandər] *adv* side by side; **~einander legen** to put next to each other; **N~eingang** *m* side entrance; **N~fach** ▲ *nt* subsidiary subject; **N~fluss** ▲ *m* tributary; **N~gebäude** *nt* annexe; **N~geräusch** *nt* (RADIO) atmospherics *pl*, interference; **~her** [ne:ban'he:r] *adv* (zusätzlich) besides; (gleichzeitig) at the same time; (daneben) alongside; **N~kosten** *pl* extra charges, extras; **N~produkt** *nt* by-product; **N~sache** *f* trifle, side issue; **~sächlich** *adj* minor, peripheral; **N~saison** *f* low season; **N~straße** *f* side street; **N~verdienst** *m* secondary income; **N~wirkung** *f* side effect; **N~zimmer** *nt* adjoining room

neblig ['ne:blɪç] *adj* foggy, misty

Necessaire [nese'sɛ:r] (-s, -s) *nt* (Nähnecessaire) needlework box; (Nagelnecessaire) manicure case

necken ['nɛkən] *vt* to tease

Neckerei [nɛkə'rai] *f* teasing

Neffe ['nɛfə] (-n, -n) *m* nephew

negativ ['ne:gati:f] *adj* negative; **N~** (-s, -e) *nt* (PHOT) negative

Neger ['ne:gər] (-s, -) *m* negro; **~in** *f* negress

nehmen ['ne:mən] (unreg) *vt* to take; **jdn zu sich ~** to take sb in; **sich ernst ~** to take o.s. seriously; **nimm dir doch bitte** please help yourself

Neid [nait] (-(e)s) *m* envy; **~er** (-s, -) *m* envier; **n~isch** ['naidɪʃ] *adj* envious, jealous

neigen ['naigən] *vt* to incline, to lean; (Kopf) to bow ♦ *vi*: **zu etw ~** to tend to sth

Neigung *f* (des Geländes) slope; (Tendenz) tendency, inclination; (Vorliebe) liking; (Zuneigung) affection

nein [nain] *adv* no

Nektarine [nɛkta'ri:nə] *f* (Frucht) nectarine

Nelke ['nɛlkə] *f* carnation, pink; (Gewürz) clove

Nenn- ['nɛn] *zW*: **n~en** (unreg) *vt* to name; (mit Namen) to call; **wie n~t man ...?** what do you call ...?; **n~enswert** *adj* worth mentioning; **~er** (-s, -) *m* denominator; **~wert** *m* nominal value; (COMM) par

Neon ['ne:ɔn] (-s) *nt* neon; **~licht** *nt* neon light; **~röhre** *f* neon tube

Nerv [nɛrf] (-s) *m* nerve; **jdm auf die ~en gehen** to get on sb's nerves; **n~enaufreibend** *adj* nerve-racking; **~enbündel** *nt* bundle of nerves; **~enheilanstalt** *f* mental home; **n~enkrank** *adj* mentally ill; **~ensäge** (umg) *f* pain (in the neck) (umg); **~ensystem** *nt* nervous system; **~enzusammenbruch** *m* nervous breakdown; **n~lich** *adj* (Belastung) affecting the nerves; **n~ös** [nɛr'vø:s] *adj* nervous; **~osität** *f* nervousness; **n~tötend** *adj* nerve-racking; (Arbeit) soul-destroying

Nerz [nɛrts] (-es, -e) *m* mink

Nessel ['nɛsl] (-, -n) *f* nettle

Nessessär ▲ [nese'sɛ:r] (-s, -s) *nt* = **Necessaire**

Nest [nɛst] (-(e)s, -er) *nt* nest; (umg: Ort) dump

nett [nɛt] *adj* nice; (freundlich) nice, kind; **~erweise** *adv* kindly

netto ['nɛto] *adv* net

Netz [nɛts] (-es, -e) *nt* net; (Gepäcknetz) rack; (Einkaufsnetz) string bag; (Spinnennetz) web; (System) network; **jdm ins ~ gehen** (fig) to fall into sb's trap; **~anschluss** ▲ *m* mains connection; **~haut** f retina

neu [nɔy] adj new; (Sprache, Geschichte) modern; **seit ~estem** (since) recently; **die ~esten Nachrichten** the latest news; **~ schreiben** to rewrite, to write again; **N~anschaffung** f new purchase od acquisition; **~artig** adj new kind of; **N~bau** m new building; **N~e(r)** f(m) the new man/woman; **~erdings** adv (kürzlich) (since) recently; (von ~em) again; **N~erscheinung** f (Buch) new publication; (Schallplatte) new release; **N~erung** f innovation, new departure; **N~gier** f curiosity; **~gierig** adj curious; **N~heit** f newness, novelty; **N~igkeit** f news sg; **N~jahr** m New Year; **~lich** adv recently, the other day; **N~ling** m novice; **N~mond** m new moon

neun [nɔyn] num nine; **~zehn** num nineteen; **~zig** num ninety

neureich adj nouveau riche; **N~e(r)** f(m) nouveau riche

neurotisch adj neurotic

Neuseeland [nɔy'ze:lant] nt New Zealand; **Neuseeländer(in)** [nɔy'ze:lɛndər(ɪn)] m(f) New Zealander

neutral [nɔy'tra:l] adj neutral; **~isieren** vt to neutralize

Neutrum [ˈnɔytrʊm] nt (-s, -a od -en) nt neuter

Neu- zW: **~wert** m purchase price; **n~wertig** adj (as) new, not used; **~zeit** f modern age; **n~zeitlich** adj modern, recent

---

nicht [nɪçt] adv 1 (Verneinung) not; **er ist es nicht** it's not him, it isn't him; **er raucht nicht** (gerade) he isn't smoking; (gewöhnlich) he doesn't smoke; **ich kann das nicht - ich auch nicht** I can't do it - neither od nor can I; **es regnet nicht mehr** it's not raining any

more; **nicht rostend** stainless

2 (Bitte, Verbot): **nicht!** don't!, no!; **nicht berühren!** do not touch!; **nicht doch!** don't!

3 (rhetorisch): **du bist müde, nicht (wahr)?** you're tired, aren't you?; **das ist schön, nicht (wahr)?** it's nice, isn't it?

4: **was du nicht sagst!** the things you say!

Nichtangriffspakt [nɪçt'|angrɪfspakt] m non-aggression pact

Nichte [ˈnɪçtə] f niece

nichtig [ˈnɪçtɪç] adj (ungültig) null, void; (wertlos) futile; **N~keit** f nullity, invalidity; (Sinnlosigkeit) futility

Nichtraucher(in) m(f) non-smoker

nichts [nɪçts] pron nothing; **für ~ und wieder ~** for nothing at all; **~ sagend** meaningless; **N~ (-)** nt nothingness; (pej: Person) nonentity

Nichtschwimmer m non-swimmer

nichts- zW: **~desto weniger** adv nevertheless; **N~nutz** (-es, -e) m good-for-nothing; **~nutzig** adj worthless, useless; **N~tun** (-s) nt idleness

Nichtzutreffende(s) nt: **~s od nicht Zutreffendes (bitte) streichen!** (please) delete where appropriate

Nickel [ˈnɪkəl] (-s) nt nickel

nicken [ˈnɪkən] vi to nod

Nickerchen [ˈnɪkərçən] nt nap

nie [niː] adv never; **~ wieder** od **mehr** never again; **~ und nimmer** never ever

nieder [ˈniːdər] adj low; (gering) inferior ♦ adv down; **N~gang** m decline; **~gedrückt** adj (deprimiert) dejected, depressed; **~gehen** vi (unreg) to descend; (AVIAT) to come down; (Regen) to fall; (Boxer) to go down; **~geschlagen** adj depressed, dejected; **N~lage** f defeat; **N~lande** pl Netherlands; **N~länder(in)** m(f) Dutchman/

Spelling Reform: ▲ new spelling △ old spelling (to be phased out)

woman); **~ländisch** adj Dutch; **~las-sen** (unreg) vr (sich setzen) to sit down; (an Ort) to settle (down); (Arzt, Rechtsanwalt) to set up a practice; **N~lassung** f settlement; (COMM) branch; **~legen** vt to lay down; (Arbeit) to stop; (Amt) to resign; **N~sachsen** nt Lower Saxony; **N~schlag** m (MET) precipitation; rainfall; **~schlagen** (unreg) vt (Gegner) to beat down; (Gegenstand) to knock down; (Augen) to lower; (Aufstand) to put down ♦ vr (CHEM) to precipitate; **~trächtig** adj base, mean; **N~trächtigkeit** f meanness, baseness; outrage; **N~ung** f (GEOG) depression; (Mündungsgebiet) flats pl

niedlich ['ni:tlɪç] adj sweet, cute
niedrig ['ni:drɪç] adj low; (Stand) lowly, humble; (Gesinnung) mean
niemals ['ni:ma:ls] adv never
niemand ['ni:mant] pron nobody, no-one
Niemandsland ['ni:mantslant] nt no-man's-land
Niere ['ni:rə] f kidney
nieseln ['ni:zəln] vi to drizzle
niesen ['ni:zən] vi to sneeze
Niete ['ni:tə] f (TECH) rivet; (Los) blank; (Reinfall) flop; (Mensch) failure; **n~n** vt to rivet

St. Nikolaus

On December 6th, St. Nikolaus visits German children to reward those who have been good by filling shoes they have left out with sweets and small presents.

Nikotin [niko'ti:n] (-s) nt nicotine
Nilpferd ['ni:l-] nt hippopotamus
Nimmersatt ['nɪmɐzat] (-(e)s, -e) m glutton
nimmst etc [nɪmst] vb siehe **nehmen**
nippen ['nɪpən] vt, vi to sip
nirgend- ['nɪrgənt] zW: **~s** adv nowhere; **~wo** adv nowhere; **~wohin**

adv nowhere
Nische ['ni:ʃə] f niche
nisten ['nɪstən] vi to nest
Niveau [ni'vo:] (-s, -s) nt level
Nixe ['nɪksə] f water nymph
nobel ['no:bəl] adj (großzügig) generous; (elegant) posh (inf)

noch [nɔx] adv 1 (weiterhin) still; **noch nicht** not yet; **noch nie** never (yet); **noch immer** od **immer noch** still; **bleiben Sie doch noch** stay a bit longer

2 (in Zukunft) still, yet; **das kann noch passieren** that might still happen; **er wird noch kommen** he'll come (yet)

3 (nicht später als): **noch vor einer Woche** only a week ago; **noch am selben Tag** the very same day; **noch im 19. Jahrhundert** as late as the 19th century; **noch heute** today

4 (zusätzlich): **wer war noch da?** who else was there?; **noch einmal** once more, again; **noch dreimal** three more times; **noch einer** another one

5 (bei Vergleichen): **noch größer** even bigger; **das ist noch besser** that's better still; **und wenn es noch so schwer ist** however hard it is

6: **Geld noch und noch** heaps (and heaps) of money; **sie hat noch und noch versucht**, ... she tried again and again to ...

♦ konj: **weder A noch B** neither A nor B

noch- zW: **~mal** ['nɔxma:l] adv again, once more; **~malig** ['nɔxma:lɪç] adj repeated; **~mals** adv again, once more
Nominativ ['no:minati:f] (-s, -e) m nominative
nominell [nomi'nɛl] adj nominal
Nonne ['nɔnə] f nun
Nord(en) ['nɔrd(ən)] (-s) m north
Nord'irland nt Northern Ireland
nordisch ['nɔrdɪʃ] adj northern

nördlich 185 **nun**

nördlich ['nœrtlɪç] *adj* northerly, northern ♦ *präp* +gen (to the) north of; ~ **von** (to the) north of

Nord- *zW:* ~**pol** *m* North Pole; ~**rhein-Westfalen** *nt* North Rhine-Westphalia; ~**see** *f* North Sea; **n~wärts** *adv* northwards

nörgeln ['nœrgəln] *vi* to grumble; **Nörgler** (-s, -) *m* grumbler

Norm [nɔrm] (-, -en) *f* norm; (Größenvorschrift) standard; **n~al** [nɔr'maːl] *adj* normal; **n~al(benzin)** *nt* ≈ 2-star petrol (BRIT), regular petrol (US); **n~alerweise** *adv* normally; **n~ali'sieren** *vt* to normalize ♦ *vr* to return to normal

normen *vt* to standardize

Norwegen ['nɔrveːgən] *nt* Norway; **norwegisch** *adj* Norwegian

Nostalgie [nɔstal'giː] *f* nostalgia

Not [noːt] (-, ⁻e) *f* need; (Mangel) want; (Mühe) trouble; (Zwang) necessity; ~ **leidend** needy; **zur** ~ if necessary; (gerade noch) just about

Notar [no'taːr] (-s, -e) *m* notary; **n~i'ell** *adj* notarial

Not- *zW:* ~**arzt** *m* emergency doctor; ~**ausgang** *m* emergency exit; ~**behelf** (-s, -e) *m* makeshift; ~**bremse** *f* emergency brake; ~**dienst** *m* (Bereitschaftsdienst) emergency service; **n~dürftig** *adj* scanty; (behelfsmäßig) makeshift

Note ['noːtə] *f* note; (SCH) mark (BRIT), grade (US)

Noten- *zW:* ~**blatt** *nt* sheet of music; ~**schlüssel** *m* clef; ~**ständer** *m* music stand

Not- *zW:* ~**fall** *m* (case of) emergency; **n~falls** *adv* if need be; **n~gedrungen** *adj* necessary, unavoidable; **etw n~gedrungen machen** to be forced to do sth

notieren [no'tiːrən] *vt* to note; (COMM) to quote

Notierung *f* (COMM) quotation

nötig ['nøːtɪç] *adj* necessary; **etw ~ haben** to need sth; **~en** [-gən] *vt* to compel, to force; **~enfalls** *adv* if necessary

Notiz [no'tiːts] (-, -en) *f* note; (Zeitungsnotiz) item; ~ **nehmen** to take notice; ~**block** *m* notepad; ~**buch** *nt* notebook

Not- *zW:* ~**lage** *f* crisis, emergency; **n~landen** *vi* to make a forced od emergency landing; **n~leidend** △ *adj* siehe **Not**; ~**lösung** *f* temporary solution; ~**lüge** *f* white lie

notorisch [no'toːrɪʃ] *adj* notorious

Not- *zW:* ~**ruf** *m* emergency call; ~**rufsäule** *f* emergency telephone; ~**stand** *m* state of emergency; ~**unterkunft** *f* emergency accommodation; ~**verband** *m* emergency dressing; ~**wendig** (-) *f* self-defence; **n~wendig** *adj* necessary; ~**wendigkeit** *f* necessity

Novelle [no'vɛlə] *f* short novel; (JUR) amendment

November [no'vɛmbər] (-s, -) *m* November

Nu [nuː] *m:* **im** ~ in an instant

Nuance [ny'ãːsə] *f* nuance

nüchtern ['nʏçtərn] *adj* sober; (Magen) empty; (Urteil) prudent; **N~heit** *f* sobriety

Nudel ['nuːdəl] (-, -n) *f* noodle; ~**n** *pl* (Teigwaren) pasta *sg*; (in Suppe) noodles

Null [nʊl] (-, -en) *f* nought, zero; (pej: Mensch) washout; ~ **num** zero; (Fehler) no; **n~ Uhr** midnight; **n~ und nichtig** null and void; ~**punkt** *m* zero; **auf dem ~punkt** at zero

numerisch [nu'meːrɪʃ] *adj* numerical

Nummer ['nʊmər] (-, -n) *f* number; (Größe) size; **n~ieren** *vt* to number; ~**nschild** *nt* (AUT) number od license (US) plate

nun [nuːn] *adv* now ♦ *excl* well; **das ist**

Spelling Reform: ▲ new spelling △ old spelling (to be phased out)

~ **mal** so that's the way it is

nur [nuːr] *adv* just, only; **wo bleibt er ~?** (just) where is he?

Nürnberg [ˈnʏrnbɛrk] (**-s**) *nt* Nuremberg

Nuss ▲ [nʊs] (**-**, **-e**) *f* nut; **~baum** *m* walnut tree; **~knacker** (**-s**, **-**) *m* nutcracker

nutz [nʊts] *adj*: **zu nichts ~ sein** to be no use for anything; **~bringend** *adj* (*Verwendung*) profitable

nütze [ˈnʏtsə] *adj* = nutz

Nutzen (**-s**) *m* usefulness; (*Gewinn*) profit; **von ~** useful; **n~** *vi* (*o Gebrauch sein*) to be of use ♦ *vt*: **etw zu etw n~** to use sth for sth; **was nutzt es?** what's the use?, what use is it?

nützen *vi*, *vt* = nutzen

nützlich [ˈnʏtslɪç] *adj* useful; **N~keit** *f* usefulness

Nutz- *zW*: **n~los** *adj* useless; **~losigkeit** *f* uselessness; **~nießer** (**-s**, **-**) *m* beneficiary

Nylon [ˈnaɪlɔn] (**-(s)**) *nt* nylon

O, o

Oase [oˈaːzə] *f* oasis

ob [ɔp] *konj* if, whether; **~ das wohl wahr ist?** can that be true?; **und ~!** you bet!

obdachlos *adj* homeless

Obdachlose(r) *f(m)* homeless person; **~nasyl** *nt* shelter for the homeless

Obduktion [ɔpdʊktsiˈoːn] *f* postmortem

obduzieren [ɔpduˈtsiːrən] *vt* to do a post-mortem on

O-Beine [ˈoːbaɪnə] *pl* bow or bandy legs

oben [ˈoːbən] *adv* above; (*in Haus*) upstairs; ~ **erwähnt**, ~ **genannt** abovementioned; **nach** ~ up; **von** ~ down; ~ **ohne** topless; **von** ~ **bis unten** ansehen to look sb up and down; **~an** *adv* at the top; **~auf** *adv* up

above, on the top ♦ *adj* (*munter*) in form; **~drein** *adv* into the bargain

Ober [ˈoːbər] (**-s**, **-**) *m* waiter; **die ~en** *pl* (*umg*) the bosses; (*ECCL*) the superiors; **~arm** *m* upper arm; **~arzt** *m* senior physician; **~aufsicht** *f* supervision; **~bayern** *nt* Upper Bavaria; **~befehl** *m* supreme command; **~befehlshaber** *m* commander-in-chief; **~bekleidung** *f* outer clothing; **~'bürgermeister** *m* lord mayor; **~deck** *nt* upper *od* top deck; **~e(r, s)** *adj* upper; **~fläche** *f* surface; **o~flächlich** *adj* superficial; **~geschoss** ▲ *nt* upper storey; **~halb** *adv* above ♦ *präp +gen* above; **~haupt** *nt* head, chief; **~haus** *nt* (*POL*) upper house, House of Lords (*BRIT*); **~hemd** *nt* shirt; **~herrschaft** *f* supremacy, sovereignty; **~in** *f* matron; (*ECCL*) Mother Superior; **~kellner** *m* head waiter; **~kiefer** *m* upper jaw; **~körper** *m* upper part of body; **~leitung** *f* direction; (*ELEK*) overhead cable; **~licht** *nt* skylight; **~lippe** *f* upper lip; **~schenkel** *m* thigh; **~schicht** *f* upper classes *pl*; **~schule** *f* grammar school (*BRIT*), high school (*US*); **~schwester** *f* (*MED*) matron

Oberst [ˈoːbərst] (**-en** *od* **-s**, **-en** *od* **-e**) *m* colonel; **o~e(r, s)** *adj* very top, topmost

Ober- *zW*: **~stufe** *f* upper school; **~teil** *nt* upper part; **~weite** *f* bust/chest measurement

obgleich [ɔpˈglaɪç] *konj* although

Obhut [ˈɔphuːt] (**-**) *f* care, protection; **in jds ~ sein** to be in sb's care

obig [ˈoːbɪç] *adj* above

Objekt [ɔpˈjɛkt] (**-(e)s**, **-e**) *nt* object; **~iv** [-ˈtiːf] (**-s**, **-e**) *nt* lens; **o~iv** *adj* objective

Objektivi'tät *f* objectivity

Oblate [oˈblaːtə] *f* (*Gebäck*) wafer; (*ECCL*) host

obligatorisch [obligaˈtoːrɪʃ] *adj* compulsory, obligatory

Obrigkeit ['oːbrɪçkaɪt] f (Behörden) authorities pl, administration; (Regierung) government

obschon [ɔp'ʃoːn] konj although

Observatorium [ɔpzɛrva'toːriʊm] nt observatory

obskur [ɔps'kuːr] adj obscure; (verdächtig) dubious

Obst [oːpst] nt (-(e)s) fruit; **~baum** m fruit tree; **~garten** m orchard; **~händler** m fruiterer, fruit merchant; **~kuchen** m fruit tart

obszön [ɔps'tsøːn] adj obscene; **O~i'tät** f obscenity

obwohl [ɔp'voːl] konj although

Ochse ['ɔksə] m (-n, -n) m ox; **o~n** (umg) vt, vi to cram, to swot (BRIT)

Ochsenschwanzsuppe f oxtail soup

Ochsenzunge f oxtongue

öd(e) ['øːd(ə)] adj (Land) waste, barren; (fig) dull; **Ö~** f desert, waste(land); (fig) tedium

oder ['oːdər] konj or; **das stimmt, ~?** that's right, isn't it?

Ofen ['oːfən] m (-s, ̈) m oven; (Heizofen) fire, heater; (Kohlenofen) stove; (Hochofen) furnace; (Herd) cooker, stove; **~rohr** nt stovepipe

offen ['ɔfən] adj open; (aufrichtig) frank; (Stelle) vacant; **~ bleiben** (Fenster) to stay open; (Frage, Entscheidung) to remain open; **~ halten** to keep open; **~ lassen** to leave open; **~ stehen** to be open; (Rechnung) to be unpaid; **es steht Ihnen ~, es zu tun** you are at liberty to do it; **~ gesagt** to be honest; **~bar** adj obvious; **~baren** [ɔfən'baːrən] vt to reveal, to manifest; **O~barung** f (REL) revelation; **O~heit** f candour, frankness; **~herzig** adj candid, frank; (Kleid) revealing; **~kundig** adj well-known, (klar) evident; **~sichtlich** adj evident, obvious

offensiv [ɔfɛn'ziːf] adj offensive; **O~e** f [-'ziːvə] f offensive

öffentlich ['œfəntlɪç] adj public; **Ö~keit** f (Leute) public; (einer Versammlung etc) public nature; **in aller Ö~keit** in public; **an die Ö~keit dringen** to reach the public ear

offiziell [ɔfitsi'ɛl] adj official

Offizier [ɔfi'tsiːr] (-s, -e) m officer; **~skasino** nt officers' mess

öffnen ['œfnən] vt, vr to open; **jdm die Tür ~** to open the door for sb

Öffner ['œfnər] (-s, -) m opener

Öffnung ['œfnʊŋ] f opening; **~szeiten** pl opening times

oft [ɔft] adv often

öfter ['œftər] adv more often od frequently; **~s** adv often, frequently

oh [oː] excl oh; **~ je!** oh dear

OHG abk (= Offene Handelsgesellschaft) general partnership

ohne ['oːnə] präp +akk without ♦ konj without; **das ist nicht ~** (umg) it's not bad; **~ weiteres** without a second thought; (sofort) immediately; **~ zu fragen** without asking; **~ dass er es wusste** without him knowing it; **~dies** [oːnə'diːs] adv anyway; **~gleichen** [oːnə'glaɪçən] adj unsurpassed, without equal; **~hin** [oːnə'hɪn] adv anyway, in any case

Ohnmacht ['oːnmaxt] f faint; (fig) impotence; **in ~ fallen** to faint

ohnmächtig ['oːnmɛçtɪç] adj in a faint, unconscious; (fig) weak, impotent; **sie ist ~** she has fainted

Ohr [oːr] (-(e)s, -en) nt ear

Öhr [øːr] (-(e)s, -e) nt eye

Ohren- zW: **~arzt** m ear specialist; **o~betäubend** adj deafening; **~schmalz** nt earwax; **~schmerzen** pl earache sg

Ohr- zW: **~feige** f slap on the face; box on the ears; **o~feigen** vt: **jdn o~feigen** to slap sb's face; to box sb's ears; **~läppchen** nt ear lobe; **~ring** m earring; **~wurm** m earwig; (MUS)

catchy tune

Öko- [øko] *zW:* **~laden** *m* wholefood shop; **ö~logisch** [-'lo:ɡɪʃ] *adj* ecological; **ö~nomisch** [-'no:mɪʃ] *adj* economical

Oktober [ɔk'to:bər] **(-s, -)** *m* October; **~fest** *nt* Munich beer festival

---
Oktoberfest

The annual beer festival, the Oktoberfest, takes place in Munich at the end of September in a huge area where beer tents and various amusements are set up. People sit at long wooden tables, drink beer from enormous beer mugs, eat pretzels and listen to brass bands. It is a great attraction for tourists and locals alike.

ökumenisch [øku'me:nɪʃ] *adj* ecumenical

Öl [ø:l] **(-(e)s, -e)** *nt* oil; **~baum** *m* olive tree; **ö~en** *vt* to oil; (*TECH*) to lubricate; **~farbe** *f* oil paint; **~feld** *nt* oilfield; **~film** *m* film of oil; **~heizung** *f* oil-fired central heating; **ö~ig** *adj* oily; **~industrie** *f* oil industry

oliv [o'li:f] *adj* olive-green; **O~e** *f* olive

Öl- *zW:* **~messstab** ▲ *m* dipstick; **~sardine** *f* sardine; **~stand** *m* oil level; **~standanzeiger** *m* (*AUT*) oil gauge; **~tanker** *m* oil tanker; **~ung** *f* lubrication; oiling; (*ECCL*) anointment; **die Letzte ~ung** Extreme Unction; **~wechsel** *m* oil change

Olymp- [o'lʏmp] *zW:* **~iade** [olʏmpi'a:də] *f* Olympic Games *pl*; **~iasieger(in)** [-iazi:ɡər(ɪn)] *m(f)* Olympic champion; **~iateilnehmer(in)** *m(f)* Olympic competitor; **o~isch** *adj* Olympic

Ölzeug *nt* oilskins *pl*

Oma [ˈoːma] **(-, -s)** (*umg*) *f* granny

Omelett [ɔm(ə)'lɛt] **(-(e)s, -s)** *nt* omelet(te)

ominös [omi'nøːs] *adj* (*unheilvoll*) ominous

Onanie [ona'ni:] *f* masturbation; **o~ren** *vi* to masturbate

Onkel [ˈɔŋkəl] **(-s, -)** *m* uncle

Opa [ˈo:pa] **(-s, -s)** (*umg*) *m* grandpa

Oper [ˈo:pər] **(-, -n)** *f* opera; opera house

Operation [operatsi'o:n] *f* operation; **~ssaal** *m* operating theatre

Operette [ope'rɛtə] *f* operetta

operieren [ope'ri:rən] *vt* to operate on ♦ *vi* to operate

Opern- *zW:* **~glas** *nt* opera glasses *pl*; **~haus** *nt* opera house

Opfer [ˈɔpfər] **(-s, -)** *nt* sacrifice; (*Mensch*) victim; **o~n** *vt* to sacrifice; **~ung** *f* sacrifice

opponieren [ɔpo'ni:rən] *vi:* **gegen jdn/etw ~** to oppose sb/sth

Opportunist [ɔportu'nɪst] *m* opportunist

Opposition [ɔpozitsi'o:n] *f* opposition; **o~ell** *adj* opposing

Optik [ˈɔptɪk] *f* optics *sg*; **~er (-s, -)** *m* optician

optimal [ɔpti'ma:l] *adj* optimal, optimum

Optimismus [ɔpti'mɪsmʊs] *m* optimism

Optimist [ɔpti'mɪst] *m* optimist; **o~isch** *adj* optimistic

optisch [ˈɔptɪʃ] *adj* optical

Orakel [o'ra:kəl] **(-s, -)** *nt* oracle

oral [o'ra:l] *adj* (*MED*) oral

Orange [o'rãːʒə] *f* orange; **o~** *adj* orange; **~ade** [orã'ʒa:də] *f* orangeade; **~at** [orã'ʒa:t] **(-s, -e)** *nt* candied peel

Orchester [ɔr'kɛstər] **(-s, -)** *nt* orchestra

Orchidee [ɔrçi'de:ə] *f* orchid

Orden [ˈɔrdən] **(-s, -)** *m* (*ECCL*) order; (*MIL*) decoration; **~sschwester** *f* nun

ordentlich [ˈɔrdəntlɪç] *adj* (*anständig*) decent, respectable; (*geordnet*) tidy, neat; (*umg: annehmbar*) not bad; (*: tüchtig*) real, proper ♦ *adv* properly; **~er Professor** (full) professor; **O~keit** *f* respectability; tidiness, neatness

ordinär [ɔrdi'nɛːr] adj common, vulgar

ordnen ['ɔrdnən] vt to order, to put in order

Ordner (-s, -) m steward; (COMM) file

Ordnung f order; (Ordnen) ordering; (Geordnetsein) tidiness; ~ **machen** to tidy up; **in** ~! okay!

Ordnungs- zW: **o~gemäß** adj proper, according to the rules; **o~liebend** adj orderly, methodical; ~**strafe** f fine; **o~widrig** adj contrary to the rules, irregular; ~**widrigkeit** [-vi:driçkaɪt] f infringement (of law or rule); ~**zahl** f ordinal number

Organ [ɔr'gaːn] (-s, -e) nt organ; (Stimme) voice; ~**isation** [-izatsi'oːn] f organization; ~**isator** [i'zaːtɔr] m organizer; **o~isch** adj organic; **o~isieren** [-i'ziːrən] vt to organize, to arrange; (umg: beschaffen) to acquire ♦ vr to organize; ~**ismus** [-'nɪsmus] m organism; ~**ist** [-'nɪst] m organist; ~**spende** f organ donation; ~**spenderausweis** m donor card

Orgasmus [ɔr'gasmos] m orgasm

Orgel ['ɔrgəl] (-, -n) f organ

Orgie ['ɔrgiə] f orgy

Orient ['oːriɛnt] (-s) m Orient, east; **o~alisch** [-'taːlɪʃ] adj oriental

orientier- zW: ~**en** [-'tiːrən] vt (örtlich) to locate; (fig) to inform ♦ vr to find one's way od bearings; to inform o.s.; **O~ung** [-'tiːrʊŋ] f orientation; (fig) information; **O~ungssinn** m sense of direction; **O~ungsstufe** f period during which pupils are selected for different schools

---

Orientierungsstufe

The **Orientierungsstufe** is the name given to the first two years spent in a Realschule or Gymnasium, during which a child is assessed as to his or her suitability for that type of school. At the end of two years it may be de-

cided to transfer the child to a school more suited to his or her ability.

---

original [origi'naːl] adj original; **O~** (-s, -e) nt original; **O~fassung** f original version; **O~i'tät** f originality

originell [origi'nɛl] adj original

Orkan [ɔr'kaːn] (-(e)s, -e) m hurricane; **o~artig** adj (Wind) gale-force; (Beifall) thunderous

Ornament [ɔrna'mɛnt] nt decoration, ornament; **o~al** [-'taːl] adj decorative, ornamental

Ort [ɔrt] (-(e)s, -e od ¨er) m place; **an** ~ **und Stelle** on the spot; **o~en** vt to locate

ortho- [ɔrto] zW: ~**dox** [-'dɔks] adj orthodox; **O~grafie** ▲ [-gra'fiː] f spelling, orthography; **o~'grafisch** ▲ adj orthographic; **O~päde** [-'pɛːdə] (-n, -n) m orthopaedist; **O~pädie** [-pɛ'diː] f orthopaedics sg; ~'**pädisch** adj orthopaedic

örtlich ['œrtlıç] adj local; **Ö~keit** f locality

ortsansässig adj local

Ortschaft f village, small town

Orts- zW: **o~fremd** adj non-local; **~gespräch** nt local (phone)call; **~name** m place name; **~netz** nt (TEL) local telephone exchange area; **~tarif** m (TEL) tariff for local calls; **~zeit** f local time

Ortung f locating

Öse ['øːzə] f loop, eye

Ost'asien [ɔs'taːziən] nt Eastern Asia

Osten ['ɔstən] (-s) m east

Oster- ['ɔstər] zW: **~ei** nt Easter egg; **~fest** nt Easter; **~glocke** f daffodil; **~hase** m Easter bunny; **~montag** m Easter Monday; **~n** (-s, -) nt Easter

Österreich ['øːstəraıç] (-s) nt Austria; **~er(in)** m(f) Austrian; **ö~isch** adj Austrian

Ostküste f east coast

östlich ['œstlıç] adj eastern, easterly

Ostsee f: die ~ the Baltic (Sea)
Ouvertüre [uver'ty:rə] f overture
oval [o'va:l] adj oval
Ovation [ovatsi'o:n] f ovation
Oxid, Oxyd [ɔ'ksy:t] (-(e)s, -e) nt oxide; **o~ieren** vt, vi to oxidize; **~ierung** f oxidization
Ozean [o:tsea:n] (-s, -e) m ocean; **~dampfer** m (ocean-going) liner
Ozon [o'tso:n] (-s) nt ozone; **~loch** nt ozone hole; **~schicht** f ozone layer

P, p

Paar [pa:r] (-(e)s, -e) nt pair; (Ehepaar) couple; ein p~ a few; die Paare a few times; **p~en** vt, vr to couple; (Tiere) to mate; **~lauf** m pair skating; **~ung** f combination; mating; **p~weise** adv in pairs; in couples
Pacht [paxt] (-, -en) f lease; **p~en** vt to lease
Pächter ['pɛçtər] (-s, -) m leaseholder, tenant
Pack¹ [pak] (-(e)s, -e od ⁼e) m bundle, pack
Pack² [pak] (-(e)s) nt (pej) mob, rabble
Päckchen ['pɛkçən] nt small package; (Zigaretten) packet; (Postpäckchen) small parcel
Pack- zW: **p~en** vt to pack; (fassen) to grasp, to seize; (umg: schaffen) to manage; (fig: fesseln) to grip; **~en** (-s, -) m bundle; (fig: Menge) heaps of; **~esel** m (auch fig) packhorse; **~papier** nt brown paper, wrapping paper; **~ung** f packet; (Pralinenpackung) box; (MED) compress; **~ungsbeilage** f enclosed instructions pl for use
Pädagog- [pɛda'go:g] zW: **~e** (-n, -n) m teacher; **~ik** f education; **p~isch** adj educational, pedagogical
Paddel ['padəl] (-s, -) nt paddle; **~boot** nt canoe; **p~n** vi to paddle
Page ['pa:ʒə] (-n, -n) m page

Paket [pa'ke:t] (-(e)s, -e) nt packet; (Postpaket) parcel; **~karte** f dispatch note; **~post** f parcel post; **~schalter** m parcels counter
Pakt [pakt] (-(e)s, -e) m pact
Palast [pa'last] (-(e)s, Paläste) m palace
Palästina [palɛ'sti:na] (-s) nt Palestine
Palme ['palmə] f palm (tree)
Pampelmuse [pampəl'mu:zə] f grapefruit
panieren [pa'ni:rən] vt (KOCH) to bread
Paniermehl [pa'ni:rme:l] nt breadcrumbs pl
Panik ['pa:nik] f panic
panisch ['pa:nɪʃ] adj panic-stricken
Panne ['panə] f (AUT etc) breakdown; (Missgeschick) slip; **~nhilfe** f breakdown service
panschen ['panʃən] vi to splash about ♦ vt to water down
Pantoffel [pan'tɔfəl] (-s, -n) m slipper
Pantomime [panto'mi:mə] f mime
Panzer ['pantsər] (-s, -) m armour; (Platte) armour plate; (Fahrzeug) tank; **~glas** nt bulletproof glass; **p~n** vt to armour ♦ vr (fig) to arm o.s.
Papa [pa'pa:] (-s, -s) (umg) m dad, daddy
Papagei [papa'gai] (-s, -en) m parrot
Papier [pa'pi:r] (-s, -e) nt paper; (Wertpapier) security; **~fabrik** f paper mill; **~geld** nt paper money; **~korb** m wastepaper basket; **~taschentuch** nt tissue
Papp- ['pap] zW: **~deckel** m cardboard; **~e** f cardboard; **~el** (-, -n) f poplar; **p~en** (umg) vt, vi to stick; **p~ig** adj sticky
Paprika ['paprika] (-s, -s) m (Gewürz) paprika; (~schote) pepper
Papst [pa:pst] (-(e)s, ⁼e) m pope
päpstlich ['pɛ:pstlɪç] adj papal
Parabel [pa'ra:bəl] (-, -n) f parable; (MATH) parabola
Parabolantenne [para'bo:lantenə] f satellite dish
Parade [pa'ra:də] f (MIL) parade, re-

view; (SPORT) parry

Paradies [para'di:s] (-es, -e) nt paradise; **p~isch** adj heavenly

Paradox [para'dɔks] (-es, -e) nt paradox; **p~** adj paradoxical

Paragraf ▲ [para'gra:f] (-en, -en) m paragraph; (JUR) section

parallel [para'le:l] adj parallel; **P~e** f parallel

Parasit [para'zi:t] (-en, -en) m (auch fig) parasite

parat [pa'ra:t] adj ready

Pärchen ['pɛːrçən] nt couple

Parfüm [par'fy:m] (-s, -s od -e) nt perfume; **~erie** [-ə'ri:] f perfumery; **p~frei** adj non-perfumed; **p~ieren** vt to scent, to perfume

parieren [pa'ri:rən] vt to parry ♦ vi (umg) to obey

Paris [pa'ri:s] (-) nt Paris; **~er** m Parisian ♦ m Parisian; **~erin** f Parisian

Park [park] (-s, -e) m park; **~anlage** f park; (um Gebäude) grounds pl; **p~en** vt, vi to park; **~ett** (-(e)s, -e) nt parquet (floor); (THEAT) stalls pl; **~gebühr** f parking fee; **~haus** nt multi-storey car park; **~lücke** f parking space; **~platz** m parking place; car park, parking lot (US); **~scheibe** f parking disc; **~schein** m car park ticket; **~uhr** f parking meter; **~verbot** nt parking ban

Parlament [parla'mɛnt] nt parliament; **~arier** [-'ta:riər] (-s, -) m parliamentarian; **p~arisch** [-'ta:rɪʃ] adj parliamentary

Parlaments- zW: **~beschluss** ▲ m vote of parliament; **~mitglied** nt member of parliament; **~sitzung** f sitting (of parliament)

Parodie [paro'di:] f parody; **p~ren** vt to parody

Parole [pa'ro:lə] f password; (Wahlspruch) motto

Partei [par'tai] f party; **~ ergreifen für**

jdn to take sb's side; **p~isch** adj partial, bias(s)ed; **p~los** adj neutral, impartial; **~mitglied** nt party member; **~programm** nt (party) manifesto; **~tag** m party conference

Parterre [par'tɛr] (-s, -s) nt ground floor; (THEAT) stalls pl

Partie [par'ti:] f part; (Spiel) game; (Ausflug) outing; (Mann, Frau) catch; (COMM) lot; **mit von der ~ sein** to join in

Partizip [parti'tsi:p] (-s, -ien) nt participle

Partner(in) ['partnər(ɪn)] (-s, -) m(f) partner; **~schaft** f partnership; (von Städten) twinning; **p~schaftlich** adj as partners; **~stadt** f twin town

Party ['pa:rti] (-, -s) f party

Pass ▲ [pas] (-es, ²e) m pass; (Ausweis) passport

passabel [pa'sa:bəl] adj passable, reasonable

Passage [pa'sa:ʒə] f passage

Passagier [pasa'ʒi:r] (-s, -e) m passenger; **~flugzeug** nt airliner

Passamt nt passport office

Passant [pa'sant] m passer-by

Passbild ▲ nt passport photograph

passen ['pasən] vi to fit; (Farbe) to go; (auf Frage, KARTEN, SPORT) to pass; **das passt mir nicht** that doesn't suit me; **~ zu** (Farbe, Kleider) to go with; **er passt nicht zu dir** he's not right for you; **~d** adj suitable; (zusammenpassend) matching; (angebracht) fitting; (Zeit) convenient

passier- [pa'si:r] zW: **~bar** adj passable; **~en** vt to pass; (durch Sieb) to strain ♦ vi to happen; **P~schein** m pass, permit

Passion [pasi'o:n] f passion; **p~iert** [-'ni:rt] adj enthusiastic, passionate; **~sspiel** nt Passion Play

passiv [pasi'f] adj passive; **P~** (-s, -e) nt passive; **P~a** pl (COMM) liabilities;

Spelling Reform: ▲ new spelling △ old spelling (to be phased out)

P~i'tät f passiveness; **P~rauchen** nt passive smoking

Pass- ▲ zW: **~kontrolle** f passport control; **~stelle** f passport office; **~straße** f (mountain) pass

Paste ['pastə] f paste

Pastete [pas'te:tə] f pie

pasteurisieren [pastøri'zi:rən] vt to pasteurize

Pastor ['pastɔr] m vicar; pastor, minister

Pate ['pa:tə] (-n, -n) m godfather; **~nkind** nt godchild

Patent [pa'tɛnt] (-(e)s, -e) nt patent; (MIL) commission; **p~** adj clever; **~amt** nt patent office

Patentante f godmother

patentieren [patɛn'ti:rən] vt to patent

Patentinhaber m patentee

pathetisch [pa'te:tiʃ] adj emotional; bombastic

Pathologe [pato'lo:gə] (-n, -n) m pathologist

pathologisch adj pathological

Pathos ['pa:tɔs] (-) nt emotiveness, emotionalism

Patient(in) [patsi'ɛnt(ɪn)] m(f) patient

Patin ['pa:tɪn] f godmother

Patriot [patri'o:t] (-en, -en) m patriot; **p~isch** adj patriotic; **~ismus** ['-tɪsmʊs] m patriotism

Patrone [pa'tro:nə] f cartridge

Patrouille [pa'troljə] f patrol

patrouillieren [patrol'ji:rən] vi to patrol

patsch [patʃ] excl splash; **P~e** (umg) f (Bedrängnis) mess, jam; **~en** vi to smack, to slap; (im Wasser) to splash; **~nass ▲** adj soaking wet

patzig ['patsɪç] (umg) adj cheeky, saucy

Pauke ['paʊkə] f kettledrum; **auf die ~ hauen** to live it up

pauken vt (intensiv lernen) to swot up (inf) ♦ vi to swot (inf), cram (inf)

pausbäckig ['paʊsbɛkɪç] adj chubby-cheeked

pauschal [paʊ'ʃa:l] adj (Kosten) inclusive; (Urteil) sweeping; **P~e** f flat rate; **P~gebühr** f flat rate; **P~preis** m all-in price; **P~reise** f package tour; **P~summe** f lump sum

Pause ['paʊzə] f break; (THEAT) interval; (Innehalten) pause; (Kopie) tracing

pausen vt to trace; **~los** adj non-stop; **P~zeichen** nt call sign; (MUS) rest

Pauspapier ['paʊspapi:r] nt tracing paper

Pavillon ['paviljõ] (-s, -s) m pavilion

Pazif- [pa'tsi:f] zW: **~ik** (-s) m Pacific; **p~istisch** adj pacifist

Pech [pɛç] (-s, -e) nt pitch; (fig) bad luck; **~ haben** to be unlucky; **p~schwarz** adj pitch-black; **~strähne** (umg) m unlucky patch; **~vogel** (umg) m unlucky person

Pedal [pe'da:l] (-s, -e) nt pedal

Pedant [pe'dant] m pedant; **~e'rie** f pedantry; **p~isch** adj pedantic

Pediküre [pedi'ky:rə] f (Fußpflege) pedicure

Pegel ['pe:gəl] (-s, -) m water gauge; **~stand** m water level

peilen ['paɪlən] vt to get a fix on

Pein [paɪn] (-) f agony, pain; **p~igen** vt to torture; (plagen) to torment; **p~lich** adj (unangenehm) embarrassing, awkward, painful; (genau) painstaking

Peitsche ['paɪtʃə] f whip; **p~n** vt to whip; (Regen) to lash

Pelle ['pɛlə] f skin; **p~n** vt to skin, to peel

Pellkartoffeln pl jacket potatoes

Pelz [pɛlts] (-es, -e) m fur

Pendel ['pɛndəl] (-s, -) nt pendulum; **p~n** vi (Zug, Fähre etc) to operate a shuttle service; (Mensch) to commute; **~verkehr** m shuttle traffic; (für Pendler) commuter traffic

Pendler ['pɛndlər] (-s, -) m commuter

penetrant [pene'trant] adj sharp; (Person) pushing

Penis ['pe:nɪs] (-, -se) m penis

pennen ['pɛnən] (umg) vi to kip

Penner (umg: pej) m (Landstreicher)

tramp

Pension [penzi'o:n] f (Geld) pension; (Ruhestand) retirement; (für Gäste) boarding od guesthouse; **~är(in)** [-'nɛ:r(ɪn)] (-s, -e) m(f) pensioner; **p~ieren** vt to pension off; **p~iert** adj retired; **~ierung** f retirement; **~sgast** m boarder, paying guest

Pensum ['pɛnzʊm] (-s, Pensen) nt quota; (SCH) curriculum

per [pɛr] präp +akk by, per; (pro) per; (bis) by

Perfekt ['pɛrfɛkt] (-(e)s, -e) nt perfect; **p~** adj perfect

perforieren [pɛrfo'ri:rən] vt to perforate

Pergament [pɛrga'mɛnt] nt parchment; **~papier** nt greaseproof paper

Periode [peri'o:də] f period; **periodisch** adj periodic; (dezimal) recurring

Perle ['pɛrlə] f (auch fig) pearl; **p~n** vi to sparkle; (Tropfen) to trickle

Perl- ['pɛrl] zW: **~mutt** (-s) nt mother-of-pearl; **~wein** m sparkling wine

perplex [pɛr'plɛks] adj dumbfounded

Person [pɛr'zo:n] (-, -en) f person; **ich für meine ~** ... personally I ...

Personal [pɛrzo'na:l] (-s) nt personnel; (Bedienung) servants pl; **~ausweis** m identity card; **~computer** m personal computer; **~ien** [-ĭən] pl particulars; **~mangel** m undermanning; **~pronomen** nt personal pronoun

personell [pɛrzo'nɛl] adj (Veränderungen) personnel

Personen- zW: **~aufzug** m lift, elevator (US); **~kraftwagen** m private motorcar; **~schaden** m injury to persons; **~zug** m stopping train; passenger train

personifizieren [pɛrzonifi'tsi:rən] vt to personify

persönlich [pɛr'zø:nlɪç] adj personal ♦ adv in person; personally; **P~keit** f personality

Perspektive [pɛrspɛk'ti:və] f perspective

Perücke [pe'rʏkə] f wig

pervers [pɛr'vɛrs] adj perverse

Pessimismus [pɛsi'mɪsmʊs] m pessimism

Pessimist [pɛsi'mɪst] m pessimist; **p~isch** adj pessimistic

Pest [pɛst] (-) f plague

Petersilie [petar'zi:liə] f parsley

Petroleum [pe'tro:leʊm] (-s) nt paraffin, kerosene (US)

Pfad [pfa:t] (-(e)s, -e) m path; **~finder** (-s, -) m boy scout; **~finderin** f girl guide

Pfahl [pfa:l] (-(e)s, ⁻e) m post, stake

Pfand [pfant] (-(e)s, ⁻er) nt pledge, security; (Flaschenpfand) deposit; (im Spiel) forfeit; **~brief** m bond

Pfänderspiel nt game of forfeits

Pfandflasche f returnable bottle

Pfandschein m pawn ticket

Pfändung ['pfɛndʊŋ] f seizure, distraint

Pfanne ['pfanə] f (frying) pan

Pfannkuchen m pancake; (Berliner) doughnut

Pfarr- ['pfar] zW: **~ei** f parish; **~er** (-s, -) m priest; (evangelisch) vicar; minister; **~haus** nt vicarage; manse

Pfau [pfaʊ] (-(e)s, -en) m peacock; **~enauge** nt peacock butterfly

Pfeffer ['pfɛfər] (-s, -) m pepper; **~kuchen** m gingerbread; **~minz** (-es, -e) nt peppermint; **~mühle** f pepper mill; **p~n** vt to pepper; (umg: werfen) to fling; **gepfefferte Preise/Witze** steep prices/spicy jokes

Pfeife ['pfaɪfə] f whistle; (Tabakpfeife, Orgelpfeife) pipe; **p~n** (unreg) vt, vi to whistle; **~r** (-s, -) m piper

Pfeil [pfaɪl] (-(e)s, -e) m arrow

Pfeiler ['pfaɪlər] (-s, -) m pillar, prop;

(*Brückenpfeiler*) pier

Pfennig ['pfɛnɪç] (-(e)s, -e) *m* pfennig (*hundredth part of a mark*)

Pferd [pfe:rt] (-(e)s, -e) *nt* horse

Pferde- ['pfe:rdə] *zW:* **~rennen** *nt* horse race; horse racing; **~schwanz** *m* (*Frisur*) ponytail; **~stall** *m* stable

Pfiff [pfɪf] (-(e)s, -e) *m* whistle

Pfifferling ['pfɪfərlɪŋ] *m* yellow chanterelle (*mushroom*); **keinen ~ wert** not worth a thing

pfiffig *adj* sly, sharp

Pfingsten ['pfɪŋstən] (-, -) *nt* Whitsun (*BRIT*), Pentecost

Pfirsich ['pfɪrzɪç] (-s, -e) *m* peach

Pflanz- ['pflants] *zW:* **~e** *f* plant; **p~en** *vt* to plant; **~enfett** *nt* vegetable fat; **p~lich** *adj* vegetable; **~ung** *f* plantation

Pflaster ['pflastər] (-s, -) *nt* plaster; (*Straße*) pavement; **p~n** *vt* to pave; **~stein** *m* paving stone

Pflaume ['pflaumə] *f* plum

Pflege ['pfle:gə] *f* care; (*von Idee*) cultivation; (*Krankenpflege*) nursing; **in ~ sein** (*Kind*) to be fostered out; **p~bedürftig** *adj* needing care; **~eltern** *pl* foster parents; **~heim** *nt* nursing home; **~kind** *nt* foster child; **p~leicht** *adj* easy-care; **~mutter** *f* foster mother; **p~n** *vt* to look after; (*Kranke*) to nurse; (*Beziehungen*) to foster; **~r (-s, -)** *m* orderly; male nurse; **~rin** *f* nurse, attendant; **~vater** *m* foster father

Pflicht [pflɪçt] (-, -en) *f* duty; (*SPORT*) compulsory section; **p~bewusst ▲** *adj* conscientious; **~fach** *nt* (*SCH*) compulsory subject; **~gefühl** *nt* sense of duty; **p~gemäß** *adj* dutiful ♦ *adv* as in duty bound; **~versicherung** *f* compulsory insurance

pflücken ['pflʏkən] *vt* to pick; (*Blumen*) to pick, to pluck

Pflug [pflu:k] (-(e)s, ⁺e) *m* plough

pflügen ['pfly:gən] *vt* to plough

Pforte ['pfɔrtə] *f* gate; door

Pförtner ['pfœrtnər] (-s, -) *m* porter, doorkeeper, doorman

Pfosten ['pfɔstən] (-s, -) *m* post

Pfote ['pfo:tə] *f* paw; (*umg: Schrift*) scrawl

Pfropfen (-s, -) *m* (*Flaschenpfropfen*) stopper; (*Blutpropfen*) clot

pfui [pfʊɪ] *excl* ugh!

Pfund [pfʊnt] (-(e)s, -e) *nt* pound

pfuschen ['pfʊʃən] (*umg*) *vi* to be sloppy; **jdm ins Handwerk ~** to interfere in sb's business

Pfuscher ['pfʊʃər] (-s, -) *m* (*umg*) sloppy worker; (*Kurpfuscher*) quack; **~ei** (*umg*) *f* sloppy work; quackery

Pfütze ['pfʏtsə] *f* puddle

Phänomen [fɛnoˈmeːn] (-s, -e) *nt* phenomenon; **p~al** [-ˈnaːl] *adj* phenomenal

Phantasie *etc* [fantaˈziː] *f* = **Fantasie** *etc*

phantastisch [fanˈtastɪʃ] *adj* = **fantastisch**

Phase ['faːzə] *f* phase

Philologie [filoloˈgiː] *f* philology

Philosoph [filoˈzoːf] (-en, -en) *m* philosopher; **~ie** [-ˈfiː] *f* philosophy; **p~isch** *adj* philosophical

phlegmatisch [fleˈgmaːtɪʃ] *adj* lethargic

Phonetik [foˈneːtɪk] *f* phonetics *sg*

phonetisch *adj* phonetic

Phosphor ['fɔsfɔr] (-s) *m* phosphorus

Photo *etc* ['foːto] (-s, -s) *nt* = **Foto** *etc*

Phrase ['fraːzə] *f* phrase; (*pej*) hollow phrase

pH-Wert [peːˈhaːvɛrt] *m* pH-value

Physik [fyˈziːk] *f* physics *sg*; **p~alisch** [-kaˈliːʒ] *adj* of physics; **~er(in)** ['fyːzɪkɐr(ɪn)] (-s, -) *m(f)* physicist

Physiologie [fyzioloˈgiː] *f* physiology

physisch ['fyːzɪʃ] *adj* physical

Pianist(in) [piaˈnɪst(ɪn)] *m(f)* pianist

Pickel ['pɪkəl] (-s, -) *m* pimple; (*Werkzeug*) pickaxe; (*Bergpickel*) ice axe; **p~ig** *adj* pimply, spotty

picken ['pɪkən] vi to pick, to peck

Picknick ['pɪknɪk] (-s, -e od -s) nt picnic; ~ **machen** to have a picnic

piepen ['piːpən] vi to chirp

piepsen ['piːpsən] vi to chirp

Piepser (umg) m pager, paging device

Pier [piːɐ] (-s, -s od -e) m od f pier

Pietät [pie'tɛːt] f piety, reverence; **p~los** adj impious, irreverent

Pigment [pɪg'mɛnt] nt pigment

Pik [piːk] (-s, -) nt (KARTEN) spades

pikant [pi'kant] adj spicy, piquant; (anzüglich) suggestive

Pilger ['pɪlgɐ] (-s, -) m pilgrim; ~**fahrt** f pilgrimage

Pille ['pɪlə] f pill

Pilot [pi'loːt] (-en, -en) m pilot

Pilz [pɪlts] (-es, -e) m fungus; (essbar) mushroom; (giftig) toadstool; ~**krankheit** f fungal disease

Pinguin ['pɪŋguiːn] (-s, -e) m penguin

Pinie ['piːniə] f pine

pinkeln ['pɪŋkəln] (umg) vi to pee

Pinnwand ['pɪnvant] f noticeboard

Pinsel ['pɪnzəl] (-s, -) m paintbrush

Pinzette [pɪn'tsɛtə] f tweezers pl

Pionier [pio'niːɐ] (-s, -e) m pioneer; (MIL) sapper, engineer

Pirat [pi'raːt] (-en, -en) m pirate

Piste ['pɪstə] f (SKI) run, piste; (AVIAT) runway

Pistole [pɪs'toːlə] f pistol

Pizza ['pɪtsa] (-, -s) f pizza

Pkw [peːkaː'veː] (-(s), -(s)) m abk = Personenkraftwagen

plädieren [plɛ'diːrən] vi to plead

Plädoyer [plɛdoa'jeː] (-s, -s) nt speech for the defence; (fig) plea

Plage ['plaːgə] f plague; (Mühe) nuisance; ~**geist** m pest, nuisance; **p~n** vt to torment ♦ vr to toil, to slave

Plakat [pla'kaːt] (-(e)s, -e) nt placard; poster

Plan [plaːn] (-(e)s, ⁼e) m plan; (Karte) map

Plane f tarpaulin

planen vt to plan; (Mord etc) to plot

Planer (-s, -) m planner

Planet [pla'neːt] (-en, -en) m planet

planieren [pla'niːrən] vt to plane, to level

Planke ['plaŋkə] f plank

plan- in zW: ~**los** adj (Vorgehen) unsystematic; (Umherlaufen) aimless; ~**mäßig** adj according to plan; systematic; (EISENB) scheduled

Plansoll (-s) nt output target

Plantage [plan'taːʒə] f plantation

Plan(t)schbecken ['plan(t)fbɛkən] nt paddling pool

plan(t)schen ['plan(t)fən] vi to splash

Planung f planning

Planwirtschaft f planned economy

plappern ['plapɐn] vi to chatter

plärren ['plɛrən] vi (Mensch) to cry, to whine; (Radio) to blare

Plasma ['plasma] (-s, Plasmen) nt plasma

Plastik¹ ['plastɪk] f sculpture

Plastik² ['plastɪk] (-s) nt (Kunststoff) plastic; ~**beutel** m plastic bag, carrier bag; ~**folie** f plastic film

plastisch ['plastɪf] adj plastic; **stell dir das ~ vor!** just picture it!

Platane [pla'taːnə] f plane (tree)

Platin ['plaːtiːn] (-s) nt platinum

platonisch [pla'toːnɪf] adj platonic

platsch [platf] excl splash; ~**en** vi to splash

plätschern ['plɛtfɐn] vi to babble

platschnass ▲ adj drenched

platt [plat] adj flat; (umg: überrascht) flabbergasted; (fig: geistlos) flat, boring; ~**deutsch** adj low German; **P~e** f (Speiseplatte, PHOT, TECH) plate; (Steinplatte) flag; (Kachel) tile; (Schallplatte) record; **P~enspieler** m record player; **P~enteller** m turntable

Platz [plats] (-es, ⁼e) m place; (Sitzplatz) seat; (Raum) space, room; (in

Stadt) square; *(Sportplatz)* playing field; **~ nehmen** to take a seat; **jdm ~ machen** to make room for sb; **~angst** *f* claustrophobia; **~anweiser(in)** (-s, -) *m(f)* usher(ette)

Plätzchen ['plɛtsçən] *nt* spot; *(Gebäck)* biscuit

platz- *zW:* **p~en** *vi* to burst; *(Bombe)* to explode; **vor Wut p~en** *(umg)* to be bursting with anger

platzieren ▲ [pla'tsi:rən] *vt* to place ♦ *vr (SPORT)* to be placed; *(TENNIS)* to be seeded

Platz- *zW:* **~karte** *f* seat reservation; **~mangel** *m* lack of space; **~patrone** *f* blank cartridge; **~regen** *m* downpour; **~reservierung** [-rezεrvi:ruɳ] *f* seat reservation; **~wunde** *f* cut

Plauderei [plaudə'rai] *f* chat, conversation; *(RADIO)* talk

plaudern ['plaudərn] *vi* to chat, to talk

plausibel [plau'zi:bəl] *adj* plausible

plazieren △ *vt, vr siehe* **platzieren**

Pleite ['plaitə] *f* bankruptcy; *(umg: Reinfall)* flop; **~ machen** to go bust; **p~** *(umg) adj* broke

Plenum ['ple:nʊm] (-s) *nt* plenum

Plombe ['plɔmbə] *f* lead seal; *(Zahnplombe)* filling

plombieren [plɔm'bi:rən] *vt* to seal; *(Zahn)* to fill

plötzlich ['plœtslɪç] *adj* sudden ♦ *adv* suddenly

plump [plʊmp] *adj* clumsy; *(Hände)* coarse; *(Körper)* shapeless; **~sen** *vi* to plump down, to fall

Plunder ['plʊndər] (-s) *m* rubbish

plündern ['plʏndərn] *vt* to plunder; *(Stadt)* to sack ♦ *vi* to plunder; **Plünderung** *f* plundering, sack, pillage

Plural ['plu:ra:l] (-s, -e) *m* plural; **p~istisch** *adj* pluralistic

Plus [plʊs] (-, -) *nt* plus; *(FIN)* profit; *(Vorteil)* advantage; **p~** *adv* plus

Plüsch [ply:ʃ] (-(e)s, -e) *m* plush

Plus- [plʊs] *zW:* **~pol** *m (ELEK)* positive

pole; **~punkt** *m* point; *(fig)* point in sb's favour

Plutonium [plu'to:niʊm] (-s) *nt* plutonium

PLZ *abk* = **Postleitzahl**

Po [po:] (-s, -s) *(umg) m* bottom, bum

Pöbel ['pø:bəl] (-s) *m* mob, rabble; **~ei** *f* vulgarity; **p~haft** *adj* low, vulgar

pochen ['pɔxən] *vi* to knock; *(Herz)* to pound; **auf etw** *akk* **~** *(fig)* to insist on sth

Pocken ['pɔkən] *pl* smallpox *sg*

Podium ['po:diʊm] *nt* podium; **~sdiskussion** *f* panel discussion

Poesie [poe'zi:] *f* poetry

Poet [po'e:t] (-en, -en) *m* poet; **p~isch** *adj* poetic

Pointe [po'ɛ̃:tə] *f* point

Pokal [po'ka:l] (-s, -e) *m* goblet; *(SPORT)* cup; **~spiel** *nt* cup tie

pökeln ['pø:kəln] *vt* to pickle, to salt

Poker ['po:kər] (-s) *nt od m* poker

Pol [po:l] (-s, -e) *m* pole; **p~ar** *adj* polar; **~arkreis** *m* Arctic circle

Pole ['po:lə] (-n, -n) *m* Pole

polemisch [po:le'mɪʃ] *adj* polemical

Polen ['po:lən] (-s) *nt* Poland

Police [po'li:s(ə)] *f* insurance policy

Polier [po'li:r] (-s, -e) *m* foreman

polieren *vt* to polish

Poliklinik [poli'kli:nɪk] *f* outpatients (department) *sg*

Polin *f* Pole

Politik [poli'ti:k] *f* politics *sg; (eine bestimmte)* policy; **~er(in)** [po'li:tɪkər(ɪn)] (-s, -) *m(f)* politician

politisch [po'li:tɪʃ] *adj* political

Politur [poli'tu:r] *f* polish

Polizei [poli'tsai] *f* police; **~beamte(r)** *m* police officer; **p~lich** *adj* police; **sich p~lich melden** to register with the police; **~revier** *nt* police station; **~staat** *m* police state; **~streife** *f* police patrol; **~stunde** *f* closing time; **~wache** *f* police station

Polizist(in) [poli'tsɪst(ɪn)] (-en, -en) *m(f)* policeman(-woman)

Pollen ['pɔlən] (-s, -) m pollen; ~**flug** m pollen count

polnisch ['pɔlnɪʃ] adj Polish

Polohemd ['poːlohɛmt] nt polo shirt

Polster ['pɔlstar] (-s, -) nt cushion; (~ung) upholstery; (in Kleidung) padding; (fig: Geld) reserves pl; ~**er** (-s, -) m upholsterer; ~**möbel** pl upholstered furniture sg; **p~n** vt to upholster; to pad

Polterabend ['pɔltəraːbənt] m party on eve of wedding

poltern vi (Krach machen) to crash; (schimpfen) to rant

Polyp [po'lyːp] (-en, -en) m polyp; (umg) cop; ~**en** pl (MED) adenoids

Pomade [po'maːdə] f pomade

Pommes frites [pɔm'frɪt] pl chips, French fried potatoes

Pomp [pɔmp] (-(e)s pomp; **p~ös** [pɔm'pøːs] adj (Auftritt, Fest, Haus) ostentatious, showy

Pony ['pɔni] (-s, -s) nt (Pferd) pony ♦ m (Frisur) fringe

Popmusik ['pɔpmuziːk] f pop music

Popo [po'poː] (-s, -s) (umg) m bottom, bum

poppig ['pɔpɪç] adj (Farbe etc) gaudy

populär [popu'lɛːr] adj popular

Popularität [populari'tɛːt] f popularity

Pore ['poːrə] f pore

Pornografie [pɔrnogra'fiː] f pornography; **pornografisch** ▲ [pɔrno'graːfɪʃ] adj pornographic ▲

porös [po'røːs] adj porous

Porree ['pɔre] (-s, -s) m leek

Portefeuille [pɔrt(ə)'føːj] nt (POL, FIN) portfolio

Portemonnaie [pɔrtmo'neː] (-s, -s) nt = Portemonnaie

Portier [pɔrti'eː] (-s, -s) m porter

Portion [pɔrtsi'oːn] f portion, helping; (umg: Anteil) amount

Portmonee ▲ [pɔrtmo'neː] nt = Portemonnaie

Porto ['pɔrto] (-s, -s) nt postage; **p~frei** adj post-free, (postage) prepaid

Portrait [pɔr'trɛː] (-s, -s) nt = Porträt; **p~ieren** vt = porträtieren

Porträt [pɔr'trɛː] (-s, -s) nt portrait; **p~ieren** vt to paint, to portray

Portugal ['pɔrtugal] (-s) nt Portugal; **Portugiese** [pɔrtu'giːzə] (-n, -n) m Portuguese; **Portu'giesin** f Portuguese; **portu'giesisch** adj Portuguese

Porzellan [pɔrtsɛ'laːn] (-s, -e) nt china, porcelain; (Geschirr) china

Posaune [po'zaunə] f trombone

Pose ['poːzə] f pose

Position [pozitsi'oːn] f position

positiv ['poːzitiːf] adj positive; **P~** (-s, -e) nt (PHOT) positive

possessiv ['pɔsɛsiːf] adj possessive; **P~pronomen** (-s, -e) nt possessive pronoun

possierlich [pɔ'siːrlɪç] adj funny

Post [pɔst] (-, -en) f post (office); (Briefe) mail; ~**amt** nt post office; ~**anweisung** f postal order, money order; ~**bote** m postman; ~**en** (-s, -) m post, position; (COMM) item; (auf Liste) entry; (MIL) sentry; (Streikposten) picket; ~**er** (-s, -(s)) nt poster; ~**fach** nt post office box; ~**karte** f postcard; **p~lagernd** adv poste restante (BRIT), general delivery (US); ~**leitzahl** f postal code; ~**scheckkonto** nt postal giro account; ~**sparbuch** nt post office savings book; ~**sparkasse** f post office savings bank; ~**stempel** m postmark; **p~wendend** adv by return of post; ~**wertzeichen** nt postage stamp

potent [po'tɛnt] adj potent

Potential △ [potentsi'aːl] (-s, -e) nt siehe Potenzial

potentiell △ [potentsi'ɛl] adj siehe potenziell

Potenz [po'tɛnts] f power; (eines Mannes) potency

Potenzial ▲ [poten'tsiaːl] (-s, -e) nt

potential

potenziell ▲ [potɛn'tsiɛl] adj potential

Pracht [praxt] (-) f splendour, magnificence; **prächtig** ['prɛçtıç] adj splendid

Prachtstück nt showpiece

prachtvoll adj splendid, magnificent

Prädikat [prɛdi'ka:t] (-(e)s, -e) nt title; (GRAM) predicate; (Zensur) distinction

prägen ['prɛ:gən] vt to stamp; (Münze) to mint; (Ausdruck) to coin; (Charakter) to form

prägnant [prɛ'gnant] adj precise, terse

Prägung ['prɛ:gʊŋ] f minting, forming; (Eigenart) character, stamp

prahlen ['pra:lən] vi to boast, to brag; **Prahlerei** f boasting

Praktik ['praktık] f practice; **p~abel** [-'ka:bəl] adj practicable; **~ant(in)** [-'kant(ın)] m(f) trainee; **~um** (-s, Praktika od Praktiken) nt practical training

praktisch ['praktıʃ] adj practical, handy; **~er Arzt** general practitioner

praktizieren [praktı'tsi:rən] vt, vi to practise

Praline [pra'li:nə] f chocolate

prall [pral] adj firmly rounded; (Segel) taut; (Arme) plump; (Sonne) blazing; **~en** vi to bounce, to rebound; (Sonne) to blaze

Prämie ['prɛ:miə] f premium; (Belohnung) award, prize; **p~ren** vt to give an award to

Präparat [prɛpa'ra:t] (-(e)s, -e) nt (BIOL) preparation; (MED) medicine

Präposition [prɛpozitsi'o:n] f preposition

Prärie [prɛ'ri:] f prairie

Präsens ['prɛ:zɛns] (-) nt present tense

präsentieren [prɛzen'ti:rən] vt to present

Präservativ [prɛzɛrva'ti:f] (-s, -e) nt contraceptive

Präsident(in) [prɛzi'dɛnt(ın)] m(f) president; **~schaft** f presidency

Präsidium [prɛ'zi:diʊm] nt presidency, chair(manship); (Polizeipräsidium) police headquarters pl

prasseln ['prasəln] vi (Feuer) to crackle; (Hagel) to drum; (Wörter) to rain down

Praxis ['praksıs] (-, Praxen) f practice; (Behandlungsraum) surgery; (von Anwalt) office

Präzedenzfall [prɛtse'dɛnts-] m precedent

präzis [prɛ'tsi:s] adj precise; **P~ion** [prɛtsizi'o:n] f precision

predigen ['prɛ:dıgən] vt, vi to preach; **Prediger** (-s, -) m preacher

Predigt ['prɛ:dıçt] (-, -en) f sermon

Preis [praıs] (-es, -e) m price; (Siegespreis) prize; **um keinen ~** not at any price; **p~bewusst** ▲ adj price-conscious

Preiselbeere f cranberry

preis- ['praız] zW: **~en** (unreg) vt to praise; **~geben** (unreg) vt to abandon; (opfern) to sacrifice; (zeigen) to expose; **~gekrönt** adj prizewinning; **P~gericht** nt jury; **~günstig** adj inexpensive; **P~lage** f price range; **~lich** adj (Lage, Unterschied) price, in price; **P~liste** f price list; **P~richter** m judge (in a competition); **P~schild** nt price tag; **P~träger(in)** m(f) prizewinner; **~wert** adj inexpensive

Prell- [prɛl] zW: **~bock** m buffers pl; **~en** vt to bump; (fig) to cheat, to swindle; **~ung** f bruise

Premiere [prəmi'e:rə] f premiere

Premierminister [prəmi'e:mınıstər] m prime minister, premier

Presse ['prɛsə] f press; **~agentur** f press agency; **~freiheit** f freedom of the press; **p~n** vt to press

Pressluft ▲ ['prɛslʊft] f compressed air; **~bohrer** m pneumatic drill

Prestige [prɛs'ti:ʒə] (-s) nt prestige

prickeln ['prıkəln] vt, vi to tingle; to tickle

Priester ['prɛ:stər] (-s, -) m priest

prima [pri:ma] adj inv first-class, excellent

primär [pri'mɛ:r] adj primary

Primel ['pri:məl] (-, -n) f primrose

primitiv [primi'ti:f] *adj* primitive

Prinz [prɪnts] (**-en, -en**) *m* prince; **~essin** *f* princess

Prinzip [prɪn'tsi:p] (**-s, -ien**) *nt* principle; **p~iell** [-i'el] *adj, adv* on principle; **p~ienlos** *adj* unprincipled

Priorität [priori'tɛːt] *f* priority

Prise ['pri:zə] *f* pinch

Prisma ['prɪsma] (**-s, Prismen**) *nt* prism

privat [pri'va:t] *adj* private; **P~besitz** *m* private property; **P~fernsehen** *nt* commercial television; **P~patient(in)** *m(f)* private patient; **P~schule** *f* public school

Privileg [privi'le:k] (**-(e)s, -ien**) *nt* privilege

Pro [pro:] (**-**) *nt* pro

pro *präp +akk* per

Probe ['pro:bə] (**-**) *f* test; (*Teststück*) sample; (*THEAT*) rehearsal; **jdn auf die ~ stellen** to put sb to the test; **~exemplar** *nt* specimen copy; **~fahrt** *f* test drive; **p~n** *vt* to try; (*THEAT*) to rehearse; **p~weise** *adv* on approval; **~zeit** *f* probation period

probieren [pro'bi:rən] *vt* to try; (*Wein, Speise*) to taste, to sample ♦ *vi* to try; to taste

Problem [pro'ble:m] (**-s, -e**) *nt* problem; **~atik** [-'ma:tɪk] *f* problem; **p~atisch** [-'ma:tʃ] *adj* problematic; **p~los** *adj* problem-free

Produkt [pro'dʊkt] (**-(e)s, -e**) *nt* product; (*AGR*) produce *no pl*; **~ion** [prodʊktsi'o:n] *f* production; output; **p~iv** [-'ti:f] *adj* productive; **~ivität** [-ivi'tɛːt] *f* productivity

Produzent [produ'tsɛnt] *m* manufacturer; (*Film*) producer

produzieren [produ'tsi:rən] *vt* to produce

Professor [pro'fɛsɔr] *m* professor

Profi ['pro:fi] (**-s, -s**) *m* (*umg*) professional

Profil [pro'fi:l] (**-s, -e**) *nt* profile; (*fig*) image

Profit [pro'fi:t] (**-(e)s, -e**) *m* profit; **p~ieren** *vi*: **p~ieren (von)** to profit (from)

Prognose [pro'gno:zə] *f* prediction, prognosis

Programm [pro'gram] (**-s, -e**) *nt* programme; (*COMPUT*) program; **p~ieren** [-'mi:rən] *vt* to programme; (*COMPUT*) to program; **~ierer(in)** (**-s, -**) *m(f)* programmer

progressiv [progrɛ'si:f] *adj* progressive

Projekt [pro'jɛkt] (**-(e)s, -e**) *nt* project; **~or** [pro'jɛktor] *m* projector

proklamieren [prokla'mi:rən] *vt* to proclaim

Prokurist(in) [proku'rɪst(ɪn)] *m(f)* company secretary

Prolet [pro'le:t] (**-en, -en**) *m* prole, pleb; **~arier** [-'ta:riər] (**-s, -**) *m* proletarian

Prolog [pro'lo:k] (**-(e)s, -e**) *m* prologue

Promenade [promə'na:də] *f* promenade

Promille [pro'mɪlə] (**-(s), -**) *nt* alcohol level

prominent [promi'nɛnt] *adj* prominent

Prominenz [promi'nɛnts] *f* VIPs *pl*

Promotion [promotsi'o:n] *f* doctorate, Ph.D.

promovieren [promo'vi:rən] *vi* to do a doctorate *or* Ph.D.

prompt [prɔmpt] *adj* prompt

Pronomen [pro'no:men] (**-s, -**) *nt* pronoun

Propaganda [propa'ganda] (**-**) *f* propaganda

Propeller [pro'pɛlɐ] (**-s, -**) *m* propeller

Prophet [pro'fe:t] (**-en, -en**) *m* prophet

prophezeien [profe'tsaɪən] *vt* to prophesy; **Prophezeiung** *f* prophecy

Proportion [proportsi'o:n] *f* proportion; **p~al** [-'na:l] *adj* proportional

proportioniert [proportsio'ni:rt] *adj*:

gut/schlecht ~ well-/badly-proportioned

Prosa ['pro:za] (-) f prose; **p~isch** ['pro:zaːɪʃ] adj prosaic

prosit ['pro:zɪt] excl cheers

Prospekt [pro'spɛkt] (-(e)s, -e) m leaflet, brochure

prost [proːst] excl cheers

Prostituierte [prostitu'iːrtə] f prostitute

Prostitution [prostitutsi'oːn] f prostitution

Protest [pro'tɛst] (-(e)s, -e) m protest; **~ant(in)** [protɛs'tant(ɪn)] m(f) Protestant; **p~antisch** [protɛs'tantɪʃ] adj Protestant; **p~ieren** [protɛs'tiːrən] vi to protest

Prothese [pro'teːzə] f artificial limb; (Zahnprothese) dentures pl

Protokoll [proto'kɔl] (-s, -e) nt register; (von Sitzung) minutes pl; (diplomatisch) protocol; (Polizeiprotokoll) statement; **p~ieren** [-'liːrən] vt to take down in the minutes

protzen ['prɔtsən] vi to show off

Proviant [provi'ant] (-s, -e) m provisions pl, supplies pl

Provinz [pro'vɪnts] (-, -en) f province; **p~iell** adj provincial

Provision [provizi'oːn] f (COMM) commission

provisorisch [provi'zoːrɪʃ] adj provisional

Provokation [provokatsi'oːn] f provocation

provozieren [provo'tsiːrən] vt to provoke

Prozedur [protse'duːr] f procedure; (pej) carry-on

Prozent [pro'tsɛnt] (-(e)s, -e) nt per cent, percentage; **~satz** m percentage; **p~ual** [-u'aːl] adj percentage cpd; as a percentage

Prozess ▲ [pro'tsɛs] (-es, -e) m trial, case

Prozession [protsesi'oːn] f procession

prüde ['pryːdə] adj prudish; **P~rie**

[-'riː] f prudery

Prüf- ['pryːf] zW: **p~en** vt to examine, to test; (nachprüfen) to check; **~er** (-s, -) m examiner; **~ling** m examinee; **~ung** f examination; checking; **~ungsausschuss** ▲ m examining board

Prügel ['pryːgəl] (-s, -) m cudgel ♦ pl (Schläge) beating; **~ei** [-'lai] f fight; **p~n** vt to beat ♦ vr to fight; **~strafe** f corporal punishment

Prunk [prʊŋk] (-(e)s) m pomp, show; **p~voll** adj splendid, magnificent

PS [pɛːˈɛs] abk (= Pferdestärke) H.P.

Psych- ['psyç] zW: **~iater** [-i'aːtər] (-s, -) m psychiatrist; **p~iatrisch** (MED) psychiatric; **p~isch** adj psychological; **~oanalyse** [-o|ana'lyːzə] f psychoanalysis; **~ploge** (-n, -n) m psychologist; **~olo'gie** f psychology; **p~ologisch** adj psychological; **~otherapeut(in)** (-, -en) m(f) psychotherapist

Pubertät [puber'tɛːt] f puberty

Publikum ['puːblikʊm] (-s) nt audience; (SPORT) crowd

publizieren [publi'tsiːrən] vt to publish, to publicize

Pudding ['pʊdɪŋ] (-s, -e od -s) m blancmange

Pudel ['puːdəl] (-s, -) m poodle

Puder ['puːdər] (-s, -) m powder; **~dose** f powder compact; **p~n** vt to powder; **~zucker** m icing sugar

Puff¹ [pʊf] (-s, -e) m (Wäschepuff) linen basket; (Sitzpuff) pouf

Puff² [pʊf] (-s, -e) (umg) m (Stoß) push

Puff³ [pʊf] (-s, -) (umg) m od nt (Bordell) brothel

Puffer (-s, -) m buffer

Pullover [pʊ'loːvər] (-s, -) m pullover, jumper

Puls [pʊls] (-es, -e) m pulse; **~ader** f artery; **p~ieren** vi to throb, to pulsate

Pult [pʊlt] (-(e)s, -e) nt desk

Pulver ['pʊlfər] (-s, -) nt powder; **p~ig** adj powdery; **~schnee** m powdery snow

pummelig ['pɔməlɪç] *adj* chubby

Pumpe ['pɔmpə] *f* pump; **p~n** *vt* to pump; (*umg*) to lend; to borrow

Punkt [pɔŋkt] (-(e)s, -e) *m* point; (*bei Muster*) dot; (*Satzzeichen*) full stop; **p~ieren** [-'ti:rən] *vt* to dot; (*MED*) to aspirate

pünktlich ['pʏŋktlɪç] *adj* punctual; **P~keit** *f* punctuality

Punktsieg *m* victory on points

Punktzahl *f* score

Punsch [pɔnʃ] (-(e)s, -e) *m* punch

Pupille [pu'pɪlə] *f* pupil

Puppe ['pɔpə] *f* doll; (*Marionette*) puppet; (*Insektenpuppe*) pupa, chrysalis

Puppen- *zW:* **~spieler** *m* puppeteer; **~stube** *f* doll's house; **~theater** *nt* puppet theatre

pur [pu:r] *adj* pure; (*völlig*) sheer; (*Whisky*) neat

Püree [py're:] (-s, -s) *nt* mashed potatoes *pl*

Purzelbaum ['pɔrtsəlbaom] *m* somersault

purzeln ['pɔrtsəln] *vi* to tumble

Puste ['pu:stə] (-) (*umg*) *f* puff; (*fig*) steam; **p~n** *vi* to puff, to blow

Pute ['pu:tə] *f* turkey hen; **~r** (-s, -) *m* turkey cock

Putsch [pɔtʃ] (-(e)s, -e) *m* revolt, putsch

Putz [pɔts] (-es) *m* (*Mörtel*) plaster, roughcast

putzen *vt* to clean; (*Nase*) to wipe, to blow ♦ *vr* to clean o.s.; to dress o.s. up

Putz- *zW:* **~frau** *f* charwoman; **p~ig** *adj* quaint, funny; **~lappen** *m* cloth

Puzzle ['pasəl] (-s, -s) *nt* jigsaw

PVC *nt abk* PVC

Pyjama [pi'dʒa:ma] (-s, -s) *m* pyjamas *pl*

Pyramide [pyra'mi:də] *f* pyramid

Pyrenäen [pyre'nɛ:ən] *pl* Pyrenees

Q, q

Quacksalber ['kvakzalbər] (-s, -) *m* quack (doctor)

Quader ['kva:dər] (-s, -) *m* square stone; (*MATH*) cuboid

Quadrat [kva'dra:t] (-(e)s, -e) *nt* square; **q~isch** *adj* square; **~meter** *m* square metre

quaken ['kva:kən] *vi* to croak; (*Ente*) to quack

quäken ['kvɛ:kən] *vi* to screech

Qual [kva:l] (-, -en) *f* pain, agony; (*seelisch*) anguish; **quälen** *vt* to torment o.s.; (*geistig*) to torment o.s.; **Quälerei** *f* torture, torment

Qualifikation [kvalifikatsi'o:n] *f* qualification

qualifizieren [kvalifi'tsi:rən] *vt* to qualify; (*einstufen*) to label ♦ *vr* to qualify

Qualität [kvali'tɛ:t] *f* quality; **~sware** *f* article of high quality

Qualle ['kvalə] *f* jellyfish

Qualm [kvalm] (-(e)s, -en) *m* thick smoke; **q~en** *vt, vi* to smoke

qualvoll ['kva:lfɔl] *adj* excruciating, painful, agonizing

Quant- ['kvant] *zW:* **~ität** [-i'tɛ:t] *f* quantity; **q~itativ** [-ita'ti:f] *adj* quantitative; **~um** (-s) *nt* quantity, amount

Quarantäne [karan'tɛ:nə] *f* quarantine

Quark [kvark] (-s) *m* curd cheese

Quartal [kvar'ta:l] (-s, -e) *nt* quarter (year)

Quartier [kvar'ti:r] (-s, -e) *nt* accommodation; (*MIL*) quarters *pl*; (*Stadtquartier*) district

Quarz [kva:rts] (-es) *m* quartz

quasseln ['kvasəln] (*umg*) *vi* to natter

Quatsch [kvatʃ] (-es) *m* rubbish; **q~en** *vi* to chat, to natter

Quecksilber ['kvɛkzɪlbər] *nt* mercury

Quelle ['kvɛlə] *f* spring; (*eines Flusses*)

source; **q~n** (unreg) vi (hervorquellen) to pour od gush forth; (schwellen) to swell

quer [kveːr] adv crossways, diagonally; (rechtwinklig) at right angles; **~ auf dem Bett** across the bed; **Q~balken** m crossbeam; **Q~flöte** f flute; **Q~format** nt (PHOT) oblong format; **Q~schnitt** m cross-section; **~schnittsgelähmt** adj paralysed below the waist; **Q~straße** f intersecting road

quetschen ['kvɛtʃən] vt to squash, to crush; (MED) to bruise

Quetschung f bruise, contusion

quieken ['kviːkən] vi to squeak

quietschen ['kviːtʃən] vi to squeak

Quintessenz ['kvɪntɛsɛnts] f quintessence

Quirl [kvɪrl] (-(e)s, -e) m whisk

quitt [kvɪt] adj quits, even

Quitte f quince

quittieren [kvɪˈtiːrən] vt to give a receipt for; (Dienst) to leave

Quittung f receipt

Quiz [kvɪs] (-, -) nt quiz

quoll etc [kvɔl] vb siehe **quellen**

Quote ['kvoːtə] f number, rate

R, r

Rabatt [raˈbat] (-(e)s, -e) m discount

Rabattmarke f trading stamp

Rabe ['raːbə] (-n, -n) m raven

rabiat [rabiˈaːt] adj furious

Rache ['raxə] f revenge, vengeance

Rachen (-s, -) m throat

rächen ['rɛçən] vt to avenge, to revenge ♦ vr to take (one's) revenge; **das wird sich ~** you'll pay for that

Rad [raːt] (-(e)s, ²er) nt wheel; (Fahrrad) bike; **~ fahren** to cycle

Radar ['raːdar] (-s) m od nt radar; **~falle** f speed trap; **~kontrolle** f radar-controlled speed trap

Radau [raˈdau] (-s) (umg) m row

radeln ['raːdəln] (umg) vi to cycle

Radfahr- zW: **r~en** △ (unreg) vi siehe **Rad**; **~er(in)** m(f) cyclist; **~weg** m cycle track od path

Radier- [raˈdiːr] zW: **r~en** vt to rub out, to erase; (KUNST) to etch; **~gummi** m rubber, eraser; **~ung** f etching

Radieschen [raˈdiːsçən] nt radish

radikal [radiˈkaːl] adj radical

Radio ['raːdio] (-s, -s) nt radio, wireless; **r~aktiv** adj radioactive; **~aktivität** f radioactivity; **~apparat** m radio, wireless set

Radius ['raːdius] (-, **Radien**) m radius

Rad- zW: **~kappe** f (AUT) hub cap; **~ler(in)** (umg) m(f) cyclist; **~rennen** nt cycle race; cycle racing; **~sport** m cycling; **~weg** m cycleway

raffen ['rafən] vt to snatch, to pick up; (Stoff) to gather (up); (Geld) to pile up, to rake in

raffiniert adj crafty, cunning

ragen ['raːgən] vi to tower, to rise

Rahm [raːm] (-s) m cream

Rahmen ['raːmən] (-s, -) m frame(work); **im ~ des Möglichen** within the bounds of possibility; **r~** vt to frame

räkeln ['rɛːkəln] vr = rekeln

Rakete [raˈkeːtə] f rocket; **~nstützpunkt** m missile base

rammen ['ramən] vt to ram

Rampe ['rampə] f ramp; **~nlicht** nt (THEAT) footlights pl

ramponieren [rampoˈniːrən] (umg) vt to damage

Ramsch [ramʃ] (-(e)s, -e) m junk

ran [ran] (umg) adv = heran

Rand [rant] (-(e)s, ²er) m edge; (von Brille, Tasse etc) rim; (Hutrand) brim; (auf Papier) margin; (Schmutzrand, unter Augen) ring; (fig) verge, brink; **außer ~ und Band** wild; **am ~e bemerkt** mentioned in passing

randalieren [randaˈliːrən] vi to (go on the) rampage

Rang [raŋ] (-(e)s, ²e) m rank; (Stand) standing; (Wert) quality; (THEAT) circle

Rangier- [rãˈʒiːr] zW: **~bahnhof**

marshalling yard; **r~en** vt (EISENB) to shunt, to switch (US) ♦ vi to rank, to be classed; **~gleis** nt siding

Ranke ['raŋkə] f tendril, shoot

ranzig ['rantsɪç] adj rancid

Rappen ['rapən] m (FIN) rappen, centime

rar [raːr] adj rare; **sich ~ machen** (umg) to keep o.s. to o.s.; **R~i'tät** f rarity; (Sammelobjekt) curio

rasant [ra'zant] adj quick, rapid

rasch [raʃ] adj quick

rascheln vi to rustle

Rasen ['raːzən] (-s, -) m lawn; grass

rasen vi to rave; (schnell) to race; **~de Kopfschmerzen** a splitting headache

Rasenmäher (-s, -) m lawnmower

Rasier- [ra'ziːr] zW: **~apparat** m shaver; **~creme** f shaving cream; **r~en** vt, vr to shave; **~klinge** f razor blade; **~messer** nt razor; **~pinsel** m shaving brush; **~schaum** m shaving foam; **~seife** f shaving soap od stick; **~wasser** nt shaving lotion

Rasse ['rasə] f race; (Tierrasse) breed; **~hund** m thoroughbred dog

rasseln ['rasəln] vi to clatter

Rassen- zW: **~hass ▲** m race od racial hatred; **~trennung** f racial segregation

Rassismus [ra'sɪsmʊs] m racism

Rast [rast] (-, -en) f rest; **r~en** vi to rest; **~hof** m (AUT) service station; **r~los** adj tireless; (unruhig) restless; **~platz** m (AUT) layby; **~stätte** f (AUT) service station

Rasur [ra'zuːr] f shaving

Rat [raːt] (-(e)s, -schläge) m advice no pl; **ein ~** a piece of advice; **keinen ~ wissen** not to know what to do; siehe zurate

Rate f instalment

raten (unreg) vt, vi to guess; (empfehlen): **jdm ~** to advise sb

Ratenzahlung f hire purchase

Ratgeber (-s, -) m adviser

Rathaus nt town hall

ratifizieren [ratifi'tsiːrən] vt to ratify

Ration [ratsi'oːn] f ration; **r~al** [-'naːl] adj rational; **r~ali'sieren** vt to rationalize; **r~ell** [-'nɛl] adj efficient; **r~ieren** [-'niːrən] vt to ration

Rat- zW: **r~los** adj at a loss, helpless; **r~sam** adj advisable; **~schlag** m (piece of) advice

Rätsel ['rɛːtsəl] (-s, -) nt puzzle; (Worträtsel) riddle; **r~haft** adj mysterious; **es ist mir r~haft** it's a mystery to me

Ratte ['ratə] f rat; **~nfänger** m ratcatcher

rattern ['ratərn] vi to rattle, to clatter

rau ▲ [rau] adj rough, coarse; (Wetter) harsh

Raub [raup] (-(e)s) m robbery; (Beute) loot, booty; **~bau** m ruthless exploitation; **r~en** ['raubən] vt to rob; (Mensch) to kidnap, to abduct

Räuber ['rɔybər] (-s, -) m robber

Raub- zW: **~mord** m robbery with murder; **~tier** nt predator; **~überfall** m robbery with violence; **~vogel** m bird of prey

Rauch [raux] (-(e)s) m smoke; **r~en** vt, vi to smoke; **r~er(in)** (-s, -) m(f) smoker; **~erabteil** nt (EISENB) smoker; **räuchern** vt to smoke, to cure; **~fleisch** nt smoked meat; **r~ig** adj smoky

rauf [rauf] (umg) adv = herauf; hinauf

raufen vt (Haare) to pull out ♦ vi, vr to fight; **Raufe'rei** f brawl, fight

Rauh △ etc [rau] adj siehe rau etc

Raum [raum] (-(e)s, Räume) m space; (Zimmer, Platz) room; (Gebiet) area

räumen ['rɔymən] vt to clear; (Wohnung, Platz) to vacate; (wegbringen) to shift, to move; (in Schrank etc) to put away

Raum- zW: **~fähre** f space shuttle;

~fahrt f space travel; **~inhalt** m cubic capacity, volume

räumlich ['rɔymlɪç] adj spatial; **R~keiten** pl premises

Raum- zW: **~pflegerin** f cleaner; **~schiff** nt spaceship; **~schiffahrt ▲** f space travel

Räumung ['rɔymʊn] f vacating, evacuation; clearing (away)

Räumungs- zW: **~arbeiten** pl clearance operations; **~verkauf** m clearance sale; (bei Geschäftsaufgabe) closing down sale

raunen ['raʊnən] vt, vi to whisper

Raupe ['raʊpə] f caterpillar; (~nkette) (caterpillar) track

Raureif ▲ ['raʊraif] m hoarfrost

raus [raʊs] (umg) adv = heraus; hinaus

Rausch [raʊʃ] (-(e)s, Räusche) m intoxication

rauschen vi (Wasser) to rush; (Baum) to rustle; (Radio etc) to hiss; (Mensch) to sweep, to sail; **~d** adj (Beifall) thunderous; (Fest) sumptuous

Rauschgift nt drug; **~süchtige(r)** f(m) drug addict

räuspern ['rɔyspərn] vr to clear one's throat

Razzia ['ratsia] (-, Razzien) f raid

Reagenzglas [rea'gɛntsglaːs] nt test tube

reagieren [rea'giːrən] vi: **~** (auf +akk) to react (to)

Reakt- zW: **~ion** [reaktsi'oːn] f reaction; **r~io'när** adj reactionary; **~or** [re'aktor] m reactor

real [re'aːl] adj real, material

reali'sieren vt (verwirklichen: Pläne) to carry out

Realismus [rea'lɪsmʊs] m realism

rea'listisch adj realistic

Realschule f secondary school

Realschule

The **Realschule** is one of the secondary schools a German schoolchild may attend after the **Grundschule**. On

the successful completion of six years of schooling in the **Realschule** pupils gain the **mittlere Reife** and usually go on to vocational training or further education.

Rebe ['reːbə] f vine

rebellieren [rebe'liːrən] vi to rebel; **Rebelli'on** f rebellion; **re'bellisch** adj rebellious

Rebhuhn ['rɛphuːn] nt (KOCH, ZOOL) partridge

Rechen ['rɛçən] (-s, -) m rake

Rechen- zW: **~fehler** m miscalculation; **~maschine** f calculating machine; **~schaft** f account; **für etw ~schaft ablegen** to account for sth; **~schieber** m slide rule

Rech- zW: **r~nen** vt, vi to calculate; **jdn/etw r~nen zu** to count sb/sth among; **r~nen mit** to reckon with; **r~nen auf** +akk to count on; **~nen** nt arithmetic; **~ner** (-s, -) m calculator; (COMPUT) computer; **~nung** f calculation(s); (COMM) bill, check (US); **jdm/etw ~nung tragen** to take sb/sth into account; **~nungsbetrag** m total amount of a bill/invoice; **~nungsjahr** nt financial year; **~nungsprüfer** m auditor

Recht [rɛçt] (-(e)s, -e) nt right; (JUR) law; **mit ~** rightly, justly; **R~ haben** to be right; **jdm R~ geben** to agree with sb; **von ~s wegen** by rights

recht adj right ♦ adv (vor Adjektiv) really, quite; **das ist mir ~** that suits me; **jetzt erst ~** now more than ever

Rechte f right (hand); (POL) Right; **r~(r, s)** adj right; (POL) right-wing; **ein ~r** a right-winger; **~(s)** nt right thing; **etwas/nichts ~s** something/nothing proper

recht- zW: **~eckig** adj rectangular; **~fertigen** vt insep to justify ♦ vr insep to justify o.s.; **R~fertigung** f justification; **~haberisch** (pej) adj (Mensch) opinionated; **~lich** adj (gesetzlich: Gleichstellung, Anspruch) legal; **~los** adj with no rights; **~mäßig** adj legal, lawful

rechts [rɛçts] adv on/to the right; **R~anwalt** m lawyer, barrister; **R~anwältin** f lawyer, barrister

Rechtschreibung f spelling

Rechts- zW: **~fall** m (law) case; **~händer** (-s, -) m right-handed person; **r~kräftig** adj valid, legal; **~kurve** f right-hand bend; **r~verbindlich** adj legally binding; **~verkehr** m driving on the right; **r~widrig** adj illegal; **~wissenschaft** f jurisprudence

rechtwinklig adj right-angled

rechtzeitig adj timely ♦ adv in time

Reck [rɛk] (-(e)s, -e) nt horizontal bar; **r~en** vt, vr to stretch

recyceln [riːˈsaɪkəln] vt to recycle; **Recycling** [riːˈsaɪklɪŋ] nt recycling

Redakteur [redakˈtøːr] m editor

Redaktion [redaktsiˈoːn] f editing; (Leute) editorial staff; (Büro) editorial office(s)

Rede [ˈreːdə] f speech; (Gespräch) talk; jdn zur ~ **stellen** to take sb to task; **~freiheit** f freedom of speech; **r~gewandt** adj eloquent; **r~n** vi to talk, to speak ♦ vt to say; (Unsinn etc) to talk; **~nsart** f set phrase

redlich [ˈreːtlɪç] adj honest

Redner (-s, -) m speaker, orator

redselig [ˈreːtzeːlɪç] adj talkative, loquacious

reduzieren [reduˈtsiːrən] vt to reduce

Reede [ˈreːdə] f protected anchorage; **~r** (-s, -) m shipowner; **~rei** f shipping line od firm

reell [reˈɛl] adj fair, honest; (MATH) real

Refer- zW: **~at** [refeˈraːt] (-(e)s, -e) nt report; (Vortrag) paper; (Gebiet) section; **~ent** [refeˈrɛnt] m speaker; (Berichterstatter) reporter; (Sachbearbeiter) expert; **r~ieren** [refeˈriːrən] vi: **~ieren über** +akk to speak od talk on

reflektieren [reflɛkˈtiːrən] vt (Licht) to reflect

Reflex [reˈflɛks] (-es, -e) m reflex; **r~iv** [-ˈksiːf] adj (GRAM) reflexive

Reform [reˈfɔrm] (-, -en) f reform; **~ati'on** f reformation; **~ationstag** m Reformation Day; **~haus** nt health food shop; **r~ieren** [-ˈmiːrən] vt to reform

Regal [reˈgaːl] (-s, -e) nt (book)shelves pl, bookcase; stand, rack

rege [ˈreːgə] adj (lebhaft: Treiben) lively; (wach, lebendig: Geist) keen

Regel [ˈreːgəl] (-, -n) f rule; (MED) period; **r~mäßig** adj regular; **~mäßigkeit** f regularity; **r~n** vt to regulate, to control; (Angelegenheit) to settle ♦ vr: **sich von selbst r~n** to take care of itself; **r~recht** adj regular, proper, thorough; **~ung** f regulation; settlement; **r~widrig** adj irregular, against the rules

Regen [ˈreːgən] (-s, -) m rain; **~bogen** m rainbow; **~bogenpresse** f tabloids pl

regenerierbar [regeneˈriːrbaːr] adj renewable

Regen- zW: **~mantel** m raincoat, mac(kintosh); **~schauer** m shower (of rain); **~schirm** m umbrella; **~wald** m (GEOG) rainforest; **~wurm** m earthworm; **~zeit** f rainy season

Regie [reˈʒiː] f (Film etc) direction; (THEAT) production

Regier- [reˈgiːr] zW: **r~en** vt, vi to govern, to rule; **~ung** f government; (Monarchie) reign; **~ungssitz** m seat of government; **~ungswechsel** m change of government; **~ungszeit** f period in government; (von König) reign

Regiment [regiˈmɛnt] (-s, -er) nt regiment

Region [regiˈoːn] f region

Regisseur [reʒiˈsøːr] m director; (THEAT) (stage) producer

Register [re'gɪstər] (-s, -) nt register; (in Buch) table of contents, index

registrieren [regɪs'triːrən] vt to register

Regler ['reːglər] (-s, -) m regulator, governor

reglos ['reːkloːs] adj motionless

regnen ['reːgnən] vi unpers to rain

regnerisch adj rainy

regulär [regu'lɛːr] adj regular

regulieren [regu'liːrən] vt to regulate; (COMM) to settle

Regung ['reːgʊŋ] f motion; (Gefühl) feeling, impulse; **r~slos** adj motionless

Reh [reː] (-(e)s, -e) nt deer, roe; **~bock** m roebuck; **~kitz** nt fawn

Reib- ['raɪb] zW: **~e** f grater; **~eisen** nt grater; **r~en** (unreg) vt to rub; (KOCH) to grate; **~fläche** f rough surface; **~ung** f friction; **r~ungslos** adj smooth

Reich (-(e)s, -e) nt empire, kingdom; (fig) realm; **das Dritte R~** the Third Reich

reich [raɪç] adj rich

reichen vi to reach; (genügen) to be enough ♦ vt to hold out; (geben) to pass, to hand; (anbieten) to offer; **jdm ~** to be enough od sufficient for sb

reich- zW: **~haltig** adj ample, rich; **~lich** adj ample, plenty of; **R~tum** (-s) m wealth; **R~weite** f range

Reif (-(e)s, -e) m (Ring) ring, hoop

reif [raɪf] adj ripe; (Mensch, Urteil) mature

Reife (-) f ripeness; maturity; **r~n** vi to mature; to ripen

Reifen (-s, -) m ring, hoop; (Fahrzeugreifen) tyre; **~druck** m tyre pressure; **~panne** f puncture

Reihe ['raɪə] f row; (von Tagen etc, umg: Anzahl) series sg; **der ~ nach** in turn; **er ist an der ~** it's his turn; **an die ~ kommen** to have one's turn

Reihen- zW: **~folge** f sequence; **alphabetische ~folge** alphabetical order; **~haus** nt terraced house

reihum [raɪ'ʊm] adv: **es geht/wir machen das ~** we take turns

Reim [raɪm] (-(e)s, -e) m rhyme; **r~en** vt to rhyme

rein¹ [raɪn] (umg) adv = **herein**; **hinein**

rein² [raɪn] adj pure; (sauber) clean ♦ adv purely; **etw ins R~e schreiben** to make a fair copy of sth; **etw ins R~e bringen** to clear up sth; **R~fall** (umg) m let-down; **R~gewinn** m net profit; **R~heit** f purity; cleanness; **~igen** vt to clean; (Wasser) to purify; **R~igung** f cleaning; purification; (Geschäft) cleaner's; **chemische R~igung** dry cleaning; dry cleaner's; **R~igungsmittel** nt cleansing agent; **~rassig** adj pedigree; **R~schrift** f fair copy

Reis [raɪs] (-es, -e) m rice

Reise ['raɪzə] f journey; (Schiffsreise) voyage; **~n** pl (Herumreisen) travels; **gute ~!** have a good journey; **~apotheke** f first-aid kit; **~büro** nt travel agency; **r~fertig** adj ready to start; **~führer** m guide(book); (Mensch) travel guide; **~gepäck** nt luggage; **~gesellschaft** f party of travellers; **~kosten** pl travelling expenses; **~leiter** m courier; **~lektüre** f reading matter for the journey; **r~n** vi to travel; **r~nach** to go to; **~nde(r)** f(m) traveller; **~pass** m passport; **~proviant** m food and drink for the journey; **~route** f route, itinerary; **~ruf** m personal message; **~scheck** m traveller's cheque; **~veranstalter** m tour operator; **~versicherung** f travel insurance; **~ziel** nt destination

Reißbrett nt drawing board

reißen ['raɪsən] (unreg) vt to tear; (ziehen) to pull, to drag; (Witz) to crack ♦ vi to tear; to pull, to drag; **etw an sich ~** to snatch sth up; (fig) to take over sth; **sich um etw ~** to scramble for sth; **~d** adj (Fluss) raging; (WIRTS: Verkauf) rapid

Reiß- zW: **~verschluss** ▲ m zip(per); zip fastener; **~zwecke** m drawing pin

(BRIT), thumbtack (US)

Reit- ['raɪt] zW: **r~en** (unreg) vt, vi to ride; **~er** (-s, -) m rider; (MIL) cavalryman, trooper; **~erin** f rider; **~hose** f riding breeches pl; **~pferd** nt saddle horse; **~stiefel** m riding boot; **~weg** m bridle path; **~zeug** nt riding outfit

Reiz [raɪts] (-es, -e) m stimulus; (angenehm) charm; (Verlockung) attraction; **r~bar** adj irritable; **~barkeit** f irritability; **r~en** vt to stimulate; (unangenehm) to irritate; (verlocken) to appeal to, to attract; **r~end** adj charming; **r~voll** adj attractive

rekeln ['re:kəln] vr to stretch out; (lümmeln) to lounge od loll about

Reklamation [reklamatsi'o:n] f complaint

Reklame [re'kla:mə] f advertising; advertisement; **~ machen für etw** to advertise sth

rekonstruieren [rekɔnstru'i:rən] vt to reconstruct

Rekord [re'kɔrt] (-(e)s, -e) m record; **~leistung** f record performance

Rektor ['rektɔr] m (UNIV) rector, vice-chancellor; (SCH) headteacher (BRIT), principal (US); **~at** [-'ra:t] (-(e)s, -e) nt rectorate, vice-chancellorship; headship; (Zimmer) rector's etc office

Relais [rə'le:] (-, -) nt relay

relativ [rela'ti:f] adj relative; **R~ität** [relativi'te:t] f relativity

relevant [rele'vant] adj relevant

Relief [reli'ɛf] (-s, -s) nt relief

Religion [religi'o:n] f religion

religiös [religi'ø:s] adj religious

Reling ['re:lɪŋ] (-, -s) f (NAUT) rail

Remoulade [remu'la:də] f remoulade

Rendezvous [rãde'vu:] (-, -) nt rendezvous

Renn- ['rɛn] zW: **~bahn** f racecourse; (AUT) circuit, race track; **r~en** (unreg) vt, vi to run, to race; **~en** (-s, -) nt running; (Wettbewerb) race; **~fahrer** m

racing driver; **~pferd** nt racehorse; **~wagen** m racing car

renommiert [renɔ'mi:rt] adj renowned

renovieren [reno'vi:rən] vt to renovate; **Renovierung** f renovation

rentabel [rɛn'ta:bəl] adj profitable, lucrative

Rentabilität [rɛntabili'tɛ:t] f profitability

Rente ['rɛntə] f pension

Rentenversicherung f pension scheme

rentieren [rɛn'ti:rən] vr to pay, to be profitable

Rentner(in) ['rɛntnər(ɪn)] (-s, -) m(f) pensioner

Reparatur [repara'tu:r] f repairing; repair; **~werkstatt** f repair shop; (AUT) garage

reparieren [repa'ri:rən] vt to repair

Reportage [repɔr'ta:ʒə] f (on-the-spot) report; (TV, RADIO) live commentary od coverage

Reporter [re'pɔrtər] (-s, -) m reporter, commentator

repräsentativ [reprezenta'ti:f] adj (stellvertretend, typisch: Menge, Gruppe) representative; (beeindruckend: Haus, Auto etc) impressive

repräsentieren [reprezen'ti:rən] vt (Staat, Firma) to represent; (darstellen: Wert) to constitute ♦ vi (gesellschaftlich) to perform official duties

Repressalie [repre'sa:liə] f reprisal

Reprivatisierung [repriva'ti:zɪrʊŋ] f denationalization

Reproduktion [reproduktsi'o:n] f reproduction

reproduzieren [reprodu'tsi:rən] vt to reproduce

Reptil [rep'ti:l] (-s, -ien) nt reptile

Republik [repu'bli:k] f republic; **r~anisch** adj republican

Reservat [rezɛr'va:t] (-(e)s, -e) nt res-

Spelling Reform: ▲ new spelling △ old spelling (to be phased out)

ervation

Reserve [re'zɛrvə] f reserve; **~rad** nt (AUT) spare wheel; **~spieler** m reserve; **~tank** m reserve tank

reservieren [rezer'viːrən] vt to reserve

Reservoir [rezervo'aːr] (-s, -e) nt reservoir

Residenz [rezi'dɛnts] f residence, seat

resignieren [rezi'gniːrən] vi to resign

resolut [rezo'luːt] adj resolute

Resonanz [rezo'nants] f resonance; (fig) response

Resozialisierung [rezotsiali'ziːrʊŋ] f rehabilitation

Respekt [re'spɛkt] (-(e)s) m respect; **r~ieren** [-'tiːrən] vt to respect; **r~los** adj disrespectful; **r~voll** adj respectful

Ressort [re'soːr] (-s, -s) nt department

Rest [rɛst] (-(e)s, -e) m remainder, rest; (Überrest) remains pl

Restaurant [rɛsto'rãː] (-s, -s) nt restaurant

restaurieren [rɛstau'riːrən] vt to restore

Rest- zW: **~betrag** m remainder, outstanding sum; **r~lich** adj remaining; **r~los** adj complete

Resultat [rezʊl'taːt] (-(e)s, -e) nt result

Retorte [re'tɔrtə] f retort

Retouren [re'tuːrən] pl (COMM) returns

retten ['rɛtən] vt to save, to rescue

Retter(in) m(f) rescuer

Rettich ['rɛtɪç] (-s, -e) m radish

Rettung f rescue; (Hilfe) help; **seine letzte ~** his last hope

Rettungs- zW: **~boot** nt lifeboat; **~dienst** m rescue service; **r~los** adj hopeless; **~ring** m lifebelt, life preserver (US); **~wagen** m ambulance

retuschieren [retu'ʃiːrən] vt (PHOT) to retouch

Reue ['rɔʏə] (-) f remorse; (Bedauern) regret; **r~n** vt: **es reut ihn** he regrets (it) and is sorry (about it)

Revanche [re'vãːʃə] f revenge; (SPORT) return match

revanchieren [revã'ʃiːrən] vr (sich

rächen) to get one's own back, to have one's revenge; (erwidern) to reciprocate, to return the compliment

Revier [re'viːr] (-s, -e) nt (Jagdrevier) preserve; (Polizeirevier) police station; beat

Revolte [re'vɔltə] f revolt

revol'tieren vi (gegen jdn/etw) to rebel

Revolution [revolutsi'oːn] f revolution; **~är** [-'nɛːr] (-s, -e) m revolutionary; **r~ieren** [-'niːrən] vt to revolutionize

Rezept [re'tsɛpt] (-(e)s, -e) nt recipe; (MED) prescription; **r~frei** adj available without prescription; **~ion** f reception; **r~pflichtig** adj available only on prescription

R-Gespräch ['ɛrgəʃprɛːç] nt reverse charge call (BRIT), collect call (US)

Rhabarber [ra'barbar] (-s) m rhubarb

Rhein [raɪn] (-s) m Rhine; **r~isch** adj Rhenish

Rheinland-Pfalz nt (GEOG) Rheinland-Pfalz, Rhineland-Palatinate

Rhesusfaktor ['reːzʊsfaktoːr] m rhesus factor

rhetorisch [re'toːrɪʃ] adj rhetorical

Rheuma ['rɔʏma] (-s) nt rheumatism; **r~tisch** [-'maːtɪʃ] adj rheumatic

rhythmisch ['rʏtmɪʃ] adj rhythmical

Rhythmus ['rʏtmʊs] m rhythm

richt- ['rɪçt] zW: **~en** vt to direct; (Waffe) to aim; (einstellen) to adjust; (instandsetzen) to repair; (zurechtmachen) to prepare; (bestrafen) to pass judgement on ♦ vr: **sich ~en nach** to go by; **~en an** +akk to direct at; (fig) to direct to; **~en auf** +akk to aim at; **R~er(in)** (-s, -) m(f) judge; **~erlich** adj judicial; **R~geschwindigkeit** f recommended speed

richtig adj right, correct; (echt) proper ♦ adv (umg: sehr) really; **bin ich hier ~?** am I in the right place?; **der/die R~e** the right one/person; **das R~e** the right thing; **etw ~ stellen** to correct sth; **R~keit** f correctness

Richt- zW: **~linie** f guideline; **~preis** m recommended price

Richtung f direction; tendency, orientation

rieb etc [ri:p] vb siehe **reiben**

riechen ['ri:çən] (unreg) vt, vi to smell; **an etw** dat **~** to smell sth; **nach etw ~** to smell of sth; **ich kann das/ihn nicht ~** (umg) I can't stand it/him

rief etc [ri:f] vb siehe **rufen**

Riegel ['ri:gəl] (-s, -) m bolt; (Schokolade usw) bar

Riemen ['ri:mən] (-s, -) m strap; (Gürtel, TECH) belt; (NAUT) oar

Riese ['ri:zə] (-n, -n) m giant

rieseln vi to trickle; (Schnee) to fall gently

Riesen- zW: **~erfolg** m enormous success; **r~groß** adj colossal, gigantic, huge; **~rad** nt big wheel

riesig ['ri:zıç] adj enormous, huge, vast

riet etc [ri:t] vb siehe **raten**

Riff [rıf] (-(e)s, -e) nt reef

Rille ['rılə] f groove

Rind [rınt] (-(e)s, -er) nt ox; cow; cattle pl; (KOCH) beef

Rinde ['rındə] f rind; (Baumrinde) bark; (Brotrinde) crust

Rind- ['rınt] zW: **~fleisch** nt beef; **~vieh** nt cattle pl; (umg) blockhead, stupid oaf

Ring [rıŋ] (-(e)s, -e) m ring; **~buch** nt ring binder; **r~en** (unreg) vi to wrestle; **~en** (-s) nt wrestling; **~finger** m ring finger; **~kampf** m wrestling bout; **~richter** m referee; **r~s** adv: **r~s um** round; **r~sherum** adv round about; **~straße** f ring road; **r~sum** adv (rundherum) round about; (überall) all round; **r~sumher** adv = **ringsum**

Rinn- ['rın] zW: **~e** f gutter, drain; **r~en** (unreg) vi to run, to trickle; **~stein** m gutter

Rippchen ['rıpçən] nt small rib; cutlet

Rippe ['rıpə] f rib

Risiko ['ri:ziko] (-s, -s od Risiken) nt risk

riskant [rıs'kant] adj risky, hazardous

riskieren [rıs'ki:rən] vt to risk

Riss [rıs] (-es, -e) m tear; (in Mauer, Tasse etc) crack; (in Haut) scratch; (TECH) design

rissig ['rısıç] adj torn; cracked; scratched

Ritt [rıt] (-(e)s, -e) m ride

ritt etc vb siehe **reiten**

Ritter ['rıtər] (-s, -) m knight; **r~lich** adj chivalrous

Ritze ['rıtsə] f crack, chink

Rivale [ri'va:lə] (-n, -n) m rival

Rivalität [rivali'tε:t] f rivalry

Robbe ['rɔbə] f seal

Roboter ['rɔbɔtər] (-s, -) m robot

robust [ro'bʊst] adj (kräftig: Mensch, Gesundheit) robust

roch etc [rɔx] vb siehe **riechen**

Rock [rɔk] (-(e)s, ⁼e) m skirt; (Jackett) jacket; (Uniformrock) tunic

Rodel ['ro:dəl] (-s, -) m toboggan; **~bahn** f toboggan run; **r~n** vi to toboggan

Rogen ['ro:gən] (-s, -) m roe, spawn

Roggen ['rɔgən] (-s, -) m rye; **~brot** nt (KOCH) rye bread

roh [ro:] adj raw; (Mensch) coarse, crude; **R~bau** m shell of a building; **R~material** nt raw material; **R~öl** nt crude oil

Rohr [ro:r] (-(e)s, -e) nt pipe, tube; (BOT) cane; (Schilf) reed; (Gewehrrohr) barrel; **~bruch** m burst pipe

Röhre ['rø:rə] f tube, pipe; (RADIO etc) valve; (Backröhre) oven

Rohr- zW: **~leitung** f pipeline; **~zucker** m cane sugar

Rohstoff m raw material

Rokoko ['rɔkoko] (-s) nt rococo

Rolladen △ m siehe **Rollladen**

Rollbahn ['rɔlba:n] f (AVIAT) runway

Rolle ['rɔlə] f roll; (THEAT, soziologisch) role; (Garnrolle etc) reel, spool; (Walze) roller; (Wäscherolle) mangle; **keine ~ spielen** not to matter; **eine (wichtige) ~ spielen bei** to play a (major) part od role in; **r~n** vt, vi to roll; (AVIAT) to taxi; **~r** (-s, -) m scooter; (Welle) roller

Roll- zW: **~kragen** m rollneck, polo neck; **~laden** ▲ m shutter; **~mops** m pickled herring; **~schuh** m roller skate; **~stuhl** m wheelchair; **~stuhlfahrer(in)** m(f) wheelchair user; **~treppe** f escalator

Rom [rɔm] (-s) nt Rome

Roman [ro'maːn] (-s, -e) m novel; **~tik** f romanticism; **~tiker** [ro'mantikər] (-s, -) m romanticist; **r~tisch** [ro'mantiʃ] adj romantic; **~ze** [ro'mantsə] f romance

Römer ['røːmər] (-s, -) m wineglass; (Mensch) Roman

römisch ['røːmiʃ] adj Roman; **~-katholisch** adj (REL) Roman Catholic

röntgen ['rœntgən] vt to X-ray; **R~bild** nt X-ray; **R~strahlen** pl X-rays

rosa ['roːza] adj inv pink, rose(-coloured)

Rose ['roːzə] f rose

Rosen- zW: **~kohl** m Brussels sprouts pl; **~kranz** m rosary; **~montag** m Monday before Ash Wednesday

rosig ['roːziç] adj rosy

Rosine [ro'ziːnə] f raisin, currant

Ross ▲ [rɔs] (-es, -e) nt horse, steed; **~kastanie** f horse chestnut

Rost [rɔst] (-(e)s, -e) m rust; (Gitter) grill, gridiron; (Bettrost) springs pl; **~braten** m roast(ed) meat, roast; **r~en** vi to rust

rösten ['rœstən] vt to roast; to toast; to grill

Rost- zW: **r~frei** adj rust-free; rustproof; stainless; **r~ig** adj rusty; **~schutz** m rust-proofing

rot [roːt] adj red; **in den ~en Zahlen** in the red

Röte ['røːtə] (-) f redness; **~ln** pl Ger-

man measles sg; **r~n** vt, vr to redden

rothaarig adj red-haired

rotieren [ro'tiːrən] vi to rotate

Rot- zW: **~kehlchen** nt robin; **~stift** m red pencil; **~wein** m red wine

Rouge [ruːʒ] nt blusher

Roulade [ru'laːdə] f (KOCH) beef olive

Route ['ruːtə] f route

Routine [ru'tiːnə] f experience; routine

Rübe ['ryːbə] f turnip; **Gelbe ~** carrot; **Rote ~** beetroot (BRIT), beet (US)

rüber ['ryːbər] (umg) adv = herüber; hinüber

Rubrik [ru'briːk] f heading; (Spalte) column

Ruck [rʊk] (-(e)s, -e) m jerk, jolt

Rück- ['ryk] zW: **~antwort** f reply, answer; **r~bezüglich** adj reflexive

Rücken ['rykən] (-s, -) m back; (Bergrücken) ridge

rücken vt, vi to move

Rücken- zW: **~mark** nt spinal cord; **~schwimmen** nt backstroke

Rück- zW: **~erstattung** f return, restitution; **~fahrkarte** f return (ticket); **~fahrt** f return journey; **~fall** m relapse; **r~fällig** adj relapsing; **r~fällig werden** to relapse; **~flug** m return flight; **~frage** f question; **r~fragen** vi to check, to inquire (further); **~gabe** f return; **~gaberecht** nt right of return; **~gang** m decline, fall; **r~gängig** adj: **etw r~gängig machen** to cancel sth; **~grat** (-(e)s, -e) nt spine, backbone; **~halt** m (Unterstützung) backing, support; **~kehr** (-, -en) f return; **~licht** nt back light; **r~lings** adv from behind; backwards; **~nahme** f taking back; **~porto** nt return postage; **~reise** f return journey; (NAUT) home voyage; **~reiseverkehr** m homebound traffic; **~ruf** m recall

Rucksack ['rʊkzak] m rucksack; **~tourist(in)** m(f) backpacker

Rück- zW: **~schau** f reflection; **~schlag** m (plötzliche Verschlechterung) setback; **~schluss** ▲ m conclusion;

~schritt m retrogression; **r~schrittlich** adj reactionary; retrograde; **~seite** f back; (von Münze etc) reverse; **~sicht** f consideration; **~sicht nehmen auf** +akk to show consideration for; (Fahren) reckless; (unbarmherzig) ruthless; **r~sichtslos** adj inconsiderate; (Fahren) reckless; (unbarmherzig) ruthless; **r~sichtsvoll** adj considerate; **~sitz** m back seat; **~spiegel** m (AUT) rear-view mirror; **~spiel** nt return match; **~sprache** f further discussion od talk; **~stand** m arrears pl; **r~ständig** adj backward, out-of-date; (Zahlungen) in arrears; **~strahler (-s, -)** m rear reflector; **~tritt** m resignation; **~trittbremse** f pedal brake; **~vergütung** f repayment; (COMM) refund; **~versicherung** f reinsurance; **r~wärtig** adj rear; **r~wärts** adv backward(s), back; **~wärtsgang** m (AUT) reverse gear; **~weg** m return journey, way back; **r~wirkend** adj retroactive; **~wirkung** f reaction; retrospective effect; **~zahlung** f repayment; **~zug** m retreat

Rudel ['ruːdəl] (-s, -) nt pack; herd

Ruder ['ruːdər] (-s, -) nt oar; (Steuer) rudder; **~boot** nt rowing boat; **r~n** vt, vi to row

Ruf [ruːf] (-(e)s, -e) m call, cry; (Ansehen) reputation; **r~en** (unreg) vt, vi to call; to cry; **~name** m usual (first) name; **~nummer** f (tele)phone number; **~säule** f (an Autobahn) emergency telephone; **~zeichen** nt (RADIO) call sign; (TEL) ringing tone

rügen ['ryːɡən] vt to rebuke

Ruhe ['ruːə] (-) f rest; (Ungestörtheit) peace, quiet; (Gelassenheit, Stille) calm; (Schweigen) silence; **jdn in ~ lassen** to leave sb alone; **sich zur ~ setzen** to retire; **~! be quiet!, silence!; **r~n** vi to rest; **~pause** f break; **~stand** m retirement; **~stätte** f: **letzte ~stätte** final resting place; **~störung** f breach of

the peace; **~tag** m (von Geschäft) closing day

ruhig ['ruːɪç] adj quiet; (bewegungslos) still; (Hand) steady; (gelassen, friedlich) calm; (Gewissen) clear; **kommen Sie ~ herein** just come on in; **tu das ~** feel free to do that

Ruhm [ruːm] (-(e)s) m fame, glory

rühmen ['ryːmən] vt to praise ♦ vr to boast

Ruhr [ryːr] zW: **~ei** nt scrambled egg; **r~en** vt, vr (auch fig) to move, to stir ♦ vi: **r~en von** to come or stem from; **r~en an** +akk to touch; (fig) to touch on; **r~end** adj touching, moving; **r~selig** adj sentimental, emotional; **~ung** f emotion

Ruin [ru'iːn] (-s, -e) m ruin; **~e** f ruin; **r~ieren** [-'iːrən] vt to ruin

rülpsen ['rʏlpsən] vi to burp, to belch

Rum [rom] (-s, -s) m rum

Rumän- [ru'mɛːn] zW: **~ien (-s)** nt Ro(u)mania; **r~isch** adj Ro(u)manian

Rummel ['roməl] (-s) (umg) m hubbub; (Jahrmarkt) fair; **~platz** m fairground, fair

Rumpf [rompf] (-(e)s, ᵉe) m trunk, torso; (AVIAT) fuselage; (NAUT) hull

rümpfen ['rʏmpfən] vt (Nase) to turn up

rund [ront] adj round ♦ adv (etwa) around; **~ um etw** round sth; **R~brief** m circular; **R~e (-, -n)** f round; (in Rennen) lap; (Gesellschaft) circle; **R~fahrt** f (round) trip

Rundfunk ['rontfoŋk] (-(e)s) m broadcasting; **im ~** on the radio; **~gerät** nt wireless set; **~sendung** f broadcast, radio programme

Rund- zW: **r~heraus** adv straight out, bluntly; **r~herum** adv round about; all round; **r~lich** adj plump, rounded; **~reise** f round trip; **r~schreiben** nt (COMM) circular; **~(wander)weg** m circular path od route

runter ['rontər] (umg) adv = herunter;

hinunter

Runzel ['rʊntsəl] (-, -n) f wrinkle; **r~ig** adj wrinkled; **r~n** vt to wrinkle; **die Stirn r~n** to frown

rupfen ['rʊpfən] vt to pluck

ruppig ['rʊpɪç] adj rough, gruff

Rüsche ['ry:ʃə] f frill

Ruß [ru:s] (-es) m soot

Russe ['rʊsə] (-n, -n) m Russian

Rüssel ['rʊsəl] (-s, -) m snout; (Elefantenrüssel) trunk

rußig ['ru:sɪç] adj sooty

Russin ['rʊsɪn] f Russian

russisch adj Russian

Rußland ▲ ['rʊslant] (-s) nt Russia

rüsten ['rʊstən] vt to prepare ♦ vi to prepare; (MIL) to arm ♦ vr to prepare (o.s.); to arm o.s.

rüstig ['rʊstɪç] adj sprightly, vigorous

Rüstung ['rʊstʊŋ] f preparation; arming; (Ritterrüstung) armour; (Waffen etc) armaments pl; **~skontrolle** f arms control

Rute ['ru:tə] f rod

Rutsch [rʊtʃ] (-(e)s, -e) m slide; (Erdrutsch) landslide; **~bahn** f slide; **r~en** vi to slide; (ausrutschen) to slip; **r~ig** adj slippery

rütteln ['rʊtəln] vt, vi to shake, to jolt

S, s

S. abk (= Seite) p.; **= Schilling**

s. abk (= siehe) see

Saal [za:l] (-(e)s, Säle) m hall; room

Saarland ['za:rlant] nt: **das ~** the Saar(land)

Saat [za:t] (-, -en) f seed; (Pflanzen) crop; (Säen) sowing

Säbel ['zɛ:bəl] (-s, -) m sabre, sword

Sabotage [zabo'ta:ʒə] f sabotage

Sach- ['zax] zW: **~bearbeiter** m specialist; **s~dienlich** adj relevant, helpful; **~e** f thing; (Angelegenheit) affair, business; (Frage) matter; (Pflicht) task; **zur ~e** to the point; **s~kundig** adj ex-

pert; **s~lich** adj matter-of-fact; objective; (Irrtum, Angabe) factual

sächlich ['zɛxlɪç] adj neuter

Sachschaden m material damage

Sachsen ['zaksən] (-s) nt Saxony

sächsisch ['zɛksɪʃ] adj Saxon

sacht(e) ['zaxt(ə)] adv softly, gently

Sachverständige(r) f(m) expert

Sack [zak] (-(e)s, ⁼e) m sack; **~gasse** f cul-de-sac, dead-end street (US)

Sadismus [za'dɪsmʊs] m sadism

Sadist [za'dɪst] m sadist

säen ['zɛ:ən] vt, vi to sow

Safersex ▲, **Safer Sex** m safe sex

Saft [zaft] (-(e)s, ⁼e) m juice; (BOT) sap; **s~ig** adj juicy; **s~los** adj dry

Sage ['za:gə] f saga

Säge ['zɛ:gə] f saw; **~mehl** nt sawdust

sagen ['za:gən] vt, vi to say; (mitteilen): **jdm ~** to tell sb; **~ Sie ihm, dass ...** tell him ...

sägen vt, vi to saw

sagenhaft adj legendary; (umg) great, smashing

sah etc [za:] vb siehe **sehen**

Sahne ['za:nə] (-) f cream

Saison [zɛ'zõ:] (-, -s) f season

Saite ['zaitə] f string

Sakko ['zako] (-s, -s) m od nt jacket

Sakrament [zakra'mɛnt] nt sacrament

Sakristei [zakrɪs'tai] f sacristy

Salat [za'la:t] (-(e)s, -e) m salad; (Kopfsalat) lettuce; **~soße** f salad dressing

Salbe ['zalbə] f ointment

Salbei ['zalbai] (-s od -) m od f sage

Saldo ['zaldo] (-s, Salden) m balance

Salmiak [zalmi'ak] (-s) m sal ammoniac; **~geist** m liquid ammonia

Salmonellenvergiftung [zalmo-'nɛlən-] f salmonella (poisoning)

salopp [za'lɔp] adj casual

Salpeter [zal'pe:tər] (-s) m saltpetre; **~säure** f nitric acid

Salz [zalts] (-es) nt salt; **s~en** (unreg) vt to salt; **s~ig** adj salty; **~kartoffeln** pl boiled potatoes; **~säure**

hydrochloric acid; **~streuer** m salt cellar; **~wasser** nt (Meerwasser) salt water

Samen ['za:mən] (-s, -) m seed; (ANAT) sperm

Sammel- ['zaməl] zW: **~band** m anthology; **~fahrschein** m multi-journey ticket; (für mehrere Personen) group ticket

sammeln ['zaməln] vt to collect ♦ vr to assemble, to gather; (konzentrieren) to concentrate

Sammlung ['zamluŋ] f collection; assembly, gathering; concentration

Samstag ['zamsta:k] m Saturday; **s~s** adv (on) Saturdays

Samt [zamt] (-(e)s, -e) m velvet; **s~** präp +dat (along) with, together with; **s~ und sonders** each and every one (of them)

sämtlich ['zɛmtlɪç] adj all (the), entire

Sand [zant] (-(e)s, -e) m sand

Sandale [zan'da:lə] f sandal

Sand- zW: **~bank** f sandbank; **s~ig** ['zandɪç] adj sandy; **~kasten** m sandpit; **~kuchen** m Madeira cake; **~papier** nt sandpaper; **~stein** m sandstone; **s~strahlen** vt, vi insep to sandblast; **~strand** m sandy beach

sandte etc ['zantə] vb siehe **senden**

sanft [zanft] adj soft, gentle; **~mütig** adj gentle, meek

sang etc [zaŋ] vb siehe **singen**

Sänger(in) ['zɛŋər(ɪn)] (-s, -) m(f) singer

Sani- zW: **s~eren** [za'ni:rən] vt to redevelop; (Betrieb) to make financially sound ♦ vr to line one's pockets; to become financially sound; **s~tär** [zani'tɛːr] adj sanitary; **s~täre Anlagen** sanitation sg; **~täter** [zani'tɛːtər] (-s, -) m first-aid attendant; (MIL) (medical) orderly

sanktionieren [zaŋktsio'ni:rən] vt to sanction

Sardelle [zar'dɛlə] f anchovy

Sardine [zar'di:nə] f sardine

Sarg [zark] (-(e)s, -e) m coffin

Sarkasmus [zar'kasmus] m sarcasm

saß etc [za:s] vb siehe **sitzen**

Satan ['za:tan] (-s, -e) m Satan; devil

Satellit [zate'li:t] (-en, -en) m satellite; **~enfernsehen** nt satellite television

Satire [za'ti:rə] f satire; **satirisch** adj satirical

satt [zat] adj full; (Farbe) rich; **jdn/etw ~ sein** od **haben** to be fed up with sb/sth; sich **~ hören/sehen an** +dat to hear/see enough of; **sich ~ essen** to eat one's fill; **~ machen** to be filling

Sattel ['zatəl] (-s, =) m saddle; (Berg) ridge; **s~n** vt to saddle; **~schlepper** m articulated lorry

sättigen ['zetɪgən] vt to satisfy; (CHEM) to saturate

Satz [zats] (-es, =e) m (GRAM) sentence; (Nebensatz, Adverbialsatz) clause; (Theorem) theorem; (MUS) movement; (TENNIS: Briefmarken etc) set; (Kaffee) grounds pl; (COMM) rate; (Sprung) jump; **~teil** m part of a sentence; **~ung** f (Statut) statute, rule; **~zeichen** nt punctuation mark

Sau [zau] (-, **Säue**) f sow; (umg) dirty pig

sauber ['zaubər] adj clean; (ironisch) fine; **~ halten** to keep clean; **S~keit** f cleanness; (einer Person) cleanliness

säuberlich ['zɔybərlɪç] adv neatly

säubern vt to clean; (POL etc) to purge; **Säuberung** f cleaning; purge

Sauce ['zo:sə] f sauce, gravy

sauer ['zauər] adj sour; (CHEM) acid; (umg) cross; **saurer Regen** acid rain; **S~braten** m braised beef marinated in vinegar

Sauerei [zauə'raɪ] (umg) f rotten state of affairs, scandal; (Schmutz etc) mess; (Unanständigkeit) obscenity

Sauerkraut nt sauerkraut, pickled cabbage

säuerlich ['zɔʏɐlɪç] adj (Geschmack) sour; (missvergnügt: Gesicht) dour

Sauer- zW: **~milch** f sour milk; **~rahm** m (KOCH) sour cream; **~stoff** m oxygen; **~teig** m leaven

saufen ['zaʊfən] (unreg) (umg) vt, vi to drink, to booze; **Säufer** ['zɔʏfɐ] (-s, -) (umg) m boozer

saugen ['zaʊɡən] (unreg) vt, vi to suck

säugen ['zɔʏɡən] vt to suckle

Sauger ['zaʊɡɐ] (-s, -) m dummy, comforter (US); (auf Flasche) teat

Säugetier ['zɔʏɡə-] nt mammal

Säugling m infant, baby

Säule ['zɔʏlə] f column, pillar

Saum [zaʊm] (-(e)s, Säume) m hem; (Naht) seam

säumen ['zɔʏmən] vt to hem; to seam ♦ vi to delay, to hesitate

Sauna ['zaʊna] (-, -s) f sauna

Säure ['zɔʏrə] f acid

sausen ['zaʊzən] vi to blow; (umg: eilen) to rush; (Ohren) to buzz; **etw ~ lassen** (umg) not to bother with sth

Saxofon, Saxophon [zakso'foːn] (-s, -e) nt saxophone

SB abk = **Selbstbedienung**

S-Bahn f abk (= Schnellbahn) high speed railway; (= Stadtbahn) suburban railway

schaben ['ʃaːbən] vt to scrape

schäbig ['ʃɛːbɪç] adj shabby

Schablone [ʃa'bloːnə] f stencil; (Muster) pattern; (fig) convention

Schach [ʃax] (-s, -s) nt chess; (Stellung) check; **~brett** nt chessboard; **~figur** f chessman; **'~matt** adj checkmate; **~spiel** nt game of chess

Schacht [ʃaxt] (-(e)s, -e) m shaft

Schachtel (-, -n) f box

schade ['ʃaːdə] adj a pity od shame ♦ excl: **(wie) ~!** (what a) pity od shame; **sich auf zu ~ sein für etw** to consider o.s. too good for sth

Schädel ['ʃɛːdəl] (-s, -) m skull; **~bruch** m fractured skull

Schaden ['ʃaːdən] (-s, -) m damage; (Verletzung) injury; (Nachteil) disadvantage; **s~** vi +dat to hurt; **einer Sache s~** to damage sth; **~ersatz** m compensation, damages pl; **~freude** f malicious glee; **s~froh** adj (Mensch, Lachen) gloating; **~sfall** m: **im ~sfall** in the event of a claim

schadhaft ['ʃaːthaft] adj faulty, damaged

schäd- ['ʃɛːt] zW: **~igen** ['ʃɛːdɪɡən] vt to damage; (Person) to do harm to, to harm; **~lich** adj: **~lich (für)** harmful (to); **S~lichkeit** f harmfulness; **S~ling** m pest

Schadstoff ['ʃaːtʃtɔf] m harmful substance; **s~arm** adj (Auto) to contain a low level of harmful substances

Schaf [ʃaːf] (-(e)s, -e) nt sheep

Schäfer ['ʃɛːfɐ] (-s, -e) m shepherd; **~hund** m Alsatian (dog) (BRIT), German shepherd (dog) (US)

schaffen ['ʃafən] (-s) vt (creative) activity

schaffen¹ ['ʃafən] (unreg) vt to create; (Platz) to make

schaffen² ['ʃafən] vt (erreichen) to manage, to do; (erledigen) to finish; (Prüfung) to pass; (transportieren) to take ♦ vi (umg: arbeiten) to work; **sich dat etw ~** to get o.s. sth; **sich an etw dat zu ~ machen** to busy o.s. with sth

Schaffner(in) ['ʃafnɐ(ɪn)] (-s, -) m(f) (Busschaffner) conductor(-tress); (EISENB) guard

Schaft [ʃaft] (-(e)s, -e) m shaft; (von Gewehr) stock; (von Stiefel) leg; (BOT) stalk; tree trunk

Schal [ʃaːl] (-s, -s od -e) m scarf

schal adj flat; (fig) insipid

Schälchen ['ʃɛːlçən] f cup, bowl

Schale ['ʃaːlə] f skin; (abgeschält) peel; (Nussschale, Muschelschale, Eischale) shell; (Geschirr) dish, bowl

schälen ['ʃɛːlən] vt to peel; to shell ♦ vr to peel

Schall [ʃal] (-(e)s, -e) m sound; ~**dämpfer** (-s, -) m (AUT) silencer; **s~dicht** adj soundproof; **s~en** vi to (re)sound; **s~end** adj resounding, loud; ~**mauer** f sound barrier; ~**platte** f (gramophone) record

Schalt- [ʃalt] zW: ~**bild** nt circuit diagram; ~**brett** nt switchboard; **s~en** vt to switch, to turn ♦ vi (AUT) to change (gear); (umg: begreifen) to catch on; ~**er** (-s, -) m counter; (an Gerät) switch; ~**erbeamte(r)** m counter clerk; ~**erstunden** pl hours of business; ~**hebel** m switch; (AUT) gear lever; ~**jahr** nt leap year; ~**ung** f switching; (ELEK) circuit; (AUT) gear change

Scham [ʃaːm] (-) f shame; (Organe) private parts pl

schämen [ˈʃɛːmən] vr to be ashamed

schamlos adj shameless

Schande [ˈʃandə] (-) f disgrace

schändlich [ˈʃɛntlɪç] adj disgraceful, shameful

Schändung [ˈʃɛndʊŋ] f violation, defilement

Schanze [ˈʃantsə] f (Sprungschanze) ski jump

Schar [ʃaːr] (-, -en) f band, company; (Vögel) flock; (Menge) crowd; in ~en in droves; **s~en** vr to assemble, to rally

scharf [ʃarf] adj sharp; (Essen) hot, spicy; (Munition) live; ~ **nachdenken** to think hard; **auf etw** akk ~ **sein** (umg) to be keen on sth

Schärfe [ˈʃɛrfə] f sharpness; (Strenge) rigour; **s~n** vt to sharpen

Scharf- zW: **s~machen** (umg) vt to stir up; ~**richter** m executioner; ~**schütze** m marksman, sharpshooter; **s~sinnig** adj astute, shrewd

Scharlach [ˈʃarlax] (-s, -e) m (~fieber) scarlet fever

Scharnier [ʃarˈniːr] (-s, -e) nt hinge

scharren [ˈʃarən] vt, vi to scrape, to scratch

Schaschlik [ˈʃaʃlɪk] (-s, -s) m od nt (shish) kebab

Schatten [ˈʃatən] (-s, -) m shadow; ~**riss** ▲ m silhouette; ~**seite** f shady side, dark side

schattieren [ʃaˈtiːrən] vt, vi to shade

schattig [ˈʃatɪç] adj shady

Schatulle [ʃaˈtʊlə] f casket; (Geldschatulle) coffer

Schatz [ʃats] (-es, -e) m treasure; (Person) darling

schätz- [ʃɛts] zW: **s~bar** adj assessable; **S~chen** nt darling, love; **s~en** vt (abschätzen) to estimate; (Gegenstand) to value; (würdigen) to value, to esteem; (vermuten) to reckon; **S~ung** f estimate; estimation; valuation; **nach meiner S~ung ...** I reckon that ...

Schau [ʃau] (-) f show; (Ausstellung) display, exhibition; **etw zur ~ stellen** to make a show of sth, to show sth off; ~**bild** nt diagram

Schauder [ˈʃaudər] (-s, -s) m shudder; (wegen Kälte) shiver; **s~haft** adj horrible; **s~n** vi to shudder; to shiver

schauen [ˈʃauən] vi to look

Schauer [ˈʃauər] (-s, -) m (Regenschauer) shower; (Schreck) shudder; ~**geschichte** f horror story; **s~lich** adj horrific, spine-chilling

Schaufel [ˈʃaufəl] (-, -n) f shovel; (NAUT) paddle; (TECH) scoop; **s~n** vt to shovel, to scoop

Schau- zW: ~**fenster** nt shop window; ~**fensterbummel** m window shopping (expedition); ~**kasten** m showcase

Schaukel [ˈʃaukəl] (-, -n) f swing; **s~n** vi to swing, to rock; ~**pferd** nt rocking horse; ~**stuhl** m rocking chair

Schaulustige(r) [ˈʃaulʊstɪɡə(r)] f(m) onlooker

Schaum [ʃaum] (-(e)s, Schäume) m foam; (Seifenschaum) lather; ~**bad** nt bubble bath

schäumen ['ʃɔymən] vi to foam

Schaum- zW: **~festiger** (-s, -) m mousse; **~gummi** m foam (rubber); **s~ig** adj frothy, foamy; **~stoff** m foam material; **~wein** m sparkling wine

Schauplatz m scene

schaurig ['ʃaurɪç] adj horrific, dreadful

Schauspiel nt spectacle; (THEAT) play; **~er(in)** m(f) actor (actress); **s~ern** vi insep to act; **Schauspielhaus** nt theatre

Scheck [ʃɛk] (-s, -s) m cheque; **~ge- bühr** f encashment fee; **~heft** nt cheque book; **~karte** f cheque card

scheffeln ['ʃɛfəln] vt to amass

Scheibe ['ʃaibə] f disc; (Brot etc) slice; (Glasscheibe) pane; (MIL) target

Scheiben- zW: **~bremse** f (AUT) disc brake; **~wischer** m (AUT) windscreen wiper

Scheide ['ʃaidə] f sheath; (Grenze) boundary; (ANAT) vagina; **s~n** (unreg) vt to separate; (Ehe) to dissolve ♦ vi to depart; to part; **sich ~n lassen** to get a divorce

Scheidung f (Ehescheidung) divorce

Schein [ʃain] (-(e)s, -e) m light; (Anschein) appearance; (Geld) (bank)note; (Bescheinigung) certificate; **zum ~** in pretence; **s~bar** adj appar- ent; **s~en** (unreg) vi to shine; (Anschein haben) to seem; **s~heilig** adj hypo- critical; **~werfer** (-s, -) m floodlight; spotlight; (Suchscheinwerfer) search- light; (AUT) headlamp

Scheiß- ['ʃais] (umg) in zW bloody

Scheiße ['ʃaisə] (-) (umg) f shit

Scheitel ['ʃaitəl] (-s, -) m top; (Haarscheitel) parting; **s~n** vt to part

scheitern ['ʃaitərn] vi to fail

Schelle ['ʃɛlə] f small bell; **s~n** vi to ring

Schellfisch ['ʃɛlfɪʃ] m haddock

Schelm [ʃɛlm] (-(e)s, -e) m rogue; **s~isch** adj mischievous, roguish

Schelte ['ʃɛltə] f scolding; **s~n** (unreg) vt to scold

Schema ['ʃeːma] (-s, -s od -ta) nt scheme, plan; (Darstellung) schema; **nach ~** quite mechanically; **s~tisch** [ʃe'maːtɪʃ] adj schematic; (pej) me- chanical

Schemel ['ʃeːml] (-s, -) m (foot)stool

Schenkel ['ʃɛŋkl] (-s, -) m thigh

schenken ['ʃɛŋkən] vt (auch fig) to give; (Getränk) to pour; **sich dat etw ~** (umg) to skip sth; **das ist geschenkt!** (billig) that's a giveaway!; (nichts wert) that's worthless!

Scherbe ['ʃɛrbə] f broken piece, frag- ment; (archäologisch) potsherd

Schere ['ʃeːrə] f scissors pl; (groß) shears pl; **s~n** (unreg) vt to cut; (Schaf) to shear; (kümmern) to bother ♦ vr to care; **scher dich zum Teufel!** get lost!; **~rei** (umg) f bother, trouble

Scherz [ʃɛrts] (-es, -e) m joke; fun; **~frage** f conundrum; **s~haft** adj jok- ing, jocular

Scheu [ʃɔy] (-) f shyness; (Angst) fear; (Ehrfurcht) awe; **s~** adj shy; **s~en** vt: **sich ~en vor** +dat to be afraid of, to shrink from ♦ vt to shun ♦ vi (Pferd) to shy

scheuern ['ʃɔyərn] vt to scour, to scrub

Scheune ['ʃɔynə] f barn

Scheusal ['ʃɔyzaːl] (-s, -e) nt monster

scheußlich ['ʃɔyslɪç] adj dreadful, frightful

Schi [ʃiː] m = Ski

Schicht [ʃɪçt] (-, -en) f layer; (Klasse) class, level; (in Fabrik etc) shift; **~arbeit** f shift work; **s~en** vt to layer, to stack

schick [ʃɪk] adj stylish, chic

schicken vt to send ♦ vr: **sich ~ (in** +akk) to resign o.s. (to) ♦ vb unpers (an- ständig sein) to be fitting

schicklich adj proper, fitting

Schicksal (-s, -e) nt fate; **~sschlag** m great misfortune, blow

Schieb- ['ʃiːb] zW: **~edach** nt (AUT) sun roof; **s~en** (unreg) vt (auch Drogen) to push; (Schuld) to put ♦ vi to push;

~etür f sliding door; **~ung** f fiddle
Schieds- ['ʃiːts] zW: **~gericht** nt court of arbitration; **~richter** m referee; umpire; (Schlichter) arbitrator

schief [ʃiːf] adj crooked; (Ebene) sloping; (Turm) leaning; (Winkel) oblique; (Blick) funny; (Vergleich) distorted ♦ adv crooked(ly); (ansehen) askance; **etw ~ stellen** to slope sth; **~ gehen** (umg) to go wrong

Schiefer ['ʃiːfər] (-s, -) m slate
schielen ['ʃiːlən] vi to squint; **nach etw ~** (fig) to eye sth
schien etc [ʃiːn] vb siehe **scheinen**
Schienbein nt shinbone
Schiene ['ʃiːnə] f rail; (MED) splint; **s~n** vt to put in splints
schier [ʃiːr] adj (fig) sheer ♦ adv nearly, almost

Schieß- ['ʃiːs] zW: **~bude** f shooting gallery; **s~en** (unreg) vt to shoot; (Ball) to kick; (Geschoss) to fire ♦ vi to shoot; (Salat etc) to run to seed; **s~en auf** +akk to shoot at; **~e'rei** f shooting incident, shoot-out; **~pulver** nt gunpowder; **~scharte** f embrasure

Schiff [ʃɪf] (-(e)s, -e) nt ship, vessel; (Kirchenschiff) nave; **s~bar** adj (Fluss) navigable; **~bruch** m shipwreck; **s~brüchig** adj shipwrecked; **~chen** nt small boat; (Weben) shuttle; (Mütze) forage cap; **~er** (-s) m bargeman, boatman; **~fahrt** ▲ f shipping; (Reise) voyage

Schikane [ʃi'kaːnə] f harassment; dirty trick; **mit allen ~n** with all the trimmings
schikanieren [ʃika'niːrən] vt to harass, to torment

Schikoree ▲ ['ʃikoreː] (-s) m od f = **Chicorée**
Schild¹ [ʃɪlt] (-(e)s, -e) m shield; **etw im ~e führen** to be up to sth
Schild² [ʃɪlt] (-(e)s, -er) nt sign; nameplate; (Etikett) label

Schilddrüse f thyroid gland
schildern ['ʃɪldərn] vt to depict, to portray
Schildkröte f tortoise; (Wasserschildkröte) turtle
Schilf [ʃɪlf] (-(e)s, -e) nt (Pflanze) reed; (Material) reeds pl, rushes pl; **~rohr** nt (Pflanze) reed
schillern ['ʃɪlərn] vi to shimmer; **~d** adj iridescent
Schilling ['ʃɪlɪŋ] m schilling
Schimmel ['ʃɪməl] (-s, -) m mould; (Pferd) white horse; **s~ig** adj mouldy; **s~n** vi to get mouldy
Schimmer ['ʃɪmər] (-s) m (Lichtsein) glimmer; (Glanz) shimmer; **s~n** vi to glimmer, to shimmer
Schimpanse [ʃɪm'panzə] (-n, -n) m chimpanzee
schimpfen ['ʃɪmpfən] vt to scold ♦ vi to curse, to complain; to scold
Schimpfwort nt term of abuse
schinden ['ʃɪndən] (unreg) vt to maltreat, to drive too hard ♦ vr: **sich ~ (mit)** to sweat and strain (at), to toil away (at); **Eindruck ~** (umg) to create an impression
Schinde'rei f grind, drudgery
Schinken ['ʃɪŋkən] (-s, -) m ham
Schirm [ʃɪrm] (-(e)s, -e) m (Regenschirm) umbrella; (Sonnenschirm) parasol, sunshade; (Wandschirm, Bildschirm) screen; (Lampenschirm) (lamp)shade; (Mützenschirm) peak; (Pilzschirm) cap; **~mütze** f peaked cap; **~ständer** m umbrella stand
schizophren [ʃitso'freːn] adj schizophrenic
Schlacht [ʃlaxt] (-, -en) f battle; **s~en** vt to slaughter, to kill; **~er** (-s, -) m butcher; **~feld** nt battlefield; **~hof** m slaughterhouse, abattoir; **~schiff** nt battleship; **~vieh** nt animals kept for meat; beef cattle
Schlaf [ʃlaːf] (-(e)s) m sleep; **~anzug** m

pyjamas *pl*

Schläfe [ˈʃlɛːfə] (ANAT) temple

schlafen [ˈʃlaːfən] (*unreg*) *vi* to sleep; ~ **gehen** to go to bed; **S~zeit** *f* bedtime

schlaff [ʃlaf] *adj* slack; (*energielos*) limp; (*erschöpft*) exhausted

Schlaf- *zW*: **~gelegenheit** *f* sleeping accommodation; **~lied** *nt* lullaby; **s~los** *adj* sleepless; **~losigkeit** *f* sleeplessness, insomnia; **~mittel** *nt* sleeping pill

schläfrig [ˈʃlɛːfrɪç] *adj* sleepy

Schlaf- *zW*: **~saal** *m* dormitory; **~sack** *m* sleeping bag; **~tablette** *f* sleeping pill; **~wagen** *m* sleeping car, sleeper; **s~wandeln** *vi insep* to sleepwalk; **~zimmer** *nt* bedroom

Schlag [ʃlaːk] (-(e)s, ¨e) *m* (*auch fig*) blow; (*auch MED*) stroke; (*Pulsschlag, Herzschlag*) beat; (ELEK) shock; (*Blitzschlag*) bolt, stroke; (*Autotür*) car door; (*umg*: *Portion*) helping; (*Art*) kind, type; **Schläge** *pl* (*Tracht Prügel*) beating *sg*; **mit einem ~** all at once; **~ auf ~** in rapid succession; **~ader** *f* artery; **~anfall** *m* stroke; **s~artig** *adj* sudden, without warning; **~baum** *m* barrier

Schlägel [ˈʃlɛːgəl] (-s, -) *m* (drum)stick; (*Hammer*) mallet, hammer

schlagen [ˈʃlaːgən] (*unreg*) *vt, vi* to strike, to hit; (*wiederholt ~, besiegen*) to beat; (*Glocke*) to ring; (*Stunde*) to strike; (*Sahne*) to whip; (*Schlacht*) to fight ♦ *vr* to fight; **nach jdm ~** (*fig*) to take after sb; **sich gut ~** (*fig*) to do well

Schlager [ˈʃlaːgər] (-s, -) *m* (*auch fig*) hit

Schläger [ˈʃlɛːgər] *m* brawler; (SPORT) bat; (TENNIS *etc*) racket; (GOLF) club; hockey stick; (*Waffe*) rapier; **Schläge'rei** *f* fight, punch-up

Schlagersänger(in) *m(f)* pop singer

Schlag- *zW*: **s~fertig** *adj* quick-witted; **~fertigkeit** *f* ready wit, quickness of repartee; **~loch** *nt* pothole; **~obers**

(ÖSTERR) *nt* = **Schlagsahne**; **~sahne** *f* (whipped) cream; **~seite** *f* (NAUT) list; **~wort** *nt* slogan, catch phrase; **~zeile** *f* headline; **~zeug** *nt* percussion; drums *pl*; **~zeuger** (-s, -) *m* drummer

Schlamassel [ʃlaˈmasəl] (-s, -) (*umg*) *m* mess

Schlamm [ʃlam] (-(e)s, -e) *m* mud; **s~ig** *adj* muddy

Schlamp- [ˈʃlamp] *zW*: **~e** (*umg*) *f* slut; **s~en** (*umg*) *vi* to be sloppy; **~e'rei** (*umg*) *f* disorder, untidiness; sloppy work; **s~ig** (*umg*) *adj* (*Mensch, Arbeit*) sloppy, messy

Schlange [ˈʃlaŋə] *f* snake; (*Menschenschlange*) queue (BRIT), line-up (US); **~ stehen** to (form a) queue, to line up

schlängeln [ˈʃlɛŋəln] *vr* (*Schlange*) to wind; (*Weg*) to wind, twist; (*Fluss*) to meander

Schlangen- *zW*: **~biss** ▲ *m* snake bite; **~gift** *nt* snake venom; **~linie** *f* wavy line

schlank [ʃlaŋk] *adj* slim, slender; **S~heit** *f* slimness, slenderness; **S~heitskur** *f* diet

schlapp [ʃlap] *adj* limp; (*locker*) slack; **S~e** (*umg*) *f* setback

Schlaraffenland [ʃlaˈrafənlant] *nt* land of milk and honey

schlau [ʃlau] *adj* crafty, cunning

Schlauch [ʃlaux] (-(e)s, Schläuche) *m* hose; (*in Reifen*) inner tube; (*umg: Anstrengung*) grind; **~boot** *nt* rubber dinghy; **s~en** (*umg*) *vt* to tell on, to exhaust

Schläue [ˈʃlɔyə] (-) *f* cunning

Schlaufe [ˈʃlaufə] *f* loop; (*Aufhänger*) hanger

Schlauheit *f* cunning

schlecht [ʃlɛçt] *adj* bad ♦ *adv* badly; **~ gelaunt** in a bad mood; **~ und recht** after a fashion; **jdm ist ~** sb feels sick *od* bad; **jdm geht es ~** sb is in a bad way; **~ machen** to run down; **S~igkeit** *f* badness; bad deed

schlecken [ˈʃlɛkən] *vt, vi* to lick

Schlegel ['ʃleːgəl] **(-s, -)** *m* (*KOCH*) leg; *siehe* **Schlägel**

schleichen ['ʃlaɪçən] (*unreg*) *vi* to creep, to crawl; **~d** *adj* gradual; creeping

Schleichwerbung *f* (*COMM*) plug

Schleier ['ʃlaɪər] **(-s, -)** *m* veil; **s~haft** (*umg*) *adj*: **jdm s~haft sein** to be a mystery to sb

Schleif- ['ʃlaɪf] *zW*: **~e** *f* loop; (*Band*) bow; **s~en¹** *vt, vi* to drag; **s~en²** (*unreg*) *vt* to grind; (*Edelstein*) to cut; **~stein** *m* grindstone

Schleim [ʃlaɪm] **(-(e)s, -e)** *m* slime; (*MED*) mucus; (*KOCH*) gruel; **~haut** *f* (*ANAT*) mucous membrane; **s~ig** *adj* slimy

Schlemm- ['ʃlɛm] *zW*: **s~en** *vi* to feast; **~er (-s, -)** *m* gourmet; **~e'rei** *f* gluttony, feasting

schlendern ['ʃlɛndərn] *vi* to stroll

schlenkern ['ʃlɛŋkərn] *vt, vi* to swing, to dangle

Schlepp- [ʃlɛp] *zW*: **~e** *f* train; **s~en** *vt* to drag; (*Auto, Schiff*) to tow; (*tragen*) to lug; **s~end** *adj* dragging, slow; **~er (-s, -)** *m* tractor; (*Schiff*) tug

Schlesien ['ʃleːziən] **(-s)** *nt* Silesia

Schleuder ['ʃlɔydər] **(-, -n)** *f* catapult; (*Wäscheschleuder*) spin-drier; (*Butterschleuder etc*) centrifuge; **~gefahr** *f* risk of skidding; **„Achtung ~gefahr"** "slippery road ahead"; **s~n** *vt* to hurl; (*Wäsche*) to spin-dry ♦ *vi* (*AUT*) to skid; **~preis** *m* give-away price; **~sitz** *m* (*AVIAT*) ejector seat; (*fig*) hot seat; **~ware** *f* cheap *od* cut-price goods *pl*

schleunigst ['ʃlɔynɪçst] *adv* straight away

Schleuse ['ʃlɔyzə] *f* lock; (*~ntor*) sluice

schlicht [ʃlɪçt] *adj* simple, plain; **~en** *vt* (*glätten*) to smooth, to dress; (*Streit*) to settle; **S~er (-s, -)** *m* mediator, arbitrator; **S~ung** *f* settlement; arbitration

Schlick [ʃlɪk] **(-(e)s, -e)** *m* mud; (*Ölschlick*) slick

schlief *etc* [ʃliːf] *vb siehe* **schlafen**

Schließ- ['ʃliːs] *zW*: **s~en** (*unreg*) *vt* to close, to shut; (*beenden*) to close; (*Freundschaft, Bündnis, Ehe*) to enter into; (*folgern*): **s~en (aus)** to infer (from) ♦ *vi, vr* to close, to shut; **etw in sich s~en** to include sth; **~fach** *nt* locker; **s~lich** *adv* finally; **s~lich doch** after all

Schliff [ʃlɪf] **(-(e)s, -e)** *m* cut(ting); (*fig*) polish

schlimm [ʃlɪm] *adj* bad; **~er** *adj* worse; **~ste(r, s)** *adj* worst; **~stenfalls** *adv* at (the) worst

Schlinge ['ʃlɪŋə] *f* loop; (*bes Henkersschlinge*) noose; (*Falle*) snare; (*MED*) sling; **s~n** (*unreg*) *vt* to wind; (*essen*) to bolt, to gobble ♦ *vi* (*essen*) to bolt one's food, to gobble

schlingern *vi* to roll

Schlips [ʃlɪps] **(-es, -e)** *m* tie

Schlitten ['ʃlɪtən] **(-s, -)** *m* sledge, sleigh; **~fahren (-s)** *nt* tobogganing

schlittern ['ʃlɪtərn] *vi* to slide

Schlittschuh ['ʃlɪtʃuː] *m* skate; **~ laufen** to skate; **~bahn** *f* skating rink; **~läufer(in)** *m(f)* skater

Schlitz [ʃlɪts] **(-es, -e)** *m* slit; (*für Münze*) slot; (*Hosenschlitz*) flies *pl*; **s~äugig** *adj* slant-eyed

Schloss ▲ [ʃlɔs] **(-es, ⸚er)** *nt* lock; (*an Schmuck etc*) clasp; (*Bau*) castle; chateau

schloss ▲ *etc vb siehe* **schließen**

Schlosser ['ʃlɔsər] **(-s, -)** *m* (*Autoschlosser*) fitter; (*für Schlüssel etc*) locksmith

Schlosserei [-'raɪ] *f* metal (working) shop

Schlot [ʃloːt] **(-(e)s, -e)** *m* chimney; (*NAUT*) funnel

schlottern ['ʃlɔtərn] *vi* to shake, to tremble; (*Kleidung*) to be baggy

Schlucht [ʃlʊxt] **(-, -en)** *f* gorge, ravine

schluchzen ['ʃlʊxtsən] *vi* to sob

Schluck [ʃlʊk] (-(e)s, -e) *m* swallow; (*Menge*) drop; ~auf (-s, -s) *m* hiccups *pl*; s~en *vt*, *vi* to swallow

schludern [ˈʃluːdərn] *vi* to skimp, to do sloppy work

schlug *etc* [ʃluːk] *vb siehe* **schlagen**

Schlummer [ˈʃlʊmər] (-s) *m* slumber; s~n *vi* to slumber

Schlund [ʃlʊnt] (-(e)s, ⁼e) *m* gullet; (*fig*) jaw

schlüpfen [ˈʃlʏpfən] *vi* to slip; (*Vogel etc*) to hatch (out)

Schlüpfer [ˈʃlʏpfər] (-s, -) *m* panties *pl*, knickers *pl*

schlüpfrig [ˈʃlʏpfrɪç] *adj* slippery; (*fig*) lewd; S~keit *f* slipperiness; (*fig*) lewdness

schlurfen [ˈʃlʊrfən] *vi* to shuffle

schlürfen [ˈʃlʏrfən] *vt*, *vi* to slurp

Schluss ▲ [ʃlʊs] (-es, ⁼e) *m* end; (~*folgerung*) conclusion; am ~ at the end; ~ machen mit to finish with

Schlüssel [ˈʃlʏsəl] (-s, -) *m* (*auch fig*) key; (*Schraubenschlüssel*) spanner, wrench; (*MUS*) clef; ~bein *nt* collarbone; ~blume *f* cowslip, primrose; ~bund *m* bunch of keys; ~dienst *m* key cutting service; ~loch *nt* keyhole; ~position *f* key position; ~wort *nt* keyword

schlüssig [ˈʃlʏsɪç] *adj* conclusive

Schluss- ▲ *zW*: ~licht *nt* taillight; (*fig*) tailender; ~strich *m* (*fig*) final stroke; ~verkauf *m* clearance sale

schmächtig [ˈʃmɛçtɪç] *adj* slight

schmackhaft [ˈʃmakhaft] *adj* tasty

schmal [ʃmaːl] *adj* narrow; (*Person, Buch etc*) slender, slim; (*karg*) meagre

schmälern [ˈʃmɛːlərn] *vt* to diminish; (*fig*) to belittle

Schmalfilm *m* cine film

Schmalz [ʃmalts] (-es, -e) *nt* dripping, lard; (*fig*) sentiment, schmaltz; s~ig *adj* (*fig*) schmaltzy

schmarotzen [ʃmaˈrɔtsən] *vi* to sponge; (*BOT*) to be parasitic; **Schmarotzer** (-s, -) *m* parasite; sponger

Schmarren [ˈʃmarən] (-s, -) *m* (*ÖSTERR*) small piece of pancake; (*fig*) rubbish, tripe

schmatzen [ˈʃmatsən] *vi* to smack one's lips; to eat noisily

schmecken [ˈʃmɛkən] *vt*, *vi* to taste; es schmeckt ihm he likes it

Schmeichel- [ˈʃmaɪçəl] *zW*: ~ei [-ˈlaɪ] *f* flattery; s~haft *adj* flattering; s~n *vi* to flatter

schmeißen [ˈʃmaɪsən] (*unreg*) (*umg*) *vt* to throw, to chuck

Schmelz [ʃmɛlts] (-es, -e) *m* enamel; (*Glasur*) glaze; (*von Stimme*) melodiousness; s~en (*unreg*) *vt* to melt; (*Erz*) to smelt ♦ *vi* to melt; ~punkt *m* melting point; ~wasser *nt* melted snow

Schmerz [ʃmɛrts] (-es, -en) *m* pain; (*Trauer*) grief; s~empfindlich *adj* sensitive to pain; s~en *vt*, *vi* to hurt; ~ensgeld *nt* compensation; s~haft *adj* painful; s~lich *adj* painful; s~los *adj* painless; ~mittel *nt* painkiller; ~tablette *f* painkiller

Schmetterling [ˈʃmɛtərlɪŋ] *m* butterfly

schmettern [ˈʃmɛtərn] *vt* (*werfen*) to hurl; (*TENNIS: Ball*) to smash; (*singen*) to belt out (*inf*)

Schmied [ʃmiːt] (-(e)s, -e) *m* blacksmith; ~e [ˈʃmiːdə] *f* smithy, forge; ~eeisen *nt* wrought iron; s~en *vt* to forge; (*Pläne*) to devise, to concoct

schmiegen [ˈʃmiːgən] *vt* to press, to nestle ♦ *vr*: sich ~ (an +akk) to cuddle up (to), to nestle (up to)

Schmier- [ˈʃmiːr] *zW*: ~e *f* grease; (*THEAT*) greasepaint, make-up; s~en *vt* to smear; (*ölen*) to lubricate, to grease; (*bestechen*) to bribe; (*schreiben*) to scrawl ♦ *vi* (*schreiben*) to scrawl; ~fett *nt* grease; ~geld *nt* bribe; s~ig *adj* greasy; ~seife *f* soft soap

Schminke [ˈʃmɪŋkə] *f* make-up; s~n *vt*, *vr* to make up

schmirgeln [ˈʃmɪrgəln] *vt* to sand (down)

Schmirgelpapier nt emery paper

schmollen ['ʃmɔlən] vi to sulk, to pout

Schmorbraten m stewed od braised meat

schmoren ['ʃmoːrən] vt to stew, to braise

Schmuck [ʃmʊk] (-(e)s, -e) m jewellery; (Verzierung) decoration

schmücken ['ʃmʏkən] vt to decorate

Schmuck- zW: **s~los** adj unadorned, plain; **~sachen** pl jewels, jewellery sg

Schmuggel ['ʃmʊgəl] (-s) m smuggling; **s~n** vt, vi to smuggle

Schmuggler (-s, -) m smuggler

schmunzeln ['ʃmʊntsəln] vi to smile benignly

schmusen ['ʃmuːzən] (umg) vi (zärtlich sein) to cuddle, to canoodle (inf)

Schmutz [ʃmʊts] (-es) m dirt, filth; **~fink** m filthy creature; **~fleck** m stain; **s~ig** adj dirty

Schnabel ['ʃnaːbəl] (-s, ⁼) m beak, bill; (Ausguss) spout

Schnalle ['ʃnalə] f buckle, clasp; **s~n** vt to buckle

Schnapp- ['ʃnap] zW: **s~en** vt to grab, to catch ♦ vi to snap; **~schloss** ▲ nt spring lock; **~schuss** ▲ m (PHOT) snapshot

Schnaps [ʃnaps] (-es, ⁼e) m spirits pl; schnapps

schnarchen ['ʃnarçən] vi to snore

schnattern ['ʃnatərn] vi (Gänse) to gabble, (Ente) to quack

schnauben ['ʃnaʊbən] vi to snort ♦ vr to blow one's nose

schnaufen ['ʃnaʊfən] vi to puff, to pant

Schnauze f snout, muzzle; (Ausguss) spout; (umg) gob

schnäuzen ▲ ['ʃnɔytsən] vr to blow one's nose

Schnecke ['ʃnɛkə] f snail; **~nhaus** nt snail's shell

Schnee [ʃneː] (-s) m snow; (Eischnee)

beaten egg white; **~ball** m snowball; **~flocke** f snowflake; **s~frei** adj free of snow; **~gestöber** nt snowstorm; **~glöckchen** nt snowdrop; **~grenze** f snow line; **~kette** f (AUT) snow chain; **~mann** m snowman; **~pflug** m snowplough; **~regen** m sleet; **~schmelze** f thaw; **~wehe** f snowdrift

Schneide ['ʃnaɪdə] f edge; (Klinge) blade; **s~n** (unreg) vt to cut; (kreuzen) to cross, to intersect with ♦ vr to cut o.s.; to cross, to intersect; **s~nd** adj cutting; **~r** (-s, -) m tailor; **~rei** f (Geschäft) tailor's; **~rin** f dressmaker; **s~rn** vt to make ♦ vi to be a tailor; **~zahn** m incisor

schneien ['ʃnaɪən] vi unpers to snow

Schneise ['ʃnaɪzə] f clearing

schnell [ʃnɛl] adj quick, fast ♦ adv quick, quickly, fast; **S~hefter** (-s, -) m loose-leaf binder; **S~igkeit** f speed; **S~imbiss** ▲ m (Lokal) snack bar; **S~kochtopf** m (Dampfkochtopf) pressure cooker; **S~reinigung** f dry cleaner's; **~stens** adv as quickly as possible; **S~straße** f expressway; **S~zug** m fast od express train

schneuzen △ ['ʃnɔytsən] vr siehe **schnäuzen**

schnippeln ['ʃnɪpəln] (umg) vt: **~ (an** +dat) to snip (at)

schnippisch ['ʃnɪpɪʃ] adj sharp-tongued

Schnitt (-(e)s, -e) m cut(ting); (~punkt) intersection; (Querschnitt) (cross) section; (Durchschnitt) average; (~muster) pattern; (an Buch) edge; (umg: Gewinn) profit

schnitt etc vb siehe **schneiden**

Schnitt- zW: **~blumen** pl cut flowers; **~e** f slice; (belegt) sandwich; **~fläche** f section; **~lauch** m chive; **~punkt** m (point of) intersection; **~stelle** f (COMPUT) interface; **~wunde** f cut

Schnitz- ['ʃnɪts] zW: **~arbeit** f wood

---

carving; **~el** (-s, -) *nt* chip; (KOCH) escalope; **s~en** *vt* to carve; **~er** (-s, -) *m* carver; (umg) blunder; **~e'rei** *f* carving; carved woodwork

schnodderig ['ʃnɔdərɪç] (umg) adj snotty

Schnorchel ['ʃnɔrçəl] (-s, -) *m* snorkel

Schnörkel ['ʃnœrkəl] (-s, -) *m* flourish; (ARCHIT) scroll

schnorren ['ʃnɔrən] *vt, vi* to cadge

schnüffeln ['ʃnʏfəln] *vi* to sniff

Schnüffler (-s, -) *m* snooper

Schnuller ['ʃnʊlər] (-s, -) *m* dummy, comforter (US)

Schnupfen ['ʃnʊpfən] (-s, -) *m* cold

schnuppern ['ʃnʊpərn] *vi* to sniff

Schnur [ʃnuːr] (-, ⸚e) *f* string, cord; (ELEK) flex

schnüren ['ʃnyːrən] *vt* to tie

schnurgerade adj straight (as a die)

Schnurrbart ['ʃnʊrbaːrt] *m* moustache

schnurren ['ʃnʊrən] *vi* to purr; (Kreisel) to hum

Schnürschuh *m* lace-up (shoe)

Schnürsenkel *m* shoelace

schnurstracks adv straight (away)

Schock [ʃɔk] (-(e)s, -e) *m* shock; **s~ieren** [ʃɔ'kiːrən] *vt* to shock, to outrage

Schöffe ['ʃœfə] (-n, -n) *m* lay magistrate; **Schöffin** *f* lay magistrate

Schokolade [ʃoko'laːdə] *f* chocolate

Scholle ['ʃɔlə] *f* clod; (Eisscholle) ice floe; (Fisch) plaice

---

SCHLÜSSELWORT

schon [ʃoːn] adv **1** (bereits) already; **er ist schon da** he's there already, he's already there; **ist er schon da?** is he there yet?; **warst du schon einmal da?** have you ever been there?; **ich war schon einmal da** I've been there before; **das war schon immer so** that has always been the case; **schon oft** often; **hast du schon gehört?** have you heard?

2 (bestimmt) all right; **du wirst schon**

sehen you'll see (all right); **das wird schon noch gut** that'll be OK

3 (bloß) just; **allein schon das Gefühl ...** just the very feeling ...; **schon der Gedanke** the very thought; **wenn ich das schon höre** I only have to hear that

4 (einschränkend): **ja schon, aber ...** yes (well), but ...

5: **schon möglich** possible; **schon gut!** OK!; **du weißt schon** you know; **komm schon!** come on!

---

schön [ʃøːn] adj beautiful; (nett) nice; **~e Grüße** best wishes; **~e Ferien** have a nice holiday; **~en Dank** (many) thanks; **sich ~ machen** to make o.s. look nice

schonen ['ʃoːnən] *vt* to look after ♦ *vr* to take it easy; **~d** adj careful, gentle

Schön- *zW*: **~heit** *f* beauty; **~heitsfehler** *m* blemish, flaw; **~heitsoperation** *f* cosmetic surgery

Schonkost (-) *f* light diet; (Spezialdiät) special diet

Schon- *zW*: **~ung** *f* good care; (Nachsicht) consideration; (Forst) plantation of young trees; **s~ungslos** adj unsparing, harsh; **~zeit** *f* close season

Schöpf- ['ʃœpf] *zW*: **s~en** *vt* to scoop, to ladle; (Mut) to summon up; (Luft) to breathe in; **~er** (-s, -) *m* creator; **s~erisch** adj creative; **~kelle** *f* ladle; **~ung** *f* creation

Schorf [ʃɔrf] (-(e)s, -e) *m* scab

Schornstein ['ʃɔrnʃtain] *m* chimney; (NAUT) funnel; **~feger** (-s, -) *m* chimney sweep

Schoß [ʃoːs] (-es, ⸚e) *m* lap

schoss ▲ etc vb siehe **schießen**

Schoßhund *m* pet dog, lapdog

Schote ['ʃoːtə] *f* pod

Schotte ['ʃɔtə] *m* Scot, Scotsman

Schotter ['ʃɔtər] (-s, -) *m* broken stone, road metal; (EISENB) ballast

Schott- [ʃɔt] *zW*: **~in** *f* Scot, Scotswoman; **s~isch** adj Scottish; Scots;

~land nt Scotland

schraffieren [ʃraˈfiːrən] vt to hatch

schräg [ʃrɛːk] adj slanting, not straight; etw **~ stellen** to put sth at an angle; **~ gegenüber** diagonally opposite; **S~e** [ˈʃrɛːgə] f slant; **S~strich** m oblique stroke

Schramme [ˈʃramə] f scratch; **s~n** vt to scratch

Schrank [ʃraŋk] (-(e)s, **~e**) m cupboard; (Kleiderschrank) wardrobe; **~e** f barrier; **~koffer** m trunk

Schraube [ˈʃraubə] f screw; **s~n** vt to screw; **~nschlüssel** m spanner; **~nzieher** (-s, -) m screwdriver

Schraubstock [ˈʃraupʃtɔk] m (TECH) vice

Schreck [ʃrɛk] (-(e)s, -e) m terror; fright; **~en** (-s, -) m terror; fright; **s~en** vt to frighten, to scare; **~gespenst** nt spectre, nightmare; **s~haft** adj jumpy, easily frightened; **s~lich** adj terrible, dreadful

Schrei [ʃrai] (-(e)s, -e) m scream; (Ruf) shout

Schreib- [ˈʃraib] zW: **~block** m writing pad; **s~en** (unreg) vt, vi to write; (buchstabieren) to spell; **~en** (-s, -) nt letter, communication; **s~faul** adj bad about writing letters; **~kraft** f typist; **~maschine** f typewriter; **~papier** nt notepaper; **~tisch** m desk; **~ung** f spelling; **~waren** pl stationery sg; **~weise** f spelling; way of writing; **~zentrale** f typing pool; **~zeug** nt writing materials pl

schreien [ˈʃraiən] (unreg) vt, vi to scream; (rufen) to shout; **~d** adj (fig) glaring; (Farbe) loud

Schrein [ʃrain] (-(e)s, -e) m shrine

Schreiner [ˈʃrainɐ] (-s, -) m joiner; (Zimmermann) carpenter; (Möbelschreiner) cabinetmaker; **~ei** [-ˈrai] f joiner's workshop

schreiten [ˈʃraitən] (unreg) vi to stride

schrieb etc [ʃriːp] vb siehe **schreiben**

Schrift [ʃrɪft] (-, -en) f writing; handwriting; (~art) script; (Gedrucktes) pamphlet, work; **~deutsch** nt written German; **~führer** m secretary; **s~lich** adj written ♦ adv in writing; **~sprache** f written language; **~steller(in)** (-s, -) m(f) writer; **~stück** nt document; **~wechsel** m correspondence

schrill [ʃrɪl] adj shrill

Schritt [ʃrɪt] (-(e)s, -e) m step; (Gangart) walk; (Tempo) pace; (von Hose) crutch; **~ fahren** to drive at walking pace; **~macher** (-s, -) m pacemaker; **~tempo** ▲ nt: im **~tempo** at a walking pace

schroff [ʃrɔf] adj steep; (zackig) jagged; (fig) brusque

schröpfen [ˈʃrœpfən] vt (fig) to fleece

Schrot [ʃroːt] (-(e)s, -e) m od nt (Blei) (small) shot; (Getreide) coarsely ground grain, groats pl; **~flinte** f shotgun

Schrott [ʃrɔt] (-(e)s, -e) m scrap metal; **~haufen** m scrap heap; **s~reif** adj ready for the scrap heap

schrubben [ˈʃrʊbən] vt to scrub

Schrubber (-s, -) m scrubbing brush

schrumpfen [ˈʃrʊmpfən] vi to shrink; (Apfel) to shrivel

Schub- [ˈʃuːb] zW: **~fach** nt drawer; **~karren** m wheelbarrow; **~lade** f drawer

Schubs [ʃuːps] (-es, -e) (umg) m shove (inf), push

schüchtern [ˈʃʏçtɐn] adj shy; **S~heit** f shyness

Schuft [ʃʊft] (-(e)s, -e) m scoundrel

schuften (umg) vi to graft, to slave away

Schuh [ʃuː] (-(e)s, -e) m shoe; **~band** nt shoelace; **~creme** f shoe polish; **~größe** f shoe size; **~löffel** m shoehorn; **~macher** (-s, -) m shoemaker

Schul- zW: **~arbeit** f homework (no

pl); **~aufgaben** pl homework sg; **~be-such** m school attendance; **~buch** nt school book

Schuld [ʃʊlt] (-, -en) f guilt; (FIN) debt; (Verschulden) fault; ~ haben (an +dat) to be to blame (for); **er hat ~** it's his fault; **jdm ~ geben** to blame sb; siehe **zuschulden; s~** adj: **s~ sein** (an +dat) to be to blame (for); **er ist s~** it's his fault; **s~en** ['ʃʊldən] vt to owe; **s~enfrei** adj free from debt; **~gefühl** nt feeling of guilt; **s~ig** adj guilty; (gebührend) due; **s~ig an etw** dat sein to be guilty of sth; **jdm etw s~ig sein** to owe sb sth; **jdm etw s~ig bleiben** not to provide sb with sth; **s~los** adj innocent, without guilt; **~ner** (-s, -) m debtor; **~schein** m promissory note, IOU

Schule ['ʃuːlə] f school; **s~n** vt to train, to school

Schüler(in) ['ʃyːlər(ın)] (-s, -) m(f) pupil; **~austausch** m school od student exchange; **~ausweis** m (school) student card

Schul- zW: **~ferien** pl school holidays; **s~frei** adj: **s~freier Tag** holiday; **s~frei sein** to be a holiday; **~hof** m playground; **~jahr** nt school year; **~kind** nt schoolchild; **s~pflichtig** adj of school age; **~schiff** nt (NAUT) training ship; **~stunde** f period, lesson; **~tasche** f school bag

Schulter ['ʃʊltər] (-, -n) f shoulder; **~blatt** nt shoulder blade; **s~n** vt to shoulder

Schulung f education, schooling

Schulzeugnis nt school report

Schund [ʃʊnt] (-(e)s) m trash, garbage

Schuppe ['ʃʊpə] f scale; **~n** pl (Haarschuppen) dandruff sg

Schuppen (-s, -) m shed

schuppig ['ʃʊpɪç] adj scaly

Schur [ʃuːr] (-, -en) f shearing

schüren ['ʃyːrən] vt to rake; (fig) to stir up

schürfen ['ʃʏrfən] vt, vi to scrape, to

scratch; (MIN) to prospect

Schurke ['ʃʊrkə] (-n, -n) m rogue

Schurwolle f: **"reine ~"** "pure new wool"

Schürze ['ʃʏrtsə] f apron

Schuss ▲ [ʃʊs] (-es, ⁻e) m shot; (WEBEN) woof; **~bereich** m effective range

Schüssel ['ʃʏsəl] (-, -n) f bowl

Schuss- ▲ zW: **~linie** f line of fire; **~verletzung** f bullet wound; **~waffe** f firearm

Schuster ['ʃuːstər] (-s, -) m cobbler, shoemaker

Schutt [ʃʊt] (-(e)s) m rubbish; (Bauschutt) rubble

Schüttelfrost m shivering

schütteln ['ʃʏtəln] vt, vr to shake

schütten ['ʃʏtən] vt to pour; (Zucker, Kies etc) to tip; (verschütten) to spill ♦ vi unpers to pour (down)

Schutthalde f dump

Schutthaufen m heap of rubble

Schutz [ʃʊts] (-es) m protection; (Unterschlupf) shelter; **jdn in ~ nehmen** to stand up for sb; **~anzug** m overalls pl; **~blech** nt mudguard

Schütze ['ʃʏtsə] (-n, -n) m gunman; (Gewehrschütze) rifleman; (Scharfschütze, Sportschütze) marksman; (ASTROL) Sagittarius

schützen ['ʃʏtsən] vt to protect; ~ **vor** +dat od **gegen** to protect from

Schützenfest nt fair featuring shooting matches

Schutz- zW: **~engel** m guardian angel; **~gebiet** nt protectorate; (Naturschutzgebiet) reserve; **~hütte** f shelter, refuge; **~impfung** f immunisation

Schützling ['ʃʏtslɪŋ] m protégé(e); (bes Kind) charge

Schutz- zW: **s~los** adj defenceless; **~mann** m policeman; **~patron** m patron saint

Schwaben ['ʃvaːbən] nt Swabia; **schwäbisch** adj Swabian

schwach [ʃvax] adj weak, feeble

Schwäche ['ʃvɛçə] f weakness; **s~n** t

to weaken

Schwachheit f weakness

schwächlich adj weakly, delicate

Schwächling m weakling

Schwach- zW: **~sinn** m imbecility; **s~sinnig** adj mentally deficient; (Idee) idiotic; **~strom** m weak current

Schwächung [ʃvɛçʊŋ] f weakening

Schwager [ʃvaːɡər] (-s, ⸚) m brother-in-law; **Schwägerin** [ʃvɛːɡərin] f sister-in-law

Schwalbe [ʃvalbə] f swallow

Schwall [ʃval] (-(e)s, -e) m surge; (Worte) flood, torrent

Schwamm [ʃvam] (-(e)s, ⸚e) m sponge; (Pilz) fungus

schwamm etc vb siehe **schwimmen**

schwammig adj spongy; (Gesicht) puffy

Schwan [ʃvaːn] (-(e)s, ⸚e) m swan

schwanger [ʃvaŋər] adj pregnant; **S~schaft** f pregnancy

schwanken vi to sway; (taumeln) to stagger, to reel; (Preise, Zahlen) to fluctuate; (zögern) to hesitate, to vacillate

Schwankung f fluctuation

Schwanz [ʃvants] (-es, ⸚e) m tail

schwänzen [ʃvɛntsən] (umg) vt to skip, to cut ♦ vi to play truant

Schwarm [ʃvarm] (-(e)s, ⸚e) m swarm; (umg) heart-throb, idol

schwärm- [ʃvɛrm] zW: **~en** vi to swarm; **~en für** to be mad od wild about; **S~erei** [-ə'raɪ] f enthusiasm; **~erisch** adj impassioned, effusive

Schwarte [ʃvartə] f hard skin; (Speck-schwarte) rind

schwarz [ʃvarts] adj black; **~es Brett** notice board; **ins S~e treffen** (auch fig) to hit the bull's eye; **in den ~en Zahlen** in the black; **~ sehen** (umg) to see the gloomy side of things; **S~arbeit** f illicit work, moonlighting; **S~brot** nt black bread; **S~e(r)** f(m)

black (man/woman)

Schwärze [ʃvɛrtsə] f blackness; (Farbe) blacking; (Druckerschwärze) printer's ink; **s~n** vt to blacken

Schwarz- zW: **s~fahren** (unreg) vi to travel without paying; to drive without a licence; **~handel** m black market (trade); **~markt** m black market; **~wald** m Black Forest; **s~weiß**, **s~-weiß** adj black and white

schwatzen [ʃvatsən] vi to chatter

schwätzen [ʃvɛtsən] vi to chatter

Schwätzer [ʃvɛtsər] (-s, -) m gasbag

schwatzhaft adj talkative, gossipy

Schwebe [ʃveːbə] f: **in der ~** (fig) in abeyance; **~bahn** f overhead railway; **s~n** vi to drift, to float; (hoch) to soar

Schwed- [ʃveːd] zW: **~e** m Swede; **~en** nt Sweden; **~in** f Swede; **s~isch** adj Swedish

Schwefel [ʃveːfəl] (-s) m sulphur; **s~ig** adj sulphurous; **~säure** f sulphuric acid

Schweig- [ʃvaɪg] zW: **~egeld** nt hush money; **~en** (-s) nt silence; **s~en** (unreg) vi to be silent; to stop talking; **~epflicht** f pledge of secrecy; (von Anwalt) requirement of confidentiality; **s~sam** [ʃvaɪkzaːm] adj silent, taciturn; **~samkeit** f taciturnity, quietness

Schwein [ʃvaɪn] (-(e)s, -e) nt pig; (umg) (good) luck

Schweine- zW: **~fleisch** nt pork; **~'rei** f mess; (Gemeinheit) dirty trick; **~stall** m pigsty

schweinisch adj filthy

Schweinsleder nt pigskin

Schweiß [ʃvaɪs] (-es) m sweat, perspiration; **s~en** vt, vi to weld; **~er** (-s) m welder; **~füße** pl sweaty feet; **~naht** f weld

Schweiz [ʃvaɪts] f Switzerland; **~er(in)** m(f) Swiss; **s~erisch** adj Swiss

schwelgen [ʃvɛlgən] vi to indulge

Schwelle ['ʃvɛlə] f (auch fig) threshold; doorstep; (EISENB) sleeper (BRIT), tie (US)

schwellen (unreg) vi to swell

Schwellung f swelling

Schwemme ['ʃvɛmə] f (WIRTS) Überangebot) surplus

Schwenk- ['ʃvɛŋk] zW: **s~bar** adj swivel-mounted; **s~en** vt to swing; (Fahne) to wave; (abspülen) to rinse ♦ vi to turn, to swivel; (MIL) to wheel; **~ung** f turn; wheel

schwer [ʃveːr] adj heavy; (schwierig) difficult, hard; (schlimm) serious, bad ♦ adv (sehr) very (much); (verletzt etc) seriously, badly; **~ erziehbar** difficult (to bring up); **jdm ~ fallen** to be difficult for sb; **jdm/sich etw ~ machen** to make sth difficult for sb/o.s.; **~ nehmen** to take to heart; **sich** dat od akk **~ tun** to have difficulties; **~ verdaulich** indigestible, heavy; **~ wiegend** weighty, important; **S~arbeiter** m manual worker, labourer; **S~behinderte(r)** f(m) seriously handicapped person; **S~e** f weight, heaviness; (PHYS) gravity; **~elos** adj weightless; (Kammer) zero-G; **~fällig** adj ponderous; **S~gewicht** nt heavyweight; (fig) emphasis; **~hörig** adj hard of hearing; **S~industrie** f heavy industry; **S~kraft** f gravity; **S~kranke(r)** f(m) person who is seriously ill; **~lich** adv hardly; **~mütig** adj melancholy; **S~punkt** m centre of gravity; (fig) emphasis, crucial point

Schwert [ʃveːrt] (-(e)s, -er) nt sword; **~lilie** f iris

schwer- zW: **S~verbrecher(in)** m(f) criminal, serious offender; **S~verletzte(r)** f(m) serious casualty; (bei Unfall usw auch) seriously injured person

Schwester ['ʃvɛstər] (-, -n) f sister; (MED) nurse; **s~lich** adj sisterly

Schwieger- ['ʃviːɡər] zW: **~eltern** pl parents-in-law; **~mutter** f mother-in-law; **~sohn** m son-in-law; **~tochter** f daughter-in-law; **~vater** m father-in-law

schwierig ['ʃviːrɪç] adj difficult, hard; **S~keit** f difficulty

Schwimm- ['ʃvɪm] zW: **~bad** nt swimming baths pl; **~becken** nt swimming pool; **s~en** (unreg) vi to swim; (treiben, nicht sinken) to float; (fig: unsicher sein) to be all at sea; **~er (-s, -)** m swimmer; (Angeln) float; **~erin** f (female) swimmer; **~lehrer** m swimming instructor; **~weste** f life jacket

Schwindel ['ʃvɪndəl] (-s) m giddiness; dizzy spell; (Betrug) swindle, fraud; (Zeug) stuff; **s~frei** adj: **s~frei sein** to have a good head for heights; **s~n** (umg) vi (lügen) to fib; (fig: schwindlig sein) **jdm s~t es** sb feels dizzy

schwinden ['ʃvɪndən] (unreg) vi to disappear; (sich verringern) to decrease; (Kräfte) to decline

Schwindler ['ʃvɪndlər] m swindler; (Lügner) liar

schwindlig adj dizzy; **mir ist ~** I feel dizzy

Schwing- ['ʃvɪŋ] zW: **s~en** (unreg) vt to swing; (Waffe etc) to brandish ♦ vi to swing; (vibrieren) to vibrate; (klingen) to sound; **~tür** f swing door(s); **~ung** f vibration; (PHYS) oscillation

Schwips [ʃvɪps] (-es, -e) m: **einen ~ haben** to be tipsy

schwirren ['ʃvɪrən] vi to buzz

schwitzen ['ʃvɪtsən] vi to sweat, to perspire

schwören ['ʃvøːrən] (unreg) vt, vi to swear

schwul [ʃvuːl] (umg) adj gay, queer

schwül [ʃvyːl] adj sultry, close; **S~e (-)** f sultriness

Schwule(r) (umg) f(m) gay (man/woman)

Schwung [ʃvʊŋ] (-(e)s, ²e) m swing; (Triebkraft) momentum; (fig: Energie) verve, energy; (umg: Menge) batch; **s~haft** adj brisk, lively; **s~voll** adj vigorous

Schwur [ʃvuːr] (-(e)s, ⁼e) m oath; **~ge-richt** nt court with a jury

sechs [zɛks] num six; **~hundert** num six hundred; **~te(r, s)** adj sixth; **S~tel** (-s, -) nt sixth

sechzehn ['zɛçtseːn] num sixteen

sechzig ['zɛçtsɪç] num sixty

See¹ [zeː] (-, -n) f sea

See² [zeː] (-s, -n) m lake

See- [zeː] zW: **~bad** nt seaside resort; **~hund** m seal; **~igel** ['zeːliːgəl] m sea urchin; **s~krank** adj seasick; **~krank-heit** f seasickness; **~lachs** m rock salmon

Seele ['zeːlə] f soul; **s~nruhig** adv calmly

Seeleute ['zeːlɔʏtə] pl seamen

Seel- zW: **s~isch** adj mental; **~sorge** f pastoral duties pl; **~sorger** (-s, -) m clergyman

See- zW: **~macht** f naval power; **~mann** (pl **-leute**) m seaman, sailor; **~meile** f nautical mile; **~möwe** f (ZOOL) seagull; **~not** f distress; **~räuber** m pirate; **~rose** f water lily; **~stern** m starfish; **s~tüchtig** adj seaworthy; **~weg** m sea route; **auf dem ~weg** by sea; **~zunge** f sole

Segel ['zeːgəl] (-s, -) nt sail; **~boot** nt yacht; **~fliegen** (-s) nt gliding; **~flie-ger** m glider pilot; **~flugzeug** nt glider; **s~n** vt, vi to sail; **~schiff** nt sailing vessel; **~sport** m sailing; **~tuch** nt canvas

Segen ['zeːgən] (-s, -) m blessing

Segler ['zeːglər] (-s, -) m sailor, yachtsman

segnen ['zeːgnən] vt to bless

Seh- ['zeː] zW: **s~behindert** adj partially sighted; **s~en** (unreg) vt, vi to see; (in bestimmter Richtung) to look; **mal s~en(, ob ...)** let's see (if ...); **siehe Seite 5** see page 5; **s~enswert** adj worth seeing; **~enswürdigkeiten** pl sights (of a town); **~fehler** m sight de-

---

fect

Sehne ['zeːnə] f sinew; (an Bogen) string

sehnen vr: **sich ~ nach** to long od yearn for

sehnig adj sinewy

Sehn- zW: **s~lich** adj ardent; **~sucht** f longing; **s~süchtig** adj longing

sehr [zeːr] adv very; (mit Verben) a lot, (very) much; **zu ~** too much; **~ geehrte(r) ...** dear ...

seicht [zaɪçt] adj (auch fig) shallow

Seide ['zaɪdə] f silk; **s~n** adj silk; **~npa-pier** nt tissue paper

seidig ['zaɪdɪç] adj silky

Seife ['zaɪfə] f soap

Seifen- zW: **~lauge** f soapsuds pl; **~schale** f soap dish; **~schaum** m lather

seihen ['zaɪən] vt to strain, to filter

Seil [zaɪl] (-(e)s, -e) nt rope; cable; **~bahn** f cable railway; **~hüpfen** (-s) nt skipping; **~springen** (-s) nt skipping; **~tänzer(in)** m(f) tightrope walker

---

SCHLÜSSELWORT

sein [zaɪn] (pt **war**, pp **gewesen**) vi 1 to be; **ich bin** I am; **du bist** you are; **er/sie/es ist** he/she/it is; **wir sind/ihr seid/sie sind** we/you/they are; **wir waren** we were; **wir sind gewesen** we have been

2: **seien Sie nicht böse** don't be angry; **sei so gut und ...** be so kind as to ...; **das wäre gut** that would od that'd be a good thing; **wenn ich Sie wäre** if I were od was you; **das wärs** that's all, that's it; **morgen bin ich in Rom** tomorrow I'll od I will od I shall be in Rome; **waren Sie mal in Rom?** have you ever been to Rome?

3: **wie ist das zu verstehen?** how is that to be understood?; **er ist nicht zu ersetzen** he cannot be replaced;

---

mit ihr ist nicht zu reden you can't talk to her

4: mir ist kalt I'm cold; **was ist?** what's the matter?, what is it?; **ist was?** is something the matter?; **es sei denn, dass ...** unless ...; **wie dem auch sei** be that as it may; **wie wäre es mit ...?** how *od* what about ...?; **lass das sein!** stop that!

sein(e) ['zaɪn(ə)] *adj* his; its; **~e(r, s)** *pron* his; its; **~er** *(gen von er)* *pron* of him; **~erseits** *adv* for his part; **~erzeit** *adv* in those days, formerly; **~esglei-chen** *pron* people like him; **~etwegen** *adv (für ihn)* for his sake; *(wegen ihm)* on his account; *(von ihm aus)* as far as he is concerned; **~etwillen** *adv*: **um ~etwillen** = seinetwegen; **~ige** *pron*: **der/die/das ~ige** *od* **S~ige** his

seit [zaɪt] *präp +dat* since ♦ *konj* since; **er ist ~ einer Woche hier** he has been here for a week; **~ langem** for a long time; **~dem** [zaɪt'deːm] *adv, konj* since

Seite ['zaɪtə] *f* side; *(Buchseite)* page; *(MIL)* flank

Seiten- *zW:* **~ansicht** *f* side view; **~hieb** *m (fig)* passing shot, dig; **s~s** *präp +gen* on the part of; **~schiff** *nt* aisle; **~sprung** *m* extramarital escapade; **~stechen** *nt (a)* stitch; **~straße** *f* side road; **~streifen** *m* verge; *(der Autobahn)* hard shoulder

seither [zaɪt'heːr] *adv, konj* since (then)

seit- *zW:* **~lich** *adj* on one *od* the other side; side *cpd;* **~wärts** *adv* sideways

Sekretär [zekre'tɛːr] *m* secretary; *(Möbel)* bureau

Sekretariat [zekretari'aːt] *(-(e)s, -e) nt* secretary's office, secretariat

Sekretärin *f* secretary

Sekt [zɛkt] *(-(e)s, -e) m* champagne

Sekte ['zɛktə] *f* sect

Sekunde [ze'kʊndə] *f* second

selber ['zɛlbər] = **selbst**

Selbst [zɛlpst] *(-) nt* self

selbst [zɛlpst] *pron* **1: ich/er/wir selbst** I myself/he himself/we ourselves; **sie ist die Tugend selbst** she's virtue itself; **er braut sein Bier selbst** he brews his own beer; **wie gehts? - gut, und selbst?** how are things? - fine, and yourself?

2 *(ohne Hilfe)* alone, on my/his/one's *etc* own; **von selbst** by itself; **er kam von selbst** he came of his own accord; **selbst gemacht** home-made

♦ *adv* even; **selbst wenn** even if; **selbst Gott** even God (himself)

selbständig *etc* ['zɛlpʃtɛndɪç] = **selbst-ständig** *etc*

Selbst- *zW:* **~auslöser** *m (PHOT)* delayed-action shutter release; **~bedienung** *f* self-service; **~befriedigung** *f* masturbation; **~beherrschung** *f* self-control; **~bestimmung** *f (POL)* self-determination; **~beteiligung** *f (VERSICHERUNG: bei Kosten)* (voluntary) excess; **s~bewusst** ▲ *adj* self-confident; **~bewusstsein** ▲ *nt* self-confidence; **~erhaltung** *f* self-preservation; **~erkenntnis** *f* self-knowledge; **s~gefällig** *adj* smug, self-satisfied; **~gespräch** *nt* conversation with o.s.; **~kostenpreis** *m* cost price; **s~los** *adj* unselfish, selfless; **~mord** *m* suicide; **~mörder(in)** *m(f)* suicide; **s~mörderisch** *adj* suicidal; **s~sicher** *adj* self-assured; **s~ständig** ▲ *adj* independent; **~ständigkeit** ▲ *f* independence; **s~süchtig** *adj (Mensch)* selfish; **~versorger (-s, -)** *m (im Urlaub etc)* self-caterer; **s~verständlich** ['zɛlpstfɛrʃtɛntlɪç] *adj* obvious ♦ *adv* naturally; **ich halte das für s~verständlich** I take that for granted; **~verteidigung** *f* self-defence; **~vertrauen** *nt* self-confidence; **~verwaltung** *f* autonomy, self-government

selig ['ze:lɪç] *adj* happy, blissful; (REL) blessed; (tot) late; **S~keit** f bliss

Sellerie ['zɛləri:] (-s, -(s) *od* -, -) *m od* f celery

selten ['zɛltən] *adj* rare ♦ *adv* seldom, rarely; **S~heit** f rarity

Selterswasser ['zɛltərsvasər] *nt* soda water

seltsam ['zɛltza:m] *adj* strange, curious; **S~keit** f strangeness

Semester [ze'mɛstər] (-s, -) *nt* semester; **~ferien** *pl* vacation *sg*

Semi- [zemi] *in ZW* semi-; **~kolon** [-'ko:lɔn] (-s, -s) *nt* semicolon

Seminar [zemi'na:r] (-s, -e) *nt* seminary; (Kurs) seminar; (UNIV: Ort) department building

Semmel ['zɛməl] (-, -n) f roll

Senat [ze'na:t] (-(e)s, -e) *m* senate, council

Sende- ['zɛndə] *in ZW*: **~bereich** *m* transmission range; **~folge** f (Serie) series; **s~n** (unreg) vt to send; (RADIO, TV) to transmit, to broadcast ♦ vi to transmit, to broadcast; **~r** (-s, -) *m* station; (Anlage) transmitter; **~reihe** f series (of broadcasts)

Sendung ['zɛndʊŋ] f consignment; (Aufgabe) mission; (RADIO, TV) transmission; (Programm) programme

Senf [zɛnf] (-(e)s, -e) *m* mustard

senil [ze'ni:l] (pej) *adj* senile

Senior(in) ['ze:niɔr(ɪn)] (-s, -en) *m(f)* (Mensch im Rentenalter) (old age) pensioner

Seniorenheim [zeni'o:rənhaɪm] *nt* old people's home

Senk- ['zɛŋk] *in ZW*: **~blei** *nt* plumb; **~e** f depression; **s~en** vt to lower ♦ vr to sink, to drop gradually; **~recht** *adj* vertical, perpendicular; **~rechte** f perpendicular; **~rechtstarter** *m* (AVIAT) vertical take-off plane; (fig) high-flyer

Sensation [zɛnzatsi'o:n] f sensation; **s~ell** [-'nɛl] *adj* sensational

sensibel [zɛn'zi:bəl] *adj* sensitive

sentimental [zɛntimɛn'ta:l] *adj* sentimental; **S~i̱tät** f sentimentality

separat [zepa'ra:t] *adj* separate

September [zɛp'tɛmbər] (-(s), -) *m* September

Serie ['ze:riə] f series

serien- *in ZW*: **~mäßig** *adj* standard; **S~mörder(in)** *m(f)* serial killer; **~weise** *adv* in series

seriös [zeri'ø:s] *adj* serious, bona fide

Service¹ [zɛr'vi:s] (-(s), -) *nt* (Geschirr) set, service

Service² (-, -s) *m* service

servieren [zɛr'vi:rən] vt, vi to serve

Serviererin [zɛr'vi:rərɪn] f waitress

Serviette [zɛrvi'ɛtə] f napkin, serviette

Servo- ['zɛrvo] *in ZW*: **~bremse** f (AUT) servo(-assisted) brake; **~lenkung** f (AUT) power steering

Sessel ['zɛsəl] (-s, -) *m* armchair; **~lift** *m* chairlift

sesshaft ▲ ['zɛshaft] *adj* settled; (ansässig) resident

setzen ['zɛtsən] vt to put, to set; (Baum etc) to plant; (Segel, TYP) to set ♦ vr to settle; (Person) to sit down ♦ vi (springen) to leap; (wetten) to bet

Setz- ['zɛts] *in ZW*: **~er** (-s, -) *m* (TYP) compositor; **~ling** *m* young plant

Seuche ['zɔʏçə] f epidemic; **~ngebiet** *nt* infected area

seufzen ['zɔʏftsən] vt, vi to sigh

Seufzer ['zɔʏftsər] (-s, -) *m* sigh

Sex [zɛks] (-es) *m* sex; **~ualität** [-uali'tɛt] f sex, sexuality; **~ualkunde** [zɛksu'a:l-] f (SCH) sex education; **s~uell** [-u'ɛl] *adj* sexual

Shampoo [ʃam'pu:] (-s, -s) *nt* shampoo

Sibirien [zi'bi:riən] *nt* Siberia

SCHLÜSSELWORT
---

sich [zɪç] *pron* 1 (akk): **er/sie/es ... sich** he/she/it ... himself/herself/itself; **sie**

pl/**man** they/one ... themselves/
oneself; **Sie ... sich** you ... yourself/
yourselves *pl*; **sich wiederholen** to repeat oneself/itself
2 (*dat*): **er/sie/es ... sich** he/she/it ...
to himself/herself/itself; **sie** *pl*/**man ...
sich** they/one ... to themselves/
oneself; **Sie ... sich** you ... to
yourself/yourselves *pl*; **sie hat sich
einen Pullover gekauft** she bought
herself a jumper; **sich die Haare waschen** to wash one's hair
3 (*mit Präposition*): **haben Sie Ihren
Ausweis bei sich?** do you have your
pass on you?; **er hat nichts bei sich**
he's got nothing on him; **sie bleiben
gern unter sich** they keep themselves
to themselves
4 (*einander*) each other, one another;
sie bekämpfen sich they fight each
other *od* one another
5: **dieses Auto fährt sich gut** this car
drives well; **hier sitzt es sich gut** it's
good to sit here

Sichel ['zɪçəl] (-, -n) *f* sickle; (*Mond-
sichel*) crescent
sicher ['zɪçər] *adj* safe; (*gewiss*) certain;
(*zuverlässig*) secure, reliable; (*selbstsicher*) confident; **vor jdm/etw ~ sein**
to be safe from sb/sth; **bist du sich/sth**
I'm not sure *od* certain; **~ nicht** surely
not; **aber ~!** of course!; **~gehen** (*unreg*) *vi* to make sure
Sicherheit ['zɪçərhaɪt] *f* safety; (*auch
FIN*) security; (*Gewissheit*) certainty;
(*Selbstsicherheit*) confidence
Sicherheits- *zW*: **~abstand** *m* safe
distance; **~glas** *nt* safety glass; **~gurt**
m safety belt; **~halber** *adv* for safety;
to be on the safe side; **~nadel** *f* safety
pin; **~schloss** ▲ *nt* safety lock; **~vor-
kehrung** *f* safety precaution
sicher- *zW*: **~lich** *adv* certainly, surely;
~n *vt* to secure; (*schützen*) to protect;
(*Waffe*) to put the safety catch on;
jdm etw ~n to secure sth for sb; **sich**

dat **etw ~n** to secure sth (for o.s.);
~stellen *vt* to impound; (*COMPUT*) to
save; **S~ung** *f* (*S~n*) securing; (*Vorrichtung*) safety device; (*an Waffen*) safety
catch; (*ELEK*) fuse; **S~ungskopie** *f*
back-up copy

Sicht [zɪçt] (-) *f* sight; (*Aussicht*) view;
auf od nach ~ at sight; **auf lange
~** on a long-term basis; **s~bar** *adj* visible; **s~en** *vt* to sight; (*auswählen*) to
sort out; **s~lich** *adj* evident, obvious;
~verhältnisse *pl* visibility *sg*; **~ver-
merk** *m* visa; **~weite** *f* visibility
sickern ['zɪkərn] *vi* to trickle, to seep
Sie [zi:] (*nom, akk*) *pron* you
sie [zi:] *pron* (*sg: nom*) she, it; (: *akk*)
her, it; (*pl: nom*) they; (: *akk*) them
Sieb [zi:p] (-(e)s, -e) *nt* sieve; (*KOCH*)
strainer; **s~en**[1] ['zi:bən] *vt* to sift; (*
Flüssigkeit*) to strain
sieben[2] *num* seven; **~hundert** *num*
seven hundred; **S~sachen** *pl* belongings
siebte(r, s) ['zi:ptə(r, s)] *adj* seventh;
S~l (-s, -) *nt* seventh
siebzehn ['zi:ptse:n] *num* seventeen
siebzig ['zi:ptsɪç] *num* seventy
siedeln ['zi:dəln] *vt* to settle
sieden ['zi:dən] *vt, vi* to boil, to simmer
Siedepunkt *m* boiling point
Siedler (-s, -) *m* settler
Siedlung *f* settlement; (*Häusersiedlung*)
housing estate
Sieg [zi:k] (-(e)s, -e) *m* victory
Siegel ['zi:gəl] (-s, -) *nt* seal; **~ring** *m*
signet ring
Sieg- *zW*: **s~en** *vi* to be victorious;
(*SPORT*) to win; **~er** (-s, -) *m* victor;
(*SPORT etc*) winner; **s~reich** *adj* victo-
rious
siehe etc ['zi:ə] *vb siehe* **sehen**
siezen ['zi:tsən] *vt* to address as "Sie"
Signal [zɪ'gna:l] (-s, -e) *nt* signal
Silbe ['zɪlbə] *f* syllable
Silber ['zɪlbər] (-s) *nt* silver; **~hochzeit**
f silver wedding (anniversary); **s~n** *adj*

silver; **~papier** nt silver paper
Silhouette [zilu'ɛta] f silhouette
Silvester [zil'vɛstɐr] (-s, -) nt New Year's Eve, Hogmanay (SCOTTISH); **~abend** m = **Silvester**

> **Silvester**
>
> **Silvester** is the German word for New Year's Eve. Although not an official holiday most businesses close early and shops shut at midday. Most Germans celebrate in the evening, and at midnight they let off fireworks and rockets; the revelry usually lasts until the early hours of the morning.

simpel ['zɪmpəl] adj simple
Sims [zɪms] (-es, -e) nt od m (Kaminsims) mantelpiece; (Fenstersims) (window)sill
simulieren [zimu'liːrən] vt to simulate; (vortäuschen) to feign ♦ vi to feign illness
simultan [zimʊl'taːn] adj simultaneous
Sinfonie [zɪnfo'niː] f symphony
singen ['zɪŋən] (unreg) vt, vi to sing
Singular ['zɪŋgulaːr] m singular
Singvogel ['zɪŋfoːgəl] m songbird
sinken ['zɪŋkən] (unreg) vi to sink; (Preise etc) to fall, to go down
Sinn [zɪn] (-(e)s, -e) m mind; (Wahrnehmungssinn) sense; (Bedeutung) sense, meaning; **~ für etw** sense of sth; **von ~ sein** to be out of one's mind; **es hat keinen ~** there's no point; **~bild** nt symbol; **s~en** (unreg) vi to ponder; **auf etw akk s~en** to contemplate sth; **~estäuschung** f illusion; **s~gemäß** adj faithful; (Wiedergabe) in one's own words; **s~ig** adj clever; **s~lich** adj sensual, sensuous; (Wahrnehmung) sensory; **~lichkeit** f sensuality; **s~los** adj senseless; meaningless; **~losigkeit** f senselessness; meaninglessness; **s~voll** adj meaning-

ful; (vernünftig) sensible
Sintflut ['zɪntfluːt] f Flood
Sippe ['zɪpə] f clan, kin
Sippschaft ['zɪpʃaft] (pej) f relations pl, tribe; (Bande) gang
Sirene [zi'reːnə] f siren
Sirup ['ziːrʊp] (-s, -e) m syrup
Sitt- ['zɪt] zW: **~e** f custom; **~en** pl (~lichkeit) morals; **~enpolizei** f vice squad; **s~sam** adj modest, demure
Situation [zituatsi'oːn] f situation
Sitz [zɪts] (-es, -e) m seat; **der Anzug hat einen guten ~** the suit is a good fit; **s~en** (unreg) vi to sit; (Bemerkung, Schlag) to strike home, to tell; (Gelerntes) to have sunk in; **s~en bleiben** to remain seated; (SCH) to have to repeat a year; **auf etw dat s~en bleiben** to be lumbered with sth; **s~en lassen** (SCH) to make (sb) repeat a year; (Mädchen) to jilt; (Wartenden) to stand up; **etw auf sich dat s~en lassen** to take sth lying down; **s~end** adj (Tätigkeit) sedentary; **~gelegenheit** f place to sit down; **~platz** m seat; **~streik** m sit-down strike; **~ung** f meeting
Sizilien [zi'tsiːliən] nt Sicily
Skala ['skaːla] (-, Skalen) f scale
Skalpell [skal'pɛl] (-s, -e) nt scalpel
Skandal [skan'daːl] (-s, -e) m scandal; **s~ös** [-'løːs] adj scandalous
Skandinav- [skandi'naːv] zW: **~ien** nt Scandinavia; **~ier(in)** m(f) Scandinavian; **s~isch** adj Scandinavian
Skelett [ske'lɛt] (-(e)s, -e) nt skeleton
Skepsis ['skɛpsɪs] (-) f scepticism
skeptisch ['skɛptɪʃ] adj sceptical
Ski [ʃiː] (-s, -er) m ski; **~ laufen** od **fahren** to ski; **~fahrer** m skier; **~gebiet** nt ski(ing) area; **~läufer** m skier; **~lehrer** m ski instructor; **~lift** m ski-lift; **~springen** nt ski-jumping; **~stock** m ski-pole
Skizze ['skɪtsə] f sketch
skizzieren [skɪ'tsiːrən] vt, vi to sketch

Sklave ['skla:və] (-n, -n) m slave; **~'rei** f slavery; **Sklavin** f slave

Skonto ['skɔnto] (-s, -s) m od nt discount

Skorpion [skɔrpi'o:n] (-s, -e) m scorpion; (ASTROL) Scorpio

Skrupel ['skru:pəl] (-s, -) m scruple; **s~los** adj unscrupulous

Skulptur [skʊlp'tu:r] f sculpture

S-Kurve ['ɛskʊrvə] f S-bend

Slip [slɪp] (-s, -s) m (under)pants; **~einlage** f panty liner

Slowakei [slova'kai] f: **die ~** Slovakia

Slowenien [slo've:nɪən] nt Slovenia

Smaragd [sma'rakt] (-(e)s, -e) m emerald

Smoking ['smo:kɪŋ] (-s, -s) m dinner jacket

SCHLÜSSELWORT

so [zo:] adv 1 (so sehr) so; **so groß/ schön** etc so big/nice etc; **so groß/ schön wie ...** as big/nice as ...; **so viel (wie)** as much as; **rede nicht so viel** don't talk so much; **so weit sein** to be ready; **so weit wie od als möglich** as far as possible; **ich bin so weit zufrieden** by and large I'm quite satisfied; **so wenig (wie)** as little (as); **das hat ihn so geärgert, dass ...** that annoyed him so much that ...; **so einer wie ich** somebody like me; **na so was!** well, well!

2 (auf diese Weise) like this; **mach es nicht so** don't do it like that; **so oder so** in one way or the other; **und so weiter** and so on; **... oder so was ...** or something like that; **das ist gut so** that's fine; **so genannt** so-called

3 (umg: umsonst): **ich habe es so bekommen** I got it for nothing

♦ konj: **so dass, sodass** so that; **so wie es jetzt ist** as things are at the moment

♦ excl: **so?** really?; **so, das wärs** so, that's it then

---

s. o. abk = **siehe oben**

Söckchen ['zœkçən] nt ankle socks

Socke ['zɔkə] f sock

Sockel ['zɔkəl] (-s, -) m pedestal, base

sodass ▲ [zo'das] konj so that

Sodawasser ['zo:davasər] nt soda water

Sodbrennen ['zo:tbrɛnən] (-s, -) nt heartburn

soeben [zo'e:bən] adv just (now)

Sofa ['zo:fa] (-s, -s) nt sofa

sofern [zo'fɛrn] konj if, provided (that)

sofort [zo'fɔrt] adv immediately, at once; **~ig** adj immediate

Sog [zo:k] (-(e)s, -e) m (Strömung) undertow

sogar [zo'ga:r] adv even

sogleich [zo'glaiç] adv straight away, at once

Sohle ['zo:lə] f sole; (Talsohle etc) bottom; (MIN) level

Sohn [zo:n] (-(e)s, ᵉe) m son

Solar- [zo'la:r] in zW solar; **~zelle** f solar cell

solch [zɔlç] pron such; **ein ~e(r, s) ...** such a ...

Soldat [zɔl'da:t] (-en, -en) m soldier

Söldner ['zœldnər] (-s, -) m mercenary

solidarisch [zoli'da:rɪʃ] adj in od with solidarity; **sich ~ erklären** to declare one's solidarity

Solidari'tät f solidarity

solid(e) [zo'li:d(ə)] adj solid; (Leben, Person) respectable

Solist(in) [zo'lɪst(ɪn)] m(f) soloist

Soll [zɔl] (-(s), -(s)) nt (FIN) debit (side); (Arbeitsmenge) quota, target

---

SCHLÜSSELWORT

sollen ['zɔlən] (pt **sollte**, pp **gesollt** od (als Hilfsverb) **sollen**) Hilfsverb 1 (Pflicht, Befehl) to be supposed to; **du hättest nicht gehen sollen** you shouldn't have gone, you oughtn't to have gone; **soll ich?** shall I?; **soll ich dir helfen?** shall I help you?; **sag ihm, er**

soll warten tell him he's to wait; **was soll ich machen?** what should I do?

2 (*Vermutung*): **sie soll verheiratet sein** she's said to be married; **was soll das heißen?** what's that supposed to mean?; **man sollte glauben, dass ...** you would think that ...; **sollte das passieren, ...** if that should happen ...

♦ *vi*: **was soll das?** what's all this?; **das sollst du nicht** you shouldn't do that; **was solls?** what the hell!

Solo ['zo:lo] (**-s**, **-s** *od* **Soli**) *nt* solo

somit [zo'mɪt] *konj* and so, therefore

Sommer ['zɔmər] (**-s**, **-**) *m* summer; **s~lich** *adj* summery; summer; **~reifen** *m* normal tyre; **~schlussverkauf** ▲ *m* summer sale; **~sprossen** *pl* freckles

Sonde ['zɔndə] *f* probe

Sonder- ['zɔndər] *in zW* special; **~angebot** *nt* special offer; **s~bar** *adj* strange, odd; **~fahrt** *f* special trip; **~fall** *m* special case; **s~lich** *adj* particular; (*außergewöhnlich*) remarkable; (*eigenartig*) peculiar; **~marke** *f* special issue stamp; **s~n** *konj* but ♦ *vt* to separate; **nicht nur ..., s~n auch** not only ..., but also; **~preis** *m* special reduced price; **~zug** *m* special train

Sonnabend ['zɔn|a:bənt] *m* Saturday

Sonne ['zɔnə] *f* sun; **s~n** *vr* to sun o.s.

Sonnen- *zW*: **~aufgang** *m* sunrise; **s~baden** *vi* to sunbathe; **~brand** *m* sunburn; **~brille** *f* sunglasses *pl*; **~creme** *f* suntan lotion; **~energie** *f* solar energy, solar power; **~finsternis** *f* solar eclipse; **~kollektor** *m* solar panel; **~schein** *m* sunshine; **~schirm** *m* parasol, sunshade; **~schutzfaktor** *m* protection factor; **~stich** *m* sunstroke; **~uhr** *f* sundial; **~untergang** *m* sunset; **~wende** *f* solstice

sonnig ['zɔnɪç] *adj* sunny

Sonntag ['zɔnta:k] *m* Sunday

sonst [zɔnst] *adv* otherwise; (*mit pron, in Fragen*) else; (*zu anderer Zeit*) at other times, normally ♦ *konj* otherwise; **~ noch etwas?** anything else?; **~ nichts** nothing else; **~ jemand** anybody (at all); **~ wo** somewhere else; **~ woher** from somewhere else; **~ wohin** somewhere else; **~ig** *adj* other

sooft [zo'|ɔft] *konj* whenever

Sopran [zo'pra:n] (**-s**, **-e**) *m* soprano

Sorge ['zɔrgə] *f* care, worry

sorgen ['zɔrgən] *vi*: **für jdn ~** to look after sb ♦ *vr*: **sich ~ (um)** to worry (about); **für etw ~** to take care of *od* see to sth; **~frei** *adj* carefree; **~voll** *adj* troubled, worried

Sorgerecht *nt* custody (of a child)

Sorg- *zW*: **~falt** (**-**) *f* care(fulness); **s~fältig** *adj* careful; **s~los** *adj* careless; (*ohne ~en*) carefree; **s~sam** *adj* careful

Sorte ['zɔrtə] *f* sort; (*Warensorte*) brand; **~n** *pl* (FIN) foreign currency *sg*

sortieren [zɔr'ti:rən] *vt* to sort (out)

Sortiment [zɔrti'mɛnt] *nt* assortment

sosehr [zo'ze:r] *konj* as much as

Soße ['zo:sə] *f* sauce; (*Bratensoße*) gravy

soufflieren [zu'fli:rən] *vt, vi* to prompt

Souterrain [zute're:] (**-s**, **-s**) *nt* basement

souverän [zuvə're:n] *adj* sovereign; (*überlegen*) superior

so- *zW*: **~viel** [zo'fi:l] *konj*: **~viel ich weiß** as far as I know; *siehe* so; **~weit** [zo'vait] *konj* as far as; *siehe* so; **~wenig** [zo've:nɪç] *konj* little as; *siehe* so; **~wie** [zo'vi:] *konj* (*~bald*) as soon as; (*ebenso*) as well as; **~wieso** [zovi'zo:] *adv* anyway

sowjetisch [zo'vjetɪʃ] *adj* Soviet

Sowjetunion *f* Soviet Union

sowohl [zo'vo:l] *konj*: **~ ... als od wie auch buch ...** *and*

sozial [zotsi'a:l] *adj* social; **S~abgaben**

pl national insurance contributions;
S~arbeiter(in) *m(f)* social worker;
S~demokrat *m* social democrat; **~demokratisch** *adj* social democratic;
S~hilfe *f* income support (*BRIT*); welfare (aid) (*US*); **~isieren** *vt* to socialize;
S~ismus [-'ʃɪsmʊs] *m* socialism; **S~ist**
[-'lɪst] *m* socialist; **~istisch** *adj* socialist;
S~politik *f* social welfare policy;
S~produkt *nt* (net) national product;
S~staat *m* welfare state;
S~versicherung *f* national insurance
(*BRIT*), social security (*US*);
S~wohnung *f* council flat

soziologisch [zotsio'lo:gɪʃ] *adj* sociological

sozusagen [zotsu'za:gən] *adv* so to
speak

Spachtel ['ʃpaxtəl] (**-s, -**) *m* spatula

spähen ['ʃpɛ:ən] *vi* to peep, to peek

Spalier [ʃpa'li:r] (**-s, -e**) *nt* (*Gerüst*) trellis; (*Leute*) guard of honour

Spalt [ʃpalt] (**-(e)s, -e**) *m* crack;
(*Türspalt*) chink; (*fig: Kluft*) split; **~e** *f*
crack, fissure; (*Gletscherspalte*) crevasse; (*in Text*) column; **s~en** *vt, vr*
(*auch fig*) to split; **~ung** *f* splitting

Span [ʃpa:n] (**-(e)s, ²e**) *m* shaving

Spanferkel *nt* sucking pig

Spange ['ʃpaŋə] *f* clasp; (*Haarspange*)
hair slide; (*Schnalle*) buckle

Spanien ['ʃpa:niən] *nt* Spain; **Spanier(in)** *m(f)* Spaniard; **spanisch** *adj*
Spanish

Spann- ['ʃpan] *zW:* **~beton** *m* prestressed concrete; **~bettuch ▲** *nt*
fitted sheet; **~e** *f* (*Zeitspanne*) space;
(*Differenz*) gap; **s~en** *vt* (*straffen*) to
tighten, to tauten; (*befestigen*) to
brace ◊ *vi* to be tight; **s~end** *adj* exciting, gripping; **~ung** *f* tension; (*ELEK*)
voltage; (*fig*) suspense; (*unangenehm*)
tension

Spar- ['ʃpa:r] *zW:* **~buch** *nt* savings
book; **~büchse** *f* money box; **s~en** *vt,
vi* to save; **sich** *dat* **etw s~en** to save
o.s. sth; (*Bemerkung*) to keep sth to

o.s.; **mit etw s~en** to be sparing with
sth; **an etw** *dat* **s~en** to economize on
sth; **~er** (**-s, -**) *m* saver

Spargel ['ʃpargəl] (**-s, -**) *m* asparagus

Sparkasse *f* savings bank

Sparkonto *nt* savings account

spärlich ['ʃpɛ:rlɪç] *adj* meagre; (*Bekleidung*) scanty

Spar- *zW:* **~preis** *m* economy price;
s~sam *adj* economical, thrifty; **~samkeit** *f* thrift, economizing; **~schwein**
nt piggy bank

Sparte ['ʃpartə] *f* field; line of business;
(*PRESSE*) column

Spaß [ʃpa:s] (**-es, ²e**) *m* joke; (*Freude*)
fun; **jdm ~ machen** to be fun (for sb);
viel ~! have fun!; **s~en** *vi* to joke; **mit
ihm ist nicht zu s~en** you can't take
liberties with him; **s~haft** *adj* funny,
droll; **s~ig** *adj* funny, droll

spät [ʃpɛ:t] *adj, adv* late; **wie ~ ist es?**
what's the time?

Spaten ['ʃpa:tən] (**-s, -**) *m* spade

später *adj, adv* later

spätestens *adv* at the latest

Spätvorstellung *f* late show

Spatz [ʃpats] (**-en, -en**) *m* sparrow

spazier- [ʃpa'tsi:r] *zW:* **~en** *vi* to stroll,
to walk; **~en fahren** to go for a drive;
~en gehen to go for a walk; **S~gang**
m walk; **S~stock** *m* walking stick;
S~weg *m* path, walk

Specht [ʃpɛçt] (**-(e)s, -e**) *m* woodpecker

Speck [ʃpɛk] (**-(e)s, -e**) *m* bacon

Spediteur [ʃpedi'tø:r] *m* carrier;
(*Möbelspediteur*) furniture remover

Spedition [ʃpeditsi'o:n] *f* carriage;
(*~sfirma*) road haulage contractor; removal firm

Speer [ʃpe:r] (**-(e)s, -e**) *m* spear; (*SPORT*)
javelin

Speiche ['ʃpaiçə] *f* spoke

Speichel ['ʃpaiçəl] (**-s**) *m* saliva,
spit(tle)

Speicher ['ʃpaiçər] (**-s, -**) *m* storehouse; (*Dachspeicher*) attic, loft; (*Korn-*

speien 235 **Spitze**

speicher) granary; *(Wasserspeicher)* tank; *(TECH)* store; *(COMPUT)* memory; **s~n** vt to store; *(COMPUT)* to save

speien ['ʃpaɪən] *(unreg)* vt, vi to spit; *(erbrechen)* to vomit; *(Vulkan)* to spew

Speise ['ʃpaɪzə] f food; *(Süße)* ice-cream; **~kammer** f larder, pantry; **~karte** f menu; **s~n** vt to feed; to eat ♦ vi to dine; **~röhre** f gullet, oesophagus; **~saal** m dining room; **~wagen** m dining car

Speku- [ʃpeku] zW: **~lant** m speculator; **~lation** [-latsi'o:n] f speculation; **s~lieren** [-'li:rən] vi (fig) to speculate; **auf etw akk s~lieren** to have hopes of sth

Spelunke [ʃpe'lʊŋkə] f dive

Spende ['ʃpɛndə] f donation; **s~n** vt to donate, to give; **~r** (-s, -) m donor, donator

spendieren [ʃpɛn'di:rən] vt to pay for, to buy; **jdm etw ~** to treat sb to sth, to stand sb sth

Sperling ['ʃpɛrlɪŋ] m sparrow

Sperma ['ʃpɛrma] (-s, Spermen) nt sperm

Sperr- ['ʃpɛr] zW: **~e** f barrier; *(Verbot)* ban; **s~en** vt to block; *(SPORT)* to suspend, to bar; *(vom Ball)* to obstruct; *(einschließen)* to lock; *(verbieten)* to ban ♦ vr to baulk, to jib(e); **~gebiet** nt prohibited area; **~holz** nt plywood; **s~ig** adj bulky; **~müll** m bulky refuse; **~sitz** m *(THEAT)* stalls pl; **~stunde** f closing time

Spesen ['ʃpe:zən] pl expenses

Spezial- [ʃpetsi'a:l] in zW special; **~gebiet** nt specialist field; **s~isieren** vr to specialize; **~isierung** f specialization; **~ist** [-'lɪst] m specialist; **~ität** f speciality

speziell [ʃpetsi'ɛl] adj special

spezifisch [ʃpe'tsi:fɪʃ] adj specific

Sphäre ['ʃfɛ:rə] f sphere

Spiegel ['ʃpi:gəl] (-s, -) m mirror; *(Was-*

serspiegel) level; *(MIL)* tab; **~bild** nt reflection; **s~bildlich** adj reversed; **~ei** nt fried egg; **s~n** vt to mirror, to reflect ♦ vr to be reflected ♦ vi to gleam; *(widerspiegeln)* to be reflective; **~ung** f reflection

Spiel [ʃpi:l] (-(e)s, -e) nt game; *(Schauspiel)* play; *(Tätigkeit)* play(ing); *(KARTEN)* deck; *(TECH)* (free) play; **s~en** vt, vi to play; *(um Geld)* to gamble; *(THEAT)* to perform, to act; **s~end** adv easily; **~er** (-s, -) m player; *(um Geld)* gambler; **s~erei** f trifling pastime; **~feld** nt pitch, field; **~film** m feature film; **~kasino** nt casino; **~plan** m *(THEAT)* programme; **~platz** m playground; **~raum** m room to manoeuvre, scope; **~regel** f rule; **~sachen** pl toys; **~uhr** f musical box; **~verderber** (-s, -) m spoilsport; **~waren** pl toys; **~zeug** nt toy(s)

Spieß [ʃpi:s] (-es, -e) m spear; *(Bratspieß)* spit; **~bürger** m bourgeois; **~er** (-s, -) m bourgeois; **s~ig** (pej) adj (petit) bourgeois

Spinat [ʃpi'na:t] (-(e)s, -e) m spinach

Spind [ʃpɪnt] (-(e)s, -e) m od nt locker

Spinn- ['ʃpɪn] zW: **~e** f spider; **s~en** *(unreg)* vt, vi to spin; *(umg)* to talk rubbish; *(verrückt sein)* to be crazy od mad; **~e'rei** f spinning mill; **~rad** nt spinning wheel; **~webe** f cobweb

Spion [ʃpi'o:n] (-s, -e) m spy; *(in Tür)* spyhole; **~age** [ʃpio'na:ʒə] f espionage; **s~ieren** [ʃpio'ni:rən] vi to spy; **~in** f (female) spy

Spirale [ʃpi'ra:lə] f spiral

Spirituosen [ʃpiritu'o:zən] pl spirits

Spiritus ['ʃpi:ritus] (-, -se) m (methylated) spirit

Spital [ʃpi'ta:l] (-s, "er) nt hospital

spitz [ʃpɪts] adj pointed; *(Winkel)* acute; *(fig: Zunge)* sharp; *(: Bemerkung)* caustic

Spitze f point, tip; *(Bergspitze)* peak;

Spelling Reform: ▲ *new spelling* △ *old spelling (to be phased out)*

(Bemerkung) taunt, dig; *(erster Platz)* lead, top; *(meist pl: Gewebe)* lace

Spitzel (-s, -) m police informer

spitzen vt to sharpen

Spitzenmarke f brand leader

spitzfindig adj (over)subtle

Spitzname m nickname

Splitter ['ʃplɪtər] (-s, -) m splinter

sponsern ['ʃpɔnzərn] vt to sponsor

spontan [ʃpɔn'taːn] adj spontaneous

Sport [ʃpɔrt] (-(e)s, -e) m sport; *(fig)* hobby; **~lehrer(in)** m(f) games od P.E. teacher; **~ler(in)** (-, -) m(f) sportsman(-woman); **s~lich** adj sporting; *(Mensch)* sporty; *(fig: playing od sports field;* **~schuh** m *(Turnschuh)* training shoe, trainer; **~stadion** nt sports stadium; **~verein** m sports club; **~wagen** m sports car

Spott [ʃpɔt] (-(e)s) m mockery, ridicule; **s~billig** adj dirt-cheap; **s~en** vi to mock; **s~en (über** +akk) to mock (at), to ridicule

spöttisch ['ʃpœtɪʃ] adj mocking

sprach etc [ʃpraːx] vb siehe **sprechen**

Sprach- zW: **s~begabt** adj good at languages; **~e** f language; **~enschule** f language school; **~fehler** m speech defect; **~führer** m phrasebook; **~gefühl** nt feeling for language; **~kenntnisse** pl linguistic proficiency sg; **~kurs** m language course; **~labor** nt language laboratory; **s~lich** adj linguistic; **~los** adj speechless

sprang etc [ʃpraŋ] vb siehe **springen**

Spray [spreː] (-s, -s) m od nt spray

Sprech- ['ʃpreç] zW: **~anlage** f intercom; **s~en** *(unreg)* vi to speak, to talk ♦ vt to say; *(Sprache)* to speak; *(Person)* to speak to; **mit jdm s~en** to speak to sb; **das spricht für ihn** that's a point in his favour; **~er(in)** (-s, -) m(f) speaker; *(für Gruppe)* spokesman(-woman); *(RADIO, TV)* announcer; **~stunde** f consultation (hour); *(doctor's)* surgery; **~stundenhilfe** f (doctor's) receptionist; **~zimmer** nt consulting room,

surgery, office *(US)*

spreizen ['ʃpraɪtsən] vt *(Beine)* to open, to spread; *(Finger, Flügel)* to spread

Spreng- ['ʃpreŋ] zW: **s~en** vt to sprinkle; *(mit ~stoff)* to blow up; *(Gestein)* to blast; *(Versammlung)* to break up; **~stoff** m explosive(s)

sprich etc [ʃprɪç] vb siehe **sprechen**

Sprichwort nt proverb; **sprichwörtlich** adj proverbial

Spring- ['ʃprɪŋ] zW: **~brunnen** m fountain; **s~en** *(unreg)* vi to jump; *(Glas)* to crack; *(mit Kopfsprung)* to dive; **~er** (-s, -) m jumper; *(Schach)* knight

Sprit [ʃprɪt] (-(e)s, -e) *(umg)* m juice, gas

Spritz- ['ʃprɪts] zW: **~e** f syringe; injection; *(an Schlauch)* nozzle; **s~en** vt to spray; *(MED)* to inject ♦ vi to splash; *(herausspritzen)* to spurt; *(MED)* to give injections; **~pistole** f spray gun; **~tour** f *(umg)* spin

spröde ['ʃprøːdə] adj brittle; *(Person)* reserved, coy

Sprosse ['ʃprɔsə] f rung

Sprössling ▲ ['ʃprœslɪŋ] *(umg)* m *(Kind)* offspring *(pl inv)*

Spruch [ʃprʊx] (-(e)s, -e) m saying, maxim; *(JUR)* judgement

Sprudel ['ʃpruːdəl] (-s, -) m mineral water; lemonade; **s~n** vi to bubble; **~wasser** nt *(KOCH)* sparkling od fizzy mineral water

Sprüh- ['ʃpryː] zW: **~dose** f aerosol (can); **s~en** vi to spray; *(fig)* to sparkle ♦ vt to spray; **~regen** m drizzle

Sprung [ʃprʊŋ] (-(e)s, -e) m jump; *(Riss)* crack; **~brett** nt springboard; **s~haft** adj erratic; *(Aufstieg)* rapid; **~schanze** f ski jump

Spucke ['ʃpʊkə] (-) f spit; **s~n** vt, vi to spit

Spuk [ʃpuːk] (-(e)s, -e) m haunting; *(fig)* nightmare; **s~en** vi *(Geist)* to walk; **hier s~t es** this place is haunted

Spülbecken ['ʃpyːlbɛkən] nt *(in Küche)*

sink

Spule ['ʃpuːlə] f spool; (ELEK) coil

Spül- ['ʃpyːl] zW: **~e** f (kitchen) sink; **s~en** vt, vi to rinse; (Geschirr) to wash up; (Toilette) to flush; **~maschine** f dishwasher; **~mittel** nt washing-up liquid; **~stein** m sink; **~ung** f rinsing; flush; (MED) irrigation

Spur [ʃpuːr] (-, -en) f trace; (Fußspur, Radspur, Tonbandspur) track; (Fährte) trail; (Fahrspur) lane

spürbar adj noticeable, perceptible

spüren ['ʃpyːrən] vt to feel

spurlos adv without (a) trace

Spurt [ʃpʊrt] (-(e)s, -s od -e) m spurt; **s~en** vi to spurt

sputen ['ʃpuːtən] vr to make haste

St. abk = Stück; (= Sankt) St.

Staat [ʃtaːt] (-(e)s, -en) m state; (Prunk) show; (Kleidung) finery; **s~enlos** adj stateless; **s~lich** adj state(-); state-run

Staats- zW: **~angehörige(r)** f(m) national; **~angehörigkeit** f nationality; **~anwalt** m public prosecutor; **~bürger** m citizen; **~dienst** m civil service; **~examen** nt (UNIV) state exam(ination); **s~feindlich** adj subversive; **~mann** (pl **-männer**) m statesman; **~oberhaupt** nt head of state

Stab [ʃtaːp] (-(e)s, ^e) m rod; (Gitterstab) bar; (Menschen) staff; **~hochsprung** m pole vault

stabil [ʃtaˈbiːl] adj stable; (Möbel) sturdy; **~isieren** vt to stabilize

Stachel ['ʃtaxəl] (-s, -n) m spike; (von Tier) spine; (von Insekten) sting; **~beere** f gooseberry; **~draht** m barbed wire; **s~ig** adj prickly; **~schwein** nt porcupine

Stadion ['ʃtaːdiɔn] (-s, Stadien) nt stadium

Stadium ['ʃtaːdiʊm] nt stage, phase

Stadt [ʃtat] (-, ^e) f town; **~autobahn** f urban motorway; **~bahn** f suburban railway; **~bücherei** f municipal library

Städt- ['ʃtɛːt] zW: **~ebau** m town planning; **~epartnerschaft** f town twinning; **~er(in)** (-s, -) m(f) town dweller; **s~isch** adj municipal; (nicht ländlich) urban

Stadt- zW: **~kern** m town centre, city centre; **~mauer** f city wall(s); **~mitte** f town centre; **~plan** m street map; **~rand** m outskirts pl; **~rat** m (Behörde) town council, city council; **~rundfahrt** f tour of a/the city; **~teil** m district, part of town; **~zentrum** nt town centre

Staffel ['ʃtafəl] (-, -n) f rung; (SPORT) relay (team); (AVIAT) squadron; **~lauf** m (SPORT) relay (race); **s~n** vt to graduate

Stahl [ʃtaːl] (-(e)s, ^e) m steel

stahl etc vb siehe **stehlen**

stak etc [ʃtaːk] vb siehe **stecken**

Stall [ʃtal] (-(e)s, ^e) m stable; (Kaninchenstall) hutch; (Schweinestall) sty; (Hühnerstall) henhouse

Stamm [ʃtam] (-(e)s, ^e) m (Baumstamm) trunk; (Menschenstamm) tribe; (GRAM) stem; **~baum** m family tree; (von Tier) pedigree; **s~eln** vt, vi to stammer; **s~en von** od **aus** to come from; **~gast** m regular (customer)

stämmig ['ʃtɛmɪç] adj sturdy; (Mensch) stocky

Stammtisch ['ʃtamtɪʃ] m table for the regulars

stampfen ['ʃtampfən] vt, vi to stamp; (stapfen) to tramp; (mit Werkzeug) to pound

Stand [ʃtant] (-(e)s, ^e) m position; (Wasserstand, Benzinstand etc) level; (Stehen) standing position; (Zustand) state; (Spielstand) score; (Messestand etc) stand; (Klasse) class; (Beruf) profession; siehe **imstande**, **zustande**

stand etc vb siehe **stehen**

Standard ['ʃtandart] (-s, -s) m standard

Ständer ['ʃtɛndɐ] (-s, -) m stand

Standes- ['ʃtandəs] zW: **~amt** nt registry office; **~beamte(r)** m registrar; **s~gemäß** adj, adv according to one's social position; **~unterschied** m social difference

Stand- zW: **s~haft** adj steadfast; **s~halten** (unreg) vi: (jdm/etw) **s~halten** to stand firm (against sb/ sth), to resist (sb/sth)

ständig ['ʃtɛndɪç] adj permanent; (ununterbrochen) constant, continual

Stand- zW: **s~licht** nt sidelights pl, parking lights pl (US); **~ort** m location; (MIL) garrison; **~punkt** m standpoint; **~spur** f hard shoulder

Stange ['ʃtaŋə] f stick; (Stab) pole, bar; rod; (Zigaretten) carton; **von der ~** (COMM) off the peg; **eine ~ Geld** (umg) quite a packet

Stängel ▲ ['ʃtɛŋəl] (-s, -) m stalk

Stapel ['ʃtaːpəl] (-s, -) m pile; (NAUT) stocks pl; **~lauf** m launch; **s~n** vt to pile (up)

Star¹ [ʃtaːr] (-(e)s, -e) m starling; (MED) cataract

Star² [ʃtaːr] (-s, -s) m (Filmstar etc) star

starb etc [ʃtarp] vb siehe **sterben**

stark [ʃtark] adj strong; (heftig, groß) heavy; (Maßangabe) thick

Stärke ['ʃtɛrkə] f strength; heaviness; thickness; (KOCH: Wäschestärke) starch; **s~n** vt to strengthen; (Wäsche) to starch

Starkstrom m heavy current

Stärkung ['ʃtɛrkʊŋ] f strengthening; (Essen) refreshment

starr [ʃtar] adj stiff; (unnachgiebig) rigid; (Blick) staring; **~en** vi to stare; **~en vor** od **von** to be covered in; (Waffen) to be bristling with; **S~heit** f rigidity; **~köpfig** adj stubborn; **S~sinn** m obstinacy

Start [ʃtart] (-(e)s, -e) m start; (AVIAT) takeoff; **~automatik** f (AUT) automatic choke; **~bahn** f runway; **s~en** vt to start ♦ vi to start; to take off; **~er** (-s,

-) m starter; **~erlaubnis** f takeoff clearance; **~hilfekabel** nt jump leads pl

Station [ʃtatsi'oːn] f station; hospital ward; **s~är** [-'nɛːr] adj (MED) inpatient attr; **s~ieren** [-'niːrən] vt to station

Statist [ʃta'tɪst] m extra, supernumerary

Statistik f statistics sg; **~er** (-s, -) m statistician

statistisch adj statistical

Stativ [ʃta'tiːf] (-s, -e) nt tripod

statt [ʃtat] konj instead of ♦ präp (+gen od dat) instead of

Stätte ['ʃtɛtə] f place

statt- zW: **s~finden** (unreg) vi to take place; (Menschen) imposing, handsome

Statue ['ʃtaːtuə] f statue

Status ['ʃtaːtos] (-, -) m status

Stau [ʃtao] (-(e)s, -e) m blockage; (Verkehrsstau) (traffic) jam

Staub [ʃtaop] (-(e)s) m dust; **~ saugen** to vacuum, to hoover®; **s~en** ['ʃtaobən] vi to be dusty; **s~ig** adj dusty; **s~saugen** vi to vacuum, to hoover®; **~sauger** m vacuum cleaner; **~tuch** nt duster

Staudamm m dam

Staude ['ʃtaodə] f shrub

stauen ['ʃtaoən] vt (Wasser) to dam up; (Blut) to stop the flow of ♦ vr (Wasser) to become dammed up; (MED: Verkehr) to become congested; (Menschen) to collect; (Gefühle) to build up

staunen ['ʃtaonən] vi to be astonished; **S~** (-s) nt amazement

Stausee ['ʃtaozeː] (-s, -en) m reservoir, man-made lake

Stauung ['ʃtaoʊŋ] f (von Wasser) damming-up; (von Blut, Verkehr) congestion

Std. abk (= Stunde) hr.

Steak [ʃteːk] nt steak

Stech- ['ʃtɛç] zW: **s~en** (unreg) vt (mit Nadel etc) to prick; (mit Messer) to stab; (mit Finger) to poke; (Biene etc)

sting; (*Mücke*) to bite; (*Sonne*) to burn; (*KARTEN*) to take; (*ART*) to engrave; (*Torf, Spargel*) to cut; **in See s~en** to put to sea; **~en (-s, -)** nt (*SPORT*) play-off; jump-off; **s~end** *adj* piercing, stabbing; (*Geruch*) pungent; **~palme** *f* holly; **~uhr** *f* time clock

Steck- ['ʃtɛk] *zW*: **~brief** *m* "wanted" poster; **~dose** *f* (*wall*) socket; **s~en** *vt* to put, to insert; (*Nadel*) to stick; (*Pflanzen*) to plant; (*beim Nähen*) to pin ♦ *vi* (*auch unreg*) to be; (*festsitzen*) to be stuck; (*Nadeln*) to stick; **s~en bleiben** to get stuck; **s~en lassen** to leave in; **~enpferd** *nt* hobby-horse; **~er (-s, -)** *m* plug; **~nadel** *f* pin

Steg [ʃteːk] **(-(e)s, -e)** *m* small bridge; (*Anlegesteg*) landing stage; **~reif** *m*: **aus dem ~reif** just like that

stehen ['ʃteːən] (*unreg*) *vi* to stand; (*sich befinden*) to be; (*in Zeitung*) to say; (*stillstehen*) to have stopped ♦ *vi unpers*: **es steht schlecht um jdn/etw** things are bad for sb/sth; (*zu*) **jdm/etw ~** to stand for sb/sth; **jdm ~** to suit sb; **wie stehts?** how are things?; (*SPORT*) what's the score?; **~ bleiben** to remain standing; (*Uhr*) to stop; (*Fehler*) to stay as it is; **~ lassen** to leave; (*Bart*) to grow

Stehlampe ['ʃteːlampə] *f* standard lamp

stehlen ['ʃteːlən] (*unreg*) *vt* to steal

Stehplatz ['ʃteːplats] *m* standing place

steif [ʃtaɪf] *adj* stiff; **S~heit** *f* stiffness

Steig- [ʃtaɪk] *zW*: **~bügel** *m* stirrup; **s~en** ['ʃtaɪɡən] (*unreg*) *vi* to rise; (*klettern*) to climb; **s~en in** +*akk/auf* +*akk* to get in/on; **s~ern** *vt* to raise; (*GRAM*) to compare ♦ *vi* (*Auktion*) to bid ♦ *vr* to increase; **~erung** *f* raising; (*GRAM*) comparison; **~ung** *f* incline, gradient, rise

steil [ʃtaɪl] *adj* steep; **S~küste** *f* steep coast; (*Klippen*) cliffs *pl*

Stein [ʃtaɪn] **(-(e)s, -e)** *m* stone; (*in Uhr*) jewel; **~bock** *m* (*ASTROL*) Capricorn; **~bruch** *m* quarry; **s~ern** *adj* (*made of*) stone; (*fig*) stony; **~gut** *nt* stoneware; **s~ig** [ʃtaɪnɪç] *adj* stony; **s~igen** *vt* to stone; (*vorgeben*) coal; **~zeit** *f* Stone Age

Stelle ['ʃtɛlə] *f* place; (*Arbeit*) post, job; (*Amt*) office; **an Ihrer/meiner ~** in your/my place; *siehe* **anstelle**

stellen *vt* to put; (*Uhr etc*) to set; (*zur Verfügung ~*) to supply; (*fassen: Dieb*) to apprehend ♦ *vr* (*sich aufstellen*) to stand; (*sich einfinden*) to present o.s.; (*bei Polizei*) to give o.s. up; (*vorgeben*) to pretend (to be); **sich zu etw ~** to have an opinion of sth

Stellen- *zW*: **~angebot** *nt* offer of a post; (*in Zeitung*) "vacancies"; **~anzeige** *f* job advertisement; **~gesuch** *nt* application for a post; **~vermittlung** *f* employment agency

Stell- *zW*: **~ung** *f* position; (*MIL*) line; **~ung nehmen zu** to comment on; **~ungnahme** *f* comment; **s~vertretend** *adj* deputy, acting; **~vertreter** *m* deputy

Stelze ['ʃtɛltsə] *f* stilt

stemmen ['ʃtɛmən] *vt* to lift (up); (*drücken*) to press; **sich ~ gegen** (*fig*) to resist, to oppose

Stempel ['ʃtɛmpəl] **(-s, -)** *m* stamp; (*BOT*) pistil; **~kissen** *nt* ink pad; **s~n** *vt* (*Briefmarke*) to cancel; **s~n gehen** (*umg*) to be on the dole

Stengel △ ['ʃtɛŋəl] **(-s, -)** *m* = **Stängel**

Steno- [ʃteno] *zW*: **~gramm** [-'ɡram] *nt* shorthand report; **~grafie** ▲ [-ɡra-'fiː] *f* shorthand; **s~grafieren** ▲ [-ɡra-'fiːrən] *vt*, *vi* to write in shorthand; **~typist(in)** [-ty'pɪst(ɪn)] *m(f)* shorthand typist

Stepp- ['ʃtɛp] *zW*: **~decke** *f* quilt; **~e** *f* prairie; steppe; **s~en** *vt* to stitch ♦ *vi* to tap-dance

Spelling Reform: ▲ *new spelling* △ *old spelling (to be phased out)*

Sterb- ['ſterb] zW: **~efall** m death; **~ehilfe** f euthanasia; **~en** (unreg) vi to die; **s~lich** ['ſterplıç] adj mortal; **~lichkeit** f mortality; **~lichkeitsziffer** f death rate

stereo- ['ſteːreo] in zW stereo(-); **S~anlage** f stereo (system); **~typ** [ſtereo'tyːp] adj stereotype

steril [ſteˈriːl] adj sterile; **~i'sieren** vt to sterilize; **S~i'sierung** f sterilization

Stern [ſtern] (-(e)s, -e) m star; **~bild** nt constellation; **~schnuppe** f meteor, falling star; **~stunde** f historic moment; **~zeichen** nt sign of the zodiac

stet [ſteːt] adj steady; **~ig** adj continual, continual; **~s** adv continually, always

Steuer¹ ['ſtɔyɐ] (-s, -) nt (NAUT) helm; (~ruder) rudder; (AUT) steering wheel

Steuer² ['ſtɔyɐ] (-, -n) f tax; **~berater(in)** m(f) tax consultant

Steuerbord (NAUT, AVIAT) starboard

Steuer- ['ſtɔyɐ] zW: **~erklärung** f tax return; **s~frei** adj tax-free; **~freibetrag** m tax allowance; **~klasse** f tax group; **~knüppel** m control column; (AVIAT, COMPUT) joystick; **~mann** (pl **-männer** od **-leute**) m helmsman; **s~n** vt, vi to steer; (Flugzeug) to pilot; (Entwicklung, Tonstärke) to control; **s~pflichtig** [-pflıçtıç] adj taxable; **~rad** nt steering wheel; **~ung** f (auch AUT) steering; piloting; control; (Vorrichtung) controls pl; **~zahler** (-s, -) m taxpayer

Steward ['ſtjuːɐt] (-s, -s) m steward; **~ess** ▲ ['ſtjuːɐdɛs] (-, -en) f stewardess; air hostess

Stich [ſtıç] (-(e)s, -e) m (Insektenstich) sting; (Messerstich) stab; (beim Nähen) stitch; (Färbung) tinge; (KARTEN) trick; (ART) engraving; **jdn im ~ lassen** to leave sb in the lurch; **s~eln** vi (fig) to jibe; **s~haltig** adj sound, tenable; **~probe** f spot check; **~straße** f cul-de-sac; **~wahl** f final ballot; **~wort** nt cue; (in Wörterbuch) headword; (für Vortrag) note

sticken ['ſtıkən] vt, vi to embroider

Sticke'rei f embroidery

stickig adj stuffy, close

Stickstoff m nitrogen

Stiefel ['ſtiːfəl] (-s, -) m boot

Stief- ['ſtiːf] in zW step

Stief- zW: **~kind** nt stepchild; (fig) Cinderella; **~mutter** f stepmother; **~mütterchen** nt pansy; **s~mütterlich** adj (fig): **jdn/etw s~mütterlich behandeln** to pay little attention to sb/sth; **~vater** m stepfather

stiehlst etc [ſtiːlst] vb siehe **stehlen**

Stiel [ſtiːl] (-(e)s, -e) m handle; (BOT) stalk

Stier [ſtiːɐ] (-(e)s, -e) m bull; (ASTROL) Taurus

stieren vi to stare

Stierkampf m bullfight

Stierkämpfer m bullfighter

Stift [ſtıft] (-(e)s, -e) m peg; (Nagel) tack; (Farbstift) crayon; (Bleistift) pencil ♦ nt (charitable) foundation; (ECCL) religious institution; **s~en** vt to found; (Unruhe) to cause; (spenden) to contribute; **~er(in)** (-s, -) m(f) founder; **~ung** f donation; (Organisation) foundation; **~zahn** m post crown

Stil [ſtiːl] (-(e)s, -e) m style

still [ſtıl] adj quiet; (unbewegt) still; (heimlich) secret; **S~er Ozean** Pacific; **~ halten** to keep still; **~ stehen** to stand still; **S~e** f stillness, quietness; **in aller S~e** quietly; **~en** vt to stop; (befriedigen) to satisfy; (Säugling) to breast-feed; **~legen** ▲ vt to close down; **~schweigen** (unreg) vi to be silent; **S~schweigen** nt silence; **~schweigend** adj silent; (Einverständnis) tacit ♦ adv silently; tacitly; **S~stand** m standstill

Stimm- [ſtım] zW: **~bänder** pl vocal cords; **s~berechtigt** adj entitled to vote; **~e** f voice; (Wahlstimme) vote; **~e** f voice nt (MUS) to tune ♦ vi to be right; **das s~te ihn traurig** that made him feel sad; **s~en für/gegen** to vote for/

against; **s~t so!** that's right; **~enmehrheit** *f* majority (of votes); **~enthaltung** *f* abstention; **~gabel** *f* tuning fork; **~recht** *nt* right to vote; **~ung** *f* mood; atmosphere; **s~ungsvoll** *adj* enjoyable; full of atmosphere; **~zettel** *m* ballot paper

stinken ['ʃtɪŋkən] (*unreg*) *vi* to stink

Stipendium [ʃti'pɛndiʊm] *nt* grant

stirbst *etc* [ʃtɪrpst] *vb siehe* **sterben**

Stirn [ʃtɪrn] (-, **-en**) *f* forehead, brow; (*Frechheit*) impudence; **~band** *nt* headband; **~höhle** *f* sinus

stöbern ['ʃtøbərn] *vi* to rummage

stochern ['stɔxərn] *vi* to poke (about)

Stock[1] [ʃtɔk] (**-(e)s, ⸚e**) *m* stick; (*BOT*) stock

Stock[2] [ʃtɔk] (**-(e)s, -** *od* **Stockwerke**) *m* storey

stocken *vi* to stop, to pause; **~d** *adj* halting

Stockung *f* stoppage

Stockwerk *nt* storey, floor

Stoff [ʃtɔf] (**-(e)s, -e**) *m* (*Gewebe*) material, cloth; (*Materie*) matter; (*von Buch etc*) subject (matter); **s~lich** *adj* material; **~tier** *nt* soft toy; **~wechsel** *m* metabolism

stöhnen ['ʃtøːnən] *vi* to groan

Stollen ['ʃtɔlən] (**-s, -**) *m* (*MIN*) gallery; (*KOCH*) *cake eaten at Christmas*; (*von Schuhen*) stud

stolpern ['ʃtɔlpərn] *vi* to stumble, to trip

Stolz [ʃtɔlts] (**-es**) *m* pride; **s~** *adj* proud; **s~ieren** [ʃtɔl'tsiːrən] *vi* to strut

stopfen ['ʃtɔpfən] *vt* (*hineinstopfen*) to stuff; (*voll stopfen*) to fill (up); (*nähen*) to darn ♦ *vi* (*MED*) to cause constipation

Stopfgarn *nt* darning thread

Stoppel ['ʃtɔpəl] (**-, -n**) *f* stubble

Stopp- ['ʃtɔp] *zW*: **s~en** *vt* to stop; (*mit Uhr*) to time ♦ *vi* to stop; **~schild** *nt* stop sign; **~uhr** *f* stopwatch

Stöpsel ['ʃtœpsəl] (**-s, -**) *m* plug; (*für Flaschen*) stopper

Storch [ʃtɔrç] (**-(e)s, ⸚e**) *m* stork

Stör- ['ʃtøːr] *zW*: **s~en** *vt* to disturb; (*behindern, RADIO*) to interfere with ♦ *vr*: **sich an etw** *dat* **s~en** to let sth bother one; **s~end** *adj* disturbing, annoying; **~enfried (-(e)s, -e)** *m* troublemaker

stornieren [ʃtɔr'niːrən] *vt* (*Auftrag*) to cancel; (*Buchung*) to reverse

Stornogebühr ['ʃtɔrno-] *f* cancellation fee

störrisch ['ʃtœrɪʃ] *adj* stubborn, perverse

Störung *f* disturbance; interference

Stoß [ʃtoːs] (**-es, ⸚e**) *m* (*Schub*) push; (*Schlag*) blow; knock; (*mit Schwert*) thrust; (*mit Fuß*) kick; (*Erdstoß*) shock; (*Haufen*) pile; **~dämpfer (-s, -)** *m* shock absorber; **s~en** (*unreg*) *vt* (*mit Druck*) to shove, to push; (*mit Schlag*) to knock, to bump; (*mit Fuß*) to kick; (*Schwert etc*) to thrust; (*anstoßen: Kopf etc*) to bump ♦ *vr* to get a knock ♦ *vi*: **s~en an** *od* **auf** *+akk* to bump into; (*finden*) to come across; (*angrenzen*) to be next to; **sich s~en an** *+dat* (*fig*) to take exception to; **~stange** *f* (*AUT*) bumper

stottern ['ʃtɔtərn] *vt, vi* to stutter

Str. *abk* (= *Straße*) St.

Straf- ['ʃtraːf] *zW*: **~anstalt** *f* penal institution; **~arbeit** *f* (*SCH*) punishment; lines *pl*; **s~bar** *adj* punishable; **~e** *f* punishment; (*JUR*) penalty; (*Gefängnisstrafe*) sentence; (*Geldstrafe*) fine; **s~en** *vt* to punish

straff [ʃtraf] *adj* tight; (*streng*) strict; (*Stil etc*) concise; (*Haltung*) erect; **~en** *vt* to tighten, to tauten

Strafgefangene(r) *f(m)* prisoner, convict

Strafgesetzbuch *nt* penal code

sträflich ['ʃtrɛːflɪç] *adj* criminal

Sträfling m convict

Straf- zW: **~porto** nt excess postage (charge); **~predigt** f telling-off; **~raum** m (SPORT) penalty area; **~recht** nt criminal law; **~stoß** m (SPORT) penalty (kick); **~tat** f punishable act; **~zettel** m ticket

Strahl [ʃtraːl] (-s, -en) m ray, beam; (Wasserstrahl) jet; **s~en** vi to radiate; (fig) to beam; **~ung** f radiation

Strähne ['ʃtrɛːnə] f strand

stramm [ʃtram] adj tight; (Haltung) erect; (Mensch) robust

strampeln ['ʃtrampəln] vi to kick (about), to fidget

Strand [ʃtrant] (-(e)s, ⸚e) m shore; (mit Sand) beach; **~bad** nt open-air swimming pool, lido; **s~en** ['ʃtrandən] vi to run aground; (fig: Mensch) to fail; **~gut** nt flotsam; **~korb** m beach chair

Strang [ʃtraŋ] (-(e)s, ⸚e) m cord, rope; (Bündel) skein

Strapaz- zW: **~e** [ʃtra'paːtsə] f strain, exertion; **s~ieren** [ʃtrapatsiːrən] vt (Material) to treat roughly, to punish; (Mensch, Kräfte) to wear out, to exhaust; **s~ierfähig** adj hard-wearing; **s~iös** [ʃtrapatsiːøːs] adj exhausting, tough

Straße ['ʃtraːsə] f street, road

Straßen- zW: **~bahn** f tram, streetcar (US); **~glätte** f slippery road surface; **~karte** f road map; **~kehrer** (-s, -) m roadsweeper; **~sperre** f roadblock; **~verkehr** m (road) traffic; **~verkehrs-ordnung** f highway code

Strateg- [ʃtra'teːg] zW: **~e** (-n, -n) m strategist; **~ie** [ʃtrate'giː] f strategy; **s~isch** adj strategic

sträuben ['ʃtrɔʏbən] vt to ruffle ♦ vr to bristle; (Mensch): **sich (gegen etw)** ~ to resist (sth)

Strauch [ʃtraux] (-(e)s, Sträucher) m bush, shrub

Strauß¹ [ʃtraus] (-es, Sträuße) m bunch; bouquet

Strauß² [ʃtraus] (-es, -e) m ostrich

Streb- [ʃtreːb] zW: **s~en** vi to strive, to endeavour; **s~en nach** to strive for; **~er** (-s, -) (pej) m pusher, climber; **~sam** (-s, -) swot (BRIT)

Strecke ['ʃtrɛkə] f stretch; (Entfernung) distance; (EISENB, MATH) line; **s~n** vt to stretch; (Waffen) to lay down; (KOCH) to eke out ♦ vr to stretch (o.s.)

Streich [ʃtraɪç] (-(e)s, -e) m trick, prank; (Hieb) blow; **s~eln** vt to stroke; **s~en** (unreg) vt (berühren) to stroke; (auftragen) to spread; (anmalen) to paint; (durchstreichen) to delete; (nicht genehmigen) to cancel ♦ vi (berühren) to brush; (schleichen) to prowl; **~holz** nt match; **~instrument** nt string instrument

Streif- ['ʃtraɪf] zW: **~e** f patrol; **s~en** vt (leicht berühren) to brush against, to graze; (Blick) to skim over; (Thema, Problem) to touch on; (abstreifen) to take off ♦ vi (gehen) to roam; **~en** (-s, -) m (Linie) stripe; (Stück) strip; (Film) film; **s~enwagen** m patrol car; **~schuss** ⸘ m graze, grazing shot; **~zug** m scouting trip

Streik [ʃtraɪk] (-(e)s, -s) m strike; **~brecher** (-s, -) m blackleg, strikebreaker; **s~en** vi to strike; **~posten** m (strike) picket

Streit [ʃtraɪt] (-(e)s, -e) m argument; dispute; **s~en** (unreg) vi, vr to argue; to dispute; **~frage** f point at issue; **s~ig** adj: **jdm etw ~ig machen** to dispute sb's right to sth; **~igkeiten** pl quarrel sg, dispute sg; **~kräfte** pl (MIL) armed forces

streng [ʃtrɛŋ] adj severe; (Lehrer, Maßnahme) strict; (Geruch etc) sharp; **~genommen** strictly speaking; **S~e** (-) f severity; strictness; sharpness; **~gläubig** adj orthodox, strict; **~stens** adv strictly

Stress ⸘ (-es, -e) m stress

stressen vt to put under stress

streuen ['ʃtrɔʏən] vt to strew, to scatter, to spread

Strich [ʃtrɪç] (-(e)s, -e) m (Linie) line; (Federstrich, Pinselstrich) stroke; (von Geweben) nap; (von Fell) pile; **auf den ~ gehen** (umg) to walk the streets; **jdm gegen den ~ gehen** to rub sb up the wrong way; **einen ~ machen durch** to cross out; (fig) to foil; **~kode** m (auf Waren) bar code; **~mädchen** nt streetwalker; **s~weise** adv here and there

Strick [ʃtrɪk] (-(e)s, -e) m rope; **s~en** vt, vi to knit; **~jacke** f cardigan; **~leiter** f rope ladder; **~nadel** f knitting needle; **~waren** pl knitwear sg

strikt [strɪkt] adj strict

strittig [ʃtrɪtɪç] adj disputed, in dispute

Stroh [ʃtroː] (-(e)s, no pl) nt straw; **~blume** f everlasting flower; **~dach** nt thatched roof; **~halm** m (drinking) straw

Strom [ʃtroːm] (-(e)s, ⸚e) m river; (fig) stream; (ELEK) current; **s~abwärts** adv downstream; **s~aufwärts** adv upstream; **~ausfall** m power failure

strömen [ʃtrøːmən] vi to stream, to pour

Strom- zW: **~kreis** m circuit; **s~linienförmig** adj streamlined; **~sperre** f power cut

Strömung [ʃtrøːmʊŋ] f current

Strophe [ʃtroːfə] f verse

strotzen [ʃtrɔtsən] vi: **~ vor** or **von** to abound in, to be full of

Strudel [ʃtruːdəl] (-s, -) m whirlpool, vortex; (KOCH) strudel

Struktur [ʃtrʊktuːr] f structure

Strumpf [ʃtrʊmpf] (-(e)s, ⸚e) m stocking; **~band** nt garter; **~hose** f (pair of) tights

Stube [ʃtuːbə] f room

Stuben- zW: **~arrest** m confinement to one's room; (MIL) confinement to quarters; **~hocker** (umg) m stay-at-home; **s~rein** adj house-trained

Stuck [ʃtʊk] (-(e)s) m stucco

Stück [ʃtʏk] (-(e)s, -e) nt piece; (etwas)

bit; (THEAT) play; **~chen** nt little piece; **~lohn** m piecework wages pl; **s~weise** adv bit by bit, piecemeal; (COMM) individually

Student(in) [ʃtuˈdɛnt(ɪn)] m(f) student; **s~isch** adj student, academic

Studie [ʃtuːdiə] f study

Studienfahrt f study trip

studieren [ʃtuˈdiːrən] vt, vi to study

Studio [ʃtuːdio] (-s, -s) nt studio

Studium [ʃtuːdiom] nt studies pl

Stufe [ʃtuːfə] f step; (Entwicklungsstufe) stage; **s~nweise** adv gradually

Stuhl [ʃtuːl] (-(e)s, ⸚e) m chair; **~gang** m bowel movement

stülpen [ʃtʏlpən] vt (umdrehen) to turn upside down; (bedecken) to put on

stumm [ʃtʊm] adj silent; (MED) dumb

Stummel [ʃtʊməl] (-s, -) m stump; (Zigarettenstummel) stub

Stummfilm m silent film

Stümper [ʃtʏmpər] (-s, -) m incompetent, duffer; **s~haft** adj bungling, incompetent; **s~n** vi to bungle

Stumpf [ʃtʊmpf] (-(e)s, ⸚e) m stump; **s~** adj blunt; (teilnahmslos, glanzlos) dull; (Winkel) obtuse; **~sinn** m tediousness; **s~sinnig** adj dull

Stunde [ʃtʊndə] f hour; (SCH) lesson

stunden vt: **jdm etw ~** to give sb time to pay sth; **S~geschwindigkeit** f average speed per hour; **S~kilometer** pl kilometres per hour; **~lang** adj for hours; **S~lohn** m hourly wage; **S~plan** m timetable; **~weise** adv by the hour; every hour

stündlich [ʃtʏntlɪç] adj hourly

Stups [ʃtʊps] (-es, -e) (umg) m push; **~nase** f snub nose

stur [ʃtuːr] adj obstinate, pigheaded

Sturm [ʃtʊrm] (-(e)s, ⸚e) m storm, gale; (MIL etc) attack, assault

stürm- [ʃtʏrm] zW: **~en** vi (Wind) to blow hard, to rage; (rennen) to storm ♦ vt (MIL, fig) to storm ♦ vb unpers: **es ~t**

---

there's a gale blowing; **S~er** (-s, -) *m* (SPORT) forward, striker; **~isch** *adj* stormy

Sturmwarnung *f* gale warning

Sturz [ʃtʊrts] (-es, -e) *m* fall; (POL) overthrow

stürzen [ʃtʏrtsən] *vt* (werfen) to hurl; (POL) to overthrow; (umkehren) to overturn ♦ *vr* to rush; (hineinstürzen) to plunge ♦ *vi* to fall; (AVIAT) to dive; (rennen) to dash

Sturzflug *m* nose dive

Sturzhelm *m* crash helmet

Stute [ʃtuːtə] *f* mare

Stützbalken *m* brace, joist

Stütze [ʃtʏtsə] *f* support; help

stutzen [ʃtʊtsən] *vt* to trim; (Ohr, Schwanz) to dock; (Flügel) to clip ♦ *vi* to hesitate; to become suspicious

stützen *vt* (auch fig) to support; (Ellbogen etc) to prop up

stutzig *adj* perplexed, puzzled; (misstrauisch) suspicious

Stützpunkt *m* point of support; (von Hebel) fulcrum; (MIL, fig) base

Styropor [ʃtyro'poːr] (®; -s) *nt* polystyrene

s. u. *abk* = siehe unten

Subjekt [zʊp'jɛkt] (-(e)s, -e) *nt* subject; **s~iv** [-'tiːf] *adj* subjective; **~ivi'tät** *f* subjectivity

Subsidiarität *f* subsidiarity

Substantiv [zʊpstan'tiːf] (-s, -e) *nt* noun

Substanz [zʊp'stants] *f* substance

subtil [zʊp'tiːl] *adj* subtle

subtrahieren [zʊptra'hiːrən] *vt* to subtract

subtropisch [zʊptro'piːʃ] *adj* subtropical

Subvention [zʊpvɛntsi'oːn] *f* subsidy; **s~ieren** *vt* to subsidize

Such- [zuːx] *zW:* **~aktion** *f* search; **~e** *f* search; **s~en** *vt* to look (for), to seek; (versuchen) to try ♦ *vi* to seek, to search; **~er** (-s, -) *m* seeker, searcher; (PHOT) viewfinder

Sucht [zʊxt] (-, -e) *f* mania; (MED) addiction, craving

süchtig [zʏçtɪç] *adj* addicted; **S~e(r)** *f(m)* addict

Süd- [zyːt] *zW:* **~en** [zyːdən] (-s) *m* south; **~früchte** *pl* Mediterranean fruit *sg;* **s~lich** *adj* southern; **s~lich von** (to the) south of; **~pol** *m* South Pole; **s~wärts** *adv* southwards

süffig [zʏfɪç] *adj* (Wein) pleasant to the taste

süffisant [zʏfi'zant] *adj* smug

suggerieren [zʊge'riːrən] *vt* to suggest

Sühne [zyːnə] *f* atonement, expiation; **s~n** *vt* to atone for, to expiate

Sultan [zʊltan] (-s, -e) *m* sultan; **~ine** [zʊlta'niːnə] *f* sultana

Sülze [zʏltsə] *f* brawn

Summe [zʊmə] *f* sum, total

summen *vt, vi* to buzz; (Lied) to hum

Sumpf [zʊmpf] (-(e)s, -e) *m* swamp, marsh; **s~ig** *adj* marshy

Sünde [zʏndə] *f* sin; **~nbock** (umg) *m* scapegoat; **~r(in)** (-s, -) *m(f)* sinner; **sündigen** *vi* to sin

Super [zuːpər] (-s) *nt* (Benzin) four star (petrol) (BRIT), premium (US); **~lativ** [-latiːf] (-s, -e) *m* superlative; **~macht** *f* superpower; **~markt** *m* supermarket

Suppe [zʊpə] *f* soup; **~nteller** *m* soup plate

süß [zyːs] *adj* sweet; **S~e** (-) *f* sweetness; **~en** *vt* to sweeten; **S~igkeit** *f* sweetness; (Bonbon etc) sweet (BRIT), candy (US); **~lich** *adj* sweetish; (fig) sugary; **~sauer** *adj* sweet-and-sour; (Sauce etc) sweet-and-sour; **S~speise** *f* pudding, sweet; **S~stoff** *m* sweetener; **S~waren** *pl* confectionery (sing); **S~wasser** *nt* fresh water

Symbol [zʏm'boːl] (-s, -e) *nt* symbol; **s~isch** *adj* symbolic(al)

Symmetrie [zʏme'triː] *f* symmetry

symmetrisch [zʏ'meːtrɪʃ] *adj* symmetrical

Sympathie [zʏmpa'tiː] *f* liking, sym-

pathy; **sympathisch** [zym'pa:tɪʃ] *adj*
likeable; **er ist mir ~** I like him; **sympathisieren** *vi* to sympathize
Symphonie [zymfo'ni:] *f* (MUS)
symphony
Symptom [zymp'to:m] (-s, -e) *nt*
symptom; **s~atisch** [zymp'to'ma:tɪʃ]
adj symptomatic
Synagoge [zyna'go:gə] *f* synagogue
synchron [zyn'kro:n] *adj* synchronous;
~i'sieren *vt* to synchronize; (Film) to
dub
Synonym [zyno'ny:m] (-s, -e) *nt* synonym; **s~** *adj* synonymous
Synthese [zyn'te:zə] *f* synthesis
synthetisch *adj* synthetic
System [zys'te:m] (-s, -e) *nt* system;
s~atisch [zyste'ma:tɪʃ] *adj* systematic; **s~ati'sieren**
vt to systematize
Szene ['stse:nə] *f* scene; **~rie**
[stsenə'ri:] *f* scenery

T, t

t *abk* (= Tonne) t
Tabak ['ta:bak] (-s, -e) *m* tobacco
Tabell- [ta'bɛl] *zW:* **t~arisch**
[tabe'la:rɪʃ] *adj* tabular; **~e** *f* table
Tablett [ta'blɛt] *nt* tray; **~e** *f* tablet, pill
Tabu [ta'bu:] *nt* taboo; **t~** *adj* taboo
Tachometer [taxo'me:tər] (-s, -) *m*
(AUT) speedometer
Tadel ['ta:dəl] (-s, -) *m* censure; scolding; (Fehler) fault, blemish; **t~los** *adj*
faultless, irreproachable; **t~n** *vt* to
scold
Tafel ['ta:fəl] (-, -n) *f* (auch MATH) table;
(Anschlagtafel) board; (Wandtafel)
blackboard; (Schiefertafel) slate; (Gedenktafel) plaque; (Illustration) plate;
(Schalttafel) panel; (Schokolade etc) bar
Tag [ta:k] (-(e)s, -e) *m* day; daylight;
unter/über ~ (MIN) underground/on
the surface; **an den ~ kommen** to

come to light; **guten ~!** good
morning/afternoon!; *siehe* zutage;
t~aus *adv:* **t~aus, ~ein** day in, day
out; **~dienst** *m* day duty
Tage- ['ta:gə] *zW:* **~buch** ['ta:gəbu:x]
nt diary, journal; **~geld** *nt* daily allowance; **t~lang** *adv* for days; **t~n** *vi* to
sit, to meet ♦ *vb unpers:* **es tagt** dawn
is breaking
Tages- *zW:* **~ablauf** *m* course of the
day; **~anbruch** *m* dawn; **~fahrt** *f* day
trip; **~karte** *f* menu of the day; (Fahrkarte) day ticket; **~licht** *nt* daylight;
~ordnung *f* agenda; **~zeit** *f* time of
day; **~zeitung** *f* daily (paper)
täglich ['tɛ:klɪç] *adj, adv* daily
tagsüber ['ta:ksy:bər] *adv* during the
day
Tagung *f* conference
Taille ['taljə] *f* waist
Takt [takt] (-(e)s, -e) *m* tact; (MUS)
time; **~gefühl** *nt* tact
Taktik [taktɪk] *f* tactics *pl*; **taktisch** *adj* tactical
Takt- *zW:* **t~los** *adj* tactless; **~losigkeit**
f tactlessness; **~stock** *m* (conductor's)
baton; **t~voll** *adj* tactful
Tal [ta:l] (-(e)s, ¨er) *nt* valley
Talent [ta'lɛnt] (-(e)s, -e) *nt* talent;
t~iert [talɛn'ti:rt] *adj* talented, gifted
Talisman ['ta:lɪsman] (-s, -e) *m* talisman
Talsohle *f* bottom of a valley
Talsperre *f* dam
Tampon ['tampɔn] (-s, -s) *m* tampon
Tandem [tandɛm] (-s, -s) *nt* tandem
Tang [taŋ] (-(e)s, -e) *m* seaweed
Tank [taŋk] (-s, -s) *m* tank; **~anzeige** *f*
fuel gauge; **t~en** *vi* to fill up with
petrol (BRIT) od gas (US); (AVIAT) to
refuel; **~er** (-s, -) *m* tanker; **~schiff** *nt*
tanker; **~stelle** *f* petrol (BRIT) od gas
(US) station; **~wart** *m* petrol pump
(BRIT) od gas station (US) attendant
Tanne ['tanə] *f* fir
Tannen- *zW:* **~baum** *m* fir tree; **~zap-**

fen m fir cone

Tante ['tantə] f aunt

Tanz [tants] m (-es, ⸚e) m dance; **t~en** m, vi to dance

Tänzer(in) ['tɛntsər(ɪn)] m (-s, -) m(f) dancer

Tanzfläche f (dance) floor

Tanzschule f dancing school

Tapete [ta'pe:tə] f wallpaper; **~nwechsel** m (fig) change of scenery

tapezieren [tape'tsi:rən] vt to (wall)paper; **Tapezierer** [tape'tsi:rər] (-s, -) m (interior) decorator

tapfer ['tapfər] adj brave; **T~keit** f courage, bravery

Tarif [ta'ri:f] (-s, -e) m tariff, (scale of) fares od charges; **~lohn** m standard wage rate; **~verhandlungen** pl wage negotiations; **~zone** f fare zone

Tarn- ['tarn] zW: **t~en** vt to camouflage; (Person, Absicht) to disguise; **~ung** f camouflaging; disguising

Tasche ['taʃə] f pocket; handbag

Taschen- in zW pocket; **~buch** nt paperback; **~dieb** m pickpocket; **~geld** nt pocket money; **~lampe** f (electric) torch, flashlight (US); **~messer** nt penknife; **~tuch** nt handkerchief

Tasse ['tasə] f cup

Tastatur [tasta'tu:r] f keyboard

Taste ['tastə] f push-button control; (an Schreibmaschine) key; **t~n** vt to feel, to touch ♦ vi to feel, to grope ♦ vr to feel one's way

Tat [ta:t] (-, -en) f act, deed, action; **in der ~** indeed, as a matter of fact; **t** etc vb siehe **tun**; **~bestand** m facts pl of the case; **t~enlos** adj inactive

Tät- ['tɛ:t] zW: **~er(in)** (-s, -) m(f) perpetrator, culprit; **t~ig** adj active; **in einer Firma t~ig sein** to work for a firm; **~igkeit** f activity; (Beruf) occupation; **t~lich** adj violent; **~lichkeit** f violence; **~lichkeiten** pl (Schläge) blows

tätowieren [teto'vi:rən] vt to tattoo

Tatsache f fact

tatsächlich adj actual ♦ adv really

Tau¹ [tau] (-(e)s, -e) nt rope

Tau² [tau] (-(e)s) m dew

taub [taup] adj deaf; (Nuss) hollow

Taube ['taubə] f dove; pigeon; **~nschlag** m dovecote; **hier geht es zu wie in einem ~nschlag** it's a hive of activity here

taub- zW: **T~heit** f deafness; **~stumm** adj deaf-and-dumb

Tauch- [taux] zW: **t~en** vt to dip ♦ vi to dive; (NAUT) to submerge; **~er** (-s, -) m diver; **~eranzug** m diving suit; **~erbrille** f diving goggles pl; **~sieder** (-s, -) m immersion coil (for boiling water)

tauen ['tauən] vt, vi to thaw ♦ vb unpers: **es taut** it's thawing

Tauf- ['tauf] zW: **~becken** nt font; **~e** f baptism; **t~en** vt to christen, to baptize; **~pate** m godfather; **~patin** f godmother; **~schein** m certificate of baptism

taug- ['taug] zW: **~en** vi to be of use; **~en für** to do for, to be good for; **nicht ~en** to be no good od useless; **T~enichts** (-es, -e) m good-for-nothing; **~lich** ['tauklɪç] adj suitable; (MIL) fit (for service)

Taumel ['tauməl] (-s) m dizziness; (fig) frenzy; **t~n** vi to reel, to stagger

Tausch [tauʃ] (-(e)s, -e) m exchange; **t~en** vt to exchange, to swap

täuschen ['tɔyʃən] vt to deceive ♦ vi to be deceptive ♦ vr to be wrong; **~d** adj deceptive

Tauschhandel m barter

Täuschung f deception; (optisch) illusion

tausend ['tauzənt] num (a) thousand

Tauwetter nt thaw

Taxi ['taksi] (-s, -(s)) nt taxi; **~fahrer** m taxi driver; **~stand** m taxi rank

Tech- ['tɛç] zW: **~nik** f technology; (Methode, Kunstfertigkeit) technique; **~niker** (-s, -) m technician; **t~nisch** adj technical; **~nolo'gie** f technology; **t~no'logisch** adj technological

Tee [te:] (-s, -s) m tea; **~beutel** m tea

bag; **~kanne** f teapot; **~löffel** m tea-spoon

Teer [teːr] (-(e)s, -e) m tar; **t~en** vt to tar

Teesieb nt tea strainer

Teich [taɪç] (-(e)s, -e) m pond

Teig [taɪk] (-(e)s, -e) m dough; **t~ig** ['taɪgɪç] adj doughy; **~waren** pl pasta sg

Teil [taɪl] (-(e)s, -e) m od nt part; (Anteil) share; (Bestandteil) component; **zum ~** partly; **t~bar** adj divisible; **t~betrag** m instalment; **~chen** nt (atomic) particle; **t~en** vt, vi to divide; (mit jdm) to share; **t~haben** (unreg) vi: **t~haben an** +dat to share in; **~haber** (-s, -) m partner; **~kaskoversicherung** f third party, fire and theft insurance; **t~möbliert** adj partially furnished; **~nahme** f participation; (Mitleid) sympathy; **t~nahmslos** adj disinterested, apathetic; **t~nehmen** (unreg) vi: **t~nehmen an** +dat to take part in; **~nehmer** (-s, -) m participant; **t~s** adv partly; **~ung** f division; **t~weise** adv partially, in part; **~zahlung** f payment by instalments; **~zeitarbeit** f part-time work

Teint [tɛ̃ː] (-s, -s) m complexion

Telearbeit ['teːlɐarbaɪt] f teleworking

Telefax ['teːlefaks] nt fax

Telefon [tele'foːn] (-s, -e) nt telephone; **~anruf** m (tele)phone call; **~at** [telefo'naːt] (-(e)s, -e) nt (tele)phone call; **~buch** nt telephone directory; **~hörer** m (telephone) receiver; **t~ieren** vi to telephone; **t~isch** [-ʃ] adj telephone; (Benachrichtigung) by telephone; **~ist(in)** [telefo'nɪst(ɪn)] m(f) telephonist; **~karte** f phonecard; **~nummer** f (tele)phone number; **~zelle** f telephone kiosk, callbox; **~zentrale** f telephone exchange

Telegraf [tele'graːf] (-en, -en) m telegraph; **~enmast** m telegraph pole;

~ie [-'fiː] f telegraphy; **t~ieren** [-'fiːrən] vt, vi to telegraph, to wire

Telegramm [tele'gram] (-s, -e) nt telegram, cable; **~adresse** f telegraphic address

Tele- zW: **~objektiv** ['teːlɛʔɔpjɛktiːf] nt telephoto lens; **t~pathisch** [tele'paːtɪʃ] adj telepathic; **~skop** [tele'skoːp] (-s, -e) nt telescope

Teller ['telɐ] (-s, -) m plate; **~gericht** nt (KOCH) one-course meal

Tempel ['tempəl] (-s, -) m temple

Temperament [tempera'ment] nt temperament; (Schwung) vivacity, liveliness; **t~voll** adj high-spirited, lively

Temperatur [tempera'tuːr] f temperature

Tempo¹ ['tempo] (-s, Tempi) nt (MUS) time

Tempo² ['tempo] (-s, -s) nt speed, pace; **~!** get a move on!; **~limit** [-limɪt] (-s, -s) nt speed limit; **~taschentuch** ® nt tissue

Tendenz [ten'dents] f tendency; (Absicht) intention; **t~iös** [-i'øːs] adj biased, tendentious

tendieren [ten'diːrən] vi: **~ zu** to show a tendency to, to incline towards

Tennis ['tenɪs] (-) nt tennis; **~ball** m tennis ball; **~platz** m tennis court; **~schläger** m tennis racket; **~schuh** m tennis shoe; **~spieler(in)** m(f) tennis player

Tenor [te'noːr] (-s, ⁺e) m tenor

Teppich ['tepɪç] (-s, -e) m carpet; **~boden** m wall-to-wall carpeting

Termin [tɛr'miːn] (-s, -e) m (Zeitpunkt) date; (Frist) time limit, deadline; (Arzttermin etc) appointment; **~kalender** m diary, appointments book; **~planer** m personal organizer

Terrasse [tɛ'rasə] f terrace

Terrine [tɛ'riːnə] f tureen

territorial [tɛritori'aːl] adj territorial

Territorium [tɛri'toːriʊm] nt territory

Spelling Reform: ▲ *new spelling* △ *old spelling (to be phased out)*

Terror ['tɛrɔr] (-s) *m* terror; reign of terror; **t~isieren** [tɛrori'ziːrən] *vt* to terrorize; **t~ismus** [-'rɪsmʊs] *m* terrorism; **~ist** [-'rɪst] *m* terrorist

Tesafilm ['tezafɪlm] ® *m* Sellotape ® (BRIT), Scotch tape ® (US)

Tessin [tɛ'siːn] (-s) *nt*: **das ~** Ticino

Test [tɛst] (-s, -s) *m* test

Testament [tɛsta'mɛnt] *nt* will, testament; (REL) Testament; **t~arisch** [-'taːrɪʃ] *adj* testamentary

Testamentsvollstrecker *m* executor (of a will)

testen *vt* to test

Tetanus ['teːtanʊs] (-) *m* tetanus; **~impfung** *f* (anti-)tetanus injection

teuer ['tɔyər] *adj* dear, expensive; **T~ung** *f* increase in prices; **T~ungszulage** *f* cost of living bonus

Teufel ['tɔyfəl] (-s, -) *m* devil; **teuflisch** ['tɔyflɪʃ] *adj* fiendish, diabolical

Text [tɛkst] (-(e)s, -e) *m* text; (Liedertext) words *pl*; **t~en** *vi* to write the words

textil [tɛks'tiːl] *adj* textile; **T~ien** *pl* textiles; **T~industrie** *f* textile industry; **T~waren** *pl* textiles

Textverarbeitung *f* word processing

Theater [te'aːtər] (-s, -) *nt* theatre; (umg) fuss; **~ spielen** (auch fig) to playact; **~besucher** *m* playgoer; **~kasse** *f* box office; **~stück** *nt* (stage) play

Theke ['teːkə] *f* (Schanktisch) bar; (Ladentisch) counter

Thema ['teːma] (-s, Themen od -ta) *nt* theme, topic, subject

Themse ['tɛmzə] *f* Thames

Theo- [teo] *zW*: **~loge** [-'loːgə] (-n, -n) *m* theologian; **~logie** [-lo'giː] *f* theology; **t~logisch** [-'loːgɪʃ] *adj* theological; **~retiker** [-'reːtikər] (-s, -) *m* theorist; **t~retisch** [-'reːtɪʃ] *adj* theoretical; **~rie** [-'riː] *f* theory

Thera- [tera] *zW*: **~peut** [-'pɔyt] (-en, -en) *m* therapist; **t~peutisch** [-'pɔytɪʃ] *adj* therapeutic; **~pie** [-'piː] *f* therapy

Therm- *zW*: **~albad** [tɛr'maːlbaːt] *nt* thermal bath; thermal spa; **~odrucker** [tɛrmo-] *m* thermal printer; **~ometer** [tɛrmo'meːtər] (-s, -) *nt* thermometer; **~osflasche** ['tɛrmɔsflaʃə] ® *f* Thermos ® flask

These ['teːzə] *f* thesis

Thrombose [trɔm'boːzə] *f* thrombosis

Thron [troːn] (-(e)s, -e) *m* throne; **t~en** *vi* to sit enthroned; (fig) to sit in state; **~folge** *f* succession (to the throne); **~folger(in)** (-s, -) *m(f)* heir to the throne

Thunfisch ['tuːnfɪʃ] *m* tuna

Thüringen ['tyːrɪŋən] (-s) *nt* Thuringia

Thymian ['tyːmiaːn] (-s) *m* thyme

Tick [tɪk] (-(e)s, -s) *m* tic; (Eigenart) quirk; (Fimmel) craze

ticken *vi* to tick

tief [tiːf] *adj* deep; (-sinnig) profound; (Ausschnitt, Preis, Ton) low; **~ greifend** far-reaching; **t~ schürfend** profound; **T~** (-s, -s) *nt* (MET) depression; **T~druck** *m* low pressure; **T~e** *f* depth; **T~ebene** *f* plain; **T~enschärfe** *f* (PHOT) depth of focus; **T~garage** *f* underground garage; **~gekühlt** *adj* frozen; **T~kühlfach** *nt* deepfreeze compartment; **T~kühlkost** *f* (deep) frozen food; **T~kühltruhe** *f* deep-freeze, freezer; **T~punkt** *m* low point; (fig) low ebb; **T~schlag** *m* (BOXEN, fig) blow below the belt; **T~see** *f* deep sea; **~sinnig** *adj* profound; melancholy; **T~stand** *m* low level; **T~stwert** *m* minimum od lowest value

Tier [tiːr] (-(e)s, -e) *nt* animal; **~arzt** *m* vet(erinary surgeon); **~garten** *m* zoo(logical gardens pl); **~heim** *nt* cat/dog home; **t~isch** *adj* animal; (auch fig) brutish; (fig: Ernst etc) deadly; **~kreis** *m* zodiac; **~kunde** *f* zoology; **t~liebend** *adj* fond of animals; **~park** *m* zoo; **~quälerei** *f* cruelty to animals; **~schutzverein** *m* society for the prevention of cruelty to animals

Tiger(in) ['tiːgər(ɪn)] (-s, -) m(f) tiger (-gress)

tilgen ['tɪlgən] vt to erase; (Sünden) to expiate; (Schulden) to pay off

Tinte ['tɪntə] f ink

Tintenfisch m cuttlefish

Tipp ▲ [tɪp] m tip; t~en vt, vi to tap, to touch; (umg: schreiben) to type; (im Lotto etc) to bet (on); auf jdn t~en (umg: raten) to tip sb, to put one's money on sb (fig)

Tipp- ['tɪp] zW: ~fehler (umg) m typing error; t~topp (umg) adj tip-top; ~zettel m (pools) coupon

Tirol [tiˈroːl] nt the Tyrol; ~er(in) m(f) Tyrolean; t~isch adj Tyrolean

Tisch [tɪʃ] (-(e)s, -e) m table; bei ~ at table; vor/nach ~ before/after eating; unter den ~ fallen (fig) to be dropped; ~decke f tablecloth; ~ler (-s, -) m carpenter, joiner; ~le'rei f joiner's workshop; (Arbeit) carpentry, joinery; t~lern vi to do carpentry etc; ~rede f after-dinner speech; ~tennis nt table tennis; ~tuch nt tablecloth

Titel ['tiːtəl] (-s, -) m title; ~bild nt cover (picture); (von Buch) frontispiece; ~rolle f title role; ~seite f cover; (Buchtitelseite) title page; ~verteidiger m defending champion, title holder

Toast [toːst] (-(e)s, -e od -s) m toast; ~brot nt bread for toasting; ~er (-s, -) m toaster

tob- ['toːb] zW: ~en vi to rage; (Kinder) to romp about; ~süchtig adj maniacal

Tochter ['tɔxtar] (-, ¨) f daughter; ~gesellschaft f subsidiary (company)

Tod [toːt] (-(e)s, -e) m death; t~ernst adj deadly serious ♦ adv in dead earnest

Todes- ['toːdəs] zW: ~angst [-aŋst] f mortal fear; ~anzeige f obituary (notice); ~fall m death; ~strafe f death penalty; ~ursache f cause of death; ~urteil nt death sentence; ~verach-

tung f utter disgust

todkrank adj dangerously ill

tödlich ['tøːtlɪç] adj deadly, fatal

tod- zW: ~müde adj dead tired; ~schick (umg) adj smart, classy; ~sicher (umg) adj absolutely od dead certain; T~sünde f deadly sin

Toilette [toaˈletə] f toilet, lavatory; (Frisiertisch) dressing table

Toiletten- zW: ~artikel pl toiletries, toilet articles; ~papier nt toilet paper; ~tisch m dressing table

toi, toi, toi ['tɔyˈtɔyˈtɔy] excl touch wood

tolerant [toleˈrant] adj tolerant

Toleranz [toleˈrants] f tolerance

tolerieren [toleˈriːrən] vt to tolerate

toll [tɔl] adj mad; (Treiben) wild; (umg) terrific; ~en vi to romp; T~kirsche f deadly nightshade; ~kühn adj daring; T~wut f rabies

Tomate [toˈmaːtə] f tomato; ~nmark nt tomato purée

Ton¹ [toːn] (-(e)s, -e) m (Erde) clay

Ton² [toːn] (-(e)s, ¨e) m (Laut) sound; (MUS) note; (Redeweise) tone; (Farbton, Nuance) shade; (Betonung) stress; t~angebend adj leading; ~art f (musical) key; ~band nt tape; ~bandgerät nt tape recorder

tönen ['tøːnən] vi to sound ♦ vt to shade; (Haare) to tint

tönern ['tøːnərn] adj clay

Ton- zW: ~fall m intonation; ~film m sound film; ~leiter f (MUS) scale; t~los adj soundless

Tonne ['tɔnə] f barrel; (Maß) ton

Ton- zW: ~taube f clay pigeon; ~waren pl pottery sg, earthenware sg

Topf [tɔpf] (-(e)s, ¨e) m pot; ~blume f pot plant

Töpfer ['tœpfar] (-s, -) m potter; ~ei [-'raɪ] f piece of pottery; potter's workshop; ~scheibe f potter's wheel

topografisch ▲ [topoˈgraːfɪʃ] adj

topographic

Tor¹ [toːr] (-en, -en) *m* fool

Tor² [toːr] (-(e)s, -e) *nt* gate; (SPORT) goal; **~bogen** *m* archway

Torf [tɔrf] (-(e)s) *m* peat

Torheit *f* foolishness; foolish deed

töricht ['tøːrɪçt] *adj* foolish

torkeln ['tɔrkəln] *vi* to stagger, to reel

Torte ['tɔrtə] *f* cake; (Obsttorte) flan, tart

Tortur [tɔr'tuːr] *f* ordeal

Torwart (-(e)s, -e) *m* goalkeeper

tosen ['toːzən] *vi* to roar

tot [toːt] *adj* dead; **~ geboren** stillborn; **sich ~ stellen** to pretend to be dead

total [to'taːl] *adj* total; **~itär** [totali'tɛːr] *adj* totalitarian; **T~schaden** *m* (AUT) complete write-off

Tote(r) *f(m)* dead person

töten ['tøːtən] *vt, vi* to kill

Toten- *zW:* **~bett** *nt* death bed; **t~blass ▲** *adj* deathly pale, white as a sheet; **~kopf** *m* skull; **~schein** *m* death certificate; **~stille** *f* deathly silence

tot- *zW:* **~fahren** (unreg) *vt* to run over; **~geboren** △ *adj* siehe **tot**; **~lachen** (umg) *vr* to laugh one's head off

Toto ['toːto] (-s, -s) *m od nt* pools *pl*; **~schein** *m* pools coupon

tot- *zW:* **T~schlag** *m* manslaughter; **~schlagen** (unreg) *vt* (auch fig) to kill; **~schweigen** (unreg) *vt* to hush up; **~stellen** △ *vr* siehe **tot**

Tötung ['tøːtʊŋ] *f* killing

Toupet [tu'peː] (-s, -s) *nt* toupee

toupieren [tu'piːrən] *vt* to backcomb

Tour [tuːr] (-, -en) *f* tour, trip; (Umdrehung) revolution; (Verhaltensart) way; **in einer ~** incessantly; **~enzähler** *m* rev counter; **~ismus** [tu'rɪsmʊs] *m* tourism; **~ist** [tu'rɪst] *m* tourist; **~istenklasse** *f* tourist class; **~nee** [tʊr'neː] (-, -n) *f* (THEAT *etc*) tour; **auf ~nee gehen** to go on tour

Trab [traːp] (-(e)s) *m* trot

Trabantenstadt *f* satellite town

traben ['traːbən] *vi* to trot

Tracht [traxt] (-, -en) *f* (Kleidung) costume, dress; **eine ~ Prügel** a sound thrashing; **t~en** *vi* (nach) to strive (for); **jdm nach dem Leben t~en** to seek to kill sb; **danach t~en, etw zu tun** to strive *od* endeavour to do sth

trächtig ['trɛçtɪç] *adj* (Tier) pregnant

Tradition [traditsi'oːn] *f* tradition; **t~ell** [-'nɛl] *adj* traditional

traf *etc* [traːf] *vb* siehe **treffen**

Tragbahre *f* stretcher

tragbar *adj* (Gerät) portable; (Kleidung) wearable; (erträglich) bearable

träge ['trɛːgə] *adj* sluggish, slow; (PHYS) inert

tragen ['traːgən] (unreg) *vt* to carry; (Kleidung, Brille) to wear; (Namen, Früchte) to bear; (erdulden) to endure ♦ *vi* (schwanger sein) to be pregnant; (Eis) to hold; **sich mit einem Gedanken ~** to have an idea in mind; **zum T~ kommen** to have an effect

Träger ['trɛːgər] (-s, -) *m* carrier; wearer; bearer; (Ordensträger) holder; (an Kleidung) (shoulder) strap; (Körperschaft etc) sponsor

Tragetasche *f* carrier bag

Tragfläche *f* (AVIAT) wing

Tragflügelboot *nt* hydrofoil

Trägheit ['trɛːkhait] *f* laziness; (PHYS) inertia

Tragik ['traːgɪk] *f* tragedy; **tragisch** *adj* tragic

Tragödie [tra'gøːdiə] *f* tragedy

Tragweite *f* range; (fig) scope

Train- ['trɛːn] *zW:* **~er** (-s, -) *m* (SPORT) trainer, coach; (Fußball) manager; **t~ieren** [trɛ'niːrən] *vt, vi* to train; (Mensch) to train, to coach; (Übung) to practise; **~ing** (-s, -s) *nt* training; **~ingsanzug** *m* track suit

Traktor ['traktɔr] *m* tractor; (von Drucker) tractor feed

trällern ['trɛlərn] *vt, vi* to trill, to sing

Tram [tram] (-, -s) *f* tram

trampeln ['trampəln] vt, vi to trample, to stamp

trampen ['trɛmpən] vi to hitch-hike

Tramper(in) [trɛmpər(ɪn)] (-s, -) m(f) hitch-hiker

Tran [traːn] (-(e)s, -e) m train oil, blubber

tranchieren [trãˈʃiːrən] vt to carve

Träne ['trɛːnə] f tear; **t~n** vi to water; **~ngas** nt teargas

trank etc [traŋk] vb siehe **trinken**

tränken ['trɛŋkən] vt (Tiere) to water

transchieren ▲ [tranˈʃiːrən] vt to carve

Trans- zW: **~formator** [transfɔrˈmaːtɔr] m transformer; **~istor** [tranˈzɪstɔr] m transistor; **~itverkehr** [tranˈziːtfɛrkeːr] m transit traffic; **~itvisum** nt transit visa; **t~parent** adj transparent; **~parent** (-(e)s, -e) nt (Bild) transparency; (Spruchband) banner; **~plantation** [transplantatsiˈoːn] f transplantation; (Hauttransplantation) graft(ing)

Transport [transˈpɔrt] (-(e)s, -e) m transport; **t~ieren** [transpɔrˈtiːrən] vt to transport; **~kosten** pl transport charges, carriage sg; **~mittel** nt means sg of transportation; **~unternehmen** nt carrier

Traube ['traubə] f grape; bunch (of grapes); **~nzucker** m glucose

trauen ['trauən] vi: **jdm/etw ~** to trust sb/sth ♦ vr to dare ♦ vt to marry

Trauer ['trauər] (-) f sorrow; (für Verstorbenen) mourning; **~fall** m death, bereavement; **~feier** f funeral service; **~kleidung** f mourning; **t~n** vi to mourn; **um jdn ~n** to mourn (for) sb; **~rand** m black border; **~spiel** nt tragedy

traulich ['traulɪç] adj cosy, intimate

Traum [traum] (-(e)s, Träume) m dream

Trauma (-s, -men) nt trauma

träum- ['trɔym] zW: **~en** vt, vi to dream; **T~er** (-s, -) m dreamer; **T~e'rei** f dreaming; **~erisch** adj dreamy

traumhaft adj dreamlike; (fig) wonderful

traurig ['trauriç] adj sad; **T~keit** f sadness

Trau- ['trau] zW: **~ring** m wedding ring; **~schein** m marriage certificate; **~ung** f wedding ceremony; **~zeuge** m witness (to a marriage); **~zeugin** f witness (to a marriage)

treffen ['trɛfən] (unreg) vt to strike, to hit; (Bemerkung) to hurt; (begegnen) to meet; (Entscheidung etc) to make; (Maßnahmen) to take ♦ vi to hit ♦ vr to meet; **er hat es gut getroffen** he did well; **~ auf** +akk to come across, to meet with; **es traf sich, dass ...** it so happened that ...; **es trifft sich gut** it's convenient; **wie es so trifft** as these things happen; **T~** (-s, -) nt meeting; **~d** adj pertinent, apposite

Treffer (-s, -) m hit; (Tor) goal; (Los) winner

Treffpunkt m meeting place

Treib- ['traib] zW: **~eis** nt drift ice; **t~en** (unreg) vt to drive; (Studien etc) to pursue; (Sport) to do, to go in for ♦ vi (Schiff etc) to drift; (Pflanzen) to sprout; (KOCH: aufgehen) to rise; (Tee, Kaffee) to be diuretic; **~haus** nt greenhouse; **~hauseffekt** m greenhouse effect; **~hausgas** nt greenhouse gas; **~stoff** m fuel

trenn- ['trɛn] zW: **~bar** adj separable; **~en** vt to separate; (teilen) to divide ♦ vr to separate; **sich ~en von** to part with; **T~ung** f separation; **T~wand** f partition (wall)

Trepp- ['trɛp] zW: **t~ab** adv downstairs; **t~auf** adv upstairs; **~e** f stair(case); **~engeländer** nt banister; **~enhaus** nt staircase

---

Spelling Reform: ▲ *new spelling* △ *old spelling (to be phased out)*

Tresor [tre'zo:r] (-s, -e) *m* safe
Tretboot *nt* pedalo, pedal boat
treten ['tre:tən] (*unreg*) *vi* to step; (*Tränen, Schweiß*) to appear ♦ *vt* (*mit Fußtritt*) to kick; (*niedertreten*) to tread, to trample; ~ **nach** to kick at; ~ **in** +*akk* to step in(to); **in Verbindung** ~ to get in contact; **in Erscheinung** ~ to appear
treu [trɔy] *adj* faithful, true; **T~e** (-) *f* loyalty, faithfulness; **T~händer** (-) *m* trustee; **T~handanstalt** *f* trustee organization; **T~handgesellschaft** *f* trust company; **~herzig** *adj* innocent; **~los** *adj* faithless

---
Treuhandanstalt

The **Treuhandanstalt** *was the organization set up in 1990 to take over the nationally-owned companies of the former* **DDR,** *break them down into smaller units and privatize them. It was based in Berlin and had nine branches. Many companies were closed down by the* **Treuhandanstalt** *because of their outdated equipment and inability to compete with Western firms which resulted in rising unemployment. Having completed its initial task, the* **Treuhandanstalt** *was closed down in 1995.*

Tribüne [tri'by:nə] *f* grandstand; (*Rednertribüne*) platform
Trichter ['trɪçtər] (-s, -) *m* funnel; (*in Boden*) crater
Trick [trɪk] (-s, -e *od* -s) *m* trick; ~**film** *m* cartoon
Trieb [tri:p] (-(e)s, -e) *m* urge, drive; (*Neigung*) inclination; (*an Baum etc*) shoot; ~ *etc vb siehe* **treiben**; ~**kraft** *f* (*fig*) drive; ~**täter** *m* sex offender; ~**werk** *nt* engine
triefen ['tri:fən] *vi* to drip
triffst *etc* [trɪfst] *vb siehe* **treffen**
triftig ['trɪftɪç] *adj* good, convincing
Trikot [tri'ko:] (-s, -s) *nt* vest; (*SPORT*)

shirt
Trimester [tri'mɛstər] (-s, -) *nt* term
trimmen ['trɪmən] *vr* to do keep fit exercises
trink- ['trɪŋk] *zW*: ~**bar** *adj* drinkable; ~**en** (*unreg*) *vt, vi* to drink; **T~er** (-s, -) *m* drinker; **T~geld** *nt* tip; **T~halle** *f* re-freshment kiosk; **T~wasser** *nt* drinking water
Tripper ['trɪpər] (-s, -) *m* gonorrhoea
Tritt [trɪt] (-(e)s, -e) *m* step; (*Fußtritt*) kick; ~**brett** *nt* (*EISENB*) step; (*AUT*) running board
Triumph [tri'ʊmf] (-(e)s, -e) *m* triumph; ~**bogen** *m* triumphal arch; **t~ieren** [triʊm'fi:rən] *vi* to triumph; (*jubeln*) to exult
trocken ['trɔkən] *adj* dry; **T~element** *nt* dry cell; **T~haube** *f* hair dryer; **T~heit** *f* dryness; ~**legen** *vt* (*Sumpf*) to drain; (*Kind*) to put a clean nappy on; **T~milch** *f* dried milk; **T~rasur** *f* dry shave, electric shave
trocknen ['trɔknən] *vt, vi* to dry
Trödel ['trø:dəl] (-s) (*umg*) *m* junk; ~**markt** *m* flea market; **t~n** (*umg*) *vi* to dawdle
Trommel ['trɔməl] (-, -n) *f* drum; ~**fell** *nt* eardrum; **t~n** *vt, vi* to drum
Trompete [trɔm'pe:tə] *f* trumpet; ~**r** (-s, -) *m* trumpeter
Tropen ['tro:pən] *pl* tropics; ~**helm** *m* sun helmet
tröpfeln ['trœpfəln] *vi* to drop, to trickle
Tropfen ['trɔpfən] (-s, -) *m* drop; **t~** *vt, vi* to drip ♦ *vb unpers*: **es tropft** a few raindrops are falling; ~**weise** *adv* in drops
Tropfsteinhöhle *f* stalactite cave
tropisch ['tro:pɪʃ] *adj* tropical
Trost [tro:st] (-es) *m* consolation, comfort
trösten ['trø:stən] *vt* to console, to comfort
trost- *zW*: ~**los** *adj* bleak; (*Verhältnisse*) wretched; **T~preis** *m* consolation

prize; **~reich** adj comforting

Trott [trɔt] (-(e)s, -e) m trot; (Routine) routine; **~el** (-s, -) (umg) m fool, dope; **t~en** vi to trot

Trotz [trɔts] (-es) m pigheadedness; **etw aus ~ tun** to do sth just to show them; **jdm zum ~** in defiance of sb; **t~** präp (+gen od dat) in spite of; **t~dem** adv nevertheless, all the same ♦ konj although; **t~en** vi (+dat) to defy; (der Kälte, Klima etc) to withstand; (der Gefahr) to brave; (t~ig sein) to be awkward; **t~ig** adj defiant, pig-headed; **~kopf** m obstinate child

trüb [try:p] adj dull; (Flüssigkeit, Glas) cloudy; (fig) gloomy

Trubel ['tru:bəl] (-s) m hurly-burly

trüb- zW: **~en** ['try:bən] vt to cloud ♦ vr to become clouded; **T~heit** f dullness; cloudiness; gloom; **T~sal** (-, -e) f distress; **~selig** adj sad, melancholy; **T~sinn** m depression; **~sinnig** adj depressed, gloomy

Trüffel ['tryfəl] (-, -n) f truffle

trug etc [tru:k] vb siehe **tragen**

trügen ['try:gən] (unreg) vt to deceive ♦ vi to be deceptive

trügerisch adj deceptive

Trugschluss ▲ ['tru:kʃlʊs] m false conclusion

Truhe ['tru:ə] f chest

Trümmer ['trymər] pl wreckage sg; (Bautrümmer) ruins; **~haufen** m heap of rubble

Trumpf [trʊmpf] (-(e)s, -e) m (auch fig) trump; **t~en** vt, vi to trump

Trunk [trʊŋk] (-(e)s, -e) m drink; **t~en** adj intoxicated; **~enheit** f intoxication; **~enheit am Steuer** drunken driving; **~sucht** f alcoholism

Trupp [trʊp] (-s, -s) m troop; **~e** f troop; (Waffengattung) force; (Schauspieltruppe) troupe; **~en** pl (MIL) troops; **~enübungsplatz** m training area

Truthahn ['tru:tha:n] m turkey

Tschech- ['tʃɛç] zW: **~e** m Czech; **~ien** (-s) nt the Czech Republic; **~in** f Czech; **t~isch** adj Czech; **~oslowakei** [-oslova'kaı] f: **die ~oslowakei** Czechoslovakia; **T~oslowakisch** [-oslo'va:kıʃ] adj Czechoslovak(ian)

tschüs(s) [tʃys] excl cheerio

T-Shirt ['ti:ʃørt] nt T-shirt

Tube ['tu:bə] f tube

Tuberkulose [tuberku'lo:zə] f tuberculosis

Tuch [tu:x] (-(e)s, -er) nt cloth; (Halstuch) scarf; (Kopftuch) headscarf; (Handtuch) towel

tüchtig ['tyçtıç] adj efficient, (cap)able; (umg: kräftig) good, sound; **T~keit** f efficiency, ability

Tücke ['tykə] f (Arglist) malice; (Trick) trick; (Schwierigkeit) difficulty, problem

tückisch ['tykıʃ] adj treacherous; (böswillig) malicious

Tugend ['tu:gənt] (-, -en) f virtue; **t~haft** adj virtuous

Tülle f spout

Tulpe ['tʊlpə] f tulip

Tumor ['tu:mɔr] (-s, -e) m tumour

Tümpel ['tympəl] (-s, -) m pool, pond

Tumult [tu'mʊlt] (-(e)s, -e) m tumult

tun [tu:n] (unreg) vt (machen) to do; (legen) to put ♦ vi to act ♦ vr: **es tut sich etwas/viel** something/a lot is happening; **jdm etw ~** (antun) to do sth to sb; **etw tut es auch** sth will do; **das tut nichts** that doesn't matter; **das tut nichts zur Sache** that's neither here nor there; **so ~ als ob** to act as if

tünchen ['tynçən] vt to whitewash

Tunfisch ▲ ['tu:nfıʃ] m = **Thunfisch**

Tunke ['tʊŋkə] f sauce; **t~n** vt to dip, to dunk

tunlichst ['tu:nlıçst] adv if at all possible; **~ bald** as soon as possible

Tunnel ['tʊnəl] (-s, -s od -) m tunnel

Tupfen ['tʊpfən] (-s, -) m dot, spot; **t~**

vt, vi to dab; (*mit Farbe*) to dot

Tür [ty:r] (-, -en) *f* door

Turbine [tʊr'biːnə] *f* turbine

Türk- [tʏrk] *zW:* **~e** *m* Turk; **~ei** [tʏr'kaɪ] *f:* **die ~ei** Turkey; **~in** *f* Turk

Türkis [tʏr'kiːs] (-es, -e) *m* turquoise; **t~** *adj* turquoise

türkisch ['tʏrkɪʃ] *adj* Turkish

Türklinke *f* doorknob, door handle

Turm [tʊrm] (-(e)s, ~e) *m* tower; (*Kirchturm*) steeple; (*Sprungturm*) diving platform; (*SCHACH*) castle, rook

türmen ['tʏrmən] *vr* to tower up ♦ *vt* to heap up ♦ *vi* (*umg*) to scarper, to bolt

Turn- ['tʊrn] *zW:* **t~en** *vi* to do gymnastic exercises ♦ *vt* to perform; **~en** (-s) *nt* gymnastics; (*SCH*) physical education, P.E.; **~er(in)** (-s, -) *m(f)* gymnast; **~halle** *f* gym(nasium); **~hose** *f* gym shorts *pl*

Turnier [tʊr'niːr] (-s, -e) *nt* tournament

Turn- *zW:* **~schuh** *m* gym shoe; **~verein** *m* gymnastics club; **~zeug** *nt* gym things *pl*

Tusche ['tʊʃə] *f* Indian ink

tuscheln ['tʊʃəln] *vt, vi* to whisper

Tuschkasten *m* paintbox

Tüte ['ty:tə] *f* bag

tuten ['tuːtən] *vi* (*AUT*) to hoot (*BRIT*), to honk (*US*)

TÜV [tʏf] (-s, -s) *m abk* (= *Technischer Überwachungs-Verein*) ≈ MOT

Typ [ty:p] (-s, -en) *m* type; **~e** *f* (*TYP*) type

Typhus ['ty:fʊs] (-) *m* typhoid (fever)

typisch ['ty:pɪʃ] *adj:* **~ (für)** typical (of)

Tyrann [ty'ran] (-en, -en) *m* tyrant; **~ei** [-'naɪ] *f* tyranny; **t~isch** *adj* tyrannical; **t~i'sieren** *vt* to tyrannize

U, u

u. a. *abk* = **unter anderem**

U-Bahn ['uːbaːn] *f* underground, tube

übel ['y:bəl] *adj* bad; (*moralisch*) bad, wicked; **jdm ist ~** sb feels sick; **~ gelaunt** bad-tempered; **jdm eine Bemerkung ~ nehmen** to be offended at sb's remark; **Ü~** (-s, -) *nt* evil; (*Krankheit*) disease; **Ü~keit** *f* nausea

üben ['y:bən] *vt, vi* to exercise, to practise

SCHLÜSSELWORT

über ['y:bər] *präp +dat* **1** (*räumlich*) over, above; **zwei Grad über null** two degrees above zero

2 (*zeitlich*) over; **über der Arbeit einschlafen** to fall asleep over one's work ♦ *präp +akk* **1** (*räumlich*) over; (*hoch über auch*) above; (*quer über auch*) across

2 (*zeitlich*) over; **über Weihnachten** over Christmas; **über kurz oder lang** sooner or later

3 (*mit Zahlen*) **Kinder über 12 Jahren** children over *od* above 12 years of age; **ein Scheck über 200 Mark** a cheque for 200 marks

4 (*auf dem Wege*) via; **nach Köln über Aachen** to Cologne via Aachen; **ich habe es über die Auskunft erfahren** I found out from information

5 (*betreffend*) about; **ein Buch über ...** a book about *od* on ...; **über jdn/etw lachen** to laugh about *od* at sb/sth

6: Macht über jdn haben to have power over sb; **sie liebt ihn über alles** she loves him more than everything

♦ *adv* over; **über und über** over and over; **den ganzen Tag über** all day long; **jdm in etw** *dat* **über sein** to be superior to sb in sth

überall [y:bər'|al] adv everywhere;
~'hin adv everywhere

überanstrengen [y:bər'|anʃtrɛŋən] vt
insep to overexert ♦ vr insep to overexert o.s.

überarbeiten [y:bər'|arbaitən] vt insep
to revise, to rework ♦ vr insep to overwork (o.s.)

überaus ['y:bər|aus] adv exceedingly

überbelichten [y:bər'bəliçtən] vt
(PHOT) to overexpose

über'bieten (unreg) vt insep to outbid;
(übertreffen) to surpass; (Rekord) to
break

Überbleibsel ['y:bərblaipsəl] (-s, -) nt
residue, remainder

Überblick ['y:bərblik] m view; (fig:
Darstellung) survey, overview;
(Fähigkeit): ~ (über +akk) grasp (of),
overall view (of); **ü~en** [-'blikən] vt insep to survey

überbring- [y:bər'brɪŋ] zW: **~en** (unreg) vt insep to deliver, to hand over;
Ü~er (-s, -) m bearer

überbrücken [y:bər'brʏkən] vt insep to
bridge (over)

überbuchen ['y:bərbu:xən] vt insep to
overbook

über'dauern vt insep to outlast

über'denken (unreg) vt insep to think
over

überdies [y:bər'di:s] adv besides

überdimensional
['y:bərdimɛnzionaːl] adj oversize

Überdruss ▲ [y:bərdrus] (-es) m
weariness; **bis zum ~** to ad nauseam

überdurchschnittlich ['y:bərdurçʃnɪtlɪç] adj above-average ♦ adv exceptionally

übereifrig [y:bər'|aifrɪç] adj over-keen

übereilt [y:bər'|aɪlt] adj (over)hasty,
premature

überein- [y:bər'|aɪn] zW: **~ander**
[y:bər|aɪ'nandər] adv one upon the
other; (sprechen) about each other;

~kommen (unreg) vi to agree;
Ü~kunft (-, **-künfte**) f agreement;
~stimmen vi to agree; **Ü~stimmung**
f agreement

überempfindlich ['y:bər|ɛmpfɪntlɪç]
adj hypersensitive

überfahren [y:bər'fa:rən] (unreg) vt insep (AUT) to run over; (fig) to walk all
over

Überfahrt ['y:bərfa:rt] f crossing

Überfall ['y:bərfal] m (Banküberfall, MIL)
raid; (auf jdn) assault; **ü~en** [-'falən]
(unreg) vt insep to attack; (Bank) to raid;
(besuchen) to drop in on, to descend
on

überfällig ['y:bərfɛlɪç] adj overdue

über'fliegen (unreg) vt insep to fly over,
to overfly; (Buch) to skim through

Überfluss ▲ ['y:bərflus] m: **~ (an** +dat)
(super)abundance (of), excess (of)

überflüssig ['y:bərflʏsɪç] adj superfluous

über'fordern vt insep to demand too
much of; (Kräfte etc) to overtax

über'führen vt insep (Leiche etc)
to transport; (Täter) to have convicted

Über'führung f transport; conviction;
(Brücke) bridge, overpass

überfüllt [y:bər'fʏlt] adj (Schulen, Straßen) overcrowded; (Kurs) oversubscribed

Übergabe ['y:bərga:bə] f handing
over; (MIL) surrender

Übergang ['y:bərgaŋ] m crossing;
(Wandel, Überleitung) transition

Übergangs- zW: **~lösung** f provisional solution, stopgap; **~zeit** f transitional period

über'geben (unreg) vt insep to hand
over; (MIL) to surrender ♦ vr insep to be
sick

übergehen ['y:bərge:ən] (unreg) vi (Besitz) to pass; (zum Feind etc) to go
over, to defect; **in +akk** to turn into;
über'gehen (unreg) vt insep to pass

over, to omit

Übergewicht ['y:bərgəvɪçt] nt excess weight; (fig) preponderance

überglücklich ['y:bərglʏklɪç] adj overjoyed

Übergröße ['y:bərɡrø:sə] f oversize

überhaupt [y:bər'haupt] adv at all; (im Allgemeinen) in general; (besonders) especially; ~ **nicht/keine** not/none at all

überheblich [y:bər'he:plɪç] adj arrogant; **Ü~keit** f arrogance

über'holen vt insep to overtake; (TECH) to overhaul

über'holt adj out-of-date, obsolete

Überholverbot [y:bər'ho:lfɛrbo:t] nt restriction on overtaking

über'hören vt insep not to hear; (absichtlich) to ignore

überirdisch [y:bər'ɪrdɪʃ] adj supernatural, unearthly

über'laden (unreg) vt insep to overload ♦ adj (fig) cluttered

über'lassen (unreg) vt insep: **jdm etw** ~ to leave sth to sb ♦ vr insep: **sich einer Sache** dat ~ to give o.s. over to sth

über'lasten vt insep to overload; (Mensch) to overtax

überlaufen [y:bər'laufən] (unreg) vi (Flüssigkeit) to flow over; (zum Feind etc) to go over, to defect; ~ **sein** to be inundated od besieged; **über'laufen** (unreg) vt insep (Schauer etc) to come over

über'leben vt insep to survive; **Über'lebende(r)** f(m) survivor

über'legen vt insep to consider ♦ adj superior; **ich muss es mir** ~ I'll have to think about it; **Über'legenheit** f superiority

Über'legung f consideration, deliberation

über'liefern vt insep to hand down, to transmit

Überlieferung f tradition

überlisten [y:bər'lɪstən] vt insep to outwit

überm ['y:bərm] = über dem

Übermacht ['y:bərmaxt] f superior force, superiority; **übermächtig** ['y:bərmɛçtɪç] adj superior (in strength); (Gefühl etc) overwhelming

übermäßig ['y:bərmɛ:sɪç] adj excessive

Übermensch ['y:bərmɛnʃ] m superman; **ü~lich** adj superhuman

übermitteln [y:bər'mɪtəln] vt insep to convey

übermorgen ['y:bərmɔrɡən] adv the day after tomorrow

Übermüdung [y:bər'my:dʊŋ] f fatigue, overtiredness

Übermut ['y:bərmu:t] m exuberance

übermütig ['y:bərmy:tɪç] adj exuberant, high-spirited; ~ **werden** to get overconfident

übernächste(r, s) [y:bər'nɛ:çstə(r, s)] adj (Jahr) next but one

übernacht- [y:bər'naxt] zW: **~en** vi insep: (**bei jdm**) **~en** to spend the night (at sb's place); **Ü~ung** f overnight stay; **Ü~ung mit Frühstück** bed and breakfast; **Ü~ungsmöglichkeit** f overnight accommodation no pl

Übernahme [y:bər'na:mə] f taking over od on, acceptance

über'nehmen (unreg) vt insep to take on, to accept; (Amt, Geschäft) to take over ♦ vr insep to take on too much

über'prüfen vt insep to examine, to check

überqueren [y:bər'kve:rən] vt insep to cross

überragen [y:bər'ra:gən] vt insep to tower above; (fig) to surpass

überraschen [y:bər'raʃən] vt insep to surprise

Überraschung f surprise

überreden [y:bər're:dən] vt insep to persuade

überreichen [y:bər'raɪçən] vt insep to present, to hand over

'Überrest m remains, remnants

überrumpeln [y:bər'rʊmpəln] vt insep to take by surprise

überrunden [y:bər'rʊndən] vt insep to lap

übers ['y:bərs] = **über das**

Überschall- ['y:bərʃal] zW: **~flugzeug** nt supersonic jet; **~geschwindigkeit** f supersonic speed

über'schätzen vt insep to overestimate

'überschäumen vi (Bier) to foam over, bubble over; (Temperament) to boil over

Überschlag ['y:bərʃla:k] m (FIN) estimate; (SPORT) somersault; **ü~en** [-'ʃla:gən] (unreg) vt insep (berechnen) to estimate; (auslassen: Seite) to omit ♦ vt insep to somersault; (Stimme) to crack; (AVIAT) to loop the loop; **'überschlagen** (unreg) vi (Wellen) to break; (Funken) to flash

überschnappen ['y:bərʃnapən] vi (Stimme) to crack; (umg: Mensch) to flip one's lid

über'schneiden (unreg) vr insep (auch fig) to overlap; (Linien) to intersect

über'schreiben (unreg) vt insep to provide with a heading; **jdm etw ~** to transfer od make over sth to sb

über'schreiten (unreg) vt insep to cross over; (fig) to exceed; (verletzen) to transgress

Überschrift ['y:bərʃrɪft] f heading, title

Überschuss ▲ ['y:bərʃʊs] m: **~ (an** +dat) surplus (of); **überschüssig** ['y:bərʃʏsɪç] adj surplus, excess

über'schütten vt insep: **jdn/etw mit etw ~** to pour sth over sb/sth; **jdn mit etw ~** (fig) to shower sb with sth

überschwänglich ▲ ['y:bərʃvɛŋlɪç] adj effusive

überschwemmen [y:bər'ʃvɛmən] vt insep to flood

Überschwemmung f flood

Übersee ['y:bərze:] f: **nach/in** ~ overseas; **ü~isch** adj overseas

über'sehen (unreg) vt insep to look

(out) over; (fig: Folgen) to see, to get an overall view of; (: nicht beachten) to overlook

über'senden (unreg) vt insep to send, to forward

übersetz- zW: **~en** [y:bər'zɛtsən] vt insep to translate; **'übersetzen** vi to cross; **Ü~er(in)** [-'zɛtsər(ɪn)] (-s, -) m(f) translator; **Ü~ung** [-'zɛtsʊŋ] f translation; (TECH) gear ratio

Übersicht ['y:bərzɪçt] f overall view; (Darstellung) survey; **ü~lich** adj clear; (Gelände) open; **~lichkeit** f clarity, lucidity

übersiedeln ['y:bərzi:dəln] vi sep to move; **über'siedeln** vi to move

überspannt adj eccentric; (Idee) wild, crazy

überspitzt [y:bər'ʃpɪtst] adj exaggerated

über'springen (unreg) vt insep to jump over; (fig) to skip

über'stehen (unreg) vt insep to overcome, to get over; (Winter etc) to survive, to get through; **'überstehen** vi to project

über'steigen (unreg) vt insep to climb over; (fig) to exceed

über'stimmen vt insep to outvote

Überstunden ['y:bərʃtʊndən] pl overtime sg

über'stürzen vt insep to rush ♦ vr insep to follow (one another) in rapid succession

überstürzt adj (over)hasty

Übertrag ['y:bərtra:k] (-(e)s, -träge) m (COMM) amount brought forward; **ü~bar** [-'tra:kba:r] adj transferable; (MED) infectious; **ü~en** [-'tra:gən] (unreg) vt insep to transfer; (RADIO) to broadcast; (übersetzen) to render; (Krankheit) to transmit ♦ vr insep to spread ♦ adj figurative; **ü~en auf** +akk to transfer to; **jdm etw ü~en** to assign sth to sb; **sich ü~en auf** +akk to spread to; **~ung** [-'tra:goŋ] f transfer(ence); (RADIO) broadcast; rendering; transmission

über'treffen (unreg) vt insep to surpass

über'treiben (unreg) vt insep to exaggerate; **Übertreibung** f exaggeration

übertreten [y:bər'tre:tən] (unreg) vi insep to cross; (Gebot etc) to break; **'übertreten** (unreg) vi (über Linie, Gebiet) to step (over); (SPORT) to overstep; (zu anderem Glauben) to be converted; **'übertreten** (in +akk) (POL) to go over (to)

Über'tretung f violation, transgression

übertrieben [y:bər'tri:bən] adj exaggerated, excessive

übervölkert [y:bər'fœlkərt] adj over-populated

übervoll ['y:bərfɔl] adj overfull

übervorteilen [y:bər'fɔrtaɪlən] vt insep to dupe, to cheat

über'wachen vt insep to supervise; (Verdächtigen) to keep under surveillance; **Überwachung** f supervision; surveillance

überwältigen [y:bər'vɛltɪgən] vt insep to overpower; **~d** adj overwhelming

überweisen [y:bər'vaɪzən] (unreg) vt insep to transfer

Überweisung f transfer; **~sauftrag** m (credit) transfer order

über'wiegen (unreg) vi insep to be predominate; **~d** adj predominant

über'winden (unreg) vt insep to overcome ♦ vr insep to make an effort, to bring o.s. (to do sth)

Überwindung f effort, strength of mind

Überzahl ['y:bərtsa:l] f superiority, superior numbers pl; **in der ~ sein** to be numerically superior

überzählig ['y:bərtsɛ:lɪç] adj surplus

über'zeugen vt insep to convince; **~d** adj convincing

Überzeugung f conviction

überziehen ['y:bərtsi:ən] (unreg) vt to put on; **über'ziehen** (unreg) vt insep to

cover; (Konto) to overdraw

Überziehungskredit m overdraft provision

Überzug ['y:bərtsu:k] m cover; (Belag) coating

üblich ['y:plɪç] adj usual

U-Boot ['u:bo:t] nt submarine

übrig ['y:brɪç] adj remaining; **für jdn etwas ~ haben** (umg) to be fond of sb; **die Ü~en the others; das Ü~e the rest; im Ü~en besides; ~ bleiben** to remain, to be left (over); **~ lassen** to leave (over); **~ens** ['y:brɪgəns] adv besides; (nebenbei bemerkt) by the way

Übung ['y:boŋ] f practice; (Turnübung, Aufgabe etc) exercise; **~ macht den Meister** practice makes perfect

Ufer ['u:fər] (-s, -) nt bank; (Meeresufer) shore

Uhr [u:r] (-, -en) f clock; (Armbanduhr) watch; **wie viel ~ ist es?** what time is it?; **1 ~** 1 o'clock; **20 ~** 8 o'clock, 20.00 (twenty hundred) hours; **~(arm)band** nt watch strap; **~band** nt watch strap; **~macher (-s, -)** m watchmaker; **~werk** nt clockwork; works of a watch; **~zeiger** m hand; **~zeigersinn** m: **im ~zeigersinn** clockwise; **entgegen dem ~zeigersinn** anticlockwise; **~zeit** f time (of day)

Uhu ['u:hu] (-s, -s) m eagle owl

UKW [u:ka:'ve:] abk (= Ultrakurzwelle) VHF

ulkig ['ʊlkɪç] adj funny

Ulme ['ʊlmə] f elm

Ultimatum [ʊlti'ma:tʊm] (-s, Ultimaten) nt ultimatum

Ultra- ['ʊltra] zW: **~schall** m (PHYS) ultrasound; **u~violett** adj ultraviolet

---

SCHLÜSSELWORT

um [ʊm] präp +akk **1** (um herum) **1** (a)round; **um Weihnachten** around Christmas; **er schlug um sich** he hit about him

2 (mit Zeitangabe) at; **um acht (Uhr)** at eight (o'clock)

3 (mit Größenangabe) by; **etw um 4 cm kürzen** to shorten sth by 4 cm; **um 10% teurer** 10% more expensive; **um vieles besser** better by far; **um nichts besser** not in the least bit better

4: **der Kampf um den Titel** the battle for the title; **um Geld spielen** to play for money; **Stunde um Stunde** hour after hour; **Auge um Auge** an eye for an eye

♦ präp +gen: **um ... willen** for the sake of ...; **um Gottes willen** for goodness' od (stärker) God's sake

♦ konj: **um ... zu** (in order) to ...; **zu klug, um zu ...** too clever to ...; siehe **umso**

♦ adv 1 (ungefähr) about; **um (die) 30 Leute** about od around 30 people

2 (vorbei): **die 2 Stunden sind um** the two hours are up

umändern ['ʊmʔɛndɐn] vt to alter
Umänderung f alteration
umarbeiten ['ʊmʔarbaitn] vt to remodel; (Buch etc) to revise, to rework
umarmen [ʊm'ʔarmən] vt insep to embrace
Umbau ['ʊmbaʊ] m (-(e)s, -e od -ten) m reconstruction, alteration(s); **u~en** vt to rebuild, to reconstruct
umbilden ['ʊmbɪldən] vt to reorganize; (POL: Kabinett) to reshuffle
umbinden ['ʊmbɪndn̩] (unreg) vt (Krawatte etc) to put on
umblättern ['ʊmblɛtɐn] vt to turn over
umblicken ['ʊmblɪkn̩] vr to look around
umbringen ['ʊmbrɪŋən] (unreg) vt to kill
umbuchen ['ʊmbuːxən] vi to change one's reservation/flight etc ♦ vt to change
umdenken ['ʊmdɛŋkən] (unreg) vi to

adjust one's views
umdrehen ['ʊmdreːən] vt to turn (round); (Hals) to wring ♦ vr to turn (round)
Um'drehung f revolution; rotation
umeinander [ʊmʔaɪ'nandɐ] adv round one another; (füreinander) for one another
umfahren ['ʊmfaːrən] (unreg) vt to run over; **um'fahren** (unreg) vt insep to drive round; to sail round
umfallen ['ʊmfalən] (unreg) vi to fall down od over
Umfang ['ʊmfaŋ] m extent; (von Buch) size; (Reichweite) range; (Fläche) area; (MATH) circumference; **u~reich** adj extensive; (Buch etc) voluminous
um'fassen vt insep to embrace; (umgeben) to surround; (enthalten) to include; **um'fassend** adj comprehensive, extensive
umformen ['ʊmfɔrmən] vt to transform
Umfrage ['ʊmfraːɡə] f poll
umfüllen ['ʊmfʏlən] vt to transfer; (Wein) to decant
umfunktionieren ['ʊmfʊŋktsioniːrən] vt to convert, to transform
Umgang ['ʊmgaŋ] m company; (mit jdm) dealings pl; (Behandlung) way of behaving
umgänglich ['ʊmgɛŋlɪç] adj sociable
Umgangs- zW: **~formen** pl manners; **~sprache** f colloquial language
umgeben [ʊm'geːbən] (unreg) vt insep to surround
Umgebung f surroundings pl; (Milieu) environment; (Personen) people in one's circle
umgehen ['ʊmgeːən] (unreg) vi to go (a)round; **im Schlosse ~** to haunt the castle; **mit jdm grob** etc **~** to treat sb roughly etc; **mit Geld sparsam ~** to be careful with one's money; **um'gehen** vt insep to bypass; (MIL) to

outflank; (*Gesetz etc*) to circumvent; (*vermeiden*) to avoid; **'umgehend** *adj* immediate

Um'gehung *f* bypassing; outflanking; circumvention; avoidance; **~sstraße** *f* bypass

umgekehrt ['ʊmgəkeːrt] *adj* reverse(d); (*gegenteilig*) opposite ♦ *adv* the other way around; **und ~** *adv* vice versa

umgraben ['ʊmgraːbən] (*unreg*) *vt* to dig up

Umhang ['ʊmhaŋ] *m* wrap, cape

umhauen ['ʊmhaʊən] *vt* to fell; (*fig*) to bowl over

umher [ʊm'heːr] *adv* about, around; **~gehen** (*unreg*) *vi* to walk about; **~ziehen** (*unreg*) *vi* to wander from place to place

umhinkönnen [ʊm'hɪnkœnən] (*unreg*) *vi*: **ich kann nicht umhin, das zu tun** I can't help doing it

umhören ['ʊmhøːrən] *vr* to ask around

Umkehr ['ʊmkeːr] (-) *f* turning back; (*Änderung*) change; **u~en** *vi* to turn back ♦ *vt* to turn round, to reverse; (*Tasche etc*) to turn inside out; (*Gefäß etc*) to turn upside down

umkippen ['ʊmkɪpən] *vt* to tip over ♦ *vi* to overturn; (*umg: Mensch*) to keel over; (*fig: Meinung ändern*) to change one's mind

Umkleide- ['ʊmklaɪdə] *zW*: **~kabine** *f* (*im Schwimmbad*) (changing) cubicle; **~raum** *m* changing *od* dressing room

umkommen ['ʊmkɔmən] (*unreg*) *vi* to die, to perish; (*Lebensmittel*) to go off

Umkreis ['ʊmkraɪs] *m* neighbourhood; **im ~ von** within a radius of

Umlage ['ʊmlaːgə] *f* share of the costs

Umlauf ['ʊmlaʊf] *m* (*Geldumlauf*) circulation; (*von Gestirn*) revolution; **~bahn** *f* orbit

Umlaut ['ʊmlaʊt] *m* umlaut

umlegen ['ʊmleːgən] *vt* to put on; (*verlegen*) to move, to shift; (*Kosten*) to

share out; (*umkippen*) to tip over; (*umg: töten*) to bump off

umleiten ['ʊmlaɪtən] *vt* to divert

Umleitung *f* diversion

umliegend ['ʊmliːgənt] *adj* surrounding

um'randen *vt insep* to border, to edge

umrechnen ['ʊmrɛçnən] *vt* to convert

Umrechnung *f* conversion; **~skurs** *m* rate of exchange

um'reißen (*unreg*) *vt insep* to outline, to sketch

Umriss ▲ ['ʊmrɪs] *m* outline

umrühren ['ʊmryːrən] *vt, vi* to stir

ums [ʊms] = **um das**

Umsatz ['ʊmzats] *m* turnover; **~steuer** *f* sales tax

umschalten ['ʊmʃaltən] *vt* to switch

umschauen *vr* to look round

Umschlag ['ʊmʃlaːk] *m* cover; (*Buchumschlag auch*) jacket; (*MED*) compress; (*Briefumschlag*) envelope; (*Wechsel*) change; (*von Hose*) turn-up; **u~en** [-gən] (*unreg*) *vi* to change; (*Boot*) to capsize ♦ *vt* to knock over; (*Ärmel*) to turn up; (*Seite*) to turn over; (*Waren*) to transfer; **~platz** *m* (*COMM*) distribution centre

umschreiben ['ʊmʃraɪbən] (*unreg*) *vt* (*neu schreiben*) to rewrite; (*übertragen*): **~ auf** *+akk* to transfer to; **um'schreiben** *vt insep* to paraphrase; (*abgrenzen*) to define

umschulen ['ʊmʃuːlən] *vt* to retrain; (*Kind*) to send to another school

Umschweife ['ʊmʃvaɪfə] *pl*: **ohne ~** without beating about the bush, straight out

Umschwung ['ʊmʃvʊŋ] *m* change (around), revolution

umsehen ['ʊmzeːən] (*unreg*) *vr* to look around *od* about; (*suchen*): **sich ~ (nach)** to look out (for)

umseitig ['ʊmzaɪtɪç] *adv* overleaf

umsichtig ['ʊmzɪçtɪç] *adj* cautious, prudent

umso ▲ ['ʊmzo] *konj*: **~ besser/**

schlimmer so much the better/worse

umsonst [om'zɔnst] adv in vain; (gratis) for nothing

umspringen ['omʃprɪŋən] (unreg) vi to change; (Wind auch) to veer; **mit jdm ~** to treat sb badly

Umstand ['omʃtant] m circumstance; **Umstände** pl (fig: Schwierigkeiten) fuss; **in anderen Umständen sein** to be pregnant; **Umstände machen** to go to a lot of trouble; **unter Umständen** possibly

umständlich ['omʃtɛntlɪç] adj (Methode) cumbersome, complicated; (Ausdrucksweise, Erklärung) long-winded; (Mensch) ponderous

Umstandskleid nt maternity dress

Umstehende(n) ['omʃtɛːəndə(n)] pl bystanders

umsteigen ['omʃtaɪɡən] (unreg) vi (EISENB) to change

umstellen ['omʃtɛlən] vt (an anderen Ort) to change round, to rearrange; (TECH) to convert ♦ vr to adapt (o.s.); **sich auf etw** akk **~** to adapt to sth; **um'stellen** vt insep to surround

Umstellung ['omʃtɛlʊŋ] f change; (Umgewöhnung) adjustment; (TECH) conversion

umstimmen ['omʃtɪmən] vt (MUS) to retune; **jdn ~** to make sb change his mind

umstoßen ['omʃtoːsən] (unreg) vt to overturn; (Plan etc) to change, to upset

umstritten [om'ʃtrɪtən] adj disputed

Umsturz ['omʃtʊrts] m overthrow

umstürzen ['omʃtvrtsən] vt (umwerfen) to overturn ♦ vi to collapse, to fall down; (Wagen) to overturn

Umtausch ['omtaoʃ] m exchange; **u~en** vt to exchange

Umverpackung ['omfɛrpakʊŋ] f packaging

umwandeln ['omvandəln] vt to

change, to convert; (ELEK) to transform

umwechseln ['omvɛksəln] vt to change

Umweg ['omveːk] m detour, roundabout way

Umwelt ['omvɛlt] f environment; **u~freundlich** adj not harmful to the environment, environment-friendly; **u~schädlich** adj ecologically harmful; **~schutz** m environmental protection; **~schützer** m environmentalist; **~verschmutzung** f environmental pollution

umwenden ['omvɛndən] (unreg) vt, vr to turn (round)

umwerfen ['omvɛrfən] (unreg) vt to upset, to overturn; (fig: erschüttern) to upset, to throw; **~d** (umg) adj fantastic

umziehen ['omtsiːən] (unreg) vt, vr to change ♦ vi to move

Umzug ['omtsuːk] m procession; (Wohnungsumzug) move, removal

unab- ['on|ap] zW: **~änderlich** adj irreversible, unalterable; **~hängig** adj independent; **U~hängigkeit** f independence; **~kömmlich** adj indispensable; **zur Zeit ~kömmlich** not free at the moment; **~lässig** adj incessant, constant; **~sehbar** adj immeasurable; (Folgen) unforeseeable; (Kosten) incalculable; **~sichtlich** adj unintentional; **~'wendbar** adj inevitable

unachtsam ['on|axtzaːm] adj careless; **U~keit** f carelessness

unan- ['on|an] zW: **~'fechtbar** adj indisputable; **~gebracht** adj uncalled-for; **~gemessen** adj inadequate; **~genehm** adj unpleasant; **U~nehmlichkeit** f inconvenience; **U~nehmlichkeiten** pl (Ärger) trouble sg; **~sehnlich** adj unsightly; **~ständig** adj indecent, improper

unappetitlich ['on|apetiːtlɪç] adj unsavoury

Unart ['on|aːrt] f bad manners pl; (An-

gewohnheit) bad habit; **u~ig** *adj* naughty, badly behaved

unauf- ['ʊnaʊf] *zW:* **~fällig** *adj* unobtrusive; *(Kleidung)* inconspicuous; **~'findbar** *adj* not to be found; **~gefordert** *adj* unasked ♦ *adv* spontaneously; **~haltsam** *adj* irresistible; **~'hörlich** *adj* incessant, continuous; **~merksam** *adj* inattentive; **~richtig** *adj* insincere

unaus- ['ʊnaʊs] *zW:* **~geglichen** *adj* unbalanced; **~'sprechlich** *adj* inexpressible; **~'stehlich** *adj* intolerable

unbarmherzig ['ʊnbarmhɛrtsɪç] *adj* pitiless, merciless

unbeabsichtigt ['ʊnbəlapzɪçtɪçt] *adj* unintentional

unbeachtet ['ʊnbəlaxtət] *adj* unnoticed, ignored

unbedenklich ['ʊnbədɛŋklɪç] *adj* *(Plan)* unobjectionable

unbedeutend ['ʊnbədɔʏtant] *adj* insignificant, unimportant; *(Fehler)* slight

unbedingt ['ʊnbədɪŋt] *adj* unconditional ♦ *adv* absolutely; **musst du ~ gehen?** do you really have to go?

unbefangen ['ʊnbəfaŋən] *adj* impartial, unprejudiced; *(ohne Hemmungen)* uninhibited; **U~heit** *f* impartiality; uninhibitedness

unbefriedigend ['ʊnbəfri:dɪgənd] *adj* unsatisfactory

unbefriedigt ['ʊnbəfri:dɪçt] *adj* unsatisfied, dissatisfied

unbefugt ['ʊnbəfu:kt] *adj* unauthorized

unbegreiflich [ʊnbə'graɪflɪç] *adj* inconceivable

unbegrenzt ['ʊnbəgrɛntst] *adj* unlimited

unbegründet ['ʊnbəgryndət] *adj* unfounded

Unbehagen ['ʊnbəha:gən] *nt* discomfort; **unbehaglich** ['ʊnbəha:klɪç] *adj* uncomfortable; *(Gefühl)* uneasy

unbeholfen ['ʊnbəhɔlfən] *adj* awkward, clumsy

unbekannt ['ʊnbəkant] *adj* unknown

unbekümmert ['ʊnbəkʏmərt] *adj* unconcerned

unbeliebt ['ʊnbəli:pt] *adj* unpopular

unbequem ['ʊnbəkve:m] *adj* *(Stuhl)* uncomfortable; *(Mensch)* bothersome; *(Regelung)* inconvenient

unberechenbar ['ʊnbə'rɛçənba:r] *adj* incalculable; *(Mensch, Verhalten)* unpredictable

unberechtigt ['ʊnbərɛçtɪçt] *adj* unjustified; *(nicht erlaubt)* unauthorized

unberührt ['ʊnbəry:rt] *adj* untouched, intact; **sie ist noch ~** she is still a virgin

unbescheiden ['ʊnbəʃaɪdən] *adj* presumptuous

unbeschreiblich [ʊnbə'ʃraɪplɪç] *adj* indescribable

unbeständig ['ʊnbəʃtɛndɪç] *adj* *(Mensch)* inconstant; *(Wetter)* unsettled; *(Lage)* unstable

unbestechlich [ʊnbə'ʃtɛçlɪç] *adj* incorruptible

unbestimmt ['ʊnbəʃtɪmt] *adj* indefinite; *(Zukunft auch)* uncertain

unbeteiligt [ʊnbə'taɪlɪçt] *adj* unconcerned, indifferent

unbeweglich ['ʊnbəve:klɪç] *adj* immovable

unbewohnt ['ʊnbəvo:nt] *adj* uninhabited; *(Wohnung)* unoccupied

unbewusst ▲ ['ʊnbəvʊst] *adj* unconscious

unbezahlt ['ʊnbətsa:lt] *adj* *(Rechnung)* outstanding, unsettled; *(Urlaub)* unpaid

unbrauchbar ['ʊnbraʊxba:r] *adj* *(Arbeit)* useless; *(Gerät auch)* unusable

und [ʊnt] *konj* and; **~ so weiter** and so on

Undank ['ʊndaŋk] *m* ingratitude; **u~bar** *adj* ungrateful

undefinierbar [ʊndefi'ni:rba:r] *adj* indefinable

undenkbar [ʊn'dɛŋkba:r] *adj* inconceivable

undeutlich ['ʊndɔytlɪç] *adj* indistinct

undicht ['ʊndɪçt] *adj* leaky

Unding ['ʊndɪŋ] *nt* absurdity

undurch- ['ʊndʊrç] *zW:* **~führbar** [-'fy:rba:r] *adj* impracticable; **~lässig** [-'lɛsɪç] *adj* waterproof, impermeable; **~sichtig** [-'zɪçtɪç] *adj* opaque; *(fig)* obscure

uneben ['ʊn|e:bən] *adj* uneven

unecht ['ʊn|ɛçt] *adj* (Schmuck) fake; (vorgetäuscht: Freundlichkeit) false

unehelich ['ʊn|e:əlɪç] *adj* illegitimate

uneinig ['ʊn|aɪnɪç] *adj* divided; **~ sein** to disagree; **U~keit** *f* discord, dissension

uneins ['ʊn|aɪns] *adj* at variance, at odds

unempfindlich ['ʊn|ɛmpfɪntlɪç] *adj* insensitive; (Stoff) practical

unendlich [ʊn|ɛntlɪç] *adj* infinite

unent- [ʊn|ɛnt] *zW:* **~behrlich** [-'be:rlɪç] *adj* indispensable; **~geltlich** [-gɛltlɪç] *adj* free (of charge); **~schieden** [-ʃi:dən] *adj* undecided; **~schieden enden** (SPORT) to end in a draw; **~schlossen** [-ʃlɔsən] *adj* undecided; irresolute; **~wegt** [-'ve:kt] *adj* unswerving; (unaufhörlich) incessant

uner- ['ʊn|e:r] *zW:* **~bittlich** [-'bɪtlɪç] *adj* unyielding, inexorable; **~fahren** [-fa:rən] *adj* inexperienced; **~freulich** [-frɔylɪç] *adj* unpleasant; **~gründlich** *adj* unfathomable; **~hört** [-hø:rt] *adj* unheard-of; (Bitte) outrageous; **~lässlich** ▲ [-'lɛslɪç] *adj* indispensable; **~laubt** *adj* unauthorized; **~messlich** ▲ *adj* immeasurable, immense; **~reichbar** *adj* (Ziel) unattainable; (Ort) inaccessible; (telefonisch) unobtainable; **~schöpflich** [-'ʃœpflɪç] *adj* inexhaustible; **~schwinglich** [-'ʃvɪŋlɪç] *adj* (Preis) exorbitant; too expensive; **~träglich** [-'trɛːklɪç] *adj* unbearable; (Frechheit) insufferable; **~wartet** *adj* unexpected; **~wünscht** *adj* undesirable, unwelcome

unfähig ['ʊnfɛːɪç] *adj* incapable, incompetent; **zu etw ~ sein** to be incapable of sth; **U~keit** *f* incapacity; incompetence

unfair ['ʊnfɛːr] *adj* unfair

Unfall ['ʊnfal] *m* accident; **~flucht** *f* hit-and-run (driving); **~schaden** *m* damages *pl*; **~station** *f* emergency ward; **~stelle** *f* scene of the accident; **~versicherung** *f* accident insurance

unfassbar ▲ [ʊn'fasba:r] *adj* inconceivable

unfehlbar [ʊn'fe:lba:r] *adj* infallible ♦ *adv* inevitably; **U~keit** *f* infallibility

unförmig ['ʊnfœrmɪç] *adj* (formlos) shapeless

unfrei ['ʊnfraɪ] *adj* not free, unfree; (Paket) unfranked; **~willig** *adj* involuntary, against one's will

unfreundlich ['ʊnfrɔyntlɪç] *adj* unfriendly; **U~keit** *f* unfriendliness

Unfriede(n) ['ʊnfri:də(n)] *m* dissension, strife

unfruchtbar ['ʊnfrʊxtba:r] *adj* infertile; (Gespräche) fruitless; **U~keit** *f* infertility; unfruitfulness

Unfug ['ʊnfu:k] (-s) *m* (Benehmen) mischief; (Unsinn) nonsense; **grober ~** (JUR) gross misconduct; malicious damage

Ungar(in) ['ʊngar(ɪn)] *m(f)* Hungarian; **u~isch** *adj* Hungarian; **~n** *nt* Hungary

ungeachtet ['ʊngə|axtət] *präp* +gen notwithstanding

ungeahnt ['ʊngə|a:nt] *adj* unsuspected, undreamt-of

ungebeten ['ʊngə|be:tən] *adj* uninvited

ungebildet ['ʊngə|bɪldət] *adj* uneducated; uncultured

ungedeckt ['ʊngədɛkt] *adj* (Scheck) uncovered

Ungeduld ['ʊngədʊlt] *f* impatience; **u~ig** [-dɪç] *adj* impatient

ungeeignet ['ʊngə|aɪgnət] *adj* unsuit-

Spelling Reform: ▲ *new spelling* △ *old spelling (to be phased out)*

able

ungefähr ['ʊngəfɛːr] *adj* rough, approximate; **das kommt nicht von ~** that's hardly surprising

ungefährlich ['ʊngəfɛːrlɪç] *adj* not dangerous, harmless

ungehalten ['ʊngəhaltən] *adj* indignant

ungeheuer ['ʊngəhɔʏər] *adj* huge ♦ *adv* (*umg*) enormously; **U~ (-s, -)** *nt* monster; **~lich** [-'hɔʏrlɪç] *adj* monstrous

ungehörig ['ʊngəhøːrɪç] *adj* impertinent, improper

ungehorsam ['ʊngəhoːrzaːm] *adj* disobedient; **U~** *m* disobedience

ungeklärt ['ʊngəklɛːrt] *adj* not cleared up; (*Rätsel*) unsolved

ungeladen ['ʊngəlaːdən] *adj* not loaded; (*Gast*) uninvited

ungelegen ['ʊngəleːgən] *adj* inconvenient

ungelernt ['ʊngəlɛrnt] *adj* unskilled

ungelogen ['ʊngəloːgən] *adv* really, honestly

ungemein ['ʊngəmaɪn] *adj* uncommon

ungemütlich ['ʊngəmyːtlɪç] *adj* uncomfortable; (*Person*) disagreeable

ungenau ['ʊngənaʊ] *adj* inaccurate; **U~igkeit** *f* inaccuracy

ungenießbar ['ʊngəniːsbaːr] *adj* inedible; undrinkable; (*umg*) unbearable

ungenügend ['ʊngənyːgənt] *adj* insufficient, inadequate

ungepflegt ['ʊngəpfleːkt] *adj* (*Garten etc*) untended; (*Person*) unkempt; (*Hände*) neglected

ungerade ['ʊngəraːdə] *adj* uneven, odd

ungerecht ['ʊngərɛçt] *adj* unjust; **~fertigt** *adj* unjustified; **U~igkeit** *f* injustice, unfairness

ungern ['ʊngɛrn] *adv* unwillingly, reluctantly

ungeschehen ['ʊngəʃeːən] *adj*: **~ machen** to undo

Ungeschicklichkeit ['ʊngəʃɪklɪçkaɪt] *f* clumsiness

ungeschickt *adj* awkward, clumsy

ungeschminkt ['ʊngəʃmɪŋkt] *adj* without make-up; (*fig*) unvarnished

ungesetzlich ['ʊngəzɛtslɪç] *adj* illegal

ungestört ['ʊngəʃtøːrt] *adj* undisturbed

ungestraft ['ʊngəʃtraːft] *adv* with impunity

ungestüm ['ʊngəʃtyːm] *adj* impetuous; tempestuous

ungesund ['ʊngəzʊnt] *adj* unhealthy

ungetrübt ['ʊngətryːpt] *adj* clear; (*fig*) untroubled; (*Freude*) unalloyed

Ungetüm ['ʊngətyːm] **(-(e)s, -e)** *nt* monster

ungewiss ▲ ['ʊngəvɪs] *adj* uncertain; **U~heit** *f* uncertainty

ungewöhnlich ['ʊngəvøːnlɪç] *adj* unusual

ungewohnt ['ʊngəvoːnt] *adj* unaccustomed

Ungeziefer ['ʊngətsiːfər] **(-s)** *nt* vermin

ungezogen ['ʊngətsoːgən] *adj* rude, impertinent; **U~heit** *f* rudeness, impertinence

ungezwungen ['ʊngətsvʊŋən] *adj* natural, unconstrained

unglaublich [ʊn'glaʊplɪç] *adj* incredible

ungleich ['ʊnglaɪç] *adj* dissimilar; unequal ♦ *adv* incomparably; **~artig** *adj* different; **U~heit** *f* dissimilarity; inequality; **~mäßig** *adj* irregular, uneven

Unglück ['ʊnglʏk] **(-(e)s, -e)** *nt* misfortune; (*Pech*) bad luck; (~sfall) calamity, disaster; (*Verkehrsunglück*) accident; **u~lich** *adj* unhappy; (*erfolglos*) unlucky; (*unerfreulich*) unfortunate; **u~licherweise** [-'vaɪzə] *adv* unfortunately; **~sfall** *m* accident, calamity

ungültig ['ʊngʏltɪç] *adj* invalid; **U~keit** *f* invalidity

ungünstig ['ʊngʏnstɪç] *adj* unfavourable

ungut ['ʊnguːt] adj (Gefühl) uneasy; **nichts für ~** no offence

unhaltbar ['ʊnhaltbaːr] adj untenable

Unheil ['ʊnhail] nt evil; (Unglück) misfortune; **~ anrichten** to cause mischief; **u~bar** adj incurable

unheimlich ['ʊnhaimlɪç] adj weird, uncanny ♦ adv (umg) tremendously

unhöflich ['ʊnhøːflɪç] adj impolite; **U~keit** f impoliteness

unhygienisch ['ʊnhygieːnɪʃ] adj unhygienic

Uni ['ʊni] (-, -s) (umg) f university

Uniform [uni'fɔrm] f uniform; **u~iert** [-'miːrt] adj uniformed

uninteressant ['ʊnɪnterɛsant] adj uninteresting

Uni- zW: **~versität** [univɛrzi'tɛːt] f university; **~versum** [uni'vɛrzɔm] (-s) nt universe

unkenntlich ['ʊnkɛntlɪç] adj unrecognizable

Unkenntnis ['ʊnkɛntnɪs] f ignorance

unklar ['ʊnklaːr] adj unclear; **im U~en sein über** +akk to be in the dark about; **U~heit** f unclarity; (Unentschiedenheit) uncertainty

unklug ['ʊnkluːk] adj unwise

Unkosten ['ʊnkɔstən] pl expense(s); **~beitrag** m contribution to costs od expenses

Unkraut ['ʊnkraʊt] nt weed; weeds pl

unkündbar ['ʊnkʏntbaːr] adj (Stelle) permanent; (Vertrag) binding

unlauter ['ʊnlaʊtər] adj unfair

unleserlich ['ʊnleːzərlɪç] adj illegible

unlogisch ['ʊnloːgɪʃ] adj illogical

unlösbar [ʊn'løːsbaːr] adj insoluble

Unlust ['ʊnlʊst] f lack of enthusiasm

Unmenge ['ʊnmɛŋə] f tremendous number, hundreds pl

Unmensch ['ʊnmɛnʃ] m ogre, brute; **u~lich** adj inhuman, brutal; (ungeheuer) awful

unmerklich [ʊn'mɛrklɪç] adj imperceptible

unmissverständlich ▲ ['ʊnmɪsfɛrʃtɛntlɪç] adj unmistakable

unmittelbar ['ʊnmɪtəlbaːr] adj immediate

unmodern ['ʊnmɔdɛrn] adj oldfashioned

unmöglich ['ʊnmøːklɪç] adj impossible; **U~keit** f impossibility

unmoralisch ['ʊnmoraːlɪʃ] adj immoral

Unmut ['ʊnmuːt] m ill humour

unnachgiebig ['ʊnnaːxgiːbɪç] adj unyielding

unnahbar [ʊn'naːbaːr] adj unapproachable

unnötig ['ʊnnøːtɪç] adj unnecessary

unnütz ['ʊnnʏts] adj useless

unordentlich ['ʊnɔrdəntlɪç] adj untidy

Unordnung ['ʊnɔrdnʊŋ] f disorder

unparteiisch ['ʊnpartaiɪʃ] adj impartial; **U~e(r)** f(m) umpire; (FUSSBALL) referee

unpassend ['ʊnpasənt] adj inappropriate; (Zeit) inopportune

unpässlich ['ʊnpɛslɪç] adj unwell

unpersönlich ['ʊnpɛrzøːnlɪç] adj impersonal

unpolitisch ['ʊnpoliːtɪʃ] adj apolitical

unpraktisch ['ʊnpraktɪʃ] adj unpractical

unpünktlich ['ʊnpʏŋktlɪç] adj unpunctual

unrationell ['ʊnratsionɛl] adj inefficient

unrealistisch ['ʊnrealɪstɪʃ] adj unrealistic

unrecht ['ʊnrɛçt] adj wrong; **U~** nt wrong; **zu U~** wrongly; **U~ haben** to be wrong; **U~mäßig** adj unlawful, illegal

unregelmäßig ['ʊnreːgəlmɛːsɪç] adj irregular; **U~keit** f irregularity

unreif ['ʊnraif] adj (Obst) unripe; (fig)

immature

unrentabel ['ʊnrɛntaːbəl] adj unprofitable

unrichtig ['ʊnrɪçtɪç] adj incorrect, wrong

Unruhe ['ʊnruːə] f unrest; **~stifter** m troublemaker

unruhig ['ʊnruːɪç] adj restless

uns [ʊns] (akk, dat von wir) pron us; ourselves

unsachlich ['ʊnzaxlɪç] adj not to the point, irrelevant

unsagbar [ʊn'zaːkbaːr] adj indescribable

unsanft ['ʊnzanft] adj rough

unsauber ['ʊnzaʊbər] adj unclean, dirty; (fig) crooked; (MUS) fuzzy

unschädlich ['ʊnʃɛːtlɪç] adj harmless; **jdn/etw ~ machen** to render sb/sth harmless

unscharf ['ʊnʃarf] adj indistinct; (Bild etc) out of focus, blurred

unscheinbar ['ʊnʃaɪnbaːr] adj insignificant; (Aussehen, Haus etc) unprepossessing

unschlagbar [ʊn'ʃlaːkbaːr] adj invincible

unschön ['ʊnʃøːn] adj (hässlich: Anblick) ugly, unattractive; (unfreundlich: Benehmen) unpleasant, ugly

Unschuld ['ʊnʃʊlt] f innocence; **u~ig** [-dɪç] adj innocent

unselbst(st)ändig ['ʊnzɛlpʃtɛndɪç] adj dependent, over-reliant on others

unser(e) ['ʊnzər(ə)] pron ours; **~einer** pron people like us; **~eins** pron = unsereiner; **~erseits** adv on our part; **~twegen** adv (für uns) for our sake; (wegen uns) on our account; **~twillen** adv: **um ~twillen = unsertwegen**

unsicher ['ʊnzɪçər] adj uncertain; (Mensch) insecure; **U~heit** f uncertainty; insecurity

unsichtbar ['ʊnzɪçtbaːr] adj invisible

Unsinn ['ʊnzɪn] m nonsense; **u~ig** adj nonsensical

Unsitte ['ʊnzɪtə] f deplorable habit

unsozial ['ʊnzotsiaːl] adj (Verhalten) antisocial

unsportlich ['ʊnʃpɔrtlɪç] adj not sporty; unfit; (Verhalten) unsporting

unsre ['ʊnzrə] = **unsere**

unsterblich ['ʊnʃtɛrplɪç] adj immortal

Unstimmigkeit ['ʊnʃtɪmɪçkaɪt] f inconsistency; (Streit) disagreement

unsympathisch ['ʊnzʏmpaːtɪʃ] adj unpleasant; **er ist mir ~** I don't like him

untätig ['ʊntɛːtɪç] adj idle

untauglich ['ʊntaʊklɪç] adj unsuitable; (MIL) unfit

unteilbar [ʊn'taɪlbaːr] adj indivisible

unten ['ʊntən] adv below; (im Haus) downstairs; (an der Treppe etc) at the bottom; **nach ~** down; **~ am Berg** etc at the bottom of the mountain etc; **ich bin bei ihm ~ durch** (umg) he's through with me

---

SCHLÜSSELWORT

unter ['ʊntər] präp +dat 1 (räumlich, mit Zahlen) under; (drunter) underneath, below; **unter 18 Jahren** under 18 years

2 (zwischen) among(st); **sie waren unter sich** they were by themselves; **einer unter ihnen** one of them; **unter anderem** among other things

♦ präp +akk under, below

Unterarm ['ʊntarʔarm] m forearm

unter- zW: **~belichten** vt (PHOT) to underexpose; **U~bewusstsein ▲** nt subconscious; **~bezahlt** adj underpaid

unterbieten [ʊntar'biːtən] (unreg) vt insep (COMM) to undercut; (Rekord) to lower

unterbrechen [ʊntar'brɛçən] (unreg) vt insep to interrupt

Unterbrechung f interruption

unterbringen ['ʊntarbrɪŋən] (unreg) vt (in Koffer) to stow; (in Zeitung) to place; (Person: in Hotel etc) to accommodate, to put up

unterdessen [ʊntar'dɛsən] *adv* meanwhile

Unterdruck ['ʊntardrʊk] *m* low pressure

unterdrücken [ʊntar'drʏkən] *vt insep* to suppress; (*Leute*) to oppress

untere(r, s) ['ʊntara(r, s)] *adj* lower

untereinander [ʊntaraɪ'nandar] *adv* with each other; among themselves *etc*

unterentwickelt ['ʊntarʔɛntvɪkəlt] *adj* underdeveloped

unterernährt ['ʊntarʔɛrnɛːrt] *adj* undernourished, underfed

Unterernährung *f* malnutrition

Unterführung *f* subway, underpass

Untergang ['ʊntargaŋ] *m* (down)fall, decline; (*NAUT*) sinking; (*von Gestirn*) setting

unter'geben *adj* subordinate

untergehen ['ʊntargeːən] (*unreg*) *vi* to go down; (*Sonne auch*) to set; (*Staat*) to fall; (*Volk*) to perish; (*Welt*) to come to an end; (*im Lärm*) to be drowned

Untergeschoss ▲ ['ʊntargəʃɔs] *nt* basement

'Untergewicht *nt* underweight

unter'gliedern *vt* to subdivide

Untergrund ['ʊntargrʊnt] *m* foundation; (*POL*) underground; **~bahn** *f* underground, tube, subway (*US*)

unterhalb ['ʊntarhalp] *präp* +*gen* below ♦ *adv* below; **~ von** below

Unterhalt ['ʊntarhalt] *m* maintenance; **u~en** (*unreg*) *vt insep* to maintain; (*belustigen*) to entertain ♦ *vr insep* to talk; (*sich belustigen*) to enjoy o.s.; **u~sam** *adj* (*Abend, Person*) entertaining, amusing; **~ung** *f* maintenance; (*Belustigung*) entertainment, amusement; (*Gespräch*) talk

Unterhändler ['ʊntarhɛntlar] *m* negotiator

Unter- *zW:* **~hemd** *nt* vest, undershirt (*US*); **~hose** *f* underpants *pl*; **~kiefer** *m*

lower jaw

unterkommen ['ʊntarkɔmən] (*unreg*) *vi* to find shelter; to find work; **das ist mir noch nie untergekommen** I've never met with that

unterkühlt [ʊntar'kyːlt] *adj* (*Körper*) affected by hypothermia

Unterkunft ['ʊntarkʊnft] (-, **-künfte**) *f* accommodation

Unterlage ['ʊntarlaːgə] *f* foundation; (*Beleg*) document; (*Schreibunterlage etc*) pad

unter'lassen (*unreg*) *vt insep* (*versäumen*) to fail to do; (*sich enthalten*) to refrain from

unterlaufen [ʊntar'laʊfən] (*unreg*) *vi insep* to happen ♦ *adj*: **mit Blut ~** suffused with blood; (*Augen*) bloodshot

unterlegen ['ʊntarleːgən] *vt* to lay *od* put under; **unter'legen** *adj* inferior; (*besiegt*) defeated

Unterleib ['ʊntarlaɪp] *m* abdomen

unter'liegen (*unreg*) *vi insep* (+*dat*) to be defeated *od* overcome (by); (*unterworfen sein*) to be subject (to)

Untermiete ['ʊntarmiːtə] *f*: **zur ~ wohnen** to be a subtenant *od* lodger; **~r(in)** *m(f)* subtenant, lodger

unternehmen (*unreg*) *vt insep* to undertake; **Unter'nehmen** (-s, -) *nt* undertaking, enterprise (*auch COMM*)

Unternehmer [ʊntar'neːmar] (-s, -) *m* entrepreneur, businessman

'unterordnen ['ʊntarɔrdnən] *vr* +*dat* to submit o.s. (to), to give o.s. second place to

Unterredung [ʊntar'reːdʊŋ] *f* discussion, talk

Unterricht ['ʊntarrɪçt] (-(e)s, -e) *m* instruction, lessons *pl*; **u~en** [ʊntar'rɪçtən] *vt insep* to instruct; (*SCH*) to teach ♦ *vr insep*: **sich u~en** (*über** +*akk*) to inform o.s. (about), to obtain information (about); **~sfach** *nt* subject (on school *etc* curriculum)

Spelling Reform: ▲ *new spelling* △ *old spelling (to be phased out)*

Unterrock ['ʊntərɔk] *m* petticoat, slip

unter'sagen *vt insep* to forbid; **jdm etw ~** to forbid sb to do sth

Untersatz ['ʊntərzats] *m* coaster, saucer

unter'schätzen *vt insep* to underestimate

unter'scheiden (*unreg*) *vt insep* to distinguish ♦ *vr insep* to differ

Unter'scheidung *f* (*Unterschied*) distinction; (*Unterscheiden*) differentiation

Unterschied ['ʊntərʃiːt] (-(e)s, -e) *m* difference, distinction; **im ~ zu** as distinct from; **u~lich** *adj* varying, differing; (*diskriminierend*) discriminatory

unterschiedslos *adv* indiscriminately

unter'schlagen (*unreg*) *vt insep* to embezzle; (*verheimlichen*) to suppress

Unterschlagung *f* embezzlement

Unterschlupf ['ʊntərʃlʊpf] (-(e)s, -schlüpfe) *m* refuge

unter'schreiben (*unreg*) *vt insep* to sign

Unterschrift ['ʊntərʃrɪft] *f* signature

Unterseeboot ['ʊntərzeːboːt] *nt* submarine

Untersetzer ['ʊntərzɛtsər] *m* tablemat; (*für Gläser*) coaster

untersetzt [ʊntər'zɛtst] *adj* stocky

unterste(r, s) ['ʊntərstə(r, s)] *adj* lowest, bottom

unterstehen [ʊntər'ʃteːən] (*unreg*) *vi insep* (+*dat*) to be under ♦ *vr insep* to dare; **'unterstehen** (*unreg*) *vi* to shelter

unterstellen [ʊntər'ʃtɛlən] *vt insep* to subordinate; (*fig*) to impute ♦ *vt* (*Auto*) to garage, to park ♦ *vr* to take shelter

unter'streichen (*unreg*) *vt insep* (auch fig) to underline

Unterstufe ['ʊntərʃtuːfə] *f* lower grade

Unter'stützen *vt insep* to support

Unter'stützung *f* support, assistance

unter'suchen *vt insep* (*MED*) to examine; (*Polizei*) to investigate

Unter'suchung *f* examination; investigation, inquiry; **~sausschuss** ▲ *m* committee of inquiry; **~shaft** *f* im-

---

prisonment on remand

Untertasse ['ʊntərtasə] *f* saucer

untertauchen ['ʊntərtauxən] *vi* to dive; (*fig*) to disappear, to go underground

Unterteil ['ʊntərtail] *nt* od *m* lower part, bottom; **u~en** [ʊntər'tailən] *vt insep* to divide up

Untertitel ['ʊntərtiːtəl] *m* subtitle

Unterwäsche ['ʊntərvɛʃə] *f* underwear

unterwegs [ʊntər'veːks] *adv* on the way

unter'werfen (*unreg*) *vt insep* to subject; (*Volk*) to subjugate ♦ *vr insep* (+*dat*) to submit (to)

unter'zeichnen *vt insep* to sign

unter'ziehen (*unreg*) *vt insep* to subject ♦ *vr insep* (+*dat*) to undergo; (*einer Prüfung*) to take

untragbar [ʊn'traːkbaːr] *adj* unbearable, intolerable

untreu ['ʊntrɔy] *adj* unfaithful; **U~e** *f* unfaithfulness

untröstlich [ʊn'trøːstlɪç] *adj* inconsolable

unüberlegt ['ʊnlyːbərleːkt] *adj* ill-considered ♦ *adv* without thinking

unübersichtlich *adj* (*Gelände*) broken; (*Kurve*) blind

unumgänglich [ʊn|ʊm'gɛŋlɪç] *adj* indispensable, vital; absolutely necessary

ununterbrochen ['ʊn|ʊntərbrɔxən] *adj* uninterrupted

unver- ['ʊnfer] *zW*: **~änderlich** [-'ɛndərlɪç] *adj* unchangeable; **~antwortlich** [-'antvɔrtlɪç] *adj* irresponsible; (*unentschuldbar*) inexcusable; **~besserlich** *adj* incorrigible; **~bindlich** *adj* not binding; (*Antwort*) curt ♦ *adv* (*COMM*) without obligation; ♦ *bleit* *ad* (*Benzin usw*) unleaded; **ich fahre ~bleit** I use unleaded; **~blümt** [-'blyːmt] *adj* plain, blunt ♦ *adv* plainly, bluntly; **~daulich** *adj* indigestible; **~einbar** *adj* incompatible; **~fänglich** [-'fɛŋlɪç] *adj* harmless; **~froren** *adj* impudent; **~gesslich** ▲ *adj* (*Tag, Erlebnis*) unforgettable; **~hofft** [-'hɔft] *adj* unexpected; **~meidlich** [-'maıtlıç] *adj* unavoidable; **~mutet** *adj* unexpected; **~nünftig** [-'nʏnftıç] *adj* foolish; **~schämt** *adj* impudent; **U~schämtheit** *f* impudence, insolence; **~sehrt** *adj* uninjured; **~söhnlich** [-'zøːnlıç] *adj* irreconcilable; **~ständlich** [-'ʃtɛntlıç] *adj* unintelligible; **~träglich** *adj* quarrelsome; (*Meinungen, MED*) incompatible; **~zeihlich** *adj* unpardonable; **~züglich** [-'tsyːklıç] *adj* immediate

unvollkommen ['ʊnfɔlkɔmən] *adj* imperfect

unvollständig *adj* incomplete

unvor- ['ʊnfoːr] *zW:* **~bereitet** *adj* unprepared; **~eingenommen** *adj* unbiased; **~hergesehen** [-heːrgəzeːən] *adj* unforeseen; **~sichtig** [-zıçtıç] *adj* careless, imprudent; **~stellbar** [-'ʃtɛlbaːr] *adj* inconceivable; **~teilhaft** *adj* disadvantageous

unwahr ['ʊnvaːr] *adj* untrue; **~scheinlich** *adj* improbable, unlikely ♦ *adv* (*umg*) incredibly

unweigerlich [ʊn'vaıgərlıç] *adj* unquestioning ♦ *adv* without fail

Unwesen ['ʊnveːzən] *nt* nuisance; (*Unfug*) mischief; **sein ~ treiben** to wreak havoc

unwesentlich *adj* inessential, unimportant; **~ besser** marginally better

Unwetter ['ʊnvɛtər] *nt* thunderstorm

unwichtig ['ʊnvıçtıç] *adj* unimportant

unwider- ['ʊnviːdər] *zW:* **~legbar** *adj* irrefutable; **~ruflich** *adj* irrevocable; **~stehlich** *adj* irresistible

unwill- ['ʊnvıl] *zW:* **U~e(n)** *m* indignation; **~ig** *adj* indignant; (*widerwillig*) reluctant; **~kürlich** [-kyːrlıç] *adj* involuntary ♦ *adv* instinctively; (*lachen*) involuntarily

unwirklich ['ʊnvırklıç] *adj* unreal

unwirksam ['ʊnvırkzaːm] *adj* (*Mittel, Methode*) ineffective

unwirtschaftlich ['ʊnvırtʃaftlıç] *adj* uneconomical

unwissen- ['ʊnvısən] *zW:* **~d** *adj* ignorant; **U~heit** *f* ignorance; **~tlich** *adv* unknowingly, unwittingly

unwohl ['ʊnvoːl] *adj* unwell, ill; **U~sein** (**-s**) *nt* indisposition

unwürdig ['ʊnvʏrdıç] *adj* unworthy

unzählig [ʊn'tsɛːlıç] *adj* innumerable, countless

unzer- [ʊntsɛr] *zW:* **~brechlich** *adj* unbreakable; **~störbar** *adj* indestructible; **~trennlich** *adj* inseparable

Unzucht ['ʊntsʊxt] *f* sexual offence

unzüchtig ['ʊntsʏçtıç] *adj* immoral; lewd

unzu- ['ʊntsu] *zW:* **~frieden** *adj* dissatisfied; **U~friedenheit** *f* discontent; **~länglich** *adj* inadequate; **~lässig** *adj* inadmissible; **~rechnungsfähig** *adj* irresponsible; **~treffend** *adj* incorrect; **~verlässig** *adj* unreliable

unzweideutig ['ʊntsvaıdɔytıç] *adj* unambiguous

üppig ['ʏpıç] *adj* (*Frau*) curvaceous; (*Busen*) full, ample; (*Essen*) sumptuous; (*Vegetation*) luxuriant, lush

Ur- ['uːr] *in zW* original

uralt ['uːr|alt] *adj* ancient, very old

Uran [u'raːn] (**-s**) *nt* uranium

Ur- *zW:* **~aufführung** *f* first performance; **~einwohner** *m* original inhabitant; **~eltern** *pl* ancestors; **~enkel(in)** *m(f)* great-grandchild, great-grandson(-daughter); **~großeltern** *pl* great-grandparents; **~heber** (**-s, -**) *m* originator; (*Autor*) author; **~heberrecht** *nt* copyright

Urin [u'riːn] (**-s, -e**) *m* urine

Urkunde ['uːrkʊndə] *f* document, deed

Urlaub ['uːrlaʊp] (**-(e)s, -e**) *m* holiday (*pl*) (*BRIT*), vacation (*US*); (*MIL etc*) leave;

~er [-'laʊbər] (-s, -) m holiday-maker (BRIT), vacationer (US); **~sort** m holiday resort; **~szeit** f holiday season

Urne ['ʊrnə] f urn

Ursache ['uːrzaxə] f cause; **keine ~** that's all right

Ursprung ['uːrʃprʊŋ] m origin, source; (von Fluss) source

ursprünglich ['uːrʃprʏŋlɪç] adj original ♦ adv originally

Ursprungsland nt country of origin

Urteil ['ʊrtail] (-s, -e) nt opinion; (JUR) sentence, judgement; **u~en** vi to judge; **~sspruch** m sentence, verdict

Urwald m jungle

Urzeit f prehistoric times pl

USA [uː'es'ʔaː] pl abk (= Vereinigte Staaten von Amerika) USA

usw. abk (= und so weiter) etc

Utensilien [uten'ziːliən] pl utensils

Utopie [uto'piː] f pipe dream

utopisch [u'toːpɪʃ] adj utopian

V, v

vag(e) [vaːk, 'vaːgə] adj vague

Vagina [va'giːna] (-, Vaginen) f vagina

Vakuum ['vaːkuʊm] (-s, Vakua od Vakuen) nt vacuum

Vampir [vam'piːr] (-s, -e) m vampire

Vanille [va'nɪljə] (-) f vanilla

Variation [variatsi'oːn] f variation

variieren [vari'iːrən] vt, vi to vary

Vase ['vaːzə] f vase

Vater ['faːtər] (-s, ◦) m father; **~land** nt native country; Fatherland

väterlich ['fɛːtərlɪç] adj fatherly

Vaterschaft f paternity

Vaterunser (-s, -) nt Lord's prayer

Vati ['faːti] m daddy

v. Chr. abk (= vor Christus) B.C.

Vegetarier(in) [vege'taːriər(ɪn)] (-s, -) m(f) vegetarian

vegetarisch [vege'taːrɪʃ] adj vegetarian

Veilchen ['faɪlçən] nt violet

Vene ['veːnə] f vein

Ventil [vɛn'tiːl] (-s, -e) nt valve

Ventilator [vɛnti'laːtər] m ventilator

verab- [fɛr'ʔap] zW: **~reden** vt to agree, to arrange ♦ vr: **sich mit jdm ~reden** to arrange to meet sb; **mit jdm ~redet sein** to have arranged to meet sb; **V~redung** f arrangement; (Treffen) appointment; **~scheuen** vt to detest, to abhor; **~schieden** vt (Gäste) to say goodbye to; (entlassen) to discharge; (Gesetz) to pass ♦ vr to take one's leave; **V~schiedung** f leave-taking; discharge; passing

ver- [fɛr] zW: **~achten** vt to despise; **~ächtlich** [-'ʔɛçtlɪç] adj contemptuous; (~achtenswert) contemptible; **jdn ~ächtlich machen** to run sb down; **V~achtung** f contempt

verallgemeinern [fɛrʔalgə'maɪnərn] vt to generalize; **Verallgemeinerung** f generalization

veralten [fɛr'ʔaltən] vi to become obsolete od out-of-date

Veranda [ve'randa] (-, Veranden) f veranda

veränder- [fɛr'ʔɛndər] zW: **~lich** adj changeable; **~n** vt, vr to change, to alter; **V~ung** f change, alteration

veran- [fɛr'ʔan] zW: **~lagt** adj with a ... nature; **V~lagung** f disposition; **~lassen** vt to cause; **Maßnahmen ~lassen** to take measures; **sich ~lasst sehen** to feel prompted; **~schaulichen** vt to illustrate; **~schlagen** vt to estimate; **~stalten** vt to organize, to arrange; **V~stalter** (-s, -) m organizer; **V~staltung** f (V~stalten) organizing; (Konzert etc) event, function

verantwort- [fɛr'ʔantvɔrt] zW: **~en** vt to answer for ♦ vr to justify o.s.; **~lich** adj responsible; **V~ung** f responsibility; **~ungsbewusst ▲** adj responsible; **~ungslos** adj irresponsible

verarbeiten [fɛr'ʔarbaɪtən] vt to process; (geistig) to assimilate; **etw zu etw ~** to make sth into sth; **Verarbeitung** f processing; assimilation

verärgern [fɛrˈʔɛrgərn] vt to annoy

verausgaben [fɛrˈʔausgaːbən] vr to run out of money; (fig) to exhaust o.s.

Verb [vɛrp] (-s, -en) nt verb

Verband [fɛrˈbant] (-(e)s, ⸚e) m (MED) bandage, dressing; (Bund) association, society; (MIL) unit; **~kasten** m medicine chest, first-aid box; **~zeug** nt bandage

verbannen [fɛrˈbanən] vt to banish

verbergen [fɛrˈbɛrgən] (unreg) vt, vr (**sich**) ~ (**vor** +dat) to hide (from)

verbessern [fɛrˈbɛsərn] vt, vr to improve; (berichtigen) to correct (o.s.)

Verbesserung f improvement; correction

verbeugen [fɛrˈbɔygən] vr to bow

Verbeugung f bow

ver'biegen (unreg) vi to bend

ver'bieten (unreg) vt to forbid; **jdm etw ~** to forbid sb to do sth

verbilligen [fɛrˈbɪlɪgn] vt to reduce the cost of; (Preis) to reduce

ver'binden (unreg) vt to connect; (kombinieren) to combine; (MED) to bandage ♦ vr (auch CHEM) to combine, to join; **jdm die Augen ~** to blindfold sb

verbindlich [fɛrˈbɪntlɪç] adj binding; (freundlich) friendly

Ver'bindung f connection; (Zusammensetzung) combination; (CHEM) compound; (UNIV) club

verbissen [fɛrˈbɪsn] adj (Kampf) bitter; (Gesichtsausdruck) grim

ver'bitten (unreg) vt: **sich** dat **etw ~** not to tolerate sth, not to stand for sth

Verbleib [fɛrˈblaip] (-(e)s) m whereabouts; **v~en** (unreg) vi to remain

verbleit [fɛrˈblait] adj (Benzin) leaded

verblüffen [fɛrˈblʏfən] vt to stagger, to amaze; **Verblüffung** f stupefaction

verblühen vi to wither, to fade

verbluten vi to bleed to death

verborgen [fɛrˈbɔrgən] adj hidden

Verbot [fɛrˈboːt] (-(e)s, -e) nt prohibition, ban; **v~en** adj forbidden; **Rauchen v~en!** no smoking; **~sschild** nt prohibitory sign

Verbrauch [fɛrˈbraux] m consumption; **v~en** vt to use up; **~er** (-s, -) m consumer; **v~t** adj used up, finished; (Luft) stale; (Mensch) worn out

Verbrechen [fɛrˈbrɛçən] (-s, -) nt crime

Verbrecher [fɛrˈbrɛçər] (-s, -) m criminal; **v~isch** adj criminal

ver'breiten vt, vr to spread; **sich über etw** akk **~** to expound on sth

verbreitern [fɛrˈbraitərn] vt to broaden

Verbreitung f spread(ing), propagation

verbrenn- [fɛrˈbrɛn] zW: **~bar** adj combustible; **~en** (unreg) vt to burn; (Leiche) to cremate; **V~ung** f burning; (in Motor) combustion; (von Leiche) cremation; **V~ungsmotor** m internal combustion engine

verbringen [fɛrˈbrɪŋən] (unreg) vt to spend

verbrühen [fɛrˈbryːən] vt to scald

verbuchen [fɛrˈbuːxən] vt (FIN) to register; (Erfolg) to enjoy; (Misserfolg) to suffer

verbunden [fɛrˈbundən] adj connected; **jdm ~ sein** to be obliged or indebted to sb; **„falsch ~"** (TEL) "wrong number"

verbünden [fɛrˈbʏndən] vr to ally o.s.; **Verbündete(r)** f(m) adj ally

ver'bürgen vr: **sich ~ für** to vouch for

ver'büßen vr: **eine Strafe ~** to serve a sentence

Verdacht [fɛrˈdaxt] (-(e)s) m suspicion

verdächtig [fɛrˈdɛçtɪç] adj suspicious, suspect; **~en** [fɛrˈdɛçtɪgən] vt to suspect

verdammen [fɛrˈdamən] vt to damn,

to condemn; **verdammt!** damn!

verdammt (umg) adj, adv damned; **~ noch mal!** damn!, dammit!

ver'dampfen vi to vaporize, to evaporate

ver'danken vt: jdm etw **~** to owe sb sth

verdau- [fɛr'dau] zW: **~en** vt (auch fig) to digest; **~lich** adj digestible; **das ist schwer ~lich** that is hard to digest; **V~ung** f digestion

Verdeck [fɛr'dɛk] (-(e)s, -e) nt (AUT) hood; (NAUT) deck; **v~en** vt to cover (up); (verbergen) to hide

Verderb- [fɛr'dɛrp] zW: **~en** [-'dɛrbən] (-s) nt ruin; **v~en** (unreg) vt to spoil; (schädigen) to ruin; (moralisch) to corrupt ♦ vi (Essen) to spoil, to rot; (Mensch) to go to the bad; **jdm v~en** to get into sb's bad books; **v~lich** adj (Einfluss) pernicious; (Lebensmittel) perishable

verdeutlichen [fɛr'dɔytlɪçən] vt to make clear

ver'dichten vt, vr to condense

ver'dienen vi to earn; (moralisch) to deserve

Ver'dienst (-(e)s, -e) m earnings pl ♦ nt merit; (Leistung): **~ (um)** service (to)

verdient [fɛr'diːnt] adj well-earned; (Person) deserving of esteem; **sich um etw ~ machen** to do a lot for sth

verdoppeln [fɛr'dɔpəln] vt to double

verdorben [fɛr'dɔrbən] adj spoilt; (geschädigt) ruined; (moralisch) corrupt

verdrängen [fɛr'drɛŋən] vt to oust, to displace (auch PHYS); (PSYCH) to repress

ver'drehen vt (auch fig) to twist; (Augen) to roll; **jdm den Kopf ~** (fig) to turn sb's head

verdrießlich [fɛr'driːslɪç] adj peevish, annoyed

Verdruss [fɛr'drus] ▲ (-es, -e) m annoyance, worry

verdummen [fɛr'dumən] vt to make stupid ♦ vi to grow stupid

verdunkeln [fɛr'dʊŋkəln] vt to darken;

(fig) to obscure ♦ vr to darken

Verdunk(e)lung f blackout; (fig) obscuring

verdünnen [fɛr'dʏnən] vt to dilute

verdunsten [fɛr'dʊnstən] vi to evaporate

verdursten [fɛr'dʊrstən] vi to die of thirst

verdutzt [fɛr'dʊtst] adj nonplussed, taken aback

verehr- [fɛr'eːr] zW: **~en** vt to venerate, to worship (auch REL); **jdm etw ~en** to present sb with sth; **V~er(in)** (-s, -) m(f) admirer, worshipper (auch REL); **~t** adj esteemed; **V~ung** f respect; (REL) worship

Verein [fɛr'ain] (-(e)s, -e) m club, association; **v~bar** adj compatible; **v~baren** vt to agree upon; **~barung** f agreement; **v~en** vt (Menschen, Länder) to unite; (Prinzipien) to reconcile; **mit v~ten Kräften** having pooled resources, having joined forces; **~te Nationen** United Nations; **v~fachen** [-faxən] vt to simplify; **v~heitlichen** [-haitlɪçən] vt to standardize; **v~igen** vt, vr to unite; **~igung** f union; (Verein) association; **v~t** adj united; **v~zelt** adj isolated

ver'eitern vi to suppurate, to fester

verengen [fɛr'ɛŋən] vr to narrow

vererb- [fɛr'ɛrp] zW: **~en** vt to bequeath; (BIOL) to transmit ♦ vr to be hereditary; **V~ung** f bequeathing; (BIOL) transmission; (Lehre) heredity

verewigen [fɛr'eːvɪgən] vt to immortalize ♦ vr (umg) to immortalize o.s.

ver'fahren (unreg) vi to act ♦ vr to get lost ♦ adj tangled; **~ mit** to deal with; **Ver'fahren** (-s, -) nt procedure; (TECH) process; (JUR) proceedings pl

Verfall [fɛr'fal] (-(e)s) m decline; (von Haus) dilapidation; (FIN) expiry; **v~en** (unreg) vi to decline; (Haus) to be falling down; (FIN) to lapse; **v~en in** +akk to lapse into; **v~en auf** +akk to hit upon; **einem Laster v~en sein** to be addicted to a vice; **~sdatum** nt expiry date; (der Haltbarkeit) sell-by date

ver'**färben** vt to change colour

ver'**fassen** [fɛr'fasən] vt (Rede) to prepare, work out

Ver'**fasser(in)** [fɛr'fasər(ɪn)] (-s, -) m(f) author, writer

Ver'**fassung** f (auch POL) constitution

Verfassungs- zW: **~gericht** nt constitutional court; **v~widrig** adj unconstitutional

ver'**faulen** vi to rot

ver'**fehlen** vt to miss; **etw für verfehlt halten** to regard sth as mistaken

ver'**feinern** [fɛr'faɪnərn] vt to refine

ver'**filmen** vt to film

ver'**flixt** [fɛr'flɪkst] (umg) adj damned, damn

ver'**fluchen** vt to curse

verfolg- [fɛr'fɔlg] zW: **~en** vt to pursue; (gerichtlich) to prosecute; (grausam, bes POL) to persecute; **V~er** (-s, -) m pursuer; **V~ung** f pursuit; prosecution; persecution

ver'**früht** [fɛr'fry:t] adj premature

verfüg- [fɛr'fy:g] zW: **~bar** adj available; **~en** vt to direct, to order ♦ vr to proceed ♦ vi: **~en über** +akk to have at one's disposal; **V~ung** f direction, order; **zur V~ung** at one's disposal; **jdm zur V~ung stehen** to be available to sb

verführ- [fɛr'fy:r] zW: **~en** vt to tempt; (sexuell) to seduce; **V~er** m tempter; seducer; **~erisch** adj seductive; **V~ung** f seduction; (Versuchung) temptation

ver'**gammeln** (umg) vi to go to seed; (Nahrung) to go off

vergangen [fɛr'ɡaŋən] adj past; **V~heit** f past

ver'**gänglich** [fɛr'ɡɛŋlɪç] adj transitory

ver'**gasen** [fɛr'ɡa:zən] vt (töten) to gas

Vergaser (-s, -) m (AUT) carburettor

Vergaß etc [fɛr'ɡa:s] vb siehe vergessen

vergeb- [fɛr'ɡe:b] zW: **~en** (unreg) vt (verzeihen) to forgive; (weggeben) to give away; **jdm etw ~en** to forgive sb (for) sth; **~ens** adv in vain; **~lich** [fɛr'ɡe:plɪç] adv in vain ♦ adj vain, futile; **V~ung** f forgiveness

ver'**gehen** (unreg) vi to pass by od away ♦ vr to commit an offence; **jdm vergeht etw** sb loses sth; **sich an jdm ~** to (sexually) assault sb; **ver'gehen** (-s, -) nt offence

ver'**gelten** (unreg) vt: **jdm etw ~** to pay sb back for sth, to repay sb for sth

Ver'**geltung** f retaliation, reprisal

ver'**gessen** [fɛr'ɡɛsən] (unreg) vt to forget; **V~heit** f oblivion

ver'**gesslich** ▲ [fɛr'ɡɛslɪç] adj forgetful; **V~keit** f forgetfulness

ver'**geuden** [fɛr'ɡɔʏdən] vt to squander, to waste

ver'**gewaltigen** [fɛrɡə'valtɪɡən] vt to rape; (fig) to violate

Ver'**gewaltigung** f rape

ver'**gewissern** [fɛrɡə'vɪsərn] vr to make sure

ver'**gießen** (unreg) vt to shed

ver'**giften** [fɛr'ɡɪftən] vt to poison

Ver'**giftung** f poisoning

Ver'**gissmeinnicht** ▲ [fɛr'ɡɪsmaɪn-nɪçt] (-(e)s, -e) nt forget-me-not

ver'**gisst** etc [fɛr'ɡɪst] vb siehe vergessen

Ver'**gleich** [fɛr'ɡlaɪç] (-(e)s, -e) m comparison; (JUR) settlement; **im ~ mit** od **zu** compared with od to; **v~bar** adj comparable; **v~en** (unreg) vt to compare ♦ vr to reach a settlement

ver'**gnügen** [fɛr'ɡny:ɡən] vr to enjoy od amuse o.s.; **V~** (-s, -) nt pleasure; **viel V~!** enjoy yourself!

ver'**gnügt** [fɛr'ɡny:kt] adj cheerful

Ver'**gnügung** f pleasure, amusement; **~spark** m amusement park

ver'**golden** [fɛr'ɡɔldən] vt to gild

ver'graben vt to bury

ver'greifen (unreg) vr: **sich an jdm ~** to lay hands on sb; **sich an etw ~** to misappropriate sth; **sich im Ton ~** to say the wrong thing

vergriffen [fɛr'grɪfən] adj (Buch) out of print; (Ware) out of stock

vergrößern [fɛr'grøːsərn] vt to enlarge; (mengenmäßig) to increase; (Lupe) to magnify

Vergrößerung f enlargement; increase; magnification; **~glas** nt magnifying glass

Vergünstigung [fɛr'gʏnstɪɡʊŋ] f concession, privilege

Vergütung f compensation

verhaften [fɛr'haftən] vt to arrest

Verhaftung f arrest

ver'halten (unreg) vr to be, to stand; (sich benehmen) to behave ♦ vt to hold od keep back; (Schritt) to check; **sich ~ (zu)** (MATH) to be in proportion (to); **Ver'halten (-s)** nt behaviour

Verhältnis [fɛr'hɛltnɪs] (-ses, -se) nt relationship; (MATH) proportion, ratio; **~se** pl (Umstände) conditions; **über seine ~se leben** to live beyond one's means; **v~mäßig** adj relative, comparative ♦ adv relatively, comparatively

verhandeln [fɛr'handəln] vi to negotiate; (JUR) to hold proceedings ♦ vt to discuss; (JUR) to hear; **über etw** akk **~** to negotiate sth od about sth

Verhandlung f negotiation; (JUR) proceedings pl; **~sbasis** f (FIN) basis for negotiations

ver'hängen vt (fig) to impose, to inflict

Verhängnis [fɛr'hɛŋnɪs] (-ses, -se) nt fate, doom; **jdm zum ~ werden** to be sb's undoing; **v~voll** adj fatal, disastrous

verharmlosen [fɛr'harmloːzən] vt to make light of, to play down

verhärten [fɛr'hɛrtən] vt to harden

verhasst ▲ [fɛr'hast] adj odious, hateful

verhauen [fɛr'havən] (unreg; umg) vt (verprügeln) to beat up

verheerend [fɛr'heːrənt] adj disastrous, devastating

verheimlichen [fɛr'haɪmlɪçən] vt: **jdm etw ~** to keep sth secret from sb

verheiratet [fɛr'haɪraːtət] adj married

ver'helfen (unreg) vi: **jdm ~ zu** to help sb to get

ver'hindern vt to prevent; **verhindert sein** to be unable to make it

verhöhnen [fɛr'høːnən] vt to mock, to sneer at

Verhör [fɛr'høːr] (-(e)s, -e) nt interrogation; (gerichtlich) (cross-) examination; **v~en** vt to interrogate; to (cross-)examine ♦ vr to misunderstand, to mishear

ver'hungern vi to starve, to die of hunger

ver'hüten vt to prevent, to avert

Ver'hütung f prevention; **~smittel** nt contraceptive

verirren [fɛr'ɪrən] vr to go astray

ver'jagen vt to drive away od off

verkalken [fɛr'kalkən] vi to calcify; (umg) to become senile

Verkauf [fɛr'kaʊf] m sale; **v~en** vt to sell

Verkäufer(in) [fɛr'kɔʏfər(ɪn)] (-s, -) m(f) seller; salesman(-woman); (in Laden) shop assistant

verkaufsoffen adj: **~er Samstag** Saturday when the shops stay open all day

Verkehr [fɛr'keːr] (-s, -e) m traffic; (Umgang, bes sexuell) intercourse; (Umlauf) circulation; **v~en** vi (Fahrzeug) to ply, to run ♦ vt, vr to turn, to transform; **v~en mit** to associate with; bei **jdm v~en** (besuchen) to visit sb regularly

Verkehrs- zW: **~ampel** f traffic lights pl; **~aufkommen** nt volume of traffic; **~beruhigung** f traffic calming; **~delikt** nt traffic offence; **~funk** m radio traffic service; **v~günstig** adj convenient; **~mittel** nt means of transport; **~schild** nt road sign; **~stauung** f traffic jam, stoppage; **~unfall** m traffic accident; **~verein** m tourist information office; **~zeichen** nt traffic sign

verkehrt adj wrong; (umgekehrt) the wrong way round

ver'kennen (unreg) vt to misjudge, not to appreciate

ver'klagen vt to take to court

verkleiden [fɛr'klaɪdən] vr to disguise (o.s.); (sich kostümieren) to get dressed up ♦ vt (Wand) to cover

Verkleidung f disguise; (ARCHIT) wainscoting

verkleinern [fɛr'klaɪnərn] vt to make smaller, to reduce in size

ver'kneifen (umg) vt: **sich dat etw ~** (Lachen) to stifle sth; (Schmerz) to hide sth; (sich versagen) to do without sth

verknüpfen [fɛr'knʏpfən] vt to tie (up), to knot; (fig) to connect

ver'kommen (unreg) vi to deteriorate, to decay; (Mensch) to go downhill, to come down in the world ♦ adj (moralisch) dissolute, depraved

verkörpern [fɛr'kœrpərn] vt to embody, to personify

verkraften [fɛr'kraftən] vt to cope with

ver'kriechen (unreg) vr to creep away, to creep into a corner

verkrüppelt [fɛr'krʏpəlt] adj crippled

ver'kühlen vr to get a chill

ver'kümmern vi to waste away

ver'künden [fɛr'kʏndən] vt to proclaim; (Urteil) to pronounce

ver'kürzen [fɛr'kʏrtsən] vt to shorten; (Wort) to abbreviate; **sich dat die Zeit ~** to while away the time

Verkürzung f shortening, abbreviation

verladen [fɛr'laːdən] (unreg) vt (Waren, Vieh) to load; (Truppen) to embark, entrain, enplane

Verlag [fɛr'laːk] (-(e)s, -e) m publishing firm

verlangen [fɛr'laŋən] vt to demand; to desire ♦ vi: **~ nach** to ask for, to desire; **~ Sie Herrn X** ask for Mr X; **V~** (-s, -) nt: **V~ (nach)** desire (for); **auf jds V~ (hin)** at sb's request

verlängern [fɛr'lɛŋərn] vt to extend; (länger machen) to lengthen

Verlängerung f extension; (SPORT) extra time; **~sschnur** f extension cable

verlangsamen [fɛr'laŋzaːmən] vt, vr to decelerate, to slow down

Verlass ▲ [fɛr'las] m: **auf ihn/das ist kein ~** he/it cannot be relied upon

ver'lassen (unreg) vt to leave ♦ vr: **sich ~ auf** +akk to depend on ♦ adj desolate; (Mensch) abandoned

verlässlich ▲ [fɛr'lɛslɪç] adj reliable

Verlauf [fɛr'laʊf] m course; **v~en** (unreg) vi (zeitlich) to pass; (Farben) to run ♦ vr to get lost; (Menschenmenge) to disperse

ver'lauten vi: **etw ~ lassen** to disclose sth; **wie verlautet** as reported

ver'legen vt to move; (verlieren) to mislay; (Buch) to publish ♦ vr: **sich auf etw akk ~** to take up od to sth ♦ adj embarrassed; **nicht ~ um** never at a loss for; **Ver'legenheit** f embarrassment; (Situation) difficulty, scrape

Verleger [fɛr'leːgər] (-s, -) m publisher

Verleih [fɛr'laɪ] (-(e)s, -e) m hire service; **v~en** (unreg) vt to lend; (Kraft, Anschein) to confer, to bestow; (Preis, Medaille) to award; **~ung** f lending; bestowal; award

ver'leiten vt to lead astray; **~ zu** to talk into, to tempt into

ver'lernen vt to forget, to unlearn

ver'lesen (unreg) vt to read out; (aussondern) to sort out ♦ vr to make a mistake in reading

verletz- [fɛr'lɛts] zW: **~en** vt (auch fig)

to injure, to hurt; (*Gesetz etc*) to violate; **~end** *adj* (*fig: Worte*) hurtful; **~lich** *adj* vulnerable, sensitive; **V~te(r)** *f(m)* injured person; **V~ung** *f* injury; (*Verstoß*) violation, infringement

verleugnen [fɛr'lɔygnən] *vt* (*Herkunft, Glauben*) to belie; (*Menschen*) to disown

verleumden [fɛr'lɔymdən] *vt* to slander; **Verleumdung** *f* slander, libel

ver'lieben *vr*: **sich ~ (in** +*akk*) to fall in love (with)

verliebt [fɛr'li:pt] *adj* in love

verlieren [fɛr'li:rən] (*unreg*) *vt, vi* to lose ♦ *vr* to get lost

Verlierer *m* loser

verlob- [fɛr'lo:p] *zW*: **~en** *vr*: **sich ~en (mit)** to get engaged (to); **V~te(r)** [fɛr'lo:pta(r)] *f(m)* fiancé *m*, fiancée *f*; **V~ung** *f* engagement

ver'locken *vt* to entice, to lure

Ver'lockung *f* temptation, attraction

verlogen [fɛr'lo:gən] *adj* untruthful

verlor *etc vb siehe* **verlieren**

verloren [fɛr'lo:rən] *adj* lost; (*Eier*) poached ♦ *vb* siehe **verlieren**; **~ geben** to give sth up for lost; **~ gehen** to get lost

verlosen [fɛr'lo:zən] *vt* to raffle, to draw lots for; **Verlosung** *f* raffle, lottery

Verlust [fɛr'lʊst] (**-(e)s, -e**) *m* loss; (*MIL*) casualty

ver'machen *vt* to bequeath, to leave

Vermächtnis [fɛr'mɛçtnɪs] (**-ses, -se**) *nt* legacy

Vermählung [fɛr'mɛ:lʊŋ] *f* wedding, marriage

vermarkten [fɛr'marktən] *vt* (*COMM: Artikel*) to market

vermehren [fɛr'me:rən] *vt, vr* to multiply; (*Menge*) to increase

Vermehrung *f* multiplying; increase

ver'meiden (*unreg*) *vt* to avoid

vermeintlich [fɛr'maɪntlɪç] *adj* supposed

Vermerk [fɛr'mɛrk] (**-(e)s, -e**) *m* note;

(*in Ausweis*) endorsement; **v~en** *vt* to note

ver'messen (*unreg*) *vt* to survey ♦ *adj* presumptuous, bold; **Ver'messenheit** *f* presumptuousness; recklessness

Ver'messung *f* survey(ing)

vermiet- [fɛr'mi:t] *zW*: **ver'mieten** *vt* to let, to rent (out); (*Auto*) to hire out, to rent; **Ver'mieter(in)** (**-s, -)** *m(f)* landlord(-lady); **Ver'mietung** *f* letting, renting (out); (*von Autos*) hiring (out)

vermindern [fɛr'mɪndərn] *vt, vr* to lessen, to decrease; (*Preise*) to reduce

Verminderung *f* reduction

ver'mischen *vt, vr* to mix, to blend

vermissen [fɛr'mɪsən] *vt* to miss

vermitt- [fɛr'mɪt] *zW*: **~eln** *vi* to mediate ♦ *vt* (*Gespräch*) to connect; **jdm etw ~eln** to help sb to obtain sth; **V~ler** (**-s, -)** *m* (*Schlichter*) agent, mediator; **V~lung** *f* procurement; (*Stellenvermittlung*) agency; (*TEL*) exchange; (*Schlichtung*) mediation; **V~lungsgebühr** *f* commission

ver'mögen (*unreg*) *vt* to be capable of; **~ zu** to be able to; **Ver'mögen** (**-s, -)** *nt* wealth; (*Fähigkeit*) ability; **ein V~ kosten** to cost a fortune; **ver'mögend** *adj* wealthy

vermuten [fɛr'mu:tən] *vt* to suppose, to guess; (*argwöhnen*) to suspect

vermutlich *adj* supposed, presumed ♦ *adv* probably

Vermutung *f* supposition; suspicion

vernachlässigen [fɛr'na:xlɛsɪgən] *vt* to neglect

ver'nehmen (*unreg*) *vt* to perceive, to hear; (*erfahren*) to learn; (*JUR*) to (cross-)examine; **dem V~ nach** from what I/we *etc* hear

Vernehmung *f* (cross-)examination

verneigen [fɛr'naɪgən] *vr* to bow

verneinen [fɛr'naɪnən] *vt* (*Frage*) to answer in the negative; (*ablehnen*) to deny; (*GRAM*) to negate; **~d** *adj* negative

Verneinung f negation

vernichten [fɛr'nɪçtən] vt to annihilate, to destroy; **~d** adj (fig) crushing; (Blick) withering; (Kritik) scathing

Vernunft [fɛr'nʊnft] (-) f reason, understanding

vernünftig [fɛr'nʏnftıç] adj sensible, reasonable

veröffentlichen [fɛr|'œfəntlıçən] vt to publish; **Veröffentlichung** f publication

verordnen [fɛr|'ɔrdnən] vt (MED) to prescribe

Verordnung f order, decree; (MED) prescription

ver'pachten vt to lease (out)

ver'packen vt to pack

Ver'packung f packing, wrapping; **~smaterial** nt packing, wrapping

ver'passen vt to miss; **jdm eine Ohrfeige ~** (umg) to give sb a clip round the ear

verpfänden [fɛr'pfɛndən] vt (Besitz) to mortgage

ver'pflanzen vt to transplant

ver'pflegen vt to feed, to cater for

Ver'pflegung f feeding, catering; (Kost) food; (in Hotel) board

verpflichten [fɛr'pflıçtən] vt to oblige, to bind; (anstellen) to engage ♦ vr to undertake; (MIL) to sign on ♦ vi to carry obligations; **jdm zu Dank verpflichtet sein** to be obliged to sb

Verpflichtung f obligation, duty

verpönt [fɛr'pø:nt] adj disapproved (of), taboo

ver'prügeln (umg) vt to beat up, to do over

Verputz [fɛr'pʊts] m plaster, roughcast; **v~en** vt to plaster; (umg: Essen) to put away

Verrat [fɛr'ra:t] (-(e)s) m treachery; (POL) treason; **v~en** (unreg) vt to betray; (Geheimnis) to divulge ♦ vr to

give o.s. away

Verräter [fɛr'rɛ:tər] (-s, -) m traitor(-tress); **v~isch** adj treacherous

ver'rechnen vt: **~ mit** to set off against ♦ vr to miscalculate

Verrechnungsscheck [fɛr'rɛçnʊŋsʃɛk] m crossed cheque

verregnet [fɛr're:gnət] adj spoilt by rain, rainy

ver'reisen vi to go away (on a journey)

verrenken [fɛr'rɛŋkən] vt to contort; (MED) to dislocate; **sich** dat **den Knöchel ~** to sprain one's ankle

ver'richten vt to do, to perform

ver'riegeln [fɛr'ri:gəln] vt to bolt up, to lock

verringern [fɛr'rɪŋərn] vt to reduce ♦ vr to diminish

Verringerung f reduction; lessening

ver'rinnen (unreg) vi to run out od away; (Zeit) to elapse

ver'rosten vi to rust

verrotten [fɛr'rɔtən] vi to rot

ver'rücken vt to move, to shift

verrückt [fɛr'rʏkt] adj crazy, mad; **V~e(r)** f(m) lunatic; **V~heit** f madness, lunacy

Verruf [fɛr'ru:f] m: **in ~ geraten/bringen** to fall/bring into disrepute; **v~en** adj notorious, disreputable

Vers [fɛrs] (-es, -e) m verse

ver'sagen vt: **jdm/sich etw ~** to deny sb/o.s. sth ♦ vi to fail; **Ver'sagen** (-s) nt failure

ver'salzen (unreg) vt to put too much salt in; (fig) to spoil

ver'sammeln vt, vr to assemble, to gather

Ver'sammlung f meeting, gathering

Versand [fɛr'zant] (-(e)s) m forwarding; dispatch; (~abteilung) dispatch department; **~haus** nt mail-order firm

ver'säumen vt to miss; (unterlassen) to neglect, to fail

ver'schaffen vt: jdm/sich etw ~ to get od procure sth for sb/o.s.

verschämt [fɛrˈʃɛːmt] adj bashful

verschandeln [fɛrˈʃandəln] (umg) vt to spoil

verschärfen [fɛrˈʃɛrfən] vt to intensify; (Lage) to aggravate ♦ vr to intensify; to become aggravated

ver'schätzen vr to be out in one's reckoning

ver'schenken vt to give away

verscheuchen [fɛrˈʃɔʏçən] vt (Tiere) to chase off od away

ver'schicken vt to send off

ver'schieben (unreg) vt to shift; (EISENB) to shunt; (Termin) to postpone

verschieden [fɛrˈʃiːdən] adj different; (pl: mehrere) various; **sie sind ~ groß** they are of different sizes; **~tlich** adv several times

verschimmeln [fɛrˈʃɪməln] vi (Nahrungsmittel) to go mouldy

verschlafen [fɛrˈʃlaːfən] (unreg) vt to sleep through; (fig: versäumen) to miss ♦ vi, vr to oversleep ♦ adj sleepy

Verschlag [fɛrˈʃlaːk] m shed; **v~en** [-gən] (unreg) vt to board up ♦ adj cunning; **jdm den Atem v~en** to take sb's breath away; **an einen Ort v~en werden** to wind up in a place

ver'schlechtern vt to make worse ♦ vr to deteriorate, to get worse; **Verschlechterung** f deterioration

Verschleiß [fɛrˈʃlaɪs] (-es, -e) m wear and tear; **v~en** (unreg) vt to wear out

ver'schleppen vt to carry off, to abduct; (Krankheit) to protract; (zeitlich) to drag out

ver'schleudern vt to squander; (COMM) to sell dirt-cheap

verschließbar adj lockable

verschließen [fɛrˈʃliːsən] (unreg) vt to close; to lock ♦ vr: **sich einer Sache dat ~** to close one's mind to sth

verschlimmern [fɛrˈʃlɪmərn] vt to make worse, to aggravate ♦ vr to get

worse, to deteriorate

verschlingen [fɛrˈʃlɪŋən] (unreg) vt to devour, to swallow up; (Fäden) to twist

verschlossen [fɛrˈʃlɔsən] adj locked; (fig) reserved; **V~heit** f reserve

ver'schlucken vt to swallow ♦ vr to choke

Verschluss ▲ [fɛrˈʃlʊs] m lock; (von Kleid etc) fastener; (PHOT) shutter; (Stöpsel) plug

verschlüsseln [fɛrˈʃlʏsəln] vt to encode

verschmieren [fɛrˈʃmiːrən] vt (verstreichen: Gips, Mörtel) to apply, spread on; (schmutzig machen: Wand etc) to smear

ver'schmutzen vt to soil; (Umwelt) to pollute

verschneit [fɛrˈʃnaɪt] adj snowed up, covered in snow

verschollen [fɛrˈʃɔlən] adj lost, missing

ver'schonen vt: **jdn mit etw ~** to spare sb sth

verschönern [fɛrˈʃøːnərn] vt to decorate; (verbessern) to improve

ver'schreiben (unreg) vt (MED) to prescribe ♦ vr to make a mistake (in writing); **sich einer Sache dat ~** to devote o.s. to sth

verschreibungspflichtig adj (Medikament) available on prescription only

ver'schrotten vt to scrap

verschuld- [fɛrˈʃʊld] zW: **~en** vt to be guilty of; **V~en** (-s) nt fault, guilt; **v~et** adj in debt; **V~ung** f fault; (Geld) debts pl

ver'schütten vt to spill; (zuschütten) to fill; (unter Trümmern) to bury

ver'schweigen (unreg) vt to keep secret; **jdm etw ~** to keep sth from sb

verschwend- [fɛrˈʃvɛnd] zW: **~en** vt to squander; **V~er** (-s, -) m spendthrift; **v~erisch** adj wasteful, extravagant; **V~ung** f waste; extravagance

verschwiegen [fɛrˈʃviːgən] adj discreet; (Ort) secluded; **V~heit** f discretion; seclusion

ver'schwimmen (*unreg*) *vi* to grow hazy, to become blurred

ver'schwinden (*unreg*) *vi* to disappear, to vanish; **Ver'schwinden** (-s) *nt* disappearance

verschwitzt [fɛr'ʃvɪtst] *adj* (*Mensch*) sweaty

verschwommen [fɛr'ʃvɔmən] *adj* hazy, vague

verschwör- [fɛr'ʃvøːr] *zW*: **~en** (*unreg*) *vr* to plot, to conspire; **V~ung** *f* conspiracy, plot

ver'sehen (*unreg*) *vt* to supply, to provide; (*Pflicht*) to carry out; (*Amt*) to fill; (*Haushalt*) to keep ♦ *vr* (*fig*) to make a mistake; **ehe er sichs ~ hatte ...** before he knew it ...; **Ver'sehen** (-s, -) *nt* oversight; **aus V~** by mistake; **~tlich** *adv* by mistake

Versehrte(r) [fɛr'zeːrtə(r)] *f(m)* disabled person

ver'senden (*unreg*) *vt* to forward, to dispatch

ver'senken *vt* to sink ♦ *vr*: **sich ~ in** +*akk* to become engrossed in

versessen [fɛr'zɛsən] *adj*: **~ auf** +*akk* mad about

ver'setzen *vt* to transfer; (*verpfänden*) to pawn; (*umg*) to stand up ♦ *vr*: **sich in jdn** *od* **in jds Lage ~** to put o.s. in sb's place; **jdm einen Tritt/Schlag ~** to kick/hit sb; **etw mit etw ~** to mix sth with sth; **jdn in gute Laune ~** to put sb in a good mood

Ver'setzung *f* transfer

verseuchen [fɛr'zɔʏçən] *vt* to contaminate

versichern [fɛr'zɪçɐn] *vt* to assure; (*mit Geld*) to insure

Versicherung *f* assurance; insurance

Versicherungs- *zW*: **~gesellschaft** *f* insurance company; **~karte** *f* insurance card; **die grüne ~karte** the green card; **~police** *f* insurance policy

ver'sinken (*unreg*) *vi* to sink

versöhnen [fɛr'zøːnən] *vt* to reconcile ♦ *vr* to become reconciled

Versöhnung *f* reconciliation

ver'sorgen *vt* to provide, to supply; (*Familie etc*) to look after

Ver'sorgung *f* provision; (*Unterhalt*) maintenance; (*Altersversorgung etc*) benefit, assistance

verspäten [fɛr'ʃpɛːtən] *vr* to be late

verspätet *adj* (*Zug, Abflug, Ankunft*) late; (*Glückwünsche*) belated

Verspätung *f* delay; **~ haben** to be late

ver'sperren *vt* to bar, to obstruct

verspielt [fɛr'ʃpiːlt] *adj* (*Kind, Tier*) playful

ver'spotten *vt* to ridicule, to scoff at

ver'sprechen (*unreg*) *vt* to promise; **sich** *dat* **etw von etw ~** to expect sth from sth; **Ver'sprechen** (-s, -) *nt* promise

verstaatlichen [fɛr'ʃtaːtlɪçən] *vt* to nationalize

Verstand [fɛr'ʃtant] *m* intelligence; mind; **den ~ verlieren** to go out of one's mind; **über jds ~ gehen** to go beyond sb

verständig [fɛr'ʃtɛndɪç] *adj* sensible; **~en** [fɛr'ʃtɛndɪgən] *vt* to inform ♦ *vr* to communicate; (*sich einigen*) to come to an understanding; **V~ung** *f* communication; (*Benachrichtigung*) informing; (*Einigung*) agreement

verständ- [fɛr'ʃtɛnt] *zW*: **~lich** *adj* understandable, comprehensible; **V~lichkeit** *f* clarity, intelligibility; **V~nis** (-ses, -se) *nt* understanding; **~nislos** *adj* uncomprehending; **~nisvoll** *adj* understanding, sympathetic

verstärk- [fɛr'ʃtɛrk] *zW*: **~en** *vt* to strengthen; (*Ton*) to amplify; (*erhöhen*) to intensify ♦ *vr* to intensify; **V~er** (-s, -) *m* amplifier; **V~ung** *f* strengthening; (*Hilfe*) reinforcements *pl*; (*von Ton*) am-

---

Spelling Reform: ▲ *new spelling* △ *old spelling (to be phased out)*

plification

verstauchen [fɛr'ʃtaoxən] vt to sprain

verstauen [fɛr'ʃtaoən] vt to stow away

Versteck [fɛr'ʃtɛk] (-(e)s, -e) nt hiding (place); **v~en** vt, vr to hide; **v~t** adj hidden

ver'stehen (unreg) vt to understand ♦ vr to get on; **das versteht sich (von selbst)** that goes without saying

versteigern [fɛr'ʃtaɪɡərn] vt to auction; **Versteigerung** f auction

verstell- [fɛr'ʃtɛl] zW: **~bar** adj adjustable, variable; **~en** vt to move, to shift; (Uhr) to adjust; (versperren) to block; (fig) to disguise ♦ vr to pretend, to put on an act; **V~ung** f pretence

versteuern [fɛr'ʃtɔʏrn] vt to pay tax on

verstimmt [fɛr'ʃtɪmt] adj out of tune; (fig) cross, put out; (Magen) upset

ver'stopfen vt to block, to stop up; (MED) to constipate

Ver'stopfung f obstruction; (MED) constipation

verstorben [fɛr'ʃtɔrbən] adj deceased, late

verstört [fɛr'ʃtøːrt] adj (Mensch) distraught

Verstoß [fɛr'ʃtoːs] m: **~ (gegen)** infringement (of), violation (of); **v~en** (unreg) vt to disown, to reject ♦ vi: **v~en gegen** to offend against

ver'streichen (unreg) vt to spread ♦ vi to elapse

ver'streuen vt to scatter (about)

verstümmeln [fɛr'ʃtʏməln] vt to maim, to mutilate (auch fig)

verstummen [fɛr'ʃtomən] vi to go silent; (Lärm) to die away

Versuch [fɛr'zuːx] (-(e)s, -e) m attempt; (SCI) experiment; **v~en** vt to try; (verlocken) to tempt; **sich an etw** dat **v~en** to try one's hand at sth; **~skaninchen** nt (fig) guinea-pig; **~ung** f temptation

vertagen [fɛr'taːɡn] vt, vi to adjourn

ver'tauschen vt to exchange; (verse-

hentlich) to mix up

verteidig- [fɛr'taɪdɪɡ] zW: **~en** vt to defend; **V~er** (-s, -) m defender; (JUR) defence counsel; **V~ung** f defence

ver'teilen vt to distribute; (Rollen) to assign; (Salbe) to spread

Verteilung f distribution, allotment

vertiefen [fɛr'tiːfən] vt to deepen ♦ vr: **sich in etw** akk **~** to become engrossed or absorbed in sth

Vertiefung f depression

vertikal [vɛrti'kaːl] adj vertical

vertilgen [fɛr'tɪlɡən] vt to exterminate; (umg) to eat up, to consume

vertonen [fɛr'toːnən] vt to set to music

Vertrag [fɛr'traːk] (-(e)s, ⁿe) m contract, agreement; (POL) treaty; **v~en** [-ɡən] (unreg) vt to tolerate, to stand ♦ vr to get along; (sich aussöhnen) to become reconciled; **v~lich** adj contractual

verträglich [fɛr'trɛːklɪç] adj goodnatured, sociable; (Speisen) easily digested; (MED) easily tolerated; **V~keit** f sociability; good nature; digestibility

Vertrags- zW: **~bruch** m breach of contract; **~händler** m appointed retailer; **~partner** m party to a contract; **~werkstatt** f appointed repair shop; **v~widrig** adj contrary to contract

vertrauen [fɛr'traoən] vi: **jdm ~** to trust sb; **~ auf** +akk to rely on; **V~** (-s) nt confidence; **V~ erweckend** inspiring trust; **~svoll** adj trustful; **~swürdig** adj trustworthy

vertraulich [fɛr'traolɪç] adj familiar; (geheim) confidential

vertraut [fɛr'traot] adj familiar; **V~heit** f familiarity

ver'treiben (unreg) vt to drive away; (aus Land) to expel; (COMM) to sell; (Zeit) to pass

vertret- [fɛr'treːt] zW: **~en** (unreg) vt to represent; (Ansicht) to hold, to advocate; **sich** dat **die Beine ~en** to stretch one's legs; **V~er** (-s, -) m representative; (Verfechter) advocate; **V~ung** f re-presentation; advocacy

Vertrieb [fer'tri:p] **(-(e)s, -e)** m market-ing (department)

ver'trocknen vi to dry up

ver'trösten vt to put off

vertun [fer'tu:n] (unreg) vt to waste ♦ vr (umg) to make a mistake

vertuschen [fer'tuʃən] vt to hush up, cover up

verübeln [fɛr'ly:bəln] vt: **jdm etw ~** to be cross od offended with sb on ac-count of sth

verüben [fɛr'ly:bən] vt to commit

verun- [fɛr'ʊn] zW: **~glimpfen** vt to disparage; **~glücken** vt to have an ac-cident; **tödlich ~glücken** to be killed in an accident; **~reinigen** vt to soil; (Umwelt) to pollute; **~sichern** vt to rattle; **~treuen** [-trɔyən] vt to embez-zle

verur- [fɛr'u:r] zW: **~sachen** vt to cause; **~teilen** [-taɪlən] vt to con-demn; **V~teilung** f condemnation; (JUR) sentence

verviel- [fɛr'fi:l] zW: **~fachen** vt to multiply; **~fältigen** [-fɛltɪgən] vt to duplicate, to copy; **V~fältigung** f dupli-cation, copying

vervollkommnen [fɛr'fɔlkɔmnən] vt to perfect

vervollständigen [fɛr'fɔlʃtɛndɪgən] vt to complete

ver'wackeln vt (Foto) to blur

ver'wählen vr (TEL) to dial the wrong number

verwahren [fɛr'va:rən] vt to keep, to lock away ♦ vr to protest

verwalt- [fɛr'valt] zW: **~en** vt to man-age; to administer; **V~er (-s, -)** m manager; (Vermögensverwalter) trustee; **V~ung** f administration; management

ver'wandeln vt to change, to trans-form ♦ vr to change; to be trans-formed; **Ver'wandlung** f change,

transformation

verwandt [fɛr'vant] adj: **~ (mit)** re-lated (to); **V~e(r)** f(m) relative, rela-tion; **V~schaft** f relationship; (Menschen) relations pl

ver'warnen vt to caution

Ver'warnung f caution

ver'wechseln vt: **~ mit** to confuse with; to mistake for; **zum V~ ähnlich** as like as two peas

Ver'wechslung f confusion, mixing up

Verwehung [fɛr'veːʊŋ] f snowdrift; sand drift

verweichlicht [fɛr'vaɪçlɪçt] adj effemi-nate, soft

ver'weigern vt: **jdm etw ~** to refuse sb sth; **den Gehorsam/die Aussage ~** to refuse to obey/testify

Ver'weigerung f refusal

Verweis [fɛr'vaɪs] **(-es, -e)** m repri-mand, rebuke; (Hinweis) reference; **v~en** (unreg) vt to refer; **jdn von der Schule v~en** to expel sb (from school); **jdn des Landes v~en** to de-port od expel sb

ver'welken vi to fade

verwend- [fɛr'vɛnd] zW: **~bar** [-'vɛnt-ba:r] adj usable; **ver'wenden** (unreg) vt to use; (Mühe, Zeit, Arbeit) to spend ♦ vr to intercede; **Ver'wendung** f use

ver'werfen (unreg) vt to reject

verwerflich [fɛr'vɛrflɪç] adj reprehen-sible

ver'werten vt to utilize

Ver'wertung f utilization

verwesen [fɛr'veːzən] vi to decay

ver'wickeln vt to tangle (up); (fig) to involve ♦ vr to get tangled (up); **jdn in etw akk ~** to involve sb in sth; **sich in etw akk ~** to get involved in sth

verwickelt [fɛr'vɪkəlt] adj (Situation, Fall) difficult, complicated

verwildern [fɛr'vɪldərn] vi to run wild

Spelling Reform: ▲ *new spelling* △ *old spelling (to be phased out)*

verwirklichen [fɛr'vɪrklɪçən] *vt* to realize, to put into effect

Verwirklichung *f* realization

verwirren [fɛr'vɪrən] *vt* to tangle (up); *(fig)* to confuse

Verwirrung *f* confusion

verwittern [fɛr'vɪtərn] *vi* to weather

verwitwet [fɛr'vɪtvət] *adj* widowed

verwöhnen [fɛr'vøːnən] *vt* to spoil

verworren [fɛr'vɔrən] *adj* confused

verwundbar [fɛr'vʊntbaːr] *adj* vulnerable

verwunden [fɛr'vʊndən] *vt* to wound

verwunder- [fɛr'vʊndər] *zW:* **~lich** *adj* surprising; **V~ung** *f* astonishment

Verwundete(r) *f(m)* injured person

Verwundung *f* wound, injury

ver'wünschen *vt* to curse

verwüsten [fɛr'vyːstən] *vt* to devastate

verzagen [fɛr'tsaːgən] *vi* to despair

ver'zählen *vt* to miscount

verzehren [fɛr'tseːrən] *vt* to consume

ver'zeichnen *vt* to list; *(Niederlage, Verlust)* to register

Verzeichnis [fɛr'tsaɪçnɪs] *(-ses, -se)* *nt* list, catalogue; *(in Buch)* index

verzeih- [fɛr'tsaɪ] *zW:* **~en** *(unreg)* *vt*, *vi* to forgive; **jdm etw ~en** to forgive sb for sth; **~lich** *adj* pardonable; **V~ung** *f* forgiveness, pardon; **V~ung!** sorry!, excuse me!

verzichten [fɛr'tsɪçtən] *vi:* **~ auf** +*akk* to forgo, to give up

ver'ziehen *(unreg)* *vi* to move ♦ *vt* to put out of shape; *(Kind)* to spoil; *(Pflanzen)* to thin out ♦ *vr* to go out of shape; *(Gesicht)* to contort; *(verschwinden)* to disappear; **das Gesicht ~** to pull a face

verzieren [fɛr'tsiːrən] *vt* to decorate, to ornament

Verzierung *f* decoration

verzinsen [fɛr'tsɪnzən] *vt* to pay interest on

ver'zögern *vt* to delay

Ver'zögerung *f* delay, time lag; **~staktik** *f* delaying tactics *pl*

verzollen [fɛr'tsɔlən] *vt* to pay duty on

Verzug [fɛr'tsuːk] *m* delay

verzweif- [fɛr'tsvaɪf] *zW:* **~eln** *vi* to despair; **~elt** *adj* desperate; **V~lung** *f* despair

Veto ['veːto] *(-s, -s)* *nt* veto

Vetter ['fɛtər] *(-s, -n)* *m* cousin

vgl. *abk (= vergleiche)* cf.

v. H. *abk (= vom Hundert)* p.c.

vibrieren [vi'briːrən] *vi* to vibrate

Video ['viːdeo] *nt* video; **~gerät** *nt* video recorder; **~rekorder** *m* video recorder

Vieh [fiː] *(-(e)s* *nt* cattle *pl;* **v~isch** *adj* bestial

viel [fiːl] *adj* a lot of, much ♦ *adv* a lot, much; **~ sagend** significant; **~ versprechend** promising; **~e** *pron pl* a lot of, many; **~ zu wenig** much too little; **~erlei** *adj* a great variety of; **~es** *pron* a lot; **~fach** *adj, adv* many times; **auf ~fachen Wunsch** at the request of many people; **V~falt** *(-)* *f* variety; **~fältig** *adj* varied, many-sided

vielleicht [fi'laɪçt] *adv* perhaps

viel- *zW:* **~mal(s)** *adv* many times; **danke ~mals** many thanks; **~mehr** *adv* rather, on the contrary; **~seitig** *adj* many-sided

vier [fiːr] *num* four; **V~eck** *(-(e)s, -e)* *nt* four-sided figure; *(gleichseitig)* square; **~eckig** *adj* four-sided; square; **V~taktmotor** *m* four-stroke engine; **~te(r, s)** ['fiːrtə(r, s)] *adj* fourth; **V~tel** ['fɪrtəl] *(-s, -)* *nt* quarter; **V~teljahr** *nt* quarter; **~teljährlich** *adj* quarterly; **~teln** *vt* to divide into four; *(Kuchen usw)* to divide into quarters; **V~telstunde** *f* quarter of an hour; **~zehn** ['fɪrtseːn] *num* fourteen; **in ~zehn Tagen** in a fortnight; **~zehntägig** *adj* fortnightly; **~zig** ['fɪrtsɪç] *num* forty

Villa ['vɪla] *(-, Villen)* *f* villa

violett [vio'lɛt] *adj* violet

Violin- [vio'liːn] *zW:* **~e** *f* violin; **~schlüssel** *m* treble clef

virtuell [vɪr'tʊɛl] adj (COMPUT) virtual; **~e Realität** virtual reality

Virus ['viːrʊs] (-, **Viren**) m od nt (auch COMPUT) virus

Visa ['viːza] pl von **Visum**

vis-a-vis ▲, **vis-à-vis** [viza'viː] adv opposite

Visen ['viːzən] pl von **Visum**

Visier [vi'ziːr] (-s, -e) nt gunsight; (am Helm) visor

Visite [vi'ziːtə] f (MED) visit; **~nkarte** f visiting card

Visum ['viːzʊm] (-s, **Visa** od **Visen**) nt visa

vital [vi'taːl] adj lively, full of life, vital

Vitamin [vita'miːn] (-s, -e) nt vitamin

Vogel ['foːgəl] (-s, ") m bird; **einen ~ haben** (umg) to have bats in the belfry; **jdm den ~ zeigen** (umg) to tap one's forehead (meaning that one thinks sb stupid); **~bauer** m birdcage; **~perspektive** f bird's-eye view; **~scheuche** f scarecrow

Vokabel [vo'kaːbəl] (-, -n) f word

Vokabular [vokabu'laːr] (-s, -e) nt vocabulary

Vokal [vo'kaːl] (-s, -e) m vowel

Volk [fɔlk] (-(e)s, "er) nt people; nation

Völker- ['fœlkər] zW: **~recht** nt international law; **~rechtlich** adj according to international law; **~verständigung** f international understanding

---

Volkshochschule

The **Volkshochschule** (VHS) is an institution which offers Adult Education classes. No set qualifications are necessary to attend. For a small fee adults can attend both vocational and non-vocational classes in the day-time or evening.

Volks- zW: **~entscheid** m referendum;

~fest nt fair; **~hochschule** f adult education classes pl; **~lied** nt folksong; **~republik** f people's republic; **~schule** f elementary school; **~tanz** m folk dance; **~vertreter(in)** m(f) people's representative; **~wirtschaft** f economics sg

voll [fɔl] adj full; **etw ~ machen** to fill sth up; **~ tanken** to fill up; **~ und ganz** completely; **jdn für ~ nehmen** (umg) to take sb seriously; **~auf** adv amply; **V~bart** m full beard; **V~beschäftigung** f full employment; **~'bringen** (unreg) vt insep to accomplish; **~'enden** vt insep to finish, to complete; **~endet** adj (~kommen) completed; **~ends** ['fɔlɛnts] adv completely; **V~'endung** f completion

Volleyball ['vɔlibal] m volleyball

Vollgas nt: **mit ~** at full throttle; **~ geben** to step on it ♦

völlig ['fœlɪç] adj complete ♦ adv completely

voll- zW: **~jährig** adj of age; **V~kaskoversicherung** ['fɔlkaskoferzɪçərʊŋ] f fully comprehensive insurance; **~'kommen** adj perfect; **V~'kommenheit** f perfection; **V~kornbrot** nt wholemeal bread; **V~macht** (-, -en) f authority, full powers pl; **V~milch** f (KOCH) full-cream milk; **V~mond** m full moon; **V~pension** f full board; **~ständig** ['fɔlʃtɛndɪç] adj complete; **~strecken** vt insep to execute; **~tanken** △ vt, vi siehe **voll**; **V~waschmittel** nt detergent; **V~wertkost** f wholefood; **~zählig** ['fɔlsɛːlɪç] adj complete; in full number; **~ziehen** (unreg) vt insep to carry out ♦ vr insep to happen; **V~'zug** m execution

Volumen [vo'luːmən] (-s, - od **Volumina**) nt volume

vom [fɔm] = **von dem**

von [fɔn] *präp +dat* 1 (*Ausgangspunkt*) from; **von ... bis** from ... to; **von morgens bis abends** from morning till night; **von ... nach ...** from ... to ...; **von ... an** from ...; **von ... aus** from ... to ...; **von dort aus** from there; **etw von sich aus tun** to do sth of one's own accord; **von mir aus** (*umg*) if you like, I don't mind; **von wo/wann ...?** where/when ... from?

2 (*Ursache, im Passiv*) by; **ein Gedicht von Schiller** a poem by Schiller; **von etw müde** tired from sth

3 (*als Genitiv*) of; **ein Freund von mir** a friend of mine; **nett von dir** nice of you; **jeweils zwei von zehn** two out of every ten

4 (*über*) about; **er erzählte vom Urlaub** he talked about his holiday

5: **von wegen!** (*umg*) no way!

voneinander *adv* from each other

vor [foːr] *präp +dat* 1 (*räumlich*) in front of; **vor der Kirche links abbiegen** turn left before the church

2 (*zeitlich*) before; **ich war vor ihm da** I was there before him; **vor 2 Tagen** 2 days ago; **5 (Minuten) vor 4** 5 (minutes) to 4; **vor kurzem** a little while ago

3 (*Ursache*) with; **vor Wut/Liebe** with rage/love; **vor Hunger sterben** to die of hunger; **vor lauter Arbeit** because of work

4: **vor allem, vor allen Dingen** most of all

♦ *präp +akk* (*räumlich*) in front of

♦ *adv*: **vor und zurück** backwards and forwards

Vorabend [foːrˈʔaːbənt] *m* evening before, eve

voran [foˈran] *adv* before, ahead;

mach ~! get on with it!; **~gehen** (*unreg*) *vi* to go ahead; **einer Sache** *dat* **~gehen** to precede sth; **~kommen** (*unreg*) *vi* to come along, to make progress

Voranschlag [ˈfoːrʔanʃlaːk] *m* estimate

Vorarbeiter [ˈfoːrʔarbaɪtər] *m* foreman

voraus [foˈraʊs] *adv* ahead; (*zeitlich*) in advance; **jdm ~ sein** to be ahead of sb; **im V~** in advance; **~gehen** (*unreg*) *vi* to go on ahead; (*fig*) to precede; **~haben** (*unreg*) *vt*: **jdm etw ~haben** to have the edge on sb in sth; **V~sage** *f* prediction; **~sagen** *vt* to predict; **~sehen** (*unreg*) *vt* to foresee; **~setzen** *vt* to assume; **~gesetzt, dass ...** provided that ...; **V~setzung** *f* requirement, prerequisite; **V~sicht** *f* foresight; **aller V~sicht nach** in all probability; **~sichtlich** *adv* probably

Vorbehalt [ˈfoːrbəhalt] (**-(e)s, -e**) *m* reservation, proviso; **~en** (*unreg*) *vt*: **sich/jdm etw V~en** to reserve sth (for o.s.)/for sb; **v~los** *adj* unconditional ♦ *adv* unconditionally

vorbei [foːrˈbaɪ] *adv* by, past; **das ist ~** that's over; **~gehen** (*unreg*) *vi* to pass by, to go past; **~kommen** (*unreg*) *vi*: **bei jdm ~kommen** to drop in *od* call in on sb

vor- *zW*: **~belastet** [ˈfoːrbəlastət] *adj* (*fig*) handicapped; **~bereiten** *vt* to prepare; **V~bereitung** *f* preparation; **V~bestellung** *f* advance order; (*von Platz, Tisch etc*) advance booking; **~bestraft** [ˈfoːrbəʃtraːft] *adj* previously convicted, with a record

vorbeugen [ˈfoːrbɔʏɡən] *vt, vr* to lean forward ♦ *vi +dat* to prevent; **~d** *adj* preventive

Vorbeugung *f* prevention; **zur ~ gegen** for the prevention of

Vorbild [ˈfoːrbɪlt] *nt* model; **sich** *dat* **jdn zum ~ nehmen** to model o.s. on sb; **v~lich** *adj* model, ideal

vorbringen [ˈfoːrbrɪŋən] (*unreg*) *vt* to advance, to state

Vorder- ['fɔrdər] zW: **~achse** f front axle; **v~e(r, s)** adj front; **~grund** m foreground; **~mann** (pl **-männer**) m man in front; **jdn auf ~mann bringen** (umg) to get sb to shape up; **~seite** f front (side); **v~ste(r, s)** adj front

vordrängen ['fɔːrdrɛŋən] vr to push to the front

voreilig ['fɔːraɪlıç] adj hasty, rash

voreinander [fɔːr'aɪnandər] adv (räumlich) in front of each other

voreingenommen ['fɔːraɪngənɔmən] adj biased; **V~heit** f bias

vorenthalten ['fɔːrɛnthaltən] (unreg) vt: **jdm etw ~** to withhold sth from sb

vorerst ['fɔːrɛrst] adv for the moment od present

Vorfahr ['fɔːrfaːr] (**-en, -en**) m ancestor

vorfahren (unreg) vi to drive (on) ahead; (vors Haus etc) to drive up

Vorfahrt f (AUT) right of way; **~ achten!** give way!

Vorfahrts- zW: **v~regel** f right of way; **~schild** nt give way sign; **~straße** f major road

Vorfall ['fɔːrfal] m incident; **v~en** (unreg) vi to occur

vorfinden ['fɔːrfındən] (unreg) vt to find

Vorfreude ['fɔːrfrɔydə] f (joyful) anticipation

vorführen ['fɔːrfyːrən] vt to show, to display; **dem Gericht ~** to bring before the court

Vorgabe ['fɔːrgaːbə] f (SPORT) start, handicap ♦ in zW (COMPUT) default

Vorgang ['fɔːrgaŋ] m course of events; (bes SCI) process

Vorgänger(in) ['fɔːrgɛŋər(ın)] (**-s, -**) m(f) predecessor

vorgeben ['fɔːrgeːbən] (unreg) vt to pretend, to use as a pretext; (SPORT) to give an advantage od a start of

vorgefertigt ['fɔːrgəfɛrtıçt] adj prefabricated

vorgehen ['fɔːrgeːən] (unreg) vi (voraus) to go (on) ahead; (nach vorn) to go up front; (handeln) to act, to proceed; (Uhr) to be fast; (Vorrang haben) to take precedence; (passieren) to go on

Vorgehen (**-s**) nt action

Vorgeschichte ['fɔːrgəʃıçtə] f past history

Vorgeschmack ['fɔːrgəʃmak] m foretaste

Vorgesetzte(r) ['fɔːrgəzɛtstə(r)] f(m) superior

vorgestern ['fɔːrgɛstərn] adv the day before yesterday

vorhaben ['fɔːrhaːbən] (unreg) vt to intend; **hast du schon was vor?** have you got anything on?; **V~** (**-s, -**) nt intention

vorhalten ['fɔːrhaltən] (unreg) vt to hold od put up ♦ vi to last; **jdm etw ~** (fig) to reproach sb for sth

vorhanden [fɔːr'handən] adj existing; (erhältlich) available

Vorhang ['fɔːrhaŋ] m curtain

Vorhängeschloss ['fɔːrhɛŋəʃlɔs] nt padlock

vorher [fɔːr'heːr] adv before(hand); **~bestimmen** vt (Schicksal) to preordain; **~gehen** (unreg) vi to precede; **~ig** adj previous

Vorherrschaft ['fɔːrhɛrʃaft] f predominance, supremacy

vorherrschen ['fɔːrhɛrʃən] vi to predominate

vorher- [fɔːr'heːr] zW: **V~sage** f forecast; **~sagen** vt to forecast, to predict; **~sehbar** adj predictable; **~sehen** (unreg) vt to foresee

vorhin [fɔːr'hın] adv not long ago, just now; **V~ein ▲** adv: **im V~ein** beforehand

---

vorig ['fo:rıç] *adj* previous, last

Vorkämpfer(in) ['fo:rkɛmpfər(ın)] *m(f)* pioneer

Vorkaufsrecht ['fo:rkaufsrɛçt] *nt* option to buy

Vorkehrung ['fo:rke:rʊŋ] *f* precaution

vorkommen ['fo:rkɔmən] (*unreg*) *vi* to come forward; (*geschehen, sich finden*) to occur; (*scheinen*) to seem (to be); **sich** *dat* **dumm etc** ~ to feel stupid *etc*; **V~ (-s, -)** *nt* occurrence

Vorkriegs- ['fo:rkri:ks] *in zW* prewar

Vorladung ['fo:rla:dʊŋ] *f* summons *sg*

Vorlage ['fo:rla:gə] *f* model, pattern; (*Gesetzvorlage*) bill; (*SPORT*) pass

vorlassen ['fo:rlasən] (*unreg*) *vt* to admit; (*vorgehen lassen*) to allow to go in front

vorläufig ['fo:rlɔyfıç] *adj* temporary, provisional

vorlaut ['fo:rlaut] *adj* impertinent, cheeky

vorlesen ['fo:rle:zən] (*unreg*) *vt* to read (out)

Vorlesung *f* (*UNIV*) lecture

vorletzte(r, s) ['fo:rlɛtstə(r, s)] *adj* last but one

vorlieb [fo:r'li:p] *adv*: ~ **nehmen mit** to make do with

Vorliebe ['fo:rli:bə] *f* preference, partiality

vorliegen ['fo:rli:gən] (*unreg*) *vi* to be (here); **etw liegt jdm vor** sb has sth; ~**d** *adj* present, at issue

vormachen ['fo:rmaxən] *vt*: **jdm etw** ~ to show sb how to do sth; (*fig*) to fool sb; to have sb on

Vormachtstellung ['fo:rmaxtʃtɛlʊŋ] *f* supremacy, hegemony

Vormarsch ['fo:rmarʃ] *m* advance

vormerken ['fo:rmɛrkən] *vt* to book

Vormittag ['fo:rmıta:k] *m* morning; **v~s** *adv* in the morning, before noon

vorn [fɔrn] *adv* in front; **von** ~ **anfangen** to start at the beginning; **nach** ~ to the front

Vorname ['fo:rna:mə] *m* first name,

Christian name

vorne ['fɔrnə] *adv* = **vorn**

vornehm ['fo:rne:m] *adj* distinguished; refined; elegant

vornehmen (*unreg*) *vt* (*fig*) to carry out; **sich** *dat* **etw** ~ to start on sth; (*beschließen*) to decide to do sth; **sich** *dat* **jdn** ~ to tell sb off

vornherein ['fɔrnhɛraın] *adv*: **von** ~ from the start

Vorort ['fo:rɔrt] *m* suburb

Vorrang ['fo:raŋ] *m* precedence, priority; **v~ig** *adj* of prime importance, primary

Vorrat ['fo:ra:t] *m* stock, supply

vorrätig ['fo:rɛ:tıç] *adj* in stock

Vorratskammer *f* pantry

Vorrecht ['fo:rrɛçt] *nt* privilege

Vorrichtung ['fo:rrıçtʊŋ] *f* device, contrivance

vorrücken ['fo:rrʏkən] *vi* to advance ♦ *vt* to move forward

Vorsaison ['fo:rzɛzɔ̃] *f* early season

Vorsatz ['fo:rzats] *m* intention; (*JUR*) intent; **einen** ~ **fassen** to make a resolution

vorsätzlich ['fo:rzɛtslıç] *adj* intentional; (*JUR*) premeditated ♦ *adv* intentionally

Vorschau ['fo:rʃau] *f* (*RADIO, TV*) (programme) preview; (*Film*) trailer

Vorschlag ['fo:rʃla:k] *m* suggestion, proposal; **v~en** (*unreg*) *vt* to suggest, to propose

vorschreiben ['fo:rʃraıbən] (*unreg*) *vt* to prescribe, to specify

Vorschrift ['fo:rʃrıft] *f* regulation(s); rule(s); (*Anweisungen*) instruction(s); **Dienst nach** ~ work-to-rule; **v~smäßig** *adj* as per regulations/instructions

Vorschuss ▲ ['fo:rʃʊs] *m* advance

vorsehen ['fo:rze:ən] (*unreg*) *vt* to provide for, to plan ♦ *vr* to take care, to be careful ♦ *vi* to be visible

Vorsehung *f* providence

Vorsicht ['fo:rzıçt] *f* caution, care; ~!

look out!, take care!; *(auf Schildern)* caution!, danger!; **~, Stufe!** mind the step!; **v~ig** *adj* cautious, careful; **v~shalber** *adv* just in case

Vorsilbe ['foːɐzɪlbə] *f* prefix

vorsingen ['foːɐzɪŋən] *vt (vor Zuhörern)* to sing (to); *(in Prüfung, für Theater etc)* to audition (for) ♦ *vi* to sing

Vorsitz ['foːɐzɪts] *m* chair(manship); **~ende(r)** *f(m)* chairman(-woman)

Vorsorge ['foːɐzɔrgə] *f* precaution(s), provision(s); **v~n** *vi*: **v~n für** to make provision(s) for; **~untersuchung** *f* check-up

vorsorglich ['foːɐzɔrklɪç] *adv* as a precaution

Vorspeise ['foːɐʃpaɪzə] *f* hors d'oeuvre, appetizer

Vorspiel ['foːɐʃpiːl] *nt* prelude

vorspielen *vt*: **jdm etw ~** *(MUS)* to play sth for *od* to sb ♦ *vi (zur Prüfung etc)* to play for *od* to sb

vorsprechen ['foːɐʃprɛçən] *(unreg) vt* to say out loud, to recite ♦ *vi*: **bei jdm ~** to call on sb

Vorsprung ['foːɐʃprʊŋ] *m* projection, ledge; *(fig)* advantage, start

Vorstadt ['foːɐʃtat] *f* suburbs *pl*

Vorstand ['foːɐʃtant] *m* executive committee; *(COMM)* board (of directors); *(Person)* director, head

vorstehen ['foːɐʃteːən] *(unreg) vi* to project; **einer Sache dat ~** *(fig)* to be the head of sth

vorstell- ['foːɐʃtɛl] *zW*: **~bar** *adj* conceivable; **~en** *vt* to put forward; *(bekannt machen)* to introduce; *(darstellen)* to represent; **~en vor** +*akk* to put in front of; **sich** *dat* **etw ~en** to imagine sth; **V~ung** *f (Bekanntmachen)* introduction; *(THEAT etc)* performance; *(Gedanke)* idea, thought

vorstoßen ['foːɐʃtoːsən] *(unreg) vi (ins Unbekannte)* to venture (forth)

Vorstrafe ['foːɐʃtraːfə] *f* previous conviction

Vortag ['foːɐtak] *m*: **am ~ einer Sache** *gen* on the day before sth

vortäuschen ['foːɐtɔʏʃən] *vt* to feign, to pretend

Vorteil ['foːɐtaɪl] *m*: **~ (gegenüber)** advantage (over); **im ~ sein** to have the advantage; **v~haft** *adj* advantageous

Vortrag ['foːɐtraːk] *m* talk, lecture; **v~en** *[-ɡən]* *(unreg, Vorträge) vt* to carry forward; *(fig)* to recite; *(Rede)* to deliver; *(Lied)* to perform; *(Meinung etc)* to express

vortreten ['foːɐtreːtən] *(unreg) vi* to step forward; *(Augen etc)* to protrude

vorüber [foːˈryːbər] *adv* past, over; **~gehen** *(unreg) vi* to pass (by); **~gehen an** +*dat (fig)* to pass over; **~gehend** *adj* temporary, passing

Vorurteil ['foːɐʔʊrtaɪl] *nt* prejudice

Vorverkauf ['foːɐfɛrkaʊf] *m* advance booking

Vorwahl ['foːɐvaːl] *f* preliminary election; *(TEL)* dialling code

Vorwand ['foːɐvant] *m* (-(e)s, **Vorwände**) *m* pretext

vorwärts ['foːɐvɛrts] *adv* forward; **~gehen** to progress; **V~gang** *m (AUT etc)* forward gear; **~ kommen** to get on, to make progress

Vorwäsche *f* prewash

vorweg [foːɐˈvɛk] *adv* in advance; **~nehmen** *(unreg) vt* to anticipate

vorweisen ['foːɐvaɪzən] *(unreg) vt* to show, to produce

vorwerfen ['foːɐvɛrfən] *(unreg) vt*: **jdm etw ~** to reproach sb for sth, to accuse sb of sth; **sich** *dat* **nichts vorzuwerfen haben** to have nothing to reproach o.s. with

vorwiegend ['foːɐviːɡənt] *adj* predominant ♦ *adv* predominantly

vorwitzig ['foːɐvɪtsɪç] *adj (Mensch, Bemerkung)* cheeky

Vorwort ['fo:rvort] (-(e)s, -e) *nt* preface

Vorwurf ['fo:rvurf] *m* reproach; jdm/ sich Vorwürfe machen to reproach sb/o.s.; **v~svoll** *adj* reproachful

vorzeigen ['fo:rtsaigən] *vt* to show, to produce

vorzeitig ['fo:rtsaitıç] *adj* premature

vorziehen ['fo:rtsi:ən] (*unreg*) *vt* to pull forward; (*Gardinen*) to draw; (*lieber haben*) to prefer

Vorzimmer ['fo:rtsımər] *nt* (*Büro*) outer office

Vorzug ['fo:rtsu:k] *m* preference; (*gute Eigenschaft*) merit, good quality; (*Vorteil*) advantage

vorzüglich [fo:r'tsy:klıç] *adj* excellent

Vorzugspreis *m* special discount price

vulgär [vul'gε:r] *adj* vulgar

Vulkan [vul'ka:n] (-s, -e) *m* volcano

W, w

Waage ['va:gə] *f* scales *pl*; (*ASTROL*) Libra; **w~recht** *adj* horizontal

Wabe ['va:bə] *f* honeycomb

wach [vax] *adj* awake; (*fig*) alert; **W~e** *f* guard, watch; **w~ halten** to keep watch; **W~e stehen** to stand guard; **~en** *vi* to be awake; (*Wache halten*) to guard

Wachs [vaks] (-es, -e) *nt* wax

wachsam ['vaxza:m] *adj* watchful, vigilant, alert

wachsen (*unreg*) *vi* to grow

Wachstuch ['vakstu:x] *nt* oilcloth

Wachstum ['vakstu:m] (-s) *nt* growth

Wächter ['vεçtər] (-s, -) *m* guard, warden, keeper; (*Parkplatzwächter*) attendant

wackel- ['vakəl] *zW*: **~ig** *adj* shaky, wobbly; **W~kontakt** *m* loose connection; **~n** *vi* to shake; (*fig: Position*) to be shaky

wacker ['vakər] *adj* valiant, stout ♦ *adv* well, bravely

Wade ['va:də] *f* (*ANAT*) calf

Waffe ['vafə] *f* weapon

Waffel ['vafəl] (-, -n) *f* waffle; wafer

Waffen- *zW*: **~schein** *m* gun licence; **~stillstand** *m* armistice, truce

Wagemut *m* daring

wagen ['va:gən] *vt* to venture, to dare

Wagen ['va:gən] (-s, -) *m* vehicle; (*Auto*) car; (*EISENB*) carriage; (*Pferdewagen*) cart; **~heber** (-s, -) *m* jack

Waggon [va'gõ:] (-s, -s) *m* carriage; (*Güterwaggon*) goods van, freight truck (*US*)

Wagnis ['va:knıs] (-ses, -se) *nt* risk

Wagon ▲ [va'gõ:, va'go:n] (-s, -s) *m* = Waggon

Wahl [va:l] (-, -en) *f* choice; (*POL*) election; **zweite ~** (*COMM*) seconds *pl*

wähl- ['vε:l] *zW*: **~bar** *adj* eligible; **~en** *vt*, *vi* to choose; (*POL*) to elect, to vote (for); (*TEL*) to dial; **W~er(in)** (-s, -) *m(f)* voter; **~erisch** *adj* fastidious, particular

Wahl- *zW*: **~fach** *nt* optional subject; **~gang** *m* ballot; **~kabine** *f* polling booth; **~kampf** *m* election campaign; **~kreis** *m* constituency; **~lokal** *nt* polling station; **~los** *adv* at random; **~recht** *nt* franchise; **~spruch** *m* motto; **~urne** *f* ballot box

Wahn [va:n] (-(e)s) *m* delusion; folly; **~sinn** *m* madness; **w~sinnig** *adj* insane, mad ♦ *adv* (*umg*) incredibly

wahr [va:r] *adj* true

wahren *vt* to maintain, to keep

während ['vε:rənt] *präp +gen* during ♦ *konj* while; **~dessen** *adv* meanwhile

wahr- *zW*: **~haben** (*unreg*) *vt*: etw nicht ~haben wollen to refuse to admit sth; **~haft** *adv* (*tatsächlich*) truly; **~haftig** [va:r'haftıç] *adj* true, real ♦ *adv* really; **W~heit** *f* truth; **~nehmen** (*unreg*) *vt* to perceive, to observe; **W~nehmung** *f* perception; **~sagen** *vi* to prophesy, to tell fortunes; **W~sager(in)** (-s, -) *m(f)* fortune teller; **~scheinlich** [va:r'ʃainlıç] *adj* probable ♦ *adv* probably; **W~'scheinlichkeit** *f* probability; **aller W~scheinlichkeit nach** in all probability

Währung ['vɛːrʊŋ] f currency

Wahrzeichen nt symbol

Waise ['vaɪzə] f orphan; **~nhaus** nt orphanage

Wald [valt] (-(e)s, ꞏer) m wood(s); (groß) forest; **~brand** m forest fire; **~sterben** nt trees dying due to pollution

Wales [weɪlz] (-) nt Wales

Wal(fisch) ['vaːl(fɪʃ)] (-(e)s, -e) m whale

Waliser [va'liːzər] (-s, -) m Welshman; **Waliserin** [va'liːzərɪn] f Welshwoman; **walisisch** [va'liːzɪʃ] adj Welsh

Walkman ['wɔːkman] (®, -s, **Walkmen**) m Walkman ®, personal stereo

Wall [val] (-(e)s, ꞏe) m embankment; (Bollwerk) rampart

Wallfahr- zW: **~er(in)** m(f) pilgrim; **~t** f pilgrimage

Walnuss ▲ ['valnʊs] f walnut

Walross ▲ ['valrɔs] nt walrus

Walze ['valtsə] f (Gerät) cylinder; (Fahrzeug) roller; **w~n** vt to roll (out)

wälzen ['vɛltsən] vt to roll (over); (Bücher) to hunt through; (Probleme) to deliberate on ♦ vr to wallow; (vor Schmerzen) to roll about; (im Bett) to toss and turn

Walzer ['valtsər] (-s, -) m waltz

Wand [vant] (-, ꞏe) f wall; (Trennwand) partition; (Bergwand) precipice

Wandel ['vandəl] (-s) m change; **w~bar** adj changeable, variable; **w~n** vt, vr to change ♦ vi (gehen) to walk

Wander- ['vandər] zW: **~er** (-s, -) m hiker, rambler; **~karte** f map of country walks; **w~n** vi to hike; (Blick) to wander; (Gedanken) to stray; **~schaft** f travelling; **~ung** f walk, hike; **~weg** m trail, walk

Wandlung f change, transformation

Wange ['vaŋə] f cheek

wanken ['vaŋkən] vi to stagger; (fig) to waver

wann [van] adv when

Wanne ['vanə] f tub

Wanze ['vantsə] f bug

Wappen ['vapən] (-s, -) nt coat of arms, crest; **~kunde** f heraldry

war etc [vaːr] vb siehe **sein**

Ware ['vaːrə] f ware

Waren- zW: **~haus** nt department store; **~lager** nt stock, store; **~muster** nt trade sample; **~probe** f sample, **~sendung** f trade sample (sent by post); **~zeichen** nt: (eingetragenes) **~zeichen** (registered) trademark

warf etc [varf] vb siehe **werfen**

warm [varm] adj warm; (Essen) hot

Wärm- zW: **~e** f warmth; **w~en** vt, vr to warm (up), to heat (up); **~flasche** f hot-water bottle

Warn- zW: **~blinkanlage** f (AUT) hazard warning lights pl; **~dreieck** nt warning triangle; **w~en** vt to warn; **~ung** f warning

warten ['vartən] vi: **~ (auf** +akk) to wait (for); **auf sich ~ lassen** to take a long time

Wärter(in) ['vɛrtər(ɪn)] (-s, -) m(f) attendant

Warte- zW: **~saal** m (EISENB) waiting room; **~zimmer** nt waiting room

Wartung f servicing; service; **~ und Instandhaltung** maintenance

warum [va'rʊm] adv why

Warze ['vartsə] f wart

was [vas] pron what; (umg: etwas) something; **~ für (ein)** ... what sort of ...

waschbar adj washable

Waschbecken nt washbasin

Wäsche ['vɛʃə] f wash(ing); (Bettwäsche) linen; (Unterwäsche) underclothing

waschecht adj colourfast; (fig) genuine

Wäsche- zW: **~klammer** f clothes peg (BRIT), clothespin (US); **~leine** f washing line (BRIT)

waschen ['vaʃən] (unreg) vt, vi to wash ♦ vr to (have a) wash; **sich auf die Hände ~** to wash one's hands

Wäsche'rei f laundry

Wasch- zW: **~gelegenheit** f washing facilities; **~küche** f laundry room; **~lappen** m face flannel, washcloth (US); (umg) sissy; **~maschine** f washing machine; **~mittel** nt detergent, washing powder; **~pulver** nt detergent, washing powder; **~raum** m washroom; **~salon** m Launderette ®

Wasser ['vasər] (-s, -) nt water; **~ball** m water polo; **w~dicht** adj waterproof; **~fall** m waterfall; **~farbe** f watercolour; **~hahn** m tap, faucet (US); **~kraftwerk** nt hydroelectric power station; **~leitung** f water pipe; **~mann** n (ASTROL) Aquarius

wässern ['vesərn] vt, vi to water

Wasser- zW: **w~scheu** adj afraid of (the) water; **~ski** ['vasərʃi:] nt waterskiing; **~stoff** m hydrogen; **~waage** f spirit level; **~zeichen** nt watermark

wässrig ▲ ['vesrɪç] adj watery

Watt [vat] (-(e)s, -en) nt mud flats pl

Watte f cotton wool, absorbent cotton (US)

WC ['ve:'tse:] (-s, -s) nt abk (= water closet) W.C.

Web- ['ve:b] zW: **w~en** (unreg) vt to weave; **~er** (-s, -) m weaver; **~e'rei** f (Betrieb) weaving mill; **~stuhl** m loom

Wechsel ['vɛksəl] (-s, -) m change; (COMM) bill of exchange; **~geld** nt change; **w~haft** adj (Wetter) variable; **~jahre** pl change of life sg; **~kurs** m rate of exchange; **w~n** vt to change; (Blicke) to exchange ♦ vi to change; to vary; (Geldwechseln) to have change; **~strom** m alternating current; **~stube** f bureau de change; **~wirkung** f interaction

Weck- ['vɛk] zW: **~dienst** m alarm call service; **w~en** vt to wake (up); to call; **~er** (-s, -) m alarm clock

wedeln ['ve:dəln] vi (mit Schwanz) to wag; (mit Fächer etc) to wave

weder ['ve:dər] konj neither; **~ ... noch** ... neither ... nor ...

Weg [ve:k] (-(e)s, -e) m way; (Pfad) path; (Route) route; **sich auf den ~ machen** to be on one's way; **jdm aus dem ~ gehen** to keep out of sb's way; siehe **zuwege**

weg [vɛk] adv away, off; **über etw** akk **~ sein** to be over sth; **er war schon ~** he had already left; **Finger ~!** hands off!

wegbleiben (unreg) vi to stay away

wegen ['ve:gən] präp +gen (umg: +dat) because of

weg- ['vɛk] zW: **~fallen** (unreg) vi to be left out; (Ferien, Bezahlung) to be cancelled; (aufhören) to cease; **~gehen** (unreg) vi to go away; to leave; **~lassen** (unreg) vt to leave out; **~laufen** (unreg) vi to run away od off; **~legen** vt to put aside; **~machen** (umg) vt to get rid of; **~müssen** (unreg; umg) vi to have to go; **~nehmen** (unreg) vt to take away; **~tun** (unreg) vt to put away; **W~weiser** (-s, -) m road sign, signpost; **~werfen** (unreg) vt to throw away

weh [ve:] adj sore; **~(e)** excl: **~(e),** **wenn du ...** woe betide you if ...; **o ~!** oh dear!; **~e!** just you dare!

wehen vt, vi to blow; (Fahnen) to flutter

weh- zW: **~leidig** adj whiny, whining; **~mütig** adj melancholy

Wehr [ve:r] (-, -en) f: **sich zur ~ setzen** to defend o.s.; **~dienst** m military service; **~dienstverweigerer** m ≈ conscientious objector; **w~en** vr to defend o.s.; **w~los** adj defenceless; **~pflicht** f compulsory military service; **w~pflichtig** adj liable for military service

Wehrdienst *is military service which is still compulsory in Germany. All young men receive their call-up papers at 18 and are required to spend 10 months in the* **Bundeswehr**. *Conscientious objectors are allowed to do* **Zivildienst** *as an alternative, after attending a hearing and presenting their case.*

wehtun ▲ ['veːtuːn] (*unreg*) *vt* to hurt, to be sore; **jdm/sich** ~ to hurt sb/o.s.

Weib [vaɪp] (-(e)s, -er) *nt* woman, female; wife; **~chen** *nt* female; **w~lich** *adj* feminine

weich [vaɪç] *adj* soft; **W~e** *f* (*EISENB*) points *pl*; **~en** (*unreg*) *vi* to yield, to give way; **W~heit** *f* softness; **~lich** *adj* soft, namby-pamby

Weide ['vaɪdə] *f* (*Baum*) willow; (*Gras*) pasture; **w~n** *vi* to graze ♦ *vr*: **sich an etw** *dat* **w~n** to delight in sth

weigern ['vaɪɡərn] *vr* to refuse

Weigerung ['vaɪɡərʊŋ] *f* refusal

Weihe ['vaɪə] *f* consecration; (*Priesterweihe*) ordination; **w~n** *vt* to consecrate; to ordain

Weihnacht *zW*: **~en** (-) *nt* Christmas; **w~lich** *adj* Christmas *cpd*

Weihnachts- *zW*: **~abend** *m* Christmas Eve; **~lied** *nt* Christmas carol; **~mann** *m* Father Christmas, Santa Claus; **~markt** *m* Christmas fair; **~tag** *m* Christmas Day; **zweiter ~tag** Boxing Day

The **Weihnachtsmarkt** *is a market held in most large towns in Germany in the weeks prior to Christmas. People visit it to buy presents, toys and Christmas decorations, and to enjoy the festive atmosphere. Traditional Christmas food and drink can also be consumed there, for example,* **Lebkuchen** *and* **Glühwein**.

Weihwasser *nt* holy water

weil [vaɪl] *konj* because

Weile ['vaɪlə] (-) *f* while, short time

Wein [vaɪn] (-(e)s, -e) *m* wine; (*Pflanze*) vine; **~bau** *m* cultivation of vines; **~berg** *m* vineyard; **~bergschnecke** *f* snail; **~brand** *m* brandy

weinen *vt, vi* to cry; **das ist zum W~** it's enough to make you cry *od* weep

Wein- *zW*: **~glas** *nt* wine glass; **~karte** *f* wine list; **~lese** *f* vintage; **~probe** *f* wine-tasting; **~rebe** *f* vine; **~rot** *adj* burgundy, claret, wine-red; **~stock** *m* vine; **~stube** *f* wine bar; **~traube** *f* grape

weise ['vaɪzə] *adj* wise

Weise ['vaɪzə] *f* manner, way; (*Lied*) tune; **auf diese ~** in this way

weisen ['vaɪzn] (*unreg*) *vt* to show

Weisheit ['vaɪshaɪt] *f* wisdom; **~zahn** *m* wisdom tooth

weiß [vaɪs] *adj* white ♦ *vb siehe* **wissen**; **W~bier** *nt* weissbier (*light, fizzy beer made using top-fermentation yeast*); **W~brot** *nt* white bread; **~en** *vt* to whitewash; **W~glut** *f* (*TECH*) incandescence; **jdn bis zur W~glut bringen** (*fig*) to make sb see red; **W~kohl** *m* (white) cabbage; **W~wein** *m* white wine; **W~wurst** *f* veal sausage

weit [vaɪt] *adj* wide; (*Begriff*) broad; (*Reise, Wurf*) long ♦ *adv*: **wie ist es ...?** how far is it ...?; **in ~er Ferne** in the far distance; **~ blickend** far-seeing; **~ reichend** long-range; (*fig*) far-reaching; **~ verbreitet** widespread; **das geht zu ~** that's going too far; **~aus** *adv* by far; **~blickend** *adj* far-seeing; **W~e** *f* width; (*Raum*) space; (*von Entfernung*) distance; **~en** *vt, vr* to widen

weiter ['vaɪtər] adj wider; broader; farther (away); (zusätzlich) further ♦ adv further; **ohne ~es** without further ado; just like that; **~ nichts/niemand** nothing/nobody else; **~arbeiten** vi to go on working; **~bilden** vt to continue one's education; **~empfehlen** (unreg) vt to recommend (to others); **W~fahrt** f continuation of the journey; **~führen** vi (Straße) to lead on (to) ♦ vt (fortsetzen) to continue, carry on; **~gehen** (unreg) vi to go on; **~hin** adv: **etw ~hin tun** to go on doing sth; **~kommen** (unreg) vi (fig: mit Arbeit) to make progress; **~leiten** vt to pass on; **~machen** vt, vi to continue

weit- zW: **~gehend** adj considerable ♦ adv largely; **~läufig** adj (Gebäude) spacious; (Erklärung) lengthy; (Verwandter) distant; **~reichend** adj long-range; (fig) far-reaching; **~schweifig** adj long-winded; **~sichtig** adj (MED) long-sighted; (fig) far-sighted; **W~sprung** m long jump; **~verbreitet** adj widespread

Weizen ['vaɪtsən] (-s, -) m wheat

welche(r, s) interrogativ pron which; **welcher von beiden?** which (one) of the two?; **welchen hast du genommen?** which one did you take?; **welche eine ...!** what a ...!; **welche Freude!** what joy!

♦ indef pron some; (in Fragen) any; **ich habe welche** I have some; **haben Sie welche?** do you have any?

♦ relativ pron (bei Menschen) who; (bei Sachen) which, that; **welche(r, s) auch immer** whoever/whichever/whatever

welk [vɛlk] adj withered; **~en** vi to wither

Welle ['vɛlə] f wave; (TECH) shaft

Wellen- zW: **~bereich** m waveband;

~länge f (auch fig) wavelength; **~linie** f wavy line; **~sittich** m budgerigar

Welt [vɛlt] (-, -en) f world; **~all** nt universe; **~anschauung** f philosophy of life; **w~berühmt** adj world-famous; **~krieg** m world war; **w~lich** adj worldly; (nicht kirchlich) secular; **~macht** f world power; **~meister** m world champion; **~raum** m space; **~reise** f trip round the world; **~stadt** f metropolis; **w~weit** adj world-wide

wem [veːm] (dat von wer) pron to whom

wen [veːn] (akk von wer) pron whom

Wende ['vɛndə] f turn; (Veränderung) change; **~kreis** m (GEOG) tropic; (AUT) turning circle; **~ltreppe** f spiral staircase; **w~n** (unreg) vt, vi, vr to turn; **sich an jdn w~n** to go/come to sb

wendig ['vɛndɪç] adj (Auto etc) manœuvrable; (fig) agile

Wendung f turn; (Redewendung) idiom

wenig ['veːnɪç] adj, adv little; **~e** pron pl few pl; **~er** adj less; (mit pl) fewer ♦ adv less; **~ste(r, s)** adj least; **am ~sten** least; **~stens** adv at least

wenn [vɛn] konj 1 (falls, bei Wünschen) if; **wenn auch ..., selbst wenn ...** even if ...; **wenn ich doch ...** if only I ...

2 (zeitlich) when; **immer wenn** whenever

wennschon ['vɛnʃoːn] adv: **na ~** so what?; **~, dennschon!** in for a penny, in for a pound

wer [veːr] pron who

Werbe- ['vɛrbə] zW: **~fernsehen** nt commercial television; **~geschenk** nt gift (from company); (zu Gekauftem) free gift; **w~n** (unreg) vt to win; (Mitglied) to recruit ♦ vi to advertise; **um jdn/etw w~n** to try to win sb/sth; **für jdn/etw w~n** to promote sb/sth

Werbung f advertising; (von Mitgliedern) recruitment; **~ um jdn/etw** promotion of sb/sth

Werdegang ['ve:ɐdəgaŋ] m (Laufbahn) development; (beruflich) career

---
SCHLÜSSELWORT
---

werden ['ve:ɐdən] (pt **wurde**, pp **geworden** od (bei Passiv) **worden**) vi to become; **was ist aus ihm/aus der Sache geworden?** what became of him/it?; **es ist nichts/gut geworden** it came to nothing/turned out well; **es wird Nacht/Tag** it's getting dark/light; **mir wird kalt** I'm getting cold; **mir wird schlecht** I feel ill; **Erster werden** to come od be first; **das muss anders werden** that'll have to change; **rot/zu Eis werden** to turn red/to ice; **was willst du (mal) werden?** what do you want to be?; **die Fotos sind gut geworden** the photos have come out nicely

♦ als Hilfsverb **1** (bei Futur): **er wird es tun** he will od he'll do it; **er wird das nicht tun** he will not od he won't do it; **es wird gleich regnen** it's going to rain

2 (bei Konjunktiv): **ich würde ...** I would ...; **er würde gern ...** he would od he'd like to ...; **ich würde lieber ...** I would od I'd rather ...

3 (bei Vermutung): **sie wird in der Küche sein** she will be in the kitchen **4** (bei Passiv): **gebraucht werden** to be used; **er ist erschossen worden** he has od he's been shot; **mir wurde gesagt, dass ...** I was told that ...

---

werfen ['vɛrfən] (unreg) vt to throw
Werft [vɛrft] (-, -en) f shipyard, dockyard
Werk [vɛrk] (-(e)s, -e) nt work; (Tätigkeit) job; (Fabrik, Mechanismus) works pl; **ans ~ gehen** to set to work; **~statt** (-, -stätten) f workshop; (AUT)

garage; **~tag** m working day; **w~tags** adv on working days; **w~tätig** adj working; **~zeug** nt tool

Wermut ['ve:rmu:t] (-(e)s) m wormwood; (Wein) vermouth

Wert [ve:rt] (-(e)s, -e) m worth; (FIN) value; **~ legen auf** +akk to attach importance to; **es hat doch keinen ~** it's useless; **w~** adj worth; (geschätzt) dear; worthy; **das ist nichts/viel w~** it's not worth anything/it's worth a lot; **das ist es/er mir w~** it's/he's worth that to me; **~angabe** f declaration of value; **~brief** m registered letter (containing sth of value); **w~en** vt to rate; **~gegenstände** mpl valuables; **w~los** adj worthless; **~papier** nt security; **w~voll** adj valuable

Wesen ['ve:zən] (-s, -) nt (Geschöpf) being; (Natur, Charakter) nature; **w~tlich** adj significant; (beträchtlich) considerable

weshalb [vɛs'halp] adv why
Wespe ['vɛspə] f wasp
wessen ['vɛsən] (gen von **wer**) pron whose
Weste ['vɛstə] f waistcoat, vest (US); (Wollweste) cardigan
West- zW: **~en** (-s) m west; **~europa** nt Western Europe; **w~lich** adj western ♦ adv to the west
weswegen [vɛs've:gən] adv why
wett [vɛt] adj even; **W~bewerb** m competition; **W~e** f bet, wager; **~en** vt, vi to bet
Wetter ['vɛtɐ] (-s, -) nt weather; **~bericht** m weather report; **~dienst** m meteorological service; **~lage** f (weather) situation; **~vorhersage** f weather forecast; **~warte** f weather station
Wett- zW: **~kampf** m contest; **~lauf** m race; **w~machen** vt to make good
wichtig ['vɪçtɪç] adj important; **W~keit** f importance

Spelling Reform: ▲ new spelling △ old spelling (to be phased out)

wickeln ['vɪkəln] *vt* to wind; (*Haare*) to set; (*Kind*) to change; **jdn/etw in etw** *akk* ~ to wrap sb/sth in sth

Wickelraum *m* mothers' (and babies') room

Widder ['vɪdər] **(-s, -)** *m* ram; (*ASTROL*) Aries

wider ['vi:dər] *präp +akk* against; ~**'fahren** (*unreg*) *vi* to happen; ~**'legen** *vt* to refute

widerlich ['vi:dərlɪç] *adj* disgusting, repulsive

wider- ['vi:dər] *zW:* ~**rechtlich** *adj* unlawful; **W~rede** *f* contradiction; ~**rufen** (*unreg*) *vt insep* to retract; (*Anordnung*) to revoke; (*Befehl*) to countermand; ~**'setzen** *vr insep:* **sich jdm/etw ~setzen** to oppose sb/sth

widerspenstig ['vi:dərʃpɛnstɪç] *adj* wilful

wider- ['vi:dər] *zW:* ~**spiegeln** *vt* (*Entwicklung, Erscheinung*) to mirror, to reflect ♦ *vr* to be reflected; ~**'sprechen** (*unreg*) *vi insep:* **jdm ~sprechen** to contradict sb

Widerspruch ['vi:dərʃprɔx] *m* contradiction; **w~slos** *adv* without arguing

Widerstand ['vi:dərʃtant] *m* resistance

Widerstands- *zW:* ~**bewegung** *f* resistance (movement); **w~fähig** *adj* resistant, tough; **w~los** *adj* unresisting

wider'stehen (*unreg*) *vi insep:* **jdm/etw ~** to withstand sb/sth

wider- ['vi:dər] *zW:* ~**wärtig** *adj* nasty, horrid; **W~wille** *m* ~**wille** (**gegen**) aversion (to); **w~willig** *adj* unwilling, reluctant

widmen ['vɪtmən] *vt* to dedicate; to devote ♦ *vr* to devote o.s.

widrig ['vi:drɪç] *adj* (*Umstände*) adverse

SCHLÜSSELWORT

wie [vi:] *adv* how; **wie groß/schnell?** how big/fast?; **wie wärs?** how about it?; **wie ist er?** what's he like?; **wie gut du das kannst!** you're very good at it; **wie bitte?** pardon?; (*entrüstet*) I

beg your pardon!; **und wie!** and how!; **wie viel** how much; **wie viel Menschen** how many people; **wie weit** to what extent

♦ *konj* **1** (*bei Vergleichen*): **so schön wie ...** as beautiful as ...; **wie ich schon sagte** as I said; **wie du** like you; **singen wie ein ...** to sing like a ...; **wie (zum Beispiel)** such as (for example)

2 (*zeitlich*): **wie er das hörte, ging er** when he heard that he left; **er hörte, wie der Regen fiel** he heard the rain falling

wieder ['vi:dər] *adv* again; ~ **da sein** to be back (again); ~ **aufbereiten** to recycle; ~ **aufnehmen** to resume; ~ **erkennen** to recognize; ~ **gutmachen** to make up for; (*Fehler*) to put right; ~ **herstellen** (*Ruhe, Frieden etc*) to restore; ~ **vereinigen** to reunite; (*POL*) to reunify; ~ **verwerten** to recycle; **gehst du schon ~?** are you off again?; ~ **ein(e)** ... another ...; **W~aufbau** *m* rebuilding; ~**bekommen** (*unreg*) *vt* to get back; **W~gabe** *f* reproduction; ~**geben** (*unreg*) *vt* (*zurückgeben*) to return; (*Erzählung etc*) to repeat; (*Gefühle etc*) to convey; **W~'gutmachung** *f* reparation; ~**'herstellen** (*Gesundheit, Gebäude*) to restore; ~**'holen** *vt insep* to repeat; **W~'holung** *f* repetition; ~**hören** *nt:* **auf W~hören** (*TEL*) goodbye; **W~kehr** (-) *f* return; (*von Vorfall*) repetition, recurrence; ~**sehen** (*unreg*) *vt* to see again; **auf W~sehen** goodbye; ~**um** *adv* again; (*andererseits*) on the other hand; **W~vereinigung** *f* (*POL*) reunification; **W~wahl** *f* re-election

Wiege ['vi:gə] *f* cradle; **w~n**[1] *vt* (*schaukeln*) to rock

wiegen[2] (*unreg*) *vt, vi* (*Gewicht*) to weigh

Wien [vi:n] *nt* Vienna

Wiese ['vi:zə] *f* meadow

Wiesel ['viːzəl] (-s, -) nt weasel

wieso [viːˈzoː] adv why

wieviel △ [viːˈfiːl] adj siehe **wie**

wievielmal [viːˈfiːlmaːl] adv how often

wievielte(r, s) adj: **zum ~n Mal?** how many times?; **den W~n haben wir?** what's the date?; **an ~r Stelle?** in what place?; **der ~ Besucher war er?** how many visitors were there before him?

wild [vɪlt] adj wild; **W~** (-(e)s) nt game; **W~e(r)** ['vɪldə(r)] f(m) savage; **~ern** vi to poach; **~'fremd** (umg) adj quite strange od unknown; **W~heit** f wildness; **W~leder** nt suede; **W~nis** (-, -se) f wilderness; **W~schwein** nt (wild) boar

will etc [vɪl] vb siehe **wollen**

Wille ['vɪlə] (-ns, -n) m will; **W~n** +gen: **um ... w~n** for the sake of ...; **w~nsstark** adj strong-willed

will- zW: **~ig** adj willing; **W~kommen** [vɪlˈkɔmən] (-s, -) nt welcome; **~kommen** adj welcome; **jdn ~kommen heißen** to welcome sb; **~kürlich** adj arbitrary; (Bewegung) voluntary

wimmeln ['vɪməln] vi: **~ (von)** to swarm (with)

wimmern ['vɪmərn] vi to whimper

Wimper ['vɪmpər] (-, -n) f eyelash

Wimperntusche f mascara

Wind [vɪnt] (-(e)s, -e) m wind; **~beutel** m cream puff; (fig) rake; **~e** f (TECH) winch, windlass; (BOT) bindweed; **~el** ['vɪndəl] (-, -n) f nappy, diaper (US); **w~en** vi unpers to be windy ♦ vt (unreg) to wind; (Kranz) to weave; (entwinden) to twist ♦ vr (unreg) (entwinden) to twist ♦ vr (unreg) (Person) to writhe; **~energie** f wind energy; **w~ig** ['vɪndɪç] adj windy; (fig) dubious; **~jacke** f windcheater; **~mühle** f windmill; **~pocken** pl chickenpox sg; **~schutzscheibe** f (AUT) windscreen (BRIT), windshield (US); **~stärke** f wind force; **w~still** adj

(Tag) still, windless; (Platz) sheltered; **~stille** f calm; **~stoß** m gust of wind

Wink [vɪŋk] (-(e)s, -e) m (mit Hand) wave; (mit Kopf) nod; (Hinweis) hint

Winkel ['vɪŋkəl] (-s, -) m (MATH) angle; (Gerät) set square; (in Raum) corner

winken ['vɪŋkən] vt, vi to wave

winseln ['vɪnzəln] vi to whine

Winter ['vɪntər] (-s, -) m winter; **w~fest** adj (Pflanze) hardy; **~garten** m conservatory; **w~lich** adj wintry; **~reifen** m winter tyre; **~sport** m winter sports pl

Winzer ['vɪntsər] (-s, -) m vine grower

winzig ['vɪntsɪç] adj tiny

Wipfel ['vɪpfəl] (-s, -) m treetop

wir [viːr] pron we; **~ alle** all of us, we all

Wirbel ['vɪrbəl] (-s, -) m whirl, swirl; (Trubel) hurly-burly; (Aufsehen) fuss; (ANAT) vertebra; **w~n** vi to whirl, to swirl; **~säule** f spine

wird [vɪrt] vb siehe **werden**

wirfst etc [vɪrfst] vb siehe **werfen**

wirken ['vɪrkən] vi to have an effect; (erfolgreich sein) to work; (scheinen) to seem ♦ vt (Wunder) to work

wirklich ['vɪrklɪç] adj real ♦ adv really; **W~keit** f reality

wirksam ['vɪrkzaːm] adj effective

Wirkstoff m (biologisch, chemisch, pflanzlich) active substance

Wirkung ['vɪrkʊŋ] f effect; **w~slos** adj ineffective; **w~slos bleiben** to have no effect; **w~svoll** adj effective

wirr [vɪr] adj confused, wild; **W~warr** (-s) m disorder, chaos

wirst [vɪrst] vb siehe **werden**

Wirt(in) [vɪrt(ɪn)] (-(e)s, -e) m(f) landlord(lady); **~schaft** f (Gaststätte) pub; (Haushalt) housekeeping; (eines Landes) economy; (umg: Durcheinander) mess; **w~schaftlich** adj economical; (POL) economic

Wirtschafts- zW: **~krise** f economic crisis; **~politik** f economic policy;

~prüfer m chartered accountant; **~wunder** nt economic miracle

Wirtshaus nt inn

wischen ['vɪʃən] vt to wipe

Wischer (-s, -) m (AUT) wiper

Wissbegier(de) ▲ ['vɪsbəgiːr(də)] f thirst for knowledge; **wissbegierig** ▲ adj inquisitive, eager for knowledge

wissen ['vɪsən] (unreg) vt to know; **was weiß ich!** I don't know!; **W~** (-s) nt knowledge; **W~schaft** f science; **W~schaftler(in)** (-s, -) m(f) scientist; **~schaftlich** adj scientific; **~swert** adj worth knowing

wittern ['vɪtərn] vt to scent; (fig) to suspect

Witterung f weather; (Geruch) scent

Witwe ['vɪtvə] f widow; **~r** (-s, -) m widower

Witz [vɪts] (-(e)s, -e) m joke; **~bold** (-(e)s, -e) m joker, wit; **~ig** adj funny

wo [voː] adv where; (umg: irgendwo) somewhere; **im Augenblick, ~** ... the moment (that) ...; **die Zeit, ~** ... the time when ...; **~anders** [voːˈandərs] adv elsewhere; **~bei** [-ˈbaɪ] adv (relativ) by/with which; (interrogativ) what ... in/by/with

Woche ['vɔxə] f week

Wochen- zW: **~ende** nt weekend; **w~lang** adj, adv for weeks; **~markt** m weekly market; **~schau** f newsreel

wöchentlich ['vœçəntlɪç] adj, adv weekly

wodurch [voˈdʊrç] adv (relativ) through which; (interrogativ) through what

wofür [voˈfyːr] adv (relativ) for which; (interrogativ) what ... for

wog etc [voːk] vb siehe **wiegen**

wo- [voː] zW: **~'gegen** adv (relativ) against which; (interrogativ) what ... against; **~her** [-ˈheːr] adv where from; **~hin** [-ˈhɪn] adv where ... to

wohl [voːl] adv 1: **sich wohl fühlen**

(zufrieden) to feel happy; (gesundheitlich) to feel well; **jdm wohl tun** to do sb good; **wohl oder übel** whether one likes it or not

2 (wahrscheinlich) probably; (gewiss) certainly; (vielleicht) perhaps; **sie ist wohl zu Hause** she's probably at home; **das ist doch wohl nicht dein Ernst!** surely you're not serious!; **das mag wohl sein** that may well be; **ob das wohl stimmt?** I wonder if that's true; **er weiß das sehr wohl** he knows that perfectly well

Wohl [voːl] (-(e)s) nt welfare; **zum ~!** cheers!; **w~auf** adv well; **~behagen** nt comfort; **~fahrt** f welfare; **~fahrtsstaat** m welfare state; **w~habend** adj wealthy; **w~ig** adj contented, comfortable; **w~schmeckend** adj delicious; **~stand** m prosperity; **~standsgesellschaft** f affluent society; **~tat** f relief; act of charity; **~täter(in)** m(f) benefactor; **w~tätig** adj charitable; **~tätigkeits-** zW charity, charitable; **w~verdient** adj well-earned, well-deserved; **w~weislich** adv prudently; **~wollen** (-s) nt good will; **w~wollend** adj benevolent

wohn- ['voːn] zW: **~en** vi to live; **W~gemeinschaft** f (Menschen) people sharing a flat; **~haft** adj resident; **W~heim** nt (für Studenten) hall of residence; (für Senioren) home; (bes für Arbeiter) hostel; **~lich** adj comfortable; **W~mobil** (-s, -e) nt camper; **W~ort** m domicile; **W~sitz** m place of residence; **W~ung** f house; (Etagenwohnung) flat, apartment (US); **W~wagen** m caravan; **W~zimmer** nt living room

wölben ['vœlbən] vt, vr to curve

Wolf [vɔlf] (-(e)s, ⸚e) m wolf

Wolke ['vɔlkə] f cloud; **~nkratzer** m skyscraper

wolkig ['vɔlkɪç] adj cloudy

Wolle ['vɔlə] f wool; **w~n¹** adj woollen

wollen 297 Wurf

SCHLÜSSELWORT

wollen² ['vɔlən] (pt **wollte**, pp **gewollt**
od als Hilfsverb) **wollen**) vt, vi to want;
ich will nach Hause I want to go
home; **er will nicht** he doesn't want
to; **er wollte das nicht** he didn't want
it; **wenn du willst** if you like; **ich will,
dass du mir zuhörst** I want you to listen to me

♦ Hilfsverb: **er will ein Haus kaufen** he
wants to buy a house; **ich wollte, ich
wäre ...** I wish I were ...; **etw gerade
tun wollen** to be going to do sth

wollüstig ['vɔlʏstɪç] adj lusty, sensual
wo- zW: **~mit** adv (relativ) with which;
(interrogativ) what ... with; **~möglich**
adv probably, I suppose; **~nach** adv
(relativ) after/for which; (interrogativ)
what ... for/after; **~ran** adv (relativ)
what ... on/at which; (interrogativ) what
on/at which; **~rauf** adv (relativ) on which; (interrogativ) what ... on; **~raus** adv (relativ) from/out of which; (interrogativ)
what ... from/out of; **~rin** adv (relativ)
in which; (interrogativ) what ... in

Wort [vɔrt] (-(e)s, -er od -e) nt word;
jdn beim ~ **nehmen** to take sb at his
word; **mit anderen ~en** in other
words; **w~brüchig** adj not true to
one's word

Wörterbuch ['vœrtərbuːx] nt dictionary

Wort- zW: **~führer** m spokesman;
w~karg adj taciturn; **~laut** m wording
wörtlich ['vœrtlɪç] adj literal

Wort- zW: **w~los** adj mute; **w~reich**
adj wordy, verbose; **~schatz** m vocabulary; **~spiel** nt play on words, pun
wo- zW: **~rüber** adv (relativ) over/
about which; (interrogativ) what ...
over/about; **~rum** adv (relativ) about/
round which; (interrogativ) what ...
about/round; **~runter** adv (relativ) un-

der which; (interrogativ) what ... under; **~von** adv (relativ) from which; (interrogativ) what ... from; **~vor** adv (relativ) in front of/before which; (interrogativ) in front of/before what; of what;
~zu adv (relativ) to/for which; (interrogativ) what ... for/to; (warum) why

Wrack [vrak] (-(e)s, -s) nt wreck

Wucher ['vuːxər] (-s) m profiteering;
~er (-s, -) m profiteer; **w~isch** adj
profiteering; **w~n** vi (Pflanzen) to
grow wild; **~ung** f (MED) growth, tumour

Wuchs [vuːks] (-es) m (Wachstum)
growth; (Statur) build

Wucht [vɔxt] (-) f force

wühlen ['vyːlən] vi to scrabble; (Tier)
to root; (Maulwurf) to burrow; (umg:
arbeiten) to slave away ♦ vt to dig

Wulst [vɔlst] (-es, ⸚e) m bulge; (an
Wunde) swelling

wund [vɔnt] adj sore, raw; **W~e** f
wound

Wunder ['vɔndər] (-s, -) nt miracle; **es
ist kein ~** it's no wonder; **w~bar** adj
wonderful, marvellous; **~kerze** f
sparkler; **~kind** nt infant prodigy;
w~lich adj odd, peculiar; **w~n** vr to
be surprised ♦ vt to surprise; **sich w~n
über** +akk to be surprised at;
w~schön adj beautiful; **w~voll** adj
wonderful

Wundstarrkrampf ['vɔntʃtarkrampf]
m tetanus, lockjaw

Wunsch [vɔnʃ] (-(e)s, ⸚e) m wish
wünschen ['vʏnʃən] vt to wish; **sich
dat etw ~** to want sth, to wish for sth;
~swert adj desirable

wurde etc ['vɔrdə] vb siehe **werden**

Würde ['vʏrdə] f dignity; (Stellung)
honour; **w~voll** adj dignified

würdig ['vʏrdɪç] adj worthy; (würdevoll)
dignified; **~en** vt to appreciate

Wurf [vɔrf] (-s, ⸚e) m throw; (Junge) lit-

Spelling Reform: ▲ *new spelling* △ *old spelling (to be phased out)*

Würfel ['vʏrfəl] (-s, -) *m* dice; (MATH) cube; **~becher** *m* (dice) cup; **w~n** *vi* to play dice ♦ *vt* to dice; **~zucker** *m* lump sugar

würgen ['vʏrgən] *vt, vi* to choke

Wurm [vʊrm] (-(e)s, *e*er) *m* worm; **w~stichig** *adj* worm-ridden

Wurst [vʊrst] (-, *e*e) *f* sausage; **das ist mir ~** (*umg*) I don't care, I don't give a damn

Würstchen ['vʏrstçən] *nt* sausage

Würze ['vʏrtsə] *f* seasoning, spice

Wurzel ['vʊrtsəl] (-, -n) *f* root

würzen ['vʏrtsən] *vt* to season, to spice

würzig *adj* spicy

wusch *etc* [vʊʃ] *vb siehe* **waschen**

wusste ▲ *etc* ['vʊstə] *vb siehe* **wissen**

wüst [vy:st] *adj* untidy, messy; (*ausschweifend*) wild; (*öde*) waste; (*umg: heftig*) terrible; **W~e** *f* desert

Wut [vu:t] (-) *f* rage, fury; **~anfall** *m* fit of rage

wüten ['vy:tən] *vi* to rage; **~d** *adj* furious, mad

X, x

X-Beine ['ɪksbaɪnə] *pl* knock-knees

x-beliebig [ɪksbə'li:bɪç] *adj* any (whatever)

xerokopieren [kseroko'pi:rən] *vt* to xerox, to photocopy

x-mal ['ɪksma:l] *adv* any number of times, n times

Xylofon ▲, **Xylophon** [ksylo'fo:n] (-s, -e) *nt* xylophone

Y, y

Yacht (-, -en) *f siehe* **Jacht**

Ypsilon ['ʏpsilɔn] (-(s), -s) *nt* the letter Y

Z, z

Zacke ['tsakə] *f* point; (*Bergzacke*) jagged peak; (*Gabelzacke*) prong; (*Kammzacke*) tooth

zackig ['tsakɪç] *adj* jagged; (*umg*) smart; (*Tempo*) brisk

zaghaft ['tsa:khaft] *adj* timid

zäh [tsɛ:] *adj* tough; (*Mensch*) tenacious; (*Flüssigkeit*) thick; (*schleppend*) sluggish; **Z~igkeit** *f* toughness; tenacity

Zahl [tsa:l] (-, -en) *f* number; **z~bar** *adj* payable; **z~en** *vt, vi* to pay; **z~en bitte!** the bill please!

zählen ['tsɛ:lən] *vt, vi* to count; **~ auf** +*akk* to count on; **~ zu** to be numbered among

Zahlenschloss ▲ *nt* combination lock

Zähler ['tsɛ:lər] (-s, -) *m* (TECH) meter; (MATH) numerator

Zahl- *zW:* **z~los** *adj* countless; **z~reich** *adj* numerous; **~tag** *m* payday; **~ung** *f* payment; **~ungsanweisung** *f* giro transfer order; **z~ungsfähig** *adj* solvent; **~wort** *nt* numeral

zahm [tsa:m] *adj* tame

zähmen ['tsɛ:mən] *vt* to tame; (*fig*) to curb

Zahn [tsa:n] (-(e)s, *e*e) *m* tooth; **~arzt** *m* dentist; **~ärztin** *f* (female) dentist; **~bürste** *f* toothbrush; **~fleisch** *nt* gums *pl*; **~pasta** *f* toothpaste; **~rad** *nt* cog(wheel); **~schmerzen** *pl* toothache *sg*; **~stein** *m* tartar; **~stocher** (-s, -) *m* toothpick

Zange ['tsaŋə] *f* pliers *pl*; (*Zuckerzange etc*) tongs *pl*; (*Beißzange*, ZOOL) pincers *pl*; (MED) forceps *pl*

zanken ['tsaŋkən] *vi, vr* to quarrel

zänkisch ['tsɛŋkɪʃ] *adj* quarrelsome

Zäpfchen ['tsɛpfçən] *nt* (ANAT) uvula; (MED) suppository

Zapfen ['tsapfən] (-s, -) *m* plug; (BOT) cone; (*Eiszapfen*) icicle

zappeln ['tsapəln] vi to wriggle; to fidget

zart [tsart] adj (weich, leise) soft; (Fleisch) tender; (fein, schwächlich) delicate; **Z~heit** f softness; tenderness; delicacy

zärtlich ['tsɛːrtlɪç] adj tender, affectionate

Zauber ['tsaubər] (-s, -) m magic; (~bann) spell; **~ei** [-'raɪ] f magic; **~er** (-s, -) m magician; conjuror; **z~haft** adj magical, enchanting; **~künstler** m conjuror; **~kunststück** nt conjuring trick; **z~n** vi to conjure, to practise magic

zaudern ['tsaudərn] vi to hesitate

Zaum [tsaum] (-(e)s, Zäume) m bridle; **etw im ~ halten** to keep sth in check

Zaun [tsaun] (-(e)s, Zäune) m fence

z. B. abk (= zum Beispiel) e.g.

Zebra ['tseːbra] nt zebra; **~streifen** m zebra crossing

Zeche ['tsɛçə] f (Rechnung) bill; (Bergbau) mine

Zeh [tseː] (-s, -en) m toe

Zehe ['tseːə] f toe; (Knoblauchzehe) clove

zehn [tseːn] num ten; **~te(r, s)** adj tenth; **Z~tel** (-s, -) nt tenth (part)

Zeich- ['tsaɪç] zW: **~en** (-s, -) nt sign; **z~nen** vt to draw; (kennzeichnen) to mark; (unterzeichnen) to sign ♦ vi to draw; to sign; **~ner** (-s, -) m artist; technischer ~ draughtsman; **~nung** f drawing; (Markierung) markings pl

Zeige- ['tsaɪgə] zW: **~finger** m index finger; **z~n** vt to show ♦ vi to point ♦ vt to show o.s.; **z~n auf** +akk to point to; to point at; **es wird sich z~n** time will tell; **es zeigte sich, dass ...** it turned out that ...; **~r** (-s, -) m pointer; (Uhrzeiger) hand

Zeile ['tsaɪlə] f line; (Häuserzeile) row

Zeit [tsaɪt] (-, -en) f time; (GRAM) tense; **sich** dat **~ lassen** to take one's time;

von ~ zu ~ from time to time; siehe zurzeit; **~alter** nt age; **~ansage** f (TEL) speaking clock; **~arbeit** f temporary job; **z~gemäß** adj in keeping with the times; **~genosse** m contemporary; **z~ig** adj early; **z~lich** adj temporal; **~lupe** f slow motion; **z~raubend** adj time-consuming; **~raum** m period; **~rechnung** f time, era; nach/vor unserer **~rechnung** A.D./B.C.; **~schrift** f periodical; **~ung** f newspaper; **~vertreib** m pastime, diversion; **z~weilig** adj temporary; **z~weise** adv for a time; **~wort** nt verb

Zelle ['tsɛlə] f cell; (Telefonzelle) callbox

Zellstoff m cellulose

Zelt [tsɛlt] (-(e)s, -e) nt tent; **z~en** vi to camp; **~platz** m camp site

Zement [tse'mɛnt] (-(e)s, -e) m cement; **z~ieren** vt to cement

zensieren [tsɛn'ziːrən] vt to censor; (SCH) to mark

Zensur [tsɛn'zuːr] f censorship; (SCH) mark

Zentimeter [tsɛnti'meːtər] m od nt centimetre

Zentner ['tsɛntnər] (-s, -) m hundredweight

zentral [tsɛn'traːl] adj central; **Z~e** f central; (TEL) exchange; **Z~heizung** f central heating

Zentrum ['tsɛntrom] (-s, Zentren) nt centre

zerbrechen [tsɛr'brɛçən] (unreg) vt, vi to break

zerbrechlich adj fragile

zer'drücken vt to squash, to crush; (Kartoffeln) to mash

Zeremonie [tseremo'niː] f ceremony

Zerfall [tsɛr'fal] m decay; **z~en** (unreg) vi to disintegrate, to decay; (sich gliedern): **z~en (in** +akk) to fall (into)

zer'gehen (unreg) vi to melt, to dissolve

zerkleinern [tsɛr'klaɪnərn] vt to reduce

to small pieces

zerlegbar [tser'le:kba:r] *adj* able to be dismantled

zerlegen [tser'le:gən] *vt* to take to pieces; (*Fleisch*) to carve; (*Satz*) to analyse

zermürben [tser'myrbən] *vt* to wear down

zerquetschen [tser'kvetʃən] *vt* to squash

Zeuge ['tsɔʏgə] (**-n, -n**) *m* witness; **z~n** *vi* to bear witness, to testify ♦ *vt* (*Kind*) to father; **es zeugt von ...** it testifies to ...; **~naussage** *f* evidence; **Zeugin** ['tsɔʏgɪn] *f* witness

zer'reißen (*unreg*) *vt* to tear to pieces ♦ *vi* to tear, to rip

zerren ['tsɛrən] *vt* to drag ♦ *vi*: ~ **(an** +*dat*) to tug (at)

Zeugnis ['tsɔʏgnɪs] (**-ses, -se**) *nt* certificate; (*SCH*) report; (*Referenz*) reference; (*Aussage*) evidence, testimony; ~ **geben von** to be evidence of, to testify to

zer'rinnen (*unreg*) *vi* to melt away

zerrissen [tser'rɪsən] *adj* torn, tattered; **Z~heit** *f* tattered state; (*POL*) disunion, discord; (*innere Z~heit*) disintegration

z. H(d). *abk* (= *zu Händen*) attn.

Zickzack ['tsɪktsak] (**-(e)s, -e**) *m* zigzag

Ziege ['tsi:gə] *f* goat

Zerrung *f* (*MED*): **eine ~** pulled muscle

Ziegel ['tsi:gəl] (**-s, -**) *m* brick; (*Dach-ziegel*) tile

zerrütten [tser'rʏtən] *vt* to wreck, to destroy

ziehen ['tsi:ən] (*unreg*) *vt* to draw; (*zerren*) to pull; (*SCHACH etc*) to move; (*züchten*) to rear ♦ *vi* to draw; (*umziehen, wandern*) to move; (*Rauch, Wolke etc*) to drift; (*reißen*) to pull ♦ *vb unpers*: **es zieht** there is a draught, it's draughty ♦ *vr* (*Gummi*) to stretch; (*Grenze etc*) to run; (*Gespräche*) to be drawn out; **etw nach sich ~** to lead to sth, to entail sth

zer'schlagen (*unreg*) *vt* to shatter, to smash ♦ *vr* to fall through

zer'schneiden (*unreg*) *vt* to cut up

zer'setzen *vt, vr* to decompose, to dissolve

zer'springen (*unreg*) *vi* to shatter, to burst

Ziehung ['tsi:ʊŋ] *f* (*Losziehung*) drawing

Zerstäuber [tser'ʃtɔʏbər] (**-s, -**) *m* atomizer

Ziel [tsi:l] (**-(e)s, -e**) *nt* (*einer Reise*) destination; (*SPORT*) finish; (*MIL*) target; (*Absicht*) goal; **z~bewusst ▲** *adj* decisive; **z~en** *vi*: **z~en (auf** +*akk*) to aim (at); **z~los** *adj* aimless; **~scheibe** *f* target; **z~strebig** *adj* purposeful

zerstören [tser'ʃtø:rən] *vt* to destroy

Zerstörung *f* destruction

zerstreu- [tser'ʃtrɔʏ] *zW*: ~**en** *vt* to disperse, to scatter; (*unterhalten*) to divert; (*Zweifel etc*) to dispel ♦ *vr* to disperse, to scatter; to be dispelled; ~**t** *adj* scattered; (*Mensch*) absentminded; **Z~theit** *f* absentmindedness; **Z~ung** *f* dispersion; (*Ablenkung*) diversion

ziemlich ['tsi:mlɪç] *adj* quite a; fair ♦ *adv* rather; quite a bit

zieren ['tsi:rən] *vr* to act coy

zierlich ['tsi:rlɪç] *adj* dainty

zerstückeln [tser'ʃtʏkəln] *vt* to cut into pieces

zer'teilen *vt* to divide into parts

Zertifikat [tsertifi'ka:t] (**-(e)s, -e**) *nt* certificate

Ziffer ['tsɪfər] (**-, -n**) *f* figure, digit; ~**blatt** *nt* dial, clock-face

zer'treten (*unreg*) *vt* to crush underfoot

zertrümmern [tser'trʏmərn] *vt* to

zig [tsɪk] (umg) adj umpteen
Zigarette [tsiga'rɛtə] f cigarette
Zigaretten- zW: **~automat** m cigarette machine; **~schachtel** f cigarette packet; **~spitze** f cigarette holder
Zigarre [tsi'garə] f cigar
Zigeuner(in) [tsi'gɔynər(ɪn)] (-s, -) m(f) gipsy
Zimmer ['tsɪmər] (-s, -) nt room; **~lautstärke** f reasonable volume; **~mädchen** nt chambermaid; **~mann** m carpenter; **z~n** vi to make (from wood); **~nachweis** m accommodation office; **~pflanze** f indoor plant; **~service** m room service
zimperlich ['tsɪmpərlɪç] adj squeamish; (pinglig) fussy, finicky
Zimt [tsɪmt] (-(e)s, -e) m cinnamon
Zink [tsɪŋk] (-(e)s) nt zinc
Zinn [tsɪn] (-(e)s) nt (Element) tin; (in ~waren) pewter; **~soldat** m tin soldier
Zins [tsɪns] (-es, -en) m interest; **~eszins** m compound interest; **~fuß** m rate of interest; **z~los** adj interest-free; **~satz** m rate of interest
Zipfel ['tsɪpfəl] (-s, -) m corner; (spitz) tip; (Hemdzipfel) tail; (Wurstzipfel) end
zirka ['tsɪrka] adv (round) about
Zirkel ['tsɪrkəl] (-s, -) m circle; (MATH) pair of compasses
Zirkus ['tsɪrkʊs] (-, -se) m circus
zischen ['tsɪʃən] vi to hiss
Zitat [tsi'ta:t] (-(e)s, -e) nt quotation, quote
zitieren [tsi'ti:rən] vt to quote
Zitrone [tsi'tro:nə] f lemon; **~nlimonade** f lemonade; **~nsaft** m lemon juice
zittern ['tsɪtərn] vi to tremble
zivil [tsi'vi:l] adj civil; (Preis) moderate; **Z~** (-s) nt plain clothes pl; (MIL) civilian clothing; **Z~courage** f courage of one's convictions; **Z~dienst** m community service; **Z~isation** [tsiviliza-

si'o:n] f civilization; **Z~isationskrankheit** f disease peculiar to civilization; **z~i'sieren** vt to civilize

Zivilist [tsivi'lɪst] m civilian
zögern ['tsø:gərn] vi to hesitate
Zoll [tsɔl] (-(e)s, "-e) m customs pl; (Abgabe) duty; **~abfertigung** f customs clearance; **~amt** nt customs office; **~beamte(r)** m customs official; **~erklärung** f customs declaration; **z~frei** adj duty-free; **~kontrolle** f customs check; **z~pflichtig** adj liable to duty, dutiable
Zone ['tso:nə] f zone
Zoo [tso:] (-s, -s) m zoo; **~loge** [tsoo'lo:gə] (-n, -n) m zoologist; **~lo'gie** f zoology; **z~'logisch** adj zoological
Zopf [tsɔpf] (-(e)s, "-e) m plait; pigtail; **alter ~** antiquated custom
Zorn [tsɔrn] (-(e)s) m anger; **z~ig** adj angry
zottig ['tsɔtɪç] adj shaggy
z. T. abk = **zum Teil**

─── SCHLÜSSELWORT ───

zu [tsu:] präp +dat **1** (örtlich) to; **zum Bahnhof/Arzt gehen** to go to the station/doctor; **zur Schule/Kirche gehen** to go to school/church; **sollen wir zu euch gehen?** shall we go to your place?; **sie sah zu ihm hin** she looked towards him; **zum Fenster herein** through the window; **zu mei-**

ner Linken to od on my left

2 (*zeitlich*) at; **zu Ostern** at Easter; **bis zum 1. Mai** until May 1st; (*nicht später als*) by May 1st; **zu meiner Zeit** in my time

3 (*Zusatz*) with; **Wein zum Essen trinken** to drink wine with one's meal; **sich zu jdm setzen** to sit down beside sb; **setz dich doch zu uns** (come and) sit with us; **Anmerkungen zu etw** notes on sth

4 (*Zweck*) for; **Wasser zum Waschen** water for washing; **Papier zum Schreiben** paper to write on; **etw zum Geburtstag bekommen** to get sth for one's birthday

5 (*Veränderung*) into; **zu etw werden** to turn into sth; **jdn zu etw machen** to make sb (into) sth; **zu Asche verbrennen** to burn to ashes

6 (*mit Zahlen*): **3 zu 2** (*SPORT*) 3-2; **das Stück zu 2 Mark** at 2 marks each; **zum ersten Mal** for the first time

7: **zu meiner Freude** *etc* to my joy *etc*; **zum Glück** luckily; **zu Fuß** on foot; **es ist zum Weinen** it's enough to make you cry

♦ *konj* to; **etw zu essen** sth to eat; **um besser sehen zu können** in order to see better; **ohne es zu wissen** without knowing it; **noch zu bezahlende Rechnungen** bills that are still to be paid

♦ *adv* **1** (*allzu*) too; **zu sehr** too much; **zu viel** too much; **zu wenig** too little

2 (*örtlich*) toward(s); **er kam auf mich zu** he came up to me

3 (*geschlossen*) shut, closed; **die Geschäfte haben zu** the shops are closed; **„auf/zu"** (*Wasserhahn etc*) "on/off"

4 (*umg: los*): **nur zu!** just keep on!; **mach zu!** hurry up!

zualler- [tsu'ʔalər] *zW:* **~erst** [-'ʔeːrst] *adv* first of all; **~letzt** [-'lɛtst] *adv* last of all

Zubehör [ˈtsuːbəhøːr] (**-(e)s, -e**) *nt* accessories *pl*

zubereiten [ˈtsuːbəraɪtən] *vt* to prepare

zubilligen [ˈtsuːbɪlɪɡən] *vt* to grant

zubinden [ˈtsuːbɪndən] (*unreg*) *vt* to tie up

zubringen [ˈtsuːbrɪŋən] (*unreg*) *vt* (*Zeit*) to spend

Zubringer (**-s, -**) *m* (*Straße*) approach *od* slip road

Zucchini [tsʊˈkiːni] *pl* (*BOT, KOCH*) courgette (*BRIT*), zucchini (*US*)

Zucht [tsʊxt] (**-, -en**) *f* (*von Tieren*) breeding; (*von Pflanzen*) cultivation; (*Rasse*) breed; (*Erziehung*) raising; (*Disziplin*) discipline

züchten [ˈtsʏçtən] *vt* (*Tiere*) to breed; (*Pflanzen*) to cultivate, to grow; **Züchter** (**-s, -**) *m* breeder; grower

Zuchthaus *nt* prison, penitentiary (*US*)

züchtigen [ˈtsʏçtɪɡən] *vt* to chastise

Züchtung *f* (*Zuchtart, Sorte: von Tier*) breed; (*von Pflanze*) variety

zucken [ˈtsʊkən] *vi* to jerk, to twitch; (*Strahl etc*) to flicker ♦ *vt* (*Schultern*) to shrug

Zucker [ˈtsʊkər] (**-s, -**) *m* sugar; (*MED*) diabetes; **~guss** ▲ *m* icing; **z~krank** *adj* diabetic; **~krankheit** *f* (*MED*) diabetes; **z~n** *vt* to sugar; **~rohr** *nt* sugar cane; **~rübe** *f* sugar beet

Zuckung [ˈtsʊkʊŋ] *f* convulsion, spasm; (*leicht*) twitch

zudecken [ˈtsuːdɛkən] *vt* to cover (up)

zudem [tsuˈdeːm] *adv* in addition (to this)

zudringlich [ˈtsuːdrɪŋlɪç] *adj* forward, pushing, obtrusive

zudrücken [ˈtsuːdrʏkən] *vt* to close; **ein Auge ~** to turn a blind eye

zueinander [tsuʔaɪˈnandər] *adv* to one other; (*in Verbindung*) together

zuerkennen [ˈtsuːʔɛrkɛnən] (*unreg*) *vt* to award; **jdm etw ~** to award sth to sb, to award sb sth

zuerst [tsuˈʔeːrst] *adv* first; (*zu Anfang*)

at first; **~ einmal** first of all

Zufahrt ['tsu:fa:rt] f approach; **~sstra-ße** f approach road; (von Autobahn etc) slip road

Zufall ['tsu:fal] m chance; (Ereignis) coincidence; **durch ~** by accident; **so ein ~** what a coincidence; **z~en** (unreg) vi to close, to shut; (Anteil, Aufgabe) to fall

zufällig ['tsu:fɛlɪç] adj chance ♦ adv by chance; (in Frage) by any chance

Zuflucht ['tsu:flʊxt] f recourse; (Ort) refuge

zufolge [tsu'fɔlgə] präp (+dat od gen) judging by; (laut) according to

zufrieden [tsu'fri:dən] adj content(ed), satisfied; **~ geben** to be content od satisfied (with); **~ stellen** to satisfy

zufrieren [tsu'fri:rən] (unreg) vi to freeze up od over

zufügen ['tsu:fy:gən] vt to add; (Leid etc): **(jdm) etw ~** to cause (sb) sth

Zufuhr ['tsu:fu:r] (-, -en) f (Herbeibringen) supplying; (MET) influx

Zug [tsu:k] (-(e)s, =e) m (EISENB) train; (Luftzug) draught; (Ziehen) pull(ing); (Gesichtszug) feature; (SCHACH etc) move; (Schriftzug) stroke; (Atemzug) breath; (Charakterzug) trait; (an Zigarette) puff, pull, drag; (Schluck) gulp; (Menschengruppe) procession; (von Vögeln) flight; (MIL) platoon; **etw in vollen Zügen genießen** to enjoy sth to the full

Zu- ['tsu:-] zW: **~gabe** f extra; (in Konzert etc) encore; **~gang** m access, approach; **z~gänglich** adj accessible; (Mensch) approachable

zugeben ['tsu:ge:bən] (unreg) vt (beifügen) to add, to throw in; (zugestehen) to admit; (erlauben) to permit

zugehen ['tsu:ge:ən] (unreg) vi (schließen) to shut; **es geht dort seltsam zu** there are strange goings-on there; **auf jdn/etw ~** to walk towards

sb/sth; **dem Ende ~** to be finishing

Zugehörigkeit ['tsu:gəhø:rɪçkaɪt] f: **~ (zu)** membership (of), belonging (to)

Zügel ['tsy:gəl] (-s, -) m rein(s); (fig) curb; **z~n** vt to curb; (Pferd) to rein in

zuge- ['tsu:gə] zW: **Z~ständnis** (-ses, -se) nt concession; **~stehen** (unreg) vt to admit; (Rechte) to concede

Zugführer m (EISENB) guard

zugig ['tsu:gɪç] adj draughty

zügig ['tsy:gɪç] adj speedy, swift

zugreifen ['tsu:graɪfən] (unreg) vi to seize od grab at; (helfen) to help; (beim Essen) to help o.s.

Zugrestaurant nt dining car

zugrunde [tsu'grʊndə] adv: **~ gehen** to collapse; (Mensch) to perish; **einer Sache dat etw ~ legen** to base sth on sth; **einer Sache dat ~ liegen** to be based on sth; **~ richten** to ruin, to destroy

zugunsten, **zu Gunsten** [tsu'gʊnstən] präp (+gen od dat) in favour of

zugute [tsu'gu:tə] adv: **jdm etw ~ halten** to concede sth to sb; **jdm ~ kommen** to be of assistance to sb

Zugvogel m migratory bird

zuhalten ['tsu:haltən] (unreg) vt to keep closed ♦ vi: **auf jdn/etw ~** to make a beeline for sb/sth

Zuhälter ['tsu:hɛltər] (-s, -) m pimp

Zuhause [tsu'haʊzə] (-) nt home

zuhause [tsu'haʊzə] adv (österreichisch, schweizerisch) at home

zuhören ['tsu:hø:rən] vi to listen

Zuhörer (-s, -) m listener

zukleben ['tsu:kle:bən] vt to paste up

zukommen ['tsu:kɔmən] (unreg) vi to come up; **auf jdn ~** to come up to sb; **jdm etw ~ lassen** to give sb sth; **etw auf sich ~ lassen** to wait and see; **jdm ~** (sich gehören) to be fitting for sb

Zukunft ['tsu:kʊnft] (-, Zukünfte) f future; **zukünftig** ['tsu:kynftɪç] *adj* future ♦ *adv* in future; **mein zukünftiger Mann** my husband ist to be

Zulage ['tsu:la:gə] *f* bonus

zulassen ['tsu:lasən] (*unreg*) *vt* (*hereinlassen*) to admit; (*erlauben*) to permit; (*Auto*) to license; (*ung: nicht öffnen*) to (keep) shut

zulässig ['tsu:lesɪç] *adj* permissible, permitted

Zulassung *f* (*amtlich*) authorization; (*von Kfz*) licensing

zulaufen ['tsu:laufən] (*unreg*) *vi* (*subj: Mensch*): ~ **auf jdn/etw** to run up to sb/sth; (: *Straße*): ~ **auf** to lead towards

zuleide, zu Leide [tsu:'laɪdə] *adv*: **jdm etw** ~ **tun** *od* harm sb

zuletzt [tsu:'letst] *adv* finally, at last

zuliebe [tsu:'li:bə] *adv*: **jdm** ~ to please sb

zum [tsʊm] = **zu dem**; ~ **dritten Mal** for the third time; ~ **Scherz** as a joke; ~ **Trinken** for drinking

zumachen ['tsu:maxən] *vt* to shut; (*Kleidung*) to do up, to fasten ♦ *vi* to shut; (*umg*) to hurry up

zu- *zW*: ~**mal** [tsu:'ma:l] *konj* especially (as); ~**meist** ['tsu:maɪst] *adv* mostly; ~**mindest** ['tsu:mɪndəst] *adv* at least

zumutbar ['tsu:mu:tba:r] *adj* reasonable

zumute, zu Mute [tsu:'mu:tə] *adv*: **wie ist ihm** ~? how does he feel?

zumuten ['tsu:mu:tən] *vt*: (**jdm**) **etw** ~ to expect *od* ask sth (of sb)

Zumutung ['tsu:mu:tʊŋ] *f* unreasonable expectation *od* demand, impertinence

zunächst [tsu:'nɛːçst] *adv* first of all; ~ **einmal** to start with

Zunahme ['tsu:na:mə] *f* increase

Zuname ['tsu:na:mə] *m* surname

Zünd- [tsynd] *zW*: **z~en** *vi* (*Feuer*) to light, to ignite; (*Motor*) to fire; (*begeistern*): **bei jdm z~en** to fire sb (with enthusiasm); **z~end** *adj* fiery; ~**er** (**-s**, **-**) *m* fuse; (*MIL*) detonator; ~**holz**

['tsynt-] *nt* match; ~**kerze** *f* (*AUT*) spark(ing) plug; ~**schloss** ▲ *nt* ignition lock; ~**schlüssel** *m* ignition key; ~**schnur** *f* fuse wire; ~**stoff** *m* (*fig*) inflammatory stuff; ~**ung** *f* ignition

zunehmen [tsu:'ne:mən] (*unreg*) *vi* to increase, to grow; (*Mensch*) to put on weight

Zuneigung ['tsu:naɪgʊŋ] *f* affection

Zunft [tsʊnft] (**-**, ⁺**e**) *f* guild

zünftig ['tsynftɪç] *adj* proper, real; (*Handwerk*) decent

Zunge ['tsʊŋə] *f* tongue

zunichte [tsu:'nɪçtə] *adv*: ~ **machen** to ruin, to destroy; ~ **werden** to come to nothing

zunutze, zu Nutze [tsu:'nʊtsə] *adv*: **sich** *dat* **etw** ~ **machen** to make use of sth

zuoberst [tsu:'o:bərst] *adv* at the top

zupfen ['tsʊpfən] *vt* to pull, to pick, to pluck; (*Gitarre*) to pluck

zur [tsu:r] = **zu der**

zurate, zu Rate [tsu:'ra:tə] *adv*: **jdn** ~ **ziehen** to consult sb

zurechnungsfähig ['tsu:rɛçnʊŋsfɛːɪç] *adj* responsible, accountable

zurecht- [tsu:'rɛçt] *zW*: ~**finden** (*unreg*) *vr* to find one's way (about); ~**kommen** (*unreg*) *vi* to (be able to) cope, to manage; ~**legen** *vt* to get ready; (*Ausrede etc*) to have ready; ~**machen** *vt* to prepare ♦ *vr* to get ready; ~**weisen** (*unreg*) *vt* to reprimand

zureden ['tsu:re:dən] *vi*: **jdm** ~ to persuade *od* urge sb

zurück [tsu'rʏk] *adv* back; ~**behalten** (*unreg*) *vt* to keep back; ~**bekommen** (*unreg*) *vt* to get back; ~**bleiben** (*unreg*) *vi* (*Mensch*) to remain behind; (*nicht nachkommen*) to fall behind, to lag; (*Schaden*) to remain; ~**bringen** (*unreg*) *vt* to bring back; ~**fahren** (*unreg*) *vi* to travel back; (*vor Schreck*) to recoil, to start ♦ *vt* to drive back; ~**finden** (*unreg*) *vi* to find one's way back; ~**fordern** *vt* to demand back; ~**führen**

to lead back; **etw auf etw akk ~führen** to trace sth back to sth; **~geben** (unreg) vt to give back; (antworten) to retort with; **~geblieben** adj retarded; **~gehen** (unreg) vi to go back; (fallen) to go down, to fall; (zeitlich): **~gehen (auf +akk)** to date back (to); **~gezogen** adj retired, withdrawn; **~halten** (unreg) vt to hold back; (Mensch) to restrain; (hindern) to prevent ♦ vr (reserviert sein) to be reserved; (im Essen) to hold back; **~haltend** adj reserved; **Z~haltung** f reserve; **~kehren** vi to return; **~kommen** (unreg) vi to come back; auf etw akk **~kommen** to return to sth; **~lassen** (unreg) vt to leave behind; **~legen** vt to put back; (Geld) to put by; (reservieren) to keep back; (Strecke) to cover; **~nehmen** (unreg) vt to take back; **~stellen** vt to put back, to replace; (aufschieben) to put off, to postpone; (Interessen) to defer; (Ware) to keep; **~treten** (unreg) vi to step back; (vom Amt) to retire; **gegenüber etw** od **hinter etw dat ~treten** to diminish in importance in view of sth; **~weisen** (unreg) vt to turn down; (Mensch) to reject; **~zahlen** vt to repay, to pay back; **~ziehen** (unreg) vt to pull back (Angebot) to withdraw ♦ vr to retire

Zuruf ['tsu:ruf] m shout, cry

zurzeit [tsʊr'tsaɪt] adv at the moment

Zusage ['tsu:za:gə] f promise; (Annahme) consent; **z~n** vt to promise ♦ vi to accept; **jdm z~n** (gefallen) to agree with od please sb

zusammen [tsu'zamən] adv together; **Z~arbeit** f cooperation; **~arbeiten** vi to cooperate; **~beißen** (unreg) vt (Zähne) to clench; **~brechen** (unreg) vi to collapse; (Mensch auch) to break down; **~bringen** (unreg) vt to bring od get together; (Geld) to get; (Sätze) to put together; **Z~bruch** m collapse;

~fassen vt to summarize; (vereinigen) to unite; **Z~fassung** f summary, résumé; **~fügen** vt to join (together), to unite; **~halten** (unreg) vt to stick together; **Z~hang** m connection; **im/ aus dem Z~hang** in/out of context; **~hängen** (unreg) vi to be connected od linked; **~kommen** (unreg) vi to meet, to assemble; (sich ereignen) to occur at once od together; **~legen** vt to put together; (stapeln) to pile up; (falten) to fold; (verbinden) to combine, to unite; (Termine, Fest) to amalgamate; (Geld) to collect; **~nehmen** (unreg) vt to summon up ♦ vr to pull o.s. together; **alles ~genommen** all in all; **~passen** vi to go well together, to match; **~schließen** (unreg) vt, vr to join (together); **Z~schluss** ▲ m amalgamation; **~schreiben** (unreg) vt to write as one word; (Bericht) to put together; **Z~sein (-s)** nt get-together; **~setzen** vt (Stoff) to be composed of; (Menschen) to get together; **Z~setzung** f composition; **~stellen** vt to put together; to compile; **Z~stoß** m collision; **~stoßen** (unreg) vi to collide; (Menschen) to meet; **~treffen** (unreg) vi to coincide; (Menschen) to meet; **Z~treffen** nt coincidence; meeting; **~zählen** vt to add up; **~ziehen** (unreg) vt (verengern) to draw together; (vereinigen) to bring together; (addieren) to add up ♦ vr to shrink; (sich bilden) to form, to develop

zusätzlich ['tsu:zɛtslɪç] adj additional ♦ adv in addition

zuschauen ['tsu:ʃaʊən] vi to watch, to look on; **Zuschauer(in) (-s, -)** m(f) spectator ♦ pl (THEAT) audience sg

zuschicken ['tsu:ʃɪkən] vt: **(jdm etw) ~** to send od to forward (sth to sb)

Zuschlag ['tsu:ʃlaːk] m extra charge, surcharge; **z~en** (unreg) vt (Tür) to slam; (Ball) to hit; (bei Auktion) to

---

zuschneiden knock down; (*Steine etc*) to knock into shape ♦ *vi* (*Fenster, Tür*) to shut; (*Mensch*) to hit, to punch; **~karte** *f* (*EISENB*) surcharge ticket; **z~pflichtig** *adj* subject to surcharge

zuschneiden ['tsu:ʃnaɪdən] (*unreg*) *vt* to cut out; to cut to size

zuschrauben ['tsu:ʃraʊbən] *vt* to screw down *od* up

zuschreiben ['tsu:ʃraɪbən] (*unreg*) *vt* (*fig*) to ascribe, to attribute; (*COMM*) to credit

Zuschrift ['tsu:ʃrɪft] *f* letter, reply

zuschulden, zu Schulden [tsu:ʃʊldən] *adv*: sich *dat* etw ~ **kommen lassen** to make o.s. guilty of sth

Zuschuss ▲ ['tsu:ʃʊs] *m* subsidy, allowance

zusehen ['tsu:ze:ən] (*unreg*) *vi* to watch; (*dafür sorgen*) to take care; **jdm/etw** ~ to watch sb/sth; **~ds** *adv* visibly

zusenden ['tsu:zɛndən] (*unreg*) *vt* to forward, to send on

zusichern ['tsu:zɪçərn] *vt*: **jdm etw** ~ to assure sb of sth

zuspielen ['tsu:ʃpi:lən] *vt, vi* to pass

zuspitzen ['tsu:ʃpɪtsən] *vt* to sharpen ♦ *vr* (*Lage*) to become critical

zusprechen ['tsu:ʃprɛçən] (*unreg*) *vt* (*zuerkennen*) to award ♦ *vi* to speak; **jdm etw** ~ to award sb sth *od* sth to sb; **jdm Trost** ~ to comfort sb; **dem Essen/Alkohol** ~ to eat/drink a lot

Zustand ['tsu:ʃtant] *m* state, condition

zustande, zu Stande [tsu:ʃtandə] *adv*: ~ **bringen** to bring about; ~ **kommen** to come about

zuständig ['tsu:ʃtɛndɪç] *adj* responsible; **Z~keit** *f* competence, responsibility

zustehen ['tsu:ʃte:ən] (*unreg*) *vi*: **jdm** ~ to be sb's right

zustellen ['tsu:ʃtɛlən] *vt* (*verstellen*) to block; (*Post etc*) to send

Zustellung ['tsu:ʃtɛlʊŋ] *f* delivery

zustimmen ['tsu:ʃtɪmən] *vi* to agree

Zustimmung *f* agreement, consent

zustoßen ['tsu:ʃto:sən] (*unreg*) *vi* (*fig*) to happen

zutage, zu Tage [tsu:ta:gə] *adv*: ~ **bringen** to bring to light; ~ **treten** to come to light

Zutaten ['tsu:ta:tən] *pl* ingredients

zuteilen ['tsu:taɪlən] *vt* (*Arbeit, Rolle*) to designate, assign; (*Aktien, Wohnung*) to allocate

zutiefst [tsu:'ti:fst] *adv* deeply

zutragen ['tsu:tra:gən] (*unreg*) *vt* to bring; (*Klatsch*) to tell ♦ *vr* to happen

zutrau- ['tsu:traʊ] *zW*: **Z~en** (-s) *nt*: **Z~en (zu)** trust (in); **~en** *vt*: **jdm etw ~en** to credit sb with sth; **~lich** *adj* trusting, friendly

zutreffen ['tsu:trɛfən] (*unreg*) *vi* to be correct; to apply; **~d** *adj* (*richtig*) accurate; **Z~des bitte unterstreichen** please underline where applicable

Zutritt ['tsu:trɪt] *m* access, admittance

Zutun ['tsu:tu:n] (-s) *nt* assistance

zuverlässig ['tsu:fɛrlɛsɪç] *adj* reliable; **Z~keit** *f* reliability

zuversichtlich ['tsu:fɛrzɪçtlɪç] *adj* confident

zuvor [tsu'fo:r] *adv* before, previously; **~kommen** (*unreg*) *vi* +*dat* to anticipate; **jdm ~kommen** to beat sb to it; **~kommend** *adj* obliging, courteous

Zuwachs ['tsu:vaks] (-es) *m* increase, growth; (*umg*) addition; **z~en** (*unreg*) *vi* to become overgrown; (*Wunde*) to heal (up)

zuwege, zu Wege [tsu:'ve:gə] *adv*: **etw** ~ **bringen** to accomplish sth

zuweilen [tsu:'vaɪlən] *adv* at times, now and then

zuweisen ['tsu:vaɪzən] (*unreg*) *vt* to assign, to allocate

zuwenden ['tsu:vɛndən] (*unreg*) *vt* (+*dat*) to turn (towards) ♦ *vr*: **sich jdm/etw** ~ to devote o.s. to sb/sth; to turn to sb/sth

zuwider [tsu:'vi:dər] *adv*: **etw ist jdm** ~ sb loathes sth, sb finds sth repugnant; **~handeln** vi: **einer Sache** dat **~handeln** to act contrary to sth; **einem Gesetz ~handeln** to contravene a law

zuziehen ['tsuːtsiːən] (unreg) vt (schließen: Vorhang) to draw, to close; (herbeirufen: Experten) to call in ◆ vi to move in, to come; **sich** dat **etw ~** (Krankheit) to catch sth; (Zorn) to incur sth

zuzüglich ['tsuːtsyːklɪç] präp +gen plus, with the addition of

Zwang [tsvaŋ] (-(e)s, ⁻e) m compulsion, coercion

zwängen ['tsvɛŋən] vt, vr to squeeze

zwanglos adj informal

Zwangs- zW: **~arbeit** f forced labour; (Strafe) hard labour; **~lage** f predicament, tight corner; **z~läufig** adj necessary, inevitable

zwanzig ['tsvantsɪç] num twenty

zwar [tsvaːr] adv to be sure, indeed; **das ist ~ ..., aber ...** that may be ... but ...; **und ~ am Sonntag** on Sunday to be precise; **und ~ so schnell, dass ...** in fact so quickly that ...

Zweck [tsvɛk] (-(e)s, -e) m purpose, aim; **es hat keinen ~** there's no point; **z~dienlich** adj practical; expedient

Zwecke f hobnail; (Heftzwecke) drawing pin, thumbtack (US)

Zweck- zW: **z~los** adj pointless; **z~mäßig** adj suitable, appropriate; **z~s** präp +gen for the purpose of

zwei [tsvai] num two; **Z~bettzimmer** nt twin room; **~deutig** adj ambiguous; (unanständig) suggestive; **~erlei** adj: **~erlei Stoff** two different kinds of material; **~erlei Meinung** of differing opinions; **~fach** adj double

Zweifel ['tsvaifəl] (-s, -) m doubt; **z~haft** adj doubtful, dubious; **z~los** adj doubtless; **z~n** vi: **(an etw** dat**) z~n** to doubt (sth)

Zweig [tsvaik] (-(e)s, -e) m branch; **~stelle** f branch (office)

zwei- zW: **~hundert** num two hundred; **~mal** adv twice; **~sprachig** adj bilingual; **~spurig** adj (AUT) two-lane; **~stimmig** adj for two voices

zweit [tsvait] adv: **zu ~** together; (bei mehreren Paaren) in twos

zweitbeste(r, s) adj second best

zweite(r, s) adj second

zweiteilig ['tsvaitailiç] adj (Gruppe) two-piece; (Fernsehfilm) two-part; (Kleidung) two-piece

zweit- zW: **~ens** adv secondly; **~größte(r, s)** adj second largest; **~klassig** adj second-class; **~letzte(r, s)** adj last but one, penultimate; **~rangig** adj second-rate

Zwerchfell ['tsvɛrçfɛl] nt diaphragm

Zwerg [tsvɛrk] (-(e)s, -e) m dwarf

Zwetsch(g)e ['tsvɛt͡ʃ(ɡ)ə] f plum

Zwieback ['tsviːbak] (-(e)s, -e) m rusk

Zwiebel ['tsviːbəl] (-, -n) f onion; (Blumenzwiebel) bulb

Zwie- ['tsviː] zW: **z~lichtig** adj shady, dubious; **z~spältig** adj (Gefühle) conflicting; (Charakter) contradictory; **~tracht** f discord, dissension

Zwilling ['tsvilɪŋ] (-s, -e) m twin; **~e** pl (ASTROL) Gemini

zwingen ['tsviŋən] (unreg) vt to force; **~d** adj (Grund etc) compelling

zwinkern ['tsviŋkərn] vi to blink; (absichtlich) to wink

Zwirn [tsvirn] (-(e)s, -e) m thread

zwischen ['tsviʃən] präp (+akk or dat) between; **Z~bemerkung** f (incidental) remark; **Z~ding** nt cross; **~durch** adv in between; (räumlich) here and there; **Z~ergebnis** nt intermediate result; **Z~fall** m incident; **Z~frage** f question; **Z~handel** m middlemen pl; middleman's trade; **Z~landung** f (AVIAT) stopover; **~menschlich** adj interpersonal; **Z~raum** m space; **Z~ruf** m interjection; **Z~stecker** m adaptor (plug); **Z~zeit** f interval; **in der Z~zeit** in the interim, meanwhile

zwitschern ['tsvɪtʃərn] vt, vi to twitter, to chirp

zwo [tsvoː] num two

zwölf [tsvœlf] num twelve

Zyklus ['tsyːklʊs] (-, **Zyklen**) m cycle

Zylinder [tsi'lɪndər] (**-s**, **-**) m cylinder; (Hut) top hat

Zyniker ['tsyːnikər] (**-s**, **-**) m cynic

zynisch ['tsyːnɪʃ] adj cynical

Zypern ['tsyːpərn] nt Cyprus

Zyste ['tsʏstə] f cyst

zz., zzt. abk = **zurzeit**

ENGLISH – GERMAN
ENGLISCH – DEUTSCH

A, a

A [eɪ] n (MUS) A nt; **~ road** Hauptverkehrsstraße f

KEYWORD

a [eɪ, ə] (before vowel or silent h: an) indef art **1** (before vowel or silent h: an) ein; eine; **a woman** eine Frau; **a book** ein Buch; **an eagle** ein Adler; **she's a doctor** sie ist Ärztin

2 (instead of the number "one") ein, eine; **a year ago** vor einem Jahr; **a hundred/thousand** etc pounds (ein) hundert/(ein) tausend etc Pfund

3 (in expressing ratios, prices etc) pro; **3 a day/week** 3 pro Tag/Woche, 3 am Tag/in der Woche; **10 km an hour** 10 km pro Stunde/in der Stunde

---

A.A. n abbr = **Alcoholics Anonymous**; (BRIT) = **Automobile Association**

A.A.A. (US) n abbr = **American Automobile Association**

aback [ə'bæk] adv: **to be taken ~** verblüfft sein

abandon [ə'bændən] vt (give up) aufgeben; (desert) verlassen ♦ n Hingabe f

abate [ə'beɪt] vi nachlassen, sich legen

abattoir ['æbətwɑːʳ] (BRIT) n Schlachthaus n

abbey ['æbɪ] n Abtei f

abbot ['æbət] n Abt m

abbreviate [ə'briːvɪeɪt] vt abkürzen; **abbreviation** [əbriːvɪ'eɪʃən] n Abkürzung f

abdicate ['æbdɪkeɪt] vt aufgeben ♦ vi abdanken

abdomen ['æbdəmən] n Unterleib m

abduct [æb'dʌkt] vt entführen

aberration [æbə'reɪʃən] n (geistige) Verwirrung f

abet [ə'bet] vt see **aid**

abeyance [ə'beɪəns] n: **in ~** in der Schwebe; (disuse) außer Kraft

abide [ə'baɪd] vt vertragen; leiden; **~ by** vt sich halten an +acc

ability [ə'bɪlɪtɪ] n (power) Fähigkeit f; (skill) Geschicklichkeit f

abject ['æbdʒekt] adj (liar) übel; (poverty) größte(r, s); (apology) zerknirscht

ablaze [ə'bleɪz] adj in Flammen

able ['eɪbl] adj geschickt, fähig; **to be ~ to do sth** etw tun können; **~-bodied** ['eɪbl'bɒdɪd] adj kräftig; (seaman) Voll-; **ably** ['eɪblɪ] adv geschickt

abnormal [æb'nɔːml] adj regelwidrig, abnorm

aboard [ə'bɔːd] adv, prep an Bord +gen

abode [ə'bəud] n: **of no fixed ~** ohne festen Wohnsitz

abolish [ə'bɒlɪʃ] vt abschaffen; **abolition** [æbə'lɪʃən] n Abschaffung f

abominable [ə'bɒmɪnəbl] adj scheußlich

aborigine [æbə'rɪdʒɪnɪ] n Ureinwohner m

abort [ə'bɔːt] vt abtreiben; fehlgebären; **~ion** [ə'bɔːʃən] n Abtreibung f; (miscarriage) Fehlgeburt f; **~ive** adj misslungen

abound [ə'baund] vi im Überfluss vorhanden sein; **to ~ in** Überfluss haben an +dat

---
KEYWORD

about [ə'baut] adv **1** (approximately) etwa, ungefähr; **about a hundred/thousand** etc etwa hundert/tausend etc; **at about 2 o'clock** etwa um 2 Uhr; **I've just about finished** ich bin gerade fertig

2 (referring to place) herum, umher; **to**

leave things lying about Sachen herumliegen lassen; **to run/walk** etc **about** herumrennen/gehen etc
3: to be about to do sth im Begriff sein, etw zu tun; **he was about to go to bed** er wollte gerade ins Bett gehen

♦ prep **1** (relating to) über +acc; **a book about London** ein Buch über London; **what is it about?** worum geht es?; (book etc) wovon handelt es?; **we talked about it** wir haben darüber geredet; **what** or **how about doing this?** wollen wir das machen?

2 (referring to place) um (... herum); **to walk about the town** in der Stadt herumgehen; **her clothes were scattered about the room** ihre Kleider waren über das ganze Zimmer verstreut

about-turn [ə'baut'tə:n] n Kehrtwendung f
above [ə'bʌv] adv oben ♦ prep über; ~ all vor allem; ~ **board** adj ehrlich
abrasive [ə'breiziv] adj Abschleif-; (personality) zermürbend, aufreibend
abreast [ə'brest] adv nebeneinander; **to keep ~ of** Schritt halten mit
abroad [ə'brɔ:d] adv (be) im Ausland; (go) ins Ausland
abrupt [ə'brʌpt] adj (sudden) abrupt, jäh; (curt) schroff; **~ly** adv abrupt
abscess ['æbsis] n Geschwür nt
abscond [əb'skɒnd] vi flüchten, sich davonmachen
abseil ['æbseil] vi (also: ~ down) sich abseilen
absence ['æbsəns] n Abwesenheit f
absent ['æbsənt] adj abwesend, nicht da; (lost in thought) geistesabwesend; **~-minded** adj zerstreut
absolute ['æbsəlu:t] adj absolut; (power) unumschränkt; (rubbish) rein; **~ly** [æbsə'lu:tli] adv absolut, vollkommen; **~ly!** ganz bestimmt!

absolve [əb'zɒlv] vt entbinden; freisprechen
absorb [əb'zɔ:b] vt aufsaugen, absorbieren; (fig) ganz in Anspruch nehmen, fesseln; **to be ~ed in a book** in ein Buch vertieft sein; **~ent cotton** (US) n Verbandwatte f; **~ing** adj aufsaugend; (fig) packend; **absorption** [əb'sɔ:pʃən] n Aufsaugung f, Absorption f; (fig) Versunkenheit f
abstain [əb'stein] vi (in voting) sich enthalten; **to ~ from** (keep from) sich enthalten +gen
abstemious [əb'sti:miəs] adj enthaltsam
abstinence ['æbstinəns] n Enthaltsamkeit f
abstract ['æbstrækt] adj abstrakt
absurd [əb'sɜ:d] adj absurd
abundance [ə'bʌndəns] n: ~ (of) Überfluss m (an +dat); **abundant** [ə'bʌndənt] adj reichlich
abuse [n ə'bju:s, vb ə'bju:z] n (rude language) Beschimpfung f; (ill usage) Missbrauch m; (bad practice) (Amts)missbrauch m ♦ vt (misuse) missbrauchen; **abusive** [ə'bju:siv] adj beleidigend, Schimpf-
abysmal [ə'bizməl] adj scheußlich; (ignorance) bodenlos
abyss [ə'bis] n Abgrund m
AC abbr (= alternating current) Wechselstrom m
academic [ækə'demik] adj akademisch; (theoretical) theoretisch ♦ n Akademiker(in) m(f)
academy [ə'kædəmi] n (school) Hochschule f; (society) Akademie f
accelerate [æk'seləreit] vi schneller werden; (AUT) Gas geben ♦ vt beschleunigen; **acceleration** [ækselə'reiʃən] n Beschleunigung f; **accelerator** [æk'seləreitə] n Gas(pedal) nt
accent ['æksent] n Akzent m, Tonfall m; (mark) Akzent m; (stress) Betonung f
accept [ək'sept] vt (take) annehmen;

(agree to) akzeptieren; **~able** adj annehmbar; **~ance** n Annahme f

access ['ækses] n Zugang m; **~ible** [æk'sesəbl] adj (easy to approach) zugänglich; (within reach) (leicht) erreichbar

accessory [æk'sesərɪ] n Zubehörteil nt; **toilet accessories** Toilettenartikel pl

accident ['æksɪdənt] n Unfall m; (coincidence) Zufall m; **by ~** zufällig; **~al** [æksɪ'dentl] adj unbeabsichtigt; **~ally** [æksɪ'dentəlɪ] adv zufällig; **~ insurance** n Unfallversicherung f; **~-prone** adj: **to be ~-prone** zu Unfällen neigen

acclaim [ə'kleɪm] vt zujubeln +dat ♦ n Beifall m

acclimatize [ə'klaɪmətaɪz] vt: **to become ~d (to)** sich gewöhnen (an +acc), sich akklimatisieren (in +dat)

accommodate [ə'kɒmədeɪt] vt unterbringen; (hold) Platz haben für; (oblige) (aus)helfen +dat

accommodating [ə'kɒmədeɪtɪŋ] adj entgegenkommend

accommodation [əkɒmə'deɪʃən] (US **accommodations**) n Unterkunft f

accompany [ə'kʌmpənɪ] vt begleiten

accomplice [ə'kʌmplɪs] n Helfershelfer m, Komplize m

accomplish [ə'kʌmplɪʃ] vt (fulfil) durchführen; (finish) vollenden; (aim) erreichen; **~ed** adj vollendet, ausgezeichnet; **~ment** n (skill) Fähigkeit f; (completion) Vollendung f; (feat) Leistung f

accord [ə'kɔːd] n Übereinstimmung f ♦ vt gewähren; **of one's own ~** freiwillig; **~ing to** nach, laut +gen; **~ance** n: **in ~ance with** in Übereinstimmung mit; **~ingly** adv danach, dementsprechend

accordion [ə'kɔːdɪən] n Akkordeon nt

accost [ə'kɒst] vt ansprechen

account [ə'kaʊnt] n (bill) Rechnung f; (narrative) Bericht m; (report) Rechenschaftsbericht m; (in bank) Konto nt; (importance) Geltung f; **~s** npl (FIN)

Bücher pl; **on ~** auf Rechnung; **of no ~** ohne Bedeutung; **on no ~** keinesfalls; **on ~ of** wegen; **to take into ~** berücksichtigen; **~ for** vt fus (expenditure) Rechenschaft ablegen für; **how do you ~ for that?** wie erklären Sie (sich) das?; **~able** adj verantwortlich; **~ancy** [ə'kaʊntənsɪ] n Buchhaltung f; **~ant** [ə'kaʊntənt] n Wirtschaftsprüfer(in) m(f); **~ number** n Kontonummer f

accumulate [ə'kjuːmjuleɪt] vt ansammeln ♦ vi sich ansammeln

accuracy ['ækjurəsɪ] n Genauigkeit f

accurate ['ækjurɪt] adj genau; **~ly** adv genau, richtig

accusation [ækju'zeɪʃən] n Anklage f, Beschuldigung f

accuse [ə'kjuːz] vt anklagen, beschuldigen; **~d** n Angeklagte(r) f(m)

accustom [ə'kʌstəm] vt: **to ~ sb (to sth)** jdn (an etw acc) gewöhnen; **~ed** adj gewohnt

ace [eɪs] n Ass nt; (cf) Ass nt, Kanone f

ache [eɪk] n Schmerz m ♦ vi (be sore) schmerzen, wehtun

achieve [ə'tʃiːv] vt zustande or zu Standen bringen; (aim) erreichen; **~ment** n Leistung f, (act) Erreichen nt

acid ['æsɪd] n Säure f ♦ adj sauer, scharf; **~ rain** n saure(r) Regen m

acknowledge [ək'nɒlɪdʒ] vt (receipt) bestätigen; (admit) zugeben; **~ment** n Anerkennung f, (letter) Empfangsbestätigung f

acne ['æknɪ] n Akne f

acorn ['eɪkɔːn] n Eichel f

acoustic [ə'kuːstɪk] adj akustisch; **~s** npl Akustik f

acquaint [ə'kweɪnt] vt vertraut machen; **to be ~ed with sb** mit jdm bekannt sein; **~ance** n (person) Bekannte(r) f(m); (knowledge) Kenntnis f

acquire [ə'kwaɪə*] vt erwerben; **acquisition** [ækwɪ'zɪʃən] n Errungenschaft f, (act) Erwerb m

acquit [ə'kwɪt] vt (free) freisprechen; **to**

~ **o.s. well** sich bewähren; **~tal** n Freispruch m

acre ['eɪkə] n Morgen m

acrid ['ækrɪd] adj (smell, taste) bitter; (smoke) beißend

acrobat ['ækrəbæt] n Akrobat m

across [ə'krɒs] prep über ~acc ♦ adv hinüber, herüber; **he lives ~ the river** er wohnt auf der anderen Seite des Flusses; **ten metres ~** zehn Meter breit; **he lives ~ from us** er wohnt uns gegenüber; **to run/swim ~** hinüberlaufen/schwimmen

acrylic [ə'krɪlɪk] adj Acryl-

act [ækt] n (deed) Tat f; (JUR) Gesetz nt; (THEAT) Akt m; (: turn) Nummer f ♦ vi (take ~ion) handeln; (behave) sich verhalten; (pretend) vorgeben; (THEAT) spielen ♦ vt (in play) spielen; **to ~ as** fungieren als; **~ing** adj stellvertretend ♦ n Schauspielkunst f; (performance) Aufführung f

action ['ækʃən] n (deed) Tat f; Handlung f; (motion) Bewegung f; (way of working) Funktionieren nt; (battle) Einsatz m, Gefecht nt; (lawsuit) Klage f, Prozess m; **out of ~** (person) nicht einsatzfähig; (thing) außer Betrieb; **to take ~** etwas unternehmen; **~ replay** n (TV) Wiederholung f

activate ['æktɪveɪt] vt (mechanism) betätigen; (CHEM, PHYS) aktivieren

active ['æktɪv] adj (brisk) rege, tatkräftig; (working) aktiv; (GRAM) aktiv, Tätigkeits-; **~ly** adv aktiv; (dislike) offen

activity [æk'tɪvɪtɪ] n Aktivität f; (doings) Unternehmungen pl; (occupation) Tätigkeit f; **~ holiday** n Aktivurlaub m

actor ['æktə] n Schauspieler m

actress ['æktrɪs] n Schauspielerin f

actual ['æktjuəl] adj wirklich; **~ly** adv tatsächlich; **~ly no** eigentlich nicht

acumen ['ækjumən] n Scharfsinn m

acute [ə'kju:t] adj (severe) heftig, akut; (keen) scharfsinnig

ad [æd] n abbr = **advertisement**

A.D. adv abbr (= Anno Domini) n. Chr.

adamant ['ædəmənt] adj eisern; hartnäckig

adapt [ə'dæpt] vt anpassen ♦ vi: **to ~ (to)** sich anpassen (an +acc); **~able** adj anpassungsfähig; **~ation** [ædæp'teɪʃən] n (THEAT etc) Bearbeitung f; (adjustment) Anpassung f; **~er, ~or** n (ELEC) Zwischenstecker m

add [æd] vt (join) hinzufügen; (numbers: also: ~ up) addieren; **~ up** vi (make sense) stimmen; **~ up to** vt fus ausmachen

adder ['ædə] n Kreuzotter f, Natter f

addict ['ædɪkt] n Süchtige(r) f(m); **~ed** [ə'dɪktɪd] adj: **~ed to** -süchtig; **~ion** [ə'dɪkʃən] n Sucht f; **~ive** [ə'dɪktɪv] adj: **to be ~ive** süchtig machen

addition [ə'dɪʃən] n Anhang m, Addition f; (MATH) Addition f, Zusammenzählen nt; **in ~** zusätzlich, außerdem; **~al** adj zusätzlich, weiter

additive ['ædɪtɪv] n Zusatz m

address [ə'dres] n Adresse f; (speech) Ansprache f ♦ vt (letter) adressieren; (speak to) ansprechen; (make speech to) eine Ansprache halten an +acc

adept ['ædept] adj geschickt; **to be ~** at gut sein in +dat

adequate ['ædɪkwɪt] adj angemessen

adhere [əd'hɪə] vi: **to ~** to haften an +dat; (fig) festhalten an +dat

adhesive [əd'hiːzɪv] adj klebend; Kleb(e)- ♦ n Klebstoff m; **~ tape** n (BRIT) Klebestreifen m; (US) Heftpflaster nt

ad hoc [æd'hɔk] adj (decision, committee) Ad-hoc- ♦ adv ad hoc

adjacent [ə'dʒeɪsənt] adj benachbart; **~ to** angrenzend an +acc

adjective ['ædʒektɪv] n Adjektiv nt, Eigenschaftswort nt

adjoining [ə'dʒɔɪnɪŋ] adj benachbart, Neben-

adjourn [ə'dʒɜːn] vt vertagen ♦ vi abbrechen

adjudicate [ə'dʒuːdɪkeɪt] vi entscheiden, ein Urteil fällen

adjust [ə'dʒʌst] vt (alter) anpassen; (put right) regulieren, richtig stellen ♦ vi sich anpassen; **~able** adj verstellbar

ad-lib [æd'lɪb] vt, vi improvisieren ♦ adv: **ad lib** aus dem Stegreif

administer [əd'mɪnɪstə*] vt (manage) verwalten; (dispense) ausüben; (justice) sprechen; (medicine) geben; **administration** [ədmɪnɪs'treɪʃən] n Verwaltung f; (POL) Regierung f; **administrative** [əd'mɪnɪstrətɪv] adj Verwaltungs-; **administrator** [əd'mɪnɪstreɪtə*] n Verwaltungsbeamte(r) f(m)

Admiralty ['ædmərəltɪ] (BRIT) n Admiralität f

admiration [ædmə'reɪʃən] n Bewunderung f

admire [əd'maɪə*] vt (respect) bewundern; (love) verehren; **~r** n Bewunderer m

admission [əd'mɪʃən] n (entrance) Einlass m; (fee) Eintritt(spreis m) m; (confession) Geständnis n; **~ charge** n Eintritt(spreis) m

admit [əd'mɪt] vt (let in) einlassen; (confess) gestehen; (accept) anerkennen; **~tance** n Zulassung f; **~tedly** adv zugegebenermaßen

admonish [əd'mɒnɪʃ] vt ermahnen

ad nauseam [æd'nɔːsɪæm] adv (repeat, talk) endlos

ado [ə'duː] n: **without more ~** ohne weitere Umstände

adolescence [ædəu'lesns] n Jugendalter nt; **adolescent** [ædəu'lesnt] adj jugendlich ♦ n Jugendliche(r) f(m)

adopt [ə'dɒpt] vt (child) adoptieren; (idea) übernehmen; **~ion** [ə'dɒpʃən] n Adoption f; Übernahme f

adore [ə'dɔː*] vt anbeten; verehren

adorn [ə'dɔːn] vt schmücken

Adriatic [eɪdrɪ'ætɪk] n: **the ~ (Sea)** die Adria

adrift [ə'drɪft] adv Wind und Wellen preisgegeben

adult ['ædʌlt] n Erwachsene(r) f(m)

adultery [ə'dʌltərɪ] n Ehebruch m

advance [əd'vɑːns] n (in progress) Vorrücken nt; (money) Vorschuss m ♦ vt (move forward) vorrücken; (money) vorschießen; (argument) vorbringen ♦ vi vorwärts gehen; **in ~** im Voraus; **~ booking** n Vorverkauf m; **~d** adj (ahead) vorgerückt; (modern) fortgeschritten; (study) für Fortgeschrittene

advantage [əd'vɑːntɪdʒ] n Vorteil m; **to have an ~ over sb** jdm gegenüber im Vorteil sein; **to take ~ of** (misuse) ausnutzen; (profit from) Nutzen ziehen aus; **~ous** [ædvən'teɪdʒəs] adj vorteilhaft

advent ['ædvənt] n Ankunft f; **A~** Advent m

adventure [əd'ventʃə*] n Abenteuer nt; **adventurous** adj abenteuerlich, waghalsig

adverb ['ædvəːb] n Adverb nt, Umstandswort nt

adversary ['ædvəsərɪ] n Gegner m

adverse ['ædvəːs] adj widrig; **adversity** [əd'vəːsɪtɪ] n Widrigkeit f, Missgeschick nt

advert ['ædvəːt] n Anzeige f; **~ise** ['ædvətaɪz] vt werben für ♦ vi annoncieren; **to ~ise for sth** etw (per Anzeige) suchen; **~isement** [əd'vəːtɪsmənt] n Anzeige f, Inserat nt; **~iser** n (in newspaper etc) Inserent m; **~ising** n Werbung f

advice [əd'vaɪs] n Rat(schlag) m

advisable [əd'vaɪzəbl] adj ratsam

advise [əd'vaɪz] vt: **to ~ (sb)** (jdm) raten; **~dly** [əd'vaɪzdlɪ] adv (deliberately) bewusst; **~r** n Berater m; **advisory** [əd'vaɪzərɪ] adj beratend, Beratungs-

advocate [vb 'ædvəkeɪt, n 'ædvəkət] vt vertreten ♦ n Befürworter(in) m(f)

Aegean [iː'dʒiːən] n: **the ~ (Sea)** die Ägäis

aerial ['ɛərɪəl] n Antenne f ♦ adj Luft-

aerobics [ɛə'rəubɪks] n Aerobic nt

aerodynamic ['ɛərəudaɪ'næmɪk] adj aerodynamisch

aeroplane ['εərəpleɪn] n Flugzeug nt

aerosol ['εərəsɔl] n Aerosol nt; Sprühdose f

aesthetic [iːs'θεtɪk] adj ästhetisch

afar [ə'fɑː] adv: **from ~** aus der Ferne

affable ['æfəbl] adj umgänglich

affair [ə'fεə] n (concern) Angelegenheit f; (event) Ereignis nt; (love ~) Verhältnis nt; **~s** npl (business) Geschäfte pl

affect [ə'fεkt] vt (influence) (ein)wirken auf +acc; (move deeply) bewegen; **this change doesn't ~ us** diese Änderung betrifft uns nicht; **~ed** adj affektiert, gekünstelt

affection [ə'fεkʃən] n Zuneigung f; **~ate** adj liebevoll

affiliated [ə'fɪlɪeɪtɪd] adj angeschlossen

affinity [ə'fɪnɪtɪ] n (attraction) gegenseitige Anziehung f; (relationship) Verwandtschaft f

affirmative [ə'fɜːmətɪv] adj bestätigend

afflict [ə'flɪkt] vt quälen, heimsuchen

affluence ['æfluəns] n (wealth) Wohlstand m; **affluent** adj wohlhabend, Wohlstands-

afford [ə'fɔːd] vt sich dat leisten; (yield) bieten, einbringen

afield [ə'fiːld] adv: **far ~** weit fort

afloat [ə'fləʊt] adj: **to be ~** schwimmen

afoot [ə'fʊt] adv im Gang

afraid [ə'freɪd] adj ängstlich; **to be ~ of** Angst haben vor +dat; **to be ~ to do sth** sich scheuen, etw zu tun; **I am ~ I have ...** ich habe leider ...; **I'm ~ so/ not** leider/leider nicht; **I am ~ that ...** ich fürchte(, dass) ...

afresh [ə'frεʃ] adv von neuem

Africa ['æfrɪkə] n Afrika nt; **~n** adj afrikanisch ♦ n Afrikaner(in) m(f)

after ['ɑːftə] prep nach; (following, seeking) hinter ... dat; (in imitation) nach, im Stil von ♦ adv: **soon ~** bald danach ♦ conj nachdem; **what are you ~?** was wollen Sie?; **he left** nachdem er gegangen war; **~ you!**

nach Ihnen!; **~ all** letzten Endes; **~ having shaved** als er sich rasiert hatte; **~effects** npl Nachwirkungen pl; **~math** n Auswirkungen pl; **~noon** n Nachmittag m; **~s** (inf) n (dessert) Nachtisch m; **~sales service** (BRIT) n Kundendienst m; **~shave (lotion)** n Rasierwasser nt; **~sun** n Aftersunlotion f; **~thought** n nachträgliche(r) Einfall m; **~wards** adv danach, nachher

again [ə'gεn] adv wieder, noch einmal; (besides) außerdem, ferner; **~ and ~** immer wieder

against [ə'gεnst] prep gegen

age [eɪdʒ] n (of person) Alter nt; (in history) Zeitalter nt ♦ vi altern, alt werden ♦ vt älter machen; **to come of ~** mündig werden; **20 years of ~** 20 Jahre alt; **it's been ~s since ...** es ist ewig her, seit ...

aged¹ [eɪdʒd] adj ... Jahre alt, -jährig

aged² [eɪdʒd] adj (elderly) betagt ♦ npl: **the ~** die Alten pl

age group n Altersgruppe f

age limit n Altersgrenze f

agency ['eɪdʒənsɪ] n Agentur f; Vermittlung f; (CHEM) Wirkung f; **through or by the ~ of** mithilfe or mit Hilfe von ...

agenda [ə'dʒεndə] n Tagesordnung f

agent ['eɪdʒənt] n (COMM) Vertreter m; (spy) Agent m

aggravate ['ægrəveɪt] vt (make worse) verschlimmern; (irritate) reizen

aggregate ['ægrɪgɪt] n Summe f

aggression [ə'grεʃən] n Aggression f;

aggressive [ə'grεsɪv] adj aggressiv

aghast [ə'gɑːst] adj entsetzt

agile ['ædʒaɪl] adj flink, agil; (mind) rege

agitate ['ædʒɪteɪt] vt rütteln; **to ~ for** sich stark machen für

AGM n abbr (= annual general meeting) JHV f

ago [ə'gəʊ] adv: **two days ~** vor zwei Tagen; **not long ~** vor kurzem; **it's so long ~** es ist schon so lange her

agog [ə'gɔg] adj gespannt

agonizing ['ægənaızıŋ] adj quälend

agony ['ægənı] n Qual f; **to be in ~** Qualen leiden

agree [ə'gri:] vt (date) vereinbaren ♦ vi (have same opinion, correspond) übereinstimmen; (consent) zustimmen; (be in harmony) sich vertragen; **to ~ to sth** einer Sache dat zustimmen; **to ~ that ...** (admit) zugeben, dass ...; **to ~ to do sth** sich bereit erklären, etw zu tun; garlic doesn't ~ with me Knoblauch vertrage ich nicht; **I ~** einverstanden, ich stimme zu; **to ~ on sth** sich auf etw acc einigen; **~able** adj (pleasing) liebenswürdig; (willing to consent) einverstanden; **~d** adj vereinbart; **~ment** n (~ing) Übereinstimmung f; (contract) Vereinbarung f, Vertrag m; **to be in ~ment** übereinstimmen

agricultural [ægrı'kʌltʃərəl] adj landwirtschaftlich, Landwirtschafts-

agriculture ['ægrıkʌltʃəʳ] n Landwirtschaft f

aground [ə'graund] adv: **to run ~** auf Grund laufen

ahead [ə'hed] adv vorwärts; **to be ~** voraus sein; **~ of time** der Zeit voraus; **go right ~ straight ~** gehen Sie geradeaus; fahren Sie geradeaus

aid [eıd] n (assistance) Hilfe f, Unterstützung f; (person) Hilfe f; (thing) Hilfsmittel nt ♦ vt unterstützen, helfen +dat; **in ~ of** zugunsten or zu Gunsten +gen; **to ~ and abet sb** jdm Beihilfe leisten

aide [eıd] n (person) Gehilfe m; (MIL) Adjutant m

AIDS [eıdz] n abbr (= acquired immune deficiency syndrome) Aids nt; **AIDS-related** aidsbedingt

ailing ['eılıŋ] adj kränkelnd

ailment ['eılmənt] n Leiden nt

aim [eım] vt (gun, camera) richten ♦ vi (with gun: also: **take ~**) zielen; (intend) beabsichtigen ♦ n (intention) Absicht f,

Ziel nt; (pointing) Zielen nt, Richten nt; **to ~ at sth** auf etw dat richten; (fig) etw anstreben; **to ~ to do sth** vorhaben, etw zu tun; **~less** adj ziellos; **~lessly** adv ziellos

ain't [eınt] (inf) = **are not; are not; is not; has not; have not**

air [ɛəʳ] n Luft f; (manner) Miene f, Anschein m; (MUS) Melodie f ♦ vt lüften; (fig) an die Öffentlichkeit bringen ♦ cpd Luft-; **by ~** (travel) auf dem Luftweg; **to be on the ~** (RADIO, TV: programme) gesendet werden; **~bed** (BRIT) n Luftmatratze f; **~-conditioned** adj mit Klimaanlage; **~-conditioning** n Klimaanlage; **~craft** n Flugzeug nt, Maschine f; **~craft carrier** n Flugzeugträger m; **~field** n Flugplatz m; **~ force** n Luftwaffe f; **~ freshener** n Raumspray nt; **~gun** n Luftgewehr nt; **~ hostess** (BRIT) n Stewardess f; **~ letter** (BRIT) n Luftpostbrief m; **~lift** n Luftbrücke f; **~line** n Luftverkehrsgesellschaft f; **~liner** n Verkehrsflugzeug nt; **~lock** n Luftblase f; **~mail** n: **by ~mail** mit Luftpost; **~ miles** npl ≈ Flugkilometer npl; **~plane** (US) n Flugzeug nt; **~port** n Flughafen m, Flugplatz m; **~ raid** n Luftangriff m; **~sick** adj luftkrank; **~space** n Luftraum m; **~strip** n Landestreifen m; **~ terminal** n Terminal m; **~tight** adj luftdicht; **~ traffic controller** n Fluglotse m; **~y** adj luftig; (manner) leichtfertig

aisle [aıl] n Gang m; **~ seat** n Sitz m am Gang

ajar [ə'dʒɑːʳ] adv angelehnt; einen Spalt offen

alarm [ə'lɑːm] n (warning) Alarm m; (bell etc) Alarmanlage f; (anxiety) Sorge f ♦ vt erschrecken; **~ call** n (in hotel etc) Weckruf m; **~ clock** n Wecker m

Albania [æl'beınıə] n Albanien nt

albeit [ɔːl'biːıt] conj obgleich

album ['ælbəm] n Album nt

alcohol ['ælkəhɔl] n Alkohol m; **~-free** adj alkoholfrei; **~ic** [ælkə'hɔlık] (drink) alkoholisch ♦ n Alkoholiker(in) m(f); **~ism** n Alkoholismus m

alert [əˈləːt] adj wachsam ♦ n Alarm m ♦ vt alarmieren; **to be on the ~** wachsam sein

Algeria [ælˈdʒɪərɪə] n Algerien nt

alias [ˈeɪlɪəs] adv alias ♦ n Deckname m

alibi [ˈælɪbaɪ] n Alibi nt

alien [ˈeɪlɪən] n Ausländer m ♦ adj (foreign) ausländisch; (strange) fremd; **~ to** fremd +dat; **~ate** vt entfremden

alight [əˈlaɪt] adj brennend; (of building) in Flammen ♦ vi (descend) aussteigen; (bird) sich setzen

align [əˈlaɪn] vt ausrichten

alike [əˈlaɪk] adj gleich, ähnlich ♦ adv gleich, ebenso; **to look ~** sich dat ähnlich sehen

alimony [ˈælɪmənɪ] n Unterhalt m, Alimente pl

alive [əˈlaɪv] adj (living) lebend; (lively) lebendig, aufgeweckt; **~ with** (full of) voll (von), wimmelnd (von)

KEYWORD

all [ɔːl] adj alle(r, s); **all day/night** den ganzen Tag/die ganze Nacht; **all men are equal** alle Menschen sind gleich; **all five came** alle fünf kamen; **all the books/food** die ganzen Bücher/das ganze Essen; **all the time** die ganze Zeit (über); **all his life** sein ganzes Leben (lang)

♦ pron 1 alles; **I ate it all, I ate all of it** ich habe alles gegessen; **all of us/the boys went** wir gingen alle/alle Jungen gingen; **we all sat down** wir setzten uns alle

2 (in phrases): **above all** vor allem; **after all** schließlich; **at all: not at all** (in answer to question) überhaupt nicht; (in answer to thanks) gern geschehen; **I'm not at all tired** ich bin überhaupt nicht müde; **anything at all will do** es ist egal, welche(r, s); **in all** alles in allem

♦ adv ganz; **all alone** ganz allein; **it's**

---

not as hard as all that so schwer ist es nun auch wieder nicht; **all the more/the better** umso mehr/besser; **all but fast**; **the score is 2 all** es steht 2 zu 2

allay [əˈleɪ] vt (fears) beschwichtigen

all clear n Entwarnung f

allegation [ælɪˈgeɪʃən] n Behauptung f

allege [əˈledʒ] vt (declare) behaupten; (falsely) vorgeben; **~dly** adv angeblich

allegiance [əˈliːdʒəns] n Treue f

allergic [əˈləːdʒɪk] adj: **~ (to)** allergisch (gegen)

allergy [ˈælədʒɪ] n Allergie f

alleviate [əˈliːvɪeɪt] vt lindern

alley [ˈælɪ] n Gasse f, Durchgang m

alliance [əˈlaɪəns] n Bund m, Allianz f

allied [ˈælaɪd] adj vereinigt; (powers) alliiert; **~ to** verwandt (mit)

all: **~-in** (BRIT) adj (also charge) alles inbegriffen, Gesamt-; **~-in wrestling** n Freistilringen nt; **~-night** adj (café, cinema) die ganze Nacht geöffnet, Nacht-

allocate [ˈæləkeɪt] vt zuteilen

allot [əˈlɒt] vt zuteilen; **~ment** n (share) Anteil m; (plot) Schrebergarten m

all-out [ˈɔːlaʊt] adj total; **all out** adv mit voller Kraft

allow [əˈlaʊ] vt (permit) erlauben, gestatten; (grant) bewilligen; (deduct) abziehen; (concede): **to ~ that ...** annehmen, dass ...; **to ~ sb to do sth** jdm erlauben or gestatten, etw zu tun; **~ for** vt fus berücksichtigen, einplanen; **~ance** n Beihilfe f; **to make ~ances for** berücksichtigen

alloy [ˈælɔɪ] n Metalllegierung f

all: **~ right** adv (well) gut; (correct) richtig; (as answer) okay; **~-round** adj (sportsman) allseitig, Allround-; (view) Rundum-, **~-time** adj (record, high) ... aller Zeiten, Höchst-

allude [əˈluːd] vi: **to ~ to** hinweisen auf +acc, anspielen auf +acc

alluring [əˈljʊərɪŋ] adj verlockend

ally [n 'ælaɪ, vb ə'laɪ] n Verbündete(r) f(m); (POL) Alliierte(r) f(m) ♦ vt: **to ~ o.s. with** sich verbünden mit

almighty [ɔːl'maɪtɪ] adj allmächtig

almond ['aːmənd] n Mandel f

almost ['ɔːlməʊst] adv fast, beinahe

alms [aːmz] npl Almosen n

alone [ə'ləʊn] adj, adv allein; **to leave sth ~** etw sein lassen; **let ~ ...** geschweige denn ...

along [ə'lɒŋ] prep entlang, längs ♦ adv (onward) vorwärts, weiter; **~ with** zusammen mit; **he was limping ~** er humpelte einher; **all ~** (all the time) die ganze Zeit; **~side** adv (walk) nebenher; (come) nebendran; (be) daneben ♦ prep (walk, compared with) neben +dat; (come) neben +acc; (be) neben +dat; (of ship) längsseits +gen

aloof [ə'luːf] adj zurückhaltend ♦ adv fern; **to stand ~** abseits stehen

aloud [ə'laʊd] adv laut

alphabet ['ælfəbet] n Alphabet nt; **~ical** [ælfə'betɪkl] adj alphabetisch

alpine ['ælpaɪn] adj alpin, Alpen-

Alps [ælps] npl: **the ~** die Alpen pl

already [ɔːl'redɪ] adv schon, bereits

alright ['ɔːl'raɪt] (BRIT) adv = **all right**

Alsatian [æl'seɪʃən] n (dog) Schäferhund m

also ['ɔːlsəʊ] adv auch, außerdem

altar ['ɔːltə'] n Altar m

alter ['ɔːltə'] vt ändern; (dress) umändern; **~ation** [ɔːltə'reɪʃən] n Änderung f; Umänderung f; (to building) Umbau m

alternate [adj ɔl'tɜːnɪt, vb 'ɔltəneɪt] adj abwechselnd ♦ vi abwechseln; **on ~ days** jeden zweiten Tag

alternating ['ɔltəneɪtɪŋ] adj: **~ current** Wechselstrom m; **alternative** [ɔl'tɜːnətɪv] adj andere(r, s) ♦ n Alternative f; **alternative medicine** Alternativmedizin f; **alternatively** adv im anderen Falle; **alternatively one could ...** oder man könnte ...; **alternator** ['ɔltɜːneɪtə'] n (AUT) Lichtmaschine f

although [ɔːl'ðəʊ] conj obwohl

altitude ['æltɪtjuːd] n Höhe f

alto ['æltəʊ] n Alt m

altogether [ɔːltə'geðə'] adv (on the whole) im Ganzen genommen; (entirely) ganz und gar

aluminium [ælju'mɪnɪəm] (BRIT) n Aluminium nt

aluminum [ə'luːmɪnəm] (US) n Aluminium nt

always ['ɔːlweɪz] adv immer

Alzheimer's (disease) ['æltshaɪməz-] n (MED) Alzheimerkrankheit f

AM n abbr (= Assembly Member) Mitglied nt der walisischen Versammlung

am [æm] see **be**

a.m. adv abbr (= ante meridiem) vormittags

amalgamate [ə'mælgəmeɪt] vi (combine) sich vereinigen ♦ vt (mix) amalgamieren

amass [ə'mæs] vt anhäufen

amateur ['æmətə'] n Amateur m; (pej) Amateur m, Stümper m; **~ish** (pej) adj dilettantisch, stümperhaft

amaze [ə'meɪz] vt erstaunen; **to be ~d (at)** erstaunt sein (über); **~ment** n höchste(s) Erstaunen nt; **amazing** adj höchst erstaunlich

Amazon ['æməzən] n (GEOG) Amazonas m

ambassador [æm'bæsədə'] n Botschafter m

amber ['æmbə'] n Bernstein m; **at ~** (BRIT: AUT) auf Gelb, gelb

ambiguous [æm'bɪgjuəs] adj zweideutig; (not clear) unklar

ambition [æm'bɪʃən] n Ehrgeiz m; **ambitious** adj ehrgeizig

amble ['æmbl] vi (usu: ~ along) schlendern

ambulance ['æmbjuləns] n Krankenwagen m; **~ man** (irreg) n Sanitäter m

ambush ['æmbuʃ] n Hinterhalt m ♦ vt (aus dem Hinterhalt) überfallen

amenable [ə'miːnəbl] adj gefügig; **~ (to)** (reason) zugänglich (+dat); (flattery) empfänglich (für)

amend [ə'mɛnd] vt (law etc) abändern, ergänzen; **to make ~s** etw wieder gutmachen; **~ment** n Abänderung f

amenities [ə'miːnɪtɪz] npl Einrichtungen pl

America [ə'mɛrɪkə] n Amerika nt; **~n** adj amerikanisch ♦ n Amerikaner(in) m(f)

amiable ['eɪmɪəbl] adj liebenswürdig

amicable ['æmɪkəbl] adj freundschaftlich; (settlement) gütlich

amid(st) [ə'mɪd(st)] prep mitten in or unter +dat

amiss [ə'mɪs] adv: **to take sth ~** etw übel nehmen; **there's something ~** da stimmt irgendetwas nicht

ammonia [ə'məunɪə] n Ammoniak nt

ammunition [æmju'nɪʃən] n Munition f

amnesia [æm'niːzɪə] n Gedächtnisverlust m

amnesty ['æmnɪstɪ] n Amnestie f

amok [ə'mɔk] adv: **to run ~** Amok laufen

among(st) [ə'mʌŋ(st)] prep unter

amoral [æ'mɔrəl] adj unmoralisch

amorous ['æmərəs] adj verliebt

amount [ə'maunt] n (of money) Betrag m; (of water, sand) Menge f ♦ vi: **to ~ to** (total) sich belaufen auf +acc; **a great ~ of time/energy** ein großer Aufwand an Zeit/Energie (dat); **this ~s to treachery** das kommt Verrat gleich; **he won't ~ to much** aus ihm wird nie was

amp(ere) ['æmp(ɛər)] n Ampere nt

amphibian [æm'fɪbɪən] n Amphibie f

amphitheatre ['æmfɪθɪətər] n Amphitheater nt

ample ['æmpl] adj (portion) reichlich; (dress) weit, groß; **~ time** genügend Zeit

amplifier ['æmplɪfaɪər] n Verstärker m

amuse [ə'mjuːz] vt (entertain) unterhalten; (make smile) belustigen; **~ment** n (feeling) Unterhaltung f; (recreation) Zeitvertreib m; **~ment arcade** n Spielhalle f; **~ment park** n Vergnügungspark m

an [æn, ən] see **a**

anaemia [ə'niːmɪə] n Anämie f; **anaemic** adj blutarm

anaesthetic [ænəs'θɛtɪk] n Betäubungsmittel nt; **under ~** unter Narkose; **anaesthetist** [æ'niːsθɪtɪst] n Anästhesist(in) m(f)

analgesic [ænæl'dʒiːsɪk] n schmerzlindernde(s) Mittel nt

analog(ue) ['ænəlɔg] adj Analog-

analogy [ə'nælədʒɪ] n Analogie f

analyse ['ænəlaɪz] (BRIT) vt analysieren

analyses [ə'næləsiːz] (BRIT) npl of **analysis**

analysis [ə'næləsɪs] (pl **analyses**) n Analyse f

analyst ['ænəlɪst] n Analytiker(in) m(f)

analytic(al) [ænə'lɪtɪk(l)] adj analytisch

analyze ['ænəlaɪz] (US) vt = **analyse**

anarchy ['ænəkɪ] n Anarchie f

anatomy [ə'nætəmɪ] n (structure) anatomische(r) Aufbau m; (study) Anatomie f

ancestor ['ænsɪstər] n Vorfahr m

anchor ['æŋkər] n Anker m ♦ vi (also: **to drop ~**) ankern, vor Anker gehen ♦ vt verankern; **to weigh ~** den Anker lichten

anchovy ['æntʃəvɪ] n Sardelle f

ancient ['eɪnʃənt] adj alt; (car etc) uralt

ancillary [æn'sɪlərɪ] adj Hilfs-

and [ænd] conj und; **~ so on** und so weiter; **try ~ come** versuche zu kommen; **better ~ better** immer besser

Andes ['ændiːz] npl: **the ~** die Anden pl

anemia etc [ə'niːmɪə] (US) n = **anaemia** etc

anesthetic etc [ænəs'θɛtɪk] (US) n = **anaesthetic** etc

anew [ə'njuː] adv von neuem

angel ['eɪndʒəl] n Engel m

anger ['æŋgər] n Zorn m ♦ vt ärgern

angina [æn'dʒaɪnə] n Angina f

angle ['æŋgl] n Winkel m; (point of view) Standpunkt m

angler ['æŋglər] n Angler m

Anglican ['æŋglɪkən] *adj* anglikanisch ♦ *n* Anglikaner(in) *m(f)*

angling ['æŋglɪŋ] *n* Angeln *nt*

angrily ['æŋgrɪlɪ] *adv* ärgerlich, böse

angry ['æŋgrɪ] *adj* ärgerlich, ungehalten, böse; (*wound*) entzündet; **to be ~ with sb** auf jdn böse sein; **to be ~ at sth** über etw *acc* verärgert sein

anguish ['æŋgwɪʃ] *n* Qual *f*

angular ['æŋgjulə*] *adj* eckig, winkelförmig; (*face*) kantig

animal ['ænɪməl] *n* Tier *nt*; (*living creature*) Lebewesen *nt* ♦ *adj* tierisch

animate [*vb* 'ænɪmeɪt, *adj* 'ænɪmɪt] *vt* beleben ♦ *adj* lebhaft; **~d** *adj* lebendig; (*film*) Zeichentrick-

animosity [ænɪ'mɔsɪtɪ] *n* Feindseligkeit *f*, Abneigung *f*

aniseed ['ænɪsiːd] *n* Anis *m*

ankle ['æŋkl] *n* (Fuß)knöchel *m*; **~ sock** *n* Söckchen *n*

annex [*n* 'æneks, *vb* ə'neks] *n* (*BRIT: also:* **~e**) Anbau *m* ♦ *vt* anfügen; (*POL*) annektieren, angliedern

annihilate [ə'naɪəleɪt] *vt* vernichten

anniversary [ænɪ'vɜːsərɪ] *n* Jahrestag *m*

announce [ə'nauns] *vt* ankündigen, anzeigen; **~ment** *n* Ankündigung *f*; (*official*) Bekanntmachung *f*; **~r** *n* Ansager(in) *m(f)*

annoy [ə'nɔɪ] *vt* ärgern; **don't get ~ed!** reg dich nicht auf!; **~ance** *n* Ärgernis *nt*, Störung *f*; **~ing** *adj* ärgerlich; (*person*) lästig

annual ['ænjuəl] *adj* jährlich; (*salary*) Jahres- ♦ *n* (*plant*) einjährige Pflanze *f*; (*book*) Jahrbuch *nt*; **~ly** *adv* jährlich

annul [ə'nʌl] *vt* aufheben, annullieren

annum ['ænəm] *n see* **per**

anonymous [ə'nɔnɪməs] *adj* anonym

anorak ['ænəræk] *n* Anorak *m*, Windjacke *f*

anorexia [ænə'reksɪə] *n* (*MED*) Magersucht *f*

another [ə'nʌðə*] *adj, pron* (*different*) ein(e) andere(r, s); (*additional*) noch eine(r, s); *see also* **one**

answer ['ɑːnsə*] *n* Antwort *f* ♦ *vi* antworten; (*on phone*) sich melden ♦ *vt* (*person*) antworten +*dat*; (*letter, question*) beantworten; (*telephone*) gehen an +*acc*, abnehmen; (*door*) öffnen; **in ~ to your letter** in Beantwortung Ihres Schreibens; **to ~ the phone** ans Telefon gehen; **to ~ the bell** *or* **the door** aufmachen; **~ back** *vi* frech sein; **~ for** *vt fus*: **to ~ for sth** für etw verantwortlich sein; **~able** *adj*: **to be ~able to sb for sth** jdm gegenüber für etw verantwortlich sein; **~ing machine** *n* Anrufbeantworter *m*

ant [ænt] *n* Ameise *f*

antagonism [æn'tægənɪzəm] *n* Antagonismus *m*

antagonize [æn'tægənaɪz] *vt* reizen

Antarctic [ænt'ɑːktɪk] *adj* antarktisch ♦ *n*: **the ~** die Antarktis

antelope ['æntɪləup] *n* Antilope *f*

antenatal ['æntɪ'neɪtl] *adj* vor der Geburt; **~ clinic** *n* Sprechstunde *f* für werdende Mütter

antenna [æn'tenə] *n* (*BIOL*) Fühler *m*; (*RAD*) Antenne *f*

antennae [æn'teniː] *npl of* **antenna**

anthem ['ænθəm] *n* Hymne *f*; **national ~** Nationalhymne *f*

anthology [æn'θɔlədʒɪ] *n* Gedichtsammlung *f*, Anthologie *f*

anti- ['æntɪ] *prefix* Gegen-, Anti-

anti-aircraft ['æntɪ'eəkrɑːft] *adj* Flugabwehr-

antibiotic ['æntɪbaɪ'ɔtɪk] *n* Antibiotikum *nt*

antibody ['æntɪbɔdɪ] *n* Antikörper *m*

anticipate [æn'tɪsɪpeɪt] *vt* (*expect: trouble, question*) erwarten, rechnen mit; (*look forward to*) sich freuen auf +*acc*; (*do first*) vorwegnehmen; (*foresee*) ahnen, vorhersehen; **anticipation** [æntɪsɪ'peɪʃən] *n* Erwartung *f*; (*foreshadowing*) Vorwegnahme *f*

anticlimax ['æntɪ'klaɪmæks] *n* Ernüchterung *f*

anticlockwise ['æntɪ'klɔkwaɪz] adv entgegen dem Uhrzeigersinn

antics ['æntɪks] npl Possen pl

anti-: ~**cyclone** n Hoch nt, Hochdruckgebiet nt; ~**depressant** n Antidepressivum nt; ~**dote** n Gegenmittel nt; ~**freeze** n Frostschutzmittel nt; ~**histamine** n Antihistamin nt

antiquated ['æntɪkweɪtɪd] adj antiquiert

antique [æn'ti:k] n Antiquität f ♦ adj antik; (old-fashioned) altmodisch; ~**shop** n Antiquitätenladen m; **antiquity** [æn'tɪkwɪtɪ] n Altertum nt

antiseptic [æntɪ'septɪk] n Antiseptikum nt ♦ adj antiseptisch

antisocial ['æntɪ'səufəl] adj (person) ungesellig; (law) unsozial

antlers ['æntləz] npl Geweih nt

anus ['eɪnəs] n After m

anvil ['ænvɪl] n Amboss m

anxiety [æŋ'zaɪətɪ] n Angst f; (worry) Sorge f; **anxious** ['æŋkʃəs] adj ängstlich; (worried) besorgt; **to be anxious to do sth** etw unbedingt tun wollen

---
KEYWORD
---

any ['enɪ] adj 1 (in questions etc): **have you any butter?** haben Sie (etwas) Butter?; **have you any children?** haben Sie Kinder?; **if there are any tickets left** falls noch Karten da sind
2 (with negative): **I haven't any money/books** ich habe kein Geld/keine Bücher
3 (no matter which) jede(r, s) (beliebige); **any colour (at all)** jede beliebige Farbe; **choose any book you like** nehmen Sie ein beliebiges Buch
4 (in phrases): **in any case** in jedem Fall; **any day now** jeden Tag; **at any moment** jeden Moment; **at any rate** auf jeden Fall
♦ pron 1 (in questions etc): **have you got any?** haben Sie welche?; **can any of you sing?** kann (irgend)einer von euch singen?

2 (with negative): **I haven't any (of them)** ich habe keinen/keines (davon)
3 (no matter which one(s)): **take any of those books (you like)** nehmen Sie irgendeines dieser Bücher
♦ adv 1 (in questions etc): **do you want any more soup/sandwiches?** möchten Sie noch Suppe/Brote?; **are you feeling any better?** fühlen Sie sich etwas besser?
2 (with negative): **I can't hear him any more** ich kann ihn nicht mehr hören

anybody ['enɪbɔdɪ] pron (no matter who) jede(r); (in questions etc) (irgend)jemand, (irgend)eine(r); (with negative): **I can't see ~** ich kann niemanden sehen

anyhow ['enɪhau] adv (at any rate): **I shall go ~** ich gehe sowieso; (haphazardly): **do it ~** machen Sie es, wie Sie wollen

anyone ['enɪwʌn] pron = anybody

KEYWORD
---

anything ['enɪθɪŋ] pron 1 (in questions etc) (irgend)etwas; **can you see anything?** können Sie etwas sehen?
2 (with negative): **I can't see anything** ich kann nichts sehen
3 (no matter what): **you can say anything you like** Sie können sagen, was Sie wollen; **anything will do** irgendetwas (wird genügen), irgendeine(r, s) (wird genügen); **he'll eat anything** er isst alles

anyway ['enɪweɪ] adv (at any rate) auf jeden Fall; (besides): ~, **I couldn't come even if I wanted to** jedenfalls könnte ich nicht kommen, selbst wenn ich wollte; **why are you phoning,** ~? warum rufst du überhaupt an?

anywhere ['enɪweə'] adv (in questions etc) irgendwo; (: with direction) irgendwohin; (no matter where) überall; (: with direction) überallhin; (with negative): **I can't see him ~** ich kann ihn nirgendwo or nirgends sehen; **can you see him ~?** siehst du ihn irgendwo?; **put the books down ~** leg die Bücher irgendwohin

apart [əˈpɑːt] adv (parted) auseinander; (away) beiseite, abseits; **10 miles ~** 10 Meilen auseinander; **to take ~** auseinander nehmen; **~ from** prep außer

apartheid [əˈpɑːteɪt] n Apartheid f

apartment [əˈpɑːtmənt] n (US) Wohnung f; **~ building** (US) n Wohnhaus nt

apathy [ˈæpəθɪ] n Teilnahmslosigkeit f, Apathie f

ape [eɪp] n (Menschen)affe m ♦ vt nachahmen

aperitif [əˈperɪtiːf] n Aperitif m

aperture [ˈæpətjuəˑ] n Öffnung f; (PHOT) Blende f

APEX [ˈeɪpeks] n abbr (AVIAT: = advance purchase excursion) APEX (im Voraus reservierte(r) Fahrkarte/Flugschein zu reduzierten Preisen)

apex [ˈeɪpeks] n Spitze f

apiece [əˈpiːs] adv pro Stück; (per person) pro Kopf

apologetic [əpɒləˈdʒetɪk] adj entschuldigend; **to be ~** sich sehr entschuldigen

apologize [əˈpɒlədʒaɪz] vi: **to ~ (for sth to sb)** sich (für etw bei jdm) entschuldigen; **apology** n Entschuldigung f

apostle [əˈpɒsl] n Apostel m

apostrophe [əˈpɒstrəfi] n Apostroph m

appal [əˈpɔːl] vt erschrecken; **~ling** adj schrecklich

apparatus [æpəˈreɪtəs] n Gerät nt

apparel [əˈpærəl] (US) n Kleidung f

apparent [əˈpærənt] adj offenbar; **~ly** adv anscheinend

apparition [æpəˈrɪʃən] n (ghost) Erscheinung f, Geist m

appeal [əˈpiːl] vi dringend ersuchen; (JUR) Berufung einlegen ♦ n Aufruf m; (JUR) Berufung f; **to ~ for** dringend bit-

ten um; **to ~ to** sich wenden an +acc; (to public) appellieren an +acc; **it doesn't ~ to me** es gefällt mir nicht; **~ing** adj ansprechend

appear [əˈpɪəˑ] vi (come into sight) erscheinen; (be seen) scheinen; (seem) scheinen; **it would ~ that ...** anscheinend ...; **~ance** n (coming into sight) Erscheinen nt; (outward show) Äußere(s) nt

appease [əˈpiːz] vt beschwichtigen

appendices [əˈpendɪsiːz] npl of **appendix**

appendicitis [əpendɪˈsaɪtɪs] n Blinddarmentzündung f

appendix [əˈpendɪks] (pl **appendices**) n (in book) Anhang m; (MED) Blinddarm m

appetite [ˈæpɪtaɪt] n Appetit m; (fig) Lust f

appetizer [ˈæpɪtaɪzəˑ] n Appetitanreger m; **appetizing** [ˈæpɪtaɪzɪŋ] adj appetitanregend

applaud [əˈplɔːd] vt Beifall klatschen, applaudieren ♦ vt Beifall klatschen +dat; **applause** [əˈplɔːz] n Beifall m, Applaus m

apple [ˈæpl] n Apfel m; **~ tree** n Apfelbaum m

appliance [əˈplaɪəns] n Gerät nt

applicable [əˈplɪkəbl] adj anwendbar; (in forms) zutreffend

applicant [ˈæplɪkənt] n Bewerber(in) m(f)

application [æplɪˈkeɪʃən] n (request) Antrag m; (for job) Bewerbung f; (putting into practice) Anwendung f; (hard work) Fleiß m; **~ form** n Bewerbungsformular nt

applied [əˈplaɪd] adj angewandt

apply [əˈplaɪ] vi (be suitable) zutreffen; (ask): **to ~ to** sich wenden an +acc; (request): **to ~ for** sich melden für +acc ♦ vt (place on) auflegen; (cream) auftragen; (put into practice) anwenden; **to ~ for sth** sich um etw bewerben; **to ~ o.s. to sth** sich bei etw anstrengen

appoint [ə'pɔint] vt (to office) ernennen, berufen; (settle) festsetzen; **~ment** n (meeting) Verabredung f; (at hairdresser etc) Bestellung f; (in business) Termin m; (choice for a position) Ernennung f; (UNIV) Berufung f

appraisal [ə'preizl] n Beurteilung f

appreciable [ə'pri:ʃəbl] adj (perceptible) merklich; (able to be estimated) abschätzbar

appreciate [ə'pri:ʃieit] vt (value) zu schätzen wissen; (understand) einsehen ♦ vi (increase in value) im Wert steigen; **appreciation** [əpri:ʃi'eiʃən] n Wertschätzung f; (COMM) Wertzuwachs m; **appreciative** [ə'pri:ʃiətiv] adj (showing thanks) dankbar; (showing liking) anerkennend

apprehend [æpri'hend] vt (arrest) festnehmen; (understand) erfassen

apprehension [æpri'henʃən] n Angst f

apprehensive [æpri'hensiv] adj furchtsam

apprentice [ə'prentis] n Lehrling m; **~ship** n Lehrzeit f

approach [ə'prəutʃ] vi sich nähern ♦ vt herantreten an +acc; (problem) herangehen an +acc ♦ n Annäherung f; (to problem) Ansatz m; (path) Zugang m, Zufahrt f; **~able** adj zugänglich

appropriate [adj ə'prəupriit, vb ə'prəuprieit] adj angemessen; (remark) angebracht ♦ vt (take for o.s.) sich aneignen; (set apart) bereitstellen

approval [ə'pru:vəl] n (show of satisfaction) Beifall m; (permission) Billigung f; **on ~** (COMM) bei Gefallen

approve [ə'pru:v] vt, vi billigen; **I don't ~ of it/him** ich halte nichts davon/von ihm; **~d school** (BRIT) n Erziehungsheim nt

approximate [adj ə'prɔksimit, vb ə'prɔksimeit] adj annähernd, ungefähr ♦ vt nahe kommen +dat; **~ly** adv rund, ungefähr

apricot ['eiprikɔt] n Aprikose f

April ['eiprəl] n April m; **~ Fools' Day** n der erste April

apron ['eiprən] n Schürze f

apt [æpt] adj (suitable) passend; (able) begabt; (likely): **to be ~ to do sth** dazu neigen, etw zu tun

aptitude ['æptitju:d] n Begabung f

aqualung ['ækwəlʌŋ] n Unterwasseratmungsgerät nt

aquarium [ə'kweəriəm] n Aquarium nt

Aquarius [ə'kweəriəs] n Wassermann m

aquatic [ə'kwætik] adj Wasser-

Arab ['ærəb] n Araber(in) m(f)

Arabia [ə'reibiə] n Arabien nt; **~n** adj arabisch

Arabic ['ærəbik] adj arabisch ♦ n Arabisch nt

arable ['ærəbl] adj bebaubar, Kulturland-

arbitrary ['ɑ:bitrəri] adj willkürlich

arbitration [ɑ:bi'treiʃən] n Schlichtung f

arc [ɑ:k] n Bogen m

arcade [ɑ:'keid] n Säulengang m; (with video games) Spielhalle f

arch [ɑ:tʃ] n Bogen m ♦ vt überwölben; (back) krumm machen

archaeologist [ɑ:ki'ɔlədʒist] n Archäologe m

archaeology [ɑ:ki'ɔlədʒi] n Archäologie f

archaic [ɑ:'keiik] adj altertümlich

archbishop [ɑ:tʃ'biʃəp] n Erzbischof m

archenemy ['ɑ:tʃ'enəmi] n Erzfeind m

archeology [ɑ:ki'ɔlədʒi] (US) = archaeology etc

archery ['ɑ:tʃəri] n Bogenschießen nt

architect ['ɑ:kitekt] n Architekt(in) m(f); **~ural** [ɑ:ki'tektʃərəl] adj architektonisch; **~ure** n Architektur f

archives ['ɑ:kaivz] npl Archiv nt

archway ['ɑ:tʃwei] n Bogen m

Arctic ['ɑ:ktik] adj arktisch ♦ n: **the ~** die Arktis

ardent ['ɑ:dənt] adj glühend

arduous ['ɑ:djuəs] adj mühsam

are [ɑ:] see be

area ['eəriə] n Fläche f; (of land) Gebiet

nt; (part of sth) Teil m, Abschnitt m

arena [əˈriːnə] n Arena f

aren't [ɑːnt] = **are not**

Argentina [ɑːdʒənˈtiːnə] n Argentinien nt; **Argentinian** [ɑːdʒənˈtɪnɪən] adj argentinisch ♦ n Argentinier(in) m(f)

arguably [ˈɑːɡjuəblɪ] adv wohl

argue [ˈɑːɡjuː] vi diskutieren; (angrily) streiten; **argument** n (theory) Argument nt; (reasoning) Argumentation f; (row) Auseinandersetzung f, Streit m; **to have an argument** sich streiten; **argumentative** [ɑːɡjuˈmentətɪv] adj streitlustig

aria [ˈɑːrɪə] n Arie f

Aries [ˈeəriːz] n Widder m

arise [əˈraɪz] vi (pt **arose**, pp **arisen**) vi aufsteigen; (get up) aufstehen; (difficulties etc) entstehen; (case) vorkommen; **to ~ from sth** herrühren von etw; **~n** [əˈrɪzn] pp of **arise**

aristocracy [ærɪsˈtɒkrəsɪ] n Adel m, Aristokratie f; **aristocrat** [ˈærɪstəkræt] n Adlige(r) f(m), Aristokrat(in) m(f)

arithmetic [əˈrɪθmətɪk] n Rechnen nt, Arithmetik f

arm [ɑːm] n Arm m; (branch of military service) Zweig m ♦ vt bewaffnen; **~s** npl (weapons) Waffen pl

armaments [ˈɑːməmənts] npl Ausrüstung f

armchair [ˈɑːmtʃeəʳ] n Lehnstuhl m

armed [ɑːmd] adj (forces) Streit-, bewaffnet; **~ robbery** n bewaffnete(r) Raubüberfall m

armistice [ˈɑːmɪstɪs] n Waffenstillstand m

armour [ˈɑːməʳ] (US **armor**) n (knight's) Rüstung f; (MIL) Panzerplatte f; **~ed car** n Panzerwagen m

armpit [ˈɑːmpɪt] n Achselhöhle f

armrest [ˈɑːmrest] n Armlehne f

army [ˈɑːmɪ] n Armee f, Heer nt; (host) Heer nt

aroma [əˈrəumə] n Duft m, Aroma nt; **~therapy** [ərəuməˈθerəpɪ] n Aromatherapie f; **~tic** [ærəˈmætɪk] adj aroma

tisch, würzig

arose [əˈrəuz] pt of **arise**

around [əˈraund] adv ringsherum; (almost) ungefähr ♦ prep um ... herum; **is he ~?** ist er hier?

arrange [əˈreɪndʒ] vt (time, meeting) festsetzen; (holidays) festlegen; (flowers, hair, objects) anordnen; **I ~d to meet him** ich habe mit ihm ausgemacht, ihn zu treffen; **it's all ~d** es ist alles arrangiert; **~ment** n (order) Reihenfolge f; (agreement) Vereinbarung f; **~ments** npl (plans) Pläne pl

array [əˈreɪ] n (collection) Ansammlung f

arrears [əˈrɪəz] npl (of debts) Rückstand m; (of work) Unerledigte(s) nt; **in ~** im Rückstand

arrest [əˈrest] vt (person) verhaften; (stop) aufhalten ♦ n Verhaftung f; **under ~** in Haft

arrival [əˈraɪvl] n Ankunft f

arrive [əˈraɪv] vi ankommen; **to ~ at** ankommen in +dat, ankommen bei

arrogance [ˈærəgəns] n Überheblichkeit f, Arroganz f; **arrogant** [ˈærəgənt] adj überheblich, arrogant

arrow [ˈærəu] n Pfeil m

arse [ɑːs] (inf!) n Arsch m (!)

arsenal [ˈɑːsɪnl] n Waffenlager nt, Zeughaus nt

arsenic [ˈɑːsnɪk] n Arsen nt

arson [ˈɑːsn] n Brandstiftung f

art [ɑːt] n Kunst f; **A~s** npl (UNIV) Geisteswissenschaft f

artery [ˈɑːtərɪ] n Schlagader f, Arterie f

art gallery n Kunstgalerie f

arthritis [ɑːˈθraɪtɪs] n Arthritis f

artichoke [ˈɑːtɪtʃəuk] n Artischocke f; **Jerusalem ~** Erdartischocke f

article [ˈɑːtɪkl] n (PRESS, GRAM) Artikel m; (thing) Gegenstand m, Artikel m; (clause) Abschnitt m, Paragraf m; **~ of clothing** n Kleidungsstück nt

articulate [adj ɑːˈtɪkjulɪt, vb ɑːˈtɪkjuleɪt] adj (able to express o.s.) re degewandt; (*speaking clearly*) deutlich, verständlich ♦ *vt* (*connect*) zusammenfügen, gliedern; **to be** ~ sich gut ausdrücken können; **~d vehicle** *n* Sattelschlepper *m*

artificial [ɑ:tɪˈfɪʃəl] *adj* künstlich, Kunst-; ~ **respiration** *n* künstliche Atmung *f*

artisan [ˈɑ:tɪzæn] *n* gelernte(r) Handwerker *m*

artist [ˈɑ:tɪst] *n* Künstler(in) *m(f)*; **~ic** [ɑ:ˈtɪstɪk] *adj* künstlerisch; **~ry** *n* künstlerische(s) Können *nt*

art school *n* Kunsthochschule *f*

KEYWORD

---

as [æz] *conj* **1** (*referring to time*) als; **as the years went by** mit den Jahren; **he came in as I was leaving** als er hereinkam, ging ich gerade; **as from tomorrow** ab morgen

2 (*in comparisons*): **as big as** so groß wie; **twice as big as** zweimal so groß wie; **as much/many** as so viel/so viele wie; **as soon as** sobald

3 (*since, because*) da; **he left early as he had to be home by 10** er ging früher, da er um 10 zu Hause sein musste

4 (*referring to manner, way*) wie; **do as you wish** mach was du willst; **as she said** wie sie sagte

5 (*concerning*): **as for** *or* **to that** was das betrifft *or* angeht

6: as if *or* **though** als ob

♦ *prep* als; **as long; he works as a driver** er arbeitet als Fahrer; *see also* **such**; **he gave it to me as a present** er hat es mir als Geschenk gegeben; *see also* **well**

a.s.a.p. *abbr* = **as soon as possible**

asbestos [æzˈbestəs] *n* Asbest *m*

ascend [əˈsend] *vi* aufsteigen ♦ *vt* besteigen; **ascent** *n* Aufstieg *m*; Besteigung *f*

ascertain [æsəˈteɪn] *vt* feststellen

ascribe [əˈskraɪb] *vt*: **to ~ sth to sth /sth to sb** etw einer Sache/jdm etw zuschreiben

ash [æʃ] *n* Asche *f*; (*tree*) Esche *f*

ashamed [əˈʃeɪmd] *adj* beschämt; **to be ~ of** sich für etw schämen

ashen [ˈæʃən] *adj* (*pale*) aschfahl

ashore [əˈʃɔ:ʳ] *adv* an Land

ashtray [ˈæʃtreɪ] *n* Aschenbecher *m*

Ash Wednesday *n* Aschermittwoch *m*

Asia [ˈeɪʃə] *n* Asien *nt*; **~n** *adj* asiatisch ♦ *n* Asiat(in) *m(f)*

aside [əˈsaɪd] *adv* beiseite

ask [ɑ:sk] *vt* fragen; (*permission*) bitten um; ~ **him his name** frage ihn nach seinem Namen; **he ~ed to see you** er wollte dich sehen; **to ~ sb to do sth** jdn bitten, etw zu tun; **to ~ sb about sth** jdn nach etw fragen; **to ~ (sb) a question** (jdn) etwas fragen; **to ~ sb out to dinner** jdn zum Essen einladen; **~ after** *vt fus* fragen nach; **~ for** *vt fus* bitten um

askance [əˈskɑ:ns] *adv*: **to look ~ at sb** jdn schief ansehen

asking price [ˈɑ:skɪŋ-] *n* Verkaufspreis *m*

asleep [əˈsli:p] *adj*: **to be ~** schlafen; **to fall ~** einschlafen

asparagus [əsˈpærəgəs] *n* Spargel *m*

aspect [ˈæspekt] *n* Aspekt *m*

aspersions [əsˈpɜ:ʃənz] *npl*: **to cast ~ on sb/sth** sich abfällig über jdn/etw äußern

asphyxiation [æsfɪksɪˈeɪʃən] *n* Erstickung *f*

aspirations [æspəˈreɪʃənz] *npl*: **to have ~ towards sth** etw anstreben

aspire [əsˈpaɪəʳ] *vi*: **to ~ to** streben nach

aspirin [ˈæsprɪn] *n* Aspirin *nt*

ass [æs] *n* (*also fig*) Esel *m*; (*US: inf!*) Arsch *m* [?]

assailant [əˈseɪlənt] *n* Angreifer *m*

assassin [əˈsæsɪn] *n* Attentäter(in) *m(f)*; **~ate** *vt* ermorden; **~ation** [əsæsɪˈneɪʃən] *n* (geglückte(s)) Attentat *nt*

assault [əˈsɔːlt] *n* Angriff *m* ♦ *vt* überfallen; (*woman*) herfallen über +*acc*

assemble [əˈsɛmbl] *vt* versammeln; (*parts*) zusammensetzen ♦ *vi* sich versammeln; **assembly** (*meeting*) Versammlung *f*; (*construction*) Zusammensetzung *f*, Montage *f*; **assembly line** *n* Fließband *nt*

assent [əˈsɛnt] *n* Zustimmung *f*

assert [əˈsɜːt] *vt* erklären; **~ion** *n* Behauptung *f*

assess [əˈsɛs] *vt* schätzen; **~ment** *n* Bewertung *f*, Einschätzung *f*; **~or** *n* Steuerberater *m*

asset [ˈæset] *n* Vorteil *m*, Wert *m*; **~s** *pl* (*FIN*) Vermögen *nt*; (*estate*) Nachlass *m*

assign [əˈsaɪn] *vt* zuweisen; **~ment** *n* Aufgabe *f*, Auftrag *m*

assimilate [əˈsɪmɪleɪt] *vt* sich aneignen, aufnehmen

assist [əˈsɪst] *vt* beistehen +*dat*; **~ance** *n* Unterstützung *f*, Hilfe *f*; **~ant** *n* Assistent(in) *m(f)*, Mitarbeiter(in) *m(f)*; (*BRIT: also:* **shop ~ant**) Verkäufer(in) *m(f)*

associate [*n* əˈsəuʃɪt, *vb* əˈsəuʃɪeɪt] *n* (*partner*) Kollege *m*, Teilhaber *m*; (*member*) außerordentliche(s) Mitglied *nt* ♦ *vt* verbinden ♦ *vi* (*keep company*) verkehren; **association** [əsəusɪˈeɪʃən] *n* Verband *m*, Verein *m*; (*PSYCH*) Assoziation *f*; (*link*) Verbindung *f*

assorted [əˈsɔːtɪd] *adj* gemischt

assortment [əˈsɔːtmənt] *n* Sammlung *f*; (*COMM*): **~ (of)** Sortiment *nt* (von), Auswahl *f* (an +*dat*)

assume [əˈsjuːm] *vt* (*take for granted*) annehmen; (*power*) an sich nehmen, sich geben; **~d name** *n* Deckname *m*

assumption [əˈsʌmpʃən] *n* Annahme *f*

assurance [əˈʃuərəns] *n* (*firm statement*) Versicherung *f*; (*confidence*) Selbstsicherheit *f*; (*insurance*) (Lebens)versicherung *f*

assure [əˈʃuər] *vt* (*make sure*) sicherstel-

len; (*convince*) versichern +*dat*; (*life*) versichern

asterisk [ˈæstərɪsk] *n* Sternchen *nt*

asthma [ˈæsmə] *n* Asthma *nt*

astonish [əˈstɒnɪʃ] *vt* erstaunen; **~ment** *n* Erstaunen *nt*

astound [əˈstaund] *vt* verblüffen

astray [əˈstreɪ] *adv* in die Irre; auf Abwege; **to go ~** (*go wrong*) sich vertun; **to lead ~** irreführen

astride [əˈstraɪd] *adv* rittlings ♦ *prep* rittlings auf

astrologer [əsˈtrɒlədʒər] *n* Astrologe *m*, Astrologin *f*; **astrology** *n* Astrologie *f*

astronaut [ˈæstrənɔːt] *n* Astronaut(in) *m(f)*

astronomer [əsˈtrɒnəmər] *n* Astronom *m*

astronomical [æstrəˈnɒmɪkl] *adj* astronomisch; (*success*) riesig

astronomy [əsˈtrɒnəmɪ] *n* Astronomie *f*

astute [əsˈtjuːt] *adj* scharfsinnig; schlau, gerissen

asylum [əˈsaɪləm] *n* (*home*) Heim *nt*; (*refuge*) Asyl *nt*

KEYWORD

at [æt] *prep* **1** (*referring to position, direction*) an +*dat*, bei +*dat*; (*with place*) in +*dat*; **at the top** an der Spitze; **at home/school** zu Hause/in der Schule; **at the baker's** beim Bäcker; **to look at sth** auf etw *acc* blicken; **to throw sth at sb** etw nach jdm werfen

2 (*referring to time*): **at 4 o'clock** um 4 Uhr; **at night** bei Nacht; **at Christmas** zu Weihnachten; **at times** manchmal

3 (*referring to rates, speed etc*): **at £1 a kilo** zu £1 pro Kilo; **two at a time** zwei auf einmal; **at 50 km/h** mit 50 km/h

4 (*referring to manner*): **at a stroke** mit einem Schlag; **at peace** in Frieden

5 (*referring to activity*): **to be at work** bei der Arbeit sein; **to play at cow-

boys Cowboy spielen; **to be good at sth** gut in etw *dat* sein
6 (*referring to cause*): **shocked/ surprised/annoyed at sth** schockiert/überrascht/verärgert über etw *acc*; **I went at his suggestion** ich ging auf seinen Vorschlag hin

ate [eɪt] *pt of* eat

atheist ['eɪθɪɪst] *n* Atheist(in) *m(f)*

Athens ['æθɪnz] *n* Athen *nt*

athlete ['æθliːt] *n* Athlet *m*, Sportler *m*

athletic [æθ'lɛtɪk] *adj* sportlich, athletisch; **~s** *n* Leichtathletik *f*

Atlantic [at'læntɪk] *adj* atlantisch ♦ *n*: **the ~ (Ocean)** der Atlantik

atlas ['ætləs] *n* Atlas *m*

ATM *abbr* (= *automated teller machine*) Geldautomat *m*

atmosphere ['ætməsfɪər] *n* Atmosphäre *f*

atom ['ætəm] *n* Atom *nt*; (*fig*) bisschen *nt*; **~ic** [ə'tɒmɪk] *adj* atomar, Atom-; **~(ic) bomb** *n* Atombombe *f*

atomizer ['ætəmaɪzə] *n* Zerstäuber *m*

atone [ə'təun] *vi* sühnen; **to ~ for sth** etw sühnen

atrocious [ə'trəuʃəs] *adj* grässlich

atrocity [ə'trɒsɪtɪ] *n* Scheußlichkeit *f*; (*deed*) Gräueltat *f*

attach [ə'tætʃ] *vt* (*fasten*) befestigen; **to be ~ed to sb/sth** an jdm/etw hängen; **to ~ importance** *etc* **to sth** Wichtigkeit *etc* auf etw *acc* legen, einer Sache *dat* Wichtigkeit *etc* beimessen

attaché case [ə'tæʃeɪ] *n* Aktenkoffer *m*

attachment [ə'tætʃmənt] *n* (*tool*) Zubehörteil *nt*; (*love*): **~ (to sb)** Zuneigung *f* (zu jdm)

attack [ə'tæk] *vt* angreifen ♦ *n* Angriff *m*; (*MED*) Anfall *m*; **~er** *n* Angreifer(in) *m(f)*

attain [ə'teɪn] *vt* erreichen; **~ments** *npl* Kenntnisse *pl*

attempt [ə'tɛmpt] *n* Versuch *m* ♦ *vt* versuchen; **~ed murder** Mordversuch *m*

attend [ə'tɛnd] *vt* (*go to*) teilnehmen (an +*dat*); (*lectures*) besuchen; **to ~ to** (*needs*) nachkommen +*dat*; (*person*) sich kümmern um; **~ance** *n* (*presence*) Anwesenheit *f*; (*people present*) Besucherzahl *f*; **good ~ance** gute Teilnahme; **~ant** *n* (*companion*) Begleiter(in) *m(f)*; Gesellschafter(in) *m(f)*; (*in car park etc*) Wächter(in) *m(f)*; (*servant*) Bedienstete(r) *mf* ♦ *adj* begleitend; (*fig*) damit verbunden

attention [ə'tɛnʃən] *n* Aufmerksamkeit *f*; (*care*) Fürsorge *f*; (*for machine etc*) Pflege *f* ♦ *excl* (MIL) Achtung!; **for the ~ of ...** zu Händen (von) ...

attentive [ə'tɛntɪv] *adj* aufmerksam

attic ['ætɪk] *n* Dachstube *f*, Mansarde *f*

attitude ['ætɪtjuːd] *n* (*mental*) Einstellung *f*

attorney [ə'tɜːnɪ] *n* (*solicitor*) Rechtsanwalt *m*; **A~ General** *n* Justizminister *m*

attract [ə'trækt] *vt* anziehen; (*attention*) erregen; **~ion** *n* Anziehungskraft *f*; (*thing*) Attraktion *f*; **~ive** *adj* attraktiv

attribute [*n* 'ætrɪbjuːt, *vb* ə'trɪbjuːt] *n* Eigenschaft *f*, Attribut *nt* ♦ *vt* zuschreiben

attrition [ə'trɪʃən] *n*: **war of ~** Zermürbungskrieg *m*

aubergine ['əubəʒiːn] *n* Aubergine *f*

auburn ['ɔːbən] *adj* kastanienbraun

auction ['ɔːkʃən] *n* (*also*: **sale by ~**) Versteigerung *f*, Auktion *f* ♦ *vt* versteigern; **~eer** [ɔːkʃə'nɪər] *n* Versteigerer *m*

audacity [ɔː'dæsɪtɪ] *n* (*boldness*) Wagemut *m*; (*impudence*) Unverfrorenheit *f*

audible ['ɔːdɪbl] *adj* hörbar

audience ['ɔːdɪəns] *n* Zuhörer *pl*, Zuschauer *pl*; (*with queen*) Audienz *f*

audiotypist ['ɔːdɪəʊtaɪpɪst] *n* Phonotypistin *f*, Fonotypistin *f*

audiovisual ['ɔːdɪəʊ'vɪzjʊəl] *adj* audiovisuell

audit ['ɔːdɪt] *vt* prüfen

audition [ɔː'dɪʃən] *n* Probe *f*

auditor ['ɔːdɪtə'] *n* (*accountant*) Rech-

nungsprüfer(in) m(f), Buchprüfer m
auditorium [ɔːdɪ'tɔːrɪəm] n Zuschauerraum m
augment [ɔːg'ment] vt vermehren
augur ['ɔːgə'] vi bedeuten, voraussagen; **this ~s well** das ist ein gutes Omen
August ['ɔːgəst] n August m
aunt [aːnt] n Tante f; **~ie** n Tantchen nt; **~y** n = **auntie**
au pair ['əu'pεə'] n (also: ~ **girl**) Aupairmädchen nt, Au-pair-Mädchen nt
aura ['ɔːrə] n Nimbus m
auspicious [ɔːs'pɪʃəs] adj günstig; verheißungsvoll
austere [ɔs'tɪə'] adj streng; (room) nüchtern; **austerity** [ɔs'terɪtɪ] n Strenge f; (POL) wirtschaftliche Einschränkung f
Australia [ɔs'treɪlɪə] n Australien nt; **~n** adj australisch ♦ n Australier(in) m(f)
Austria ['ɔstrɪə] n Österreich nt; **~n** adj österreichisch ♦ n Österreicher(in) m(f)
authentic [ɔː'θentɪk] adj echt, authentisch
author ['ɔːθə'] n Autor m, Schriftsteller m; (beginner) Urheber m, Schöpfer m
authoritarian [ɔːθɒrɪ'tεərɪən] adj autoritär
authoritative [ɔː'θɒrɪtətɪv] adj (account) maßgeblich; (manner) herrisch
authority [ɔː'θɒrɪtɪ] n (power) Autorität f; (expert) Autorität f, Fachmann m; **the authorities** npl (ruling body) die Behörden pl
authorize ['ɔːθəraɪz] vt bevollmächtigen; (permit) genehmigen
auto ['ɔːtəu] (US) n Auto nt, Wagen m
autobiography [ɔːtəbaɪ'ɒgrəfɪ] n Autobiografie f
autograph ['ɔːtəgrɑːf] n (of celebrity) Autogramm nt ♦ vt mit Autogramm versehen
automatic [ɔːtə'mætɪk] adj automatisch ♦ n (gun) Selbstladepistole f; (car) Automatik m; **~ally** adv automatisch
automation [ɔːtə'meɪʃən] n Automati-

sierung f
automobile ['ɔːtəməbiːl] (US) n Auto(mobil) nt
autonomous [ɔː'tɒnəməs] adj autonom; **autonomy** n Autonomie f
autumn ['ɔːtəm] n Herbst m
auxiliary [ɔːg'zɪlɪərɪ] adj Hilfs-
Av. abbr = **avenue**
avail [ə'veɪl] vt: **to ~ o.s. of sth** sich einer Sache gen bedienen ♦ n: **to no ~** nutzlos
availability [əveɪlə'bɪlɪtɪ] n Erhältlichkeit f, Vorhandensein nt
available [ə'veɪləbl] adj erhältlich; zur Verfügung stehend; (person) erreichbar, abkömmlich
avalanche ['ævəlɑːnʃ] n Lawine f
Ave. abbr = **avenue**
avenge [ə'vendʒ] vt rächen, sühnen
avenue ['ævənjuː] n Allee f
average ['ævərɪdʒ] n Durchschnitt m ♦ adj durchschnittlich, Durchschnitts- ♦ vt (figures) den Durchschnitt nehmen von; (perform) durchschnittlich leisten; (in car etc) im Schnitt fahren; **on ~** durchschnittlich, im Durchschnitt; **~ out** vi: **to ~ out at** im Durchschnitt betragen
averse [ə'vɜːs] adj: **to be ~ to doing sth** eine Abneigung dagegen haben, etw zu tun
avert [ə'vɜːt] vt (turn away) abkehren; (prevent) abwehren
aviary ['eɪvɪərɪ] n Vogelhaus nt
aviation [eɪvɪ'eɪʃən] n Luftfahrt f, Flugwesen nt
avid ['ævɪd] adj: **~ (for)** gierig (auf +acc)
avocado [ævə'kɑːdəu] n (BRIT: also: ~ **pear**) Avocado(birne) f
avoid [ə'vɔɪd] vt vermeiden
await [ə'weɪt] vt erwarten, entgegensehen +dat
awake [ə'weɪk] (pt awoke, pp awoken or awaked) adj wach ♦ vt (auf)wecken ♦ vi aufwachen; **to be ~** wach sein; **~ning** n Erwachen nt
award [ə'wɔːd] n (prize) Preis m ♦ vt: **to**

~ (sb sth) (jdm etw) zuerkennen

aware [ə'wɛər] *adj* bewusst; **to be ~** sich bewusst sein; **~ness** *n* Bewusstsein *nt*

awash [ə'wɔʃ] *adj* überflutet

away [ə'weɪ] *adv* weg, fort; **two hours ~ by car** zwei Autostunden entfernt; **the holiday was two weeks ~** es war noch zwei Wochen bis zum Urlaub; **two kilometres ~** zwei Kilometer entfernt; **~ match** *n* (SPORT) Auswärtsspiel *nt*

awe [ɔː] *n* Ehrfurcht *f*; **~-inspiring** *adj* Ehrfurcht gebietend; **~some** *adj* Ehrfurcht gebietend

awful ['ɔːfəl] *adj* (*very bad*) furchtbar; **~ly** *adv* furchtbar, sehr

awhile [ə'waɪl] *adv* eine Weile

awkward ['ɔːkwəd] *adj* (*clumsy*) ungeschickt, linkisch; (*embarrassing*) peinlich

awning ['ɔːnɪŋ] *n* Markise *f*

awoke [ə'wəʊk] *pt of* **awake**; **~n** *pp of* **awake**

awry [ə'raɪ] *adv* schief; (*plans*) schief gehen

axe [æks] (*US* **ax**) *n* Axt *f*, Beil *nt* ♦ *vt* (*end suddenly*) streichen

axes¹ ['æksɪz] *npl of* **axe**

axes² ['æksiːz] *npl of* **axis**

axis ['æksɪs] (*pl* **axes**) *n* Achse *f*

axle ['æksl] *n* Achse *f*

ay(e) [aɪ] *excl* (*yes*) ja

azalea [ə'zeɪlɪə] *n* Azalee *f*

B, b

B [biː] *n* (MUS) H *nt*; **~ road** (BRIT) Landstraße *f*

B.A. *n abbr* = **Bachelor of Arts**

babble ['bæbl] *vi* schwätzen

baby ['beɪbɪ] *n* Baby *nt*; **~ carriage** (US) *n* Kinderwagen *m*; **~ food** *n* Babynahrung *f*; **~-sit** *vi* Kinder hüten, babysitten; **~-sitter** *n* Babysitter *m*; **~sitting** *n* Babysitten *nt*, Babysitting *nt*; **~ wipe**

n Ölpflegetuch *nt*

bachelor ['bætʃələr] *n* Junggeselle *m*; **B~ of Arts** Bakkalaureus *m* der philosophischen Fakultät; **B~ of Science** Bakkalaureus *m* der Naturwissenschaften

back [bæk] *n* (*of person, horse*) Rücken *m*; (*of house*) Rückseite *f*; (*of train*) Ende *nt*; (FOOTBALL) Verteidiger *m* ♦ *vt* (*support*) unterstützen; (*wager*) wetten auf +*acc*; (*car*) rückwärts fahren ♦ *vi* (*go ~wards*) rückwärts gehen *or* fahren ♦ *adj* hintere(r, s) ♦ *adv* zurück; (*to the rear*) nach hinten; **~ down** *vi* zurückstecken; **~ out** *vi* sich zurückziehen; (*inf*) kneifen; **~ up** *vt* (*support*) unterstützen; (*car*) zurücksetzen; (COMPUT) eine Sicherungskopie machen von; **~ache** *n* Rückenschmerzen *pl*; **~bencher** (BRIT) *n* Parlamentarier(in) *m(f)*; **~bone** *n* Rückgrat *nt*; (*support*) Rückhalt *m*; **~cloth** *n* Hintergrund *m*; **~date** *vt* rückdatieren; **~drop** *n* = **backcloth**; (*~ground*) Hintergrund *m*; **~fire** *vi* (*plan*) fehlschlagen; (TECH) fehlzünden; **~ground** *n* Hintergrund *m*; (*person's education*) Vorbildung *f*; **~ family ~ground** Familienverhältnisse *pl*; **~hand** *n* (TENNIS: *also:* **~hand stroke**) Rückhand *f*; **~hander** (BRIT) *n* (*bribe*) Schmiergeld *nt*; **~ing** *n* (*support*) Unterstützung *f*; **~lash** *n* (*fig*) Gegenschlag *m*; **~log** *n* (*of work*) Rückstand *m*; **~ number** *n* (PRESS) alte Nummer *f*; **~pack** *n* Rucksack *m*; **~packer** *n* Rucksacktourist(in) *m(f)*; **~ pain** *n* Rückenschmerzen *pl*; **~ pay** *n* (Gehalts- *or* Lohn)nachzahlung *f*; **~ payments** *npl* Zahlungsrückstände *pl*; **~ seat** *n* (AUT) Rücksitz *m*; **~side** (*inf*) *n* Hintern *m*; **~stage** *adv* hinter den Kulissen; **~stroke** *n* Rückenschwimmen *nt*; **~up** *adj* (COMPUT) Sicherungs- ♦ *n* (COMPUT) Sicherungskopie *f*; **~ward** *adj* (*less developed*) zurückgeblieben; (*primitive*) rückständig; **~wards** *adv* rückwärts; ~**water** n (fig) Kaff nt; ~**yard** n Hinterhof m

bacon ['beɪkən] n Schinkenspeck m

bacteria [bæk'tɪərɪə] npl Bakterien pl

bad [bæd] adj schlecht, schlimm; **to go** ~ schlecht werden

bade [bæd] pt of **bid**

badge [bædʒ] n Abzeichen nt

badger ['bædʒəʳ] n Dachs m

badly ['bædlɪ] adv schlecht, schlimm; ~ **wounded** schwer verwundet; **he needs it** ~ er braucht es dringend; **to be** ~ **off (for money)** dringend Geld nötig haben

badminton ['bædmɪntən] n Federball m, Badminton nt

bad-tempered ['bæd'tempəd] adj schlecht gelaunt

baffle ['bæfl] vt (puzzle) verblüffen

bag [bæg] n (sack) Beutel m; (paper) Tüte f; (handbag) Tasche f; (suitcase) Koffer m; (inf: old woman) alte Schachtel f ♦ vt (put in sack) in einen Sack stecken; (hunting) erlegen; ~**s of** (inf: lots of) eine Menge +acc; ~**gage** ['bægɪdʒ] n Gepäck nt; ~ **allowance** n Freigepäck nt; ~ **reclaim** n Gepäckausgabe f; ~**gy** ['bægɪ] adj bauschig, sackartig

bagpipes ['bægpaɪps] npl Dudelsack m

bail [beɪl] n (money) Kaution f ♦ vt (prisoner: usu. grant: ~) gegen Kaution freilassen; (boat: also: ~ **out**) ausschöpfen; (on ~ (prisoner) gegen Kaution freigelassen; **to** ~ **sb out** die Kaution für jdn stellen; see also **bale**

bailiff ['beɪlɪf] n Gerichtsvollzieher(in) m(f)

bait [beɪt] n Köder m ♦ vt mit einem Köder versehen; (fig) ködern

bake [beɪk] vt, vi backen; ~**d beans** npl gebackene Bohnen pl; ~**d potatoes** npl in der Schale gebackene Kartoffeln pl; ~**r** n Bäcker m; ~**ry** n Bäckerei f; **baking** n Backen nt; **baking powder** n Backpulver nt

balance ['bæləns] n (scales) Waage f; (equilibrium) Gleichgewicht nt; (FIN: state of account) Bilanz f; (difference) Bilanz f; (amount remaining) Restbetrag m ♦ vt (weigh) wägen; (make equal) ausgleichen; ~ **of trade/payments** Handels-/Zahlungsbilanz f; ~**d** adj ausgeglichen; ~ **sheet** n Bilanz f, Rechnungsabschluss m

balcony ['bælkənɪ] n Balkon m

bald [bɔːld] adj kahl; (statement) knapp

bale [beɪl] n Ballen m; **bale out** vi (from a plane) abspringen

ball [bɔːl] n Ball m; ~ **bearing** n Kugellager nt

ballet ['bæleɪ] n Ballett nt; ~ **dancer** n Balletttänzer(in) m(f); ~ **shoe** n Ballettschuh m

balloon [bə'luːn] n (Luft)ballon m

ballot ['bælət] n (geheime) Abstimmung f

ballpoint (pen) ['bɔːlpɔɪnt-] n Kugelschreiber m

ballroom ['bɔːlrum] n Tanzsaal m

Baltic ['bɔːltɪk] n: **the** ~ **(Sea)** die Ostsee

bamboo [bæm'buː] n Bambus m

ban [bæn] n Verbot nt ♦ vt verbieten

banana [bə'nɑːnə] n Banane f

band [bænd] n Band nt; (group) Gruppe f; (of criminals) Bande f; (MUS) Kapelle f, Band f; ~ **together** vi sich zusammentun

bandage ['bændɪdʒ] n Verband m; (elastic) Bandage f ♦ vt (cut) verbinden; (broken limb) bandagieren

Bandaid ['bændeɪd] (® US) n Heftpflaster nt

bandit ['bændɪt] n Bandit m, Räuber m

bandwagon ['bændwægən] n: **to jump on the** ~ (fig) auf den fahrenden Zug aufspringen

bandy ['bændɪ] vt wechseln; ~-**legged** adj o-beinig, O-beinig

bang [bæŋ] n (explosion) Knall m; (blow) Hieb m ♦ vt, vi knallen

Bangladesh [bæŋglə'deʃ] n Bangladesch nt

bangle ['bæŋgl] *n* Armspange *f*

bangs [bæŋz] *(US)* npl *(fringe)* Pony *m*

banish ['bænɪʃ] *vt* verbannen

banister(s) ['bænɪstə(z)] *n(pl)* (Treppen)geländer *nt*

bank [bæŋk] *n (raised ground)* Erdwall *m; (of lake etc)* Ufer *nt, (FIN)* Bank *f* ♦ *vt (tilt: AVIAT)* in die Kurve bringen; *(money)* einzahlen; **~ on** *vt fus:* **to ~ on sth** mit etw rechnen; **~ account** *n* Bankkonto *nt;* **~ card** *n* Scheckkarte *f;* **~er** *n* Bankier *m;* **~er's card** *(BRIT) n =* **bank card;** **B~ holiday** *(BRIT) n* gesetzliche(r) Feiertag *m;* **~ing** *n* Bankwesen *nt;* **~note** *n* Banknote *f;* **~ rate** *n* Banksatz *m*

---

bank holiday

Als **bank holiday** wird in Großbritannien ein gesetzlicher Feiertag bezeichnet, an dem die Banken geschlossen sind. Die meisten dieser Feiertage, abgesehen von Weihnachten und Ostern, fallen auf Montage im Mai und August. An diesen langen Wochenenden (bank holiday weekends) fahren viele Briten in Urlaub, so dass dann auf den Straßen, Flughäfen und bei der Bahn sehr viel Betrieb ist.

---

bankrupt ['bæŋkrʌpt] *adj:* **to be ~** bankrott sein; **to go ~** Bankrott machen; **~cy** *n* Bankrott *m*

bank statement *n* Kontoauszug *m*

banned [bænd] *adj:* **he was ~ from driving** *(BRIT)* ihm wurde Fahrverbot erteilt

banner ['bænə] *n* Banner *nt*

banns [bænz] *npl* Aufgebot *nt*

baptism ['bæptɪzəm] *n* Taufe *f*

baptize [bæp'taɪz] *vt* taufen

bar [baː] *n (rod)* Stange *f; (obstacle)* Hindernis *nt; (of chocolate)* Tafel *f; (of soap)* Stück *nt; (for drink, food)* Buffet *nt,* Bar *f; (pub)* Wirtschaft *f; (MUS)* Takt(strich) *m* ♦ *vt (fasten)* verriegeln; *(hinder)* versperren; *(exclude)* ausschlie-

ßen; **behind ~s** hinter Gittern; **the B~:** **to be called to the B~** als Anwalt zugelassen werden; **~ none** ohne Ausnahme

barbaric [baː'bærɪk] *adj* primitiv, unkultiviert

barbecue ['baːbɪkjuː] *n* Barbecue *nt*

barbed wire ['baːbd-] *n* Stacheldraht *m*

barber ['baːbə] *n* Herrenfriseur *m*

bar code *n (COMM)* Registrierkode *f*

bare [bɛə] *adj* nackt; *(trees, country)* kahl; *(mere)* bloß ♦ *vt* entblößen; **~back** *adv* ungesattelt; **~faced** *adj* unverfroren; **~foot** *adj, adv* barfuß; **~ly** *adv* kaum, knapp

bargain ['baːgɪn] *n (sth cheap)* günstiger Kauf; *(agreement: written)* Kaufvertrag *m; (: oral)* Geschäft *nt;* **into the ~** obendrein; **~ for** *vt:* **he got more than he ~ed for** er erlebte sein blaues Wunder

barge [baːdʒ] *n* Lastkahn *m;* **~ in** *vi* hereinplatzen; **~ into** *vt* rennen gegen

bark [baːk] *n (of tree)* Rinde *f; (of dog)* Bellen *nt* ♦ *vi (dog)* bellen

barley ['baːlɪ] *n* Gerste *f;* **~ sugar** *n* Malzbonbon *nt*

bar: **~maid** *n* Bardame *f;* **~man** *(irreg) n* Barkellner *m;* **~ meal** *n* einfaches Essen *nt* in einem Pub

barn [baːn] *n* Scheune *f*

barometer [bə'rɔmɪtə] *n* Barometer *nt*

baron ['bærən] *n* Baron *m;* **~ess** *n* Baronin *f*

barracks ['bærəks] *npl* Kaserne *f*

barrage ['bæraːʒ] *n (gunfire)* Sperrfeuer *nt; (dam)* Staudamm *m;* Talsperre *f*

barrel ['bærəl] *n* Fass *nt; (of gun)* Lauf *m*

barren ['bærən] *adj* unfruchtbar

barricade [bærɪ'keɪd] *n* Barrikade *f* ♦ *vt* verbarrikadieren

barrier ['bærɪə] *n (obstruction)* Hindernis *nt; (fence)* Schranke *f*

barring ['baːrɪŋ] *prep* außer im Falle +gen

barrister ['bærɪstə] *(BRIT) n* Rechtsanwalt m

barrow ['bærəu] n (cart) Schubkarren m

bartender ['bɑ:tendər] n (US) Barmann or -kellner m

barter ['bɑ:tər] vt handeln

base [beɪs] n (bottom) Boden m, Basis f; (MIL) Stützpunkt ♦ vt gründen; (opinion, theory): **to be ~d on** basieren auf +dat ♦ adj (low) gemein; **I'm ~d in London** ich wohne in London; **~ball** ['beɪsbɔːl] n Baseball m; **~ment** ['beɪsmənt] n Kellergeschoss nt

bases¹ ['beɪsɪz] npl of **base**

bases² ['beɪsiːz] npl of **basis**

bash [bæʃ] (inf) vt (heftig) schlagen

bashful ['bæʃful] adj schüchtern

basic ['beɪsɪk] adj grundlegend; **~s** npl: **the ~s** das Wesentliche sg; **~ally** adv im Grunde

basil ['bæzl] n Basilikum nt

basin ['beɪsn] n (dish) Schüssel f; (for washing, also valley) Becken nt; (dock) (Trocken)becken nt

basis ['beɪsɪs] n (pl **bases**) n Basis f, Grundlage f

bask [bɑːsk] vi: **to ~ in the sun** sich sonnen

basket ['bɑːskɪt] n Korb m; **~ball** n Basketball m

bass [beɪs] n (MUS, also instrument) Bass m; (voice) Bassstimme f; **~ drum** n große Trommel

bassoon [bə'suːn] n Fagott nt

bastard ['bɑːstəd] n Bastard m; (inf!) Arschloch nt (!)

bat [bæt] n (SPORT) Schlagholz nt; Schläger m; (ZOOL) Fledermaus f ♦ vt: **he didn't ~ an eyelid** er hat nicht mit der Wimper gezuckt

batch [bætʃ] n (of letters) Stoß m; (of samples) Satz m

bated ['beɪtɪd] adj: **with ~ breath** mit angehaltenem Atem

bath [bɑːθ] n Bad nt; (~ tub) Badewanne f ♦ vt baden; **to have a ~** baden; see also **baths**

bathe [beɪð] vt, vi baden; **~r** n Badende(r) f(m)

bathing ['beɪðɪŋ] n Baden nt; **~ cap** n Badekappe f; **~ costume** n Badeanzug m; **~ suit** (US) n Badeanzug m; **~ trunks** npl Badehose f

bath: **~robe** n Bademantel m; **~room** n Bad(ezimmer nt) nt; **~s** npl (Schwimm)bad nt; **~ towel** n Badetuch nt

baton ['bætən] n (of police) Gummiknüppel m; (MUS) Taktstock m

batter ['bætər] vt verprügeln ♦ n Schlagteig m; (for cake) Biskuitteig m; **~ed** adj (hat, pan) verbeult

battery ['bætərɪ] n (ELEC) Batterie f; (MIL) Geschützbatterie f

battery farming n (Hühneretc)batterien pl

battle ['bætl] n Schlacht f; (small) Gefecht m ♦ vi kämpfen; **~field** n Schlachtfeld nt; **~ship** n Schlachtschiff nt

Bavaria [bə'veərɪə] n Bayern nt; **~n** adj bay(e)risch ♦ n (person) Bayer(in) m(f)

bawdy ['bɔːdɪ] adj unflätig

bawl [bɔːl] vi brüllen

bay [beɪ] n (of sea) Bucht f ♦ vi bellen; **to keep at ~** unter Kontrolle halten; **~ window** n Erkerfenster nt

bazaar [bə'zɑː] n Basar m

B. & B. abbr = **bed and breakfast**

BBC n abbr (= British Broadcasting Corporation) BBC f or m

B.C. adv abbr (= before Christ) v. Chr.

KEYWORD

be [biː] (pt **was**, **were**, pp **been**) aux vb **1** (with present participle: forming continuous tenses): **what are you doing?** was machst du (gerade)?; **it is raining** es regnet; **I've been waiting for you for hours** ich warte schon seit Stunden auf dich

2 (with pp: forming passives): **to be killed** getötet werden; **the thief was nowhere to be seen** der Dieb war nirgendwo zu sehen

3 (*in tag questions*): **it was fun, wasn't it?** es hat Spaß gemacht, nicht wahr?

4 (+*to* +*infin*): **the house is to be sold** das Haus soll verkauft werden; **he's not to open it** er darf es nicht öffnen

♦ *vb* +*complement* 1 (*usu*) sein; **I'm tired** ich bin müde; **I'm hot/cold** mir ist heiß/kalt; **I'm a doctor** ich bin Arzt; **2 and 2 are 4** 2 und 2 ist *or* sind 4; **she's tall/pretty** sie ist groß/hübsch; **be careful/quiet** sei vorsichtig/ruhig

2 (*of health*): **how are you?** wie geht es dir?; **he's very ill** er ist sehr krank; **I'm fine now** jetzt geht es mir gut

3 (*of age*): **how old are you?** wie alt bist du?; **I'm sixteen (years old)** ich bin sechzehn (Jahre alt)

4 (*cost*): **how much was the meal?** was *or* wie viel hat das Essen gekostet?; **that'll be £5.75, please** das macht £5.75, bitte

♦ *vi* 1 (*exist, occur etc*) sein; **is there a God?** gibt es einen Gott?; **be that as it may** wie dem auch sei; **so be it** also gut

2 (*referring to place*) sein; **I won't be here tomorrow** iche werde morgen nicht hier sein

3 (*referring to movement*): **where have you been?** wo bist du gewesen?; **I've been in the garden** ich war im Garten

♦ *impers vb* 1 (*referring to time, distance, weather*) sein; **it's 5 o'clock** es ist 5 Uhr; **it's 10 km to the village** es sind 10 km bis zum Dorf; **it's too hot/cold** es ist zu heiß/kalt

2 (*emphatic*): **it's me** ich bins; **it's the postman** es ist der Briefträger

beach [biːtʃ] *n* Strand *m* ♦ *vt* (*ship*) auf den Strand setzen

beacon ['biːkən] *n* (*signal*) Leuchtfeuer *nt*; (*traffic ~*) Bake *f*

bead [biːd] *n* Perle *f*; (*drop*) Tropfen *m*

beak [biːk] *n* Schnabel *m*

beaker ['biːkər] *n* Becher *m*

beam [biːm] *n* (*of wood*) Balken *m*; (*of light*) Strahl *m*; (*smile*) strahlende(s) Lächeln *nt* ♦ *vi* strahlen

bean [biːn] *n* Bohne *f*; (*also:* **baked ~s**) gebackene Bohnen *pl*; **~ sprouts** *npl* Sojasprossen *pl*

bear [beər] (*pt* bore, *pp* borne) *n* Bär *m* ♦ *vt* (*weight, crops*) tragen; (*tolerate*) ertragen; (*young*) gebären ♦ *vi*: **to ~ right/left** sich rechts/links halten; **~ out** *vt* (*suspicions etc*) bestätigen; **~ up** *vi* sich halten

beard [biəd] *n* Bart *m*; **~ed** *adj* bärtig

bearer ['beərər] *n* Träger *m*

bearing ['beəriŋ] *n* (*posture*) Haltung *f*; (*relevance*) Relevanz *f*; (*relation*) Bedeutung *f*; (*TECH*) Kugellager *nt*; **~s** *npl* (*direction*) Orientierung *f*; (*also:* **ball ~s**) (Kugel)lager *nt*

beast [biːst] *n* Tier *nt*, Vieh *nt*; (*person*) Biest *nt*

beat [biːt] (*pt* beat, *pp* beaten) *n* (*stroke*) Schlag *m*; (*pulsation*) (Herz)schlag *m*; (*police round*) Runde *f*; Revier *nt*; (*MUS*) Takt *m*; Beat *m* ♦ *vt, vi* schlagen; **to ~ it** abhauen; (*off*) **the ~en track** abgelegen; **~ off** *vt* abschlagen; **~ up** *vt* zusammenschlagen; **~en up** *pp* of beat; **~ing** *n* Prügel *pl*

beautiful ['bjuːtiful] *adj* schön; **~ly** *adv* ausgezeichnet

beauty ['bjuːtɪ] *n* Schönheit *f*; **~ salon** *n* Schönheitssalon *m*; **~ spot** *n* Schönheitsfleck *m*; (*BRIT: TOURISM*) (besonders) schöne(r) Ort *m*

beaver ['biːvər] *n* Biber *m*

became [bɪ'keɪm] *pt* of become

because [bɪ'kɔz] *conj* weil ♦ *prep*: **~ of** wegen +*gen*, wegen +*dat* (*inf*)

beck [bek] *n*: **to be at the ~ and call of sb** nach jds Pfeife tanzen

beckon ['bekən] *vt, vi*: **to ~ to sb** jdm ein Zeichen geben

become [bɪ'kʌm] (*irreg: like* come) *vi* werden ♦ *vt* werden; (*clothes*) stehen +*dat*

becoming 333 believe

becoming [bɪˈkʌmɪŋ] adj (suitable) schicklich; (clothes) kleidsam

bed [bed] n Bett nt; (of river) Flussbett nt; (foundation) Schicht f; (in garden) Beet nt; **to go to ~** zu Bett gehen; **~ and breakfast** n Übernachtung f mit Frühstück; **~clothes** npl Bettwäsche f; **~ding** n Bettzeug nt

Bed and Breakfast

Bed and Breakfast bedeutet „Übernachtung mit Frühstück", wobei sich dies in Großbritannien nicht auf Hotels, sondern auf kleinere Pensionen, Privathäuser und Bauernhöfe bezieht, wo man wesentlich preisgünstiger übernachten kann als in Hotels. Oft wird für Bed and Breakfast, auch B & B genannt, durch ein entsprechendes Schild im Garten oder an der Einfahrt geworben.

bedlam [ˈbedləm] n (uproar) tolle(s) Durcheinander nt

bed linen n Bettwäsche f

bedraggled [bɪˈdrægld] adj ramponiert

bed: **~ridden** adj bettlägerig; **~room** n Schlafzimmer nt; **~side** n: **at the ~side** am Bett; **~sit(ter)** (BRIT) n Einzimmerwohnung f, möblierte(s) Zimmer nt; **~spread** n Tagesdecke f; **~time** n Schlafenszeit f

bee [biː] n Biene f

beech [biːtʃ] n Buche f

beef [biːf] n Rindfleisch nt; **roast ~** Roastbeef nt; **~burger** n Hamburger m

beehive [ˈbiːhaɪv] n Bienenstock m

beeline [ˈbiːlaɪn] n: **to make a ~ for** schnurstracks zugehen auf +acc

been [biːn] pp of be

beer [bɪəʳ] n Bier nt

beet [biːt] n (vegetable) Rübe f; (US: also: **red ~**) Rote Bete for Rübe f

beetle [ˈbiːtl] n Käfer m

beetroot [ˈbiːtruːt] (BRIT) n Rote Bete f

before [bɪˈfɔːʳ] prep vor ♦ conj bevor ♦ adv (of time) zuvor; früher; **the week**

~ die Woche zuvor or vorher; **I've done it ~** das hab ich schon mal getan; ~ **going** bevor er/sie etc geht/ ging; ~ **she goes** bevor sie geht; **~hand** adv im Voraus

beg [beg] vt, vi (implore) dringend bitten; (alms) betteln

began [bɪˈgæn] pt of begin

beggar [ˈbegəʳ] n Bettler(in) m(f)

begin [bɪˈgɪn] (pt began, pp begun) vt, vi anfangen, beginnen; (found) gründen; to ~ **doing** or **to do sth** anfangen or beginnen, etw zu tun; **to ~ with** zunächst (einmal); **~ner** n Anfänger m; **~ning** n Anfang m

begun [bɪˈgʌn] pp of begin

behalf [bɪˈhɑːf] n: **on ~ of** im Namen +gen; **on my ~** für mich

behave [bɪˈheɪv] vi sich benehmen; **behaviour** [bɪˈheɪvjəʳ] (US behavior) n Benehmen nt

beheld [bɪˈheld] pt, pp of behold

behind [bɪˈhaɪnd] prep hinter ♦ adv (late) im Rückstand; (in the rear) hinten ♦ n (inf) Hinterteil nt; **the ~ scenes** (fig) hinter den Kulissen

behold [bɪˈhəʊld] (irreg: like hold) vt erblicken

beige [beɪʒ] adj beige

Beijing [ˈbeɪˈdʒɪŋ] n Peking nt

being [ˈbiːɪŋ] n (existence) (Da)sein nt; (person) Wesen nt; **to come into ~** entstehen

Belarus [belaˈruːs] n Weißrussland nt

belated [bɪˈleɪtɪd] adj verspätet

belch [beltʃ] vi rülpsen ♦ vt (smoke) ausspeien

belfry [ˈbelfrɪ] n Glockenturm m

Belgian [ˈbeldʒən] adj belgisch ♦ n Belgier(in) m(f)

Belgium [ˈbeldʒəm] n Belgien nt

belie [bɪˈlaɪ] vt Lügen strafen +acc

belief [bɪˈliːf] n Glaube m; (conviction) Überzeugung f; **~ in sb/sth** Glaube an jdn/etw

believe [bɪˈliːv] vt glauben +dat; (think) glauben, meinen, denken ♦ vi (have faith) glauben; **to ~ in** sth an etw acc glauben; **~r** n Gläubige(r) f(m)

belittle [bɪ'lɪtl] vt herabsetzen

bell [bel] n Glocke f

belligerent [bɪ'lɪdʒərənt] adj (person) streitsüchtig; (country) Krieg führend

bellow ['beləu] vt, vi brüllen

bellows ['beləuz] npl (TECH) Gebläse nt; (for fire) Blasebalg m

belly ['belɪ] n Bauch m

belong [bɪ'lɒŋ] vi gehören; **to ~ to** sb jdm gehören; **to ~ to a club** etc einem Klub etc angehören; **~ings** npl Habe f

beloved [bɪ'lʌvɪd] adj innig geliebt ♦ n Geliebte(r) f(m)

below [bɪ'ləu] prep unter ♦ adv unten

belt [belt] n (band) Riemen m; (round waist) Gürtel m ♦ vt (fasten) mit Riemen befestigen; (inf: beat) schlagen; **~way** (US) n (AUT: ring road) Umgehungsstraße f

bemused [bɪ'mju:zd] adj verwirrt

bench [bentʃ] n (seat) Bank f; (workshop) Werkbank f; (judge's seat) Richterbank f; (judges) Richter pl

bend [bend] (pt, pp bent) vt (curve) biegen; (stoop) beugen ♦ vi sich biegen; sich beugen ♦ n Biegung f; (BRIT: in road) Kurve f; **~ down** or **over** vi sich bücken

beneath [bɪ'ni:θ] prep unter ♦ adv darunter

benefactor ['benɪfæktə*] n Wohltäter(in) m(f)

beneficial [benɪ'fɪʃəl] adj vorteilhaft; (to health) heilsam

benefit ['benɪfɪt] n (advantage) Nutzen m ♦ vt fördern ♦ vi: **to ~ (from)** Nutzen ziehen (aus)

Benelux ['benɪlʌks] n Beneluxstaaten pl

benevolent [bɪ'nevələnt] adj wohlwollend

benign [bɪ'naɪn] adj (person) gütig; (climate) mild

bent [bent] pt, pp of **bend** ♦ n (inclination) Neigung f ♦ adj (inf: dishonest)

unehrlich; **to be ~ on** versessen sein auf +acc

bequest [bɪ'kwest] n Vermächtnis nt

bereaved [bɪ'ri:vd] npl: **the ~** die Hinterbliebenen pl

beret ['bereɪ] n Baskenmütze f

Berlin [bə:'lɪn] n Berlin nt

berm [bə:m] (US) n (AUT) Seitenstreifen m

berry ['berɪ] n Beere f

berserk [bə'sə:k] adj: **to go ~** wild werden

berth [bə:θ] n (for ship) Ankerplatz m; (in ship) Koje f; (in train) Bett nt ♦ vt am Kai festmachen ♦ vi anlegen

beseech [bɪ'si:tʃ] (pt, pp besought) vt anflehen

beset [bɪ'set] (pt, pp beset) vt bedrängen

beside [bɪ'saɪd] prep neben, bei; (except) außer; **to be ~ o.s. (with)** außer sich sein (vor +dat); **that's ~ the point** das tut nichts zur Sache

besides [bɪ'saɪdz] prep außer, neben ♦ adv außerdem

besiege [bɪ'si:dʒ] vt (MIL) belagern; (surround) umlagern, bedrängen

besought [bɪ'sɔ:t] pt, pp of **beseech**

best [best] adj best(e, r) s ♦ adv am besten; **the ~ part of** (quantity) das meiste +gen; **at ~** höchstens; **to make the ~ of it** das Beste daraus machen; **to do one's ~** sein Bestes tun; **to the ~ of my knowledge** meines Wissens; **to the ~ of my ability** so gut ich kann; **for the ~** zum Besten; **~-before date** n Mindesthaltbarkeitsdatum nt; **~ man** n Trauzeuge m

bestow [bɪ'stəu] vt verleihen

bet [bet] (pt, pp bet or betted) n Wette f ♦ vt, vi wetten

betray [bɪ'treɪ] vt verraten

better ['betə*] adj, adv besser ♦ vt verbessern ♦ n: **to get the ~ of** sb jdn überwinden; **he thought ~ of it** er hat sich eines Besseren besonnen; **you had ~ leave** Sie gehen jetzt wohl besser; **to get ~** (MED) gesund werden; **~ off** adj (richer) wohlhabender

betting ['betɪŋ] n Wetten nt; **~ shop** (BRIT) n Wettbüro nt

between [bɪ'twiːn] prep zwischen; (among) unter ♦ adv dazwischen

beverage ['bevərɪdʒ] n Getränk nt

bevy ['bevɪ] n Schar f

beware [bɪ'weəʳ] vt, vi sich hüten vor +dat; **"~ of the dog"** „Vorsicht, bissiger Hund!"

bewildered [bɪ'wɪldəd] adj verwirrt

beyond [bɪ'jɒnd] prep (place) jenseits +gen; (time) über ... hinaus; (out of reach) außerhalb +gen ♦ adv darüber hinaus; **~ doubt** ohne Zweifel; **~ repair** nicht mehr zu reparieren

bias ['baɪəs] n (slant) Neigung f; (prejudice) Vorurteil nt; **~(s)ed** adj voreingenommen

bib [bɪb] n Latz m

Bible ['baɪbl] n Bibel f

bicarbonate of soda [baɪ'kɑːbənɪt-] n Natron nt

bicker ['bɪkəʳ] vi zanken

bicycle ['baɪsɪkl] n Fahrrad nt

bid [bɪd] (pt **bade** or **bid**, pp **bid(den)**) n (offer) Gebot nt; (attempt) Versuch m ♦ vt, vi (offer) bieten; **to ~ farewell** Lebewohl sagen; **~der** n (person) Steigerer m; **the highest ~der** der Meistbietende; **~ding** n (command) Geheiß nt

bide [baɪd] vt: **to ~ one's time** abwarten

bifocals [baɪ'fəʊklz] npl Bifokalbrille f

big [bɪg] adj groß; **~ dipper** [-'dɪpəʳ] n Achterbahn f; **~headed** ['bɪg'hedɪd] adj eingebildet

bigot ['bɪgət] n Frömmler m; **~ed** adj bigott; **~ry** n Bigotterie f

big top n Zirkuszelt nt

bike [baɪk] n Rad nt

bikini [bɪ'kiːnɪ] n Bikini m

bile [baɪl] n (BIOL) Galle f

bilingual [baɪ'lɪŋgwəl] adj zweisprachig

bill [bɪl] n (account) Rechnung f; (POL) Gesetzentwurf m; (US: FIN) Geldschein m; **to fit** or **fill the ~** (fig) der/die/das Richtige sein; **"post no ~s"** „Plakate ankleben verboten"; **~board** ['bɪlbɔːd] n Reklameschild nt

billet ['bɪlɪt] n Quartier nt

billfold ['bɪlfəʊld] (US) n Geldscheintasche f

billiards ['bɪljədz] n Billard nt

billion ['bɪljən] n (BRIT) Billion f; (US) Milliarde f

bimbo ['bɪmbəʊ] (inf: pej) n Puppe f, Häschen n

bin [bɪn] n Kasten m; (dustbin) (Abfall)eimer m

bind [baɪnd] (pt, pp **bound**) vt (tie) binden; (tie together) zusammenbinden; (oblige) verpflichten; **~ing** n (Buch)einband m ♦ adj verbindlich

binge [bɪndʒ] (inf) n Sauferei f

bingo ['bɪŋgəʊ] n Bingo nt

binoculars [bɪ'nɒkjuləz] npl Fernglas nt

bio... [baɪəʊ] prefix: **~chemistry** n Biochemie f; **~degradable** adj biologisch abbaubar; **~graphy** n Biografie f; **~logical** [baɪə'lɒdʒɪkl] adj biologisch; **~logy** [baɪ'ɒlədʒɪ] n Biologie f

birch [bɜːtʃ] n Birke f

bird [bɜːd] n Vogel m; (BRIT: inf: girl) Mädchen nt; **~'s-eye view** n Vogelschau f; **~ watcher** n Vogelbeobachter(in) m(f); **~ watching** n Vogelbeobachten nt

Biro ['baɪərəʊ] ® n Kugelschreiber m

birth [bɜːθ] n Geburt f; **to give ~ to** zur Welt bringen; **~ certificate** n Geburtsurkunde f; **~ control** n Geburtenkontrolle f; **~day** n Geburtstag m; **~day card** n Geburtstagskarte f; **~place** n Geburtsort m; **~ rate** n Geburtenrate f

biscuit ['bɪskɪt] n Keks m

bisect [baɪ'sekt] vt halbieren

bishop ['bɪʃəp] n Bischof m

bit [bɪt] pt of **bite** ♦ n bisschen, Stückchen n; (horse's) Gebiss nt; (COMPUT) Bit nt; **a ~ tired** etwas müde

bitch 336 **blimey**

bitch [bɪtʃ] n (dog) Hündin f; (unpleasant woman) Weibsstück nt

bite [baɪt] (pt bit, pp bitten) vt, vi beißen ♦ n Biss m; (mouthful) Bissen m; **to ~ one's nails** Nägel kauen; **let's have a ~** to eat lass uns etwas essen

bitten ['bɪtn] pp of bite

bitter ['bɪtər] adj bitter; (memory etc) schmerzlich; (person) verbittert ♦ n (BRIT: beer) dunkle(s) Bier nt; **~ness** n Bitterkeit f

blab [blæb] vi klatschen ♦ vt (also: **~out**) ausplaudern

black [blæk] adj schwarz; (night) finster ♦ vt schwärzen; (shoes) wichsen; (eye) blau schlagen; (BRIT: INDUSTRY) boykottieren; **to give sb a ~ eye** jdm ein blaues Auge schlagen; **in the ~** (bank account) in den schwarzen Zahlen; **~ and blue** adj grün und blau; **~berry** n Brombeere f; **~bird** n Amsel f; **~board** n (Wand)tafel f; **~ coffee** n schwarze(r) Kaffee m; **~currant** n schwarze Johannisbeere f; **~en** vt schwärzen; (fig) verunglimpfen; **B~ Forest** n Schwarzwald m; **~ ice** n Glatteis nt; **~leg** (BRIT) n Streikbrecher(in) m(f); **~list** n schwarze Liste f; **~mail** n Erpressung f ♦ vt erpressen; **~ market** n Schwarzmarkt m; **~out** n Verdunkelung f; (MED): **to have a ~out** bewusstlos werden; (fig) Ohnmachtsanfall m; **~ pudding** n ≈ Blutwurst f; **B~ Sea** n: **the B~ Sea** das Schwarze Meer; **~ sheep** n schwarze(s) Schaf nt; **~smith** n Schmied m; **~ spot** n (AUT) Gefahrenstelle f; (for unemployment etc) schwer betroffene(s) Gebiet nt

bladder ['blædər] n Blase f

blade [bleɪd] n (of weapon) Klinge f; (of grass) Halm m; (of oar) Ruderblatt nt

blame [bleɪm] n Tadel m, Schuld f ♦ vt Vorwürfe machen +dat; **to ~ sb for sth** jdm die Schuld an etw dat geben; **he is to ~** er ist daran schuld

bland [blænd] adj mild

blank [blæŋk] adj leer, unbeschrieben; (look) verdutzt; (verse) Blank- ♦ n

(space) Lücke f; Zwischenraum m; (cartridge) Platzpatrone f; **~ cheque** n Blankoscheck m; (fig) Freibrief m

blanket ['blæŋkɪt] n (Woll)decke f

blare [blɛər] vi (radio) plärren; (horn) tuten; (MUS) schmettern

blasé ['blɑːzeɪ] adj blasiert

blast [blɑːst] n Explosion f; (of wind) Windstoß m ♦ vt (blow up) sprengen; **~!** (inf) verflixt!; **~off** n (SPACE) (Raketen)abschuss m

blatant ['bleɪtənt] adj offenkundig

blaze [bleɪz] n (fire) lodernde(s) Feuer nt ♦ vi lodern ♦ vt: **to ~ a trail** Bahn brechen

blazer ['bleɪzər] n Blazer m

bleach [bliːtʃ] n (also: household ~) Bleichmittel nt ♦ vt bleichen; **~ed** adj gebleicht

bleachers ['bliːtʃəz] (US) npl (SPORT) unüberdachte Tribüne f

bleak [bliːk] adj kahl, rau; (future) trostlos

bleary-eyed ['blɪərˈaɪd] adj triefäugig; (on waking up) mit verschlafenen Augen

bleat [bliːt] vi blöken; (fig: complain) meckern

bled [bled] pt, pp of bleed

bleed [bliːd] (pt, pp bled) vi bluten ♦ vt (draw blood) zur Ader lassen; **to ~ to death** verbluten

bleeper ['bliːpər] n (of doctor etc) Funkrufempfänger m

blemish ['blemɪʃ] n Makel m ♦ vt verunstalten

blend [blend] n Mischung f ♦ vt mischen ♦ vi sich mischen; **~er** n Mixer m, Mixgerät nt

bless [bles] (pt, pp blessed) vt segnen; (give thanks) preisen; (make happy) glücklich machen; **~ you!** Gesundheit!; **~ing** n Segen m; (at table) Tischgebet nt; (happiness) Wohltat f; Segen m; (good wish) Glück nt

blew [bluː] pt of blow

blimey ['blaɪmɪ] (BRIT: inf) excl verflucht

blind [blaɪnd] adj blind; (corner) unübersichtlich ♦ n (for window) Rouleau n ♦ vt blenden; ~ **alley** n Sackgasse f; ~**fold** n Augenbinde f ♦ adj, adv mit verbundenen Augen ♦ vt: to ~**fold sb** jdm die Augen verbinden; ~**ly** adv blind; (fig) blindlings; ~**ness** n Blindheit f; ~ **spot** n (AUT) tote(r) Winkel m; (fig) schwache(r) Punkt m

blink [blɪŋk] vi blinzeln; ~**ers** npl Scheuklappen pl

bliss [blɪs] n (Glück)seligkeit f

blister ['blɪstər] n Blase f ♦ vi Blasen werfen

blitz [blɪts] n Luftkrieg m

blizzard ['blɪzəd] n Schneesturm m

bloated ['bləʊtɪd] adj aufgedunsen; (inf: full) nudelsatt

blob [blɒb] n Klümpchen nt

bloc [blɒk] n (POL) Block m

block [blɒk] n (of wood) Block m, Klotz m; (of houses) Häuserblock m ♦ vt hemmen; ~**ade** [blɒ'keɪd] n Blockade f ♦ vt blockieren; ~**age** n Verstopfung f; ~**buster** n Knüller m; ~ **letters** npl Blockbuchstaben pl; ~ **of flats** (BRIT) n Häuserblock m

bloke [bləʊk] (BRIT: inf) n Kerl m, Typ m

blond(e) [blɒnd] adj blond ♦ n Blondine f

blood [blʌd] n Blut nt; ~ **donor** n Blutspender m; ~ **group** n Blutgruppe f; ~ **poisoning** n Blutvergiftung f; ~ **pressure** n Blutdruck m; ~**shed** n Blutvergießen nt; ~**shot** adj blutunterlaufen; ~ **sports** npl Jagdsport, Hahnenkampf etc; ~**stained** adj blutbefleckt; ~**stream** n Blut nt, Blutkreislauf m; ~ **test** n Blutprobe f; ~**thirsty** adj blutrünstig; ~ **vessel** n Blutgefäß nt; ~**y** adj blutig; (BRIT: inf) verdammt; ~**y-minded** (BRIT: inf) adj stur

bloom [bluːm] n Blüte f; (freshness) Glanz m ♦ vi blühen

blossom ['blɒsəm] n Blüte f ♦ vi blühen

blot [blɒt] n Klecks m ♦ vt beklecksen;

(ink) (ab)löschen; ~ **out** vt auslöschen

blotchy ['blɒtʃi] adj fleckig

blotting paper ['blɒtɪŋ-] n Löschpapier nt

blouse [blaʊz] n Bluse f

blow [bləʊ] (pt **blew**, pp **blown**) n Schlag m ♦ vt blasen ♦ vi (wind) wehen; **to ~ one's nose** sich dat die Nase putzen; ~ **away** vt wegblasen; ~ **down** vt umwehen; ~ **off** vt wegwehen ♦ vi wegfliegen; ~ **out** vi ausgehen; ~ **over** vi vorübergehen; ~ **up** vi explodieren ♦ vt sprengen; ~**dry** n: to **have a ~-dry** sich föhnen lassen ♦ vt föhnen; ~**lamp** (BRIT) n Lötlampe f; ~**n** pp of **blow**; ~**out** n (AUT) geplatzte(r) Reifen m; ~**torch** n = **blowlamp**

blue [bluː] adj blau; (inf: unhappy) niedergeschlagen; (obscene) pornografisch; (joke) anzüglich ♦ n: **out of the ~** (fig) aus heiterem Himmel; **to have the ~s** traurig sein; ~**bell** n Glockenblume f; ~**bottle** n Schmeißfliege f; ~**film** n Pornofilm m; ~**print** n (fig) Entwurf m

bluff [blʌf] vi bluffen, täuschen ♦ n (deception) Bluff m; **to call sb's ~** es darauf ankommen lassen

blunder ['blʌndər] n grobe(r) Fehler m, Schnitzer m ♦ vi einen groben Fehler machen

blunt [blʌnt] adj (knife) stumpf; (talk) unverblümt ♦ vt abstumpfen

blur [blɜː] n Fleck m ♦ vt verschwommen machen

blurb [blɜːb] n Waschzettel m

blush [blʌʃ] vi erröten

blustery ['blʌstəri] adj stürmisch

boar [bɔː] n Keiler m, Eber m

board [bɔːd] n (of wood) Brett nt; (of card) Pappe f; (committee) Ausschuss m; (of firm) Aufsichtsrat m; (SCH) Direktorium nt ♦ vt (train) einsteigen in +acc; (ship) an Bord gehen +gen; on ~ (AVIAT, NAUT) an Bord; ~ **and lodging** Unterkunft f und Verpflegung; **full/half ~** (BRIT) Voll-/Halbpension f; **to go by**

the ~ flachfallen, über Bord gehen; ~ **up** vt mit Brettern vernageln; **~er** n Kostgänger m; (SCH) Internatsschüler(in) m(f); ~ **game** n Brettspiel nt; **~ing card** n (AVIAT, NAUT) Bordkarte f; **~ing house** n Pension f; **~ing school** n Internat nt; **~ room** n Sitzungszimmer nt

boast [bəust] vi prahlen ♦ vt sich rühmen +gen ♦ n Großtuerei f; Prahlerei f; **to ~ about** or **of sth** mit etw prahlen

boat [bəut] n Boot nt; (ship) Schiff nt; **~er** n (hat) Kreissäge f = bosun; **~swain** [bəusn] n = bosun; **~ train** n Zug m mit Fährenanschluss

bob [bɔb] vi sich auf und nieder bewegen; **~ up** vi auftauchen

bobbin ['bɔbɪn] n Spule f

bobby ['bɔbɪ] (BRIT: inf) n Bobby m

bobsleigh ['bɔbsleɪ] n Bob m

bode [bəud] vi: **to ~ well/ill** ein gutes/schlechtes Zeichen sein

bodily ['bɔdɪlɪ] adj, adv körperlich

body ['bɔdɪ] n Körper m; (dead) Leiche f; (group) Mannschaft f; (AUT) Karosserie f; (trunk) Rumpf m; **~ building** n Bodybuilding nt; **~guard** n Leibwache f; **~work** n Karosserie f

bog [bɔg] n Sumpf m ♦ vt: **to get ~ged down** sich festfahren

boggle ['bɔgl] vi stutzen; **the mind ~s** es ist kaum auszumalen

bog-standard adj stinknormal (inf)

bogus ['bəugəs] adj unecht, Schein-

boil [bɔɪl] vt, vi kochen ♦ n (MED) Geschwür nt; **to come to the** (BRIT) or **a** (US) ~ zu kochen anfangen; **~ down to** (fig) hinauslaufen auf +acc; **~ over** vi überkochen; **~ed egg** n (weich) gekochtes Ei nt; **~ed potatoes** npl Salzkartoffeln pl; **~er** n Boiler m; **~er suit** (BRIT) n Arbeitsanzug m; **~ing point** n Siedepunkt m

boisterous ['bɔɪstərəs] adj ungestüm

bold [bəuld] adj (fearless) unerschrocken; (handwriting) fest und klar

bollard ['bɔləd] n (NAUT) Poller m; (BRIT: AUT) Pfosten m

bolt [bəult] n Bolzen m; (lock) Riegel m ♦ adv: **~ upright** kerzengerade ♦ vt verriegeln; (swallow) verschlingen ♦ vi (horse) durchgehen

bomb [bɔm] n Bombe f ♦ vt bombardieren; **~ard** [bɔm'baːd] vt bombardieren; **~ardment** [bɔm'baːdmənt] n Beschießung f; **~ disposal** n: **~ disposal unit** Bombenräumkommando nt; **~er** n Bomber m; (terrorist) Bombenattentäter(in) m(f); **~ing** n Bombenabwurf m; **~shell** n (fig) Bombe f

bona fide ['bəunə'faɪdɪ] adj echt

bond [bɔnd] n (link) Band nt; (FIN) Schuldverschreibung f

bondage ['bɔndɪdʒ] n Sklaverei f

bone [bəun] n Knochen m; (of fish) Gräte f; (piece of ~) Knochensplitter m ♦ vt die Knochen herausnehmen +dat; (fish) entgräten; **~ dry** adj (inf) knochentrocken; **~ idle** adj stinkfaul; **~ marrow** n (ANAT) Knochenmark nt

bonfire ['bɔnfaɪə] n Feuer nt im Freien

bonnet ['bɔnɪt] n Haube f; (for baby) Häubchen nt; (BRIT: AUT) Motorhaube f

bonus ['bəunəs] n Bonus m; (annual ~) Prämie f

bony ['bəunɪ] adj knochig, knochenähnlich

boo [buː] vt auspfeifen

booby trap ['buːbɪ-] n Falle f

book [buk] n Buch nt; (ticket etc) vorbestellen; (person) verwarnen; **~s** npl (COMM) Bücher pl; **~case** n Bücherregal nt, Bücherschrank m; **~ing office** n (RAIL) Fahrkartenschalter m; (THEAT) Vorverkaufsstelle f; **~keeping** n Buchhaltung f; **~let** n Broschüre f; **~maker** n Buchmacher m; **~seller** n Buchhändler m; **~shelf** n Bücherbord nt; **~shop** ['bukʃɔp], **~store** n Buchhandlung f

boom [buːm] n (noise) Dröhnen m; (busy period) Hochkonjunktur f ♦ vi dröhnen

boon [buːn] n Wohltat f, Segen m

boost [buːst] n Auftrieb m, (fig) Reklame f ♦ vt Auftrieb geben; **~er** n (MED) Wiederholungsimpfung f

boot [buːt] n Stiefel m; (BRIT: AUT) Kofferraum m ♦ vt (kick) einen Fußtritt geben; (COMPUT) laden; **to ~** (in addition) obendrein

booth [buːð] n (at fair) Bude f; (telephone ~) Zelle f; (voting ~) Kabine f

booze [buːz] (inf) n Alkohol m, Schnaps m ♦ vi saufen

border ['bɔːdə] n Grenze f; (edge) Kante f; (in garden) (Blumen)rabatte f ♦ adj Grenz-; **the B~s** Grenzregion zwischen England und Schottland; **~ on** vt grenzen an +acc; **~line** n Grenze f; **~line case** n Grenzfall m

bore [bɔː] pt of bear ♦ vt bohren; (weary) langweilen ♦ n (person) Langweiler m; (thing) langweilige Sache f; (of gun) Kaliber nt; **I am ~d** ich langweile mich; **~dom** n Langeweile f

boring ['bɔːrɪŋ] adj langweilig

born [bɔːn] adj: **to be ~** geboren werden

borne [bɔːn] pp of bear

borough ['bʌrə] n Stadt(gemeinde) f, Stadtbezirk m

borrow ['bɔrəʊ] vt borgen

Bosnia (and) Herzegovina ['bɒznɪə (ənd) hɜːtsəgəʊ'viːnə] n Bosnien und Herzegowina nt; **~n** n Bosnier(in) m(f) ♦ adj bosnisch

bosom ['bʊzəm] n Busen m

boss [bɒs] n Chef m, Boss m ♦ vt: **to ~ around** or about herumkommandieren; **~y** adj herrisch

bosun ['bəʊsn] n Bootsmann m

botany ['bɒtənɪ] n Botanik f

botch [bɒtʃ] vt (also: ~ up) verpfuschen

both [bəʊθ] adj beide(s) ♦ pron beide(s) ♦ adv: **~ X and Y** sowohl X wie or als auch Y; **~ (of) the books** beide Bücher; **~ of us went, we ~ went** wir gingen beide

bother ['bɒðə] vt (pester) quälen ♦ vi

(fuss) sich aufregen ♦ n Mühe f, Umstand m; **to ~ doing sth** sich die Mühe machen, etw zu tun; **what a ~!** wie ärgerlich!

bottle ['bɒtl] n Flasche f ♦ vt (in Flaschen) abfüllen; **~ up** vt aufstauen; **~ bank** n Altglascontainer m; **~d beer** n Flaschenbier nt; **~d water** n in Flaschen abgefülltes Wasser; **~neck** n (also fig) Engpass m; **~ opener** n Flaschenöffner m

bottom ['bɒtəm] n Boden m; (of person) Hintern m; (riverbed) Flussbett m ♦ adj unterste(r, s)

bough [baʊ] n Zweig m, Ast m

bought [bɔːt] pt, pp of buy

boulder ['bəʊldə] n Felsbrocken m

bounce [baʊns] vi (person) herumhüpfen; (ball) hochspringen; (cheque) platzen ♦ vt (auf)springen lassen ♦ n (rebound) Aufprall m; **~r** n Rausschmeißer m

bound [baʊnd] pt, pp of bind ♦ n Grenze f; (leap) Sprung m ♦ vi (spring, leap) (auf)springen ♦ adj (obliged) gebunden, verpflichtet; **out of ~s** Zutritt verboten; **to be ~ to do sth** verpflichtet sein, etw zu tun; **it's ~ to happen** es muss so kommen; **to be ~ for ...** nach ... fahren

boundary ['baʊndrɪ] n Grenze f

bouquet ['bʊkeɪ] n Strauß m; (of wine) Blume f

bourgeois ['bʊəʒwɑː] adj kleinbürgerlich, bourgeois ♦ n Spießbürger(in) m(f)

bout [baʊt] n (of illness) Anfall m; (of contest) Kampf m

bow¹ [bəʊ] n (ribbon) Schleife f; (weapon, MUS) Bogen m

bow² [baʊ] n (with head, body) Verbeugung f; (of ship) Bug m ♦ vi sich verbeugen; (submit): **to ~ to** sich beugen +dat

bowels ['baʊəlz] npl (ANAT) Darm m

bowl [bəʊl] n (basin) Schüssel f; (of pipe) (Pfeifen)kopf m; (wooden ball)

(Holz)kugel f ♦ vt, vi (die Kugel) rollen
bow-legged ['bəʊ'legɪd] adj o-beinig, O-beinig
bowler ['bəʊlə*] n Werfer m; (BRIT: also: ~ hat) Melone f
bowling ['bəʊlɪŋ] n Kegeln nt; ~ **alley** n Kegelbahn f; ~ **green** n Rasen m zum Bowlingspiel
bowls n (game) Bowlsspiel nt
bow tie [bəʊ-] n Fliege f
box [bɒks] n (also: **cardboard** ~) Schachtel f, (bigger) Kasten m, (THEAT) Loge f ♦ vt einpacken ♦ vi boxen; ~**er** n Boxer m; ~**er shorts** (BRIT) npl Boxershorts pl; ~**ing** n (SPORT) Boxen nt; **B~ing Day** (BRIT) n zweite(r) Weihnachtsfeiertag m; ~**ing gloves** npl Boxhandschuhe pl; ~**ing ring** n Boxring m; ~ **office** n (Theater)kasse f; ~**room** n Rumpelkammer f

---

Boxing Day

Boxing Day (26.12.) ist ein Feiertag in Großbritannien. Wenn Weihnachten auf ein Wochenende fällt, wird der Feiertag am nächsten darauf folgenden Wochentag nachgeholt. Der Name geht auf einen alten Brauch zurück; früher erhielten Händler und Lieferanten an diesem Tag ein Geschenk, die so genannte Christmas Box.

---

boy [bɔɪ] n Junge m
boycott ['bɔɪkɒt] n Boykott m ♦ vt boykottieren
boyfriend ['bɔɪfrend] n Freund m
boyish ['bɔɪɪʃ] adj jungenhaft
B.R. n abbr = **British Rail**
bra [brɑː] n BH m
brace [breɪs] n (TECH) Stütze f, (MED) Klammer f ♦ vt stützen; ~**s** npl (BRIT) Hosenträger pl; **to ~ o.s. for sth** (fig) sich auf etw acc gefasst machen
bracelet ['breɪslɪt] n Armband nt
bracing ['breɪsɪŋ] adj kräftigend
bracken ['brækən] n Farnkraut nt
bracket ['brækɪt] n Halter m, Klammer

f; (in punctuation) Klammer f; (group) Gruppe f ♦ vt einklammern; (fig) in dieselbe Gruppe einordnen
brag [bræg] vi sich rühmen
braid [breɪd] n (hair) Flechte f, (trim) Borte f
Braille [breɪl] n Blindenschrift f
brain [breɪn] n (ANAT) Gehirn nt; (intellect) Intelligenz f, Verstand m; (person) kluge(r) Kopf m; ~**s** npl (intelligence) Verstand m; ~**child** n Erfindung f; ~**wash** vt eine Gehirnwäsche vornehmen bei; ~**wave** n Geistesblitz m; ~**y** adj gescheit
braise [breɪz] vt schmoren
brake [breɪk] n Bremse f ♦ vt, vi bremsen; ~ **fluid** n Bremsflüssigkeit f; ~ **light** n Bremslicht nt
bramble ['bræmbl] n Brombeere f
bran [bræn] n Kleie f; (food) Frühstücksflocken pl
branch [brɑːntʃ] n Ast m; (division) Zweig m ♦ vi (also: ~ **out**: road) sich verzweigen
brand [brænd] n (COMM) Marke f, Sorte f; (on cattle) Brandmal nt ♦ vt brandmarken; (COMM) ein Warenzeichen geben +dat
brandish ['brændɪʃ] vt (drohend) schwingen
brand-new ['brænd'njuː] adj funkelnagelneu
brandy ['brændɪ] n Weinbrand m, Kognak m
brash [bræʃ] adj unverschämt
brass [brɑːs] n Messing nt; **the ~** (MUS) das Blech; ~ **band** n Blaskapelle f
brassière ['bræsɪə*] n Büstenhalter m
brat [bræt] n Gör nt
bravado [brə'vɑːdəʊ] n Tollkühnheit f
brave [breɪv] adj tapfer ♦ vt die Stirn bieten +dat; ~**ry** n Tapferkeit f
brawl [brɔːl] n Rauferei f
brawn [brɔːn] n (ANAT) Muskeln pl; (strength) Muskelkraft f
bray [breɪ] vi schreien
brazen ['breɪzn] adj (shameless) unver-

schämt ♦ vt: **to ~ it out** sich mit Lügen und Betrügen durchsetzen

brazier ['breɪzɪə*] n (of workmen) offene(r) Kohlenofen m

Brazil [brə'zɪl] n Brasilien nt; **~ian** adj brasilianisch ♦ n Brasilianer(in) m(f)

breach [briːtʃ] n (gap) Lücke f, (MIL) Durchbruch m; (of discipline) Verstoß m (gegen die Disziplin); (of faith) Vertrauensbruch m ♦ vt durchbrechen; **~ of contract** Vertragsbruch m; **~ of the peace** öffentliche Ruhestörung f

bread [bred] n Brot nt; **~ and butter** Butterbrot nt; **~bin** n Brotkasten m; **~ box** (US) n Brotkasten m; **~crumbs** n Brotkrumen pl; (COOK) Paniermehl nt; **~line** n: **on the ~line** sich gerade so durchschlagen

breadth [bretθ] n Breite f

breadwinner ['bredwɪnə*] n Ernährer m

break [breɪk] (pt **broke**, pp **broken**) vt (destroy) (ab- or zer)brechen; (promise) brechen, nicht einhalten ♦ vi (fall apart) auseinander brechen; (collapse) zusammenbrechen; (dawn) anbrechen ♦ n (gap) Lücke f; (chance) Chance f, Gelegenheit f; (fracture) Bruch m; (rest) Pause f; **~ down** vt (figures, data) aufschlüsseln; (undermine) überwinden ♦ vi (car) eine Panne haben; (person) zusammenbrechen; **~ even** vi die Kosten decken; **~ free** vi sich losreißen; **~ in** vt (horse) zureiten ♦ vi (burglar) einbrechen; **~ into** vt fus (house) einbrechen in +acc; **~ loose** vi sich losreißen; **~ off** vi abbrechen; **~ open** vt (door etc) aufbrechen; **~ out** vi ausbrechen; **to ~ out in spots** Pickel bekommen; **~ up** vi zerbrechen; (fig) sich zerstreuen; (BRIT: SCH) in die Ferien gehen ♦ vt brechen; **~age** n Bruch m, Beschädigung f; **~down** n (TECH) Panne f; (MED: also: **nervous ~down**) Zusammenbruch m; **~down van** (BRIT) n Abschleppwagen m; **~er** n Brecher m

breakfast ['brekfəst] n Frühstück nt

break: **~in** n Einbruch m; **~ing** n: **~ing and entering** (JUR) Einbruch m; **~through** n Durchbruch m; **~water** n Wellenbrecher m

breast [brest] n Brust f; **~-feed** (irreg: like **feed**) vt, vi stillen; **~-stroke** n Brustschwimmen nt

breath [breθ] n Atem m; **out of ~** außer Atem; **under one's ~** flüsternd

Breathalyzer ['breθəlaɪzə*] ® n Röhrchen nt

breathe [briːð] vt, vi atmen; **~ in** vt, vi einatmen; **~ out** vt, vi ausatmen; **~r** n Verschnaufpause f; **breathing** n Atmung f

breathless ['breθlɪs] adj atemlos

breathtaking ['breθteɪkɪŋ] adj atemberaubend

bred [bred] pt, pp of **breed**

breed [briːd] (pt, pp **bred**) vi sich vermehren ♦ vt züchten ♦ n (race) Rasse f, Zucht f; **~ing** n Züchtung f; (upbringing) Erziehung f

breeze [briːz] n Brise f; **breezy** adj windig; (manner) munter

brevity ['brevɪtɪ] n Kürze f

brew [bruː] vt (beer) brauen ♦ vi (storm) sich zusammenziehen; **~ery** n Brauerei f

bribe [braɪb] n Bestechungsgeld nt, Bestechungsgeschenk nt ♦ vt bestechen; **~ry** ['braɪbərɪ] n Bestechung f

bric-a-brac ['brɪkəbræk] n Nippes pl

brick [brɪk] n Backstein m; **~layer** n Maurer m; **~works** n Ziegelei f

bridal ['braɪdl] adj Braut-

bride [braɪd] n Braut f; **~groom** n Bräutigam m; **~smaid** n Brautjungfer f

bridge [brɪdʒ] n Brücke f; (NAUT) Kommandobrücke f; (CARDS) Bridge nt; (ANAT) Nasenrücken m ♦ vt eine Brücke schlagen über +acc; (fig) überbrücken

bridle ['braɪdl] n Zaum m ♦ vt (fig) zügeln; (horse) aufzäumen; **~ path** n Reitweg m

brief [briːf] adj kurz ♦ n (JUR) Akten pl ♦ vt instruieren; **~s** npl (underwear)

Schlüpfer *m*, Slip *m*; **~case** *n* Aktentasche *f*; **~ing** *n* (genaue) Anweisung *f*; **~ly** *adv* kurz

brigadier [brɪgəˈdɪəʳ] *n* Brigadegeneral *m*

bright [braɪt] *adj* hell; (*cheerful*) heiter; (*idea*) klug; **~en (up)** [ˈbraɪtn] *vt* aufhellen; (*person*) aufheitern ♦ *vi* sich aufheitern

brilliance [ˈbrɪljəns] *n* Glanz *m*; (*of person*) Scharfsinn *m*

brilliant [ˈbrɪljənt] *adj* glänzend

brim [brɪm] *n* Rand *m*

brine [braɪn] *n* Salzwasser *nt*

bring [brɪŋ] (*pt, pp* brought) *vt* bringen; **~ about** *vt* zustande *or* zu Stande bringen; **~ back** *vt* zurückbringen; **~ down** *vt* (*price*) senken; **~ forward** *vt* (*meeting*) vorverlegen; (*comm*) übertragen; **~ in** *vt* hereinbringen; (*harvest*) einbringen; **~ off** *vt* davontragen; (*success*) erzielen; **~ out** *vt* (*object*) herausbringen; **~ round** *or* **to** *vt* wieder zu sich bringen; **~ up** *vt* aufziehen; (*question*) zur Sprache bringen

brink [brɪŋk] *n* Rand *m*

brisk [brɪsk] *adj* lebhaft

bristle [ˈbrɪsl] *n* Borste *f* ♦ *vi* sich sträuben; **bristling with** strotzend vor +*dat*

Britain [ˈbrɪtən] *n* (*also: Great ~*) Großbritannien *nt*

British [ˈbrɪtɪʃ] *adj* britisch ♦ *npl*: **the ~** die Briten *pl*; **~ Isles** *npl*: **the ~ Isles** die Britischen Inseln *pl*; **~ Rail** *n* die Britischen Eisenbahnen

Briton [ˈbrɪtən] *n* Brite *m*, Britin *f*

Brittany [ˈbrɪtənɪ] *n* die Bretagne

brittle [ˈbrɪtl] *adj* spröde

broach [brəʊtʃ] *vt* (*subject*) anschneiden

broad [brɔːd] *adj* breit; (*hint*) deutlich; (*general*) allgemein; (*accent*) stark; **in ~ daylight** am helllichten Tag; **~cast** (*pt, pp* broadcast) *n* Rundfunkübertragung *f* ♦ *vt* übertragen, senden; **~en** *vt* erweitern ♦ *vi* sich erweitern; **~ly** *adv* allgemein gesagt; **~-**

minded *adj* tolerant

broccoli [ˈbrɒkəlɪ] *n* Brokkoli *pl*

brochure [ˈbrəʊʃjʊəʳ] *n* Broschüre *f*

broil [brɔɪl] *vt* (*grill*) grillen

broke [brəʊk] *pt of* break ♦ *adj* (*inf*) pleite

broken [ˈbrəʊkn] *pp of* break ♦ *adj*: **~ leg** gebrochenes Bein; **in ~ English** in gebrochenem Englisch; **~-hearted** *adj* untröstlich

broker [ˈbrəʊkəʳ] *n* Makler *m*

brolly [ˈbrɒlɪ] (*BRIT: inf*) *n* Schirm *m*

bronchitis [brɒŋˈkaɪtɪs] *n* Bronchitis *f*

bronze [brɒnz] *n* Bronze *f*

brooch [brəʊtʃ] *n* Brosche *f*

brood [bruːd] *n* Brut *f* ♦ *vi* brüten

brook [brʊk] *n* Bach *m*

broom [bruːm] *n* Besen *m*

Bros. *abbr* = **Brothers**

broth [brɒθ] *n* Suppe *f*, Fleischbrühe *f*

brothel [ˈbrɒθl] *n* Bordell *nt*

brother [ˈbrʌðəʳ] *n* Bruder *m*; **~-in-law** *n* Schwager *m*

brought [brɔːt] *pt, pp of* bring

brow [braʊ] *n* (*eyebrow*) (Augen)braue *f*; (*forehead*) Stirn *f*; (*of hill*) Bergkuppe *f*

brown [braʊn] *adj* braun ♦ *n* Braun *nt* ♦ *vt* bräunen; **~ bread** *n* Mischbrot *nt*; **B~ie** *n* Wichtel *m*; **~ paper** *n* Packpapier *nt*; **~ sugar** *n* braune(r) Zucker *m*

browse [braʊz] *vi* (*in books*) blättern; (*in shop*) schmökern, herumschauen; **~r** *n* (*INTERNET*) Browser *m*

bruise [bruːz] *n* Bluterguss *m*, blaue(r) Fleck *m* ♦ *vt* einen blauen Fleck geben ♦ *vi* einen blauen Fleck bekommen

brunt [brʌnt] *n* volle Wucht *f*

brush [brʌʃ] *n* Bürste *f*; (*for sweeping*) Handbesen *m*; (*for painting*) Pinsel *m*; (*fight*) kurze(r) Kampf *m*; (*MIL*) Scharmützel *nt*; (*fig*) Auseinandersetzung *f* ♦ *vt* (*clean*) bürsten; (*sweep*) fegen; (*usu: ~ past, ~ against*) streifen; **~ aside** *vt* abtun; **~ up** *vt* (*knowledge*) auffrischen; **~wood** *n* Gestrüpp *nt*

brusque [bruːsk] *adj* schroff

Brussels 343 **bulletproof**

Brussels ['brʌslz] n Brüssel nt; ~ **sprout** n Rosenkohl m

brutal ['bru:tl] adj brutal

brute [bru:t] n (person) Scheusal nt ♦ adj: **by** ~ **force** mit roher Kraft

B.Sc. n abbr = **Bachelor of Science**

BSE n abbr (= bovine spongiform encephalopathy) BSE f

bubble ['bʌbl] n (Luft)blase f ♦ vi sprudeln; (with joy) überspudeln; ~ **bath** n Schaumbad nt; ~ **gum** n Kaugummi m or nt

buck [bʌk] n Bock m; (US: inf) Dollar m ♦ vi bocken; **to pass the ~ (to sb)** die Verantwortung (auf jdn) abschieben; ~ **up** (inf) vi sich zusammenreißen

bucket ['bʌkɪt] n Eimer m

Buckingham Palace

Buckingham Palace ist die offizielle Londoner Residenz der britischen Monarchen und liegt am St James Park. Der Palast wurde 1703 für den Herzog von Buckingham erbaut, 1762 von George III. gekauft, zwischen 1821 und 1836 von John Nash umgebaut, und Anfang des 20. Jahrhunderts teilweise neu gestaltet. Teile des Buckingham Palace sind heute der Öffentlichkeit zugänglich.

buckle ['bʌkl] n Schnalle f ♦ vt (an- or zusammen)schnallen ♦ vi (bend) sich verziehen

bud [bʌd] n Knospe f ♦ vi knospen, keimen

Buddhism ['budɪzəm] n Buddhismus m; **Buddhist** adj buddhistisch ♦ n Buddhist(in) m(f)

budding ['bʌdɪŋ] adj angehend

buddy ['bʌdɪ] (inf) n Kumpel m

budge [bʌdʒ] vt, vi (sich) von der Stelle rühren

budgerigar ['bʌdʒərɪgɑːr] n Wellensittich m

budget ['bʌdʒɪt] n Budget nt; (POL) Haushalt m ♦ vi: **to ~ for sth** etw einplanen

budgie ['bʌdʒɪ] n = budgerigar

buff [bʌf] adj (colour) lederfarben ♦ n (enthusiast) Fan m

buffalo ['bʌfələu] (pl ~ or ~es) n (BRIT) Büffel m; (US: bison) Bison m

buffer ['bʌfər] n Puffer m; (COMPUT) Pufferspeicher m; ~ **zone** n Pufferzone f

buffet1 ['bʌfɪt] n (blow) Schlag m ♦ vt (herum)stossen

buffet2 ['bufeɪ] (BRIT) n (bar) Imbissraum m, Erfrischungsraum m; (food) (kaltes) Büfett nt; ~ **car** (BRIT) n Speisewagen m

bug [bʌg] n (also fig) Wanze f ♦ vt verwanzen; **the room is bugged** das Zimmer ist verwanzt

bugle ['bju:gl] n Jagdhorn nt; (MIL: MUS) Bügelhorn n

build [bɪld] (pt, pp built) vt bauen ♦ n Körperbau m; ~ **up** vi aufbauen; ~**er** n Bauunternehmer m; ~**ing** n Gebäude nt; ~**ing society** (BRIT) n Bausparkasse f

built [bɪlt] pt, pp of **build**; ~**-in** adj (cupboard) eingebaut; ~**-up area** n Wohngebiet nt

bulb [bʌlb] n (BOT) (Blumen)zwiebel f; (ELEC) Glühlampe f, Birne f

Bulgaria [bʌl'gɛərɪə] n Bulgarien nt; ~**n** adj bulgarisch ♦ n Bulgare m, Bulgarin f; (LING) Bulgarisch nt

bulge [bʌldʒ] n Wölbung f ♦ vi sich wölben

bulk [bʌlk] n Größe f, Masse f; (greater part) Großteil m; **in** ~ (COMM) en gros; **the ~ of** der größte Teil +gen; ~**head** n Schott nt; ~**y** adj (sehr) umfangreich; (goods) sperrig

bull [bul] n Bulle m; (cattle) Stier m; ~**dog** n Bulldogge f

bulldozer ['buldəuzər] n Planierraupe f

bullet ['bulɪt] n Kugel f

bulletin ['bulɪtɪn] n Bulletin nt, Bekanntmachung f

bulletproof ['bulɪtpru:f] adj kugelsicher

bullfight ['bulfaɪt] n Stierkampf m; **~er** n Stierkämpfer m; **~ing** n Stierkampf m

bullion ['buljən] n Barren m

bullock ['bulək] n Ochse m

bullring ['bulrɪŋ] n Stierkampfarena f

bull's-eye ['bulzaɪ] n Zentrum nt

bully ['bulɪ] n Raufbold m ♦ vt einschüchtern

bum [bʌm] n (inf: backside) Hintern m; (tramp) Landstreicher m

bumblebee ['bʌmblbiː] n Hummel f

bump [bʌmp] n (blow) Stoß m; (swelling) Beule f ♦ vt, vi stoßen, prallen; **~into** vt fus stoßen gegen + akk (person) treffen; **~er** n (AUT) Stoßstange f ♦ adj (edition) dick; (harvest) Rekord-

bumpy ['bʌmpɪ] adj holprig

bun [bʌn] n Korinthenbrötchen nt

bunch [bʌntʃ] n (of flowers) Strauß m; (of keys) Bund m; (of people) Haufen m; **~es** npl (in hair) Zöpfe pl

bundle ['bʌndl] n Bündel nt ♦ vt (also: **~up**) bündeln

bungalow ['bʌngələʊ] n einstöckige(s) Haus nt, Bungalow m

bungle ['bʌngl] vt verpfuschen

bunion ['bʌnjən] n entzündete(r) Fußballen m

bunk [bʌnk] n Schlafkoje f; **~ beds** npl Etagenbett nt

bunker ['bʌnkər] n (coal store) Kohlenbunker m; (GOLF) Sandloch nt

bunny ['bʌnɪ] n (also: **~ rabbit**) Häschen n

bunting ['bʌntɪŋ] n Fahnentuch nt

buoy [bɔɪ] n Boje f; (lifebuoy) Rettungsboje f; **~ant** adj (floating) schwimmend; (fig) heiter

burden ['bɜːdn] n (weight) Ladung f, Last f; (fig) Bürde f ♦ vt belasten

bureau ['bjʊərəʊ] (pl **~x**) n (BRIT: writing desk) Sekretär m; (US: chest of drawers) Kommode f; (for information etc) Büro nt

bureaucracy [bjʊəˈrɒkrəsɪ] n Bürokratie f

bureaucrat ['bjʊərəkræt] n Büro-

krat(in) m(f)

bureaux [bjʊəˈrəʊz] npl of bureau

burglar ['bɜːglər] n Einbrecher m; **~ alarm** n Einbruchssicherung f; **~y** n Einbruch m

burial ['berɪəl] n Beerdigung f

burly ['bɜːlɪ] adj stämmig

Burma ['bɜːmə] n Birma n

burn [bɜːn] (pt, pp **burned** or **burnt**) vt verbrennen ♦ vi brennen ♦ n Brandwunde f; **~ down** vt, vi abbrennen; **~er** n Brenner m; **~ing** adj brennend; **~t** [bɜːnt] pt, pp of burn

burrow ['bʌrəʊ] n (of fox) Bau m; (of rabbit) Höhle f ♦ vt eingraben

bursar ['bɜːsər] n Kassenverwalter m, Quästor m; **~y** (BRIT) n Stipendium f

burst [bɜːst] (pt, pp **burst**) vt zerbrechen ♦ vi platzen ♦ n Explosion f; (outbreak) Ausbruch m; (in pipe) Bruch(stelle f) m; to **~ into flames** in Flammen aufgehen; to **~ into tears** in Tränen ausbrechen; to **~ out laughing** in Gelächter ausbrechen; **~ into** vt fus (room etc) platzen in +acc; **~ open** vi aufbrechen

bury ['berɪ] vt vergraben; (in grave) beerdigen

bus [bʌs] n (Auto)bus m, Omnibus m

bush [buʃ] n Busch m; to **beat about the ~** wie die Katze um den heißen Brei herumgehen; **~y** ['buʃɪ] adj buschig

busily ['bɪzɪlɪ] adv geschäftig

business ['bɪznɪs] n Geschäft nt; (concern) Angelegenheit f; **it's none of your ~** es geht dich nichts an; to **mean ~** es ernst meinen; to **be away on ~** geschäftlich verreist sein; **it's my ~ to ...** es ist meine Sache, zu ...; **~like** adj geschäftsmäßig; **~man** (irreg) n Geschäftsmann m; **~ trip** n Geschäftsreise f; **~woman** (irreg) n Geschäftsfrau f

busker ['bʌskər] (BRIT) n Straßenmusikant m

bus: ~ shelter n Wartehäuschen nt; **~**

bust   345   by

station n Busbahnhof m; **~ stop** n Bushaltestelle f

bust [bʌst] n Büste f ♦ adj (broken) kaputt(gegangen); (business) pleite; **to go ~** Pleite machen

bustle ['bʌsl] n Getriebe nt ♦ vi hasten

bustling ['bʌslɪŋ] adj geschäftig

busy ['bɪzɪ] adj beschäftigt; (road) belebt ♦ vt: **to ~ o.s.** sich beschäftigen; **~body** n Übereifrige(r) mf; **~ signal** (US) n (TEL) Besetztzeichen nt

---

KEYWORD

but [bʌt] conj 1 (yet) aber; **not X but Y** nicht X sondern Y

2 (however): **I'd love to come, but I'm busy** ich würde gern kommen, bin aber beschäftigt

3 (showing disagreement, surprise etc): **but that's fantastic!** (aber) das ist ja fantastisch!

♦ prep (apart from, except): **nothing but trouble** nichts als Ärger; **no-one but him can do it** niemand außer ihm kann es machen; **but for you/your help** ohne dich/deine Hilfe; **anything but that** alles, nur das nicht

♦ adv (just, only): **she's but a child** sie ist noch ein Kind; **had I but known** wenn ich es nur gewusst hätte; **I can but try** ich kann es immerhin versuchen; **all but finished** so gut wie fertig

---

butcher ['bʊtʃəʳ] n Metzger m; (murderer) Schlächter m ♦ vt schlachten; (kill) abschlachten; **~'s (shop)** n Metzgerei f

butler ['bʌtləʳ] n Butler m

butt [bʌt] n (cask) große(s) Fass nt; (BRIT: fig: target) Zielscheibe f; (of gun) Kolben m; (of cigarette) Stummel m ♦ vt (mit dem Kopf) stoßen; **~ in** vi sich einmischen

butter ['bʌtəʳ] n Butter f ♦ vt buttern; **~ bean** n Wachsbohne f; **~cup** n Butterblume f

butterfly ['bʌtəflaɪ] n Schmetterling m; (SWIMMING: also: **~ stroke**) Butterflystil m

buttocks ['bʌtəks] npl Gesäß nt

button ['bʌtn] n Knopf m ♦ vt, vi (also: **~ up**) zuknöpfen

buttress ['bʌtrɪs] n Strebepfeiler m; Stützbogen m

buxom ['bʌksəm] adj drall

buy [baɪ] (pt, pp **bought**) vt kaufen ♦ n Kauf m; **to ~ sb a drink** jdm einen Drink spendieren; **~er** n Käufer(in) m(f)

buzz [bʌz] n Summen nt ♦ vi summen; **~er** ['bʌzəʳ] n Summer m; **~ word** n Modewort nt

---

KEYWORD

by [baɪ] prep 1 (referring to cause, agent) of, durch; **killed by lightning** vom Blitz getötet; **a painting by Picasso** ein Gemälde von Picasso

2 (referring to method, manner): **by bus/car/train** mit dem Bus/Auto/Zug; **to pay by cheque** per Scheck bezahlen; **by moonlight** bei Mondschein; **by saving hard, he ...** indem er eisern sparte, ... er ...

3 (via, through) über +acc; **he came in by the back door** er kam durch die Hintertür herein

4 (close to, past) bei, an +dat; **a holiday by the sea** ein Urlaub am Meer; **she rushed by me** sie eilte an mir vorbei

5 (not later than): **by 4 o'clock** bis 4 Uhr; **by this time tomorrow** morgen um diese Zeit; **by the time I got here it was too late** als ich hier ankam, war es zu spät

6 (during): **by day** bei Tag

7 (amount): **by the kilo/metre** kiloweise/meterweise; **paid by the hour** stundenweise bezahlt

8 (MATH, measure): **to divide by 3** durch 3 teilen; **to multiply by 3** mit 3 malnehmen; **a room 3 metres by 4** ein Zimmer 3 mal 4 Meter; **it's broad-**

er by a metre es ist (um) einem Meter breiter
9 (according to) nach; **it's all right by me** von mir aus gern
10: (all) **by oneself** etc ganz allein
11: **by the way** übrigens
♦ adv 1 see go; pass etc
2: **by and by** irgendwann; (with past tenses) nach einiger Zeit; **by and large** (on the whole) im Großen und Ganzen

bye(-bye) ['baɪ('baɪ)] excl (auf) Wiedersehen
by(e)-law ['baɪlɔː] n Verordnung f
by-election ['baɪɪlekʃən] (BRIT) n Nachwahl f
bygone ['baɪgɒn] adj vergangen ♦ n: **let ~s be ~s** lass(t) das Vergangene vergangen sein
bypass ['baɪpɑːs] n Umgehungsstraße f ♦ vt umgehen
by-product ['baɪprɒdʌkt] n Nebenprodukt nt
bystander ['baɪstændə*] n Zuschauer m
byte [baɪt] n (COMPUT) Byte nt
byword ['baɪwɜːd] n Inbegriff m

C, c

C [siː] n (MUS) C nt
C. abbr (= centigrade) C
C.A. abbr = chartered accountant
cab [kæb] n Taxi nt; (of train) Führerstand m; (of truck) Führersitz m
cabaret ['kæbəreɪ] n Kabarett nt
cabbage ['kæbɪdʒ] n Kohl(kopf) m
cabin ['kæbɪn] n Hütte f; (NAUT) Kajüte f; (AVIAT) Kabine f; **~ crew** n (AVIAT) Flugbegleitpersonal nt; **~ cruiser** n Motorjacht f
cabinet ['kæbɪnɪt] n Schrank m; (for china) Vitrine f; (POL) Kabinett nt; **~maker** n Kunsttischler m
cable ['keɪbl] n Drahtseil nt, Tau nt; (TEL) (Leitungs)kabel nt; (telegram) Ka-

bel nt ♦ vt kabeln, telegrafieren; **~ car** n Seilbahn f; **~ television** n Kabelfernsehen nt
cache [kæʃ] n geheime(s) (Waffen)lager nt; geheime(s) (Proviant)lager nt
cackle ['kækl] vi gackern
cacti ['kæktaɪ] npl of **cactus**
cactus ['kæktəs] (pl **cacti**) n Kaktus m, Kaktee f
caddie ['kædɪ] n (GOLF) Golfjunge m
caddy ['kædɪ] n = **caddie**
cadet [kə'det] n Kadett m
cadge [kædʒ] vt schmarotzen
Caesarean [siː'zeərɪən] adj: **~ (section)** n Kaiserschnitt m
café ['kæfeɪ] n Café nt, Restaurant nt
cafeteria [kæfɪ'tɪərɪə] n Selbstbedienungsrestaurant nt
caffein(e) ['kæfiːn] n Koffein nt
cage [keɪdʒ] n Käfig m ♦ vt einsperren
cagey ['keɪdʒɪ] adj geheimnistuerisch, zurückhaltend
cagoule [kə'guːl] n Windhemd nt
Cairo ['kaɪərəʊ] n Kairo nt
cajole [kə'dʒəʊl] vt überreden
cake [keɪk] n Kuchen m; (of soap) Stück nt; **~d** adj verkrustet
calamity [kə'læmɪtɪ] n Unglück nt, (Schicksals)schlag m
calcium ['kælsɪəm] n Kalzium nt
calculate ['kælkjʊleɪt] vt berechnen, kalkulieren; **calculating** adj berechnend; **calculation** [kælkjʊ'leɪʃən] n Berechnung f; **calculator** n Rechner m
calendar ['kælɪndə*] n Kalender m; **~ month** n Kalendermonat m
calf [kɑːf] (pl **calves**) n Kalb nt; (also: **~skin**) Kalbsleder nt; (ANAT) Wade f
calibre ['kælɪbə*] (US **caliber**) n Kaliber nt
call [kɔːl] vt rufen; (name) nennen; (meeting) einberufen; (awaken) wecken; (TEL) anrufen ♦ vi (shout) rufen; (visit: also: **~ in**, **~ round**) vorbeikommen ♦ n (shout) Ruf m; (TEL) Anruf m; **to be ~ed** heißen; **on ~** in Bereit-

callous   347   cannabis

schaft; **~ back** vi (return) wiederkommen; (TEL) zurückrufen; **~ for** vt fus (demand) erfordern, verlangen; (fetch) abholen; **~ off** vt (cancel) absagen; **~ on** vt fus (visit) besuchen; (turn to) bitten; **~ out** vi rufen; **~ up** vt (MIL) einberufen; **~box** (BRIT) n Telefonzelle f; **~ centre** n Telefoncenter nt, Callcenter nt; **~er** n Besucher(in) m(f); (TEL) Anrufer m; **~ girl** n Callgirl nt; **~-in** (US) n (phone-in) Phone-in nt; **~ing** n (vocation) Berufung f; **~ing card** (US) n Visitenkarte f

callous ['kæləs] adj herzlos

calm [kɑːm] n Ruhe f; (NAUT) Flaute f ♦ vt beruhigen ♦ adj ruhig; (person) gelassen; **~ down** vi sich beruhigen ♦ vt beruhigen

Calor gas ['kælər-] ® n Propangas nt

calorie ['kælərɪ] n Kalorie f

calves [kɑːvz] npl of **calf**

Cambodia [kæm'bəudɪə] n Kambodscha nt

camcorder ['kæmkɔːdər] n Camcorder m

came [keɪm] pt of **come**

cameo ['kæmɪəu] n Kamee f

camera ['kæmərə] n Fotoapparat m; (CINE, TV) Kamera f; **in ~** unter Ausschluss der Öffentlichkeit; **~man** (irreg) n Kameramann m

camouflage ['kæməflɑːʒ] n Tarnung f ♦ vt tarnen

camp [kæmp] n Lager nt ♦ vi zelten, campen ♦ adj affektiert

campaign [kæm'peɪn] n Kampagne f; (MIL) Feldzug m ♦ vi (MIL) Krieg führen; (fig) werben, Propaganda machen; (POL) den Wahlkampf führen

camp: **~ bed** [kæmp'bed] (BRIT) n Campingbett nt; **~er** ['kæmpər] n Camper(in) m(f); (vehicle) Wohnwagen m; **~ing** ['kæmpɪŋ] n: **to go ~ing** zelten, Camping machen; **~ing gas** (US) n Campinggas nt; **~site** ['kæmpsaɪt] n Campingplatz m

campus ['kæmpəs] n Universi-

tätsgelände nt, Campus m

can¹ [kæn] n Büchse f, Dose f; (for water) Kanne f ♦ vt konservieren, in Büchsen einmachen

can² [kæn] (negative **cannot**, **can't**, conditional **could**) aux vb **1** (be able to, know how to) können; **I can see you tomorrow, if you like** ich könnte Sie morgen sehen, wenn Sie wollen; **I can swim** ich kann schwimmen; **can you speak German?** sprechen Sie Deutsch?

2 (may) können, dürfen; **could I have a word with you?** könnte ich Sie kurz sprechen?

Canada ['kænədə] n Kanada nt; **Canadian** [kə'neɪdɪən] adj kanadisch ♦ n Kanadier(in) m(f)

canal [kə'næl] n Kanal m

canapé ['kænəpeɪ] n Cocktail- or Appetithappen m

canary [kə'neərɪ] n Kanarienvogel m

cancel ['kænsəl] vt absagen; (delete) durchstreichen; (train) streichen; **~lation** [kænsə'leɪʃən] n Absage f; Streichung f

cancer ['kænsər] n (ASTROL: C~) Krebs m

candid ['kændɪd] adj offen, ehrlich

candidate ['kændɪdeɪt] n Kandidat(in) m(f)

candle ['kændl] n Kerze f; **~light** n Kerzenlicht nt; **~stick** n (also: **~ holder**) Kerzenhalter m

candour ['kændər] (US **candor**) n Offenheit f

candy ['kændɪ] n Kandis(zucker) m; (US) Bonbons pl; **~floss** (BRIT) n Zuckerwatte f

cane [keɪn] n (BOT) Rohr nt; (stick) Stock m ♦ vt (BRIT: beat) schlagen

canine ['keɪnaɪn] adj Hunde-

canister ['kænɪstər] n Blechdose f

cannabis ['kænəbɪs] n Hanf m, Haschisch m

canned [kænd] *adj* Büchsen-, eingemacht

cannon ['kænən] (*pl ~ or ~s*) *n* Kanone *f*

cannot ['kænɒt] = **can not**

canny ['kænɪ] *adj* schlau

canoe [kə'nuː] *n* Kanu *nt*; **~ing** *n* Kanusport *m*, Kanufahren *nt*

canon ['kænən] *n* (*clergyman*) Domherr *m*; (*standard*) Grundsatz *m*

can-opener ['kænəupnə'] *n* Büchsenöffner *m*

canopy ['kænəpɪ] *n* Baldachin *m*

can't [kænt] = **can not**

cantankerous [kæn'tæŋkərəs] *adj* zänkisch, mürrisch

canteen [kæn'tiːn] *n* Kantine *f*; (*BRIT: of cutlery*) Besteckkasten *m*

canter ['kæntə'] *n* Kanter *m* ♦ *vi* in kurzem Galopp reiten

canvas ['kænvəs] *n* Segeltuch *nt*, (*sail*) Segel *nt*; (*for painting*) Leinwand *f*; **under ~** (*camping*) in Zelten

canvass ['kænvəs] *vi* um Stimmen werben; **~ing** *n* Wahlwerbung *f*

canyon ['kænjən] *n* Felsenschlucht *f*

cap [kæp] *n* Mütze *f*; (*of pen*) Kappe *f*; (*of bottle*) Deckel *m* ♦ *vt* (*surpass*) übertreffen; (*SPORT*) aufstellen; (*put limit on*) einen Höchstsatz festlegen für

capability [keɪpə'bɪlɪtɪ] *n* Fähigkeit *f*

capable ['keɪpəbl] *adj* fähig

capacity [kə'pæsɪtɪ] *n* Fassungsvermögen *nt*; (*ability*) Fähigkeit *f*; (*position*) Eigenschaft *f*

cape [keɪp] *n* (*garment*) Cape *nt*, Umhang *m*; (*GEOG*) Kap *nt*

caper ['keɪpə'] *n* (*COOK: usu: ~s*) Kaper *f*; (*prank*) Kapriole *f*

capital ['kæpɪtl] *n* (*~ city*) Hauptstadt *f*; (*FIN*) Kapital *nt*; (*~ letter*) Großbuchstabe *m*; **~ gains tax** *n* Kapitalertragssteuer *f*; **~ism** *n* Kapitalismus *m*; **~ist** *adj* kapitalistisch ♦ *n* Kapitalist(in) *m(f)*; **~ize** *vi*: **to ~ize on** Kapital schlagen aus; **~ punishment** *n* Todesstrafe *f*

Capricorn ['kæprɪkɔːn] *n* Steinbock *m*

capsize [kæp'saɪz] *vt, vi* kentern

capsule ['kæpsjuːl] *n* Kapsel *f*

captain ['kæptɪn] *n* Kapitän *m*, (*MIL*) Hauptmann *m* ♦ *vt* anführen

caption ['kæpʃən] *n* (*heading*) Überschrift *f*; (*to picture*) Unterschrift *f*

captivate ['kæptɪveɪt] *vt* fesseln

captive ['kæptɪv] *n* Gefangene(r) *f(m)* ♦ *adj* gefangen (gehalten); **captivity** [kæp'tɪvɪtɪ] *n* Gefangenschaft *f*

capture ['kæptʃə'] *vt* gefangen nehmen; (*place*) erobern; (*attention*) erregen ♦ *n* Gefangennahme *f*; (*data ~*) Erfassung *f*

car [kɑː'] *n* Auto *nt*, Wagen *m*; (*RAIL*) Wagen *m*

caramel ['kærəməl] *n* Karamelle *f*, Karamellbonbon *m or nt*; (*burnt sugar*) Karamell *m*

carat ['kærət] *n* Karat *nt*

caravan ['kærəvæn] *n* (*BRIT*) Wohnwagen *m*; (*in desert*) Karawane *f*; **~ning** *n* Caravaning *nt*, Urlaub *m* im Wohnwagen; **~ site** (*BRIT*) *n* Campingplatz *m* für Wohnwagen

carbohydrate [kɑːbəu'haɪdreɪt] *n* Kohlenhydrat *nt*

carbon ['kɑːbən] *n* Kohlenstoff *m*; **~ copy** *n* Durchschlag *m*; **~ dioxide** *n* Kohlendioxyd *nt*; **~ monoxide** *n* Kohlenmonoxyd *nt*; **~ paper** *n* Kohlepapier *nt*

car boot sale *n* auf einem Parkplatz stattfindender Flohmarkt mit dem Kofferraum als Auslage

carburettor [kɑːbju'retə'] (*US* **carbure-**

tor) n Vergaser m

carcass ['kɑːkəs] n Kadaver m

card [kɑːd] n Karte f; **~board** n Pappe f; **~ game** n Kartenspiel nt

cardiac ['kɑːdæk] adj Herz-

cardigan ['kɑːdɪɡən] n Strickjacke f

cardinal ['kɑːdɪnl] adj: **~ number** Kardinalzahl f ♦ n (REL) Kardinal m

card index n Kartei f; (in library) Katalog m

cardphone n Kartentelefon nt

care [kɛəʳ] n (of teeth, car etc) Pflege f; (of children) Fürsorge f; (~fulness) Sorgfalt f; (worry) Sorge f ♦ vi: **to ~ about** sich kümmern um; **~ of** bei; **in sb's ~** in jds Obhut; **I don't ~** das ist mir egal; **I couldn't ~ less** es ist mir doch völlig egal; **to take ~** aufpassen; **to take ~ of** sorgen für; **to take ~ to do** sth bemühen, etw zu tun; **~ for** vt sorgen für; (like) mögen

career [kəˈrɪəʳ] n Karriere f, Laufbahn f ♦ vi (also: **~ along**) rasen; **~ woman** (irreg) n Karrierefrau f

care: **~free** adj sorgenfrei; **~ful** adj sorgfältig; (be) **~ful!** pass auf!; **~fully** adv vorsichtig; (methodically) sorgfältig; **~less** adj nachlässig; **~lessness** n Nachlässigkeit f; **~r** n (MED) Betreuer(in) m(f)

caress [kəˈrɛs] n Liebkosung f ♦ vt liebkosen

caretaker ['kɛəteɪkəʳ] n Hausmeister m

car ferry n Autofähre f

cargo ['kɑːɡəʊ] (pl **~es**) n Schiffsladung f

car hire n Autovermietung f

Caribbean [kærɪˈbiːən] n: **the ~ (Sea)** die Karibik

caricature ['kærɪkətjʊəʳ] n Karikatur f

caring ['kɛərɪŋ] adj (society, organization) sozial eingestellt; (person) liebevoll

carnage ['kɑːnɪdʒ] n Blutbad nt

carnation [kɑːˈneɪʃən] n Nelke f

carnival ['kɑːnɪvl] n Karneval m, Fasching m; (US: fun fair) Kirmes f

carnivorous [kɑːˈnɪvərəs] adj Fleisch fressend

carol ['kærəl] n: **(Christmas) ~** (Weihnachts)lied nt

carp [kɑːp] n (fish) Karpfen m

car park (BRIT) n Parkplatz m; (covered) Parkhaus n

carpenter ['kɑːpɪntəʳ] n Zimmermann m; **carpentry** ['kɑːpɪntrɪ] n Zimmerei f

carpet ['kɑːpɪt] n Teppich m ♦ vt mit einem Teppich auslegen; **~ bombing** n Flächenbombardierung f; **~ slippers** npl Pantoffeln pl; **~ sweeper** ['kɑːpɪtswiːpəʳ] n Teppichkehrer m

car phone n (TEL) Autotelefon nt

car rental (US) n Autovermietung f

carriage ['kærɪdʒ] n Kutsche f; (RAIL of typewriter) Wagen m; (of goods) Beförderung f; (bearing) Haltung f; **~ return** n (of typewriter) Rücklauftaste f; **~way** (BRIT) n (part of road) Fahrbahn f

carrier ['kærɪəʳ] n Träger(in) m(f); (COMM) Spediteur m; **~ bag** (BRIT) n Tragetasche m

carrot ['kærət] n Möhre f, Karotte f

carry ['kærɪ] vt, vi tragen; **to get carried away** (fig) sich nicht mehr bremsen können; **~ on** vi (continue) weitermachen; (inf: complain) Theater machen; **~ out** vt (orders) ausführen; (investigation) durchführen; **~cot** (BRIT) n Babytragetasche f; **~on** (inf) n (fuss) Theater nt

cart [kɑːt] n Wagen m, Karren m ♦ vt schleppen

cartilage ['kɑːtɪlɪdʒ] n Knorpel m

carton ['kɑːtən] n Karton m; (of milk) Tüte f

cartoon [kɑːˈtuːn] n (PRESS) Karikatur f; (comic strip) Comics pl; (CINE) (Zeichen)trickfilm m

cartridge ['kɑːtrɪdʒ] n Patrone f

carve [kɑːv] vt (wood) schnitzen; (stone) meißeln; (meat) (vor)schneiden; **~ up** vt aufschneiden; **carving** ['kɑːvɪŋ] n Schnitzerei f; **carving knife** n Tran(s)chiermesser nt

car wash 350 Catholic

car wash n Autowäsche f

cascade ['kæskeɪd] n Wasserfall m ♦ vi kaskadenartig herabfallen

case [keɪs] n (box) Kasten m; (BRIT: also: **suitcase**) Koffer m; (JUR, matter) Fall m; **in ~** falls, im Falle; **in any ~** jedenfalls, auf jeden Fall

cash [kæʃ] n (Bar)geld nt ♦ vt einlösen; **~ on delivery** per Nachnahme; **~ book** n Kassenbuch nt; **~ card** n Scheckkarte f; **~ desk** (BRIT) n Kasse f; **~ dispenser** n Geldautomat m

cashew [kæ'ʃuː] n (also: **~ nut**) Cashewnuss f

cash flow n Cashflow m

cashier [kæ'ʃɪə*] n Kassierer(in) m(f)

cashmere ['kæʃmɪə*] n Kaschmirwolle f

cash register n Registrierkasse f

casing ['keɪsɪŋ] n Gehäuse nt

casino [kə'siːnəu] n Kasino nt

casket ['kɑːskɪt] n Kästchen nt; (US: coffin) Sarg m

casserole ['kæsərəul] n Kasserolle f; (food) Auflauf m

cassette [kæ'set] n Kassette f; **~ player** n Kassettengerät nt

cast [kɑːst] (pt, pp **cast**) vt werfen; (horns) verlieren; (metal) abgeben; (THEAT) besetzen; (vote) abgeben ♦ n (THEAT) Besetzung f; (also: **plaster ~**) Gipsverband m; **~ off** vi (NAUT) losmachen

castaway ['kɑːstəweɪ] n Schiffbrüchige(r) f(m)

caste [kɑːst] n Kaste f

caster sugar ['kɑːstə-] (BRIT) n Raffinade f

casting vote ['kɑːstɪŋ-] (BRIT) n entscheidende Stimme f

cast iron n Gusseisen nt

castle ['kɑːsl] n Burg f; Schloss nt; (CHESS) Turm m

castor ['kɑːstə*] n (wheel) Laufrolle f

castor oil n Rizinusöl nt

castrate [kæs'treɪt] vt kastrieren

casual ['kæʒjul] adj (attitude) nachlässig; (dress) leger; (meeting) zufällig; (work) Gelegenheits-; **~ly** adv (dress) zwanglos, leger; (remark) beiläufig

casualty ['kæʒjultɪ] n Verletzte(r) f(m); (dead) Tote(r) f(m); (also: **~ department**) Unfallstation f

cat [kæt] n Katze f

catalogue ['kætəlɒg] (US **catalog**) n Katalog m ♦ vt katalogisieren

catalyst ['kætəlɪst] n Katalysator m

catalytic converter [kætə'lɪtɪk kən'vɜːtə*] n Katalysator m

catapult ['kætəpʌlt] n Schleuder f

cataract ['kætərækt] n (MED) graue(r) Star m

catarrh [kə'tɑː*] n Katarr(h) m

catastrophe [kə'tæstrəfɪ] n Katastrophe f

catch [kætʃ] (pt, pp **caught**) vt fangen; (arrest) festnehmen; (train) erreichen; (person: by surprise) ertappen; (also: **~ up**) einholen ♦ vi (fire) in Gang kommen; (in branches etc) hängen bleiben ♦ n (fish etc) Fang m; (trick) Haken m; (of lock) Sperrhaken m; **to ~ an illness** sich dat eine Krankheit holen; **to ~ fire** Feuer fangen; **to ~ on** vi (understand) begreifen; (grow popular) ankommen; **~ up** vi (fig) aufholen; **~ing** ['kætʃɪŋ] adj ansteckend; **~ment area** ['kætʃmənt-] (BRIT) n Einzugsgebiet nt; **~ phrase** n Slogan m; **~y** ['kætʃɪ] adj (tune) eingängig

categoric(al) [kætɪ'gɒrɪk(l)] adj kategorisch

category ['kætɪgərɪ] n Kategorie f

cater ['keɪtə*] vi versorgen; **~ for** (BRIT) vt fus (party) ausrichten; (needs) eingestellt sein auf +acc; **~er** n Lieferant(in) m(f) von Speisen und Getränken; **~ing** n Gastronomie f

caterpillar ['kætəpɪlə*] n Raupe f; **~ track** ® n Gleiskette f

cathedral [kə'θiːdrəl] n Kathedrale f, Dom m

Catholic ['kæθəlɪk] adj (REL) katholisch ♦ n Katholik(in) m(f); **c~** adj (tastes etc) vielseitig

CAT scan [kæt-] n Computertomografie f

Catseye ['kæts'aɪ] (BRIT: ®) n (AUT) Katzenauge nt

cattle ['kætl] npl Vieh nt

catty ['kætɪ] adj gehässig

caucus ['kɔːkəs] n (POL) Gremium nt; (US: meeting) Sitzung f

caught [kɔːt] pt, pp of **catch**

cauliflower ['kɒlɪflaʊə] n Blumenkohl m

cause [kɔːz] n Ursache f; (purpose) Sache f ♦ vt verursachen

causeway ['kɔːzweɪ] n Damm m

caustic ['kɔːstɪk] adj ätzend; (fig) bissig

caution ['kɔːʃən] n Vorsicht f; (warning) Verwarnung f ♦ vt verwarnen; **cautious** ['kɔːʃəs] adj vorsichtig

cavalry ['kævəlrɪ] n Kavallerie f

cave [keɪv] n Höhle f; **~ in** vi einstürzen; **~man** (irreg) n Höhlenmensch m

cavern ['kævən] n Höhle f

caviar(e) ['kævɪɑː] n Kaviar m

cavity ['kævɪtɪ] n Loch nt

cavort [kə'vɔːt] vi umherspringen

C.B. n abbr (= Citizens' Band (Radio)) CB

C.B.I. n abbr (= Confederation of British Industry) ≈ BDI m

cc n abbr = **carbon copy**; **cubic centimetres**

CD n abbr (= compact disc) CD f

CDI n abbr (= Compact Disk Interactive) CD-I f

CD player n CD-Spieler m

CD-ROM n abbr (= compact disc read-only memory) CD-Rom f

cease [siːs] vi aufhören ♦ vt beenden; **~fire** n Feuereinstellung f; **~less** adj unaufhörlich

cedar ['siːdə] n Zeder f

ceiling ['siːlɪŋ] n Decke f; (fig) Höchstgrenze f

celebrate ['selɪbreɪt] vt, vi feiern; **~d** adj gefeiert; **celebration** [selɪ'breɪʃən] n Feier f

celebrity [sɪ'lebrɪtɪ] n gefeierte Persönlichkeit f

celery ['selərɪ] n Sellerie m or f

celibacy ['selɪbəsɪ] n Zölibat nt or m

cell [sel] n Zelle f; (ELEC) Element nt

cellar ['selə] n Keller m

cello ['tʃeləʊ] n Cello nt

Cellophane ['seləfeɪn] ® n Cellophan nt ®

cellphone ['selfəʊn] n Funktelefon nt

cellular ['seljʊlə] adj zellular

cellulose ['seljʊləʊs] n Zellulose f

Celt [kelt, selt] n Kelte m, Keltin f; **~ic** ['keltɪk, 'seltɪk] adj keltisch

cement [sə'ment] n Zement m ♦ vt zementieren; **~ mixer** n Betonmischmaschine f

cemetery ['semɪtrɪ] n Friedhof m

censor ['sensə] n Zensor m ♦ vt zensieren; **~ship** n Zensur f

censure ['senʃə] vt rügen

census ['sensəs] n Volkszählung f

cent [sent] n (US: coin) Cent m; see also **per cent**

centenary [sen'tiːnərɪ] n Jahrhundertfeier f

center ['sentə] (US) n = **centre**

centigrade ['sentɪgreɪd] adj Celsius

centimetre ['sentɪmiːtə] (US **centimeter**) n Zentimeter nt

centipede ['sentɪpiːd] n Tausendfüßler m

central ['sentrəl] adj zentral; **C~ America** n Mittelamerika nt; **~ heating** n Zentralheizung f; **~ize** vt zentralisieren; **~ reservation** (BRIT) n (AUT) Mittelstreifen m

centre ['sentə] (US **center**) n Zentrum nt ♦ vt zentrieren; **~-forward** n (SPORT) Mittelstürmer m; **~-half** n (SPORT) Stopper m

century ['sentjʊrɪ] n Jahrhundert nt

ceramic [sɪ'ræmɪk] adj keramisch; **~s** npl Keramiken pl

cereal ['sɪːrɪəl] n (grain) Getreide nt; (at breakfast) Getreideflocken pl

cerebral ['serɪbrəl] adj zerebral; (intellectual) geistig

ceremony ['serɪmənɪ] n Zeremonie f;
to stand on ~ förmlich sein

certain ['sɜːtən] adj sicher; (particular)
gewiß; **for ~** ganz bestimmt; **~ly** adv
sicher, bestimmt; **~ty** n Gewißheit f

certificate [sə'tɪfɪkɪt] n Bescheinigung
f; (SCH etc) Zeugnis nt

certified mail ['sɜːtɪfaɪd-] (US) n Einschreiben nt

certified public accountant
['sɜːtɪfaɪd-] (US) n geprüfte(r) Buchhal-
ter m

certify ['sɜːtɪfaɪ] vt bescheinigen

cervical ['sɜːvɪkl] adj (smear, cancer)
Gebärmutterhals-

cervix ['sɜːvɪks] n Gebärmutterhals m

cf. abbr (= compare) vgl.

CFC n abbr (= chlorofluorocarbon) FCKW
m

ch. abbr (= chapter) Kap.

chafe [tʃeɪf] vt scheuern

chaffinch ['tʃæfɪntʃ] n Buchfink m

chain [tʃeɪn] n Kette f ♦ vt (also: ~ up)
anketten; **~ reaction** n Kettenreaktion
f; **~-smoke** vi kettenrauchen; **~ store**
n Kettenladen m

chair [tʃeəᵊ] n Stuhl m; (armchair) Sessel
m; (UNIV) Lehrstuhl m ♦ vt (meeting)
den Vorsitz führen bei; **~lift** n Sessellift
m; **~man** (irreg) n Vorsitzende(r) m

chalet ['ʃæleɪ] n Chalet m

chalk [tʃɔːk] n Kreide f

challenge ['tʃælɪndʒ] n Herausforde-
rung f ♦ vt herausfordern; (contest) bestreiten; **challenging** adj (tone) her-
ausfordernd; (work) anspruchsvoll

chamber ['tʃeɪmbəᵊ] n Kammer f; **~ of
commerce** Handelskammer f; **~maid**
n Zimmermädchen nt; **~ music** n
Kammermusik f

chamois ['ʃæmwɑː] n Gämse f

champagne [ʃæm'peɪn] n Champagner m, Sekt m

champion ['tʃæmpɪən] n (SPORT) Meis-
ter(in) m(f); (of cause) Verfechter m
m(f); **~ship** n Meisterschaft f

chance [tʃɑːns] n (luck) Zufall m; (possibility) Möglichkeit f; (opportunity) Gelegenheit f, Chance f; (risk) Risiko nt
♦ adj zufällig ♦ vt: **to ~ it** es darauf ankommen lassen; **by ~** zufällig; **to take
a ~** ein Risiko eingehen

chancellor ['tʃɑːnsələᵊ] n Kanzler m;
C~ of the Exchequer (BRIT) n Schatz-
kanzler m

chandelier [ʃændə'lɪəᵊ] n Kronleuchter
m

change [tʃeɪndʒ] vt ändern; (replace,
COMM: money) wechseln; (exchange)
umtauschen; (transform) verwandeln
♦ vi sich ändern; (~ trains) umsteigen;
(~ clothes) sich umziehen ♦ n Veränderung f; (money returned) Wechsel-
geld nt; (coins) Kleingeld nt; **to ~ one's
mind** es sich dat anders überlegen; **to
~ into sth** (be transformed) sich in etw
acc verwandeln; **for a ~** zur Abwechslung; **~able** adj (weather) wechselhaft;
~ machine n Geldwechselautomat m;
~over n Umstellung f

changing ['tʃeɪndʒɪŋ] adj veränderlich;
~ room (BRIT) n Umkleideraum m

channel ['tʃænl] n (stream) Bachbett nt;
(NAUT) Straße f; (TV) Kanal m; (fig) Weg
m ♦ vt (efforts) lenken; **the (English)
C~** der Ärmelkanal; **~-hopping** n (TV)
ständiges Umschalten; **C~ Islands** npl:
the C~ Islands die Kanalinseln pl; **C~
Tunnel** n: **the C~ Tunnel** der Kanal-
tunnel

chant [tʃɑːnt] n Gesang m; (of fans)
Sprechchor m ♦ vt intonieren

chaos ['keɪɒs] n Chaos nt

chap [tʃæp] (inf) n Kerl m

chapel ['tʃæpl] n Kapelle f

chaperon ['ʃæpərəʊn] n Anstandsda-
me f

chaplain ['tʃæplɪn] n Kaplan m

chapped [tʃæpt] adj (skin, lips) spröde

chapter ['tʃæptəᵊ] n Kapitel nt

char [tʃɑːᵊ] vt (burn) verkohlen

character ['kærɪktəᵊ] n Charakter m,
Wesen nt; (in novel, film) Figur f; **~istic**

[kærɪktə'rɪstɪk] *adj:* **~istic (of sb/sth)** (für jdn/etw) charakteristisch ♦ *n* Kennzeichen *nt;* **~ize** *vt* charakterisieren, kennzeichnen

charade [ʃə'rɑːd] *n* Scharade *f*

charcoal ['tʃɑːkəul] *n* Holzkohle *f*

charge [tʃɑːdʒ] *n* (*cost*) Preis *m;* (*JUR*) Anklage *f;* (*explosive*) Ladung *f;* (*attack*) Angriff *m* ♦ *vt* (*gun, battery*) laden; (*price*) verlangen; (*JUR*) anklagen; (*MIL*) angreifen ♦ *vi* (*rush*) (an)stürmen; **bank ~s** Bankgebühren *pl;* **free of ~** kostenlos; **to reverse the ~s** (*TEL*) ein R-Gespräch führen; **to be in ~ of** verantwortlich sein für; **to take ~** (die Verantwortung) übernehmen; **~ sth (up) to sb's account** jdm etw in Rechnung stellen; **~ card** *n* Kundenkarte *f*

charitable ['tʃærɪtəbl] *adj* wohltätig; (*lenient*) nachsichtig

charity ['tʃærɪtɪ] *n* (*institution*) Hilfswerk *nt;* (*attitude*) Nächstenliebe *f*

charm [tʃɑːm] *n* Charme *m;* (*spell*) Bann *m;* (*object*) Talisman *m* ♦ *vt* bezaubern; **~ing** *adj* reizend

chart [tʃɑːt] *n* Tabelle *f;* (*NAUT*) Seekarte *f* ♦ *vt* (*course*) abstecken

charter ['tʃɑːtə'] *vt* chartern ♦ *n* Schutzbrief *m;* **~ed accountant** ♦ *n* Wirtschaftsprüfer(in) *m(f);* **~ flight** *n* Charterflug *m*

chase [tʃeɪs] *vt* jagen, verfolgen ♦ *n* Jagd *f*

chasm ['kæzəm] *n* Kluft *f*

chassis ['ʃæsɪ] *n* Fahrgestell *nt*

chat [tʃæt] *vi* (*also:* **have a ~**) plaudern ♦ *n* Plauderei *f;* **~ show** (*BRIT*) *n* Talkshow *f*

chatter ['tʃætə'] *vi* schwatzen; (*teeth*) klappern ♦ *n* Geschwätz *nt;* **~box** *n* Quasselstrippe *f*

chatty ['tʃætɪ] *adj* geschwätzig

chauffeur ['ʃəufə'] *n* Chauffeur *m*

chauvinist ['ʃəuvɪnɪst] *n* (*male ~*) Chauvi *m* (*inf*)

cheap [tʃiːp] *adj, adv* billig; **~ day re-**

turn *n* Tagesrückfahrkarte *f* (*zu einem günstigeren Tarif*); **~ly** *adv* billig

cheat [tʃiːt] *vt, vi* betrügen; (*SCH*) mogeln ♦ *n* Betrüger(in) *m(f)*

check [tʃek] *vt* (*examine*) prüfen; (*make sure*) nachsehen; (*control*) kontrollieren; (*restrain*) zügeln; (*stop*) anhalten ♦ *n* (*examination, restraint*) Kontrolle *f;* (*bill*) Rechnung *f;* (*pattern*) Karo(muster) *nt;* (*US*) = **cheque** ♦ *adj* (*pattern, cloth*) kariert; **~ in** *vi* (*in hotel, airport*) einchecken ♦ *vt* (*luggage*) abfertigen lassen; **~ out** *vi* (*of hotel*) abreisen; **~ up** *vi* nachschauen; **~ up on** *vt* kontrollieren; **~ered** (*US*) *adj* = **chequered**; **~ers** (*US*) *n* (*draughts*) Damespiel *nt;* **~-in (desk)** *n* Abfertigung *f;* **~ing account** (*US*) *n* (*current account*) Girokonto *nt;* **~mate** *n* Schachmatt *nt;* **~out** *n* Kasse *f;* **~point** *n* Kontrollpunkt *m;* **~ room** (*US*) *n* (*left-luggage office*) Gepäckaufbewahrung *f;* **~up** *n* (Nach)prüfung *f;* (*MED*) (ärztliche) Untersuchung *f*

cheek [tʃiːk] *n* Backe *f;* (*fig*) Frechheit *f;* **~bone** *n* Backenknochen *m;* **~y** *adj* frech

cheep [tʃiːp] *vi* piepsen

cheer [tʃɪə'] *n* (*usu pl*) Hurra- or Beifallsruf *m* ♦ *vt* zujubeln; (*encourage*) aufmuntern ♦ *vi* jauchzen; **~s!** Prost!; **~ up** *vi* bessere Laune bekommen ♦ *vt* aufmuntern; **~ up!** nun lach doch mal!; **~ful** *adj* fröhlich

cheerio [tʃɪərɪ'əu] (*BRIT*) *excl* tschüss!

cheese [tʃiːz] *n* Käse *m;* **~board** *n* (gemischte) Käseplatte *f*

cheetah ['tʃiːtə] *n* Gepard *m*

chef [ʃef] *n* Küchenchef *m*

chemical ['kemɪkl] *adj* chemisch ♦ *n* Chemikalie *f*

chemist ['kemɪst] *n* (*BRIT: pharmacist*) Apotheker, Drogist *m;* (*scientist*) Chemiker *m;* **~ry** *n* Chemie *f;* **~'s (shop)** (*BRIT*) *n* Apotheke *f;* Drogerie *f*

cheque [tʃek] (*BRIT*) *n* Scheck *m;* **~book** *n* Scheckbuch *nt;* **~ card** *n* Scheckkarte *f*

f
chequered ['tʃekəd] adj (fig) bewegt
cherish ['tʃerɪʃ] vt (person) lieben;
(hope) hegen
cherry ['tʃerɪ] n Kirsche f
chess [tʃes] n Schach nt; **~board** n
Schachbrett nt; **~man** (irreg) n
Schachfigur f
chest [tʃest] n (ANAT) Brust f; (box) Kiste
f; **~ of drawers** Kommode f
chestnut ['tʃesnʌt] n Kastanie f
chew [tʃu:] vt, vi kauen; **~ing gum** n
Kaugummi m
chic [ʃi:k] adj schick, elegant
chick [tʃɪk] n Küken nt; (US: inf: girl) Biene f
chicken ['tʃɪkɪn] n Huhn nt; (food)
Hähnchen nt; **~ out** vi (inf) kneifen
chickenpox ['tʃɪkɪnpɒks] n Windpo-
cken pl
chicory ['tʃɪkərɪ] n (in coffee) Zichorie f;
(plant) Chicorée f, Schikoree f
chief [tʃi:f] n (of tribe) Häuptling m;
(COMM) Chef m ♦ adj Haupt-; **~ executive** n Geschäftsführer(in) m(f); **~ly**
adv hauptsächlich
chilblain ['tʃɪlbleɪn] n Frostbeule f
child [tʃaɪld] (pl **~ren**) n Kind nt; **~birth**
n Entbindung f; **~hood** n Kindheit f;
~ish adj kindisch; **~like** adj kindlich; **~
minder** (BRIT) n Tagesmutter f; **~ren**
['tʃɪldrən] npl of **child**; **~ seat** n Kin-
dersitz m
Chile ['tʃɪlɪ] n Chile nt; **~an** adj chile-
nisch
chill [tʃɪl] n Kühle f; (MED) Erkältung f
♦ vt (COOK) kühlen
chilli ['tʃɪlɪ] n Peperoni pl; (meal, spice)
Chili m
chilly ['tʃɪlɪ] adj kühl, frostig
chime [tʃaɪm] n Geläut nt ♦ vi ertönen
chimney ['tʃɪmnɪ] n Schornstein m; **~
sweep** n Schornsteinfeger(in) m(f)
chimpanzee [tʃɪmpæn'zi:] n Schimpanse m
chin [tʃɪn] n Kinn nt
China ['tʃaɪnə] n China nt

china ['tʃaɪnə] n Porzellan nt
Chinese [tʃaɪ'ni:z] adj chinesisch ♦ n
(inv) Chinese m, Chinesin f; (LING) Chinesisch nt
chink [tʃɪŋk] n (opening) Ritze f; (noise)
Klirren nt
chip [tʃɪp] n (of wood etc) Splitter m; (in
poker etc; US: crisp) Chip m ♦ vt absplit-
tern; **~s** npl (BRIT: COOK) Pommes frites
pl; **~ in** vi Zwischenbemerkungen machen

Chip shop

Chip shop, auch fish-and-chip shop,
ist die traditionelle britische Imbissbu-
de, in der vor allem frittierte Fischfilets
und Pommes frites, aber auch andere
einfache Mahlzeiten angeboten werden. Früher wurde das Essen zum Mitnehmen in Zeitungspapier verpackt.
Manche chip shops haben auch einen
Essraum.

---

chiropodist [kɪ'rɒpədɪst] (BRIT) n Fuß-
pfleger(in) m(f)
chirp [tʃɜ:p] vi zwitschern
chisel ['tʃɪzl] n Meißel m
chit [tʃɪt] n Notiz f
chivalrous ['ʃɪvəlrəs] adj ritterlich;
chivalry ['ʃɪvəlrɪ] n Ritterlichkeit f
chives [tʃaɪvz] npl Schnittlauch m
chlorine ['klɔ:ri:n] n Chlor nt
chock-a-block ['tʃɒkə'blɒk] adj voll
gepfropft
chock-full [tʃɒk'ful] adj voll gepfropft
chocolate ['tʃɒklɪt] n Schokolade f
choice [tʃɔɪs] n Wahl f; (of goods) Auswahl f ♦ adj Qualitäts-
choir ['kwaɪə] n Chor m; **~boy** n
Chorknabe m
choke [tʃəuk] vi ersticken ♦ vt erdrosseln; (block) (ab)drosseln ♦ n (AUT)
Starterklappe f
cholera ['kɒlərə] n Cholera f
cholesterol [kə'lestərɒl] n Cholesterin
nt
choose [tʃu:z] (pt **chose**, pp **chosen**) vt

wählen; **choosy** ['tʃuːzɪ] *adj* wählerisch

chop [tʃɒp] *vt* (wood) spalten; (COOK: also: ~ up) (zer)hacken ♦ *n* Hieb *m*; (COOK) Kotelett *nt*; **~s** *npl* (jaws) Lefzen *pl*

chopper ['tʃɒpə'] *n* (helicopter) Hubschrauber *m*

choppy ['tʃɒpɪ] *adj* (sea) bewegt

chopsticks ['tʃɒpstɪks] *npl* (Ess)stäbchen *pl*

choral ['kɔːrəl] *adj* Chor-

chord [kɔːd] *n* Akkord *m*

chore [tʃɔː'] *n* Pflicht *f*; **~s** *npl* (housework) Hausarbeit *f*

choreographer [kɒrɪ'ɒgrəfə'] *n* Choreograf(in) *m(f)*

chorister ['kɒrɪstə'] *n* Chorsänger(in) *m(f)*

chortle ['tʃɔːtl] *vi* glucksen

chorus ['kɔːrəs] *n* Chor *m*; (in song) Refrain *m*

chose [tʃəʊz] *pt of* **choose**

chosen ['tʃəʊzn] *pp of* **choose**

chowder ['tʃaʊdə'] *n* (US) sämige Fischsuppe *f*

Christ [kraɪst] *n* Christus *m*

christen ['krɪsn] *vt* taufen; **~ing** *n* Taufe *f*

Christian ['krɪstɪən] *adj* christlich ♦ *n* Christ(in) *m(f)*; **~ity** [krɪstɪ'ænɪtɪ] *n* Christentum *nt*; **~ name** *n* Vorname *m*

Christmas ['krɪsməs] *n* Weihnachten *pl*; **Happy** *or* **Merry ~!** frohe *or* fröhliche Weihnachten!; **~ card** *n* Weihnachtskarte *f*; **~ Day** *n* der erste Weihnachtstag; **~ Eve** *n* Heiligabend *m*; **~ tree** *n* Weihnachtsbaum *m*

chrome [krəʊm] *n* Verchromung *f*

chromium ['krəʊmɪəm] *n* Chrom *nt*

chronic ['krɒnɪk] *adj* chronisch

chronicle ['krɒnɪkl] *n* Chronik *f*

chronological [krɒnə'lɒdʒɪkl] *adj* chronologisch

chubby ['tʃʌbɪ] *adj* rundlich

chuck [tʃʌk] *vt* werfen; (BRIT: also: ~ up) hinwerfen; **~ out** *vt* (person) rauswerfen; (old clothes etc) wegwerfen

chuckle ['tʃʌkl] *vi* in sich hineinlachen

chug [tʃʌg] *vi* tuckern

chunk [tʃʌŋk] *n* Klumpen *m*; (of food) Brocken *m*

church [tʃɜːtʃ] *n* Kirche *f*; **~yard** *n* Kirchhof *m*

churn [tʃɜːn] *n* (for butter) Butterfass *nt*; (for milk) Milchkanne *f*; **~ out** (inf) *vt* produzieren

chute [ʃuːt] *n* Rutsche *f*; (rubbish ~) Müllschlucker *m*

chutney ['tʃʌtnɪ] *n* Chutney *nt*

CIA (US) *n abbr* (= Central Intelligence Agency) CIA *m*

CID (BRIT) *n abbr* (= Criminal Investigation Department) ≃ Kripo *f*

cider ['saɪdə'] *n* Apfelwein *m*

cigar [sɪ'gɑː'] *n* Zigarre *f*

cigarette [sɪgə'ret] *n* Zigarette *f*; **~ case** *n* Zigarettenetui *nt*; **~ end** *n* Zigarettenstummel *m*

Cinderella [sɪndə'relə] *n* Aschenbrödel *nt*

cinders ['sɪndəz] *npl* Asche *f*

cine camera ['sɪnɪ-] (BRIT) *n* Filmkamera *f*

cine film (BRIT) *n* Schmalfilm *m*

cinema ['sɪnəmə] *n* Kino *nt*

cinnamon ['sɪnəmən] *n* Zimt *m*

circle ['sɜːkl] *n* Kreis *m*; (in cinema etc) Rang *m* ♦ *vi* kreisen ♦ *vt* (surround) umgeben; (move round) kreisen um

circuit ['sɜːkɪt] *n* (track) Rennbahn *f*; (lap) Runde *f*; (ELEC) Stromkreis *m*

circular ['sɜːkjʊlə'] *adj* rund ♦ *n* Rundschreiben *nt*

circulate ['sɜːkjʊleɪt] *vi* zirkulieren ♦ *vt* in Umlauf setzen; **circulation** [sɜːkjʊ'leɪʃən] *n* (of blood) Kreislauf *m*; (of newspaper) Auflage *f*; (of money) Umlauf *m*

circumcise ['sɜːkəmsaɪz] *vt* beschneiden

circumference [sə'kʌmfərəns] *n* (Kreis)umfang *m*

circumspect ['sɜːkəmspekt] *adj* umsichtig

circumstances ['sɜːkəmstənsɪz] npl Umstände pl; (financial) Verhältnisse pl

circumvent [sɜːkəm'vent] vt umgehen

circus ['sɜːkəs] n Zirkus m

CIS n abbr (= Commonwealth of Independent States) GUS f

cistern ['sɪstən] n Zisterne f; (of W.C.) Spülkasten m

cite [saɪt] vt zitieren, anführen

citizen ['sɪtɪzn] n Bürger(in) m(f); **~ship** n Staatsbürgerschaft f

citrus fruit ['sɪtrəs-] n Zitrusfrucht f

city ['sɪtɪ] n Großstadt f; **the C~** die City, das Finanzzentrum Londons

city technology college n ≈ Technische Fachschule f

civic ['sɪvɪk] adj (of town) städtisch; (of citizen) Bürger-; **~ centre** (BRIT) n Stadtverwaltung f

civil ['sɪvl] adj bürgerlich; (not military) zivil; (polite) höflich; **~ engineer** n Bauingenieur m; **~ian** [sɪ'vɪlɪən] n Zivilperson f ♦ adj zivil, Zivil-

civilization [sɪvɪlaɪ'zeɪʃən] n Zivilisation f

civilized ['sɪvɪlaɪzd] adj zivilisiert

civil: ~ law n Zivilrecht nt; **~ servant** n Staatsbeamte(r) m; **C~ Service** n Staatsdienst m; **~ war** n Bürgerkrieg m

clad [klæd] adj: **~ in** gehüllt in +acc

claim [kleɪm] vt beanspruchen; (have opinion) behaupten ♦ vi (for insurance) Ansprüche geltend machen ♦ n (demand) Forderung f; (right) Anspruch m; (pretension) Behauptung f; **~ant** n Antragsteller(in) m(f)

clairvoyant [kleə'vɔɪənt] n Hellseher(in) m(f)

clam [klæm] n Venusmuschel f

clamber ['klæmbə*] vi kraxeln

clammy ['klæmɪ] adj klamm

clamour ['klæmə*] vi: **to ~ for sth** nach etw verlangen

clamp [klæmp] n Schraubzwinge f ♦ vt einspannen; (AUT: wheel) krallen; **~ down on** vt fus Maßnahmen ergreifen gegen

clan [klæn] n Clan m

clandestine [klæn'destɪn] adj geheim

clang [klæŋ] vi scheppern

clap [klæp] vi klatschen ♦ vt Beifall klatschen +dat ♦ n (of hands) Klatschen nt; (of thunder) Donnerschlag m; **~ping** n Klatschen nt

claret ['klærət] n rote(r) Bordeaux(wein) m

clarify ['klærɪfaɪ] vt klären, erklären

clarinet [klærɪ'net] n Klarinette f

clarity ['klærɪtɪ] n Klarheit f

clash [klæʃ] n (fig) Konflikt m ♦ vi zusammenprallen; (colours) sich beißen; (argue) sich streiten

clasp [klɑːsp] n Griff m; (on jewels, bag) Verschluss m ♦ vt umklammern

class [klɑːs] n Klasse f ♦ vt einordnen; **~-conscious** adj klassenbewusst

classic ['klæsɪk] n Klassiker m ♦ adj klassisch; **~al** adj klassisch

classified ['klæsɪfaɪd] adj (information) Geheim-; **~ advertisement** n Kleinanzeige f

classify ['klæsɪfaɪ] vt klassifizieren

classmate ['klɑːsmeɪt] n Klassenkamerad(in) m(f)

classroom ['klɑːsrʊm] n Klassenzimmer nt

clatter ['klætə*] n klappern; (feet) trappeln

clause [klɔːz] n (JUR) Klausel f; (GRAM) Satz m

claustrophobia [klɔːstrə'fəʊbɪə] n Platzangst f

claw [klɔː] n Kralle f ♦ vt (zer)kratzen

clay [kleɪ] n Lehm m; (for pots) Ton m

clean [kliːn] adj sauber ♦ vt putzen; (clothes) reinigen; **~ out** vt gründlich putzen; **~ up** vt aufräumen; **~-cut** adj (person) adrett; (clear) klar; **~er** n (person) Putzfrau f; **~er's** n (also: dry **~er's**) Reinigung f; **~ing** n Putzen nt; (clothes) Reinigung f; **~liness** ['klenlɪnɪs] n Reinlichkeit f

cleanse [klenz] vt reinigen; **~r** n (for

face) Reinigungsmilch f

clean-shaven ['kliːn'ʃeɪvn] *adj* glatt rasiert

cleansing department ['klenzɪŋ-] *(BRIT) n* Stadtreinigung f

clear [klɪə'] *adj* klar; *(road)* frei ♦ *vt (road etc)* freimachen; *(obstacle)* beseitigen; *(JUR: suspect)* freisprechen ♦ *vi* klar werden; *(fog)* sich lichten ♦ *adv:* ~ **of** von ... entfernt; **to** ~ **the table** den Tisch abräumen; ~ **up** *vt* aufräumen; *(solve)* aufklären; **~ance** ['klɪərəns] *n (removal)* Räumung f; *(free space)* Lichtung f; *(permission)* Freigabe f; **~cut** *adj (case)* eindeutig; **~ing** *n* Lichtung f; **~ing bank** *(BRIT) n* Clearingbank f; **~ly** *adv* klar; *(obviously)* eindeutig; **~way** *(BRIT) n* (Straße f mit) Halteverbot nt

cleaver ['kliːvə'] *n* Hackbeil f

cleft [kleft] *n (in rock)* Spalte f

clementine ['kleməntaɪn] *n (fruit)* Klementine f

clench [klentʃ] *vt (teeth)* zusammenbeißen; *(fist)* ballen

clergy ['klɜːdʒɪ] *n* Geistliche(n) *pl;* **~man** *(irreg) n* Geistliche(r) *m*

clerical ['klerɪkl] *adj (office)* Schreib-, Büro-; *(REL)* geistlich

clerk [klɑːk, *(US)* klɜːrk] *n (in office)* Büroangestellte(r) *m/f;* *(US: sales person)* Verkäufer(in) *m(f)*

clever ['klevə'] *adj* klug; *(crafty)* schlau

cliché ['kliːʃeɪ] *n* Klischee nt

click [klɪk] *vt (tongue)* schnalzen mit; *(heels)* zusammenknacken

client ['klaɪənt] *n* Klient(in) *m(f);* **~ele** [kliːɑ:n'tel] *n* Kundschaft f

cliff [klɪf] *n* Klippe f

climate ['klaɪmɪt] *n* Klima nt

climax ['klaɪmæks] *n* Höhepunkt m

climb [klaɪm] *vt* besteigen ♦ *vi* steigen, klettern ♦ *n* Aufstieg m; **~-down** *n* Abstieg m; **~er** *n* Bergsteiger(in) *m(f);* **~ing** *n* Bergsteigen nt

clinch [klɪntʃ] *vt (decide)* entscheiden; *(deal)* festmachen

cling [klɪŋ] *(pt, pp* **clung)** *vi (clothes)* eng anliegen; **to** ~ **to** sich festklammern an +*dat*

clinic ['klɪnɪk] *n* Klinik f; **~al** *adj* klinisch

clink [klɪŋk] *vi* klimpern

clip [klɪp] *n* Spange f; *(also:* **paper** ~) Klammer f ♦ *vt (papers)* heften; *(hair, hedge)* stutzen; **~pers** *npl (for hedge)* Heckenschere f; *(for hair)* Haarschneidemaschine f; **~ping** *n* Ausschnitt m

cloak [kləuk] *n* Umhang m ♦ *vt* hüllen; **~room** *n (for coats)* Garderobe f; *(BRIT: W.C.)* Toilette f

clock [klɒk] *n* Uhr f; ~ **in** *or* **on** *vi* stempeln; ~ **off** *or* **out** *vi* stempeln; **~wise** *adv* im Uhrzeigersinn; **~work** *n* Uhrwerk nt ♦ *adj* zum Aufziehen

clog [klɒg] *n* Holzschuh m ♦ *vt* verstopfen

cloister ['klɔɪstə'] *n* Kreuzgang m

clone [kləun] *n* Klon m

close¹ [kləus] *adj (near)* in der Nähe; *(friend, connection, print)* eng; *(relative)* nahe; *(result)* knapp; *(examination)* eingehend; *(weather)* schwül; *(room)* stickig ♦ *adv* nahe, dicht; ~ **by** in der Nähe; ~ **at hand** in der Nähe; **to have a** ~ **shave** *(fig)* mit knapper Not davonkommen

close² [kləuz] *vt (shut)* schließen; *(end)* beenden ♦ *vi (shop etc)* schließen; *(door etc)* sich schließen ♦ *n* Ende nt; ~ **down** *vi* schließen; **~d** *adj (shop etc)* geschlossen; **~d shop** *n* Gewerkschaftszwang m

close-knit ['kləus'nɪt] *adj* eng zusammengewachsen

closely ['kləuslɪ] *adv* eng; *(carefully)* genau

closet ['klɒzɪt] *n* Schrank m

close-up ['kləuzʌp] *n* Nahaufnahme f

closure ['kləuʒə'] *n* Schließung f

clot [klɒt] *n (of blood)* Blutgerinnsel nt; *(fool)* Blödmann m ♦ *vi* gerinnen

cloth [klɒθ] *n (material)* Tuch nt; *(rag)* Lappen m

clothe [kləuð] *vt* kleiden

clothes   358   coffee

clothes [kləuðz] *npl* Kleider *pl*; ~ **brush** *n* Kleiderbürste *f*; ~ **line** *n* Wäscheleine *f*; ~ **peg**, ~ **pin** (*US*) *n* Wäscheklammer *f*

clothing ['kləuðɪŋ] *n* Kleidung *f*

clotted cream ['klɔtɪd-] (*BRIT*) *n* Sahne *f aus erhitzter Milch*

cloud [klaud] *n* Wolke *f*; **~burst** *n* Wolkenbruch *m*; **~y** *adj* bewölkt; (*liquid*) trüb

clout [klaut] *vt* hauen

clove [kləuv] *n* Gewürznelke *f*; ~ **of garlic** Knoblauchzehe *f*

clover ['kləuvə^r] *n* Klee *m*

clown [klaun] *n* Clown *m* ♦ *vi* (*also:* ~ **about**, ~ **around**) kaspern

cloying ['klɔɪɪŋ] *adj* (*taste, smell*) übersüß

club [klʌb] *n* (*weapon*) Knüppel *m*; (*society*) Klub *m*; (*also:* **golf** ~) Golfschläger *m* ♦ *vt* prügeln ♦ *vi*: **to** ~ **together** zusammenlegen; **~s** *npl* (*CARDS*) Kreuz *nt*; ~ **car** (*US*) *n* (*RAIL*) Speisewagen *m*; ~ **class** *n* (*AVIAT*) Club-Klasse *f*; **~house** *n* Klubhaus *nt*

cluck [klʌk] *vi* glucken

clue [klu:] *n* Anhaltspunkt *m*; (*in crosswords*) Frage *f*; **I haven't a** ~ (ich hab) keine Ahnung

clump [klʌmp] *n* Gruppe *f*

clumsy ['klʌmzɪ] *adj* (*person*) unbeholfen; (*shape*) unförmig

clung [klʌŋ] *pt, pp of* **cling**

cluster ['klʌstə^r] *n* (*of trees etc*) Gruppe *f* ♦ *vi* sich drängen, sich scharen

clutch [klʌtʃ] *n* Griff *m*; (*AUT*) Kupplung *f* ♦ *vt* sich festklammern an +*dat*

clutter ['klʌtə^r] *vt* voll pfropfen; (*desk*) übersäen

CND *n abbr* = **Campaign for Nuclear Disarmament**

Co. *abbr* = **county; company**

c/o *abbr* (= *care of*) c/o

coach [kəutʃ] *n* (*bus*) Reisebus *m*; (*horse-drawn*) Kutsche *f*; (*RAIL*) (Personen)wagen *m*; (*trainer*) Trainer *m* ♦ *vt* (*SCH*) Nachhilfeunterricht geben +*dat*;

(*SPORT*) trainieren; ~ **trip** *n* Busfahrt *f*

coal [kəul] *n* Kohle *f*; ~ **face** *n* Streb *m*

coalition [kəuə'lɪʃən] *n* Koalition *f*

coalman ['kəulmən] (*irreg*) *n* Kohlenhändler *m*

coal mine *n* Kohlenbergwerk *nt*

coarse [kɔ:s] *adj* grob; (*fig*) ordinär

coast [kəust] *n* Küste *f* ♦ *vi* dahinrollen; (*AUT*) im Leerlauf fahren; (*AUT*) **Küsten-**; **~guard** *n* Küstenwache *f*; **~line** *n* Küste(nlinie) *f*

coat [kəut] *n* Mantel *m*; (*on animals*) Fell *nt*; (*of paint*) Schicht *f* ♦ *vt* überstreichen; **~hanger** *n* Kleiderbügel *m*; **~ing** *n* Überzug *m*; (*of paint*) Schicht *f*; ~ **of arms** *n* Wappen *nt*

cob [kɔb] *n see* **corn**

cobbler ['kɔblə^r] *n* Schuster *m*

cobbles ['kɔblz] *npl* Pflastersteine *pl*

cobweb ['kɔbweb] *n* Spinnennetz *nt*

cocaine [kə'keɪn] *n* Kokain *nt*

cock [kɔk] *n* Hahn *m* ♦ *vt* (*gun*) entsichern; **~erel** ['kɔkərl] *n* junge(r) Hahn *m*; **~eyed** (*fig*) verrückt

cockle ['kɔkl] *n* Herzmuschel *f*

cockney ['kɔknɪ] *n* echte(r) Londoner *m*

cockpit ['kɔkpɪt] *n* (*AVIAT*) Pilotenkanzel *f*

cockroach ['kɔkrəutʃ] *n* Küchenschabe *f*

cocktail ['kɔkteɪl] *n* Cocktail *m*; ~ **cabinet** *n* Hausbar *f*; ~ **party** *n* Cocktailparty *f*

cocoa ['kəukəu] *n* Kakao *m*

coconut ['kəukənʌt] *n* Kokosnuss *f*

cocoon [kə'ku:n] *n* Kokon *m*

cod [kɔd] *n* Kabeljau *m*

C.O.D. *abbr* = **cash on delivery**

code [kəud] *n* Kode *m*; (*JUR*) Kodex *m*

cod-liver oil ['kɔdlɪvə-] *n* Lebertran *m*

coercion [kəu'ə:ʃən] *n* Zwang *m*

coffee ['kɔfɪ] *n* Kaffee *m*; ~ **bar** (*BRIT*) *n* Café *nt*; ~ **bean** *n* Kaffeebohne *f*; ~ **break** *n* Kaffeepause *f*; **~pot** *n* Kaffeekanne *f*; ~ **table** *n* Couchtisch *m*

coffin
359
come

coffin ['kɔfɪn] n Sarg m

cog [kɔg] n (Rad)zahn m

cognac ['kɔnjæk] n Kognak m

coherent [kəu'hɪərənt] adj zusammenhängend; (person) verständlich

coil [kɔɪl] n Rolle f; (ELEC) Spule f; (contraceptive) Spirale ♦ vt aufwickeln

coin [kɔɪn] n Münze f ♦ vt prägen; **~age** ['kɔɪnɪdʒ] n (word) Prägung f; **~ box** (BRIT) n Münzfernsprecher m

coincide [kəuɪn'saɪd] vi (happen together) zusammenfallen; (agree) übereinstimmen; **~nce** [kəu'ɪnsɪdəns] n Zufall m

coinphone ['kɔɪnfəun] n Münzfernsprecher m

Coke [kəuk] ® n (drink) Coca-Cola ® f

coke [kəuk] n Koks m

colander ['kɔləndə*] n Durchschlag m

cold [kəuld] adj kalt ♦ n Kälte f; (MED) Erkältung f; **I'm ~** mir ist kalt; **to catch ~** sich erkälten; **in ~ blood** kaltblütig; **to give sb the ~ shoulder** jdm die kalte Schulter zeigen; **~ly** adv kalt; **~-shoulder** vt die kalte Schulter zeigen +dat; **~ sore** n Erkältungsbläschen nt

coleslaw ['kəulslɔ:] n Krautsalat m

colic ['kɔlɪk] n Kolik f

collaborate [kə'læbəreɪt] vi zusammenarbeiten

collapse [kə'læps] vi (people) zusammenbrechen; (things) einstürzen ♦ n Zusammenbruch m; Einsturz m; **collapsible** adj zusammenklappbar, Klapp-

collar ['kɔlə*] n Kragen m; **~bone** n Schlüsselbein nt

collateral [kə'lætərl] n (zusätzliche) Sicherheit f

colleague ['kɔli:g] n Kollege m, Kollegin f

collect [kə'lɛkt] vt sammeln; (BRIT: call and pick up) abholen ♦ vi sich sammeln ♦ adv: **to call ~** (US: TEL) ein R-Gespräch führen; **~ion** [kə'lɛkʃən] n Sammlung f; (REL) Kollekte f; (of post)

Leerung f; **~ive** [kə'lɛktɪv] adj gemeinsam; (POL) kollektiv; **~or** [kə'lɛktə*] n Sammler m; (tax ~or) (Steuer)einnehmer m

college ['kɔlɪdʒ] n (UNIV) College nt; (TECH) Fach-, Berufsschule f

collide [kə'laɪd] vi zusammenstoßen

collie ['kɔlɪ] n Collie m

colliery ['kɔlɪərɪ] (BRIT) n Zeche f

collision [kə'lɪʒən] n Zusammenstoß m

colloquial [kə'ləukwɪəl] adj umgangssprachlich

colon ['kəulən] n Doppelpunkt m; (MED) Dickdarm m

colonel ['kɜ:nl] n Oberst m

colonial [kə'ləunɪəl] adj Kolonial-

colonize ['kɔlənaɪz] vt kolonisieren

colony ['kɔlənɪ] n Kolonie f

colour ['kʌlə*] (US color) n Farbe f ♦ vt (also fig) färben ♦ vi sich verfärben; **~s** npl (of club) Fahne f; **~ bar** n Rassenschranke f; **~-blind** adj farbenblind; **~ed** adj farbig; **~ film** n Farbfilm m; **~ful** adj bunt; (personality) schillernd; **~ing** n (complexion) Gesichtsfarbe f; (substance) Farbstoff m; **~ scheme** n Farbgebung f; **~ television** n Farbfernsehen nt

colt [kəult] n Fohlen nt

column ['kɔləm] n Säule f; (MIL) Kolonne f; (of print) Spalte f; **~ist** ['kɔləmnɪst] n Kolumnist m

coma ['kəumə] n Koma nt

comb [kəum] n Kamm m ♦ vt kämmen; (search) durchkämmen

combat ['kɔmbæt] n Kampf m ♦ vt bekämpfen

combination [kɔmbɪ'neɪʃən] n Kombination f

combine [vb kəm'baɪn, n 'kɔmbaɪn] vt verbinden ♦ vi sich vereinigen ♦ n (COMM) Konzern m; **~ (harvester)** n Mähdrescher m

combustion [kəm'bʌstʃən] n Verbrennung f

come [kʌm] (pt came, pp come) vi kommen; **to ~ undone** aufgehen; **~**

about vi geschehen; **~ across** vt fus (find) stoßen auf +acc; **~ away** vi (person) weggehen; (handle etc) abgehen; **~ back** vi zurückkommen; **~ by** vt fus (find): **to ~ by sth** zu etw kommen; **~ down** vi (price) fallen; **~ forward** vi (volunteer) sich melden; **~ from** vt fus (result) kommen von; **where do you come from?** wo kommen Sie her?; **I ~ from London** ich komme aus London; **~ in** vi hereinkommen; (train) einfahren; **in for** vt fus abkriegen; **~ into** vt fus (inherit) erben; **~ off** vi (handle) abgehen; (succeed) klappen; **~ on** vi (progress) vorankommen; **~ on!** komm!; (hurry) beeil dich!; **~ out** vi herauskommen; **~ round** vi (MED) wieder zu sich kommen; **~ to** vi (MED) wieder zu sich kommen ♦ vt fus (bill) sich belaufen auf +acc; **~ up** vi hochkommen; (sun) aufgehen; (problem) auftauchen; **~ up against** vt fus (resistance, difficulties) stoßen auf +acc; **~ upon** vt fus stoßen auf +acc; **~ up with** vt fus sich einfallen lassen

comedian [kə'mi:diən] n Komiker m; **comedienne** [kəmi:dr'en] n Komikerin f

comedown ['kʌmdaun] n Abstieg m

comedy ['kɔmidi] n Komödie f

comet ['kɔmit] n Komet m

comeuppance [kʌm'ʌpəns] n: **to get one's ~** seine Quittung bekommen

comfort ['kʌmfət] n Komfort m; (consolation) Trost m ♦ vt trösten; **~able** adj bequem; **~ably** adv (sit etc) bequem; (live) angenehm; **~ station** (US) n öffentliche Toilette f

comic ['kɔmik] n Comic(heft) nt; (comedian) Komiker m ♦ adj (also: **~al**) komisch; **~ strip** n Comicstrip m

coming ['kʌmiŋ] n Kommen nt; **~(s) and going(s)** n(pl) Kommen und Gehen nt

comma ['kɔmə] n Komma nt

command [kə'mɑ:nd] n Befehl m; (control) Führung f; (MIL) Kommando nt; (mastery) Beherrschung f ♦ vt befehlen +dat; (MIL) kommandieren; (be able to get) verfügen über +acc; **~er** [kə'mɑːndə[r]] vt requirieren; **~er** n Kommandant m; **~ment** n (REL) Gebot nt

commando [kə'mɑːndəu] n Kommandotruppe nt; (person) Mitglied nt einer Kommandotruppe

commemorate [kə'meməreit] vt gedenken +gen

commence [kə'mens] vt, vi beginnen

commend [kə'mend] vt (recommend) empfehlen; (praise) loben

commensurate [kə'menʃərit] adj: **~ with sth** einer Sache dat entsprechend

comment ['kɔment] n Bemerkung f ♦ vi: **to ~ (on)** sich äußern (zu); **~ary** n Kommentar m; **~ator** n Kommentator m; (TV) Reporter(in) m(f)

commerce ['kɔmə:s] n Handel m

commercial [kə'mə:ʃəl] adj kommerziell, geschäftlich; (training) kaufmännisch ♦ n (TV) Fernsehwerbung f; **~ break** n Werbespot m; **~ize** vt kommerzialisieren

commiserate [kə'mizəreit] vi: **to ~ with** Mitleid haben mit

commission [kə'miʃən] n (act) Auftrag m; (fee) Provision f; (body) Kommission f ♦ vt beauftragen; (MIL) zum Offizier ernennen; (work of art) in Auftrag geben; **out of ~** außer Betrieb; **~er** n (POLICE) Polizeipräsident m

commit [kə'mit] vt (crime) begehen; (entrust) anvertrauen; **to ~ o.s.** sich festlegen; **~ment** n Verpflichtung f

committee [kə'miti] n Ausschuss m

commodity [kə'mɔditi] n Ware f

common ['kɔmən] adj (cause) gemeinsam; (pej) gewöhnlich; (widespread) üblich, häufig ♦ n Gemeindeland nt; **the C~s** das Unterhaus; **~er** n Bürgerliche(r) mf; **~ law** n Gewohnheitsrecht nt; **~ly** adv gewöhnlich; **C~ Market** n Gemeinsame(r) Markt m; **~place** adj alltäglich;

room n Gemeinschaftsraum m; **~ sense** n gesunde(r) Menschenverstand m; **C~wealth** n: **the C~wealth** das Commonwealth

commotion [kə'məʊʃən] n Aufsehen nt

communal ['kɔmjuːnl] adj Gemeinde-; Gemeinschafts-

commune n ['kɔmjuːn, vb kə'mjuːn] n Kommune f ♦ vi: **to ~ with** sich mitteilen +dat

communicate [kə'mjuːnɪkeɪt] vt (transmit) übertragen ♦ vi (be in touch) in Verbindung stehen; (make self understood) sich verständlich machen; **communication** [kəmjuːnɪ'keɪʃən] n (message) Mitteilung f; (making understood) Kommunikation f; **communication cord** (BRIT) n Notbremse f

communion [kə'mjuːniən] n (also: **Holy C~**) Abendmahl nt, Kommunion f

communism ['kɔmjunɪzəm] n Kommunismus m; **communist** ['kɔmjunɪst] n Kommunist(in) m(f) ♦ adj kommunistisch

community [kə'mjuːnɪtɪ] n Gemeinschaft f; **~ centre** n Gemeinschaftszentrum nt; **~ chest** (US) n Wohltätigkeitsfonds m; **~ home** (BRIT) n Erziehungsheim nt

commutation ticket [kɔmju'teɪʃən-] (US) n Zeitkarte f

commute [kə'mjuːt] vi pendeln ♦ vt umwandeln; **~r** n Pendler m

compact [adj kəm'pækt, n 'kɔmpækt] adj kompakt ♦ n (for make-up) Puderdose f; **~ disc** n Compactdisc f, Compact Disc f; **~ disc player** n CD-Spieler m

companion [kəm'pænjən] n Begleiter(in) m(f); **~ship** n Gesellschaft f

company ['kʌmpənɪ] n Gesellschaft f; (COMM) Firma f, Gesellschaft f; **to keep sb ~** jdm Gesellschaft leisten; **~ secretary** (BRIT) n ≈ Prokurist(in) m(f)

comparable ['kɔmpərəbl] adj ver-

gleichbar

comparative [kəm'pærətɪv] adj (relative) relativ; **~ly** adv verhältnismäßig

compare [kəm'pɛə*] vt vergleichen ♦ vi sich vergleichen lassen; **comparison** [kəm'pærɪsn] n Vergleich m; **in comparison (with)** im Vergleich (mit or zu)

compartment [kəm'pɑːtmənt] n (RAIL) Abteil nt; (in drawer) Fach nt

compass ['kʌmpəs] n Kompass m; **~es** npl (MATH etc: also: **pair of ~es**) Zirkel m

compassion [kəm'pæʃən] n Mitleid nt; **~ate** adj mitfühlend

compatible [kəm'pætɪbl] adj vereinbar; (COMPUT) kompatibel

compel [kəm'pɛl] vt zwingen

compensate ['kɔmpənseɪt] vt entschädigen ♦ vi: **to ~ for** Ersatz leisten für; **compensation** [kɔmpən'seɪʃən] n Entschädigung f

compère ['kɔmpɛə*] n Conférencier m

compete [kəm'piːt] vi (take part) teilnehmen; (vie with) konkurrieren

competent ['kɔmpɪtənt] adj kompetent

competition [kɔmpɪ'tɪʃən] n (contest) Wettbewerb m; (COMM, rivalry) Konkurrenz f; **competitive** [kəm'petɪtɪv] adj (COMM) konkurrenzfähig; **competitor** [kəm'petɪtə*] n (COMM) Konkurrent(in) m(f); (participant) Teilnehmer(in) m(f)

compile [kəm'paɪl] vt zusammenstellen

complacency [kəm'pleɪsnsɪ] n Selbstzufriedenheit f

complacent [kəm'pleɪsnt] adj selbstzufrieden

complain [kəm'pleɪn] vi sich beklagen; (formally) sich beschweren; **~t** n Klage f; (formal ~t) Beschwerde f; (MED) Leiden nt

complement [n 'kɔmplɪmənt, vb 'kɔmplɪmɛnt] n Ergänzung f; (ship's crew etc) Bemannung f ♦ vt ergänzen; **~ary** [kɔmplɪ'mɛntərɪ] adj (sich) ergänzend

complete [kəm'pli:t] adj (full) vollkommen, ganz; (finished) fertig ♦ vt vervollständigen; (finish) beenden; (fill in: form) ausfüllen; **~ly** adv ganz; **completion** [kəm'pli:ʃən] n Fertigstellung f; (of contract etc) Abschluss m

complex ['kɒmpleks] adj kompliziert

complexion [kəm'plekʃən] n Gesichtsfarbe f; (fig) Aspekt m

complexity [kəm'pleksɪti] n Kompliziertheit f

compliance [kəm'plaɪəns] n Fügsamkeit f, Einwilligung f; **in ~ with** sth einer Sache dat gemäß

complicate ['kɒmplɪkeɪt] vt komplizieren; **~d** adj kompliziert; **complication** [kɒmplɪ'keɪʃən] n Komplikation f

compliment [n 'kɒmplɪmənt, vb 'kɒmplɪment] n Kompliment nt ♦ vt ein Kompliment machen +dat; **~s** npl (greetings) Grüße pl; **to pay sb a ~** jdm ein Kompliment machen; **~ary** [kɒmplɪ'mentərɪ] adj schmeichelhaft; (free) Frei-, Gratis-

comply [kəm'plaɪ] vi: **to ~ with** erfüllen +acc; entsprechen +dat

component [kəm'pəʊnənt] adj Teil- ♦ n Bestandteil m

compose [kəm'pəʊz] vt (music) komponieren; (poetry) verfassen; **to ~ o.s.** sich sammeln; **~d** adj gefasst; **~r** n Komponist(in) m(f); **composition** [kɒmpə'zɪʃən] n (MUS) Komposition f; (SCH) Aufsatz m; (structure) Zusammensetzung f, Aufbau m

composure [kəm'pəʊʒə*] n Fassung f

compound ['kɒmpaʊnd] n (CHEM) Verbindung f; (enclosure) Lager nt; (LING) Kompositum nt ♦ adj zusammengesetzt; (fracture) kompliziert; **~ interest** n Zinseszins m

comprehend [kɒmprɪ'hend] vt begreifen; **comprehension** n Verständnis nt

comprehensive [kɒmprɪ'hensɪv] adj umfassend ♦ n = **comprehensive school; ~ insurance** n Vollkasko nt; **~**

school (BRIT) n Gesamtschule f

compress [vb kəm'pres, n 'kɒmpres] vt komprimieren ♦ n (MED) Kompresse f

comprise [kəm'praɪz] vt (also: **be ~d of**) umfassen, bestehen aus

compromise ['kɒmprəmaɪz] n Kompromiss m ♦ vi kompromittieren ♦ vi einen Kompromiss schließen

compulsion [kəm'pʌlʃən] n Zwang m; **compulsive** [kəm'pʌlsɪv] adj zwanghaft; (smoker) süchtig; **compulsory** [kəm'pʌlsərɪ] adj obligatorisch

computer [kəm'pju:tə*] n Computer m, Rechner m; **~ game** n Computerspiel nt; **~-generated** adj computergeneriert; **~ize** vt (information) computerisieren; (company, accounts) auf Computer umstellen; **~ programmer** n Programmierer(in) m(f); **~ programming** n Programmieren nt; **~ science** n Informatik f; **computing** [kəm'pju:tɪŋ] n (science) Informatik f; (work) Computerei f

comrade ['kɒmrɪd] n Kamerad m; (POL) Genosse m

con [kɒn] vt hereinlegen ♦ n Schwindel nt

concave ['kɒnkeɪv] adj konkav

conceal [kən'si:l] vt (secret) verschweigen; (hide) verbergen

concede [kən'si:d] vt (grant) gewähren; (point) zugeben ♦ vi (admit defeat) nachgeben

conceit [kən'si:t] n Einbildung f; **~ed** adj eingebildet

conceivable [kən'si:vəbl] adj vorstellbar

conceive [kən'si:v] vt (idea) ausdenken; (imagine) sich vorstellen; (baby) empfangen ♦ vi empfangen

concentrate ['kɒnsəntreɪt] vi sich konzentrieren ♦ vt konzentrieren; **to ~ on** sth sich auf etw acc konzentrieren; **concentration** [kɒnsən'treɪʃən] n Konzentration f; **concentration camp** n Konzentrationslager nt, KZ nt

concept ['kɒnsept] n Begriff m

conception [kən'sɛpʃən] n (idea) Vorstellung f; (BIOL) Empfängnis f

concern [kən'sɜːn] n (affair) Angelegenheit f; (COMM) Unternehmen nt; (worry) Sorge f ♦ vt (interest) angehen; (be about) handeln von; (have connection with) betreffen; **to be ~ed (about)** sich Sorgen machen (um); **~ing** prep hinsichtlich +gen

concert ['kɒnsət] n Konzert nt

concerted [kən'sɜːtɪd] adj gemeinsam

concert hall n Konzerthalle f

concertina [kɒnsə'tiːnə] n Handharmonika f

concerto [kən'tʃɜːtəʊ] n Konzert nt

concession [kən'sɛʃən] n (yielding) Zugeständnis nt; **tax ~** Steuerkonzession f

conciliation [kənsɪlɪ'eɪʃən] n Versöhnung f; (official) Schlichtung f

concise [kən'saɪs] adj präzis

conclude [kən'kluːd] vt (end) beenden; (treaty) (ab)schließen; (decide) schließen, folgern; **conclusion** [kən'kluːʒən] n (Ab)schluss m; (deduction) Schluss m; **conclusive** [kən'kluːsɪv] adj schlüssig

concoct [kən'kɒkt] vt zusammenbrauen; **~ion** [kən'kɒkʃən] n Gebräu nt

concourse ['kɒŋkɔːs] n (Bahnhofs)halle f, Vorplatz m

concrete ['kɒnkriːt] n Beton m ♦ adj konkret

concur [kən'kɜːʳ] vi übereinstimmen

concurrently [kən'kʌrntlɪ] adv gleichzeitig

concussion [kən'kʌʃən] n (Gehirn)erschütterung f

condemn [kən'dɛm] vt (JUR) verurteilen; (building) abbruchreif erklären

condensation [kɒndɛn'seɪʃən] n Kondensation f

condense [kən'dɛns] vi (CHEM) kondensieren ♦ vt (fig) zusammendrängen; **~d milk** n Kondensmilch f

condescending [kɒndɪ'sɛndɪŋ] adj herablassend

condition [kən'dɪʃən] n (state) Zustand m; (presupposition) Bedingung f ♦ vt (hair etc) behandeln; (accustom) gewöhnen; **~s** npl (circumstances) Verhältnisse pl; **on ~ that ...** unter der Bedingung, dass ...; **~al** adj bedingt; **~er** n (for hair) Spülung f (for fabrics) Weichspüler m

condolences [kən'dəʊlənsɪz] npl Beileid nt

condom ['kɒndəm] n Kondom nt or m

condominium [kɒndə'mɪnɪəm] (US) n Eigentumswohnung f; (block) Eigentumsblock m

condone [kən'dəʊn] vt gutheißen

conducive [kən'djuːsɪv] adj: **~ to** dienlich +dat

conduct [n 'kɒndʌkt, vb kən'dʌkt] n (behaviour) Verhalten nt; (management) Führung f ♦ vt führen; (MUS) dirigieren; **~ed tour** n Führung f; **~or** [kən'dʌktəʳ] n (of orchestra) Dirigent m; (in bus, US: on train) Schaffner m; (ELEC) Leiter m; **~ress** [kən'dʌktrɪs] n (in bus) Schaffnerin f

cone [kəʊn] n (MATH) Kegel m; (for ice cream) (Waffel)tüte f; (BOT) Tannenzapfen m

confectioner's (shop) [kən'fɛkʃənəz-] n Konditorei f; **~y** [kən'fɛkʃənrɪ] n Süßigkeiten pl

confederation [kənfɛdə'reɪʃən] n Bund m

confer [kən'fɜːʳ] vt (degree) verleihen ♦ vi (discuss) konferieren, verhandeln; **~ence** ['kɒnfərəns] n Konferenz f

confess [kən'fɛs] vt, vi gestehen; (ECCL) beichten; **~ion** [kən'fɛʃən] n Geständnis nt; (ECCL) Beichte f; **~ional** n Beichtstuhl m

confide [kən'faɪd] vi: **to ~ in** (sich) anvertrauen +dat

confidence ['kɒnfɪdns] n Vertrauen nt; (assurance) Selbstvertrauen nt; (secret) Geheimnis nt; **in ~** (speak, write) vertraulich; **~ trick** n Schwindel m

confident ['kɒnfɪdənt] adj (sure)

überzeugt; (*self-assured*) selbstsicher

confidential [kɒnfɪˈdenʃəl] *adj* vertraulich

confine [kənˈfaɪn] *vt* (*limit*) beschränken; (*lock up*) einsperren; **~d** *adj* (*space*) eng; **~ment** *n* (*in prison*) Haft *f*; (MED) Wochenbett *nt*; **~s** [ˈkɒnfaɪnz] *npl* Grenzen *pl*

confirm [kənˈfɜːm] *vt* bestätigen; **~ation** [kɒnfəˈmeɪʃən] *n* Bestätigung *f*; (REL) Konfirmation *f*; **~ed** *adj* unverbesserlich; (*bachelor*) eingefleischt

confiscate [ˈkɒnfɪskeɪt] *vt* beschlagnahmen

conflict [*n* ˈkɒnflɪkt, *vb* kənˈflɪkt] *n* Konflikt *m* ♦ *vi* im Widerspruch stehen; **~ing** [kənˈflɪktɪŋ] *adj* widersprüchlich

conform [kənˈfɔːm] *vi*: **to ~ (to)** (*things*) entsprechen +*dat*; (*people*) sich anpassen +*dat*; (*to rules*) sich richten (nach)

confound [kənˈfaʊnd] *vt* verblüffen; (*confuse*) durcheinander bringen

confront [kənˈfrʌnt] *vt* (*enemy*) entgegentreten +*dat*; (*problems*) sich stellen +*dat*; **to ~ sb with sth** jdn mit etw konfrontieren; **~ation** [kɒnfrənˈteɪʃən] *n* Konfrontation *f*

confuse [kənˈfjuːz] *vt* verwirren; (*sth with sth*) verwechseln; **~d** *adj* verwirrt; **confusing** *adj* verwirrend; **confusion** [kənˈfjuːʒən] *n* (*perplexity*) Verwirrung *f*; (*mixing up*) Verwechslung *f*; (*tumult*) Aufruhr *m*

congeal [kənˈdʒiːl] *vi* (*freeze*) gefrieren; (*clot*) gerinnen

congested [kənˈdʒestɪd] *adj* überfüllt

congestion [kənˈdʒestʃən] *n* Stau *m*

conglomerate [*n* (COMM, GEOL) Konglomerat *nt*

conglomeration [kɒnglɒməˈreɪʃən] *n* Anhäufung *f*

congratulate [kənˈɡrætjʊleɪt] *vt*: **to ~ sb (on sth)** jdn (zu etw) beglückwünschen; **congratulations** [kənɡrætjʊˈleɪʃənz] *npl* Glückwünsche *pl*; **congratulations!** gratuliere!, herzli-

chen Glückwunsch!

congregate [ˈkɒŋɡrɪɡeɪt] *vi* sich versammeln; **congregation** [kɒŋɡrɪˈɡeɪʃən] *n* Gemeinde *f*

congress [ˈkɒŋɡres] *n* Kongress *m*; **C~man** (*irreg*: US) *n* Mitglied *nt* des amerikanischen Repräsentantenhauses

conifer [ˈkɒnɪfəʳ] *n* Nadelbaum *m*

conjunction [kənˈdʒʌŋkʃən] *n* Verbindung *f*; (GRAM) Konjunktion *f*

conjunctivitis [kəndʒʌŋktɪˈvaɪtɪs] *n* Bindehautentzündung *f*

conjure [ˈkʌndʒəʳ] *vi* zaubern; **~ up** *vt* heraufbeschwören; **~r** *n* Zauberkünstler(in) *m(f)*

conk out [kɒŋk-] (*inf*) *vi* den Geist aufgeben

con man (*irreg*) *n* Schwindler *m*

connect [kəˈnekt] *vt* verbinden; (ELEC) anschließen; **to be ~ed with** eine Beziehung haben zu; (*be related to*) verwandt sein mit; **~ion** [kəˈnekʃən] *n* Verbindung *f*; (*relation*) Zusammenhang *m*; (ELEC, TEL, RAIL) Anschluss *m*

connive [kəˈnaɪv] *vi*: **to ~ at** stillschweigend dulden

connoisseur [kɒnɪˈsɜːʳ] *n* Kenner *m*

conquer [ˈkɒŋkəʳ] *vt* (*feelings*) überwinden; (*enemy*) besiegen; (*country*) erobern; **~or** *n* Eroberer *m*

conquest [ˈkɒŋkwest] *n* Eroberung *f*

cons [kɒnz] *npl see* **convenience**; **pro**

conscience [ˈkɒnʃəns] *n* Gewissen *nt*

conscientious [kɒnʃɪˈenʃəs] *adj* gewissenhaft

conscious [ˈkɒnʃəs] *adj* bewusst; (MED) bei Bewusstsein; **~ness** *n* Bewusstsein *nt*

conscript [ˈkɒnskrɪpt] *n* Wehrpflichtige(r) *m*; **~ion** [kənˈskrɪpʃən] *n* Wehrpflicht *f*

consecutive [kənˈsekjʊtɪv] *adj* aufeinander folgend

consensus [kənˈsensəs] *n* allgemeine Übereinstimmung *f*

consent [kənˈsent] *n* Zustimmung *f* ♦ *vi* zustimmen

consequence ['kɔnsɪkwəns] n (importance) Bedeutung f; (effect) Folge f

consequently ['kɔnsɪkwəntlɪ] adv folglich

conservation [kɔnsə'veɪʃən] n Erhaltung f; (nature ~) Umweltschutz m

conservative [kən'sɜːvətɪv] adj konservativ; **C~** (BRIT) adj konservativ ♦ n Konservative(r) mf

conservatory [kən'sɜːvətrɪ] n (room) Wintergarten m

conserve [kən'sɜːv] vt erhalten

consider [kən'sɪdə*] vt überlegen; (take into account) in Betracht ziehen; (regard as) halten für; **to ~ doing sth** daran denken, etw zu tun; **~able** [kən'sɪdərəbl] adj beträchtlich; **~ably** adv beträchtlich; **~ate** adj rücksichtsvoll; **~ation** [kənsɪdə'reɪʃən] n Rücksicht(nahme) f; (thought) Erwägung f; **~ing** prep in Anbetracht +gen

consign [kən'saɪn] vt übergeben; **~ment** n Sendung f

consist [kən'sɪst] vi: **to ~ of** bestehen aus

consistency [kən'sɪstənsɪ] n (of material) Konsistenz f; (of argument, person) Konsequenz f

consistent [kən'sɪstənt] adj (person) konsequent; (argument) folgerichtig

consolation [kɔnsə'leɪʃən] n Trost m

console¹ [kən'səul] vt trösten

console² ['kɔnsəul] n Kontrollpult nt

consolidate [kən'sɔlɪdeɪt] vt festigen

consommé [kən'sɔmeɪ] n Fleischbrühe f

consonant ['kɔnsənənt] n Konsonant m, Mitlaut m

conspicuous [kən'spɪkjuəs] adj (prominent) auffällig; (visible) deutlich sichtbar

conspiracy [kən'spɪrəsɪ] n Verschwörung f

conspire [kən'spaɪə*] vi sich verschwören

constable ['kʌnstəbl] (BRIT) n Poli-

zist(in) m(f); **chief ~** Polizeipräsident m; **constabulary** [kən'stæbjulərɪ] n Polizei f

constant ['kɔnstənt] adj (continuous) ständig; (unchanging) konstant; **~ly** adv ständig

constellation [kɔnstə'leɪʃən] n Sternbild nt

consternation [kɔnstə'neɪʃən] n Bestürzung f

constipated ['kɔnstɪpeɪtɪd] adj verstopft; **constipation** [kɔnstɪ'peɪʃən] n Verstopfung f

constituency [kən'stɪtjuənsɪ] n Wahlkreis m

constituent [kən'stɪtjuənt] n (person) Wähler m; (part) Bestandteil m

constitute ['kɔnstɪtjuːt] vt (make up) bilden; (amount to) darstellen

constitution [kɔnstɪ'tjuːʃən] n Verfassung f; **~al** adj Verfassungs-

constraint [kən'streɪnt] n Zwang m; (shyness) Befangenheit f

construct [kən'strʌkt] vt bauen; **~ion** [kən'strʌkʃən] n Konstruktion f; (building) Bau m; **~ive** adj konstruktiv

construe [kən'struː] vt deuten

consul ['kɔnsl] n Konsul m; **~ate** n Konsulat nt

consult [kən'sʌlt] vt um Rat fragen; (doctor) konsultieren; (book) nachschlagen in +dat; **~ant** n (MED) Facharzt m; (other specialist) Gutachter m; **~ation** [kɔnsəl'teɪʃən] n Beratung f; (MED) Konsultation f; **~ing room** n Sprechzimmer nt

consume [kən'sjuːm] vt verbrauchen; (food) konsumieren; (drink) verzehren m; **~r** n Verbraucher m; **~r goods** npl Konsumgüter pl; **~rism** n Konsum m; **~r society** n Konsumgesellschaft f

consummate ['kɔnsʌmeɪt] vt (marriage) vollziehen

consumption [kən'sʌmpʃən] n Verbrauch m; (of food) Konsum m

cont. abbr (= continued) Forts.

contact ['kɔntækt] n (touch) Berührung

f; (connection) Verbindung f; (person)
Kontakt m ♦ vt sich in Verbindung setzen mit; **~ lenses** npl Kontaktlinsen pl
contagious [kənˈteɪdʒəs] adj ansteckend
contain [kənˈteɪn] vt enthalten; **to ~
o.s.** sich zügeln; **~er** n Behälter m;
(transport) Container m
contaminate [kənˈtæmɪneɪt] vt verunreinigen
cont'd abbr (= continued) Forts.
contemplate [ˈkɒntəmpleɪt] vt (look
at) (nachdenklich) betrachten; (think
about) überdenken; (plan) vorhaben
contemporary [kənˈtempərəri] adj
zeitgenössisch ♦ n Zeitgenosse m
contempt [kənˈtempt] n Verachtung f;
~ of court (JUR) Missachtung f des Ge-
richts; **~ible** adj verachtenswert;
~uous adj verächtlich
contend [kənˈtend] vt (argue) behaupten ♦ vi kämpfen; **~er** n (for post) Be-
werber(in) m(f); (SPORT) Wett-
kämpfer(in) m(f)
content [adj, vb kənˈtent, n ˈkɒntent]
adj zufrieden ♦ vt befriedigen ♦ n (also:
~s) Inhalt m; **~ed** adj zufrieden
contention [kənˈtenʃən] n (dispute)
Streit m; (argument) Behauptung f
contentment [kənˈtentmənt] n Zufrie-
denheit f
contest [n ˈkɒntest, vb kənˈtest] n
(Wett)kampf m ♦ vt (dispute) bestreiten; (JUR) anfechten; (POL) kandidieren
in +dat; **~ant** [kənˈtestənt] n Bewer-
ber(in) m(f)
context [ˈkɒntekst] n Zusammenhang
m
continent [ˈkɒntɪnənt] n Kontinent m;
the C~ (BRIT) das europäische Festland; **~al** [kɒntɪˈnentl] adj kontinental;
~al breakfast n kleines Frühstück nt;
~al quilt (BRIT) n Federbett nt
contingency [kənˈtɪndʒənsɪ] n
Möglichkeit f
contingent [kənˈtɪndʒənt] n Kontingent nt

continual [kənˈtɪnjʊəl] adj (endless)
fortwährend; (repeated) immer wiederkehrend; **~ly** adv immer wieder
continuation [kəntɪnjʊˈeɪʃən] n Fortsetzung f
continue [kənˈtɪnjuː] vi (person) weitermachen; (thing) weitergehen ♦ vt
fortsetzen
continuity [kɒntɪˈnjuːɪtɪ] n Kontinuität
f
continuous [kənˈtɪnjʊəs] adj ununterbrochen; **~ stationery** n Endlospapier
nt
contort [kənˈtɔːt] vt verdrehen; **~ion**
[kənˈtɔːʃən] n Verzerrung f
contour [ˈkɒntʊəʳ] n Umriss m; (also: **~
line**) Höhenlinie f
contraband [ˈkɒntrəbænd] n Schmug-
gelware f
contraception [kɒntrəˈsepʃən] n Emp-
fängnisverhütung f
contraceptive [kɒntrəˈseptɪv] n emp-
fängnisverhütende(s) Mittel nt ♦ adj
empfängnisverhütend
contract [n ˈkɒntrækt, vb kənˈtrækt] n
Vertrag m ♦ vi (muscle, metal) sich zusammenziehen ♦ vt zusammenziehen;
to ~ to do sth (COMM) sich vertraglich
verpflichten, etw zu tun; **~ion**
[kənˈtrækʃən] n (shortening) Verkürzung f; **~or** [kənˈtræktəʳ] n Unternehmer m
contradict [kɒntrəˈdɪkt] vt widersprechen +dat; **~ion** [kɒntrəˈdɪkʃən] n Widerspruch m
contraflow [ˈkɒntrəfləʊ] n (AUT)
Gegenverkehr m
contraption [kənˈtræpʃən] (inf) n Apparat m
contrary[1] [ˈkɒntrərɪ] adj (opposite) entgegengesetzt ♦ n Gegenteil nt; **on
the ~** im Gegenteil
contrary[2] [kənˈtreərɪ] adj (obstinate)
widerspenstig
contrast [n ˈkɒntrɑːst, vb kənˈtrɑːst] n
Kontrast m ♦ vt entgegensetzen; **~ing**
[kənˈtrɑːstɪŋ] adj Kontrast-

contravene [kɒntrə'viːn] vt verstoßen gegen

contribute [kən'trɪbjuːt] vt, vi: **to ~ to** beitragen zu; **contribution** [kɒntrɪ'bjuːʃən] n Beitrag m; **contributor** [kən'trɪbjutə[r]] n Beitragende(r) f(m)

contrive [kən'traɪv] vt ersinnen ♦ vi: **to ~ to do sth** es schaffen, etw zu tun

control [kən'trəʊl] vt (direct, test) kontrollieren ♦ n Kontrolle f; ~s npl (of vehicle) Steuerung f; (of engine) Schalttafel f; **to be in ~ of** (business, office) leiten; (group of children) beaufsichtigen; **out of ~** außer Kontrolle; **under ~** unter Kontrolle; **~led substance** n verschreibungspflichtiges Medikament; **~ panel** n Schalttafel f; **~ room** n Kontrollraum m; **~ tower** n (AVIAT) Kontrollturm m

controversial [kɒntrə'vɜːʃl] adj umstritten; **controversy** ['kɒntrəvɜːsɪ] n Kontroverse f

conurbation [kɒnə'beɪʃən] n Ballungsgebiet nt

convalesce [kɒnvə'les] vi genesen; **~nce** [kɒnvə'lesns] n Genesung f

convector [kən'vektə[r]] n Heizlüfter m

convene [kən'viːn] vt zusammenrufen ♦ vi sich versammeln

convenience [kən'viːnɪəns] n Annehmlichkeit f; **all modern ~s** or (BRIT) **mod cons** mit allem Komfort; **at your ~** wann es Ihnen passt

convenient [kən'viːnɪənt] adj günstig

convent ['kɒnvənt] n Kloster nt

convention [kən'venʃən] n Versammlung f; (custom) Konvention f; **~al** adj konventionell

convent school n Klosterschule f

converge [kən'vɜːdʒ] vi zusammenlaufen

conversant [kən'vɜːsnt] adj: **to be ~ with** bewandert sein in +dat

conversation [kɒnvə'seɪʃən] n Gespräch nt; **~al** adj Unterhaltungs-

converse [n 'kɒnvɜːs, vb kən'vɜːs] n

Gegenteil nt ♦ vi sich unterhalten

conversion [kən'vɜːʃən] n Umwandlung f; (REL) Bekehrung f

convert [vb kən'vɜːt, n 'kɒnvɜːt] vt (change) umwandeln; (REL) bekehren ♦ n Bekehrte(r) mf; Konvertit(in) m(f); **~ible** n (AUT) Kabriolett nt ♦ adj umwandelbar; (FIN) konvertierbar

convex ['kɒnveks] adj konvex

convey [kən'veɪ] vt (carry) befördern; (feelings) vermitteln; **~or belt** n Fließband nt

convict [vb kən'vɪkt, n 'kɒnvɪkt] vt verurteilen ♦ n Häftling m; **~ion** [kən'vɪkʃən] n (verdict) Verurteilung f; (belief) Überzeugung f

convince [kən'vɪns] vt überzeugen; **~d** adj: **~d that** überzeugt davon, dass; **convincing** adj überzeugend

convoluted ['kɒnvəluːtɪd] adj verwickelt; (style) gewunden

convoy ['kɒnvɔɪ] n (of vehicles) Kolonne f; (protected) Konvoi m

convulse [kən'vʌls] vt zusammenzucken lassen; **to be ~d with laughter** sich vor Lachen krümmen; **convulsion** [kən'vʌlʃən] n (esp MED) Zuckung f, Krampf m

coo [kuː] vi gurren

cook [kuk] vt, vi kochen ♦ n Koch m, Köchin f; **~ book** n Kochbuch nt; **~er** n Herd m; **~ery** n Kochkunst f; **~ery book** (BRIT) n = **cook book**; **~ie** (US) n Plätzchen nt; **~ing** n Kochen nt

cool [kuːl] adj kühl ♦ vt, vi (ab)kühlen; **~ down** vt, vi (fig) sich beruhigen; **~ness** n Kühle f; (of temperament) kühle(r) Kopf m

coop [kuːp] n Hühnerstall m ♦ vt: **~ up** (fig) einpferchen

cooperate [kəʊ'ɒpəreɪt] vi zusammenarbeiten; **cooperation** [kəʊɒpə'reɪʃən] n Zusammenarbeit f

cooperative [kəʊ'ɒpərətɪv] adj hilfsbereit; (COMM) genossenschaftlich ♦ n (of farmers) Genossenschaft f; (~ store) Konsumladen m

coordinate [vb kəʊˈɔːdɪneɪt, n kəʊˈɔːdɪnət] n (MATH) Koordinate f; **~s** npl (clothes) Kombinationen pl; **coordination** [kəʊːdɪˈneɪʃən] n Koordination f

cop [kɒp] (inf) n Polyp m, Bulle m

cope [kəʊp] vi: **to ~ with** fertig werden mit

copious [ˈkəʊpɪəs] adj reichhaltig

copper [ˈkɒpər] n (metal) Kupfer nt; (inf: policeman) Polyp m, Bulle m; **~s** npl (money) Kleingeld nt

copse [kɒps] n Unterholz nt

copy [ˈkɒpɪ] n (imitation) Kopie f; (of book etc) Exemplar nt; (of newspaper) Nummer f ♦ vt kopieren, abschreiben; **~right** n Copyright nt

coral [ˈkɒrəl] n Koralle f; **~ reef** n Korallenriff nt

cord [kɔːd] n Schnur f; (ELEC) Kabel nt

cordial [ˈkɔːdɪəl] adj herzlich ♦ n Fruchtsaft m

cordon [ˈkɔːdn] n Absperrkette f; **~ off** vt abriegeln

corduroy [ˈkɔːdərɔɪ] n Kord(samt) m

core [kɔːr] n Kern m ♦ vt entkernen

cork [kɔːk] n (bark) Korkrinde f; (stopper) Korken m; **~screw** n Korkenzieher m

corn [kɔːn] n (BRIT: wheat) Getreide nt, Korn nt; (US: maize) Mais m; (on foot) Hühnerauge nt; **~ on the cob** Maiskolben m

corned beef [ˈkɔːnd-] n Cornedbeef nt, Corned Beef nt

corner [ˈkɔːnər] n Ecke f; (on road) Kurve f ♦ vt in die Enge treiben; (market) monopolisieren ♦ vi (AUT) in die Kurve gehen; **~stone** n Eckstein m

cornet [ˈkɔːnɪt] n (MUS) Kornett nt; (BRIT: of ice cream) Eistüte f

corn: ~flakes [ˈkɔːnfleɪks] npl Cornflakes pl ®; **~flour** [ˈkɔːnflaʊər] (BRIT) n Maizena nt ®, **~starch** [ˈkɔːnstɑːtʃ] (US) n Maizena nt ®

corny [ˈkɔːnɪ] adj (joke) blöd(e)

coronary [ˈkɒrənərɪ] n (also: **~ throm-**

bosis) Herzinfarkt m

coronation [kɒrəˈneɪʃən] n Krönung f

coroner [ˈkɒrənər] n Untersuchungsrichter m

corporal [ˈkɔːpərl] n Obergefreite(r) m ♦ adj: **~ punishment** Prügelstrafe f

corporate [ˈkɔːpərɪt] adj gemeinschaftlich, korporativ

corporation [kɔːpəˈreɪʃən] n (of town) Gemeinde f; (COMM) Körperschaft f, Aktiengesellschaft f

corps [kɔːr] (pl **~**) n (Armee)korps nt

corpse [kɔːps] n Leiche f

correct [kəˈrekt] adj (accurate) richtig; (proper) korrekt ♦ vt korrigieren; **~ion** [kəˈrekʃən] n Berichtigung f

correlation [kɒrɪˈleɪʃən] n Wechselbeziehung f

correspond [kɒrɪsˈpɒnd] vi (agree) übereinstimmen; (exchange letters) korrespondieren; **~ence** n (similarity) Entsprechung f; (letters) Briefwechsel m, Korrespondenz f; **~ence course** n Fernkurs m; **~ent** n (PRESS) Berichterstatter m

corridor [ˈkɒrɪdɔːr] n Gang m

corroborate [kəˈrɒbəreɪt] vt bestätigen

corrode [kəˈrəʊd] vt zerfressen ♦ vi rosten

corrosion [kəˈrəʊʒən] n Korrosion f

corrugated [ˈkɒrəgeɪtɪd] adj gewellt; **~ iron** n Wellblech nt

corrupt [kəˈrʌpt] adj korrupt ♦ vt verderben; (bribe) bestechen; **~ion** [kəˈrʌpʃən] n Verdorbenheit f; (bribery) Bestechung f

corset [ˈkɔːsɪt] n Korsett nt

Corsica [ˈkɔːsɪkə] n Korsika f

cosmetics [kɒzˈmetɪks] npl Kosmetika pl

cosmic [ˈkɒzmɪk] adj kosmisch

cosmonaut [ˈkɒzmənɔːt] n Kosmonaut(in) m(f)

cosmopolitan [kɒzməˈpɒlɪtn] adj international; (city) Welt-

cosmos [ˈkɒzmɒs] n Kosmos m

cost [kɔst] (*pt, pp* **cost**) *n* Kosten *pl*,
Preis *m* ♦ *vt, vi* kosten; **~s** *npl* (JUR) Kosten *pl*; **how much does it ~?** wie viel
kostet das?; **at all ~s** um jeden Preis

co-star ['kəustɑː] *n* zweite(r) *or* weitere(r) Hauptdarsteller(in) *m(f)*

cost: ~-effective *adj* rentabel; **~ly**
['kɔstlɪ] *adj* kostspielig; **~-of-living**
['kɔstə'lɪvɪŋ] *adj* (*index*)
Lebenshaltungskosten-; **~ price** (BRIT)
n Selbstkostenpreis *m*

costume ['kɔstjuːm] *n* Kostüm *nt*; (*fancy dress*) Maskenkostüm *nt*; (BRIT: also:
swimming ~) Badeanzug *m*; **~ jewellery** *n* Modeschmuck *m*

cosy ['kəuzɪ] (BRIT) *adj* behaglich; (*atmosphere*) gemütlich

cot [kɔt] *n* (BRIT: *child's*) Kinderbett(chen) *nt*; (US: *camp bed*) Feldbett
nt

cottage ['kɔtɪdʒ] *n* kleine(s) Haus *nt*; **~
cheese** *n* Hüttenkäse *m*; **~ industry** *n*
Heimindustrie *f*; **~ pie** *n* Auflauf *mit*
Hackfleisch und Kartoffelbrei

cotton ['kɔtn] *n* Baumwolle *f*; (*thread*)
Garn *nt*; **~ on to** (*inf*) *vi* kapieren; **~
candy** (US) *n* Zuckerwatte *f*; **~ wool**
(BRIT) *n* Watte *f*

couch [kautʃ] *n* Couch *f*

couchette [kuː'ʃet] *n* (*on train, boat*)
Liegewagenplatz *m*

cough [kɔf] *vi* husten ♦ *n* Husten *m*; **~
drop** *n* Hustenbonbon *nt*

could [kud] *pt of* can²

couldn't ['kudnt] = **could not**

council ['kaunsl] *n* (*of town*) Stadtrat
m; **~ estate** (BRIT) *n* Siedlung *f* des sozialen Wohnungsbaus; **~ house** (BRIT)
n Haus *nt* des sozialen Wohnungsbaus;
~lor ['kaunslə] *n* Stadtrat *m*/-rätin *f*

counsel ['kaunsl] *n* (*barrister*) Anwalt
m; (*advice*) Rat(schlag) *m* ♦ *vt* beraten;
~lor ['kaunslə] *n* Berater *m*

count [kaunt] *vt, vi* zählen ♦ *n* (*reckoning*) Abrechnung *f*; (*nobleman*) Graf
m; **~ on** *vt* zählen auf +*acc*

countenance ['kauntinəns] *n* (*old*)

Antlitz *nt* ♦ *vt* (*tolerate*) gutheißen

counter ['kauntə] *n* (*in shop*) Ladentisch *m*; (*in café*) Theke *f*; (*in bank, post office*) Schalter *m* ♦ *vt* entgegnen

counteract ['kauntər'ækt] *vt* entgegenwirken +*dat*

counterfeit ['kauntəfɪt] *n* Fälschung *f*
♦ *vt* fälschen ♦ *adj* gefälscht

counterfoil ['kauntəfɔɪl] *n* (Kontroll)abschnitt *m*

counterpart ['kauntəpɑːt] *n* (*object*)
Gegenstück *nt*; (*person*) Gegenüber *nt*

counterproductive ['kauntəprə'dʌktɪv] *adj* destruktiv

countersign ['kauntəsaɪn] *vt* gegenzeichnen

countess ['kauntɪs] *n* Gräfin *f*

countless ['kauntlɪs] *adj* zahllos, unzählig

country ['kʌntrɪ] *n* Land *nt*; **~ dancing**
(BRIT) *n* Volkstanz *m*; **~ house** *n* Landhaus *nt*; **~man** (*irreg*) *n* (*national*)
Landsmann *m*; (*rural*) Bauer *m*; **~side**
n Landschaft *f*

county ['kauntɪ] *n* Landkreis *m*; (BRIT)
Grafschaft *f*

coup [kuː] (*pl* **~s**) *n* Coup *m*; (*also:* **~
d'état**) Staatsstreich *m*, Putsch *m*

couple ['kʌpl] *n* Paar *nt* ♦ *vt* koppeln; **a
~ of** ein paar

coupon ['kuːpɔn] *n* Gutschein *m*

coups [kuː] *npl of* **coup**

courage ['kʌrɪdʒ] *n* Mut *m*; **~ous**
[kə'reɪdʒəs] *adj* mutig

courgette [kuə'ʒet] (BRIT) *n* Zucchini *f*
or pl

courier ['kurɪə] *n* (*for holiday*) Reiseleiter *m*; (*messenger*) Kurier *m*

course [kɔːs] *n* (*race*) Bahn *f*; (*of
stream*) Lauf *m*; (*golf ~*) Platz *m*; (NAUT,
SCH) Kurs *m*; (*in meal*) Gang *m*; **of ~**
natürlich

court [kɔːt] *n* (*royal*) Hof *m*; (JUR) Gericht *nt*; (*sport*) Platz *m* ♦ *vt* (*woman*) gehen mit; (*danger*) herausfordern; **to take to ~** vor
Gericht bringen

courteous ['kɜːtɪəs] *adj* höflich

courtesy ['kɔːtəsɪ] n Höflichkeit f

courtesy bus, courtesy coach n gebührenfreier Bus m

court: ~ **house** (US) n Gerichtsgebäude nt; **~ier** ['kɔːtɪər] n Höfling m; ~ **martial** ['kɔːt'mɑːʃəl] (pl **~s martial**) n Kriegsgericht nt ♦ vt vor ein Kriegsgericht stellen; **~room** n Gerichtssaal m; **~s martial** npl of **court martial**; **~yard** ['kɔːtjɑːd] n Hof m

cousin ['kʌzn] n Cousin m, Vetter m; Kusine f

cove [kəuv] n kleine Bucht f

covenant ['kʌvənənt] n (ECCL) Bund m; (JUR) Verpflichtung f

cover ['kʌvə'] vt (spread over) bedecken; (shield) abschirmen; (include) sich erstrecken über +acc; (protect) decken; (distance) zurücklegen; (report on) berichten über +acc ♦ n (lid) Deckel m; (for bed) Decke f; (MIL) Bedeckung f; (of book) Einband m; (of magazine) Umschlag m; (insurance) Versicherung f; **to take ~** (from rain) sich unterstellen; (MIL) in Deckung gehen; **under ~** (indoors) drinnen; **under ~ of** im Schutze +gen; **under separate ~** (COMM) mit getrennter Post; **to ~ up for sb** jdn decken; **~age** n (PRESS: reports) Berichterstattung f; (distribution) Verbreitung f; **~ charge** n Bedienungsgeld nt; **~ing** n Bedeckung f; **~ing letter** (US **~ letter**) n Begleitbrief m; **~ note** n (INSURANCE) vorläufige(r) Versicherungsschein m

covert ['kʌvət] adj geheim

cover-up ['kʌvərʌp] n Vertuschung f

cow [kau] n Kuh f ♦ vt einschüchtern

coward ['kauəd] n Feigling m; **~ice** ['kauədɪs] n Feigheit f; **~ly** adj feige

cower ['kauə'] vi kauern

coy [kɔɪ] adj schüchtern

coyote [kɔɪ'əutɪ] n Präriewolf m

cozy ['kəuzɪ] (US) adj = **cosy**

CPA (US) n abbr = **certified public accountant**

crab [kræb] n Krebs m

crab apple n Holzapfel m

crack [kræk] n Riss m, Sprung m; (noise) Knall m; (drug) Crack nt ♦ vt (break) springen lassen; (joke) reißen; (nut, safe) knacken; (whip) knallen lassen ♦ vi springen; (noise) knacken ♦ adj (troops) Elite-; **~ down** vi: **to ~ down (on)** hart durchgreifen (bei); **~ up** vi (fig) zusammenbrechen

cracked [krækt] adj (glass, plate, ice) gesprungen; (rib, bone) gebrochen, angeknackst (umg); (broken) gebrochen; (surface, walls) rissig; (inf: mad) übergeschnappt

cracker ['krækə'] n (firework) Knallkörper m, Kracher m; (biscuit) Keks m; (Christmas ~) Knallbonbon nt

crackle ['krækl] vi knistern; (fire) prasseln

cradle ['kreɪdl] n Wiege f

craft [krɑːft] n (skill) (Hand- or Kunst)fertigkeit f; (trade) Handwerk nt; (NAUT) Schiff nt; **~sman** (irreg) n Handwerker m; **~smanship** n (quality) handwerkliche Ausführung f; (ability) handwerkliche(s) Können nt

crafty ['krɑːftɪ] adj schlau

crag [kræg] n Klippe f

cram [kræm] vt voll stopfen ♦ vi (learn) pauken; **to ~ sth into sth** etw in etw acc stopfen

cramp [kræmp] n Krampf m ♦ vt (limit) einengen; (hinder) hemmen; **~ed** adj (position) verkrampft; (space) eng

crampon ['kræmpən] n Steigeisen nt

cranberry ['krænbərɪ] n Preiselbeere f

crane [kreɪn] n (machine) Kran m; (bird) Kranich m

crank [kræŋk] n (lever) Kurbel f; (person) Spinner m; **~shaft** n Kurbelwelle f

cranny ['krænɪ] n see **nook**

crash [kræʃ] n (noise) Krachen nt; (with cars) Zusammenstoß m; (with plane) Absturz m; (COMM) Zusammenbruch m ♦ vt (plane) abstürzen mit ♦ vi (cars) zusammenstoßen; (plane) abstürzen; (economy) zusammenbrechen; (noise) knallen; **~ course** n Schnellkurs m; **~ helmet** n Sturzhelm m; **~ landing** n Bruchlandung f

crass [kræs] adj krass

crate [kreɪt] n (also fig) Kiste f

crater ['kreɪtə'] n Krater m

cravat(e) [krə'væt] n Halstuch nt

crave [kreɪv] vt verlangen nach

crawl [krɔːl] vi kriechen; (baby) krabbeln ♦ n Kriechen nt; (swim) Kraul nt

crayfish ['kreɪfɪʃ] n inv (freshwater) Krebs m; (saltwater) Languste f

crayon ['kreɪən] n Buntstift m

craze [kreɪz] n Fimmel m

crazy ['kreɪzɪ] adj verrückt

creak [kriːk] vi knarren

cream [kriːm] n (from milk) Rahm m, Sahne f; (polish, cosmetic) Creme f; (fig: people) Elite f ♦ adj cremefarbig; **~ cake** n Sahnetorte f; **~ cheese** n Rahmquark m; **~y** adj sahnig

crease [kriːs] n Falte f ♦ vt falten; (wrinkle) zerknittern ♦ vi (wrinkle up) knittern; **~d** adj zerknittert, faltig

create [kriː'eɪt] vt erschaffen; (cause) verursachen; **creation** [kriː'eɪʃən] n Schöpfung f; **creative** adj kreativ; **creator** n Schöpfer m

creature ['kriːtʃə'] n Geschöpf nt

crèche [kreʃ] n Krippe f

credence ['kriːdns] n: **to lend** or **give ~ to sth** etw dat Glauben schenken

credentials [krɪ'denʃlz] npl Beglaubigungsschreiben nt

credibility [kredɪ'bɪlɪtɪ] n Glaubwürdigkeit f

credible ['kredɪbl] adj (person) glaubwürdig; (story) glaubhaft

credit ['kredɪt] n (also COMM) Kredit m ♦ vt Glauben schenken +dat; (COMM) gutschreiben; **~s** npl (of film) Mitwirkende pl; **~able** adj rühmlich, ehrenhaft; **~ card** n Kreditkarte f; **~or** n Gläubiger m

creed [kriːd] n Glaubensbekenntnis nt

creek [kriːk] n (inlet) kleine Bucht f; (US: river) kleine(r) Wasserlauf m

creep [kriːp] (pt, pp **crept**) vi kriechen;

~er n Kletterpflanze f; **~y** adj (frightening) gruselig

cremate [krɪ'meɪt] vt einäschern; **cremation** [krɪ'meɪʃən] n Einäscherung f; **crematorium** [kremə'tɔːrɪəm] n Krematorium nt

crêpe [kreɪp] n Krepp m; **~ bandage** (BRIT) n Elastikbinde f

crept [krept] pt, pp of **creep**

crescent ['kresnt] n (of moon) Halbmond m

cress [kres] n Kresse f

crest [krest] n (of cock) Kamm m; (of wave) Wellenkamm m; (coat of arms) Wappen nt

crestfallen ['krestfɔːlən] adj niedergeschlagen

Crete [kriːt] n Kreta f

crevice ['krevɪs] n Riss m

crew [kruː] n Besatzung f, Mannschaft f; **~-cut** n Bürstenschnitt m; **~ neck** n runde(r) Ausschnitt m

crib [krɪb] n (bed) Krippe f ♦ vt (inf) spicken

crick [krɪk] n Muskelkrampf m

cricket ['krɪkɪt] n (insect) Grille f; (game) Kricket m

crime [kraɪm] n Verbrechen nt

criminal ['krɪmɪnl] n Verbrecher m ♦ adj kriminell; (act) strafbar

crimson ['krɪmzn] adj leuchtend rot

cringe [krɪndʒ] vi sich ducken

crinkle ['krɪŋkl] vt zerknittern

cripple ['krɪpl] n Krüppel m ♦ vt lahm legen; (MED) verkrüppeln

crisis ['kraɪsɪs] (pl **crises**) n Krise f

crisp [krɪsp] adj knusprig; **~s** (BRIT) npl Chips pl

crisscross ['krɪskrɔs] adj gekreuzt, Kreuz-

criteria [kraɪ'tɪərɪə] npl of **criterion**

criterion [kraɪ'tɪərɪən] (pl **criteria**) n Kriterium nt

critic ['krɪtɪk] n Kritiker(in) m(f); **~al** adj kritisch; **~ally** adv kritisch; (ill) gefährlich; **~ism** ['krɪtɪsɪzəm] n Kritik f; **~ize** ['krɪtɪsaɪz] vt kritisieren

croak [krəuk] vi krächzen; (frog) quaken

Croatia [krəu'eɪʃə] n Kroatien nt

crochet ['krəuʃeɪ] n Häkelei f

crockery ['krɔkərɪ] n Geschirr nt

crocodile ['krɔkədaɪl] n Krokodil nt

crocus ['krəukəs] n Krokus m

croft [krɔft] (BRIT) n kleine(s) Pachtgut nt

crony ['krəunɪ] (inf) n Kumpel m

crook [kruk] n (criminal) Gauner m; (stick) Hirtenstab m

crooked ['krukɪd] adj krumm

crop [krɔp] n (harvest) Ernte f; (riding ~) Reitpeitsche f ♦ vt ernten; **~ up** vi passieren

croquet ['krəukeɪ] n Krocket nt

croquette [krə'ket] n Krokette f

cross [krɔs] n Kreuz nt ♦ vt (road) überqueren; (legs) übereinander legen; kreuzen ♦ adj (annoyed) böse; **~ out** vt streichen; **~ over** vi hinübergehen; **~bar** n Querstange f; **~-country** (race) n Geländelauf m; **~-examine** vt ins Kreuzverhör nehmen; **~-eyed** adj: **to be ~-eyed** schielen; **~fire** n Kreuzfeuer nt; **~ing** n (~roads) (Straßen)kreuzung f; (of ship) Überfahrt f; (for pedestrians) Fußgängerüberweg m; **~ing guard** (US) n Schülerlotse m; **~ purposes** npl: **to be at ~ purposes** aneinander vorbeireden; **~-reference** n Querverweis m; **~roads** n Straßenkreuzung f; (fig) Scheideweg m; **~ section** n Querschnitt m; **~walk** (US) n Fußgängerüberweg m; **~wind** n Seitenwind m; **~word** (puzzle) n Kreuzworträtsel m

crotch [krɔtʃ] n Zwickel m; (ANAT) Unterleib m

crouch [krautʃ] vi hocken

crow [krəu] n (bird) Krähe f; (of cock) Krähen nt ♦ vi krähen

crowbar ['krəuba:ʳ] n Stemmeisen nt

crowd [kraud] n Menge f ♦ vt (fill) überfüllen ♦ vi drängen; **~ed** adj überfüllt

crown [kraun] n Krone f; (of head, hat) Kopf m ♦ vt krönen; **~ jewels** npl Kronjuwelen pl; **~ prince** n Kronprinz m

crow's-feet ['krəuzfi:t] npl Krähenfüße pl

crucial ['kru:ʃl] adj entscheidend

crucifix ['kru:sɪfɪks] n Kruzifix nt; **~ion** [kru:sɪ'fɪkʃən] n Kreuzigung f

crude [kru:d] adj (raw) roh; (humour, behaviour) grob; (basic) primitiv; **~ (oil)** n Rohöl nt

cruel ['kruəl] adj grausam; **~ty** n Grausamkeit f

cruise [kru:z] n Kreuzfahrt f ♦ vi kreuzen; **~r** n (MIL) Kreuzer m

crumb [krʌm] n Krume f

crumble ['krʌmbl] vt, vi zerbröckeln; **crumbly** adj krümelig

crumpet ['krʌmpɪt] n Tee(pfann)kuchen m

crumple ['krʌmpl] vt zerknittern

crunch [krʌntʃ] n: **the ~** (fig) der Knackpunkt ♦ vt knirschen; **~y** adj knusprig

crusade [kru:'seɪd] n Kreuzzug m

crush [krʌʃ] n Gedränge nt ♦ vt zerdrücken; (rebellion) unterdrücken

crust [krʌst] n Kruste f

crutch [krʌtʃ] n Krücke f

crux [krʌks] n springende(r) Punkt m

cry [kraɪ] vi (shout) schreien; (weep) weinen ♦ n (call) Schrei m; **~ off** vi (plötzlich) absagen

crypt [krɪpt] n Krypta f

cryptic ['krɪptɪk] adj hintergründig

crystal ['krɪstl] n Kristall m; (glass) Kristallglas nt; (mineral) Bergkristall m; **~-clear** adj kristallklar

crystallize ['krɪstəlaɪz] vt, vi kristallisieren; (fig) klären

CSA n abbr (= Child Support Agency) Amt zur Regelung von Unterhaltszahlungen für Kinder

CTC (BRIT) n abbr = **city technology college**

cub [kʌb] n Junge(s) nt; (also: **C~ scout**) Wölfling m

Cuba ['kju:bə] n Kuba nt f; **~n** adj kubanisch ♦ n Kubaner(in) m(f)

cubbyhole ['kʌbɪhəʊl] n Eckchen nt

cube [kju:b] n Würfel m ♦ vt (MATH) hoch drei nehmen

cubic ['kju:bɪk] adj würfelförmig; (centimetre etc) Kubik-; **~ capacity** n Fassungsvermögen nt

cubicle ['kju:bɪkl] n Kabine f

cuckoo ['kuku:] n Kuckuck m; **~ clock** n Kuckucksuhr f

cucumber ['kju:kʌmbə*] n Gurke f

cuddle ['kʌdl] vt, vi herzen, drücken (inf)

cue [kju:] n (THEAT) Stichwort nt; (snooker~) Billardstock m

cuff [kʌf] n (BRIT: of shirt, coat etc) Manschette f; (US) Aufschlag m; **off the ~** aus dem Handgelenk; **~link** n Manschettenknopf m

cuisine [kwɪ'zi:n] n Kochkunst f, Küche f

cul-de-sac ['kʌldəsæk] n Sackgasse f

culinary ['kʌlɪnərɪ] adj Koch-

cull [kʌl] vt (select) auswählen

culminate ['kʌlmɪneɪt] vi gipfeln; **culmination** [kʌlmɪ'neɪʃən] n Höhepunkt m

culottes [kju:'lɒts] n Hosenrock m

culpable ['kʌlpəbl] adj schuldig

culprit ['kʌlprɪt] n Täter m

cult [kʌlt] n Kult m

cultivate ['kʌltɪveɪt] vt (AGR) bebauen; (mind) bilden; **cultivation** [kʌltɪ'veɪʃən] n (AGR) Bebauung f; (of person) Bildung f

cultural ['kʌltʃərəl] adj kulturell, Kultur-

culture ['kʌltʃə*] n Kultur f; **~d** adj gebildet

cumbersome ['kʌmbəsəm] adj (object) sperrig

cumulative ['kju:mjʊlətɪv] adj gehäuft

cunning ['kʌnɪŋ] n Verschlagenheit f ♦ adj schlau

cup [kʌp] n Tasse f; (prize) Pokal m

cupboard ['kʌbəd] n Schrank m

cup tie (BRIT) n Pokalspiel nt

curate ['kjʊarɪt] n (Catholic) Kurat m; (Protestant) Vikar m

curator [kjʊə'reɪtə*] n Kustos m

curb [kə:b] vt zügeln ♦ n (on spending etc) Einschränkung f; (US) Bordstein m

curdle ['kə:dl] vi gerinnen

cure [kjʊə*] n Heilmittel nt; (process) Heilverfahren nt ♦ vt heilen

curfew ['kə:fju:] n Ausgangssperre f; Sperrstunde f

curio ['kjʊərɪəʊ] n Kuriosität f

curiosity [kjʊərɪ'ɒsɪtɪ] n Neugier f

curious ['kjʊərɪəs] adj neugierig; (strange) seltsam

curl [kə:l] n Locke f ♦ vt locken ♦ vi sich locken; **~ up** vi sich zusammenrollen; (person) sich ankuscheln; **~er** n Lockenwickler m; **~y** ['kə:lɪ] adj lockig

currant ['kʌrnt] n Korinthe f

currency ['kʌrnsɪ] n Währung f; **to gain ~** an Popularität gewinnen

current ['kʌrnt] n Strömung f ♦ adj (expression) gängig, üblich; (issue) neueste; **~ account** n Girokonto nt; **~ affairs** npl Zeitgeschehen nt; **~ly** adv zurzeit

curricula [kə'rɪkjʊlə] npl of curriculum

curriculum [kə'rɪkjʊləm] (pl **~s** or **curricula**) n Lehrplan m; **~ vitae** [-'vi:taɪ] n Lebenslauf m

curry ['kʌrɪ] n Currygericht nt ♦ vt: **to ~ favour with** sich einschmeicheln bei; **~ powder** n Curry(pulver) nt

curse [kə:s] vi (swear): **to ~ (at)** fluchen (auf or über +acc) ♦ vt (insult) verwünschen ♦ n Fluch m

cursor ['kə:sə*] n (COMPUT) Cursor m

cursory ['kə:sərɪ] adj flüchtig

curt [kə:t] adj schroff

curtail [kə:'teɪl] vt abkürzen; (rights) einschränken

curtain ['kə:tn] n Vorhang m

curts(e)y ['kə:tsɪ] n Knicks m ♦ vi knicksen

curve [kə:v] n Kurve f; (of body, vase

cushion ['kuʃən] n Kissen nt ♦ vt dämpfen

custard ['kʌstəd] n Vanillesoße f

custodian [kʌs'təudiən] n Kustos m, Verwalter(in) m(f)

custody ['kʌstədi] n Aufsicht f; (police ~) Haft f; **to take into ~** verhaften

custom ['kʌstəm] n (tradition) Brauch m; (COMM) Kundschaft f; **~ary** adj üblich

customer ['kʌstəmə*] n Kunde m, Kundin f

customized ['kʌstəmaizd] adj (car etc) mit Spezialausrüstung

custom-made ['kʌstəm'meid] adj speziell angefertigt

customs ['kʌstəmz] npl Zoll m; **~ duty** n Zollabgabe f; **~ officer** n Zollbeamte(r) m, Zollbeamtin f

cut [kʌt] (pt, pp **cut**) vt schneiden; (wages) kürzen; (prices) heruntersetzen ♦ vi schneiden; (intersect) sich schneiden ♦ n Schnitt m; (wound) Schnittwunde f; (in income etc) Kürzung f; (share) Anteil m; **to ~ a tooth** zahnen; **~ down** vt (tree) fällen; (reduce) einschränken; **~ off** vt (also fig) abschneiden; (allowance) sperren; **~ out** vt (shape) ausschneiden; (delete) streichen; **~ up** vt (meat) aufschneiden; **~back** n Kürzung f

cute [kju:t] adj niedlich

cuticle ['kju:tikl] n Nagelhaut f

cutlery ['kʌtləri] n Besteck nt

cutlet ['kʌtlit] n (pork) Kotelett nt; (veal) Schnitzel nt

cut: ~out n (cardboard ~out) Ausschneidemodell nt; **~-price**, (US) **~-rate** adj verbilligt; **~throat** n Verbrechertyp m ♦ adj mörderisch

cutting ['kʌtiŋ] adj schneidend ♦ n (BRIT: PRESS) Ausschnitt m; (: RAIL) Durchstich m

CV n abbr = **curriculum vitae**

cwt abbr = **hundredweight(s)**

cyanide ['saiənaid] n Zyankali nt

cybercafé ['saibəkæfei] n Internetcafé nt, Cybercafé nt

cyberspace ['saibəspeis] n Cyberspace m

cycle ['saikl] n Fahrrad nt; (series) Reihe f ♦ vi Rad fahren; **~ hire** n Fahrradverleih m; **~ lane**, **~ path** n (Fahr)radweg m; **cycling** n Radfahren nt; **cyclist** n Radfahrer(in) m(f)

cyclone ['saikləun] n Zyklon m

cygnet ['signit] n junge(r) Schwan m

cylinder ['silində*] n Zylinder m; (TECH) Walze f; **~ head gasket** n Zylinderkopfdichtung f

cymbals ['simblz] npl Becken nt

cynic ['sinik] n Zyniker(in) m(f); **~al** adj zynisch; **~ism** ['sinisizəm] n Zynismus m

cypress ['saiprəs] n Zypresse f

Cyprus ['saiprəs] n Zypern nt

cystitis [sis'taitis] n Blasenentzündung f

czar [zɑ:*] n Zar m

Czech [tʃek] adj tschechisch ♦ n Tscheche m, Tschechin f

Czechoslovakia [tʃekəslə'vækiə] (HIST) n die Tschechoslowakei; **~n** adj tschechoslowakisch ♦ n Tschechoslowake m, Tschechoslowakin f

D, d

D [di:] n (MUS) D nt

dab [dæb] vt (wound, paint) betupfen ♦ n (little bit) bisschen nt; (of paint) Tupfer m

dabble ['dæbl] vi: **to ~ in sth** in etw dat machen

dad [dæd] n Papa m, Vati m; **~dy** ['dædi] n Papa m, Vati m; **~dy-long-legs** n Weberknecht m

daffodil ['dæfədil] n Osterglocke f

daft [dɑ:ft] (inf) adj blöd(e), doof

dagger ['dægə*] n Dolch m

daily ['deili] adj täglich ♦ n (PRESS) Tageszeitung f; (BRIT: cleaner) Haushaltshilfe f ♦ adv täglich

dainty ['deɪntɪ] adj zierlich

dairy ['dɛərɪ] n (shop) Milchgeschäft nt; (on farm) Molkerei f ♦ adj Milch-; ~ **farm** n Hof m mit Milchwirtschaft; ~ **produce** n Molkereiprodukte pl; ~ **products** npl Milchprodukte pl, Molkereiprodukte pl; ~ **store** (US) n Milchgeschäft nt

dais ['deɪs] n Podium nt

daisy ['deɪzɪ] n Gänseblümchen nt

dale [deɪl] n Tal nt

dam [dæm] n (Stau)damm m ♦ vt stauen

damage ['dæmɪdʒ] n Schaden m ♦ vt beschädigen; ~**s** npl (JUR) Schaden(s)ersatz m

damn [dæm] vt verdammen ♦ n (inf): I don't give a ~ das ist mir total egal ♦ adj (inf: also: ~ed) verdammt; ~ **it!** verflucht!; ~**ing** adj vernichtend

damp [dæmp] adj feucht ♦ n Feuchtigkeit f ♦ vt (also: ~**en**) befeuchten; (discourage) dämpfen

damson ['dæmzən] n Damaszenerpflaume f

dance [dɑːns] n Tanz m ♦ vi tanzen; ~ **hall** n Tanzlokal nt; ~**r** n Tänzer(in) m(f); **dancing** n Tanzen nt

dandelion ['dændɪlaɪən] n Löwenzahn m

dandruff ['dændrəf] n (Kopf)schuppen pl

Dane [deɪn] n Däne m, Dänin f

danger ['deɪndʒər] n Gefahr f; ~! (sign) Achtung!; **to be in ~ of doing sth** Gefahr laufen, etw zu tun; ~**ous** adj gefährlich

dangle ['dæŋgl] vi baumeln ♦ vt herabhängen lassen

Danish ['deɪnɪʃ] adj dänisch ♦ n Dänisch nt

dare [dɛər] vt herausfordern ♦ vi: **to ~ (to) do sth** es wagen, etw zu tun; I ~ **say** ich würde sagen; **daring** ['dɛərɪŋ] adj (audacious) verwegen; (bold) wage-

mutig; (dress) gewagt ♦ n Mut m

dark [dɑːk] adj dunkel; (fig) düster, trübe; (deep colour) dunkel- ♦ n Dunkelheit f; **to be left in the ~ about** etw +acc) nach Anbruch der Dunkelheit; **~en** vt, vi verdunkeln; ~ **glasses** npl Sonnenbrille f; **~ness** n Finsternis nt; **~room** n Dunkelkammer f

darling ['dɑːlɪŋ] n Liebling m ♦ adj lieb

darn [dɑːn] vt stopfen

dart [dɑːt] n (weapon) Pfeil m; (in sewing) Abnäher m ♦ vi sausen; ~**s** n (game) Pfeilwerfen nt; **~board** n Zielscheibe f

dash [dæʃ] n Sprung m; (mark) (Gedanken)strich m; (small amount) bisschen nt ♦ vt (hopes) zunichte machen; (rush) stürzen; ~ **away** vi davonstürzen; ~ **off** vi davonstürzen

dashboard ['dæʃbɔːd] n Armaturenbrett nt

dashing ['dæʃɪŋ] adj schneidig

data ['deɪtə] npl Einzelheiten pl, Daten pl; **~base** n Datenbank f; ~ **processing** n Datenverarbeitung f

date [deɪt] n Datum nt; (for meeting etc) Termin m; (with person) Verabredung f; (fruit) Dattel f ♦ vt (letter etc) datieren; (person) gehen mit; ~ **of birth** Geburtsdatum nt; **to ~** bis heute; **out of ~** überholt; **up to ~** (clothes) modisch; (report) up-to-date; (with news) auf dem Laufenden; **~d** adj altmodisch; **~ rape** n Vergewaltigung f nach einem Rendezvous

daub [dɔːb] vt beschmieren; (paint) schmieren

daughter ['dɔːtər] n Tochter f; **~-in-law** n Schwiegertochter f

daunting ['dɔːntɪŋ] adj entmutigend

dawdle ['dɔːdl] vi trödeln

dawn [dɔːn] n Morgendämmerung f ♦ vi dämmern; (fig): **it ~ed on him that ...** es dämmerte ihm, dass ...

day [deɪ] n Tag m; **the ~ before/after** am Tag zuvor/danach; **the ~ after to-**

morrow übermorgen; **the ~ before yesterday** vorgestern; **by ~** am Tage; **~break** n Tagesanbruch m; **~dream** vi mit offenen Augen träumen; **~light** n Tageslicht nt; **~return** (BRIT) n Tagesrückfahrkarte f; **~time** n Tageszeit f; **~-to~** adj alltäglich

daze [deɪz] vt betäuben ♦ n Betäubung f; **in a ~** benommen

dazzle ['dæzl] vt blenden

DC abbr (= direct current) Gleichstrom m

D-day ['diːdeɪ] n (HIST) Tag der Invasion durch die Alliierten (6.6.44); (fig) der Tag X

deacon ['diːkən] n Diakon m

dead [ded] adj tot; (without feeling) gefühllos ♦ adv ganz; (exactly) genau ♦ npl: **the ~** die Toten pl; **to shoot sb ~** jdn erschießen; **~ tired** todmüde; **to stop ~** abrupt stehen bleiben; **~en** vt (pain) abtöten; (sound) ersticken; **~ end** n Sackgasse f; **~ heat** n tote(s) Rennen nt; **~line** n Stichtag m; **~lock** n Stillstand m; **~ loss** (inf) n: **to be a ~ loss** ein hoffnungslose(r) Fall sein; **~ly** adj tödlich; **~pan** adj undurchdringlich; **D~ Sea** n: **the D~ Sea** das Tote Meer

deaf [def] adj taub; **~en** vt taub machen; **~ening** adj (noise) ohrenbetäubend; (noise) lautstark; **~-mute** n Taubstumme(r) mf; **~ness** n Taubheit f

deal [diːl] (pt, pp **dealt**) n Geschäft nt ♦ vt austeilen; (CARDS) geben; **a great ~ of** sehr viel; **~ in** vt fus handeln mit; **~ with** vt fus (person) behandeln; (subject) sich befassen mit; (problem) in Angriff nehmen; **~er** n (COMM) Händler m; (CARDS) Kartengeber m; **~ings** npl (FIN) Geschäfte pl; (relations) Beziehungen pl; **~t** [delt] pt, pp of **deal**

dean [diːn] n (Protestant) Superintendent m; (Catholic) Dechant m; (UNIV) Dekan m

dear [dɪəʳ] adj lieb; (expensive) teuer ♦ n Liebling m ♦ excl: **~ me!** du liebe Zeit!;

D~ Sir Sehr geehrter Herr!; **D~ John** Lieber John!; **~ly** adv (love) herzlich; (pay) teuer

death [deθ] n Tod m; (statistic) Todesfall m; **~ certificate** n Totenschein m; **~ly** adj totenähnlich, Toten-; **~ penalty** n Todesstrafe f; **~ rate** n Sterblichkeitsziffer f

debar [dɪ'baːʳ] vt ausschließen

debase [dɪ'beɪs] vt entwerten

debatable [dɪ'beɪtəbl] adj anfechtbar

debate [dɪ'beɪt] n Debatte f ♦ vt debattieren, diskutieren; (consider) überlegen

debilitating [dɪ'bɪlɪteɪtɪŋ] adj schwächend

debit ['debɪt] n Schuldposten m ♦ vt belasten

debris ['debriː] n Trümmer pl

debt [det] n Schuld f; **to be in ~** verschuldet sein; **~or** n Schuldner m

debunk [diː'bʌŋk] vt entlarven

decade ['dekeɪd] n Jahrzehnt m

decadence ['dekədəns] n Dekadenz f

decaff ['diːkæf] (inf) n koffeinfreier Kaffee

decaffeinated [diː'kæfɪneɪtɪd] adj koffeinfrei

decanter [dɪ'kæntəʳ] n Karaffe f

decay [dɪ'keɪ] n Verfall m; (tooth ~) Karies m ♦ vi verfallen; (teeth, meat etc) faulen; (leaves etc) verrotten

deceased [dɪ'siːst] adj verstorben

deceit [dɪ'siːt] n Betrug m; **~ful** adj falsch

deceive [dɪ'siːv] vt täuschen

December [dɪ'sembəʳ] n Dezember m

decency ['diːsənsɪ] n Anstand m

decent ['diːsənt] adj (respectable) anständig; (pleasant) annehmbar

deception [dɪ'sepʃən] n Betrug m

deceptive [dɪ'septɪv] adj irreführend

decibel ['desɪbel] n Dezibel nt

decide [dɪ'saɪd] vt entscheiden ♦ vi sich entscheiden; **to ~ on sth** etw beschließen; **~d** adj entscheiden; **~dly** [dɪ'saɪdɪdlɪ] adv entschieden

deciduous [dɪ'sɪdjuəs] adj Laub-

decimal ['desɪməl] adj dezimal ♦ n Dezimalzahl f; **~ point** n Komma nt

decipher [dɪ'saɪfər] vt entziffern

decision [dɪ'sɪʒən] n Entscheidung f, Entschluss m

decisive [dɪ'saɪsɪv] adj entscheidend; (person) entschlossen

deck [dek] n (NAUT) Deck nt; (of cards) Pack m; **~chair** n Liegestuhl m

declaration [deklə'reɪʃən] n Erklärung f

declare [dɪ'klɛər] vt erklären; (CUSTOMS) verzollen

decline [dɪ'klaɪn] n (decay) Verfall m; (lessening) Rückgang m ♦ vt (invitation) ablehnen ♦ vi (say no) ablehnen; (of strength) nachlassen

decode ['di:'kəʊd] vt entschlüsseln; **~r** n (TV) Decoder m

decompose [di:kəm'pəʊz] vi (sich) zersetzen

décor ['deɪkɔːr] n Ausstattung f

decorate ['dekəreɪt] vt (room: paper) tapezieren; (: paint) streichen; (adorn) (aus)schmücken; (cake) verzieren; (honour) auszeichnen; **decoration** [dekə'reɪʃən] n (of house) (Wand)dekoration f; (medal) Orden m; **decorator** ['dekəreɪtər] n Maler m, Anstreicher m

decorum [dɪ'kɔːrəm] n Anstand m

decoy ['di:kɔɪ] n Lockvogel m

decrease [n 'di:kri:s, vb di:'kri:s] n Abnahme f ♦ vt verringern ♦ vi abnehmen

decree [dɪ'kri:] n Erlass m; **~ nisi** n vorläufige(s) Scheidungsurteil nt

decrepit [dɪ'krepɪt] adj hinfällig

dedicate ['dedɪkeɪt] vt widmen; **~d** adj hingebungsvoll, engagiert; (COMPUT) dediziert; **dedication** [dedɪ'keɪʃən] n (devotion) Ergebenheit f; (in book) Widmung f

deduce [dɪ'dju:s] vt: **to ~ sth (from sth)** etw (aus etw) ableiten, etw (aus etw) schließen

deduct [dɪ'dʌkt] vt abziehen; **~ion**

[dɪ'dʌkʃən] n (of money) Abzug m; (conclusion) (Schluss)folgerung f

deed [di:d] n Tat f; (document) Urkunde f

deem [di:m] vt: **to ~ sb/sth (to be)** sth jdn/etw für etw halten

deep [di:p] adj tief ♦ adv: **the spectators stood 20 ~** die Zuschauer standen in 20 Reihen hintereinander; **to be 4m ~** 4 Meter tief sein; **~en** vt vertiefen ♦ vi (darkness) tiefer werden; **~end** n: **the ~ end** (of swimming pool) das Tiefe; **~-freeze** n Tiefkühlung f; **~-fry** vt frittieren; **~ly** adv tief; **~-sea diving** n Tiefseetauchen nt; **~-seated** adj tief sitzend

deer [dɪər] n Reh nt; **~skin** n Hirsch-/ Rehleder nt

deface [dɪ'feɪs] vt entstellen

defamation [defə'meɪʃən] n Verleumdung f

default [dɪ'fɔːlt] n Versäumnis nt; (COMPUT) Standardwert m ♦ vi versäumen; **by ~** durch Nichterstehen

defeat [dɪ'fi:t] n Niederlage f ♦ vt schlagen; **~ist** adj defätistisch ♦ n Defätist m

defect [n 'di:fekt, vb dɪ'fekt] n Fehler m ♦ vi überlaufen; (to dɪ'fektɪv] adj fehlerhaft

defence [dɪ'fens] n Verteidigung f; **~less** adj wehrlos

defend [dɪ'fend] vt verteidigen; **~ant** n Angeklagte(r) mf; **~er** n Verteidiger m

defense [dɪ'fens] (US) n = **defence**

defensive [dɪ'fensɪv] adj defensiv ♦ n: **on the ~** in der Defensive

defer [dɪ'fɜːr] vt verschieben

deference ['defərəns] n Rücksichtnahme f

defiance [dɪ'faɪəns] n Trotz m, Unnachgiebigkeit f; **in ~ of sth** einer Sache dat zum Trotz

defiant [dɪ'faɪənt] adj trotzig, unnachgiebig

deficiency [dɪ'fɪʃənsɪ] n (lack) Mangel m; (weakness) Schwäche f

deficient [dɪ'fɪʃənt] *adj* mangelhaft

deficit ['defɪsɪt] *n* Defizit *nt*

defile [*vb* dɪ'faɪl, *n* 'di:faɪl] *vt* beschmutzen ♦ *n* Hohlweg *m*

define [dɪ'faɪn] *vt* bestimmen; *(explain)* definieren

definite ['defɪnɪt] *adj (fixed)* definitiv; *(clear)* eindeutig; **~ly** *adv* bestimmt

definition [defɪ'nɪʃən] *n* Definition *f*

deflate [di:'fleɪt] *vt* die Luft ablassen aus

deflect [dɪ'flekt] *vt* ablenken

deformity [dɪ'fɔ:mɪtɪ] *n* Missbildung *f*

defraud [dɪ'frɔ:d] *vt* betrügen

defrost [di:'frɒst] *vt (fridge)* abtauen; *(food)* auftauen; **~er** *(US) n (demister)* Gebläse *nt*

deft [deft] *adj* geschickt

defunct [dɪ'fʌŋkt] *adj* verstorben

defuse [di:'fju:z] *vt* entschärfen

defy [dɪ'faɪ] *vt (disobey)* sich widersetzen +*dat*; *(orders, death)* trotzen +*dat*; *(challenge)* herausfordern

degenerate [*v* dɪ'dʒenəreɪt, *adj* dɪ'dʒenərɪt] *vi* degenerieren ♦ *adj* degeneriert

degrading [dɪ'greɪdɪŋ] *adj* erniedrigend

degree [dɪ'gri:] *n* Grad *m*; *(UNIV)* Universitätsabschluss *m*; **by ~s** allmählich; **to some ~** zu einem gewissen Grad

dehydrated [di:haɪ'dreɪtɪd] *adj (person)* ausgetrocknet

de-ice ['di:'aɪs] *vt* enteisen

deign [deɪn] *vi* sich herablassen

deity ['di:ɪtɪ] *n* Gottheit *f*

dejected [dɪ'dʒektɪd] *adj* niedergeschlagen

delay [dɪ'leɪ] *vt (hold back)* aufschieben ♦ *vi (linger)* sich aufhalten ♦ *n* Aufschub *m*, Verzögerung *f*; *(of train etc)* Verspätung *f*; **to be ~ed** *(train)* Verspätung haben; **without ~** unverzüglich

delectable [dɪ'lektəbl] *adj* köstlich; *(fig)* reizend

delegate [*n* 'delɪgɪt, *vb* 'delɪgeɪt] *n* Delegierte(r) *mf* ♦ *vt* delegieren

delete [dɪ'li:t] *vt* (aus)streichen

deliberate [*adj* dɪ'lɪbərɪt, *vb* dɪ'lɪbəreɪt] *adj (intentional)* absichtlich; *(slow)* bedächtig ♦ *vi (consider)* überlegen; *(debate)* sich beraten; **~ly** *adv* absichtlich

delicacy ['delɪkəsɪ] *n* Zartheit *f*; *(weakness)* Anfälligkeit *f*; *(food)* Delikatesse *f*

delicate ['delɪkɪt] *adj (fine)* fein; *(fragile)* zart; *(situation)* heikel; *(MED)* empfindlich

delicatessen [delɪkə'tesn] *n* Feinkostgeschäft *nt*

delicious [dɪ'lɪʃəs] *adj* lecker

delight [dɪ'laɪt] *n* Wonne *f* ♦ *vt* entzücken; **to take ~ in sth** Freude an etw *dat* haben; **~ed** *adj*: **~ed (at** *or* **with sth)** entzückt (über +*acc* etw); **~ed to do sth** etw sehr gern tun; **~ful** *adj* entzückend, herrlich

delinquency [dɪ'lɪŋkwənsɪ] *n* Kriminalität *f*

delinquent [dɪ'lɪŋkwənt] *n* Straffällige(r) *mf* ♦ *adj* straffällig

delirious [dɪ'lɪrɪəs] *adj* im Fieberwahn

deliver [dɪ'lɪvər] *vt (goods)* (ab)liefern; *(letter)* zustellen; *(speech)* halten; **~y** *n* (Ab)lieferung *f*; *(of letter)* Zustellung *f*; *(of speech)* Vortragsweise *f*; *(MED)* Entbindung *f*; **to take ~y of** in Empfang nehmen

delude [dɪ'lu:d] *vt* täuschen

deluge ['delju:dʒ] *n* Überschwemmung *f*; *(fig)* Flut *f* ♦ *vt (fig)* überfluten

delusion [dɪ'lu:ʒən] *n* (Selbst)täuschung *f*

de luxe [də'lʌks] *adj* Luxus-

delve [delv] *vi*: **to ~ into** sich vertiefen in +*acc*

demand [dɪ'mɑ:nd] *vt* verlangen ♦ *n (request)* Verlangen *nt*; *(COMM)* Nachfrage *f*; **in ~** gefragt; **on ~** auf Verlangen; **~ing** *adj* anspruchsvoll

demean [dɪ'mi:n] *vt*: **to ~ o.s.** sich erniedrigen

demeanour [dɪ'mi:nər] *(US* **de**

meanor) *n* Benehmen *nt*

demented [dɪˈmɛntɪd] *adj* wahnsinnig

demister [diːˈmɪstə*] *n* (AUT) Gebläse *nt*

demo [ˈdɛməʊ] (*inf*) *n abbr* (= demon-stration) Demo *f*

democracy [dɪˈmɒkrəsɪ] *n* Demokratie *f*

democrat [ˈdɛməkræt] *n* Demokrat *m*; **democratic** [dɛməˈkrætɪk] *adj* demo-kratisch

demolish [dɪˈmɒlɪʃ] *vt* abreißen; (*fig*) vernichten

demolition [dɛməˈlɪʃən] *n* Abbruch *m*

demon [ˈdiːmən] *n* Dämon *m*

demonstrate [ˈdɛmənstreɪt] *vt*, *vi* de-monstrieren; **demonstration** [dɛmənˈstreɪʃən] *n* Demonstration *f*; **demonstrator** [ˈdɛmənstreɪtə*] *n* (POL) Demonstrant(in) *m(f)*

demote [dɪˈməʊt] *vt* degradieren

demure [dɪˈmjʊə*] *adj* ernst

den [dɛn] *n* (*of animal*) Höhle *f*; (*study*) Bude *f*

denatured alcohol [diːˈneɪtʃəd-] (US) *n* ungenießbar gemachte(r) Alkohol *m*

denial [dɪˈnaɪəl] *n* Leugnung *f*; **official ~** *n* Dementi *nt*

denim [ˈdɛnɪm] *adj* Denim-; **~s** *npl* De-nimjeans *pl*

Denmark [ˈdɛnmɑːk] *n* Dänemark *nt*

denomination [dɪnɒmɪˈneɪʃən] *n* (ECCL) Bekenntnis *nt*; (*type*) Klasse *f*; (FIN) Wert *m*

denote [dɪˈnəʊt] *vt* bedeuten

denounce [dɪˈnaʊns] *vt* brandmarken

dense [dɛns] *adj* dicht; (*stupid*) schwer von Begriff; **~ly** *adv* dicht; **density** [ˈdɛnsɪtɪ] *n* Dichte *f*; **single/double density disk** Diskette *f* mit einfacher/doppelter Dichte

dent [dɛnt] *n* Delle *f* ♦ *vt* (*also*: **make a ~ in**) einbeulen

dental [ˈdɛntl] *adj* Zahn-; **~ surgeon** *n* = dentist

dentist [ˈdɛntɪst] *n* Zahnarzt(ärztin) *m(f)*

dentures [ˈdɛntʃəz] *npl* Gebiss *nt*

deny [dɪˈnaɪ] *vt* leugnen; (*officially*) de-mentieren; (*help*) abschlagen

deodorant [diːˈəʊdərənt] *n* Deodorant *nt*

depart [dɪˈpɑːt] *vi* abfahren; **to ~ from** (*fig*: *differ from*) abweichen von

department [dɪˈpɑːtmənt] *n* (COMM) Abteilung *f*; (UNIV) Seminar *nt*; (POL) Ministerium *nt*; **~ store** *n* Warenhaus *nt*

departure [dɪˈpɑːtʃə*] *n* (*of person*) Abreise *f*; (*of train*) Abfahrt *f*; (*of plane*) Abflug *m*; **new ~** Neuerung *f*; **~ lounge** *n* (*at airport*) Abflughalle *f*

depend [dɪˈpɛnd] *vi*: **to ~ on** ab-hängen von; (*rely on*) angewiesen sein auf *+acc*; **it ~s** es kommt darauf an; **~ing on the result ...** abhängend vom Resultat ...; **~able** *adj* zuverlässig; **~ant** *n* Angehörige(r) *f(m)*; **~ence** *n* Abhängigkeit *f*; **~ent** *adj* abhängig ♦ *n* = dependant; **~ent on** abhängig von

depict [dɪˈpɪkt] *vt* schildern

depleted [dɪˈpliːtɪd] *adj* aufgebraucht

deplorable [dɪˈplɔːrəbl] *adj* bedauer-lich

deploy [dɪˈplɔɪ] *vt* einsetzen

depopulation [ˈdiːpɒpjuˈleɪʃən] *n* Ent-völkerung *f*

deport [dɪˈpɔːt] *vt* deportieren; **~ation** [diːpɔːˈteɪʃən] *n* Abschiebung *f*

deportment [dɪˈpɔːtmənt] *n* Betragen *nt*

deposit [dɪˈpɒzɪt] *n* (*in bank*) Guthaben *nt*; (*down payment*) Anzahlung *f*; (*security*) Kaution *f*; (CHEM) Niederschlag *m* ♦ *vt* (*in bank*) deponieren; (*put down*) niederlegen; **~ account** *n* Sparkonto *nt*

depot [ˈdɛpəʊ] *n* Depot *nt*

depraved [dɪˈpreɪvd] *adj* verkommen

depreciate [dɪˈpriːʃɪeɪt] *vi* im Wert sin-ken; **depreciation** [dɪpriːʃɪˈeɪʃən] *n* Wertminderung *f*

depress [dɪˈprɛs] *vt* (*press down*) nie-derdrücken; (*in mood*) deprimieren; **~ed** *adj* deprimiert; **~ion** [dɪˈprɛʃən] *n* (mood) Depression f; (in trade) Wirtschaftskrise f; (hollow) Vertiefung f; (MET) Tief(druckgebiet) nt

deprivation [deprɪˈveɪʃən] n Not f

deprive [dɪˈpraɪv] vt: **to ~ sb of sth** jdn einer Sache gen berauben; **~d** (child) sozial benachteiligt; (area) unterentwickelt

depth [depθ] n Tiefe f; **in the ~s of despair** in tiefster Verzweiflung

deputation [depjʊˈteɪʃən] n Abordnung f

deputize [ˈdepjʊtaɪz] vi: **to ~ (for sb)** (jdn) vertreten

deputy [ˈdepjʊtɪ] adj stellvertretend ♦ n (Stell)vertreter m; **~ head** (BRIT: SCOL) n Konrektor(in) m(f)

derail [dɪˈreɪl] vt: **to be ~ed** entgleisen; **~ment** n Entgleisung f

deranged [dɪˈreɪndʒd] adj verrückt

derby [ˈdɑːbɪ] (US) n Melone f

derelict [ˈderɪlɪkt] adj verlassen

deride [dɪˈraɪd] vt auslachen

derisory [dɪˈraɪsərɪ] adj spöttisch

derivative [dɪˈrɪvətɪv] n Derivat nt ♦ adj abgeleitet

derive [dɪˈraɪv] vt (get) gewinnen; (deduce) ableiten ♦ vi (come from) abstammen

dermatitis [dəːməˈtaɪtɪs] n Hautentzündung f

derogatory [dɪˈrɒgətərɪ] adj geringschätzig

derrick [ˈderɪk] n Drehkran m

descend [dɪˈsend] vt, vi hinuntersteigen; **to ~ from** abstammen von; **~ant** n Nachkomme m; **descent** [dɪˈsent] n (coming down) Abstieg m; (origin) Abstammung f

describe [dɪsˈkraɪb] vt beschreiben

description [dɪsˈkrɪpʃən] n Beschreibung f; (sort) Art f

descriptive [dɪsˈkrɪptɪv] adj beschreibend; (word) anschaulich

desecrate [ˈdesɪkreɪt] vt schänden

desert [n ˈdezət, vb dɪˈzəːt] n Wüste f ♦ vt verlassen; (temporarily) im Stich

lassen ♦ vi (MIL) desertieren; **~s** npl (what one deserves): **to get one's just ~s** seinen gerechten Lohn bekommen; **~er** n Deserteur m; **~ion** [dɪˈzəːʃən] n (of wife) Verlassen nt; (MIL) Fahnenflucht f; **~ island** n einsame Insel f

deserve [dɪˈzəːv] vt verdienen; **deserving** adj verdienstvoll

design [dɪˈzaɪn] n (plan) Entwurf m; (planning) Design nt ♦ vt entwerfen

designate [vb ˈdezɪgneɪt, adj ˈdezɪgnɪt] vt bestimmen ♦ adj designiert

designer [dɪˈzaɪnəʳ] n Designer(in) m(f); (TECH) Konstrukteur(in) m(f); (fashion ~) Modeschöpfer(in) m(f)

desirable [dɪˈzaɪərəbl] adj wünschenswert

desire [dɪˈzaɪəʳ] n Wunsch m, Verlangen nt ♦ vt (lust) begehren; (ask for) wollen

desk [desk] n Schreibtisch m; (BRIT: in shop, restaurant) Kasse f; **~top publishing** n Desktop-Publishing nt

desolate [ˈdesəlɪt] adj öde; (sad) trostlos; **desolation** [desəˈleɪʃən] n Trostlosigkeit f

despair [dɪsˈpeəʳ] n Verzweiflung f ♦ vi: **to ~ (of)** verzweifeln (an +dat)

despatch [dɪsˈpætʃ] n, vt = **dispatch**

desperate [ˈdespərɪt] adj verzweifelt; **~ly** adv verzweifelt; **desperation** [despəˈreɪʃən] n Verzweiflung f

despicable [dɪsˈpɪkəbl] adj abscheulich

despise [dɪsˈpaɪz] vt verachten

despite [dɪsˈpaɪt] prep trotz +gen

despondent [dɪsˈpɒndənt] adj mutlos

dessert [dɪˈzəːt] n Nachtisch m; **~spoon** n Dessertlöffel m

destination [destɪˈneɪʃən] n (of person) (Reise)ziel nt; (of goods) Bestimmungsort m

destiny [ˈdestɪnɪ] n Schicksal nt

destitute [ˈdestɪtjuːt] adj Not leidend

destroy [dɪsˈtrɔɪ] vt zerstören; **~er** n (NAUT) Zerstörer m

destruction [dɪsˈtrʌkʃən] n Zerstörung f

destructive [dɪs'trʌktɪv] adj zerstörend

detach [dɪ'tætʃ] vt loslösen; **~able** adj abtrennbar; **~ed** adj (attitude) distanziert; (house) Einzel-; **~ment** n (fig) Abstand m; (MIL) Sonderkommando nt

detail ['diːteɪl] n Einzelheit f, Detail m ♦ vt (relate) ausführlich berichten; (appoint) abkommandieren; **in ~** im Detail; **~ed** adj detailliert

detain [dɪ'teɪn] vt aufhalten; (imprison) in Haft halten

detect [dɪ'tekt] vt entdecken; **~ion** [dɪ'tekʃən] n Aufdeckung f; **~ive** n Detektiv m; **~ive story** n Kriminalgeschichte f, Krimi m

détente [deɪ'tɑːnt] n Entspannung f

detention [dɪ'tenʃən] n Haft f; (SCH) Nachsitzen nt

deter [dɪ'tɜː*] vt abschrecken

detergent [dɪ'tɜːdʒənt] n Waschmittel nt

deteriorate [dɪ'tɪərɪəreɪt] vi sich verschlechtern; **deterioration** [dɪtɪərɪə'reɪʃən] n Verschlechterung f

determination [dɪtɜːmɪ'neɪʃən] n Entschlossenheit f

determine [dɪ'tɜːmɪn] vt bestimmen; **~d** adj entschlossen

deterrent [dɪ'terənt] n Abschreckungsmittel nt

detest [dɪ'test] vt verabscheuen

detonate ['detəneɪt] vt explodieren lassen ♦ vi detonieren

detour ['diːtuə*] n Umweg m; (US: AUT: diversion) Umleitung f ♦ vt (US: AUT: traffic) umleiten

detract [dɪ'trækt] vi: **to ~ from** schmälern

detriment ['detrɪmənt] n: **to the ~ of** zum Schaden +gen; **~al** [detrɪ'mentl] adj schädlich

devaluation [dɪvæljuˈeɪʃən] n Abwertung f

devastate ['devəsteɪt] vt verwüsten; (fig: shock): **to be ~d by** niedergeschmettert sein von; **devastating** adj verheerend

develop [dɪ'veləp] vt entwickeln; (resources) erschließen ♦ vi sich entwickeln; **~ing country** n Entwicklungsland nt; **~ment** n Entwicklung f

deviate ['diːvɪeɪt] vi abweichen

device [dɪ'vaɪs] n Gerät nt

devil ['devl] n Teufel m

devious ['diːvɪəs] adj (means) krumm; (person) verschlagen

devise [dɪ'vaɪz] vt entwickeln

devoid [dɪ'vɔɪd] adj: **~ of** ohne

devolution [diːvə'luːʃən] n (POL) Dezentralisierung f

devote [dɪ'vəʊt] vt: **to ~ sth (to sth)** etw (einer Sache dat) widmen; **~d** adj ergeben; **~e** [devəʊ'tiː] n Anhänger(in) m(f), Verehrer(in) m(f); **devotion** [dɪ'vəʊʃən] n (piety) Andacht f; (loyalty) Ergebenheit f, Hingabe f

devour [dɪ'vaʊə*] vt verschlingen

devout [dɪ'vaʊt] adj andächtig

dew [djuː] n Tau m

dexterity [deks'terɪtɪ] n Geschicklichkeit f

DHSS (BRIT) n abbr = **Department of Health and Social Security**

diabetes [daɪə'biːtiːz] n Zuckerkrankheit f

diabetic [daɪə'betɪk] adj zuckerkrank; (food) Diabetiker- ♦ n Diabetiker m

diabolical [daɪə'bɒlɪkl] (inf) adj (weather, behaviour) saumäßig

diagnose [daɪəg'nəʊz] vt diagnostizieren

diagnoses [daɪəg'nəʊsiːz] npl of **diagnosis**

diagnosis [daɪəg'nəʊsɪs] n Diagnose f

diagonal [daɪ'ægənl] adj diagonal ♦ n Diagonale f

diagram ['daɪəgræm] n Diagramm nt, Schaubild nt

dial ['daɪəl] n (TEL) Wählscheibe f; (of clock) Zifferblatt nt ♦ vt wählen

dialect ['daɪəlekt] n Dialekt m

dialling code ['daɪəlɪŋ-] n Vorwahl f

dialling tone n Amtszeichen nt

dialogue ['daɪəlɒg] n Dialog m

dial tone (US) n = **dialling tone**

diameter [daɪˈæmɪtə*] n Durchmesser m

diamond [ˈdaɪəmənd] n Diamant m; **~s** npl (CARDS) Karo nt

diaper [ˈdaɪəpə*] (US) n Windel f

diaphragm [ˈdaɪəfræm] n Zwerchfell nt

diarrhoea [daɪəˈrɪːə], (US **diarrhea**) n Durchfall m

diary [ˈdaɪərɪ] n Taschenkalender m; (account) Tagebuch nt

dice [daɪs] n Würfel pl ♦ vt in Würfel schneiden

dictate [dɪkˈteɪt] vt diktieren; **~s** [ˈdɪkteɪts] npl Gebote pl; **dictation** [dɪkˈteɪʃən] n Diktat nt

dictator [dɪkˈteɪtə*] n Diktator m; **~ship** [dɪkˈteɪtəʃɪp] n Diktatur f

dictionary [ˈdɪkʃənrɪ] n Wörterbuch nt

did [dɪd] pt of **do**

didn't [ˈdɪdnt] = **did not**

die [daɪ] vi sterben; **to be dying for sth** etw unbedingt haben wollen; **to be dying to do sth** darauf brennen, etw zu tun; **~ away** vi schwächer werden; **~ down** vi nachlassen; **~ out** vi aussterben

diesel [ˈdiːzl] n (car) Diesel m; **~ engine** n Dieselmotor m; **~ oil** n Dieselkraftstoff m

diet [ˈdaɪət] n Nahrung f; (special food) Diät f; (slimming) Abmagerungskur f ♦ vi (also: **be on a ~**) eine Abmagerungskur machen

differ [ˈdɪfə*] vi sich unterscheiden; (disagree) anderer Meinung sein; **~ence** n Unterschied m; **~ent** adj anders; (two things) verschieden; **~entiate** [dɪfəˈrɛnʃɪeɪt] vt, vi unterscheiden; **~ently** adv anders; (from one another) unterschiedlich

difficult [ˈdɪfɪkəlt] adj schwierig; **~y** n Schwierigkeit f

diffident [ˈdɪfɪdənt] adj schüchtern

diffuse [adj dɪˈfjuːs, vb dɪˈfjuːz] adj langatmig ♦ vt verbreiten

dig [dɪg] (pt, pp **dug**) vt graben ♦ n

(prod) Stoß m; (remark) Spitze f; (archaeological) Ausgrabung f; **~ in** vi (MIL) sich eingraben; **~ into** vt fus (savings) angreifen; **~ up** vt ausgraben; (fig) aufgabeln

digest [vb dɪˈdʒɛst, n ˈdaɪdʒɛst] vt verdauen ♦ n Auslese f; **~ion** [dɪˈdʒɛstʃən] n Verdauung f

digit [ˈdɪdʒɪt] n Ziffer f; (ANAT) Finger m; **~al** adj digital, Digital-; **~al TV** n Digitalfernsehen nt

dignified [ˈdɪgnɪfaɪd] adj würdevoll

dignity [ˈdɪgnɪtɪ] n Würde f

digress [daɪˈgrɛs] vi abschweifen

digs [dɪgz] (BRIT: inf) npl Bude f

dilapidated [dɪˈlæpɪdeɪtɪd] adj baufällig

dilate [daɪˈleɪt] vt weiten ♦ vi sich weiten

dilemma [daɪˈlɛmə] n Dilemma nt

diligent [ˈdɪlɪdʒənt] adj fleißig

dilute [daɪˈluːt] vt verdünnen

dim [dɪm] adj trübe; (stupid) schwer von Begriff ♦ vt verdunkeln; (AUT): **to ~ one's headlights** (esp US) abblenden

dime [daɪm] (US) n Zehncentstück nt

dimension [daɪˈmɛnʃən] n Dimension f

diminish [dɪˈmɪnɪʃ] vt, vi verringern

diminutive [dɪˈmɪnjutɪv] adj winzig ♦ n Verkleinerungsform f

dimmer [ˈdɪmə*] (US) n (AUT) Abblendschalter m; **~s** npl Abblendlicht nt; (sidelights) Begrenzungsleuchten pl

dimple [ˈdɪmpl] n Grübchen nt

din [dɪn] n Getöse nt

dine [daɪn] vi speisen; **~r** n Tischgast m; (RAIL) Speisewagen m

dinghy [ˈdɪŋgɪ] n Dingi nt; **rubber ~** Schlauchboot nt

dingy [ˈdɪndʒɪ] adj armselig

dining car (BRIT) n Speisewagen m

dining room [ˈdaɪnɪŋ-] n Esszimmer nt; (in hotel) Speisezimmer nt

dinner [ˈdɪnə*] n (lunch) Mittagessen nt; (evening) Abendessen nt; (public) Festessen nt; **~ jacket** n Smoking m; **~**

party n Tischgesellschaft f; **~ time** n Tischzeit f

dinosaur ['daɪnəsɔ:ʳ] n Dinosaurier m

dint [dɪnt] n: **by ~ of** durch

diocese ['daɪəsɪs] n Diözese f

dip [dɪp] n (hollow) Senkung f; (bathe) kurze(s) Baden nt ♦ vt eintauchen; (BRIT: AUT) abblenden ♦ vi (slope) sich senken, abfallen

diploma [dɪ'pləʊmə] n Diplom nt

diplomacy [dɪ'pləʊməsɪ] n Diplomatie f

diplomat ['dɪpləmæt] n Diplomat(in) m(f); **~ic** [dɪplə'mætɪk] adj diplomatisch

dip stick n Ölmessstab m

dipswitch ['dɪpswɪtʃ] (BRIT) n (AUT) Abblendschalter m

dire [daɪəʳ] adj schrecklich

direct [daɪ'rekt] adj direkt ♦ vt leiten; (film) die Regie führen +gen; (aim) richten; (order) anweisen; **can you ~ me to ...?** können Sie mir sagen, wie ich zu ... komme?; **~ debit** n (BRIT) Einzugsauftrag m; (transaction) automatische Abbuchung f

direction [dɪ'rekʃən] n Richtung f; (CINE) Regie f; Leitung f; **~s** npl (for use) Gebrauchsanleitung f; (orders) Anweisungen pl; **sense of ~** Orientierungssinn m

directly [dɪ'rektlɪ] adv direkt; (at once) sofort

director [dɪ'rektəʳ] n Direktor m; (of film) Regisseur m

directory [dɪ'rektərɪ] n (TEL) Telefonbuch nt; **~ enquiries**, **~ assistance** (US) n (Fernsprech)auskunft f

dirt [dɜːt] n Schmutz m, Dreck m; **~-cheap** adj spottbillig; **~y** adj schmutzig ♦ vt beschmutzen; **~y trick** n gemeine(r) Trick m

disability [dɪsə'bɪlɪtɪ] n Körperbehinderung f

disabled [dɪs'eɪbld] adj körperbehindert

disadvantage [dɪsəd'vɑ:ntɪdʒ] n

Nachteil m

disagree [dɪsə'gri:] vi nicht übereinstimmen; (quarrel) (sich) streiten; (food): **to ~ with sb** jdm nicht bekommen; **~able** adj unangenehm; **~ment** n (between persons) Streit m; (between things) Widerspruch m

disallow [dɪsə'laʊ] vt nicht zulassen

disappear [dɪsə'pɪəʳ] vi verschwinden; **~ance** n Verschwinden nt

disappoint [dɪsə'pɔɪnt] vt enttäuschen; **~ed** adj enttäuscht; **~ment** n Enttäuschung f

disapproval [dɪsə'pru:vəl] n Missbilligung f

disapprove [dɪsə'pru:v] vi: **to ~ of** missbilligen

disarm [dɪs'ɑ:m] vt entwaffnen; (POL) abrüsten; **~ament** n Abrüstung f

disarray [dɪsə'reɪ] n: **in ~** (army) in Auflösung (begriffen) sein; (clothes) in unordentlichem Zustand sein

disaster [dɪ'zɑ:stəʳ] n Katastrophe f; **disastrous** [dɪ'zɑ:strəs] adj verhängnisvoll

disband [dɪs'bænd] vt auflösen ♦ vi auseinander gehen

disbelief ['dɪsbə'li:f] n Ungläubigkeit f

disc [dɪsk] n Scheibe f; (record) (Schall)platte f; (COMPUT) = **disk**

discard [dɪs'kɑ:d] vt ablegen

discern [dɪ'sɜːn] vt erkennen; **~ing** adj scharfsinnig

discharge [vb dɪs'tʃɑ:dʒ, n 'dɪstʃɑ:dʒ] vt (ship) entladen; (duties) nachkommen +dat; (dismiss) entlassen; (gun) abschießen; (JUR) freisprechen ♦ n (of ship, ELEC) Entladung f; (dismissal) Entlassung f; (MED) Ausfluss m

disciple [dɪ'saɪpl] n Jünger m

discipline ['dɪsɪplɪn] n Disziplin f ♦ vt (train) schulen; (punish) bestrafen

disc jockey n Diskjockey m

disclaim [dɪs'kleɪm] vt nicht anerkennen

disclose [dɪs'kləʊz] vt enthüllen; **disclosure** [dɪs'kləʊʒəʳ] n Enthüllung f

disco ['dɪskəu] n abbr = **discotheque**

discoloured [dɪs'kʌləd] (US **discoloured**) adj verfärbt

discomfort [dɪs'kʌmfət] n Unbehagen nt

disconcert [dɪskən'sɜːt] vt aus der Fassung bringen

disconnect [dɪskə'nekt] vt abtrennen

disconnect [dɪskə'nekt] vt abtrennen

discontent [dɪskən'tent] n Unzufriedenheit f; **~ed** adj unzufrieden

discontinue [dɪskən'tɪnjuː] vt einstellen

discord ['dɪskɔːd] n Zwietracht f; (noise) Dissonanz f

discotheque ['dɪskəutek] n Diskothek f

discount [n 'dɪskaunt, vb dɪs'kaunt] n Rabatt m ♦ vt außer Acht lassen

discourage [dɪs'kʌrɪdʒ] vt entmutigen; (prevent) abraten

discourteous [dɪs'kɜːtɪəs] adj unhöflich

discover [dɪs'kʌvər] vt entdecken; **~y** n Entdeckung f

discredit [dɪs'kredɪt] vt in Verruf bringen

discreet [dɪs'kriːt] adj diskret

discrepancy [dɪs'krepənsɪ] n Diskrepanz f

discriminate [dɪs'krɪmɪneɪt] vi unterscheiden; **to ~ against** diskriminieren; **discriminating** adj anspruchsvoll; **discrimination** [dɪskrɪmɪ'neɪʃən] n Urteilsvermögen nt; (pej) Diskriminierung f

discuss [dɪs'kʌs] vt diskutieren, besprechen; **~ion** [dɪs'kʌʃən] n Diskussion f, Besprechung f

disdain [dɪs'deɪn] n Verachtung f

disease [dɪ'ziːz] n Krankheit f

disembark [dɪsɪm'bɑːk] vi von Bord gehen

disenchanted [dɪsɪn'tʃɑːntɪd] adj desillusioniert

disengage [dɪsɪn'geɪdʒ] vt (AUT) auskuppeln

disentangle [dɪsɪn'tæŋgl] vt entwirren

disfigure [dɪs'fɪgər] vt entstellen

disgrace [dɪs'greɪs] n Schande f ♦ vt Schande bringen über +acc; **~ful** adj unerhört

disgruntled [dɪs'grʌntld] adj verärgert

disguise [dɪs'gaɪz] vt verkleiden; (feelings) verhehlen ♦ n Verkleidung f; **in ~** verkleidet, maskiert

disgust [dɪs'gʌst] n Abscheu f ♦ vt anwidern; **~ed** adj angeekelt; (at sb's behaviour) empört; **~ing** adj widerlich

dish [dɪʃ] n Schüssel f; (food) Gericht nt; **to do** or **wash the ~es** abwaschen; **~ up** vt auftischen; **~ cloth** n Spüllappen m

dishearten [dɪs'hɑːtn] vt entmutigen

dishevelled [dɪ'ʃevəld] adj (hair) zerzaust; (clothing) ungepflegt

dishonest [dɪs'ɔnɪst] adj unehrlich

dishonour [dɪs'ɔnər] (US **dishonor**) n Unehre f; **~able** adj unehrenhaft

dishtowel ['dɪʃtauəl] n Geschirrtuch nt

dishwasher ['dɪʃwɔʃər] n Geschirrspülmaschine f

disillusion [dɪsɪ'luːʒən] vt enttäuschen, desillusionieren

disincentive [dɪsɪn'sentɪv] n Entmutigung f

disinfect [dɪsɪn'fekt] vt desinfizieren; **~ant** n Desinfektionsmittel nt

disintegrate [dɪs'ɪntɪgreɪt] vi sich auflösen

disinterested [dɪs'ɪntrəstɪd] adj uneigennützig; (inf) uninteressiert

disjointed [dɪs'dʒɔɪntɪd] adj unzusammenhängend

disk [dɪsk] n (COMPUT) Diskette f; **single/double sided ~** einseitige/ beidseitige Diskette; **~ drive** n Diskettenlaufwerk nt; **~ette** [dɪs'ket] (US) n = **disk**

dislike [dɪs'laɪk] n Abneigung f ♦ vt nicht leiden können

dislocate ['dɪsləkeɪt] vt auskugeln

dislodge [dɪs'lɔdʒ] vt verschieben; (MIL) aus der Stellung werfen

disloyal [dɪs'lɔɪəl] adj treulos

dismal ['dɪzml] adj trostlos, trübe

dismantle [dɪs'mæntl] *vt* demontieren

dismay [dɪs'meɪ] *n* Bestürzung *f* ♦ *vt* bestürzen

dismiss [dɪs'mɪs] *vt* (*employee*) entlassen; (*idea*) von sich weisen; (*send away*) wegschicken; (*JUR*) abweisen; **~al** *n* Entlassung *f*

dismount [dɪs'maunt] *vi* absteigen

disobedience [dɪsə'biːdɪəns] *n* Ungehorsam *m*; **disobedient** *adj* ungehorsam

disobey [dɪsə'beɪ] *vt* nicht gehorchen +*dat*

disorder [dɪs'ɔːdəʳ] *n* (*confusion*) Verwirrung *f*; (*commotion*) Aufruhr *m*; (*MED*) Erkrankung *f*

disorderly [dɪs'ɔːdəlɪ] *adj* (*untidy*) unordentlich; (*unruly*) ordnungswidrig

disorganized [dɪs'ɔːgənaɪzd] *adj* unordentlich

disorientated [dɪs'ɔːrɪəntertɪd] *adj* (*person: after journey*) verwirrt

disown [dɪs'əun] *vt* (*child*) verstoßen

disparaging [dɪs'pærɪdʒɪŋ] *adj* geringschätzig

dispassionate [dɪs'pæʃənət] *adj* objektiv

dispatch [dɪs'pætʃ] *vt* (*goods*) abschicken, abfertigen ♦ *n* Absendung *f*; (*esp* MIL) Meldung *f*

dispel [dɪs'pel] *vt* zerstreuen

dispensary [dɪs'pensərɪ] *n* Apotheke *f*

dispense [dɪs'pens] *vt* verteilen, austeilen; **~ with** *vt fus* verzichten auf +*acc*; **~r** *n* (*container*) Spender *m*; **dispensing** *adj*: **dispensing chemist** (BRIT) Apotheker *m*

dispersal [dɪs'pɜːsl] *n* Zerstreuung *f*

disperse [dɪs'pɜːs] *vt* zerstreuen ♦ *vi* sich verteilen

dispirited [dɪs'pɪrɪtɪd] *adj* niedergeschlagen

displace [dɪs'pleɪs] *vt* verschieben; **~d person** *n* Verschleppte(r) *mf*

display [dɪs'pleɪ] *n* (*of goods*) Auslage *f*; (*of feeling*) Zurschaustellung *f* ♦ *vt* zeigen; (*ostentatiously*) vorführen; (*goods*) ausstellen

displease [dɪs'pliːz] *vt* missfallen +*dat*

displeasure [dɪs'pleʒəʳ] *n* Missfallen *nt*

disposable [dɪs'pəuzəbl] *adj* Wegwerf-; **~ nappy** *n* Papierwindel *f*

disposal [dɪs'pəuzl] *n* (*of property*) Verkauf *m*; (*throwing away*) Beseitigung *f*; **to be at one's ~** einem zur Verfügung stehen

dispose [dɪs'pəuz] *vi*: **to ~ of** loswerden; **~d** *adj* geneigt

disposition [dɪspə'zɪʃən] *n* Wesen *nt*

disproportionate [dɪsprə'pɔːʃənət] *adj* unverhältnismäßig

disprove [dɪs'pruːv] *vt* widerlegen

dispute [dɪs'pjuːt] *n* Streit *m*; (*also*: **industrial ~**) Arbeitskampf *m* ♦ *vt* bestreiten

disqualify [dɪs'kwɔlɪfaɪ] *vt* disqualifizieren

disquiet [dɪs'kwaɪət] *n* Unruhe *f*

disregard [dɪsrɪ'gɑːd] *vt* nicht (be)achten

disrepair ['dɪsrɪ'peəʳ] *n*: **to fall into ~** verfallen

disreputable [dɪs'repjutəbl] *adj* verrufen

disrespectful [dɪsrɪ'spektful] *adj* respektlos

disrupt [dɪs'rʌpt] *vt* stören; (*service*) unterbrechen; **~ion** [dɪs'rʌpʃən] *n* Störung *f*; Unterbrechung *f*

dissatisfaction [dɪssætɪs'fækʃən] *n* Unzufriedenheit *f*; **dissatisfied** [dɪs'sætɪsfaɪd] *adj* unzufrieden

dissect [dɪ'sekt] *vt* zerlegen, sezieren

dissent [dɪ'sent] *n* abweichende Meinung *f*

dissertation [dɪsə'teɪʃən] *n* wissenschaftliche Arbeit *f*; (*Ph.D.*) Doktorarbeit *f*

disservice [dɪs'sɜːvɪs] *n*: **to do sb a ~** jdm einen schlechten Dienst erweisen

dissident ['dɪsɪdnt] *adj* anders denkend ♦ *n* Dissident *m*

dissimilar [dɪ'sɪmɪləʳ] *adj*: **~ (to sb/ sth)** (jdm/etw) unähnlich

dissipate 386 **do**

dissipate ['dɪsɪpeɪt] vt (waste) verschwenden; (scatter) zerstreuen

dissociate [dɪ'səʊʃɪeɪt] vt trennen

dissolve [dɪ'zɒlv] vt auflösen ♦ vi sich auflösen

dissuade [dɪ'sweɪd] vt: **to ~ sb from doing sth** jdn davon abbringen, etw zu tun

distance ['dɪstns] n Entfernung f; **in the ~** in der Ferne; **distant** adj entfernt, fern; (with time) fern

distaste [dɪs'teɪst] n Abneigung f; **~ful** adj widerlich

distended [dɪs'tendɪd] adj (stomach) aufgebläht

distil [dɪs'tɪl] vt destillieren; **~lery** n Brennerei f

distinct [dɪs'tɪŋkt] adj (separate) getrennt; (clear) klar, deutlich; **as ~ from** im Unterschied zu; **~ion** [dɪs'tɪŋkʃən] n Unterscheidung f; (eminence) Auszeichnung f; **~ive** adj bezeichnend

distinguish [dɪs'tɪŋgwɪʃ] vt unterscheiden; **~ed** adj (eminent) berühmt; **~ing** adj bezeichnend

distort [dɪs'tɔːt] vt verdrehen; (misrepresent) entstellen; **~ion** [dɪs'tɔːʃən] n Verzerrung f

distract [dɪs'trækt] vt ablenken; **~ing** adj verwirrend; **~ion** [dɪs'trækʃən] n (distress) Raserei f; (diversion) Zerstreuung f

distraught [dɪs'trɔːt] adj bestürzt

distress [dɪs'tres] n Not f; (suffering) Qual f ♦ vt quälen; **~ing** adj erschütternd; **~ signal** n Notsignal nt

distribute [dɪs'trɪbjuːt] vt verteilen; **distribution** [dɪstrɪ'bjuːʃən] n Verteilung f; **distributor** n Verteiler m

district ['dɪstrɪkt] n (of country) Kreis m; (of town) Bezirk m; **~ attorney** (US) n Oberstaatsanwalt m; **~ nurse** n Kreiskrankenschwester f

distrust [dɪs'trʌst] n Misstrauen nt ♦ vt misstrauen +dat

disturb [dɪs'tɜːb] vt stören; (agitate) erregen; **~ance** n Störung f; **~ed** adj

beunruhigt; **emotionally ~ed** emotional gestört; **~ing** adj beunruhigend

disuse [dɪs'juːs] n: **to fall into ~** außer Gebrauch kommen; **~d** [dɪs'juːzd] adj außer Gebrauch, (mine, railway line) stillgelegt

ditch [dɪtʃ] n Graben m ♦ vt (person) loswerden; (plan) fallen lassen

dither ['dɪðə] vi verdattert sein

ditto ['dɪtəʊ] adv dito, ebenfalls

divan [dɪ'væn] n Liegesofa nt

dive [daɪv] n (into water) Kopfsprung m; (AVIAT) Sturzflug m ♦ vi tauchen; **~r** n Taucher m

diverge [daɪ'vɜːdʒ] vi auseinander gehen

diverse [daɪ'vɜːs] adj verschieden

diversion [daɪ'vɜːʃən] n Ablenkung f; (BRIT: AUT) Umleitung f

diversity [daɪ'vɜːsɪti] n Vielfalt f

divert [daɪ'vɜːt] vt ablenken; (traffic) umleiten

divide [dɪ'vaɪd] vt teilen ♦ vi sich teilen; **~d highway** (US) n Schnellstraße f

divine [dɪ'vaɪn] adj göttlich

diving ['daɪvɪŋ] n (SPORT) Turmspringen nt; (underwater ~) Tauchen nt; **~board** n Sprungbrett nt

divinity [dɪ'vɪnɪti] n Gottheit f; (subject) Religion f

division [dɪ'vɪʒən] n Teilung f; (MIL) Division f; (part) Abteilung f; (in opinion) Uneinigkeit f; (BRIT: POL) (Abstimmung f durch) Hammelsprung f

divorce [dɪ'vɔːs] n (Ehe)scheidung f ♦ vt scheiden; **~d** adj geschieden; **~e** [dɪvɔː'siː] n Geschiedene(r) f(m)

divulge [daɪ'vʌldʒ] vt preisgeben

DIY (BRIT) n abbr = **do-it-yourself**

dizzy ['dɪzɪ] adj schwindlig

DJ n abbr = **disc jockey**

DNA fingerprinting n genetische Fingerabdrücke pl

───────────────
│ **KEYWORD** │
───────────────

do [duː] (pt **did**, pp **done**) n (inf: party etc) Fete f

♦ *aux vb* **1** (*in negative constructions and questions*): **I don't understand** ich verstehe nicht; **didn't you know?** wusstest du das nicht?; **what do you think?** was meinen Sie?

2 (*for emphasis, in polite phrases*): **she does seem rather tired** sie scheint wirklich sehr müde zu sein; **do sit down/help yourself** setzen Sie sich doch hin/greifen Sie doch zu

3 (*used to avoid repeating vb*): **she swims better than I do** sie schwimmt besser als ich; **she lives in Glasgow - so do I** sie wohnt in Glasgow - ich auch

4 (*in tag questions*): **you like him, don't you?** du magst ihn doch, oder?

♦ *vt* **1** (*carry out, perform etc*) tun, machen; **what are you doing tonight?** was machst du heute Abend?; **I've got nothing to do** ich habe nichts zu tun; **to do one's hair/nails** sich die Haare/Nägel machen

2 (*AUT etc*) fahren

♦ *vi* **1** (*act, behave*): **do as I do** mach es wie ich

2 (*get on, fare*): **he's doing well/badly at school** er ist gut/schlecht in der Schule; **how do you do?** guten Tag

3 (*be suitable*) gehen; (*be sufficient*) reichen; **to make do (with)** auskommen mit

  do away with *vt* (*kill*) umbringen; (*abolish: law etc*) abschaffen

  do up *vt* (*laces, dress, buttons*) zumachen; (*room, house*) renovieren

  do with *vt* (*need*) brauchen; (*be connected*) zu tun haben mit

  do without *vt, vi* auskommen ohne

docile ['dəʊsaɪl] *adj* gefügig

dock [dɒk] *n* Dock *nt*; (*JUR*) Anklagebank *f* ♦ *vi* ins Dock gehen; **~er** *n* Hafenarbeiter *m*; **~yard** *n* Werft *f*

doctor ['dɒktəʳ] *n* Arzt *m*, Ärztin *f*; (*UNIV*) Doktor *m* ♦ *vt* (*fig*) fälschen; (*drink etc*) etw beimischen +*dat*; **D~ of**

Philosophy *n* Doktor *m* der Philosophie

document ['dɒkjumənt] *n* Dokument *nt*; **~ary** [dɒkju'mentərɪ] *n* Dokumentarbericht *m*; (*film*) Dokumentarfilm *m* ♦ *adj* dokumentarisch; **~ation** [dɒkjumən'teɪʃən] *n* dokumentarische(r) Nachweis *m*

dodge [dɒdʒ] *n* Kniff *m* ♦ *vt* ausweichen +*dat*

dodgems ['dɒdʒəmz] (*BRIT*) *npl* Autoskooter *m*

doe [dəʊ] *n* (*roe deer*) Ricke *f*; (*red deer*) Hirschkuh *f*; (*rabbit*) Weibchen *nt*

does [dʌz] *vb see* **do**; **~n't = does not**

dog [dɒg] *n* Hund *m*; **~ collar** *n* Hundehalsband *nt*; (*ECCL*) Kragen *m* des Geistlichen; **~-eared** *adj* mit Eselsohren

dogged ['dɒgɪd] *adj* hartnäckig

dogsbody ['dɒgzbɒdɪ] *n* Mädchen *nt* für alles

doings ['duːɪŋz] *npl* (*activities*) Treiben *nt*

do-it-yourself ['duːɪtjɔː'self] *n* Do-it-yourself *nt*

doldrums ['dɒldrəmz] *npl*: **to be in the ~** (*business*) Flaute haben; (*person*) deprimiert sein

dole [dəʊl] (*BRIT*) *n* Stempelgeld *nt*; **to be on the ~** stempeln gehen; **~ out** *vt* ausgeben, austeilen

doleful ['dəʊlful] *adj* traurig

doll [dɒl] *n* Puppe *f* ♦ *vt*: **to ~ o.s. up** sich aufdonnern

dollar ['dɒləʳ] *n* Dollar *m*

dolphin ['dɒlfɪn] *n* Delfin *m*, Delphin *m*

dome [dəʊm] *n* Kuppel *f*

domestic [də'mestɪk] *adj* häuslich; (*within country*) Innen-, Binnen-; (*animal*) Haus-; **~ated** *adj* (*person*) häuslich; (*animal*) zahm

dominant ['dɒmɪnənt] *adj* vorherrschend

dominate ['dɒmɪneɪt] *vt* beherrschen

domineering [dɒmɪ'nɪərɪŋ] *adj* herrisch

dominion [də'mɪnɪən] *n* (*rule*) Regie-

domino ['dɒmɪnəʊ] (*pl* **~es**) *n* Dominostein *m*; **~es** *n* (*game*) Domino(spiel) *nt*

don [dɒn] (*BRIT*) *n* akademische(r) Lehrer *m*

donate [də'neɪt] *vt* (*blood, money*) spenden; (*lot of money*) stiften; **donation** [də'neɪʃən] *n* Spende *f*

done [dʌn] *pp of* **do**

donkey ['dɒŋkɪ] *n* Esel *m*

donor ['dəʊnə*] *n* Spender *m*; **~ card** *n* Organspenderausweis *m*

don't [dəʊnt] = **do not**

doodle ['du:dl] *vi* kritzeln

doom [du:m] *n* böse(s) Geschick *nt*; (*downfall*) Verderben *nt* ♦ *vt*: **to be ~ed** zum Untergang verurteilt sein; **~sday** *n* der Jüngste Tag

door [dɔ:*] *n* Tür *f*; **~bell** *n* Türklingel *f*; **~ handle** *n* Türklinke *f* (*man, irreg*) *n* Türsteher *m*; **~mat** *n* Fußmatte *f*; **~step** *n* Türstufe *f*; **~way** *n* Türöffnung *f*

dope [dəʊp] *n* (*drug*) Aufputschmittel *nt* ♦ *vt* (*horse*) dopen

dopey ['dəʊpɪ] (*inf*) *adj* bekloppt

dormant ['dɔ:mənt] *adj* latent

dormitory ['dɔ:mɪtrɪ] *n* Schlafsaal *m*

dormouse ['dɔ:maʊs] (*pl* **-mice**) *n* Haselmaus *f*

DOS [dɒs] *n abbr* (= *disk operating system*) DOS *nt*

dosage ['dəʊsɪdʒ] *n* Dosierung *f*

dose [dəʊs] *n* Dosis *f*

dosh [dɒʃ] (*inf*) *n* (*money*) Moos *nt*, Knete *f*

doss house ['dɒs-] (*BRIT*) *n* Bleibe *f*

dot [dɒt] *n* Punkt *m*; **~ted with** übersät mit; **on the ~** pünktlich

dote [dəʊt]: **to ~ on** *vt fus* vernarrt sein in *+acc*

dotted line ['dɒtɪd-] *n* punktierte Linie *f*

double ['dʌbl] *adj, adv* doppelt ♦ *n* Doppelgänger *m* ♦ *vt* verdoppeln ♦ *vi*

sich verdoppeln; **~s** *npl* (*TENNIS*) Doppel *nt*; **on** *or* **at the ~** im Laufschritt; **~ bass** *n* Kontrabass *m*; **~ bed** *n* Doppelbett *nt*; **~ bend** (*BRIT*) *n* S-Kurve *f*; **~-breasted** *adj* zweireihig; **~-cross** *vt* hintergehen; **~-decker** *n* Doppeldecker *m*; **~ glazing** (*BRIT*) *n* Doppelverglasung *f*; **~ room** *n* Doppelzimmer *nt*

doubly ['dʌblɪ] *adv* doppelt

doubt [daʊt] *n* Zweifel *m* ♦ *vt* bezweifeln; **~ful** *adj* zweifelhaft; **~less** *adv* ohne Zweifel

dough [dəʊ] *n* Teig *m*; **~nut** *n* Berliner *m*

douse [daʊz] *vt* (*drench*) mit Wasser begießen, durchtränken; (*extinguish*) ausmachen

dove [dʌv] *n* Taube *f*

dovetail ['dʌvteɪl] *vi* (*plans*) übereinstimmen

dowdy ['daʊdɪ] *adj* unmodern

down [daʊn] *n* (*fluff*) Flaum *m*; (*hill*) Hügel *m* ♦ *adv* unten; (*motion*) herunter; hinunter ♦ *prep*: **to go ~ the street** die Straße hinuntergehen ♦ *vt* niederschlagen; **~ with X!** nieder mit X!; **~-and-out** *n* Tramp *m*; **~-at-heel** *adj* schäbig; **~cast** *adj* niedergeschlagen; **~fall** *n* Sturz *m*; **~hearted** *adj* niedergeschlagen; **~hill** *adv* bergab; **~ payment** *n* Anzahlung *f*; **~pour** *n* Platzregen *m*; **~right** *adj* ausgesprochen; **~size** *vi* (*ECON: company*) sich verkleinern

---

Downing Street

Downing Street *ist die Straße in London, die von Whitehall zum St James Park führt und in der sich der offizielle Wohnsitz des Premierministers (Nr. 10) und des Finanzministers (Nr. 11) befindet. Im weiteren Sinne bezieht sich der Begriff Downing Street auf die britische Regierung.*

Down's syndrome [daʊnz-] *n* (*MED*) Down-Syndrom *nt*

down: ~**stairs** adv unten; (motion) nach unten; ~**stream** adv flussabwärts; ~**-to-earth** adj praktisch; ~**town** adv in der Innenstadt; (motion) in die Innenstadt; ~ **under** (BRIT: inf) adv in/nach Australien/Neuseeland; ~**ward** adj Abwärts-, nach unten ♦ adv abwärts, nach unten; ~**wards** adv abwärts, nach unten

dowry ['dauri] n Mitgift f

doz. abbr (= dozen) Dtzd.

doze [dauz] vi dösen; ~ **off** vi einnicken

dozen ['dʌzn] n Dutzend nt; **a** ~ **books** ein Dutzend Bücher; ~**s of** dutzende or Dutzende von

Dr. abbr = doctor; drive

drab [dræb] adj düster, eintönig

draft [dra:ft] n Entwurf m; (FIN) Wechsel m; (US: MIL) Einberufung f ♦ vt skizzieren; see also **draught**

draftsman ['dra:ftsmən] (US: irreg) n = **draughtsman**

drag [dræg] vt schleppen; (river) mit einem Schleppnetz absuchen ♦ vi sich (dahin)schleppen ♦ n (bore) etwas Blödes; **in** ~ als Tunte; **a man in** ~ eine Tunte; ~ **on** vi sich in die Länge ziehen; ~ **and drop** vt (COMPUT) Drag & Drop nt

dragon ['drægn] n Drache m; ~**fly** ['drægnflai] n Libelle f

drain [drein] n Abfluss m; (fig: burden) Belastung f ♦ vt ableiten; (exhaust) erschöpfen ♦ vi (of water) abfließen; ~**age** n Kanalisation f; ~**ing board** (US **~board**) n Ablaufbrett nt; ~**pipe** n Abflussrohr nt

dram [dræm] n Schluck m

drama ['dra:mə] n Drama nt; ~**tic** [drə'mætik] adj dramatisch; ~**tist** ['dræmətist] n Dramatiker m; ~**tize** ['dræmətaiz] vt (events) dramatisieren; (for TV etc) bearbeiten

drank [dræŋk] pt of **drink**

drape [dreip] vt drapieren; ~**s** (US) npl Vorhänge pl

drastic ['dræstik] adj drastisch

draught [dra:ft] (US **draft**) n Zug m; (NAUT) Tiefgang m; ~**s** n Damespiel nt; **on** ~ (beer) vom Fass; ~ **beer** n Bier nt vom Fass; ~**board** (BRIT) n Zeichenbrett n

draughtsman ['dra:ftsmən] (irreg) n technische(r) Zeichner m

draw [dro:] (pt **drew**, pp **drawn**) vt ziehen; (crowd) anlocken; (picture) zeichnen; (money) abheben; (water) schöpfen ♦ vi (SPORT) unentschieden spielen ♦ n (SPORT) Unentschieden nt; (lottery) Ziehung f; ~ **near** vi näher rücken; ~ **out** vi (train) ausfahren; (lengthen) sich hinziehen; ~ **up** vi (stop) halten ♦ vt (document) aufsetzen

drawback ['dro:bæk] n Nachteil m

drawbridge ['dro:bridʒ] n Zugbrücke f

drawer [dro:r] n Schublade f

drawing ['dro:iŋ] n Zeichnung f; Zeichnen nt; ~**board** n Reißbrett nt; ~**pin** (BRIT) n Reißzwecke f; ~ **room** n Salon m

drawl [dro:l] n schleppende Sprechweise f

drawn [dro:n] pp of **draw**

dread [dred] n Furcht f ♦ vt fürchten; ~**ful** adj furchtbar

dream [dri:m] (pt, pp **dreamed** or **dreamt**) n Traum m ♦ vt träumen ♦ vi: **to** ~ (**about**) träumen (von); ~**er** n Träumer m; ~**t** [dremt] pt, pp of **dream**; ~**y** adj verträumt

dreary ['driəri] adj trostlos, öde

dredge [dredʒ] vt ausbaggern

dregs [dregz] npl Bodensatz m; (fig) Abschaum m

drench [drentʃ] vt durchnässen

dress [dres] n Kleidung f; (garment) Kleid nt ♦ vt anziehen; (MED) verbinden; **to get** ~**ed** sich anziehen; ~ **up** vi sich fein machen; ~ **circle** (BRIT) n erste(r) Rang m; ~**er** n (furniture) Anrichte f; ~**ing** n (MED) Verband m; (COOK) Soße f; ~**ing gown** (BRIT) n Morgenrock m; ~**ing room** n (THEAT)

Garderobe f; (SPORT) Umkleideraum m; **~ing table** n Toilettentisch m; **~maker** n Schneiderin f; **~ rehearsal** n Generalprobe f

drew [dru:] pt of **draw**

dribble ['drɪbl] vi sabbern ♦ vt (ball) dribbeln

dried [draɪd] adj getrocknet; (fruit) Dörr-, gedörrte(r, s); **~ milk** n Milchpulver nt

drier ['draɪə*] n = **dryer**

drift [drɪft] n Strömung f; (snowdrift) Schneewehe f; (fig) Richtung f ♦ vi sich treiben lassen; **~wood** n Treibholz nt

drill [drɪl] n Bohrer m; (MIL) Drill m ♦ vt bohren; (MIL) ausbilden ♦ vi: **to ~ (for)** bohren (nach)

drink [drɪŋk] (pt **drank**, pp **drunk**) n Getränk nt; (spirits) Drink m ♦ vt, vi trinken; **to have a ~** etwas trinken; **~er** n Trinker m; **~ing water** n Trinkwasser nt

drip [drɪp] n Tropfen m ♦ vi tropfen; **~dry** adj bügelfrei; **~ping** n Bratenfett nt

drive [draɪv] (pt **drove**, pp **driven**) n Fahrt f; (road) Einfahrt f; (campaign) Aktion f; (energy) Schwung m; (SPORT) Schlag m; (also: **disk ~**) Diskettenlaufwerk nt ♦ vt (car) fahren; (animals, people, objects) treiben; (power) antreiben ♦ vi fahren; **left-/right-hand ~** Links-/Rechtssteuerung f; **to ~ sb mad** jdn verrückt machen; **~-by shooting** n Schusswaffenangriff aus einem vorbeifahrenden Wagen

drivel ['drɪvl] n Faselei f

driven ['drɪvn] pp of **drive**

driver ['draɪvə*] n Fahrer m; **~'s license** (US) n Führerschein m

driveway ['draɪvweɪ] n Auffahrt f; (longer) Zufahrtsstraße f

driving ['draɪvɪŋ] adj (rain) stürmisch; **~ instructor** n Fahrlehrer m; **~ lesson** n Fahrstunde f; **~ licence** (BRIT) n Führerschein m; **~ school** n Fahrschule f; **~ test** n Fahrprüfung f

drizzle ['drɪzl] n Nieselregen m ♦ vi nieseln

droll [drəʊl] adj drollig

drone [drəʊn] n (sound) Brummen nt; (bee) Drohne f

drool [dru:l] vi (schlaff) herabhängen

droop [dru:p] vi (schlaff) herabhängen

drop [drɒp] n (of liquid) Tropfen m; (fall) Fall m ♦ vt fallen lassen; (lower) senken; (abandon) fallen lassen ♦ vi fallen; herunterfallen; **~s** npl (MED) Tropfen pl; **~ off** vi (sleep) einschlafen ♦ vt (passenger) absetzen; **~ out** vi (withdraw) ausscheiden; **~-out** n Aussteiger m; **~per** n Pipette f; **~pings** npl Kot m

drought [draʊt] n Dürre f

drove [drəʊv] pt of **drive**

drown [draʊn] vt ertränken; (sound) übertönen ♦ vi ertrinken

drowsy ['draʊzɪ] adj schläfrig

drudgery ['drʌdʒərɪ] n Plackerei f

drug [drʌg] n (MED) Arznei f; (narcotic) Rauschgift nt ♦ vt betäuben; **~ addict** n Rauschgiftsüchtige(r) f(m); **~gist** (US) n Drogist(in) m(f); **~store** (US) n Drogerie f

drum [drʌm] n Trommel f ♦ vi trommeln; **~s** npl (MUS) Schlagzeug nt; **~mer** n Trommler m

drunk [drʌŋk] pp of **drink** ♦ adj betrunken ♦ n (also: **~ard**) Trinker(in) m(f); **~en** adj betrunken

dry [draɪ] adj trocken ♦ vt abtrocknen ♦ vi trocknen; **~ up** vi austrocknen ♦ vt (dishes) abtrocknen; **~ cleaner's** n chemische Reinigung f; **~ cleaning** n chemische Reinigung f; **~er** n Trockner m; (US: spin-dryer) (Wäsche)schleuder f; **~ goods store** (US) n Kurzwarengeschäft nt; **~ness** n Trockenheit f; **~ rot** n Hausschwamm m

DSS (BRIT) n abbr (= Department of Social Security) ≈ Sozialministerium nt

DTP n abbr (= desktop publishing) DTP nt

dual ['djuːəl] adj doppelt; **~ carriageway** (BRIT) n zweispurige Fahrbahn f

nationality n doppelte Staatsangehörigkeit f; **~-purpose** adj Mehrzweck-

dubbed [dʌbd] adj (film) synchronisiert

dubious ['djuːbɪəs] adj zweifelhaft

duchess ['dʌtʃɪs] n Herzogin f

duck [dʌk] n Ente f ♦ vi sich ducken; **~ling** n Entchen nt

duct [dʌkt] n Röhre f

dud [dʌd] n Niete f ♦ adj (cheque) ungedeckt

due [djuː] adj fällig; (fitting) angemessen ♦ n Gebühr f; (right) Recht nt ♦ adv (south etc) genau; **~s** npl (for club) Beitrag m; (NAUT) Gebühren pl; **~ to** wegen +gen

duel ['djuəl] n Duell nt

duet [djuː'et] n Duett nt

duffel ['dʌfl] adj: **~ bag** Matchbeutel m, Matchsack m

dug [dʌg] pt, pp of **dig**

duke [djuːk] n Herzog m

dull [dʌl] adj (colour, weather) trübe; (stupid) schwer von Begriff; (boring) langweilig ♦ vt abstumpfen

duly ['djuːlɪ] adv ordnungsgemäß

dumb [dʌm] adj stumm; (inf: stupid) doof, blöde; **~founded** [dʌm'faundɪd] adj verblüfft

dummy ['dʌmɪ] n Schneiderpuppe f; (substitute) Attrappe f; (BRIT: for baby) Schnuller m ♦ adj Schein-

dump [dʌmp] n Abfallhaufen m; (MIL) Stapelplatz m; (inf: place) Nest nt ♦ vt abladen, auskippen; **~ing** n (COMM) Schleuderexport m; (of rubbish) Schuttabladen nt

dumpling ['dʌmplɪŋ] n Kloß m, Knödel m

dumpy ['dʌmpɪ] adj pummelig

dunce [dʌns] n Dummkopf m

dune [djuːn] n Düne f

dung [dʌŋ] n Dünger m

dungarees [dʌŋgə'riːz] npl Latzhose f

dungeon ['dʌndʒən] n Kerker m

dupe [djuːp] n Gefoppte(r) m ♦ vt hintergehen, anführen

duplex ['djuːpleks] (US) n zweistöckige Wohnung f

duplicate [n 'djuːplɪkət, vb 'djuːplɪkeɪt] n Duplikat nt ♦ vt verdoppeln; (make copies) kopieren; **in ~** in doppelter Ausführung

duplicity [djuː'plɪsɪtɪ] n Doppelspiel nt

durable ['djuərəbl] adj haltbar

duration [djuə'reɪʃən] n Dauer f

duress [djuə'res] n: **under ~** unter Zwang

during ['djuərɪŋ] prep während +gen

dusk [dʌsk] n Abenddämmerung f

dust [dʌst] n Staub m ♦ vt abstauben; (sprinkle) bestäuben; **~bin** (BRIT) n Mülleimer m; **~er** n Staubtuch nt; **~jacket** n Schutzumschlag m; **~man** (BRIT: irreg) n Müllmann m; **~y** adj staubig

Dutch [dʌtʃ] adj holländisch, niederländisch ♦ n (LING) Holländisch nt, Niederländisch nt; **the ~** npl (people) die Holländer pl, die Niederländer pl; **to go ~** getrennte Kasse machen; **~man/woman** (irreg) n Holländer(in) m(f), Niederländer(in) m(f)

dutiful ['djuːtɪful] adj pflichtbewusst

duty ['djuːtɪ] n Pflicht f; (job) Aufgabe f; (tax) Einfuhrzoll m; **on ~** im Dienst; **~ chemist's** n Apotheke f im Bereitschaftsdienst; **~-free** adj zollfrei

duvet ['duːveɪ] (BRIT) n Daunendecke f

DVD n abbr (= digital versatile disc) DVD f

dwarf [dwɔːf] (pl **dwarves**) n Zwerg m ♦ vt überragen

dwell [dwel] (pt, pp **dwelt**) vi wohnen; **~ on** vt fus verweilen bei; **~ing** n Wohnung f

dwelt [dwelt] pt, pp of **dwell**

dwindle ['dwɪndl] vi schwinden

dye [daɪ] n Farbstoff m ♦ vt färben

dying ['daɪɪŋ] adj (person) sterbend; (moments) letzt

dyke [daɪk] (BRIT) n (channel) Kanal m; (barrier) Deich m, Damm m

dynamic [daɪ'næmɪk] adj dynamisch

dynamite ['daɪnəmaɪt] n Dynamit nt

dynamo ['daɪnəməʊ] n Dynamo m

dyslexia [dɪs'lɛksɪə] n Legasthenie f

E, e

E [iː] n (MUS) E nt

each [iːtʃ] adj jeder/jede/jedes ♦ pron (ein) jeder/(eine) jede/(ein) jedes; ~ **other** einander, sich; **they have two books** → sie haben je 2 Bücher

eager ['iːgə*] adj eifrig

eagle ['iːgl] n Adler m

ear [ɪə*] n Ohr nt; (of corn) Ähre f; **~ache** n Ohrenschmerzen pl; **~drum** n Trommelfell nt

earl [əːl] n Graf m

earlier ['əːlɪə*] adj, adv früher; **I can't come any ~** ich kann nicht früher or eher kommen

early ['əːlɪ] adj, adv früh; **~ retirement** n vorzeitige Pensionierung

earmark ['ɪəmɑːk] vt vorsehen

earn [əːn] vt verdienen

earnest ['əːnɪst] adj ernst; **in ~** im Ernst

earnings ['əːnɪŋz] npl Verdienst m

ear: ~phones ['ɪəfəʊnz] npl Kopfhörer pl; **~ring** ['ɪərɪŋ] n Ohrring m; **~shot** ['ɪəʃɒt] n Hörweite f

earth [əːθ] n Erde f; (BRIT: ELEC) Erdung f ♦ vt erden; **~enware** n Steingut nt; **~quake** n Erdbeben nt; **~y** adj roh

earwig ['ɪəwɪg] n Ohrwurm m

ease [iːz] n (simplicity) Leichtigkeit f; (social) Ungezwungenheit f ♦ vt (pain) lindern; (burden) erleichtern; **at ~** ungezwungen; (MIL) rührt euch!; **~ off** or **up** vi nachlassen

easel ['iːzl] n Staffelei f

easily ['iːzɪlɪ] adv leicht

east [iːst] n Osten m ♦ adj östlich ♦ adv nach Osten

Easter ['iːstə*] n Ostern nt; **~ egg** n Osterei nt

east: ~erly adj östlich, Ost-; **~ern** adj östlich; **~ward(s)** adv ostwärts

easy ['iːzɪ] adj (task) einfach; (life) bequem; (manner) ungezwungen, na-

türlich ♦ adv leicht; **~ chair** n Sessel m; **~-going** adj gelassen; (lax) lässig

eat [iːt] (pt **ate**, pp **eaten**) vt essen; (animals) fressen; (destroy) (zer)fressen ♦ vi essen; fressen; **~ away** vt zerfressen; **~ into** vt fus zerfressen; **~en** pp of **eat**

eau de Cologne ['əʊdəkə'ləʊn] n Kölnischwasser nt

eaves [iːvz] npl Dachrand m

eavesdrop ['iːvzdrɒp] vi lauschen; **to ~ on sb** jdn belauschen

ebb [ɛb] n Ebbe f ♦ vi (fig: also: **~ away**) (ab)ebben

ebony ['ɛbənɪ] n Ebenholz nt

EC n abbr (= European Community) EG f

ECB n abbr (= European Central Bank) EZB f

eccentric [ɪk'sɛntrɪk] adj exzentrisch ♦ n Exzentriker(in) m(f)

ecclesiastical [ɪkliːzɪ'æstɪkl] adj kirchlich

echo ['ɛkəʊ] (pl **~es**) n Echo nt ♦ vt zurückwerfen; (fig) nachbeten ♦ vi widerhallen

eclipse [ɪ'klɪps] n Finsternis f ♦ vt verfinstern

ecology [ɪ'kɒlədʒɪ] n Ökologie f

e-commerce [iː'kɒmɜːs] n Onlinehandel m

economic [iːkə'nɒmɪk] adj wirtschaftlich; **~al** adj wirtschaftlich; (person) sparsam; **~ refugee** n Wirtschaftsflüchtling m; **~s** n Volkswirtschaft f

economist [ɪ'kɒnəmɪst] n Volkswirt(schaftler) m

economize [ɪ'kɒnəmaɪz] vi sparen

economy [ɪ'kɒnəmɪ] n (thrift) Sparsamkeit f; (of country) Wirtschaft f; **~ class** n Touristenklasse f

ecstasy ['ɛkstəsɪ] n Ekstase f; (drug) Ecstasy nt; **ecstatic** [ɛks'tætɪk] adj hingerissen

ECU ['eɪkjuː] n abbr (= European Currency Unit) ECU m

eczema ['ɛksɪmə] n Ekzem nt

edge [ɛdʒ] n Rand m; (of knife) Schneide f ♦ vt (SEWING) einfassen; **on ~** (fig)

= **edgy; to ~ away from** langsam abrücken von; **~ways** *adv:* **he couldn't get a word in ~ways** er kam überhaupt nicht zu Wort

edgy ['edʒɪ] *adj* nervös

edible ['edɪbl] *adj* essbar

edict ['iːdɪkt] *n* Erlass *m*

edit ['edɪt] *vt* redigieren; **~ion** [ɪ'dɪʃən] *n* Ausgabe *f*; **~or** *n* (*of newspaper*) Redakteur *m*; (*of book*) Lektor *m*

editorial [edɪ'tɔːrɪəl] *adj* Redaktions- ♦ *n* Leitartikel *m*

educate ['edjʊkeɪt] *vt* erziehen, (aus)bilden; **~d** *adj* gebildet; **education** [edjʊ'keɪʃən] *n* (*teaching*) Unterricht *m*; (*system*) Schulwesen *nt*; (*schooling*) Erziehung *f*; Bildung *f*; **educational** *adj* pädagogisch

eel [iːl] *n* Aal *m*

eerie ['ɪərɪ] *adj* unheimlich

effect [ɪ'fekt] *n* Wirkung *f* ♦ *vt* bewirken; **~s** *npl* (*sound, visual*) Effekte *pl*; **in** ~ in der Tat; **to take ~** (*law*) in Kraft treten; (*drug*) wirken; **~ive** *adj* wirksam, effektiv; **~ively** *adv* wirksam, effektiv, effektiv

effeminate [ɪ'femɪnɪt] *adj* weibisch

effervescent [efə'vesnt] *adj* (*also fig*) sprudelnd

efficiency [ɪ'fɪʃənsɪ] *n* Leistungsfähigkeit *f*

efficient [ɪ'fɪʃənt] *adj* tüchtig; (*TECH*) leistungsfähig; (*method*) wirksam

effigy ['efɪdʒɪ] *n* Abbild *nt*

effort ['efət] *n* Anstrengung *f*; **~less** *adj* mühelos

effusive [ɪ'fjuːsɪv] *adj* überschwänglich

e.g. *adv abbr* (= *exempli gratia*) z. B.

egg [eg] *n* Ei *nt*; **~ on** *vt* anstacheln; **~cup** *n* Eierbecher *m*; **~plant** (*esp US*) *n* Aubergine *f*; **~shell** *n* Eierschale *f*

ego ['iːgəʊ] *n* Ich, Selbst *nt*; **~tism** ['egəʊtɪzəm] *n* Ichbezogenheit *f*; **~tist** ['egəʊtɪst] *n* Egozentriker *m*

Egypt ['iːdʒɪpt] *n* Ägypten *nt*; **~ian** [ɪ'dʒɪpʃən] *adj* ägyptisch ♦ *n* Ägypter(in) *m(f)*

eiderdown ['aɪdədaʊn] *n* Daunende-

cke *f*

eight [eɪt] *num* acht; **~een** *num* achtzehn; **~h** [eɪtθ] *adj* achte(r, s) ♦ *n* Achtel *nt*; **~y** *num* achtzig

Eire ['eərə] *n* Irland *nt*

either ['aɪðə] *conj*: **~ ... or** entweder ... oder ♦ *pron*: **~ of the two** eine(r, s) von beiden ♦ *adj*: **on ~ side** auf beiden Seiten ♦ *adv*: **I don't ~** ich auch nicht; **I don't want ~** ich will keins von beiden

eject [ɪ'dʒekt] *vt* ausstoßen, vertreiben

eke [iːk] *vt*: **to ~ out** strecken

elaborate [*adj* ɪ'læbərɪt, *vb* ɪ'læbəreɪt] *adj* sorgfältig ausgearbeitet, ausführlich ♦ *vt* sorgfältig ausarbeiten, ausführlich darstellen

elapse [ɪ'læps] *vi* vergehen

elastic [ɪ'læstɪk] *n* Gummiband *m* ♦ *adj* elastisch; **~ band** (*BRIT*) *n* Gummiband *nt*

elated [ɪ'leɪtɪd] *adj* froh

elation [ɪ'leɪʃən] *n* gehobene Stimmung *f*

elbow ['elbəʊ] *n* Ellbogen *m*

elder ['eldə] *adj* älter ♦ *n* Ältere(r) *f(m)*; **~ly** *adj* ältere(r, s) ♦ *npl*: **the ~ly** die Älteren *pl*; **eldest** ['eldɪst] *adj* älteste(r, s) ♦ *n* Älteste(r) *f(m)*

elect [ɪ'lekt] *vt* wählen ♦ *adj* zukünftig; **~ion** [ɪ'lekʃən] *n* Wahl *f*; **~ioneering** [ɪlekʃə'nɪərɪŋ] *n* Wahlpropaganda *f*; **~or** *n* Wähler *m*; **~oral** *adj* Wahl-; **~orate** *n* Wähler *pl*, Wählerschaft *f*

electric [ɪ'lektrɪk] *adj* elektrisch, Elektro-; **~al** *adj* elektrisch; **~ blanket** *n* Heizdecke *f*; **~ chair** *n* elektrische(r) Stuhl *m*; **~ fire** *n* elektrische(r) Heizofen *m*

electrician [ɪlek'trɪʃən] *n* Elektriker *m*

electricity [ɪlek'trɪsɪtɪ] *n* Elektrizität *f*

electrify [ɪ'lektrɪfaɪ] *vt* elektrifizieren; (*fig*) elektrisieren

electrocute [ɪ'lektrəkjuːt] *vt* durch elektrischen Strom töten

electronic [ɪlek'trɒnɪk] *adj* elektronisch, Elektronen-; **~ mail** *n* elektronische(r) Briefkasten *m*; **~s** *n* Elektronik *f*

elegance ['eligəns] *n* Eleganz *f*; **elegant** ['eligənt] *adj* elegant

element ['elimənt] *n* Element *nt*; **~ary** [eli'mentəri] *adj* einfach; (*primary*) Grund-

elephant ['elifənt] *n* Elefant *m*

elevate ['eliveit] *vt* emporheben; **elevation** [eli'veiʃən] *n* (*height*) Erhebung *f*; (ARCHIT) (Quer)schnitt *m*; **elevator** (US) *n* Fahrstuhl *m*, Aufzug *m*

eleven [i'levn] *num* elf; **~ses** (BRIT) *npl* ≈ zweite(s) Frühstück *nt*; **~th** *adj* elfte(r, s)

elicit [i'lisit] *vt* herausbekommen

eligible ['elidʒəbl] *adj* wählbar; **to be ~ for a pension** pensionsberechtigt sein

eliminate [i'limineit] *vt* ausschalten

elite [ei'li:t] *n* Elite *f*

elm [elm] *n* Ulme *f*

elocution [elə'kju:ʃən] *n* Sprecherziehung *f*

elongated ['i:lɔŋgeitid] *adj* verlängert

elope [i'ləup] *vi* entlaufen

eloquence ['eləkwəns] *n* Beredsamkeit *f*; **eloquent** *adj* redegewandt

else [els] *adv* sonst; **who ~?** wer sonst?; **somebody ~** jemand anders; **or ~** sonst; **~where** *adv* anderswo, woanders

elude [i'lu:d] *vt* entgehen +*dat*

elusive [i'lu:siv] *adj* schwer fassbar

emaciated [i'meisieitid] *adj* abgezehrt

E-mail ['i:meil] *n abbr* (= *electronic mail*) E-Mail *f*

emancipation [imænsi'peiʃən] *n* Emanzipation *f*; Freilassung *f*

embankment [im'bæŋkmənt] *n* (*of river*) Uferböschung *f*; (*of road*) Straßendamm *m*

embargo [im'bɑ:gəu] (*pl* **~es**) *n* Embargo *nt*

embark [im'bɑ:k] *vi* sich einschiffen; **~ on** *vt fus* unternehmen; **~ation** [embɑ:'keiʃən] *n* Einschiffung *f*

embarrass [im'bærəs] *vt* in Verlegenheit bringen; **~ed** *adj* verlegen; **~ing**

adj peinlich; **~ment** *n* Verlegenheit *f*

embassy ['embəsi] *n* Botschaft *f*

embed [im'bed] *vt* einbetten

embellish [im'beliʃ] *vt* verschönern

embers ['embəz] *npl* Glut(asche) *f*

embezzle [im'bezl] *vt* unterschlagen; **~ment** *n* Unterschlagung *f*

embitter [im'bitər] *vt* verbittern

embody [im'bɔdi] *vt* (*ideas*) verkörpern; (*new features*) (in sich) vereinigen

embossed [im'bɔst] *adj* geprägt

embrace [im'breis] *vt* umarmen; (*include*) einschließen ♦ *vi* sich umarmen ♦ *n* Umarmung *f*

embroider [im'brɔidər] *vt* (be)sticken; (*story*) ausschmücken; **~y** *n* Stickerei *f*

emerald ['emərəld] *n* Smaragd *m*

emerge [i'mɜ:dʒ] *vi* auftauchen; (*truth*) herauskommen; **~nce** *n* Erscheinen *nt*

emergency [i'mɜ:dʒənsi] *n* Notfall *m*; **~ cord** (US) *n* Notbremse *f*; **~ exit** *n* Notausgang *m*; **~ landing** *n* Notlandung *f*; **~ services** *npl* Notdienste *pl*

emery board ['eməri-] *n* Papiernagelfeile *f*

emigrant ['emigrənt] *n* Auswanderer *m*

emigrate ['emigreit] *vi* auswandern; **emigration** [emi'greiʃən] *n* Auswanderung *f*

eminence ['eminəns] *n* hohe(r) Rang *m*

eminent ['eminənt] *adj* bedeutend

emission [i'miʃən] *n* Ausströmen *nt*; **~s** *npl* Emissionen *pl*

emit [i'mit] *vt* von sich *dat* geben

emotion [i'məuʃən] *n* Emotion *f*, Gefühl *nt*; **~al** *adj* (*person*) emotional; (*scene*) ergreifend

emotive [i'məutiv] *adj* gefühlsbetont

emperor ['empərər] *n* Kaiser *m*

emphases ['emfəsi:z] *npl of* **emphasis**

emphasis ['emfəsis] *n* (LING) Betonung *f*; (*fig*) Nachdruck *m*; **emphasize** ['emfəsaiz] *vt* betonen

emphatic [em'fætik] *adj* nach-

drücklich; **~ally** *adv* nachdrücklich
empire ['empaɪə¹] *n* Reich *nt*
empirical [em'pɪrɪkl] *adj* empirisch
employ [ɪm'plɔɪ] *vt* (*use*) anstellen; (*use*) verwenden; **~ee** [ɪmplɔɪ'i:] *n* Angestellte(r) *f(m)*; **~er** *n* Arbeitgeber(in) *m(f)*; **~ment** *n* Beschäftigung *f*; **~ment agency** *n* Stellenvermittlung *f*
empower [ɪm'paʊə¹] *vt* to ~ sb to do sth jdn ermächtigen, etw zu tun
empress ['emprɪs] *n* Kaiserin *f*
emptiness ['emptɪnɪs] *n* Leere *f*
empty ['emptɪ] *adj* leer ♦ *vt* (*bottle*) Leergut *nt* ♦ *vt* (*contents*) leeren; (*container*) ausleeren ♦ *vi* (*water*) abfließen; (*river*) münden; (*house*) sich leeren; **~handed** *adj* mit leeren Händen
EMU ['i:mju:] *n abbr* (= *economic and monetary union*) EWU *f*
emulate ['emjʊleɪt] *vt* nacheifern +*dat*
emulsion [ɪ'mʌlʃən] *n* Emulsion *f*
enable [ɪ'neɪbl] *vt* to ~ sb to do sth es jdm ermöglichen, etw zu tun
enact [ɪ'nækt] *vt* (*law*) erlassen; (*play*) aufführen; (*role*) spielen
enamel [ɪ'næməl] *n* Email *nt*, (*of teeth*) (Zahn)schmelz *m*
encased [ɪn'keɪst] *adj*: **~ in** (*enclosed*) eingeschlossen in +*dat*; (*covered*) verkleidet mit
enchant [ɪn'tʃɑːnt] *vt* bezaubern; **~ing** *adj* entzückend
encircle [ɪn'sɜːkl] *vt* umringen
encl. *abbr* (= *enclosed*) Anl.
enclose [ɪn'kləʊz] *vt* einschließen; to ~ sth (in *or* with a letter) etw (einem Brief) beilegen; **~d** (*in letter*) beiliegend, anbei; **enclosure** [ɪn'kləʊʒə¹] *n* Einfriedung *f*; (*in letter*) Anlage *f*
encompass [ɪn'kʌmpəs] *vt* (*include*) umfassen
encore [ɒŋ'kɔː¹] *n* Zugabe *f*
encounter [ɪn'kaʊntə¹] *n* Begegnung *f*; (*MIL*) Zusammenstoß *m* ♦ *vt* treffen; (*resistance*) stoßen auf +*acc*
encourage [ɪn'kʌrɪdʒ] *vt* ermutigen; **~ment** *n* Ermutigung *f*, Förderung *f*;

encouraging *adj* ermutigend, viel versprechend
encroach [ɪn'krəʊtʃ] *vi*: to ~ (up)on eindringen in +*acc*; (*time*) in Anspruch nehmen
encrusted [ɪn'krʌstɪd] *adj*: **~ with** besetzt mit
encyclop(a)edia [ensaɪkləʊ'piːdɪə] *n* Konversationslexikon *nt*
end [end] *n* Ende *nt*, Schluss *m*; (*purpose*) Zweck *m* ♦ *vt* (*also*: **bring to an ~**, **put an ~ to**) beenden ♦ *vi* zu Ende gehen; **in the ~** zum Schluss; **on ~** (*object*) hochkant; **to stand on ~** (*hair*) zu Berge stehen; **for hours on ~** stundenlang; **~ up** *vi* landen
endanger [ɪn'deɪndʒə¹] *vt* gefährden; **~ed species** *n* eine vom Aussterben bedrohte Art
endearing [ɪn'dɪərɪŋ] *adj* gewinnend
endeavour [ɪn'devə¹] (*US* **endeavor**) *n* Bestrebung *f* ♦ *vi* sich bemühen
ending ['endɪŋ] *n* Ende *nt*
endless ['endlɪs] *adj* endlos
endorse [ɪn'dɔːs] *vt* unterzeichnen; (*approve*) unterstützen; **~ment** *n* (*AUT*) Eintrag *m*
endow [ɪn'daʊ] *vt*: to ~ sb with sth jdm etw verleihen; (*with money*) jdm etw stiften
endurance [ɪn'djʊərəns] *n* Ausdauer *f*
endure [ɪn'djʊə¹] *vt* ertragen ♦ *vi* (*last*) (fort)dauern
enemy ['enəmɪ] *n* Feind *m* ♦ *adj* feindlich
energetic [enə'dʒetɪk] *adj* tatkräftig
energy ['enədʒɪ] *n* Energie *f*
enforce [ɪn'fɔːs] *vt* durchsetzen
engage [ɪn'geɪdʒ] *vt* (*employ*) einstellen; (*in conversation*) verwickeln; (*TECH*) einschalten ♦ *vt* (*TECH*) ineinander greifen; (*clutch*) fassen; **to ~ in** sich beteiligen an +*dat*; **~d** *adj* verlobt; (*BRIT: TEL, toilet*) besetzt; (: *busy*) beschäftigt; **to get ~d** sich verloben; **~d tone** (*BRIT*) *n* (*TEL*) Besetztzeichen *nt*; **~ment** *n* (*appointment*) Verabredung *f*; (*to marry*)

Verlobung f; (MIL) Gefecht nt; **~ment ring** n Verlobungsring m; **engaging** adj gewinnend

engender [ɪn'dʒendər] vt hervorrufen

engine ['endʒɪn] n (AUT) Motor m; (RAIL) Lokomotive f; **~ driver** n Lok(omotiv)führer(in) m(f)

engineer [endʒɪ'nɪər] n Ingenieur m; (US: RAIL) Lok(omotiv)führer(in) m(f); **~ing** [endʒɪ'nɪərɪŋ] n Technik f

England ['ɪŋglənd] n England nt

English ['ɪŋglɪʃ] adj englisch ♦ n (LING) Englisch nt; the **~** npl (people) die Engländer pl; **~ Channel** n: the **~ Channel** der Ärmelkanal m; **~man/woman** (irreg) n Engländer(in) m(f)

engraving [ɪn'greɪvɪŋ] n Stich m

engrossed [ɪn'grəʊst] adj vertieft

engulf [ɪn'gʌlf] vt verschlingen

enhance [ɪn'hɑːns] vt steigern, heben

enigma [ɪ'nɪgmə] n Rätsel nt; **~tic** [enɪg'mætɪk] adj rätselhaft

enjoy [ɪn'dʒɔɪ] vt genießen; (privilege) besitzen; **to ~ o.s.** sich amüsieren; **~able** adj erfreulich; **~ment** n Genuss m, Freude f

enlarge [ɪn'lɑːdʒ] vt erweitern; (PHOT) vergrößern ♦ vi: **to ~ on sth** etw weiter ausführen; **~ment** n Vergrößerung f

enlighten [ɪn'laɪtn] vt aufklären; **~ment** n: the **E~ment** (HIST) die Aufklärung

enlist [ɪn'lɪst] vt gewinnen ♦ vi (MIL) sich melden

enmity ['enmɪtɪ] n Feindschaft f

enormity [ɪ'nɔːmɪtɪ] n Ungeheuerlichkeit f

enormous [ɪ'nɔːməs] adj ungeheuer

enough [ɪ'nʌf] adj, adv genug; **funnily ~** komischerweise

enquire [ɪn'kwaɪər] vt, vi = **inquire**

enrage [ɪn'reɪdʒ] vt wütend machen

enrich [ɪn'rɪtʃ] vt bereichern

enrol [ɪn'rəʊl] vt einschreiben ♦ vi (register) sich anmelden; **~ment** n (for course) Anmeldung f

en route [ɒn'ruːt] adv unterwegs

ensign ['ensaɪn, 'ensən] n (NAUT) Flagge f; (MIL) Fähnrich m

enslave [ɪn'sleɪv] vt versklaven

ensue [ɪn'sjuː] vi folgen, sich ergeben

en suite [ɒnswiːt] adj: **room with ~ bathroom** Zimmer nt mit eigenem Bad

ensure [ɪn'ʃʊər] vt garantieren

entail [ɪn'teɪl] vt mit sich bringen

entangle [ɪn'tæŋgl] vt verwirren, verstricken; **~d** adj: **to become ~d (in)** (in net, rope etc) sich verfangen (in +dat)

enter ['entər] vt betreten in +dat, betreten; (club) beitreten +dat; (in book) eintragen ♦ vi hereinkommen, hineingehen; **~ for** vt fus sich beteiligen an +dat; **~ into** vt fus (agreement) eingehen; (plans) eine Rolle spielen bei; **~ (up)on** vt fus beginnen

enterprise ['entəpraɪz] n (in person) Initiative f; (COMM) Unternehmen nt; **enterprising** ['entəpraɪzɪŋ] adj unternehmungslustig

entertain [entə'teɪn] vt (guest) bewirten; (amuse) unterhalten; **~er** n Unterhaltungskünstler(in) m(f); **~ing** adj unterhaltsam; **~ment** n Unterhaltung f

enthralled [ɪn'θrɔːld] adj gefesselt

enthusiasm [ɪn'θjuːzɪæzəm] n Begeisterung f

enthusiast [ɪn'θjuːzɪæst] n Enthusiast m; **~ic** [ɪnθjuːzɪ'æstɪk] adj begeistert

entice [ɪn'taɪs] vt verleiten, locken

entire [ɪn'taɪər] adj ganz; **~ly** adv ganz, völlig; **~ty** [ɪn'taɪərətɪ] n: **in its ~ty** in seiner Gesamtheit

entitle [ɪn'taɪtl] vt (allow) berechtigen; (name) betiteln; **~d** adj (book) mit dem Titel; **to be ~d to sth** das Recht auf etw acc haben; **to be ~d to do sth** das Recht haben, etw zu tun

entity ['entɪtɪ] n Ding nt, Wesen nt

entourage [ɒntuˈrɑːʒ] n Gefolge nt

entrails ['entreɪlz] npl Eingeweide pl

entrance [n 'entrns, vb ɪn'trɑːns] n Eingang m; (entering) Eintritt m ♦ vt hinreißen; **~ examination** n Aufnahmeprüfung f; **~ fee** n Eintrittsgeld nt; **~ ramp** (US) n (AUT) Einfahrt f

entrant ['entrnt] n (for exam) Kandidat m; (in race) Teilnehmer m

entreat [en'tri:t] vt anflehen

entrenched [en'trentʃt] adj (fig) verwurzelt

entrepreneur ['ɔntrəprə'nə:r] n Unternehmer(in) m(f)

entrust [in'trʌst] vt: **to ~ sb with sth** or **sth to sb** jdm etw anvertrauen

entry ['entri] n Eingang m; (THEAT) Auftritt m; (in account) Eintragung f; (in dictionary) Eintrag m; **"no ~"** „Eintritt verboten"; (for cars) „Einfahrt verboten"; **~ form** n Anmeldeformular nt; **~ phone** n Sprechanlage f

enumerate [ɪ'nju:məreit] vt aufzählen

enunciate [ɪ'nʌnsieit] vt aussprechen

envelop [in'veləp] vt einhüllen

envelope ['envələup] n Umschlag m

enviable ['enviəbl] adj beneidenswert

envious ['enviəs] adj neidisch

environment [in'vaiərnmənt] n Umgebung f; (ECOLOGY) Umwelt f; **~al** [invaiərn'mentl] adj Umwelt-; **~friendly** adj umweltfreundlich

envisage [in'vizidʒ] vt sich dat vorstellen

envoy ['envɔi] n Gesandte(r) mf

envy ['envi] n Neid m ♦ vt: **to ~ sb sth** jdn um etw beneiden

enzyme ['enzaim] n Enzym nt

epic ['epik] n Epos nt ♦ adj episch

epidemic [epi'demik] n Epidemie f

epilepsy ['epilepsi] n Epilepsie f; **epileptic** [epi'leptik] adj epileptisch ♦ n Epileptiker(in) m(f)

episode ['episəud] n (incident) Vorfall m; (story) Episode f

epitaph ['epita:f] n Grabinschrift f

epitomize [ɪ'pitəmaiz] vt verkörpern

equable ['ekwəbl] adj ausgeglichen

equal ['i:kwəl] adj gleich ♦ n Gleichgestellte(r) mf ♦ vt gleichkommen +dat; **~**

to the task der Aufgabe gewachsen;

equality [i:'kwɔliti] n Gleichheit f; (equal rights) Gleichberechtigung f; **~ize** vt gleichmachen ♦ vi (SPORT) ausgleichen; **~izer** n (SPORT) Ausgleich(streffer) m; **~ly** adv gleich

equanimity [ekwə'nimiti] n Gleichmut m

equate [ɪ'kweit] vt gleichsetzen

equation [ɪ'kweiʃən] n Gleichung f

equator [ɪ'kweitər] n Äquator m

equestrian [ɪ'kwestriən] adj Reit-

equilibrium [i:kwi'libriəm] n Gleichgewicht nt

equinox ['i:kwinɔks] n Tagundnachtgleiche f

equip [ɪ'kwip] vt ausrüsten; **to be well ~ped** gut ausgerüstet sein; **~ment** n Ausrüstung f; (TECH) Gerät nt

equitable ['ekwitəbl] adj gerecht, billig

equities ['ekwitiz] (BRIT) npl (FIN) Stammaktien pl

equivalent [ɪ'kwivələnt] adj gleichwertig, entsprechend ♦ n Äquivalent nt; (in money) Gegenwert m; **~ to** gleichwertig +dat, entsprechend +dat

equivocal [ɪ'kwivəkl] adj zweideutig

era ['iərə] n Epoche f, Ära f

eradicate [ɪ'rædikeit] vt ausrotten

erase [ɪ'reiz] vt ausradieren; (tape) löschen; **~r** n Radiergummi m

erect [ɪ'rekt] adj aufrecht ♦ vt errichten; **~ion** [ɪ'rekʃən] n Errichtung f; (ANAT) Erektion f

ERM n abbr (= Exchange Rate Mechanism) Wechselkursmechanismus m

erode [ɪ'rəud] vt zerfressen; (land) auswaschen

erotic [ɪ'rɔtik] adj erotisch

err [ə:r] vi sich irren

errand ['erənd] n Besorgung f

erratic [ɪ'rætik] adj unberechenbar

erroneous [ɪ'rəuniəs] adj irrig

error ['erər] n Fehler m

erupt [ɪ'rʌpt] vi ausbrechen; **~ion** [ɪ'rʌpʃən] n Ausbruch m

escalate ['eskəleit] vi sich steigern

escalator ['eskəleitə^r] n Rolltreppe f

escape [is'keip] n Flucht f; (of gas) Entweichen nt ♦ vi entkommen; (prisoners) fliehen; (leak) entweichen ♦ vt entkommen +dat; **escapism** n Flucht f (vor der Wirklichkeit)

escort [n 'eskɔ:t, vb is'kɔ:t] n (person accompanying) Begleiter m; (guard) Eskorte f ♦ vt (lady) begleiten; (MIL) eskortieren

Eskimo ['eskiməu] n Eskimo(frau) m(f)

especially [is'peʃli] adv besonders

espionage ['espiəna:ʒ] n Spionage f

esplanade [esplə'neid] n Promenade f

Esquire [is'kwaiə^r] n: **J. Brown ~** Herrn J. Brown

essay ['esei] n Aufsatz m; (LITER) Essay m

essence ['esns] n (quality) Wesen nt; (extract) Essenz f

essential [i'senʃl] adj (necessary) unentbehrlich; (basic) wesentlich ♦ n Allernötigste(s) nt; **~ly** adv eigentlich

establish [is'tæbliʃ] vt (set up) gründen; (prove) nachweisen; **~ed** adj anerkannt; (belief, laws etc) herrschend; **~ment** n (setting up) Einrichtung f

estate [is'teit] n Gut nt; (BRIT: housing ~) Siedlung f; (will) Nachlass m; **~ agent** (BRIT) n Grundstücksmakler m; **~ car** (BRIT) n Kombiwagen m

esteem [is'ti:m] n Wertschätzung f

esthetic [is'θetik] (US) adj = **aesthetic**

estimate [n 'estimət, vb 'estimeit] n Schätzung f; (of price) (Kosten)voranschlag m ♦ vt schätzen; **estimation** [esti'meiʃən] n Einschätzung f; (esteem) Achtung f

estranged [is'treindʒd] adj entfremdet

estuary ['estjuəri] n Mündung f

etc abbr (= et cetera) usw

etching ['etʃiŋ] n Kupferstich m

eternal [i'tə:nl] adj ewig

eternity [i'tə:niti] n Ewigkeit f

ether ['i:θə^r] n Äther m

ethical ['eθikl] adj ethisch

ethics ['eθiks] n Ethik f ♦ npl Moral f

Ethiopia [i:θi'əupiə] n Äthiopien nt

ethnic ['eθnik] adj Volks-, ethnisch; **~ minority** n ethnische Minderheit f

ethos ['i:θɔs] n Gesinnung f

etiquette ['etiket] n Etikette f

EU abbr (= European Union) EU f

euphemism ['ju:fəmizəm] n Euphemismus m

euro ['juərəu] n (FIN) Euro m

Eurocheque ['juərəutʃek] n Euroscheck m

Euroland ['juərəulænd] n Eurozone f; Euroland nt

Europe ['juərəp] n Europa nt; **~an** [juərə'pi:ən] adj europäisch ♦ n Europäer(in) m(f); **~an Community** n: the **~an Community** die Europäische Gemeinschaft

Euro-sceptic ['juərəuskeptik] n Kritiker der Europäischen Gemeinschaft

evacuate [i'vækjueit] vt (place) räumen; (people) evakuieren; **evacuation** [ivækju'eiʃən] n Räumung f; Evakuierung f

evade [i'veid] vt (escape) entkommen +dat; (avoid) meiden; (duty) sich entziehen +dat

evaluate [i'væljueit] vt bewerten; (information) auswerten

evaporate [i'væpəreit] vi verdampfen ♦ vt verdampfen lassen; **~d milk** n Kondensmilch f

evasion [i'veiʒən] n Umgehung f

evasive [i'veisiv] adj ausweichend

eve [i:v] n: **on the ~ of** am Vorabend +gen

even ['i:vn] adj eben; gleichmäßig; (score etc) unentschieden; (number) gerade ♦ adv: **~ you** sogar du; to **get ~ with sb** jdm heimzahlen; **~ if** selbst wenn; **~ so** dennoch; **~ though** obwohl; **~ more** sogar noch mehr; **~ out** vi sich ausgleichen

evening ['i:vniŋ] n Abend m; **in the ~** abends, am Abend; **~ class** n Abendschule f; **~ dress** n (no pl) (man's) Gesellschaftsanzug m; (woman's) Abendkleid nt

event [i'vent] n (happening) Ereignis nt;

(SPORT) Disziplin f; **in the ~ of** im Falle +gen; **~ful** adj ereignisreich

eventual [ɪ'ventʃuəl] adj (final) schließlich; **~ity** [ɪventʃu'ælɪtɪ] n Möglichkeit f; **~ly** adv am Ende; (given time) schließlich

ever ['evə'] adv (always) immer; (at any time) jemals ♦ conj seit; **have you ~ seen it?** haben Sie es je gesehen?; **~green** n Immergrün nt; **~lasting** adj immer während

every ['evrɪ] adj jede(r, s); **~ other/ third day** jeden zweiten/dritten Tag; **~ one of them** alle; **I have ~ confidence in him** ich habe uneingeschränktes Vertrauen in ihn; **we wish you ~ success** wir wünschen Ihnen viel Erfolg; **he's ~ bit as clever as his brother** er ist genauso klug wie sein Bruder; **~ now and then** ab und zu; **~body** pron = everyone; **~day** adj (daily) täglich; (commonplace) alltäglich, Alltags-; **~one** pron jeder, alle pl; **~thing** pron alles; **~where** adv überall(hin); (wherever) wohin; **~where you go** wohin du auch gehst

evict [ɪ'vɪkt] vt ausweisen; **~ion** [ɪ'vɪkʃən] n Ausweisung f

evidence ['evɪdns] n (sign) Spur f; (proof) Beweis m; (testimony) Aussage f

evident ['evɪdnt] adj augenscheinlich; **~ly** adv offensichtlich

evil ['iːvl] adj böse ♦ n Böse nt

evocative [ɪ'vɔkətɪv] adj: **to be ~ of sth** an etw acc erinnern

evoke [ɪ'vəuk] vt hervorrufen

evolution [iːvə'luːʃən] n Entwicklung f; (of life) Evolution f

evolve [ɪ'vɔlv] vt entwickeln ♦ vi sich entwickeln

ewe [juː] n Mutterschaf nt

ex- [eks] prefix Ex-, Alt-, ehemalig

exacerbate [eks'æsəbeɪt] vt verschlimmern

exact [ɪg'zækt] adj genau ♦ vt (demand) verlangen; **~ing** adj anspruchsvoll; **~ly** adv genau

exaggerate [ɪg'zædʒəreɪt] vt, vi übertreiben; **exaggeration** [ɪgzædʒə'reɪʃən] n Übertreibung f

exalted [ɪg'zɔːltɪd] adj (position, style) hoch; (person) exaltiert

exam [ɪg'zæm] n abbr (SCH) = **examination**

examination [ɪgzæmɪ'neɪʃən] n Untersuchung f; (SCH) Prüfung f, Examen nt; (customs) Kontrolle f

examine [ɪg'zæmɪn] vt untersuchen; (SCH) prüfen; (consider) erwägen; **~r** n Prüfer m

example [ɪg'zɑːmpl] n Beispiel nt; **for ~** zum Beispiel

exasperate [ɪg'zɑːspəreɪt] vt zur Verzweiflung bringen; **exasperating** adj ärgerlich, zum Verzweifeln bringend; **exasperation** [ɪgzɑːspə'reɪʃən] n Verzweiflung f

excavate ['ekskəveɪt] vt ausgraben; **excavation** [ekskə'veɪʃən] n Ausgrabung f

exceed [ɪk'siːd] vt überschreiten; (hopes) übertreffen; **~ingly** adv äußerst

excel [ɪk'sel] vi sich auszeichnen; **~lence** ['eksələns] n Vortrefflichkeit f; **E~lency** ['eksələnsɪ] n: **His E~lency** Seine Exzellenz f; **~lent** ['eksələnt] adj ausgezeichnet

except [ɪk'sept] prep (also: **~ for, ~ing**) außer +dat ♦ vt ausnehmen; **~ion** [ɪk'sepʃən] n Ausnahme f; **to take ~ion to** Anstoß nehmen an +dat; **~ional** [ɪk'sepʃənl] adj außergewöhnlich

excerpt ['eksəːpt] n Auszug m

excess [ɪk'ses] n Übermaß nt; **an ~ of** ein Übermaß an +dat; **~ baggage** n Mehrgepäck nt; **~ fare** n Nachlösegebühr f; **~ive** adj übermäßig

exchange [ɪks'tʃeɪndʒ] n Austausch m; (also: **telephone ~**) Zentrale f ♦ vt (goods) tauschen; (greetings) austauschen; (money, blows) wechseln; **~ rate** n Wechselkurs m

Exchequer [ɪks'tʃekə'] (BRIT) n: **the ~** das Schatzamt

excise ['ɛksaɪz] n Verbrauchssteuer f

excite [ɪk'saɪt] vt erregen; **to get ~d** sich aufregen; **~ment** n Aufregung f; **exciting** adj spannend

exclaim [ɪks'kleɪm] vi ausrufen

exclamation [ɛksklə'meɪʃən] n Ausruf m; **~ mark** n Ausrufezeichen nt

exclude [ɪks'kluːd] vt ausschließen

exclusion [ɪks'kluːʒən] n Ausschluss m; **~ zone** n Sperrzone f

exclusive [ɪks'kluːsɪv] adj (select) exklusiv; (sole) ausschließlich, Allein-; **~ of** exklusive +gen; **~ly** adv nur, ausschließlich

excommunicate [ɛkskə'mjuːnɪkeɪt] vt exkommunizieren

excrement ['ɛkskrəmənt] n Kot m

excruciating [ɪks'kruːʃieɪtɪŋ] adj qualvoll

excursion [ɪks'kəːʃən] n Ausflug m

excusable [ɪks'kjuːzəbl] adj entschuldbar

excuse [n ɪks'kjuːs, vb ɪks'kjuːz] n Entschuldigung f ♦ vt entschuldigen; **~ me!** entschuldigen Sie!

ex-directory ['ɛksdɪ'rɛktərɪ] (BRIT) adj: **to be ~** nicht im Telefonbuch stehen

execute ['ɛksɪkjuːt] vt (carry out) ausführen; (kill) hinrichten; **execution** [ɛksɪ'kjuːʃən] n Ausführung f; (killing) Hinrichtung f; **executioner** [ɛksɪ-'kjuːʃnə*] n Scharfrichter m

executive [ɪg'zɛkjutɪv] n (COMM) Geschäftsführer m; (POL) Exekutive f ♦ adj Exekutiv-, ausführend

executor [ɪg'zɛkjutə*] n Testamentsvollstrecker m

exemplary [ɪg'zɛmplərɪ] adj musterhaft

exemplify [ɪg'zɛmplɪfaɪ] vt veranschaulichen

exempt [ɪg'zɛmpt] adj befreit ♦ vt befreien; **~ion** [ɪg'zɛmpʃən] n Befreiung f

exercise ['ɛksəsaɪz] n Übung f n (power) ausüben; (muscle, patience) üben; (dog) ausführen ♦ vi Sport treiben; **~ bike** n Heimtrainer m; **~ book**

n (Schul)heft nt

exert [ɪg'zəːt] vt (influence) ausüben; **to ~ o.s.** sich anstrengen; **~ion** [ɪg'zəːʃən] n Anstrengung f

exhale [ɛks'heɪl] vt, vi ausatmen

exhaust [ɪg'zɔːst] n (fumes) Abgase pl; (pipe) Auspuffrohr nt ♦ vt erschöpfen; **~ed** adj erschöpft; **~ion** [ɪg'zɔːstʃən] n Erschöpfung f; **~ive** adj erschöpfend

exhibit [ɪg'zɪbɪt] n (JUR) Beweisstück nt; (ART) Ausstellungsstück nt ♦ vt ausstellen; **~ion** [ɛksɪ'bɪʃən] n (ART) Ausstellung f; (of temper etc) Zurschaustellung f; **~ionist** [ɛksɪ'bɪʃənɪst] n Exhibitionist m

exhilarating [ɪg'zɪləreɪtɪŋ] adj erhebend

ex-husband n Ehemann m

exile ['ɛksaɪl] n Exil nt; (person) Verbannte(r) f(m) ♦ vt verbannen

exist [ɪg'zɪst] vi existieren; **~ence** n Existenz f; **~ing** adj bestehend

exit ['ɛksɪt] n Ausgang m; (THEAT) Abgang m ♦ vi (THEAT) abtreten; (COMPUT) aus einem Programm herausgehen; **~ poll** n bei Wahlen unmittelbar nach Verlassen der Wahllokale durchgeführte Umfrage; **~ ramp** n (US) n (AUT) Ausfahrt f

exodus ['ɛksədəs] n Auszug m

exonerate [ɪg'zɔnəreɪt] vt entlasten

exorbitant [ɪg'zɔːbɪtnt] adj übermäßig; (price) Fantasie-

exotic [ɪg'zɔtɪk] adj exotisch

expand [ɪks'pænd] vt ausdehnen ♦ vi sich ausdehnen

expanse [ɪks'pæns] n Fläche f

expansion [ɪks'pænʃən] n Erweiterung f

expatriate [ɛks'pætrɪət] n Ausländer(in) m(f)

expect [ɪks'pɛkt] vt erwarten; (suppose) annehmen ♦ vi: **to be ~ing** ein Kind erwarten; **~ancy** n Erwartung f; **~ant mother** n werdende Mutter f; **~ation** [ɛkspɛk'teɪʃən] n Hoffnung f

expedient [ɪks'piːdɪənt] adj zweckdienlich ♦ n (Hilfs)mittel nt

expedition [ɛkspə'dɪʃən] n Expedition f

expel [ɪks'pel] vt ausweisen; (student) (ver)weisen

expend [ɪks'pend] vt (effort) aufwenden; **~iture** n Ausgaben pl

expense [ɪks'pens] n Kosten pl; ~s npl (COMM) Spesen pl; **at the ~ of** auf Kosten von; **~ account** n Spesenkonto nt; **expensive** [ɪks'pensɪv] adj teuer

experience [ɪks'pɪərɪəns] n (incident) Erlebnis nt; (practice) Erfahrung f ♦ vt erleben; **~d** adj erfahren

experiment [ɪks'perɪmənt] n Versuch m, Experiment nt ♦ vi experimentieren; **~al** [ɪksperɪ'mentl] adj experimentell

expert ['ɛkspɜːt] n Fachmann m, (official) Sachverständige(r) m ♦ adj erfahren; **~ise** [ɛkspɜː'tiːz] n Sachkenntnis f

expire [ɪks'paɪə'] vi (end) ablaufen; (ticket) verfallen; (die) sterben; **expiry** n Ablauf m

explain [ɪks'pleɪn] vt erklären

explanation [ɛksplə'neɪʃən] n Erklärung f; **explanatory** [ɪks'plænətrɪ] adj erklärend

explicit [ɪks'plɪsɪt] adj ausdrücklich

explode [ɪks'pləud] vi explodieren ♦ vt (bomb) sprengen

exploit [n 'ɛksplɔɪt, vb ɪks'plɔɪt] n (Helden)tat f ♦ vt ausbeuten; **~ation** [ɛksplɔɪ'teɪʃən] n Ausbeutung f

exploration [ɛksplə'reɪʃən] n Erforschung f

exploratory [ɪks'plɔrətrɪ] adj Probe-

explore [ɪks'plɔː'] vt (travel) erforschen; (search) untersuchen; **~r** n Erforscher(in) m(f)

explosion [ɪks'pləuʒən] n Explosion f; (fig) Ausbruch m

explosive [ɪks'pləusɪv] adj explosiv, Spreng- ♦ n Sprengstoff m

export [vb ɛks'pɔːt, n 'ɛkspɔːt] vt exportieren ♦ n Export m ♦ cpd (trade) Export-; **~er** [ɛks'pɔːtə'] n Exporteur m

expose [ɪks'pəuz] vt (to danger etc) aus-

setzen; (impostor) entlarven; **to ~ sb to sth** jdn einer Sache dat aussetzen; **~d** adj (position) exponiert

exposure [ɪks'pəuʒə'] n (MED) Unterkühlung f; (PHOT) Belichtung f; **exposure meter** n Belichtungsmesser m

express [ɪks'pres] adj ausdrücklich; (speedy) Express-, Eil- ♦ n (RAIL) Schnellzug m ♦ adv (send) per Express ♦ vt ausdrücken; **to ~ o.s.** sich ausdrücken; **~ion** [ɪks'preʃən] n Ausdruck m; **~ive** adj ausdrucksvoll; **~ly** adv ausdrücklich; **~way** (US) n (urban motorway) Schnellstraße f

expulsion [ɪks'pʌlʃən] n Ausweisung f

exquisite [ɛks'kwɪzɪt] adj erlesen

extend [ɪks'tend] vt (visit etc) verlängern; (building) ausbauen; (hand) ausstrecken; (welcome) bieten ♦ vi (land) sich erstrecken

extension [ɪks'tenʃən] n Erweiterung f; (of building) Anbau m; (TEL) Apparat m

extensive [ɪks'tensɪv] adj (knowledge) umfassend; (use) weitgehend, weit gehend

extent [ɪks'tent] n Ausdehnung f; (fig) Ausmaß nt; **to a certain ~** bis zu einem gewissen Grade; **to such an ~ that ...** dermaßen, dass ...; **to what ~?** inwieweit?

extenuating [ɪks'tenjueɪtɪŋ] adj mildernd

exterior [ɛks'tɪərɪə'] adj äußere(r, s), Außen- ♦ n Äußere(s) nt

exterminate [ɪks'tɜːmɪneɪt] vt ausrotten

external [ɛks'tɜːnl] adj äußere(r, s), Außen-

extinct [ɪks'tɪŋkt] adj ausgestorben; **~ion** [ɪks'tɪŋkʃən] n Aussterben nt

extinguish [ɪks'tɪŋgwɪʃ] vt (aus)löschen

extort [ɪks'tɔːt] vt erpressen; **~ion** [ɪks'tɔːʃən] n Erpressung f; **~ionate** [ɪks'tɔːʃnɪt] adj überhöht, erpresserisch

extra ['ɛkstrə] adj zusätzlich ♦ adv besonders ♦ n (for car etc) Extra nt;

(*charge*) Zuschlag *m*; (THEAT) Statist *m* ♦ *prefix* außer...

extract [*v* ɪksˈtrækt, *n* ˈekstrækt] *vt* (heraus)ziehen ♦ *n* (*from book etc*) Auszug *m*; (COOK) Extrakt *m*

extracurricular [ˈekstrəkəˈrɪkjʊləʳ] *adj* außerhalb des Stundenplans

extradite [ˈekstrədaɪt] *vt* ausliefern

extramarital [ˈekstrəˈmærɪtl] *adj* außerehelich

extramural [ˈekstrəˈmjʊərl] *adj* (*course*) Volkshochschul-

extraordinary [ɪksˈtrɔːdnrɪ] *adj* außerordentlich; (*amazing*) erstaunlich

extravagance [ɪksˈtrævəgəns] *n* Verschwendung *f*; (*lack of restraint*) Zügellosigkeit *f*; (*an ~*) Extravaganz *f*

extravagant [ɪksˈtrævəgənt] *adj* extravagant

extreme [ɪksˈtriːm] *adj* (*edge*) äußerste(r, s), hinterste(r, s); (*cold*) äußerste(r, s); (*behaviour*) außergewöhnlich, übertrieben ♦ *n* Extrem *nt*; **~ly** *adv* äußerst, höchst; **extremist** *n* Extremist(in) *m(f)*

extremity [ɪksˈtremɪtɪ] *n* (*end*) Spitze *f*, äußerste(s) Ende *nt*; (*hardship*) bitterste Not *f*; (ANAT) Hand *f*, Fuß *m*

extricate [ˈekstrɪkeɪt] *vt* losmachen, befreien

extrovert [ˈekstrəvəːt] *n* extrovertierte(r) Mensch *m*

exuberant [ɪgˈzjuːbərnt] *adj* ausgelassen

exude [ɪgˈzjuːd] *vt* absondern

eye [aɪ] *n* Auge *nt*; (*of needle*) Öhr *nt* ♦ *vt* betrachten; (*up and down*) mustern; **to keep an ~ on** aufpassen auf +*acc*; **~ball** *n* Augapfel *m*; **~bath** *n* Augenbad *nt*; **~brow** *n* Augenbraue *f*; **~brow pencil** *n* Augenbrauenstift *m*; **~drops** *npl* Augentropfen *pl*; **~lash** *n* Augenwimper *f*; **~lid** *n* Augenlid *nt*; **~liner** *n* Eyeliner *m*; **~opener** *n*: **that was an ~-opener** das hat mir/ihm *etc* die Augen geöffnet; **~shadow** *n* Lidschatten *m*; **~sight** *n* Sehkraft *f*; **~sore**

n Schandfleck *m*; **~ witness** *n* Augenzeuge *m*

F, f

F [ef] *n* (MUS) F *nt*

F. *abbr* (= *Fahrenheit*) F

fable [ˈfeɪbl] *n* Fabel *f*

fabric [ˈfæbrɪk] *n* Stoff *m*; (*fig*) Gefüge *nt*

fabrication [fæbrɪˈkeɪʃən] *n* Erfindung *f*

fabulous [ˈfæbjuləs] *adj* sagenhaft

face [feɪs] *n* Gesicht *nt*; (*surface*) Oberfläche *f*; (*of clock*) Zifferblatt *nt* ♦ *vt* (*point towards*) liegen nach; (*situation, difficulty*) sich stellen +*dat*; **~ down** (*person*) mit dem Gesicht nach unten; (*card*) mit der Vorderseite nach unten; **to make** *or* **pull a ~** das Gesicht verziehen; **in the ~ of** angesichts +*gen*; **on the ~ of it** so, wie es aussieht; **~ to ~** Auge in Auge; **to ~ up to sth** einer Sache *dat* ins Auge sehen; **~ cloth** (BRIT) *n* Waschlappen *m*; **~ cream** *n* Gesichtscreme *f*; **~ lift** *n* Facelifting *nt*; **~ powder** *n* (Gesichts)puder *m*

facet [ˈfæsɪt] *n* Aspekt *m*; (*of gem*) Facette *f*, Fassette *f*

facetious [fəˈsiːʃəs] *adj* witzig

face value *n* Nennwert *m*; **to take sth at (its) ~** (*fig*) etw für bare Münze nehmen

facial [ˈfeɪʃl] *adj* Gesichts-

facile [ˈfæsaɪl] *adj* (*easy*) leicht

facilitate [fəˈsɪlɪteɪt] *vt* erleichtern

facilities [fəˈsɪlɪtɪz] *npl* Einrichtungen *pl*; **credit ~** Kreditmöglichkeiten *pl*

facing [ˈfeɪsɪŋ] *adj* zugekehrt ♦ *prep* gegenüber

facsimile [fækˈsɪmɪlɪ] *n* Faksimile *nt*; (*machine*) Telekopierer *m*

fact [fækt] *n* Tatsache *f*; **in ~** in der Tat

faction [ˈfækʃən] *n* Splittergruppe *f*

factor [ˈfæktəʳ] *n* Faktor *m*

factory [ˈfæktərɪ] *n* Fabrik *f*

factual [ˈfæktjuəl] *adj* sachlich

faculty 403 fancy

faculty ['fækəltɪ] n Fähigkeit f; (UNIV) Fakultät f; (US: teaching staff) Lehrpersonal nt

fad [fæd] n Tick m; (fashion) Masche f

fade [feɪd] vi (lose colour) verblassen; (dim) nachlassen; (sound, memory) schwächer werden; (wilt) verwelken

fag [fæg] (inf) n (cigarette) Kippe f

fail [feɪl] vt (exam) nicht bestehen; (student) durchfallen lassen; (courage) verlassen; (memory) im Stich lassen ♦ vi (supplies) zu Ende gehen; (student) durchfallen; (eyesight) nachlassen; (light) schwächer werden; (crop) fehlschlagen; (remedy) nicht wirken; **to do sth** (neglect) es unterlassen, etw zu tun; (be unable) es nicht schaffen, etw zu tun; **without ~** unbedingt; **~ing** n Schwäche f ♦ prep mangels +gen; **~ure** ['feɪljə*] n (person) Versager m; (act) Versagen nt; (TECH) Defekt m

faint [feɪnt] adj schwach ♦ n Ohnmacht f ♦ vi ohnmächtig werden

fair [feə*] adj (just) gerecht, fair; (hair) blond; (skin) hell; (weather) schön; (not very good) mittelmäßig; (sizeable) ansehnlich ♦ adv (play) fair ♦ n (COMM) Messe f; (BRIT: funfair) Jahrmarkt m; **~ly** adv (honestly) gerecht, fair; (rather) ziemlich; **~ness** n Fairness f

fairy ['feərɪ] n Fee f; **~ tale** n Märchen nt

faith [feɪθ] n Glaube m; (trust) Vertrauen nt; (sect) Bekenntnis nt; **~ful** adj treu; **~fully** adv treu; **yours ~fully** (BRIT) hochachtungsvoll

fake [feɪk] n (thing) Fälschung f; (person) Schwindler m ♦ adj vorgetäuscht ♦ vt fälschen

falcon ['fɔ:lkən] n Falke m

fall [fɔ:l] (pt fell, pp fallen) n Fall m, Sturz m; (decrease) Fallen nt; (of snow) (Schnee)fall m; (US: autumn) Herbst m; **~s** npl (waterfall) Fälle pl; **to ~ flat** platt hinfallen; (joke) nicht ankommen; **~ back** vi zurückweichen; **~ back on** vt fus zurückgreifen auf +acc; **~ behind** vi zurückbleiben; **~ down** vi (person) hinfallen; (building) einstürzen; **~ for** vt fus (trick) hereinfallen auf +acc; (person) sich verknallen in +acc; **~ in** vi (roof) einstürzen; **~ off** vi herunterfallen; (diminish) sich vermindern; **~ out** vi sich streiten; (MIL) wegtreten; **~ through** vi (plan) ins Wasser fallen

fallacy ['fæləsɪ] n Trugschluss m

fallen ['fɔ:lən] pp of **fall**

fallible ['fæləbl] adj fehlbar

fallout ['fɔ:laut] n radioaktive(r) Niederschlag m; **~ shelter** n Atombunker m

fallow ['fæləu] adj brach(liegend)

false [fɔ:ls] adj falsch; (artificial) künstlich; **under ~ pretences** unter Vorspiegelung falscher Tatsachen; **~ alarm** n Fehlalarm m; **~ teeth** (BRIT) npl Gebiss nt

falter ['fɔ:ltə*] vi schwanken; (in speech) stocken

fame [feɪm] n Ruhm m

familiar [fə'mɪlɪə*] adj bekannt; (intimate) familiär; **to be ~ with** vertraut sein mit; **~ize** vt vertraut machen

family ['fæmɪlɪ] n Familie f; (relations) Verwandtschaft f; **~ business** n Familienunternehmen nt; **~ doctor** n Hausarzt m

famine ['fæmɪn] n Hungersnot f

famished ['fæmɪʃt] adj ausgehungert

famous ['feɪməs] adj berühmt

fan [fæn] n (folding) Fächer m; (ELEC) Ventilator m; (admirer) Fan m ♦ vt fächeln; **~ out** vi sich fächerförmig ausbreiten

fanatic [fə'nætɪk] n Fanatiker(in) m(f)

fan belt n Keilriemen m

fanciful ['fænsɪful] adj (odd) seltsam; (imaginative) fantasievoll

fancy ['fænsɪ] n (liking) Neigung f; (imagination) Einbildung f ♦ adj schick ♦ vt (like) gern haben; wollen; (imagine) sich einbilden; **he fancies her** er

mag sie; **~ dress** n Maskenkostüm nt;
~-dress ball n Maskenball m

fang [fæŋ] n Fangzahn m; (of snake)
Giftzahn m

fantastic [fæn'tæstik] adj fantastisch

fantasy ['fæntəsɪ] n Fantasie f

far [faːʳ] adj weit ♦ adv weit entfernt;
(very much) weitaus; **by ~** bei weitem;
so ~ so weit; bis jetzt; **go as ~ as the
station** gehen Sie bis zum Bahnhof;
as ~ as I know soweit or soviel ich
weiß; **~away** adj weit entfernt

farce [faːs] n Farce f; **farcical** ['faːsɪkl]
adj lächerlich

fare [feəʳ] n Fahrpreis m; (food) Kost f;
half/full ~ halber/voller
Fahrpreis m

Far East n: the **~** der Ferne Osten

farewell [feə'wel] n Abschied(sgruß) m
♦ excl lebe wohl!

farm [faːm] n Bauernhof m, Farm f ♦ vt
bewirtschaften; **~er** n Bauer m, Land-
wirt m; **~hand** n Landarbeiter m;
~house n Bauernhaus nt; **~ing** n
Landwirtschaft f; **~land** n Ackerland
nt; **~yard** n Hof m

far-reaching ['faː'riːtʃɪŋ] adj (reform,
effect) weitreichend, weit reichend

fart [faːt] (inf!) n Furz m ♦ vi furzen

farther ['faːðəʳ] adv weiter; **farthest**
['faːðɪst] adj fernste(r, s) ♦ adv am wei-
testen

fascinate ['fæsɪneɪt] vt faszinieren; **fascinating** adj faszinierend; **fascination**
[fæsɪ'neɪʃən] n Faszination f

fascism ['fæʃɪzəm] n Faschismus m

fashion ['fæʃən] n (of clothes) Mode f;
(manner) Art f (und Weise f) ♦ vt machen; **in ~** in Mode; **out of ~** unmo-
disch; **~able** adj (clothes) modisch;
(place) elegant; **~ show** n
Mode(n)schau f

fast [faːst] adj schnell; (firm) fest ♦ adv
schnell; fest ♦ n Fasten nt ♦ vi fasten;
to be ~ (clock) vorgehen

fasten ['faːsn] vt (attach) befestigen;
(with rope) zuschnüren; (seat belt) festmachen; (coat) zumachen ♦ vi sich
schließen lassen; **~er** n Verschluss m;
~ing n Verschluss m

fast food n Fastfood nt, Fast Food nt

fastidious [fæs'tɪdɪəs] adj wählerisch

fat [fæt] adj dick ♦ n Fett nt

fatal ['feɪtl] adj tödlich; (disastrous) verhängnisvoll; **~ity** [fə'tælɪtɪ] n (road
death etc) Todesopfer nt; **~ly** adv
tödlich

fate [feɪt] n Schicksal nt; **~ful** adj (pro-
phetic) schicksalsschwer; (important)
schicksalhaft

father ['faːðəʳ] n Vater m; (REL) Pater m;
~-in-law n Schwiegervater m; **~ly** adj
väterlich

fathom ['fæðəm] n Klafter m ♦ vt auslo-
ten; (fig) ergründen

fatigue [fə'tiːg] n Ermüdung f

fatten ['fætn] vt dick machen; (animals)
mästen ♦ vi dick werden

fatty ['fætɪ] adj fettig ♦ n (inf) Dicker-
chen nt

fatuous ['fætjuəs] adj albern, affig

faucet ['fɔːsɪt] (US) n Wasserhahn m

fault [fɔːlt] n (defect) Defekt m; (ELEC)
Störung f; (blame) Schuld f; (GEOG)
Verwerfung f; **it's your ~** du bist daran schuld; **to find ~ with (sth/sb)** etwas auszusetzen haben an (etw/jdm);
at ~ im Unrecht; **~less** adj tadellos; **~y**
adj fehlerhaft, defekt

fauna ['fɔːnə] n Fauna f

favour ['feɪvəʳ] (US favor) n (approval)
Wohlwollen nt; (kindness) Gefallen m
♦ vt (prefer) vorziehen (f); **in ~ of** zugunsten or zu Gunsten +gen; **to find ~
with sb** bei jdm Anklang finden;
~able ['feɪvrəbl] adj günstig; **~ite**
['feɪvrɪt] adj Lieblings- ♦ n (child) Liebling m; (SPORT) Favorit m

fawn [fɔːn] adj rehbraun ♦ n (animal)
(Reh)kitz nt ♦ vi: **to ~ (up)on** (fig) katz-
buckeln vor +dat

fax [fæks] n (document) Fax nt; (machine) Telefax nt ♦ vt: **to ~ sth to sb**
jdm etw faxen

FBI (US) n abbr (= Federal Bureau of Investigation) FBI nt

fear [fɪəʳ] n Furcht f ♦ vt fürchten; **~ful** adj (timid) furchtsam; (terrible) fürchterlich; **~less** adj furchtlos

feasible ['fiːzəbl] adj durchführbar

feast [fiːst] n Festmahl nt; (REL: also: **~day**) Feiertag m ♦ vi: **to ~** (on) sich gütlich tun (an +dat)

feat [fiːt] n Leistung f

feather ['feðəʳ] n Feder f

feature ['fiːtʃəʳ] n (Gesichts)zug m; (important part) Grundzug m; (CINE, PRESS) Feature nt ♦ vt darstellen; (advertising etc) groß herausbringen ♦ vi vorkommen; **featuring X** mit X; **~ film** n Spielfilm m

February ['fɛbruəri] n Februar m

fed [fɛd] pt, pp of **feed**

federal ['fɛdərəl] adj Bundes-

federation [fɛdə'reɪʃən] n (society) Verband m; (of states) Staatenbund m

fed up adj: **to be ~ with** etw satt haben; **I'm ~** ich habe die Nase voll

fee [fiː] n Gebühr f

feeble ['fiːbl] adj (person) schwach; (excuse) lahm

feed [fiːd] (pt, pp **fed**) n (for animals) Futter nt ♦ vt füttern; (support) ernähren; (data) eingeben; **to ~ on** fressen; **~back** n (information) Feed-back nt, Feedback nt; **~ing bottle** (BRIT) n Flasche f

feel [fiːl] (pt, pp **felt**) n: **it has a soft ~** es fühlt sich weich an ♦ vt (sense) fühlen; (touch) anfassen; (think) meinen ♦ vi (person) sich fühlen; (thing) sich anfühlen; **to get the ~ of sth** sich an etw acc gewöhnen; **I ~ cold** mir ist kalt; **I ~ like a cup of tea** ich habe Lust auf eine Tasse Tee; **~ about** or **around** vi herumsuchen; **~er** n Fühler m; **~ing** n Gefühl nt; (opinion) Meinung f

feet [fiːt] npl of **foot**

feign [feɪn] vt vortäuschen

feline ['fiːlaɪn] adj katzenartig

fell [fɛl] pt of **fall** ♦ vt (tree) fällen

fellow ['fɛləu] n (man) Kerl m; **~ citizen** n Mitbürger(in) m(f); **~ countryman** (irreg) n Landsmann m; **~ men** npl Mitmenschen pl; **~ship** n (group) Körperschaft f; (friendliness) Kameradschaft f; (scholarship) Forschungsstipendium nt; **~ student** n Kommilitone m, Kommilitonin f

felony ['fɛləni] n schwere(s) Verbrechen nt

felt [fɛlt] pt, pp of **feel** ♦ n Filz m; **~-tip pen** n Filzstift m

female ['fiːmeɪl] n (of animals) Weibchen nt ♦ adj weiblich

feminine ['fɛmɪnɪn] adj (LING) weiblich; (qualities) fraulich

feminist ['fɛmɪnɪst] n Feminist(in) m(f)

fence [fɛns] n Zaun m ♦ vt (also: **~ in**) einzäunen ♦ vi fechten; **fencing** ['fɛnsɪŋ] n Zaun m; (SPORT) Fechten nt

fend [fɛnd] vi: **to ~ for o.s.** sich (allein) durchschlagen; **~ off** vt abwehren

fender ['fɛndəʳ] n Kaminvorsetzer m; (US: AUT) Kotflügel m

ferment [vb fə'mɛnt, n 'fɜːmɛnt] vi (CHEM) gären ♦ n (unrest) Unruhe f

fern [fɜːn] n Farn m

ferocious [fə'rəuʃəs] adj wild, grausam

ferret ['fɛrɪt] n Frettchen nt ♦ vt: **to ~ out** aufspüren

ferry ['fɛrɪ] n Fähre f ♦ vt übersetzen

fertile ['fɜːtaɪl] adj fruchtbar

fertilize ['fɜːtɪlaɪz] vt (AGR) düngen; (BIOL) befruchten; **~r** n (Kunst)dünger m

fervent ['fɜːvənt] adj (admirer) glühend; (hope) sehnlich

fervour ['fɜːvəʳ] (US **fervor**) n Leidenschaft f

fester ['fɛstəʳ] vi eitern

festival ['fɛstɪvəl] n (REL etc) Fest nt; (ART, MUS) Festspiele pl

festive ['fɛstɪv] adj festlich; **the ~ season** (Christmas) die Festzeit; **festivities** [fɛs'tɪvɪtɪz] npl Feierlichkeiten pl

festoon [fɛs'tuːn] vt: **to ~ with**

schmücken mit

fetch [fetʃ] vt holen; (in sale) einbringen

fetching [ˈfetʃɪŋ] adj reizend

fête [feɪt] n Fest nt

fetus [ˈfiːtəs] (esp US) n = **foetus**

feud [fjuːd] n Fehde f

feudal [ˈfjuːdl] adj Feudal-

fever [ˈfiːvəʳ] n Fieber nt; **~ish** adj (MED) fiebrig; (fig) fieberhaft

few [fjuː] adj wenig; **a ~** einige; **~er** adj weniger; **~est** adj wenigste(r,s)

fiancé [fɪˈɑːnseɪ] n Verlobte(r) m; **~e** n Verlobte f

fib [fɪb] n Flunkerei f ♦ vi flunkern

fibre [ˈfaɪbəʳ] (US **fiber**) n Faser f; **~glass** n Glaswolle f

fickle [ˈfɪkl] adj unbeständig

fiction [ˈfɪkʃən] n (novels) Romanliteratur f; (story) Erdichtung f; **~al** adj erfunden

fictitious [fɪkˈtɪʃəs] adj erfunden, fingiert

fiddle [ˈfɪdl] n Geige f; (trick) Schwindelei f ♦ vt (BRIT: accounts) frisieren; **~ with** vt fus herumfummeln an +dat

fidelity [fɪˈdelɪtɪ] n Treue f

fidget [ˈfɪdʒɪt] vi zappeln

field [fiːld] n Feld nt; (range) Gebiet nt; **~ marshal** n Feldmarschall m; **~work** n Feldforschung f

fiend [fiːnd] n Teufel m

fierce [fɪəs] adj wild

fiery [ˈfaɪərɪ] adj (person) hitzig

fifteen [fɪfˈtiːn] num fünfzehn

fifth [fɪfθ] adj fünfte(r, s) ♦ n Fünftel nt

fifty [ˈfɪftɪ] num fünfzig; **~-fifty** adj, adv halbe-halbe, fifty-fifty (inf)

fig [fɪg] n Feige f

fight [faɪt] (pt, pp **fought**) n Kampf m; (brawl) Schlägerei f; (argument) Streit m ♦ vt kämpfen gegen; sich schlagen mit; (fig) bekämpfen ♦ vi kämpfen; sich schlagen; streiten; **~er** n Kämpfer(in) m(f); (plane) Jagdflugzeug nt; **~ing** n Kämpfen nt; (war) Kampfhandlungen pl

figment [ˈfɪgmənt] n: **~ of the imagination** reine Einbildung f

figurative [ˈfɪgjʊrətɪv] adj bildlich

figure [ˈfɪgəʳ] n (of person) Figur f; (person) Gestalt f; (number) Ziffer f ♦ vt (US: imagine) glauben ♦ vi (appear) erscheinen; **~ out** vt herauskommen; **~head** n (NAUT, fig) Galionsfigur f; **~ of speech** n Redensart f

file [faɪl] n (tool) Feile f; (dossier) Akte f; (folder) Aktenordner m; (COMPUT) Datei f; (row) Reihe f ♦ vt (metal, nails) feilen; (papers) abheften; (claim) einreichen ♦ vi: **to ~ in/out** hintereinander hereinkommen/hinausgehen; **to ~ past** vorbeimarschieren; **filing** [ˈfaɪlɪŋ] n Ablage f; **filing cabinet** n Aktenschrank m

fill [fɪl] vt füllen; (occupy) ausfüllen; (satisfy) sättigen ♦ n: **to eat one's ~** sich richtig satt essen; **~ in** vt (hole) (auf)füllen; (form) ausfüllen; **~ up** vt (container) auffüllen; (form) ausfüllen ♦ vt (AUT) tanken

fillet [ˈfɪlɪt] n Filet nt; **~ steak** n Filetsteak nt

filling [ˈfɪlɪŋ] n (COOK) Füllung f; (for tooth) (Zahn)plombe f; **~ station** n Tankstelle f

film [fɪlm] n Film m ♦ vt (scene) filmen; **~ star** n Filmstar m

filter [ˈfɪltəʳ] n Filter m ♦ vt filtern; **~ lane** (BRIT) n Abbiegespur f; **~-tipped** adj Filter-

filth [fɪlθ] n Dreck m; **~y** adj dreckig; (weather) scheußlich

fin [fɪn] n Flosse f

final [ˈfaɪnl] adj letzte(r, s); End-; (conclusive) endgültig ♦ n (FOOTBALL etc) Endspiel nt; **~s** npl (UNIV) Abschlussexamen nt; (SPORT) Schlussrunde f

finale [fɪˈnɑːlɪ] n (MUS) Finale nt

finalist [ˈfaɪnəlɪst] n (SPORT) Schlussrundenteilnehmer m; **~ize** vt endgültige Form geben +dat; abschließen; **~ly** adv (lastly) zuletzt; (eventually) endlich; (irrevocably) endgültig

finance [faɪˈnæns] n Finanzwesen nt ♦ vt finanzieren; ~s npl (funds) Finanzen pl; **financial** [faɪˈnænʃəl] adj Finanz-; finanziell

find [faɪnd] (pt, pp found) vt finden ♦ n Fund m; **to ~ sb guilty** jdn für schuldig erklären; **~ out** vt herausfinden; **~ings** npl (JUR) Ermittlungsergebnis nt; (of report) Befund m

fine [faɪn] adj fein; (good) gut; (weather) schön ♦ adv (well) gut; (small) klein ♦ n (JUR) Geldstrafe f ♦ vt (JUR) mit einer Geldstrafe belegen; **~ arts** npl schöne(n) Künste pl

finger [ˈfɪŋgər] n Finger m ♦ vt befühlen; **~nail** n Fingernagel m; **~print** n Fingerabdruck m; **~tip** n Fingerspitze f

finicky [ˈfɪnɪkɪ] adj pingelig

finish [ˈfɪnɪʃ] n Ende nt; (SPORT) Ziel nt; (of object) Verarbeitung f; (of paint) Oberflächenwirkung f ♦ vt (book) zu Ende lesen ♦ vi aufhören; (SPORT) ans Ziel kommen; **to be ~ed with sth** fertig sein mit etw; **to ~ doing sth** mit etw fertig werden; **~ off** vt (complete) fertig machen; (kill) den Gnadenstoß geben +dat; (knock out) erledigen (umg); **~ up** vt (food) aufessen; (drink) austrinken ♦ vi (end up) enden; **~ing line** n Ziellinie f; **~ing school** n Mädchenpensionat nt

finite [ˈfaɪnaɪt] adj endlich, begrenzt

Finland [ˈfɪnlənd] n Finnland nt

Finn [fɪn] n Finne m, Finnin f; **~ish** adj finnisch ♦ n (LING) Finnisch nt

fir [fɜːr] n Tanne f

fire [faɪər] n Feuer nt; (in house etc) Brand m ♦ vt (gun) abfeuern; (imagination) entzünden; (dismiss) hinausfeuern ♦ vi (AUT) zünden; **to be on ~** brennen; **~ alarm** n Feueralarm m; **~arm** n Schusswaffe f; **~ brigade** (BRIT) n Feuerwehr f; **~ department** (US) n Feuerwehr f; **~ engine** n Feuerwehrauto nt; **~ escape** n Feuerleiter f; **~ extinguisher** n Löschgerät nt;

~man (irreg) n Feuerwehrmann m; **~place** n Kamin m; **~side** n Kamin m; **~ station** n Feuerwache f; **~wood** n Brennholz nt; **~works** npl Feuerwerk nt; **~ squad** n Exekutionskommando nt

firm [fɜːm] adj fest ♦ n Firma f; **~ly** [ˈfɜːmlɪ] adv (grasp, speak) fest; (push, tug) energisch; (decide) endgültig

first [fɜːst] adj erste(r, s) ♦ adv zuerst; (arrive) als Erste(r); (happen) zum ersten Mal ♦ n (person: in race) Erste(r) mf; (UNIV) Eins f; (AUT) erster Gang m; **at ~** zuerst; **~ of all** zuallererst; **~ aid** n erste Hilfe f; **~-aid kit** n Verbandskasten m; **~-class** adj erstklassig; (travel) erster Klasse; **~-hand** adj aus erster Hand; **~ lady** (US) n First Lady f; **~ly** adv erstens; **~ name** n Vorname m; **~ rate** adj erstklassig

fiscal [ˈfɪskl] adj Finanz-

fish [fɪʃ] n inv Fisch m ♦ vi fischen; angeln; **to go ~ing** angeln gehen; (in sea) fischen gehen; **~erman** (irreg) n Fischer m; **~ farm** n Fischzucht f; **~ fingers** (BRIT) npl Fischstäbchen pl; **~ing boat** n Fischerboot nt; **~ing line** n Angelschnur f; **~ing rod** n Angel(rute) f; **~ing tackle** n (for sport) Angelgeräte pl; **~monger's (shop)** n Fischhändler m; **~ slice** n Fischvorlegemesser nt; **~ sticks** (US) npl = **fish fingers**

fishy [ˈfɪʃɪ] (inf) adj (suspicious) faul

fission [ˈfɪʃən] n Spaltung f

fissure [ˈfɪʃər] n Riss m

fist [fɪst] n Faust f

fit [fɪt] adj (MED) gesund; (SPORT) in Form, fit; (suitable) geeignet ♦ vt passen +dat; (insert, attach) einsetzen ♦ vi passen; (in space, gap) hineinpassen ♦ n (of clothes) Sitz m; (MED, of anger) Anfall m; (of laughter) Krampf m; **by ~s and starts** (move) ruckweise; (work) unregelmäßig; **~ in** vi hineinpassen; (fig: person) passen; **~ out** vt (also: **~ up**) ausstatten; **~ful** adj (sleep) unruhig; **~ment** n Einrichtungsgegenstand m; **~ness** n (suitability) Eignung f; (MED) Gesundheit f; (SPORT) Fitness f; **~ted carpet** n Teppichboden m; **~ted kitchen** n Einbauküche f; **~ter** n (TECH) Monteur m; **~ting** adj passend ♦ n (of dress) Anprobe f; (piece of equipment) (Ersatz)teil nt; **~tings** npl (equipment) Zubehör nt; **~ting room** n Anproberaum m

five [faɪv] num fünf; **~r** n (inf) (BRIT) Fünfpfundnote f; (US) Fünfdollarnote f

fix [fɪks] vt befestigen; (settle) festsetzen; (repair) reparieren ♦ n: in a ~ in der Klemme; **to ~ sb up with sth** jdm etw acc verschaffen; **~ation** [fɪkˈseɪʃən] n Fixierung f; **~ed** [fɪkst] adj fest; **~ture** [ˈfɪkstʃəʳ] n Installationsteil nt; (SPORT) Spiel nt

fizzy [ˈfɪzɪ] adj Sprudel-, sprudelnd

flabbergasted [ˈflæbəgɑːstɪd] (inf) adj platt

flabby [ˈflæbɪ] adj wabbelig

flag [flæg] n Fahne f ♦ vi (strength) nachlassen; (spirit) erlahmen; **~ down** vt anhalten; **~pole** [ˈflægpəʊl] n Fahnenstange f

flair [flɛəʳ] n Talent nt

flak [flæk] n Flakfeuer nt

flake [fleɪk] n (of snow) Flocke f; (of rust) Schuppe f ♦ vi (also: ~ off) abblättern

flamboyant [flæmˈbɔɪənt] adj extravagant

flame [fleɪm] n Flamme f

flamingo [fləˈmɪŋgəʊ] n Flamingo m

flammable [ˈflæməbl] adj brennbar

flan [flæn] (BRIT) n Obsttorte f

flank [flæŋk] n Flanke f ♦ vt flankieren

flannel [ˈflænl] n Flanell m; (BRIT: also: face ~) Waschlappen m; (: inf) Geschwafel nt; **~s** npl (trousers) Flanellhose f

flap [flæp] n Klappe f; (inf: crisis) (helle) Aufregung f ♦ vt (wings) schlagen mit ♦ vi flattern

flare [flɛəʳ] n (signal) Leuchtsignal nt; (in skirt etc) Weite f; **~ up** vi aufflammen; (fig) aufbrausen; (revolt) (plötzlich) ausbrechen

flash [flæʃ] n Blitz m; (also: news ~) Kurzmeldung f; (PHOT) Blitzlicht nt ♦ vt aufleuchten lassen ♦ vi aufleuchten; **in a ~** im Nu; **~ by** or **past** vi vorbeirasen; **~back** n Rückblende f; **~bulb** n Blitzlichtbirne f; **~ cube** n Blitzwürfel m; **~light** n Blitzlicht nt

flashy [ˈflæʃɪ] (pej) adj knallig

flask [flɑːsk] n (CHEM) Kolben m; (also: vacuum ~) Thermosflasche f ®

flat [flæt] adj flach; (dull) matt; (tyre) niedrigt; (beer) schal; (tyre) platt ♦ n (BRIT: rooms) Wohnung f; (MUS) b nt; (AUT) Platte(r) m; **to work ~ out** auf Hochtouren arbeiten; **~ly** adv glatt; **~screen** adj (TV, COMPUT) mit flachem Bildschirm; **~ten** vt (also: **~ten out**) ebnen

flatter [ˈflætəʳ] vt schmeicheln +dat; **~ing** adj schmeichelhaft; **~y** n Schmeichelei f

flatulence [ˈflætjʊləns] n Blähungen pl

flaunt [flɔːnt] vt prunken mit

flavour [ˈfleɪvəʳ] (US flavor) n Geschmack m ♦ vt würzen; **~ed** adj: **strawberry-~ed** mit Erdbeergeschmack; **~ing** n Würze f

flaw [flɔː] n Fehler m; **~less** adj einwandfrei

flax [flæks] n Flachs m; **~en** adj flachsfarben

flea [fliː] n Floh m

fleck [flek] n (mark) Fleck m; (pattern) Tupfen m

fled [fled] pt, pp of **flee**

flee [fliː] (pt, pp fled) vi fliehen ♦ vt fliehen vor +dat; (country) fliehen aus

fleece [fliːs] n Vlies nt ♦ vt (inf) schröpfen

fleet [fliːt] n Flotte f

fleeting [ˈfliːtɪŋ] adj flüchtig

Flemish [ˈflemɪʃ] adj flämisch

flesh [fleʃ] n Fleisch nt; **~ wound** n

Fleischwunde f

flew [fluː] pt of **fly**

flex [fleks] n Kabel nt ♦ vt beugen; **~ibility** [fleksɪ'bɪlɪti] n Biegsamkeit f; (fig) Flexibilität f; **~ible** adj biegsam; (plans) flexibel

flick [flɪk] n leichte(r) Schlag m ♦ vt leicht schlagen; **~ through** vt fus durchblättern

flicker ['flɪkə*] n Flackern nt ♦ vi flackern

flier ['flaɪə*] n Flieger m

flight [flaɪt] n Flug m; (fleeing) Flucht f; (also: **~ of steps**) Treppe f; **to take ~** die Flucht ergreifen; **~ attendant** [a] n Steward(ess) m(f); **~ deck** n Flugdeck nt

flimsy ['flɪmzi] adj (thin) hauchdünn; (excuse) fadenscheinig

flinch [flɪntʃ] vi: **to ~ (away from)** zurückschrecken (vor +dat)

fling [flɪŋ] (pt, pp **flung**) vt schleudern

flint [flɪnt] n Feuerstein m

flip [flɪp] vt werfen

flippant ['flɪpənt] adj schnippisch

flipper ['flɪpə*] n Flosse f

flirt [flɜːt] vi flirten ♦ n: **he/she is a ~** er/sie flirtet gern

flit [flɪt] vi flitzen

float [fləʊt] n (FISHING) Schwimmer m; (esp in procession) Plattformwagen m ♦ vi schwimmen; (in air) schweben ♦ vt (COMM) gründen; (currency) floaten

flock [flɒk] n (of sheep, REL) Herde f; (of birds) Schwarm m

flog [flɒg] vt prügeln; (inf: sell) verkaufen

flood [flʌd] n Überschwemmung f; (fig) Flut f ♦ vt überschwemmen; **~ing** n Überschwemmung f; **~light** n Flutlicht nt

floor [flɔː*] n (Fuß)boden m; (storey) Stock m ♦ vt (person) zu Boden schlagen; **ground ~** (BRIT) Erdgeschoss nt; **first ~** (BRIT) erste(r) Stock m; (US) Erdgeschoss nt; **~board** n Diele f; **~ show** n Kabarettvorstellung f

flop [flɒp] n Plumps m; (failure) Reinfall m ♦ vi (fail) durchfallen

floppy ['flɒpɪ] adj hängend; **~ (disk)** n (COMPUT) Diskette f

flora ['flɔːrə] n Flora f; **~l** adj Blumen-

florist ['flɒrɪst] n Blumenhändler(in) m(f); **~'s (shop)** n Blumengeschäft nt

flotation [fləʊ'teɪʃən] n (FIN) Auflegung f

flounce [flaʊns] n Volant m

flounder ['flaʊndə*] vi (fig) ins Schleudern kommen ♦ n (ZOOL) Flunder f

flour ['flaʊə*] n Mehl nt

flourish ['flʌrɪʃ] vi blühen; gedeihen ♦ n (waving) Schwingen nt; (of trumpets) Tusch m, Fanfare f

flout [flaʊt] vt missachten

flow [fləʊ] n Fließen nt; (of sea) Flut f ♦ vi fließen; **~ chart** n Flussdiagramm nt

flower ['flaʊə*] n Blume f ♦ vi blühen; **~ bed** n Blumenbeet nt; **~pot** n Blumentopf m; **~y** adj (style) blumenreich

flown [fləʊn] pp of **fly**

flu [fluː] n Grippe f

fluctuate ['flʌktjʊeɪt] vi schwanken; **fluctuation** [flʌktjʊ'eɪʃən] n Schwankung f

fluency ['fluːənsɪ] n Flüssigkeit f

fluent ['fluːənt] adj fließend; **~ly** adv fließend

fluff [flʌf] n Fussel f; **~y** adj flaumig

fluid ['fluːɪd] n Flüssigkeit f ♦ adj flüssig; (fig: plans) veränderbar

fluke [fluːk] (inf) n Dusel m

flung [flʌŋ] pt, pp of **fling**

fluoride ['fluəraɪd] n Fluorid nt; **~ toothpaste** n Fluorzahnpasta f

flurry ['flʌrɪ] n (of snow) Gestöber nt; (of activity) Aufregung f

flush [flʌʃ] n Erröten nt; (of excitement) Glühen nt ♦ vt (aus)spülen ♦ vi erröten ♦ adj glatt; **~ out** vt aufstöbern; **~ed** adj rot

flustered ['flʌstəd] adj verwirrt

flute [fluːt] n Querflöte f

flutter ['flʌtə*] n Flattern nt ♦ vi flattern

flux [flʌks] n: **in a state of ~** im Fluss

fly [flaɪ] *(pt* **flew,** *pp* **flown)** *n (insect)* Fliege *f;* (on trousers: also: **flies)** (Hosen)schlitz *m* ♦ *vi* fliegen; *(flee)* fliehen; *(flag)* wehen; **~ away** *or* **off** *vi (bird, insect)* wegfliegen; **~drive** *n:* **~drive holiday** Fly & Drive-Urlaub *m;* **~ing** *n* Fliegen *nt* ♦ *adj:* **with ~ing colours** mit fliegenden Fahnen; **~ing start** gute(r) Start *m;* **~ing visit** Stippvisite *f;* **~ing saucer** *n* fliegende Untertasse *f;* **~over** *(BRIT) n* Überführung *f;* **~sheet** *n (for tent)* Regendach *nt*

foal [fəʊl] *n* Fohlen *nt*

foam [fəʊm] *n* Schaum *m* ♦ *vi* schäumen; **~ rubber** *n* Schaumgummi *m*

fob [fɔb] *vt:* **to ~ sb off with sth** jdm etw andrehen; *(with promise)* jdn mit etw abspeisen

focal ['fəʊkl] *adj* Brenn-; **~ point** *n (of room, activity)* Mittelpunkt *m*

focus ['fəʊkəs] *(pl* **~es)** *n* Brennpunkt *m* ♦ *vt (attention)* konzentrieren; *(camera)* scharf einstellen ♦ *vi:* **to ~ (on)** sich konzentrieren (auf *+acc);* **in ~** scharf eingestellt; **out of ~** unscharf

fodder ['fɔdə*r*] *n* Futter *nt*

foe [fəʊ] *n* Feind *m*

foetus ['fiːtəs] *(US* **fetus)** *n* Fötus *m*

fog [fɔg] *n* Nebel *m;* **~ lamp** *(BRIT),* **~ light** *(US) n (AUT)* Nebelscheinwerfer *m*

foil [fɔɪl] *vt* vereiteln ♦ *n (metal, also fig)* Folie *f;* *(FENCING)* Florett *nt*

fold [fəʊld] *n (bend, crease)* Falte *f;* *(AGR)* Pferch *m* ♦ *vt* falten; **~ up** *vi (map etc)* zusammenfalten ♦ *vi (business)* eingehen; **~er** *n* Schnellhefter *m;* **~ing** *adj (chair etc)* Klapp-

foliage ['fəʊlɪidʒ] *n* Laubwerk *nt*

folk [fəʊk] *npl* Leute *pl* ♦ *adj* Volks-; **~s** *npl (family)* Leute *pl;* **~lore** ['fəʊklɔːr] *n (study)* Volkskunde *f;* *(tradition)* Folklore *f;* **~ song** *n* Volkslied *nt;* (modern) Folksong *m*

follow ['fɔləʊ] *vt* folgen *+dat; (fashion)*

mitmachen ♦ *vi* folgen; **~ up** *vt* verfolgen; **~er** *n* Anhänger(in) *m(f);* **~ing** *adj* folgend ♦ *n (people)* Gefolgschaft *f;* **~ on call** *n* weiteres Gespräch zu einer Telefonzelle um Guthaben zu verbrauchen

folly ['fɔlɪ] *n* Torheit *f*

fond [fɔnd] *adj:* **to be ~ of** gern haben

fondle ['fɔndl] *vt* streicheln

font [fɔnt] *n* Taufbecken *nt*

food [fuːd] *n* Essen *nt;* *(fodder)* Futter *nt;* **~ mixer** *n* Küchenmixer *m;* **~ poisoning** *n* Lebensmittelvergiftung *f;* **~ processor** *n* Küchenmaschine *f;* **~stuffs** *npl* Lebensmittel *pl*

fool [fuːl] *n* Narr *m,* Närrin *f* ♦ *vt (deceive)* hereinlegen ♦ *vi (also: ~ around)* (herum)albern; **~hardy** *adj* tollkühn; **~ish** *adj* albern; **~proof** *adj* idiotensicher

foot [fʊt] *(pl* **feet)** *n* Fuß *m* ♦ *vt (bill)* bezahlen; **on ~** zu Fuß

footage ['fʊtɪdʒ] *n (CINE)* Filmmaterial *nt*

football ['fʊtbɔːl] *n* Fußball *m;* *(game: BRIT)* Fußball *m;* (: *US)* Football *m;* **~ player** *n (BRIT: also:* **~er)** Fußballspieler *m,* Fußballer *m;* *(US)* Footballer *m*

Football Pools

Football Pools, umgangssprachlich auch **the pools** genannt, ist das in Großbritannien weit verbreitete Fußballtoto, bei dem auf die Ergebnisse der samstäglichen Fußballspiele gewettet wird. Teilnehmer schicken ihren ausgefüllten Totoschein vor den Spielen an die Totogesellschaft und vergleichen nach den Spielen die Ergebnisse mit ihrem Schein. Die Gewinne können sehr hoch sein und gelegentlich Millionen von Pfund betragen.

---

foot: ~brake *n* Fußbremse *f;* **~bridge** *n* Fußgängerbrücke *f;* **~hills** *npl* Ausläufer *pl;* **~hold** *n* Halt *m;* **~ing** *n* Halt *m;* *(fig)* Verhältnis *nt;* **~lights** *npl* Rampenlich nt; **~man** (irreg) n Bedienstete(r) m; **~note** n Fußnote f; **~path** n Fußweg m; **~print** n Fußabdruck m; **~sore** adj fußkrank; **~step** n Schritt m; **~wear** n Schuhzeug nt

---

KEYWORD

---

for [fɔːʳ] prep **1** für; **is this for me?** ist das für mich?; **the train for London** der Zug nach London; **he went for the paper** er ging die Zeitung holen; **give it to me – what for?** gib es mir – warum?

2 (because of) wegen; **for this reason** aus diesem Grunde

3 (referring to distance): **there are roadworks for 5 km** die Baustelle ist 5 km lang; **we walked for miles** wir sind meilenweit gegangen

4 (referring to time) seit; (: with future sense) für; **he was away for 2 years** er war zwei Jahre lang weg

5 (+infin clauses): **it is not for me to decide** das kann ich nicht entscheiden; **for this to be possible ...** damit dies möglich wird/würde ...

6 (in spite of) trotz +gen or (inf) dat ; **for all his complaints** obwohl er sich ständig beschwert

♦ conj denn

forage ['fɔrɪdʒ] n (Vieh)futter nt

foray ['fɔreɪ] n Raubzug m

forbad(e) [fə'bæd] pt of **forbid**

forbid(e) [fə'bɪd] (pt **forbad(e)**, pp **forbidden**) vt verbieten; **~ding** adj einschüchternd

force [fɔːs] n Kraft f; (compulsion) Zwang m ♦ vt zwingen; (lock) aufbrechen; **the F~s** npl (BRIT) die Streitkräfte; **in ~** (rule) gültig; (group) in großer Stärke; **~d** adj (smile) gezwungen; (landing) Not-; **~feed** vt zwangsernähren; **~ful** adj (speech) kraftvoll; (personality) resolut

forceps ['fɔːseps] npl Zange f

forcibly ['fɔːsəblɪ] adv zwangsweise

ford [fɔːd] n Furt f ♦ vt durchwaten

fore [fɔːʳ] n: **to the ~** in den Vordergrund; **~arm** ['fɔːrɑːm] n Unterarm m; **~boding** [fɔː'bəudɪŋ] n Vorahnung f; **~cast** ['fɔːkɑːst] (irreg: like **cast**) n Vorhersage f ♦ vt voraussagen; **~court** ['fɔːkɔːt] n (of garage) Vorplatz m; **~fathers** ['fɔːfɑːðəz] npl Vorfahren pl; **~finger** ['fɔːfɪŋgəʳ] n Zeigefinger m; **~front** ['fɔːfrʌnt] n Spitze f

forego [fɔː'gəu] (irreg: like **go**) vt verzichten auf +acc

fore: **~gone** [fɔː'gɔn] adj: **it's a ~gone conclusion** es steht von vornherein fest; **~ground** ['fɔːgraund] n Vordergrund m; **~head** ['fɔrɪd] n Stirn f

foreign ['fɔrɪn] adj Auslands-; (accent) ausländisch; (trade) Außen-; (body) Fremd-; **~er** n Ausländer(in) m(f); **~ exchange** n Devisen pl; **F~ Office** (BRIT) n Außenministerium nt; **F~ Secretary** (BRIT) n Außenminister m

fore [fɔː-]: **~leg** n Vorderbein nt; **~man** (irreg) n Vorarbeiter m; **~most** adj erste(r, s) ♦ adv: **first and ~most** vor allem

forensic [fə'rensɪk] adj gerichtsmedizinisch

fore ['fɔː-]: **~runner** n Vorläufer m; **~see** [fɔː'siː] (irreg: like **see**) vt vorhersehen; **~seeable** adj absehbar; **~shadow** [fɔː'ʃædəu] vt andeuten; **~sight** ['fɔːsaɪt] n Voraussicht f

forest ['fɔrɪst] n Wald m

forestall [fɔː'stɔːl] vt zuvorkommen +dat

forestry ['fɔrɪstrɪ] n Forstwirtschaft f

foretaste ['fɔːteɪst] n Vorgeschmack m

foretell [fɔː'tel] (irreg: like **tell**) vt vorhersagen

forever [fə'revəʳ] adv für immer

foreword ['fɔːwəːd] n Vorwort nt

forfeit ['fɔːfɪt] n Einbuße f ♦ vt verwirken

forgave [fə'geɪv] pt of **forgive**

forge [fɔːdʒ] n Schmiede f ♦ vt fälschen; (iron) schmieden; **~ ahead**

vi Fortschritte machen; **~d** *adj* gefälscht; **~d banknotes** Blüten (*inf*) *pl*; **~r** *n* Fälscher *m*; **~ry** *n* Fälschung *f*

forget [fə'gɛt] (*pt* **forgot**, *pp* **forgotten**) *vt, vi* vergessen; **~ful** *adj* vergesslich; **~-me-not** *n* Vergissmeinnicht *nt*

forgive [fə'gɪv] (*pt* **forgave**, *pp* **forgiven**) *vt* vergeben; **to ~ sb** (**for sth**) jdm (etw) verzeihen; **~ness** *n* Verzeihung *f*

forgot [fə'gɒt] *pt of* **forget**; **~ten** *pp of* **forget**

fork [fɔːk] *n* Gabel *f*; (*in road*) Gabelung *f* ♦ *vi* (*road*) sich gabeln; **~ out** (*inf*) *vt* (*pay*) blechen; **~-lift truck** *n* Gabelstapler *m*

forlorn [fə'lɔːn] *adj* (*person*) verlassen; (*hope*) vergeblich

form [fɔːm] *n* Form *f*; (*type*) Art *f*; (*figure*) Gestalt *f*; (*SCH*) Klasse *f*; (*bench*) (Schul)bank *f*; (*document*) Formular *nt* ♦ *vt* formen; (*be part of*) bilden

formal ['fɔːməl] *adj* formell; (*occasion*) offiziell; **~ly** *adv* (*ceremoniously*) formell; (*officially*) offiziell

format ['fɔːmæt] *n* Format *nt* ♦ *vt* (*COMPUT*) formatieren

formation [fɔː'meɪʃən] *n* Bildung *f*; (*AVIAT*) Formation *f*

formative ['fɔːmətɪv] *adj* (*years*) formend

former ['fɔːmə*] *adj* früher; (*opposite of latter*) erstere(r, s); **~ly** *adv* früher

formidable ['fɔːmɪdəbl] *adj* furchtbar

formula ['fɔːmjʊlə] (*pl* **~e** *or* **~s**) *n* Formel *f*; **~e** ['fɔːmjʊliː] *npl of* **formula**; **~te** ['fɔːmjʊleɪt] *vt* formulieren

fort [fɔːt] *n* Feste *f*, Fort *nt*

forte ['fɔːtɪ] *n* Stärke *f*, starke Seite *f*

forth [fɔːθ] *adv*: **and so ~** und so weiter; **~coming** *adj* kommend; (*character*) entgegenkommend; **~right** *adj* offen; **~with** *adv* umgehend

fortify ['fɔːtɪfaɪ] *vt* (ver)stärken; (*protect*) befestigen

fortitude ['fɔːtɪtjuːd] *n* Seelenstärke *f*

fortnight ['fɔːtnaɪt] (*BRIT*) *n* vierzehn

Tage *pl*; **~ly** (*BRIT*) *adj* zweiwöchentlich ♦ *adv* alle vierzehn Tage

fortress ['fɔːtrɪs] *n* Festung *f*

fortunate ['fɔːtʃənɪt] *adj* glücklich; **~ly** *adv* glücklicherweise, zum Glück

fortune ['fɔːtʃən] *n* Glück *nt*; (*money*) Vermögen *nt*; **~-teller** *n* Wahrsager(in) *m(f)*

forty ['fɔːtɪ] *num* vierzig

forum ['fɔːrəm] *n* Forum *nt*

forward ['fɔːwəd] *adj* vordere(r, s); (*movement*) Vorwärts-; (*person*) vorlaut; (*planning*) Voraus- ♦ *adv* vorwärts ♦ *n* (*SPORT*) Stürmer *m* ♦ *vt* (*send*) schicken; (*help*) fördern; **~s** *adv* vorwärts

fossil ['fɒsl] *n* Fossil *nt*, Versteinerung *f*

foster ['fɒstə*] *vt* (*talent*) fördern; **~ child** *n* Pflegekind *nt*; **~ mother** *n* Pflegemutter *f*

fought [fɔːt] *pt, pp of* **fight**

foul [faʊl] *adj* schmutzig; (*language*) gemein; (*weather*) schlecht ♦ *n* (*SPORT*) Foul *nt* ♦ *vt* (*mechanism*) blockieren; (*SPORT*) foulen; **~ play** *n* (*SPORT*) Foulspiel *nt*; (*LAW*) Verbrechen *nt*

found [faʊnd] *pt, pp of* **find** ♦ *vt* gründen; **~ation** [faʊn'deɪʃən] *n* (*act*) Gründung *f*; (*fig*) Fundament *nt*; (*also*: **~ation cream**) Grundierungscreme *f*; **~ations** *npl* (*of house*) Fundament *nt*; **~er** *n* Gründer(in) *m(f)* ♦ *vi* sinken

foundry ['faʊndrɪ] *n* Gießerei *f*

fountain ['faʊntɪn] *n* (Spring)brunnen *m*; **~ pen** *n* Füllfederhalter *m*

four [fɔː*] *num* vier; **on all ~s** auf allen vieren; **~-poster** *n* Himmelbett *nt*; **~some** *n* Quartett *nt*; **~teen** *num* vierzehn; **~teenth** *adj* vierzehnte(r, s); **~th** *adj* vierte(r, s)

fowl [faʊl] *n* Huhn *nt*; (*food*) Geflügel *nt*

fox [fɒks] *n* Fuchs *m* ♦ *vt* täuschen

foyer ['fɔɪeɪ] *n* Foyer *nt*, Vorhalle *f*

fraction ['frækʃən] *n* (*MATH*) Bruch *m*; (*part*) Bruchteil *m*

fracture ['fræktʃə*] *n* (*MED*) Bruch *m* ♦ *vt* brechen

fragile ['frædʒaɪl] *adj* zerbrechlich

fragment ['frægmənt] n Bruchstück nt; (small part) Splitter m

fragrance ['freɪɡrəns] n Duft m; **fragrant** ['freɪɡrənt] adj duftend

frail [freɪl] adj schwach, gebrechlich

frame [freɪm] n Rahmen m; (of spectacles: also: **~s**) Gestell nt; (body) Gestalt f ♦ vt einrahmen; **to ~ sb** (inf: incriminate) jdm etwas anhängen; **~ of mind** Verfassung f; **~work** n Rahmen m; (of society) Gefüge nt

France [frɑːns] n Frankreich nt

franchise ['fræntʃaɪz] n (POL) aktives Wahlrecht nt; (COMM) Lizenz f

frank [fræŋk] adj offen ♦ vt (letter) frankieren; **~ly** adv offen gesagt

frantic ['fræntɪk] adj verzweifelt

fraternal [frə'tɜːnl] adj brüderlich

fraternity [frə'tɜːnɪtɪ] n (club) Vereinigung f; (spirit) Brüderlichkeit f; (US: SCH) Studentenverbindung f

fraternize ['frætənaɪz] vi fraternisieren

fraud [frɔːd] n (trickery) Betrug m; (person) Schwindler(in) m(f); **~ulent** ['frɔːdjulənt] adj betrügerisch

fraught [frɔːt] adj: **~ with** voller +gen

fray [freɪ] vt, vi ausfransen; **tempers were ~ed** die Gemüter waren erhitzt

freak [friːk] n Monstrosität f ♦ cpd (storm etc) anormal

freckle ['frekl] n Sommersprosse f

free [friː] adj frei; (loose) lose; (liberal) freigebig ♦ vt (set ~) befreien; (unblock) freimachen; **~ (of charge)** gratis, umsonst; **for ~** gratis, umsonst; **~dom** ['friːdəm] n Freiheit f; **F~fone** ® n: **call F~fone 0800 ...** rufen Sie gebührenfrei 0800 ... an; **~-for-all** n (fight) allgemein(es) Handgemenge nt; **~ gift** n Geschenk nt; **~ kick** n Freistoß m; **~lance** adj frei; (artist) freischaffend; **~ly** adv frei; (admit) offen; **F~post** ® n ≈ Gebühr zahlt Empfänger; **~-range** adj (hen) Farmhof-; (eggs) Land-; **~ trade** n Freihandel m; **~way** (US) n Autobahn f; **~wheel** vi im Freilauf fahren; **~ will** n: **of one's**

own ~ will aus freien Stücken

freeze [friːz] (pt froze, pp frozen) vi gefrieren; (feel cold) frieren ♦ vt (also fig) einfrieren ♦ n (fig, FIN) Stopp m; **~r** n Tiefkühltruhe f, (in fridge) Gefrierfach nt; **freezing** adj eisig; (freezing cold) eiskalt; **freezing point** n Gefrierpunkt m

freight [freɪt] n Fracht f; **~ train** n Güterzug m

French [frentʃ] adj französisch ♦ n (LING) Französisch nt; **the ~** npl (people) die Franzosen pl; **~ bean** n grüne Bohne f; **~ fried potatoes** (BRIT) npl Pommes frites pl; **~ fries** (US) npl Pommes frites pl; **~ horn** n (MUS) (Wald)horn nt; **~ kiss** n Zungenkuss m; **~ loaf** n Baguette f; **~man/woman** (irreg) n Franzose m/Französin f; **~ window** n Verandatür f

frenzy ['frenzɪ] n Raserei f

frequency ['friːkwənsɪ] n Häufigkeit f; (PHYS) Frequenz f

frequent [adj 'friːkwənt, vb frɪ'kwent] adj häufig ♦ vt (regelmäßig) besuchen; **~ly** adv (often) häufig, oft

fresh [freʃ] adj frisch; **~en** vi (also: **~en up**) (sich) auffrischen; (person) sich frisch machen; **~er** (inf: BRIT) n (UNIV) Erstsemester nt; **~ly** adv gerade; **~man** (irreg) (US) n = fresher; **~ness** n Frische f; **~water** adj (fish) Süßwasser-

fret [fret] vi sich dat Sorgen machen

friar ['fraɪə*] n Klosterbruder m

friction ['frɪkʃən] n (also fig) Reibung f

Friday ['fraɪdɪ] n Freitag m

fridge [frɪdʒ] (BRIT) n Kühlschrank m

fried [fraɪd] adj gebraten

friend [frend] n Freund(in) m(f); **~ly** adj freundlich; (relations) freundschaftlich; **~ly fire** n Beschuss m durch die eigene Seite; **~ship** n Freundschaft f

frieze [friːz] n Fries m

frigate ['frɪɡɪt] n Fregatte f

fright [fraɪt] n Schrecken m; **to take ~** es mit der Angst zu tun bekommen; **~en** vt erschrecken; **to be ~ened**

Angst haben; **~ening** adj schrecklich; **~ful** (inf) furchtbar

frigid ['frɪdʒɪd] adj frigide

frill [frɪl] n Rüsche f

fringe [frɪndʒ] n Besatz m; (BRIT: of hair) Pony m; (fig) Peripherie f; **~ benefits** npl zusätzliche Leistungen pl

Frisbee ['frɪzbɪ] ® n Frisbee ® nt

frisk [frɪsk] vt durchsuchen

frisky ['frɪskɪ] adj lebendig, ausgelassen

fritter ['frɪtə'] vt: **to ~** vergeuden

frivolous ['frɪvələs] adj frivol

frizzy ['frɪzɪ] adj kraus

fro [frəʊ] adv see to

frock [frɒk] n Kleid nt

frog [frɒg] n Frosch m; **~man** (irreg) n Froschmann m

frolic ['frɒlɪk] vi ausgelassen sein

KEYWORD

from [frɒm] prep **1** (indicating starting place) of; (indicating origin etc) aus +dat; **a letter/telephone call from my sister** ein Brief/Anruf von meiner Schwester; **where do you come from?** woher kommen Sie?; **to drink from the bottle** aus der Flasche trinken

2 (indicating time) von ... an; (: past) seit; **from one o'clock to or until or till two** von ein Uhr bis zwei; **from January (on)** ab Januar

3 (indicating distance) von ... (entfernt)

4 (indicating price, number etc) ab +dat; **from £10** ab £10; **there were from 20 to 30 people there** es waren zwischen 20 und 30 Leute da

5 (indicating difference) **he can't tell red from green** er kann nicht zwischen Rot und Grün unterscheiden; **to be different from sb/sth** anders sein als jd/etw

6 (because of, based on): **from what he says** nach dem, was er sagt; **weak from hunger** schwach vor Hunger

---

front [frʌnt] n Vorderseite f; (of house) Fassade f; (promenade: also: **sea ~**)

Strandpromenade f; (MIL, POL, MET) Front f; (fig: appearances) Fassade f ♦ adj (forward) vordere(r, s), Vorder-; (first) vorderste(r, s); **in ~** vorne; **in ~ of** vor; **~age** ['frʌntɪdʒ] n Vorderfront f; **~ door** n Haustür f; **~ier** ['frʌntɪə'] n Grenze f; **~ page** n Titelseite f; **~ room** (BRIT) n Wohnzimmer nt; **~-wheel drive** n Vorderradantrieb m

frost [frɒst] n Frost m; **~bite** n Erfrierung f; **~ed** adj (glass) Milch-; **~y** adj frostig

froth [frɒθ] n Schaum m

frown [fraʊn] n Stirnrunzeln nt ♦ vi die Stirn runzeln

froze [frəʊz] pt of freeze

frozen ['frəʊzn] pp of freeze

frugal ['fru:gl] adj sparsam, bescheiden

fruit [fru:t] n inv (as collective) Obst nt; (particular) Frucht f; **~ful** adj fruchtbar; **~ion** [fru:'ɪʃən] n: **to come to ~ion** in Erfüllung gehen; **~ juice** n Fruchtsaft m; **~ machine** (BRIT) n Spielautomat m; **~ salad** n Obstsalat m

frustrate [frʌs'treɪt] vt vereiteln; **~d** adj gehemmt; (PSYCH) frustriert

fry [fraɪ] (pt, pp **fried**) vt braten ♦ npl: **small ~** kleine Fische pl; **~ing pan** n Bratpfanne f

ft. abbr = **foot; feet**

fuddy-duddy ['fʌdɪdʌdɪ] n altmodische(r) Kauz m

fudge [fʌdʒ] n Fondant m

fuel ['fjʊəl] n Treibstoff m; (for heating) Brennstoff m; (for lighter) Benzin nt; **~ oil** n (diesel fuel) Heizöl nt; **~ tank** n Tank m

fugitive ['fju:dʒɪtɪv] n Flüchtling m

fulfil [fʊl'fɪl] vt (duty) erfüllen; (promise) einhalten; **~ment** n Erfüllung f

full [fʊl] adj (box, bottle, price) voll; (person: satisfied) satt; (member, power, employment) Voll-; (complete) vollständig, Voll-; (speed) höchste(r, s); (skirt) weit ♦ adv: **~ well** sehr wohl; **in ~** vollständig; **a ~ two hours** volle zwei Stunden; **~-length** adj (lifesize) lebensgroß; **a ~-length photograph** *n* Ganzaufnahme; **~ moon** *n* Vollmond *m*; **~-scale** *adj (attack)* General-; *(drawing)* in Originalgröße; **~ stop** *n* Punkt *m*; **~-time** *adj (job)* Ganztags- ♦ *adv (work)* ganztags ♦ *n (SPORT)* Spielschluss *nt*; **~ly** *adv* völlig; **~ly fledged** *adj (also fig)* flügge; **~ly licensed** *adj (hotel, restaurant)* mit voller Schankkonzession *or* -erlaubnis

fumble ['fʌmbl] *vi*: **to ~ (with)** herumfummeln (an *+dat*)

fume [fjuːm] *vi* qualmen; *(fig)* kochen *(inf)*; **~s** *npl (of fuel, car)* Abgase *pl*

fumigate ['fjuːmɪgeɪt] *vt* ausräuchern

fun [fʌn] *n* Spaß *m*; **to make ~ of** sich lustig machen über *+acc*

function ['fʌŋkʃən] *n* Funktion *f*; *(occasion)* Veranstaltung *f* ♦ *vi* funktionieren; **~al** *adj* funktionell

fund [fʌnd] *n (money)* Geldmittel *pl*, Fonds *m*; *(store)* Vorrat *m*; **~s** *npl (resources)* Mittel *pl*

fundamental [fʌndə'mentl] *adj* fundamental, grundlegend

funeral ['fjuːnərəl] *n* Beerdigung *f*; **~ parlour** *n* Leichenhalle *f*; **~ service** *n* Trauergottesdienst *m*

funfair ['fʌnfeəᵣ] *(BRIT) n* Jahrmarkt *m*

fungi ['fʌŋgaɪ] *npl of* **fungus**

fungus ['fʌŋgəs] *n* Pilz *m*

funnel ['fʌnl] *n* Trichter *m*; *(NAUT)* Schornstein *m*

funny ['fʌnɪ] *adj* komisch

fur [fɜːᵣ] *n* Pelz *m*; **~ coat** *n* Pelzmantel *m*

furious ['fjuərɪəs] *adj* wütend; *(attempt)* heftig

furlong ['fɜːlɒŋ] *n* = 201.17 m

furnace ['fɜːnɪs] *n (Brenn)ofen m*

furnish ['fɜːnɪʃ] *vt* einrichten; *(supply)* versehen; **~ings** *npl* Einrichtung *f*

furniture ['fɜːnɪtʃəᵣ] *n* Möbel *pl*; **piece of ~** Möbelstück *nt*

furrow ['fʌrəu] *n* Furche *f*

furry ['fɜːrɪ] *adj (tongue)* pelzig; *(animal)* Pelz-

further ['fɜːðəᵣ] *adj* weitere(r, s) ♦ *adv* weiter ♦ *vt* fördern; **~ education** *n* Weiterbildung *f*; Erwachsenenbildung *f*; **~more** *adv* ferner

furthest ['fɜːðɪst] *superl of* **far**

furtive ['fɜːtɪv] *adj* verstohlen

fury ['fjuərɪ] *n* Wut *f*, Zorn *m*

fuse [fjuːz] *(US* **fuze)** *n (ELEC)* Sicherung *f*; *(of bomb)* Zünder *m* ♦ *vt* verschmelzen ♦ *vi (BRIT: ELEC)* durchbrennen; **~ box** *n* Sicherungskasten *m*

fuselage ['fjuːzəlɑːʒ] *n* Flugzeugrumpf *m*

fusion ['fjuːʒən] *n* Verschmelzung *f*

fuss [fʌs] *n* Theater *nt*; **~y** *adj* kleinlich

futile ['fjuːtaɪl] *adj* zwecklos, sinnlos; **futility** [fjuː'tɪlɪtɪ] *n* Zwecklosigkeit *f*

future ['fjuːtʃəᵣ] *adj* zukünftig ♦ *n* Zukunft *f*; **in (the) ~** in Zukunft

fuze [fjuːz] *(US)* = **fuse**

fuzzy ['fʌzɪ] *adj (indistinct)* verschwommen; *(hair)* kraus

G, g

G [dʒiː] *n (MUS)* G *nt*

G7 *n abbr (= Group of Seven)* G7 *f*

gabble ['gæbl] *vi* plappern

gable ['geɪbl] *n* Giebel *m*

gadget ['gædʒɪt] *n* Vorrichtung *f*

Gaelic ['geɪlɪk] *adj* gälisch ♦ *n (LING)* Gälisch *nt*

gaffe [gæf] *n* Fauxpas *m*

gag [gæg] *n* Knebel *m*; *(THEAT)* Gag *m* ♦ *vt* knebeln

gaiety ['geɪtɪ] *n* Fröhlichkeit *f*

gain [geɪn] *vt (obtain)* erhalten; *(win)* gewinnen ♦ *vi (clock)* vorgehen ♦ *n* Gewinn *m*; **to ~ in sth** an etw *dat* gewinnen; **~ on** *vt fus* einholen

gait [geɪt] *n* Gang *m*

gal. *abbr* = **gallon**

gala ['gɑːlə] *n* Fest *nt*

galaxy ['gæləksɪ] *n* Sternsystem *nt*

gale [geɪl] *n* Sturm *m*

gallant ['gælənt] *adj* tapfer; *(polite)* galant

gallbladder ['gɔːl-] n Gallenblase f

gallery ['gælərɪ] n (also: **art ~**) Galerie f

galley ['gælɪ] n (ship's kitchen) Kombüse f; (ship) Galeere f

gallon ['gælən] n Gallone f

gallop ['gæləp] n Galopp m ♦ vi galoppieren

gallows ['gæləuz] n Galgen m

gallstone ['gɔːlstəun] n Gallenstein m

galore [gə'lɔː] adv in Hülle und Fülle

galvanize ['gælvənaɪz] vt (metal) galvanisieren; (fig) elektrisieren

gambit ['gæmbɪt] n (fig): **opening ~** (einleitende(r)) Schachzug m

gamble ['gæmbl] vi (um Geld) spielen ♦ vt (risk) aufs Spiel setzen ♦ n Risiko nt; **~r** n Spieler(in) m(f); **gambling** n Glücksspiel nt

game [geɪm] n Spiel nt; (hunting) Wild nt ♦ adj: **~ (for)** bereit (zu); **~keeper** n Wildhüter m; **~s console** n (COMPUT) Gameboy m ®, Konsole f

gammon ['gæmən] n geräucherte(r) Schinken m

gamut ['gæmət] n Tonskala f

gang [gæŋ] n (of criminals, youths) Bande f; (of workmen) Kolonne f ♦ vi: **to ~ up on sb** sich gegen jdn verschwören

gangrene ['gæŋgriːn] n Brand m

gangster ['gæŋstə] n Gangster m

gangway ['gæŋweɪ] n (NAUT) Laufplanke f; (aisle) Gang m

gaol [dʒeɪl] (BRIT) n, vt = **jail**

gap [gæp] n Lücke f

gape [geɪp] vi glotzen; **gaping** ['geɪpɪŋ] adj (wound) klaffend; (hole) gähnend

garage ['gærɑːʒ] n Garage f; (for repair) (Auto)reparaturwerkstatt f; (for petrol) Tankstelle f

garbage ['gɑːbɪdʒ] n Abfall m; **~ can** (US) n Mülltonne f

garbled ['gɑːbld] adj (story) verdreht

garden ['gɑːdn] n Garten m; **~s** npl (public park) Park m; (private) Gartenanlagen pl; **~er** n Gärtner(in) m(f);

~ing n Gärtnern nt

gargle ['gɑːgl] vi gurgeln

gargoyle ['gɑːgɔɪl] n Wasserspeier m

garish ['gɛərɪʃ] adj grell

garland ['gɑːlənd] n Girlande f

garlic ['gɑːlɪk] n Knoblauch m

garment ['gɑːmənt] n Kleidungsstück nt

garnish ['gɑːnɪʃ] vt (food) garnieren

garrison ['gærɪsn] n Garnison f

garter ['gɑːtə] n Strumpfband nt; (US) Strumpfhalter m

gas [gæs] n Gas nt; (esp US: petrol) Benzin nt ♦ vt vergasen; **~ cooker** (BRIT) n Gasherd m; **~ cylinder** n Gasflasche f; **~ fire** n Gasofen m

gash [gæʃ] n klaffende Wunde f ♦ vt sich verwunden

gasket ['gæskɪt] n Dichtungsring m

gas mask n Gasmaske f

gas meter n Gaszähler m

gasoline ['gæsəliːn] (US) n Benzin nt

gasp [gɑːsp] vi keuchen; (in surprise) tief Luft holen ♦ n Keuchen nt

gas: ~ ring n Gasring m; **~ station** (US) n Tankstelle f; **~ tap** n Gashahn m

gastric ['gæstrɪk] adj Magen-

gate [geɪt] n Tor nt; (barrier) Schranke f

gateau ['gætəu] (pl **~x**) n Torte f

gatecrash ['geɪtkræʃ] (BRIT) vt (party) platzen in +acc

gateway ['geɪtweɪ] n Toreingang m

gather ['gæðə] vt (people) versammeln; (things) sammeln; (understand) annehmen ♦ vi (assemble) sich versammeln; **to ~ speed** schneller werden; **to ~ (from)** schließen (aus), **~ing** n Versammlung f

gauche [gəuʃ] adj linkisch

gaudy ['gɔːdɪ] adj schreiend

gauge [geɪdʒ] n (instrument) Messgerät nt; (RAIL) Spurweite f; (dial) Anzeiger m; (measure) Maß nt ♦ vt (ab)messen; (fig) abschätzen

gaunt [gɔːnt] adj hager

gauze [gɔːz] n Gaze f

gave [geɪv] pt of **give**

gay [geɪ] adj (homosexual) schwul; (lively) lustig

gaze [geɪz] n Blick m ♦ vi starren; **to ~ at sth** etw dat anstarren

gazelle [gə'zɛl] n Gazelle f

gazumping [gə'zʌmpɪŋ] (BRIT) n Hausverkauf an Höherbietenden trotz Zusage an anderen

GB n abbr = **Great Britain**

GCE (BRIT) n abbr = **General Certificate of Education**

GCSE (BRIT) n abbr = **General Certificate of Secondary Education**

gear [gɪəʳ] n Getriebe nt; (equipment) Ausrüstung f; (AUT) Gang m ♦ vt (fig: adapt): **to be ~ed to** ausgerichtet sein auf +acc; **top ~** höchste(r) Gang m; **high ~** (US) höchste(r) Gang m; **low ~** niedrige(r) Gang m; **in ~** eingekuppelt; **~ box** n Getriebe(gehäuse) nt; **~ lever** n Schalthebel m; **~ shift** (US) n Schalthebel m

geese [giːs] npl of **goose**

gel [dʒɛl] n Gel nt

gelatin(e) ['dʒɛlətiːn] n Gelatine f

gem [dʒɛm] n Edelstein m; (fig) Juwel nt

Gemini ['dʒɛmɪnaɪ] n Zwillinge pl

gender ['dʒɛndəʳ] n (GRAM) Geschlecht nt

gene [dʒiːn] n Gen nt

general ['dʒɛnərəl] n General m ♦ adj allgemein; **~ delivery** (US) n Ausgabe(schalter) m f postlagernder Sendungen; **~ election** n allgemeine Wahlen pl; **~ize** vi verallgemeinern; **~ knowledge** n Allgemeinwissen nt; **~ly** adv allgemein, im Allgemeinen; **~ practitioner** n praktische(r) Arzt m, praktische Ärztin f

generate ['dʒɛnəreɪt] vt erzeugen

generation [dʒɛnə'reɪʃən] n Generation f; (act) Erzeugung f

generator ['dʒɛnəreɪtəʳ] n Generator m

generosity [dʒɛnə'rɒsɪtɪ] n Großzügigkeit f

generous ['dʒɛnərəs] adj großzügig

genetic [dʒɪ'nɛtɪk] adj genetisch; **~ally** adv genetisch; **~ally modified** genmanipuliert; **~ engineering** n Gentechnik f; **~ fingerprinting** [-'fɪŋgəprɪntɪŋ] n genetische Fingerabdrücke pl

genetics [dʒɪ'nɛtɪks] n Genetik f

Geneva [dʒɪ'niːvə] n Genf nt

genial ['dʒiːnɪəl] adj freundlich, jovial

genitals ['dʒɛnɪtlz] npl Genitalien pl

genius ['dʒiːnɪəs] n Genie nt

genocide ['dʒɛnəusaɪd] n Völkermord m

gent [dʒɛnt] n abbr = **gentleman**

genteel [dʒɛn'tiːl] adj (polite) wohlanständig; (affected) affektiert

gentle ['dʒɛntl] adj sanft, zart

gentleman ['dʒɛntlmən] (irreg) n Herr m; (polite) Gentleman m

gentleness ['dʒɛntlnɪs] n Zartheit f, Milde f

gently ['dʒɛntlɪ] adv zart, sanft

gentry ['dʒɛntrɪ] n Landadel m

gents [dʒɛnts] n: **G~** (lavatory) Herren pl

genuine ['dʒɛnjuɪn] adj echt

geographic(al) [dʒɪə'græfɪk(l)] adj geografisch

geography [dʒɪ'ɒgrəfɪ] n Geografie f

geological [dʒɪə'lɒdʒɪkl] adj geologisch

geology [dʒɪ'ɒlədʒɪ] n Geologie f

geometric(al) [dʒɪə'mɛtrɪk(l)] adj geometrisch

geometry [dʒɪ'ɒmətrɪ] n Geometrie f

geranium [dʒɪ'reɪnɪəm] n Geranie f

geriatric [dʒɛrɪ'ætrɪk] adj Alten- ♦ n Greis(in) m(f)

germ [dʒɜːm] n Keim m; (MED) Bazillus m

German ['dʒɜːmən] adj deutsch ♦ n Deutsche(r) f(m); (LING) Deutsch nt; **~ measles** n Röteln pl; **~y** n Deutschland nt

germination [dʒɜːmɪ'neɪʃən] n Keimen nt

gesticulate [dʒɛsˈtɪkjuleɪt] *vi* gestiku-
lieren

gesture [ˈdʒɛstjəʳ] *n* Geste *f*

get [gɛt] (*pt, pp* **got,** *pp* **gotten** (*US*)) *vi* **1**
(*become, be*) werden; **to get old/tired**
alt/müde werden; **to get married** heiraten

2 (*go*) (an)kommen, gehen

3 (*begin*): **to get to know sb** jdn kennen lernen; **let's get going** *or* **started!**
fangen wir an!

4 (*modal aux vb*): **you've got to do it**
du musst es tun

♦ *vt* **1: to get sth done** (*do*) etw machen; (*have done*) etw machen lassen;
to get sth going *or* **to go** etw in Gang
bringen *or* bekommen; **to get sb to**
do sth jdn dazu bringen, etw zu tun

2 (*obtain: money, permission, results*) erhalten; (*find: job, flat*) finden; (*fetch:*
person, object) holen; **to get sth for sb**
jdm etw besorgen; **get me Mr Jones,**
please (*TEL*) verbinden Sie mich bitte
mit Mr Jones

3 (*receive: present, letter*) bekommen,
kriegen; (*acquire: reputation etc*) erwerben

4 (*catch*) bekommen, kriegen; (*hit: tar-*
get etc) treffen, erwischen; **get him!**
(*to dog*) fass!

5 (*take, move*) bringen; **to get sth to**
sb jdm etw bringen

6 (*understand*) verstehen; (*hear*) mitbekommen; **I've got it!** ich hab's!

7 (*have, possess*): **to have got sth** etw
haben

get about *vi* herumkommen; (*news*)
sich verbreiten

get along *vi* (*people*) (gut) zurechtkommen; (*depart*) sich *acc* auf den
Weg machen

get at *vt* (*facts*) herausbekommen; **to**
get at sb (*nag*) an jdm herumnörgeln

get away *vi* (*leave*) sich *acc* davonmachen; (*escape*): **to get away from sth**

von etw *dat* entkommen; **to get away**
with sth mit etw davonkommen

get back *vi* (*return*) zurückkommen
♦ *vt* zurückbekommen

get by *vi* (*pass*) vorbeikommen;
(*manage*) zurechtkommen

get down *vi* (*her*)untergehen ♦ *vt*
(*depress*) fertig machen; **to get down**
to in Angriff nehmen; (*find time to do*)
kommen zu

get in *vi* (*train*) ankommen; (*arrive*
home) heimkommen

get into *vt* (*enter*) hinein-/
hereinkommen in +*acc*; (: *car, train etc*)
einsteigen in +*acc*; (*clothes*) anziehen

get off *vi* (*from train etc*) aussteigen;
(*from horse*) absteigen ♦ *vt* aussteigen
aus; absteigen von

get on *vi* (*progress*) vorankommen;
(*be friends*) auskommen; (*age*) alt werden; (*onto train etc*) einsteigen; (*onto*
horse) aufsteigen ♦ *vt* einsteigen in
+*acc*; auf etw *acc* aufsteigen

get out *vi* (*of house*) herauskommen;
(*of vehicle*) aussteigen ♦ *vt* (*take out*)
herausholen

get out of *vt* (*duty etc*) herumkommen um

get over *vt* (*illness*) sich *acc* erholen
von; (*surprise*) verkraften; (*news*) fassen; (*loss*) sich abfinden mit

get round *vt* herumkommen; (*fig:*
person) herumkriegen

get through to *vt* (*TEL*) durchkommen zu

get together *vi* zusammenkommen

get up *vi* aufstehen ♦ *vt* hinaufbrin-
gen; (*go up*) hinaufgehen; (*organize*)
auf die Beine stellen

get up to *vt* (*reach*) erreichen; (*prank*
etc) anstellen

getaway [ˈɡetəweɪ] *n* Flucht *f*

get-up [ˈɡetʌp] (*inf*) *n* Aufzug *m*

geyser [ˈɡiːzəʳ] *n* Geiser *m*; (*heater*)
Durchlauferhitzer *m*

ghastly [ˈɡɑːstlɪ] *adj* grässlich

gherkin ['gɜːkɪn] n Gewürzgurke f

ghetto ['gɛtəu] n G(h)etto nt; ~ **blaster** n (große(r)) Radiorekorder m

ghost [gəust] n Gespenst nt

giant ['dʒaɪənt] n Riese m ♦ adj riesig, Riesen-

gibberish ['dʒɪbərɪʃ] n dumme(s) Geschwätz nt

gibe [dʒaɪb] n spöttische Bemerkung f

giblets ['dʒɪblɪts] npl Geflügelinnereien pl

giddiness ['gɪdɪnɪs] n Schwindelgefühl nt

giddy ['gɪdɪ] adj schwindlig

gift [gɪft] n Geschenk nt; (ability) Begabung f; ~**ed** adj begabt; ~ **shop** n Geschenkladen m; ~ **token**, ~ **voucher** n Geschenkgutschein m

gigantic [dʒaɪ'gæntɪk] adj riesenhaft

giggle ['gɪgl] vi kichern ♦ n Gekicher nt

gild [gɪld] vt vergolden

gill [dʒɪl] n (1/4 pint) Viertelpinte f

gills [gɪlz] npl (of fish) Kiemen pl

gilt [gɪlt] n Vergoldung f ♦ adj vergoldet; ~**edged** adj mündelsicher

gimmick ['gɪmɪk] n Gag m

gin [dʒɪn] n Gin m

ginger ['dʒɪndʒə*] n Ingwer m; ~ **ale** n Ingwerbier nt; ~ **beer** n Ingwerbier nt; ~**bread** n Pfefferkuchen m; ~**haired** adj rothaarig

gingerly ['dʒɪndʒəlɪ] adv behutsam

gipsy ['dʒɪpsɪ] n Zigeuner(in) m(f)

giraffe [dʒɪ'rɑːf] n Giraffe f

girder ['gɜːdə*] n Eisenträger m

girdle ['gɜːdl] n Hüftgürtel m

girl [gɜːl] n Mädchen nt; **an English ~** eine (junge) Engländerin; ~**friend** n Freundin f; ~**ish** adj mädchenhaft

giro ['dʒaɪrəu] n (bank ~) Giro nt; (post office ~) Postscheckverkehr m

girth [gɜːθ] n (measure) Umfang m; (strap) Sattelgurt m

gist [dʒɪst] n Wesentliche(s) nt

give [gɪv] (pt **gave**, pp **given**) vt geben ♦ vi (break) nachgeben; ~ **away** vt verschenken; (betray) verraten; ~

back vt zurückgeben; ~ **in** vi nachgeben ♦ vt (hand in) abgeben; ~ **off** vt abgeben; ~ **out** vt verteilen; (announce) bekannt geben; ~ **up** vt, vi aufgeben; **to ~ o.s. up** sich stellen; (after siege) sich ergeben; **to ~ way** (BRIT: traffic) Vorfahrt lassen; (to feelings): **to ~ way to** nachgeben +dat

glacier ['glæsɪə*] n Gletscher m

glad [glæd] adj froh; ~**ly** ['glædlɪ] adv gern(e)

glamorous ['glæmərəs] adj reizvoll

glamour ['glæmə*] n Glanz m

glance [glɑːns] n Blick m ♦ vi: **to ~ (at)** (hin)blicken (auf +acc); ~ **off** vt fus (fly off) abprallen von; **glancing** ['glɑːnsɪŋ] adj (blow) Streif-

gland [glænd] n Drüse f

glare [glɛə*] n (light) grelle(s) Licht nt; (stare) wilde(r) Blick m ♦ vi grell scheinen; (angrily): **to ~ at** böse ansehen; **glaring** ['glɛərɪŋ] adj (injustice) schreiend; (mistake) krass

glass [glɑːs] n Glas nt; (mirror: also: **looking ~**) Spiegel m; ~**es** npl (spectacles) Brille f; ~**house** n Gewächshaus nt; ~**ware** n Glaswaren pl; ~**y** adj glasig

glaze [gleɪz] vt verglasen; (finish with a ~) glasieren ♦ n Glasur f; ~**d** adj (eye) glasig; (pot) glasiert; **glazier** ['gleɪzɪə*] n Glaser m

gleam [gliːm] n Schimmer m ♦ vi schimmern

glean [gliːn] vt (fig) ausfindig machen

glen [glɛn] n Bergtal nt

glib [glɪb] adj oberflächlich

glide [glaɪd] vi gleiten; ~**r** n (AVIAT) Segelflugzeug nt; **gliding** ['glaɪdɪŋ] n Segelfliegen nt

glimmer ['glɪmə*] n Schimmer m

glimpse [glɪmps] n flüchtige(r) Blick m ♦ vt flüchtig erblicken

glint [glɪnt] n Glitzern nt ♦ vi glitzern

glisten ['glɪsn] vi glänzen

glitter ['glɪtə*] vi funkeln ♦ n Funkeln nt

gloat [gləut] vi: **to ~ over** sich weiden an +dat

global ['gləʊbl] *adj*: ~ **warming** globale(r) Temperaturanstieg *m*

globe [gləʊb] *n* Erdball *m*; *(sphere)* Globus *m*

gloom [glu:m] *n (darkness)* Dunkel *nt*; *(depression)* düstere Stimmung *f*; **~y** *adj* düster

glorify ['glɔ:rɪfaɪ] *vt* verherrlichen

glorious ['glɔ:rɪəs] *adj* glorreich

glory ['glɔ:rɪ] *n* Ruhm *m*

gloss [glɒs] *n (shine)* Glanz *m*; ~ **over** *vt fus* übertünchen

glossary ['glɒsərɪ] *n* Glossar *nt*

glossy ['glɒsɪ] *adj (surface)* glänzend

glove [glʌv] *n* Handschuh *m*; ~ **compartment** *n (AUT)* Handschuhfach *nt*

glow [gləʊ] *vi* glühen ♦ *n* Glühen *nt*

glower ['glaʊə*] *vi*: **to ~ at** finster anblicken

glucose ['glu:kəʊs] *n* Traubenzucker *m*

glue [glu:] *n* Klebstoff *m* ♦ *vt* kleben

glum [glʌm] *adj* bedrückt

glut [glʌt] *n* Überfluss *m*

glutton ['glʌtn] *n* Vielfraß *m*; **a ~ for work** ein Arbeitstier *nt*

glycerin(e) ['glɪsəri:n] *n* Glyzerin *nt*

GM *abbr* = **genetically modified**

gnarled [nɑ:ld] *adj* knorrig

gnat [næt] *n* Stechmücke *f*

gnaw [nɔ:] *vt* nagen an +*dat*

gnome [nəʊm] *n* Gnom *m*

go [gəʊ] *(pt* **went**, *pp* **gone**, *pl* ~**es)** *vi* gehen; *(travel)* reisen, fahren; *(depart: train)* (ab)fahren; *(be sold)* verkauft werden; *(work)* gehen, funktionieren; *(fit, suit)* passen; *(become)* werden; *(break etc)* nachgeben ♦ *n (energy)* Schwung *m*; *(attempt)* Versuch *m*; **he's ~ing to do it** er wird es tun; **to ~ for a walk** spazieren gehen; **to ~ dancing** tanzen gehen; **how did it ~?** wie war's?; **to ~ with** *(be suitable)* passen zu; **to have a ~ at sth** etw versuchen; **to be on the ~** auf Trab sein; **whose ~ is it?** wer ist dran?; ~ **about** *vi (rumour)* umgehen ♦ *vt fus*: **how do I ~ about this?** wie packe ich das an?; ~

after *vt fus (pursue: person)* nachgehen +*dat*; ~ **ahead** *vi (proceed)* weitergehen; ~ **along** *vi* dahingehen, dahinziehen ♦ *vt fus* entlanggehen, entlangfahren; **to ~ along with** *(support)* zustimmen +*dat*; ~ **away** *vi (depart)* weggehen; ~ **back** *vi (return)* zurückgehen; ~ **back on** *vt fus (promise)* nicht halten; ~ **by** *vi (years, time)* vergehen ♦ *vt fus* sich richten nach; ~ **down** *vi (sun)* untergehen ♦ *vt fus* hinuntergehen, hinunterfahren; ~ **for** *vt fus (fetch)* holen *(gehen)*; *(like)* mögen; *(attack)* sich stürzen auf +*acc*; ~ **in** *vi* hineingehen; ~ **in for** *vt fus (competition)* teilnehmen an; ~ **into** *vt fus (enter)* hineingehen in +*acc*; *(study)* sich befassen mit; ~ **off** *vi (depart)* weggehen; *(lights)* ausgehen; *(milk etc)* sauer werden; *(explode)* losgehen ♦ *vt fus (dislike)* nicht mehr mögen; ~ **on** *vi (continue)* weitergehen; *(inf: complain)* meckern; *(lights)* angehen; **to ~ on with sth** mit etw weitermachen; ~ **out** *vi (of fire, light)* ausgehen; *(of house)* hinausgehen; ~ **over** *vi (ship)* kentern ♦ *vt fus (examine, check)* durchgehen; ~ **past** *vi*: **to ~ past sth** an etw +*dat* vorbeigehen; ~ **round** *vi (visit)*: **to ~ round (to sb's)** (bei jdm) vorbeigehen; ~ **through** *vt fus (town etc)* durchgehen, durchfahren; ~ **up** *vi (price)* steigen; ~ **with** *vt fus (suit)* zu etw passen; ~ **without** *vt fus* sich behelfen ohne; *(food)* entbehren

goad [gəʊd] *vt* anstacheln

go-ahead ['gəʊəhed] *adj* zielstrebig; *(progressive)* fortschrittlich ♦ *n* grünes Licht *nt*

goal [gəʊl] *n* Ziel *nt*; *(SPORT)* Tor *nt*; ~**keeper** *n* Torwart *m*; ~ **post** *n* Torpfosten *m*

goat [gəʊt] *n* Ziege *f*

gobble ['gɒbl] *vt (also*: ~ **down**, ~ **up)** hinunterschlingen

go-between ['gəʊbɪtwi:n] *n* Mittelsmann *m*

god [gɔd] n Gott m; **G~** n Gott m;
~child n Patenkind nt; **~daughter** n
Patentochter f; **~dess** n Göttin f;
~father n Pate m; **~forsaken** adj gott-
verlassen; **~mother** n Patin f; **~send** n
Geschenk nt des Himmels; **~son** n Pa-
tensohn m

goggles ['gɔglz] npl Schutzbrille f

going ['gəʊɪŋ] n (HORSE-RACING) Bahn f
♦ adj (rate) gängig; (concern) gut gehend; **it's hard ~** es ist schwierig

gold [gəʊld] n Gold m ♦ adj golden;
~en adj golden, Gold-; **~fish** n
Goldfisch m; **~ mine** n Goldgrube f;
~plated adj vergoldet; **~smith** n
Goldschmied(in) m(f)

golf [gɔlf] n Golf nt; **~ ball** n Golfball
m; (on typewriter) Kugelkopf m; **~ club**
n (society) Golfklub m; (stick) Golfschläger m; **~ course** n Golfplatz m;
~er n Golfspieler(in) m(f)

gondola ['gɔndələ] n Gondel f

gone [gɔn] pp of **go**

gong [gɔŋ] n Gong m

good [gʊd] n (benefit) Wohl nt; (moral
excellence) Güte f ♦ adj gut; **~s** npl
(merchandise etc) Waren pl, Güter pl; **a
~ deal (of)** ziemlich viel; **a ~ many**
ziemlich viele; **~ morning!** guten Morgen!; **~ afternoon!** guten Tag!; **~
evening!** guten Abend!; **~ night!** gute
Nacht!; **would you be ~ enough to
...?** könnten Sie bitte ...?

goodbye [gʊd'baɪ] excl auf Wiedersehen!

good: G~ Friday n Karfreitag m; **~-
looking** adj gut aussehend; **~-
natured** adj gutmütig; (joke) harmlos;
~ness n Güte f; (virtue) Tugend f; **~
train** (BRIT) n Güterzug m; **~will** n (favour) Wohlwollen nt; (COMM) Firmen-
ansehen nt

goose [guːs] n (pl **geese**) n Gans f

gooseberry ['gʊzbərɪ] n Stachelbeere f

gooseflesh ['guːsfleʃ] n Gänsehaut f

goose pimples npl Gänsehaut f

gore [gɔːr] vt aufspießen ♦ n Blut nt

gorge [gɔːdʒ] n Schlucht f ♦ vt: **to ~
o.s.** (sich voll) fressen

gorgeous ['gɔːdʒəs] adj prächtig

gorilla [gə'rɪlə] n Gorilla m

gorse [gɔːs] n Stechginster m

gory ['gɔːrɪ] adj blutig

go-slow ['gəʊ'sləʊ] (BRIT) n Bummel-
streik m

gospel ['gɔspl] n Evangelium nt

gossip ['gɔsɪp] n Klatsch m; (person)
Klatschbase f ♦ vi klatschen

got [gɔt] pt, pp of **get**

gotten ['gɔtn] (US) pp of **get**

gout [gaʊt] n Gicht f

govern ['gʌvən] vt regieren; verwalten

governess ['gʌvənɪs] n Gouvernante f

government ['gʌvnmənt] n Regierung f

governor ['gʌvənər] n Gouverneur m

gown [gaʊn] n Gewand nt; (UNIV) Robe
f

G.P. n abbr = **general practitioner**

grab [græb] vt packen

grace [greɪs] n Anmut f; (blessing) Gnade f; (prayer) Tischgebet nt ♦ vt (adorn)
zieren; (honour) auszeichnen; **5 days'
~** 5 Tage Aufschub; **~ful** adj anmutig

gracious ['greɪʃəs] adj gnädig; (kind)
freundlich

grade [greɪd] n Grad m; (slope) Gefälle
nt ♦ vt (classify) einstufen; **~ crossing**
(US) n Bahnübergang m; **~ school** (US)
n Grundschule f

gradient ['greɪdɪənt] n Steigung f; Gefälle nt

gradual ['grædjʊəl] adj allmählich; **~ly**
adv allmählich

graduate [n 'grædjʊət, vb 'grædjʊeɪt]
n: **to be a ~** das Staatsexamen haben
♦ vi das Staatsexamen machen; **gra-
duation** [grædjʊ'eɪʃən] n Abschluss-
feier f

graffiti [grə'fiːtɪ] npl Graffiti pl

graft [grɑːft] n (hard work) Schufterei f;
(MED) Verpflanzung f ♦ vt pfropfen;
(fig) aufpfropfen; (MED) verpflanzen

grain [greɪn] n Korn nt; (in wood) Mase-

rung f
gram [græm] n Gramm nt
grammar ['græmə'] n Grammatik f; ~
school (BRIT) n Gymnasium nt; **grammatical** [grə'mætɪkl] adj grammat(ikal)isch
gramme [græm] n = **gram**
granary ['grænərɪ] n Kornspeicher m
grand [grænd] adj großartig; **~child** (pl
~children) n Enkelkind nt, Enkel(in)
m(f); **~dad** n Opa m; **~daughter** n Enkelin f; **~eur** ['grændjə'] n Erhabenheit
f; **~father** n Großvater m; **~iose**
['grændɪəus] adj (imposing) großartig;
(pompous) schwülstig; **~ma** n Oma f;
~mother n Großmutter f; **~pa** n =
granddad; **~parents** npl Großeltern
pl; **~ piano** n Flügel m; **~son** n Enkel
m; **~stand** n Haupttribüne f
granite ['grænɪt] n Granit m
granny ['grænɪ] n Oma f
grant [grɑːnt] vt gewähren ♦ n Unterstützung f; (UNIV) Stipendium nt; **to
take sth for ~ed** etw als selbstverständlich (an)nehmen
granulated sugar ['grænjuleɪtɪd-] n
Zuckerraffinade f
granule ['grænjuːl] n Körnchen nt
grape [greɪp] n (Wein)traube f
grapefruit ['greɪpfruːt] n Pampelmuse
f, Grapefruit f
graph [grɑːf] n Schaubild nt; **~ic**
['græfɪk] adj (descriptive) anschaulich;
(drawing) grafisch; **~ics** npl Grafik f
grapple ['græpl] vi: **to ~ with** kämpfen
mit
grasp [grɑːsp] vt ergreifen; (understand)
begreifen ♦ n Griff m; (of subject) Beherrschung f; **~ing** adj habgierig
grass [grɑːs] n Gras nt; **~hopper** n
Heuschrecke f; **~land** n Weideland nt;
~roots adj an der Basis; **~ snake** n
Ringelnatter f
grate [greɪt] n Kamin m ♦ vi (sound)
knirschen ♦ vt (cheese etc) reiben; **to ~
on the nerves** auf die Nerven gehen
grateful ['greɪtful] adj dankbar

grater ['greɪtə'] n Reibe f
gratify ['grætɪfaɪ] vt befriedigen; **~ing**
adj erfreulich
grating ['greɪtɪŋ] n (iron bars) Gitter nt
♦ adj (noise) knirschend
gratitude ['grætɪtjuːd] n Dankbarkeit f
gratuity [grə'tjuːɪtɪ] n Gratifikation f
grave [greɪv] n Grab nt ♦ adj (serious)
ernst
gravel ['grævl] n Kies m
gravestone ['greɪvstəun] n Grabstein
m
graveyard ['greɪvjɑːd] n Friedhof m
gravity ['grævɪtɪ] n Schwerkraft f; (seriousness) Schwere f
gravy ['greɪvɪ] n (Braten)soße f
gray [greɪ] adj = **grey**
graze [greɪz] vi grasen ♦ vt (touch) streifen; (MED) abschürfen ♦ n Abschürfung
f
grease [griːs] n (fat) Fett nt; (lubricant)
Schmiere f ♦ vt (ab)schmieren; **~proof**
(BRIT) adj (paper) Butterbrot-; **greasy**
['griːsɪ] adj fettig
great [greɪt] adj groß; (inf: good) prima;
G~ Britain n Großbritannien nt; **~
grandfather** n Urgroßvater m; **~
grandmother** n Urgroßmutter f; **~ly**
adv sehr
Greece [griːs] n Griechenland nt
greed [griːd] n (also: **~iness**) Gier f;
(meanness) Geiz m; **~(iness) for** Gier
nach; **~y** adj gierig
Greek [griːk] adj griechisch ♦ n Grieche
m, Griechin f; (LING) Griechisch nt
green [griːn] adj grün ♦ n (village ~)
Dorfwiese f; **~ belt** n Grüngürtel m; **~
card** n (AUT) grüne Versicherungskarte
f; **~ery** n Grün nt; **grüne(s) Laub nt**;
~gage n Reneklode f, Reineclaude f;
~grocer (BRIT) n Obst- und Gemüsehändler m; **~house** n Gewächshaus nt; **~house effect** n Treibhauseffekt m; **~house gas** n Treibhausgas nt
Greenland ['griːnlənd] n Grönland nt
greet [griːt] vt grüßen; **~ing** n Gruß m

~ing(s) card n Glückwunschkarte f

gregarious [grə'gɛəriəs] adj gesellig

grenade [grə'neɪd] n Granate f

grew [gru:] pt of **grow**

grey [greɪ] adj grau; **~-haired** adj grauhaarig; **~hound** n Windhund m

grid [grɪd] n Gitter nt; (ELEC) Leitungsnetz nt; (on map) Gitternetz nt

gridlock ['grɪdlɔk] n (AUT: traffic jam) totale(r) Stau m; **~ed** adj: **to be ~ed** (roads) total verstopft sein; (talks etc) festgefahren sein

grief [gri:f] n Gram m, Kummer m

grievance ['gri:vəns] n Beschwerde f

grieve [gri:v] vi sich grämen ♦ vt betrüben

grievous ['gri:vəs] adj: **~ bodily harm** (JUR) schwere Körperverletzung f

grill [grɪl] n Grill m ♦ vt (question) in die Mangel nehmen

grille [grɪl] n (AUT) (Kühler)gitter nt

grim [grɪm] adj grimmig; (situation) düster

grimace [grɪ'meɪs] n Grimasse f ♦ vi Grimassen schneiden

grime [graɪm] n Schmutz m; **grimy** ['graɪmɪ] adj schmutzig

grin [grɪn] n Grinsen nt ♦ vi grinsen

grind [graɪnd] (pt, pp ground) vt mahlen; (US: meat) durch den Fleischwolf drehen; (sharpen) schleifen; (teeth) knirschen mit ♦ n (bore) Plackerei f

grip [grɪp] n Griff m; (suitcase) Handkoffer m ♦ vt packen; **~ping** adj (exciting) spannend

grisly ['grɪzlɪ] adj grässlich

gristle ['grɪsl] n Knorpel m

grit [grɪt] n Splitt m; (courage) Mut m ♦ vt (teeth) zusammenbeißen; (road) (mit Splitt be)streuen

groan [grəun] n Stöhnen nt ♦ vi stöhnen

grocer ['grəusə'] n Lebensmittelhändler m; **~ies** npl Lebensmittel pl; **~'s (shop)** n Lebensmittelgeschäft nt

groggy ['grɔgɪ] adj benommen

groin [grɔɪn] n Leistengegend f

groom [gru:m] n (also: **bridegroom**) Bräutigam m; (for horses) Pferdeknecht m ♦ vt (horse) striegeln; **(well-)~ed** adj gepflegt

groove [gru:v] n Rille f, Furche f

grope [grəup] vi tasten; **~ for** vt fus suchen nach

gross [grəus] adj (coarse) dick, plump; (bad) grob, schwer; (COMM) brutto; **~ly** adv höchst

grotesque [grə'tɛsk] adj grotesk

grotto ['grɔtəu] n Grotte f

ground [graund] pt, pp of **grind** ♦ n Boden m; (land) Grundbesitz m; (reason) Grund m; (US: also: **~ wire**) Erdung f ♦ vi (run ashore) stranden, auflaufen; **~s** pl (dregs) Bodensatz m; (around house) (Garten)anlagen pl; **on the ~** am Boden; **to the ~** zu Boden; **to gain/lose ~** Boden gewinnen/ verlieren; **~ cloth** (US) n = **groundsheet**; **~ing** n (instruction) Anfangsunterricht m; **~less** adj grundlos; **~sheet** (BRIT) n Zeltboden m; **~ staff** n Bodenpersonal nt; **~work** n Grundlage f

group [gru:p] n Gruppe f ♦ vt (also: **~ together**) gruppieren ♦ vi sich gruppieren

grouse [graus] n inv (bird) schottische(s) Moorhuhn nt

grove [grəuv] n Gehölz nt, Hain m

grovel ['grɔvl] vi (fig) kriechen

grow [grəu] (pt grew, pp grown) vi wachsen; (become) werden ♦ vt (raise) anbauen; **~ up** vi aufwachsen; **~er** n Züchter m; **~ing** adj zunehmend

growl [graul] vi knurren

grown [grəun] pp of **grow**; **~-up** n Erwachsene(r) mf

growth [grəuθ] n Wachstum nt; (increase) Zunahme f; (of beard etc) Wuchs m

grub [grʌb] n Made f, Larve f; (inf: food) Futter nt; **~by** ['grʌbɪ] adj schmutzig

grudge [grʌdʒ] n Groll m ♦ vt: **to ~ sb sth** jdm etw missgönnen; **to bear sb**

a ~ einen Groll gegen jdn hegen

gruelling ['gruəlɪŋ] *adj (climb, race)* mörderisch

gruesome ['gru:səm] *adj* grauenhaft

gruff [grʌf] *adj* barsch

grumble ['grʌmbl] *vi* murren

grumpy ['grʌmpɪ] *adj* verdrießlich

grunt [grʌnt] *vi* grunzen ♦ *n* Grunzen *nt*

G-string ['dʒi:strɪŋ] *n* Minislip *m*

guarantee [gærən'ti:] *n* Garantie *f* ♦ *vt* garantieren

guard [gɑ:d] *n (sentry)* Wache *f; (BRIT: RAIL)* Zugbegleiter *m* ♦ *vt* bewachen; **~ed** *adj* vorsichtig; **~ian** *n* Vormund *m; (keeper)* Hüter *m*; **~'s van** *(BRIT)* *n (RAIL)* Dienstwagen *m*

guerrilla [gə'rɪlə] *n* Guerilla(kämpfer) *m*; **~ warfare** *n* Guerillakrieg *m*

guess [ges] *vt, vi* (er)raten, schätzen ♦ *n* Vermutung *f*; **~work** *n* Raterei *f*

guest [gest] *n* Gast *m*; **~ house** *n* Pension *f*; **~ room** *n* Gastzimmer *nt*

guffaw [gʌ'fɔ:] *vi* schallend lachen

guidance ['gaɪdəns] *n (control)* Leitung *f; (advice)* Beratung *f*

guide [gaɪd] *n* Führer *m; (also: girl ~)* Pfadfinderin *f* ♦ *vt* führen; **~book** *n* Reiseführer *m*; **~ dog** *n* Blindenhund *m*; **~lines** *npl* Richtlinien *pl*

guild [gɪld] *n (HIST)* Gilde *f*

guillotine ['gɪləti:n] *n* Guillotine *f*

guilt [gɪlt] *n* Schuld *f*; **~y** *adj* schuldig

guinea pig ['gɪnɪ-] *n* Meerschweinchen *nt; (fig)* Versuchskaninchen *nt*

guise [gaɪz] *n*: **in the ~ of** in der Form +gen

guitar [gɪ'tɑ:] *n* Gitarre *f*

gulf [gʌlf] *n* Golf *m; (fig)* Abgrund *m*

gull [gʌl] *n* Möwe *f*

gullet ['gʌlɪt] *n* Schlund *m*

gullible ['gʌlɪbl] *adj* leichtgläubig

gully ['gʌlɪ] *n (Wasser)*rinne *f*

gulp [gʌlp] *vt (also: ~ down)* hinunterschlucken ♦ *vi (gasp)* schlucken

gum [gʌm] *n (around teeth)* Zahnfleisch *nt; (glue)* Klebstoff *m; (also: chewing ~)*

Kaugummi *m* ♦ *vt* gummieren; **~boots** *(BRIT)* *npl* Gummistiefel *pl*

gun [gʌn] *n* Schusswaffe *f*; **~boat** *n* Kanonenboot *nt*; **~fire** *n* Geschützfeuer *nt*; **~man** *(irreg)* *n* bewaffnete(r) Verbrecher *m*; **~point** *n*: **at ~point** mit Waffengewalt; **~powder** *n* Schießpulver *nt*; **~shot** *n* Schuss *m*

gurgle ['gɜ:gl] *vi* gluckern

gush [gʌʃ] *n (rush out)* hervorströmen; *(fig)* schwärmen

gust [gʌst] *n* Windstoß *m*, Bö *f*

gusto ['gʌstəu] *n* Genuss *m*, Lust *f*

gut [gʌt] *n (ANAT)* Gedärme *pl; (string)* Darm *m*; **~s** *npl (fig)* Schneid *m*

gutter ['gʌtə] *n* Dachrinne *f; (in street)* Gosse *f*

guttural ['gʌtərl] *adj* guttural, Kehl-

guy [gaɪ] *n (also: ~rope)* Halteseil *nt; (man)* Typ *m*, Kerl *m*

Guy Fawkes' Night, auch *bonfire night* genannt, erinnert an den Gunpowder Plot, einen Attentatsversuch auf James I. und sein Parlament am 5. November 1605. Einer der Verschwörer, Guy Fawkes, wurde auf frischer Tat ertappt, als er das Parlamentsgebäude in die Luft sprengen wollte. Vor der Guy Fawkes' Night basteln Kinder in Großbritannien eine Puppe des Guy Fawkes, mit der sie Geld für Feuerwerkskörper von Passanten erbetteln, und die dann am 5. November auf einem Lagerfeuer mit Feuerwerk verbrannt wird.

guzzle ['gʌzl] *vt, vi (drink)* saufen; *(eat)* fressen

gym [dʒɪm] *n (also: ~nasium)* Turnhalle *f; (also: ~nastics)* Turnen *nt*; **~nast** ['dʒɪmnæst] *n* Turner(in) *m(f)*; **~nastics** [dʒɪm'næstɪks] *n* Turnen *nt*, Gymnastik *f*; **~ shoes** *npl* Turnschuhe *pl*

gynaecologist [gaɪnɪ'kɔlədʒɪst] *(US* **gynecologist)** *n* Frauenarzt(ärztin) *m(f)* gypsy ['dʒɪpsɪ] n = gipsy

gyrate [dʒər'reɪt] vi kreisen

H, h

haberdashery ['hæbə'dæʃərɪ] (BRIT) n Kurzwaren pl

habit ['hæbɪt] n (An)gewohnheit f; (monk's) Habit nt or m

habitable ['hæbɪtəbl] adj bewohnbar

habitat ['hæbɪtæt] n Lebensraum m

habitual [hə'bɪtjuəl] adj gewohnheitsmäßig; ~ly adv gewöhnlich

hack [hæk] vt hacken ♦ n Hieb m; (writer) Schreiberling m

hacker ['hækə'] n (COMPUT) Hacker m

hackneyed ['hæknɪd] adj abgedroschen

had [hæd] pt, pp of have

haddock ['hædək] (pl ~ or ~s) n Schellfisch m

hadn't ['hædnt] = had not

haemorrhage ['heməndʒ] (US hemorrhage) n Blutung f

haemorrhoids ['heməroidz] (US hemorrhoids) npl Hämorr(ho)iden pl

haggard ['hægəd] adj abgekämpft

haggle ['hægl] vi feilschen

Hague [heɪg] n: The ~ Den Haag m

hail [heɪl] n Hagel m ♦ vt umjubeln ♦ vi hageln; ~stone n Hagelkorn nt

hair [heə'] n Haar nt, Haare pl; (one ~) Haar nt; ~brush n Haarbürste f; ~cut n Haarschnitt m; to get a ~cut sich dat die Haare schneiden lassen; ~do n Frisur f; ~dresser n Friseur m, Friseuse f; ~dresser's n Friseursalon m; ~ dryer n Trockenhaube f; (hand-held) Föhn m, Fön m ®; ~ gel n Haargel nt; ~grip n Klemme f; ~net n Haarnetz nt; ~pin n Haarnadel f; ~pin bend (US ~pin curve) n Haarnadelkurve f; ~-raising adj haarsträubend; ~ removing cream n Enthaarungscreme nt; ~ spray n Haarspray nt; ~style n Frisur f; ~y adj haarig

hake [heɪk] n Seehecht m

half [hɑːf] (pl halves) n Hälfte f ♦ adj halb ♦ adv halb, zur Hälfte; ~ an hour eine halbe Stunde; two and a ~ zweieinhalb; to cut sth in ~ etw halbieren; ~ a dozen ein halbes Dutzend, sechs; ~ board n Halbpension f; ~-caste n Mischling m; ~ fare n halbe(r) Fahrpreis m; ~-hearted adj lustlos; ~ hour n halbe Stunde f; ~-price n: (at) ~-price zum halben Preis; ~ term (BRIT) n (SCH) Ferien pl in der Mitte des Trimesters; ~-time n Halbzeit f; ~way adv halbwegs, auf halbem Wege

halibut ['hælɪbət] n inv Heilbutt m

hall [hɔːl] n Saal m; (entrance ~) Hausflur m; (building) Halle f; ~ of residence (BRIT) n Studentenwohnheim nt

hallmark ['hɔːlmɑːk] n Stempel m

hallo [hə'ləu] excl = hello

Hallowe'en ['hæləu'iːn] n Tag m vor Allerheiligen

Hallowe'en

Hallowe'en ist der 31. Oktober, der Vorabend von Allerheiligen und nach altem Glauben der Abend, an dem man Geister und Hexen sehen kann. In Großbritannien und Amerika ist dies ein Anlass zum Feiern vor allem in den USA feiern die Kinder Hallowe'en, indem sie sich verkleiden und mit selbst gemachten Laternen aus Kürbissen von Tür zu Tür ziehen.

hallucination [həluːsɪ'neɪʃən] n Halluzination f

hallway ['hɔːlweɪ] n Korridor m

halo ['heɪləu] n Heiligenschein m

halt [hɔːlt] n Halt m ♦ vt, vi anhalten

halve [hɑːv] vt halbieren

ham [hæm] n Schinken m

hamburger ['hæmbəːgə'] n Hamburger m

hamlet ['hæmlɪt] n Weiler m

hammer ['hæmə'] n Hammer m ♦ vt, vi hämmern

hammock ['hæmək] n Hängematte f

hamper ['hæmpə'] vt (be)hindern ♦ n Picknickkorb m

hamster ['hæmstə'] n Hamster m

hand [hænd] n Hand f; (of clock) (Uhr)zeiger m; (worker) Arbeiter m ♦ vt (pass) geben; **to give sb a** ~ jdm helfen; **at** ~ nahe; **to** ~ zur Hand; **in** ~ (under control) unter Kontrolle; (being done) im Gange; (extra) übrig; **on** ~ zur Verfügung; **on the one** ~ ..., **on the other** ~ ... einerseits ..., andererseits ...; ~ **in** vt abgeben; (forms) einreichen; ~ **out** vt austeilen; ~ **over** vt (deliver) übergeben; (surrender) abgeben; (: prisoner) ausliefern; ~**bag** n Handtasche f; ~**book** n Handbuch nt; ~**brake** n Handbremse f; ~**cuffs** npl Handschellen pl; ~**ful** n Hand f voll; (inf: person) Plage f

handicap ['hændikæp] n Handikap nt ♦ vt benachteiligen; **mentally/physically** ~**ped** geistig/körperlich behindert

handicraft ['hændikrɑːft] n Kunsthandwerk nt

handiwork ['hændiwɜːk] n Arbeit f; (fig) Werk nt

handkerchief ['hæŋkətʃif] n Taschentuch nt

handle ['hændl] n (of door etc) Klinke f; (of cup etc) Henkel m; (for winding) Kurbel f ♦ vt (touch) anfassen; (deal with: things) sich befassen mit; (: people) umgehen mit; ~**bar(s)** n(pl) Lenkstange f

hand: ~ **luggage** n Handgepäck nt; ~**made** adj handgefertigt; ~**out** n (distribution) Verteilung f; (charity) Geldzuwendung f; (leaflet) Flugblatt nt; ~**rail** n Geländer nt; (on ship) Reling f; ~**set** n (TEL) Hörer m; **please replace the** ~**set** bitte legen Sie auf; ~**shake** n Händedruck f

handsome ['hænsəm] adj gut aussehend

handwriting ['hændraitiŋ] n Hand-

schrift f

handy ['hændi] adj praktisch; (shops) leicht erreichbar; ~**man** ['hændimæn] (irreg) n Bastler m

hang [hæŋ] (pt, pp hung) vt aufhängen; (pt, pp **hanged**: criminal) hängen ♦ vi hängen ♦ n: **to get the** ~ **of sth** (inf) den richtigen Dreh bei etw herauskriegen; ~ **about,** ~ **around** vi sich herumtreiben; ~ **on** vi (wait) warten; ~ **up** vi (TEL) auflegen

hangar ['hæŋə'] n Hangar m

hanger ['hæŋə'] n Kleiderbügel m

hanger-on [hæŋər'ɔn] n Anhänger(in) m(f)

hang ['hæŋ-]: ~**gliding** n Drachenfliegen nt; ~**over** n Kater m; ~**up** n Komplex m

hanker ['hæŋkə'] vi: **to** ~ **for** or **after** sich sehnen nach

hankie ['hæŋki] n abbr = **handkerchief**

hanky ['hæŋki] n abbr = **handkerchief**

haphazard [hæp'hæzəd] adj zufällig

happen ['hæpən] vi sich ereignen, passieren; **as I** ~**s I'm going there today** zufällig(erweise) gehe ich heute (dort)hin; ~**ing** n Ereignis nt

happily ['hæpili] adv glücklich; (fortunately) glücklicherweise

happiness ['hæpinis] n Glück nt

happy ['hæpi] adj glücklich; ~ **birthday!** alles Gute zum Geburtstag!; ~**go-lucky** adj sorglos; ~ **hour** n Happy Hour f

harass ['hærəs] vt plagen; ~**ment** n Belästigung f

harbour ['hɑːbə'] (US **harbor**) n Hafen m ♦ vt (hope etc) hegen; (criminal etc) Unterschlupf gewähren

hard [hɑːd] adj (firm) hart; (difficult) schwer; (harsh) hart(herzig) ♦ adv (work) hart; (try) sehr; (push, hit) fest; **no** ~ **feelings!** ich nehme es dir nicht übel; ~ **of hearing** schwerhörig; **to be** ~ **done by** übel dran sein; ~**back** n kartonierte Ausgabe f; ~ **cash** n Bargeld nt; ~ **disk** n (COMPUT) Festplatte f;

~en vt erhärten; (fig) verhärten ♦ vi hart werden; (fig) sich verhärten; **~-headed** adj nüchtern; **~ labour** n Zwangsarbeit f

hardly ['hɑːdlɪ] adv kaum

hard: ~ship n Not f; **~ shoulder** (BRIT) n (AUT) Seitenstreifen m; **~ up** adj knapp bei Kasse; **~ware** n Eisenwaren pl; (COMPUT) Hardware f; **~ware shop** n Eisenwarenhandlung f; **~-wearing** adj strapazierfähig; **~-working** adj fleißig

hardy ['hɑːdɪ] adj widerstandsfähig

hare [heəʳ] n Hase m; **~-brained** adj schwachsinnig

harm [hɑːm] n Schaden m ♦ vt schaden +dat; **out of ~'s way** in Sicherheit; **~ful** adj schädlich; **~less** adj harmlos

harmonica [hɑːˈmɒnɪkə] n Mundharmonika f

harmonious [hɑːˈməunɪəs] adj harmonisch

harmonize ['hɑːmənaɪz] vt abstimmen ♦ vi harmonieren

harmony ['hɑːmənɪ] n Harmonie f

harness ['hɑːnɪs] n Geschirr nt ♦ vt (horse) anschirren; (fig) nutzbar machen

harp [hɑːp] n Harfe f ♦ vi: **to ~ on about sth** auf etw dat herumreiten

harpoon [hɑːˈpuːn] n Harpune f

harrowing ['hærəuɪŋ] adj nervenaufreibend

harsh [hɑːʃ] adj (rough) rau; (severe) streng; **~ness** n Härte f

harvest ['hɑːvɪst] n Ernte f ♦ vt, vi ernten

has [hæz] vb see **have**

hash [hæʃ] vt klein hacken ♦ n (mess) Kuddelmuddel m

hashish ['hæʃɪʃ] n Haschisch nt

hasn't ['hæznt] = **has not**

hassle ['hæsl] (inf) n Theater nt

haste [heɪst] n Eile f; **~n** ['heɪsn] vt beschleunigen ♦ vi eilen; **hasty** adj hastig; (rash) vorschnell

hat [hæt] n Hut m

hatch [hætʃ] n (NAUT: also: **~way**) Luke f; (in house) Durchreiche f ♦ vi (young) ausschlüpfen ♦ vt (brood) ausbrüten; (plot) aushecken; **~back** n (AUT) (Auto nt mit) Heckklappe f

hatchet ['hætʃɪt] n Beil nt

hate [heɪt] vt hassen ♦ n Hass m; **~ful** adj verhasst

hatred ['heɪtrɪd] n Hass m

haughty ['hɔːtɪ] adj hochnäsig, überheblich

haul [hɔːl] vt ziehen ♦ n (catch) Fang m; **~age** n Spedition f; **~ier** (US **hauler**) n Spediteur m

haunch [hɔːntʃ] n Lende f

haunt [hɔːnt] vt (ghost) spuken in +dat; (memory) verfolgen; (pub) häufig besuchen ♦ n Lieblingsplatz m; **the castle is ~ed** in dem Schloss spukt es

---

KEYWORD

have [hæv] (pt, pp **had**) aux vb **1** haben; (esp with vbs of motion) sein; **to have arrived/slept** angekommen sein/geschlafen haben; **to have been** gewesen sein; **having eaten** or **when he had eaten**, **he left** nachdem er gegessen hatte, ging er

2 (in tag questions): **you've done it, haven't you?** du hast es doch gemacht, oder nicht?

3 (in short answers and questions): **you've made a mistake – so I have/ no I haven't** du hast einen Fehler gemacht – ja, stimmt/nein; **we haven't paid – yes we have!** wir haben nicht bezahlt – doch; **I've been there before, have you?** ich war schon einmal da, du auch?

♦ modal aux vb (be obliged): **to have (got) to do sth** etw tun müssen; **you haven't to tell her** du darfst es ihr nicht erzählen

♦ vt **1** (possess) haben; **he has (got) blue eyes** er hat blaue Augen; **he has (got) an idea** ich habe eine Idee

2 (referring to meals etc): **to have**

breakfast/a cigarette frühstücken/
eine Zigarette rauchen

3 (*receive, obtain etc*) haben; **may I
have your address?** kann ich Ihre
Adresse haben?; **to have a baby** ein
Kind bekommen

4 (*maintain, allow*): **he will have it
that he is right** er besteht darauf,
dass er Recht hat; **I won't have it** das
lasse ich hier nicht bieten

5: to have sth done etw machen lassen; **to have sb do sth** jdn etw machen lassen; **he soon had them all
laughing** er brachte sie alle zum Lachen

6 (*experience, suffer*): **she had her bag
stolen** man hat ihr die Tasche gestohlen; **he had his arm broken** er hat
sich den Arm gebrochen

7 (*+noun: take, hold etc*): **to have a
walk/rest** spazieren gehen/sich ausruhen; **to have a meeting/party** eine
Besprechung/Party haben

have out *vt*: **to have it out with sb**
(*settle problem*) etw mit jdm bereden

---

haven ['heɪvn] *n* Zufluchtsort *m*

haven't ['hævnt] = **have not**

havoc ['hævək] *n* Verwüstung *f*

hawk [hɔːk] *n* Habicht *m*

hay [heɪ] *n* Heu *nt*; **~ fever** *n* Heu-
schnupfen *m*; **~stack** *n* Heuschober *m*

haywire ['heɪweəʳ] (*inf*) *adj* durcheinander

hazard ['hæzəd] *n* Risiko *nt* ♦ *vt* aufs
Spiel setzen; **~ous** *adj* gefährlich; **~
(warning) lights** *npl* (AUT) Warnblink-
licht *nt*

haze [heɪz] *n* Dunst *m*

hazelnut ['heɪzlnʌt] *n* Haselnuss *f*

hazy ['heɪzɪ] *adj* (*misty*) dunstig;
(*vague*) verschwommen

he [hiː] *pron* er

head [hed] *n* Kopf *m*; (*leader*) Leiter *m*
♦ *vt* (an)führen, leiten; (*ball*) köpfen;
~s (or tails) Kopf (oder Zahl); **~ first**
mit dem Kopf nach unten; **~ over**

heels kopfüber; **~ for** *vt fus* zugehen
auf *+acc*; **~ache** *n* Kopfschmerzen *pl*;
~dress *n* Kopfschmuck *m*; **~ing** *n*
Überschrift *f*; **~lamp** (BRIT) *n* Scheinwerfer *m*; **~land** *n* Landspitze *f*; **~light**
n Scheinwerfer *m*; **~line** *n* Schlagzeile
f; **~long** *adv* kopfüber; **~master** *n* (*of
primary school*) Rektor *m*; (*of secondary
school*) Direktor *m*; **~mistress** *n* Rekto-
rin *f*; Direktorin *f*; **~ office** *n* Zentrale
f; **~-on** *adj* Frontal-; **~phones** *npl*
Kopfhörer *pl*; **~quarters** *npl* Zentrale *f*;
(MIL) Hauptquartier *nt*; **~rest** *n* Kopf-
stütze *f*; **~room** *n* (*of bridges etc*) lichte
Höhe *f*; **~scarf** *n* Kopftuch *nt*;
~strong *adj* eigenwillig; **~teacher**
(BRIT) *n* Schulleiter(in) *m(f)*; (*of secondary school also*) Direktor(in) *m*; **~wait-
er** *n* Oberkellner *m*; **~way** *n* Fortschritte *pl*; **~wind** *n* Gegenwind *m*; **~y** *adj*
berauschend

heal [hiːl] *vt* heilen ♦ *vi* verheilen

health [helθ] *n* Gesundheit *f*; **~ food** *n*
Reformkost *f*; **H~ Service** (BRIT) *n* the
H~ Service die Gesundheitswesen; **~y**
adj gesund

heap [hiːp] *n* Haufen *m* ♦ *vt* häufen

hear [hɪəʳ] (*pt, pp* **heard**) *vt* hören; (*listen to*) anhören ♦ *vi* hören; **~d** [hɜːd]
pt, pp of **hear**; **~ing** *n* Gehör *nt*; (JUR)
Verhandlung *f*; **~ing aid** *n* Hörapparat
m; **~say** *n* Hörensagen *nt*

hearse [hɜːs] *n* Leichenwagen *m*

heart [hɑːt] *n* Herz *nt*; **~s** *npl* (CARDS)
Herz *nt*; **by ~** auswendig; **~ attack** *n*
Herzanfall *m*; **~beat** *n* Herzschlag *m*;
~breaking *adj* herzzerbrechend;
~broken *adj* untröstlich; **~burn** *n* Sodbrennen *nt*; **~ failure** *n* Herzschlag *m*;
~felt *adj* aufrichtig

hearth [hɑːθ] *n* Herd *m*

heartily ['hɑːtɪlɪ] *adv* herzlich; (*eat*)
herzhaft

heartless ['hɑːtlɪs] *adj* herzlos

hearty ['hɑːtɪ] *adj* kräftig; (*friendly*)
freundlich

heat [hiːt] *n* Hitze *f*; (*of food, water etc*)

Wärme f; (SPORT: also: **qualifying ~**) Ausscheidungsrunde f ♦ vt (house) heizen; (substance) heiß machen, erhitzen; **~ up** vi warm werden ♦ vt erwärmen; **~ed** adj erhitzt; (fig) hitzig; **~er** n (Heiz)ofen m

heath [hi:θ] (BRIT) n Heide f

heathen ['hi:ðn] n Heide m/Heidin f ♦ adj heidnisch, Heiden-

heather ['heðə'] n Heidekraut nt

heat: ~ing n Heizung f; **~-seeking** adj Wärme suchend; **~stroke** n Hitzschlag m; **~ wave** n Hitzewelle f

heave [hi:v] vt hochheben; (sigh) ausstoßen ♦ vi wogen; (breast) sich heben ♦ n Heben nt

heaven [hevn] n Himmel m; **~ly** adj himmlisch

heavily ['hevɪlɪ] adv schwer

heavy ['hevɪ] adj schwer; **~ goods vehicle** n Lastkraftwagen m; **~weight** n (SPORT) Schwergewicht nt

Hebrew ['hi:bru:] adj hebräisch ♦ n (LING) Hebräisch nt

Hebrides ['hebrɪdi:z] npl Hebriden pl

heckle ['hekl] vt unterbrechen

hectic ['hektɪk] adj hektisch

he'd [hi:d] = he had; he would

hedge [hedʒ] n Hecke f ♦ vt einzäunen ♦ vi (fig) ausweichen; **to ~ one's bets** sich absichern

hedgehog ['hedʒhɔg] n Igel m

heed [hi:d] vt (also: **take ~ of**) beachten ♦ n Beachtung f; **~less** adj achtlos

heel [hi:l] n Ferse f; (of shoe) Absatz m ♦ vt mit Absätzen versehen

hefty ['heftɪ] adj (person) stämmig; (portion) reichlich

heifer ['hefə'] n Färse f

height [haɪt] n (of person) Größe f; (of object) Höhe f; **~en** vt erhöhen

heir [ɛə'] n Erbe m; **~ess** ['ɛərɛs] n Erbin f; **~loom** n Erbstück nt

held [held] pt, pp of **hold**

helicopter ['helɪkɔptə'] n Hubschrauber m

heliport ['helɪpɔ:t] n Hubschrauberlan-

deplatz m

hell [hel] n Hölle f ♦ excl verdammt!

he'll [hi:l] = he will; he shall

hellish ['helɪʃ] adj höllisch, verteufelt

hello [hə'ləu] excl hallo

helm [helm] n Ruder nt, Steuer nt

helmet ['helmɪt] n Helm m

help [help] n Hilfe f ♦ vt helfen +dat; I can't **~ it** ich kann nichts dafür; **~ yourself** bedienen Sie sich; **~er** n Helfer m; **~ful** adj hilfreich; **~ing** n Portion f; **~less** adj hilflos

hem [hem] n Saum m ♦ vt säumen; **~ in** vt einengen

hemorrhage ['hemərɪdʒ] (US) n = **haemorrhage**

hemorrhoids ['hemərɔɪdz] (US) npl = **haemorrhoids**

hen [hen] n Henne f

hence [hens] adv von jetzt an; (therefore) daher; **~forth** adv von nun an; (from then on) von da an

henchman ['hentʃmən] (irreg) n Gefolgsmann m

her [hə:'] pron (acc) sie; (dat) ihr ♦ adj ihr; see also **me; my**

herald ['herəld] n (Vor)bote m ♦ vt verkünden

heraldry ['herəldrɪ] n Wappenkunde f

herb [hə:b] n Kraut nt

herd [hə:d] n Herde f

here [hɪə'] adv hier; (to this place) hierher; **~after** [hɪər'a:ftə'] adv hernach, künftig ♦ n Jenseits nt; **~by** [hɪə'baɪ] adv hiermit

hereditary [hɪ'redɪtrɪ] adj erblich

heredity [hɪ'redɪtɪ] n Vererbung f

heritage ['herɪtɪdʒ] n Erbe nt

hermit ['hə:mɪt] n Einsiedler m

hernia ['hə:nɪə] n Bruch m

hero ['hɪərəu] (pl **~es**) n Held m; **~ic** [hɪ'rəuɪk] adj heroisch

heroin ['herəuɪn] n Heroin nt

heroine ['herəuɪn] n Heldin f

heroism ['herəuɪzəm] n Heldentum nt

heron ['herən] n Reiher m

herring ['herɪŋ] n Hering m

hers [hə:z] *pron* ihre(r, s); *see also* **mine²**

herself [hə:'self] *pron* sich (selbst); *(emphatic)* selbst; *see also* **oneself**

he's [hi:z] = **he is**; **he has**

hesitant ['hezitənt] *adj* zögernd

hesitate ['heziteit] *vi* zögern; **hesitation** [hezi'teiʃən] *n* Zögern *nt*

heterosexual ['hetərəu'seksjuəl] *adj* heterosexuell ♦ *n* Heterosexuelle(r) *mf*

hew [hju:] *(pt* **hewed**, *pp* **hewn** *or* **hewed)** *vt* hauen, hacken

hexagonal [hek'sægənl] *adj* sechseckig

heyday ['heidei] *n* Blüte *f*, Höhepunkt *m*

HGV *n abbr* = **heavy goods vehicle**

hi [hai] *excl* he, hallo

hibernate ['haibəneit] *vi* Winterschlaf *m* halten; **hibernation** [haibə'neiʃən] *n* Winterschlaf *m*

hiccough ['hikʌp] *vi* den Schluckauf haben; **~s** *npl* Schluckauf *m*

hiccup ['hikʌp] = **hiccough**

hid [hid] *pt of* **hide**; **~den** ['hidn] *pp of* **hide**

hide [haid] *(pt* **hid**, *pp* **hidden)** *n (skin)* Haut *f*, Fell *nt* ♦ *vt* verstecken ♦ *vi* sich verstecken; **~-and-seek** *n* Versteckspiel *nt*; **~away** *n* Versteck *nt*

hideous ['hidiəs] *adj* abscheulich

hiding ['haidiŋ] *n (beating)* Tracht *f* Prügel; **to be in ~** *(concealed)* sich versteckt halten; **~ place** *n* Versteck *nt*

hi-fi ['haifai] *n* Hi-Fi *nt* ♦ *adj* Hi-Fi-

high [hai] *adj* hoch; *(wind)* stark ♦ *adv* hoch; **it is 20m ~** es ist 20 Meter hoch; **~brow** *adj* (betont) intellektuell; **~chair** *n* Hochstuhl *m*; **~er education** *n* Hochschulbildung *f*; **~-handed** *adj* eigenmächtig; **~-heeled** *adj* hochhackig; **~ jump** *n (SPORT)* Hochsprung *m*; **H~lands** *npl*: **the H~lands** das schottische Hochland; **~light** *n (fig)* Höhepunkt *m* ♦ *vt* hervorheben; **~ly** *adv* höchst; **~ly strung** *adj* überempfindlich; **~ness** *n* Höhe *f*; **Her H~ness** Ihre Hoheit *f*; **~-pitched**

adj hoch; **~-rise block** *n* Hochhaus *nt*; **~ school** *(US)* *n* Oberschule *f*; **~ season** *(BRIT)* *n* Hochsaison *f*; **~ street** *(BRIT)* *n* Hauptstraße *f*

highway ['haiwei] *n* Landstraße *f*; **H~ Code** *(BRIT)* *n* Straßenverkehrsordnung *f*

hijack ['haidʒæk] *vt* entführen; **~er** *n* Entführer(in) *m(f)*

hike [haik] *vi* wandern ♦ *n* Wanderung *f*; **~r** *n* Wanderer *m*; **hiking** *n* Wandern *nt*

hilarious [hi'lɛəriəs] *adj* lustig

hill [hil] *n* Berg *m*; **~side** *n* (Berg)hang *m*; **~ walking** *n* Bergwandern *nt*; **~y** *adj* hügelig

hilt [hilt] *n* Heft *nt*; **(up) to the ~** ganz und gar

him [him] *pron (acc)* ihn; *(dat)* ihm; *see also* **me**; **~self** *pron* sich (selbst); *(emphatic)* selbst; *see also* **oneself**

hind [haind] *adj* hinter, Hinter-

hinder ['hində] *vt (stop)* hindern; *(delay)* behindern; **hindrance** *n (delay)* Behinderung *f*; *(obstacle)* Hindernis *nt*

hindsight ['haindsait] *n*: **with ~** im nachhinein

Hindu ['hindu:] *n* Hindu *m*

hinge [hindʒ] *n* Scharnier *nt*; *(on door)* Türangel *f* ♦ *vi (fig)*: **to ~ on** abhängen von

hint [hint] *n* Tipp *m*; *(trace)* Anflug *m* ♦ *vt*: **to ~ that** andeuten, dass ♦ *vi*: **to ~ at** andeuten

hip [hip] *n* Hüfte *f*

hippie ['hipi] *n* Hippie *m*

hippo ['hipəu] *(inf)* *n* Nilpferd *nt*

hippopotami [hipə'pɔtəmai] *npl of* **hippopotamus**

hippopotamus [hipə'pɔtəməs] *(pl* **~es** *or* **hippopotami)** *n* Nilpferd *nt*

hire ['haiə] *vt (worker)* anstellen; *(BRIT: car)* mieten ♦ *n* Miete *f*; **for ~** *(taxi)* frei; **~(d) car** *(BRIT)* *n* Mietwagen *m*, Leihwagen *m*; **~ purchase** *(BRIT)* *n* Teilzahlungskauf *m*

his [hiz] *adj* sein ♦ *pron* seine(r, s); *see*

also **my; mine²**

hiss [hɪs] vi zischen ♦ n Zischen nt
historian [hɪˈstɔːrɪən] n Historiker m
historic [hɪˈstɒrɪk] adj historisch; **~al**
adj historisch, geschichtlich
history [ˈhɪstərɪ] n Geschichte f
hit [hɪt] (pt, pp **hit**) vt schlagen; (injure)
treffen ♦ n (blow) Schlag m; (success)
Erfolg m; (MUS) Hit m; **to ~ it off with
sb** prima mit jdm auskommen; **~-
and-run driver** n jemand, der Fahrer-
flucht begeht
hitch [hɪtʃ] vt festbinden; (also: **~ up**)
hochziehen ♦ n (difficulty) Haken m; **to ~
a lift** trampen; **~hike** vi trampen; **~hi-
ker** n Tramper m; **~hiking** n Trampen nt
hi-tech [ˈhaɪˈtek] adj Hightech- ♦ n
Spitzentechnologie f
hitherto [hɪðəˈtuː] adv bislang
hit man (inf) (irreg) n Killer m
HIV n abbr: **HIV-negative/-positive**
HIV-negativ/-positiv
hive [haɪv] n Bienenkorb m
HMS abbr = **His/Her Majesty's Ship**
hoard [hɔːd] n Schatz m ♦ vt horten,
hamstern
hoarding [ˈhɔːdɪŋ] n Bretterzaun m;
(BRIT: for posters) Reklamewand f
hoarse [hɔːs] adj heiser, rau
hoax [həʊks] n Streich m
hob [hɒb] n Kochmulde f
hobble [ˈhɒbl] vi humpeln
hobby [ˈhɒbɪ] n Hobby nt
hobby-horse [ˈhɒbɪhɔːs] n (fig) Stek-
kenpferd nt
hobo [ˈhəʊbəʊ] (US) n Tippelbruder m
hockey [ˈhɒkɪ] n Hockey nt
hoe [həʊ] n Hacke f ♦ vt hacken
hog [hɒg] n Schlachtschwein nt ♦ vt mit
Beschlag belegen; **to go the whole ~**
aufs Ganze gehen
hoist [hɔɪst] n Winde f ♦ vt hochziehen
hold [həʊld] (pt, pp **held**) vt halten;
(contain) enthalten; (be able to contain)
fassen; (breath) anhalten; (meeting) abhalten ♦ vi (withstand pressure) aushalten ♦ n (grasp) Halt m; (NAUT) Schiffs-

raum m; **~ the line!** (TEL) bleiben Sie
am Apparat!; **to ~ one's own** sich behaupten; **~ back** vt zurückhalten; **~
down** vt niederhalten; (job) behalten;
~ off vt (enemy) abwehren; **~ on** vi
sich festhalten; (resist) durchhalten;
(wait) warten; **~ on to** vt fus festhalten
an +dat; (keep) behalten; **~ out** vt hin-
halten ♦ vi aushalten; **~ up** vt (delay)
aufhalten; (rob) überfallen; **~all** (BRIT) n
Reisetasche f; **~er** n Behälter m; **~ing** n
(share) (Aktien)anteil m; **~up** n (BRIT: in
traffic) Stockung f; (robbery) Überfall
m; (delay) Verzögerung f
hole [həʊl] n Loch nt; **~ in the wall**
(inf) n (cash dispenser) Geldautomat m
holiday [ˈhɒlɪdeɪ] n (day) Feiertag m;
freie(r) Tag m; (vacation) Urlaub m;
(SCH) Ferien pl; **~-maker** (BRIT) n Urlau-
ber(in) m(f); **~ resort** n Ferienort m
Holland [ˈhɒlənd] n Holland nt
hollow [ˈhɒləʊ] adj hohl; (fig) leer ♦ n
Vertiefung f; **~ out** vt aushöhlen
holly [ˈhɒlɪ] n Stechpalme f
holocaust [ˈhɒləkɔːst] n Inferno nt
holster [ˈhəʊlstə*] n Pistolenhalfter m
holy [ˈhəʊlɪ] adj heilig; **H~ Ghost** or
Spirit n: **the H~ Ghost** or **Spirit** der
Heilige Geist
homage [ˈhɒmɪdʒ] n Huldigung f; **to
pay ~ to** huldigen +dat
home [həʊm] n Zuhause nt; (institution) Heim nt, Anstalt f ♦ adj einheimisch; (POL) inner ♦ adv heim, nach
Hause; **at ~** zu Hause; **~ address** n
Heimatadresse f; **~coming** n Heim-
kehr f; **~land** n Heimat(land) nt(f);
~less adj obdachlos; **~ly** adj häuslich;
(US: ugly) unscheinbar; **~made** adj
selbst gemacht; **~ match** adj Heim-
spiel nt; **H~ Office** (BRIT) n Innenmini-
sterium nt; **~ page** n (COMPUT) Home-
page f; **~ rule** n Selbstverwaltung f;
H~ Secretary (BRIT) n Innenmini-
ster(in) m(f); **~sick** adj: **to be ~sick**
Heimweh haben; **~ town** n Heimat-
stadt f; **~ward** adj (journey) Heim-

~work n Hausaufgaben pl

homicide ['hɒmɪsaɪd] (US) n Totschlag m

homoeopathic [həʊmɪə'pæθɪk] (US **homeopathic**) adj homöopathisch; **homoeopathy** [həʊmɪ'ɒpəθɪ] (US **homeopathy**) n Homöopathie f

homogeneous [həʊmə'dʒiːnɪəs] adj homogen

homosexual [həʊmə'seksjuəl] adj homosexuell ♦ n Homosexuelle(r) mf

honest ['ɒnɪst] adj ehrlich; **~ly** adv ehrlich; **~y** n Ehrlichkeit f

honey ['hʌnɪ] n Honig m; **~comb** n Honigwabe f; **~moon** n Flitterwochen pl, Hochzeitsreise f; **~suckle** ['hʌnɪsʌkl] n Geißblatt nt

honk [hɒŋk] vi hupen

honor etc ['ɒnər] (US) vt, n = **honour** etc

honorary ['ɒnərərɪ] adj Ehren-

honour ['ɒnər] (US **honor**) vt ehren; (cheque) einlösen ♦ n Ehre f; **~able** adj ehrenwert; (intention) ehrenhaft; **~s degree** n (UNIV) akademischer Grad mit Prüfung im Spezialfach

hood [hʊd] n Kapuze f; (BRIT: AUT) Verdeck nt; (US: AUT) Kühlerhaube f

hoof [huːf] (pl **hooves**) n Huf m

hook [hʊk] n Haken m ♦ vt einhaken

hooligan ['huːlɪgən] n Rowdy m

hoop [huːp] n Reifen m

hooray [huː'reɪ] excl = **hurrah**

hoot [huːt] vi (AUT) hupen; **~er** n (NAUT) Dampfpfeife f; (BRIT: AUT) (Auto)hupe f

Hoover ['huːvər] (®; BRIT) n Staubsauger m ♦ vt: **to h~** staubsaugen, Staub saugen

hooves [huːvz] pl of **hoof**

hop [hɒp] vi hüpfen, hopsen ♦ n (jump) Hopser m

hope [həʊp] vt, vi hoffen ♦ n Hoffnung f; **I ~ so/not** hoffentlich/hoffentlich nicht; **~ful** adj hoffnungsvoll; (promising) viel versprechend; **~fully** adv hoffentlich; **~less** adj hoffnungslos

hops [hɒps] npl Hopfen m

horizon [hə'raɪzn] n Horizont m; **~tal**

[hɒrɪ'zɒntl] adj horizontal

hormone ['hɔːməʊn] n Hormon nt

horn [hɔːn] n Horn nt; (AUT) Hupe f

hornet ['hɔːnɪt] n Hornisse f

horny ['hɔːnɪ] adj schwielig; (US: inf) scharf

horoscope ['hɒrəskəʊp] n Horoskop nt

horrendous [hə'rendəs] adj (crime) abscheulich; (error) schrecklich

horrible ['hɒrɪbl] adj fürchterlich

horrid ['hɒrɪd] adj scheußlich

horrify ['hɒrɪfaɪ] vt entsetzen

horror ['hɒrər] n Schrecken m; **~ film** n Horrorfilm m

hors d'oeuvre [ɔː'dɜːvrə] n Vorspeise f

horse [hɔːs] n Pferd nt; **~back** n: **on ~back** berittem; **~chestnut** n Rosskastanie f; **~man/woman** (irreg) n Reiter(in) m(f); **~power** n Pferdestärke f; **~racing** n Pferderennen nt; **~radish** n Meerrettich m; **~shoe** n Hufeisen nt

horticulture ['hɔːtɪkʌltʃər] n Gartenbau m

hose [həʊz] n (also: **~pipe**) Schlauch m

hosiery ['həʊzɪərɪ] n Strumpfwaren pl

hospitable ['hɒspɪtəbl] adj gastfreundlich

hospital ['hɒspɪtl] n Krankenhaus nt

hospitality [hɒspɪ'tælɪtɪ] n Gastfreundschaft f

host [həʊst] n Gastgeber m; (innkeeper) (Gast)wirt m; (large number) Heerschar f; (ECCL) Hostie f

hostage ['hɒstɪdʒ] n Geisel f

hostel ['hɒstl] n Herberge f; (also: **youth ~**) Jugendherberge f

hostess ['həʊstɪs] n Gastgeberin f

hostile ['hɒstaɪl] adj feindlich; **hostility** [hɒ'stɪlɪtɪ] n Feindschaft f; **hostilities** npl (fighting) Feindseligkeiten pl

hot [hɒt] adj heiß; (food, water) warm; (spiced) scharf; **I'm ~** mir ist heiß; **~bed** n (fig) Nährboden m; **~ dog** n heiße(s) Würstchen nt

hotel [həʊ'tel] n Hotel nt; **~ier** [həʊ'telɪər] n Hotelier m

hot: ~house n Treibhaus nt; **~ line** n

(POL) heiße(r) Draht m; **~ly** adv (argue) hitzig; **~plate** n Kochplatte f; **~pot** ['hɔtpɔt] (BRIT) n Fleischeintopf m; **~ water bottle** n Wärmflasche f

hound [haund] n Jagdhund m ♦ vt hetzen

hour ['auəʳ] n Stunde f; (time of day) (Tages)zeit f; **~ly** adj, adv stündlich

house [n haus, vb hauz] n Haus n ♦ vt unterbringen; **on the ~** auf Kosten des Hauses; **~ arrest** n (POL, MIL) Hausarrest m; **~boat** n Hausboot nt; **~breaking** n Einbruch m; **~coat** n Morgenmantel m; **~hold** n Haushalt m; **~keeper** n Haushälterin f; **~keeping** n Haushaltung f; **~-warming party** n Einweihungsparty f; **~wife** (irreg) n Hausfrau f; **~work** n Hausarbeit f

housing ['hauziŋ] n (act) Unterbringung f; (houses) Wohnungen pl; (POL) Wohnungsbau m; (covering) Gehäuse nt; **~ estate** (US **~ development**) n (Wohn)siedlung f

hovel ['hɔvl] n elende Hütte f

hover ['hɔvəʳ] vi (bird) schweben; (person) herumstehen; **~craft** n Luftkissenfahrzeug nt

how [hau] adv wie; **~ are you?** wie geht es Ihnen?; **~ much milk?** wie viel Milch?; **~ many people?** wie viele Leute?

however [hau'ɛvəʳ] adv (but) (je)doch, aber; **~ you phrase it** wie Sie es auch ausdrücken

howl [haul] n Heulen nt ♦ vi heulen

H.P. abbr = **hire purchase**

h.p. abbr = **horsepower**

H.Q. abbr = **headquarters**

hub [hʌb] n Radnabe f

hubbub ['hʌbʌb] n Tumult m

hubcap ['hʌbkæp] n Radkappe f

huddle ['hʌdl] vi: **to ~ together** sich zusammendrängen

hue [hju:] n Färbung f; **~ and cry** n Zetergeschrei nt

huff [hʌf] n: **to go into a ~** einschnappen

hug [hʌg] vt umarmen ♦ n Umarmung f

huge [hju:dʒ] adj groß, riesig

hulk [hʌlk] n (ship) abgetakelte(s) Schiff nt; (person) Moloch m

hull [hʌl] n Schiffsrumpf m

hullo [hə'ləu] excl = **hello**

hum [hʌm] vt, vi summen

human ['hju:mən] adj menschlich ♦ n (also: ~ being) Mensch m

humane [hju:'mein] adj human

humanitarian [hju:mæni'tɛəriən] adj humanitär

humanity [hju:'mæniti] n Menschheit f; (kindliness) Menschlichkeit f

humble ['hʌmbl] adj demütig; (modest) bescheiden ♦ vt demütigen

humbug ['hʌmbʌg] n Humbug m; (BRIT: sweet) Pfefferminzbonbon m

humdrum ['hʌmdrʌm] adj stumpfsinnig

humid ['hju:mid] adj feucht; **~ity** [hju:'miditi] n Feuchtigkeit f

humiliate [hju:'milieit] vt demütigen; **humiliation** [hju:mili'eiʃən] n Demütigung f

humility [hju:'militi] n Demut f

humor ['hju:məʳ] (US) n, vt = **humour**

humorous ['hju:mərəs] adj humorvoll

humour ['hju:məʳ] (US **humor**) n (fun) Humor m; (mood) Stimmung f ♦ vt bei Stimmung halten

hump [hʌmp] n Buckel m

hunch [hʌntʃ] n Buckel m; (premonition) (Vor)ahnung f; **~back** n Bucklige(r) mf; **~ed** adj gekrümmt

hundred ['hʌndrəd] num hundert; **~weight** n Zentner m (BRIT = 50.8 kg; US = 45.3 kg)

hung [hʌŋ] pt, pp of **hang**

Hungarian [hʌŋ'gɛəriən] adj ungarisch ♦ n Ungar(in) m(f); (LING) Ungarisch nt

Hungary ['hʌŋgəri] n Ungarn nt

hunger ['hʌŋgəʳ] n Hunger m ♦ vi hungern

hungry ['hʌŋgri] adj hungrig; **to be ~** Hunger haben

hunk [hʌŋk] n (of bread) Stück nt

hunt [hʌnt] vt, vi jagen ♦ n Jagd f; **to ~ for** suchen; **~er** n Jäger m; **~ing** n Jagd f

hurdle ['hɜːdl] n (also fig) Hürde f

hurl [hɜːl] vt schleudern

hurrah [hu'rɑː] n Hurra nt

hurray [hu'reɪ] n Hurra nt

hurricane ['hʌrɪkən] n Orkan m

hurried ['hʌrɪd] adj eilig; (hasty) übereilt; **~ly** adv übereilt, hastig

hurry ['hʌrɪ] n Eile f ♦ vi sich beeilen ♦ vt (an)treiben; (job) übereilen; **to be in a ~** es eilig haben; **~ up** vi sich beeilen ♦ vt (person) zur Eile antreiben; (work) vorantreiben

hurt [hɜːt] (pt, pp **hurt**) vt wehtun +dat; (injure, fig) verletzen ♦ vi wehtun; **~ful** adj schädlich; (remark) verletzend

hurtle ['hɜːtl] vi sausen

husband ['hʌzbənd] n (Ehe)mann m

hush [hʌʃ] n Stille f ♦ vt zur Ruhe bringen ♦ excl pst, still

husky ['hʌskɪ] adj (voice) rau ♦ n Eskimohund m

hustle ['hʌsl] vt (push) stoßen; (hurry) antreiben ♦ n: **~ and bustle** Geschäftigkeit f

hut [hʌt] n Hütte f

hutch [hʌtʃ] n (Kaninchen)stall m

hyacinth ['haɪəsɪnθ] n Hyazinthe f

hydrant ['haɪdrənt] n (also: **fire ~**) Hydrant m

hydraulic [haɪ'drɔːlɪk] adj hydraulisch

hydroelectric ['haɪdrəu'lektrɪk] adj (energy) durch Wasserkraft erzeugt; **~ power station** n Wasserkraftwerk nt

hydrofoil ['haɪdrəfɔɪl] n Tragflügelboot nt

hydrogen ['haɪdrədʒən] n Wasserstoff m

hyena [haɪ'iːnə] n Hyäne f

hygiene ['haɪdʒiːn] n Hygiene f; **hygienic** [haɪ'dʒiːnɪk] adj hygienisch

hymn [hɪm] n Kirchenlied nt

hype [haɪp] (inf) n Publicity f

hypermarket ['haɪpəmɑːkɪt] (BRIT) n Hypermarkt m

hypertext ['haɪpətekst] n Hypertext m

hyphen ['haɪfn] n Bindestrich m

hypnosis [hɪp'nəusɪs] n Hypnose f

hypnotize ['hɪpnətaɪz] vt hypnotisieren

hypocrisy [hɪ'pɒkrɪsɪ] n Heuchelei f

hypocrite ['hɪpəkrɪt] n Heuchler m; **hypocritical** [hɪpə'krɪtɪkl] adj scheinheilig, heuchlerisch

hypothermia [haɪpə'θɜːmɪə] n Unterkühlung f

hypotheses [haɪ'pɒθɪsiːz] npl of **hypothesis**

hypothesis [haɪ'pɒθɪsɪs] (pl **hypotheses**) n Hypothese f

hypothetic(al) [haɪpəu'θetɪk(l)] adj hypothetisch

hysterical [hɪ'sterɪkl] adj hysterisch

hysterics [hɪ'sterɪks] npl hysterische(r) Anfall m

I, i

I [aɪ] pron ich

ice [aɪs] n Eis nt ♦ vt (COOK) mit Zuckerguss überziehen ♦ vi (also: **~ up**) vereisen; **~ axe** n Eispickel m; **~berg** n Eisberg m; **~box** (US) n Kühlschrank m; **~cream** n Eis nt; **~ cube** n Eiswürfel m; **~d** [aɪst] adj (cake) mit Zuckerguss überzogen, glasiert; (tea, coffee) Eis-; **~ hockey** n Eishockey nt

Iceland ['aɪslənd] n Island nt

ice: **~ lolly** (BRIT) n Eis am Stiel; **~ rink** n (Kunst)eisbahn f; **~ skating** n Schlittschuhlaufen nt

icicle ['aɪsɪkl] n Eiszapfen m

icing ['aɪsɪŋ] n (on cake) Zuckerguss m; (on window) Vereisung f; **~ sugar** (BRIT) n Puderzucker m

icon ['aɪkɒn] n Ikone f

icy ['aɪsɪ] adj (slippery) vereist; (cold) eisig

I'd [aɪd] = I would; I had

idea [aɪ'dɪə] n Idee f

ideal [aɪ'dɪəl] n Ideal nt ♦ adj ideal

identical [aɪ'dentɪkl] *adj* identisch; *(twins)* eineiig

identification [aɪdentɪfɪ'keɪʃən] *n* Identifizierung *f*; **means of ~** Ausweispapiere *pl*

identify [aɪ'dentɪfaɪ] *vt* identifizieren; *(regard as the same)* gleichsetzen

Identikit [aɪ'dentɪkɪt] ® *n*: **~ picture** Phantombild *nt*

identity [aɪ'dentɪtɪ] *n* Identität *f*; **~ card** *n* Personalausweis *m*

ideology [aɪdɪ'ɔlədʒɪ] *n* Ideologie *f*

idiom ['ɪdɪəm] *n (expression)* Redewendung *f*; *(dialect)* Idiom *nt*; **~atic** [ɪdɪə'mætɪk] *adj* idiomatisch

idiosyncrasy [ɪdɪəʊ'sɪŋkrəsɪ] *n* Eigenart *f*

idiot ['ɪdɪət] *n* Idiot(in) *m(f)*; **~ic** [ɪdɪ'ɔtɪk] *adj* idiotisch

idle ['aɪdl] *adj (doing nothing)* untätig; *(lazy)* faul; *(useless)* nutzlos; *(machine)* still(stehend); *(threat, talk)* leer ♦ *vi (machine)* leer laufen ♦ *vt*: **to ~ away the time** die Zeit vertrödeln; **~ness** *n* Müßiggang *m*; Faulheit *f*

idol ['aɪdl] *n* Idol *nt*; **~ize** *vt* vergöttern

i.e. *abbr* (= *id est*) d. h.

KEYWORD
---

if [ɪf] *conj* **1** wenn; *(in case also)* falls; **if I were you** wenn ich Sie wäre

2 *(although)*: **(even) if** (selbst *or* auch) wenn

3 *(whether)* ob

4: **if so/not** wenn ja/nicht; **if only ...** wenn ... doch nur ...; **if only I could** wenn ich doch nur könnte; *see also* **as**

---

ignite [ɪg'naɪt] *vt* (an)zünden ♦ *vi* sich entzünden; **ignition** [ɪg'nɪʃən] *n* Zündung *f*; **to switch on/off the ignition** den Motor anlassen/abstellen; **ignition key** *n* (AUT) Zündschlüssel *m*

ignorance ['ɪgnərəns] *n* Unwissenheit *f*

ignorant ['ɪgnərənt] *adj* unwissend; **to be ~ of** nicht wissen

ignore [ɪg'nɔː] *vt* ignorieren

I'll [aɪl] = **I will; I shall**

ill [ɪl] *adj* krank ♦ *n* Übel *nt* ♦ *adv* schlecht; **~-advised** *adj* unklug; **~-at-ease** *adj* unbehaglich

illegal [ɪ'liːgl] *adj* illegal

illegible [ɪ'ledʒɪbl] *adj* unleserlich

illegitimate [ɪlɪ'dʒɪtɪmət] *adj* unehelich

ill-fated [ɪl'feɪtɪd] *adj* unselig

ill feeling *n* Verstimmung *f*

illicit [ɪ'lɪsɪt] *adj* verboten

illiterate [ɪ'lɪtərət] *adj* ungebildet

ill-mannered [ɪl'mænəd] *adj* ungehobelt

illness ['ɪlnɪs] *n* Krankheit *f*

illogical [ɪ'lɔdʒɪkl] *adj* unlogisch

ill-treat [ɪl'triːt] *vt* misshandeln

illuminate [ɪ'luːmɪneɪt] *vt* beleuchten; **illumination** [ɪluːmɪ'neɪʃən] *n* Beleuchtung *f*, **illuminations** *pl (decorative lights)* festliche Beleuchtung *f*

illusion [ɪ'luːʒən] *n* Illusion *f*; **to be under the ~ that ...** sich *dat* einbilden, dass ...

illustrate ['ɪləstreɪt] *vt (book)* illustrieren; *(explain)* veranschaulichen; **illustration** [ɪlə'streɪʃən] *n* Illustration *f*, *(explanation)* Veranschaulichung *f*

illustrious [ɪ'lʌstrɪəs] *adj* berühmt

I'm [aɪm] = **I am**

image ['ɪmɪdʒ] *n* Bild *nt*; *(public ~)* Image *nt*; **~ry** *n* Symbolik *f*

imaginary [ɪ'mædʒɪnərɪ] *adj* eingebildet; *(world)* Fantasie-

imagination [ɪmædʒɪ'neɪʃən] *n* Einbildung *f*; *(creative)* Fantasie *f*

imaginative [ɪ'mædʒɪnətɪv] *adj* fantasiereich, einfallsreich

imagine [ɪ'mædʒɪn] *vt* sich vorstellen; *(wrongly)* sich einbilden

imbalance [ɪm'bæləns] *n* Unausgeglichenheit *f*

imbecile ['ɪmbəsiːl] *n* Schwachsinnige(r) *m/f*

imitate ['ɪmɪteɪt] *vt* imitieren; **imitation** [ɪmɪ'teɪʃən] *n* Imitation *f*

immaculate [ɪ'mækjulət] *adj* makellos; *(dress)* tadellos; *(ECCL)* unbefleckt

immaterial [ɪmə'tɪərɪəl] adj unwesentlich; **it is ~ whether ...** es ist unwichtig, ob ...

immature [ɪmə'tjuə] adj unreif

immediate [ɪ'miːdɪət] adj (instant) sofortig; (near) unmittelbar; (relatives) nächste(r, s); (needs) dringlich; **~ly** adv sofort; **~ly next to** direkt neben

immense [ɪ'mɛns] adj unermesslich

immerse [ɪ'mɜːs] vt eintauchen; **to be ~d in** (fig) vertieft sein in +acc

immersion heater [ɪ'mɜːʃən-] (BRIT) n Boiler m

immigrant ['ɪmɪɡrənt] n Einwanderer m

immigrate ['ɪmɪɡreɪt] vi einwandern; **immigration** [ɪmɪ'ɡreɪʃən] n Einwanderung f

imminent ['ɪmɪnənt] adj bevorstehend

immobile [ɪ'məʊbaɪl] adj unbeweglich; **immobilize** [ɪ'məʊbɪlaɪz] vt lähmen

immoral [ɪ'mɒrl] adj unmoralisch; **~ity** [ɪmə'rælɪtɪ] n Unsittlichkeit f

immortal [ɪ'mɔːtl] adj unsterblich

immune [ɪ'mjuːn] adj (secure) sicher; (MED) immun; **~ from** sicher vor +dat; **immunity** n (MED, JUR) Immunität f; (fig) Freiheit f; **immunize** ['ɪmjunaɪz] vt immunisieren

impact ['ɪmpækt] n Aufprall m; (fig) Wirkung f

impair [ɪm'peə] vt beeinträchtigen

impart [ɪm'pɑːt] vt mitteilen; (knowledge) vermitteln; (exude) abgeben

impartial [ɪm'pɑːʃl] adj unparteiisch

impassable [ɪm'pɑːsəbl] adj unpassierbar

impassive [ɪm'pæsɪv] adj gelassen

impatience [ɪm'peɪʃəns] n Ungeduld f; **impatient** adj ungeduldig; **impatiently** adv ungeduldig

impeccable [ɪm'pekəbl] adj tadellos

impede [ɪm'piːd] vt (be)hindern; **impediment** [ɪm'pedɪmənt] n Hindernis nt; **speech impediment** Sprachfehler m

impending [ɪm'pendɪŋ] adj bevorstehend

impenetrable [ɪm'penɪtrəbl] adj (also fig) undurchdringlich

imperative [ɪm'perətɪv] adj (necessary) unbedingt erforderlich

imperceptible [ɪmpə'septɪbl] adj nicht wahrnehmbar

imperfect [ɪm'pɜːfɪkt] adj (faulty) fehlerhaft; **~ion** [ɪmpə'fekʃən] n Unvollkommenheit f; (fault) Fehler m

imperial [ɪm'pɪərɪəl] adj kaiserlich

impersonal [ɪm'pɜːsnl] adj unpersönlich

impersonate [ɪm'pɜːsəneɪt] vt sich ausgeben als; (for fun) imitieren

impertinent [ɪm'pɜːtɪnənt] adj unverschämt, frech

impervious [ɪm'pɜːvɪəs] adj (fig): **~ (to)** unempfänglich (für)

impetuous [ɪm'petjuəs] adj ungestüm

impetus ['ɪmpətəs] n Triebkraft f; (fig) Auftrieb m

impinge [ɪm'pɪndʒ]: **~ on** vt beeinträchtigen

implacable [ɪm'plækəbl] adj unerbittlich

implement [n 'ɪmplɪmənt, vb 'ɪmplɪment] n Werkzeug nt ♦ vt ausführen

implicate ['ɪmplɪkeɪt] vt verwickeln; **implication** [ɪmplɪ'keɪʃən] n (effect) Auswirkung f; (in crime) Verwicklung f

implicit [ɪm'plɪsɪt] adj (suggested) unausgesprochen; (utter) vorbehaltlos

implore [ɪm'plɔː] vt anflehen

imply [ɪm'plaɪ] vt (hint) andeuten; (be evidence for) schließen lassen auf +acc

impolite [ɪmpə'laɪt] adj unhöflich

import [vb ɪm'pɔːt, n 'ɪmpɔːt] vt einführen ♦ n Einfuhr f; (meaning) Bedeutung f

importance [ɪm'pɔːtns] n Bedeutung f

important [ɪm'pɔːtnt] adj wichtig; **it's not ~** es ist unwichtig

importer [ɪm'pɔːtə] n Importeur m

impose [ɪm'pəʊz] vt, vi: **to ~ (on)** erlegen (+dat); (penalty, sanctions) verhängen (gegen); **to ~ (o.s.) on sb** sich jdm aufdrängen

imposing [ɪmˈpəʊzɪŋ] *adj* eindrucksvoll

imposition [ɪmpəˈzɪʃən] *n (of burden, fine)* Auferlegung *f*; **to be an ~** *(on person)* eine Zumutung sein

impossible [ɪmˈpɒsɪbl] *adj* unmöglich

impostor [ɪmˈpɒstəʳ] *n* Hochstapler *m*

impotent [ˈɪmpətənt] *adj* machtlos; *(sexually)* impotent

impound [ɪmˈpaʊnd] *vt* beschlagnahmen

impoverished [ɪmˈpɒvərɪʃt] *adj* verarmt

impracticable [ɪmˈpræktɪkəbl] *adj* undurchführbar

impractical [ɪmˈpræktɪkl] *adj* unpraktisch

imprecise [ɪmprɪˈsaɪs] *adj* ungenau

impregnable [ɪmˈpregnəbl] *adj (castle)* uneinnehmbar

impregnate [ˈɪmpregneɪt] *vt (saturate)* sättigen; *(fertilize)* befruchten

impress [ɪmˈpres] *vt (influence)* beeindrucken; *(imprint)* (auf)drücken; **to ~ sth on sb** jdm etw einschärfen; **~ed** *adj* beeindruckt; **~ion** [ɪmˈpreʃən] *n* Eindruck *m*; *(on wax, footprint)* Abdruck *m*; *(of book)* Auflage *f*; *(take-off)* Nachahmung *f*; **I was under the ~ion** ich hatte den Eindruck; **~ionable** *adj* leicht zu beeindrucken; **~ive** *adj* eindrucksvoll

imprint [ˈɪmprɪnt] *n* Abdruck *m*

imprison [ɪmˈprɪzn] *vt* ins Gefängnis schicken; **~ment** *n* Inhaftierung *f*

improbable [ɪmˈprɒbəbl] *adj* unwahrscheinlich

impromptu [ɪmˈprɒmptjuː] *adj, adv* aus dem Stegreif, improvisiert

improper [ɪmˈprɒpəʳ] *adj (indecent)* unanständig; *(unsuitable)* unpassend

improve [ɪmˈpruːv] *vt* verbessern ♦ *vi* besser werden; **~ment** *n* (Ver)besserung *f*

improvise [ˈɪmprəvaɪz] *vt, vi* improvisieren

imprudent [ɪmˈpruːdnt] *adj* unklug

impudent [ˈɪmpjʊdnt] *adj* unverschämt

impulse [ˈɪmpʌls] *n* Impuls *m*; **to act on ~** spontan handeln; **impulsive** [ɪmˈpʌlsɪv] *adj* impulsiv

impure [ɪmˈpjʊəʳ] *adj (dirty)* verunreinigt; *(bad)* unsauber; **impurity** [ɪmˈpjʊərɪtɪ] *n* Unreinheit *f*; *(TECH)* Verunreinigung *f*

KEYWORD

in [ɪn] *prep* **1** *(indicating place, position)* in +*dat*; *(with motion)* in +*acc*; **in here/ there** hier/dort; **in London** in London; **in the United States** in den Vereinigten Staaten

2 *(indicating time: during)* in +*dat*; **in summer** im Sommer; **in 1988** (in Jahre) 1988; **in the afternoon** nachmittags, am Nachmittag

3 *(indicating time: in the space of)* innerhalb von; **I'll see you in 2 weeks** *or* **in 2 weeks' time** ich sehe Sie in zwei Wochen

4 *(indicating manner, circumstances, state etc)* in +*dat*; **in the sun/rain** in der Sonne/im Regen; **in English/French** auf Englisch/Französisch; **in a loud/ soft voice** mit lauter/leiser Stimme

5 *(with ratios, numbers)*: **1 in 10** jeder Zehnte; **20 pence in the pound** 20 Pence pro Pfund; **they lined up in twos** sie stellten sich in Zweierreihe auf

6 *(referring to people, works)*: **the disease is common in children** die Krankheit ist bei Kindern häufig; **in Dickens** bei Dickens; **we have a loyal friend in him** an ihm ist uns ein treuer Freund

7 *(indicating profession etc)*: **to be in teaching/the army** Lehrer(in)/beim Militär sein; **to be in publishing** im Verlagswesen arbeiten

8 *(with present participle)*: **in saying this, I ...** wenn ich das sage, ... ich; **in**

accepting this view, he ... weil er diese Meinung akzeptierte, ... ♦ *adv*: **to be in** (*person: at home, work*) da sein; (*train, ship, plane*) angekommen sein; (*in fashion*) in sein; **to ask sb in** jdn hereinbitten; **to run/limp** *etc* **in** hereingerannt/gehumpelt *etc* kommen
♦ *n*: **the ins and outs** (*of proposal, situation etc*) die Feinheiten

in. *abbr* = **inch**

inability [ɪnə'bɪlɪtɪ] *n* Unfähigkeit *f*

inaccessible [ɪnək'sesɪbl] *adj* unzugänglich

inaccurate [ɪn'ækjurət] *adj* ungenau; (*wrong*) unrichtig

inactivity [ɪnæk'tɪvɪtɪ] *n* Untätigkeit *f*

inadequate [ɪn'ædɪkwət] *adj* unzulänglich

inadvertently [ɪnəd'vɜːtntlɪ] *adv* unabsichtlich

inadvisable [ɪnəd'vaɪzəbl] *adj* nicht ratsam

inane [ɪ'neɪn] *adj* dumm, albern

inanimate [ɪn'ænɪmət] *adj* leblos

inappropriate [ɪnə'prəuprɪət] *adj* (*clothing*) ungeeignet; (*remark*) unangebracht

inarticulate [ɪnɑː'tɪkjulət] *adj* unklar

inasmuch as [ɪnəz'mʌtʃ-] *adv* da; (*in so far as*) so weit

inaudible [ɪn'ɔːdɪbl] *adj* unhörbar

inauguration [ɪnɔːgju'reɪʃən] *n* Eröffnung *f*; (*feierliche*) Amtseinführung *f*

inborn [ɪn'bɔːn] *adj* angeboren

inbred [ɪn'bred] *adj* angeboren

Inc. *abbr* = **incorporated**

incalculable [ɪn'kælkjuləbl] *adj* (*consequences*) unabsehbar

incapable [ɪn'keɪpəbl] *adj*: ~ **(of doing sth)** unfähig(, etw zu tun)

incapacitate [ɪnkə'pæsɪtet] *vt* untauglich machen

incapacity [ɪnkə'pæsɪtɪ] *n* Unfähigkeit *f*

incarcerate [ɪn'kɑːsəret] *vt* einkerkern

incarnation [ɪnkɑː'neɪʃən] *n* (*ECCL*) Menschwerdung *f*; (*fig*) Inbegriff *m*

incendiary [ɪn'sendɪərɪ] *adj* Brand-

incense [*n* 'ɪnsens, *vb* ɪn'sens] *n* Weihrauch *m* ♦ *vt* erzürnen

incentive [ɪn'sentɪv] *n* Anreiz *m*

incessant [ɪn'sesnt] *adj* unaufhörlich

incest ['ɪnsest] *n* Inzest *m*

inch [ɪntʃ] *n* Zoll *m* ♦ *vi*: **to ~ forward** sich Stückchen für Stückchen vorwärts bewegen; **to be within an ~ of** kurz davor sein; **he didn't give an ~** er gab keinen Zentimeter nach

incidence ['ɪnsɪdns] *n* Auftreten *nt*; (*of crime*) Quote *f*

incident ['ɪnsɪdnt] *n* Vorfall *m*; (*disturbance*) Zwischenfall *m*

incidental [ɪnsɪ'dentl] *adj* (*music*) Begleit-; (*unimportant*) nebensächlich; (*remark*) beiläufig; **~ly** *adv* übrigens

incinerator [ɪn'sɪnəretə] *n* Verbrennungsofen *m*

incision [ɪn'sɪʒən] *n* Einschnitt *m*

incisive [ɪn'saɪsɪv] *adj* (*style*) treffend; (*person*) scharfsinnig

incite [ɪn'saɪt] *vt* anstacheln

inclination [ɪnklɪ'neɪʃən] *n* Neigung *f*

incline [*n* 'ɪnklaɪn, *vb* ɪn'klaɪn] *n* Abhang *m* ♦ *vt* neigen; (*fig*) veranlassen ♦ *vi* sich neigen; **to be ~d to do sth** dazu neigen, etw zu tun

include [ɪn'kluːd] *vt* einschließen; (*on list, in group*) aufnehmen; **including** *prep*: **including X** inbegriffen; **inclusion** [ɪn'kluːʒən] *n* Aufnahme *f*, Einschluß *m*; **inclusive** [ɪn'kluːsɪv] *adj* einschließlich; (*COMM*) inclusive; **inclusive of** einschließlich +*gen*

incoherent [ɪnkəu'hɪərənt] *adj* zusammenhanglos

income ['ɪnkʌm] *n* Einkommen *nt*; (*from business*) Einkünfte *pl*; ~ **tax** *n* Lohnsteuer *f*; (*of self-employed*) Einkommenssteuer *f*

incoming ['ɪnkʌmɪŋ] *adj*: ~ **flight** eintreffende Maschine *f*

incomparable [ɪn'kɒmprəbl] *adj* unvergleichlich

incompatible [ɪnkəm'pætɪbl] adj unvereinbar; (people) unverträglich

incompetence [ɪn'kɔmpɪtns] n Unfähigkeit f; **incompetent** adj unfähig

incomplete [ɪnkəm'pliːt] adj unvollständig

incomprehensible [ɪnkɔmprɪ'hensɪbl] adj unverständlich

inconceivable [ɪnkən'siːvəbl] adj unvorstellbar

incongruous [ɪn'kɔŋgruəs] adj seltsam; (remark) unangebracht

inconsiderate [ɪnkən'sɪdərət] adj rücksichtslos

inconsistency [ɪnkən'sɪstənsɪ] n Widersprüchlichkeit f; (state) Unbeständigkeit f

inconsistent [ɪnkən'sɪstnt] adj (action, speech) widersprüchlich; (person, work) unbeständig; **~ with** nicht übereinstimmend mit

inconspicuous [ɪnkən'spɪkjuəs] adj unauffällig

incontinent [ɪn'kɔntɪnənt] adj (MED) nicht fähig, Stuhl und Harn zurückzuhalten

inconvenience [ɪnkən'viːnjəns] n Unbequemlichkeit f; (trouble to others) Unannehmlichkeiten pl

inconvenient [ɪnkən'viːnjənt] adj ungelegen; (journey) unbequem

incorporate [ɪn'kɔːpəreɪt] vt (include) aufnehmen; (contain) enthalten; **~d** adj: **~d company** (US) eingetragene Aktiengesellschaft f

incorrect [ɪnkə'rekt] adj unrichtig

incorrigible [ɪn'kɔrɪdʒɪbl] adj unverbesserlich

incorruptible [ɪnkə'rʌptɪbl] adj unzerstörbar; (person) unbestechlich

increase [n 'ɪnkriːs, vb ɪn'kriːs] n Zunahme f; (pay ~) Gehaltserhöhung f; (in size) Vergrößerung f ♦ vt erhöhen; (wealth, rage) vermehren; (business) erweitern ♦ vi zunehmen; (prices) steigen; (in size) größer werden; (in num-

ber) sich vermehren; **increasing** adj (number) steigend; **increasingly** [ɪn'kriːsɪŋlɪ] adv zunehmend

incredible [ɪn'kredɪbl] adj unglaublich

incredulous [ɪn'kredjuləs] adj ungläubig

increment ['ɪnkrɪmənt] n Zulage f

incriminate [ɪn'krɪmɪneɪt] vt belasten

incubation [ɪnkju'beɪʃən] n Ausbrüten nt

incubator ['ɪnkjubeɪtəʳ] n Brutkasten m

incumbent [ɪn'kʌmbənt] n ♦ adj: **it is ~ on him to ...** es obliegt ihm, ...

incur [ɪn'kɜːʳ] vt sich zuziehen; (debts) machen

incurable [ɪn'kjuərəbl] adj unheilbar

indebted [ɪn'detɪd] adj (obliged): **~ (to sb)** (jdm) verpflichtet

indecent [ɪn'diːsnt] adj unanständig; **~ assault** (BRIT) n Notzucht f; **~ exposure** n Exhibitionismus m

indecisive [ɪndɪ'saɪsɪv] adj (battle) nicht entscheidend; (person) unentschlossen

indeed [ɪn'diːd] adv tatsächlich, in der Tat; **yes ~!** allerdings!

indefinite [ɪn'defɪnɪt] adj unbestimmt; **~ly** adv auf unbestimmte Zeit; (wait) unbegrenzt lange

indelible [ɪn'delɪbl] adj unauslöschlich

indemnity [ɪn'demnɪtɪ] n (insurance) Versicherung f; (compensation) Entschädigung f

independence [ɪndɪ'pendns] n Unabhängigkeit f; **independent** adj unabhängig

---

Independence Day

Independence Day (der 4. Juli) ist in den USA ein gesetzlicher Feiertag zum Gedenken an die Unabhängigkeitserklärung am 4. Juli 1776, mit der die 13 amerikanischen Kolonien ihre Freiheit und Unabhängigkeit von Großbritannien erklärten.

indestructible [ɪndɪs'trʌktəbl] *adj* unzerstörbar

indeterminate [ɪndɪ'tə:mɪnɪt] *adj* unbestimmt

index ['ɪndɛks] (*pl* **~es** *or* **indices**) *n* Index *m*; **~ card** *n* Karteikarte *f*; **~ finger** *n* Zeigefinger *m*; **~-linked** (*US* **~ed**) *adj* (*salaries*) der Inflationsrate *dat* angeglichen; (*pensions*) dynamisch

India ['ɪndɪə] *n* Indien *nt*; **~n** *adj* indisch ♦ *n* Inder(in) *m(f)*; **American ~n** Indianer(in) *m(f)*; **~n Ocean** *n*: **the ~n Ocean** der Indische Ozean

indicate ['ɪndɪkeɪt] *vt* anzeigen; (*hint*) andeuten; **indication** [ɪndɪ'keɪʃən] *n* Anzeichen *nt*; (*information*) Angabe *f*; **indicative** [ɪn'dɪkətɪv] *adj*: **indicative of** bezeichnend für; **indicator** *n* (An)zeichen *nt*; (*AUT*) Richtungsanzeiger *m*

indict [ɪn'daɪt] *vt* anklagen; **~ment** *n* Anklage *f*

indifference [ɪn'dɪfrəns] *n* Gleichgültigkeit *f*; Unwichtigkeit *f*; **indifferent** *adj* gleichgültig; (*mediocre*) mäßig

indigenous [ɪn'dɪdʒɪnəs] *adj* einheimisch

indigestion [ɪndɪ'dʒɛstʃən] *n* Verdauungsstörung *f*

indignant [ɪn'dɪgnənt] *adj*: **to be ~ about sth** über etw *acc* empört sein

indignation [ɪndɪg'neɪʃən] *n* Entrüstung *f*

indignity [ɪn'dɪgnɪtɪ] *n* Demütigung *f*

indirect [ɪndɪ'rɛkt] *adj* indirekt

indiscreet [ɪndɪs'kri:t] *adj* (*insensitive*) taktlos; (*telling secrets*) indiskret; **indiscretion** [ɪndɪs'krɛʃən] *n* Taktlosigkeit *f*; Indiskretion *f*

indiscriminate [ɪndɪs'krɪmɪnət] *adj* wahllos; kritiklos

indispensable [ɪndɪs'pɛnsəbl] *adj* unentbehrlich

indisposed [ɪndɪs'pəʊzd] *adj* unpässlich

indisputable [ɪndɪs'pju:təbl] *adj* unbestreitbar; (*evidence*) unanfechtbar

indistinct [ɪndɪs'tɪŋkt] *adj* undeutlich

individual [ɪndɪ'vɪdjuəl] *n* Individuum *nt* ♦ *adj* individuell; (*case*) Einzel-; (*of, for one person*) eigen, individuell; (*characteristic*) eigentümlich; **~ly** *adv* einzeln, individuell

indivisible [ɪndɪ'vɪzɪbl] *adj* unteilbar

indoctrinate [ɪn'dɒktrɪneɪt] *vt* indoktrinieren

Indonesia [ɪndə'ni:zɪə] *n* Indonesien *nt*

indoor ['ɪndɔ:] *adj* Haus-; Zimmer-; Innen-; (*SPORT*) Hallen-; **~s** [ɪn'dɔ:z] *adv* drinnen, im Haus

induce [ɪn'dju:s] *vt* dazu bewegen; (*reaction*) herbeiführen

induction course [ɪn'dʌkʃən-] (*BRIT*) *n* Einführungskurs *m*

indulge [ɪn'dʌldʒ] *vt* (*give way*) nachgeben +*dat*; (*gratify*) frönen +*dat* ♦ *vi*: **to ~ (in)** frönen (+*dat*); **~nce** *n* Nachsicht *f*; (*enjoyment*) Genuss *m*; **~nt** *adj* nachsichtig; (*pej*) nachgiebig

industrial [ɪn'dʌstrɪəl] *adj* Industrie-, industriell; (*dispute, injury*) Arbeits-; **~ action** *n* Arbeitskampfmaßnahmen *pl*; **~ estate** (*BRIT*) *n* Industriegebiet *nt*; **~ist** *n* Industrielle(r) *mf*; **~ize** *vt* industrialisieren; **~ park** (*US*) *n* Industriegebiet *nt*

industrious [ɪn'dʌstrɪəs] *adj* fleißig

industry ['ɪndəstrɪ] *n* Industrie *f*; (*diligence*) Fleiß *m*

inebriated [ɪn'i:brɪeɪtɪd] *adj* betrunken

inedible [ɪn'ɛdɪbl] *adj* ungenießbar

ineffective [ɪnɪ'fɛktɪv] *adj* unwirksam; (*person*) untauglich

ineffectual [ɪnɪ'fɛktʃuəl] *adj* = **ineffective**

inefficiency [ɪnɪ'fɪʃənsɪ] *n* Ineffizienz *f*

inefficient [ɪnɪ'fɪʃənt] *adj* ineffizient; (*ineffective*) unwirksam

inept [ɪ'nɛpt] *adj* (*remark*) unpassend; (*person*) ungeeignet

inequality [ɪnɪ'kwɒlɪtɪ] *n* Ungleichheit *f*

inert [ɪ'nə:t] *adj* träge; (*CHEM*) inaktiv; (*motionless*) unbeweglich

inescapable [ɪnɪ'skeɪpəbl] *adj* unvermeidbar

inevitable [ɪn'evɪtəbl] *adj* unvermeidlich; **inevitably** *adv* zwangsläufig

inexcusable [ɪnɪks'kjuːzəbl] *adj* unverzeihlich

inexhaustible [ɪnɪg'zɔːstɪbl] *adj* unerschöpflich

inexpensive [ɪnɪk'spensɪv] *adj* preiswert

inexperience [ɪnɪk'spɪərɪəns] *n* Unerfahrenheit *f*; **~d** *adj* unerfahren

inexplicable [ɪnɪk'splɪkəbl] *adj* unerklärlich

inextricably [ɪnɪk'strɪkəblɪ] *adv* untrennbar

infallible [ɪn'fælɪbl] *adj* unfehlbar

infamous ['ɪnfəməs] *adj* (*deed*) schändlich; (*person*) niederträchtig

infancy ['ɪnfənsɪ] *n* frühe Kindheit *f*; (*fig*) Anfangsstadium *nt*

infant ['ɪnfənt] *n* kleine(s) Kind *nt*, Säugling *m*; **~ile** [-aɪl] *adj* kindisch, infantil; **~ school** (*BRIT*) *n* Vorschule *f*

infatuated [ɪn'fætjʊeɪtɪd] *adj* vernarrt; **to become ~ with** sich vernarren in +*acc*; **infatuation** [ɪnfætjʊ'eɪʃən] *n*: **infatuation (with)** Vernarrtheit *f* (in +*acc*)

infect [ɪn'fekt] *vt* anstecken (*also fig*); **~ed with** (*illness*) infiziert mit; **~ion** [ɪn'fekʃən] *n* Infektion *f*; **~ious** [ɪn'fekʃəs] *adj* ansteckend

infer [ɪn'fɜː*] *vt* schließen

inferior [ɪn'fɪərɪə*] *adj* (*rank*) untergeordnet; (*quality*) minderwertig ♦ *n* Untergebene(r) *m*; **~ity** [ɪnfɪərɪ'ɔrətɪ] *n* Minderwertigkeit *f*; (*in rank*) untergeordnete Stellung *f*; **~ity complex** *n* Minderwertigkeitskomplex *m*

infernal [ɪn'fɜːnl] *adj* höllisch

infertile [ɪn'fɜːtaɪl] *adj* unfruchtbar; **infertility** [ɪnfəː'tɪlɪtɪ] *n* Unfruchtbarkeit *f*

infested [ɪn'festɪd] *adj*: **to be ~ with** wimmeln von

infidelity [ɪnfɪ'delɪtɪ] *n* Untreue *f*

infighting ['ɪnfaɪtɪŋ] *n* Nahkampf *m*

infiltrate ['ɪnfɪltreɪt] *vt* infiltrieren; (*spies*) einschleusen ♦ *vi* (*MIL, liquid*) einsickern; (*POL*): **to ~ (into)** unterwandern (+*acc*)

infinite ['ɪnfɪnɪt] *adj* unendlich

infinitive [ɪn'fɪnɪtɪv] *n* Infinitiv *m*

infinity [ɪn'fɪnɪtɪ] *n* Unendlichkeit *f*

infirm [ɪn'fɜːm] *adj* gebrechlich; **~ary** *n* Krankenhaus *nt*

inflamed [ɪn'fleɪmd] *adj* entzündet

inflammable [ɪn'flæməbl] (*BRIT*) *adj* feuergefährlich

inflammation [ɪnflə'meɪʃən] *n* Entzündung *f*

inflatable [ɪn'fleɪtəbl] *adj* aufblasbar

inflate [ɪn'fleɪt] *vt* aufblasen; (*tyre*) aufpumpen; (*prices*) hoch treiben; **inflation** [ɪn'fleɪʃən] *n* Inflation *f*; **inflationary** [ɪn'fleɪʃənərɪ] *adj* (*increase*) inflationistisch; (*situation*) inflationär

inflexible [ɪn'fleksɪbl] *adj* (*person*) nicht flexibel; (*opinion*) starr; (*thing*) unbiegsam

inflict [ɪn'flɪkt] *vt*: **to ~ sth on sb** jdm etw zufügen; (*wound*) jdm etw beibringen

influence ['ɪnfluəns] *n* Einfluss *m* ♦ *vt* beeinflussen

influential [ɪnflu'enʃl] *adj* einflussreich

influenza [ɪnflu'enzə] *n* Grippe *f*

influx ['ɪnflʌks] *n* (*of people*) Zustrom *m*; (*of ideas*) Eindringen *nt*

infomercial ['ɪnfəʊməːʃl] *n* Werbeinformationssendung *f*

inform [ɪn'fɔːm] *vt* informieren ♦ *vi*: **to ~ on sb** jdn anzeigen; **to keep sb ~ed** jdn auf dem Laufenden halten

informal [ɪn'fɔːml] *adj* zwanglos; **~ity** [ɪnfɔː'mælɪtɪ] *n* Ungezwungenheit *f*

informant [ɪn'fɔːmənt] *n* Informant(in) *m(f)*

information [ɪnfə'meɪʃən] *n* Auskunft *f*, Information *f*; **a piece of ~** eine Auskunft, eine Information; **~ desk** *n* Auskunftsschalter *m*; **~ office** *n* Informationsbüro *nt*

informative [ɪn'fɔːmətɪv] adj informativ; (person) mitteilsam

informer [ɪn'fɔːmə^r] n Denunziant(in) m(f)

infra-red [ɪnfrə'red] adj infrarot

infrequent [ɪn'friːkwənt] adj selten

infringe [ɪn'frɪndʒ] vt (law) verstoßen gegen; ~ **upon** vt verletzen; ~**ment** n Verstoß m, Verletzung f

infuriating [ɪn'fjuərɪeɪtɪŋ] adj ärgerlich

ingenuity [ɪndʒɪ'njuːɪtɪ] n Genialität f

ingenuous [ɪn'dʒenjuəs] adj aufrichtig; (naive) naiv

ingot ['ɪŋgət] n Barren m

ingrained [ɪn'greɪnd] adj tief sitzend

ingratiate [ɪn'greɪʃɪeɪt] vt: **to ~ o.s. with sb** sich bei jdm einschmeicheln

ingratitude [ɪn'grætɪtjuːd] n Undankbarkeit f

ingredient [ɪn'griːdɪənt] n Bestandteil m; (COOK) Zutat f

inhabit [ɪn'hæbɪt] vt bewohnen; ~**ant** n Bewohner(in) m(f); (of island, town) Einwohner(in) m(f)

inhale [ɪn'heɪl] vt einatmen; (MED, cigarettes) inhalieren

inherent [ɪn'hɪərənt] adj: ~ **(in)** innewohnend (+dat)

inherit [ɪn'herɪt] vt erben; ~**ance** n Erbe nt, Erbschaft f

inhibit [ɪn'hɪbɪt] vt hemmen; **to ~ sb from doing sth** jdn daran hindern, etw zu tun; ~**ion** [ɪnhɪ'bɪʃən] n Hemmung f

inhospitable [ɪnhɔs'pɪtəbl] adj (person) ungastlich; (country) unwirtlich

inhuman [ɪn'hjuːmən] adj unmenschlich

initial [ɪ'nɪʃl] adj anfänglich, Anfangs-♦ n Initiale f ♦ vt abzeichnen; (POL) paraphieren; ~**ly** adv anfangs

initiate [ɪ'nɪʃɪeɪt] vt einführen; (negotiations) einleiten; **to ~ proceedings against sb** (JUR) gerichtliche Schritte gegen jdn einleiten; **initiation** [ɪnɪʃɪ'eɪʃən] n Einführung f; Einleitung f

initiative [ɪ'nɪʃətɪv] n Initiative f

inject [ɪn'dʒekt] vt einspritzen; einflößen; ~**ion** [ɪn'dʒekʃən] n Spritze f

injunction [ɪn'dʒʌŋkʃən] n Verfügung f

injure ['ɪndʒə^r] vt verletzen; ~**d** adj (person, arm) verletzt; **injury** ['ɪndʒərɪ] n Verletzung f; **to play injury time** (SPORT) nachspielen

injustice [ɪn'dʒʌstɪs] n Ungerechtigkeit f

ink [ɪŋk] n Tinte f

inkling ['ɪŋklɪŋ] n (dunkle) Ahnung f

inlaid ['ɪnleɪd] adj eingelegt, Einlege-

inland [adj 'ɪnlənd, adv ɪn'lænd] adj Binnen-; (domestic) Inlands- ♦ adv landeinwärts; **~ revenue** (BRIT) n Fiskus m

in-laws ['ɪnlɔːz] npl (parents-in-law) Schwiegereltern pl; (others) angeheiratete Verwandte pl

inlet ['ɪnlet] n Einlass m; (bay) kleine Bucht f

inmate ['ɪnmeɪt] n Insasse m

inn [ɪn] n Gasthaus m, Wirtshaus nt

innate [ɪ'neɪt] adj angeboren

inner ['ɪnə^r] adj inner, Innen-; (fig) verborgen; ~ **city** n Innenstadt f; ~ **tube** n (of tyre) Schlauch m

innings ['ɪnɪŋz] n (CRICKET) Innenrunde f

innocence ['ɪnəsns] n Unschuld f; (ignorance) Unkenntnis f

innocent ['ɪnəsnt] adj unschuldig

innocuous [ɪ'nɔkjuəs] adj harmlos

innovation [ɪnəu'veɪʃən] n Neuerung f

innuendo [ɪnju'endəu] n (versteckte) Anspielung f

innumerable [ɪ'njuːmrəbl] adj unzählig

inoculation [ɪnɔkju'leɪʃən] n Impfung f

inopportune [ɪn'ɔpətjuːn] adj (remark) unangebracht; (visit) ungelegen

inordinately [ɪ'nɔːdɪnətlɪ] adv unmäßig

inpatient ['ɪnpeɪʃənt] n stationäre(r) Patient m/stationäre Patientin f

input ['ɪnput] n (COMPUT) Eingabe f

(power ~) Energiezufuhr f; (of energy, work) Aufwand m

inquest ['ɪnkwest] n gerichtliche Untersuchung f

inquire [ɪn'kwaɪəʳ] vi sich erkundigen ♦ vt (price) sich erkundigen nach; ~ **into** vt untersuchen; **inquiry** [ɪn'kwaɪərɪ] n (question) Erkundigung f; (investigation) Untersuchung f; **inquiries** Auskunft f; **inquiry office** (BRIT) n Auskunft(sbüro n) f

inquisitive [ɪn'kwɪzɪtɪv] adj neugierig

ins. abbr = **inches**

insane [ɪn'seɪn] adj wahnsinnig; (MED) geisteskrank; **insanity** [ɪn'sænɪtɪ] n Wahnsinn m

insatiable [ɪn'seɪʃəbl] adj unersättlich

inscribe [ɪn'skraɪb] vt eingravieren; **inscription** [ɪn'skrɪpʃən] n (on stone) Inschrift f; (in book) Widmung f

insect ['ɪnsekt] n Insekt nt; ~**icide** [ɪn'sektɪsaɪd] n Insektenvertilgungsmittel nt; ~ **repellent** n Insektenbekämpfungsmittel nt

insecure [ɪnsɪ'kjuəʳ] adj (person) unsicher; (thing) nicht fest or sicher; in~**security** [ɪnsɪ'kjuərɪtɪ] n Unsicherheit f

insemination [ɪnsemɪ'neɪʃən] n: **artificial** ~ künstliche Befruchtung f

insensible [ɪn'sensɪbl] adj (unconscious) bewusstlos

insensitive [ɪn'sensɪtɪv] adj (to pain) unempfindlich; (unfeeling) gefühllos

inseparable [ɪn'sepərəbl] adj (people) unzertrennlich; (word) untrennbar

insert [vb ɪn'sɜːt, n 'ɪnsɜːt] vt einfügen; (coin) einwerfen; (stick into) hineinstecken; (advertisement) aufgeben ♦ n (in book) Einlage f; (in magazine) Beilage f; ~**ion** [ɪn'sɜːʃən] n Einfügung f; (PRESS) Inserat nt

in-service [ɪn'sɜːvɪs] adj (training) berufsbegleitend

inshore [ɪn'ʃɔːʳ] adj Küsten- ♦ adv an der Küste

inside ['ɪn'saɪd] n Innenseite f, Innere(s) nt ♦ adj innere(r, s), Innen- ♦ adv

(place) innen; (direction) nach innen, hinein ♦ prep (place) in +dat; (direction) in +acc ... hinein; (time) innerhalb +gen; ~**s** npl (inf) Eingeweide pl; ~ **10 minutes** unter 10 Minuten; ~ **information** n interne Informationen pl; ~ **lane** n (AUT: in Britain) linke Spur; ~ **out** adv linksherum; (know) in- und auswendig

insider dealing, insider trading [ɪn'saɪdə-] n (STOCK EXCHANGE) Insiderhandel m

insidious [ɪn'sɪdɪəs] adj heimtückisch

insight ['ɪnsaɪt] n Einsicht f; ~ **into** Einblick m in +acc

insignificant [ɪnsɪg'nɪfɪknt] adj unbedeutend

insincere [ɪnsɪn'sɪəʳ] adj unaufrichtig

insinuate [ɪn'sɪnjueɪt] vt (hint) andeuten

insipid [ɪn'sɪpɪd] adj fad(e)

insist [ɪn'sɪst] vi: **to** ~ **(on)** bestehen (auf +acc); ~**ence** n Bestehen nt; ~**ent** adj hartnäckig; (urgent) dringend

insole ['ɪnsəʊl] n Einlegesohle f

insolence ['ɪnsələns] n Frechheit f

insolent ['ɪnsələnt] adj frech

insoluble [ɪn'sɔljubl] adj unlösbar; (CHEM) unlöslich

insolvent [ɪn'sɔlvənt] adj zahlungsunfähig

insomnia [ɪn'sɔmnɪə] n Schlaflosigkeit f

inspect [ɪn'spekt] vt prüfen; (officially) inspizieren; ~**ion** [ɪn'spekʃən] n Inspektion f; ~**or** n (official) Inspektor m; (police) Polizeikommissar m; (BRIT: on buses, trains) Kontrolleur m

inspiration [ɪnspə'reɪʃən] n Inspiration f

inspire [ɪn'spaɪəʳ] vt (person) inspirieren; **to** ~ **sth in sb** (respect) jdm etw einflößen; (hope) etw in jdm wecken

instability [ɪnstə'bɪlɪtɪ] n Unbeständigkeit f, Labilität f

install [ɪn'stɔːl] vt (put in) installieren; (telephone) anschließen; (establish) einsetzen; **~ation** [ɪnstə'leɪʃən] n (of person) (Amts)einsetzung f; (of machinery) Installierung f; (machines etc) Anlage f

instalment [ɪn'stɔːlmənt] (US **installment**) n Rate f; (of story) Fortsetzung f; **to pay in ~s** in Raten zahlen

instance ['ɪnstəns] n Fall m; (example) Beispiel nt; **for ~** zum Beispiel; **in the first ~** zunächst

instant ['ɪnstənt] n Augenblick m ♦ adj augenblicklich, sofortig; **~aneous** [ɪnstən'teɪnɪəs] adj unmittelbar; **~ coffee** n Pulverkaffee m; **~ly** adv sofort

instead [ɪn'sted] adv stattdessen; **~ of** prep anstatt +gen

instep ['ɪnstep] n Spann m; (of shoe) Blatt nt

instil [ɪn'stɪl] vt (fig): **to ~ sth in sb** jdm etw beibringen

instinct ['ɪnstɪŋkt] n Instinkt m; **~ive** [ɪn'stɪŋktɪv] adj instinktiv

institute ['ɪnstɪtjuːt] n Institut m ♦ vt einführen; (search) einleiten

institution [ɪnstɪ'tjuːʃən] n Institution f; (home) Anstalt f

instruct [ɪn'strʌkt] vt anweisen; (officially) instruieren; **~ion** [ɪn'strʌkʃən] n Unterricht m; **~ions** npl (orders) Anweisungen pl; (for use) Gebrauchsanweisung f; **~or** n Lehrer m

instrument ['ɪnstrəmənt] n Instrument nt; **~al** [ɪnstru'mentl] adj (MUS) Instrumental-; (helpful): **to be ~al** in behilflich (bei); **~ panel** n Armaturenbrett nt

insubordinate [ɪnsə'bɔːdɪnɪt] adj aufsässig, widersetzlich

insufferable [ɪn'sʌfrəbl] adj unerträglich

insufficient [ɪnsə'fɪʃənt] adj ungenügend

insular ['ɪnsjulə] adj (fig) engstirnig

insulate ['ɪnsjuleɪt] vt (ELEC) isolieren; (fig): **to ~ (from)** abschirmen (vor +dat); **insulating tape** n Isolierband nt; **insulation** [ɪnsju'leɪʃən] n Isolierung f

insulin ['ɪnsjulɪn] n Insulin n

insult [n 'ɪnsʌlt, vb ɪn'sʌlt] n Beleidigung f ♦ vt beleidigen

insurance [ɪn'ʃuərəns] n Versicherung f; **fire/life ~** Feuer-/Lebensversicherung; **~ agent** n Versicherungsvertreter m; **~ policy** n Versicherungspolice f

insure [ɪn'ʃuə] vt versichern

intact [ɪn'tækt] adj unversehrt

intake ['ɪnteɪk] n (place) Einlassöffnung f; (act) Aufnahme f; (BRIT: SCH): **an ~ of 200 a year** ein Neuzugang von 200 im Jahr

intangible [ɪn'tændʒəbl] adj nicht greifbar

integral ['ɪntɪgrəl] adj (essential) wesentlich; (complete) vollständig; (MATH) Integral-

integrate ['ɪntɪgreɪt] vt integrieren ♦ vi sich integrieren

integrity [ɪn'tegrɪtɪ] n (honesty) Redlichkeit f, Integrität f

intellect ['ɪntəlekt] n Intellekt m; **~ual** [ɪntə'lektjuəl] adj geistig, intellektuell ♦ n Intellektuelle(r) mf

intelligence [ɪn'telɪdʒəns] n (understanding) Intelligenz f; (news) Information f; (MIL) Geheimdienst m; **~ ser-vice** n Nachrichtendienst m, Geheimdienst m

intelligent [ɪn'telɪdʒənt] adj intelligent; **~ly** adv klug; (write, speak) verständlich

intelligentsia [ɪntelɪ'dʒentsɪə] n Intelligenz f

intelligible [ɪn'telɪdʒɪbl] adj verständlich

intend [ɪn'tend] vt beabsichtigen; **that was ~ed for you** das war für dich gedacht

intense [ɪn'tens] adj stark, intensiv; (person) ernsthaft; **~ly** adv äußerst; (study) intensiv

intensify [ɪn'tensɪfaɪ] vt verstärken, intensivieren

intensity [ɪn'tensɪtɪ] n Intensität f

intensive [ɪn'tɛnsɪv] *adj* intensiv; **~ care unit** *n* Intensivstation *f*

intent [ɪn'tɛnt] *n* Absicht *f* ♦ *adj*: **to be ~ on doing sth** fest entschlossen sein, etw zu tun; **to all ~s and purposes** praktisch

intention [ɪn'tɛnʃən] *n* Absicht *f*; **~al** *adj* absichtlich

intently [ɪn'tɛntlɪ] *adv* konzentriert

interact [ɪntər'ækt] *vi* aufeinander einwirken; **~ion** [ɪntər'ækʃən] *n* Wechselwirkung *f*; **~ive** *adj* (COMPUT) interaktiv

intercept [ɪntə'sɛpt] *vt* abfangen

interchange [*n* 'ɪntətʃeɪndʒ], *vb* [ɪntə'tʃeɪndʒ] *n* (exchange) Austausch *m*; (on roads) Verkehrskreuz *nt* ♦ *vt* austauschen; **~able** [ɪntə'tʃeɪndʒəbl] *adj* austauschbar

intercom ['ɪntəkɒm] *n* (Gegen)sprechanlage *f*

intercourse ['ɪntəkɔːs] *n* (exchange) Beziehungen *pl*; (sexual) Geschlechtsverkehr *m*

interest ['ɪntrɪst] *n* Interesse *nt*; (FIN) Zinsen *pl*; (COMM: share) Anteil *m*; (group) Interessengruppe *f* ♦ *vt* interessieren; **~ed** *adj* (having claims) beteiligt; (attentive) interessiert; **to be ~ed in** sich interessieren für; **~ing** *adj* interessant; **~ rate** *n* Zinssatz *m*

interface ['ɪntəfeɪs] *n* (COMPUT) Schnittstelle *f*, Interface *nt*

interfere [ɪntə'fɪə] *vi*: **to ~ (with)** (meddle) sich einmischen (in +acc); (disrupt) stören +acc; **~nce** [ɪntə'fɪərəns] *n* Einmischung *f*; (TV) Störung *f*

interim ['ɪntərɪm] *n*: **in the ~** inzwischen

interior [ɪn'tɪərɪə] *n* Innere(s) *nt* ♦ *adj* innere(r, s), Innen-; **~ designer** *n* Innenarchitekt(in) *m(f)*

interjection [ɪntə'dʒɛkʃən] *n* Ausruf *m*

interlock [ɪntə'lɒk] *vi* ineinander greifen

interlude ['ɪntəluːd] *n* Pause *f*

intermediary [ɪntə'miːdɪərɪ] *n* Ver-

intermediate [ɪntə'miːdɪət] *adj* Zwischen-, Mittel-

interminable [ɪn'tɜːmɪnəbl] *adj* endlos

intermission [ɪntə'mɪʃən] *n* Pause *f*

intermittent [ɪntə'mɪtnt] *adj* periodisch, stoßweise

intern [*vb* ɪn'tɜːn, *n* 'ɪntɜːn] *vt* internieren ♦ *n* (US) Assistenzarzt *m*/-ärztin *f*

internal [ɪn'tɜːnl] *adj* (inside) innere(r, s); (domestic) Inlands-; **~ly** *adv* innen; (MED) innerlich; **"not to be taken ~ly"** "nur zur äußerlichen Anwendung"; **Internal Revenue Service** (US) *n* Finanzamt *nt*

international [ɪntə'næʃənl] *adj* international; *n* (SPORT) Nationalspieler(in) *m(f)*; (: match) internationale(s) Spiel *nt*

Internet ['ɪntənɛt] *n*: **the ~** das Internet; **~ café** *n* Internet-Café *nt*

interplay ['ɪntəpleɪ] *n* Wechselspiel *nt*

interpret [ɪn'tɜːprɪt] *vt* (explain) auslegen, interpretieren; (translate) dolmetschen; **~er** *n* Dolmetscher(in) *m(f)*

interrelated [ɪntərɪ'leɪtɪd] *adj* untereinander zusammenhängend

interrogate [ɪn'tɛrəgeɪt] *vt* verhören; **interrogation** [ɪntɛrə'geɪʃən] *n* Verhör *nt*

interrupt [ɪntə'rʌpt] *vt* unterbrechen; **~ion** [ɪntə'rʌpʃən] *n* Unterbrechung *f*

intersect [ɪntə'sɛkt] *vt* (durch)schneiden ♦ *vi* sich schneiden; **~ion** [ɪntə'sɛkʃən] *n* (of roads) Kreuzung *f*; (of lines) Schnittpunkt *m*

intersperse [ɪntə'spɜːs] *vt*: **to ~ sth with sth** etw mit etw durchsetzen

intertwine [ɪntə'twaɪn] *vt* verflechten ♦ *vi* sich verflechten

interval ['ɪntəvl] *n* Abstand *m*; (BRIT: THEAT, SPORT) Pause *f*; **at ~s** in Abständen

intervene [ɪntə'viːn] *vi* dazwischenliegen; (act): **to ~ (in)** einschreiten (gegen); **intervention** [ɪntə'vɛnʃən] *n* Eingreifen *nt*, Intervention *f*

interview ['ɪntəvjuː] *n* (PRESS etc) Interview *nt*; (*for job*) Vorstellungsgespräch *nt* ♦ *vt* interviewen; **~er** *n* Interviewer *m*

intestine [ɪn'testɪn] *n*: **large/small ~** Dick-/Dünndarm *m*

intimacy ['ɪntɪməsɪ] *n* Intimität *f*

intimate [*adj* 'ɪntɪmət, *vb* 'ɪntɪmeɪt] *adj* (*inmost*) innerste(r, s); (*knowledge*) eingehend; (*familiar*) vertraut; (*friends*) eng ♦ *vt* andeuten

intimidate [ɪn'tɪmɪdeɪt] *vt* einschüchtern

into ['ɪntʊ] *prep* (*motion*) in *+acc* ... hinein; **5 ~ 25** 25 durch 5

intolerable [ɪn'tɔlərəbl] *adj* unerträglich

intolerant [ɪn'tɔlrnt] *adj*: **~ of** unduldsam gegen(über)

intoxicate [ɪn'tɔksɪkeɪt] *vt* berauschen; **~d** *adj* betrunken; **intoxication** [ɪntɔksɪ'keɪʃən] *n* Rausch *m*

intractable [ɪn'træktəbl] *adj* schwer zu handhaben; (*problem*) schwer lösbar

intranet [ɪn'trænət] *n* (COMPUT) Intranet *nt*

intransitive [ɪn'trænsɪtɪv] *adj* intransitiv

intravenous [ɪntrə'viːnəs] *adj* intravenös

in-tray ['ɪntreɪ] *n* Eingangskorb *m*

intrepid [ɪn'trepɪd] *adj* unerschrocken

intricate ['ɪntrɪkət] *adj* kompliziert

intrigue [ɪn'triːg] *n* Intrige *f* ♦ *vt* faszinieren ♦ *vi* intrigieren

intrinsic [ɪn'trɪnsɪk] *adj* innere(r, s); (*difference*) wesentlich

introduce [ɪntrə'djuːs] *vt* (*person*) vorstellen; (*sth new*) einführen; (*subject*) anschneiden; **to ~ sb to sb** jdm jdn vorstellen; **to ~ sb to sth** jdn in etw *acc* einführen; **introduction** [ɪntrə'dʌkʃən] *n* Einführung *f*; (*to book*) Einleitung *f*; **introductory** [ɪntrə-'dʌktərɪ] *adj* Einführungs-, Vor-

introspective [ɪntrə'spektɪv] *adj* nach innen gekehrt

introvert ['ɪntrəuvɜːt] *n* Introvertier-

te(r) *mf* ♦ *adj* introvertiert

intrude [ɪn'truːd] *vi*: **to ~ (on sb/sth)** (jdn/etw) stören; **~r** *n* Eindringling *m*

intrusion [ɪn'truːʒən] *n* Störung *f*

intrusive [ɪn'truːsɪv] *adj* aufdringlich

intuition [ɪntjuː'ɪʃən] *n* Intuition *f*

inundate ['ɪnʌndeɪt] *vt* (*also fig*) überschwemmen

invade [ɪn'veɪd] *vt* einfallen in *+acc*; **~r** *n* Eindringling *m*

invalid¹ ['ɪnvəlɪd] *n* (*disabled*) Invalide *m* ♦ *adj* (*ill*) krank; (*disabled*) invalide

invalid² [ɪn'vælɪd] *adj* (*not valid*) ungültig

invaluable [ɪn'væljuəbl] *adj* unschätzbar

invariable [ɪn'vɛərɪəbl] *adj* unveränderlich; **invariably** *adv* ausnahmslos

invent [ɪn'vent] *vt* erfinden; **~ion** [ɪn'venʃən] *n* Erfindung *f*; **~ive** *adj* erfinderisch; **~or** *n* Erfinder *m*

inventory ['ɪnvəntrɪ] *n* Inventar *nt*

inverse [ɪn'vɜːs] *n* Umkehrung *f* ♦ *adj* umgekehrt

invert [ɪn'vɜːt] *vt* umdrehen; **~ed commas** (BRIT) *npl* Anführungsstriche *pl*

invest [ɪn'vest] *vt* investieren

investigate [ɪn'vestɪgeɪt] *vt* untersuchen; **investigation** [ɪnvestɪ'geɪʃən] *n* Untersuchung *f*; **investigator** [ɪn'vestɪgeɪtə'] *n* Untersuchungsbeamte(r) *m*

investiture [ɪn'vestɪtʃə'] *n* Amtseinsetzung *f*

investment [ɪn'vestmənt] *n* Investition *f*

investor [ɪn'vestə'] *n* (Geld)anleger *m*

invigilate [ɪn'vɪdʒɪleɪt] *vi* (*in exam*) Aufsicht führen ♦ *vt* Aufsicht führen bei; **invigilator** *n* Aufsicht *f*

invigorating [ɪn'vɪgəreɪtɪŋ] *adj* stärkend

invincible [ɪn'vɪnsɪbl] *adj* unbesiegbar

invisible [ɪn'vɪzɪbl] *adj* unsichtbar

invitation [ɪnvɪ'teɪʃən] *n* Einladung *f*

invite [ɪn'vaɪt] *vt* einladen

invoice ['ɪnvɔɪs] *n* Rechnung *f* ♦ *vt*

(goods): **to ~ sb for sth** jdm etw acc in Rechnung stellen

invoke [ɪnˈvəʊk] vt anrufen

involuntary [ɪnˈvɒləntrɪ] adj unabsichtlich

involve [ɪnˈvɒlv] vt (entangle) verwickeln; (entail) mit sich bringen; **~d** adj verwickelt; **~ment** n Verwicklung f

inward [ˈɪnwəd] adj innere(r, s); (curve) Innen- ♦ adv nach innen; **~ly** adv im Innern; **~s** adv nach innen

I/O abbr (COMPUT) (= input/output) I/O

iodine [ˈaɪəʊdiːn] n Jod nt

ioniser [ˈaɪənaɪzə] n Ionisator m

iota [aɪˈəʊtə] n (fig) bisschen nt

IOU n abbr (= I owe you) Schuldschein m

IQ n abbr (= intelligence quotient) IQ m

IRA n abbr (= Irish Republican Army) IRA f

Iran [ɪˈrɑːn] n Iran m; **~ian** [ɪˈreɪnɪən] adj iranisch ♦ n Iraner(in) f(m); (LING) Iranisch nt

Iraq [ɪˈrɑːk] n Irak m; **~i** adj irakisch ♦ n Iraker(in) m(f)

irate [aɪˈreɪt] adj zornig

Ireland [ˈaɪələnd] n Irland nt

iris [ˈaɪrɪs] (pl **~es**) n Iris f

Irish [ˈaɪrɪʃ] adj irisch ♦ npl: **the ~** die Iren pl, die Irländer pl; **~man** (irreg) n Ire m, Irländer m; **~ Sea** n: **the ~ Sea** die Irische See f; **~woman** (irreg) n Irin f, Irländerin f

irksome [ˈəːksəm] adj lästig

iron [ˈaɪən] n Eisen nt; (for ~ing) Bügeleisen nt ♦ adj eisern ♦ vt bügeln; **~ out** vt (also fig) ausbügeln; **Iron Curtain** n (HIST) Eiserne(r) Vorhang m

ironic(al) [aɪˈrɒnɪk(l)] adj ironisch; (coincidence) witzig

iron: ~ing n Bügeln nt; (laundry) Bügelwäsche f; **~ing board** n Bügelbrett nt; **~monger's (shop)** n Eisen- und Haushaltswarenhandlung f

irony [ˈaɪrənɪ] n Ironie f

irrational [ɪˈræʃənl] adj irrational

irreconcilable [ɪrekənˈsaɪləbl] adj unvereinbar

irrefutable [ɪrɪˈfjuːtəbl] adj unwider-

legbar

irregular [ɪˈregjʊlə] adj unregelmäßig; (shape) ungleich(mäßig); (fig) unüblich; (: behaviour) ungehörig

irrelevant [ɪˈreləvənt] adj belanglos, irrelevant

irreparable [ɪˈreprəbl] adj nicht wieder gutzumachen

irreplaceable [ɪrɪˈpleɪsəbl] adj unersetzlich

irresistible [ɪrɪˈzɪstɪbl] adj unwiderstehlich

irrespective [ɪrɪˈspektɪv]: **~ of** prep ungeachtet +gen

irresponsible [ɪrɪˈspɒnsɪbl] adj verantwortungslos

irreverent [ɪˈrevərənt] adj respektlos

irrevocable [ɪˈrevəkəbl] adj unwiderrufbar

irrigate [ˈɪrɪgeɪt] vt bewässern

irritable [ˈɪrɪtəbl] adj reizbar

irritate [ˈɪrɪteɪt] vt irritieren, reizen (also MED); **irritating** adj ärgerlich, irritierend; **he is irritating** er kann einem auf die Nerven gehen; **irritation** [ɪrɪˈteɪʃən] n (anger) Ärger m; (MED) Reizung f

IRS n abbr = Internal Revenue Service

is [ɪz] vb see **be**

Islam [ˈɪzlɑːm] n Islam m; **~ic** [ɪzˈlæmɪk] adj islamisch

island [ˈaɪlənd] n Insel f; **~er** n Inselbewohner(in) m(f)

isle [aɪl] n (kleine) Insel f

isn't [ɪznt] = **is not**

isolate [ˈaɪsəleɪt] vt isolieren; **~d** adj isoliert; (case) Einzel-; **isolation** [aɪsəˈleɪʃən] n Isolierung f

Israel [ˈɪzreɪl] n Israel nt; **~i** [ɪzˈreɪlɪ] adj israelisch ♦ n Israeli mf

issue [ˈɪʃuː] n (matter) Frage f; (outcome) Ausgang m; (of newspaper, shares) Ausgabe f; (offspring) Nachkommenschaft f ♦ vt ausgeben; (warrant) erlassen; (documents) ausstellen; (orders) erteilen; (books) herausgeben; (verdict) aussprechen; **to be at ~** zur Debatte stehen; **to take ~ with sb over sth** jdm in etw *dat* widersprechen

KEYWORD

it [ɪt] *pron* **1** (*specific: subject*) er/sie/es; (*: direct object*) ihn/sie/es; (*: indirect object*) ihm/ihr/ihm; **about/from/in/of it** darüber/davon/darin/davon
2 (*impers*) es; **it's raining** es regnet; **it's Friday tomorrow** morgen ist Freitag; **who is it? – it's me** wer ist da? – ich (bins)

Italian [ɪ'tæljən] *adj* italienisch ♦ *n* Italiener(in) *m(f)*; (*LING*) Italienisch *nt*
italic [ɪ'tælɪk] *adj* kursiv; **~s** *npl* Kursivschrift *f*
Italy ['ɪtəlɪ] *n* Italien *nt*
itch [ɪtʃ] *n* Juckreiz *m*; (*fig*) Lust *f* ♦ *vi* jucken; **to be ~ing to do sth** darauf brennen, etw zu tun; **~y** *adj* juckend
it'd ['ɪtd] = **it would**; **it had**
item ['aɪtəm] *n* Gegenstand *m*; (*on list*) Posten *m*; (*in programme*) Nummer *f*; (*in agenda*) (Programm)punkt *m*; (*in newspaper*) (Zeitungs)notiz *f*; **~ize** *vt* verzeichnen
itinerant [ɪ'tɪnərənt] *adj* (*person*) umherreisend
itinerary [aɪ'tɪnərərɪ] *n* Reiseroute *f*
it'll ['ɪtl] = **it will**; **it shall**
its [ɪts] *adj* (*masculine, neuter*) sein; (*feminine*) ihr
it's [ɪts] = **it is**; **it has**
itself [ɪt'self] *pron* sich (selbst); (*emphatic*) selbst
ITV (*BRIT*) *n abbr* = **Independent Television**
I.U.D. *n abbr* (= *intra-uterine device*) Pessar *nt*
I've [aɪv] = **I have**
ivory ['aɪvərɪ] *n* Elfenbein *nt*
ivy ['aɪvɪ] *n* Efeu *m*

J, j

jab [dʒæb] *vt* (hinein)stechen ♦ *n* Stich *m*, Stoß *m*; (*inf*) Spritze *f*
jack [dʒæk] *n* (*AUT*) (Wagen)heber *m*; (*CARDS*) Bube *m*; **~ up** *vt* aufbocken
jackal ['dʒækl] *n* (*ZOOL*) Schakal *m*
jackdaw ['dʒækdɔ:] *n* Dohle *f*
jacket ['dʒækɪt] *n* Jacke *f*; (*of book*) Schutzumschlag *m*; (*TECH*) Ummantelung *f*; **~ potatoes** *npl* in der Schale gebackene Kartoffeln *pl*
jackknife ['dʒæknaɪf] *vi* (*truck*) sich zusammenschieben
jack plug *n* (*ELEC*) Buchsenstecker *m*
jackpot ['dʒækpɔt] *n* Haupttreffer *m*
jaded ['dʒeɪdɪd] *adj* ermattet
jagged ['dʒægɪd] *adj* zackig
jail [dʒeɪl] *n* Gefängnis *nt* ♦ *vt* einsperren; **~er** *n* Gefängniswärter *m*
jam [dʒæm] *n* Marmelade *f*; (*also: traffic ~*) (Verkehrs)stau *m*; (*inf: trouble*) Klemme *f* ♦ *vt* (*wedge*) einklemmen; (*cram*) hineinzwängen; (*obstruct*) blockieren ♦ *vi* sich verklemmen; **to ~ sth into sth** etw in etw *acc* hineinstopfen
Jamaica [dʒə'meɪkə] *n* Jamaika *f*
jam jar *n* Marmeladenglas *nt*
jammed [dʒæmd] *adj*: **it's ~** es klemmt
jam-packed [dʒæm'pækt] *adj* überfüllt, proppenvoll
jangle ['dʒæŋgl] *vt*, *vi* klimpern
janitor ['dʒænɪtə*] *n* Hausmeister *m*
January ['dʒænjʊərɪ] *n* Januar *m*
Japan [dʒə'pæn] *n* Japan *nt*; **~ese** [dʒæpə'ni:z] *adj* japanisch ♦ *n inv* Japaner(in) *m(f)*; (*LING*) Japanisch *nt*
jar [dʒɑ:*] *n* Glas *nt* ♦ *vi* kreischen; (*colours etc*) nicht harmonieren
jargon ['dʒɑ:gən] *n* Fachsprache *f*, Jargon *m*
jaundice ['dʒɔ:ndɪs] *n* Gelbsucht *f*; **~d** *adj* (*fig*) missgünstig
jaunt [dʒɔ:nt] *n* Spritztour *f*

javelin ['dʒævlɪn] n Speer m

jaw [dʒɔː] n Kiefer m

jay [dʒeɪ] n (ZOOL) Eichelhäher m

jaywalker ['dʒeɪwɔːkə(r)] n unvorsichtige(r) Fußgänger m

jazz [dʒæz] n Jazz m; **~ up** vt (MUS) verjazzen; (enliven) aufpolieren

jealous ['dʒeləs] adj (envious) missgünstig; (husband) eifersüchtig; **~y** n Missgunst f; Eifersucht f

jeans [dʒiːnz] npl Jeans pl

Jeep [dʒiːp] ® n Jeep m ®

jeer [dʒɪə(r)] vi: **to ~ (at sb)** (über jdn) höhnisch lachen, (jdn) verspotten

Jehovah's Witness [dʒɪ'həʊvəz-] n Zeuge m/Zeugin f Jehovas

jelly ['dʒelɪ] n Gelee nt; (dessert) Grütze f; **~fish** n Qualle f

jeopardize ['dʒepədaɪz] vt gefährden

jeopardy ['dʒepədɪ] n: **to be in jeopardy** in Gefahr sein

jerk [dʒɜːk] n Ruck m; (inf: idiot) Trottel m ♦ vt ruckartig bewegen ♦ vi sich ruckartig bewegen

jerky ['dʒɜːkɪ] adj (movement) ruckartig; (ride) rüttelnd

jersey ['dʒɜːzɪ] n Pullover m

jest [dʒest] n Scherz m ♦ vi spaßen; **in ~** im Spaß

Jesus ['dʒiːzəs] n Jesus m

jet [dʒet] n (stream of water etc) Strahl m; (spout) Düse f; (AVIAT) Düsenflugzeug nt; **~-black** adj rabenschwarz; **~ engine** n Düsenmotor m; **~ lag** n Jetlag m

jettison ['dʒetɪsn] vt über Bord werfen

jetty ['dʒetɪ] n Landesteg m, Mole f

Jew [dʒuː] n Jude m

jewel ['dʒuːəl] n (also fig) Juwel nt; **~ler** (US **jeweler**) n Juwelier m; **~ler's (shop)** n Juwelier m, **~lery** (US **jewelry**) n Schmuck m

Jewess ['dʒuːɪs] n Jüdin f

Jewish ['dʒuːɪʃ] adj jüdisch

jibe [dʒaɪb] n spöttische Bemerkung f

jiffy ['dʒɪfɪ] (inf) n: **in a ~** sofort

jigsaw ['dʒɪgsɔː] n (also: **~ puzzle**) Puzzle(spiel) nt

jilt [dʒɪlt] vt den Laufpass geben +dat

jingle ['dʒɪŋgl] n (advertisement) Werbesong m ♦ vi klimpern; (bells) bimmeln ♦ vt klimpern mit; bimmeln lassen

jinx [dʒɪŋks] n: **there's a ~ on it** es ist verhext

jitters ['dʒɪtəz] (inf) npl: **to get the ~** einen Bammel kriegen

job [dʒɒb] n (piece of work) Arbeit f; (position) Stellung f; (duty) Aufgabe f; (difficulty) Mühe f; **it's a good ~ he ...** es ist ein Glück, dass er ...; **just the ~** genau das Richtige; **J~centre** (BRIT) n Arbeitsamt nt; **~less** adj arbeitslos

jockey ['dʒɒkɪ] n Jockei m, Jockey m ♦ vi: **to ~ for position** sich in eine gute Position drängeln

jocular ['dʒɒkjʊlə(r)] adj scherzhaft

jog [dʒɒg] vt (an)stoßen ♦ vi (run) joggen; **to ~ along** vor sich acc hinwursteln; (work) seinen Gang gehen; **~ging** n Jogging nt

join [dʒɔɪn] vt (club) beitreten +dat; (person) sich anschließen +dat; (fasten); **to ~ (sth to sth)** (etw mit etw) verbinden ♦ vi (unite) sich vereinigen ♦ n Verbindungsstelle f, Naht f; **~ in** vt, vi: **to ~ in (sth)** (bei etw) mitmachen; **~ up** vi (MIL) zur Armee gehen

joiner ['dʒɔɪnə(r)] n Schreiner m; **~y** n Schreinerei f

joint [dʒɔɪnt] n (TECH) Fuge f; (of bones) Gelenk nt; (of meat) Braten m; (inf: place) Lokal nt ♦ adj gemeinsam; **~ account** n (with bank etc) gemeinsame(s) Konto nt; **~ly** adv gemeinsam

joke [dʒəʊk] n Witz m ♦ vi Witze machen; **to play a ~ on sb** jdm einen Streich spielen; **~r** n Witzbold m; (CARDS) Joker m

jolly ['dʒɒlɪ] adj lustig ♦ adv (inf) ganz schön

jolt [dʒəʊlt] n (shock) Schock m; (jerk) Stoß m ♦ vt (push) stoßen; (shake) durchschütteln; (fig) aufrütteln ♦ vi holpern

Jordan ['dʒɔːdən] n Jordanien nt

jostle ['dʒɒsl] vt anrempeln

jot [dʒɒt] n: **not one ~** kein Jota nt; **~ down** vt notieren; **~ter** (BRIT) n Notizblock m

journal ['dʒɜːnl] n (diary) Tagebuch nt; (magazine) Zeitschrift f; (of journalism m; **~ist** n Journalist(in) m(f)

journey ['dʒɜːnɪ] n Reise f

jovial ['dʒəuvɪəl] adj jovial

joy [dʒɔɪ] n Freude f; **~ful** adj freudig; **~ous** adj freudig; **~ ride** n Schwarzfahrt f; **~rider** n Autodieb, der den Wagen nur für eine Spritztour stiehlt; **~stick** n Steuerknüppel m; (COMPUT) Joystick m

J.P. n abbr = Justice of the Peace

Jr abbr = junior

jubilant ['dʒuːbɪlnt] adj triumphierend

jubilee ['dʒuːbɪliː] n Jubiläum nt

judge [dʒʌdʒ] n Richter m; (fig) Kenner m ♦ vt (JUR: person) die Verhandlung führen über +acc; (case) verhandeln; (assess) beurteilen; (estimate) einschätzen; **~ment** n (JUR) Urteil nt; (ECCL) Gericht nt; (ability) Urteilsvermögen nt

judicial [dʒuːˈdɪʃl] adj gerichtlich, Justiz-

judiciary [dʒuːˈdɪʃɪərɪ] n Gerichtsbehörden pl; (judges) Richterstand m

judicious [dʒuːˈdɪʃəs] adj weise

judo ['dʒuːdəu] n Judo nt

jug [dʒʌg] n Krug m

juggernaut ['dʒʌgənɔːt] (BRIT) n (huge truck) Schwertransporter m

juggle ['dʒʌgl] vi jonglieren; **~r** n Jongleur m

Jugoslav etc ['juːgəuˈslɑːv] = **Yugoslav** etc

juice [dʒuːs] n Saft m; **juicy** ['dʒuːsɪ] adj (also fig) saftig

jukebox ['dʒuːkbɒks] n Musikautomat m

July [dʒuːˈlaɪ] n Juli m

jumble ['dʒʌmbl] n Durcheinander nt

♦ vt (also: **~ up**) durcheinander werfen; (facts) durcheinander bringen; **~ sale** (BRIT) n Basar m, Flohmarkt m

---
Jumble sale

Jumble sale ist ein Wohltätigkeitsbasar, meist in einer Aula oder einem Gemeindehaus abgehalten, bei dem alle möglichen Gebrauchtwaren (vor allem Kleidung, Spielzeug, Bücher, Geschirr und Möbel) verkauft werden. Der Erlös fließt entweder einer Wohltätigkeitsorganisation zu oder wird für örtliche Zwecke verwendet, z.B. die Pfadfinder, die Grundschule, Reparatur der Kirche usw.

jumbo (jet) ['dʒʌmbəu-] n Jumbo(jet) m

jump [dʒʌmp] vi springen; (nervously) zusammenzucken ♦ vt überspringen ♦ n Sprung m; **to ~ the queue** (BRIT) sich vordrängeln

jumper ['dʒʌmpə*] n (BRIT: pullover) Pullover m; (US: dress) Trägerkleid nt

jump leads, jumper cables US npl Überbrückungskabel nt

jumpy ['dʒʌmpɪ] adj nervös

Jun. abbr = junior

junction ['dʒʌŋkʃən] n (BRIT: of roads) (Straßen)kreuzung f; (RAIL) Knotenpunkt m

juncture ['dʒʌŋktʃə*] n: **at this ~** in diesem Augenblick

June [dʒuːn] n Juni m

jungle ['dʒʌŋgl] n Dschungel m

junior ['dʒuːnɪə*] adj (younger) jünger; (after name) junior; (SPORT) Junioren-; (lower position) untergeordnet; (for young people) Junioren- ♦ n Jüngere(r) mf; **~ school** (BRIT) n Grundschule f

junk [dʒʌŋk] n (rubbish) Plunder m; (ship) Dschunke f; **~ bond** n (COMM) niedrig eingestufte Wertpapier mit hohen Ertragschancen bei erhöhtem Risiko; **~ food** n Junk food nt; **~ mail** n Reklame, die unangefordert in den

Briefkasten gesteckt wird; ~ **shop** *n*
Ramschladen *m*

Junr *abbr* = **junior**

jurisdiction [dʒuərɪs'dɪkʃən] *n* Gerichtsbarkeit *f;* *(range of authority)* Zuständigkeit(sbereich *m*) *f*

juror ['dʒuərər] *n* Geschworene(r) *mf;* *(in competition)* Preisrichter *m*

jury ['dʒuərɪ] *n (court)* Geschworene *pl;* *(panel)* Jury *f*

just [dʒʌst] *adj* gerecht ♦ *adv (recently, now)* gerade, eben; *(barely)* gerade noch; *(exactly)* genau, gerade; *(only)* nur, bloß; *(a small distance)* gleich; *(absolutely)* einfach; ~ **as I arrived** gerade als ich ankam; ~ **as nice** genauso nett; ~ **as well** umso besser; ~ **now** soeben, gerade; ~ **try** versuch es mal; **she's ~ left** sie ist gerade *or* (so)eben gegangen; **he's ~ done it** er hat es gerade *or* (so)eben getan; ~ **before** gerade *or* kurz bevor; ~ **enough** gerade genug; **he ~ missed** er hat fast *or* beinahe getroffen

justice ['dʒʌstɪs] *n (fairness)* Gerechtigkeit *f;* **J~ of the Peace** *n* Friedensrichter *m*

justifiable [dʒʌstɪ'faɪəbl] *adj* berechtigt

justification [dʒʌstɪfɪ'keɪʃən] *n* Rechtfertigung *f*

justify ['dʒʌstɪfaɪ] *vt* rechtfertigen; *(text)* justieren

justly ['dʒʌstlɪ] *adv (say)* mit Recht; *(condemn)* gerecht

jut [dʒʌt] *vi (also:* ~ **out)** herausragen, vorstehen

juvenile ['dʒuːvənaɪl] *adj (young)* jugendlich; *(for the young)* Jugend- ♦ *n* Jugendliche(r) *mf*

juxtapose ['dʒʌkstəpəuz] *vt* nebeneinander stellen

K, k

K [keɪ] *abbr* (= *one thousand*) Tsd.; (= *kilobyte*) K

kangaroo [kæŋgə'ruː] *n* Känguru *nt*

karate [kə'rɑːtɪ] *n* Karate *nt*

kebab [kə'bæb] *n* Kebab *m*

keel [kiːl] *n* Kiel *m;* **on an even ~** *(fig)* im Lot

keen [kiːn] *adj* begeistert; *(wind, blade, intelligence)* scharf; *(sight, hearing)* gut; **to be ~ to do** *or* **on doing sth** wild *or* unbedingt tun wollen; **to be ~ on sth/ sb** scharf auf etw/jdn sein

keep [kiːp] *(pt, pp* **kept)** *vt (retain)* behalten; *(have)* haben; *(animals, one's word)* halten; *(support)* versorgen; *(maintain in state)* halten; *(preserve)* aufbewahren; *(restrain)* abhalten ♦ *vi (continue in direction)* sich halten; *(food)* sich halten; *(remain: quiet etc)* bleiben ♦ *n* Unterhalt *m;* *(tower)* Burgfried *m;* *(inf):* **for ~s** für immer; **to ~ sth to o.s.** etw für sich behalten; **it ~s happening** es passiert immer wieder; ~ **back** *vt* fern halten; *(information)* verschweigen; ~ **on** *vi:* ~ **on doing sth** etw immer wieder tun; ~ **out** *vt* nicht hereinlassen; **"~ out"** "Eintritt verboten!"; ~ **up** *vi* Schritt halten ♦ *vt* aufrechterhalten; *(continue)* weitermachen; **to ~ up with** Schritt halten mit; **~er** *n* Wärter(in) *m(f);* *(goalkeeper)* Torhüter(in) *m(f);* **~-fit** *n* Keep-fit *nt;* **~ing** *n (care)* Obhut *f;* **in ~ing with** in Übereinstimmung mit; **~sake** *n* Andenken *nt*

keg [keg] *n* Fass *nt*

kennel ['kenl] *n* Hundehütte *f;* **~s** *npl:* **to put a dog in ~s** *(for boarding)* einen Hund in Pflege geben

Kenya ['kenjə] *n* Kenia *nt;* **~n** *adj* kenianisch ♦ *n* Kenianer(in) *m(f)*

kept [kept] *pt, pp of* **keep**

kerb [kəːb] *(BRIT)* *n* Bordstein *m*

kernel ['kɜːnl] n Kern m

kerosene ['kerəsiːn] n Kerosin nt

kettle ['ketl] n Kessel m; **~drum** n Pauke f

key [kiː] n Schlüssel m; (of piano, typewriter) Taste f; (MUS) Tonart f ♦ vt (also: **~ in**) eingeben; **~board** n Tastatur f; **~ed up** adj (person) überdreht; **~hole** n Schlüsselloch nt; **~hole surgery** n minimal invasive Chirurgie f, Schlüssellochchirurgie f; **~note** n Grundton m; **~ring** n Schlüsselring m

khaki ['kɑːkɪ] n K(h)aki nt ♦ adj k(h)aki(farben)

kick [kɪk] vt einen Fußtritt geben +dat, treten ♦ vi treten; (baby) strampeln; (horse) ausschlagen ♦ n (Fuß)tritt m; (thrill) Spaß m; **he does it for ~s** er macht das aus Jux; **~ off** vi (SPORT) anstoßen; **~-off** n (SPORT) Anstoß m

kid [kɪd] n (inf: child) Kind nt; (goat) Zicklein nt; (leather) Glacéleder nt, Glaceeleder nt ♦ vi (inf) Witze machen

kidnap ['kɪdnæp] vt entführen; **~per** n Entführer m; **~ping** n Entführung f

kidney ['kɪdnɪ] n Niere f

kill [kɪl] vt töten, umbringen ♦ vi töten ♦ n (hunting) (Jagd)beute f; **~er** n Mörder(in) m(f); **~ing** n Mord m; **~joy** n Spaßverderber(in) m(f)

kiln [kɪln] n Brennofen m

kilo ['kiːləu] n Kilo nt; **~byte** n (COMPUT) Kilobyte nt; **~gram(me)** n Kilogramm nt; **~metre** ['kɪləmiːtə*] (US **kilometer**) n Kilometer m; **~watt** n Kilowatt nt

kilt [kɪlt] n Schottenrock m

kind [kaɪnd] adj freundlich ♦ n Art f, a ~ of eine Art von; **(two) of a ~** (zwei) von der gleichen Art; **in ~** auf dieselbe Art; (in goods) in Naturalien

kindergarten ['kɪndəgɑːtn] n Kindergarten m

kind-hearted [kaɪnd'hɑːtɪd] adj gutherzig

kindle ['kɪndl] vt (set on fire) anzünden; (rouse) reizen, (er)wecken

kindly ['kaɪndlɪ] adj freundlich ♦ adv

liebenswürdig(erweise); **would you ~ ...?** wären Sie so freundlich und ...?

kindness ['kaɪndnɪs] n Freundlichkeit f

kindred ['kɪndrɪd] adj: **~ spirit** Gleichgesinnte(r) mf

king [kɪŋ] n König m; **~dom** n Königreich nt

kingfisher ['kɪŋfɪʃə*] n Eisvogel m

king-size(d) ['kɪŋsaɪz(d)] adj (cigarette) Kingsize

kinky ['kɪŋkɪ] (inf) adj (person, ideas) verrückt; (sexual) abartig

kiosk ['kiːɔsk] (BRIT) n (TEL) Telefonhäuschen nt

kipper ['kɪpə*] n Räucherhering m

kiss [kɪs] n Kuss m ♦ vt küssen ♦ vi: **they ~ed** sie küssten sich; **~ of life** (BRIT) n: **the ~ of life** Mund-zu-Mund-Beatmung f

kit [kɪt] n Ausrüstung f; (tools) Werkzeug nt

kitchen ['kɪtʃɪn] n Küche f; **~ sink** n Spülbecken nt

kite [kaɪt] n Drachen m

kitten ['kɪtn] n Kätzchen nt

kitty ['kɪtɪ] n (money) Kasse f

km abbr (= kilometre) km

knack [næk] n Dreh m, Trick m

knapsack ['næpsæk] n Rucksack m; (MIL) Tornister m

knead [niːd] vt kneten

knee [niː] n Knie nt; **~cap** n Kniescheibe f

kneel [niːl] (pt, pp **knelt**) vi (also: **~ down**) knien

knelt [nelt] pt, pp of **kneel**

knew [njuː] pt of **know**

knickers ['nɪkəz] (BRIT) npl Schlüpfer m

knife [naɪf] (pl **knives**) n Messer nt ♦ vt erstechen

knight [naɪt] n Ritter m; (chess) Springer m; **~hood** n (title): **to get a ~hood** zum Ritter geschlagen werden

knit [nɪt] vt stricken ♦ vi stricken; (bones) zusammenwachsen; **~ting** n (occupation) Stricken nt; (work) Strickzeug nt; **~ting needle** n Stricknadel f

~wear n Strickwaren pl

knives [naɪvz] pl of **knife**

knob [nɔb] n Knauf m; (on instrument) Knopf m; (BRIT: of butter etc) kleine(s) Stück nt

knock [nɔk] vt schlagen; (criticize) heruntermachen ♦ vi: **to ~ at** or **on the door** an die Tür klopfen ♦ n Schlag m; (on door) Klopfen nt; **~ down** vt umwerfen; (with car) anfahren; **~ off** vi (do quickly) hinhauen; (inf: steal) klauen ♦ vi (finish) Feierabend machen; **~ out** vt ausschlagen; (BOXING) k. o. schlagen; **~ over** vt (person, object) umwerfen; (with car) anfahren; **~er** n (on door) Türklopfer m; **~out** n K.-o.-Schlag m; (fig) Sensation f

knot [nɔt] n Knoten m ♦ vt (ver)knoten

knotty ['nɔtɪ] adj (fig) kompliziert

know [nəu] (pt **knew**, pp **known**) vt, vi wissen; (be able to) können; (be acquainted with) kennen; (recognize) erkennen; **to ~ how to do sth** wissen, wie man etw macht, etw tun können; **to ~ about** or **of sth/sb** von/jdn kennen; **~-all** n Alleswisser m; **~-how** n Kenntnis f, Know-how nt; **~ing** adj (look, smile) wissend; **~ingly** adv wissentlich; (intentionally) wissentlich

knowledge ['nɔlɪdʒ] n Wissen nt, Kenntnis f; **~able** adj informiert

known [nəun] pp of **know**

knuckle ['nʌkl] n Fingerknöchel m

K.O. n abbr = knockout

Koran [kɔ'rɑːn] n Koran m

Korea [kə'rɪə] n Korea nt

kosher ['kəuʃər] adj koscher

L, l

L [ɛl] abbr (BRIT: AUT) (= learner) am Auto angebrachtes Kennzeichen für Fahrschüler; **= lake**; (= large) gr.; (= left) l.

l. abbr = litre

lab [læb] n (inf) n Labor m

label ['leɪbl] n Etikett nt ♦ vt etikettieren

labor etc ['leɪbər] (US) = **labour** etc

laboratory [lə'bɔrətərɪ] n Laboratorium nt

laborious [lə'bɔːrɪəs] adj mühsam

labour ['leɪbər] (US **labor**) n Arbeit f; (workmen) Arbeitskräfte pl; (MED) Wehen pl ♦ vi: **to ~ (at)** sich abmühen (mit) ♦ vt breittreten (inf); **in ~** (MED) in den Wehen; **L~** (BRIT: also: **the L~ party**) die Labour Party; **~ed** adj (movement) gequält; (style) schwerfällig; **~er** n Arbeiter m; **farm ~er** n (Land)arbeiter m

lace [leɪs] n (fabric) Spitze f; (of shoe) Schnürsenkel m; (braid) Litze f ♦ vt (also: **~ up**) (zu)schnüren

lack [læk] n Mangel m ♦ vt nicht haben; **sb ~s sth** jdm fehlt etw nom; **to be ~ing** fehlen; **sb is ~ing in sth** es fehlt jdm an etw dat; **for** or **through ~ of** aus Mangel an +dat

lacquer ['lækər] n Lack m

lad [læd] n Junge m

ladder ['lædər] n Leiter f; (BRIT: in tights) Laufmasche f ♦ vt (BRIT: tights) Laufmaschen bekommen in +dat

laden ['leɪdn] adj beladen, voll

ladle ['leɪdl] n Schöpfkelle f

lady ['leɪdɪ] n Dame f; (title) Lady f; **young ~** junge Dame; **the ladies' (room)** die Damentoilette; **~bird** (US **~bug**) n Marienkäfer m; **~like** adj damenhaft, vornehm; **~ship** n: **your L~ship** Ihre Ladyschaft

lag [læg] vi (also: **~ behind**) zurückbleiben ♦ vt (pipes) verkleiden

lager ['lɑːgər] n helle(s) Bier nt

lagging ['lægɪŋ] n Isolierung f

lagoon [lə'guːn] n Lagune f

laid [leɪd] pt, pp of **lay**; **~ back** (inf) adj cool

lain [leɪn] pp of **lie**

lair [lɛər] n Lager nt

lake [leɪk] n See m

lamb [læm] n Lamm nt; (meat) Lammfleisch nt; **~ chop** n Lammkotelett nt; **~swool** n Lammwolle f

lame [leɪm] *adj* lahm; *(excuse)* faul

lament [lə'ment] *n* Klage *f* ♦ *vt* beklagen

laminated ['læmɪneɪtɪd] *adj* beschichtet

lamp [læmp] *n* Lampe *f*; *(in street)* Straßenlaterne *f*; **~post** *n* Laternenpfahl *m*; **~shade** *n* Lampenschirm *m*

lance [lɑːns] *n* Lanze *f*; **~ corporal** *(BRIT)* *n* Obergefreite(r) *m*

land [lænd] *n* Land *nt* ♦ *vi* *(from ship)* an Land gehen; *(AVIAT, end up)* landen ♦ *vt* *(obtain)* kriegen; *(passengers)* absetzen; *(goods)* abladen; *(troops, space probe)* landen; **~fill site** *n* ['lændfɪl-] *n* Mülldeponie *f*; **~ing** *n* Landung *f*; *(on stairs)* Treppen)absatz *m*; **~ing gear** *n* Fahrgestell *nt*; **~ing stage** *(BRIT)* *n* Landesteg *m*; **~ing strip** *n* Landebahn *f*, **~lady** *n* (Haus)wirtin *f*; **~locked** *adj* landumschlossen, Binnen-; **~lord** *n* *(of house)* Hauswirt *m*, Besitzer *m*; *(of pub)* Gastwirt *m*; *(of area)* Grundbesitzer *m*; **~mark** *n* Wahrzeichen *nt*; *(fig)* Meilenstein *m*; **~owner** *n* Grundbesitzer *m*; **~scape** *n* Landschaft *f*; **~scape gardener** *n* Landschaftsgärtner(in) *m(f)*; **~slide** *n* *(GEOG)* Erdrutsch *m*; *(POL)* überwältigende(r) Sieg *m*

lane [leɪn] *n* *(in town)* Gasse *f*; *(in country)* Weg *m*; *(of motorway)* Fahrbahn *f*, Spur *f*; *(SPORT)* Bahn *f*; **"get in ~"** "bitte einordnen"

language ['læŋgwɪdʒ] *n* Sprache *f*; **bad ~** unanständige Ausdrücke *pl*; **~ laboratory** *n* Sprachlabor *nt*

languish ['læŋgwɪʃ] *vi* schmachten

lank [læŋk] *adj* dürr

lanky ['læŋkɪ] *adj* schlaksig

lantern ['læntən] *n* Laterne *f*

lap [læp] *n* Schoß *m*; *(SPORT)* Runde *f* ♦ *vt* *(also:* **~ up)** auflecken ♦ *vi* *(water)* plätschern

lapel [lə'pel] *n* Revers *nt or m*

Lapland ['læplænd] *n* Lappland *nt*

lapse [læps] *n* *(moral)* Fehltritt *m* ♦ *vi* *(decline)* nachlassen; *(expire)* ablaufen;

(claims) erlöschen; **to ~ into bad habits** sich schlechte Gewohnheiten angewöhnen

laptop (computer) ['læptɔp-] *n* Laptop-(Computer) *m*

lard [lɑːd] *n* Schweineschmalz *nt*

larder ['lɑːdər] *n* Speisekammer *f*

large [lɑːdʒ] *adj* groß; **at ~** auf freiem Fuß; **~ly** *adv* zum größten Teil; **~scale** *adj* groß angelegt, Groß-

lark [lɑːk] *n* *(bird)* Lerche *f*; *(joke)* Jux *m*; **~ about** *(inf)* *vi* herumalbern

laryngitis [lærɪn'dʒaɪtɪs] *n* Kehlkopfentzündung *f*

laser ['leɪzər] *n* Laser *m*; **~ printer** *n* Laserdrucker *m*

lash [læʃ] *n* Peitschenhieb *m*; *(eyelash)* Wimper *f* ♦ *vt* *(rain)* schlagen gegen; *(whip)* peitschen; *(bind)* festbinden; **~ out** *vi* *(with fists)* um sich schlagen

lass [læs] *n* Mädchen *nt*

lasso [læ'suː] *n* Lasso *nt*

last [lɑːst] *adj* letzte(r, s) ♦ *adv* zuletzt; *(~ time)* das letzte Mal ♦ *vi* *(continue)* dauern; *(remain good)* sich halten; *(money)* ausreichen; **at ~** endlich; **~ night** gestern Abend; **~ week** letzte Woche; **~ but one** vorletzte(r, s); **~ditch** *(attempt)* in letzter Minute; **~ing** *adj* dauerhaft; *(shame etc)* andauernd; **~ly** *adv* schließlich; **~ minute** *adj* in letzter Minute

latch [lætʃ] *n* Riegel *m*

late [leɪt] *adj* spät; *(dead)* verstorben ♦ *adv* spät; *(after proper time)* zu spät; **to be ~** zu spät kommen; **of ~** in letzter Zeit; **in ~ May** Ende Mai; **~comer** *n* Nachzügler(in) *m(f)*; **~ly** *adv* in letzter Zeit; **later** ['leɪtər] *adj* *(date)* später; *(version)* neuer ♦ *adv* später

lateral ['lætərəl] *adj* seitlich

latest ['leɪtɪst] *adj* *(fashion)* neueste(r, s) ♦ *n* *(news)* Neu(e)ste(s) *nt*; **at the ~** spätestens

lathe [leɪð] *n* Drehbank *f*

lather ['lɑːðər] *n* (Seifen)schaum *m* ♦ *vt* einschäumen ♦ *vi* schäumen

Latin ['lætɪn] n Latein nt ♦ adj lateinisch; (Roman) römisch; ~ **America** n Lateinamerika nt; ~ **American** adj lateinamerikanisch

latitude ['lætɪtjuːd] n (GEOG) Breite f; (freedom) Spielraum m

latter ['lætə*] adj (second of two) letztere; (coming at end) letzte(r, s), später ♦ n: **the** ~ der/die/das letztere, die letzteren; ~**ly** adv in letzter Zeit

lattice ['lætɪs] n Gitter nt

laudable ['lɔːdəbl] adj löblich

laugh [lɑːf] n Lachen nt ♦ vi lachen; ~ **at** vt lachen über +acc; ~ **off** vt lachend abtun; ~**able** adj lachhaft; ~ing **stock** n Zielscheibe f des Spottes; ~**ter** n Gelächter nt

launch [lɔːntʃ] n (of ship) Stapellauf m; (rocket) Abschuss m; (boat) Barkasse f; (of product) Einführung f ♦ vt (set afloat) vom Stapel lassen; (rocket) (ab)schießen; (product) auf den Markt bringen; ~(ing) **pad** n Abschussrampe f

launder ['lɔːndə*] vt waschen

Launderette [lɔːn'drɛt] (® BRIT) n Waschsalon m

Laundromat ['lɔːndrəmæt] (® US) n Waschsalon m

laundry ['lɔːndrɪ] n (place) Wäscherei f; (clothes) Wäsche f; **to do the** ~ waschen

laureate ['lɔːrɪət] adj see poet

laurel ['lɒrl] n Lorbeer m

lava ['lɑːvə] n Lava f

lavatory ['lævətərɪ] n Toilette f

lavender ['lævəndə*] n Lavendel m

lavish ['lævɪʃ] adj (extravagant) verschwenderisch; (generous) großzügig ♦ vt (money): **to** ~ **sth on sb** etw auf jdn verschwenden; (attention, gifts): **to** ~ **sth on sb** jdn mit etw überschütten

law [lɔː] n Gesetz nt; (system) Recht nt; (as studies) Jura no art; ~**-abiding** adj gesetzestreu; ~ **and order** n Recht und Ordnung f; ~ **court** n Gerichtshof

m; ~**ful** adj gesetzlich; ~**less** adj gesetzlos

lawn [lɔːn] n Rasen m; ~**mower** n Rasenmäher m; ~ **tennis** n Rasentennis m

law: ~ **school** n Rechtsakademie f; ~**suit** n Prozess m; ~**yer** n Rechtsanwalt m, Rechtsanwältin f

lax [læks] adj (behaviour) nachlässig; (standards) lasch

laxative ['læksətɪv] n Abführmittel nt

lay [leɪ] (pt, pp **laid**) pt of **lie** ♦ adj Laien- ♦ vt (place) legen; (table) decken; (egg) legen; (trap) stellen; (money) wetten; ~ **aside** vt zurücklegen; ~ **by** vt (set aside) beiseite legen; ~ **down** vt hinlegen; (rules) vorschreiben; (arms) strecken; **to** ~ **down the law** Vorschriften machen; ~ **off** vt (workers) (vorübergehend) entlassen; ~ **on** vt (water, gas) anschließen; (concert etc) veranstalten; ~ **out** vt (her)auslegen; (money) ausgeben; (corpse) aufbahren; ~ **up** vt (subj: illness) ans Bett fesseln; ~**about** n Faulenzer m; ~**-by** (BRIT) n Parkbucht f; (bigger) Rastplatz m

layer ['leɪə*] n Schicht f

layman ['leɪmən] (irreg) n Laie m

layout ['leɪaʊt] n Anlage f; (ART) Lay-out nt, Layout nt

laze [leɪz] vi faulenzen

laziness ['leɪzɪnɪs] n Faulheit f

lazy ['leɪzɪ] adj faul; (slow-moving) träge

lb. abbr = **pound** (weight)

lead[1] [lɛd] n (chemical) Blei nt; (of pencil) (Bleistift)mine f ♦ adj bleiern, Blei-

lead[2] [liːd] (pt, pp **led**) n (front position) Führung f; (distance, time ahead) Vorsprung f; (example) Vorbild nt; (clue) Tipp m; (of police) Spur f; (THEAT) Hauptrolle f; (dog's) Leine f ♦ vt (guide) führen; (group etc) leiten ♦ vi (be first) führen; **in the** ~ (SPORT, fig) in Führung; ~ **astray** vt irreführen; ~ **away** vt wegführen; (prisoner) abführen; ~ **back** vi zurückführen; ~ **on** vt anführen; ~ **on to** vt (induce) dazu bringen; ~ **in** vt (street) (hin)führen nach; (result in) führen zu; ~ **up to** vt (drive) führen zu; (speaker etc) hinführen auf +acc

leaded petrol ['lɛdəd-] n verbleites Benzin nt

leaden ['lɛdn] adj (sky, sea) bleiern; (heavy: footsteps) bleischwer

leader ['liːdəʳ] n Führer m, Leiter m; (of party) Vorsitzende(r) m; (PRESS) Leitartikel m; **~ship** n (office) Leitung f; (quality) Führerschaft f

lead-free ['lɛdfriː] adj (petrol) bleifrei ♦ vt pachten

leading ['liːdɪŋ] adj führend; ~ **lady** n (THEAT) Hauptdarstellerin f; ~ **light** n (person) führende(r) Geist m

lead singer [liːd-] n Leadsänger(in) m(f)

leaf [liːf] (pl **leaves**) n Blatt nt ♦ vi: to ~ **through** durchblättern; **to turn over a new ~** einen neuen Anfang machen

leaflet ['liːflɪt] n (advertisement) Prospekt m; (pamphlet) Flugblatt nt; (for information) Merkblatt nt

league [liːg] n (union) Bund m; (SPORT) Liga f; **to be in ~ with** unter einer Decke stecken mit

leak [liːk] n undichte Stelle f; (in ship) Leck nt ♦ vt (liquid etc) durchlassen ♦ vi (pipe etc) undicht sein; (liquid etc) auslaufen; **the information was ~ed to the enemy** die Information wurde dem Feind zugespielt; ~ **out** vi (liquid etc) auslaufen; (information) durchsickern; **~y** ['liːkɪ] adj undicht

lean [liːn] (pt, pp **leaned** or **leant**) adj mager ♦ vi sich neigen ♦ vt (an)lehnen; **to ~ against sth** an etw dat angelehnt sein; sich an etw acc anlehnen; ~ **back** vi sich zurücklehnen; ~ **forward** vi sich vorbeugen; ~ **on** vt fus sich stützen auf +acc; ~ **out** vi sich hinauslehnen; ~ **over** vi sich hinüberbeugen; **~ing** n Neigung f ♦ adj schief; **~t** [lɛnt] pt, pp of **lean**; **~-to** n Anbau m

leap [liːp] (pt, pp **leaped** or **leapt**) n Sprung m ♦ vi springen; **~frog** n Bockspringen nt; **~t** [lɛpt] pt, pp of **leap**; **~ year** n Schaltjahr nt

learn [ləːn] (pt, pp **learned** or **learnt**) vt, vi lernen; (find out) erfahren; to ~ **how to do sth** etw (er)lernen; **~ed** ['ləːnɪd] adj gelehrt; **~er** n Anfänger(in) m(f); (AUT: BRIT: also: **~er driver**) Fahrschüler(in) m(f); **~ing** n Gelehrsamkeit f; **~t** [ləːnt] pt, pp of **learn**

lease [liːs] n (of property) Mietvertrag m ♦ vt pachten

leash [liːʃ] n Leine f

least [liːst] adj geringste(r, s) ♦ adv am wenigsten ♦ n Mindeste(s) nt; **the ~ possible effort** möglichst geringer Aufwand; **at ~** zumindest; **not in the ~!** durchaus nicht!

leather ['lɛðəʳ] n Leder nt

leave [liːv] (pt, pp **left**) vt verlassen; (~ behind) zurücklassen; (forget) vergessen; (allow to remain) lassen; (after death) hinterlassen; (entrust): **to ~ sth to sb** jdm etw überlassen ♦ vi weggehen, wegfahren; (for journey) abreisen; (bus, train) abfahren ♦ n Erlaubnis f; (MIL) Urlaub m; **to be left** (remain) übrig bleiben; **there's some milk left over** es ist noch etwas Milch übrig; **on ~** auf Urlaub; **~ behind** vt (person, object) dalassen; (forget) liegen lassen, stehen lassen; **~ out** vt auslassen; **~ of absence** n Urlaub m

leaves [liːvz] pl of **leaf**

Lebanon ['lɛbənən] n Libanon m

lecherous ['lɛtʃərəs] adj lüstern

lecture ['lɛktʃəʳ] n Vortrag m; (UNIV) Vorlesung f ♦ vi einen Vortrag halten; (UNIV) lesen ♦ vt (scold) abkanzeln; **to give a ~ on sth** einen Vortrag über etwas halten; **~r** ['lɛktʃərəʳ] n Vortragende(r) mf; (BRIT: UNIV) Dozent(in) m(f)

led [lɛd] pt, pp of **lead**²

ledge [lɛdʒ] n Leiste f; (window ~) Sims m or nt; (of mountain) (Fels)vorsprung m

ledger ['lɛdʒər] n Hauptbuch nt

leech [li:tʃ] n Blutegel m

leek [li:k] n Lauch m

leer [lɪər] vi: to ~ (at sb) (nach jdm) schielen

leeway ['li:weɪ] n (fig): to have some ~ etwas Spielraum haben

left [lɛft] pt, pp of **leave** ♦ adj linke(r, s) ♦ n (side) linke Seite ♦ adv links; on the ~ links; to the ~ nach links; the L~ (POL) die Linke f; ~-hand adj: ~-hand drive mit Linkssteuerung; ~-handed adj linkshändig; ~-hand side n linke Seite f; ~-luggage locker n Gepäckschließfach nt; ~-luggage (office) (BRIT) n Gepäckaufbewahrung f; ~-overs npl Reste pl; ~-wing adj linke(r, s)

leg [lɛg] n Bein nt; (of meat) Keule f; (stage) Etappe f; **1st/2nd ~** (SPORT) 1./ 2. Etappe

legacy ['lɛgəsɪ] n Erbe nt, Erbschaft f

legal ['li:gl] adj gesetzlich; (allowed) legal; ~ **holiday** (US) n gesetzliche(r) Feiertag m; ~**ize** vt legalisieren; ~**ly** adv gesetzlich; legal; ~ **tender** n gesetzliche(s) Zahlungsmittel nt

legend ['lɛdʒənd] n Legende f; ~**ary** adj legendär

leggings ['lɛgɪŋz] npl Leggings pl

legible ['lɛdʒəbl] adj leserlich

legislation [lɛdʒɪs'leɪʃən] n Gesetzgebung f; **legislative** ['lɛdʒɪslətɪv] adj gesetzgebend; **legislature** ['lɛdʒɪslətʃər] n Legislative f

legitimate [lɪ'dʒɪtɪmət] adj rechtmäßig, legitim; (child) ehelich

legroom ['lɛgru:m] n Platz m für die Beine

leisure ['lɛʒər] n Freizeit f; to be at ~ Zeit haben; ~ **centre** n Freizeitzentrum nt; ~**ly** adj gemächlich

lemon ['lɛmən] n Zitrone f; (colour) Zitronengelb nt; ~**ade** [lɛmə'neɪd] n Limonade f; ~ **tea** n Zitronentee m

lend [lɛnd] (pt, pp **lent**) vt leihen; to ~ sb sth jdm etw leihen; ~**ing library** n Leihbibliothek f

length [lɛŋθ] n Länge f; (of road, pipe etc) Strecke f; (of material) Stück nt; at ~ (lengthily) ausführlich; (at last) schließlich; ~**en** vt verlängern ♦ vi länger werden; ~**ways** adv längs; ~**y** adj sehr lang, langatmig

lenient ['li:nɪənt] adj nachsichtig

lens [lɛnz] n Linse f; (PHOT) Objektiv nt

Lent [lɛnt] n Fastenzeit f

lent [lɛnt] pt, pp of **lend**

lentil ['lɛntɪl] n Linse f

Leo ['li:əu] n Löwe m

leotard ['li:əta:d] n Trikot nt, Gymnastikanzug m

leper ['lɛpər] n Leprakranke(r) f(m)

leprosy ['lɛprəsɪ] n Lepra f

lesbian ['lɛzbɪən] adj lesbisch ♦ n Lesbierin f

less [lɛs] adj, adv weniger ♦ n weniger ♦ pron weniger; ~ **than half** weniger als die Hälfte; ~ **than ever** weniger denn je; ~ **and** ~ immer weniger; **the ~ he works** je weniger er arbeitet; ~**en** ['lɛsn] vi abnehmen ♦ vt verringern, verkleinern; ~**er** ['lɛsər] adj kleiner, geringer; to a ~er **extent** in geringerem Maße

lesson ['lɛsn] n (SCH) Stunde f; (unit of study) Lektion f; (fig) Lehre f; (ECCL) Lesung f; **a maths** ~ eine Mathestunde

lest [lɛst] conj: ~ **it happen** damit es nicht passiert

let [lɛt] (pt, pp **let**) vt lassen; (BRIT: lease) vermieten; to ~ sb do sth jdn etw tun lassen; to ~ sb know sth jdn etw wissen lassen; ~'s go! gehen wir!; ~ him come soll er doch kommen; ~ down vt hinunterlassen; (disappoint) enttäuschen; ~ go vi loslassen ♦ vt (things) loslassen; (person) gehen lassen; ~ in vt hereinlassen; (water) durchlassen; ~ off vt (gun) abfeuern; (steam) ablassen; (forgive) laufen lassen; ~ on vi durchblicken lassen; (pretend) vorgeben; ~ out vt herauslassen;

(scream) fahren lassen; **~ up** vi nachlassen; *(stop)* aufhören

lethal ['li:θl] adj tödlich

lethargic [lɛ'θɑːdʒɪk] adj lethargisch

letter ['lɛtər] n Brief m; *(of alphabet)* Buchstabe m; **~ bomb** n Briefbombe f; **~box** (BRIT) n Briefkasten m; **~ing** n Beschriftung f; **~ of credit** n Akkreditiv m

lettuce ['lɛtɪs] n (Kopf)salat m

let-up ['lɛtʌp] (inf) n Nachlassen nt

leukaemia [luː'kiːmɪə] (US **leukemia**) n Leukämie f

level ['lɛvl] adj *(ground)* eben; *(at same height)* auf gleicher Höhe; *(equal)* gleich gut; *(head)* kühl ♦ adv auf gleicher Höhe ♦ n *(instrument)* Wasserwaage f; *(altitude)* Höhe f; *(flat place)* ebene Fläche f; *(position on scale)* Niveau nt; *(amount, degree)* Grad m ♦ vt *(ground)* einebnen; **to draw ~ with** gleichziehen mit; **to be ~ with** auf einer Höhe sein mit; **A ~s** (BRIT) ≃ Abitur nt; **O ~s** (BRIT) ≃ mittlere Reife f; **on the ~** *(fig: honest)* ehrlich; **to ~ sth at sb** *(blow)* jdm etw versetzen; *(remark)* etw gegen jdn richten; **~ off** or **out** vi flach or eben werden; *(fig)* sich ausgleichen; *(plane)* horizontal fliegen ♦ vt *(ground)* planieren; *(differences)* ausgleichen; **~ crossing** (BRIT) n Bahnübergang m; **~-headed** adj vernünftig

lever ['liːvər] n Hebel m; *(fig)* Druckmittel m ♦ vt *(hoch)stemmen;* **~age** n Hebelkraft f; *(fig)* Einfluss m

levy ['lɛvɪ] n *(of taxes)* Erhebung f; *(tax)* Abgaben pl; *(MIL)* Aushebung f ♦ vt erheben; *(MIL)* ausheben

lewd [luːd] adj unzüchtig, unanständig

liability [laɪə'bɪlɪtɪ] n *(burden)* Belastung f; *(duty)* Pflicht f; *(debt)* Verpflichtung f; *(responsibility)* Haftung f; *(proneness)* Anfälligkeit f

liable ['laɪəbl] adj *(responsible)* haftbar; *(prone)* anfällig; **to be ~ for sth** etw dat unterliegen; **it's ~ to happen** es

kann leicht vorkommen

liaise [liː'eɪz] vi: **to ~ (with sb)** *(mit jdm)* zusammenarbeiten; **liaison** n Verbindung f

liar ['laɪər] n Lügner m

libel ['laɪbl] n Verleumdung f ♦ vt verleumden

liberal ['lɪbərl] adj *(generous)* großzügig; *(open-minded)* aufgeschlossen; *(POL)* liberal

liberate ['lɪbəreɪt] vt befreien; **liberation** [lɪbə'reɪʃən] n Befreiung f

liberty ['lɪbətɪ] n Freiheit f; *(permission)* Erlaubnis f; **to be at ~ to do sth** etw tun dürfen; **to take the ~ of doing sth** sich dat erlauben, etw zu tun

librarian [laɪ'brɛərɪən] n Bibliothekar(in) m(f)

library ['laɪbrərɪ] n Bibliothek f; *(lending ~)* Bücherei f

Libya ['lɪbɪə] n Libyen nt; **~n** adj libysch ♦ n Libyer(in) m(f)

lice [laɪs] npl of **louse**

licence ['laɪsns] (US **license**) n *(permit)* Erlaubnis f; *(also: driving ~, (US) driver's ~)* Führerschein m

license ['laɪsns] n *(US)* = **licence** f ♦ vt genehmigen, konzessionieren; **~d** adj *(for alcohol)* konzessioniert *(für den Alkoholausschank);* **~ plate** *(US)* n *(AUT)* Nummernschild nt

lichen ['laɪkən] n Flechte f

lick [lɪk] vt lecken ♦ n Lecken nt; **a ~ of paint** ein bisschen Farbe

licorice ['lɪkərɪs] (US) n = **liquorice**

lid [lɪd] n Deckel m; *(eyelid)* Lid nt

lie [laɪ] *(pt* **lay***, pt* **lain***)* vi *(rest, be situated)* liegen; *(put o.s. in position)* sich legen; *(pt, pp* **lied***: tell lies)* lügen ♦ n Lüge f; **to ~ low** *(fig)* untertauchen; **~ about** or *(things)* herumliegen; *(people)* faulenzen; **~-down** (BRIT) n: **to have a ~-down** ein Nickerchen machen; **~-in** (BRIT) n: **to have a ~-in** sich ausschlafen

lieu [luː] n: **in ~ of** anstatt +gen

lieutenant [lɛf'tɛnənt, (US) luː'tɛnənt] n Leutnant m

life [laɪf] (pl **lives**) n Leben nt; **~ assurance** (BRIT) n = **life insurance**; **~belt** (BRIT) n Rettungsring m; **~boat** n Rettungsboot nt; **~guard** n Rettungsschwimmer m; **~ insurance** n Lebensversicherung f; **~ jacket** n Schwimmweste f; **~less** adj (dead) leblos; (dull) langweilig; **~like** adj lebensnah, naturgetreu; **~line** n Rettungsleine f; (fig) Rettungsanker m; **~long** adj lebenslang; **~ preserver** (US) n = **lifebelt**; **~ saver** n Lebensretter(in) m(f); **~ saving** adj lebensrettend, Rettungs-; **~ sentence** n lebenslängliche Freiheitsstrafe f; **~ span** n Lebensspanne f; **~style** n Lebensstil m; **~ support system** n (MED) Lebenserhaltungssystem nt; **~time** n: **in his ~time** während er lebte; **once in a ~time** einmal im Leben

lift [lɪft] vt hochheben ♦ vi sich heben ♦ n (BRIT: elevator) Aufzug m, Lift m; **to give sb a ~** jdn mitnehmen; **~-off** n Abheben nt (vom Boden)

ligament ['lɪgəmənt] n Band nt

light [laɪt] (pt, pp **lighted** or **lit**) n Licht nt; (for cigarette etc): **have you got a ~?** haben Sie Feuer? ♦ vt beleuchten; (lamp) anmachen; (fire, cigarette) anzünden ♦ adj (bright) hell; (pale) hell-; (not heavy, easy) leicht; (punishment) milde; (touch) leicht; **~s** npl (AUT) Beleuchtung f; **~ up** vi (lamp) angehen; (face) aufleuchten ♦ vt (illuminate) beleuchten; (~s) anmachen; **~ bulb** n Glühbirne f; **~en** vi (brighten) hell werden; (~ning) blitzen ♦ vt (give ~ to) erhellen; (hair) aufhellen; (gloom) aufheitern; (make less heavy) leichter machen; (fig) erleichtern; **~er** n Feuerzeug nt; **~-headed** adj (thoughtless) leichtsinnig; (giddy) schwindlig; **~-hearted** adj leichtherzig, fröhlich; **~house** n Leuchtturm m; **~ing** n Beleuchtung f; **~ly** adv leicht; (irrespon-

sibly) leichtfertig; **to get off ~ly** mit einem blauen Auge davonkommen; **~ness** n (of weight) Leichtigkeit f; (of colour) Helle f

lightning ['laɪtnɪŋ] n Blitz m; **~ conductor** (US **~ rod**) n Blitzableiter m

light: **~ pen** n Lichtstift m; **~weight** adj (suit) leicht; **~weight** n (BOXING) Leichtgewichtler m; **~ year** n Lichtjahr nt

like [laɪk] vt mögen, gern haben ♦ prep wie ♦ adj (similar) ähnlich; (equal) gleich ♦ n: **the ~** dergleichen; **I would** or **I'd ~** ich möchte gern; **would you ~ a coffee?** möchten Sie einen Kaffee?; **to be** or **look ~ sb/sth** jdm/etw ähnlich sein; **that's just ~ him** das ist typisch für ihn; **do it ~ this** mach es so; **it is nothing ~ ...** es ist nicht zu vergleichen mit ...; **what does it look ~?** wie sieht es aus?; **what does it sound ~?** wie hört es sich an?; **what does it taste ~?** wie schmeckt es?; **his ~s and dislikes** was er mag und was er nicht mag; **~able** adj sympathisch

likelihood ['laɪklɪhʊd] n Wahrscheinlichkeit f

likely ['laɪklɪ] adj wahrscheinlich; **he's ~ to leave** er geht möglicherweise; **not ~!** wohl kaum!

likeness ['laɪknɪs] n Ähnlichkeit f; (portrait) Bild nt

likewise ['laɪkwaɪz] adv ebenso

liking ['laɪkɪŋ] n Zuneigung f; (taste) Vorliebe f

lilac ['laɪlək] n Flieder m ♦ adj (colour) fliederfarben

lily ['lɪlɪ] n Lilie f; **~ of the valley** n Maiglöckchen nt

limb [lɪm] n Glied nt

limber up ['lɪmbər-] vi sich auflockern; (fig) sich vorbereiten

limbo ['lɪmbəʊ] n: **to be in ~** (fig) in der Schwebe sein

lime [laɪm] n (tree) Linde f; (fruit) Limone f; (substance) Kalk m

limelight ['laɪmlaɪt] n: **to be in the ~**

limitstone 460 literal

(fig) im Rampenlicht stehen

limestone ['laɪmstəʊn] *n* Kalkstein *m*

limit ['lɪmɪt] *n* Grenze *f*; *(inf)* Höhe *f* ♦ *vt* begrenzen, einschränken; **~ation** [lɪmɪ'teɪʃən] *n* Einschränkung *f*; **~ed** *adj* beschränkt; **to be ~ed to** sich beschränken auf *+acc*; **~ed (liability) company** *(BRIT)* *n* Gesellschaft *f* mit beschränkter Haftung

limousine ['lɪməziːn] *n* Limousine *f*

limp [lɪmp] *n* Hinken *nt* ♦ *vi* hinken ♦ *adj* schlaff

limpet ['lɪmpɪt] *n (fig)* Klette *f*

line [laɪn] *n* Linie *f*; *(rope)* Leine *f*; *(on face)* Falte *f*; *(row)* Reihe *f*; *(of hills)* Kette *f*; *(US: queue)* Schlange *f*; *(company)* Linie *f*, Gesellschaft *f*; *(RAIL)* Strecke *f*; *(TEL)* Leitung *f*; *(written)* Zeile *f*; *(direction)* Richtung *f*; *(fig: business)* Branche *f*; *(range of items)* Kollektion *f* ♦ *vt (coat)* füttern; *(border)* säumen; **~s** *npl (RAIL)* Gleise *pl*; **in ~ with** in Übereinstimmung mit; **~ up** *vi* sich aufstellen ♦ *vt* aufstellen; *(prepare)* sorgen für; *(support)* mobilisieren; *(surprise)* planen; **~ar** [] *adj* gerade; *(measure)* Längen-; **~d** *adj (face)* faltig; *(paper)* liniert

linen ['lɪnɪn] *n* Leinen *nt*; *(sheets etc)* Wäsche *f*

liner ['laɪnər] *n* Überseedampfer *m*

linesman ['laɪnzmən] *(irreg) n (SPORT)* Linienrichter *m*

line-up ['laɪnʌp] *n* Aufstellung *f*

linger ['lɪŋgər] *vi (remain long)* verweilen; *(taste)* (zurück)bleiben; *(delay)* zögern, verharren

lingerie ['lænʒəriː] *n* Damenunterwäsche *f*

lingering ['lɪŋgərɪŋ] *adj (doubt)* zurückbleibend; *(disease)* langwierig; *(taste)* nachhaltend; *(look)* lang

lingo ['lɪŋgəʊ] *(pl* **~es)** *(inf) n* Sprache *f*

linguist ['lɪŋgwɪst] *n* Sprachkundige(r) *mf*; *(UNIV)* Sprachwissenschaftler(in) *m(f)*; **~ic** [lɪŋ'gwɪstɪk] *adj* sprachlich, sprachwissenschaftlich; **~ics** *n* Sprach-

lining ['laɪnɪŋ] *n* Futter *nt*

link [lɪŋk] *n* Glied *nt*; *(connection)* Verbindung *f* ♦ *vt* verbinden; **~s** *npl (GOLF)* Golfplatz *m*; **~ up** *vt* verbinden ♦ *vi* zusammenkommen; *(companies)* sich zusammenschließen; **~up** *n (TEL)* Verbindung *f*; *(of spaceships)* Kopplung *f*

lino ['laɪnəʊ] *n* **linoleum**

linoleum [lɪ'nəʊlɪəm] *n* Linoleum *nt*

linseed oil ['lɪnsiːd-] *n* Leinöl *nt*

lion ['laɪən] *n* Löwe *m*; **~ess** *n* Löwin *f*

lip [lɪp] *n* Lippe *f*; *(of jug)* Schnabel *m*; **to pay ~ service (to)** ein Lippenbekenntnis ablegen (zu)

liposuction ['lɪpəʊsʌkʃən] *n* Fettabsaugen *nt*

lip: ~read *(irreg) vi* von den Lippen ablesen; **~ salve** *n* Lippenbalsam *m*; **~stick** *n* Lippenstift *m*

liqueur [lɪ'kjʊər] *n* Likör *m*

liquid ['lɪkwɪd] *n* Flüssigkeit *f* ♦ *adj* flüssig

liquidate ['lɪkwɪdeɪt] *vt* liquidieren

liquidize ['lɪkwɪdaɪz] *vt (COOK)* (im Mixer) pürieren; **~r** ['lɪkwɪdaɪzər] *n* Mixgerät *nt*

liquor ['lɪkər] *n* Alkohol *m*

liquorice ['lɪkərɪs] *(BRIT) n* Lakritze *f*

liquor store *(US) n* Spirituosengeschäft *nt*

Lisbon ['lɪzbən] *n* Lissabon *nt*

lisp [lɪsp] *n* Lispeln *nt* ♦ *vi* lispeln

list [lɪst] *n* Liste *f*, Verzeichnis *nt*; *(of ship)* Schlagseite *f* ♦ *vt (write down)* eine Liste machen von; *(verbally)* aufzählen ♦ *vi (ship)* Schlagseite haben

listen ['lɪsn] *vi* hören; **~ to** *vt* zuhören *+dat*; **~er** *n* (Zu)hörer(in) *m(f)*

listless ['lɪstlɪs] *adj* lustlos

lit [lɪt] *pt, pp of* **light**

liter ['liːtər] *(US) n* = **litre**

literacy ['lɪtərəsɪ] *n* Fähigkeit *f* zu lesen und zu schreiben

literal ['lɪtərəl] *adj* buchstäblich; *(translation)* wortwörtlich; **~ly** *adv* wörtlich; buchstäblich

literary ['lɪtərərɪ] adj literarisch

literate ['lɪtərət] adj des Lesens und Schreibens kundig

literature ['lɪtrɪtʃəʳ] n Literatur f

litigation [lɪtɪ'geɪʃən] n Prozess m

litre ['liːtəʳ] (US **liter**) n Liter m

litter ['lɪtəʳ] n (rubbish) Abfall m; (of animals) Wurf m ♦ vt in Unordnung bringen; **to be ~ed with** übersät sein mit; **~ bin** (BRIT) n Abfalleimer m

little ['lɪtl] adj klein ♦ adv, n wenig; **a ~** ein bisschen; **~ by ~** nach und nach

live¹ [laɪv] adj lebendig; (MIL) scharf; (ELEC) geladen; (broadcast) live

live² [lɪv] vi leben; (dwell) wohnen ♦ vt (life) führen; **~ down** vt: **I'll never ~ it down** das wird man mir nie vergessen; **~ on** vi weiterleben ♦ vt fus: **to ~ on sth** von etw leben; **~ together** vi zusammenleben; (share a flat) zusammenwohnen; **~ up to** vt (standards) gerecht werden +dat; (principles) anstreben; (hopes) entsprechen +dat

livelihood ['laɪvlɪhʊd] n Lebensunterhalt m

lively ['laɪvlɪ] adj lebhaft, lebendig

liven up ['laɪvn-] vt beleben

liver ['lɪvəʳ] n (ANAT) Leber f

lives [laɪvz] pl of **life**

livestock ['laɪvstɔk] n Vieh nt

livid ['lɪvɪd] adj bläulich; (furious) fuchsteufelswild

living ['lɪvɪŋ] n (Lebens)unterhalt m ♦ adj lebendig; (language etc) lebend; **to earn** or **make a ~** sich dat seinen Lebensunterhalt verdienen; **~ conditions** npl Wohnverhältnisse pl; **~ room** n Wohnzimmer nt; **~ standards** npl Lebensstandard m; **~ wage** n ausreichender Lohn m

lizard ['lɪzəd] n Eidechse f

load [ləʊd] n (burden) Last f; (amount) Ladung f ♦ vt (also: **~ up**) (be)laden; (COMPUT) laden; (camera) Film einlegen in +acc; (gun) laden; **a ~ of, ~s of** (fig) jede Menge; **~ed** adj beladen; (dice) präpariert; (question) Fang-; (inf: rich)

steinreich; **~ing bay** n Ladeplatz m

loaf [ləʊf] (pl **loaves**) n Brot nt ♦ vi (also: **~ about, ~ around**) herumlungern, faulenzen

loan [ləʊn] n Leihgabe f; (FIN) Darlehen nt ♦ vt leihen; **on ~** geliehen

loath [ləʊθ] adj: **to be ~ to do sth** etw ungern tun

loathe [ləʊð] vt verabscheuen

loaves [ləʊvz] pl of **loaf**

lobby ['lɔbɪ] n Vorhalle f; (POL) Lobby f ♦ vt politisch beeinflussen (wollen)

lobster ['lɔbstəʳ] n Hummer m

local ['ləʊkəl] adj ortsansässig, Orts- ♦ n (pub) Stammwirtschaft f; **the ~s** npl (people) die Ortsansässigen pl; **~ anaesthetic** n (MED) örtliche Betäubung f; **~ authority** n städtische Behörden pl; **~ call** n (TEL) Ortsgespräch m; **~ government** n Gemeinde-/Kreisverwaltung f; **~ity** [ləʊ'kælɪtɪ] n Ort m; **~ly** adv örtlich, am Ort

locate [ləʊ'keɪt] vt ausfindig machen; (establish) errichten; **location** [ləʊ'keɪʃən] n Platz m, Lage f; **on location** (CINE) auf Außenaufnahme

loch [lɔx] (SCOTTISH) n See m

lock [lɔk] n Schloss nt; (NAUT) Schleuse f; (of hair) Locke f ♦ vt (fasten) (ver)schließen ♦ vi (door etc) sich schließen (lassen); (wheels) blockieren; **~ up** vt (criminal, mental patient) einsperren; (house) abschließen

locker ['lɔkəʳ] n Spind m

locket ['lɔkɪt] n Medaillon nt

lock ['lɔk-]: **~out** n Aussperrung f; **~smith** n Schlosser(in) m(f); **~up** n (jail) Gefängnis nt; (garage) Garage f

locum ['ləʊkəm] n (MED) Vertreter(in) m(f)

lodge [lɔdʒ] n (gatehouse) Pförtnerhaus nt; (freemasons') Loge f ♦ vi (get stuck) stecken (bleiben); (in Untermiete): **to ~ (with)** wohnen (bei) ♦ vt (protest) einreichen; **~r** n (Unter)mieter m; **lodgings** n (Miet)wohnung f

loft [lɒft] n (Dach)boden m

lofty ['lɒftɪ] adj hoch(ragend); (proud) hochmütig

log [lɒg] n Klotz m; (book) = **logbook**

logbook ['lɒgbʊk] n Bordbuch nt; (for lorry) Fahrtenschreiber m; (AUT) Kraftfahrzeugbrief m

loggerheads ['lɒgəhedz] npl: **to be at ~** sich in den Haaren liegen

logic ['lɒdʒɪk] n Logik f; **~al** adj logisch

logistics [lɒ'dʒɪstɪks] npl Logistik f

logo ['lougou] n Firmenzeichen nt

loin [lɔɪn] n Lende f

loiter ['lɔɪtə*] vi herumstehen

loll [lɒl] vi (also: **~ about**) sich rekeln or räkeln

lollipop ['lɒlɪpɒp] n (Dauer)lutscher m; **~ man/lady** (irreg; BRIT) n ≈ Schülerlotse m

---
Lollipop man/lady

Lollipop man/lady heißen in Großbritannien die Männer bzw. Frauen, die mit Hilfe eines runden Stoppschildes den Verkehr anhalten, damit Schulkinder die Straße gefahrlos überqueren können. Der Name bezieht sich auf die Form des Schildes, die an einen Lutscher erinnert.

---

lolly ['lɒlɪ] (inf) n (sweet) Lutscher m

London ['lʌndən] n London nt; **~er** n Londoner(in) m(f)

lone [ləʊn] adj einsam

loneliness ['ləʊnlɪnɪs] n Einsamkeit f

lonely ['ləʊnlɪ] adj einsam

loner ['ləʊnə*] adj lang; (distance) weit ♦ adv lange ♦ vi: **to ~ for** sich sehnen nach; **before ~** bald; **as ~ as** solange; **in the ~ run** auf die Dauer; **don't be ~!** beeil dich!; **how ~ is the street?** wie lang ist die Straße?; **how ~ is the lesson?** wie lange dauert die Stunde?; **5 metres ~** 6 Meter lang; **6 months ~** 6 Monate lang; **all night ~** die ganze Nacht; **he no ~er comes** er kommt nicht mehr; **~ ago** vor langer Zeit; **~ before** lange vorher; **at ~ last** endlich; **~-distance** adj Fern-

longevity [lɒn'dʒevɪtɪ] n Langlebigkeit f

long: ~-haired adj langhaarig; **~hand** n Langschrift f; **~ing** n Sehnsucht f ♦ adj sehnsüchtig

longitude ['lɒŋgɪtjuːd] n Längengrad m

long: ~ jump n Weitsprung m; **~-life** adj (batteries etc) mit langer Lebensdauer; **~-lost** adj längst verloren geglaubt; **~-playing record** n Langspielplatte f; **~-range** adj Langstrecken-, Fern-; **~-sighted** adj weitsichtig; **~-standing** adj alt, seit langer Zeit bestehend; **~-suffering** adj schwer geprüft; **~-term** adj langfristig; **~ wave** n Langwelle f; **~-winded** adj langatmig

loo [luː] (BRIT: inf) n Klo nt

look [lʊk] vi schauen; (seem) aussehen; (building etc): **to ~ on to the sea** nach Meer gehen ♦ n Blick m; **~s** npl (appearance) Aussehen nt; **~ after** vt (care for) sorgen für; (watch) aufpassen auf +acc; **~ at** vt ansehen; (consider) sich überlegen; **~ back** vi sich umsehen; (fig) zurückblicken; **~ down on** vt (fig) herabsehen auf +acc; **~ for** vt (seek) suchen; **~ forward to** vt sich freuen auf +acc; (in letters): **we ~ forward to hearing from you** wir hoffen, bald von Ihnen zu hören; **~ into** vt untersuchen; **~ on** vi zusehen; **~ out** vi hinaussehen; (take care) aufpassen; **~ out for** vt Ausschau halten nach; (be careful) Acht geben auf +acc; **~ round** vi sich umsehen; **~ to** vt (take care of) Acht geben auf +acc; (rely on) sich verlassen auf +acc; **~ up** vi aufblicken; (improve) sich bessern ♦ vt (word) nachschlagen; (person) besuchen; **~ up to** vt aufsehen zu; **~out** n (watch) Ausschau f; (person) Wachposten m; (place) Ausguck m; (prospect

Aussichten pl; **to be on the ~ out for sth** nach etw Ausschau halten

loom [luːm] n Webstuhl m ♦ vi sich abzeichnen

loony ['luːnɪ] (inf) n Verrückte(r)

loop [luːp] n Schlaufe f; **~hole** n (fig) Hintertürchen nt

loose [luːs] adj lose, locker; (free) frei; (inexact) unpräzise ♦ vt lösen, losbinden; **~ change** n Kleingeld nt; **~ chippings** npl (on road) Rollsplitt m; **~ end** n: **to be at a ~ end** (BRIT) or **at ~ ends** (US) nicht wissen, was man tun soll; **~ly** adv locker, lose; **~n** vt lockern, losmachen

loot [luːt] n Beute f ♦ vt plündern

lop off [lɔp-] vt abhacken

lopsided ['lɔp'saɪdɪd] adj schief

lord [lɔːd] n (ruler) Herr m; (BRIT: title) Lord m; **the L~** (God) der Herr; (**House of**) **L~s** den Oberhaus; **~ship** n: **Your L~ship** Eure Lordschaft

lorry ['lɔrɪ] (BRIT) n Lastwagen m; **~ driver** (BRIT) n Lastwagenfahrer(in) m(f)

lose [luːz] (pt, pp lost) vt verlieren; (chance) verpassen ♦ vi verlieren; **to ~ (time)** (clock) nachgehen; **~r** n Verlierer m

loss [lɔs] n Verlust m; **at a ~** (COMM) mit Verlust; (unable) außerstande, außer Stande

lost [lɔst] pt, pp of **lose** ♦ adj verloren; **~ property** (US - **and found**) n Fundsachen pl

lot [lɔt] n (quantity) Menge f; (fate, at auction) Los nt; (inf: people, things) Haufen m; **the ~** alles; (people) alle; **a ~ of** (with sg) viel; (with pl) viele; **~s of** massenhaft, viel(e); **I read a ~** ich lese viel; **to draw ~s for sth** etw verlosen

lotion ['ləʊʃən] n Lotion f

lottery ['lɔtərɪ] n Lotterie f

loud [laud] adj laut; (showy) schreiend ♦ adv laut; **~ly** adv laut; **~speaker** n Lautsprecher m

lounge [laundʒ] n (in hotel) Gesellschaftsraum m; (in house) Wohnzimmer nt ♦ vi sich herumlümmeln

louse [laus] (pl lice) n Laus f

lousy ['lauzɪ] adj (fig) miserabel

lout [laut] n Lümmel m

louvre ['luːvər] (US **louver**) adj (door, window) Jalousie-.

lovable ['lʌvəbl] adj liebenswert

love [lʌv] n Liebe f; (person) Liebling m; (SPORT) null; **(person)** lieben; (activity) gerne mögen; **to be in ~ with sb** in jdn verliebt sein; **to make ~** sich lieben; **for the ~ of** aus Liebe zu; **"15 ~"** (TENNIS) „15 null"; **to ~ to do sth** etw (sehr) gerne tun; **~ affair** n (Liebes)verhältnis nt; **~ letter** n Liebesbrief m; **~ life** n Liebesleben nt

lovely ['lʌvlɪ] adj schön

lover ['lʌvər] n Liebhaber(in) m(f)

loving ['lʌvɪŋ] adj liebend, liebevoll

low [ləʊ] adj niedrig; (rank) niedere(r, s); (level, note, neckline) tief; (intelligence, density) gering; (vulgar) ordinär; (not loud) leise; (depressed) gedrückt ♦ adv (not high) niedrig; (not loudly) leise ♦ n (~ point) Tiefstand m; (MET) Tief nt; **to feel ~** sich mies fühlen; **to turn (down)** ~ leiser stellen; **~ alcohol** adj alkoholarm; **~-calorie** adj kalorienarm; **~-cut** adj (dress) tief ausgeschnitten; **~er** n herunterlassen; (eyes, gun) senken; (reduce) herabsetzen, senken ♦ vr: **to ~er o.s.** (fig) sich herablassen zu; **~er sixth** (BRIT) n (SCOL) ≈ zwölfte Klasse; **~-fat** adj fettarm, Mager-; **~lands** npl (GEOG) Flachland nt; **~ly** adj bescheiden; **~-lying** adj tief gelegen

loyal ['lɔɪəl] adj treu; **~ty** n Treue f; **~ty card** n Kundenkarte f

lozenge ['lɔzɪndʒ] n Pastille f

L-plates ['elpleɪts] (BRIT) npl L-Schild nt (für Fahrschüler)

L-Plates

Als **L-Plates** werden in Großbritannien die weißen Schilder mit einem roten „L" bezeichnet, die vorne und hinten an jedem von einem Fahrschüler geführten Fahrzeug befestigt werden *müssen. Fahrschüler müssen einen vorläufigen Führerschein beantragen und dürfen damit unter der Aufsicht eines erfahrenen Autofahrers auf allen Straßen außer Autobahnen fahren.*

Ltd *abbr* (= *limited company*) GmbH

lubricant ['lu:brɪkənt] *n* Schmiermittel *nt*

lubricate ['lu:brɪkeɪt] *vt* schmieren

lucid ['lu:sɪd] *adj* klar; (*sane*) bei klarem Verstand; (*moment*) licht

luck [lʌk] *n* Glück *nt*; **bad** or **hard** or **tough ~!** (so ein) Pech!; **good ~!** viel Glück!; **~ily** *adv* glücklicherweise, zum Glück; **~y** *adj* Glücks-; **to be ~y** Glück haben

lucrative ['lu:krətɪv] *adj* einträglich

ludicrous ['lu:dɪkrəs] *adj* grotesk

lug [lʌg] *vt* schleppen

luggage ['lʌgɪdʒ] *n* Gepäck *nt*; **~ rack** *n* Gepäcknetz *nt*

lukewarm ['lu:kwɔ:m] *adj* lauwarm; (*indifferent*) lau

lull [lʌl] *n* Flaute *f* ♦ *vt* einlullen; (*calm*) beruhigen

lullaby ['lʌləbaɪ] *n* Schlaflied *nt*

lumbago [lʌm'beɪgəu] *n* Hexenschuss *m*

lumber ['lʌmbə*] *n* Plunder *m*; (*wood*) Holz *nt*; **~jack** *n* Holzfäller *m*

luminous ['lu:mɪnəs] *adj* Leucht-

lump [lʌmp] *n* Klumpen *m*; (*MED*) Schwellung *f*; (*in breast*) Knoten *m*; (*of sugar*) Stück *nt* ♦ *vt* (*also*: **~ together**) zusammentun; (*judge together*) in einen Topf werfen; **~ sum** *n* Pauschalsumme *f*; **~y** *adj* klumpig

lunacy ['lu:nəsɪ] *n* Irrsinn *m*

lunar ['lu:nə*] *adj* Mond-

lunatic ['lu:nətɪk] *n* Wahnsinnige(r) *mf* ♦ *adj* wahnsinnig, irr

lunch [lʌntʃ] *n* Mittagessen *nt*; **~eon** ['lʌntʃən] *n* Mittagessen *nt*; **~eon meat** *n* Frühstücksfleisch *nt*; **~eon voucher** (*BRIT*) *n* Essenmarke *f*; **~time** *n* Mittagszeit *f*

lung [lʌŋ] *n* Lunge *f*

lunge [lʌndʒ] *vi* (*also*: **~ forward**) (los)stürzen; **to ~ at** sich stürzen auf *+acc*

lurch [lə:tʃ] *vi* taumeln; (*NAUT*) schlingern ♦ *n* Ruck *m*; (*NAUT*) Schlingern *nt*; **to leave sb in the ~** jdn im Stich lassen

lure [luə*] *n* Köder *m*; (*fig*) Lockung *f* ♦ *vt* (ver)locken

lurid ['luərɪd] *adj* (*shocking*) grausig, widerlich; (*colour*) grell

lurk [lə:k] *vi* lauern

luscious ['lʌʃəs] *adj* köstlich

lush [lʌʃ] *adj* satt; (*vegetation*) üppig

lust [lʌst] *n* Wollust *f*; (*greed*) Gier *f* ♦ *vi*: **to ~ after** gieren nach

lustre ['lʌstə*] (*US* **luster**) *n* Glanz *m*

Luxembourg ['lʌksəmbə:g] *n* Luxemburg *nt*

luxuriant [lʌg'zjuərɪənt] *adj* üppig

luxurious [lʌg'zjuərɪəs] *adj* luxuriös, Luxus-

luxury ['lʌkʃərɪ] *n* Luxus *m* ♦ *cpd* Luxus-

lying ['laɪɪŋ] *n* Lügen *nt* ♦ *adj* verlogen

lynx [lɪŋks] *n* Luchs *m*

lyric ['lɪrɪk] *n* Lyrik *f* ♦ *adj* lyrisch; **~s** *pl* (*words for song*) (Lied)text *m*; **~al** *adj* lyrisch, gefühlvoll

M, m

m *abbr* = **metre**; **mile**; **million**

M.A. *abbr* = **Master of Arts**

mac [mæk] (*BRIT: inf*) *n* Regenmantel *m*

macaroni [mækə'rəunɪ] *n* Makkaroni *pl*

machine [mə'ʃi:n] *n* Maschine *f* ♦ *vt* (*dress etc*) mit der Maschine nähen; **~ gun** *n* Maschinengewehr *nt*; **~ language** *n* (*COMPUT*) Maschinensprache *f*; **~ry** *n* Maschinerie *f*

macho ['mætʃəu] *adj* macho

mackerel ['mækrəl] *n* Makrele *f*

mackintosh ['mækɪntɒʃ] *n* Regenmantel *m*

mad [mæd] *adj* verrückt; (*dog*) tollwütig; (*angry*) wütend; ~ **about** (*fond of*) verrückt nach, versessen auf +*acc*

madam ['mædəm] *n* gnädige Frau *f*

madden ['mædn] *vt* verrückt machen; (*make angry*) ärgern

made [meɪd] *pt, pp of* **make**

made-to-measure ['meɪdtə'meʒə'] (*BRIT*) *adj* Maß-

mad ['mæd]: ~**ly** *adv* wahnsinnig; ~**man** (*irreg*) *n* Verrückte(r) *m*, Irre(r) *m*; ~**ness** *n* Wahnsinn *m*

magazine [mægə'ziːn] *n* Zeitschrift *f*; (*in gun*) Magazin *nt*

maggot ['mægət] *n* Made *f*

magic ['mædʒɪk] *n* Zauberei *f*, Magie *f*; (*fig*) Zauber *m* ♦ *adj* magisch, Zauber-; ~**al** *adj* magisch; ~**ian** [mə'dʒɪʃən] *n* Zauberer *m*

magistrate ['mædʒɪstreɪt] *n* (*Friedens*)richter *m*

magnanimous [mæg'nænɪməs] *adj* großmütig

magnet ['mægnɪt] *n* Magnet *m*; ~**ic** [mæg'netɪk] *adj* magnetisch; ~ **tape** *n* Magnetband *nt*; ~**ism** *n* Magnetismus *m*; (*fig*) Ausstrahlungskraft *f*

magnificent [mæg'nɪfɪsnt] *adj* großartig

magnify ['mægnɪfaɪ] *vt* vergrößern; ~**ing glass** *n* Lupe *f*

magnitude ['mægnɪtjuːd] *n* (*size*) Größe *f*; (*importance*) Ausmaß *nt*

magpie ['mægpaɪ] *n* Elster *f*

mahogany [mə'hɔgənɪ] *n* Mahagoni *nt* ♦ *cpd* Mahagoni-

maid [meɪd] *n* Dienstmädchen *nt*; **old** ~ alte Jungfer *f*

maiden ['meɪdn] *n* Maid *f* ♦ *adj* (*flight, speech*) Jungfern-; ~ **name** *n* Mädchenname *m*

mail [meɪl] *n* Post *f* ♦ *vt* aufgeben; ~ **box** (*US*) *n* Briefkasten *m*; ~**ing list** *n* Anschreibeliste *f*; ~ **order** *n* Bestellung *f* durch die Post; ~ **order firm** *n* Versandhaus *nt*

maim [meɪm] *vt* verstümmeln

main [meɪn] *adj* hauptsächlich, Haupt-

♦ *n* (*pipe*) Hauptleitung *f*; **the ~s** *npl* (*ELEC*) das Stromnetz; **in the** ~ im Großen und Ganzen; ~**frame** *n* (*COMPUT*) Großrechner *m*; ~**land** *n* Festland *nt*; ~**ly** *adv* hauptsächlich; ~ **road** *n* Hauptstraße *f*; ~**stay** *n* (*fig*) Hauptstütze *f*; ~**stream** *n* Hauptrichtung *f*

maintain [meɪn'teɪn] *vt* (*machine, roads*) instand *or* in Stand halten; (*support*) unterhalten; (*keep up*) aufrechterhalten; (*claim*) behaupten; (*innocence*) beteuern

maintenance ['meɪntənəns] *n* (*TECH*) Wartung *f*; (*of family*) Unterhalt *m*

maize [meɪz] *n* Mais *m*

majestic [mə'dʒestɪk] *adj* majestätisch

majesty ['mædʒɪstɪ] *n* Majestät *f*

major ['meɪdʒə'] *n* Major *m* (*MUS*) Dur; (*more important*) Haupt-; (*bigger*) größer

Majorca [mə'jɔːkə] *n* Mallorca *nt*

majority [mə'dʒɔrɪtɪ] *n* Mehrheit *f*; (*JUR*) Volljährigkeit *f*

make [meɪk] (*pt, pp* **made**) *vt* machen; (*appoint*) ernennen (zu); (*cause to do sth*) veranlassen; (*reach*) erreichen; (*in time*) schaffen; (*earn*) verdienen ♦ *n* Marke *f*; **to ~ sth happen** *etw* geschehen lassen; **to ~ it** es schaffen; **what time do you ~ it?** wie spät hast du es?; **to ~ do with** auskommen mit; ~ **for** *vi* gehen/fahren nach; ~ **out** *vt* (*write out*) ausstellen; (*understand*) verstehen; ~ **up** *vt* machen; (*face*) schminken; (*quarrel*) beilegen; (*story etc*) erfinden ♦ *vi* sich versöhnen; ~ **up for** *vt* wieder gutmachen; (*COMM*) vergüten; ~**believe** *n* Fantasie *f*; ~**r** *n* (*COMM*) Hersteller *m*; ~**shift** *adj* behelfsmäßig, Not-; ~**up** *n* Schminke *f*, Make-up *nt*; ~**up remover** *n* Make-up-Entferner *m*; **making** *n*: **in the making** im Entstehen; **to have the makings of** das Zeug haben zu

malaria [mə'leərɪə] *n* Malaria *f*

Malaysia [mə'leɪzɪə] *n* Malaysia *nt*

male [meɪl] *n* Mann *m*; (*animal*)

Männlichen m ♦ *adj* männlich

malevolent [mə'levələnt] *adj* übelwollend

malfunction [mæl'fʌŋkʃən] *n* (MED) Funktionsstörung *f*; (*of machine*) Defekt *m*

malice ['mælɪs] *n* Bosheit *f*; **malicious** [mə'lɪʃəs] *adj* böswillig, gehässig

malign [mə'laɪn] *vt* verleumden ♦ *adj* böse

malignant [mə'lɪgnənt] *adj* bösartig

mall [mɔːl] *n* (*also:* **shopping ~**) Einkaufszentrum *nt*

malleable ['mælɪəbl] *adj* formbar

mallet ['mælɪt] *n* Holzhammer *m*

malnutrition [mælnjuː'trɪʃən] *n* Unterernährung *f*

malpractice [mæl'præktɪs] *n* Amtsvergehen *nt*

malt [mɔːlt] *n* Malz *nt*

Malta ['mɔːltə] *n* Malta *nt*; **Maltese** [mɔːl'tiːz] *adj inv* maltesisch ♦ *n inv* Malteser(in) *m(f)*

maltreat [mæl'triːt] *vt* misshandeln

mammal ['mæml] *n* Säugetier *nt*

mammoth ['mæməθ] *n* Mammut *nt* ♦ *adj* Mammut-

man [mæn-] (*pl* **men**) *n* Mann *m*; (*human race*) der Mensch, die Menschen *pl* ♦ *vt* bemannen; **an old ~** ein alter Mann, ein Greis *m*; **~ and wife** Mann und Frau

manage ['mænɪdʒ] *vi* zurechtkommen ♦ *vt* (*control*) führen, leiten; (*cope with*) fertig werden mit; **~able** *adj* (*person, animal*) fügsam; (*object*) handlich; **~ment** *n* (*control*) Führung *f*, Leitung *f*; (*directors*) Management *nt*; **~r** *n* Geschäftsführer *m*; **~ress** [mænɪdʒə'res] *n* Geschäftsführerin *f*; **~rial** [mænɪ-'dʒɪərɪəl] *adj* (*post*) leitend; (*problem etc*) Management-; **managing** ['mænɪdʒɪŋ] *adj*: **managing director** Betriebsleiter *m*

mandarin ['mændərɪn] *n* (*fruit*) Mandarine *f*

mandatory ['mændətərɪ] *adj* obligatorisch

mane [meɪn] *n* Mähne *f*

maneuver [mə'nuːvər] (*US*) = **manoeuvre**

manfully ['mænfəlɪ] *adv* mannhaft

mangle ['mæŋgl] *vt* verstümmeln ♦ *n* Mangel *f*

mango ['mæŋgəʊ] (*pl* **~es**) *n* Mango(pflaume) *f*

mangy ['meɪndʒɪ] *adj* (*dog*) räudig

man [mæn-]: **~handle** *vt* grob behandeln; **~hole** *n* (Straßen)schacht *m*; **~hood** *n* Mannesalter *nt*; (*~liness*) Männlichkeit *f*; **~hour** *n* Arbeitsstunde *f*; **~hunt** *n* Fahndung *f*

mania ['meɪnɪə] *n* Manie *f*; **~c** ['meɪnɪæk] *n* Wahnsinnige(r) *mf*

manic ['mænɪk] *adj* (*behaviour, activity*) hektisch

manicure ['mænɪkjʊər] *n* Maniküre *f*; **~ set** *n* Necessaire *nt*, Nessessär *nt*

manifest ['mænɪfest] *vt* offenbaren ♦ *adj* offenkundig; **~ation** [mænɪfes-'teɪʃən] *n* (*sign*) Anzeichen *nt*

manifesto [mænɪ'festəʊ] *n* Manifest *nt*

manipulate [mə'nɪpjʊleɪt] *vt* handhaben; (*fig*) manipulieren

man [mæn-]: **~kind** *n* Menschheit *f*; **~ly** ['mænlɪ] *adj* männlich; mannhaft; **~made** *adj* (*fibre*) künstlich

manner ['mænər] *n* Art *f*, Weise *f*; **~s** *npl* (*behaviour*) Manieren *pl*; **in a ~ of speaking** sozusagen; **~ism** *n* (*of person*) Angewohnheit *f*, (*of style*) Manieriertheit *f*

manoeuvre [mə'nuːvər] (*US* **maneuver**) *vt, vi* manövrieren ♦ *n* (*MIL*) Feldzug *m*; (*general*) Manöver *nt*, Schachzug *m*

manor ['mænər] *n* Landgut *nt*

manpower ['mænpaʊər] *n* Arbeitskräfte *pl*

mansion ['mænʃən] *n* Villa *f*

manslaughter ['mænslɔːtər] *n* Totschlag *m*

mantelpiece ['mæntlpiːs] *n* Kaminsims *m*

manual [ˈmænjuəl] adj manuell, Hand- ♦ n Handbuch nt

manufacture [mænjuˈfæktʃəʳ] vt herstellen ♦ n Herstellung f; **~r** n Hersteller m

manure [məˈnjuəʳ] n Dünger m

manuscript [ˈmænjuskrɪpt] n Manuskript nt

Manx [mæŋks] adj der Insel Man

many [ˈmɛnɪ] adj, pron viele; **a great ~** sehr viele; **~ a time** oft

map [mæp] n (Land)karte f; (of town) Stadtplan m ♦ vt eine Karte machen von; **~ out** vt (fig) ausarbeiten

maple [ˈmeɪpl] n Ahorn m

mar [mɑːʳ] vt verderben

marathon [ˈmærəθən] n (SPORT) Marathonlauf m; (fig) Marathon m

marble [ˈmɑːbl] n Marmor m; (for game) Murmel f

March [mɑːtʃ] n März m

march [mɑːtʃ] vi marschieren ♦ n Marsch m

mare [mɛəʳ] n Stute f

margarine [mɑːdʒəˈriːn] n Margarine f

margin [ˈmɑːdʒɪn] n Rand m; (extra amount) Spielraum m; (COMM) Spanne f; **~al** adj (note) Rand-; (difference etc) geringfügig; **~al (seat)** n (POL) Wahlkreis, der nur mit knapper Mehrheit gehalten wird

marigold [ˈmærɪgəuld] n Ringelblume f

marijuana [mærɪˈwɑːnə] n Marihuana nt

marina [məˈriːnə] n Jachthafen m

marinate [ˈmærɪneɪt] vt marinieren

marine [məˈriːn] adj Meeres-, See- ♦ n (MIL) Marineinfanterist m

marital [ˈmærɪtl] adj ehelich, Ehe-; **~ status** n Familienstand m

maritime [ˈmærɪtaɪm] adj See-

mark [mɑːk] n (coin) Mark f; (spot) Fleck m; (scar) Kratzer m; (sign) Zeichen nt; (target) Ziel nt; (SCH) Note f ♦ vt (make ~ on) Flecken/Kratzer machen auf +acc; (indicate) markieren;

(exam) korrigieren; **to ~ time** (also fig) auf der Stelle treten; **~ out** vt bestimmen; (area) abstecken; **~ed** adj deutlich; **~er** n (in book) (Lese)zeichen nt; (on road) Schild nt

market [ˈmɑːkɪt] n Markt m; (stock ~) Börse f ♦ vt (COMM: new product) auf den Markt bringen; (sell) vertreiben; **~ garden** (BRIT) n Handelsgärtnerei f; **~ing** n Marketing nt; **~ research** n Marktforschung f; **~ value** n Marktwert m

marksman [ˈmɑːksmən] (irreg) n Scharfschütze m

marmalade [ˈmɑːməleɪd] n Orangenmarmelade f

maroon [məˈruːn] vt aussetzen ♦ adj (colour) kastanienbraun

marquee [mɑːˈkiː] n große(s) Zelt nt

marriage [ˈmærɪdʒ] n Ehe f; (wedding) Heirat f; **~ bureau** n Heiratsinstitut nt; **~ certificate** n Heiratsurkunde f

married [ˈmærɪd] adj (person) verheiratet; (couple, life) Ehe-

marrow [ˈmærəu] n (Knochen)mark nt; (BOT) Kürbis m

marry [ˈmærɪ] vt (join) trauen; (take as husband, wife) heiraten ♦ vi (also: **get married**) heiraten

marsh [mɑːʃ] n Sumpf m

marshal [ˈmɑːʃl] n (US) Bezirkspolizeichef m ♦ vt (an)ordnen, arrangieren

marshy [ˈmɑːʃɪ] adj sumpfig

martial law [ˈmɑːʃl] n Kriegsrecht nt

martyr [ˈmɑːtəʳ] n (also fig) Märtyrer(in) m(f) ♦ vt zum Märtyrer machen; **~dom** n Martyrium nt

marvel [ˈmɑːvl] n Wunder nt ♦ vi: **to ~ (at)** sich wundern (über +acc); **~lous** (US **~ous**) adj wunderbar

Marxist [ˈmɑːksɪst] n Marxist(in) m(f)

marzipan [ˈmɑːzɪpæn] n Marzipan nt

mascara [mæsˈkɑːrə] n Wimperntusche f

mascot [ˈmæskət] n Maskottchen nt

masculine [ˈmæskjulɪn] adj männlich

mash [mæʃ] n Brei m; **~ed potatoes**

npl Kartoffelbrei *m or* -püree *nt*

mask [mɑːsk] *n (also fig)* Maske *f* ♦ *vt* maskieren, verdecken

mason ['meɪsn] *n (stonemason)* Steinmetz *m; (freemason)* Freimaurer *m;* **~ry** *n* Mauerwerk *nt*

masquerade [mæskə'reɪd] *n* Maskerade *f* ♦ *vi:* **to ~ as** sich ausgeben als

mass [mæs] *n* Masse *f; (greater part)* Mehrheit *f; (REL)* Messe *f* ♦ *vi* sich sammeln; **the ~es** *npl (people)* die Masse(n) *f(pl)*

massacre ['mæsəkə*] *n* Blutbad *nt* ♦ *vt* niedermetzeln, massakrieren

massage ['mæsɑːʒ] *n* Massage *f* ♦ *vt* massieren

massive ['mæsɪv] *adj* gewaltig, massiv

mass media *npl* Massenmedien *pl*

mass production *n* Massenproduktion *f*

mast [mɑːst] *n* Mast *m*

master ['mɑːstə*] *n* Herr *m; (NAUT)* Kapitän *m; (teacher)* Lehrer *m; (artist)* Meister *m* ♦ *vt* meistern; *(language etc)* beherrschen; **~ly** *adj* meisterhaft; **~mind** *n* Kapazität *f* ♦ *vt* geschickt lenken; **M~ of Arts** *n* Magister *m* der philosophischen Fakultät; **M~ of Science** *n* Magister *m* der naturwissenschaftlichen Fakultät; **~piece** *n* Meisterwerk *nt;* **~ plan** *n* kluge(r) Plan *m;* **~y** *n* Können *nt*

masturbate ['mæstəbeɪt] *vi* masturbieren, onanieren

mat [mæt] *n* Matte *f; (for table)* Untersetzer *m* ♦ *adj =* **matt**

match [mætʃ] *n* Streichholz *nt; (sth corresponding)* Pendant *nt; (SPORT)* Wettkampf *m; (ball games)* Spiel *nt* ♦ *vt (be like, suit)* passen zu; *(equal)* gleichkommen *+dat* ♦ *vi* zusammenpassen; **it's a good ~ (for)** es passt gut (zu); **~box** *n* Streichholzschachtel *f;* **~ing** *adj* passend

mate [meɪt] *n (companion)* Kamerad *m; (spouse)* Lebensgefährte *m; (of animal)* Weibchen *nt/*Männchen *nt; (NAUT)*

Schiffsoffizier *m* ♦ *vi (animals)* sich paaren ♦ *vt (animals)* paaren

material [mə'tɪərɪəl] *n* Material *nt; (for book, cloth)* Stoff *m* ♦ *adj (important)* wesentlich; *(damage)* Sach-; *(comforts etc)* materiell; **~s** *npl (for building etc)* Materialien *pl;* **~istic** [mətɪərə'lɪstɪk] *adj* materialistisch; **~ize** *vi* sich verwirklichen, zustande *or* zu Stande kommen

maternal [mə'tɜːnl] *adj* mütterlich, Mutter-

maternity [mə'tɜːnɪtɪ] *adj (dress)* Umstands-; *(benefit)* Wochen-; **~ hospital** *n* Entbindungsheim *nt*

math [mæθ] *(US) n =* **maths**

mathematical [mæθə'mætɪkl] *adj* mathematisch; **mathematics** *n* Mathematik *f;* **maths** *(US* math*) n* Mathe *f*

matinée ['mætɪneɪ] *n* Matinee *f*

matrices ['meɪtrɪsɪz] *npl of* **matrix**

matriculation [mətrɪkju'leɪʃən] *n* Immatrikulation *f*

matrimonial [mætrɪ'məunɪəl] *adj* ehelich, Ehe-

matrimony ['mætrɪmənɪ] *n* Ehestand *m*

matrix ['meɪtrɪks] *(pl* **matrices***) n* Matrize *f; (GEOL etc)* Matrix *f*

matron ['meɪtrən] *n (MED)* Oberin *f; (SCH)* Hausmutter *f*

matt [mæt] *adj (paint)* matt

matted ['mætɪd] *adj* verfilzt

matter ['mætə*] *n (substance)* Materie *f; (affair)* Angelegenheit *f* ♦ *vi* darauf ankommen; **no ~ how/what** egal wie/was; **what is the ~?** was ist los?; **as a ~ of course** selbstverständlich; **as a ~ of fact** eigentlich; **it doesn't ~** es macht nichts; **~-of-fact** *adj* sachlich, nüchtern

mattress ['mætrɪs] *n* Matratze *f*

mature [mə'tjuə*] *adj* reif ♦ *vi* reif werden; **maturity** [mə'tjuərɪtɪ] *n* Reife *f*

maul [mɔːl] *vt* übel zurichten

maxima ['mæksɪmə] *npl of* **maximum**

maximum ['mæksɪməm] *(pl* **maxima***) adj* Höchst-, Maximal- ♦ *n* Maximum *nt*

May [meɪ] *n* Mai *m*

may [meɪ] (*conditional* **might**) *vi* (*be possible*) können; (*have permission*) dürfen; **he ~ come** er kommt vielleicht; **~be** ['meɪbiː] *adv* vielleicht

May Day *n* der 1. Mai

mayhem ['meɪhem] *n* Chaos *nt*; (*US*) Körperverletzung *f*

mayonnaise [meɪə'neɪz] *n* Majonäse *f*, Mayonnaise *f*

mayor [mɛəˀ] *n* Bürgermeister *m*; **~ess** *n* Bürgermeisterin *f*; (*wife*) (die) Frau *f* Bürgermeister

maypole ['meɪpəʊl] *n* Maibaum *m*

maze [meɪz] *n* Irrgarten *m*; (*fig*) Wirrwarr *nt*

M.D. *abbr* = **Doctor of Medicine**

KEYWORD

---

me [miː] *pron* **1** (*direct*) mich; **it's me** ich bins

2 (*indirect*) mir; **give them to me** gib sie mir

3 (*after prep: +acc*) mich; (: *+dat*) mir; **with/without me** mit mir/ohne mich

---

meadow ['medəʊ] *n* Wiese *f*

meagre ['miːgəˀ] (*US* **meager**) *adj* dürftig, spärlich

meal [miːl] *n* Essen *nt*, Mahlzeit *f*; (*grain*) Schrotmehl *nt*; **to have a ~** essen (gehen); **~time** *n* Essenszeit *f*

mean [miːn] (*pt, pp* **meant**) *adj* (*stingy*) geizig; (*spiteful*) gemein; (*average*) durchschnittlich, Durchschnitts- ♦ *vt* (*signify*) bedeuten; (*intend*) vorhaben, beabsichtigen ♦ *n* (*average*) Durchschnitt *m*; **~s** *npl* (*wherewithal*) Mittel *pl*; (*wealth*) Vermögen *nt*; **do you ~ me?** meinst du mich?; **do you ~ it?** meinst du das ernst?; **what do you ~?** was willst du damit sagen?; **to be ~t for sb/sth** für jdn/etw bestimmt sein; **by ~s of** durch; **by all ~s** selbstverständlich; **by no ~s** keineswegs

meander [mɪˈændəˀ] *vi* sich schlängeln

meaning ['miːnɪŋ] *n* Bedeutung *f*; (*of life*) Sinn *m*; **~ful** *adj* bedeutungsvoll; (*life*) sinnvoll; **~less** *adj* sinnlos

meanness [miːnnɪs] *n* (*stinginess*) Geiz *m*; (*pettiness*) Gemeinheit *f*

meant [ment] *pt, pp of* **mean**

meantime ['miːntaɪm] *adv* inzwischen

meanwhile ['miːnwaɪl] *adv* inzwischen

measles ['miːzlz] *n* Masern *pl*

measly ['miːzli] (*inf*) *adj* poplig

measure ['meʒəˀ] *vt, vi* messen ♦ *n* Maß *nt*; (*step*) Maßnahme *f*; **~ments** *npl* Maße *pl*

meat [miːt] *n* Fleisch *nt*; **cold ~** Aufschnitt *m*; **~ ball** *n* Fleischkloß *m*; **~ pie** *n* Fleischpastete *f*; **~y** *adj* fleischig; (*fig*) gehaltvoll

Mecca ['mekə] *n* Mekka *nt* (*also fig*)

mechanic [mɪˈkænɪk] *n* Mechaniker *m*; **~al** *adj* mechanisch; **~s** *n* Mechanik *f* ♦ *npl* Technik *f*

mechanism ['mekənɪzəm] *n* Mechanismus *m*

mechanize ['mekənaɪz] *vt* mechanisieren

medal ['medl] *n* Medaille *f*; (*decoration*) Orden *m*; **~list** (*US* **medalist**) *n* Medaillengewinner(in) *m(f)*

meddle ['medl] *vi*: **to ~ (in)** sich einmischen (in *+acc*); **to ~ with sth** sich an etw *dat* zu schaffen machen

media ['miːdɪə] *npl* Medien *pl*

mediaeval [medɪˈiːvl] *adj* = **medieval**

median ['miːdɪən] (*US*) *n* (*also*: **~ strip**) Mittelstreifen *m*

mediate ['miːdɪeɪt] *vi* vermitteln; **mediator** *n* Vermittler *m*

Medicaid ['medɪkeɪd] (®) *US*) *n* medizinisches Versorgungsprogramm für sozial Schwache

medical ['medɪkl] *adj* medizinisch; Medizin-; ärztlich ♦ *n* (ärztliche) Untersuchung *f*

Medicare ['medɪkɛəˀ] (*US*) *n* staatliche Krankenversicherung besonders für Ältere

medicated ['medɪkeɪtɪd] *adj* medizinisch

medication [mɛdɪ'keɪʃən] n (drugs etc) Medikamente pl

medicinal [mɛ'dɪsɪnl] adj medizinisch, Heil-

medicine ['mɛdsɪn] n Medizin f; (drugs) Arznei f

medieval [mɛdɪ'iːvl] adj mittelalterlich

mediocre [miːdɪ'əʊkə'] adj mittelmäßig

meditate ['mɛdɪteɪt] vi meditieren; **to ~ (on sth)** (über etw acc) nachdenken; **(on sth)** [mɛdɪ'teɪʃən] n Nachsinnen nt; Meditation f

Mediterranean [mɛdɪtə'reɪnɪən] adj Mittelmeer-; (person) südländisch; **the ~ (Sea)** das Mittelmeer

medium ['miːdɪəm] adj mittlere(r, s), Mittel-, mittel- ♦ n Mitte f; (means) Mittel nt; (person) Medium nt; **happy ~** goldener Mittelweg; **~-sized** adj mittelgroß; **~ wave** Mittelwelle f

medley ['mɛdlɪ] n Gemisch nt

meek [miːk] adj sanft(mütig); (pej) duckmäuserisch

meet [miːt] (pt, pp **met**) vt (encounter) treffen, begegnen +dat; (by arrangement) sich treffen mit; (difficulties) stoßen auf +acc; (get to know) kennen lernen; (fetch) abholen; (join) zusammentreffen mit; (satisfy) entsprechen +dat ♦ vi sich treffen; (become acquainted) sich kennen lernen; **~ with** vt (problems) stoßen auf +acc; (US: people) zusammentreffen mit; **~ing** n Treffen nt; (business ~ing) Besprechung f; (of committee) Sitzung f; (assembly) Versammlung f

mega- ['mɛgə-] (inf) prefix Mega-; **~byte** n (COMPUT) Megabyte nt; **~phone** n Megafon nt, Megaphon nt

melancholy ['mɛlənkəlɪ] adj (person) melancholisch; (sight, event) traurig

mellow ['mɛləʊ] adj mild, weich; (fruit) reif; (fig) gesetzt ♦ vi reif werden

melodious [mɪ'ləʊdɪəs] adj wohlklingend

melody ['mɛlədɪ] n Melodie f

melon ['mɛlən] n Melone f

melt [mɛlt] vi schmelzen; (anger) verfliegen ♦ vt schmelzen; **~ away** vi dahinschmelzen; **~ down** vt einschmelzen; **~down** n (in nuclear reactor) Kernschmelze f; **~ing point** n Schmelzpunkt m; **~ing pot** n (fig) Schmelztiegel m

member ['mɛmbə'] n Mitglied nt; (of tribe, species) Angehörige(r) f(m); (ANAT) Glied nt; **M~ of Parliament** (BRIT) n Parlamentsmitglied nt; **M~ of the European Parliament** (BRIT) n Mitglied nt des Europäischen Parlaments; **~ship** n Mitgliedschaft f; **to seek ~ship** of einen Antrag auf Mitgliedschaft stellen; **~ship card** n Mitgliedskarte f

memento [mə'mɛntəʊ] n Andenken nt

memo ['mɛməʊ] n Mitteilung f

memoirs ['mɛmwɑːz] npl Memoiren pl

memorable ['mɛmərəbl] adj denkwürdig

memoranda [mɛmə'rændə] npl of **memorandum**

memorandum [mɛmə'rændəm] (pl **memoranda**) n Mitteilung f

memorial [mɪ'mɔːrɪəl] n Denkmal n ♦ adj Gedenk-

memorize ['mɛməraɪz] vt sich einprägen

memory ['mɛmərɪ] n Gedächtnis nt; (of computer) Speicher m; (sth recalled) Erinnerung f

men [mɛn] pl of **man** ♦ n (human race) die Menschen pl

menace ['mɛnɪs] n Drohung f; Gefahr f ♦ vt bedrohen; **menacing** adj drohend

menagerie [mɪ'nædʒərɪ] n Tierschau f

mend [mɛnd] vt reparieren, flicken ♦ vi (ver)heilen ♦ n ausgebesserte Stelle f; **on the ~** auf dem Wege der Besserung; **~ing** n (articles) Flickarbeit f

menial ['miːnɪəl] adj niedrig

meningitis [mɛnɪn'dʒaɪtɪs] n Hirnhautentzündung f, Meningitis f

menopause ['menəupɔːz] n Wechseljahre pl, Menopause f

menstruation [menstru'eɪʃən] n Menstruation f

mental ['mentl] adj geistig, Geistes-; (arithmetic) Kopf-; (hospital) Nerven-; (cruelty) seelisch; (inf: abnormal) verrückt; **~ity** [men'tælɪtɪ] n Mentalität f

menthol ['menθɔl] n Menthol nt

mention ['menʃən] n Erwähnung f ♦ vt erwähnen; **don't ~ it!** bitte (sehr), gern geschehen

mentor ['mentɔː] n Mentor m

menu ['menjuː] n Speisekarte f

MEP n abbr = **Member of the European Parliament**

mercenary ['mɜːsɪnərɪ] adj (person) geldgierig ♦ n Söldner m

merchandise ['mɜːtʃəndaɪz] n (Handels)ware f

merchant ['mɜːtʃənt] n Kaufmann m; **~ bank** (BRIT) n Handelsbank f; **~ navy** (US **~ marine**) n Handelsmarine f

merciful ['mɜːsɪful] adj gnädig

merciless ['mɜːsɪlɪs] adj erbarmungslos

mercury ['mɜːkjurɪ] n Quecksilber nt

mercy ['mɜːsɪ] n Erbarmen nt; Gnade f; **at the ~ of** ausgeliefert +dat

mere [mɪə] adj bloß; **~ly** adv bloß

merge [mɜːdʒ] vt verbinden; (COMM) fusionieren ♦ vi verschmelzen; (roads) zusammenlaufen; (COMM) fusionieren; **~r** n (COMM) Fusion f

meringue [mə'ræŋ] n Baiser nt

merit ['merɪt] n Verdienst nt; (advantage) Vorzug m ♦ vt verdienen

mermaid ['mɜːmeɪd] n Wassernixe f

merry ['merɪ] adj fröhlich; **~-go-round** n Karussell nt

mesh [meʃ] n Masche f

mesmerize ['mezməraɪz] vt hypnotisieren; (fig) faszinieren

mess [mes] n Unordnung f; (dirt) Schmutz m; (trouble) Schwierigkeiten pl; (MIL) Messe f; **~ about** or **around** vi (play the fool) herumalbern; (do nothing in particular) herumgammeln; **~ about** or **around with** vt fus (tinker with) herummurksen an +dat; **~ up** vt verpfuschen; (make untidy) in Unordnung bringen

message ['mesɪdʒ] n Mitteilung f; **to get the ~** kapieren

messenger ['mesɪndʒəʳ] n Bote m

Messrs ['mesəz] abbr (on letters) die Herren

messy ['mesɪ] adj schmutzig; (untidy) unordentlich

met [met] pt, pp of **meet**

metabolism [me'tæbəlɪzəm] n Stoffwechsel m

metal ['metl] n Metall nt; **~lic** adj metallisch; (made of ~) aus Metall

metaphor ['metəfəʳ] n Metapher f

meteorology [miːtɪə'rɒlədʒɪ] n Meteorologie f

meter ['miːtəʳ] n Zähler m; (US) = **metre**

method ['meθəd] n Methode f; **~ical** [mɪ'θɒdɪkl] adj methodisch; **M~ist** ['meθədɪst] adj methodistisch ♦ n Methodist(in) m(f); **~ology** [meθə'dɒlədʒɪ] n Methodik f

meths [meθs] (BRIT) n(pl) = **methylated spirit(s)**

methylated spirit(s) ['meθɪleɪtɪd-] (BRIT) n (Brenn)spiritus m

meticulous [mɪ'tɪkjuləs] adj (über)genau

metre ['miːtəʳ] (US **meter**) n Meter m or nt

metric ['metrɪk] adj (also: **~al**) metrisch

metropolitan [metrə'pɒlɪtn] adj der Großstadt; **M~ Police** (BRIT) n: **the M~ Police** die Londoner Polizei

mettle ['metl] n Mut m

mew [mjuː] vi (cat) miauen

mews [mjuːz] n: **~ cottage** ehemaliges Kutscherhäuschen

Mexican ['meksɪkən] adj mexikanisch ♦ n Mexikaner(in) m(f)

Mexico ['meksɪkəu] n Mexiko nt

miaow [miː'au] vi miauen

mice [maɪs] pl of **mouse**

micro ['maɪkrəu] n (also: **~computer**) Mikrocomputer m; **~chip** n Mikrochip m; **~cosm** ['maɪkrəukɔzəm] n Mikrokosmos m; **~phone** n Mikrofon m, Mikrophon nt; **~scope** n Mikroskop nt; **~wave** n (also: **~wave oven**) Mikrowelle(nherd m) f

mid [mɪd] adj: **in ~ afternoon** am Nachmittag; **in ~ air** in der Luft; **in ~ May** Mitte Mai

midday [mɪd'deɪ] n Mittag m

middle ['mɪdl] n Mitte f; (waist) Taille f ♦ adj mittlere(r, s), Mittel-; **in the ~ of** mitten in +dat; **~aged** adj mittleren Alters; **M~ Ages** npl: **the M~ Ages** das Mittelalter; **~class** adj Mittelstands-; **M~ East** n: **the M~ East** der Nahe Osten; **~man** (irreg) n (COMM) Zwischenhändler m; **~ name** n zweiter Vorname m; **~ weight** n (BOXING) Mittelgewicht nt

middling ['mɪdlɪŋ] adj mittelmäßig

midge [mɪdʒ] n Mücke f

midget ['mɪdʒɪt] n Liliputaner(in) m(f)

midnight ['mɪdnaɪt] n Mitternacht f

midriff ['mɪdrɪf] n Taille f

midst [mɪdst] n: **in the ~ of** (persons) mitten unter +dat; (things) mitten in +dat

mid [mɪd'-]: **~summer** n Hochsommer m; **~way** adv auf halbem Wege ♦ adj Mittel-; **~week** adv in der Mitte der Woche

midwife ['mɪdwaɪf] (irreg) n Hebamme f; **~ry** ['mɪdwɪfərɪ] n Geburtshilfe f

midwinter [mɪd'wɪntə'] n tiefste(r) Winter m

might [maɪt] vi see **may** ♦ n Macht f, Kraft f; **I ~ come** ich komme vielleicht; **~y** adj, adv mächtig

migraine ['miːgreɪn] n Migräne f

migrant ['maɪgrənt] adj Wander-; (bird) Zug-

migrate [maɪ'greɪt] vi (ab)wandern; (birds) (fort)ziehen; **migration** [maɪ'greɪʃən] n Wanderung f, Zug m

mike [maɪk] n = **microphone**

Milan [mɪ'læn] n Mailand n

mild [maɪld] adj mild; (medicine, interest) leicht; (person) sanft ♦ n (beer) leichtes dunkles Bier

mildew ['mɪldjuː] n (on plants) Mehltau m; (on food) Schimmel m

mildly ['maɪldlɪ] adv leicht; **to put it ~** gelinde gesagt

mile [maɪl] n Meile f; **~age** n Meilenzahl f; **~ometer** n = **milometer**; **~stone** n (also fig) Meilenstein m

militant ['mɪlɪtnt] adj militant ♦ n Militante(r) m/f

military ['mɪlɪtərɪ] adj militärisch, Militär-, Wehr-

militate ['mɪlɪteɪt] vi: **to ~ against** entgegenwirken +dat

militia [mɪ'lɪʃə] n Miliz f

milk [mɪlk] n Milch f ♦ vt (also fig) melken; **~ chocolate** n Milchschokolade f; **~man** (irreg) n Milchmann m; **~ shake** n Milchmixgetränk nt; **~y** adj milchig; **M~y Way** n Milchstraße f

mill [mɪl] n Mühle f; (factory) Fabrik f ♦ vt mahlen ♦ vi umherlaufen

millennia [mɪ'lenɪə] npl of **millennium**

millennium [mɪ'lenɪəm] (pl **~s** or **millennia**) n Jahrtausend nt; **~ bug** n (COMPUT) Jahrtausendfehler m

miller ['mɪlə'] n Müller m

milligram(me) ['mɪlɪgræm] n Milligramm nt

millimetre ['mɪlɪmiːtə'] (US **millimeter**) n Millimeter m

million ['mɪljən] n Million f; **a ~ times** tausendmal; **~aire** [mɪljə'neə'] n Millionär(in) m(f)

millstone ['mɪlstəun] n Mühlstein m

milometer [maɪ'lɔmɪtə'] n ≃ Kilometerzähler m

mime [maɪm] n Pantomime f ♦ vt, vi mimen

mimic ['mɪmɪk] n Mimiker m ♦ vt, vi nachahmen; **~ry** n Nachahmung f; (BIOL) Mimikry f

min. abbr = **minutes; minimum**

mince [mɪns] vt (zer)hacken ♦ n (meat)

Hackfleisch nt; **~meat** n süße Pastetenfüllung f; **~ pie** n gefüllte (süße) Pastete f; **~r** n Fleischwolf m

mind [maɪnd] n Verstand m, Geist m; (opinion) Meinung f ♦ vt aufpassen auf +acc; (object to) etwas haben gegen; **on my ~** auf dem Herzen; **to my ~** meiner Meinung nach; **to be out of one's ~** wahnsinnig sein; **to bear or keep in ~** bedenken; **to change one's ~** es sich dat anders überlegen; **to make up one's ~** sich entschließen; **I don't ~** das macht mir nichts aus; **~ you, ...** allerdings ...; **never ~!** macht nichts!; **"~ the step"** „Vorsicht Stufe"; **~ your own business** kümmern Sie sich um Ihre eigenen Angelegenheiten; **~er** n Aufpasser(in f)(r); **~ful** adj: **~ful of** achtsam auf +acc; **~less** adj sinnlos

mine¹ [maɪn] n (coalmine) Bergwerk nt; (MIL) Mine f ♦ vt abbauen; (MIL) verminen

mine² [maɪn] pron meine(r, s); **that book is ~** das Buch gehört mir; **a friend of ~** ein Freund von mir

minefield ['maɪnfiːld] n Minenfeld nt

miner ['maɪnə*] n Bergarbeiter m

mineral ['mɪnərəl] adj mineralisch, Mineral- ♦ n Mineral nt; **~s** npl (BRIT: soft drinks) alkoholfreie Getränke pl; **~ water** n Mineralwasser nt

minesweeper ['maɪnswiːpə*] n Minensuchboot nt

mingle ['mɪŋgl] vi: **to ~ (with)** sich mischen (unter +acc)

miniature ['mɪnətʃə*] adj Miniatur- ♦ n Miniatur f

minibus ['mɪnɪbʌs] n Kleinbus m

minimal ['mɪnɪml] adj minimal

minimize ['mɪnɪmaɪz] vt auf das Mindestmaß beschränken

minimum ['mɪnɪməm] (pl **minima**) n Minimum nt ♦ adj Mindest-

mining ['maɪnɪŋ] n Bergbau m ♦ adj Bergbau-, Berg-

miniskirt ['mɪnɪskɜːt] n Minirock m

minister ['mɪnɪstə*] n (BRIT: POL) Minister m; (ECCL) Pfarrer m ♦ vi: **to ~ to sb/ sb's needs** sich um jdn kümmern; **~ial** [mɪnɪs'tɪərɪəl] adj ministeriell, Minister-

ministry ['mɪnɪstrɪ] n (BRIT: POL) Ministerium nt; (ECCL: office) geistliche(s) Amt nt

mink [mɪŋk] n Nerz m

minnow ['mɪnəʊ] n Elritze f

minor ['maɪnə*] adj kleiner; (operation) leicht; (problem, poet) unbedeutend; (MUS) Moll ♦ n (BRIT: under 18) Minderjährige(r) mf

minority [maɪ'nɔrɪtɪ, maɪ'nɒrɪtɪ] n Minderheit f

mint [mɪnt] n (plant) Minze f; (sweet) Pfefferminzbonbon m ♦ vt (coins) prägen; **the (Royal** (BRIT) **or US** (US)) **M~** die Münzanstalt; **in ~ condition** in tadellosem Zustand

minus ['maɪnəs] n Minuszeichen nt; (amount) Minusbetrag m ♦ prep minus, weniger

minuscule ['mɪnəskjuːl] adj winzig

minute¹ [maɪ'njuːt] adj winzig; (detailed) minutiös, minuziös

minute² ['mɪnɪt] n Minute f; (moment) Augenblick m; **~s** npl (of meeting etc) Protokoll nt

miracle ['mɪrəkl] n Wunder nt

miraculous [mɪ'rækjʊləs] adj wunderbar

mirage ['mɪrɑːʒ] n Fata Morgana f

mire ['maɪə*] n Morast m

mirror ['mɪrə*] n Spiegel m ♦ vt (wider)spiegeln

mirth [mɜːθ] n Heiterkeit f

misadventure [mɪsəd'ventʃə*] n Missgeschick nt, Unfall m

misanthropist [mɪ'zænθrəpɪst] n Menschenfeind m

misapprehension ['mɪsæprɪ'henʃən] n Missverständnis nt

misbehave [mɪsbɪ'heɪv] vi sich schlecht benehmen

miscalculate [mɪs'kælkjuleɪt] vt falsch

berechnen

miscarriage ['mɪskærɪdʒ] n (MED) Fehlgeburt f; **~ of justice** Fehlurteil nt

miscellaneous [mɪsɪ'leɪnɪəs] adj verschieden

mischief ['mɪstʃɪf] n Unfug m; **mischievous** ['mɪstʃɪvəs] adj (person) durchtrieben; (glance) verschmitzt; (rumour) bösartig

misconception ['mɪskən'sepʃən] n fälschliche Annahme f

misconduct [mɪs'kɔndʌkt] n Vergehen nt; **professional ~** Berufsvergehen nt

misconstrue [mɪskən'struː] vt missverstehen

misdemeanour [mɪsdɪ'miːnə^r] (US **misdemeanor**) n Vergehen nt

miser ['maɪzə^r] n Geizhals m

miserable ['mɪzərəbl] adj (unhappy) unglücklich; (headache, weather) fürchterlich; (poor) elend; (contemptible) erbärmlich

miserly ['maɪzəlɪ] adj geizig

misery ['mɪzərɪ] n Elend nt, Qual f

misfire [mɪs'faɪə^r] vi (gun) versagen; (engine) fehlzünden; (plan) fehlgehen

misfit ['mɪsfɪt] n Außenseiter m

misfortune [mɪs'fɔːtʃən] n Unglück nt

misgiving(s) [mɪs'gɪvɪŋ(z)] n(pl) Bedenken pl

misguided [mɪs'gaɪdɪd] adj fehlgeleitet; (opinions) irrig

mishandle [mɪs'hændl] vt falsch handhaben

mishap ['mɪshæp] n Missgeschick nt

misinform [mɪsɪn'fɔːm] vt falsch unterrichten

misinterpret [mɪsɪn'tɜːprɪt] vt falsch auffassen

misjudge [mɪs'dʒʌdʒ] vt falsch beurteilen

mislay [mɪs'leɪ] (irreg: like lay) vt verlegen

mislead [mɪs'liːd] (irreg: like lead[2]) vt (deceive) irreführen; **~ing** adj irreführend

mismanage [mɪs'mænɪdʒ] vt schlecht verwalten

misnomer [mɪs'nəʊmə^r] n falsche Bezeichnung f

misplace [mɪs'pleɪs] vt verlegen

misprint ['mɪsprɪnt] n Druckfehler m

Miss [mɪs] n Fräulein nt

miss [mɪs] vt (fail to hit, catch) verfehlen; (not notice) verpassen; (be too late) versäumen, verpassen; (omit) auslassen; (regret the absence of) vermissen ♦ vi fehlen ♦ n (shot) Fehlschuss m; (failure) Fehlschlag m; **I ~ you** du fehlst mir; **~ out** vt auslassen

misshapen [mɪs'ʃeɪpən] adj missgestaltet

missile ['mɪsaɪl] n Rakete f

missing ['mɪsɪŋ] adj (person) vermisst; (thing) fehlend; **to be ~** fehlen

mission ['mɪʃən] n (work) Auftrag m; (people) Delegation f; (REL) Mission f; **~ary** n Missionar(in) m(f); **~ statement** n Kurzdarstellung f der Firmenphilosophie

misspell ['mɪs'spel] (irreg: like spell) vt falsch schreiben

misspent ['mɪs'spent] adj (youth) vergeudet

mist [mɪst] n Dunst m, Nebel m ♦ vi (also: **~ over**, **~ up**) sich trüben; (BRIT: windows) sich beschlagen

mistake [mɪs'teɪk] (irreg: like take) n Fehler m ♦ vt (misunderstand) missverstehen; (mix up): **to ~ (sth for sth)** (etw mit etw) verwechseln; **to make a ~** einen Fehler machen; **by ~** aus Versehen; **to ~ A for B** A mit B verwechseln; **~n** pp of **mistake** ♦ adj (idea) falsch; **to be ~n** sich irren

mister ['mɪstə^r] n (inf) Herr m; see **Mr**

mistletoe ['mɪsltəʊ] n Mistel f

mistook [mɪs'tʊk] pt of **mistake**

mistress ['mɪstrɪs] n (teacher) Lehrerin f; (in house) Herrin f; (lover) Geliebte f; see **Mrs**

mistrust [mɪs'trʌst] vt misstrauen +dat

misty ['mɪstɪ] adj neblig

misunderstand [mɪsʌndə'stænd] (*irreg: like* **understand**) *vt, vi* missverstehen, falsch verstehen; **~ing** *n* Missverständnis *nt*; (*disagreement*) Meinungsverschiedenheit *f*

misuse [*n* mɪs'juːs, *vb* mɪs'juːz] *n* falsche(r) Gebrauch *m* ♦ *vt* falsch gebrauchen

mitigate ['mɪtɪgeɪt] *vt* mildern

mitt(en) ['mɪt(n)] *n* Fausthandschuh *m*

mix [mɪks] *vt* (*blend*) (ver)mischen ♦ *vi* (*liquids*) sich (ver)mischen lassen; (*people: get on*) sich vertragen; (: *associate*) Kontakt haben ♦ *n* (~*ture*) Mischung *f*; **~ up** *vt* zusammenmischen; (*confuse*) verwechseln; **~ed** *adj* gemischt; **~ed-up** *adj* durcheinander; **~er** *n* (*for food*) Mixer *m*; **~ture** *n* Mischung *f*; **~-up** *n* Durcheinander *nt*

mm *abbr* (= *millimetre(s)*) mm

moan [məʊn] *n* Stöhnen *nt*; (*complaint*) Klage *f* ♦ *vi* stöhnen; (*complain*) maulen

moat [məʊt] *n* (Burg)graben *m*

mob [mɔb] *n* Mob *m*; (*the masses*) Pöbel *m* ♦ *vt* herfallen über +*acc*

mobile ['məʊbaɪl] *adj* beweglich; (*library etc*) fahrbar ♦ *n* (*decoration*) Mobile *nt*; **~ home** *n* Wohnwagen *m*; **~ phone** *n* (TEL) Mobiltelefon *nt*; **mobility** [məʊ'bɪlɪtɪ] *n* Beweglichkeit *f*; **mobilize** ['məʊbɪlaɪz] *vt* mobilisieren

mock [mɔk] *vt* verspotten; (*defy*) trotzen +*dat* ♦ *adj* Schein-; **~ery** *n* Spott *m*; (*person*) Gespött *nt*

mod [mɔd] *adj see* **convenience**

mode [məʊd] *n* (Art *f und*) Weise *f*

model ['mɔdl] *n* Modell *nt*; (*example*) Vorbild *nt*; (*in fashion*) Mannequin *nt* ♦ *adj* (*railway*) Modell-; (*perfect*) Muster-; vorbildlich ♦ *vt* (*make*) bilden; (*clothes*) vorführen ♦ *vi* als Mannequin arbeiten

modem ['məʊdɛm] *n* (COMPUT) Modem *nt*

moderate [*adj, n* 'mɔdərət, *vb* 'mɔdəreɪt] *adj* gemäßigt ♦ *n* (POL) Gemäßigte(r) *mf* ♦ *vi* sich mäßigen ♦ *vt*

mäßigen; **moderation** [mɔdə'reɪʃən] *n* Mäßigung *f*; **in moderation** mit Maßen

modern ['mɔdən] *adj* modern; (*history, languages*) neuere(r, s); **~ize** *vt* modernisieren

modest ['mɔdɪst] *adj* bescheiden; **~y** *n* Bescheidenheit *f*

modicum ['mɔdɪkəm] *n* bisschen *nt*

modification [mɔdɪfɪ'keɪʃən] *n* (Ab-)änderung *f*

modify ['mɔdɪfaɪ] *vt* abändern

module ['mɔdjuːl] *n* (*component*) (Bau)element *nt*; (SPACE) (Raum)kapsel *f*

mogul ['məʊgl] *n* (*fig*) Mogul *m*

mohair ['məʊhɛə⁺] *n* Mohär *m*, Mohair *m*

moist [mɔɪst] *adj* feucht; **~en** ['mɔɪsn] *vt* befeuchten; **~ure** ['mɔɪstʃə⁺] *n* Feuchtigkeit *f*; **~urizer** ['mɔɪstʃəraɪzə⁺] *n* Feuchtigkeitscreme *f*

molar ['məʊlə⁺] *n* Backenzahn *m*

molasses [mə'læsɪz] *n* Melasse *f*

mold [məʊld] (US) = **mould**

mole [məʊl] *n* (*spot*) Leberfleck *m*; (*animal*) Maulwurf *m*; (*pier*) Mole *f*

molecule ['mɔlɪkjuːl] *n* Molekül *nt*

molest [məʊ'lɛst] *vt* belästigen

mollycoddle ['mɔlɪkɔdl] *vt* verhätscheln

molt [məʊlt] (US) *vi* = **moult**

molten ['məʊltən] *adj* geschmolzen

mom [mɔm] (US) *n* = **mum**

moment ['məʊmənt] *n* Moment *m*, Augenblick *m*; (*importance*) Tragweite *f*; **at the ~** im Augenblick; **~ary** *adj* kurz; **~ous** [məʊ'mɛntəs] *adj* folgenschwer

momentum [məʊ'mɛntəm] *n* Schwung *m*; **to gather ~** in Fahrt kommen

mommy ['mɔmɪ] (US) *n* = **mummy**

Monaco ['mɔnəkəʊ] *n* Monaco *nt*

monarch ['mɔnək] *n* Herrscher(in) *m(f)*; **~y** *n* Monarchie *f*

monastery ['mɔnəstərɪ] *n* Kloster *nt*

monastic [mə'næstɪk] *adj* klösterlich

Monday ['mʌndɪ] n Montag m

monetary ['mʌnɪtərɪ] adj Geld-; (of currency) Währungs-

money ['mʌnɪ] n Geld nt; **to make ~** Geld verdienen; **~ belt** n Geldgürtel nt; **~lender** n Geldverleiher m; **~ order** n Postanweisung f; **~-spinner** (inf) n Verkaufsschlager m

mongol ['mɔŋgəl] n (MED) mongoloide(s) Kind m ♦ adj mongolisch; (MED) mongoloid

mongrel ['mʌŋgrəl] n Promenadenmischung f

monitor ['mɔnɪtə'] n (SCH) Klassenordner m; (television ~) Monitor m ♦ vt (broadcasts) abhören; (control) überwachen

monk [mʌŋk] n Mönch m

monkey ['mʌŋkɪ] n Affe m; **~ nut** (BRIT) n Erdnuss f; **~ wrench** n (TECH) Engländer m, Franzose m

monochrome ['mɔnəkrəum] adj schwarz-weiß, schwarzweiß

monopolize [mə'nɔpəlaɪz] vt beherrschen

monopoly [mə'nɔpəlɪ] n Monopol nt

monosyllable ['mɔnəsɪləbl] n einsilbige(s) Wort nt

monotone ['mɔnətəun] n gleich bleibende(r) Ton(fall) m; **to speak in a ~** monoton sprechen; **monotonous** [mə'nɔtənəs] adj eintönig; **monotony** [mə'nɔtənɪ] n Eintönigkeit f, Monotonie f

monsoon [mɔn'suːn] n Monsun m

monster ['mɔnstə'] n Ungeheuer nt; (person) Scheusal nt

monstrosity [mɔn'strɔsɪtɪ] n Ungeheuerlichkeit f; (thing) Monstrosität f

monstrous ['mɔnstrəs] adj (shocking) grässlich, ungeheuerlich; (huge) riesig

month [mʌnθ] n Monat m; **~ly** adj monatlich, Monats- ♦ adv einmal im Monat ♦ n (magazine) Monatsschrift f

monument ['mɔnjumənt] n Denkmal nt; **~al** [mɔnju'mɛntl] adj (huge) gewaltig; (ignorance) ungeheuer

moo [muː] vi muhen

mood [muːd] n Stimmung f, Laune f; **to be in a good/bad ~** gute/schlechte Laune haben; **~y** adj launisch

moon [muːn] n Mond m; **~light** n Mondlicht nt; **~lighting** n Schwarzarbeit f; **~lit** adj mondhell

moor [muə'] n Heide f, Hochmoor nt ♦ vt (ship) festmachen, verankern ♦ vi anlegen; **~ings** npl Liegeplatz m; **~land** ['muələnd] n Heidemoor nt

moose [muːs] n Elch m

mop [mɔp] n Mopp m ♦ vt (auf)wischen; **~ up** vt aufwischen

mope [məup] vi Trübsal blasen

moped ['məupɛd] n Moped nt

moral ['mɔrəl] adj moralisch; (values) sittlich; (virtuous) tugendhaft ♦ n Moral f; **~s** npl (ethics) Moral f

morale [mɔ'rɑːl] n Moral f

morality [mə'rælɪtɪ] n Sittlichkeit f

morass [mə'ræs] n Sumpf m

morbid ['mɔːbɪd] adj krankhaft; (jokes) makaber

KEYWORD

more [mɔː'] adj (greater in number etc) mehr; (additional) noch mehr; **do you want (some) more tea?** möchten Sie noch etwas Tee?; **I have no** or **I don't have any more money** ich habe kein Geld mehr

♦ pron (greater amount) mehr; (further or additional amount) noch mehr; **is there any more?** gibt es noch mehr?; (left over) ist noch etwas da?; **there's no more** es ist nichts mehr da

♦ adv mehr; **more dangerous/easily etc (than)** gefährlicher/einfacher etc (als); **more and more** immer mehr; **more and more excited** immer aufgeregter; **more or less** mehr oder weniger; **more than ever** mehr denn je; **more beautiful than ever** schöner denn je

moreover [mɔː'rəʊvə] adv überdies

morgue [mɔːg] n Leichenschauhaus nt

Mormon ['mɔːmən] n Mormone m, Mormonin f

morning ['mɔːnɪŋ] n Morgen m; in the ~ am Morgen; 7 o'clock in the ~ 7 Uhr morgens; ~ sickness n (Schwangerschafts)übelkeit f

Morocco [mə'rɒkəʊ] n Marokko nt

moron ['mɔːrɒn] n Schwachsinnige(r) mf

morose [mə'rəʊs] adj mürrisch

morphine ['mɔːfiːn] n Morphium nt

Morse [mɔːs] n (also: ~ code) Morsealphabet nt

morsel ['mɔːsl] n Bissen m

mortal ['mɔːtl] adj sterblich; (deadly) tödlich; (very great) Todes- ♦ n (human being) Sterbliche(r) mf; ~ity [mɔː'tælɪtɪ] n Sterblichkeit f; (death rate) Sterblichkeitsziffer f

mortar ['mɔːtə] n (for building) Mörtel m; (MIL) Granatwerfer m

mortgage ['mɔːgɪdʒ] n Hypothek f ♦ vt hypothekarisch belasten; ~ company (US) n ≈ Bausparkasse f

mortify ['mɔːtɪfaɪ] vt beschämen

mortuary ['mɔːtjʊərɪ] n Leichenhalle f

mosaic [məʊ'zeɪɪk] n Mosaik nt

Moscow ['mɒskəʊ] n Moskau nt

Moslem ['mɒzləm] = **Muslim**

mosque [mɒsk] n Moschee f

mosquito [mɒs'kiːtəʊ] (pl ~es) n Moskito m

moss [mɒs] n Moos m

most [məʊst] adj meiste(r, s) ♦ adv am meisten; (very) höchst ♦ n das meiste, der größte Teil; (people) die meisten; ~ men die meisten Männer; at the (very) ~ allerhöchstens; to make the ~ of das Beste machen aus; a ~ interesting book ein höchstinteressantes Buch; ~ly adv größtenteils

MOT (BRIT) n abbr (= Ministry of Transport): the MOT (test) ≈ der TÜV

motel [məʊ'tel] n Motel nt

moth [mɒθ] n Nachtfalter m; (wooleating) Motte f; ~ball n Mottenkugel f

mother ['mʌðə] n Mutter f ♦ vt bemuttern; ~hood n Mutterschaft f; ~-in-law n Schwiegermutter f; ~ly adj mütterlich; ~-of-pearl n Perlmutt nt; M~'s Day n Muttertag m; ~-to-be n werdende Mutter f; ~ tongue n Muttersprache f

motif [məʊ'tiːf] n Motiv nt

motion ['məʊʃən] n Bewegung f; (in meeting) Antrag m ♦ vt, vi: to ~ (to) sb jdm winken, jdm zu verstehen geben; ~less adj regungslos; ~ picture n Film m

motivated ['məʊtɪveɪtɪd] adj motiviert

motivation [məʊtɪ'veɪʃən] n Motivierung f

motive ['məʊtɪv] n Motiv nt, Beweggrund m ♦ adj treibend

motley ['mɒtlɪ] adj bunt

motor ['məʊtə] n Motor m; (BRIT: inf: vehicle) Auto nt ♦ adj Motor-; ~bike n Motorrad nt; ~boat n Motorboot nt; ~car (BRIT) n Auto nt; ~cycle n Motorrad nt; ~cyclist n Motorradfahrer(in) m(f); ~ing (BRIT) n Autofahren nt ♦ adj Auto-; ~ist n Autofahrer(in) m(f); ~ mechanic n Kraftfahrzeugmechaniker(in) m(f), Kfz-Mechaniker(in) m(f); ~ racing (BRIT) n Autorennen nt; ~ vehicle n Kraftfahrzeug nt; ~way (BRIT) n Autobahn f

mottled ['mɒtld] adj gesprenkelt

mould [məʊld] (US **mold**) n Form f; (mildew) Schimmel m ♦ vt (also fig) formen; ~y adj schimmelig

moult [məʊlt] (US **molt**) vi sich mausern

mound [maʊnd] n (Erd)hügel m

mount [maʊnt] n (liter: hill) Berg m; (horse) Pferd nt; (for jewel etc) Fassung f ♦ vt (horse) steigen auf +acc; (put in setting) fassen; (exhibition) veranstalten; (attack) unternehmen ♦ vi (also: ~ up) sich häufen; (on horse) aufsitzen

mountain ['maʊntɪn] n Berg m ♦ cpd

mourn 478 **mug**

Berg-; **~ bike** n Mountainbike nt; **~eer** n Bergsteiger(in) m(f); **~eering** [maunti'niəriŋ] n Bergsteigen nt; **~ous** adj bergig; **~ rescue team** n Bergwacht f; **~side** n Berg(ab)hang m

mourn [mɔːn] vt betrauern, beklagen ♦ vi: **to ~ (for sb)** (um jdn) trauern; **~er** n Trauernde(r) mf; **~ful** adj traurig; **~ing** n (grief) Trauer f ♦ cpd (dress) Trauer-; **in ~ing** (period etc) in Trauer; (dress) in Trauerkleidung f

mouse [maus] (pl **mice**) n Maus f; **~trap** n Mausefalle f

mousse [muːs] n (COOK) Creme f; (cosmetic) Schaumfestiger m

moustache [mas'tɑːʃ] n Schnurrbart m

mousy ['mausɪ] adj (colour) mausgrau; (person) schüchtern

mouth [mauθ] n Mund m; (opening) Öffnung f; (of river) Mündung f; **~ful** n Mund m voll; **~organ** n Mundharmonika f; **~piece** n Mundstück nt; (fig) Sprachrohr nt; **~wash** n Mundwasser nt; **~watering** adj lecker, appetitlich

movable ['muːvəbl] adj beweglich

move [muːv] n (~ment) Bewegung f; (in game) Zug m; (step) Schritt m; (of house) Umzug m ♦ vt (emotionally) bewegen ♦ vi sich bewegen; (vehicle, ship) fahren; (~ house) umziehen; **to get a ~ on** sich beeilen; **to ~ sb to do sth** jdn veranlassen, etw zu tun; **~ about or around** vi sich hin und her bewegen; (travel) unterwegs sein; **~ along** vi weitergehen; (cars) weiterfahren; **~ away** vi weggehen; **~ back** vi zurückgehen; (to the rear) zurückweichen; **~ forward** vi vorwärts gehen, sich vorwärts bewegen ♦ vt vorschieben; (time) vorverlegen; **~ in** vi (to house) einziehen; (troops) einrücken; **~ on** vi weitergehen ♦ vt weitergehen lassen; **~ out** vi (of house) ausziehen; (troops) abziehen; **~ over** vi zur Seite rücken; **~ up** vi aufsteigen; (in job) befördert werden ♦ vt nach

oben bewegen; (in job) befördern; **~ment** ['muːvmənt] n Bewegung f

movie ['muːvɪ] n Film m; **to go to the ~s** ins Kino gehen; **~ camera** n Filmkamera f

moving ['muːvɪŋ] adj beweglich; (touching) ergreifend

mow [məu] (pt **mowed**, pp **mowed** or **mown**) vt mähen; **~ down** vt (fig) niedermähen; **~er** n (lawnmower) Rasenmäher m; **~n** pp of **mow**

MP n abbr = **Member of Parliament**

m.p.h. abbr = **miles per hour**

Mr ['mɪstəʳ] (US **Mr.**) n Herr m

Mrs ['mɪsɪz] (US **Mrs.**) n Frau f

Ms [mɪz] (US **Ms.**) n (= Miss or Mrs) Frau f

M.Sc. n abbr = **Master of Science**

MSP n abbr = (Member of the Scottish Parliament) Mitglied nt des schottischen Parlaments

much [mʌtʃ] adj viel ♦ adv sehr; viel ♦ n viel, eine Menge; **how ~ is it?** wie viel kostet das?; **too ~** zu viel; **it's not ~** es ist nicht viel; **as ~ as** so sehr, so viel; **however ~ he tries** sosehr er es auch versucht

muck [mʌk] n Mist m; (fig) Schmutz m; **~ about or around** (inf) vi: **to ~ about or around (with sth)** (an etw dat) herumalbern; **~ up** vt (inf: ruin) vermasseln; (dirty) dreckig machen; **~y** adj (dirty) dreckig

mud [mʌd] n Schlamm m

muddle ['mʌdl] n Durcheinander nt ♦ vt (also: **~ up**) durcheinander bringen; **~ through** vi sich durchwursteln

mud ['mʌd-]: **~dy** adj schlammig; **~guard** n Schutzblech nt; **~slinging** (inf) n Verleumdung f

muesli ['mjuːzlɪ] n Müsli m

muffin ['mʌfɪn] n süße(s) Teilchen nt

muffle ['mʌfl] vt (sound) dämpfen; (wrap up) einhüllen; **~d** adj gedämpft; **~r** (US) n (AUT) Schalldämpfer m

mug [mʌg] n (cup) Becher m; (inf: face) Visage f; (: fool) Trottel m ♦ vt überfallen und ausrauben; **~ger** *n* Straßenräuber *m*; **~ging** *n* Überfall *m*

muggy ['mʌgɪ] *adj* (weather) schwül

mule [mju:l] *n* Maulesel *m*

mull [mʌl]: **~ over** *vt* nachdenken über +acc

multicoloured ['mʌltɪkʌləd] (US **multicolored**) *adj* mehrfarbig

multi-level ['mʌltɪlevl] (US) *adj* = **multistorey**

multiple ['mʌltɪpl] *n* Vielfache(s) *nt* ♦ *adj* mehrfach; (many) mehrere; **~ sclerosis** *n* multiple Sklerose *f*

multiplex cinema ['mʌltɪpleks-] *n* Kinocenter *nt*

multiplication [mʌltɪplɪ'keɪʃən] *n* Multiplikation *f*; (increase) Vervielfachung *f*

multiply ['mʌltɪplaɪ] *vt*: **to ~ (by)** multiplizieren (mit) ♦ *vi* (BIOL) sich vermehren

multistorey ['mʌltɪ'stɔ:rɪ] (BRIT) *adj* (building, car park) mehrstöckig

multitude ['mʌltɪtju:d] *n* Menge *f*

mum [mʌm] *n* (BRIT: inf) Mutti *f* ♦ *adj*: **to keep ~ (about)** den Mund halten (über +acc)

mumble ['mʌmbl] *vt*, *vi* murmeln ♦ *n* Gemurmel *nt*

mummy ['mʌmɪ] *n* (dead body) Mumie *f*; (BRIT: inf) Mami *f*

mumps [mʌmps] *n* Mumps *m*

munch [mʌntʃ] *vt*, *vi* mampfen

mundane [mʌn'deɪn] *adj* banal

municipal [mju:'nɪsɪpl] *adj* städtisch, Stadt-

mural ['mjuərl] *n* Wandgemälde *nt*

murder ['mɜ:dər] *n* Mord *m* ♦ *vt* ermorden; **~er** *n* Mörder *m*; **~ous** *adj* Mord-; (fig) mörderisch

murky ['mɜ:kɪ] *adj* finster

murmur ['mɜ:mər] *n* Murmeln *nt*; (of water, wind) Rauschen *nt* ♦ *vt*, *vi* murmeln

muscle ['mʌsl] *n* Muskel *m*; **~ in** *vi* mitmischen; **muscular** ['mʌskjulər] *adj* Muskel-; (strong) muskulös

museum [mju:'zɪəm] *n* Museum *nt*

mushroom ['mʌʃrum] *n* Champignon *m*; Pilz *m* ♦ *vi* (fig) emporschießen

music ['mju:zɪk] *n* Musik *f*; (printed) Noten *pl*; **~al** *adj* (sound) melodisch; (person) musikalisch ♦ *n* (show) Musical *nt*; **~al instrument** *n* Musikinstrument *nt*; **~ hall** (BRIT) *n* Varietee *nt*, Varieté *f*; **~ian** [mju:'zɪʃən] *n* Musiker(in) *m(f)*

Muslim ['mʌzlɪm] *adj* moslemisch ♦ *n* Moslem *m*

muslin ['mʌzlɪn] *n* Musselin *m*

mussel ['mʌsl] *n* Miesmuschel *f*

must [mʌst] *vb aux* müssen; (in negation) dürfen ♦ *n* Muss *nt*; **the film is a ~** den Film muss man gesehen haben

mustard ['mʌstəd] *n* Senf *m*

muster ['mʌstər] *vt* (MIL) antreten lassen; (courage) zusammennehmen

mustn't ['mʌsnt] = **must not**

musty ['mʌstɪ] *adj* muffig

mute [mju:t] *adj* stumm ♦ *n* (person) Stumme(r) *m(f)*; (MUS) Dämpfer *m*; **~d** *adj* gedämpft

mutilate ['mju:tɪleɪt] *vt* verstümmeln

mutiny ['mju:tɪnɪ] *n* Meuterei *f* ♦ *vi* meutern

mutter ['mʌtər] *vt*, *vi* murmeln

mutton ['mʌtn] *n* Hammelfleisch *nt*

mutual ['mju:tʃuəl] *adj* gegenseitig; beiderseitig; **~ly** *adv* gegenseitig; für beide Seiten

muzzle ['mʌzl] *n* (of animal) Schnauze *f*; (for animal) Maulkorb *m*; (of gun) Mündung *f* ♦ *vt* einen Maulkorb anlegen +dat

my [maɪ] *adj* mein; **this is ~ car** das ist mein Auto; **I've washed ~ hair** ich habe mir die Haare gewaschen

myself [maɪ'self] *pron* mich acc; mir dat; (emphatic) selbst; see also **oneself**

mysterious [mɪs'tɪərɪəs] *adj* geheimnisvoll

mystery ['mɪstərɪ] *n* (secret) Geheimnis *nt*; (sth difficult) Rätsel *nt*

mystify ['mɪstɪfaɪ] *vt* ein Rätsel sein +dat; verblüffen

mystique [mɪs'ti:k] *n* geheimnisvolle

Natur f

myth [mɪθ] n Mythos m; (fig) Erfindung f; **~ology** [mɪˈθɔlədʒɪ] n Mythologie f

N, n

n/a abbr (= not applicable) nicht zutreffend

nab [næb] (inf) vt schnappen

naff [næf] (BRIT: inf) adj blöd

nag [næg] n (horse) Gaul m; (person) Nörgler(in) m(f) ♦ vt, vi: to ~ (at) sb an jdm herumnörgeln; **~ging** adj (doubt) nagend ♦ n Nörgelei f

nail [neɪl] n Nagel m ♦ vt nageln; to ~ sb down to doing sth jdn darauf festnageln, etw zu tun; **~brush** n Nagelbürste f; **~file** n Nagelfeile f; **~ polish** n Nagellack m; **~ polish remover** n Nagellackentferner m; **~ scissors** npl Nagelschere f; **~ varnish** (BRIT) n = **nail polish**

naïve [naɪˈiːv] adj naiv

naked [ˈneɪkɪd] adj nackt

name [neɪm] n Name m; (reputation) Ruf m ♦ vt nennen; (sth new) benennen; (appoint) ernennen; **by ~** mit Namen; **I know him only by ~** ich kenne ihn nur dem Namen nach; **what's your ~?** wie heißen Sie?; **in the ~ of** im Namen +gen; (for the sake of) um +gen ... willen; **~less** adj namenlos; **~ly** adv nämlich; **~sake** n Namensvetter m

nanny [ˈnænɪ] n Kindermädchen nt

nap [næp] n (sleep) Nickerchen nt; (on cloth) Strich m ♦ vi: **to be caught ~ping** (fig) überrumpelt werden

nape [neɪp] n Nacken m

napkin [ˈnæpkɪn] n (at table) Serviette f; (BRIT: for baby) Windel f

nappy [ˈnæpɪ] (BRIT) n (for baby) Windel f; **~ rash** n wunde Stellen pl

narcotic [nɑːˈkɔtɪk] adj betäubend ♦ n Betäubungsmittel nt

narrative [ˈnærətɪv] n Erzählung f ♦ adj erzählend

narrator [nəˈreɪtə*] n Erzähler(in) m(f)

narrow [ˈnærəʊ] adj eng, schmal; (limited) beschränkt ♦ vi sich verengen; **to have a ~ escape** mit knapper Not davonkommen; **to ~ sth down to sth** etw auf etw acc einschränken; **~ly** adv (miss) knapp; (escape) mit knapper Not; **~minded** adj engstirnig

nasty [ˈnɑːstɪ] adj ekelhaft, fies; (business, wound) schlimm

nation [ˈneɪʃən] n Nation f, Volk nt; **~al** [ˈnæʃənl] adj national, National-, Landes- ♦ n Staatsangehörige(r) mf; **~al anthem** (BRIT) n Nationalhymne f; **~al dress** n Tracht f; **N~al Health Service** n staatliche(r) Gesundheitsdienst m; **N~al Insurance** (BRIT) n Sozialversicherung f; **~alism** [ˈnæʃnəlɪzəm] n Nationalismus m; **~alist** [ˈnæʃnəlɪst] n Nationalist(in) m(f) ♦ adj nationalistisch; **~ality** [næʃəˈnælɪtɪ] n Staatsangehörigkeit f; **~alize** [ˈnæʃnəlaɪz] vt verstaatlichen; **~ally** [ˈnæʃnəlɪ] adv national, auf Staatsebene; **~al park** (BRIT) n Nationalpark m; **~wide** [ˈneɪʃənwaɪd], adv allgemein, landesweit

---

National Trust

Der **National Trust** ist ein 1895 gegründeter Natur- und Denkmalschutzverband in Großbritannien, der Gebäude und Gelände von besonderem historischem oder ästhetischem Interesse erhält und der Öffentlichkeit zugänglich macht. Viele Gebäude im Besitz des National Trust sind (z.T. gegen ein Eintrittsgeld) zu besichtigen.

---

native [ˈneɪtɪv] n (born in) Einheimische(r) mf; (original inhabitant) Eingeborene(r) mf ♦ adj einheimisch; (belonging by birth) heimatlich, Heimat-; (inborn) angeboren, natürlich; **a ~ of Germany** ein gebürtiger Deutscher; **a ~ speaker of French** ein französischer Muttersprachler; **N~ American** n Indianer(in) *m(f)*, Ureinwohner(in) *m(f)* Amerikas; **~ language** n Muttersprache *f*

Nativity [nə'tıvıtı] n: **the ~** Christi Geburt *no art*

NATO ['neɪtəʊ] n abbr (= North Atlantic Treaty Organization) NATO *f*

natural ['nætʃrəl] adj natürlich; Natur-; *(inborn)* (an)geboren; **~ gas** n Erdgas *nt*; **~ist** n Naturkundler(in) *m(f)*; **~ly** adv natürlich

nature ['neɪtʃə'] n Natur *f*; **by ~** von Natur (aus)

naught [nɔːt] n = nought

naughty ['nɔːtɪ] adj *(child)* unartig, ungezogen; *(action)* ungehörig

nausea ['nɔːsɪə] n *(sickness)* Übelkeit *f*; *(disgust)* Ekel *m*; **~te** ['nɔːsɪeɪt] vt anekeln

nautical ['nɔːtɪkl] adj nautisch; See-; *(expression)* seemännisch

naval ['neɪvl] adj Marine-, Flotten-; **~ officer** n Marineoffizier *m*

nave [neɪv] n Kirchen(haupt)schiff *nt*

navel ['neɪvl] n Nabel *m*

navigate ['nævɪgeɪt] vi navigieren; **navigation** [nævɪ'geɪʃən] n Navigation *f*; **navigator** ['nævɪgeɪtə'] n Steuermann *m*; *(AVIAT)* Navigator *m* *(AUT)* Beifahrer(in) *m(f)*

navvy ['nævɪ] *(BRIT)* n Straßenarbeiter *m*

navy ['neɪvɪ] n (Kriegs)marine *f* ♦ adj *(also: ~* **blue)** marineblau

Nazi ['nɑːtsɪ] n Nazi *m*

NB abbr (= nota bene) NB

near [nɪə'] adj nah ♦ prep *(also: ~* **to:** space) in der Nähe +gen; *(also: ~* time) um +acc ... herum ♦ vt sich nähern +dat; **~ miss** knapp daneben; **~by** adj nahe (gelegen) ♦ adv in der Nähe; **~ly** adv fast; **I ~ly fell** ich wäre fast gefallen; **~side** n *(AUT)* Beifahrerseite *f* ♦ adj auf der Bei-

fahrerseite; **~sighted** adj kurzsichtig

neat [niːt] adj *(tidy)* ordentlich; *(solution)* sauber; *(pure)* pur; **~ly** adv *(tidily)* ordentlich

necessarily ['nesɪsrɪlɪ] adv notwendig

necessary ['nesɪsrɪ] adj notwendig, nötig; **he did all that was ~** er erledigte alles, was nötig war; **it is ~ to/ that ...** man muss ...

necessitate [nɪ'sesɪteɪt] vt erforderlich machen

necessity [nɪ'sesɪtɪ] n *(need)* Not *f*; *(compulsion)* Notwendigkeit *f*; **necessities** npl *(things needed)* das Notwendigste

neck [nek] n Hals *m* ♦ vi *(inf)* knutschen; **~ and ~** Kopf an Kopf; **~lace** ['neklɪs] n Halskette *f*; **~line** ['neklaɪn] n Ausschnitt *m*; **~tie** ['nektaɪ] *(US)* n Krawatte *f*

née [neɪ] adj geborene

need [niːd] n Bedürfnis *nt*; *(lack)* Mangel *m*; *(necessity)* Notwendigkeit *f*; *(poverty)* Not *f* ♦ vt brauchen; **I ~ to do it** ich muss es tun; **you don't ~ to go** du brauchst nicht zu gehen

needle ['niːdl] n Nadel *f* ♦ vt *(fig: inf)* ärgern

needless ['niːdlɪs] adj unnötig; **~ to say** natürlich

needlework ['niːdlwəːk] n Handarbeit *f*

needn't ['niːdnt] = need not

needy ['niːdɪ] adj bedürftig

negative ['negətɪv] n *(PHOT)* Negativ *nt* ♦ adj negativ; *(answer)* abschlägig; **~ equity** n Differenz zwischen gefallenem Wert und hypothekarischer Belastung eines Wohneigentums

neglect [nɪ'glekt] vt vernachlässigen ♦ n Vernachlässigung *f*; **~ed** adj vernachlässigt

negligee ['neglɪʒeɪ] n Negligee *nt*, Negligé *nt*

negligence ['neglɪdʒəns] n Nachlässigkeit *f*

negligible ['neglɪdʒɪbl] adj unbedeutend, geringfügig

negotiable [nɪ'gəʊʃɪəbl] adj (cheque) übertragbar, einlösbar

negotiate [nɪ'gəʊʃɪeɪt] vi verhandeln ♦ vt (treaty) abschließen; (difficulty) überwinden; (corner) nehmen; **negotiation** [nɪgəʊʃɪ'eɪʃən] n Verhandlung f; **negotiator** n Unterhändler m

neigh [neɪ] vi wiehern

neighbour ['neɪbə*] (US **neighbor**) n Nachbar(in) m(f); **~hood** n Nachbarschaft f; Umgebung f; **~ing** adj benachbart, angrenzend; **~ly** adj (person, attitude) nachbarlich

neither ['naɪðə*] adj, pron keine(r, s) (von beiden) ♦ conj: **he can't do it, and ~ can I** er kann es nicht und ich auch nicht ♦ adv: **~ good nor bad** weder gut noch schlecht; **~ story is true** keine der beiden Geschichten stimmt

neon ['niːɔn] n Neon nt; **~ light** n Neonlampe f

nephew ['nevjuː] n Neffe m

nerve [nɜːv] n Nerv m; (courage) Mut m; (impudence) Frechheit f; **to have a fit of ~s** in Panik geraten; **~-racking** adj nervenaufreibend

nervous ['nɜːvəs] adj (of the nerves) Nerven-; (timid) nervös, ängstlich; **~ breakdown** n Nervenzusammenbruch m; **~ness** n Nervosität f

nest [nest] n Nest nt ♦ vi nisten; **~ egg** n (fig) Notgroschen m

nestle ['nesl] vi sich kuscheln

net [net] n Netz nt ♦ adj netto, Netto- ♦ vt netto einnehmen; **the N~** (INTERNET) das Internet; **~ball** n Netzball m

Netherlands ['neðələndz] npl: **the ~** die Niederlande pl

nett [net] adj = **net**

netting ['netɪŋ] n Netz(werk) nt

nettle ['netl] n Nessel f

network ['netwɜːk] n Netz nt

neurotic ['njʊə'rɒtɪk] adj neurotisch

neuter ['njuːtə*] adj (BIOL) geschlechtslos; (GRAM) sächlich ♦ vt kastrieren

neutral ['njuːtrəl] adj neutral ♦ n (AUT)

Leerlauf m; **~ity** [njuː'trælɪtɪ] n Neutralität f; **~ize** vt (fig) ausgleichen

never ['nevə*] adv nie(mals); **I ~ went** ich bin gar nicht gegangen; **~ in my life** nie im Leben; **~-ending** adj endlos; **~theless** [nevəðə'les] adv trotzdem, dennoch

new [njuː] adj neu; **N~ Age** n Newage-, New-Age-; **~born** adj neugeboren; **~comer** ['njuːkʌmə*] n Neuankömmling m; **~fangled** (pej) adj neumodisch; **~found** adj neu entdeckt; **~ly** adv frisch, neu; **~ly-weds** npl Frischvermählte pl; **~ moon** n Neumond m

news [njuːz] n Nachricht f; (RAD, TV) Nachrichten pl; **a piece of ~** eine Nachricht; **~ agency** n Nachrichtenagentur f; **~agent** (BRIT) n Zeitungshändler m; **~caster** n Nachrichtensprecher(in) m(f); **~ flash** n Kurzmeldung f; **~letter** n Rundschreiben nt; **~paper** n Zeitung f; **~print** n Zeitungspapier nt; **~reader** n = **newscaster**; **~reel** n Wochenschau f; **~ stand** n Zeitungsstand m

newt [njuːt] n Wassermolch m

New Year n Neujahr nt; **~'s Day** n Neujahrstag m; **~'s Eve** n Silvester(abend m) nt

New Zealand [-'ziːlənd] n Neuseeland nt; **~er** n Neuseeländer(in) m(f)

next [nekst] adj nächste(r, s) ♦ adv (after) dann, darauf; (~ time) das nächste Mal; **the ~ day** am nächsten or folgenden Tag; **~ time** das nächste Mal; **~ year** nächstes Jahr; **~ door** adv nebenan ♦ adj (neighbour, flat) von nebenan; **~ of kin** n nächste(r) Verwandte(r) mf; **~ to** prep neben; **~ to nothing** so gut wie nichts

NHS n abbr = **National Health Service**

nib [nɪb] n Spitze f

nibble ['nɪbl] vt knabbern an +dat

nice [naɪs] adj (person) nett; (thing) schön; (subtle) fein; **~-looking** adj nett aussehend; **~ly** adv gut, nett; **~ties**

['naɪsɪtɪz] npl Feinheiten pl

nick [nɪk] n Einkerbung f ♦ vt (inf: steal) klauen; **in the ~ of time** gerade rechtzeitig

nickel ['nɪkl] n Nickel nt; (US) Nickel m (5 cents)

nickname ['nɪkneɪm] n Spitzname m ♦ vt taufen

nicotine patch ['nɪkəti:n-] n Nikotinpflaster nt

niece [ni:s] n Nichte f

Nigeria [naɪ'dʒɪərɪə] n Nigeria nt

niggling ['nɪglɪŋ] adj pedantisch; (doubt, worry) quälend

night [naɪt] n Nacht f; (evening) Abend m; **the ~ before last** vorletzte Nacht; **at or by ~** (before midnight) abends; (after midnight) nachts; **~cap** n (drink) Schlummertrunk m; **~club** n Nachtlokal nt; **~dress** n Nachthemd nt; **~fall** n Einbruch m der Nacht; **~ gown** n = **nightdress; ~ie** (inf) n Nachthemd nt

nightingale ['naɪtɪŋgeɪl] n Nachtigall f

night: **~life** ['naɪtlaɪf] n Nachtleben nt; **~ly** ['naɪtlɪ] adj, adv jeden Abend; jede Nacht; **~mare** ['naɪtmeəʳ] n Albtraum m; **~ porter** n Nachtportier m; **~ school** n Abendschule f; **~ shift** n Nachtschicht f; **~time** n Nacht f

nil [nɪl] n Null f

Nile [naɪl] n: **the ~** der Nil

nimble ['nɪmbl] adj beweglich

nine [naɪn] num neun; **~teen** num neunzehn; **~ty** num neunzig

ninth [naɪnθ] adj neunte(r, s)

nip [nɪp] vt kneifen ♦ n Kneifen nt

nipple ['nɪpl] n Brustwarze f

nippy ['nɪpɪ] (inf) adj (person) flink; (BRIT: car) flott; (: cold) frisch

nitrogen ['naɪtrədʒən] n Stickstoff m

KEYWORD

no [nəʊ] (pl noes) adv (opposite of yes) nein; (to answer no (to question) mit Nein antworten; (to request) Nein or nein sagen; **no thank you** nein, danke ♦ adj (not any) kein(e); **I have no**

money/time ich habe kein Geld/keine Zeit; **"no smoking"** „Rauchen verboten"

♦ n Nein nt; (no vote) Neinstimme f

nobility [nəʊ'bɪlɪtɪ] n Adel m

noble ['nəʊbl] adj (rank) adlig; (splendid) nobel, edel

nobody ['nəʊbədɪ] pron niemand, keiner

nocturnal [nɔk'tə:nl] adj (tour, visit) nächtlich; (animal) Nacht-

nod [nɔd] vi nicken ♦ vt nicken mit ♦ n Nicken nt; **~ off** vi einnicken

noise [nɔɪz] n (sound) Geräusch nt; (unpleasant, loud) Lärm m; **noisy** ['nɔɪzɪ] adj laut; (crowd) lärmend

nominal ['nɔmɪnl] adj nominell

nominate ['nɔmɪneɪt] vt (suggest) vorschlagen; (in election) aufstellen; (appoint) ernennen; **nomination** [nɔmɪ'neɪʃən] n (election) Nominierung f; (appointment) Ernennung f; **nominee** [nɔmɪ'ni:] n Kandidat(in) m(f)

non... [nɔn] prefix Nicht-, un-; **~alcoholic** adj alkoholfrei

nonchalant ['nɔnʃələnt] adj lässig

non-committal [nɔnkə'mɪtl] adj (reserved) zurückhaltend; (uncommitted) unverbindlich

nondescript ['nɔndɪskrɪpt] adj mittelmäßig

none [nʌn] adj, pron kein(e, er, es) ♦ adv: **he's ~ the worse for it** es hat ihm nicht geschadet; **~ of you** keiner von euch; **I've ~ left** ich habe keinen mehr

nonentity [nɔ'nentɪtɪ] n Null f (inf)

nonetheless ['nʌnðə'les] adv nichtsdestoweniger

non-existent [nɔnɪg'zɪstənt] adj nicht vorhanden

non-fiction [nɔn'fɪkʃən] n Sachbücher pl

nonplussed [nɔn'plʌst] adj verdutzt

nonsense ['nɔnsəns] n Unsinn m

non: **~-smoker** n Nichtraucher m

noodles

m(f); **~-smoking** *adj* Nichtraucher-; **~-stick** *adj* (pan, surface) Teflon- ®; **~-stop** *adj* Nonstop-, Non-Stop-

noodles ['nu:dlz] *npl* Nudeln *pl*

nook [nuk] *n* Winkel *m*; **~s and crannies** Ecken und Winkel

noon [nu:n] *n* (12 Uhr) Mittag *m*

no one ['nəuwʌn] *pron* = **nobody**

noose [nu:s] *n* Schlinge *f*

nor [nɔ:ᵊ] *conj* = **neither** ♦ *adv* see **neither**

norm [nɔ:m] *n* (convention) Norm *f*; (rule, requirement) Vorschrift *f*

normal ['nɔ:məl] *adj* normal; **~ly** *adv* normal; (usually) normalerweise

Normandy ['nɔ:məndɪ] *n* Normandie *f*

north [nɔ:θ] *n* Norden *m* ♦ *adj* nördlich, Nord- ♦ *adv* nördlich, nach or im Norden; **N~ Africa** *n* Nordafrika *nt*; **N~ America** *n* Nordamerika *nt*; **~east** *n* Nordosten *m*; **~erly** ['nɔ:ðəlɪ] *adj* nördlich; **~ern** ['nɔ:ðən] *adj* nördlich, Nord-; **N~ern Ireland** *n* Nordirland *nt*; **N~ Pole** *n* Nordpol *m*; **N~ Sea** *n* Nordsee *f*; **~ward(s)** ['nɔ:θwəd(z)] *adv* nach Norden; **~west** *n* Nordwesten *m*

Norway ['nɔ:weɪ] *n* Norwegen *nt*

Norwegian [nɔ:'wi:dʒən] *adj* norwegisch ♦ *n* Norweger(in) *m(f)*; (LING) Norwegisch *nt*

nose [nəuz] *n* Nase *f* ♦ *vi*: **to ~ about** herumschnüffeln; **~bleed** *n* Nasenbluten *nt*; **~ dive** *n* Sturzflug *m*; **~y** *adj* = **nosy**

nostalgia [nɔs'tældʒɪə] *n* Nostalgie *f*; **nostalgic** *adj* nostalgisch

nostril ['nɔstrɪl] *n* Nasenloch *nt*

nosy ['nəuzɪ] (inf) *adj* neugierig

not [nɔt] *adv* nicht; **~ at all** gar nicht; (don't mention it) keine Ursache, bitte sehr; **~ yet/now** noch nicht; jetzt/noch nicht; see also **all**; **only**

notably ['nəutəblɪ] *adv* (especially) besonders; (noticeably) bemerkenswert

notary ['nəutərɪ] *n* Notar(in) *m(f)*

notch [nɔtʃ] *n* Kerbe *f*, Einschnitt *m*

note [nəut] *n* (MUS) Note *f*, Ton *m*; (short letter) Nachricht *f*; (POL) Note *f*; (comment, attention) Notiz *f*; (of lecture etc) Aufzeichnung *f*; (banknote) Schein *m*; (fame) Ruf *m* ♦ *vt* (observe) bemerken; (also: ~ **down**) notieren; **~book** *n* Notizbuch *nt*; **~d** *adj* bekannt; **~pad** *n* Notizblock *m*; **~paper** *n* Briefpapier *nt*

nothing ['nʌθɪŋ] *n* nichts; **~ new/much** nichts Neues/nicht viel; **for ~** umsonst

notice ['nəutɪs] *n* (announcement) Bekanntmachung *f*; (warning) Ankündigung *f*, (dismissal) Kündigung *f* ♦ *vt* bemerken; **to take ~ of** beachten; **at short ~** kurzfristig; **until further ~** bis auf weiteres; **to hand in one's ~** kündigen; **~able** *adj* merklich; **~ board** *n* Anschlagtafel *f*

notify ['nəutɪfaɪ] *vt* benachrichtigen

notion ['nəuʃən] *n* Idee *f*

notorious [nəu'tɔ:rɪəs] *adj* berüchtigt

notwithstanding [nɔtwɪθ'stændɪŋ] *adv* trotzdem; **~ this** ungeachtet dessen

nought [nɔ:t] *n* Null *f*

noun [naun] *n* Substantiv *nt*

nourish ['nʌrɪʃ] *vt* nähren; **~ing** *adj* nahrhaft; **~ment** *n* Nahrung *f*

novel ['nɔvl] *n* Roman *m* ♦ *adj* neu(artig); **~ist** *n* Schriftsteller(in) *m(f)*; **~ty** *n* Neuheit *f*

November [nəu'vembəᵊ] *n* November *m*

novice ['nɔvɪs] *n* Neuling *m*

now [nau] *adv* jetzt; **right ~** jetzt, gerade; **by ~** inzwischen; **just ~** gerade; **~ and then, ~ and again** ab und zu, manchmal; **from ~ on** von jetzt an; **~adays** *adv* heutzutage

nowhere ['nəuweəᵊ] *adv* nirgends

nozzle ['nɔzl] *n* Düse *f*

nuclear ['nju:klɪəᵊ] *adj* (energy etc) Atom-, Kern-

nuclei ['nju:klɪaɪ] *npl* of **nucleus**

nucleus ['nju:klɪəs] *n* Kern *m*

nude [njuːd] *adj* nackt ♦ *n* (ART) Akt *m*; **in the ~** nackt

nudge [nʌdʒ] *vt* leicht anstoßen

nudist ['njuːdɪst] *n* Nudist(in) *m(f)*

nudity ['njuːdɪtɪ] *n* Nacktheit *f*

nuisance ['njuːsns] *n* Ärgernis *nt*; **what a ~!** wie ärgerlich!

nuke [njuːk] (inf) *n* Kernkraftwerk *nt* ♦ *vt* atomar vernichten

null [nʌl] *adj*: **~ and void** null und nichtig

numb [nʌm] *adj* taub, gefühllos ♦ *vt* betäuben

number ['nʌmbə*] *n* Nummer *f*; (numeral also) Zahl *f*; (quantity) (An)zahl *f* ♦ *vt* nummerieren; (amount to) sein; **to be ~ed among** gezählt werden zu; **a ~ of** (several) einige; **they were ten in ~** sie waren zehn an der Zahl; **~ plate** (BRIT) *n* (AUT) Nummernschild *nt*

numeral ['njuːmərəl] *n* Ziffer *f*

numerate ['njuːmərɪt] *adj* rechenkundig

numerical [njuː'merɪkl] *adj* (order) zahlenmäßig

numerous ['njuːmərəs] *adj* zahlreich

nun [nʌn] *n* Nonne *f*

nurse [nəːs] *n* Krankenschwester *f*; (for children) Kindermädchen *nt* ♦ *vt* (patient) pflegen; (doubt etc) hegen

nursery ['nəːsərɪ] *n* (for children) Kinderzimmer *nt*; (for plants) Gärtnerei *f*; (for trees) Baumschule *f*; **~ rhyme** *n* Kinderreim *m*; **~ school** *n* Kindergarten *m*; **~ slope** (BRIT) *n* (SKI) Idiotenhügel *m* (inf), Anfängerhügel *m*

nursing ['nəːsɪŋ] *n* (profession) Krankenpflege *f*; **~ home** *n* Privatklinik *f*

nurture ['nəːtʃə*] *vt* aufziehen

nut [nʌt] *n* Nuss *f*; (TECH) Schraubenmutter *f*; (inf) Verrückte(r) *m/f*; **he's ~s** er ist verrückt; **~crackers** ['nʌtkrækəz] *npl* Nussknacker *m*

nutmeg ['nʌtmeg] *n* Muskat(nuss *f*) *m*

nutrient ['njuːtrɪənt] *n* Nährstoff *m*

nutrition [njuː'trɪʃən] *n* Nahrung *f*

nutritious [njuː'trɪʃəs] *adj* nahrhaft

nutshell ['nʌtʃel] *n* Nussschale *f*; **in a ~** (fig) kurz gesagt

nutter ['nʌtə*] (BRIT: inf) *n* Spinner(in) *m(f)*

nylon ['naɪlɔn] *n* Nylon *nt* ♦ *adj* Nylon-

O, o

oak [əuk] *n* Eiche *f* ♦ *adj* Eichen(holz)-

O.A.P. *abbr* = **old-age pensioner**

oar [ɔː*] *n* Ruder *nt*

oases [əu'eɪsiːz] *npl of* **oasis**

oasis [əu'eɪsɪs] *n* Oase *f*

oath [əuθ] *n* (statement) Eid *m*, Schwur *m*; (swearword) Fluch *m*

oatmeal ['əutmiːl] *n* Haferschrot *m*

oats [əuts] *npl* Hafer *m*

obedience [ə'biːdɪəns] *n* Gehorsam *m*

obedient [ə'biːdɪənt] *adj* gehorsam

obesity [əu'biːsɪtɪ] *n* Fettleibigkeit *f*

obey [ə'beɪ] *vt, vi*: **to ~ (sb)** (jdm) gehorchen

obituary [ə'bɪtjuərɪ] *n* Nachruf *m*

object [*n* 'ɔbdʒɪkt, *vb* əb'dʒekt] *n* (thing) Gegenstand *m*, Objekt *nt*; (purpose) Ziel *nt* ♦ *vi* dagegen sein; **expense is no ~** Ausgaben spielen keine Rolle; **I ~!** ich protestiere!; **to ~ to sth** Einwände gegen etw haben; (morally) Anstoß an etw *acc* nehmen; **to ~ that** einwenden, dass; **~ion** [əb'dʒekʃən] *n* (reason against) Einwand *m*, Einspruch *m*; (dislike) Abneigung *f*; **I have no ~ion to ...** ich habe nichts gegen ...; einzuwenden; **~ionable** [əb'dʒekʃənəbl] *adj* nicht einwandfrei; (language) anstößig

objective [əb'dʒektɪv] *n* Ziel *nt* ♦ *adj* objektiv

obligation [ɔblɪ'geɪʃən] *n* Verpflichtung *f*; **without ~** unverbindlich; **obligatory** [ə'blɪgətərɪ] *adj* obligatorisch

oblige [ə'blaɪdʒ] *vt* (compel) zwingen; (do a favour) einen Gefallen tun *+dat*; **to be ~d to sb for sth** jdm für etw verbunden sein

obliging [ə'blaɪdʒɪŋ] *adj* entgegenkommend

oblique [ə'bliːk] *adj* schräg, schief ♦ *n* Schrägstrich *m*

obliterate [ə'blɪtəreɪt] *vt* auslöschen

oblivion [ə'blɪvɪən] *n* Vergessenheit *f*

oblivious [ə'blɪvɪəs] *adj* nicht bewusst

oblong ['ɔblɔŋ] *n* Rechteck *nt* ♦ *adj* länglich

obnoxious [əb'nɔkʃəs] *adj* widerlich

oboe ['əubəu] *n* Oboe *f*

obscene [əb'siːn] *adj* obszön; **obscenity** [əb'senɪtɪ] *n* Obszönität *f*; **obscenities** *npl* (*oaths*) Zoten *pl*

obscure [əb'skjuər] *adj* unklar; (*indistinct*) undeutlich; (*unknown*) unbekannt, obskur; (*dark*) düster ♦ *vt* verdunkeln; (*view*) verbergen; (*confuse*) verwirren; **obscurity** [əb'skjuərɪtɪ] *n* Unklarheit *f*; (*darkness*) Dunkelheit *f*

observance [əb'zɜːvəns] *n* Befolgung *f*

observant [əb'zɜːvənt] *adj* aufmerksam

observation [ɔbzə'veɪʃən] *n* (*noticing*) Beobachtung *f*; (*surveillance*) Überwachung *f*; (*remark*) Bemerkung *f*

observatory [əb'zɜːvətrɪ] *n* Sternwarte *f*, Observatorium *nt*

observe [əb'zɜːv] *vt* (*notice*) bemerken; (*watch*) beobachten; (*customs*) einhalten; **~r** *n* Beobachter(in) *m(f)*

obsess [əb'ses] *vt* verfolgen, quälen; **~ion** [əb'seʃən] *n* Besessenheit *f*, Wahn *m*; **~ive** *adj* krankhaft

obsolete ['ɔbsəliːt] *adj* überholt, veraltet

obstacle ['ɔbstəkl] *n* Hindernis *nt*; **~ race** *n* Hindernisrennen *nt*

obstetrics [ɔb'stetrɪks] *n* Geburtshilfe *f*

obstinate ['ɔbstɪnɪt] *adj* hartnäckig, stur

obstruct [əb'strʌkt] *vt* versperren; (*pipe*) verstopfen; (*hinder*) hemmen; **~ion** [əb'strʌkʃən] *n* Versperrung *f*, Verstopfung *f*; (*obstacle*) Hindernis *nt*

obtain [əb'teɪn] *vt* erhalten, bekommen; (*result*) erzielen

obtrusive [əb'truːsɪv] *adj* aufdringlich

obvious ['ɔbvɪəs] *adj* offenbar, offensichtlich; **~ly** *adv* offensichtlich

occasion [ə'keɪʒən] *n* Gelegenheit *f*; (*special event*) Ereignis *nt*; (*reason*) Anlass *m* ♦ *vt* veranlassen; **~al** *adj* gelegentlich; **~ally** *adv* gelegentlich

occupant ['ɔkjupənt] *n* Inhaber(in) *m(f)*; (*of house*) Bewohner(in) *m(f)*

occupation [ɔkju'peɪʃən] *n* (*employment*) Tätigkeit *f*, Beruf *m*; (*pastime*) Beschäftigung *f*; (*of country*) Besetzung *f*, Okkupation *f*; **~al hazard** *n* Berufsrisiko *nt*

occupier ['ɔkjupaɪər] *n* Bewohner(in) *m(f)*

occupy ['ɔkjupaɪ] *vt* (*take possession of*) besetzen; (*seat*) belegen; (*live in*) bewohnen; (*position, office*) bekleiden; (*position in sb's life*) einnehmen; (*time*) beanspruchen; **to ~ o.s. with sth** sich mit etw beschäftigen; **to ~ o.s. by doing sth** sich damit beschäftigen, etw zu tun

occur [ə'kɜːr] *vi* vorkommen; **to ~ to sb** jdm einfallen; **~rence** *n* (*event*) Ereignis *nt*; (*appearing*) Auftreten *nt*

ocean ['əuʃən] *n* Ozean *m*, Meer *nt*; **~going** *adj* Hochsee-

o'clock [ə'klɔk] *adv*: **it is 5 ~** es ist 5 Uhr

OCR *n abbr* = **optical character reader**

octagonal [ɔk'tægənl] *adj* achteckig

October [ɔk'təubər] *n* Oktober *m*

octopus ['ɔktəpəs] *n* Krake *f*; (*small*) Tintenfisch *m*

odd [ɔd] *adj* (*strange*) sonderbar; (*not even*) ungerade; (*sock etc*) einzeln; (*surplus*) übrig; **60-~** so um die 60; **at ~ times** ab und zu; **to be the ~ one out** (*person*) das fünfte Rad am Wagen sein; (*thing*) nicht dazugehören; **~ity** *n* (*strangeness*) Merkwürdigkeit *f*; (*queer person*) seltsame(r) Kauz *m*; (*thing*) Kuriosität *f*; **~-job man** (*irreg*) *n* Mädchen *nt* für alles; **~ jobs** *npl* gelegentlich anfallende Arbeiten; **~ly** *adv* seltsam;

~ments npl Reste pl; ~s npl Chancen pl; (betting) Gewinnchancen pl; **it makes no** ~ **s** es spielt keine Rolle; **at** ~ uneinig; ~**s and ends** npl Krimskrams m

odometer [ɔ'dɔmɪtə] n (esp US) n Tacho(meter) m

odour ['əudə] (US **odor**) n Geruch m

KEYWORD

of [ɔv, əv] prep **1** von +dat; use of gen; **the history of Germany** die Geschichte Deutschlands; **a friend of ours** ein Freund von uns; **a boy of 10** ein 10-jähriger Junge; **that was kind of you** das war sehr freundlich von Ihnen

2 (expressing quantity, amount, dates etc): **a kilo of flour** ein Kilo Mehl; **how much of this do you need?** wie viel brauchen Sie (davon)?; **there were 3 of them** sie waren zu dritt; (objects) es gab 3 (davon); **a cup of tea/vase of flowers** eine Tasse Tee/Vase mit Blumen; **the 5th of July** der 5. Juli

3 (from, out of) aus; **a bridge made of wood** eine Holzbrücke, eine Brücke aus Holz

---

off [ɔf] adj, adv (absent) weg, fort; (switch) aus(geschaltet), ab(geschaltet); (BRIT: food: bad) schlecht; (cancelled) abgesagt ♦ prep von +dat; **to be** ~ (to leave) gehen; **to be** ~ **sick** krank sein; **a day** ~ ein freier Tag; **to have an** ~ **day** einen schlechten Tag haben; **he had his coat** ~ er hatte seinen Mantel aus; **10%** ~ (COMM) 10% Rabatt; **5 km** ~ **(the road)** 5 km (von der Straße) entfernt; ~ **the coast** vor der Küste; **I'm** ~ **meat** (no longer eat it) ich esse kein Fleisch mehr; (no longer like it) ich mag kein Fleisch mehr; **on the** ~ **chance** auf gut Glück

offal ['ɔfl] n Innereien pl

off-colour ['ɔf'kʌlə] adj nicht wohl

offence [ə'fens] (US **offense**) n (crime) Vergehen nt, Straftat f; (insult) Beleidigung f; **to take** ~ **at** gekränkt sein wegen

offend [ə'fend] vt beleidigen; ~**er** n Gesetzesübertreter m

offense [ə'fens] (US) n = offence

offensive [ə'fensɪv] adj (unpleasant) übel, abstoßend; (weapon) Kampf-; (remark) verletzend ♦ n Angriff m

offer ['ɔfə] n Angebot f ♦ vt anbieten; (opinion) äußern; (resistance) leisten; **on** ~ zum Verkauf angeboten; ~**ing** n Gabe f

offhand [ɔf'hænd] adj lässig ♦ adv ohne weiteres

office ['ɔfɪs] n Büro nt; (position) Amt nt; **doctor's** ~ (US) Praxis f; **to take** ~ sein Amt antreten; (POL) die Regierung übernehmen; ~ **automation** n Büroautomatisierung f; ~ **block** (US: **building**) n Büro(hoch)haus nt; ~ **hours** npl Dienstzeit f; (US: MED) Sprechstunde f

officer ['ɔfɪsə] n (MIL) Offizier m; (public ~) Beamte(r) m

official [ə'fɪʃl] adj offiziell, amtlich ♦ n Beamte(r) m; ~**dom** n Beamtentum nt

officiate [ə'fɪʃɪeɪt] vi amtieren

officious [ə'fɪʃəs] adj aufdringlich

offing ['ɔfɪŋ] n: **in the** ~ in (Aus)sicht

Off-licence

Off-licence ist ein Geschäft (oder eine Theke in einer Gaststätte), wo man alkoholische Getränke kaufen kann, die aber anderswo konsumiert werden müssen. In solchen Geschäften, die oft von landesweiten Ketten betrieben werden, kann man auch andere Getränke, Süßigkeiten, Zigaretten und Knabbereien kaufen.

---

off: ~**licence** (BRIT) n (shop) Wein- und Spirituosenhandlung f; ~**line** adj (COMPUT) Offline- ♦ adv (COMPUT) offline; **~peak** adj (charges) verbilligt; **~-putting** (BRIT) adj (person, remark etc) abstoßend; **~-road vehicle** n Geländefahrzeug nt; **~season** adj außer Saison; **~set** (irreg: like set) vt ausgleichen ♦ n (also: **~set printing**) Offset(druck) m; **~shoot** n (fig: of organization) Zweig m; (: of discussion etc) Randergebnis nt; **~shore** adj in einiger Entfernung vor der Küste ♦ adv küstennah, Küsten-; **~side** adj (SPORT) im Abseits ♦ adv abseits ♦ n (AUT) Fahrerseite f; **~spring** n Nachkommenschaft f; (one) Sprössling m; **~stage** adv hinter den Kulissen; **~-the-cuff** adj unvorbereitet, aus dem Stegreif; **~-the-peg** (US **~-the-rack**) adv von der Stange; **~-white** adj naturweiß

Oftel [ˈɔftɛl] n Überwachungsgremium zum Verbraucherschutz nach Privatisierung der Telekommunikationsindustrie

often [ˈɔfn] adv oft

Ofwat [ˈɔfwɔt] n Überwachungsgremium zum Verbraucherschutz nach Privatisierung der Wasserindustrie

ogle [ˈəugl] vt liebäugeln mit

oil [ɔil] n Öl nt ♦ vt ölen; **~can** n Ölkännchen nt; **~field** n Ölfeld nt; **~filter** n (AUT) Ölfilter m; **~-fired** adj Öl-; **~ painting** n Ölgemälde nt; **~ rig** n Ölplattform f; **~skins** npl Ölzeug nt; **~ slick** n Ölteppich m; **~ tanker** n (Öl)tanker m; **~ well** n Ölquelle f; **~y** adj ölig; (dirty) ölbeschmiert

ointment [ˈɔintmənt] n Salbe f

O.K. [ˈəuˈkei] excl in Ordnung, O. K., o. k. ♦ adj in Ordnung ♦ vt genehmigen

okay [ˈəuˈkei] = **O.K.**

old [əuld] adj alt; **how ~ are you?** wie alt bist du?; **he's 10 years ~** er ist 10 Jahre alt; **~er brother** ältere(r) Bruder m; **~ age** n Alter nt; **~-age pensioner** (BRIT) n Rentner(in) m(f); **~-fashioned** adj altmodisch

olive [ˈɔliv] n (fruit) Olive f; (colour) Oli-ve nt ♦ adj Oliven-; (coloured) olivenfarbig; **~ oil** n Olivenöl nt

Olympic [əuˈlimpik] adj olympisch; **the ~ Games, the ~s** die Olympischen Spiele

omelet(te) [ˈɔmlit] n Omelett nt

omen [ˈəumən] n Omen nt

ominous [ˈɔminəs] adj bedrohlich

omission [əuˈmiʃən] n Auslassung f; (neglect) Versäumnis nt

omit [əuˈmit] vt auslassen; (fail to do) versäumen

KEYWORD

---

on [ɔn] prep 1 (indicating position) auf +dat; (with vb of motion) auf +acc; (on vertical surface, part of body) an +dat/acc; **it's on the table** es ist auf dem Tisch; **she put the book on the table** sie legte das Buch auf den Tisch; **on the left** links

2 (indicating means, method, condition etc): **on foot** (go, be) zu Fuß; **on the train/plane** (go, be) mit dem Zug/Flugzeug; (be) im Zug/Flugzeug; **on the telephone/television** am Telefon/im Fernsehen; **to be on drugs** Drogen nehmen; **to be on holiday/business** im Urlaub/auf Geschäftsreise sein

3 (referring to time): **on Friday** (am) Freitag; **on Fridays** freitags; **on June 20th** am 20. Juni; **a week on Friday** Freitag in einer Woche; **on arrival** he ... als er ankam, ... er ...

4 (about, concerning) über +acc

♦ adv 1 (referring to dress) an; **she put her boots/hat on** sie zog ihre Stiefel an/setzte ihren Hut auf

2 (further, continuously) weiter; **to walk on** weitergehen

♦ adj 1 (functioning, in operation: machine, TV, light) an; (: tap) aufgedreht; (: brakes) angezogen; **is the meeting still on?** findet die Versammlung noch statt?; **there's a good film on** es läuft ein guter Film

2: **that's not on!** (inf: of behaviour) das liegt nicht drin!

once [wʌns] adv einmal ♦ conj wenn ... einmal; **~ he had left/it was done** nachdem er gegangen war/es fertig war; **at ~** sofort; (at the same time) gleichzeitig; **~ a week** einmal in der Woche; **~ more** noch einmal; **~ and for all** ein für alle Mal; **~ upon a time** es war einmal

oncoming ['ɒnkʌmɪŋ] adj (traffic) Gegen-, entgegenkommend

KEYWORD

one [wʌn] num eins; (with noun, referring back to noun) eine/eine/ein; **it is one (o'clock)** es ist eins, es ist ein Uhr; **one hundred and fifty** einhundertfünfzig

♦ adj 1 (sole) einzige(r, s); **the one book which** das einzige Buch, welches

2 (same) derselbe/dieselbe/dasselbe; **they came in the one car** sie kamen alle in dem einen Auto

3 (indef): **one day I discovered ...** eines Tages bemerkte ich ...

♦ pron 1 eine(r, s); **do you have a red one?** haben Sie einen roten/eine rote/ein rotes?; **this one** diese(r, s); **that one** der/die/das; **which one?** welche(r, s)?; **one by one** einzeln

2: **one another** einander; **do you two ever see one another?** seht ihr beide euch manchmal?

3 (impers) man; **one never knows** man kann nie wissen; **to cut one's finger** sich in den Finger schneiden

one: ~-armed bandit n einarmiger Bandit m; **~-day excursion** (US: day return) Tagesrückfahrkarte f; **~-man** adj Einmann-; **~-man band** n Einmannkapelle f; (fig) Einmannbetrieb m; **~-off** (BRIT: inf) n Einzelfall m

oneself [wʌn'sɛlf] pron (reflexive: after

prep) sich; (~ personally) sich selber or selber; (emphatic) (sich) selbst; **to hurt ~** sich verletzen

one: ~-sided adj (argument) einseitig; **~-to-~** adj (relationship) eins-zu-eins; **~-upmanship** n die Kunst, anderen um eine Nasenlänge voraus zu sein; **~-way** adj (street) Einbahn-

ongoing ['ɒngəʊɪŋ] adj momentan; (progressing) sich entwickelnd

onion ['ʌnjən] n Zwiebel f

on-line ['ɒnlaɪn] adj (COMPUT) Online-

onlooker ['ɒnlʊkə*] n Zuschauer(in) m(f)

only ['əʊnlɪ] adv nur, bloß ♦ adj einzige(r, s) ♦ conj nur, bloß; **an ~ child** ein Einzelkind; **not ~ ... but also ...** nicht nur ..., sondern auch ...

onset ['ɒnsɛt] n (start) Beginn m

onshore ['ɒnʃɔ:*] adj (wind) See-

onslaught ['ɒnslɔ:t] n Angriff m

onto ['ɒntʊ] prep = on to

onus ['əʊnəs] n Last f, Pflicht f

onward(s) ['ɒnwəd(z)] adv (place) voran, vorwärts; **from that day ~** von dem Tag an; **from today ~** ab heute

ooze [u:z] vi sickern

opaque [əʊ'peɪk] adj undurchsichtig

OPEC ['əʊpɛk] n abbr (= Organization of Petroleum-Exporting Countries) OPEC f

open ['əʊpn] adj offen; (public) öffentlich; (mind) aufgeschlossen ♦ vt öffnen, aufmachen; (trial, motorway, account) eröffnen ♦ vi (begin) anfangen; (shop) aufmachen; (door, flower) aufgehen; (play) Premiere haben; **in the ~ (air)** im Freien; **~ on to** vt fus sich öffnen auf +acc; **~ up** vt (route) erschließen; (shop, prospects) eröffnen ♦ vi öffnen; **~ing** n (hole) Öffnung f; (beginning) Anfang m; (good chance) Gelegenheit f; **~ing hours** npl Öffnungszeiten pl; **~ learning centre** n Weiterbildungseinrichtung auf Teilzeitbasis; **~ly** adv offen; (publicly) öffentlich; **~-minded** adj aufgeschlossen; **~-necked** adj offen; **~-plan**

(office) Großraum-; *(flat etc)* offen angelegt

Open University

Open University *ist eine 1969 in Großbritannien gegründete Fernuniversität für Spätstudierende. Der Unterricht findet durch Fernseh- und Radiosendungen statt, schriftliche Arbeiten werden mit der Post verschickt, und der Besuch von Sommerkursen ist Pflicht. Die Studenten eine bestimmte Anzahl von Unterrichtseinheiten in einem bestimmten Zeitraum absolvieren und für die Verleihung eines akademischen Grades eine Mindestzahl von Scheinen machen.*

---

opera ['ɔpərə] n Oper f; **~ house** n Opernhaus nt

operate ['ɔpəreɪt] vt *(machine)* bedienen; *(brakes, light)* betätigen ♦ vi *(machine)* laufen, in Betrieb sein; *(person)* arbeiten; *(MED):* **to ~ on** operieren

operatic [ɔpə'rætɪk] adj Opern-

operating ['ɔpəreɪtɪŋ] adj: **~ table/theatre** Operationstisch m/-saal m

operation [ɔpə'reɪʃən] n *(working)* Betrieb m; *(MED)* Operation f; *(undertaking)* Unternehmen nt; *(MIL)* Einsatz m; **to be in ~** *(JUR)* gelten; *(machine)* in Betrieb sein; **to have an ~** *(MED)* operiert werden; **~al** adj einsatzbereit

operative ['ɔpərətɪv] adj wirksam

operator ['ɔpəreɪtə*] n *(of machine)* Arbeiter m; *(TEL)* Telefonist(in) m(f)

opinion [ə'pɪnjən] n Meinung f; **in my ~** meiner Meinung nach; **~ated** adj starrsinnig; **~ poll** n Meinungsumfrage f

opponent [ə'pəunənt] n Gegner m

opportunity [ɔpə'tjuːnɪtɪ] n Gelegenheit f, Möglichkeit f; **to take the ~ of doing sth** die Gelegenheit ergreifen, etw zu tun

oppose [ə'pəuz] vt entgegentreten +dat; *(argument, idea)* ablehnen; *(plan)*

bekämpfen; **to be ~d to** sth gegen etw sein; **as ~d to** im Gegensatz zu; **opposing** adj gegnerisch; *(points of view)* entgegengesetzt

opposite ['ɔpəzɪt] adj *(house)* gegenüberliegend; *(direction)* entgegengesetzt ♦ adv gegenüber ♦ prep gegenüber ♦ n Gegenteil nt

opposition [ɔpə'zɪʃən] n *(resistance)* Widerstand m; *(POL)* Opposition f; *(contrast)* Gegensatz m

oppress [ə'pres] vt unterdrücken; *(heat etc)* bedrücken; **~ion** [ə'preʃən] n Unterdrückung f; **~ive** adj *(authority, law)* repressiv; *(burden, thought)* bedrückend; *(heat)* drückend

opt [ɔpt] vi: **to ~ for** sich entscheiden für; **to ~ to do sth** sich entschließen, etw zu tun; **to ~ out of** sich drücken vor +dat

optical ['ɔptɪkl] adj optisch; **~ character reader** n optische(s) Lesegerät nt

optician [ɔp'tɪʃən] n Optiker m

optimist ['ɔptɪmɪst] n Optimist m; **~ic** [ɔptɪ'mɪstɪk] adj optimistisch

optimum ['ɔptɪməm] adj optimal

option ['ɔpʃən] n Wahl f; *(COMM)* Option f; **to keep one's ~s open** sich alle Möglichkeiten offen halten; **~al** adj freiwillig; *(subject)* wahlfrei; **~al extras** npl Extras auf Wunsch

or [ɔː*] conj oder; **he could not read ~ write** er konnte weder lesen noch schreiben; **~ else** sonst

oral ['ɔːrəl] adj mündlich ♦ n *(exam)* mündliche Prüfung f

orange ['ɔrɪndʒ] n *(fruit)* Apfelsine f, Orange f; *(colour)* Orange nt ♦ adj orange

orator ['ɔrətə*] n Redner(in) m(f)

orbit ['ɔːbɪt] n Umlaufbahn f

orbital (motorway) ['ɔːbɪtl-] n Ringautobahn f

orchard ['ɔːtʃəd] n Obstgarten m

orchestra ['ɔːkɪstrə] n Orchester nt; *(US: seating)* Parkett nt; **~l** [ɔː'kestrəl] adj Orchester-, orchestral

orchid ['ɔːkɪd] n Orchidee f

ordain [ɔː'deɪn] vt (ECCL) weihen

ordeal [ɔː'diːl] n Qual f

order ['ɔːdə*] n (sequence) Reihenfolge f; (good arrangement) Ordnung f; (command) Befehl m; (JUR) Anordnung f; (peace) Ordnung f; (condition) Zustand m; (rank) Klasse f; (COMM) Bestellung f; (ECCL, honour) Orden m ♦ vt (also: put in ~) ordnen; (command) befehlen; (COMM) bestellen; in ~ in der Reihenfolge; in (working) ~ in gutem Zustand; in ~ to do sth um etw zu tun; on ~ (COMM) auf Bestellung; to ~ sb to do sth jdm befehlen, etw zu tun; to ~ sth (command) etw acc befehlen; ~ form n Bestellschein m; ~ly n (MIL) Sanitäter m; (MED) Pfleger m ♦ adj (tidy) ordentlich; (well-behaved) ruhig

ordinary ['ɔːdnrɪ] adj gewöhnlich ♦ n: out of the ~ außergewöhnlich

Ordnance Survey ['ɔːdnəns] (BRIT) n amtliche(r) Kartografiedienst m

ore [ɔː*] n Erz nt

organ ['ɔːgən] n (MUS) Orgel f; (BIOL, fig) Organ nt

organic [ɔː'gænɪk] adj (food, farming etc) biodynamisch

organization [ˌɔːgənaɪ'zeɪʃən] n Organisation f; (make-up) Struktur f

organize ['ɔːgənaɪz] vt organisieren; ~r n Organisator m, Veranstalter m

orgasm ['ɔːgæzəm] n Orgasmus m

orgy ['ɔːdʒɪ] n Orgie f

Orient ['ɔːrɪənt] n Orient m; **o~al** [ɔːrɪ'entl] adj orientalisch

origin ['ɒrɪdʒɪn] n Ursprung m; (of the world) Anfang m, Entstehung f; ~al [ə'rɪdʒɪnl] adj (first) ursprünglich; (painting) original; (idea) originell ♦ n Original nt; ~ally adv ursprünglich; originell; ~ate [ə'rɪdʒɪneɪt] vi entstehen ♦ vt ins Leben rufen; to ~ate from stammen aus

Orkney ['ɔːknɪ] npl (also: the ~ Islands) die Orkneyinseln pl

ornament ['ɔːnəmənt] n Schmuck m;

(on mantelpiece) Nippesfigur f; **~al** [ɔːnə'mentl] adj Zier-

ornate [ɔː'neɪt] adj reich verziert

orphan ['ɔːfn] n Waise f, Waisenkind nt ♦ vt: to be ~ed Waise werden; ~age n Waisenhaus nt

orthodox ['ɔːθədɒks] adj orthodox; **~y** n Orthodoxie f; (fig) Konventionalität f

orthopaedic [ɔːθə'piːdɪk] (US **orthopedic**) adj orthopädisch

ostentatious [ɒsten'teɪʃəs] adj großtuerisch, protzig

ostracize ['ɒstrəsaɪz] vt ausstoßen

ostrich ['ɒstrɪtʃ] n Strauß m

other ['ʌðə*] adj andere(r, s) ♦ pron andere(r, s) ♦ adv: ~ than anders als; the ~ (one) der/die/das andere; the ~ day neulich; ~s (~ people) andere; ~wise adv (in a different way) anders; (or else) sonst

otter ['ɒtə*] n Otter m

ouch [autʃ] excl aua

ought [ɔːt] vb aux sollen; I ~ to do it ich sollte es tun; this ~ to have been corrected das hätte korrigiert werden sollen

ounce [auns] n Unze f

our ['auə*] adj unser; see also **my**; **~s** pron unsere(r, s); see also **mine²**; **~selves** pron uns (selbst); (emphatic) (wir) selbst; see also **oneself**

oust [aust] vt verdrängen

out [aut] adv hinaus/heraus; (not indoors) draußen; (not alight) aus; (unconscious) bewusstlos; (results) bekannt gegeben; to eat/go ~ auswärts essen/ausgehen; ~ there da draußen; he is ~ (absent) er ist nicht da; he was ~ in his calculations seine Berechnungen waren nicht richtig; ~ loud laut; ~ of aus; (away from) außerhalb +gen; to be ~ of milk etc keine Milch etc mehr haben; ~ of order außer Betrieb; ~-and-~ adj (liar, thief etc) ausgemacht; ~back n Hinterland nt; ~board (motor) n Außenbordmotor m; ~break n Ausbruch m; ~burst *n* Ausbruch *m*; **~cast** *n* Ausgestoßene(r) *m(f)*; **~come** *n* Ergebnis *nt*; **~crop** *n* (*of rock*) Felsnase *f*; **~cry** *n* Protest *m*; **~dated** *adj* überholt; **~do** (*irreg: like do*) *vt* übertrumpfen; **~door** *adj* Außen-; (*SPORT*) im Freien; **~doors** *adv* draußen, im Freien

outer ['autə⟋] *adj* äußere(r, s); **~ space** *n* Weltraum *m*

outfit ['autfɪt] *n* Kleidung *f*

out: ~going *adj* (*character*) aufgeschlossen; **~goings** (*BRIT*) *npl* Ausgaben *pl*; **~grow** (*irreg: like grow*) *vt* (*clothes*) herauswachsen aus; (*habit*) ablegen; **~house** *n* Nebengebäude *nt*

outing ['autɪŋ] *n* Ausflug *m*

outlandish [aut'lændɪʃ] *adj* eigenartig

out: ~law *n* Geächtete(r) *f(m)* ♦ *vt* ächten; (*thing*) verbieten; **~lay** *n* Auslage *f*; **~let** *n* Auslass *m*, Abfluss *m*; (*also: retail ~let*) Absatzmarkt *m*; (*US: ELEC*) Steckdose *f*; (*for emotions*) Ventil *nt*

outline ['autlaɪn] *n* Umriss *m*

out: ~live *vt* überleben; **~look** *n* (*also fig*) Aussicht *f*; (*attitude*) Einstellung *f*; **~lying** *adj* entlegen; (*district*) Außen-; **~moded** *adj* veraltet; **~number** *vt* zahlenmäßig überlegen sein +*dat*; **~of-date** *adj* (*passport*) abgelaufen; (*clothes etc*) altmodisch; (*ideas etc*) überholt; **~of-the-way** *adj* abgelegen; **~patient** *n* ambulante(r) Patient *m*/ambulante Patientin *f*; **~post** (*MIL, fig*) *n* Vorposten *m*; **~put** *n* Leistung *f*, Produktion *f*; (*COMPUT*) Ausgabe *f*

outrage ['autreɪdʒ] *n* (*cruel deed*) Ausschreitung *f*; (*indecency*) Skandal *m* ♦ *vt* (*morals*) verstoßen gegen; (*person*) empören; **~ous** [aut'reɪdʒəs] *adj* unerhört

outreach worker ['autri:tʃ-] *n* Streetworker(in) *m(f)*

outright [*adv* aut'raɪt, *adj* 'autraɪt] *adv* (*at once*) sofort; (*openly*) ohne Umschweife ♦ *adj* (*denial*) völlig; (*sale*) Total-; (*winner*) unbestritten

outset ['autset] *n* Beginn *m*

outside [aut'saɪd] *n* Außenseite *f* ♦ *adj* äußere(r, s), Außen-; (*chance*) gering ♦ *adv* außen ♦ *prep* außerhalb +*gen*; **at the ~** (*fig*) maximal; (*time*) spätestens; **to go ~** nach draußen gehen; **~ lane** *n* (*AUT*) äußere Spur *f*; **~ line** *n* (*TEL*) Amtsanschluss *m*; **~r** *n* Außenseiter(in) *m(f)*

out: ~size *adj* übergroß; **~skirts** *npl* Stadtrand *m*; **~spoken** *adj* freimütig; **~standing** *adj* hervorragend; (*debts etc*) ausstehend; **~stay** *vt*: **to ~stay one's welcome** länger bleiben als erwünscht; **~stretched** *adj* ausgestreckt; **~strip** *vt* übertreffen; **~ tray** *n* Ausgangskorb *m*

outward ['autwəd] *adj* äußere(r, s); (*journey*) Hin-; (*freight*) ausgehend ♦ *adv* nach außen; **~ly** *adv* äußerlich

outweigh [aut'weɪ] *vt* (*fig*) überwiegen

outwit [aut'wɪt] *vt* überlisten

oval ['əuvl] *adj* oval ♦ *n* Oval *nt*

Oval Office

Oval Office, *ein großer ovaler Raum im Weißen Haus, ist das private Büro des amerikanischen Präsidenten. Im weiteren Sinne bezieht sich dieser Begriff auf die Präsidentschaft selbst.*

---

ovary ['əuvəri] *n* Eierstock *m*

ovation [əu'veɪʃən] *n* Beifallssturm *m*

oven ['ʌvn] *n* Backofen *m*; **~proof** *adj* feuerfest

over ['əuvə⟋] *adv* (*across*) hinüber/herüber; (*finished*) vorbei; (*left*) übrig; (*again*) wieder, noch einmal ♦ *prep* über ♦ *prefix* (*excessively*) übermäßig; **~ here** hier(hin); **~ there** dort(hin); **all ~** (*everywhere*) überall; (*finished*) vorbei; **~ and ~** immer wieder; **~ and above** darüber hinaus; **to ask sb ~** jdn einladen; **to bend ~** sich bücken

overall [*adj, n* 'əuvərɔ:l, *adv* əuvər'ɔ:l] *adj* (*situation*) allgemein; (*length*) Gesamt- ♦ *n* (*BRIT*) Kittel *m* ♦ *adv* insgesamt; **~s** npl (for man) Overall m

over: ~awe vt (frighten) einschüchtern; (make impression) überwältigen; **~balance** vi Übergewicht bekommen; **~bearing** adj aufdringlich; **~board** adv über Bord; **~book** vi überbuchen

overcast ['əuvəkɑːst] adj bedeckt

overcharge [əuvə'tʃɑːdʒ] vt: **to ~ sb** von jdm zu viel verlangen

overcoat ['əuvəkəut] n Mantel m

overcome [əuvə'kʌm] (irreg: like come) vt überwinden

over: ~crowded adj überfüllt; **~crowding** n Überfüllung f; **~do** (irreg: like do) vt (cook too much) verkochen; (exaggerate) übertreiben; **~done** adj übertrieben; (COOK) verbraten, verkocht; **~dose** n Überdosis f; **~draft** n (Konto)überziehung f; **~drawn** adj (account) überzogen; **~due** adj überfällig; **~estimate** vt überschätzen; **~excited** adj überreizt; (children) aufgeregt

overflow [əuvə'fləu] vi überfließen ♦ n ['əuvəfləu] (excess) Überschuss m; (also: **~ pipe**) Überlaufrohr nt

overgrown [əuvə'grəun] adj (garden) verwildert

overhaul [vb əuvə'hɔːl, n 'əuvəhɔːl] vt (car) überholen; (plans) überprüfen ♦ n ['əuvəhɔːl] Überholung f

overhead [adv əuvə'hed, adj, n 'əuvəhed] adv oben ♦ adj Hoch-; (lighting) Decken- ♦ n (US) = **overheads**; **~s** npl (costs) allgemeine Unkosten pl; **~ projector** n Overheadprojektor m

over: ~hear (irreg: like hear) vt (mit an)hören; **~heat** vi (engine) heiß laufen; **~joyed** adj überglücklich; **~kill** n (fig) Rundumschlag m

overland ['əuvəlænd] adj Überland- ♦ adv (travel) über Land

overlap [vb əuvə'læp, n 'əuvəlæp] vi sich überschneiden; (objects) sich teilweise decken ♦ n Überschneidung f

over: ~leaf adv umseitig; **~load** vt

überladen; **~look** vt (view from above) überblicken; (not notice) übersehen; (pardon) hinwegsehen über +acc

overnight [adv əuvə'naɪt, adj 'əuvənaɪt] adv über Nacht ♦ adj (journey) Nacht-; **~ stay** Übernachtung f; **to stay ~** übernachten

overpass ['əuvəpɑːs] n Überführung f

overpower [əuvə'pauə] vt überwältigen

over: ~rate vt überschätzen; **~ride** (irreg: like ride) vt (order, decision) aufheben; (objection) übergehen; **~riding** adj vorherrschend; **~rule** vt verwerfen; **~run** (irreg: like run) vt (country) einfallen in; (time limit) überziehen

overseas [əuvə'siːz] adv nach/in Übersee ♦ adj überseeisch, Übersee-

overseer ['əuvəsiːə] n Aufseher m

overshadow [əuvə'ʃædəu] vt überschatten

overshoot [əuvə'ʃuːt] (irreg: like shoot) vt (runway) hinausschießen über +acc

oversight ['əuvəsaɪt] n (mistake) Versehen nt

over: ~sleep (irreg: like sleep) vi verschlafen; **~spill** n (Bevölkerungs)überschuss m; **~state** vt übertreiben; **~step** vt: **to ~step the mark** zu weit gehen

overt [əu'vɜːt] adj offen(kundig)

overtake [əuvə'teɪk] (irreg: like take) vt, vi überholen

over: ~throw (irreg: like throw) vt (POL) stürzen; **~time** n Überstunden pl; **~tone** n (fig) Note f

overture ['əuvətʃuə] n Ouvertüre f

over: ~turn vt, vi umkippen; **~weight** adj zu dick; **~whelm** vt überwältigen; **~work** n Überarbeitung f ♦ vt überlasten ♦ vi sich überarbeiten; **~wrought** adj überreizt

owe [əu] vt schulden; **to ~ sth to sb** (money) jdm etw schulden; (favour etc) jdm etw verdanken; **owing to** prep wegen +gen

owl [aul] n Eule f

own [əun] vt besitzen ♦ adj eigen; **a room of my ~** mein eigenes Zimmer; **to get one's ~ back** sich rächen; **on one's ~** allein; **~ up** vi: **to ~ up (to sth)** (etw) zugeben; **~er** n Besitzer(in) m(f); **~ership** n Besitz m

ox [ɔks] n (pl **~en**) n Ochse m

oxtail ['ɔksteɪl] n: **~ soup** Ochsenschwanzsuppe f

oxygen ['ɔksɪdʒən] n Sauerstoff m; **~ mask** n Sauerstoffmaske f; **~ tent** n Sauerstoffzelt nt

oyster ['ɔɪstə'] n Auster f

oz. abbr = **ounce(s)**

ozone ['əuzəun] n Ozon nt; **~-friendly** adj (aerosol) ohne Treibgas; (fridge) FCKW-frei; **~ hole** n Ozonloch nt; **~ layer** n Ozonschicht f

P, p

p abbr = **penny; pence**

pa [pɑː] (inf) n Papa m

P.A. n abbr = **personal assistant; public address system**

p.a. abbr = **per annum**

pace [peɪs] n Schritt m; (speed) Tempo nt ♦ vi schreiten; **to keep ~ with** Schritt halten mit; **~maker** n Schrittmacher m

pacific [pə'sɪfɪk] adj pazifisch ♦ n: **the P~ (Ocean)** der Pazifik

pacifist ['pæsɪfɪst] n Pazifist m

pacify ['pæsɪfaɪ] vt befrieden; (calm) beruhigen

pack [pæk] n (of goods) Packung f; (of hounds) Meute f; (of cards) Spiel n; (gang) Bande f ♦ vt (case) packen; (clothes) einpacken ♦ vi packen; **to ~ sb off to ...** jdn nach ... schicken; **~ it in!** lass es gut sein!

package ['pækɪdʒ] n Paket nt; **~ tour** n Pauschalreise f

packed [pækt] adj abgepackt; **~ lunch** n Lunchpaket nt

packet ['pækɪt] n Päckchen nt

packing ['pækɪŋ] n (action) Packen nt; (material) Verpackung f; **~ case** n (Pack)kiste f

pact [pækt] n Pakt m, Vertrag m

pad [pæd] n (of paper) (Schreib)block m; (stuffing) Polster nt ♦ vt polstern; **~ding** n Polsterung f

paddle ['pædl] n Paddel nt; (US: SPORT) Schläger m ♦ vt (boat) paddeln ♦ vi (in sea) plan(t)schen; **~ steamer** n Raddampfer m

paddling pool ['pædlɪŋ-] (BRIT) n Plan(t)schbecken nt

paddock ['pædək] n Koppel f

paddy field ['pædɪ-] n Reisfeld nt

padlock ['pædlɔk] n Vorhängeschloss nt ♦ vt verschließen

paediatrics [piːdɪ'ætrɪks] (US **pediatrics**) n Kinderheilkunde f

pagan ['peɪgən] adj heidnisch ♦ n Heide m, Heidin f

page [peɪdʒ] n Seite f; (person) Page m ♦ vt (in hotel) ausrufen lassen

pageant ['pædʒənt] n Festzug m, ~ry n Gepränge f

pager ['peɪdʒə'] n (TEL) Funkrufempfänger m, Piepser m (inf)

paging device ['peɪdʒɪŋ-] n (TEL) = **pager**

paid [peɪd] pt, pp of **pay** ♦ adj bezahlt; **to put ~ to** (BRIT) zunichte machen

pail [peɪl] n Eimer m

pain [peɪn] n Schmerz m; **to be in ~** Schmerzen haben; **on ~ of death** bei Todesstrafe; **to take ~s to do sth** sich Mühe geben, etw zu tun; **~ed** adj (expression) gequält; **~ful** adj (physically) schmerzhaft; (embarrassing) peinlich; (difficult) mühsam; **~fully** adv (fig: very) schrecklich; **~killer** n Schmerzmittel nt; **~less** adj schmerzlos; **~staking** ['zteɪkɪŋ] adj gewissenhaft

paint [peɪnt] n Farbe f ♦ vt anstreichen; (picture) malen; **to ~ the door blue** die Tür blau streichen; **~brush** n Pinsel m; **~er** n Maler m; **~ing** n Malerei f; (picture) Gemälde nt; **~work** n Anstrich *m*; (*of car*) Lack *m*

pair [peər] *n* Paar *nt*; ~ **of scissors** Schere *f*; ~ **of trousers** Hose *f*

pajamas [pə'dʒɑːməz] (*US*) *npl* Schlafanzug *m*

Pakistan [pɑːkɪ'stɑːn] *n* Pakistan *nt*; ~**i** *adj* pakistanisch ♦ *n* Pakistani *mf*

pal [pæl] (*inf*) *n* Kumpel *m*

palace ['pælɪs] *n* Palast *m*, Schloss *nt*

palatable ['pælɪtəbl] *adj* schmackhaft

palate ['pælɪt] *n* Gaumen *m*

palatial [pə'leɪʃəl] *adj* palastartig

pale [peɪl] *adj* blass, bleich ♦ *n*: **to be beyond the** ~ die Grenzen überschreiten

Palestine ['pælɪstaɪn] *n* Palästina *n*; **Palestinian** [pælɪs'tɪnɪən] *adj* palästinensisch ♦ *n* Palästinenser(in) *m(f)*

palette ['pælɪt] *n* Palette *f*

paling ['peɪlɪŋ] *n* (*stake*) Zaunpfahl *m*; (*fence*) Lattenzaun *m*

pall [pɔːl] *vi* jeden Reiz verlieren, verblassen

pallet ['pælɪt] *n* (*for goods*) Palette *f*

pallid ['pælɪd] *adj* blass, bleich

pallor ['pælər] *n* Blässe *f*

palm [pɑːm] *n* (*of hand*) Handfläche *f*; (*also*: ~ **tree**) Palme *f* ♦ *vt*: **to** ~ **sth off on sb** jdm etw andrehen; **P~ Sunday** *n* Palmsonntag *m*

palpable ['pælpəbl] *adj* (*also fig*) greifbar

palpitation [pælpɪ'teɪʃən] *n* Herzklopfen *nt*

paltry ['pɔːltrɪ] *adj* armselig

pamper ['pæmpər] *vt* verhätscheln

pamphlet ['pæmflɪt] *n* Broschüre *f*

pan [pæn] *n* Pfanne *f* ♦ *vi* (*CINE*) schwenken

panache [pə'næʃ] *n* Schwung *m*

pancake ['pænkeɪk] *n* Pfannkuchen *m*

pancreas ['pæŋkrɪəs] *n* Bauchspeicheldrüse *f*

panda ['pændə] *n* Panda *m*; ~ **car** (*BRIT*) *n* (Funk)streifenwagen *m*

pandemonium [pændɪ'məʊnɪəm] *n* Hölle *f*; (*noise*) Höllenlärm *m*

pander ['pændər] *vi*: **to** ~ **to** sich richten nach

pane [peɪn] *n* (Fenster)scheibe *f*

panel ['pænl] *n* (*of wood*) Tafel *f*; (*TV*) Diskussionsrunde *f*; ~**ling** (*US* **paneling**) *n* Täfelung *f*

pang [pæŋ] *n*: ~**s of hunger** quälende(r) Hunger *m*; ~**s of conscience** Gewissensbisse *pl*

panic ['pænɪk] *n* Panik *f* ♦ *vi* in Panik geraten; **don't** ~ (nur) keine Panik; ~**ky** *adj* (*person*) überängstlich; ~**stricken** *adj* von panischem Schrecken erfasst; (*look*) panisch

pansy ['pænzɪ] *n* Stiefmütterchen *nt*; (*inf*) Schwule(r) *m*

pant [pænt] *vi* keuchen; (*dog*) hecheln

panther ['pænθər] *n* Pant(h)er *m*

panties ['pæntɪz] *npl* (Damen)slip *m*

pantihose ['pæntɪhəʊz] (*US*) *n* Strumpfhose *f*

pantomime ['pæntəmaɪm] (*BRIT*) *n* Märchenkomödie *f* um Weihnachten

---

Pantomime

Pantomime *oder umgangssprachlich* panto *ist im Großbritannien ein zur Weihnachtszeit aufgeführtes Märchenspiel mit possenhaften Elementen, Musik, Standardrollen (eine als Frau verkleideter Mann, ein Junge, ein Bösewicht) und aktuellen Witzen. Publikumsbeteiligung wird gern gesehen (z.B. warnen die Kinder den Helden mit dem Ruf „He's behind you" vor einer drohenden Gefahr), und viele der Witze sprechen vor allem Erwachsene an, so dass pantomimes Unterhaltung für die ganze Familie bieten.*

---

pantry ['pæntrɪ] *n* Vorratskammer *f*

pants [pænts] *npl* (*BRIT*: *woman's*) Schlüpfer *m*; (: *man's*) Unterhose *f*; (*US*: *trousers*) Hose *f*

papal ['peɪpəl] *adj* päpstlich

paper ['peɪpər] *n* Papier *nt*; (*newspaper*) Zeitung *f*; (*essay*) Referat *nt* ♦ *adj*

Papier-, aus Papier ♦ vt (wall) tapezieren; **~s** npl (identity ~s) Ausweis(papiere pl) m; **~back** n Taschenbuch nt; **~ bag** n Tüte f; **~ clip** n Büroklammer f; **~ hankie** n Tempotaschentuch nt ®; **~weight** n Briefbeschwerer m; **~work** n Schreibarbeit f

par [pɑːˈ] n (COMM) Nennwert m; (GOLF) Par nt; **on a ~ with** ebenbürtig +dat

parable [ˈpærəbl] n (REL) Gleichnis nt

parachute [ˈpærəʃuːt] n Fallschirm m ♦ vi (mit dem Fallschirm) abspringen

parade [pəˈreɪd] n Parade f ♦ vt aufmarschieren lassen; (fig) zur Schau stellen ♦ vi paradieren, vorbeimarschieren

paradise [ˈpærədaɪs] n Paradies nt

paradox [ˈpærədɒks] n Paradox n; **~ically** [pærəˈdɒksɪklɪ] adv paradoxerweise

paraffin [ˈpærəfɪn] (BRIT) n Paraffin nt

paragraph [ˈpærəɡrɑːf] n Absatz m

parallel [ˈpærəlel] adj parallel ♦ n Parallele f

paralyse [ˈpærəlaɪz] (US **paralyze**) vt (MED) lähmen, paralysieren; (fig: organization, production etc) lahm legen; **~d** gelähmt; **paralysis** [pəˈrælɪsɪs] n Lähmung f

paralyze [ˈpærəlaɪz] (US) = **paralyse**

parameter [pəˈræmɪtəˈ] n Parameter m; **~s** npl (framework, limits) Rahmen m

paramount [ˈpærəmaʊnt] adj höchste(r, s), oberste(r, s)

paranoid [ˈpærənɔɪd] adj (person) an Verfolgungswahn leidend, paranoid; (feeling) krankhaft

parapet [ˈpærəpɪt] n Brüstung f

paraphernalia [pærəfəˈneɪlɪə] n Zubehör nt, Utensilien pl

paraphrase [ˈpærəfreɪz] vt umschreiben

paraplegic [pærəˈpliːdʒɪk] n Querschnittsgelähmte(r) f(m)

parasite [ˈpærəsaɪt] n (also fig) Schmarotzer m, Parasit m

parasol [ˈpærəsɒl] n Sonnenschirm m

paratrooper [ˈpærətruːpəˈ] n Fallschirmjäger m

parcel [ˈpɑːsl] n Paket n ♦ vt (also: ~ up) einpacken

parch [pɑːtʃ] vt (aus)dörren; **~ed** adj ausgetrocknet; (person) am Verdursten

parchment [ˈpɑːtʃmənt] n Pergament nt

pardon [ˈpɑːdn] n Verzeihung f ♦ vt (JUR) begnadigen; **~ me!, I beg your ~!** verzeihen Sie bitte!; **~ me?** (US) wie bitte?; **(I beg your) ~?** wie bitte?

parent [ˈpɛərənt] n Elternteil m; **~s** npl (mother and father) Eltern pl; **~al** [pəˈrentl] adj elterlich, Eltern-

parentheses [pəˈrenθɪsiːz] npl of **parenthesis**

parenthesis [pəˈrenθɪsɪs] n Klammer f; (sentence) Parenthese f

Paris [ˈpærɪs] n Paris nt

parish [ˈpærɪʃ] n Gemeinde f

park [pɑːk] n Park m ♦ vt, vi parken

parking [ˈpɑːkɪŋ] n Parken nt; **"no ~"** "Parken verboten"; **~ lot** (US) n Parkplatz m; **~ meter** n Parkuhr f; **~ ticket** n Strafzettel m

parlance [ˈpɑːləns] n Sprachgebrauch m

parliament [ˈpɑːləmənt] n Parlament nt; **~ary** [pɑːləˈmentərɪ] adj parlamentarisch, Parlaments-

parlour [ˈpɑːləˈ] (US **parlor**) n Salon m

parochial [pəˈrəʊkɪəl] adj (narrowminded) eng(stirnig)

parole [pəˈrəʊl] n: **on ~** (prisoner) auf Bewährung

parrot [ˈpærət] n Papagei m

parry [ˈpærɪ] vt parieren, abwehren

parsley [ˈpɑːslɪ] n Petersilie f

parsnip [ˈpɑːsnɪp] n Pastinake f

parson [ˈpɑːsn] n Pfarrer m

part [pɑːt] n (piece) Teil m; (THEAT) Rolle f; (of machine) Teil n ♦ adv = **partly**; ♦ vt trennen; (hair) scheiteln ♦ vi sich trennen; **to take ~ in** teilnehmen an +dat; **to take sth in good ~** etw nicht übel nehmen; **to take sb's**

~ sich auf jds Seite *acc* stellen; **for my** ~ ich für meinen Teil; **for the most** ~ meistens, größtenteils; **in ~ exchange** (*BRIT*) in Zahlung; **~ with** *vt* fus hergeben; (*renounce*) aufgeben; **~ial** ['pɑ:ʃl] *adj* (*incomplete*) teilweise; (*biased*) parteiisch; **to be ~ial to** eine (besondere) Vorliebe haben für

participant [pɑ:'tɪsɪpənt] *n* Teilnehmer(in) *m(f)*

participate [pɑ:'tɪsɪpeɪt] *vi*: **to ~ (in)** teilnehmen (an +*dat*); **participation** [pɑ:tɪsɪ'peɪʃən] *n* Teilnahme *f*; (*sharing*) Beteiligung *f*

participle ['pɑ:tɪsɪpl] *n* Partizip *nt*

particle ['pɑ:tɪkl] *n* Teilchen *nt*

particular [pə'tɪkjulə*] *adj* bestimmt; (*exact*) genau; (*fussy*) eigen; **in ~** besonders; **~ly** *adv* besonders

particulars *npl* (*details*) Einzelheiten *pl*; (*of person*) Personalien *pl*

parting ['pɑ:tɪŋ] *n* (*separation*) Abschied *m*; (*BRIT: of hair*) Scheitel *m* ♦ *adj* Abschieds-

partition [pɑ:'tɪʃən] *n* (*wall*) Trennwand *f*; (*division*) Teilung *f* ♦ *vt* aufteilen

partly ['pɑ:tlɪ] *adv* zum Teil, teilweise

partner ['pɑ:tnə*] *n* Partner *m* ♦ *vt* der Partner sein von; **~ship** *n* Partnerschaft *f*; (*COMM*) Teilhaberschaft *f*

partridge ['pɑ:trɪdʒ] *n* Rebhuhn *nt*

part-time ['pɑ:t'taɪm] *adj* Teilzeit- ♦ *adv* stundenweise

party ['pɑ:tɪ] *n* (*POL, JUR*) Partei *f*; (*group*) Gesellschaft *f*; (*celebration*) Party *f* ♦ *adj* (*dress*) Party-; (*politics*) Partei-; **~ line** *n* (*TEL*) Gemeinschaftsanschluss *m*

pass [pɑ:s] *vt* (*on foot*) vorbeigehen an +*dat*; (*driving*) vorbeifahren an +*dat*; (*surpass*) übersteigen; (*hand on*) weitergeben; (*approve*) genehmigen; (*time*) verbringen; (*exam*) bestehen ♦ *vi* (*go by*) vorbeigehen, vorbeifahren; (*years*) vergehen; (*be successful*) bestehen ♦ *n* (*in mountains, SPORT*) Pass *m*; (*permission*) Passierschein *m*; (*in exam*):

to get a ~ bestehen. **~ to** ~ **through sth** etw durch etw führen; **to make a ~ at sb** (*inf*) bei jdm Annäherungsversuche machen; **~ away** *vi* (*euph*) verscheiden; **~ by** *vi* vorbeigehen; vorbeifahren; (*years*) vergehen; **~ on** *vt* weitergeben; **~ out** *vi* (*faint*) ohnmächtig werden; **~ up** *vt* vorübergehen lassen; **~able** *adj* (*road*) passierbar; (*fairly good*) passabel

passage ['pæsɪdʒ] *n* (*corridor*) Gang *m*; (*in book*) (*Text*)stelle *f*; (*voyage*) Überfahrt *f*; **~way** *n* Durchgang *m*

passbook ['pɑ:sbuk] *n* Sparbuch *nt*

passenger ['pæsɪndʒə*] *n* Passagier *m*; (*on bus*) Fahrgast *m*

passer-by [pɑ:sə'baɪ] *n* Passant(in) *m(f)*

passing ['pɑ:sɪŋ] *adj* (*car*) vorbeifahrend; (*thought, affair*) momentan ♦ *n*: **in ~** beiläufig; **~ place** *n* (*AUT*) Ausweichstelle *f*

passion ['pæʃən] *n* Leidenschaft *f*; **~ate** *adj* leidenschaftlich

passive ['pæsɪv] *adj* passiv; (*LING*) passivisch; **~ smoking** *n* Passivrauchen *nt*

Passover ['pɑ:səuvə*] *n* Passahfest *nt*

passport ['pɑ:spɔ:t] *n* (*Reise*)pass *m*; **~ control** *n* Passkontrolle *f*; **~ office** *n* Passamt *nt*

password ['pɑ:swɜ:d] *n* Parole *f*, Kennwort *nt*, Losung *f*

past [pɑ:st] *prep* (*motion*) an +*dat* ... vorbei; (*position*) hinter +*dat*; (*later than*) nach ♦ *adj* (*years*) vergangen; (*president etc*) ehemalig ♦ *n* Vergangenheit *f*; **he's ~ forty** er ist über vierzig; **for the ~ few/3 days** in den letzten paar/3 Tagen; **to run ~** vorbeilaufen; **ten/quarter ~ eight** zehn/Viertel nach acht

pasta ['pæstə] *n* Teigwaren *pl*

paste [peɪst] *n* (*fish ~ etc*) Paste *f*; (*glue*) Kleister *m* ♦ *vt* kleben

pasteurized ['pæstʃəraɪzd] *adj* pasteurisiert

pastime ['pɑ:staɪm] *n* Zeitvertreib *m*

pastor ['pɑ:stə*] *n* Pfarrer *m*

pastry ['peɪstrɪ] n Blätterteig m; **pastries** npl (tarts etc) Stückchen pl

pasture ['pɑːstʃər] n Weide f

pasty [n 'pæstɪ, adj 'peɪstɪ] n (Fleisch)pastete f ♦ adj blässlich, käsig

pat [pæt] n leichte(r) Schlag m, Klaps m ♦ vt tätscheln

patch [pætʃ] n Fleck m ♦ vt flicken; **(to go through) a bad ~** eine Pechsträhne (haben); **~ up** vt flicken; (quarrel) beilegen; **~ed** adj geflickt; **~y** adj (irregular) ungleichmäßig

pâté ['pæteɪ] n Pastete f

patent ['peɪtnt] n Patent nt ♦ vt patentieren lassen; (by authorities) patentieren ♦ adj offenkundig; **~ leather** n Lackleder nt

paternal [pə'tɜːnl] adj väterlich

paternity [pə'tɜːnɪtɪ] n Vaterschaft f

path [pɑːθ] n Pfad m; Weg m

pathetic [pə'θetɪk] adj (very bad) kläglich

pathological [pæθə'lɒdʒɪkl] adj pathologisch

pathology [pə'θɒlədʒɪ] n Pathologie f

pathos ['peɪθɒs] n Rührseligkeit f

pathway ['pɑːθweɪ] n Weg m

patience ['peɪʃns] n Geduld f; (BRIT: CARDS) Patience f

patient ['peɪʃnt] n Patient(in) m(f), Kranke(r) mf ♦ adj geduldig

patio ['pætɪəʊ] n Terrasse f

patriotic [pætrɪ'ɒtɪk] adj patriotisch

patrol [pə'trəʊl] n Patrouille f; (police) Streife f ♦ vt patrouillieren in +dat ♦ vi (police) Runde machen; (MIL) patrouillieren; **~ car** n Streifenwagen m; **~man** (US) (irreg) n (Streifen)polizist m

patron ['peɪtrən] n (in shop) (Stamm)kunde m; (in hotel) (Stamm)gast m; (supporter) Förderer m; **~ of the arts** Mäzen m; **~age** ['pætrənɪdʒ] n Schirmherrschaft f; **~ize** ['pætrənaɪz] vt (support) unterstützen; (shop) besuchen; (treat condescendingly) von oben herab behandeln; **~ saint** n Schutzpatron(in) m(f)

patter ['pætər] n (sound: of feet) Trappeln nt; (: of rain) Prasseln nt; (sales talk) Gerede nt ♦ vi (feet) trappeln; (rain) prasseln

pattern ['pætən] n Muster nt; (SEWING) Schnittmuster nt; (KNITTING) Strickanleitung f

pauper ['pɔːpər] n Arme(r) mf

pause [pɔːz] n Pause f ♦ vi innehalten

pave [peɪv] vt pflastern; **to ~ the way for** den Weg bahnen für

pavement ['peɪvmənt] n (BRIT) Bürgersteig m

pavilion [pə'vɪlɪən] n Pavillon m; (SPORT) Klubhaus nt

paving ['peɪvɪŋ] n Straßenpflaster nt; **~ stone** n Pflasterstein m

paw [pɔː] n Pfote f; (: of big cats) Tatze f, Pranke f ♦ vt (scrape) scharren; (handle) betatschen

pawn [pɔːn] n Pfand nt; (chess) Bauer m ♦ vt verpfänden; **~broker** n Pfandleiher m; **~shop** n Pfandhaus nt

pay [peɪ] (pt, pp paid) n Bezahlung f, Lohn m ♦ vt bezahlen ♦ vi zahlen; (be profitable) sich bezahlt machen; **to ~ attention (to)** Acht geben (auf +acc); **to ~ sb a visit** jdn besuchen; **~ back** vt zurückzahlen; **~ for** vt fus bezahlen; **~ in** vt einzahlen; **~ off** vt abzahlen ♦ vi (scheme, decision) sich bezahlt machen; **~ up** vt bezahlen; **~able** adj zahlbar, fällig; **~ee** n Zahlungsempfänger m; **~ envelope** (US) n Lohntüte f; **~ment** n Bezahlung f; **advance ~ment** Vorauszahlung f; **monthly ~ment** monatliche Rate f; **~ packet** (BRIT) n Lohntüte f; **~phone** n Münzfernsprecher m; **~roll** n Lohnliste f; **~ slip** n Lohn-/Gehaltsstreifen m; **~ television** n Abonnenten-Fernsehen nt

PC n abbr = **personal computer**

p.c. abbr = **per cent**

pea [piː] n Erbse f

peace [piːs] n Friede(n) m; **~able** adj friedlich; **~ful** adj friedlich, ruhig;

~keeping adj Friedens-

peach [pi:tʃ] n Pfirsich m

peacock ['pi:kɔk] n Pfau m

peak [pi:k] n Spitze f; (of mountain) Gipfel m; (fig) Höhepunkt m; **~ hours** npl (traffic) Hauptverkehrszeit f; (telephone, electricity) Hauptbelastungszeit f; **~ period** n Stoßzeit f, Hauptzeit f

peal [pi:l] n (Glocken)läuten nt; **~s of laughter** schallende(s) Gelächter nt

peanut ['pi:nʌt] n Erdnuss f; **~ butter** n Erdnussbutter f

pear [pɛə⁴] n Birne f

pearl [pɜ:l] n Perle f

peasant ['pɛznt] n Bauer m

peat [pi:t] n Torf m

pebble ['pɛbl] n Kiesel m

peck [pɛk] vt, vi picken ♦ n (with beak) Schnabelhieb m; (kiss) flüchtige(r) Kuss m; **~ing order** n Hackordnung f; **~ish** (inf) adj ein bisschen hungrig

peculiar [pɪ'kju:lɪə⁴] adj (odd) seltsam; **~ to** charakteristisch für; **~ity** [pɪkjuːlɪ'ærɪtɪ] n (singular quality) Besonderheit f; (strangeness) Eigenartigkeit f

pedal ['pɛdl] n Pedal nt ♦ vt, vi (cycle) fahren, Rad fahren

pedantic [pɪ'dæntɪk] adj pedantisch

peddler ['pɛdlə⁴] n Hausierer(in) m(f); (of drugs) Drogenhändler(in) m(f)

pedestal ['pɛdəstl] n Sockel m

pedestrian [pɪ'dɛstrɪən] n Fußgänger m ♦ adj Fußgänger-; (humdrum) langweilig; **~ crossing** (BRIT) n Fußgängerübergang m; **~ized** in eine Fußgängerzone umgewandelt; **~ precinct** (BRIT), **~ zone** (US) n Fußgängerzone f

pediatrics [pi:dɪ'ætrɪks] (US) n = **paediatrics**

pedigree ['pɛdɪgri:] n Stammbaum m ♦ cpd (animal) reinrassig, Zucht-

pee [pi:] (inf) vi pissen, pinkeln

peek [pi:k] vi gucken

peel [pi:l] n Schale f ♦ vt schälen ♦ vi (paint etc) abblättern; (skin) sich

schälen

peep [pi:p] n (BRIT: look) kurze(r) Blick m; (sound) Piepsen nt ♦ vi (BRIT: look) gucken; **~ out** vi herausgucken; **~hole** n Guckloch nt

peer [pɪə⁴] vi starren; (peep) gucken ♦ n (nobleman) Peer m; (equal) Ebenbürtige(r) m; **~age** n Peerswürde f

peeved [pi:vd] adj (person) sauer

peg [pɛg] n (stake) Pflock m; (BRIT: also: clothes) **~** Wäscheklammer f

Pekinese [pi:kɪ'ni:z] n (dog) Pekinese m

pelican ['pɛlɪkən] n Pelikan m; **~ crossing** (BRIT) n (AUT) Ampelüberweg m

pellet ['pɛlɪt] n Kügelchen nt

pelmet ['pɛlmɪt] n Blende f

pelt [pɛlt] vt bewerfen ♦ vi (rain) schütten ♦ n Pelz m, Fell nt

pelvis ['pɛlvɪs] n Becken nt

pen [pɛn] n (fountain ~) Federhalter m; (ball-point ~) Kuli m; (for sheep) Pferch m

penal ['pi:nl] adj Straf-; **~ize** vt (punish) bestrafen; (disadvantage) benachteiligen

penalty ['pɛnltɪ] n Strafe f; (FOOTBALL) Elfmeter m; **~ (kick)** n Elfmeter m

penance ['pɛnəns] n Buße f

pence [pɛns] (BRIT) npl of **penny**

pencil ['pɛnsl] n Bleistift m; **~ case** n Federmäppchen nt; **~ sharpener** n Bleistiftspitzer m

pendant ['pɛndnt] n Anhänger m

pending ['pɛndɪŋ] prep bis zu ♦ adj unentschieden, noch offen

pendulum ['pɛndjuləm] n Pendel m

penetrate ['pɛnɪtreɪt] vt durchdringen; (enter into) eindringen in +acc; **penetration** [pɛnɪ'treɪʃən] n Durchdringen nt; Eindringen nt

penfriend ['pɛnfrɛnd] (BRIT) n Brieffreund(in) m(f)

penguin ['pɛŋgwɪn] n Pinguin m

penicillin [pɛnɪ'sɪlɪn] n Penizillin nt

peninsula [pə'nɪnsjulə] n Halbinsel f

penis ['piːnɪs] n Penis m

penitentiary [penɪ'tenʃərɪ] (US) n Zuchthaus nt

penknife ['pennaɪf] n Federmesser nt

pen name n Pseudonym nt

penniless ['penɪlɪs] adj mittellos

penny ['penɪ] (pl **pennies** or (BRIT) **pence**) n Penny m; (US) Centstück nt

penpal ['penpæl] n Brieffreund(in) m(f)

pension ['penʃən] n Rente f; **~er** (BRIT) n Rentner(in) m(f); **~ fund** n Rentenfonds m; **~ plan** n Rentenversicherung f

pensive ['pensɪv] adj nachdenklich

Pentagon

Pentagon heißt das fünfeckige Gebäude in Arlington, Virginia, in dem das amerikanische Verteidigungsministerium untergebracht ist. Im weiteren Sinne bezieht sich dieses Wort auf die amerikanische Militärführung.

---

pentathlon [pen'tæθlən] n Fünfkampf m

Pentecost ['pentɪkɒst] n Pfingsten pl or nt

penthouse ['penthaʊs] n Dachterrassenwohnung f

pent-up ['pentʌp] adj (feelings) angestaut

penultimate [pe'nʌltɪmət] adj vorletzte(r, s)

people ['piːpl] n (nation) Volk ♦ npl (persons) Leute pl; (inhabitants) Bevölkerung f ♦ vt besiedeln; **several ~ came** mehrere Leute kamen; **~ say that ...** man sagt, dass ...

pepper ['pepə'] n Pfeffer m; (vegetable) Paprika m ♦ vt (pelt) bombardieren; **~mill** n Pfeffermühle f; **~mint** n (plant) Pfefferminze f; (sweet) Pfefferminz nt

pep talk n (inf) n Anstachelung f

per [pɜː'] prep pro; **~ day/person** n pro Tag/Person; **~ annum** adv pro Jahr; **~ capita** (income) Pro-Kopf-♦ adj pro Kopf

---

perceive [pə'siːv] vt (realize) wahrnehmen; (understand) verstehen

per cent n Prozent nt; **percentage** [pə'sentɪdʒ] n Prozentsatz m

perception [pə'sepʃən] n Wahrnehmung f; (insight) Einsicht f

perceptive [pə'septɪv] adj (person) aufmerksam; (analysis) tief gehend

perch [pɜːtʃ] n Stange f; (fish) Flussbarsch m ♦ vi sitzen, hocken

percolator ['pɜːkəleɪtə'] n Kaffeemaschine f

percussion [pə'kʌʃən] n (MUS) Schlagzeug nt

perennial [pə'renɪəl] adj wiederkehrend; (everlasting) unvergänglich

perfect [adj, n 'pɜːfɪkt, vb pə'fekt] adj vollkommen; (crime, solution) perfekt ♦ n (GRAM) Perfekt nt ♦ vt vervollkommnen; **~ion** n Vollkommenheit f; **~ly** adv vollkommen, perfekt; (quite) ganz, einfach

perforate ['pɜːfəreɪt] vt durchlöchern; **perforation** [pɜːfə'reɪʃən] n Perforieren nt; (line of holes) Perforation f

perform [pə'fɔːm] vt (carry out) durchoder ausführen; (task) verrichten; (THEAT) spielen, geben ♦ vi (THEAT) auftreten; **~ance** n Durchführung f; (efficiency) Leistung f; (show) Vorstellung f; **~er** n Künstler(in) m(f)

perfume ['pɜːfjuːm] n Duft m; (lady's) Parfüm nt

perhaps [pə'hæps] adv vielleicht

peril ['perɪl] n Gefahr f

perimeter [pə'rɪmɪtə'] n Peripherie f; (of circle etc) Umfang m

period ['pɪərɪəd] n Periode f; (GRAM) Punkt m; (MED) Periode f ♦ adj (costume) historisch; **~ic** [pɪərɪ'ɒdɪk] adj periodisch; **~ical** [pɪərɪ'ɒdɪkl] n Zeitschrift f; **~ically** [pɪərɪ'ɒdɪklɪ] adv periodisch

peripheral [pə'rɪfərəl] adj Rand-, peripher ♦ n (COMPUT) Peripheriegerät nt

perish ['perɪʃ] vi umkommen; (fruit) verderben; **~able** adj leicht verderblich

perjury ['pɜːdʒərɪ] n Meineid m

perk [pɜːk] (inf) n (fringe benefit) Vergünstigung f; ~ **up** vi munter werden; ~**y** adj keck

perm [pɜːm] n Dauerwelle f

permanent ['pɜːmənənt] adj dauernd, ständig

permeate ['pɜːmɪeɪt] vt, vi durchdringen

permissible [pə'mɪsɪbl] adj zulässig

permission [pə'mɪʃən] n Erlaubnis f

permissive [pə'mɪsɪv] adj nachgiebig; **the ~ society** die permissive Gesellschaft

permit [n 'pɜːmɪt, vb pə'mɪt] n Zulassung f ♦ vt erlauben, zulassen

perpendicular [pɜːpən'dɪkjuləʳ] adj senkrecht

perpetrate ['pɜːpɪtreɪt] vt begehen

perpetual [pə'petjuəl] adj dauernd, ständig

perpetuate [pə'petjueɪt] vt verewigen, bewahren

perplex [pə'pleks] vt verblüffen

persecute ['pɜːsɪkjuːt] vt verfolgen; **persecution** [pɜːsɪ'kjuːʃən] n Verfolgung f

perseverance [pɜːsɪ'vɪərns] n Ausdauer f

persevere [pɜːsɪ'vɪəʳ] vi durchhalten

Persian ['pɜːʒən] adj persisch ♦ n Perser(in) m(f); **the (Persian) Gulf** der Persische Golf

persist [pə'sɪst] vi (in belief etc) bleiben; (rain, smell) andauern; (continue) nicht aufhören; **to ~ in** bleiben bei; ~**ence** n Beharrlichkeit f; ~**ent** adj beharrlich; (unending) ständig

person ['pɜːsn] n Person f; **in ~** persönlich; ~**able** adj gut aussehend; ~**al** adj persönlich; (private) privat; ~**al assistant** n Assistent(in) m(f); ~**al column** n private Kleinanzeigen pl; ~**al computer** n Personalcomputer m; ~**ality** [pɜːsə'nælɪtɪ] n Persönlichkeit f; ~**ally** adv persönlich; ~**al organizer** n Ter-

minplaner m, Zeitplaner m; (electronic) elektronisches Notizbuch nt; ~**al stereo** n Walkman ® ®; ~**ify** [pə'sɒnɪfaɪ] vt verkörpern

personnel [pɜːsə'nel] n Personal nt

perspective [pə'spektɪv] n Perspektive f

Perspex ['pɜːspeks] ® n Acrylglas nt, Akrylglas nt

perspiration [pɜːspɪ'reɪʃən] n Transpiration f

perspire [pə'spaɪəʳ] vi transpirieren

persuade [pə'sweɪd] vt überreden; (convince) überzeugen

persuasion [pə'sweɪʒən] n Überredung f; Überzeugung f

persuasive [pə'sweɪsɪv] adj überzeugend

pert [pɜːt] adj keck

pertaining [pɜː'teɪnɪŋ]: ~ **to** prep betreffend +acc

pertinent ['pɜːtɪnənt] adj relevant

perturb [pə'tɜːb] vt beunruhigen

pervade [pə'veɪd] vt erfüllen

perverse [pə'vɜːs] adj pervers; (obstinate) eigensinnig

pervert [n 'pɜːvɜːt, vb pə'vɜːt] n perverse(r) Mensch m ♦ vt verdrehen; (morally) verderben

pessimist ['pesɪmɪst] n Pessimist m; ~**ic** adj pessimistisch

pest [pest] n (insect) Schädling m; (fig: person) Nervensäge f; (: thing) Plage f; ~**er** ['pestəʳ] vt plagen; ~**icide** ['pestɪsaɪd] n Insektenvertilgungsmittel nt

pet [pet] n (animal) Haustier nt ♦ vt liebkosen, streicheln

petal ['petl] n Blütenblatt nt

peter out ['piːtə-] vi allmählich zu Ende gehen

petite [pə'tiːt] adj zierlich

petition [pə'tɪʃən] n Bittschrift f

petrified ['petrɪfaɪd] adj versteinert; (person) starr (vor Schreck)

petrify ['petrɪfaɪ] vt versteinern; (person) erstarren lassen

petrol ['petrəl] (BRIT) n Benzin nt, Kraftstoff m; **two-/four-star ~** ≈ Normal-/Superbenzin nt; **~ can** n Benzinkanister m

petroleum [pə'trəuliəm] n Petroleum nt

petrol: ~ pump (BRIT) n (in car) Benzinpumpe f; (at garage) Zapfsäule f; **~ station** n Tankstelle f; **~ tank** (BRIT) n Benzintank m

petticoat ['petikəut] n Unterrock m

petty ['peti] adj (unimportant) unbedeutend; (mean) kleinlich; **~ cash** n Portokasse f; **~ officer** n Maat m

pew [pju:] n Kirchenbank f

pewter ['pju:tər] n Zinn nt

phantom ['fæntəm] n Phantom nt

pharmacist ['fɑ:məsist] n Pharmazeut m; (druggist) Apotheker m

pharmacy ['fɑ:məsi] n Pharmazie f; (shop) Apotheke f

phase [feiz] n Phase f ♦ vt: **to ~ sth in** etw allmählich einführen; **to ~ sth out** etw auslaufen lassen

Ph.D. n abbr = Doctor of Philosophy

pheasant ['feznt] n Fasan m

phenomena [fə'nɔminə] npl of **phenomenon**

phenomenon [fə'nɔminən] n Phänomen nt

philanthropist [fi'lænθrəpist] n Philanthrop m, Menschenfreund m

Philippines ['filipi:nz] npl: **the ~** die Philippinen pl

philosopher [fi'lɔsəfər] n Philosoph m; **philosophical** [filə'sɔfikl] adj philosophisch; **philosophy** [fi'lɔsəfi] n Philosophie f

phlegm [flem] n (MED) Schleim m

phobia ['fəubiə] n (irrational fear: of insects, flying, water etc) Phobie f

phone [fəun] n Telefon nt ♦ vt, vi telefonieren, anrufen; **to be on the ~** telefonieren; **~ back** vt, vi zurückrufen; **~ up** vt, vi anrufen; **~ bill** n Telefonrechnung f; **~ book** n Telefonbuch nt; **~ booth** n Telefonzelle f; **~ box** n Te-

lefonzelle f; **~ call** n Telefonanruf m; **~card** n (TEL) Telefonkarte f; **~-in** n (RAD, TV) Phone-in nt; **~ number** n Telefonnummer f

phonetics [fə'netiks] n Phonetik f

phoney ['fəuni] (inf) adj unecht ♦ n (person) Schwindler m; (thing) Fälschung f; (banknote) Blüte f

phony ['fəuni] adj, n = **phoney**

photo ['fəutəu] n Foto nt; **~copier** ['fəutəukɔpiər] n Kopiergerät nt; **~copy** ['fəutəukɔpi] n Fotokopie f ♦ vt fotokopieren; **~genic** [fəutəu'dʒenik] adj fotogen; **~graph** n Fotografie f, Aufnahme f ♦ vt fotografieren; **~grapher** [fə'tɔɡrəfər] n Fotograf m; **~graphic** [fəutə'græfik] adj fotografisch; **~graphy** [fə'tɔɡrəfi] n Fotografie f

phrase [freiz] n Satz m; (expression) Ausdruck m ♦ vt ausdrücken, formulieren; **~ book** n Sprachführer m

physical ['fizikl] adj physikalisch; (bodily) körperlich, physisch; **~ education** n Turnen nt; **~ly** adv physikalisch

physician [fi'ziʃən] n Arzt m

physicist ['fizisist] n Physiker(in) m(f)

physics ['fiziks] n Physik f

physiotherapist [fiziəu'θerəpist] n Physiotherapeut(in) m(f)

physiotherapy [fiziəu'θerəpi] n Heilgymnastik f, Physiotherapie f

physique [fi'zi:k] n Körperbau m

pianist ['piænist] n Pianist(in) m(f)

piano [pi'ænəu] n Klavier nt

pick [pik] n (tool) Pickel m; (choice) Auswahl f ♦ vt (fruit) pflücken; (choice) aussuchen; **take your ~** such dir etwas aus; **to ~ sb's pocket** jdn bestehlen; **~ on** vt fus (person) herumhacken auf +dat; **~ out** vt auswählen; **~ up** vi (improve) sich erholen ♦ vt (lift up) aufheben; (learn) (schnell) mitbekommen; (collect) abholen; (girl) (sich dat) anlachen; (AUT: passenger) mitnehmen; (speed) gewinnen an +dat; **to ~ o.s. up** aufstehen

picket ['pikit] n (striker) Streikposten m

♦ vt (factory) (Streik)posten aufstellen vor +dat ♦ vi (Streik)posten stehen

pickle ['pɪkl] n (salty mixture) Pökel m; (inf) Klemme f ♦ vt (in Essig) einlegen; einpökeln

pickpocket ['pɪkpɔkɪt] n Taschendieb m

pick-up ['pɪkʌp] n (BRIT: on record player) Tonabnehmer m; (small truck) Lieferwagen m

picnic ['pɪknɪk] n Picknick nt ♦ vi picknicken; **~ area** n Rastplatz m

pictorial [pɪk'tɔːrɪəl] adj in Bildern

picture ['pɪktʃər] n Bild nt ♦ vt (visualize) sich dat vorstellen; **the ~s** npl (BRIT) das Kino; **~ book** n Bilderbuch nt

picturesque [pɪktʃə'resk] adj malerisch

pie [paɪ] n (meat) Pastete f; (fruit) Torte f

piece [piːs] n Stück nt ♦ vt: **to ~ together** zusammenstückeln; (fig) sich dat zusammenreimen; **to take to ~s** in Einzelteile zerlegen; **~meal** adv stückweise, Stück für Stück; **~work** n Akkordarbeit f

pie chart n Kreisdiagramm nt

pier [pɪər] n Pier m, Mole f

pierce [pɪəs] vt durchstechen, durchbohren (also look); **~d** adj durchgestochen; **piercing** ['pɪəsɪŋ] adj (cry) durchdringend

pig [pɪg] n Schwein nt

pigeon ['pɪdʒən] n Taube f; **~hole** n (compartment) Ablegefach nt

piggy bank ['pɪgɪ-] n Sparschwein nt

pig: ~headed ['pɪg'hedɪd] adj dickköpfig; **~let** ['pɪglɪt] n Ferkel nt; **~skin** ['pɪgskɪn] n Schweinsleder nt; **~sty** ['pɪgstaɪ] n Schweinestall m; **~tail** ['pɪgteɪl] n Zopf m

pike [paɪk] n Pike f; (fish) Hecht m

pilchard ['pɪltʃəd] n Sardine f

pile [paɪl] n Haufen m; (of books, wood) Stapel m; (in ground) Pfahl m; (on carpet) Flausch m ♦ vt (also: **~ up**) anhäufen ♦ vi (also: **~ up**) sich anhäufen

piles [paɪlz] npl Hämorr(ho)iden pl

pile-up ['paɪlʌp] n (AUT) Massenzusammenstoß m

pilfering ['pɪlfərɪŋ] n Diebstahl m

pilgrim ['pɪlgrɪm] n Pilger(in) m(f); **~age** n Wallfahrt f

pill [pɪl] n Tablette f, Pille f; **the ~** die (Antibaby)pille

pillage ['pɪlɪdʒ] vt plündern

pillar ['pɪlər] n Pfeiler m, Säule f (also fig); **~ box** (BRIT) n Briefkasten m

pillion ['pɪljən] n Soziussitz m

pillow ['pɪləu] n Kissen nt, ~**case** n Kissenbezug m

pilot ['paɪlət] n Pilot m; (NAUT) Lotse m ♦ adj (scheme etc) Versuchs- ♦ vt führen; (ship) lotsen; **~ light** n Zündflamme f

pimp [pɪmp] n Zuhälter m

pimple ['pɪmpl] n Pickel m

PIN [pɪn] n abbr (= personal identification number) PIN f

pin [pɪn] n Nadel f; (for sewing) Stecknadel f; (TECH) Stift m, Bolzen m ♦ vt stecken; (keep in one position) pressen, drücken; **to ~ sth to sth** etw an etw acc heften; **to ~ sth on sb** (fig) jdm etw anhängen; **~s and needles** Kribbeln nt; **~ down** vt (fig: person): **to ~ sb down (to sth)** jdn (auf etw acc) festnageln

pinafore ['pɪnəfɔːr] n Schürze f; **~ dress** n Kleiderrock m

pinball ['pɪnbɔːl] n Flipper m

pincers ['pɪnsəz] npl Kneif- or Beißzange f; (MED) Pinzette f

pinch [pɪntʃ] n Zwicken nt, Kneifen nt; (of salt) Prise f ♦ vt zwicken, kneifen; (inf: steal) klauen ♦ vi (shoe) drücken; **at a ~** notfalls, zur Not

pincushion ['pɪnkuʃən] n Nadelkissen nt

pine [paɪn] n (also: ~ **tree**) Kiefer f ♦ vi: **to ~ for** sich sehnen nach; **~ away** vi sich zu Tode sehnen

pineapple ['paɪnæpl] n Ananas f

ping [pɪŋ] n Klingeln nt; **~pong** ® n Pingpong nt

pink [pɪŋk] *adj* rosa *inv* ♦ *n* Rosa *nt*; (BOT) Nelke *f*

pinnacle ['pɪnəkl] *n* Spitze *f*

PIN (number) *n* Geheimnummer *f*

pinpoint ['pɪnpɔɪnt] *vt* festlegen

pinstripe ['pɪnstraɪp] *n* Nadelstreifen *m*

pint [paɪnt] *n* Pint *nt*; (BRIT: inf: of beer) große(s) Bier *nt*

pioneer [paɪə'nɪə*] *n* Pionier *m*; (fig also) Bahnbrecher *m*

pious ['paɪəs] *adj* fromm

pip [pɪp] *n* Kern *m*; **the ~s** *npl* (BRIT: RAD) das Zeitzeichen

pipe [paɪp] *n* (smoking) Pfeife *f*; (tube) Rohr *nt*; (in house) (Rohr)leitung *f* ♦ *vt* (durch Rohre) leiten; (MUS) blasen; **~s** *npl* (also: **bagpipes**) Dudelsack *m*; **~ down** *vi* (be quiet) die Luft anhalten; **~ cleaner** *n* Pfeifenreiniger *m*; **~ dream** *n* Luftschloss *nt*; **~line** *n* (for oil) Pipeline *f*; **~r** *n* Pfeifer *m*; (bagpipes) Dudelsackbläser *m*

piping ['paɪpɪŋ] *adv*: **~ hot** siedend heiß

pique ['piːk] *n* gekränkte(r) Stolz *m*

pirate ['paɪərət] *n* Pirat *m*, Seeräuber *m*; **~d** *adj*: **~d version** Raubkopie *f*; **~ radio** (BRIT) *n* Piratensender *m*

Pisces ['paɪsiːz] *n* Fische *pl*

piss [pɪs] (inf) *vi* pissen; **~ed** (inf) *adj* (drunk) voll

pistol ['pɪstl] *n* Pistole *f*

piston ['pɪstən] *n* Kolben *m*

pit [pɪt] *n* Grube *f*; (THEAT) Parterre *nt*; (orchestra ~) Orchestergraben *m* ♦ *vt* (mark with scars) zerfressen; (compare): **to ~ sb against** sb jdn an jdm messen; **the ~s** *npl* (MOTOR RACING) die Boxen *pl*

pitch [pɪtʃ] *n* Wurf *m*; (of trader) Stand *m*; (SPORT) (Spiel)feld *nt*; (MUS) Tonlage *f*; (substance) Pech *nt* ♦ *vt* (set up) aufschlagen ♦ *vi* (NAUT) rollen; **to ~ a tent** ein Zelt aufbauen; **~-black** *adj* pechschwarz; **~ed battle** *n* offene Schlacht *f*

piteous ['pɪtɪəs] *adj* kläglich, erbärmlich

pitfall ['pɪtfɔːl] *n* (fig) Falle *f*

pith [pɪθ] *n* Mark *nt*

pithy ['pɪθɪ] *adj* prägnant

pitiful ['pɪtɪful] *adj* (deserving pity) bedauernswert; (contemptible) jämmerlich

pitiless ['pɪtɪlɪs] *adj* erbarmungslos

pittance ['pɪtns] *n* Hungerlohn *m*

pity ['pɪtɪ] *n* (sympathy) Mitleid *nt* ♦ *vt* Mitleid haben mit; **what a ~!** wie schade!

pivot ['pɪvət] *n* Drehpunkt *m* ♦ *vi*: **to ~ (on)** sich drehen (um)

pizza ['piːtsə] *n* Pizza *f*

placard ['plækɑːd] *n* Plakat *nt*, Anschlag *m*

placate [plə'keɪt] *vt* beschwichtigen

place [pleɪs] *n* Platz *m*; (spot) Stelle *f*; (town etc) Ort *m* ♦ *vt* setzen, stellen, legen; (order) aufgeben; (SPORT) platzieren; (identify) unterbringen; **to take ~** stattfinden; **out of ~** nicht am rechten Platz; (fig: remark) unangebracht; **in the first ~** erstens; **to change ~s with sb** mit jdm den Platz tauschen; **to be ~d third** (in race, exam) auf dem dritten Platz liegen

placid ['plæsɪd] *adj* gelassen, ruhig

plagiarism ['pleɪdʒjərɪzəm] *n* Plagiat *nt*

plague [pleɪg] *n* Pest *f*; (fig) Plage *f* ♦ *vt* plagen

plaice [pleɪs] *n* Scholle *f*

plaid [plæd] *n* Plaid *nt*

plain [pleɪn] *adj* (clear) klar, deutlich; (simple) einfach, schlicht; (not beautiful) alltäglich ♦ *n* Ebene *f*; **in ~ clothes** (police) in Zivil(kleidung); **~ chocolate** *n* Bitterschokolade *f*

plaintiff ['pleɪntɪf] *n* Kläger *m*

plaintive ['pleɪntɪv] *adj* wehleidig

plait [plæt] *n* Zopf *m* ♦ *vt* flechten

plan [plæn] *n* Plan *m* ♦ *vt*, *vi* planen; **according to ~** planmäßig; **to ~ to do sth** vorhaben, etw zu tun

plane [pleɪn] n Ebene f; (AVIAT) Flugzeug nt; (tool) Hobel m; (tree) Platane f

planet ['plænɪt] n Planet m

plank [plæŋk] n Brett nt

planning ['plænɪŋ] n Planung f; **family ~** Familienplanung f; **~ permission** n Baugenehmigung f

plant [plɑːnt] n Pflanze f; (TECH) (Maschinen)anlage f; (factory) Fabrik f, Werk nt ♦ vt pflanzen; (set firmly) stellen; **~ation** [plænˈteɪʃən] n Plantage f

plaque [plæk] n Gedenktafel f; (on teeth) (Zahn)belag m

plaster ['plɑːstə*] n Gips m; (in house) Verputz m; (BRIT: also: sticking ~) Pflaster nt; (for fracture: ~ of Paris) Gipsverband m ♦ vt gipsen; (hole) zugipsen; (ceiling) verputzen; (fig: with pictures etc) bekleben, verkleben; **~ed** (inf) adj besoffen; **~er** n Gipser m

plastic ['plæstɪk] n Plastik nt or f ♦ adj (made of ~) Plastik-; (art) plastisch, bildend; **~ bag** n Plastiktüte f

plasticine ['plæstɪsiːn] ®️ n Plastilin nt

plastic surgery n plastische Chirurgie f

plate [pleɪt] n Teller m; (gold/silver ~) vergoldete(s)/versilberte(s) Tafelgeschirr nt; (in book) (Bild)tafel f

plateau ['plætəʊ] (pl ~s or ~x) n (GEOG) Plateau nt, Hochebene f

plateaux ['plætəʊz] npl of **plateau**

plate glass n Tafelglas nt

platform ['plætfɔːm] n (at meeting) Plattform f, Podium nt; (RAIL) Bahnsteig m; (POL) Parteiprogramm nt; **~ ticket** n Bahnsteigkarte f

platinum ['plætɪnəm] n Platin nt

platoon [pləˈtuːn] n (MIL) Zug m

platter ['plætə*] n Platte f

plausible ['plɔːzɪbl] adj (theory, excuse, statement) plausibel; (person) überzeugend

play [pleɪ] n (also TECH) Spiel nt; (THEAT) (Theater)stück nt ♦ vt spielen; (another team) spielen gegen ♦ vi spielen; **to ~ safe** auf Nummer sicher or Sicher gehen; **~ down** vt herunterspielen; **~ up** vi (cause trouble) frech werden; (bad leg etc) wehtun ♦ vt (person) plagen; **to ~ up to sb** jdm flattieren; **~acting** n Schauspielerei f; **~er** n Spieler(in) m(f); **~ful** adj spielerisch; **~ground** n Spielplatz m; **~group** n Kindergarten m; **~ing card** n Spielkarte f; **~ing field** n Sportplatz m; **~mate** n Spielkamerad m; **~off** n (SPORT) Entscheidungsspiel nt; **~pen** n Laufstall m; **~school** n = **playgroup**; **~thing** n Spielzeug nt; **~time** n (kleine) Pause f; **~wright** ['pleɪraɪt] n Theaterschriftsteller m

plc abbr (= public limited company) AG

plea [pliː] n Bitte f; (general appeal) Appell m; (JUR) Plädoyer nt; **~ bargaining** n (LAW) Aushandeln der Strafe zwischen Staatsanwaltschaft und Verteidigung

plead [pliːd] vt (poverty) zur Entschuldigung anführen; (JUR: sb's case) vertreten ♦ vi (beg) dringend bitten; (JUR) plädieren; **to ~ with sb** jdn dringend bitten

pleasant ['pleznt] adj angenehm; **~ries** npl (polite remarks) Nettigkeiten pl

please [pliːz] vt, vi (be agreeable to) gefallen +dat; **~!** bitte!; **~ yourself!** wie du willst!; **~d** adj zufrieden; (glad): **~d (about sth)** erfreut (über etw acc); **~d to meet you** angenehm; **pleasing** ['pliːzɪŋ] adj erfreulich

pleasure ['pleʒə*] n Freude f ♦ cpd Vergnügungs-; **"it's a ~"** "gern geschehen"

pleat [pliːt] n Falte f

plectrum ['plektrəm] n Plektron nt

pledge [pledʒ] n Pfand nt; (promise) Versprechen nt ♦ vt verpfänden; (promise) geloben, versprechen

plentiful ['plentɪful] adj reichlich

plenty ['plentɪ] n Fülle f, Überfluss m; **~ of** eine Menge, viel

pleurisy ['plʊərɪsɪ] n Rippenfellentzündung f

pliable 506 **point**

pliable ['plaɪəbl] *adj* biegsam; *(person)* beeinflussbar

pliers ['plaɪəz] *npl* (Kneif)zange f

plight [plaɪt] *n* (Not)lage f

plimsolls ['plɪmsəlz] (BRIT) *npl* Turnschuhe *pl*

plinth [plɪnθ] *n* Sockel *m*

P.L.O. *n abbr* (= Palestine Liberation Organization) PLO f

plod [plɒd] *vi (work)* sich abplagen; *(walk)* trotten

plonk [plɒŋk] *n* (BRIT: inf: wine) billige(r) Wein *m* ♦ *vt*: **to ~ sth down** etw hinknallen

plot [plɒt] *n* Komplott *nt*; *(story)* Handlung f; *(of land)* Grundstück *nt* ♦ *vt* markieren; *(curve)* zeichnen; *(movements)* nachzeichnen ♦ *vi (plan secretly)* sich verschwören

plough [plaʊ] (US **plow**) *n* Pflug *m* ♦ *vt* pflügen; **~ back** *vt* (COMM) wieder in das Geschäft stecken; **~ through** *vt fus (water)* durchpflügen; *(book)* sich kämpfen durch

plow [plaʊ] (US) = **plough**

ploy [plɔɪ] *n* Masche f

pluck [plʌk] *vt (fruit)* pflücken; *(guitar)* zupfen; *(goose etc)* rupfen ♦ *n* Mut *m*; **to ~ up courage** all seinen Mut zusammennehmen

plug [plʌg] *n* Stöpsel *m*; *(inf: publicity)* Schleichwerbung f; *(AUT)* Zündkerze f ♦ *vt* (zu)stopfen; *(inf: advertise)* Reklame machen für; **~ in** *vt* (ELEC) anschließen

plum [plʌm] *n* Pflaume f, Zwetsch(g)e f

plumage ['pluːmɪdʒ] *n* Gefieder *nt*

plumber ['plʌmə*] *n* Klempner *m*, Installateur *m*; **plumbing** ['plʌmɪŋ] *n* (craft) Installieren *nt*; *(fittings)* Leitungen *pl*

plummet ['plʌmɪt] *vi* (ab)stürzen

plump [plʌmp] *adj* rundlich, füllig ♦ *vt* plumpsen lassen; **~ for** *(inf: choose)* sich entscheiden für

plunder ['plʌndə*] *n* Plünderung f;

(loot) Beute f ♦ *vt* plündern

plunge [plʌndʒ] *n* Sturz *m* ♦ *vt* stoßen ♦ *vi* (sich) stürzen; **to take the ~** den Sprung wagen; **plunging** ['plʌndʒɪŋ] *adj (neckline)* offenherzig

plural ['pluərl] *n* Plural *m*, Mehrzahl f

plus [plʌs] *n (also: ~ sign)* Plus(zeichen) *nt* ♦ *prep* plus, und; **ten/twenty ~** mehr als zehn/zwanzig

plush [plʌʃ] *adj (also: ~y: inf)* feudal

ply [plaɪ] *vt (trade)* betreiben; *(with questions)* zusetzen *+dat*; *(ship, taxi)* befahren ♦ *vi (ship, taxi)* verkehren ♦ *n*: **three~** *(wool)* Dreifach-; **to ~ sb with drink** jdn zum Trinken animieren; **~wood** *n* Sperrholz *nt*

P.M. *n abbr* = **prime minister**

p.m. *adv abbr* (= post meridiem) nachmittags

pneumatic drill *n* Presslufthammer *m*

pneumonia [njuː'məʊnɪə] *n* Lungenentzündung f

poach [pəʊtʃ] *vt* (COOK) pochieren; *(game)* stehlen ♦ *vi (steal)* wildern; **~ed** *adj (egg)* verloren; **~er** *n* Wilddieb *m*

P.O. Box *n abbr* = **Post Office Box**

pocket ['pɒkɪt] *n* Tasche f; *(of resistance)* (Widerstands)nest *nt* ♦ *vt* einstecken; **to be out of ~** (BRIT) draufzahlen; **~book** *n* Taschenbuch *nt*; **~ calculator** *n* Taschenrechner *m*; **~ knife** *n* Taschenmesser *nt*; **~ money** *n* Taschengeld *nt*

pod [pɒd] *n* Hülse f; *(of peas also)* Schote f

podgy ['pɒdʒɪ] *adj* pummelig

podiatrist [pɒ'diːətrɪst] *(US) n* Fußpfleger *m(f)*

poem ['pəʊɪm] *n* Gedicht *nt*

poet ['pəʊɪt] *n* Dichter *m*, Poet *m*; **~ic** [pəʊ'etɪk] *adj* poetisch, dichterisch; **~ laureate** *n* Hofdichter *m*; **~ry** *n* Poesie f; *(poems)* Gedichte *pl*

poignant ['pɔɪnjənt] *adj (touching)* ergreifend

point [pɔɪnt] *n* (also in discussion, scoring) Punkt *m*; *(spot)* Punkt *m*, Stelle f;

(*sharpened tip*) Spitze f; (*moment*) (Zeit)punkt m; (*purpose*) Zweck m; (*idea*) Argument nt; (*decimal*) Dezimalstelle f; (*personal characteristic*) Seite f ♦ vt zeigen mit; (*gun*) richten ♦ vi zeigen; **~s** npl (RAIL) Weichen pl; **to be on the ~ of doing sth** drauf und dran sein, etw zu tun; **to make a ~ of** Wert darauf legen; **to get the ~** verstehen, worum es geht; **to come to the ~** zur Sache kommen; **there's no ~** (*in doing sth*) es hat keinen Sinn(, etw zu tun); **~ out** vt hinweisen auf +acc; vi (*fig*) fus zeigen auf +acc; **~-blank** adv (*at close range*) aus nächster Entfernung; (*bluntly*) unverblümt; **~ed** adj (*also fig*) spitz, scharf; **~edly** adv (*fig*) spitz; **~er** n Zeigestock m; (*on dial*) Zeiger m; **~less** adj sinnlos; **~ of view** n Stand- or Gesichtspunkt m

poise [pɔɪz] n Haltung f; (*fig*) Gelassenheit f

poison ['pɔɪzn] n (*also fig*) Gift nt ♦ vt vergiften; **~ing** n Vergiftung f; **~ous** adj giftig, Gift-

poke [pəʊk] vt stoßen; (*put*) stecken; (*fire*) schüren; (*hole*) bohren; **~ about** vi herumstochern; (*nose around*) herumwühlen

poker ['pəʊkə*] n Schürhaken m; (CARDS) Poker nt

poky ['pəʊki] adj eng

Poland ['pəʊlənd] n Polen nt

polar ['pəʊlə*] adj Polar-, polar; **~ bear** n Eisbär m

Pole [pəʊl] n Pole m, Polin f

pole [pəʊl] n Stange f, Pfosten m; (*flagpole, telegraph ~*) Stange f, Mast m; (ELEC, GEOG) Pol m; (SPORT: *vaulting ~*) Stab m; (*ski ~*) Stock m; **~ bean** n (US) Stangenbohne f; **~ vault** n Stabhochsprung m

police [pə'liːs] n Polizei f ♦ vt kontrollieren; **~ car** n Polizeiwagen m; **~man** (*irreg*) n Polizist m; **~ state** n Polizeistaat m; **~ station** n (Polizei)revier nt, Wache f; **~woman** (*irreg*) n Polizistin f

policy ['pɔlɪsi] n Politik f; (*insurance*) (Versicherungs)police f

polio ['pəʊlɪəʊ] n (*spinale*) Kinderlähmung f, Polio f

Polish ['pəʊlɪʃ] adj polnisch ♦ n (LING) Polnisch nt

polish ['pɔlɪʃ] n Politur f; (*for floor*) Wachs nt; (*for shoes*) Creme f; (*for nails*) Lack m; (*shine*) Glanz m; (*of furniture*) Politur f; (*fig*) Schliff m ♦ vt polieren; (*shoes*) putzen; (*fig*) den letzten Schliff geben +dat; **~ off** vt (*inf: food*) wegputzen; (: *drink*) hinunterschütten; **~ed** adj glänzend; (*manners*) verfeinert

polite [pə'laɪt] adj höflich; **~ly** adv höflich; **~ness** n Höflichkeit f

politic ['pɔlɪtɪk] adj: **~al** [pə'lɪtɪkl] adj politisch; **~ally** [pə'lɪtɪkli] adv politisch; **~ally correct** politisch korrekt; **~ian** [pɔlɪ'tɪʃən] n Politiker m; **~s** npl Politik f

polka dot ['pɔlkə-] n Tupfen m

poll [pəʊl] n (*in election*) Wahl f; (*votes cast*) Wahlbeteiligung f; (*opinion ~*) Umfrage f ♦ vt (*votes*) erhalten

pollen ['pɔlən] n (BOT) Blütenstaub m, Pollen m

polling ['pəʊlɪŋ-]: **~ booth** (BRIT) n Wahlkabine f; **~ day** (BRIT) n Wahltag m; **~ station** (BRIT) n Wahllokal nt

pollute [pə'luːt] vt verschmutzen, verunreinigen; **~d** adj verschmutzt; **pollution** [pə'luːʃən] n Verschmutzung f

polo ['pəʊləʊ] n Polo nt; **~ neck** n (*also:* **~-necked sweater**) Rollkragen m; Rollkragenpullover m; **~ shirt** n Polohemd nt

polystyrene [pɔlɪ'staɪriːn] n Styropor nt

polytechnic [pɔlɪ'teknɪk] n technische Hochschule f

polythene ['pɔlɪθiːn] n Plastik nt; **~ bag** n Plastiktüte f

pomegranate ['pɔmɪɡrænɪt] n Granatapfel m

pompom ['pɔmpɔm] n Troddel f, Pompon m

pompous ['pɔmpəs] adj aufgeblasen; (language) geschwollen

pond [pɔnd] n Teich m, Weiher m

ponder ['pɔndəʳ] vt nachdenken über +acc; **~ous** adj schwerfällig

pong [pɔŋ] (BRIT: inf) n Mief m

pontiff ['pɔntɪf] n Pontifex m

pontoon [pɔn'tu:n] n Ponton m; (CARDS) 17-und-4 nt

pony ['pəunɪ] n Pony nt; **~tail** n Pferdeschwanz m; **~ trekking** (BRIT) n Ponyreiten nt

poodle ['pu:dl] n Pudel m

pool [pu:l] n (swimming ~) Schwimmbad nt; (: private) Swimmingpool m; (of liquid, blood) Lache f; (fund) (gemeinsame) Kasse f; (billiards) Poolspiel nt ♦ vt (money etc) zusammenlegen; (football) **~s** Toto nt

poor [puəʳ] adj arm; (not good) schlecht ♦ npl: **the ~** die Armen pl; **~ in** (resources) arm an +dat; **~ly** adv schlecht; (dressed) ärmlich ♦ adj schlecht

pop [pɔp] n Knall m; (music) Popmusik f; (drink) Limo(nade) f; (US: inf) Pa m ♦ vt (put) stecken; (balloon) platzen lassen ♦ vi knallen; **~ in** vi kurz vorbeigehen or vorbeikommen; **~ out** vi (person) kurz rausgehen; (thing) herausspringen; **~ up** vi auftauchen; **~corn** n Puffmais m

pope [pəup] n Papst m

poplar ['pɔplaʳ] n Pappel f

poppy ['pɔpɪ] n Mohn m

Popsicle ['pɔpsɪkl] (® US) n (ice lolly) Eis nt am Stiel

populace ['pɔpjuləs] n Volk nt

popular ['pɔpjuləʳ] adj beliebt, populär; (of the people) volkstümlich; (widespread) allgemein; **~ity** [pɔpju'lerɪtɪ] n Beliebtheit f, Popularität f; **~ly** adv allgemein, überall

population [pɔpju'leɪʃən] n Bevölkerung f; (of town) Einwohner pl

populous ['pɔpjuləs] adj dicht besiedelt

porcelain ['pɔ:slɪn] n Porzellan nt

porch [pɔ:tʃ] n Vorbau m, Veranda f

porcupine ['pɔ:kjupaɪn] n Stachelschwein nt

pore [pɔ:ʳ] n Pore f ♦ vi: **to ~ over** brüten über +dat

pork [pɔ:k] n Schweinefleisch nt

porn [pɔ:n] n Porno m; **~ographic** [pɔ:nə'græfɪk] adj pornografisch; **~ography** [pɔ:'nɔgrəfɪ] n Pornografie f

porous ['pɔ:rəs] adj porös; (skin) porig

porpoise ['pɔ:pəs] n Tümmler m

porridge ['pɔrɪdʒ] n Haferbrei m

port [pɔ:t] n Hafen m; (town) Hafenstadt f; (NAUT: left side) Backbord nt; (wine) Portwein m; **~ of call** Anlaufhafen m

portable ['pɔ:təbl] adj tragbar

porter ['pɔ:təʳ] n Pförtner(in) m(f); (for luggage) Gepäckträger m

portfolio [pɔ:t'fəuliəu] n (case) Mappe f; (POL) Geschäftsbereich m; (FIN) Portefeuille nt; (of artist) Kollektion f

porthole ['pɔ:thəul] n Bullauge nt

portion ['pɔ:ʃən] n Teil m, Stück nt; (of food) Portion f

portrait ['pɔ:treɪt] n Porträt nt

portray [pɔ:'treɪ] vt darstellen; **~al** n Darstellung f

Portugal ['pɔ:tjugl] n Portugal nt

Portuguese [pɔ:tju'gi:z] adj portugiesisch ♦ n inv Portugiese m, Portugiesin f; (LING) Portugiesisch nt

pose [pəuz] n Stellung f, Pose f; (affectation) Pose f ♦ vi posieren ♦ vt stellen

posh [pɔʃ] (inf) adj (piek)fein

position [pə'zɪʃən] n Stellung f; (place) Lage f; (job) Stelle f; (attitude) Standpunkt m ♦ vt aufstellen

positive ['pɔzɪtɪv] adj positiv; (convinced) sicher; (definite) eindeutig

posse ['pɔsɪ] (US) n Aufgebot nt

possess [pə'zes] vt besitzen; **~ion** [pə'zeʃən] n Besitz m; **~ive** adj besitzergreifend, eigensüchtig

possibility [pɔsɪ'bɪlɪtɪ] n Möglichkeit f

possible ['pɔsɪbl] adj möglich; **as big**

as ~ so groß wie möglich, möglichst groß; **possibly** adv möglicherweise, vielleicht; **I cannot possibly come** ich kann unmöglich kommen

post [pəʊst] n (BRIT: letters, delivery) Post f; (pole) Pfosten m, Pfahl m; (place of duty) Posten m; (job) Stelle f ♦ vt (notice) anschlagen; (BRIT: letters) aufgeben; (: appoint) versetzen; (soldiers) aufstellen; **~age** n Postgebühr f, Porto nt; **~al** adj Post-; **~al order** n Postanweisung f; **~box** (BRIT) n Briefkasten m; **~card** n Postkarte f; **~code** (BRIT) n Postleitzahl f

postdate ['pəʊst'deɪt] vt (cheque) nachdatieren

poster ['pəʊstəʳ] n Plakat nt, Poster nt

poste restante [pəʊst'restɑːnt] n Aufbewahrungsstelle f für postlagernde Sendungen

posterior [pɒs'tɪərɪəʳ] (inf) n Hintern m

posterity [pɒs'terɪtɪ] n Nachwelt f

postgraduate ['pəʊst'grædjuət] n Weiterstudierende(r) mf

posthumous ['pɒstjʊməs] adj post(h)um

postman ['pəʊstmən] (irreg) n Briefträger m

postmark ['pəʊstmɑːk] n Poststempel m

post-mortem [pəʊst'mɔːtəm] n Autopsie f

post office n Postamt nt, Post f; (organization) Post f; **Post Office Box** n Postfach nt

postpone [pəʊs'pəʊn] vt verschieben

postscript ['pəʊstskrɪpt] n Postskript nt; (to affair) Nachspiel nt

posture ['pɒstʃəʳ] n Haltung f ♦ vi posieren

postwar ['pəʊst'wɔːʳ] adj Nachkriegs-

postwoman ['pəʊstwʊmən] (irreg) n Briefträgerin f

posy ['pəʊzɪ] n Blumenstrauß m

pot [pɒt] n Topf m; (teapot) Kanne f; (inf: marijuana) Hasch m ♦ vt (plant) eintopfen; **to go to ~** (inf: work) auf

den Hund kommen

potato [pə'teɪtəʊ] (pl **~es**) n Kartoffel f; **~ peeler** n Kartoffelschäler m

potent ['pəʊtnt] adj stark; (argument) zwingend

potential [pə'tenʃl] adj potenziell, potentiell ♦ n Potenzial nt, Potential nt; **~ly** adv potenziell, potentiell

pothole ['pɒthəʊl] n (in road) Schlagloch nt; (BRIT: underground) Höhle f; **potholing** (BRIT) n: **to go potholing** Höhlen erforschen

potion ['pəʊʃən] n Trank m

potluck [pɒt'lʌk] n: **to take ~ with sth** etw auf gut Glück nehmen

pot plant n Topfpflanze f

potter ['pɒtəʳ] n Töpfer m ♦ vi herumhantieren; **~y** n Töpferwaren pl; (place) Töpferei f

potty ['pɒtɪ] adj (inf: mad) verrückt ♦ n Töpfchen nt

pouch [paʊtʃ] n Beutel m

pouf(fe) [puːf] n Sitzkissen nt

poultry ['pəʊltrɪ] n Geflügel nt

pounce [paʊns] vi sich stürzen ♦ n Sprung m, Satz m; **to ~ on** sich stürzen auf +acc

pound [paʊnd] n (FIN, weight) Pfund nt; (for cars, animals) Auslösestelle f ♦ vt (zer)stampfen ♦ vi klopfen, hämmern; **~ sterling** n Pfund Sterling nt

pour [pɔːʳ] vt gießen, schütten ♦ vi gießen; (crowds etc) strömen; **~ away** vt abgießen; **~ in** vi (people) hereinströmen; **~ off** vt abgießen; **~ out** vi (people) herausströmen ♦ vt (drink) einschenken; **~ing** adj: **~ing rain** strömende(r) Regen m

pout [paʊt] vi schmollen

poverty ['pɒvətɪ] n Armut f; **~-stricken** adj verarmt, sehr arm

powder ['paʊdəʳ] n Pulver nt; (cosmetic) Puder m ♦ vt pulverisieren; **to ~ one's nose** sich auf die Nase pudern; **~ compact** n Puderdose f; **~ed milk** n Milchpulver nt; **~ room** n Damentoilette f; **~y** adj pulverig

power ['pauə] n (also POL) Macht f; (ability) Fähigkeit f; (strength) Stärke f; (MATH) Potenz f; (ELEC) Strom m ♦ vt betreiben, antreiben; **to be in ~** (POL etc) an der Macht sein; **~ cut** n Stromausfall m; **~ed** adj: **~ed by** betrieben mit; **~ failure** (US) n Stromausfall m; **~ful** adj (person) mächtig; (engine, government) stark; **~less** adj machtlos; **~ point** (BRIT) n elektrische(r) Anschluss m; **~ station** n Elektrizitätswerk nt; **~ struggle** n Machtkampf m

p.p. abbr (= per procurationem): **p.p. J. Smith** i. A. J. Smith

PR n abbr = **public relations**

practicable ['præktɪkəbl] adj durchführbar

practical ['præktɪkl] adj praktisch; **~ity** [præktɪ'kælɪtɪ] n (of person) praktische Veranlagung f; (of situation etc) Durchführbarkeit f; **~ joke** n Streich m; **~ly** adv praktisch

practice ['præktɪs] n Übung f; (reality, also of doctor, lawyer) Praxis f; (custom) Brauch m; (in business) Usus m ♦ vt, vi (US) = **practise**; **in ~** (in reality) in der Praxis; **out of ~** außer Übung; **practicing** (US) adj = **practising**

practise ['præktɪs] (US **practice**) vt üben; (profession) ausüben ♦ vi (sich) üben; (doctor, lawyer) praktizieren; **practising** (US **practicing**) adj praktizierend; (Christian etc) aktiv

practitioner [præk'tɪʃənə] n praktische(r) Arzt m, praktische Ärztin f

pragmatic [præg'mætɪk] adj pragmatisch

prairie ['prɛərɪ] n Prärie f, Steppe f

praise [preɪz] n Lob m ♦ vt loben; **~worthy** adj lobenswert

pram [præm] (BRIT) n Kinderwagen m

prance [prɑːns] vi (horse) tänzeln; (person) stolzieren

prank [præŋk] n Streich m

prawn [prɔːn] n Garnele f, Krabbe f; **~ cocktail** n Krabbencocktail m

pray [preɪ] vi beten; **~er** [prɛə] n Ge-

bet nt

preach [priːtʃ] vi predigen; **~er** n Prediger m

preamble [prɪ'æmbl] n Einleitung f

precarious [prɪ'kɛərɪəs] adj prekär, unsicher

precaution [prɪ'kɔːʃən] n (Vorsichts-) maßnahme f

precede [prɪ'siːd] vi vorausgehen ♦ vt vorausgehen +dat; **~nce** ['presɪdəns] n Vorrang m; **~nt** ['presɪdənt] n Präzedenzfall m; **preceding** [prɪ'siːdɪŋ] adj vorhergehend

precinct ['priːsɪŋkt] n (US: district) Bezirk m; (round building) Gelände nt; (area, environs) Umgebung f; **pedestrian ~** Fußgängerzone f; **shopping ~** Geschäftsviertel nt

precious ['preʃəs] adj kostbar, wertvoll; (affected) pretiös, preziös, geziert

precipice ['presɪpɪs] n Abgrund m

precipitate [adj prɪ'sɪpɪtɪt, vb prɪ'sɪpɪteɪt] adj überstürzt, übereilt ♦ vt hinunterstürzen; (events) heraufbeschwören

precise [prɪ'saɪs] adj genau, präzis; **~ly** adv genau, präzis

precision [prɪ'sɪʒən] n Präzision f

preclude [prɪ'kluːd] vt ausschließen

precocious [prɪ'kəuʃəs] adj frühreif

preconceived [priːkən'siːvd] adj (idea) vorgefasst

precondition [priːkən'dɪʃən] n Vorbedingung f, Voraussetzung f

precursor [priː'kɜːsə] n Vorläufer m

predator ['predətə] n Raubtier m

predecessor ['priːdɪsesə] n Vorgänger m

predicament [prɪ'dɪkəmənt] n missliche Lage f

predict [prɪ'dɪkt] vt voraussagen; **~able** adj vorhersagbar; **~ion** [prɪ'dɪkʃən] n Voraussage f

predominantly [prɪ'dɒmɪnəntlɪ] adv überwiegend, hauptsächlich

predominate [prɪ'dɒmɪneɪt] vi vorherrschen; (fig) vorherrschen, überwiegen

pre-eminent [prɪ'emɪnənt] *adj* hervorragend, herausragend

pre-empt [prɪ'emt] *vt* (*action, decision*) vorwegnehmen

preen [priːn] *vt* putzen; **to ~ o.s.** (*person*) sich brüsten

prefab ['priːfæb] *n* Fertighaus *nt*

preface ['prefəs] *n* Vorwort *nt*

prefect ['priːfekt] *n* Präfekt *m*; (*SCH*) Aufsichtsschüler(in) *m(f)*

prefer [prɪ'fɜː'] *vt* vorziehen, lieber mögen; **to ~ to do** etw lieber tun; **~ably** ['prefrəblɪ] *adv* vorzugsweise, am liebsten; **~ence** ['prefrəns] *n* Präferenz *f*, Vorzug *m*; **~ential** [prefə'renʃəl] *adj* bevorzugt, Vorzugs-

prefix ['priːfɪks] *n* Vorsilbe *f*, Präfix *nt*

pregnancy ['pregnənsɪ] *n* Schwangerschaft *f*

pregnant ['pregnənt] *adj* schwanger

prehistoric ['priːhɪs'tɒrɪk] *adj* prähistorisch, vorgeschichtlich

prejudice ['predʒʊdɪs] *n* (*bias*) Voreingenommenheit *f*; (*opinion*) Vorurteil *nt*; (*harm*) Schaden *m* ♦ *vt* beeinträchtigen; **~d** *adj* (*person*) voreingenommen

preliminary [prɪ'lɪmɪnərɪ] *adj* einleitend, Vor-

prelude ['preljuːd] *n* Vorspiel *nt*; (*fig*) Auftakt *m*

premarital ['priː'mærɪtl] *adj* vorehelich

premature ['prematʃʊə'] *adj* vorzeitig, verfrüht; (*birth*) Früh-

premeditated [priː'medɪteɪtɪd] *adj* geplant; (*murder*) vorsätzlich

premenstrual syndrome [priː'menstrual-] *n* prämenstruelles Syndrom *nt*

premier ['premɪə'] *adj* erste(r, s) ♦ *n* Premier *m*

première ['premɪeə'] *n* Premiere *f*, Uraufführung *f*

Premier League [-liːg] *n* ≈ 1. Bundesliga (*höchste Spielklasse im Fußball*)

premise ['premɪs] *n* Voraussetzung *f*,

Prämisse *f*; **~s** *npl* (*shop*) Räumlichkeiten *pl*; (*grounds*) Gelände *nt*; **on the ~s** im Hause

premium ['priːmɪəm] *n* Prämie *f*; **to be at a ~** über pari stehen; **~ bond** (*BRIT*) *n* Prämienanleihe *f*

premonition [premə'nɪʃən] *n* Vorahnung *f*

preoccupation [priːɒkju'peɪʃən] *n* Sorge *f*

preoccupied [priː'ɒkjupaɪd] *adj* (*look*) geistesabwesend

prep [prep] *n* (*SCH*) Hausaufgabe *f*

prepaid [priː'peɪd] *adj* vorausbezahlt; (*letter*) frankiert

preparation [prepə'reɪʃən] *n* Vorbereitung *f*

preparatory [prɪ'pærətərɪ] *adj* Vor(bereitungs)-; **~ school** *n* (*BRIT*) *private Vorbereitungsschule für die Public School*; (*US*) *private Vorbereitungsschule für die Hochschule*

prepare [prɪ'peə'] *vt* vorbereiten ♦ *vi* sich vorbereiten; **to ~ for/prepare sth for** sich/etw vorbereiten auf +*acc*; **to be ~d to ...** bereit sein zu ...

preponderance [prɪ'pɒndərns] *n* Übergewicht *nt*

preposition [prepə'zɪʃən] *n* Präposition *f*, Verhältniswort *nt*

preposterous [prɪ'pɒstərəs] *adj* absurd

prep school *n* = preparatory school

prerequisite [priː'rekwɪzɪt] *n* (unerlässliche) Voraussetzung *f*

prerogative [prɪ'rɒgətɪv] *n* Vorrecht *nt*

Presbyterian [prezbɪ'tɪərɪən] *adj* presbyterianisch ♦ *n* Presbyterier(in) *m(f)*

preschool ['priː'skuːl] *adj* Vorschul-

prescribe [prɪ'skraɪb] *vt* vorschreiben; (*MED*) verschreiben

prescription [prɪ'skrɪpʃən] *n* (*MED*) Rezept *nt*

presence ['prezns] *n* Gegenwart *f*; **~ of mind** Geistesgegenwart *f*

present [*adj, n* 'preznt, *vb* prɪ'zent] *adj* (*here*) anwesend; (*current*) gegenwärtig ♦ *n* Gegenwart *f*; (*gift*) Geschenk *nt* ♦ *vt* vorlegen; *(introduce)* vorstellen; *(show)* zeigen; *(give)*: **to ~ sb with sth** jdm etw überreichen; **at ~** im Augenblick; **to give sb a ~** jdm ein Geschenk machen; **~able** [prɪˈzɛntəbl] *adj* präsentabel; **~ation** [prɛznˈteɪʃən] *n* Überreichung *f*; **~day** *adj* heutig; **~er** [prɪˈzɛntəʳ] *n (RAD, TV)* Moderator(in) *m(f)*; **~ly** *adv* bald; *(at ~)* im Augenblick

preservation [prɛzəˈveɪʃən] *n* Erhaltung *f*

preservative [prɪˈzɜːvətɪv] *n* Konservierungsmittel *nt*

preserve [prɪˈzɜːv] *vt* erhalten; *(food)* einmachen ♦ *n (jam)* Eingemachte(s) *nt*; *(reserve)* Schutzgebiet *nt*

preside [prɪˈzaɪd] *vi* den Vorsitz haben

president [ˈprɛzɪdənt] *n* Präsident *m*; **~ial** [prɛzɪˈdɛnʃl] *adj* Präsidenten-; *(election)* Präsidentschafts-; *(system)* Präsidial-

press [prɛs] *n* Presse *f*; *(printing house)* Druckerei *f* ♦ *vt* drücken; *(iron)* bügeln; *(urge)* (be)drängen ♦ *vi (push)* drücken; **to be ~ed for time** unter Zeitdruck stehen; **to ~ for sth** drängen auf etw *acc*; **~ on** *vi* vorwärts drängen; **~ agency** *n* Presseagentur *f*; **~ conference** *n* Pressekonferenz *f*; **~ed** *adj (clothes)* gebügelt; **~ing** *adj* dringend; **~ stud** *(BRIT)* *n* Druckknopf *m*; **~-up** *(BRIT)* *n* Liegestütz *m*

pressure [ˈprɛʃəʳ] *n* Druck *m*; **~ cooker** *n* Schnellkochtopf *m*; **~ gauge** *n* Druckmesser *m*

pressurized [ˈprɛʃəraɪzd] *adj* Druck-

prestige [prɛsˈtiːʒ] *n* Prestige *nt*; **prestigious** [prɛsˈtɪdʒəs] *adj* Prestige-

presumably [prɪˈzjuːməblɪ] *adv* vermutlich

presume [prɪˈzjuːm] *vt*, *vi* annehmen; **to ~ to do sth** sich erlauben, etw zu tun; **presumption** [prɪˈzʌmpʃən] *n* Annahme *f*; **presumptuous** [prɪˈzʌmpʃəs] *adj* anmaßend

pretence [prɪˈtɛns] *(US* **pretense)**

Vorgabe *f*, Vortäuschung *f*; *(false claim)* Vorwand *m*

pretend [prɪˈtɛnd] *vt* vorgeben, so tun als ob ... ♦ *vi* **to ~ to sth** Anspruch erheben auf etw *acc*

pretense [prɪˈtɛns] *(US)* *n* = **pretence**

pretension [prɪˈtɛnʃən] *n* Anspruch *m*; *(impudent claim)* Anmaßung *f*

pretentious [prɪˈtɛnʃəs] *adj* angeberisch

pretext [ˈpriːtɛkst] *n* Vorwand *m*

pretty [ˈprɪtɪ] *adj* hübsch ♦ *adv (inf)* ganz schön

prevail [prɪˈveɪl] *vi* siegen; *(custom)* vorherrschen; **to ~ against** *or* **over** siegen über +*acc*; **to ~ (up)on sb to do sth** jdn dazu bewegen, etw zu tun; **~ing** *adj* vorherrschend

prevalent [ˈprɛvələnt] *adj* vorherrschend

prevent [prɪˈvɛnt] *vt (stop)* verhindern, verhüten; **to ~ sb from doing sth** jdn (daran) hindern, etw zu tun; **~ative** *n* Vorbeugungsmittel *nt*; **~ion** [prɪˈvɛnʃən] *n* Verhütung *f*; **~ive** *adj* vorbeugend, Schutz-

preview [ˈpriːvjuː] *n* private Voraufführung *f*; *(trailer)* Vorschau *f*

previous [ˈpriːvɪəs] *adj* früher, vorherig; **~ly** *adv* früher

prewar [priːˈwɔːʳ] *adj nur* Vorkriegs-

prey [preɪ] *n* Beute *f*; **~ on** *vt fus* Jagd machen auf +*acc*; **it was ~ing on his mind** es quälte sein Gewissen

price [praɪs] *n* Preis *m*; *(value)* Wert *m* ♦ *vt (label)* auszeichnen; **~less** *adj (also fig)* unbezahlbar; **~ list** *n* Preisliste *f*

prick [prɪk] *n* Stich *m* ♦ *vt*, *vi* stechen; **to ~ up one's ears** die Ohren spitzen

prickle [ˈprɪkl] *n* Stachel *m*, Dorn *m*

prickly [ˈprɪklɪ] *adj* stachelig; *(fig: person)* reizbar; **~ heat** *n* Hitzebläschen *pl*

pride [praɪd] *n* Stolz *m*; *(arrogance)* Hochmut *m* ♦ *vt*: **to ~ o.s. on sth** stolz sein auf etw *acc*

priest [priːst] *n* Priester *m*; **~hood** *n* Priesteramt *nt*

prim [prɪm] *adj* prüde

primarily ['praɪmərɪlɪ] *adv* vorwiegend

primary ['praɪmərɪ] *adj (main)* Haupt-; *(SCH)* Grund-; **~ school** *(BRIT)* n Grundschule f

prime [praɪm] *adj* erste(r, s); *(excellent)* erstklassig ♦ *vt* vorbereiten; *(gun)* laden; **in the ~ of life** in der Blüte des Jahres; **~ minister** n Premierminister m, Ministerpräsident m; **~r** ['praɪmə] n Fibel f

primeval [praɪ'miːvl] *adj* vorzeitlich; *(forests)* Ur-

primitive ['prɪmɪtɪv] *adj* primitiv

primrose ['prɪmrəʊz] n *(gelbe)* Primel f

primus (stove) ['praɪməs-] (® *BRIT*) n Primuskocher m

prince [prɪns] n Prinz m; *(ruler)* Fürst m;

princess [prɪn'ses] n Prinzessin f; Fürstin f

principal ['prɪnsɪpl] *adj* Haupt- ♦ n *(SCH)* (Schul)direktor m, Rektor m; *(money)* (Grund)kapital nt

principle ['prɪnsɪpl] n Grundsatz m, Prinzip nt; **in ~** im Prinzip; **on ~** aus Prinzip, prinzipiell

print [prɪnt] n Druck m; *(made by feet, fingers)* Abdruck m; *(PHOT)* Abzug m ♦ *vt* drucken; *(name)* in Druckbuchstaben schreiben; *(PHOT)* abziehen; **out of ~** vergriffen; **~ed matter** n Drucksache f; **~er** n Drucker m; **~ing** n Drucken nt; *(of photos)* Abziehen nt; **~out** n *(COMPUT)* Ausdruck m

prior ['praɪə] *adj* früher ♦ n Prior m; **~ to sth** vor etw *dat*; **~ to going abroad, she had ...** bevor sie ins Ausland ging, hatte sie ...

priority [praɪ'ɒrɪtɪ] n Vorrang m, Priorität f

prise [praɪz] *vt*: **to ~ open** aufbrechen

prison ['prɪzn] n Gefängnis nt ♦ *adj* Gefängnis-; *(system etc)* Strafvollzugs-; **~er** n Gefangene(r) mf

pristine ['prɪstiːn] *adj* makellos

privacy ['prɪvəsɪ] n Ungestörtheit f,

Ruhe f; Privatleben nt

private ['praɪvɪt] *adj* privat, Privat-; *(secret)* vertraulich, geheim ♦ n einfache(r) Soldat m; **"~"** *(on envelope)* „persönlich"; *(on door)* „Privat"; **in ~** privat, unter vier Augen; **~ enterprise** n Privatunternehmen nt; **~ eye** n Privatdetektiv m; **~ property** n Privatbesitz m; **~ school** n Privatschule f; **privatize** *vt* privatisieren

privet ['prɪvɪt] n Liguster m

privilege ['prɪvɪlɪdʒ] n Privileg nt; **~d** *adj* bevorzugt, privilegiert

privy ['prɪvɪ] *adj* geheim, privat; **P~ Council** n Geheime(r) Staatsrat m

prize [praɪz] n Preis m ♦ *adj (example)* erstklassig; *(idiot)* Voll- ♦ *vt* (hoch)schätzen; **~-giving** n Preisverteilung f; **~winner** n Preisträger(in) m(f)

pro [prəʊ] n *(~fessional)* Profi m; **the ~s and cons** das Für und Wider

probability [prɒbə'bɪlɪtɪ] n Wahrscheinlichkeit f

probable ['prɒbəbl] *adj* wahrscheinlich; **probably** *adv* wahrscheinlich

probation [prə'beɪʃən] n Probe(zeit) f; *(JUR)* Bewährung f; **on ~** auf Probe; auf Bewährung

probe [prəʊb] n Sonde f; *(enquiry)* Untersuchung f ♦ *vt, vi* erforschen

problem ['prɒbləm] n Problem nt; **~atic** [prɒblə'mætɪk] *adj* problematisch

procedure [prə'siːdʒə] n Verfahren nt

proceed [prə'siːd] *vi (advance)* vorrücken; *(start)* anfangen; *(carry on)* fortfahren; *(set about)* vorgehen; **~ings** *npl* Verfahren nt

proceeds ['prəʊsiːdz] *npl* Erlös m

process ['prəʊses] n Prozess m; *(method)* Verfahren nt ♦ *vt* bearbeiten; *(food)* verarbeiten; *(film)* entwickeln; **~ing** n *(PHOT)* Entwickeln nt

procession [prə'seʃən] n Prozession f, Umzug m; **funeral ~** Trauerprozession f

pro-choice   514   prom

pro-choice [prəʊ'tʃɔɪs] *adj (movement)* Pro-Abtreibungs-; **~ campaigner** Abtreibungsbefürworter(in) *m(f)*

proclaim [prə'kleɪm] *vt* verkünden

procrastinate [prəʊ'kræstɪneɪt] *vi* zaudern

procure [prə'kjʊə] *vt* beschaffen

prod [prɒd] *vt* stoßen ♦ *n* Stoß *m*

prodigal ['prɒdɪgl] *adj*: **~ (with *or* of)** verschwenderisch (mit)

prodigy ['prɒdɪdʒɪ] *n* Wunder *nt*

produce [*n* 'prɒdjuːs, *vb* prə'djuːs] *n (AGR)* (Boden)produkte *pl*, (Natur)erzeugnis *nt* ♦ *vt* herstellen, produzieren; *(cause)* hervorrufen; *(farmer)* erzeugen; *(yield)* liefern, bringen; *(play)* inszenieren; **~r** *n* Hersteller *m*, Produzent *m* (also CINE); Erzeuger *m*

product ['prɒdʌkt] *n* Produkt *nt*, Erzeugnis *nt*; **~ion** [prə'dʌkʃən] *n* Produktion *f*, Herstellung *f*; *(thing)* Erzeugnis *nt*, Produkt *nt*; *(THEAT)* Inszenierung *f*; **~ion line** *n* Fließband *nt*; **~ive** [prə'dʌktɪv] *adj* produktiv; *(fertile)* ertragreich, fruchtbar

productivity [prɒdʌk'tɪvɪtɪ] *n* Produktivität *f*

profane [prə'feɪn] *adj* weltlich, profan; *(language etc)* gotteslästerlich

profess [prə'fes] *vt* bekennen; *(show)* zeigen; *(claim to be)* vorgeben

profession [prə'feʃən] *n* Beruf *m*; *(declaration)* Bekenntnis *nt*; **~al** *n* Fachmann *m*; *(SPORT)* Berufsspieler(in) *m(f)* ♦ *adj* Berufs-; *(expert)* fachlich; *(player)* professionell; **~ally** *adv* beruflich, fachmännisch

professor [prə'fesə] *n* Professor *m*

proficiency [prə'fɪʃənsɪ] *n* Können *nt*

proficient [prə'fɪʃənt] *adj* fähig

profile ['prəʊfaɪl] *n* Profil *nt*; *(fig: report)* Kurzbiografie *f*

profit ['prɒfɪt] *n* Gewinn *m* ♦ *vi*: **to ~ (by *or* from)** profitieren (von); **~ability** [prɒfɪtə'bɪlɪtɪ] *n* Rentabilität *f*; **~able** *adj* einträglich, rentabel; **~eering** [prɒfɪ'tɪərɪŋ] *n* Profitmacherei *f*

profound [prə'faʊnd] *adj* tief

profuse [prə'fjuːs] *adj* überreich; **~ly** [prə'fjuːslɪ] *adv* überschwänglich; *(sweat)* reichlich; **profusion** [prə'fjuːʒən] *n*: **profusion (of)** Überfülle *f* (von), Überfluss *m* (an +*dat*)

program ['prəʊgræm] *n (COMPUT)* Programm *nt* ♦ *vt (machine)* programmieren; **~me** *(US* **program)** *n* Programm *nt* ♦ *vt* planen; *(computer)* programmieren; **~mer** *(US* **programer)** *n* Programmierer(in) *m(f)*

progress [*n* 'prəʊgres, *vb* prə'gres] *n* Fortschritt *m* ♦ *vi* fortschreiten, weitergehen; **in ~** im Gang; **~ion** [prə'greʃən] *n* Folge *f*; **~ive** [prə'gresɪv] *adj* fortschrittlich, progressiv

prohibit [prə'hɪbɪt] *vt* verbieten; **to ~ sb from doing sth** jdm untersagen, etw zu tun; **~ion** [prəʊɪ'bɪʃən] *n* Verbot *nt*; *(US)* Alkoholverbot *nt*, Prohibition *f*; **~ive** *adj* unerschwinglich

project [*n* 'prɒdʒekt, *vb* prə'dʒekt] *n* Projekt *nt* ♦ *vt* vorausplanen; *(film etc)* projizieren; *(personality, voice)* zum Tragen bringen ♦ *vi (stick out)* hervorragen, (her)vorstehen

projectile [prə'dʒektaɪl] *n* Geschoss *nt*

projection [prə'dʒekʃən] *n* Projektion *f*; *(sth prominent)* Vorsprung *m*

projector [prə'dʒektə] *n* Projektor *m*

proletariat [prəʊlɪ'teərɪət] *n* Proletariat *nt*

pro-life [prəʊ'laɪf] *adj (movement)* Anti-Abtreibungs-; **~ campaigner** Abtreibungsgegner(in) *m(f)*

prolific [prə'lɪfɪk] *adj* fruchtbar; *(author etc)* produktiv

prologue ['prəʊlɒg] *n* Prolog *m*; *(event)* Vorspiel *nt*

prolong [prə'lɒŋ] *vt* verlängern

prom [prɒm] *n abbr* = **promenade**; **promenade concert**

Prom

Prom *(promenade concert)* ist in Großbritannien ein Konzert, bei dem

*ein Teil des Zuhörer steht (ur-
sprünglich spazieren ging). Die seit
1895 alljährlich stattfindenden Proms
(seit 1941 immer in der Londoner
Royal Albert Hall) zählen zu den be-
deutendsten Musikereignissen in England. Der letzte Abend der Proms steht
ganz im Zeichen des Patriotismus und
gipfelt im Singen des Lieds „Land of
Hope and Glory". In den USA und Kanada steht das Wort für promenade,
ein Ball an einer High School oder
einem College.*

promenade [prɔmə'nɑːd] *n* Promenade *f*; ~ **concert** *n* Promenadenkonzert
nt

prominence ['prɔminəns] *n* (große)
Bedeutung *f*

prominent ['prɔminənt] *adj* bedeutend; (*politician*) prominent; (*easily
seen*) herausragend, auffallend

promiscuous [prə'miskjuəs] *adj* lose

promise ['prɔmis] *n* Versprechen *nt*;
(*hope*: ~ *of sth*) Aussicht *f* auf *etw acc*
♦ *vt, vi* versprechen; **promising** *adj*
viel versprechend

promontory ['prɔməntri] *n* Vorsprung
m

promote [prə'məut] *vt* befördern;
(*help on*) fördern, unterstützen; ~**r** *n*
(*in entertainment, sport*) Veranstalter *m*;
(*for charity etc*) Organisator *m*; **promotion** [prə'məuʃən] *n* (*in rank*) Beförderung *f*; (*furtherance*) Förderung *f*;
(*COMM*): **promotion (of)** *n* Werbung *f*
(*für*)

prompt [prɔmpt] *adj* prompt, schnell
♦ *adv* (*punctually*) genau ♦ *n* (*COMPUT*)
Meldung *f* ♦ *vt* (*THEAT*)
souffllieren +*dat*; **to ~ sb to do sth** jdn
dazu veranlassen, etw zu tun; ~**ly** *adv*
sofort

prone [prəun] *adj* hingestreckt; **to be ~
to sth** zu etw neigen

prong [prɔŋ] *n* Zinke *f*

pronoun ['prəunaun] *n* Fürwort *nt*

pronounce [prə'nauns] *vt* aussprechen; (*JUR*) verkünden ♦ *vi*: **to ~ (on)**
sich äußern (zu)

pronunciation [prənʌnsi'eiʃən] *n* Aussprache *f*

proof [pruːf] *n* Beweis *m*; (*PRINT*) Kor-
rekturfahne *f*; (*of alcohol*) Alkoholge-
halt *m* ♦ *adj* sicher

prop [prɔp] *n* (*also fig*) Stütze *f*; (*THEAT*)
Requisit *nt* ♦ *vt* (*also: ~ up*) (ab)stützen

propaganda [prɔpə'gændə] *n* Propaganda *f*

propel [prə'pel] *vt* (an)treiben; ~**ler** *n*
Propeller *m*; ~**ling pencil** (*BRIT*) *n*
Drehbleistift *m*

propensity [prə'pensiti] *n* Tendenz *f*

proper ['prɔpə*] *adj* richtig; (*seemly*)
schicklich; ~**ly** *adv* richtig; ~ **noun** *n*
Eigenname *m*

property ['prɔpəti] *n* Eigentum *nt*;
(*quality*) Eigenschaft *f*; (*land*) Grundbesitz *m*; ~ **owner** *n* Grundbesitzer *m*

prophecy ['prɔfisi] *n* Prophezeiung *f*

prophesy ['prɔfisai] *vt* prophezeien

prophet ['prɔfit] *n* Prophet *m*

proportion [prə'pɔːʃən] *n* Verhältnis
nt; (*share*) Teil *m* ♦ *vt*: **to ~ (to)** abstimmen (auf +*acc*); ~**al** *adj* proportional;
~**ate** *adj* verhältnismäßig

proposal [prə'pəuzl] *n* Vorschlag *m*; (*of
marriage*) Heiratsantrag *m*

propose [prə'pəuz] *vt* vorschlagen;
(*toast*) ausbringen ♦ *vi* (*offer marriage*)
einen Heiratsantrag machen; **to ~ to
do sth** beabsichtigen, etw zu tun

proposition [prɔpə'ziʃən] *n* Angebot
nt; (*statement*) Satz *m*

proprietor [prə'praiətə*] *n* Besitzer *m*,
Eigentümer *m*

propriety [prə'praiəti] *n* Anstand *m*

pro rata [prəu'rɑːtə] *adv* anteilmäßig

prose [prəuz] *n* Prosa *f*

prosecute ['prɔsikjuːt] *vt* (strafrecht-
lich) verfolgen; **prosecution** [prɔsi-
'kjuːʃən] *n* (*JUR*) strafrechtliche Verfolgung *f*; (*party*) Anklage *f*; **prosecutor**
n Vertreter *m* der Anklage; **Public**

prospect 516 **psychological**

Prosecutor Staatsanwalt *m*

prospect [*n* 'prɒspekt, *vb* prə'spekt] *n* Aussicht *f* ♦ *vt* auf Bodenschätze hin untersuchen ♦ *vi*: **to ~ (for)** suchen (nach); **~ing** ['prɒspektıŋ] *n* (*for minerals*) Suche *f*; **~ive** [prə'spektıv] *adj* (*son-in-law etc*) zukünftig; (*customer, candidate*) voraussichtlich

prospectus [prə'spektəs] *n* (Werbe)prospekt *m*

prosper ['prɒspə*] *vi* blühen, gedeihen; (*person*) erfolgreich sein; **~ity** [prɒ'sperıtı] *n* Wohlstand *m*; **~ous** *adj* wohlhabend, reich

prostitute ['prɒstıtju:t] *n* Prostituierte *f*

prostrate ['prɒstreıt] *adj* ausgestreckt (liegend)

protagonist [prə'tægənıst] *n* Hauptperson *f*, Held *m*

protect [prə'tekt] *vt* (be)schützen; **~ed species** *n* geschützte Art; **~ion** [prə'tekʃən] *n* Schutz *m*; **~ive** *adj* Schutz-, (be)schützend

protégé ['prɒutεʒeı] *n* Schützling *m*

protein [prə'ti:n] *n* Protein *m*, Eiweiß *nt*

protest [*n* 'prəutεst, *vb* prə'tεst] *n* Protest *m* ♦ *vi* protestieren ♦ *vt* (*affirm*) beteuern

Protestant ['prɒtıstənt] *adj* protestantisch ♦ *n* Protestant(in) *m(f)*

protester [prə'tεstə*] *n* (*demonstrator*) Demonstrant(in) *m(f)*

protracted [prə'træktıd] *adj* sich hinziehend

protrude [prə'tru:d] *vi* (her)vorstehen

proud [praud] *adj*: **~ (of)** stolz (auf *+acc*)

prove [pru:v] *vt* beweisen ♦ *vi*: **to ~ (to be) correct** sich als richtig erweisen; **to ~ o.s.** sich bewähren

proverb ['prɒvə:b] *n* Sprichwort *nt*; **~ial** [prə'və:bıəl] *adj* sprichwörtlich

provide [prə'vaıd] *vt* versehen; (*supply*) besorgen; **to ~ sb with sth** jdn mit etw versorgen; **~ for** *vt fus* sorgen für; (*emergency*) Vorkehrungen treffen für;

~d (that) *conj* vorausgesetzt(, dass)

providing [prə'vaıdıŋ] *conj* vorausgesetzt (, dass)

province ['prɒvıns] *n* Provinz *f*; (*division of work*) Bereich *m*; **provincial** [prə'vınʃəl] *adj* provinziell, Provinz

provision [prə'vıʒən] *n* Vorkehrung *f*; (*condition*) Bestimmung *f*; **~s** *npl* (*food*) Vorräte *pl*, Proviant *m*; **~al** *adj* provisorisch

proviso [prə'vaızəu] *n* Bedingung *f*

provocative [prə'vɒkətıv] *adj* provozierend

provoke [prə'vəuk] *vt* provozieren; (*cause*) hervorrufen

prowess ['prauıs] *n* überragende(s) Können *nt*

prowl [praul] *vi* herumstreichen; (*animal*) schleichen ♦ *n*: **on the ~** umherstreifend; **~er** *n* Herumtreiber(in) *m(f)*

proximity [prɒk'sımıtı] *n* Nähe *f*

proxy ['prɒksı] *n* (Stell)vertreter *m*; (*authority, document*) Vollmacht *f*; **by ~** durch einen Stellvertreter

prudent ['pru:dnt] *adj* klug, umsichtig

prudish ['pru:dıʃ] *adj* prüde

prune [pru:n] *n* Backpflaume *f* ♦ *vt* ausputzen; (*fig*) zurechtstutzen

pry [praı] *vi*: **to ~ (into)** seine Nase stecken (in *+acc*)

PS *n abbr* (= *postscript*) PS

pseudonym ['sju:dənım] *n* Pseudonym *nt*, Deckname *m*

psychiatric [saıkı'ætrık] *adj* psychiatrisch

psychiatrist [saı'kaıətrıst] *n* Psychiater *m*

psychic ['saıkık] *adj* (*also*: **~al**) übersinnlich; (*person*) paranormal begabt

psychoanalyse [saıkəu'ænəlaız] (*US* **psychoanalyze**) *vt* psychoanalytisch behandeln; **psychoanalyst** [saıkəu'ænəlıst] *n* Psychoanalytiker(in) *m(f)*

psychological [saıkə'lɒdʒıkl] *adj* psychologisch; **psychologist** [saı'kɒlədʒɪst] *n* Psychologe *m*, Psychologin *f*; **psychology** [saɪˈkɒlədʒɪ] *n* Psychologie *f*

PTO *abbr* = **please turn over**

pub [pʌb] *n abbr* (= public house) Kneipe *f*

Pub

Pub ist ein Gasthaus mit einer Lizenz zum Ausschank von alkoholischen Getränken. Ein Pub besteht meist aus verschiedenen gemütlichen (lounge, snug) oder einfacheren Räumen (public bar), in denen auch Spiele wie Darts, Domino und Poolbillard zur Verfügung stehen. In Pubs werden vor allem mittags oft auch Mahlzeiten angeboten. Pubs sind normalerweise von 11 bis 23 Uhr geöffnet, aber manchmal nachmittags geschlossen.

---

pubic [ˈpjuːbɪk] *adj* Scham-
public [ˈpʌblɪk] *adj* öffentlich ♦ *n* (*also:* **general ~**) Öffentlichkeit *f*; **in ~** in der Öffentlichkeit; **~ address system** *n* Lautsprecheranlage *f*
publican [ˈpʌblɪkən] *n* Wirt *m*
publication [pʌblɪˈkeɪʃən] *n* Veröffentlichung *f*
public: **~ company** *n* Aktiengesellschaft *f*; **~ convenience** (BRIT) *n* öffentliche Toiletten *pl*; **~ holiday** *n* gesetzliche(r) Feiertag *m*; **~ house** (BRIT) *n* Lokal *nt*, Kneipe *f*
publicity [pʌbˈlɪsɪtɪ] *n* Publicity *f*, Werbung *f*
publicize [ˈpʌblɪsaɪz] *vt* bekannt machen; (*advertise*) Publicity machen für
publicly [ˈpʌblɪklɪ] *adv* öffentlich
public: **~ opinion** *n* öffentliche Meinung *f*; **~ relations** *npl* Publicrelations *pl*, Public Relations *pl*; **~ school** *n* (BRIT) Privatschule *f*; (US) staatliche Schule *f*; **~-spirited** *adj* mit Gemeinschaftssinn; **~ transport** *n* öffentliche Verkehrsmittel *pl*
publish [ˈpʌblɪʃ] *vt* veröffentlichen;

(*event*) bekannt geben; **~er** *n* Verleger *m*; **~ing** *n* (*business*) Verlagswesen *nt*
pub lunch *n* in Pubs servierter Imbiss
pucker [ˈpʌkəʳ] *vt* (*face*) verziehen; (*lips*) kräuseln
pudding [ˈpʊdɪŋ] *n* (BRIT: *course*) Nachtisch *m*; Pudding *m*; **black ~** *n* Blutwurst *f*
puddle [ˈpʌdl] *n* Pfütze *f*
puff [pʌf] *n* (*of wind etc*) Stoß *m*; (*cosmetic*) Puderquaste *f* ♦ *vt* blasen, pusten; (*pipe*) paffen ♦ *vi* keuchen, schnaufen; (*smoke*) paffen; **to ~ out smoke** Rauch ausstoßen; **~ pastry** (US **~ paste**) *n* Blätterteig *m*; **~y** *adj* aufgedunsen
pull [pʊl] *n* Ruck *m*; (*influence*) Beziehung *f* ♦ *vt* ziehen; (*trigger*) abdrücken ♦ *vi* ziehen; **to ~ sb's leg** jdn auf den Arm nehmen; **to ~ to pieces** in Stücke reißen; (*fig*) verreißen; **to ~ one's punches** sich zurückhalten; **to ~ one's weight** sich in die Riemen legen; **to ~ o.s. together** sich zusammenreißen; **~ apart** *vt* (*break*) zerreißen; (*dismantle*) auseinander nehmen; (*separate*) trennen; **~ down** *vt* (*house*) abreißen; **~ in** *vi* hineinfahren; (*stop*) anhalten; (RAIL) einfahren; **~ off** *vt* (*deal etc*) abschließen; **~ out** *vi* (*car*) herausfahren; (*fig: partner*) aussteigen ♦ *vt* herausziehen; **~ over** *vi* (AUT) an die Seite fahren; **~ through** *vi* durchkommen; **~ up** *vi* anhalten ♦ *vt* (*uproot*) herausreißen; (*stop*) anhalten
pulley [ˈpʊlɪ] *n* Rolle *f*, Flaschenzug *m*
pullover [ˈpʊləʊvəʳ] *n* Pullover *m*
pulp [pʌlp] *n* Brei *m*; (*of fruit*) Fruchtfleisch *nt*
pulpit [ˈpʊlpɪt] *n* Kanzel *f*
pulsate [pʌlˈseɪt] *vi* pulsieren
pulse [pʌls] *n* Puls *m*; **~s** *npl* (BOT) Hülsenfrüchte *pl*
pummel [ˈpʌml] *vt* mit den Fäusten bearbeiten
pump [pʌmp] *n* Pumpe *f*; (*shoe*) leichter (Tanz)schuh *m* ♦ *vt* pumpen; **~ up**

vt (tyre) aufpumpen

pumpkin ['pʌmpkɪn] *n* Kürbis *m*

pun [pʌn] *n* Wortspiel *nt*

punch [pʌntʃ] *n (tool)* Locher *m; (blow)* (Faust)schlag *m; (drink)* Punsch *m,* Bowle *f ♦ vt* lochen; *(strike)* schlagen, boxen; ~ **line** *n* Pointe *f;* **~-up** *(BRIT: inf) n* Keilerei *f*

punctual ['pʌŋktjuəl] *adj* pünktlich

punctuate ['pʌŋktjueɪt] *vt* mit Satzzeichen versehen; *(fig)* unterbrechen; **punctuation** [pʌŋktju'eɪʃən] *n* Zeichensetzung *f,* Interpunktion *f*

puncture ['pʌŋktʃər] *n* Loch *nt; (AUT)* Reifenpanne *f ♦ vt* durchbohren

pundit ['pʌndɪt] *n* Gelehrte(r) *m*

pungent ['pʌndʒənt] *adj* scharf

punish ['pʌnɪʃ] *vt* bestrafen; *(in boxing etc)* übel zurichten; **~ment** *n* Strafe *f; (action)* Bestrafung *f*

punk [pʌŋk] *n (also:* ~ **rocker**) Punker(in) *m(f); (also:* ~ **rock**) Punk *m; (US: inf: hoodlum)* Ganove *m*

punt [pʌnt] *n* Stechkahn *m*

punter ['pʌntər] *(BRIT) n (better)* Wetter *m*

puny ['pjuːnɪ] *adj* kümmerlich

pup [pʌp] *n* = **puppy**

pupil ['pjuːpɪl] *n* Schüler(in) *m(f); (in eye)* Pupille *f*

puppet ['pʌpɪt] *n* Puppe *f,* Marionette *f*

puppy ['pʌpɪ] *n* junge(r) Hund *m*

purchase ['pɜːtʃɪs] *n* Kauf *m; (grip)* Halt *m ♦ vt* kaufen, erwerben; **~r** *n* Käufer(in) *m(f)*

pure [pjuər] *adj (also fig)* rein; **~ly** ['pjuəlɪ] *adv* rein

purgatory ['pɜːgətərɪ] *n* Fegefeuer *nt*

purge [pɜːdʒ] *n (also POL)* Säuberung *f ♦ vt* reinigen; *(body)* entschlacken

purify ['pjuərɪfaɪ] *vt* reinigen

purity ['pjuərɪtɪ] *n* Reinheit *f*

purple ['pɜːpl] *adj* violett; *(face)* dunkelrot

purport [pɜː'pɔːt] *vi* vorgeben

purpose ['pɜːpəs] *n* Zweck *m,* Ziel *nt;*

(of person) Absicht *f;* **on** ~ absichtlich; **~ful** *adj* zielbewusst, entschlossen

purr [pɜːr] *n* Schnurren *nt ♦ vi* schnurren

purse [pɜːs] *n* Portemonnaie *nt,* Portmonee *nt,* Geldbeutel *m ♦ vt (lips)* zusammenpressen, schürzen

purser ['pɜːsər] *n* Zahlmeister *m*

pursue [pə'sjuː] *vt* verfolgen; *(study)* nachgehen *+dat;* **~r** *n* Verfolger *m;*

pursuit [pə'sjuːt] *n* Verfolgung *f; (occupation)* Beschäftigung *f*

pus [pʌs] *n* Eiter *m*

push [puʃ] *n* Stoß *m,* Schub *m; (MIL)* Vorstoß *m ♦ vt* stoßen, schieben; *(button)* drücken; *(idea)* durchsetzen *♦ vi* stoßen, schieben; ~ **aside** *vt* beiseite schieben; ~ **off** *(inf) vi* abschieben; ~ **on** *vi* weitermachen; ~ **through** *vt* durchsetzen; ~ **up** *vt (total)* erhöhen; *(prices)* hochtreiben; **~chair** *(BRIT) n* (Kinder)sportwagen *m;* **~er** *n (drug dealer)* Pusher *m;* **~over** *(inf) n* Kinderspiel *nt;* **~-up** *(US) n (press-up)* Liegestütz *m;* **~y** *(inf) adj* aufdringlich

puss [pus] *n* Mieze(katze) *f;* **~y(cat)** *n* Mieze(katze) *f*

put [put] *(pt, pp* **put**) *vt* setzen, stellen, legen; *(express)* ausdrücken, sagen; *(write)* schreiben; ~ **about** *vi (turn back)* wenden *♦ vt (spread)* verbreiten; ~ **across** *vt (explain)* erklären; ~ **away** *vt* weglegen; *(store)* beiseite legen; ~ **back** *vt* zurückstellen *or* -legen; ~ **by** *vt* zurücklegen, sparen; ~ **down** *vt* hinstellen *or* -legen; *(rebellion)* niederschlagen; *(animal)* einschläfern; *(in writing)* niederschreiben; ~ **forward** *vt (idea)* vorbringen; *(clock)* vorstellen; ~ **in** *vt (application, complaint)* einreichen; **to** ~ **off** *vt* verschieben; *(discourage)* **to** ~ **sb off sth** jdn von etw abbringen; ~ **on** *vt (clothes etc)* anziehen; *(light etc)* anschalten, anmachen; *(play etc)* aufführen; *(brake)* anziehen; ~ **out** *vt (hand etc)* (her)ausstrecken;

(*news, rumour*) verbreiten; (*light etc*) ausschalten, ausmachen; **~ through** *vt* (*TEL: person*) verbinden; (: *call*) durchstellen; **~ up** *vt* (*tent*) aufstellen; (*building*) errichten; (*price*) erhöhen; (*person*) unterbringen; **~ up with** *vt fus* sich abfinden mit

putrid ['pju:trɪd] *adj* faul

putt [pʌt] *vt* (*golf*) putten ♦ *n* (*golf*) Putten *nt*; **~ing green** *n* kleine(r) Golfplatz *m* nur zum Putten

putty ['pʌtɪ] *n* Kitt *m*; (*fig*) Wachs *nt*

put-up ['putʌp] *adj*: **~ job** abgekartete(s) Spiel *nt*

puzzle ['pʌzl] *n* Rätsel *nt*; (*toy*) Geduldspiel *nt* ♦ *vt* verwirren ♦ *vi* sich den Kopf zerbrechen; **~d** *adj* verdutzt, verblüfft; **puzzling** *adj* rätselhaft, verwirrend

pyjamas [pə'dʒɑːməz] (*BRIT*) *npl* Schlafanzug *m*, Pyjama *m*

pylon ['paɪlən] *n* Mast *m*

pyramid ['pɪrəmɪd] *n* Pyramide *f*

Q, q

quack [kwæk] *n* Quaken *nt*; (*doctor*) Quacksalber *m* ♦ *vi* quaken

quad [kwɒd] *n abbr* = **quadrangle; quadruplet**

quadrangle ['kwɒdræŋgl] *n* (*court*) Hof *m*; (*MATH*) Viereck *nt*

quadruple [kwɒ'dru:pl] *adj* ♦ *vi* sich vervierfachen ♦ *vt* vervierfachen

quadruplets [kwɒ'dru:plɪts] *npl* Vierlinge *pl*

quagmire ['kwægmaɪər] *n* Morast *m*

quail [kweɪl] *n* (*bird*) Wachtel *f* ♦ *vi* (*vor Angst*) zittern

quaint [kweɪnt] *adj* kurios; malerisch

quake [kweɪk] *vi* beben, zittern ♦ *n abbr* = **earthquake**

qualification [kwɒlɪfɪ'keɪʃən] *n* Qualifikation *f*; (*sth which limits*) Einschränkung *f*

qualified ['kwɒlɪfaɪd] *adj* (*competent*)

qualifiziert; (*limited*) bedingt

qualify ['kwɒlɪfaɪ] *vt* (*prepare*) befähigen; (*limit*) einschränken ♦ *vi* sich qualifizieren; **to ~ as** (*exam passed*) sein medizinisches/juristisches Staatsexamen machen

quality ['kwɒlɪtɪ] *n* Qualität *f*; (*characteristic*) Eigenschaft *f*

Quality press

Quality press bezeichnet die seriösen Tages- und Wochenzeitungen, im Gegensatz zu den Massenblättern. Diese Zeitungen sind fast alle großformatig und wenden sich an den anspruchsvolleren Leser, der voll informiert sein möchte und bereit ist, für die Zeitungslektüre viel Zeit aufzuwenden. Siehe auch **tabloid press**.

quality time *n* intensiv genutzte Zeit

qualm [kwɑːm] *n* Bedenken *nt*

quandary ['kwɒndrɪ] *n*: **to be in a ~** in Verlegenheit sein

quantity ['kwɒntɪtɪ] *n* Menge *f*; **~ surveyor** *n* Baukostenkalkulator *m*

quarantine ['kwɒrntiːn] *n* Quarantäne *f*

quarrel ['kwɒrəl] *n* Streit *m* ♦ *vi* sich streiten; **~some** *adj* streitsüchtig

quarry ['kwɒrɪ] *n* Steinbruch *m*; (*animal*) Wild *nt*; (*fig*) Opfer *nt*

quart ['kwɔːtər] *n* Viertel *nt*; (*of year*) Quartal *nt* ♦ *vt* (*divide*) teilen; (*MIL*) einquartieren; **~s** *npl* (*esp MIL*) Quartier *nt*; **~ of an hour** Viertelstunde *f*; **~-final** *n* Viertelfinale *nt*; **~ly** *adj* vierteljährlich

quartet(te) [kwɔː'tet] *n* Quartett *nt*

quartz [kwɔːts] *n* Quarz *m*

quash [kwɒʃ] *vt* (*verdict*) aufheben

quaver ['kweɪvər] *vi* (*tremble*) zittern

quay [kiː] *n* Kai *m*

queasy ['kwiːzɪ] *adj* übel

queen [kwiːn] *n* Königin *f*; **~ mother** *n* Königinmutter *f*

queer [kwɪər] *adj* seltsam ♦ *n* (*inf: ho-*

mosexual) Schwule(r) *m*

quell [kwɛl] *vt* unterdrücken

quench [kwɛntʃ] *vt (thirst)* löschen

querulous ['kwɛrʊləs] *adj* nörglerisch

query ['kwɪərɪ] *n (question)* (An)frage *f*; *(question mark)* Fragezeichen *nt* ♦ *vt* in Zweifel ziehen, infrage *or* in Frage stellen

quest [kwɛst] *n* Suche *f*

question ['kwɛstʃən] *n* Frage *f* ♦ *vt (ask)* (be)fragen; *(suspect)* verhören; *(doubt)* infrage *or* in Frage stellen, bezweifeln; **beyond ~** ohne Frage; **out of the ~** ausgeschlossen; **~able** *adj* zweifelhaft; **~ mark** *n* Fragezeichen *nt*

questionnaire [kwɛstʃə'nɛəʳ] *n* Fragebogen *m*

queue [kjuː] *(BRIT) n* Schlange *f* ♦ *vi (also: ~ up)* Schlange stehen

quibble ['kwɪbl] *vi* kleinlich sein

quick [kwɪk] *adj* schnell ♦ *n (of nail)* Nagelhaut *f*; **be ~!** mach schnell!; **cut to the ~** *(fig)* tief getroffen; **~en** *vt (hasten)* beschleunigen ♦ *vi* sich beschleunigen; **~ly** *adv* schnell; **~sand** *n* Treibsand *m*; **~witted** *adj* schlagfertig

quid [kwɪd] *(BRIT: inf) n* Pfund *nt*

quiet ['kwaɪət] *adj (without noise)* leise; *(peaceful, calm)* still, ruhig ♦ *n* Stille *f*, Ruhe *f* ♦ *vt, vi (US)* = **quieten**; **keep ~!** sei still!; **~en** *vi (also: ~en down)* ruhig werden ♦ *vt (also: ~ down)* beruhigen; **~ly** *adv* leise, ruhig; **~ness** *n* Ruhe *f*, Stille *f*

quilt [kwɪlt] *n (continental or US)* Steppdecke *f*

quin [kwɪn] *n abbr* = **quintuplet**

quintuplets [kwɪn'tjuːplɪts] *npl* Fünflinge *pl*

quip [kwɪp] *n* witzige Bemerkung *f*

quirk [kwɜːk] *n (oddity)* Eigenart *f*

quit [kwɪt] *(pt, pp* quit *or* quitted) *vt* verlassen ♦ *vi* aufhören

quite [kwaɪt] *adv (completely)* ganz, völlig; *(fairly)* ziemlich; **~ a few of** them ziemlich viele von ihnen; **~ (so)!** richtig!

quits [kwɪts] *adj* quitt; **let's call it ~**

lassen wirs gut sein

quiver ['kwɪvəʳ] *vi* zittern ♦ *n (for arrows)* Köcher *m*

quiz [kwɪz] *n (competition)* Quiz *nt* ♦ *vt* prüfen; **~zical** *adj* fragend

quota ['kwəʊtə] *n* Anteil *m*; *(COMM)* Quote *f*

quotation [kwəʊ'teɪʃən] *n* Zitat *nt*; *(price)* Kostenvoranschlag *m*; **~ marks** *npl* Anführungszeichen *pl*

quote [kwəʊt] *n* = **quotation** ♦ *vi (from book)* zitieren; *(price)* angeben

R, r

rabbi ['ræbaɪ] *n* Rabbiner *m*; *(title)* Rabbi *m*

rabbit ['ræbɪt] *n* Kaninchen *nt*; **~ hole** *n* Kaninchenbau *m*; **~ hutch** *n* Kaninchenstall *m*

rabble ['ræbl] *n* Pöbel *m*

rabies ['reɪbiːz] *n* Tollwut *f*

RAC *(BRIT) n abbr* = **Royal Automobile Club**

raccoon [rə'kuːn] *n* Waschbär *m*

race [reɪs] *n (species)* Rasse *f*; *(competition)* Rennen *nt*; *(on foot)* Rennen *nt*, Wettlauf *m*; *(rush)* Hetze *f* ♦ *vt* um die Wette laufen mit; *(horses)* laufen lassen ♦ *vi (run)* rennen; *(in contest)* an Rennen teilnehmen; **~ car** *(US) n* = **racing car**; **~ car driver** *(US) n* = **racing driver**; **~course** *n (for horses)* Rennbahn *f*; **~horse** *n* Rennpferd *nt*; **~r** *n (person)* Rennfahrer(in) *m(f)*; *(car)* Rennwagen *m*; **~track** *n (for cars etc)* Rennstrecke *f*

racial ['reɪʃl] *adj* Rassen-

racing ['reɪsɪŋ] *n* Rennen *nt*; **~ car** *(BRIT) n* Rennwagen *m*; **~ driver** *(BRIT) n* Rennfahrer *m*

racism ['reɪsɪzəm] *n* Rassismus *m*; **racist** ['reɪsɪst] *n* Rassist *m* ♦ *adj* rassistisch

rack [ræk] *n* Ständer *m*, Gestell *nt* ♦ *vt*

plagen; **to go to ~ and ruin** verfallen; **to ~ one's brains** sich auf den Kopf zerbrechen

racket ['rækɪt] n (din) Krach m; (scheme) (Schwindel)geschäft nt; (TENNIS) (Tennis)schläger m

racquet ['rækɪt] n (Tennis)schläger m

racy ['reɪsɪ] adj gewagt; (style) spritzig

radar ['reɪdɑː] n Radar nt or m

radial ['reɪdɪəl] adj (also: US: ~-ply) radial

radiant ['reɪdɪənt] adj strahlend; (giving out rays) Strahlungs-

radiate ['reɪdɪeɪt] vi ausstrahlen; (roads, lines) strahlenförmig wegführen ♦ vt ausstrahlen; **radiation** [reɪdɪ'eɪʃən] n (Aus)strahlung f

radiator ['reɪdɪeɪtə] n (for heating) Heizkörper m; (AUT) Kühler m

radical ['rædɪkl] adj radikal

radii ['reɪdɪaɪ] npl of **radius**

radio ['reɪdɪəʊ] n Rundfunk m, Radio nt; (set) Radio nt, Radioapparat m; **on the ~** im Radio; **~active** ['reɪdɪəʊ'æktɪv] adj radioaktiv; **~ cassette** n Radiorekorder m; **~-controlled** adj ferngesteuert; **~logy** [reɪdɪ'ɒlədʒɪ] n Strahlenkunde f; **~ station** n Rundfunkstation f; **~therapy** ['reɪdɪəʊ'θerəpɪ] n Röntgentherapie f

radish ['rædɪʃ] n (big) Rettich m; (small) Radieschen nt

radius ['reɪdɪəs] n (pl **radii**) n Radius m; (area) Umkreis m

RAF n abbr = **Royal Air Force**

raffle ['ræfl] n Verlosung f, Tombola f ♦ vt verlosen

raft [rɑːft] n Floß nt

rafter ['rɑːftə] n Dachsparren m

rag [ræg] n (cloth) Lumpen m, Lappen m; (inf: newspaper) Käseblatt nt; (UNIV: for charity) studentische Sammelaktion f ♦ vt (BRIT) auf den Arm nehmen; ~ npl (cloth) Lumpen pl; ~ **doll** n Flickenpuppe f

rage [reɪdʒ] n Wut f; (fashion) große Mode f ♦ vi wüten, toben

ragged ['rægɪd] adj (edge) gezackt; (clothes) zerlumpt

raid [reɪd] n Überfall m; (MIL) Angriff m; (by police) Razzia f ♦ vt überfallen

rail [reɪl] n (also RAIL) Schiene f; (on stair) Geländer nt; (of ship) Reling f; ~s npl (RAIL) Geleise pl; **by ~** per Bahn; **~ing(s)** n(pl) Geländer nt; **~road** (US) n Eisenbahn f; **~way** (BRIT) n Eisenbahn f; **~way line** (BRIT) n (Eisen)bahnlinie f; (track) Gleis nt; **~wayman** (irreg; BRIT) n Eisenbahner m; **~way station** (BRIT) n Bahnhof m

rain [reɪn] n Regen m ♦ vt, vi regnen; **in the ~** im Regen; **it's ~ing** es regnet; **~bow** n Regenbogen m; **~coat** n Regenmantel m; **~drop** n Regentropfen m; **~fall** n Niederschlag m; **~forest** n Regenwald m; **~y** adj (region, season) Regen-; (day) regnerisch, verregnet

raise [reɪz] n (esp US: increase) (Gehalts)erhöhung f ♦ vt (lift) (hoch)heben; (increase) erhöhen; (question) aufwerfen; (doubts) äußern; (funds) beschaffen; (family) großziehen; (livestock) züchten; **to ~ one's voice** die Stimme erheben

raisin ['reɪzn] n Rosine f

rake [reɪk] n Rechen m, Harke f; (person) Wüstling m ♦ vt rechen, harken; (search) durchsuchen

rally ['rælɪ] n (POL etc) Kundgebung f; (AUT) Rallye f ♦ vt (MIL) sammeln ♦ vi Kräfte sammeln; **~ round** vt fus (sich) scharen um; (help) zu Hilfe kommen +dat ♦ vi zu Hilfe kommen

RAM [ræm] n abbr (= random access memory) RAM m

ram [ræm] n Widder m ♦ vt (hit) rammen; (stuff) (hinein)stopfen

ramble ['ræmbl] n Wanderung f ♦ vi (talk) schwafeln; **~r** n Wanderer m; **rambling** adj (speech) weitschweifig; (town) ausgedehnt

ramp [ræmp] n Rampe f; **on/off ~** (US: AUT) Ein-/Ausfahrt f

rampage [ræm'peɪdʒ] n: **to be on the**

rampant ['ræmpənt] *adj* wild wuchernd

rampart ['ræmpɑ:t] *n* (Schutz)wall *m*

ram raid *n* Raubüberfall, *bei dem eine Geschäftsfront mit einem Fahrzeug gerammt wird*

ramshackle ['ræmʃækl] *adj* baufällig

ran [ræn] *pt of* **run**

ranch [rɑ:ntʃ] *n* Ranch *f*

rancid ['rænsid] *adj* ranzig

rancour ['ræŋkə*] (*US* **rancor**) *n* Verbitterung *f*, Groll *m*

random ['rændəm] *adj* ziellos, wahllos ♦ *n*: **at ~** aufs Geratewohl; **~ access** *n* (*COMPUT*) wahlfreie(r) Zugriff *m*

randy ['rændɪ] (*BRIT: inf*) *adj* geil, scharf

rang [ræŋ] *pt of* **ring**

range [reɪndʒ] *n* Reihe *f*; (*of mountains*) Kette *f*; (*COMM*) Sortiment *nt*; (*reach*) (Reich)weite *f*; (*of gun*) Schussweite *f*; (*for shooting practice*) Schießplatz *m*; (*stove*) (großer) Herd *m* ♦ *vt* (*set in row*) anordnen, aufstellen; (*roam*) durchstreifen ♦ *vi*: **to ~ over** (*wander*) umherstreifen in +*dat*; (*extend*) sich erstrecken auf +*acc*; **a ~** (*of selection*) eine (große) Auswahl an +*dat*; **prices ranging from £5 to £10** Preise, die sich zwischen £5 und £10 bewegen; **~r** ['reɪndʒə*] *n* Förster *m*

rank [ræŋk] *n* (*row*) Reihe *f*; (*BRIT: also*: **taxi ~**) (Taxi)stand *m*; (*MIL*) Rang *m*; (*social position*) Stand *m* ♦ *vi* (*have ~*): **to ~ among** gehören zu ♦ *adj* (*strong-smelling*) stinkend; (*extreme*) kraß; **the ~ and file** (*fig*) die breite Masse

rankle ['ræŋkl] *vi* nagen

ransack ['rænsæk] *vt* (*plunder*) plündern; (*search*) durchwühlen

ransom ['rænsəm] *n* Lösegeld *nt*; **to hold sb to ~** jdn gegen Lösegeld festhalten

rant [rænt] *vi* hochtrabend reden

rap [ræp] *n* Schlag *m*; (*music*) Rap *m* ♦ *vt* klopfen

rape [reɪp] *n* Vergewaltigung *f*; (*BOT*)

Raps *m* ♦ *vt* vergewaltigen; **~(seed) oil** *n* Rapsöl *nt*

rapid ['ræpɪd] *adj* rasch, schnell; **~ity** [rə'pɪdɪtɪ] *n* Schnelligkeit *f*; **~s** *npl* Stromschnellen *pl*

rapist ['reɪpɪst] *n* Vergewaltiger *m*

rapport [ræ'pɔ:r] *n* gute(s) Verhältnis *nt*

rapture ['ræptʃə*] *n* Entzücken *nt*; **rapturous** ['ræptʃərəs] *adj* (*applause*) stürmisch; (*expression*) verzückt

rare [reə*] *adj* selten, rar; (*underdone*) nicht durchgebraten; **~ly** ['reəlɪ] *adv* selten

raring ['reərɪŋ] *adj*: **to be ~ to go** (*inf*) es kaum erwarten können, bis es losgeht

rarity ['reərɪtɪ] *n* Seltenheit *f*

rascal ['rɑ:skl] *n* Schuft *m*

rash [ræʃ] *adj* übereilt; (*reckless*) unbesonnen ♦ *n* (Haut)ausschlag *m*

rasher ['ræʃə*] *n* Speckscheibe *f*

raspberry ['rɑ:zbərɪ] *n* Himbeere *f*

rasping ['rɑ:spɪŋ] *adj* (*noise*) kratzend; (*voice*) krächzend

rat [ræt] *n* (*animal*) Ratte *f*; (*person*) Halunke *m*

rate [reɪt] *n* (*proportion*) Rate *f*; (*price*) Tarif *m*; (*speed*) Tempo *nt* ♦ *vt* (*ein*)schätzen; **~s** *npl* (*BRIT: tax*) Grundsteuer *f*; **to ~ as** für etw halten; **~able** ['reɪtəbl] *n* Einheitswert *m* (*als Bemessungsgrundlage*); **~payer** (*BRIT*) *n* Steuerzahler(in) *m(f)*

rather ['rɑ:ðə*] *adv* (*in preference*) lieber, eher; (*to some extent*) ziemlich; **I would** *or* **I'd ~ go** ich würde lieber gehen; **it's ~ expensive** (*quite*) es ist ziemlich teuer; (*too*) es ist etwas zu teuer; **there's ~ a lot** es ist ziemlich viel

ratify ['rætɪfaɪ] *vt* (*POL*) ratifizieren

rating ['reɪtɪŋ] *n* Klasse *f*

ratio ['reɪʃɪəʊ] *n* Verhältnis *nt*; **in the ~ of 100 to 1** im Verhältnis 100 zu 1

ration ['ræʃən] *n* (*usu pl*) Ration *f* ♦ *vt* rationieren

rational ['ræʃənl] *adj* rational

rationale [ræʃəˈnɑːl] *n* Grundprinzip *nt*

rationalize [ˈræʃnəlaɪz] *vt* rationalisieren

rat race *n* Konkurrenzkampf *m*

rattle [ˈrætl] *n* (*sound*) Rasseln *nt*; (*toy*) Rassel *f* ♦ *vi* rattein, klappern ♦ *vt* rasseln mit; **~snake** *n* Klapperschlange *f*

raucous [ˈrɔːkəs] *adj* heiser, rau

rave [reɪv] *vi* (*talk wildly*) fantasieren; (*rage*) toben ♦ *n* (BRIT: inf: *party*) Rave *m*, Fete *f*

raven [ˈreɪvən] *n* Rabe *m*

ravenous [ˈrævənəs] *adj* heißhungrig

ravine [rəˈviːn] *n* Schlucht *f*

raving [ˈreɪvɪŋ] *adj*: **~ lunatic** völlig Wahnsinnige(r) *mf*

ravishing [ˈrævɪʃɪŋ] *adj* atemberaubend

raw [rɔː] *adj* roh; (*tender*) wund (gerieben); (*inexperienced*) unerfahren; **to get a ~ deal** (*inf*) schlecht wegkommen; **~ material** *n* Rohmaterial *nt*

ray [reɪ] *n* (*of light*) Strahl *m*; **~ of hope** Hoffnungsschimmer *m*

raze [reɪz] *vt* (*also*: **~ to the ground**) dem Erdboden gleichmachen

razor [ˈreɪzəˀ] *n* Rasierapparat *m*; **~ blade** *n* Rasierklinge *f*

Rd *abbr* = **road**

RE (BRIT: SCH) *abbr* (= *religious education*) Religionsunterricht *m*

re [riː] *prep* (COMM) betreffs +gen

reach [riːtʃ] *n* Reichweite *f*; (*of river*) Strecke *f* ♦ *vt* (*arrive at*) erreichen; (*give*) reichen ♦ *vi* (*stretch*) sich erstrecken; **within ~** (*shops* etc) in erreichbarer Weite *or* Entfernung; **out of ~** außer Reichweite; **to ~ for** (*try to get*) langen nach; **~ out** *vi* die Hand ausstrecken; **to ~ out for sth** nach etw greifen

react [riːˈækt] *vi* reagieren; **~ion** [riːˈækʃən] *n* Reaktion *f*; **~or** [riːˈæktəˀ] *n* Reaktor *m*

read¹ [red] *pt, pp* of **read²**

read² [riːd] (*pt, pp* **read**) *vt, vi* lesen; (*aloud*) vorlesen; **~ out** *vt* vorlesen;

~able *adj* leserlich; (*worth ~ing*) lesenswert; **~er** *n* (*person*) Leser(in) *m(f)*; **~ership** *n* Leserschaft *f*

readily [ˈredɪlɪ] *adv* (*willingly*) bereitwillig; (*easily*) prompt

readiness [ˈredɪnɪs] *n* (*willingness*) Bereitwilligkeit *f*; (*being ready*) Bereitschaft *f*; **in ~** (*prepared*) bereit

reading [ˈriːdɪŋ] *n* Lesen *nt*

readjust [riːəˈdʒʌst] *vt* neu einstellen ♦ *vi* (*person*): **to ~** to sich wieder anpassen an +acc

ready [ˈredɪ] *adj* (*prepared, willing*) bereit ♦ *adv*: **~-cooked** vorgekocht ♦ *n*: **at the ~** bereit; **~-made** *adj* gebrauchsfertig, Fertig-; (*clothes*) Konfektions-; **~ money** *n* Bargeld *nt*; **~-to-wear** *adj* Konfektions-

real [rɪəl] *adj* wirklich; (*actual*) eigentlich; (*not fake*) echt; **in ~ terms** effektiv; **~ estate** *n* Grundbesitz *m*; **~istic** [rɪəˈlɪstɪk] *adj* realistisch

reality [riːˈælɪtɪ] *n* Wirklichkeit *f*, Realität *f*; **in ~** in Wirklichkeit

realization [rɪəlaɪˈzeɪʃən] *n* (*understanding*) Erkenntnis *f*; (*fulfilment*) Verwirklichung *f*

realize [ˈrɪəlaɪz] *vt* (*understand*) begreifen; (*make real*) verwirklichen; **I didn't ~** ... ich wusste nicht, ...

really [ˈrɪəlɪ] *adv* wirklich; **~?** (*indicating interest*) tatsächlich?; (*expressing surprise*) wirklich?

realm [relm] *n* Reich *nt*

realtor [ˈrɪəltɔːˀ] (US) *n* Grundstücksmakler(in) *m(f)*

reap [riːp] *vt* ernten

reappear [riːəˈpɪəˀ] *vi* wieder erscheinen

rear [rɪəˀ] *adj* hintere(r, s), Rück- ♦ *n* Rückseite *f*; (*last part*) Schluss *m* ♦ *vt* (*bring up*) aufziehen ♦ *vi* (*horse*) sich aufbäumen; **~guard** *n* Nachhut *f*

rearmament [riːˈɑːməmənt] *n* Wiederaufrüstung *f*

rearrange [riːəˈreɪndʒ] *vt* umordnen

rear-view mirror ['rɪəvjuː-] n Rückspiegel m

reason ['riːzn] n (cause) Grund m; (ability to think) Verstand m; (sensible thoughts) Vernunft f ♦ vi (think) denken; (use arguments) argumentieren; **it stands to ~ that** es ist logisch, dass; **to ~ with sb** mit jdm diskutieren; **~able** adj vernünftig; **~ably** adv vernünftig; (fairly) ziemlich; **~ed** adj (argument) durchdacht; **~ing** n Urteilen nt; (argumentation) Beweisführung f

reassurance [riːəˈʃuərəns] n Beruhigung f; (confirmation) Bestätigung f; **reassure** [riːəˈʃuə] vt beruhigen; **to reassure sb of sth** jdm etw versichern

rebate ['riːbeɪt] n Rückzahlung f

rebel [n 'rebl, vb rɪ'bel] n Rebell m ♦ vi rebellieren; **~lion** [rɪ'beljən] n Rebellion f, Aufstand m; **~lious** [rɪ'beljəs] adj rebellisch

rebirth [riː'bəːθ] n Wiedergeburt f

rebound [vb rɪ'baund, n 'riːbaund] vi zurückprallen ♦ n Rückprall m

rebuff [rɪ'bʌf] n Abfuhr f ♦ vt abblitzen lassen

rebuild [riː'bɪld] (irreg) vt wieder aufbauen; (fig) wieder herstellen

rebuke [rɪ'bjuːk] n Tadel m ♦ vt tadeln, rügen

rebut [rɪ'bʌt] vt widerlegen

recall [vb rɪ'kɔːl, n 'riːkɔl] vt (call back) zurückrufen; (remember) sich erinnern an +acc ♦ n Rückruf m

recap ['riːkæp] vt, vi wiederholen

rec'd abbr (= received) Eing.

recede [rɪ'siːd] vi zurückweichen; **receding** adj: **receding hairline** Stirnglatze f

receipt [rɪ'siːt] n (document) Quittung f; (receiving) Empfang m; **~s** npl (ECON) Einnahmen pl

receive [rɪ'siːv] vt erhalten; (visitors etc) empfangen; **~r** n (TEL) Hörer m

recent ['riːsnt] adj vor kurzem (geschehen), neuerlich; (modern) neu; **~ly** adv kürzlich, neulich

receptacle [rɪ'septɪkl] n Behälter m

reception [rɪ'sepʃən] n Empfang m; **~ desk** n Empfang m; (in hotel) Rezeption f; **~ist** n (in hotel) Empfangschef m, Empfangsdame f; (MED) Sprechstundenhilfe f

receptive [rɪ'septɪv] adj aufnahmebereit

recess [rɪ'ses] n (break) Ferien pl; (hollow) Nische f

recession [rɪ'seʃən] n Rezession f

recharge [riː'tʃɑːdʒ] vt (battery) aufladen

recipe ['resɪpɪ] n Rezept nt

recipient [rɪ'sɪpɪənt] n Empfänger m

reciprocal [rɪ'sɪprəkl] adj gegenseitig; (mutual) wechselseitig

recital [rɪ'saɪtl] n Vortrag m

recite [rɪ'saɪt] vt vortragen, aufsagen

reckless ['rekləs] adj leichtsinnig; (driving) fahrlässig

reckon ['rekən] vt (count) rechnen, errechnen; (estimate) schätzen; (think): **I ~ that ...** ich nehme an, dass ...; **~ on** vt fus rechnen mit; **~ing** n (calculation) Rechnen nt

reclaim [rɪ'kleɪm] vt (expenses) zurückverlangen; (land): **to ~ (from sth)** (etw dat) gewinnen; **reclamation** [reklə'meɪʃən] n (of land) Gewinnung f

recline [rɪ'klaɪn] vi sich zurücklehnen; **reclining** adj Liege-

recluse [rɪ'kluːs] n Einsiedler m

recognition [rekəg'nɪʃən] n (recognizing) Erkennen nt; (acknowledgement) Anerkennung f; **transformed beyond ~** völlig verändert

recognizable ['rekəgnaɪzəbl] adj erkennbar

recognize ['rekəgnaɪz] vt erkennen; (POL approve) anerkennen; **to ~ as** anerkennen als; **to ~ by** erkennen an +dat

recoil [rɪ'kɔɪl] vi (in horror) zurückschrecken; (rebound) zurückprallen; (person): **to ~ from doing sth** davor zurückschrecken, etw zu tun

recollect [rɛkə'lɛkt] vt sich erinnern an +acc; **~ion** [rɛkə'lɛkʃən] n Erinnerung f

recommend [rɛkə'mɛnd] vt empfehlen; **~ation** [rɛkəmɛn'deɪʃən] n Empfehlung f

recompense ['rɛkəmpɛns] n (compensation) Entschädigung f; (reward) Belohnung f ♦ vt entschädigen; belohnen

reconcile ['rɛkənsaɪl] vt (facts) vereinbaren; (people) versöhnen; **to ~ o.s. to sth** sich mit etw abfinden; **reconciliation** [rɛkənsɪlɪ'eɪʃən] n Versöhnung f

recondition [ri:kən'dɪʃən] vt (machine) generalüberholen

reconnoitre [rɛkə'nɔɪtər] (US **reconnoiter**) vt erkunden ♦ vi aufklären

reconsider [ri:kən'sɪdər] vt von neuem erwägen, noch einmal überdenken ♦ vi es noch einmal überdenken

reconstruct [ri:kən'strʌkt] vt wieder aufbauen; (crime) rekonstruieren

record [n 'rɛkɔːd, vb rɪ'kɔːd] n Aufzeichnung f; (MUS) Schallplatte f; (best performance) Rekord m ♦ vt aufzeichnen; (music etc) aufnehmen; **off the ~** vertraulich, im Vertrauen; **in ~ time** in Rekordzeit; **~ card** n (in file) Karteikarte f; **~ed delivery** (BRIT) n (POST) Einschreiben nt; **~er** n (TECH) Registriergerät nt; (MUS) Blockflöte f; **~ holder** n (SPORT) Rekordinhaber m; **~ing** n (MUS) Aufnahme f; **~ player** n Plattenspieler m

recount [rɪ'kaʊnt] vt (tell) berichten

re-count ['ri:kaʊnt] n Nachzählung f

recoup [rɪ'ku:p] vt: **to ~ one's losses** seinen Verlust wieder gutmachen

recourse [rɪ'kɔːs] n: **to have ~ to** Zuflucht nehmen zu or bei

recover [rɪ'kʌvər] vt (get back) zurückerhalten ♦ vi sich erholen

re-cover [ri:'kʌvər] vt (quilt etc) neu überziehen

recovery [rɪ'kʌvərɪ] n Wiedererlangung f; (of health) Erholung f

recreate [ri:krɪ'eɪt] vt wieder herstellen

recreation [rɛkrɪ'eɪʃən] n Erholung f; **~al** adj Erholungs-; **~al drug** n Freizeitdroge f

recrimination [rɪkrɪmɪ'neɪʃən] n Gegenbeschuldigung f

recruit [rɪ'kruːt] n Rekrut m ♦ vt rekrutieren; **~ment** n Rekrutierung f

rectangle ['rɛktæŋgl] n Rechteck nt; **rectangular** [rɛk'tæŋgjʊlər] adj rechteckig, rechtwinklig

rectify ['rɛktɪfaɪ] vt berichtigen

rector ['rɛktər] n (REL) Pfarrer m; (SCH) Direktor(in) m(f); **~y** ['rɛktərɪ] n Pfarrhaus nt

recuperate [rɪ'kjuːpəreɪt] vi sich erholen

recur [rɪ'kɜːr] vi sich wiederholen; **~rence** n Wiederholung f; **~rent** adj wiederkehrend

recycle [ri:'saɪkl] vt wieder verwerten, wieder aufbereiten; **recycling** n Recycling nt

red [rɛd] n Rot nt; (POL) Rote(r) m ♦ adj rot; **in the ~** in den roten Zahlen; **~ carpet treatment** n Sonderbehandlung f, große(r) Bahnhof m; **R~ Cross** n Rote(s) Kreuz nt; **~currant** n rote Johannisbeere f; **~den** vi sich röten; (blush) erröten ♦ vt röten; **~dish** adj rötlich

redecorate [ri:'dɛkəreɪt] vt neu tapezieren, neu streichen

redeem [rɪ'diːm] vt (COMM) einlösen; (save) retten; **~ing** adj: **~ing feature** versöhnende(s) Moment nt

redeploy [ri:dɪ'plɔɪ] vt (resources) umverteilen

red: **~-haired** [rɛd'hɛəd] adj rothaarig; **~-handed** [rɛd'hændɪd] adv: **to be caught ~-handed** auf frischer Tat ertappt werden; **~head** ['rɛdhɛd] n Rothaarige(r) mf; **~ herring** n Ablenkungsmanöver nt; **~-hot** [rɛd'hɔt] adj rot glühend

redirect [ri:daɪ'rɛkt] vt umleiten

red light n: **to go through a ~** (AUT) bei Rot über die Ampel fahren; **red-**

light district n Strichviertel nt

redo [riː'duː] (irreg: like **do**) vt nochmals machen

redolent ['redəlnt] adj: **~ of** (fig) erinnernd an +acc

redouble [riː'dʌbl] vt: **to ~ one's efforts** seine Anstrengungen verdoppeln

redress [rɪ'dres] vt wieder gutmachen

red: R~ Sea n: **the R~ Sea** das Rote Meer; **~skin** n Rothaut f; **~ tape** n Bürokratismus m

reduce [rɪ'djuːs] vt (speed, temperature) vermindern; (photo) verkleinern; **"~ speed now"** "langsam"; **to ~ the price (to)** den Preis herabsetzen (auf +acc); **at a ~d price** zum ermäßigten Preis

reduction [rɪ'dʌkʃən] n Verminderung f; Verkleinerung f; Herabsetzung f; (amount of money) Nachlass m

redundancy [rɪ'dʌndənsɪ] n Überflüssigkeit f; (of workers) Entlassung f

redundant [rɪ'dʌndnt] adj überflüssig; (workers) ohne Arbeitsplatz; **to be made ~** arbeitslos werden

reed [riːd] n Schilf nt; (MUS) Rohrblatt nt

reef [riːf] n Riff nt

reek [riːk] vi: **to ~ (of)** stinken (nach)

reel [riːl] n Spule f, Rolle f ♦ vt (also: **~ in**) wickeln, spulen ♦ vi (stagger) taumeln

ref [ref] (inf) n abbr (= referee) Schiri m

refectory [rɪ'fektərɪ] n (UNIV) Mensa f; (SCH) Speisesaal m; (ECCL) Refektorium nt

refer [rɪ'fɜː] vt: **to ~ sb to sb/sth** jdn an jdn/etw verweisen ♦ vi: **to ~ to** (allude to) nachschlagen in +dat; (mention) sich beziehen auf +acc

referee [refə'riː] n Schiedsrichter m; (BRIT: for job) Referenz f ♦ vt schiedsrichtern

reference ['refrəns] n (for job) Referenz f; (in book) Verweis m; (number, code) Aktenzeichen nt; (allusion): **~ (to)** Anspielung (auf +acc); **with ~ to** in Bezug auf +acc; **~ book** n Nachschlagewerk nt; **~ number** n Aktenzeichen nt

referenda [refə'rendə] npl of **referendum**

referendum [refə'rendəm] (pl **-da**) n Volksabstimmung f

refill [vb riː'fɪl, n 'riːfɪl] vt nachfüllen ♦ n (for pen) Ersatzmine f

refine [rɪ'faɪn] vt (purify) raffinieren; **~d** adj kultiviert; **~ment** n Kultiviertheit f; **~ry** n Raffinerie f

reflect [rɪ'flekt] vt (light) reflektieren; (fig) (wider)spiegeln ♦ vi (meditate): **to ~ (on)** nachdenken (über +acc); **it ~s badly/well on him** das stellt ihn in ein schlechtes/gutes Licht; **~ion** [rɪ'flekʃən] n Reflexion f; (image) Spiegelbild nt; (thought) Überlegung f; **on ~ion** wenn man sich dat das recht überlegt

reflex [rɪ'fleks] adj Reflex- ♦ n Reflex m; **~ive** [rɪ'fleksɪv] adj reflexiv

reform [rɪ'fɔːm] n Reform f ♦ vt (person) bessern; **~atory** (US) n Besserungsanstalt f

refrain [rɪ'freɪn] vi: **to ~ from** unterlassen ♦ n Refrain m

refresh [rɪ'freʃ] vt erfrischen; **~er course** (BRIT) n Wiederholungskurs m; **~ing** adj erfrischend; **~ments** npl Erfrischungen pl

refrigeration [rɪfrɪdʒə'reɪʃən] n Kühlung f

refrigerator [rɪ'frɪdʒəreɪtə] n Kühlschrank m

refuel [riː'fjuəl] vt, vi auftanken

refuge ['refjuːdʒ] n Zuflucht f; **to take ~ in** sich flüchten in +acc; **~e** [refju'dʒiː] n Flüchtling m

refund [n 'riːfʌnd, vb rɪ'fʌnd] n Rückvergütung f ♦ vt zurückerstatten

refurbish [riː'fɜːbɪʃ] vt aufpolieren

refusal [rɪ'fjuːzl] n (Ver)weigerung f; **first ~** Vorkaufsrecht nt

refuse[^1] [rɪ'fjuːz] vt abschlagen ♦ vi sich weigern

refuse² ['refju:s] *n* Abfall *m*, Müll *m*; **~ collection** *n* Müllabfuhr *f*

refute [rɪ'fju:t] *vt* widerlegen

regain [rɪ'geɪn] *vt* wiedergewinnen; *(consciousness)* wiedererlangen

regal ['ri:gl] *adj* königlich

regalia [rɪ'geɪlɪə] *npl* Insignien *pl*

regard [rɪ'gɑ:d] *n* Achtung *f* ♦ *vt* ansehen; **to send one's ~s to sb** jdn grüßen lassen; **"with kindest ~s"** "mit freundlichen Grüßen"; **as ~s** or **with ~ to** bezüglich +gen, in Bezug auf +acc; **~less** *adj*: **~less of** ohne Rücksicht auf +acc ♦ *adv* trotzdem

regenerate [rɪ'dʒenəreɪt] *vt* erneuern

régime [reɪ'ʒi:m] *n* Regime *nt*

regiment [*n* 'redʒɪmənt, *vb* 'redʒɪment] *n* Regiment *nt* ♦ *vt* (fig) reglementieren; **~al** [redʒɪ'mentl] *adj* Regiments-

region ['ri:dʒən] *n* Region *f*; **in the ~ of** (fig) so um; **~al** *adj* örtlich, regional

register ['redʒɪstə*] *n* Register *nt* ♦ *vt* (list) registrieren; (emotion) zeigen; (write down) eintragen ♦ *vi* (at hotel) sich eintragen; (with police) sich melden; (make impression) wirken, ankommen; **~ed** (BRIT) *adj* (letter) Einschreibe-, eingeschrieben; **~ed trademark** *n* eingetragene(s) Warenzeichen *nt*

registrar ['redʒɪstrɑ:*] *n* Standesbeamte(r) *m*

registration [redʒɪs'treɪʃən] *n* (act) Registrierung *f*; (AUT: also: **~ number**) polizeiliche(s) Kennzeichen *nt*

registry ['redʒɪstrɪ] *n* Sekretariat *nt*; **~ office** (BRIT) *n* Standesamt *nt*; **to get married in a ~ office** standesamtlich heiraten

regret [rɪ'gret] *n* Bedauern *nt* ♦ *vt* bedauern; **~fully** *adv* mit Bedauern, ungern; **~table** *adj* bedauerlich

regroup [ri:'gru:p] *vt* umgruppieren ♦ *vi* sich umgruppieren

regular ['regjulə*] *adj* regelmäßig; (usual) üblich; (inf) regelrecht ♦ *n* (client etc) Stammkunde *m*; **~ity**

[regju'lærɪtɪ**]** *n* Regelmäßigkeit *f*; **~ly** *adv* regelmäßig

regulate ['regjuleɪt] *vt* regeln, regulieren; **regulation** [regju'leɪʃən] *n* (rule) Vorschrift *f*; (control) Regulierung *f*

rehabilitation ['ri:əbɪlɪ'teɪʃən] *n* (of criminal) Resozialisierung *f*

rehearsal [rɪ'hə:səl] *n* Probe *f*

rehearse [rɪ'hə:s] *vt* proben

reign [reɪn] *n* Herrschaft *f* ♦ *vi* herrschen

reimburse [ri:ɪm'bə:s] *vt*: **to ~ sb for sth** jdn für etw entschädigen, jdm etw zurückzahlen

rein [reɪn] *n* Zügel *m*

reincarnation [ri:ɪnkɑ:'neɪʃən] *n* Wiedergeburt *f*

reindeer ['reɪndɪə*] *n* Ren *nt*

reinforce [ri:ɪn'fɔ:s] *vt* verstärken; **~d concrete** *n* Stahlbeton *m*; **~ment** *n* Verstärkung *f*; **~ments** *npl* (MIL) Verstärkungstruppen *pl*

reinstate [ri:ɪn'steɪt] *vt* wieder einsetzen

reissue [ri:'ɪʃju:] *vt* neu herausgeben

reiterate [ri:'ɪtəreɪt] *vt* wiederholen

reject [*n* 'ri:dʒekt, *vb* rɪ'dʒekt] *n* (COMM) Ausschuss(artikel) *m* ♦ *vt* ablehnen; **~ion** [rɪ'dʒekʃən] *n* Zurückweisung *f*

rejoice [rɪ'dʒɔɪs] *vi*: **to ~ at** or **over** sich freuen über +acc

rejuvenate [rɪ'dʒu:vəneɪt] *vt* verjüngen

rekindle [ri:'kɪndl] *vt* wieder anfachen

relapse [rɪ'læps] *n* Rückfall *m*

relate [rɪ'leɪt] *vt* (tell) erzählen; (connect) verbinden ♦ *vi*: **to ~** zu zusammenhängen mit; (form relationship) eine Beziehung aufbauen zu; **~d** *adj*: **~d** (to) verwandt (mit); relating *prep*: **relating to** bezüglich +gen; **relation** [rɪ'leɪʃən] *n* Verwandte(r) *mf*; (connection) Beziehung *f*; **relationship** *n* Verhältnis *nt*, Beziehung *f*

relative ['relətɪv] *n* Verwandte(r) *mf* ♦ *adj* relativ; **~ly** *adv* verhältnismäßig

relax [rɪ'læks] *vi* (slacken) sich lockern;

(muscles, person) sich entspannen ♦ *vt (ease)* lockern, entspannen; **~ation** [ri:læk'seɪʃən] *n* Entspannung *f;* **~ed** *adj* entspannt, locker; **~ing** *adj* entspannend

relay [*n* 'ri:leɪ, *vb* rɪ'leɪ] *n (SPORT)* Staffel *f* ♦ *vt (message)* weiterleiten; *(RAD, TV)* übertragen

release [rɪ'li:s] *n (freedom)* Entlassung *f;* *(TECH)* Auslöser *m* ♦ *vt* befreien; *(prisoner)* entlassen; *(report, news)* verlautbaren, bekannt geben

relegate ['relɪgeɪt] *vt (SPORT):* **to be ~d** absteigen

relent [rɪ'lent] *vi* nachgeben; **~less** *adj* unnachgiebig

relevant ['reləvənt] *adj* wichtig, relevant; **~ to** relevant für

reliability [rɪlaɪə'bɪlɪtɪ] *n* Zuverlässigkeit *f*

reliable [rɪ'laɪəbl] *adj* zuverlässig; **reliably** *adv* zuverlässig; **to be reliably informed** that ... aus zuverlässiger Quelle wissen, dass ...

reliance [rɪ'laɪəns] *n:* **~ (on)** Abhängigkeit *f* (von)

relic ['relɪk] *n (from past)* Überbleibsel *nt;* *(REL)* Reliquie *f*

relief [rɪ'li:f] *n* Erleichterung *f;* *(help)* Hilfe *f;* *(person)* Ablösung *f*

relieve [rɪ'li:v] *vt (ease)* erleichtern; *(help)* entlasten; *(person)* ablösen; **to ~ sb of sth** jdm etw abnehmen; **to ~ o.s.** *(euph)* sich erleichtern *(euph)*; **~d** *adj* erleichtert

religion [rɪ'lɪdʒən] *n* Religion *f;* **religious** [rɪ'lɪdʒəs] *adj* religiös

relinquish [rɪ'lɪŋkwɪʃ] *vt* aufgeben

relish ['relɪʃ] *n* Würze *f* ♦ *vt* genießen; **to ~ doing** gern tun

relocate [ri:ləu'keɪt] *vt* verlegen ♦ *vi* umziehen

reluctance [rɪ'lʌktəns] *n* Widerstreben *nt,* Abneigung *f*

reluctant [rɪ'lʌktənt] *adj* widerwillig; **~ly** *adv* ungern

rely [rɪ'laɪ] *vt fus:* **to ~ on** sich verlassen

auf +*acc*

remain [rɪ'meɪn] *vi (be left)* übrig bleiben; *(stay)* bleiben; **~der** *n* Rest *m;* **~ing** *adj* übrig *(geblieben)*; **~s** *npl* Überreste *pl*

remake ['ri:meɪk] *n (CINE)* Neuverfilmung *f*

remand [rɪ'mɑ:nd] *n:* **on ~** in Untersuchungshaft ♦ *vt:* **to ~ in custody** in Untersuchungshaft schicken; **~ home** *(BRIT)* *n* Untersuchungsgefängnis *nt* für Jugendliche

remark [rɪ'mɑ:k] *n* Bemerkung *f* ♦ *vt* bemerken; **~able** *adj* bemerkenswert; **remarkably** *adv* außergewöhnlich

remarry [ri:'mærɪ] *vi* sich wieder verheiraten

remedial [rɪ'mi:dɪəl] *adj* Heil-; *(teaching)* Hilfsschul-

remedy ['remədɪ] *n* Mittel *nt* ♦ *vt (pain)* abhelfen +*dat;* *(trouble)* in Ordnung bringen

remember [rɪ'membə'] *vt* sich erinnern an +*acc;* **remembrance** [rɪ'membrəns] *n* Erinnerung *f;* *(official)* Gedenken *nt;* **R~ Day** *n* ≈ Volkstrauertag *m*

Remembrance Day

Remembrance Day *oder* **Remembrance Sunday** *ist der britische Gedenktag für die Gefallenen der beiden Weltkriege und anderer Konflikte. Er fällt auf einen Sonntag vor oder nach dem 11. November (am 11. November 1918 endete der erste Weltkrieg) und wird mit einer Schweigeminute, Kranzniederlegungen an Kriegerdenkmälern und dem Tragen von Anstecknadeln in Form einer Mohnblume begangen.*

remind [rɪ'maɪnd] *vt:* **to ~ sb to do sth** jdn daran erinnern, etw zu tun; **to ~ sb of sth** jdn an etw *acc* erinnern; **she ~s me of her mother** sie erinnert mich an ihre Mutter; **~er** *n* Mahnung *f*

reminisce [remɪ'nɪs] *vi* in Erinnerungen schwelgen; **~nt** [rɪˈmɪnsnt] adj: **to be ~nt of sth** an etw acc erinnern

remiss [rɪˈmɪs] adj nachlässig

remission [rɪˈmɪʃən] n Nachlass m; (of debt, sentence) Erlass m

remit [rɪˈmɪt] vt (money): **to ~ (to)** überweisen (an +acc); **~tance** n Geldanweisung f

remnant [ˈremnənt] n Rest m; **~s** npl (COMM) Einzelstücke pl

remorse [rɪˈmɔːs] n Gewissensbisse pl; **~ful** adj reumütig; **~less** adj unbarmherzig

remote [rɪˈməʊt] adj abgelegen; (slight) gering; **~ control** n Fernsteuerung f; **~ly** adv entfernt

remould [ˈriːməʊld] (BRIT) n runderneuerte(r) Reifen m

removable [rɪˈmuːvəbl] adj entfernbar

removal [rɪˈmuːvəl] n Beseitigung f; (of furniture) Umzug m; (from office) Entlassung f; **~ van** (BRIT) n Möbelwagen m

remove [rɪˈmuːv] vt beseitigen, entfernen; **~rs** npl Möbelspedition f

remuneration [rɪmjuːnəˈreɪʃən] n Vergütung f, Honorar nt

render [ˈrendər] vt machen; (translate) übersetzen; **~ing** n (MUS) Wiedergabe f

rendezvous [ˈrɒndɪvuː] n (meeting) Rendezvous nt; (place) Treffpunkt m ♦ vi sich treffen

renew [rɪˈnjuː] vt erneuern; (contract, licence) verlängern; (replace) ersetzen; **~able** adj regenerierbar; **~al** n Erneuerung f; Verlängerung f

renounce [rɪˈnaʊns] vt (give up) verzichten auf +acc; (disown) verstoßen

renovate [ˈrenəveɪt] vt renovieren; (building) restaurieren

renown [rɪˈnaʊn] n Ruf m; **~ed** adj namhaft

rent [rent] n Miete f; (for land) Pacht f ♦ vt (hold as tenant) mieten; pachten; (let) vermieten; verpachten; (car etc) mieten; (firm) vermieten; **~al** n Miete f

renunciation [rɪnʌnsɪˈeɪʃən] n: **~ (of)**

Verzicht m (auf +acc)

reorganize [riːˈɔːɡənaɪz] vt umgestalten, reorganisieren

rep [rep] n abbr (COMM) = **representative**; (THEAT) = **repertory**

repair [rɪˈpeər] n Reparatur f ♦ vt reparieren; (damage) wieder gutmachen; **in good/bad ~** in gutem/schlechtem Zustand; **~ kit** n Werkzeugkasten m

repartee [repɑːˈtiː] n Witzeleien pl

repatriate [riːˈpætrɪeɪt] vt in die Heimat zurückschicken

repay [riːˈpeɪ] (irreg) vt zurückzahlen; (reward) vergelten; **~ment** n Rückzahlung f; (fig) Vergeltung f

repeal [rɪˈpiːl] vt aufheben

repeat [rɪˈpiːt] n (RAD, TV) Wiederholung(ssendung) f ♦ vt wiederholen; **~edly** adv wiederholt

repel [rɪˈpel] vt (drive back) zurückschlagen; (disgust) abstoßen; **~lent** adj abstoßend ♦ n: **insect ~lent** Insektenmittel nt

repent [rɪˈpent] vt, vi: **to ~ (of)** bereuen; **~ance** n Reue f

repercussion [riːpəˈkʌʃən] n Auswirkung f; **to have ~s** ein Nachspiel haben

repertory [ˈrepətərɪ] n Repertoire m

repetition [repɪˈtɪʃən] n Wiederholung f

repetitive [rɪˈpetɪtɪv] adj sich wiederholend

replace [rɪˈpleɪs] vt ersetzen; (put back) zurückstellen; **~ment** n Ersatz m

replay [ˈriːpleɪ] n (of match) Wiederholungsspiel nt; (of tape, film) Wiederholung f

replenish [rɪˈplenɪʃ] vt auffüllen, ergänzen

replica [ˈreplɪkə] n Kopie f

reply [rɪˈplaɪ] n Antwort f ♦ vi antworten; **~ coupon** n Antwortschein f

report [rɪˈpɔːt] n Bericht m; (BRIT: SCH) Zeugnis nt ♦ vt (tell) berichten; (give information against) melden; (to police) anzeigen ♦ vi (make ~) Bericht erstatten; (present o.s.): **to ~ (to sb)** sich (bei jdm) melden; **~ card** (US, SCOTTISH) n

Zeugnis nt; **~edly** adv wie verlautet;
~er n Reporter m

reprehensible [reprɪ'hensɪbl] adj tadelnswert

represent [reprɪ'zent] vt darstellen; (speak for) vertreten; **~ation** [reprɪzen'teɪʃən] n Darstellung f; (being ~ed) Vertretung f; **~ations** npl (protest) Vorhaltungen pl; **~ative** n (person) Vertreter m; (US: POL) Abgeordnete(r) mf ♦ adj repräsentativ

repress [rɪ'pres] vt unterdrücken; **~ion** [rɪ'preʃən] n Unterdrückung f

reprieve [rɪ'priːv] n (JUR) Begnadigung f; (fig) Gnadenfrist f ♦ vt (JUR) begnadigen

reprimand ['reprɪmɑːnd] n Verweis m ♦ vt einen Verweis erteilen +dat

reprint [n 'riːprɪnt, vb riː'prɪnt] n Neudruck m ♦ vt wieder abdrucken

reprisal [rɪ'praɪzl] n Vergeltung f

reproach [rɪ'prəʊtʃ] n Vorwurf m ♦ vt Vorwürfe machen +dat; **to ~ sb with sth** jdm etw vorwerfen; **~ful** adj vorwurfsvoll

reproduce [riːprə'djuːs] vt reproduzieren ♦ vi (have offspring) sich vermehren; **reproduction** [riːprə'dʌkʃən] n (ART, PHOT) Reproduktion f; (breeding) Fortpflanzung f; **reproductive** [riːprə'dʌktɪv] adj reproduktiv; (breeding) Fortpflanzungs-

reprove [rɪ'pruːv] vt tadeln

reptile ['reptaɪl] n Reptil nt

republic [rɪ'pʌblɪk] n Republik f

repudiate [rɪ'pjuːdɪeɪt] vt zurückweisen

repugnant [rɪ'pʌgnənt] adj widerlich

repulse [rɪ'pʌls] vt (drive back) zurückschlagen; (reject) abweisen

repulsive [rɪ'pʌlsɪv] adj abstoßend

reputable ['repjʊtəbl] adj angesehen

reputation [repjʊ'teɪʃən] n Ruf m

reputed [rɪ'pjuːtɪd] adj angeblich; **~ly** [rɪ'pjuːtɪdlɪ] adv angeblich

request [rɪ'kwest] n Bitte f ♦ vt (thing) erbitten; **to ~ sth of** or **from sb** jdn

um etw bitten; (formally) jdn um etw ersuchen; **~ stop** (BRIT) n Bedarfshaltestelle f

require [rɪ'kwaɪə*] vt (need) brauchen; (demand) erfordern; **~ment** n (condition) Anforderung f; (need) Bedarf m

requisite ['rekwɪzɪt] adj erforderlich

requisition [rekwɪ'zɪʃən] n Anforderung f ♦ vt beschlagnahmen

rescue ['reskjuː] n Rettung f ♦ vt retten; **~ party** n Rettungsmannschaft f; **~r** n Retter m

research [rɪ'sɜːtʃ] n Forschung f ♦ vi forschen ♦ vt erforschen; **~er** n Forscher m

resemblance [rɪ'zembləns] n Ähnlichkeit f

resemble [rɪ'zembl] vt ähneln +dat

resent [rɪ'zent] vt übel nehmen; **~ful** adj nachtragend, empfindlich; **~ment** n Verstimmung f, Unwille m

reservation [rezə'veɪʃən] n (booking) Reservierung f; (THEAT) Vorbestellung f; (doubt) Vorbehalt m; (land) Reservat nt

reserve [rɪ'zɜːv] n (store) Vorrat m, Reserve f; (manner) Zurückhaltung f; (game) Naturschutzgebiet nt; (SPORT) Ersatzspieler(in) m(f) ♦ vt reservieren; (judgement) sich dat vorbehalten; **~s** npl (MIL) Reserve f; **in ~** in Reserve f; **~d** adj reserviert

reshuffle [riː'ʃʌfl] n (POL): **cabinet ~** Kabinettsumbildung f ♦ vt (POL) umbilden

reside [rɪ'zaɪd] vi wohnen, ansässig sein

residence ['rezɪdəns] n (house) Wohnsitz m; (living) Aufenthalt m; **~ permit** (BRIT) n Aufenthaltserlaubnis f

resident ['rezɪdənt] n (in house) Bewohner m; (in area) Einwohner m ♦ adj wohnhaft, ansässig; **~ial** [rezɪ'denʃəl] adj Wohn-

residue ['rezɪdjuː] n Rest m; (CHEM) Rückstand m; (fig) Bodensatz m

resign [rɪ'zaɪn] vt (office) aufgeben, zurücktreten von ♦ vi (from office) zurücktreten; (*employee*) kündigen; **to be ~ed to sth, to ~ o.s. to sth** sich mit etw abfinden; **~ation** [rɛzɪɡ'neɪʃən] *n* (*from job*) Kündigung *f*; (*POL*) Rücktritt *m*; (*submission*) Resignation *f*; **~ed** *adj* resigniert

resilience [rɪ'zɪlɪəns] *n* Spannkraft *f*; (*of person*) Unverwüstlichkeit *f*; **resilient** [rɪ'zɪlɪənt] *adj* unverwüstlich

resin ['rɛzɪn] *n* Harz *nt*

resist [rɪ'zɪst] *vt* widerstehen +*dat*; **~ance** *n* Widerstand *m*

resit [*vb* riː'sɪt, *n* 'riːsɪt] *vt* (*exam*) wiederholen ♦ *n* Wiederholung(sprüfung) *f*

resolute ['rɛzəluːt] *adj* entschlossen, resolut; **resolution** [rɛzə'luːʃən] *n* (*firmness*) Entschlossenheit *f*; (*intention*) Vorsatz *m*; (*decision*) Beschluss *m*

resolve [rɪ'zɒlv] *n* Entschlossenheit *f* ♦ *vt* (*decide*) beschließen ♦ *vi* sich lösen; **~d** *adj* (*fest*) entschlossen

resonant ['rɛzənənt] *adj* voll

resort [rɪ'zɔːt] *n* (*holiday place*) Erholungsort *m*; (*help*) Zuflucht *f* ♦ *vi*: **to ~ to** Zuflucht nehmen zu; **as a last ~** als letzter Ausweg

resound [rɪ'zaund] *vi*: **to ~ (with)** widerhallen (von); **~ing** *adj* nachhallend; (*success*) groß

resource [rɪ'sɔːs] *n* Findigkeit *f*; **~s** *npl* (*financial*) Geldmittel *pl*; (*natural*) Bodenschätze *pl*; **~ful** *adj* findig

respect [rɪs'pɛkt] *n* Respekt *m* ♦ *vt* achten, respektieren; **~s** *npl* (*regards*) Grüße *pl*; **with ~ to** in Bezug auf +*acc*, hinsichtlich +*gen*; **in this ~** in dieser Hinsicht; **~able** *adj* anständig; (*not bad*) leidlich; **~ful** *adj* höflich

respective [rɪs'pɛktɪv] *adj* jeweilig; **~ly** *adv* beziehungsweise

respiration [rɛspɪ'reɪʃən] *n* Atmung *f*

respite ['rɛspaɪt] *n* Ruhepause *f*

resplendent [rɪs'plɛndənt] *adj* strahlend

respond [rɪs'pɒnd] *vi* antworten; (*react*): **to ~ (to)** reagieren (auf +*acc*);

response [rɪs'pɒns] *n* Antwort *f*; Reaktion *f*; (*to advert*) Resonanz *f*

responsibility [rɪspɒnsɪ'bɪlɪtɪ] *n* Verantwortung *f*

responsible [rɪs'pɒnsɪbl] *adj* verantwortlich; (*reliable*) verantwortungsvoll

responsive [rɪs'pɒnsɪv] *adj* empfänglich

rest [rɛst] *n* Ruhe *f*; (*break*) Pause *f*; (*remainder*) Rest *m* ♦ *vi* sich ausruhen; (*be supported*) (auf)liegen ♦ *vt* (*lean*): **to sth on/against sth** etw gegen etw *acc* lehnen; **the ~ of them** die Übrigen; **it ~s with him to ...** es liegt bei ihm, zu ...

restaurant ['rɛstərɒŋ] *n* Restaurant *nt*; **~ car** (*BRIT*) *n* Speisewagen *m*

restful ['rɛstful] *adj* erholsam, ruhig

rest home *n* Erholungsheim *nt*

restive ['rɛstɪv] *adj* unruhig

restless ['rɛstlɪs] *adj* unruhig

restoration [rɛstə'reɪʃən] *n* Rückgabe *f*; (*of building etc*) Rückerstattung *f*

restore [rɪs'tɔː] *vt* (*order*) wieder herstellen; (*customs*) wieder einführen; (*person to position*) wieder einsetzen; (*give back*) zurückgeben; (*renovate*) restaurieren

restrain [rɪs'treɪn] *vt* zurückhalten; (*curiosity etc*) beherrschen; (*person*): **to ~ sb from doing sth** jdn davon abhalten, etw zu tun; **~ed** *adj* (*style etc*) gedämpft, verhalten; **~t** *n* (*self-control*) Zurückhaltung *f*

restrict [rɪs'trɪkt] *vt* einschränken; **~ion** *n* Einschränkung *f*; **~ive** *adj* einschränkend

rest room (*US*) *n* Toilette *f*

restructure [riː'strʌktʃər] *vt* umstrukturieren

result [rɪ'zʌlt] *n* Resultat *nt*, Folge *f*; (*of exam, game*) Ergebnis *nt* ♦ *vi*: **to ~ in** sth etw zur Folge haben; **as a ~ of** als Folge +*gen*

resume [rɪ'zjuːm] *vt* fortsetzen; (*occupy again*) wieder einnehmen ♦ *vi* (*work etc*) wieder beginnen

résumé ['reɪzjuːmeɪ] n Zusammenfassung f

resumption [rɪ'zʌmpʃən] n Wiederaufnahme f

resurgence [rɪ'sɜːdʒəns] n Wiedererwachen nt

resurrection [rezə'rekʃən] n Auferstehung f

resuscitate [rɪ'sʌsɪteɪt] vt wieder beleben; **resuscitation** [rɪsʌsɪ'teɪʃən] n Wiederbelebung f

retail [n, adj 'riːteɪl, vb rɪ'teɪl] n Einzelhandel m ♦ adj Einzelhandels- ♦ vi im Kleinen verkaufen ♦ vi im Einzelhandel kosten; **~er** [rɪ'riːteɪlə] n Einzelhändler m, Kleinhändler m; **~ price** n Ladenpreis m

retain [rɪ'teɪn] vt (keep) (zurück)behalten; **~er** n (fee) (Honorar)vorschuss m

retaliate [rɪ'tælɪeɪt] vi zum Vergeltungsschlag ausholen; **retaliation** [rɪtælɪ'eɪʃən] n Vergeltung f

retarded [rɪ'tɑːdɪd] adj zurückgeblieben

retch [retʃ] vi würgen

retentive [rɪ'tentɪv] adj (memory) gut

reticent ['retɪsnt] adj schweigsam

retina ['retɪnə] n Netzhaut f

retire [rɪ'taɪə] vi (from work) in den Ruhestand treten; (withdraw) sich zurückziehen; (go to bed) schlafen gehen; **~d** adj (person) pensioniert, im Ruhestand; **~ment** n Ruhestand m

retiring [rɪ'taɪərɪŋ] adj zurückhaltend

retort [rɪ'tɔːt] n (reply) Erwiderung f ♦ vi (scharf) erwidern

retrace [riː'treɪs] vt (events) zurückverfolgen; **to ~ one's steps** denselben Weg zurückgehen

retract [rɪ'trækt] vt (statement) zurücknehmen; (claws) einziehen ♦ vi einen Rückzieher machen; **~able** adj (aerial) ausziehbar

retrain [riː'treɪn] vt umschulen

retread ['riːtred] n (tyre) Reifen m mit erneuerter Lauffläche

retreat [rɪ'triːt] n Rückzug m; (place) Zufluchtsort m ♦ vi sich zurückziehen

retribution [retrɪ'bjuːʃən] n Strafe f

retrieval [rɪ'triːvəl] n Wiedergewinnung f

retrieve [rɪ'triːv] vt wiederbekommen; (rescue) retten; **~r** n Apportierhund m

retrograde ['retrəɡreɪd] adj (step) Rück-; (policy) rückschrittlich

retrospect ['retrəspekt] n: **in ~** im Rückblick, rückblickend; **~ive** [retrə'spektɪv] adj (action) rückwirkend; (look) rückblickend

return [rɪ'tɜːn] n Rückkehr f; (profits) Ertrag m; (BRIT: rail ticket etc) Rückfahrkarte f; (: plane ticket) Rückflugkarte f ♦ adj (journey, match) Rück- ♦ vi zurückkehren, zurückkommen ♦ vt zurückgeben, zurücksenden; (pay back) zurückzahlen; (elect) wählen; (verdict) aussprechen; **~s** npl (COMM) Gewinn m; (receipts) Einkünfte pl; **in ~** dafür; **by ~ of post** postwendend; **many happy ~s!** herzlichen Glückwunsch zum Geburtstag!

reunion [riː'juːnɪən] n Wiedervereinigung f; (SCH etc) Treffen nt

reunite [riːjuː'naɪt] vt wieder vereinigen

reuse [riː'juːz] vt wieder verwenden, wieder verwerten

rev [rev] n abbr (AUT: = revolution) Drehzahl f

revamp [riː'væmp] vt aufpolieren

reveal [rɪ'viːl] vt enthüllen; **~ing** adj aufschlussreich

revel ['revl] vi: **to ~ in sth/in doing sth** seine Freude an etw dat haben/daran haben, etw zu tun

revelation [revə'leɪʃən] n Offenbarung f

revelry ['revlrɪ] n Rummel m

revenge [rɪ'vendʒ] n Rache f; **to take ~ on** sich rächen an +dat

revenue ['revənjuː] n Einnahmen pl

reverberate [rɪ'vɜːbəreɪt] vi widerhallen

revere [rɪ'vɪər] vt (ver)ehren; **~nce** n Ehrfurcht f

Reverend ['revərənd] adj: **the ~ Robert Martin** ≃ Pfarrer Robert Martin

reversal [rɪ'vɜːsl] n Umkehrung f

reverse [rɪ'vɜːs] n Rückseite f; (AUT: gear) Rückwärtsgang m ♦ adj (order, direction) entgegengesetzt ♦ vt umkehren ♦ vi (BRIT: AUT) rückwärts fahren; **~-charge call** (BRIT) n R-Gespräch nt; **reversing lights** npl (AUT) Rückfahrscheinwerfer pl

revert [rɪ'vɜːt] vi: **to ~ to** zurückkehren zu; (to bad state) zurückfallen in +acc

review [rɪ'vjuː] n (of book) Rezension f; (magazine) Zeitschrift f; Rückschau halten auf +acc; (MIL) mustern; (book) rezensieren; (reexamine) von neuem untersuchen; **~er** n (critic) Rezensent m

revise [rɪ'vaɪz] vt (book) überarbeiten; (reconsider) ändern, revidieren; **revision** [rɪ'vɪʒən] n Prüfung f; (COMM) Revision f; (SCH) Wiederholung f

revitalize [riː'vaɪtəlaɪz] vt neu beleben

revival [rɪ'vaɪvl] n Wiederbelebung f; (REL) Erweckung f; (THEAT) Wiederaufnahme f

revive [rɪ'vaɪv] vt wieder beleben; (fig) wieder auffrischen ♦ vi wieder erwachen; (fig) wieder aufleben

revoke [rɪ'vəuk] vt aufheben

revolt [rɪ'vəult] n Aufstand m, Revolte f ♦ vi sich auflehnen ♦ vt entsetzen; **~ing** adj widerlich

revolution [revə'luːʃən] n (turn) Umdrehung f; (POL) Revolution f; **~ary** adj revolutionär ♦ n Revolutionär m; **~ize** vt revolutionieren

revolve [rɪ'vɒlv] vi kreisen; (on own axis) sich drehen

revolver [rɪ'vɒlvər] n Revolver m

revolving door [rɪ'vɒlvɪŋ-] n Drehtür f

revulsion [rɪ'vʌlʃən] n Ekel m

reward [rɪ'wɔːd] n Belohnung f ♦ vt belohnen; **~ing** adj lohnend

rewind [riː'waɪnd] (irreg: like wind) vt (tape etc) zurückspulen

rewire [riː'waɪər] vt (house) neu verkabeln

reword [riː'wɜːd] vt anders formulieren

rewrite [riː'raɪt] (irreg: like write) vt umarbeiten, neu schreiben

rheumatism ['ruːmətɪzəm] n Rheumatismus m, Rheuma nt

Rhine [raɪn] n: **the ~** der Rhein

rhinoceros [raɪ'nɒsərəs] n Nashorn nt

Rhone [rəun] n: **the ~** die Rhone

rhubarb ['ruːbɑːb] n Rhabarber m

rhyme [raɪm] n Reim m

rhythm ['rɪðm] n Rhythmus m

rib [rɪb] n Rippe f ♦ vt (mock) hänseln, aufziehen

ribbon ['rɪbən] n Band nt; **in ~s** (torn) in Fetzen

rice [raɪs] n Reis m; **~ pudding** n Milchreis m

rich [rɪtʃ] adj reich; (food) reichhaltig ♦ npl: **the ~** die Reichen pl; **~es** npl Reichtum m; **~ly** adv reich; (deserve) völlig

rickets ['rɪkɪts] n Rachitis f

rickety ['rɪkɪtɪ] adj wack(e)lig

rickshaw ['rɪkʃɔː] n Rikscha f

ricochet ['rɪkəʃeɪ] n Abprallen m; (shot) Querschläger m ♦ vi abprallen

rid [rɪd] (pt, pp **rid**) vt befreien; **to get ~ of** loswerden

riddle ['rɪdl] n Rätsel nt ♦ vt: **to be ~d with** völlig durchlöchert sein von

ride [raɪd] (pt **rode**, pp **ridden**) n (in vehicle) Fahrt f; (on horse) Ritt m ♦ vt (horse) reiten; (bicycle) fahren ♦ vi fahren, reiten; **to take sb for a ~** mit jdm eine Fahrt etc machen; (fig) jdn aufs Glatteis führen; **~r** n Reiter m

ridge [rɪdʒ] n Kamm m; (of roof) First m

ridicule ['rɪdɪkjuːl] n Spott m ♦ vt lächerlich machen

ridiculous [rɪ'dɪkjuləs] adj lächerlich

riding ['raɪdɪŋ] n Reiten nt; **~ school** n Reitschule f

rife [raɪf] adj weit verbreitet; **to be ~** grassieren; **to be ~ with** voll sein von

riffraff ['rɪfræf] n Pöbel m

rifle ['raɪfl] n Gewehr nt ♦ vt berauben; **~ range** n Schießstand m

rift [nft] n Spalte f; (fig) Bruch m

rig [rɪg] n (oil ~) Bohrinsel f ♦ vt (election etc) manipulieren; **~ out** (BRIT) vt ausstatten; **~ up** vt zusammenbasteln; **~ging** n Takelage f

right [raɪt] adj (correct, just) richtig, recht; (~ side) rechte(r, s) ♦ n Recht nt; (not left, POL) Rechte f ♦ adv (on the ~) rechts; (to the ~) nach rechts; (look, work) richtig, recht; (directly) gerade; (exactly) genau ♦ vt in Ordnung bringen, korrigieren ♦ excl gut; on the ~ rechts; to be in the ~ im Recht sein; by ~s von Rechts wegen; to be ~ Recht haben; ~ away sofort; ~ now in diesem Augenblick, eben; ~ in the middle genau in der Mitte; ~ angle n rechte(r) Winkel m; **~eous** ['raɪtʃəs] adj rechtschaffen; **~ful** adj rechtmäßig; **~-hand** adj: ~-hand drive mit Rechtssteuerung; **~-handed** adj rechtshändig; ~-hand man (irreg) n rechte Hand f; ~-hand side n rechte Seite f; **~ly** adv mit Recht; ~ of way n Vorfahrt f; **~-wing** adj rechtsorientiert

rigid ['rɪdʒɪd] adj (stiff) starr, steif; (strict) streng; **~ity** [rɪ'dʒɪdɪtɪ] n Starrheit f, Strenge f

rigmarole ['rɪgmərəʊl] n Gewäsch n

rigor ['rɪgə] (US) n = **rigour**

rigorous ['rɪgərəs] adj streng

rigour ['rɪgə] (US **rigor**) n Strenge f, Härte f

rile [raɪl] vt ärgern

rim [rɪm] n (edge) Rand m; (of wheel) Felge f

rind [raɪnd] n Rinde f

ring [rɪŋ] n (pt rang, pp rung) n Ring m; (of people) Kreis m; (arena) Manege f; (of telephone) Klingeln nt ♦ vt, vi (bell) läuten; (BRIT) anrufen; **~ back** (BRIT) vt, vi zurückrufen; **~ off** (BRIT) vi aufhängen; **~ up** (BRIT) vt anrufen; **~ binder** n Ringbuch nt; **~ing** n Klingeln nt; (of large bell) Läuten nt; (in ears)

Klingen nt; **~ing tone** n (TEL) Rufzeichen nt

ringleader ['rɪŋliːdə] n Anführer m, Rädelsführer m

ringlets ['rɪŋlɪts] npl Ringellocken pl

ring road (BRIT) n Umgehungsstraße f

rink [rɪŋk] n (ice ~) Eisbahn f

rinse [rɪns] n Spülen nt ♦ vt spülen

riot ['raɪət] n Aufruhr m ♦ vi randalieren; **to run ~** (people) randalieren; (vegetation) wuchern; **~er** n Aufrührer m; **~ous** adj aufrührerisch; (noisy) lärmend

rip [rɪp] n Schlitz m, Riss m ♦ vt, vi (zer)reißen; **~cord** n Reißleine f

ripe [raɪp] adj reif; **~n** vi reifen ♦ vt reifen lassen

rip-off ['rɪpɒf] (inf) n: it's a ~~! das ist Wucher!

ripple ['rɪpl] n kleine Welle f ♦ vt kräuseln ♦ vi sich kräuseln

rise [raɪz] (pt rose, pp risen) n (slope) Steigung f; (esp in wages: BRIT) Erhöhung f; (growth) Aufstieg m ♦ vi (sun) aufgehen; (smoke) aufsteigen; (mountain) sich erheben; (ground) ansteigen; (prices) steigen; (in revolt) sich erheben; to give ~ to Anlass geben zu; to ~ to the occasion sich der Lage gewachsen zeigen; **~n** [rɪzn] pp of **rise**; **~r** ['raɪzə] n: to be an early ~r ein(e) Frühaufsteher(in) m(f) sein; **rising** ['raɪzɪŋ] adj (tide, prices) steigend; (sun, moon) aufgehend ♦ n (uprising) Aufstand m

risk [rɪsk] n Gefahr f, Risiko nt ♦ vt (venture) wagen; (chance loss of) riskieren, aufs Spiel setzen; **to take ~ or run the ~ of doing sth** das Risiko eingehen, etw zu tun; **at ~** in Gefahr; **at one's own ~** auf eigene Gefahr; **~y** adj riskant

risqué ['riːskeɪ] adj gewagt

rissole ['rɪsəʊl] n Fleischklößchen nt

rite [raɪt] n Ritus m; **last ~s** Letzte Ölung f

ritual ['rɪtjʊəl] n Ritual m ♦ adj ritual, Ritual-; (fig) rituell

rival ['raɪvl] n Rivale m, Konkurrent m ♦ adj rivalisierend ♦ vt rivalisieren mit; (COMM) konkurrieren mit; **~ry** n Rivalität f, Konkurrenz f

river ['rɪvə*] n Fluss m, Strom m ♦ cpd (port, traffic) Fluss-; **up/down** ~ flussaufwärts/-abwärts; **~bank** n Flussufer nt; **~bed** n Flussbett nt

rivet ['rɪvɪt] n Niete f ♦ vt (fasten) (ver)nieten

Riviera [rɪvɪ'ɛərə] n: **the** ~ die Riviera

road [rəud] n Straße f ♦ cpd Straßen-; **major/minor** ~ Haupt-/Nebenstraße f; **~ accident** n Verkehrsunfall m; **~block** n Straßensperre f; **~hog** n Verkehrsrowdy m; **~ map** n Straßenkarte f; **~ rage** n Aggressivität im Straßenverkehr; **~ safety** n Verkehrssicherheit f; **~side** n Straßenrand m ♦ adj an der Landstraße (gelegen); **~ sign** n Straßenschild nt; **~ user** n Verkehrsteilnehmer m; **~way** n Fahrbahn f; **~works** npl Straßenbauarbeiten pl; **~worthy** adj verkehrssicher

roam [rəum] vi (umher)streifen ♦ vt durchstreifen

roar [rɔ:*] n Brüllen nt, Gebrüll nt ♦ vi brüllen; **to** ~ **with laughter** vor Lachen brüllen; **to do a ~ing trade** ein Riesengeschäft machen

roast [rəust] n Braten m ♦ vt braten, schmoren; **~ beef** n Roastbeef nt

rob [rɔb] vt bestehlen, berauben; (bank) ausrauben; **to ~ sb of sth** jdm etw rauben; **~ber** n Räuber m; **~bery** n Raub m

robe [rəub] n (dress) Gewand nt; (US) Hauskleid nt; (judge's) Robe f

robin ['rɔbɪn] n Rotkehlchen nt

robot ['rəubɔt] n Roboter m

robust [rəu'bʌst] adj (person) robust; (appetite, economy) gesund

rock [rɔk] n Felsen m, (BRIT: sweet) Zuckerstange f ♦ vt, vi wiegen, schaukeln; **on the ~s** (drink) mit Eis(würfeln); (marriage) gescheitert; (ship) aufgelaufen; **~ and roll** n Rock and Roll m; **~-**

bottom n (fig) Tiefpunkt m; **~ery** n Steingarten m

rocket ['rɔkɪt] n Rakete f

rocking chair ['rɔkɪŋ-] n Schaukelstuhl m

rocking horse n Schaukelpferd nt

rocky ['rɔkɪ] adj felsig

rod [rɔd] n (bar) Stange f; (stick) Rute f

rode [rəud] pt of **ride**

rodent ['rəudnt] n Nagetier nt

roe [rəu] n (also: ~ **deer**) Reh nt; (of fish: also: **hard** ~) Rogen m; **soft** ~ Milch f

rogue [rəug] n Schurke m

role [rəul] n Rolle f; **~ play** n Rollenspiel nt

roll [rəul] n Rolle f; (bread) Brötchen nt; (list) (Namens)liste f; (of drum) Wirbel m ♦ vt (turn) rollen, (herum)wälzen; (grass etc) walzen ♦ vi (swing) schlingern; (sound) rollen, grollen; **~ about** or **around** vi herumkugeln; (ship) schlingern; (dog etc) sich wälzen; **~ by** vi (time) verfließen; **~ over** vi sich (herum)drehen; **~ up** vi (arrive) kommen, auftauchen ♦ vt (carpet) aufrollen; **~ call** n Namensaufruf m; **~er** n Rolle f, Walze f; (road ~er) Straßenwalze f; **~blade** n Rollerblade m; **~er coaster** n Achterbahn f; **~er skates** npl Rollschuhe pl; **~-skating** n Rollschuhlaufen nt

rolling ['rəulɪŋ] adj (landscape) wellig; **~ pin** n Nudel- or Wellholz nt; **~ stock** n Wagenmaterial nt

ROM [rɔm] n abbr (= read only memory) ROM m

Roman ['rəumən] adj römisch ♦ n Römer(in) m(f); **~ Catholic** adj römisch-katholisch ♦ n Katholik(in) m(f)

romance [rə'mæns] n Romanze f; (story) (Liebes)roman m

Romania [rəu'meɪnɪə] n = **Rumania**; **~n** n = **Rumanian**

Roman numeral n römische Ziffer

romantic [rə'mæntɪk] adj romantisch; **~ism** [rə'mæntɪsɪzəm] n Romantik f

Rome [rəʊm] n Rom nt

romp [rɒmp] n Tollen nt ♦ vi (also: ~ **about**) herumtollen

rompers ['rɒmpəz] npl Spielanzug m

roof [ru:f] (pl ~s) n Dach nt; (of mouth) Gaumen m ♦ vt überdachen, überdecken; ~**ing** n Deckmaterial nt; ~ **rack** n (AUT) Dachgepäckträger m

rook [rʊk] n (bird) Saatkrähe f; (chess) Turm m

room [ru:m] n Zimmer nt, Raum m; (space) Platz m; (fig) Spielraum m; ~s npl (accommodation) Wohnung f; "~s to let (BRIT) or for rent (US)" „Zimmer zu vermieten"; **single/double** ~ Einzel-/Doppelzimmer nt; ~**ing house** (US) n Mietshaus nt (mit möblierten Wohnungen); ~**mate** n Mitbewohner(in) m(f); ~ **service** n Zimmerbedienung f; ~**y** adj geräumig

roost [ru:st] n Hühnerstange f ♦ vi auf der Stange hocken

rooster ['ru:stə*] n Hahn m

root [ru:t] n (also fig) Wurzel f ♦ vi (plant, belief) Wurzeln schlagen; ~ **about** vi (fig) herumwühlen; ~ **for** vt fus Stimmung machen für; ~ **out** vt ausjäten; (fig) ausrotten

rope [rəʊp] n Seil nt ♦ vt (tie) festschnüren; **to know the** ~**s** sich auskennen; **to** ~ **sb in** jdn gewinnen; ~ **off** vt absperren; ~ **ladder** n Strickleiter f

rosary ['rəʊzərɪ] n Rosenkranz m

rose [rəʊz] pt of **rise** ♦ n Rose f ♦ adj Rosen-, rosenrot

rosé ['rəʊzeɪ] n Rosé m

rosebud ['rəʊzbʌd] n Rosenknospe f

rosebush ['rəʊzbʊʃ] n Rosenstock m

rosemary ['rəʊzmərɪ] n Rosmarin m

rosette [rəʊ'zɛt] n Rosette f

roster ['rɒstə*] n Dienstplan m

rostrum ['rɒstrəm] n Rednerbühne f

rosy ['rəʊzɪ] adj rosig

rot [rɒt] n Fäulnis f; (nonsense) Quatsch m ♦ vi verfaulen ♦ vt verfaulen lassen

rota ['rəʊtə] n Dienstliste f

rotary ['rəʊtərɪ] adj rotierend

rotate [rəʊ'teɪt] vt rotieren lassen; (take turns) turnusmäßig wechseln ♦ vi rotieren; **rotating** adj rotierend; **rotation** [rəʊ'teɪʃən] n Umdrehung f

rote [rəʊt] n: **by** ~ auswendig

rotten ['rɒtn] adj faul; (fig) schlecht, gemein; **to feel** ~ (ill) sich elend fühlen

rotund [rəʊ'tʌnd] adj rundlich

rouble ['ru:bl] (US **ruble**) n Rubel m

rough [rʌf] adj (not smooth) rau; (path) uneben; (violent) roh, grob; (crossing) stürmisch; (without comforts) hart, unbequem; (unfinished, makeshift) grob; (approximate) ungefähr ♦ n (BRIT: person) Rowdy m, Rohling m; (GOLF): **in the** ~ im Rau ♦ vt: **to** ~ **it** primitiv leben; **to sleep** ~ im Freien schlafen; ~**age** n Ballaststoffe pl; ~**and-ready** adj provisorisch; (work) zusammengehauen; ~ **copy** n Entwurf m; ~ **draft** n Entwurf m; ~**ly** adv grob; (about) ungefähr; ~**ness** n Rauheit f; (of manner) Ungeschliffenheit f

roulette [ru:'lɛt] n Roulett(e) nt

Roumania [ru:'meɪnɪə] n = **Rumania**

round [raʊnd] adj rund; (figures) aufgerundet ♦ adv (in a circle) rundherum ♦ prep um ... herum ♦ n Runde f; (of ammunition) Magazin nt ♦ vt (corner) biegen um; **all** ~ überall; **the long way** ~ der Umweg; **all the year** ~ das ganze Jahr über; **it's just** ~ **the corner** (fig) es ist gerade um die Ecke; ~ **the clock** rund um die Uhr; **to go** ~ **to sb's (house)** jdn besuchen; **to go** ~ **the back** hintenherum gehen; **enough to go** ~ genug für alle; **to go the** ~**s** (story) die Runde machen; **a** ~ **of applause** eine Beifall m; **a** ~ **of drinks** eine Runde Drinks; **a** ~ **of sandwiches** ein Sandwich nt or m, ein belegtes Brot; ~ **off** vt abrunden; ~ **up** vt (end) abschließen; (figures) aufrunden; (criminals) hochtreiben; ~**about** n (BRIT: traffic) Kreisverkehr m; (: merry-go-~) Karussell m ♦ adj schließ-

Umwegen; **~ers** npl (game) ≈ Schlagball m; **~ly** adv (fig) gründlich; **~shouldered** adj mit abfallenden Schultern; **~ trip** n Rundreise f; **~up** n Zusammentreiben nt, Sammeln nt

rouse [rauz] vt (awaken) (auf)wecken; (stir up) erregen; **rousing** adj (welcome) stürmisch; (speech) zündend

route [ru:t] n Weg m, Route f; **~ map** (BRIT) n (for journey) Streckenkarte f

routine [ru:'ti:n] n Routine f ♦ adj Routine-

row¹ [rau] n (noise) Lärm m, (dispute) Streit m ♦ vi sich streiten

row² [rəu] n (line) Reihe f ♦ vt, vi (boat) rudern; **in a ~** (fig) hintereinander; **~boat** ['rəubəut] (US) n Ruderboot nt

rowdy ['raudɪ] adj rüpelhaft ♦ n (person) Rowdy m

rowing ['rəuɪŋ] n Rudern nt, (SPORT) Rudersport m; **~ boat** (BRIT) n Ruderboot nt

royal ['rɔɪəl] adj königlich, Königs-; **R~ Air Force** n Königliche Luftwaffe f; **~ty** ['rɔɪəltɪ] n (family) königliche Familie f; (for novel etc) Tantieme f

rpm abbr (= revs per minute) U/min

R.S.V.P. abbr (= répondez s'il vous plaît) u. A. w. g.

Rt. Hon. (BRIT) abbr (= Right Honourable) Abgeordnete(r) mf

rub [rʌb] n (with cloth) Polieren nt; (on person) Reiben nt ♦ vt reiben; **to ~ sb up** (BRIT) or **to ~ sb** (US) **the wrong way** jdn aufreizen; **~ off** vi (also fig): **to ~ off (on)** abfärben (auf +acc); **~ out** vt herausreiben; (with eraser) ausradieren

rubber ['rʌbə*] n Gummi m; (BRIT) Radiergummi m; **~ band** n Gummiband nt; **~ plant** n Gummibaum m

rubbish ['rʌbɪʃ] n (waste) Abfall m; (nonsense) Blödsinn m, Quatsch m; **~ bin** (BRIT) n Mülleimer m; **~ dump** n Müllabladeplatz m

rubble ['rʌbl] n (Stein)schutt m

ruby ['ru:bɪ] n Rubin m ♦ adj rubinrot

rucksack ['rʌksæk] n Rucksack m

rudder ['rʌdə*] n Steuerruder nt

ruddy ['rʌdɪ] adj (colour) rötlich; (inf: bloody) verdammt

rude [ru:d] adj unverschämt; (shock) hart; (awakening) unsanft; (unrefined, rough) grob; **~ness** n Unverschämtheit f; Grobheit f

rudiment ['ru:dɪmənt] n Grundlage f

rueful ['ru:ful] adj reuevoll

ruffian ['rʌfɪən] n Rohling m

ruffle ['rʌfl] vt kräuseln

rug [rʌg] n Brücke f; (in bedroom) Bettvorleger m, (BRIT: for knees) (Reise)decke f

rugby ['rʌgbɪ] n (also: ~ football) Rugby nt

rugged ['rʌgɪd] adj (coastline) zerklüftet; (features) markig

rugger ['rʌgə*] (BRIT: inf) n = **rugby**

ruin ['ru:ɪn] n Ruine f; (downfall) Ruin m ♦ vt ruinieren; **~s** npl (fig) Trümmer pl; **~ous** adj ruinierend

rule [ru:l] n Regel f; (government) Regierung f; (for measuring) Lineal nt ♦ vt (govern) herrschen über +acc, regieren; (decide) anordnen, entscheiden; (make lines on) linieren ♦ vi herrschen, regieren; entscheiden; **as a ~** in der Regel; **~ out** vt ausschließen; **~d** adj (paper) liniert; **~r** n Lineal nt; Herrscher m; **ruling** ['ru:lɪŋ] adj (party) Regierungs-; (class) herrschend ♦ n (JUR) Entscheid m

rum [rʌm] n Rum m

Rumania [ru:'meɪnɪə] n Rumänien m; **~n** adj rumänisch ♦ n Rumäne m, Rumänin f; (LING) Rumänisch nt

rumble ['rʌmbl] n Rumpeln nt; (of thunder) Grollen nt ♦ vi rumpeln; grollen

rummage ['rʌmɪdʒ] vi durchstöbern

rumour ['ru:mə*] (US **rumor**) n Gerücht nt ♦ vt: **it is ~ed that** man sagt or man munkelt, dass

rump [rʌmp] n Hinterteil nt; **~ steak** n Rumpsteak nt

rumpus ['rʌmpəs] n Spektakel m

run [rʌn] (pt **ran**, pp **run**) n Lauf m; (in car) (Spazier)fahrt f; (series) Serie f, Reihe f; (ski ~) (Ski)abfahrt f; (in stocking) Laufmasche f ♦ vt (cause to ~) laufen lassen; (car, train, bus) fahren; (race, distance) laufen, rennen; (manage) leiten; (COMPUT) laufen lassen; (pass: hand, eye) gleiten lassen ♦ vi laufen; (move quickly) laufen, rennen; (bus, train) fahren; (flow) fließen, laufen; (colours) (ab)färben; **there was a ~ on** (credit, tickets) es gab einen Ansturm auf +acc; **on the ~** auf der Flucht; **in the long ~** auf die Dauer; **I'll ~ you to the station** ich fahre dich zum Bahnhof; **to ~ a risk** ein Risiko eingehen; **~ about** or **around** vi (children) umherspringen; **~ across** vt fus (find) stoßen auf +acc; **~ away** vi weglaufen; **~ down** vi (clock) ablaufen ♦ vt (production, factory) allmählich auflösen; (with car) überfahren; (talk against) heruntermachen; **to be ~ down** erschöpft or abgespannt sein; **~ in** (BRIT) vt (car) einfahren; **~ into** vt fus (meet: person) zufällig treffen; (trouble) bekommen; (collide with) rennen gegen; fahren gegen; **~ off** vi fortlaufen; **~ out** vi (person) hinausrennen; (liquid) auslaufen; (lease) ablaufen; (money) ausgehen; **he ran out of money/petrol** ihm ging das Geld/ Benzin aus; **~ over** vt (in accident) überfahren; **~ through** vt (instructions) durchgehen; **~ up** vt (debt, bill) machen; **~ up against** vt fus (difficulties) stoßen auf +acc; **~away** adj (horse) ausgebrochen; (person) flüchtig

rung [rʌŋ] pp of **ring** ♦ n Sprosse f

runner ['rʌnə*] n Läufer(in) m(f); (for sleigh) Kufe f; **~ bean** (BRIT) n Stangenbohne f; **~-up** n Zweite(r) m

running ['rʌnɪŋ] n (of business) Leitung f; (of machine) Betrieb m ♦ adj (water) fließend; (commentary) laufend; **to be in/out of the ~ for sth** im/aus dem Rennen für etw sein; **3 days ~** 3 Tage lang or hintereinander; **~ costs** pl (of car, machine) Unterhaltungskosten pl

runny ['rʌnɪ] adj dünn; (nose) laufend

run-of-the-mill ['rʌnəvðə'mɪl] adj gewöhnlich, alltäglich

runt [rʌnt] n (animal) Kümmerer m

run-up ['rʌnʌp] n: **the ~~ to** (election etc) die Endphase vor +dat

runway ['rʌnweɪ] n Startbahn f

rupture ['rʌptʃə*] n (MED) Bruch m

rural ['ruərl] adj ländlich, Land-

ruse [ruːz] n Kniff m, List f

rush [rʌʃ] n Eile f, Hetze f; (FIN) starke Nachfrage f; (of water) rasche f ♦ vt (carry along) auf dem schnellsten Wege schaffen or transportieren; (attack) losstürmen auf +acc ♦ vi (hurry) eilen, stürzen; **don't ~ me** dräng mich nicht; **~ hour** n Hauptverkehrszeit f

rusk [rʌsk] n Zwieback m

Russia ['rʌʃə] n Rußland nt; **~n** adj russisch ♦ n Russe m, Russin f; (LING) Russisch nt

rust [rʌst] n Rost m ♦ vi rosten

rustic ['rʌstɪk] adj bäuerlich, ländlich

rustle ['rʌsl] vi rauschen, rascheln ♦ vt rascheln lassen

rustproof ['rʌstpruːf] adj rostfrei

rusty ['rʌstɪ] adj rostig

rut [rʌt] n (in track) Radspur f; **to be in a ~** im Trott stecken

ruthless ['ruːθlɪs] adj rücksichtslos

rye [raɪ] n Roggen m; **~ bread** n Roggenbrot nt

S, s

sabbath ['sæbəθ] n Sabbat m

sabotage ['sæbətɑːʒ] n Sabotage f ♦ vt sabotieren

saccharin ['sækərɪn] n Sa(c)charin nt

sachet ['sæʃeɪ] n (of shampoo etc) Briefchen nt, Kissen nt

sack [sæk] n Sack m ♦ vt (inf) hinauswerfen; (pillage) plündern; **to get the**

~ rausfliegen; **~ing** n (material) Sackleinen nt; (inf) Rausschmiss m

sacrament ['sækrəmənt] n Sakrament nt

sacred ['seɪkrɪd] adj heilig

sacrifice ['sækrɪfaɪs] n Opfer nt ♦ vt (also fig) opfern

sacrilege ['sækrɪlɪdʒ] n Schändung f

sad [sæd] adj traurig; **~den** vt traurig machen, betrüben

saddle ['sædl] n Sattel m ♦ vt (burden): **to ~ sb with sth** jdm etw aufhalsen; **~bag** n Satteltasche f

sadistic [sə'dɪstɪk] adj sadistisch

sadly ['sædlɪ] adv traurig; (unfortunately) leider

sadness ['sædnɪs] n Traurigkeit f

s.a.e. abbr (= stamped addressed envelope) adressierte(r) Rückumschlag m

safe [seɪf] adj (careful) vorsichtig ♦ n Safe m; **~ and sound** gesund und wohl; (just) **to be on the ~ side** um ganz sicherzugehen; **~ from** (attack) sicher vor +dat; **~-conduct** n freie(s) Geleit nt; **~-deposit** n (vault) Tresorraum m; (box) Banksafe m; **~guard** n Sicherung f ♦ vt sichern, schützen; **~keeping** n sichere Verwahrung f; **~ly** adv sicher; (arrive) wohlbehalten; **~ sex** n geschützter Sex m

safety ['seɪftɪ] n Sicherheit f; **~ belt** n Sicherheitsgurt m; **~ pin** n Sicherheitsnadel f; **~ valve** n Sicherheitsventil nt

sag [sæg] vi (durch)sacken

sage [seɪdʒ] n (herb) Salbei m; (person) Weise(r) mf

Sagittarius [sædʒɪ'tɛərɪəs] n Schütze m

Sahara [sə'hɑːrə] n: **the ~ (Desert)** die (Wüste) Sahara

said [sed] pt, pp of **say**

sail [seɪl] n Segel nt; (trip) Fahrt f ♦ vi segeln ♦ vi segeln; (begin voyage: person) abfahren; (: ship) auslaufen; (fig: cloud etc) dahinsegeln; **to go for a ~** segeln gehen; **they ~ed into Copenhagen** sie liefen in Kopenhagen ein; **~ through** vt fus, vi (fig) (es) spielend

schaffen; **~boat** (US) n Segelboot nt; **~ing** n Segeln nt; **~ing ship** n Segelschiff nt; **~or** n Matrose m, Seemann m

saint [seɪnt] n Heilige(r) mf; **~ly** adj heilig, fromm

sake [seɪk] n: **for the ~ of** um +gen willen

salad ['sæləd] n Salat m; **~ bowl** n Salatschüssel f; **~ cream** (BRIT) n Salatmayonnaise f, Salatmajonäse f; **~ dressing** n Salatsoße f

salary ['sælərɪ] n Gehalt nt

sale [seɪl] n Verkauf m; (reduced prices) Schlussverkauf m; **"for ~"** „zu verkaufen"; **on ~** zu verkaufen; **~room** n Verkaufsraum m; **~s assistant** n Verkäufer(in) m(f); **~s clerk** (US) n Verkäufer(in) m(f); **~sman** (irreg) n Verkäufer m; (representative) Vertreter m; **~s rep** n (COMM) Vertreter(in) m(f); **~swoman** (irreg) n Verkäuferin f

salient ['seɪlɪənt] adj bemerkenswert

saliva [sə'laɪvə] n Speichel m

sallow ['sæləʊ] adj fahl; (face) bleich

salmon ['sæmən] n Lachs m

salon ['sælɔn] n Salon m

saloon [sə'luːn] n (BRIT: AUT) Limousine f; (ship's lounge) Salon m; **~ car** (BRIT) n Limousine f

salt [sɔːlt] n Salz nt ♦ vt (cure) einsalzen; (flavour) salzen; **~cellar** n Salzfass nt; **~water** adj Salzwasser-; **~y** adj salzig

salute [sə'luːt] n (MIL) Gruß m; (with guns) Salutschüsse pl ♦ vt (MIL) salutieren

salvage ['sælvɪdʒ] n (from ship) Bergung f; (property) Rettung f ♦ vt bergen; retten

salvation [sæl'veɪʃən] n Rettung f; **S~ Army** n Heilsarmee f

same [seɪm] adj, pron (similar) gleiche(r, s); (identical) derselbe/dieselbe/dasselbe; **the ~ book** as das gleiche Buch wie; **at the ~ time** zur gleichen Zeit, gleichzeitig; (however) zugleich, andererseits; **all** or **just the ~** trotzdem; **the ~ to you!** gleichfalls!; **to do**

the ~ **(as sb)** das Gleiche tun (wie jd)

sample ['sɑːmpl] n Probe f ♦ vt probieren

sanctify ['sæŋktɪfaɪ] vt weihen

sanctimonious [sæŋktɪ'məunɪəs] adj scheinheilig

sanction ['sæŋkʃən] n Sanktion f

sanctity ['sæŋktɪtɪ] n Heiligkeit f; (fig) Unverletzlichkeit f

sanctuary ['sæŋktjuərɪ] n (for fugitive) Asyl nt; (refuge) Zufluchtsort m; (for animals) Schutzgebiet nt

sand [sænd] n Sand m ♦ vt (furniture) schmirgeln

sandal ['sændl] n Sandale f

sand: ~box (US) n = **sandpit**; **~castle** n Sandburg f; ~ **dune** n (Sand)düne f; **~paper** n Sandpapier nt; **~pit** n Sandkasten m; **~stone** n Sandstein m

sandwich ['sændwɪtʃ] n Sandwich m or nt ♦ vt (also: ~ **in**) einklemmen; **cheese/ham** ~ Käse-/Schinkenbrot; **~ed between** eingeklemmt zwischen; ~ **board** n Reklametafel f; ~ **course** (BRIT) n Theorie und Praxis abwechselnde(r) Ausbildungsgang m

sandy ['sændɪ] adj sandig; (hair) rotblond

sane [seɪn] adj geistig gesund or normal; (sensible) vernünftig, gescheit

sang [sæŋ] pt of **sing**

sanitary ['sænɪtərɪ] adj hygienisch; ~ **towel** n (Monats)binde f

sanitation [sænɪ'teɪʃən] n sanitäre Einrichtungen pl; ~ **department** (US) n Stadtreinigung f

sanity ['sænɪtɪ] n geistige Gesundheit f; (sense) Vernunft f

sank [sæŋk] pt of **sink**

Santa Claus [sæntə'klɔːz] n Nikolaus m, Weihnachtsmann m

sap [sæp] n (of plants) Saft m ♦ vt (strength) schwächen

sapling ['sæplɪŋ] n junge(r) Baum m

sapphire ['sæfaɪə*] n Saphir m

sarcasm ['sɑːkæzm] n Sarkasmus m

sarcastic [sɑː'kæstɪk] adj sarkastisch

sardine [sɑː'diːn] n Sardine f

Sardinia [sɑː'dɪnɪə] n Sardinien nt

sardonic [sɑː'dɒnɪk] adj zynisch

sash [sæʃ] n Schärpe f

sat [sæt] pt, pp of **sit**

Satan ['seɪtn] n Satan m

satchel ['sætʃl] n (for school) Schulmappe f

satellite ['sætəlaɪt] n Satellit m; ~ **dish** n (TECH) Parabolantenne f, Satellitenantenne f; ~ **television** n Satellitenfernsehen nt

satisfaction [sætɪs'fækʃən] n Befriedigung f, Genugtuung f; **satisfactory** [sætɪs'fæktərɪ] adj zufrieden stellend, befriedigend; **satisfied** adj befriedigt

satisfy ['sætɪsfaɪ] vt befriedigen, zufrieden stellen; (convince) überzeugen; (conditions) erfüllen; **~ing** adj befriedigend; (meal) sättigend

saturate ['sætʃəreɪt] vt (durch)tränken

Saturday ['sætədɪ] n Samstag m, Sonnabend m

sauce [sɔːs] n Soße f, Sauce f; **~pan** n Kasserolle f

saucer ['sɔːsə*] n Untertasse f

saucy ['sɔːsɪ] adj frech, keck

Saudi: ['saudɪ] ~ **Arabia** n Saudi-Arabien nt; ~ **(Arabian)** adj saudiarabisch ♦ n Saudi-Araber(in) m(f)

sauna ['sɔːnə] n Sauna f

saunter ['sɔːntə*] vi schlendern

sausage ['sɒsɪdʒ] n Wurst f; ~ **roll** n Wurst f im Schlafrock, Wurstpastete f

sauté ['səuteɪ] adj Röst-

savage ['sævɪdʒ] adj wild ♦ n Wilde(r) mf ♦ vt (animals) zerfleischen

save [seɪv] vt retten; (money, electricity etc) sparen; (strength etc) aufsparen; (COMPUT) speichern ♦ vi (also: ~ **up**) sparen ♦ n (SPORT) (Ball)abwehr f ♦ prep, conj außer, ausgenommen

saving ['seɪvɪŋ] adj: the ~ **grace** of das Versöhnende an +dat ♦ n Sparen nt, Ersparnis f; **~s** npl (money) Ersparnisse pl; **~s account** n Sparkonto nt; **~s bank** n Sparkasse f

saviour ['seɪvjəʳ] (US **savior**) n (REL) Erlöser m

savour ['seɪvəʳ] (US **savor**) vt (taste) schmecken; (fig) genießen; **~y** adj pikant, würzig

saw [sɔː] (pt **sawed**, pp **sawed** or **sawn**) pt of **see** ♦ n (tool) Säge f ♦ vt, vi sägen; **~dust** n Sägemehl nt; **~mill** n Sägewerk nt; **~n pp** of **saw**; **~n-off shotgun** n Gewehr nt mit abgesägtem Lauf

sax [sæks] (inf) n Saxofon nt, Saxophon nt

saxophone ['sæksəfəʊn] n Saxofon nt, Saxophon nt

say [seɪ] (pt, pp **said**) n: **to have a/no ~ in sth** Mitspracherecht/kein Mitspracherecht bei etw haben ♦ vt, vi sagen; **let him have his ~** lass ihn doch reden; **to ~ yes/no** ja/Nein or ja sagen; **that goes without ~ing** das versteht sich von selbst; **that is to ~** das heißt; **~ing** n Sprichwort nt

scab [skæb] n Schorf m; (pej) Streikbrecher m

scaffold ['skæfəld] n (for execution) Schafott nt; **~ing** n (Bau)gerüst nt

scald [skɔːld] n Verbrühung f ♦ vt (burn) verbrühen

scale [skeɪl] n (of fish) Schuppe f; (MUS) Tonleiter f; (on map, size) Maßstab m; (gradation) Skala f; (climb) erklimmen; **~s** npl (balance) Waage f; **on a large ~** (fig) im Großen, in großem Umfang; **~ of charges** Gebührenordnung f; **~ down** vt verkleinern; **~ model** n maßstabgetreu(e)s Modell nt

scallop ['skɒləp] n Kammmuschel f

scalp [skælp] n Kopfhaut f

scamper ['skæmpəʳ] vi: **to ~ away** or **off** sich davonmachen

scampi ['skæmpɪ] npl Scampi pl

scan [skæn] vt genau prüfen; (quickly) überfliegen; (horizon) absuchen

scandal ['skændl] n Skandal m; (piece of gossip) Skandalgeschichte f

Scandinavia [skændɪ'neɪvɪə] n Skandinavien nt; **~n** adj skandinavisch ♦ n Skandinavier(in) m(f)

scant [skænt] adj knapp; **~ily** adv knapp, dürftig; **~y** adj knapp, unzureichend

scapegoat ['skeɪpgəʊt] n Sündenbock m

scar [skɑːʳ] n Narbe f ♦ vt durch Narben entstellen

scarce [skeəs] adj selten, rar; (goods) knapp; **~ly** adv kaum; **scarcity** n Mangel m

scare [skeəʳ] n Schrecken m ♦ vt erschrecken; **bomb ~** Bombendrohung f; **to ~ sb stiff** jdn zu Tode erschrecken; **to be ~d** Angst haben; **~ away** vt (animal) verscheuchen; **~ off** vt = **scare away**; **~crow** n Vogelscheuche f

scarf [skɑːf] (pl **scarves**) n Schal m; (headscarf) Kopftuch nt

scarlet ['skɑːlɪt] adj scharlachrot ♦ n Scharlachrot nt; **~ fever** n Scharlach m

scarves [skɑːvz] npl of **scarf**

scary ['skeərɪ] (inf) adj schaurig

scathing ['skeɪðɪŋ] adj scharf, vernichtend

scatter ['skætəʳ] vt (sprinkle) (ver)streuen; (disperse) zerstreuen ♦ vi sich zerstreuen; **~brained** adj flatterhaft, schusselig

scavenger ['skævəndʒəʳ] n (animal) Aasfresser m

scenario [sɪ'nɑːrɪəʊ] n (THEAT, CINE) Szenarium nt; (fig) Szenario n

scene [siːn] n (of happening) Ort m; (of play, incident) Szene f; (view) Anblick m; (argument) Szene f; Auftritt m; **~ry** ['siːnərɪ] n (THEAT) Bühnenbild n; (landscape) Landschaft f

scenic ['siːnɪk] adj landschaftlich

scent [sent] n Parfüm nt; (smell) Duft m ♦ vt parfümieren

sceptical ['skeptɪkl] (US **skeptical**) adj skeptisch

schedule ['ʃedjuːl], (US) ['skedjuːl] n (list) Liste f; (plan) Programm nt; (of work)

scheme 542 **scrap**

Zeitplan m ♦ vt planen; **on ~ pünktlich; to be ahead of/behind ~** dem Zeitplan voraus/im Rückstand sein; **~d flight** n (not charter) Linienflug m

scheme [skiːm] n Schema nt; (dishonest) Intrige f; (plan of action) Plan m ♦ vi intrigieren ♦ vt planen; **scheming** ['skiːmɪŋ] adj intrigierend

scholar ['skɔlə'] n Gelehrte(r) m; (holding ~ship) Stipendiat m; **~ly** adj gelehrt; **~ship** n Gelehrsamkeit f; (grant) Stipendium nt

school [skuːl] n Schule f; (UNIV) Fakultät f ♦ vt schulen; **~ age** n schulpflichtige(s) Alter nt; **~book** n Schulbuch nt; **~boy** n Schüler m; **~children** npl Schüler pl, Schulkinder pl; **~days** npl (alte) Schulzeit f; **~girl** n Schülerin f; **~ing** n Schulung f, Ausbildung f; **~master** n Lehrer m; **~mistress** n Lehrerin f; **~teacher** n Lehrer(in) m(f)

sciatica [saɪ'ætɪkə] n Ischias m or nt

science ['saɪəns] n Wissenschaft f; (natural ~s) Naturwissenschaften; **~ fiction** n Sciencefiction f; **scientific** [saɪən'tɪfɪk] adj wissenschaftlich; (natural ~s) naturwissenschaftlich; **scientist** ['saɪəntɪst] n Wissenschaftler(in) m(f)

scintillating ['sɪntɪleɪtɪŋ] adj sprühend

scissors ['sɪzəz] npl Schere f; **a pair of ~** eine Schere

scoff [skɔf] vt (BRIT: inf: eat) fressen ♦ vi (mock): **to ~ (at)** spotten (über +acc)

scold [skəuld] vt schimpfen

scone [skɔn] n weiche(s) Teegebäck nt

scoop [skuːp] n Schaufel f; (news) sensationelle Erstmeldung f; **~ out** vt herausschaufeln; **~ up** vt aufschaufeln; (liquid) aufschöpfen

scooter ['skuːtə'] n Motorroller m; (child's) Roller m

scope [skəup] n Ausmaß nt; (opportunity) (Spiel)raum m

scorch [skɔːtʃ] n Brandstelle f ♦ vt versengen; **~ing** adj brennend

score [skɔː'] n (in game) Punktzahl f;

(final ~) (Spiel)ergebnis nt; (MUS) Partitur f; (line) Kratzer m; (twenty) zwanzig, zwanzig Stück ♦ vt (goal) schießen; (points) machen; (mark) einritzen ♦ vi (keep record) Punkte zählen; **on that ~** in dieser Hinsicht; **why the ~?** wie steht's?; **to ~ 6 out of 10** 6 von 10 Punkten erzielen; **~board** n Anschreibetafel f; **~r** n Torschütze m; (recorder) (Auf)schreiber m

scorn [skɔːn] n Verachtung f ♦ vt verhöhnen; **~ful** adj verächtlich

Scorpio ['skɔːpɪəu] n Skorpion m

Scot [skɔt] n Schotte m, Schottin f

Scotch [skɔtʃ] n Scotch m

scotch [skɔtʃ] vt (end) unterbinden

scot-free ['skɔt'friː] adv: **to get off ~~** (unpunished) ungeschoren davonkommen

Scotland ['skɔtlənd] n Schottland nt

Scots [skɔts] adj schottisch; **~man/woman** (irreg) n Schotte m/Schottin f

Scottish ['skɔtɪʃ] adj schottisch; **~ Parliament** n schottisches Parlament nt

scoundrel ['skaundrəl] n Schuft m

scour ['skauə'] vt (search) absuchen; (clean) schrubben

scourge [skɜːdʒ] n (whip) Geißel f; (plague) Qual f

scout [skaut] n (MIL) Späher m; (also: **boy ~**) Pfadfinder m; **~ around** vi: **to ~ around (for)** sich umsehen (nach)

scowl [skaul] n finstere(r) Blick m ♦ vi finster blicken

scrabble ['skræbl] vi (also: **~ around**: search) (herum)tasten; (claw): **to ~ (at)** kratzen (an +dat) ♦ n: **S~** ® Scrabble nt ®

scraggy ['skrægɪ] adj dürr, hager

scram [skræm] (inf) vi abhauen

scramble ['skræmbl] n (climb) Kletterei f; (struggle) Kampf m ♦ vi klettern; (fight) sich schlagen; **to ~ out/through** krabbeln aus/durch; **to ~ for** sth sich um etw raufen; **~d eggs** npl Rührei nt

scrap [skræp] n (bit) Stückchen n,

(fight) Keilerei f; (also: ~ iron) Schrott
m ♦ vt verwerfen ♦ vi (fight) streiten,
sich prügeln; ~s npl (leftovers) Reste pl;
(waste) Abfall m; ~book n Einklebeal-
bum nt; ~ dealer n Schrotthändler(in)
m(f)

scrape [skreɪp] n Kratzen nt; (trouble)
Klemme f ♦ vt kratzen; (car) zerkratzen; (clean) abkratzen ♦ vi (make harsh
noise) kratzen; to ~ through gerade
noch durchkommen; ~r n Kratzer m

scrap: ~ heap n Schrotthaufen m; on
the ~ heap (fig) beim alten Eisen; ~
iron n Schrott m; ~ merchant (BRIT) n
Altwarenhändler(in) m(f); ~ paper n
Schmierpapier nt

scrappy ['skræpɪ] adj zusammenge-
stoppelt

scratch [skrætʃ] n (wound) Kratzer m,
Schramme f ♦ vt kratzen; ~ team zusam-
mengewürfelte Mannschaft f ♦ adj: ~
(car) zerkratzen ♦ vi (sich) kratzen; to
start from ~ ganz von vorne anfangen; to be up to ~ den Anforderungen entsprechen

scrawl [skrɔːl] n Gekritzel nt ♦ vt, vi kritzeln

scrawny ['skrɔːnɪ] adj (person, neck)
dürr

scream [skriːm] n Schrei m ♦ vi
schreien

scree [skriː] n Geröll(halde f) nt

screech [skriːtʃ] n Schrei m ♦ vi kreischen

screen [skriːn] n (protective) Schutz-
schirm m; (CINE) Leinwand f; (TV) Bildschirm m; (shelter) (be)schirmen;
(film) zeigen, vorführen; ~ing n (MED)
Untersuchung f; ~play n Drehbuch nt;
~ saver n (COMPUT) Bildschirmschoner
m

screw [skruː] n Schraube f ♦ vt (fasten)
schrauben; (vulgar) bumsen; ~ up vt
(paper etc) zerknüllen; (inf: ruin) vermasseln (inf); ~driver n Schrauben-
zieher m

scribble ['skrɪbl] n Gekritzel nt ♦ vt krit-

zeln

script [skrɪpt] n (handwriting) Hand-
schrift f; (for film) Drehbuch nt; (THEAT)
Manuskript nt, Text m

Scripture ['skrɪptʃəʳ] n Heilige Schrift f

scroll [skrəʊl] n Schriftrolle f

scrounge [skraʊndʒ] (inf) vt: to ~ sth
off or from sb etw bei jdm abstauben
♦ n: on the ~ beim Schnorren

scrub [skrʌb] n (clean) Schrubben nt;
(in countryside) Gestrüpp nt ♦ vt (clean)
schrubben

scruff [skrʌf] n: by the ~ of the neck
am Genick

scruffy ['skrʌfɪ] adj unordentlich, ver-
gammelt

scrum(mage) ['skrʌm(ɪdʒ)] n Ge-
tümmel nt

scruple ['skruːpl] n Skrupel m, Bedenken nt

scrupulous ['skruːpjʊləs] adj peinlich
genau, gewissenhaft

scrutinize ['skruːtɪnaɪz] vt genau
prüfen; **scrutiny** ['skruːtɪnɪ] n genaue
Untersuchung f

scuff [skʌf] vt (shoes) abstoßen

scuffle ['skʌfl] n Handgemenge nt

sculptor ['skʌlptəʳ] n Bildhauer(in) m(f)

sculpture ['skʌlptʃəʳ] n (ART) Bildhaue-
rei f; (statue) Skulptur f

scum [skʌm] n (also fig) Abschaum m

scurry ['skʌrɪ] vi huschen

scuttle ['skʌtl] n (also: coal ~) Kohlen-
eimer m ♦ vt (ship) versenken ♦ vi
(scamper): to ~ away or off sich davonmachen

scythe [saɪð] n Sense f

SDP (BRIT) n abbr = Social Democratic
Party

sea [siː] n Meer nt, See f; (fig) Meer nt
♦ adj Meeres-, See-; by ~ (travel) auf
dem Seeweg; on the ~ (boat) auf
dem Meer; (town) am Meer; out to ~
aufs Meer hinaus; out at ~ aufs Meer;
~board n Küste f; ~food n Meeresfrüchte pl; ~ front n Strandpromenade f; ~going adj seetüchtig, Hochsee-;

~gull n Möwe f

seal [si:l] n (animal) Robbe f, Seehund m; (stamp, impression) Siegel nt ♦ vt versiegeln; (~ off) (place) abriegeln

sea level n Meeresspiegel m

sea lion n Seelöwe m

seam [si:m] n Saum m; (edges joining) Naht f; (of coal) Flöz nt

seaman [si:mən] n (irreg) Seemann m

seaplane [si:pleɪn] n Wasserflugzeug nt

seaport [si:pɔ:t] n Seehafen m

search [sɜ:tʃ] n (for person, thing) Suche f; (of drawer, pockets, house) Durchsuchung f ♦ vi suchen ♦ vt durchsuchen; **in ~ of** auf der Suche nach; **to ~ for** suchen nach; **to ~ through** vt durchsuchen; **~ing** adj (look) forschend; **~light** n Scheinwerfer m; **~ party** n Suchmannschaft f; **~ warrant** n Durchsuchungsbefehl m

sea: **~shore** n Meeresküste f; **~sick** [si:sɪk] adj seekrank; **~side** [si:saɪd] n Küste f; **~side resort** n Badeort m

season [si:zn] n Jahreszeit f; (Christmas etc) Zeit f, Saison f ♦ vt (flavour) würzen; **~al** adj Saison-; **~ed** adj (fig) erfahren; **~ing** n Gewürz nt, Würze f; **~ ticket** n (RAIL) Zeitkarte f; (THEAT) Abonnement nt

seat [si:t] n Sitz m, Platz m; (in Parliament) Sitz m; (part of body) Gesäß nt; (of trousers) Hosenboden m ♦ vt (place) setzen; (have space for) Sitzplätze bieten für; **to be ~ed** sitzen; **~ belt** n Sicherheitsgurt m

sea: **~ water** n Meerwasser nt; **~weed** [si:wi:d] n (See)tang m; **~worthy** [si:wɜ:ðɪ] adj seetüchtig

sec. abbr (= second(s)) Sek.

secluded [sɪ'klu:dɪd] adj abgelegen

seclusion [sɪ'klu:ʒən] n Zurückgezogenheit f

second [sekənd] adj zweite(r,s) ♦ adv (in ~ position) an zweiter Stelle ♦ n Sekunde f; (person) Zweite(r) mf; (COMM:

imperfect) zweite Wahl f; (SPORT) Sekundant m; (AUT: also: **~ gear**) zweite(r) Gang m; (BRIT: UNIV: degree) mittlere Note bei Abschlußprüfungen ♦ vt (support) unterstützen; **~ary** adj zweitrangig; **~ary school** n höhere Schule f, Mittelschule f; **~class** adj zweiter Klasse; **~hand** adj aus zweiter Hand; (car etc) gebraucht; **~ hand** n (on clock) Sekundenzeiger m; **~ly** adv zweitens

secondment [sɪ'kɒndmənt] (BRIT) n Abordnung f

second-rate [sekənd'reɪt] adj mittelmäßig

second thoughts npl: **to have ~** es sich dat anders überlegen; **on ~** (BRIT) or thinking (US) oder lieber (nicht)

secrecy [si:krəsɪ] n Geheimhaltung f

secret [si:krɪt] n Geheimnis nt ♦ adj geheim, Geheim-; **in ~** geheim

secretarial [sekrɪ'teərɪəl] adj Sekretärinnen-

secretary [sekrətərɪ] n Sekretär(in) m(f); **S~ of State** (BRIT) n (POL): **S~ of State (for)** Minister(in) m(f) (für)

secretion [sɪ'kri:ʃən] n Absonderung f

secretive [si:krɪtɪv] adj geheimtuerisch

secretly [si:krɪtlɪ] adv geheim

sectarian [sek'teərɪən] adj (riots etc) Konfessions-, zwischen den Konfessionen

section [sekʃən] n Teil m; (department) Abteilung f; (of document) Abschnitt m

sector [sektə*] n Sektor m

secular [sekjulə*] adj weltlich, profan

secure [sɪ'kjuə*] adj (safe) sicher; (firmly fixed) fest ♦ vt (make firm) befestigen, sichern; (obtain) sichern; **security** [sɪ'kjuərɪtɪ] n Sicherheit f; (pledge) Pfand nt; (document) Wertpapier nt; (national security) Staatssicherheit f

security guard n Sicherheitsbeamte(r) m, Wächter m, Wache f

sedan [sə'dæn] (US) n (AUT) Limousine f

sedate [sɪ'deɪt] adj gesetzt ♦ vt (MED)

ein Beruhigungsmittel geben +dat; **se-dation** [sɪ'deɪʃən] n (MED) Einfluss m von Beruhigungsmitteln; **sedative** ['sedɪtɪv] n Beruhigungsmittel nt ♦ adj beruhigend, einschläfernd

sediment ['sedɪmənt] n (Boden)satz m

seduce [sɪ'djuːs] vt verführen; **seductive** [sɪ'dʌktɪv] adj verführerisch

see [siː] (pt **saw**, pp **seen**) vt sehen; (understand) (ein)sehen, erkennen; (visit) besuchen ♦ vi (be aware) sehen; (find out) nachsehen ♦ n (ECCL: R.C.) Bistum nt; (: Protestant) Kirchenkreis m; **to ~ sb to the door** jdn hinausbegleiten; **to ~ that** (ensure) dafür sorgen, dass; **~ you soon!** bis bald!; **~ about** vt fus sich kümmern um; **~ off** vt: **to ~ sb off** jdn zum Zug etc begleiten; **~ through** vt: **to ~ sth through** etw durchfechten; **to ~ through sb/sth** jdn/etw durchschauen; ♦ **to ~** vt fus: **to ~ to it** dafür sorgen

seed [siːd] n Samen m ♦ vt (TENNIS) platzieren; **to go to ~** (plant) schießen; (fig) herunterkommen; **~ling** n Setzling m; **~y** adj (café) übel; (person) zweifelhaft

seeing ['siːɪŋ] conj: **~ (that)** da

seek [siːk] (pt, pp **sought**) vt suchen

seem [siːm] vi scheinen; **it ~s that ...** es scheint, dass ...; **~ingly** adv anscheinend

seen [siːn] pp of **see**

seep [siːp] vi sickern

seesaw ['siːsɔː] n Wippe f

seethe [siːð] vi: **to ~ with anger** vor Wut kochen

see-through ['siːθruː] adj (dress etc) durchsichtig

segment ['segmənt] n Teil m; (of circle) Ausschnitt m

segregate ['segrɪgeɪt] vt trennen

seize [siːz] vt (grasp) (er)greifen, packen; (power) ergreifen; (take legally) beschlagnahmen; **~ (up)on** vt fus stürzen auf +acc; **~ up** vi (TECH) sich festfressen; **seizure** ['siːʒə] n (illness)

Anfall m

seldom ['seldəm] adv selten

select [sɪ'lekt] adj ausgewählt ♦ vt auswählen; **~ion** [sɪ'lekʃən] n Auswahl f; **~ive** adj (person) wählerisch

self [self] (pl **selves**) pron selbst ♦ n Selbst nt, Ich nt; **the ~** das Ich; **~assured** adj selbstbewusst; **~catering** (BRIT) adj für Selbstversorger; **~-centred** (US **self-centered**) adj egozentrisch; **~-coloured** (US **self-colored**) adj (of one colour) einfarbig, uni; **~-confidence** n Selbstvertrauen nt, Selbstbewusstsein nt; **~-conscious** adj gehemmt, befangen; **~-contained** adj (complete) (in sich) geschlossen; (person) verschlossen; (BRIT: flat) separat; **~-control** n Selbstbeherrschung f; **~-defence** (US **self-defense**) n Selbstverteidigung f; (JUR) Notwehr f; **~-discipline** n Selbstdisziplin f; **~-employed** adj frei(schaffend); **~-evident** adj offensichtlich; **~-governing** adj selbst verwaltet; **~-indulgent** adj zügellos; **~-interest** n Eigennutz m

selfish ['selfɪʃ] adj egoistisch, selbstsüchtig; **~ness** n Egoismus m, Selbstsucht f

self: **~-lessly** adv selbstlos; **~-made** adj: **~-made man** Selfmademan m; **~-pity** n Selbstmitleid nt; **~-portrait** n Selbstbildnis nt; **~-possessed** adj selbstbeherrscht; **~-preservation** n Selbsterhaltung f; **~-reliant** adj unabhängig; **~-respect** n Selbstachtung f; **~-righteous** adj selbstgerecht; **~sacrifice** n Selbstaufopferung f; **~satisfied** adj selbstzufrieden; **~service** adj Selbstbedienungs-; **~sufficient** adj selbstgenügsam; **~taught** adj selbst erlernt; **~-taught person** Autodidakt m

sell [sel] (pt, pp **sold**) vt verkaufen ♦ vi verkaufen; (goods) sich verkaufen; **to ~ at or for £10** für £10 verkaufen; **~ off** vt verkaufen; **~ out** vi alles verkaufen

~-by date n Verfallsdatum nt; **~er** n Verkäufer m; **~ing price** n Verkaufspreis m

Sellotape ['seləʊteɪp] (®) n Tesafilm m ®

sellout ['selaʊt] n (of tickets): **it was a ~** es war ausverkauft

selves [selvz] npl of **self**

semaphore ['seməfɔː] n Winkzeichen pl

semblance ['sembləns] n Anschein m

semen ['siːmən] n Sperma nt

semester [sɪ'mestər] n (US) n Semester nt

semi ['semɪ] n = **semidetached house**; **~circle** n Halbkreis m; **~colon** n Semikolon nt; **~conductor** n Halbleiter m; **~detached house** (BRIT) n halbe(s) Doppelhaus nt; **~final** n Halbfinale nt

seminary ['semɪnərɪ] n (REL) Priesterseminar nt

semiskilled [semɪ'skɪld] adj angelernt

semi-skimmed [semɪ'skɪmd] adj (milk) teilentrahmt, Halbfett-

senate ['senɪt] n Senat m; **senator** n Senator m

send [send] (pt, pp **sent**) vt senden, schicken; (inf: inspire) hinreißen; **~ away** vt wegschicken; **~ away for** vt fus anfordern; **~ back** vt zurückschicken; **~ for** vt fus holen lassen; **~ off** vt (goods) abschicken; (BRIT: SPORT: player) vom Feld schicken; **~ out** vt (invitation) aussenden; **~ up** vt hinaufsenden; (BRIT: parody) verulken; **~er** n Absender m; **~-off** n: **to give sb a good ~-off** jdn (ganz) groß verabschieden

senior ['siːnɪər] adj (older) älter; (higher rank) Ober- ♦ n (older person) Ältere(r) mf; (higher ranking) Rangälteste(r) mf; **~ citizen** n ältere(r) Mitbürger(in) m(f); **~ity** [siːnɪ'ɔrɪtɪ] n (of age) höhere(s) Alter nt; (in rank) höhere(r) Dienstgrad m

sensation [sen'seɪʃən] n Gefühl nt; (excitement) Sensation f, Aufsehen nt; **~al** adj (wonderful) wunderbar; (result) sen-

sationell; (headlines etc) reißerisch

sense [sens] n Sinn m; (understanding) Verstand m, Vernunft f; (feeling) Gefühl nt ♦ vt fühlen, spüren; **~ of humour** Humor m; **to make ~** Sinn ergeben; **~less** adj sinnlos; (unconscious) besinnungslos

sensibility [sensɪ'bɪlɪtɪ] n Empfindsamkeit f; (feeling hurt) Empfindlichkeit f; **sensibilities** npl (feelings) Zartgefühl nt

sensible ['sensɪbl] adj vernünftig

sensitive ['sensɪtɪv] adj: **~ (to)** empfindlich (gegen); **sensitivity** [sensɪ'tɪvɪtɪ] n Empfindlichkeit f; (artistic) Feingefühl nt; (tact) Feinfühligkeit f

sensual ['sensjʊəl] adj sinnlich

sensuous ['sensjʊəs] adj sinnlich

sent [sent] pt, pp of **send**

sentence ['sentəns] n Satz m; (JUR) Strafe f; Urteil nt ♦ vt: **to ~ sb to death/to 5 years** jdn zum Tode/zu 5 Jahren verurteilen

sentiment ['sentɪmənt] n Gefühl nt; (thought) Gedanke m; **~al** [sentɪ'mentl] adj sentimental; (of feelings rather than reason) gefühlsmäßig

sentry ['sentrɪ] n (Schild)wache f

separate [adj 'seprɪt, vb 'sepəreɪt] adj getrennt, separat ♦ vt trennen ♦ vi sich trennen; **~ly** adv getrennt; **~s** npl (clothes) Röcke, Pullover etc; **separation** [sepə'reɪʃən] n Trennung f

September [sep'tembər] n September m

septic ['septɪk] adj vereitert, septisch; **~ tank** n Klärbehälter m

sequel ['siːkwl] n Folge f

sequence ['siːkwəns] n (Reihen)folge f

sequin ['siːkwɪn] n Paillette f

Serbia ['sɜːbɪə] n Serbien f

serene [sɪ'riːn] adj heiter

sergeant ['sɑːdʒənt] n Feldwebel m; (POLICE) (Polizei)wachtmeister m

serial ['sɪərɪəl] n Fortsetzungsroman m; (TV) Fernsehserie f ♦ adj (number) (fort)laufend; **~ize** n in Fortsetzungen veröffentlichen; in Fortsetzungen senden

series ['sɪəriːz] *n inv* Serie *f*, Reihe *f*

serious ['sɪərɪəs] *adj* ernst; *(injury)* schwer; **~ly** *adv* ernst(haft); *(hurt)* schwer; **~ness** *n* Ernst *m*, Ernsthaftigkeit *f*

sermon ['sɜːmən] *n* Predigt *f*

serrated [sɪ'reɪtɪd] *adj* gezackt

servant ['sɜːvənt] *n* Diener(in) *m(f)*

serve [sɜːv] *vt* dienen +*dat*; *(guest, customer)* bedienen; *(food)* dienen, nützen; *(at table)* bedienen; *(TENNIS)* geben, aufschlagen ♦ *vi* dienen, nützen; *(at table)* bedienen; *(TENNIS)* geben, aufschlagen; **it ~s him right** das geschieht ihm recht; **that'll ~ as a table** das geht so als Tisch; **to ~ a summons** *(on sb)* (jdn) vor Gericht laden; **~ out** *or* **up** *vt (food)* auftragen, servieren

service ['sɜːvɪs] *n (help)* Dienst *m*; *(trains etc)* Verbindung *f*; *(hotel)* Service *m*, Bedienung *f*; *(set of dishes)* Service *nt*; *(REL)* Gottesdienst *m*; *(car)* Inspektion *f*; *(for TVs etc)* Kundendienst *m*; *(TENNIS)* Aufschlag *m* ♦ *vt (AUT, TECH)* warten, überholen; **the S~s** *npl (armed forces)* die Streitkräfte *pl*; **to be of ~ to sb** jdm einen großen Dienst erweisen; **~ included/not included** Bedienung inbegriffen/nicht inbegriffen; **~able** *adj* brauchbar; **~ area** *n (on motorway)* Raststätte *f*; **~ charge** *(BRIT)* *n* Bedienung *f*; **~man** *(irreg)* *n (soldier etc)* Soldat *m*; **~ station** *n (Groß)*tankstelle *f*

serviette [sɜːvɪ'et] *n* Serviette *f*

servile ['sɜːvaɪl] *adj* unterwürfig

session ['seʃən] *n* Sitzung *f*; *(POL)* Sitzungsperiode *f*; **to be in ~** tagen

set [set] *(pt, pp* **set**) *n (collection of things)* Satz *m*, Set *nt*; *(RAD, TV)* Apparat *m*; *(TENNIS)* Satz *m*; *(group of people)* Kreis *m*; *(CINE)* Szene *f*; *(THEAT)* Bühnenbild *nt* ♦ *adj* festgelegt; *(ready)* bereit ♦ *vt (place)* setzen, stellen, legen; *(arrange)* anordnen; *(table)* decken; *(time, price)* festsetzen; *(alarm, watch, task)* stellen; *(jewels)*

(ein)fassen; *(exam)* ausarbeiten ♦ *vi (sun)* untergehen; *(become hard)* fest werden; *(bone)* zusammenwachsen; **to be ~ on doing sth** unbedingt tun wollen; **to ~ to music** vertonen; **to ~ on fire** anstecken; **to ~ free** freilassen; **to ~ sth going** etw in Gang bringen; **to ~ sail** losfahren; **~ about** *vt fus (task)* anpacken; **~ aside** *vt* beiseite legen; **~ back** *vt:* **to ~ back (by)** zurückwerfen (um); **~ off** *vi* aufbrechen ♦ *vt (explode)* sprengen; *(alarm)* losgehen lassen; *(show up well)* hervorheben; **~ out** *vi:* **to ~ out to do sth** vorhaben, etw zu tun ♦ *vt (arrange)* anlegen, arrangieren; *(state)* darlegen; **~ up** *vt (organization)* aufziehen; *(record)* aufstellen; *(monument)* erstellen; **~back** *n* Rückschlag *m*; **~ meal** *n* Menü *nt*; **~ menu** *n* Tageskarte *f*

settee [se'tiː] *n* Sofa *nt*

setting ['setɪŋ] *n* Hintergrund *m*

settle ['setl] *vt* beruhigen; *(pay)* begleichen, bezahlen; *(agree)* regeln ♦ *vi* sich einleben; *(come to rest)* sich niederlassen; *(sink)* sich setzen; *(calm down)* sich beruhigen; **to ~ for sth** sich mit etw zufrieden geben; **to ~ on sth** sich für etw entscheiden; **to ~ up with sb** mit jdm abrechnen; **~ down** *vi (feel at home)* sich einleben; *(calm down)* sich beruhigen; **~ in** *vi* sich eingewöhnen; **~ment** *n* Regelung *f*; *(payment)* Begleichung *f*; *(colony)* Siedlung *f*; **~r** *n* Siedler *m*

setup ['setʌp] *n (situation)* Lage *f*

seven ['sevn] *num* sieben; **~teen** *num* siebzehn; **~th** *adj* siebte(r, s) ♦ *n* Siebtel *nt*; **~ty** *num* siebzig

sever ['sevə'] *vt* abtrennen

several ['sevrəl] *adj* mehrere, verschiedene ♦ *pron* mehrere; **~ of us** einige von uns

severance ['sevərəns] *n:* **~ pay** Abfindung *f*

severe [sɪ'vɪə'] *adj (strict)* streng; *(serious)* schwer; *(climate)* rau; **severity**

[sɪ'verɪtɪ] n Strenge f; Schwere f; Rauheit f

sew [səu] (pt **sewed**, pp **sewn**) vt, vi nähen; **~ up** vt zunähen

sewage ['sju:ɪdʒ] n Abwässer pl

sewer ['suːə] n (Abwasser)kanal m

sewing ['səuɪŋ] n Näharbeit f; **~ machine** n Nähmaschine f

sewn [səun] pp of **sew**

sex [sɛks] n Sex m; (gender) Geschlecht nt; **to have ~ with sb** mit jdm Geschlechtsverkehr haben; **~ism** n Sexismus m; **~ist** adj sexistisch ♦ n Sexist(in) m(f); **~ual** ['sɛksjuəl] adj sexuell, geschlechtlich, Geschlechts-; **~uality** [sɛksjuˈælɪtɪ] n Sexualität f; **~y** adj sexy

shabby ['ʃæbɪ] adj (also fig) schäbig

shack [ʃæk] n Hütte f

shackles ['ʃæklz] npl (also fig) Fesseln pl, Ketten pl

shade [ʃeɪd] n Schatten m; (for lamp) Lampenschirm m; (colour) Farbton m ♦ vt abschirmen; **in the ~** im Schatten; **a ~ smaller** ein bisschen kleiner

shadow ['ʃædəu] n Schatten m ♦ vt (follow) beschatten ♦ adj: **~ cabinet** (BRIT: POL) Schattenkabinett nt; **~y** adj schattig

shady ['ʃeɪdɪ] adj schattig; (fig) zwielichtig

shaft [ʃɑːft] n (of spear etc) Schaft m; (in mine) Schacht m; (TECH) Welle f; (of light) Strahl m

shaggy ['ʃægɪ] adj struppig

shake [ʃeɪk] (pt **shook**, pp **shaken**) vt schütteln, rütteln; (shock) erschüttern ♦ vi (move) schwanken; (tremble) zittern, beben ♦ n (jerk) Schütteln nt, Rütteln nt; **to ~ hands** mit die Hand geben +dat; **to ~ one's head** den Kopf schütteln; **~ off** vt abschütteln; **~ up** vt aufschütteln; (fig) aufrütteln; **~n** ['ʃeɪkn] pp of **shake**; **shaky** ['ʃeɪkɪ] adj zittrig; (weak) unsicher

shall [ʃæl] vb aux: **I ~ go** ich werde gehen; **~ I open the door?** soll ich die Tür öffnen?; **I'll buy some cake, ~ I?**

soll ich Kuchen kaufen?, ich kaufe Kuchen, oder?

shallow ['ʃæləu] adj seicht

sham [ʃæm] n Schein m ♦ adj unecht, falsch

shambles ['ʃæmblz] n Durcheinander nt

shame [ʃeɪm] n Scham f; (disgrace, pity) Schande f ♦ vt beschämen; **it is a ~ that** es ist schade, dass; **it is a ~ to do ...** es ist eine Schande, ... zu tun; **what a ~!** wie schade!; **~faced** adj beschämt; **~ful** adj schändlich; **~less** adj schamlos

shampoo [ʃæm'puː] n Shampoo(n) nt ♦ vt (hair) waschen; **~ and set** n Waschen nt und Legen

shamrock ['ʃæmrɔk] n Kleeblatt nt

shandy ['ʃændɪ] n Bier nt mit Limonade

shan't [ʃɑːnt] = shall not

shantytown ['ʃæntɪtaun] n Bidonville f

shape [ʃeɪp] n Form f ♦ vt formen, gestalten ♦ vi (also: **~ up**) sich entwickeln; **to take ~** Gestalt annehmen; **~d** suffix: **heart~d** herzförmig; **~less** adj formlos; **~ly** adj wohlproportioniert

share [ʃɛə] n (An)teil m; (FIN) Aktie f ♦ vt teilen; **to ~ out (among/between)** verteilen (unter/zwischen); **~holder** n Aktionär(in) m(f)

shark [ʃɑːk] n Hai(fisch) m; (swindler) Gauner m

sharp [ʃɑːp] adj scharf; (pin) spitz; (person) clever; (MUS) erhöht ♦ n Kreuz nt ♦ adv zu hoch; **nine o'clock ~** Punkt neun; **~en** vt schärfen; (pencil) spitzen; **~ener** n (also: **pencil ~ener**) Anspitzer m; **~-eyed** adj scharfsichtig; **~ly** adv (turn, stop) plötzlich; (stand out, contrast) deutlich; (criticize, retort) scharf

shatter ['ʃætə] vt zerschmettern; (fig) zerstören ♦ vi zerspringen

shave [ʃeɪv] n Rasur f ♦ vt rasieren ♦ vi sich rasieren; **to have a ~** sich rasieren (lassen); **~r** n (also: **electric ~r**) Rasierapparat m

shaving ['ʃeɪvɪŋ] n (action) Rasieren nt

~s *npl* (*of wood etc*) Späne *pl*; ~ **brush** *n* Rasierpinsel *m*; ~ **cream** *n* Rasiercreme *f*; ~ **foam** *n* Rasierschaum *m*

shawl [ʃɔːl] *n* Schal *m*, Umhang *m*

she [ʃiː] *pron* sie ♦ *adj* weiblich

sheaf [ʃiːf] (*pl* **sheaves**) *n* Garbe *f*

shear [ʃɪə*] (*pt* **sheared**, *pp* **sheared** *or* **shorn**) *vt* scheren; ~ **off** *vi* abbrechen; ~s *npl* Heckenschere *f*

sheath [ʃiːθ] *n* Scheide *f*; (*condom*) Kondom *m or nt*

sheaves [ʃiːvz] *npl of* **sheaf**

shed [ʃed] (*pt, pp* **shed**) *n* Schuppen *m*; (*for animals*) Stall *m* ♦ *vt* (*leaves etc*) verlieren; (*tears*) vergießen

she'd [ʃiːd] = **she had; she would**

sheen [ʃiːn] *n* Glanz *m*

sheep [ʃiːp] *n inv* Schaf *nt*; ~**dog** *n* Schäferhund *m*; ~**ish** *adj* verlegen; ~**skin** *n* Schaffell *nt*

sheer [ʃɪə*] *adj* bloß, rein; (*steep*) steil; (*transparent*) (hauch)dünn ♦ *adv* (*directly*) direkt

sheet [ʃiːt] *n* Betttuch *nt*, Bettlaken *nt*; (*of paper*) Blatt *nt*; (*of metal etc*) Platte *f*; (*of ice*) Fläche *f*

sheik(h) [ʃeɪk] *n* Scheich *m*

shelf [ʃelf] (*pl* **shelves**) *n* Bord *nt*, Regal *nt*

shell [ʃel] *n* Schale *f*; (*seashell*) Muschel *f*; (*explosive*) Granate *f* ♦ *vt* (*peas*) schälen; (*fire on*) beschießen

she'll [ʃiːl] = **she will; she shall**

shellfish [ˈʃelfɪʃ] *n* Schalentier *nt*; (*as food*) Meeresfrüchte *pl*

shell suit *n* Ballonseidenanzug *m*

shelter [ˈʃeltə*] *n* Schutz *m*; (*air-raid* ~) Bunker *m* ♦ *vt* schützen, bedecken; (*refugees*) aufnehmen ♦ *vi* sich unterstellen; ~**ed** *adj* (*life*) behütet; (*spot*) geschützt; ~ **housing** *n* (*for old people*) Altenwohnungen *pl*; (*for handicapped people*) Behindertenwohnungen *pl*

shelve [ʃelv] *vt* aufschieben ♦ *vi* abfallen

shelves [ʃelvz] *npl of* **shelf**

shepherd [ˈʃepəd] *n* Schäfer *m* ♦ *vt* trei-

ben, führen; ~**'s pie** *n* Auflauf *aus Hackfleisch und Kartoffelbrei*

sheriff [ˈʃerɪf] *n* Sheriff *m*; (*SCOTTISH*) Friedensrichter *m*

she's [ʃiːz] = **she is; she has**

Shetland [ˈʃetlənd] *n* (*also:* **the ~s, the ~ Isles**) die Shetlandinseln *pl*

shield [ʃiːld] *n* Schild *m*; (*fig*) Schirm *m* ♦ *vt* (be)schirmen; (*TECH*) abschirmen

shift [ʃɪft] *n* Verschiebung *f*; (*work*) Schicht *f* ♦ *vt* (ver)rücken, verschieben; (*arm*) wegnehmen ♦ *vi* sich verschieben; ~**less** *adj* (*person*) träge; ~ **work** *n* Schichtarbeit *f*; ~**y** *adj* verschlagen

shilly-shally [ˈʃɪlɪʃælɪ] *vi* zögern

shin [ʃɪn] *n* Schienbein *nt*

shine [ʃaɪn] (*pt, pp* **shone**) *n* Glanz *m*, Schein *m* ♦ *vi* scheinen; *vt* scheinen; (*fig*) glänzen; **to ~ a torch on sb** jdn (mit einer Lampe) anleuchten

shingle [ˈʃɪŋgl] *n* Strandkies *m*; ~**s** *npl* (*MED*) Gürtelrose *f*

shiny [ˈʃaɪnɪ] *adj* glänzend

ship [ʃɪp] *n* Schiff *nt* ♦ *vt* verschiffen; ~**building** *n* Schiffbau *m*; ~**ment** *n* Schiffsladung *f*; ~**per** *n* Verschiffer *m*; ~**ping** *n* (*act*) Verschiffung *f*; (~*s*) Schifffahrt *f*; ~**wreck** *n* Schiffbruch *m*; (*destroyed*) ♦ *Wrack nt* ♦ *vt*: **to be** ~**wrecked** Schiffbruch erleiden; ~**yard** *n* Werft *f*

shire [ˈʃaɪə*] (*BRIT*) *n* Grafschaft *f*

shirk [ʃɜːk] *vt* ausweichen +*dat*

shirt [ʃɜːt] *n* (Ober)hemd *nt*; **in ~ sleeves** in Hemdsärmeln

shit [ʃɪt] (*infl*) *excl* Scheiße (*!*)

shiver [ˈʃɪvə*] *n* Schauer *m* ♦ *vi* frösteln, zittern

shoal [ʃəul] *n* (*Fisch*)schwarm *m*

shock [ʃɔk] *n* Erschütterung *f*; (*mental*) Schock *m*; (*ELEC*) Schlag *m* ♦ *vt* erschüttern; (*offend*) schockieren; ~ **absorber** *n* Stoßdämpfer *m*; ~**ed** *adj* geschockt, schockiert; ~**ing** *adj* unerhört

shod [ʃɔd] *pt, pp of* **shoe**

shoddy [ˈʃɔdɪ] *adj* schäbig

shoe [ʃuː] (*pt, pp* **shod**) *n* Schuh *m*; (*of horse*) Hufeisen *nt* ♦ *vt* (*horse*) beschlagen; **~brush** *n* Schuhbürste *f*; **~horn** *n* Schuhlöffel *m*; **~lace** *n* Schnürsenkel *m*; **~ polish** *n* Schuhcreme *f*; **~ shop** *n* Schuhgeschäft *nt*; **~string** *n* (*fig*): on a **~string** mit sehr wenig Geld

shone [ʃɔn] *pt, pp* of **shine**

shoo [ʃuː] *excl* sch; (*to dog etc*) pfui

shook [ʃʊk] *pt* of **shake**

shoot [ʃuːt] *n* (*branch*) Schössling *m* ♦ *vt* (*gun*) abfeuern; (*goal, arrow*) schießen; (*person*) anschießen; (*kill*) erschießen; (*film*) drehen ♦ *vi* (*move quickly*) schießen; to **~ (at)** schießen (auf +*acc*); **~ down** *vt* abschießen; **~ in** *vi* hineinschießen; **~ out** *vi* hinausschießen; **~ up** *vi* (*fig*) aus dem Boden schießen; **~ing** *n* Schießerei *f*; **~ing star** *n* Sternschnuppe *f*

shop [ʃɔp] *n* (*esp BRIT*) Geschäft *nt*, Laden *m*; (*workshop*) Werkstatt *f* ♦ *vi* (*also*: **go ~ping**) einkaufen gehen; **~ assistant** (*BRIT*) *n* Verkäufer(in) *m(f)*; **~ floor** (*BRIT*) *n* Werkstatt *f*; **~keeper** *n* Geschäftsinhaber *m*; **~lifting** *n* Ladendiebstahl *m*; **~per** *n* Käufer(in) *m(f)*; **~ping** *n* Einkaufen *nt*, Einkauf *m*; **~ping bag** *n* Einkaufstasche *f*; **~ping centre** (*US* **shopping center**) *n* Einkaufszentrum *nt*; **~-soiled** *adj* angeschmutzt; **~ steward** (*BRIT*) *n* (*INDUSTRY*) Betriebsrat *m*; **~ window** *n* Schaufenster *nt*

shore [ʃɔːr] *n* Ufer *nt*; (*of sea*) Strand *m* ♦ *vt*: to **~ up** abstützen

shorn [ʃɔːn] *pp* of **shear**

short [ʃɔːt] *adj* (*person*) klein; (*curt*) kurz angebunden; (*measure*) so knapp ♦ *n* (*also*: **~ film**) Kurzfilm *m* ♦ *adv* (*suddenly*) plötzlich ♦ *vi* (*ELEC*) einen Kurzschluss haben; **~s** *pl* (*clothes*) Shorts *pl*; to **be ~ of sth** nicht genug von etw haben; **in ~** kurz gesagt; **~ of doing sth** ohne so weit zu gehen, etw zu tun; **everything ~ of ...** alles

außer; **it is ~ for** das ist die Kurzform von; to **cut ~** abkürzen; to **fall ~ of sth** etw nicht erreichen; to **stop ~** plötzlich anhalten; to **stop ~ of** Halt machen vor; **~age** *n* Knappheit *f*, Mangel *m*; **~bread** *n* Mürbegebäck *nt*; **~change** *vt*: to **~change sb** jdm zu wenig herausgeben; **~circuit** *n* Kurzschluss *m* ♦ *vi* einen Kurzschluss haben ♦ *vt* kurzschließen; **~coming** *n* Mangel *m*; **~(crust) pastry** (*BRIT*) *n* Mürbeteig *m*; **~cut** *n* Abkürzung *f*; **~en** *vt* (*ab*)kürzen; (*clothes*) kürzer machen; **~fall** *n* Defizit *nt*; **~hand** *n* Stenografie *f*; **~hand typist** (*BRIT*) *n* Stenotypistin *f*; **~list** (*BRIT*) *n* (*for job*) engere Wahl *f*; **~lived** *adj* kurzlebig; **~ly** *adv* bald; **~ notice** *n*: at **~ notice** kurzfristig; **~sighted** (*BRIT*) *adj* (*also fig*) kurzsichtig; **~staffed** *adj*: to **be ~staffed** zu wenig Personal haben; **~stay** *n* (*car park*) Kurzparken *nt*; **~ story** *n* Kurzgeschichte *f*; **~tempered** *adj* leicht aufbrausend; **~term** *adj* (*effect*) kurzfristig; **~wave** *n* (*RAD*) Kurzwelle *f*

shot [ʃɔt] *pt, pp* of **shoot** ♦ *n* (*from gun*) Schuss *m*; (*person*) Schütze *m*; (*try*) Versuch *m*; (*injection*) Spritze *f*; (*PHOT*) Aufnahme *f*; **like a ~** wie der Blitz; **~gun** *n* Schrotflinte *f*

should [ʃʊd] *vb aux*: **I ~ go now** ich sollte jetzt gehen; **he ~ be there now** er sollte eigentlich schon da sein; **I ~ go if I were you** ich würde gehen, wenn ich du wäre; **I ~ like to** ich möchte gerne

shoulder [ˈʃəʊldər] *n* Schulter *f*; (*BRIT*: *of road*) **hard ~** Seitenstreifen *m* ♦ *vt* (*rifle*) schultern; (*fig*) auf sich nehmen; **~ bag** *n* Umhängetasche *f*; **~ blade** *n* Schulterblatt *nt*; **~ strap** *n* (*of dress etc*) Träger *m*

shouldn't [ˈʃʊdnt] = **should not**

shout [ʃaʊt] *n* Schrei *m*; (*call*) Ruf *m* ♦ *vi* rufen ♦ *vi* schreien; **~ down** *vt* niederbrüllen; **~ing** *n* Geschrei *nt*

shove [ʃʌv] n Schubs m, Stoß m ♦ vt schieben, stoßen, schubsen; (inf: put): **to ~ sth in(to) sth** etw in etw acc hineinschieben; **~ off** vi (NAUT) abstoßen; (fig: inf) abhauen

shovel [ʃʌvl] n Schaufel f ♦ vt schaufeln

show [ʃəu] (pt showed, pp shown) n (display) Schau f; (exhibition) Ausstellung f; (CINE, THEAT) Vorstellung f, Show f ♦ vt zeigen; (kindness) erweisen ♦ vi zu sehen sein; **to be on ~** (exhibits etc) ausgestellt sein; **to ~ sb in** jdn hereinführen; **to ~ sb out** jdn hinausbegleiten; **~ off** vi (pej) angeben ♦ vt (display) ausstellen; **~ up** vi (stand out) sich abheben; (arrive) erscheinen ♦ vt aufzeigen; (unmask) bloßstellen; **~ business** n Showbusiness nt; **~down** n Kraftprobe f

shower [ʃauəʳ] n Schauer m; (of stones) (Stein)hagel m; (~ bath) Dusche f ♦ vi duschen ♦ vt: **to ~ sb with sth** jdn mit etw überschütten; **~proof** adj Wasser abstoßend

showing [ʃəuɪŋ] n Vorführung f

show jumping n Turnierreiten nt

shown [ʃəun] pp of show

show-off [ʃəuɔf] n Angeber(in) m(f); **~piece** [ʃəupiːs] n Paradestück nt; **~room** [ʃəurum] n Ausstellungsraum m

shrank [ʃræŋk] pt of shrink

shred [ʃred] n Fetzen m ♦ vt zerfetzen; (COOK) raspeln; **~der** n (COOK) Gemüseschneider m; (for documents) Reißwolf m

shrewd [ʃruːd] adj clever

shriek [ʃriːk] n Schrei m ♦ vi kreischen, schreien

shrill [ʃrɪl] adj schrill

shrimp [ʃrɪmp] n Krabbe f, Garnele f

shrine [ʃraɪn] n Schrein m; (fig) Gedenkstätte f

shrink [ʃrɪŋk] (pt shrank, pp shrunk) vi schrumpfen, eingehen ♦ vt einschrumpfen lassen; **to ~ from doing**

sth davor zurückschrecken, etw zu tun; **~age** n Schrumpfung f; **~wrap** vt einschweißen

shrivel [ʃrɪvl] vt, vi (also: ~ up) schrumpfen, schrumpeln

shroud [ʃraud] n Leichentuch m ♦ vt: **~ed in mystery** mit einem Geheimnis umgeben

Shrove Tuesday [ʃrəuv-] n Fastnachtsdienstag m

shrub [ʃrʌb] n Busch m, Strauch m; **~bery** n Gebüsch nt

shrug [ʃrʌg] n Achselzucken nt ♦ vt, vi: **to ~ (one's shoulders)** die Achseln zucken; **~ off** vt auf die leichte Schulter nehmen

shrunk [ʃrʌŋk] pp of shrink

shudder [ʃʌdəʳ] n Schauder m ♦ vi schaudern

shuffle [ʃʌfl] vt (cards) mischen; **to ~ (one's feet)** schlurfen

shun [ʃʌn] vt scheuen, (ver)meiden

shunt [ʃʌnt] vt rangieren

shut [ʃʌt] (pt, pp shut) vt schließen, zumachen ♦ vi sich schließen (lassen); **~ down** vt, vi schließen; **~ off** vt (supply) abdrehen; **~ up** vi (keep quiet) den Mund halten ♦ vt (close) zuschließen; **~ter** n Fensterladen m; (PHOT) Verschluss m

shuttle [ʃʌtl] n (plane, train etc) Pendelflugzeug nt/-zug m etc; (space ~) Raumtransporter m; (also: ~ **service**) Pendelverkehr m; **~cock** [ʃʌtlkɔk] n Federball m; **~ diplomacy** n Pendeldiplomatie f

shy [ʃaɪ] adj schüchtern; **~ness** n Schüchternheit f

Siamese [saɪəˈmiːz] adj: **~ cat** Siamkatze f

Siberia [saɪˈbɪərɪə] n Sibirien nt

sibling [sɪblɪŋ] n Geschwister nt

Sicily [sɪsɪlɪ] n Sizilien nt

sick [sɪk] adj krank; (joke) makaber; **I feel ~** mir ist schlecht; **I was ~** ich habe gebrochen; **to be ~ of sb/sth** jdn/etw satt haben; **~ bay** n

(Schiffs)lazarett nt; **~en** vt (disgust) krank machen ♦ vi krank werden; **~ening** adj (annoying) zum Weinen

sickle ['sɪkl] n Sichel f

sick: **~ leave** n: **to be on ~ leave** krankgeschrieben sein; **~ly** adj kränklich, blass; (causing nausea) widerlich; **~ness** n Krankheit f; (vomiting) Übelkeit f, Erbrechen nt; **~ note** n Arbeitsunfähigkeitsbescheinigung f; **~ pay** n Krankengeld nt

side [saɪd] n Seite f ♦ adj (door, entrance) Seiten-, Neben- f ♦ vi: **to ~ with sb** jds Partei ergreifen; **by the ~ of** neben; **~ by ~** nebeneinander; **on all ~s** von allen Seiten; **to take ~s (with)** Partei nehmen (für); **from all ~s** von allen Seiten; **~board** n Sideboard nt; **~boards** (BRIT) npl Koteletten pl; **~burns** npl Koteletten pl; **~car** n Beiwagen m; ~ **drum** n (MUS) kleine Trommel; **~effect** n Nebenwirkung f; **~light** n (AUT) Parkleuchte f; **~line** n (SPORT) Seitenlinie f; (fig: hobby) Nebenbeschäftigung f; **~long** adj Seiten-; ~ **order** n Beilage f; **~saddle** adv im Damensattel; **~ show** n Nebenausstellung f; **~step** vt (fig) ausweichen; **~ street** n Seitenstraße f; **~track** vt (fig) ablenken; **~walk** (US) n Bürgersteig m; **~ways** adv seitwärts

siding ['saɪdɪŋ] n Nebengleis nt

sidle ['saɪdl] vi: **to ~ up (to)** sich heranmachen (an +acc)

siege [siːdʒ] n Belagerung f

sieve [sɪv] n Sieb nt ♦ vt sieben

sift [sɪft] vt sieben; (fig) sichten

sigh [saɪ] n Seufzer m ♦ vi seufzen

sight [saɪt] n (power of seeing) Sehvermögen nt; (look) Blick m; (fact of seeing) Anblick m; (of gun) Visier nt ♦ vt sichten; **in ~** in Sicht; **out of ~** außer Sicht; **~seeing** n Besuch m von Sehenswürdigkeiten; **to go ~seeing** Sehenswürdigkeiten besichtigen

sign [saɪn] n Zeichen nt; (notice, road etc) Schild nt ♦ vt unterschreiben; **to ~**

sth **over to** sb jdm etw überschreiben; **~ on** vi (as unemployed) sich (arbeitslos) melden ♦ (employee) anstellen ♦ vt sich verpflichten ♦ vt verpflichten

signal ['sɪgnl] n Signal nt ♦ vt ein Zeichen geben +dat; **~man** (irreg) n (RAIL) Stellwerkswärter m

signature ['sɪgnətʃə] n Unterschrift f; **~ tune** n Erkennungsmelodie f

signet ring ['sɪgnət-] n Siegelring m

significance [sɪg'nɪfɪkəns] n Bedeutung f

significant [sɪg'nɪfɪkənt] adj (meaning sth) bedeutsam; (important) bedeutend

signify ['sɪgnɪfaɪ] vt bedeuten; (show) andeuten, zu verstehen geben

sign language n Zeichensprache f, Fingersprache f

signpost ['saɪnpəʊst] n Wegweiser m

silence ['saɪləns] n Stille f; (of person) Schweigen nt ♦ vt zum Schweigen bringen; **~r** n (on gun) Schalldämpfer m; (BRIT: AUT) Auspufftopf m

silent ['saɪlənt] adj still; (person) schweigsam; **to remain ~** schweigen; ~ **partner** n (COMM) stille(r) Teilhaber m

silicon chip ['sɪlɪkən-] n Siliciumchip m, Siliziumchip m

silk [sɪlk] n Seide f ♦ adj seiden, Seiden-; **~y** adj seidig

silly ['sɪlɪ] adj dumm, albern

silt [sɪlt] n Schlamm m, Schlick m

silver ['sɪlvə] n Silber nt ♦ adj silbern, Silber-; ~ **paper** (BRIT) n Silberpapier nt; **~plated** adj versilbert; **~smith** n Silberschmied m; **~ware** n Silber nt; **~y** adj silbern

similar ['sɪmɪlə] adj: **~ (to)** ähnlich (+dat); **~ity** [sɪmɪ'lærɪtɪ] n Ähnlichkeit f; **~ly** adv in ähnlicher Weise

simmer ['sɪmə] vi sieden ♦ vt sieden lassen

simple ['sɪmpl] adj einfach; **~(-minded)** adj einfältig

simplicity [sɪm'plɪsɪtɪ] n Einfachheit f; (of person) Einfältigkeit f

simplify ['sɪmplɪfaɪ] vt vereinfachen

simply ['sɪmplɪ] adv einfach

simulate ['sɪmjʊleɪt] vt simulieren

simultaneous [sɪməl'teɪnɪəs] adj gleichzeitig

sin [sɪn] n Sünde f ♦ vi sündigen

since [sɪns] adv seither ♦ prep seit, seitdem ♦ conj (time) seit; (because) da, weil; ~ **then** seitdem

sincere [sɪn'sɪə] adj aufrichtig; ~**ly** adv: **yours** ~**ly** mit freundlichen Grüßen; **sincerity** [sɪn'serɪtɪ] n Aufrichtigkeit f

sinew ['sɪnjuː] n Sehne f

sinful ['sɪnfʊl] adj sündig, sündhaft

sing [sɪŋ] (pt **sang**, pp **sung**) vt, vi singen

Singapore [sɪŋgə'pɔː] n Singapur nt

singe [sɪndʒ] vt versengen

singer ['sɪŋə] n Sänger(in) m(f)

singing ['sɪŋɪŋ] n Singen nt, Gesang m

single ['sɪŋgl] adj (one only) einzig; (bed, room) Einzel-, einzeln; (unmarried) ledig; (BRIT: ticket) einfach; (having one part only) einzeln ♦ n (BRIT: also: ~ **ticket**) einfache Fahrkarte f; **in** ~ **file** hintereinander; ~ **out** vt aussuchen, auswählen; ~ **bed** n Einzelbett nt; ~ **breasted** adj einreihig; ~**handed** adj allein; ~**minded** adj zielstrebig; ~ **parent** n Alleinerziehende(r) f(m); ~ **room** n Einzelzimmer nt; ~**s** n (TENNIS) Einzel nt; ~**track road** n einspurige Straße (mit Ausweichstellen); **singly** adv einzeln, allein

singular ['sɪŋgjʊlə] adj (odd) merkwürdig, seltsam ♦ n (GRAM) Einzahl f, Singular m

sinister ['sɪnɪstə] adj (evil) böse; (ghostly) unheimlich

sink [sɪŋk] (pt **sank**, pp **sunk**) n Spülbecken nt ♦ vt (ship) versenken ♦ vi sinken; **to** ~ **sth into** (teeth, claws) etw schlagen in +acc; ~ **in** vi (news etc) eingehen

sinner ['sɪnə] n Sünder(in) m(f)

sinus ['saɪnəs] n (ANAT) Sinus m

sip [sɪp] n Schlückchen nt ♦ vt nippen an +dat

siphon ['saɪfən] n Siphon(flasche f) m; ~ **off** vt absaugen; (fig) abschöpfen

sir [sɜː] n (respect) Herr m; (knight) Sir m; **S~ John Smith** Sir John Smith; **yes** ~ ja(wohl, mein Herr)

siren ['saɪərn] n Sirene f

sirloin ['sɜːlɔɪn] n Lendenstück nt

sissy ['sɪsɪ] (inf) n Waschlappen m

sister ['sɪstə] n Schwester f; (BRIT: nurse) Oberschwester f; (nun) Ordensschwester f; ~**in-law** n Schwägerin f

sit [sɪt] (pt, pp **sat**) vi sitzen; (hold session) tagen ♦ vt (exam) machen; ~ **down** vi sich setzen; ~ **in on** vt fus dabei sein bei; ~ **up** vi (after lying) sich aufsetzen; (straight) sich gerade setzen; (at night) aufbleiben

sitcom ['sɪtkɒm] n abbr (= situation comedy) Situationskomödie f

site [saɪt] n Platz m; (also: **building** ~) Baustelle f ♦ vt legen

sitting ['sɪtɪŋ] n (meeting) Sitzung f; ~ **room** n Wohnzimmer nt

situated ['sɪtjʊeɪtɪd] adj: **to be** ~ liegen

situation [sɪtjʊ'eɪʃən] n Situation f, Lage f; (place) Lage f; (employment) Stelle f; "~**s vacant**" (BRIT) "Stellenangebote"

six [sɪks] num sechs; ~**teen** num sechzehn; ~**th** adj sechste(r, s) ♦ n Sechstel nt; ~**ty** num sechzig

size [saɪz] n Größe f; (of project) Umfang m; ~ **up** vt (assess) abschätzen, einschätzen; ~**able** adj ziemlich groß, ansehnlich

sizzle ['sɪzl] vi zischen; (COOK) brutzeln

skate [skeɪt] n Schlittschuh m; (fish: pl inv) Rochen m ♦ vi Schlittschuh laufen; ~**board** n Skateboard nt; ~**boarding** n Skateboardfahren nt; ~**r** n Schlittschuhläufer(in) m(f); **skating** ['skeɪtɪŋ] n Eislauf m; **to go skating** Eis laufen gehen; **skating rink** n Eisbahn f

skeleton ['skelɪtn] n Skelett nt; (fig)
Gerüst nt; **~ key** n Dietrich m; **~ staff**
n Notbesetzung f

skeptical ['skeptɪkl] (US) adj = **sceptical**

sketch [sketʃ] n Skizze f; (THEAT) Sketch
m ♦ vt skizzieren; **~book** n Skizzenbuch nt; **~y** adj skizzenhaft

skewer ['skjuːəʳ] n Fleischspieß m

ski [skiː] n Ski m, Schi m ♦ vi Ski or Schi
laufen; **~ boot** n Skistiefel m

skid [skɪd] n (AUT) Schleudern ♦ vi
rutschen; (AUT) schleudern

ski: **~er** ['skiːəʳ] n Skiläufer(in) m(f);
~ing ['skiːɪŋ] n: **to go ~ing** Ski laufen
gehen; **~jump** n Sprungschanze f ♦ vi
Ski springen

skilful ['skɪlful] adj geschickt

ski-lift n Skilift m

skill [skɪl] n Können nt; **~ed** adj geschickt; (worker) Fach-, gelernt

skim [skɪm] vt (liquid) abschöpfen;
(glide over) gleiten über +acc ♦ vi: **~
through** (book) überfliegen; **~med
milk** n Magermilch f

skimp [skɪmp] vt (a. do carelessly) oberflächlich tun; **~y** adj (dress) knapp

skin [skɪn] n Haut f; (peel) Schale f ♦ vt
abhäuten; schälen; **~ cancer** n Hautkrebs m; **~-deep** adj oberflächlich; **~-
diving** n Schwimmtauchen nt; **~head**
n Skinhead m; **~ny** adj dünn; **~tight**
adj (dress etc) hauteng

skip [skɪp] n Sprung m ♦ vi hüpfen;
(with rope) Seil springen ♦ vt (pass over)
übergehen

ski: **~ pants** npl Skihosen pl; **~ pass** n
Skipass m; **~ pole** n Skistock m

skipper ['skɪpəʳ] n Kapitän m ♦ vt
führen

skipping rope ['skɪpɪŋ-] (BRIT) n
Hüpfseil nt

skirmish ['skɜːmɪʃ] n Scharmützel nt

skirt [skɜːt] n Rock m ♦ vt herumgehen
um; (fig) umgehen; **~ing board** (BRIT)
n Fußleiste f

ski suit n Skianzug m

skit [skɪt] n Parodie f

ski tow n Schlepplift m

skittle ['skɪtl] n Kegel m; **~s** n (game)
Kegeln nt

skive [skaɪv] (BRIT: inf) vi schwänzen

skulk [skʌlk] vi sich herumdrücken

skull [skʌl] n Schädel m

skunk [skʌŋk] n Stinktier nt

sky [skaɪ] n Himmel m; **~light** n Oberlicht nt; **~scraper** n Wolkenkratzer m

slab [slæb] n (of stone) Platte f

slack [slæk] adj (loose) locker; (business)
flau; (careless) nachlässig, lasch ♦ vi
nachlässig sein ♦ n: **to take up the ~**
straff ziehen; **~s** npl (trousers) Hose(n
pl) f; **~en** vi (also: **~en off**) locker werden; (: slow down) stocken, nachlassen
♦ vt (: loosen) lockern

slag [slæg] (BRIT) vt: **~ off** (criticize)
(he)runtermachen

slag heap [slæg-] n Halde f

slain [sleɪn] pp of **slay**

slam [slæm] n Knall m ♦ vt (door) zuschlagen; (throw down) knallen ♦ vi zuschlagen

slander ['slɑːndəʳ] n Verleumdung f
♦ vt verleumden

slang [slæŋ] n Slang m; (jargon) Jargon
m

slant [slɑːnt] n Schräge f; (fig) Tendenz
f ♦ vt schräg legen ♦ vi schräg liegen;
~ed adj schräg; **~ing** adj schräg

slap [slæp] n Klaps m ♦ vt einen Klaps
geben +dat ♦ adv (directly) geradewegs;
~dash adj salopp; **~stick** n (comedy)
Klamauk m; **~-up** (BRIT) adj (meal) erstklassig, prima

slash [slæʃ] n Schnittwunde f ♦ vt
(auf)schlitzen

slat [slæt] n Leiste f

slate [sleɪt] n (stone) Schiefer m;
(roofing) Dachziegel m ♦ vt (criticize)
verreißen

slaughter ['slɔːtəʳ] n (of animals)
Schlachten nt; (of people) Gemetzel nt
♦ vt schlachten; (people) niedermetzeln; **~house** n Schlachthof m

Slav [slɑːv] adj slawisch

slave [sleɪv] n Sklave m, Sklavin f ♦ vi schuften, sich schinden; **~ry** n Sklaverei f

slay [sleɪ] (pt **slew**, pp **slain**) vt ermorden

sleazy ['sliːzɪ] adj (place) schmierig

sledge [sledʒ] n Schlitten m

sledgehammer ['sledʒhæmər] n Schmiedehammer m

sledging n Schlittenfahren nt

sleek [sliːk] adj glatt; (shape) rassig

sleep [sliːp] (pt, pp **slept**) n Schlaf m ♦ vi schlafen; **to go to ~** einschlafen; **~ in** vi ausschlafen; (oversleep) verschlafen; **~er** n (person) Schläfer m; (BRIT: RAIL) Schlafwagen m; (: beam) Schwelle f; **~ing bag** n Schlafsack m; **~ing car** n Schlafwagen m; **~ing partner** n = **silent partner**; **~ing pill** n Schlaftablette f; **~less** adj (night) schlaflos; **~walker** n Schlafwandler(in) m(f); **~y** adj schläfrig

sleet [sliːt] n Schneeregen m

sleeve [sliːv] n Ärmel m; (of record) Umschlag m; **~less** adj ärmellos

sleigh [sleɪ] n Pferdeschlitten m

sleight [slaɪt] n: **~ of hand** Fingerfertigkeit f

slender ['slendər] adj schlank; (fig) gering

slept [slept] pt, pp of **sleep**

slew [sluː] vi (veer) (herum)schwenken ♦ pt of **slay**

slice [slaɪs] n Scheibe f ♦ vt in Scheiben schneiden

slick [slɪk] adj (clever) raffiniert, aalglatt ♦ n Ölteppich m

slid [slɪd] pt, pp of **slide**

slide [slaɪd] (pt, pp **slid**) n Rutschbahn f; (PHOT) Dia(positiv) nt; (BRIT: for hair) (Haar)spange f ♦ vt schieben ♦ vi (slip) gleiten, rutschen; **sliding** ['slaɪdɪŋ] adj (door) Schiebe-; **sliding scale** n gleitende Skala f

slight [slaɪt] adj zierlich; (trivial) geringfügig; (small) gering ♦ n Kränkung f

♦ vt (offend) kränken; **not in the ~est** nicht im Geringsten; **~ly** adv etwas, ein bisschen

slim [slɪm] adj schlank; (book) dünn; (chance) gering ♦ vi eine Schlankheitskur machen

slime [slaɪm] n Schleim m

slimming ['slɪmɪŋ] n Schlankheitskur f

slimy ['slaɪmɪ] adj glitschig; (dirty) schlammig; (person) schmierig

sling [slɪŋ] (pt, pp **slung**) n Schlinge f; (weapon) Schleuder f ♦ vt schleudern

slip [slɪp] n (mistake) Flüchtigkeitsfehler m; (petticoat) Unterrock m; (of paper) Zettel m ♦ vt (put) stecken, schieben ♦ vi (lose balance) ausrutschen; (move) gleiten, rutschen; (decline) nachlassen; (move smoothly): **to ~ in/out** (person) hinein-/hinausschlüpfen; **to give sb the ~** jdm entwischen; **~ of the tongue** Versprecher m; **it ~ped my mind** das ist mir entfallen; **to ~ sth on/off** etw über-/abstreifen; **~ away** vi sich wegstehlen; **~ in** vt hineingleiten lassen ♦ vi (errors) sich einschleichen; **~ped disc** n Bandscheibenschaden m

slipper ['slɪpər] n Hausschuh m

slippery ['slɪpərɪ] adj glatt

slip: **~ road** (BRIT) n Auffahrt f/Ausfahrt f; **~shod** adj schlampig; **~-up** n Panne f; **~way** n Auslaufbahn f

slit [slɪt] (pt, pp **slit**) n Schlitz m ♦ vt aufschlitzen

slither ['slɪðər] vi schlittern; (snake) sich schlängeln

sliver ['slɪvər] n (of glass, wood) Splitter m; (of cheese) Scheibchen nt

slob [slɒb] (inf) n Klotz m

slog [slɒg] vi (work hard) schuften ♦ n: **it was a ~** es war eine Plackerei

slogan ['sləugən] n Schlagwort nt; (COMM) Werbespruch m

slop [slɒp] vi (also: **~ over**) überschwappen ♦ vt verschütten

slope [sləup] n Neigung f; (of mountains) (Ab)hang m ♦ vi: **to ~ down** sich senken; **to ~ up** ansteigen; **sloping** ['sləupıŋ] *adj* schräg

sloppy ['slɔpı] *adj* schlampig

slot [slɔt] *n* Schlitz *m* ♦ *vt*: **to ~ sth in** etw einlegen

sloth [sləuθ] *n* (*laziness*) Faulheit *f*

slot machine *n* (*BRIT*) Automat *m*; (*for gambling*) Spielautomat *m*

slouch [slautʃ] *vi*: **to ~ about** (*laze*) herumhängen (*inf*)

slovenly ['slʌvənlı] *adj* schlampig; (*speech*) salopp

slow [sləu] *adj* langsam ♦ *adv* langsam; **to be ~** (*clock*) nachgehen; (*stupid*) begriffsstutzig sein; (*road sign*) „Langsam"; **in ~ motion** in Zeitlupe; **~ down** *vi* langsamer werden ♦ *vt* verlangsamen; **~ up** *vi* sich verlangsamen, sich verzögern ♦ *vt* aufhalten, langsamer machen; **~ly** *adv* langsam

sludge [slʌdʒ] *n* Schlamm *m*

slug [slʌg] *n* Nacktschnecke *f*; (*inf: bullet*) Kugel *f*

sluggish ['slʌgıʃ] *adj* träge; (*COMM*) schleppend

sluice [slu:s] *n* Schleuse *f*

slum [slʌm] *n* (*house*) Elendsquartier *nt*

slump [slʌmp] *n* Rückgang *m* ♦ *vi* fallen, stürzen

slung [slʌŋ] *pt*, *pp of* **sling**

slur [slə:ʳ] *n* Undeutlichkeit *f*; (*insult*) Verleumdung *f*; **~red** [slə:d] *adj* (*pronunciation*) undeutlich

slush [slʌʃ] *n* (*snow*) Schneematsch *m*; **~ fund** *n* Schmiergeldfonds *m*

slut [slʌt] *n* Schlampe *f*

sly [slaı] *adj* schlau

smack [smæk] *n* Klaps *m* ♦ *vt* einen Klaps geben +*dat* ♦ *vi*: **to ~ of** riechen nach; **to ~ one's lips** schmatzen, sich *dat* die Lippen lecken

small [smɔ:l] *adj* klein; **in the ~ hours** in den frühen Morgenstunden; **~ ads** (*BRIT*) *npl* Kleinanzeigen *pl*; **~ change** *n* Kleingeld *nt*; **~holder** *n* Kleinbauer *m*; **~pox** *n* Pocken *pl*; **~ talk** *n* Geplauder *nt*

smart [smɑ:t] *adj* (*fashionable*) elegant, schick; (*neat*) adrett; (*clever*) clever; (*quick*) scharf ♦ *vi* brennen, schmerzen; **~ card** *n* Chipkarte *f*; **~en up** *vi* sich in Schale werfen ♦ *vt* herausputzen

smash [smæʃ] *n* Zusammenstoß *m*; (*TENNIS*) Schmetterball *m* ♦ *vt* (*break*) zerschmettern; (*destroy*) vernichten ♦ *vi* (*break*) zersplittern, zerspringen; **~ing** (*inf*) *adj* toll

smattering ['smætərıŋ] *n* oberflächliche Kenntnis *f*

smear [smıəʳ] *n* Fleck *m* ♦ *vt* beschmieren

smell [smɛl] (*pt*, *pp* **smelt** *or* **smelled**) *n* Geruch *m*; (*sense*) Geruchssinn *m* ♦ *vt* riechen ♦ *vi*: **to ~ (of)** riechen (nach); (*fragrantly*) duften (nach); **~y** *adj* übel riechend

smile [smaıl] *n* Lächeln *nt* ♦ *vi* lächeln

smiling ['smaılıŋ] *adj* lächelnd

smirk [smə:k] *n* blöde(s) Grinsen *nt*

smock [smɔk] *n* Kittel *m*

smoke [sməuk] *n* Rauch *m* ♦ *vt* rauchen; (*food*) räuchern ♦ *vi* rauchen; **~d** (*bacon*) geräuchert; (*glass*) Rauch-; **~r** *n* Raucher(in) *m(f)*; (*RAIL*) Raucherabteil *nt*; **~ screen** *n* Rauchwand *f*

smoking ['sməukıŋ] *n*: **"no ~"** „Rauchen verboten"; **~ compartment** (*BRIT*), **~ car** (*US*) *n* Raucherabteil *nt*

smoky ['sməukı] *adj* rauchig; (*room*) verraucht; (*taste*) geräuchert

smolder ['sməuldəʳ] (*US*) *vi* = **smoulder**

smooth [smu:ð] *adj* glatt ♦ *vt* (*also: ~ out*) glätten, glatt streichen

smother ['smʌðəʳ] *vt* ersticken

smoulder ['sməuldəʳ] (*US* **smolder**) *vi* schwelen

smudge [smʌdʒ] *n* Schmutzfleck *m* ♦ *vt* beschmieren

smug [smʌg] *adj* selbstgefällig

smuggle ['smʌgl] *vt* schmuggeln; **~r** *n* Schmuggler *m*

smuggling ['smʌglıŋ] *n* Schmuggel *m*

smutty ['smʌtɪ] adj schmutzig

snack [snæk] n Imbiss m; **~ bar** n Imbissstube f

snag [snæg] n Haken m

snail [sneɪl] n Schnecke f

snake [sneɪk] n Schlange f

snap [snæp] n Schnappen nt; (photograph) Schnappschuss m ♦ adj (decision) schnell ♦ vt (break) zerbrechen; (PHOT) knipsen ♦ vi (break) brechen; (speak) anfauchen; **to ~ shut** zuschnappen; **~ at** vt fus schnappen nach; **~ off** vt (break) abbrechen ♦ vt aufschnappen; **~shot** n Schnappschuss m

snare [snɛəʳ] n Schlinge f ♦ vt mit einer Schlinge fangen

snarl [snɑːl] n Zähnefletschen nt; (dog) knurren

snatch [snætʃ] n (small amount) Bruchteil m ♦ vt schnappen, packen

sneak [sniːk] vi schleichen ♦ n (inf) Petze(r) mf; **~ers** ['sniːkəz] (US) npl Freizeitschuhe pl; **~y** ['sniːkɪ] adj raffiniert

sneer [snɪəʳ] n Hohnlächeln nt ♦ vi spötteln

sneeze [sniːz] n Niesen nt ♦ vi niesen

sniff [snɪf] n Schnüffeln nt ♦ vi schnieben; (smell) schnüffeln ♦ vt schnuppern

snigger ['snɪgəʳ] n Kichern nt ♦ vi hämisch kichern

snip [snɪp] n Schnippel m, Schnipsel m ♦ vt schnippeln

sniper ['snaɪpəʳ] n Heckenschütze m

snippet ['snɪpɪt] n Schnipsel m; (of conversation) Fetzen m

snivelling ['snɪvlɪŋ] adj weinerlich

snob [snɒb] n Snob m

snooker ['snuːkəʳ] n Snooker nt

snoop [snuːp] vi: **to ~ about** herumschnüffeln

snooze [snuːz] n Nickerchen nt ♦ vi ein Nickerchen machen, dösen

snore [snɔːʳ] vi schnarchen ♦ n Schnarchen nt

snorkel ['snɔːkl] n Schnorchel m

snort [snɔːt] n Schnauben nt ♦ vi schnauben

snout [snaut] n Schnauze f

snow [snəu] n Schnee m ♦ vi schneien; **~ball** n Schneeball m ♦ vi eskalieren; **~bound** adj eingeschneit; **~drift** n Schneewehe f; **~drop** n Schneeglöckchen nt; **~fall** n Schneefall m; **~flake** n Schneeflocke f; **~man** (irreg) n Schneemann m; **~plough** (US snowplow) n Schneepflug m; **~ shoe** n Schneeschuh m; **~storm** n Schneesturm m

snub [snʌb] vt schroff abfertigen ♦ n Verweis m; **~-nosed** adj stupsnasig

snuff [snʌf] n Schnupftabak m

snug [snʌg] adj gemütlich, behaglich

snuggle ['snʌgl] vi: **to ~ up to sb** sich an jdn kuscheln

KEYWORD

so [səu] adv 1 (thus) so; (likewise) auch; **so saying he walked away** indem er das sagte, ging er; **if so** wenn ja; **I didn't do it - you did so!** ich hab das nicht gemacht - hast du wohl!; **so do I, so am I** etc ich auch; **so it is!** tatsächlich!; **I hope/think so** hoffentlich/ich glaube schon; **so far** bis jetzt

2 (in comparisons etc: to such a degree) so; **so quickly/big (that)** so schnell/ groß, dass; **I'm so glad to see you** ich freue mich so, dich zu sehen

3: **so many** so viele; **so much work** so viel Arbeit; **I love you so much** ich liebe dich so sehr

4 (phrases): **10 or so** etwa 10; **so long!** (inf: goodbye) tschüss!

♦ conj 1 (expressing purpose): **so as to** um ... zu; **so (that)** damit

2 (expressing result) also; **so I was right after all** ich hatte also doch Recht; **so you see** ... wie du siehst ...

---

soak [səuk] vt durchnässen; (leave in liquid) einweichen ♦ vi (ein)weichen; **~**

so-and-so in vi einsickern; **~ up** vt aufsaugen; **~ed** adj völlig durchnässt; **~ing** adj klitschnass, patschnass

so-and-so ['səuənsəu] n (somebody) Soundso m

soap [səup] n Seife f; **~flakes** npl Seifenflocken pl; **~ opera** n Familienserie f (im Fernsehen, Radio); **~ powder** n Waschpulver nt; **~y** adj seifig, Seifen-

soar [sɔːr] vi aufsteigen; (prices) in die Höhe schnellen

sob [sɔb] n Schluchzen nt ♦ vi schluchzen

sober ['səubər] adj (also fig) nüchtern; **~ up** vi nüchtern werden

so-called ['səu'kɔːld] adj so genannt

soccer ['sɔkər] n Fußball m

sociable ['səuʃəbl] adj gesellig

social ['səuʃl] adj sozial; (friendly, living with others) gesellig ♦ n gesellig(er) Abend m; **~ club** n Verein m (für Freizeitgestaltung); **~ism** n Sozialismus m; **~ist** n Sozialist(in) m(f) ♦ adj sozialistisch; **~ize** vi (be with people) (gesellschaftlich verkehren mit); **~ly** adv gesellschaftlich, privat; **~ security** n Sozialversicherung f; **~ work** n Sozialarbeit f; **~ worker** n Sozialarbeiter(in) m(f)

society [sə'saiəti] n Gesellschaft f; (fashionable world) die große Welt

sociology [səusi'ɔlədʒi] n Soziologie f

sock [sɔk] n Socke f

socket ['sɔkit] n (ELEC) Steckdose f; (of eye) Augenhöhle f

sod [sɔd] n Rasenstück nt; (inf!) Sauerkerl m (!)

soda ['səudə] n Soda f; (also: **~ water**) Soda(wasser) nt; (US: also: **~ pop**) Limonade f

sodden ['sɔdn] adj durchweicht

sodium ['səudiəm] n Natrium nt

sofa ['səufə] n Sofa nt

soft [sɔft] adj weich; (not loud) leise; (weak) nachgiebig; **~ drink** n alkoholfreie(s) Getränk nt; **~en** ['sɔfn] vt weich machen; (blow) abschwächen;

mildern ♦ vi weich werden; **~ly** adv sanft; leise; **~ness** n Weichheit f; (fig) Sanftheit f

software ['sɔftweər] n (COMPUT) Software f

soggy ['sɔgi] adj (ground) sumpfig; (bread) aufgeweicht

soil [sɔil] n Erde f ♦ vt beschmutzen

solace ['sɔlis] n Trost m

solar ['səulər] adj Sonnen-; **~ cell** n Solarzelle f; **~ energy** n Sonnenenergie f; **~ panel** n Sonnenkollektor m; **~ power** n Sonnenenergie f

sold [səuld] pt, pp of **sell**; **~ out** (COMM) ausverkauft

solder ['səuldər] vt löten

soldier ['səuldʒər] n Soldat m

sole [səul] n Sohle f; (fish) Seezunge f ♦ adj alleinig, Allein-; **~ly** adv ausschließlich

solemn ['sɔləm] adj feierlich

sole trader n (COMM) Einzelunternehmen nt

solicit [sə'lisit] vt (request) bitten um ♦ vi (prostitute) Kunden anwerben

solicitor [sə'lisitər] n Rechtsanwalt m/-anwältin f

solid ['sɔlid] adj (hard) fest; (of same material, not hollow) massiv; (without break) voll, ganz; (reliable, sensible) solide ♦ n Festkörper m; **~arity** [sɔli'dæriti] n Solidarität f; **~ify** [sə'lidifai] vi fest werden

solitary ['sɔlitəri] adj einsam, einzeln; **~ confinement** n Einzelhaft f

solitude ['sɔlitjuːd] n Einsamkeit f

solo ['səuləu] n Solo nt; **~ist** ['səuləuist] n Solist(in) m(f)

soluble ['sɔljubl] adj (substance) löslich; (problem) (auf)lösbar

solution [sə'luːʃən] n (also fig) Lösung f; (of mystery) Erklärung f

solve [sɔlv] vt (auf)lösen

solvent ['sɔlvənt] adj (FIN) zahlungsfähig ♦ n (CHEM) Lösungsmittel nt

sombre ['sɔmbər] (US **somber**) adj düster

KEYWORD

---

some [sʌm] adj 1 (a certain amount or number of) einige; (a few) ein paar; (with singular nouns) etwas; **some tea/biscuits** etwas Tee/ein paar Plätzchen; **I've got some money, but not much** ich habe ein bisschen Geld, aber nicht viel

2 (certain: in contrasts) manche(r, s); **some people say that ...** manche Leute sagen, dass ...

3 (unspecified) irgendein(e); **some woman was asking for you** da hat eine Frau nach Ihnen gefragt; **some day** eines Tages; **some day next week** irgendwann nächste Woche

♦ pron 1 (a certain number) einige; **have you got some?** haben Sie welche?

2 (a certain amount) etwas; **I've read some of the book** ich habe das Buch teilweise gelesen

♦ adv: **some 10 people** etwa 10 Leute

somebody ['sʌmbədɪ] pron = **someone**

somehow ['sʌmhaʊ] adv (in some way, for some reason) irgendwie

someone ['sʌmwʌn] pron jemand; (direct obj) jemand(en); (indirect obj) jemandem

someplace ['sʌmpleɪs] (US) adv = **somewhere**

somersault ['sʌməsɔːlt] n Salto m ♦ vi einen Salto machen

something ['sʌmθɪŋ] pron etwas

sometime ['sʌmtaɪm] adv (ir-gend)einmal

sometimes ['sʌmtaɪmz] adv manchmal

somewhat ['sʌmwɔt] adv etwas

somewhere ['sʌmwɛəʳ] adv irgendwo; (to a place) irgendwohin; **~ else** irgendwo anders

son [sʌn] n Sohn m

sonar ['səʊnɑːʳ] n Echolot nt

song [sɒŋ] n Lied nt

sonic boom ['sɒnɪk-] n Überschallknall m

son-in-law ['sʌnɪnlɔː] n Schwiegersohn m

soon [suːn] adv bald; **~ afterwards** kurz danach; **~er** adv (time) früher; (for preference) lieber; **~er or later** früher oder später

soot [sʊt] n Ruß m

soothe [suːð] vt (person) beruhigen; (pain) lindern

sophisticated [sə'fɪstɪkeɪtɪd] adj (person) kultiviert; (machinery) hoch entwickelt

sophomore ['sɒfəmɔːʳ] (US) n College-student m im 2. Jahr

soporific [sɒpə'rɪfɪk] adj einschläfernd

sopping ['sɒpɪŋ] adj patschnass

soppy ['sɒpɪ] (inf) adj schmalzig

soprano [sə'prɑːnəʊ] n Sopran m

sorcerer ['sɔːsərəʳ] n Hexenmeister m

sordid ['sɔːdɪd] adj erbärmlich

sore [sɔːʳ] adj schmerzend; (point) wund ♦ n Wunde f; **~ly** adv (tempted) stark, sehr

sorrow ['sɒrəʊ] n Kummer m, Leid nt; **~ful** adj sorgenvoll

sorry ['sɒrɪ] adj traurig, erbärmlich; **~!** Entschuldigung!; **to feel ~ for sb** jdn bemitleiden; **I feel ~ for him** er tut mir Leid; **~?** (pardon) wie bitte?

sort [sɔːt] n Art f, Sorte f ♦ vt (also: **~ out**: papers) sortieren; (: problems) sichten, in Ordnung bringen; **~ing office** n Sortierstelle f

SOS n SOS nt

so-so ['səʊsəʊ] adv so(-so) lala

sought [sɔːt] pt, pp of **seek**

soul [səʊl] n Seele f; (music) Soul m; **~-destroying** adj trostlos; **~ful** adj seelenvoll

sound [saʊnd] adj (healthy) gesund; (safe) sicher; (sensible) vernünftig; (theory) stichhaltig; (thorough) tüchtig, gehörig ♦ adv: **to be ~ asleep** fest schlafen ♦ n (noise) Geräusch nt, Laut m; (GEOG) Sund m ♦ vt erschallen lassen; (alarm) (Alarm) schlagen ♦ vi (make a ~) schallen, tönen; (seem) klingen; **to ~ like** sich anhören wie; **~ out** vt erforschen; (person) auf den Zahn fühlen +dat; **~ barrier** n Schallmauer f; **~ bite** n (RAD, TV) prägnante(s) Zitat nt; **~ effects** npl Toneffekte pl; **~ly** adv (sleep) fest; (beat) tüchtig; **~proof** adj (room) schalldicht; **~ track** n Tonstreifen m; (music) Filmmusik f

soup [su:p] n Suppe f; **~ plate** n Suppenteller m; **~spoon** n Suppenlöffel m

sour ['sauər] adj (also fig) sauer; **it's ~ grapes** (fig) die Trauben hängen zu hoch

source [sɔ:s] n (also fig) Quelle f

south [sauθ] n Süden m ♦ adj Süd-, südlich ♦ adv nach Süden, südwärts; **S~ Africa** n Südafrika nt; **S~ African** adj südafrikanisch ♦ n Südafrikaner(in) m(f); **S~ America** n Südamerika nt; **S~ American** adj südamerikanisch ♦ n Südamerikaner(in) m(f); **~-east** n Südosten m; **~erly** ['sʌðəlɪ] adj südlich; **~ern** ['sʌðən] adj südlich, Süd-; **S~ Pole** n Südpol m; **S~ Wales** n Südwales nt; **~ward(s)** adv südwärts, nach Süden; **~-west** n Südwesten m

souvenir [su:və'nɪər] n Souvenir nt

sovereign ['sɔvrɪn] n (ruler) Herrscher(in) m(f) ♦ adj (independent) souverän

soviet ['səuvɪət] adj sowjetisch; **the S~ Union** die Sowjetunion

sow[1] [sau] n Sau f

sow[2] [səu] (pt sowed, pp sown) vt (also fig) säen

soya ['sɔɪə] (US **soy**) n: **~ bean** Sojabohne f; **~ sauce** Sojasauce f

spa [spa:] n (place) Kurort m

space [speɪs] n Platz m, Raum m; (universe) Weltraum m, All nt; (length of time) Abstand m ♦ vt (also: **~ out**) verteilen; **~craft** n Raumschiff nt; **~man** (irreg) n Raumfahrer m; **~ ship** n Raum-

schiff nt

spacing ['speɪsɪŋ] n Abstand m; (also: **~ out**) Verteilung f

spacious ['speɪʃəs] adj geräumig, weit

spade [speɪd] n Spaten m; **~s** npl (CARDS) Pik nt

Spain [speɪn] n Spanien nt

span [spæn] n Spanne f; (of bridge etc) Spannweite f ♦ vt überspannen

Spaniard ['spænjəd] n Spanier(in) m(f)

spaniel ['spænjəl] n Spaniel m

Spanish ['spænɪʃ] adj spanisch ♦ n (LING) Spanisch nt; **the ~** npl (people) die Spanier pl

spank [spæŋk] vt verhauen, versohlen

spanner ['spænər] n (BRIT) Schraubenschlüssel m

spar [spa:r] n (NAUT) Sparren m ♦ vi (BOXING) einen Sparring machen

spare [speər] adj Ersatz-; n = **spare part** ♦ vt (lives, feelings) verschonen; (trouble) ersparen; **to ~** (surplus) übrig; **~ part** n Ersatzteil nt; **~ time** n Freizeit f; **~ wheel** n (AUT) Reservereifen m

sparing ['speərɪŋ] adj: **to be ~ with** geizen mit; **~ly** adv sparsam; (eat, spend etc) in Maßen

spark [spa:k] n Funken m; **~(ing) plug** n Zündkerze f

sparkle ['spa:kl] n Funkeln nt; (gaiety) Schwung m ♦ vi funkeln; **sparkling** adj funkelnd; (wine) Schaum-; (mineral water) mit Kohlensäure; (conversation) spritzig, geistreich

sparrow ['spærəu] n Spatz m

sparse [spa:s] adj spärlich

spasm ['spæzəm] n (MED) Krampf m; (fig) Anfall m; **~odic** [spæz'mɔdɪk] adj (fig) sprunghaft

spastic ['spæstɪk] (old) n Spastiker(in) m(f) ♦ adj spastisch

spat [spæt] pt, pp of **spit**

spate [speɪt] n (fig) Flut f, Schwall m; **in ~** (river) angeschwollen

spatter ['spætər] vt bespritzen, verspritzen

spatula 561 spinal

spatula [ˈspætjʊlə] n Spatel m

spawn [spɔːn] vi laichen ♦ n Laich m

speak [spiːk] (pt **spoke**, pp **spoken**) vt sprechen, reden; (truth) sagen; (language) sprechen ♦ vi: **to ~ (to)** sprechen (mit or zu); **to ~ to sb of** or **about sth** mit jdm über etw acc sprechen; **~ up!** sprich lauter!; **~er** n Sprecher(in) m(f), Redner(in) m(f); (loudspeaker) Lautsprecher m; (POL): **the S~er** der Vorsitzende des Parlaments (BRIT) or des Kongresses (US)

spear [spɪər] n Speer m ♦ vt aufspießen; **~head** vt (attack etc) anführen

spec [spek] (inf) n: **on ~** auf gut Glück

special [ˈspeʃl] adj besondere(r, s); **~ist** n (TECH) Fachmann m; (MED) Facharzt m/Fachärztin f; **~ity** [speʃɪˈælɪtɪ] n Spezialität f; (study) Spezialgebiet nt; **~ize** vi: **to ~ize (in)** sich spezialisieren (auf +acc); **~ly** adv besonders; (explicitly) extra; **~ needs** adj: **~ needs children** behinderte Kinder pl; **~ty** (esp US) n = **speciality**

species [ˈspiːʃiːz] n Art f

specific [spəˈsɪfɪk] adj spezifisch; **~ally** adv spezifisch

specification [spesɪfɪˈkeɪʃən] n Angabe f; (stipulation) Bedingung f; **~s** npl (TECH) technische Daten pl

specify [ˈspesɪfaɪ] vt genau angeben

specimen [ˈspesɪmən] n Probe f

speck [spek] n Fleckchen nt

speckled [ˈspekld] adj gesprenkelt

specs [speks] (inf) npl Brille f

spectacle [ˈspektəkl] n Schauspiel m; **~s** npl (glasses) Brille f

spectacular [spekˈtækjʊlər] adj sensationell; (success etc) spektakulär

spectator [spekˈteɪtər] n Zuschauer(in) m(f)

spectre [ˈspektər] (US **specter**) n Geist m, Gespenst nt

speculate [ˈspekjʊleɪt] vi spekulieren

speech [spiːtʃ] n Sprache f; (address) Rede f; (way one speaks) Sprechweise f; **~less** adj sprachlos

speed [spiːd] n Geschwindigkeit f; (gear) Gang m ♦ vi (JUR) (zu) schnell fahren; **at full** or **top ~** mit Höchstgeschwindigkeit; **~ up** ♦ vt beschleunigen ♦ vi schneller werden; schneller fahren; **~boat** n Schnellboot nt; **~ily** adv schleunigst; **~ing** n Geschwindigkeitsüberschreitung f; **~ limit** n Geschwindigkeitsbegrenzung f; **~ometer** [spɪˈdɒmɪtər] n Tachometer m; **~way** n (bike racing) Motorradrennstrecke f; **~y** adj schnell

spell [spel] (pt, pp **spelt** (BRIT) or **spelled**) n (magic) Bann m; (period of time) (eine) Zeit lang ♦ vt buchstabieren; (imply) bedeuten; **to cast a ~ on sb** jdn verzaubern; **~bound** adj (wie) gebannt; **~ing** n Rechtschreibung f

spelt [spelt] (BRIT) pt, pp of **spell**

spend [spend] (pt, pp **spent**) vt (money) ausgeben; (time) verbringen; **~thrift** n Verschwender(in) m(f)

spent [spent] pt, pp of **spend**

sperm [spɜːm] n (BIOL) Samenflüssigkeit f

spew [spjuː] vt (er)brechen

sphere [sfɪər] n (globe) Kugel f; (fig) Sphäre f, Gebiet nt; **spherical** [ˈsferɪk] adj kugelförmig

spice [spaɪs] n Gewürz nt ♦ vt würzen

spick-and-span [ˈspɪkənˈspæn] adj blitzblank

spicy [ˈspaɪsɪ] adj (food) stark gewürzt; (fig) pikant

spider [ˈspaɪdər] n Spinne f

spike [spaɪk] n Dorn m, Spitze f

spill [spɪl] (pt, pp **spilt** or **spilled**) vt verschütten ♦ vi sich ergießen; **~ over** vi überlaufen; (fig) sich ausbreiten

spilt [spɪlt] pt, pp of **spill**

spin [spɪn] (pt, pp **spun**) n (trip in car) Spazierfahrt f; (AVIAT) (Ab)trudeln nt; (on ball) Drall m ♦ vt (thread) spinnen; (like top) (herum)wirbeln ♦ vi sich drehen; **~ out** vt in die Länge ziehen

spinach [ˈspɪnɪtʃ] n Spinat m

spinal [ˈspaɪnl] adj Rückgrat-; **~ cord** n

Rückenmark nt

spindly ['spɪndlɪ] adj spindeldürr

spin doctor n PR-Fachmann m, PR-Fachfrau f

spin-dryer [spɪn'draɪə'] (BRIT) n Wäscheschleuder f

spine [spaɪn] n Rückgrat nt; (thorn) Stachel m; **~less** adj (also fig) rückgratlos

spinning ['spɪnɪŋ] n Spinnen nt; **~ top** n Kreisel m; **~ wheel** n Spinnrad nt

spin-off ['spɪnɒf] n Nebenprodukt nt

spinster ['spɪnstə'] n unverheiratete Frau f; (pej) alte Jungfer f

spiral ['spaɪərl] n Spirale f ♦ adj spiralförmig; (movement etc) in Spiralen ♦ vi sich (hoch)winden; **~ staircase** n Wendeltreppe f

spire [spaɪə'] n Turm m

spirit ['spɪrɪt] n Geist m; (humour, mood) Stimmung f; (courage) Mut m; (verve) Elan m; (alcohol) Alkohol m; **~s** npl (drink) Spirituosen pl; in **good ~s** gut aufgelegt; **~ed** adj beherzt; **~ level** n Wasserwaage f

spiritual ['spɪrɪtjuəl] adj geistig, seelisch; (REL) geistlich ♦ n Spiritual nt

spit [spɪt] (pt, pp spat) n (for roasting) (Brat)spieß m; (saliva) Spucke f ♦ vi spucken; (rain) sprühen; (make a sound) zischen; (cat) fauchen

spite [spaɪt] n Gehässigkeit f ♦ vt kränken; **in ~ of** trotz; **~ful** adj gehässig

spittle ['spɪtl] n Speichel m, Spucke f

splash [splæʃ] n Spritzer m; (of colour) (Farb)fleck m ♦ vt bespritzen ♦ vi spritzen

spleen [spli:n] n (ANAT) Milz f

splendid ['splendɪd] adj glänzend

splendour ['splendə'] (US splendor) n Pracht f

splint [splɪnt] n Schiene f

splinter ['splɪntə'] n Splitter m ♦ vi (zer)splittern

split [splɪt] (pt, pp split) n Spalte f; (fig) Spaltung f; (division) Trennung f ♦ vt spalten vi ♦ vi (divide) reißen; **~ up** vi

sich trennen

splutter ['splʌtə'] vi stottern

spoil [spɔɪl] (pt, pp spoilt or spoiled) vt (ruin) verderben; (child) verwöhnen; **~s** npl Beute f; **~sport** n Spielverderber m; **~t** pt, pp of spoil

spoke [spəuk] pt of speak ♦ n Speiche f; **~n** pp of speak

spokesman ['spəuksmən] (irreg) n Sprecher m; **spokeswoman** ['spəukswumən] (irreg) n Sprecherin f

sponge [spʌndʒ] n Schwamm m ♦ vt abwaschen ♦ vi: **to ~ on** auf Kosten +gen leben; **~ bag** (BRIT) n Kulturbeutel m; **~ cake** n Rührkuchen m

sponsor ['spɒnsə'] n Sponsor m ♦ vt fördern; **~ship** n Finanzierung f; (public) Schirmherrschaft f

spontaneous [spɒn'teɪnɪəs] adj spontan

spooky ['spu:kɪ] (inf) adj gespenstisch

spool [spu:l] n Spule f, Rolle f

spoon [spu:n] n Löffel m; **~-feed** (irreg) vt mit dem Löffel füttern; (fig) hochpäppeln; **~ful** n Löffel m (voll)

sport [spɔ:t] n Sport m; (person) feine(r) Kerl m; **~ing** adj (fair) sportlich, fair; **to give sb a ~ing chance** jdm eine faire Chance geben; **~ jacket** (US) n = **sports jacket**; **~s car** n Sportwagen m; **~s jacket** n Sportjackett nt; **~sman** (irreg) n Sportler m; **~smanship** n Sportlichkeit f; **~swear** n Sportkleidung f; **~swoman** (irreg) n Sportlerin f; **~y** adj sportlich

spot [spɒt] n Punkt m; (dirty) Fleck(en) m; (place) Stelle f; (MED) Pickel m ♦ vt erspähen; (mistake) bemerken; **on the ~** an Ort und Stelle; (at once) auf der Stelle; **~ check** n Stichprobe f; **~less** adj fleckenlos; **~light** n Scheinwerferlicht nt; (lamp) Scheinwerfer m; **~ted** adj gefleckt; **~ty** adj (face) pickelig

spouse [spaus] n Gatte m/Gattin f

spout [spaut] n (of pot) Tülle f; (jet) Wasserstrahl m ♦ vi speien

sprain [spreɪn] n Verrenkung f ♦ vt verrenken

sprang [spræŋ] *pt of* **spring**

sprawl [sprɔːl] *vi* sich strecken

spray [spreɪ] *n* Spray *m* ♦; *(off sea)* Gischt *f*; *(of flowers)* Zweig *m* ♦ *vt* besprühen, sprayen

spread [spred] *(pt, pp spread) n (extent)* Verbreitung *f*; *(inf: meal)* Schmaus *m*; *(for bread)* Aufstrich *m* ♦ *vt* ausbreiten; *(scatter)* verbreiten; *(butter)* streichen ♦ *vi* sich ausbreiten; **~-eagled** ['spredixgld] *adj*: **to be ~-eagled** die vier von sich strecken; **~ out** *(move apart)* sich verteilen; **~sheet** *n* Tabellenkalkulation *f*

spree [spriː] *n (shopping)* Einkaufsbummel *m*; **to go on a ~** einen draufmachen

sprightly ['spraɪtlɪ] *adj* munter, lebhaft

spring [sprɪŋ] *(pt* **sprang***, pp* **sprung***) n (leap)* Sprung *m*; *(TECH)* Feder *f*; *(season)* Frühling *m*; *(water)* Quelle *f* ♦ *vi (leap)* springen; **~ up** *(problem)* auftauchen; **~board** *n* Sprungbrett *nt*; **~-clean** *n (also:* **~-cleaning)** Frühjahrsputz *m*; **~time** *n* Frühling *m*; **~y** *adj* federnd, elastisch

sprinkle ['sprɪŋkl] *vt* streuen; **to ~ water on, to ~ with water** mit Wasser besprengen; **~r** ['sprɪŋklə^r] *n (for lawn)* Sprenger *m*; *(for fire fighting)* Sprinkler *m*

sprint [sprɪnt] *n (race)* Sprint *m* ♦ *vi (run fast)* rennen; *(SPORT)* sprinten; **~er** *n* Sprinter(in) *m(f)*

sprout [spraʊt] *vi* sprießen

sprouts [spraʊts] *npl (also:* **Brussels ~)** Rosenkohl *m*

spruce [spruːs] *n* Fichte *f* ♦ *adj* schmuck, adrett

sprung [sprʌŋ] *pp of* **spring**

spry [spraɪ] *adj* flink, rege

spun [spʌn] *pt, pp of* **spin**

spur [spɜː^r] *n* Sporn *m*; *(fig)* Ansporn *m* ♦ *vt (also:* **~ on***: fig)* anspornen; **on the ~ of the moment** spontan

spurious ['spjʊərɪəs] *adj* falsch

spurn [spɜːn] *vt* verschmähen

spurt [spɜːt] *n (jet)* Strahl *m*; *(acceleration)* Spurt *m* ♦ *vi (liquid)* schießen

spy [spaɪ] *n* Spion(in) *m(f)* ♦ *vi* spionieren ♦ *vt* erspähen; **~ing** *n* Spionage *f*

sq. *abbr =* **square**

squabble ['skwɒbl] *n* Zank *m* ♦ *vi* sich zanken

squad [skwɒd] *n (MIL)* Abteilung *f*; *(POLICE)* Kommando *nt*

squadron ['skwɒdrn] *n (cavalry)* Schwadron *f*; *(NAUT)* Geschwader *nt*; *(air force)* Staffel *f*

squalid ['skwɒlɪd] *adj* verkommen

squall [skwɔːl] *n* Bö(e) *f*, Windstoß *m*

squalor ['skwɒlə^r] *n* Verwahrlosung *f*

squander ['skwɒndə^r] *vt* verschwenden

square [skweə^r] *n* Quadrat *nt*; *(open space)* Platz *m*; *(instrument)* Winkel *m*; *(inf: person)* Spießer *m* ♦ *adj* viereckig; *(inf: ideas, tastes)* spießig ♦ *vt (arrange)* ausmachen; *(MATH)* ins Quadrat erheben ♦ *vi (agree)* übereinstimmen; **all ~** quitt; **a ~ meal** eine ordentliche Mahlzeit; **2 metres ~** 2 Meter im Quadrat; **1 ~ metre** 1 Quadratmeter; **~ly** *adv* fest, gerade

squash [skwɒʃ] *n (BRIT: drink)* Saft *m*; *(game)* Squash *nt* ♦ *vt* zerquetschen

squat [skwɒt] *adj* untersetzt ♦ *vi* hocken; **~ter** *n* Hausbesetzer(in) *m(f)*

squawk [skwɔːk] *vi* kreischen

squeak [skwiːk] *vi* quiek(s)en; *(spring, door etc)* quietschen

squeal [skwiːl] *vi* schrill schreien

squeamish ['skwiːmɪʃ] *adj* empfindlich

squeeze [skwiːz] *vt* pressen, drücken; *(orange)* auspressen; **~ out** *vt* ausquetschen

squelch [skweltʃ] *vi* platschen

squib [skwɪb] *n* Knallfrosch *m*

squid [skwɪd] *n* Tintenfisch *m*

squiggle ['skwɪgl] *n* Schnörkel *m*

squint [skwɪnt] *vi* schielen ♦ *n*: **to have a ~** schielen; **to ~ at sb/sth** nach jdm/etw schielen

squirm [skwə:m] *vi* sich winden

squirrel ['skwɪrəl] *n* Eichhörnchen *nt*

squirt [skwə:t] *vt, vi* spritzen

Sr *abbr* (= *senior*) sen.

St *abbr* (= *saint*) hl., St.; (= *street*) Str.

stab [stæb] *n* (*blow*) Stich *m*; (*inf: try*) Versuch *m* ♦ *vt* erstechen

stabilize ['steɪbɪlaɪz] *vt* stabilisieren ♦ *vi* sich stabilisieren

stable ['steɪbl] *adj* stabil ♦ *n* Stall *m*

stack [stæk] *n* Stapel *m* ♦ *vt* stapeln

stadium ['steɪdɪəm] *n* Stadion *nt*

staff [sta:f] *n* (*stick, mil*) Stab *m*; (*personnel*) Personal *nt*; (*BRIT: SCH*) Lehrkräfte *pl* ♦ *vt* besetzen

stag [stæg] *n* Hirsch *m*

stage [steɪdʒ] *n* Bühne *f*; (*of journey*) Etappe *f*; (*degree*) Stufe *f*; (*point*) Stadium *nt* ♦ *vt* (*put on*) aufführen; (*simulate*) inszenieren; (*demonstration*) veranstalten; **in ~s** etappenweise; **~coach** *n* Postkutsche *f*; **~ door** *n* Bühneneingang *m*; **~ manager** *n* Intendant *m*

stagger ['stægə*] *vi* wanken, taumeln ♦ *vt* (*amaze*) verblüffen; (*hours*) staffeln; **~ing** *adj* unglaublich

stagnant ['stægnənt] *adj* stagnierend; (*water*) stehend; **stagnate** [stæg'neɪt] *vi* stagnieren

stag party *n* Männerabend *m* (*vom Bräutigam vor der Hochzeit gegeben*)

staid [steɪd] *adj* gesetzt

stain [steɪn] *n* Fleck *m* ♦ *vt* beflecken; **~ed glass window** *buntes* Glasfenster *nt*; **~less** *adj* (*steel*) rostfrei; **~ remover** *n* Fleckentferner *m*

stair [steə*] *n* (Treppen)stufe *f*; **~s** *npl* (*flight of steps*) Treppe *f*; **~case** *n* Treppenhaus *nt*, Treppe *f*; **~way** *n* Treppenaufgang *m*

stake [steɪk] *n* (*post*) Pfahl *m*; (*money*) Einsatz *m* ♦ *vt* (*bet: money*) setzen; **to be at ~** auf dem Spiel stehen

stale [steɪl] *adj* alt; (*bread*) altbacken

stalemate ['steɪlmeɪt] *n* (*CHESS*) Patt *nt*; (*fig*) Stillstand *m*

stalk [stɔ:k] *n* Stängel *m*, Stiel *m* ♦ *vt* (*game*) jagen; **~ off** *vi* abstolzieren

stall [stɔ:l] *n* (*in stable*) Stand *m*, Box *f*; (*in market*) (Verkaufs)stand *m* ♦ *vt* (*AUT*) abwürgen ♦ *vi* (*AUT*) stehen bleiben; (*fig*) Ausflüchte machen; **~s** *npl* (*BRIT: THEAT*) Parkett *nt*

stallion ['stæljən] *n* Zuchthengst *m*

stalwart ['stɔ:lwət] *n* treue(r) Anhänger *m*

stamina ['stæmɪnə] *n* Durchhaltevermögen *nt*, Zähigkeit *f*

stammer ['stæmə*] *n* Stottern *nt* ♦ *vt, vi* stottern, stammeln

stamp [stæmp] *n* Briefmarke *f*; (*for document*) Stempel *m* ♦ *vi* stampfen ♦ *vt* (*mail*) stempeln; (*mail*) frankieren; (*foot*) stampfen mit; **~ album** *n* Briefmarkenalbum *nt*; **~ collecting** *n* Briefmarkensammeln *nt*

stampede [stæm'pi:d] *n* panische Flucht *f*

stance [stæns] *n* Haltung *f*

stand [stænd] *n* (*pt, pp* **stood**) *n* (*for objects*) Gestell *nt*; (*seats*) Tribüne *f* ♦ *vi* stehen; (*rise*) aufstehen; (*decision*) feststehen ♦ *vt* setzen, stellen; (*endure*) aushalten; (*person*) ausstehen; (*nonsense*) dulden; **to make a ~** Widerstand leisten; **to ~ for parliament** (*BRIT*) für das Parlament kandidieren; **~ by** *vi* (*be ready*) bereitstehen ♦ *vt fus* (*opinion*) treu bleiben +*dat*; **~ down** *vi* (*withdraw*) zurücktreten; **~ for** *vt fus* (*signify*) stehen für; (*permit, tolerate*) hinnehmen; **~ in for** *vt fus* einspringen für; **~ out** *vi* (*be prominent*) hervorstechen; **~ up** *vi* (*rise*) aufstehen; **~ up for** *vt fus* sich einsetzen für; **~ up to** *vt fus*: **to ~ up to sth** einer Sache *dat* gewachsen sein; **to ~ up to sb** sich jdm gegenüber behaupten

standard ['stændəd] *n* (*measure*) Norm *f*; (*flag*) Fahne *f* ♦ *adj* (*size etc*) Normal-; **~s** *npl* (*morals*) Maßstäbe *pl*; **~ize** *vt* vereinheitlichen; **~ lamp** (*BRIT*) *n* Stehlampe *f*; **~ of living** *n* Lebensstandard *m*

stand: **~by** *n* Reserve *f*; **to be on ~by** in Bereitschaft sein; **~by ticket** *n* (AVIAT) Standbyticket *nt*; **~in** ['stænd-ɪn] *n* Ersatz *m*

standing ['stændɪŋ] *adj* (erect) stehend; (permanent) ständig; (invitation) offen ♦ *n* (duration) Dauer *f*; (reputation) Ansehen *nt*; **of many years' ~** langjährig; **~ order** (BRIT) *n* (at bank) Dauerauftrag *m*; **~ room** *n* Stehplatz *m*

stand: **~-offish** [stænd'ɔfɪʃ] *adj* zurückhaltend, sehr reserviert; **~point** ['stændpɔɪnt] *n* Standpunkt *m*; **~still** ['stændstɪl] *n*: **to be at a ~still** stillstehen; **to come to a ~still** zum Stillstand kommen

stank [stæŋk] *pt of* **stink**

staple ['steɪpl] *n* (in paper) Heftklammer *f*; (article) Haupterzeugnis *nt* ♦ *adj* Grund-, Haupt- ♦ *vt* (fest)klammern; **~r** *n* Heftmaschine *f*

star [stɑː*] *n* Stern *m*; (person) Star *m* ♦ *vi* die Hauptrolle spielen ♦ *vt*: **~ring ...** in der Hauptrolle/den Hauptrollen ...

starboard ['stɑːbəd] *n* Steuerbord *nt*

starch [stɑːtʃ] *n* Stärke *f*

stardom ['stɑːdəm] *n* Berühmtheit *f*

stare [stɛə*] *n* starre(r) Blick *m* ♦ *vi*: **to ~ at** starren auf +*acc*, anstarren

starfish ['stɑːfɪʃ] *n* Seestern *m*

stark [stɑːk] *adj* öde ♦ *adv*: **~ naked** splitternackt

starling ['stɑːlɪŋ] *n* Star *m*

starry ['stɑːrɪ] *adj* Sternen-; **~-eyed** *adj* (innocent) blauäugig

start [stɑːt] *n* Anfang *m*; (SPORT) Start *m*; (lead) Vorsprung *m* ♦ *vi* in Gang setzen; (car) anlassen ♦ *vi* anfangen; (car) anspringen; (on journey) aufbrechen; (SPORT) starten; (with fright) zusammenfahren; **to ~ doing** *or* **to do sth** anfangen, etw zu tun; **~ off** *vi* anfangen; (begin moving) losgehen; losfahren; **~ up** *vi* anfangen ♦ *vt* beginnen; (car) anlassen; (engine) starten;

~er *n* (AUT) Anlasser *m*; (for race) Starter *m*; (BRIT: COOK) Vorspeise *f*; **~ing point** *n* Ausgangspunkt *m*

startle ['stɑːtl] *vt* erschrecken; **startling** *adj* erschreckend

starvation [stɑː'veɪʃən] *n* Verhungern *nt*

starve [stɑːv] *vi* verhungern ♦ *vt* verhungern lassen; **I'm starving** ich sterbe vor Hunger

state [steɪt] *n* (condition) Zustand *m*; (POL) Staat *m*; (facts) angeben; **the S~s** (USA) die Staaten (*pl*); **to be in a ~** durchdrehen; **~ly** *adj* würdevoll; **~ly home** *n* herrschaftliches Anwesen *nt*, Schloss *nt*; **~ment** *n* Aussage *f*; (POL) Erklärung *f*; **~sman** (*irreg*) *n* Staatsmann *m*

static ['stætɪk] *n* (also: **~ electricity**) Reibungselektrizität *f*

station ['steɪʃən] *n* (RAIL etc) Bahnhof *m*; (police etc) Wache *f*; (in society) Stand *m* ♦ *vt* stationieren

stationary ['steɪʃnərɪ] *adj* stillstehend; (car) parkend

stationer's (*shop*) *n* Schreibwarengeschäft *nt*; **~y** *n* Schreibwaren (*pl*)

station master *n* Bahnhofsvorsteher *m*

station wagon *n* Kombiwagen *m*

statistics [stə'tɪstɪks] *n* Statistik *f*

statue ['stætjuː] *n* Statue *f*

stature ['stætʃə*] *n* Größe *f*

status ['steɪtəs] *n* Status *m*

statute ['stætjuːt] *n* Gesetz *nt*; **statutory** ['stætjutrɪ] *adj* gesetzlich

staunch [stɔːntʃ] *adj* standhaft

stay [steɪ] *n* Aufenthalt *m* ♦ *vi* bleiben; (reside) wohnen; **to ~ put** an Ort und Stelle bleiben; **to ~ the night** übernachten; **~ behind** *vi* zurückbleiben; **~ in** *vi* (at home) zu Hause bleiben; **~ on** *vi* (continue) länger bleiben; **~ out** *vi* (of house) wegbleiben; **~ up** *vi* (at night) aufbleiben; **~ing power** *n* Durchhaltevermögen *nt*

stead [sted] n: **in sb's~** an jds Stelle dat; **to stand sb in good ~** jdm zugute kommen

steadfast ['stedfɑ:st] adj standhaft, treu

steadily ['stedɪlɪ] adv stetig, regelmäßig

steady ['stedɪ] adj (firm) fest, stabil; (regular) gleichmäßig; (reliable) beständig; (hand) ruhig; (job, boyfriend) fest ♦ vt festigen; **to ~ o.s. on/against sth** sich stützen auf/gegen etw acc

steak [steɪk] n Steak nt; (fish) Filet nt

steal [sti:l] (pt **stole**, pp **stolen**) vt stehlen ♦ vi stehlen; (go quietly) sich stehlen

stealth [stelθ] n Heimlichkeit f; **~y** adj verstohlen, heimlich

steam [sti:m] n Dampf m ♦ vt (COOK) im Dampfbad erhitzen ♦ vi dampfen; **~ engine** n Dampfmaschine f; **~er** n Dampfer m; (COOK) Dampfwalze f; **~ship** n = **steamer**; **~y** adj dampfig

steel [sti:l] n Stahl m ♦ adj Stahl-; (fig) stählern; **~works** n Stahlwerke pl

steep [sti:p] adj steil; (price) gepfeffert ♦ vt einweichen

steeple ['sti:pl] n Kirchturm m; **~chase** n Hindernisrennen nt

steer [stɪər] vt, vi steuern; (car etc) lenken; **~ing** n (AUT) Steuerung f; **~ing wheel** n Steuer- od Lenkrad nt

stem [stem] n Stiel m ♦ vt aufhalten; **~ from** vt fus abstammen von

stench [stentʃ] n Gestank m

stencil ['stensl] n Schablone f ♦ vt (auf)drucken

stenographer [ste'nɔgrəfər] (US) n Stenograf(in) m(f)

step [step] n Schritt m; (stair) Stufe f ♦ vi treten, schreiten; **~s** npl (BRIT) = **stepladder**; **to take ~s** Schritte unternehmen; **in/out of ~ (with)** im/nicht im Gleichklang (mit); **~ down** vi (fig) abtreten; **~ off** vt fus aussteigen aus; **~ up** vt steigern

stepbrother ['stepbrʌðər] n Stiefbru-

der m

stepdaughter ['stepdɔːtər] n Stieftochter f

stepfather ['stepfɑ:ðər] n Stiefvater m

stepladder ['steplædər] n Trittleiter f

stepmother ['stepmʌðər] n Stiefmutter f

stepping stone ['stepɪŋ-] n Stein m; (fig) Sprungbrett n

stepsister ['stepsɪstər] n Stiefschwester f

stepson ['stepsʌn] n Stiefsohn m

stereo ['stɛrɪəʊ] n Stereoanlage f ♦ adj (also: **~phonic**) stereofonisch, stereophonisch

stereotype ['stɪərɪətaɪp] n (fig) Klischee nt ♦ vt stereotypieren; (fig) stereotyp machen

sterile ['stɛraɪl] adj steril; (person) unfruchtbar; **sterilize** vt sterilisieren

sterling ['stɜːlɪŋ] adj (FIN) Sterling-; (character) gediegen ♦ n (ECON) das Pfund Sterling; **a pound ~** ein Pfund Sterling

stern [stɜːn] adj streng ♦ n Heck nt, Achtersteil nt

stew [stju:] n Eintopf m ♦ vt, vi schmoren

steward ['stju:əd] n Steward m; **~ess** n Stewardess f

stick [stɪk] (pt, pp **stuck**) n Stock m; (of chalk etc) Stück nt ♦ vt (stab) stechen; (fix) stecken; (put) stellen; (gum) (an)kleben; (inf: tolerate) vertragen ♦ vi (stop) stecken bleiben; (get stuck) klemmen; (hold fast) kleben, haften; **~ out** vi (project) hervorstehen; **~ up** vi (project) in die Höhe stehen; **~ up for** vt fus (defend) eintreten für; **~er** n Aufkleber m; **~ing plaster** n Heftpflaster nt

stickler ['stɪklər] n: **~ (for)** Pedant m (in +acc)

stick-up ['stɪkʌp] (inf) n (Raub)überfall m

sticky ['stɪkɪ] adj klebrig; (atmosphere) stickig

stiff [stɪf] adj steif; (difficult) hart; (paste) dick; (drink) stark; **to have a ~ neck** einen steifen Hals haben; **~en** vt verstärken, (ver)stärken ♦ vi sich versteifen

stifle ['staɪfl] vt unterdrücken; **stifling** adj drückend

stigma ['stɪgmə] (pl BOT, MED, REL **~ta**; fig **~s**) n Stigma nt

stigmata [stɪg'mɑ:tə] npl of **stigma**

stile [staɪl] n Steige f

stiletto [stɪ'letəu] (BRIT) n (also: **~ heel**) Pfennigabsatz m

still [stɪl] adj still ♦ adv (immer) noch; (anyhow) immerhin; **~born** adj tot geboren; **~ life** n Stilleben nt

stilt [stɪlt] n Stelze f

stilted ['stɪltɪd] adj gestelzt

stimulate ['stɪmjuleɪt] vt anregen, stimulieren

stimuli ['stɪmjulaɪ] npl of **stimulus**

stimulus ['stɪmjuləs] (pl **-li**) n Anregung f, Reiz m

sting [stɪŋ] (pt, pp **stung**) n Stich m; (organ) Stachel m ♦ vt stechen; (on skin) brennen ♦ vt stechen

stingy ['stɪndʒɪ] adj geizig, knauserig

stink [stɪŋk] (pt **stank**, pp **stunk**) n Gestank m ♦ vi stinken; **~ing** adj (fig) widerlich

stint [stɪnt] n (period) Betätigung f; **to do one's ~** seine Arbeit tun; (share) seinen Teil beitragen

stipulate ['stɪpjuleɪt] vt festsetzen

stir [stə:r] n Bewegung f; (COOK) Rühren nt; (sensation) Aufsehen nt ♦ vt (um)rühren ♦ vi sich rühren; **~ up** vt (mob) aufhetzen; (mixture) umrühren; (dust) aufwirbeln

stirrup ['stɪrəp] n Steigbügel m

stitch [stɪtʃ] n (with needle) Stich m; (MED) Faden m; (of knitting) Masche f; (pain) Stich m ♦ vt nähen

stoat [stəut] n Wiesel nt

stock [stɔk] n (COMM) (Waren)lager nt; (livestock) Vieh nt; (COOK) Brühe f; (FIN) Grundkapital nt ♦ adj stets vorrätig; (standard) Normal- ♦ vt

(in shop) führen; **~s** npl (FIN) Aktien pl; **in/out of ~** vorrätig/nicht vorrätig; **to take ~ of** Inventur machen von; (fig) Bilanz ziehen aus; **~s and shares** Effekten pl; **~ up** vi: **to ~ up (with)** Reserven anlegen (von); **~broker** ['stɔkbrəukər] n Börsenmakler m; **~ cube** n Brühwürfel m; **~ exchange** n Börse f

stocking ['stɔkɪŋ] n Strumpf m

stock: ~ market n Börse f; **~ phrase** n Standardsatz m; **~pile** n Vorrat m ♦ vt aufstapeln; **~taking** (BRIT) n (COMM) Inventur f, Bestandsaufnahme f

stocky ['stɔkɪ] adj untersetzt

stodgy ['stɔdʒɪ] adj pampig

stoke [stəuk] vt schüren

stole [stəul] pt of **steal** ♦ n Stola f

stolen ['stəuln] pp of **steal**

stomach ['stʌmək] n Bauch m, Magen m ♦ vt vertragen; **~-ache** n Magen- or Bauchschmerzen pl

stone [stəun] n Stein m; (BRIT: weight) Gewichtseinheit = 6.35 kg ♦ vt (olive) entkernen; (kill) steinigen; **~-cold** adj eiskalt; **~-deaf** adj stocktaub; **~work** n Mauerwerk nt; **stony** ['stəunɪ] adj steinig

stood [stud] pt, pp of **stand**

stool [stu:l] n Hocker m

stoop [stu:p] vi sich bücken

stop [stɔp] n Halt m; (bus ~) Haltestelle f; (punctuation) Punkt m ♦ vt anhalten; (bring to an end) aufhören (mit), ein lassen ♦ vi aufhören; (clock) stehen bleiben; (remain) bleiben; **to ~ doing sth** aufhören, etw zu tun; **to ~ dead** innehalten; **~ off** vi kurz Halt machen; **~ up** vt (hole) zustopfen, verstopfen; **~gap** n Notlösung f; **~lights** npl (AUT) Bremslichter pl; **~over** n (on journey) Zwischenaufenthalt m; (type) ['stɔp-ɪdʒ] n (An)halten nt; (traffic) Verkehrsstockung f; (strike) Arbeitseinstellung f; **~per** ['stɔpər] n Propfen m, Stöpsel m; **~ press** n letzte Meldung f; **~watch** ['stɔpwɔtʃ] n Stoppuhr f

storage ['stɔ:rɪdʒ] n Lagerung f; **~ heater** n (Nachtstrom)speicherofen m

store [stɔ:r] n Vorrat m; (place) Lager nt, Warenhaus nt; (BRIT: large shop) Kaufhaus nt; (US) Laden m ♦ vt lagern; **~s** npl (supplies) Vorräte pl; **~ up** vt sich eindecken mit; **~room** n Lagerraum m, Vorratsraum m

storey ['stɔ:rɪ] (US **story**) n Stock m

stork [stɔ:k] n Storch m

storm [stɔ:m] n (also fig) Sturm m ♦ vt, vi stürmen; **~y** adj stürmisch

story ['stɔ:rɪ] n Geschichte f; (lie) Märchen nt; (US) = **storey**; **~book** n Geschichtenbuch nt; **~teller** n Geschichtenerzähler m

stout [staut] adj (bold) tapfer; (fat) beleibt ♦ n Starkbier nt; (also: sweet ~) ≈ Malzbier nt

stove [stəuv] n (Koch)herd m; (for heating) Ofen m

stow [stəu] vt verstauen; **~away** n blinde(r) Passagier m

straddle ['strædl] vt (horse, fence) rittlings sitzen auf +dat; (fig) überbrücken

straggle ['strægl] vi (people) nachhinken; **~r** n Nachzügler m; **straggly** adj (hair) zottig

straight [streɪt] adj gerade; (honest) offen, ehrlich; (drink) pur ♦ adv (direct) direkt, geradewegs; **to put** or **get sth ~** etw in Ordnung bringen; **~ away** sofort; **~ off** sofort; **~en** (also: **~ out**) gerade machen; (fig) klarstellen; **~-faced** adj to be ~-faced keine Miene verziehen ♦ adj: **to be ~-faced** keine Miene verziehen; **~forward** adj einfach, unkompliziert

strain [streɪn] n Belastung f; (streak, trace) Zug m; (of music) Fetzen m ♦ vt überanstrengen; (stretch) anspannen; (muscle) zerren; (filter) (durch)seihen ♦ vi sich anstrengen; **~ed** adj (laugh) gezwungen; (relations) gespannt; **~er** n Sieb nt

strait [streɪt] n Straße f, Meerenge f; **~jacket** n Zwangsjacke f; **~laced** adj engherzig, streng

strand [strænd] n (of hair) Strähne f; (also fig) Faden m

stranded ['strændɪd] adj (also fig) gestrandet

strange [streɪndʒ] adj fremd; (unusual) seltsam; **~r** n Fremde(r) mf

strangle ['stræŋgl] vt erwürgen; **~hold** n (fig) Umklammerung f

strap [stræp] n Riemen m; (on clothes) Träger m ♦ vt (fasten) festschnallen

strapping ['stræpɪŋ] adj stramm

strata ['strɑːtə] npl of **stratum**

strategic [strə'tiːdʒɪk] adj strategisch

strategy ['strætɪdʒɪ] n Strategie f

stratum ['strɑːtəm] (pl **-ta**) n Schicht f

straw [strɔ:] n Stroh nt; (single stalk, drinking ~) Strohhalm m; **that's the ~** nt das ist der Gipfel!

strawberry ['strɔ:bərɪ] n Erdbeere f

stray [streɪ] adj (animal) verirrt ♦ vi herumstreunen

streak [striːk] n Streifen m; (in character) Einschlag m; (in hair) Strähne f ♦ vt streifen ♦ vi zucken; (move quickly) flitzen; **~ of bad luck** Pechsträhne f; **~y** adj gestreift; (bacon) durchwachsen

stream [striːm] n (brook) Bach m; (fig) Strom m ♦ vt (SCH) in (Leistungs)gruppen einteilen ♦ vi strömen; **to ~ in/out** (people) hinein-/hinausströmen

streamer ['striːmər] n (flag) Wimpel m; (of paper) Luftschlange f

streamlined ['striːmlaɪnd] adj stromlinienförmig; (effective) rationell

street [striːt] n Straße f ♦ adj Straßen-; **~car** n (US) Straßenbahn f; **~ lamp** n Straßenlaterne f; **~ plan** n Stadtplan m; **~wise** (inf) adj: **to be ~wise** wissen, wo es langgeht

strength [streŋθ] n (also fig) Stärke f, Kraft f; **~en** n (ver)stärken

strenuous ['strenjuəs] adj anstrengend

stress [stres] n Druck m; (mental) Stress m; (GRAM) Betonung f ♦ vt betonen

stretch [stretʃ] n Strecke f ♦ vt ausdehnen, strecken **♦** vi sich erstrecken; *(person)* sich strecken; **~ out** vi sich strecken **♦** vt ausstrecken

stretcher ['stretʃə*r*] n Tragbahre f

stretchy ['stretʃɪ] adj elastisch, dehnbar

strewn [struːn] adj: **~ with** übersät mit

stricken ['strɪkən] adj *(person)* ergriffen; *(city, country)* heimgesucht; **~ with** *(disease)* leidend unter +dat

strict [strɪkt] adj *(exact)* genau; *(severe)* streng; **~ly** adv streng, genau

stride [straɪd] *(pt* **strode**, *pp* **stridden)** n lange(r) Schritt m **♦** vi schreiten

strident ['straɪdnt] adj schneidend, durchdringend

strife [straɪf] n Streit m

strike [straɪk] *(pt, pp* **struck**) n Streik m; *(attack)* Schlag m **♦** vt *(hit)* schlagen; *(collide)* stoßen gegen; *(come to mind)* einfallen +dat; *(stand out)* auffallen +dat; *(find)* finden **♦** vi *(stop work)* streiken; *(attack)* zuschlagen; *(clock)* schlagen; **on ~** *(workers)* im Streik; **to ~ a match** ein Streichholz anzünden; **~ down** vt *(lay low)* niederschlagen; **~ out** vt *(cross out)* ausstreichen; **~ up** vt *(music)* anstimmen; *(friendship)* schließen; **~r** n Streikende(r) mf; **striking** ['straɪkɪŋ] adj auffallend

string [strɪŋ] *(pt, pp* **strung)** n Schnur f; *(row)* Reihe f; *(MUS)* Saite f **♦** vt: **to ~ together** aneinander reihen **♦** vi: **to ~ out** sich verteilen; **the ~s** npl *(MUS)* die Streichinstrumente pl; **to pull ~s** *(fig)* Fäden ziehen; **~ bean** n grüne Bohne f; **~(ed) instrument** n *(MUS)* Saiteninstrument nt

stringent ['strɪndʒənt] adj streng

strip [strɪp] n Streifen m **♦** vt *(uncover)* abstreifen, abziehen; *(clothes)* ausziehen; *(TECH)* auseinander nehmen **♦** vi *(undress)* sich ausziehen; **~ cartoon** n Bildserie f

stripe [straɪp] n Streifen m; **~d** adj gestreift

strip lighting n Neonlicht nt

stripper ['strɪpə*r*] n Stripteasetänzerin f

strip-search ['strɪpsɜːtʃ] n Leibesvisitation f *(bei der man sich ausziehen muss)* **♦** vt: **to be ~~ed** sich ausziehen müssen und durchsucht werden

stripy ['straɪpɪ] adj gestreift

strive [straɪv] *(pt* **strove**, *pp* **striven)** vi: **to ~ (for)** streben (nach)

strode [strəud] pt of **stride**

stroke [strəuk] n Schlag m; *(SWIMMING, ROWING)* Stoß m; *(MED)* Schlaganfall m; *(caress)* Streicheln n **♦** vt streicheln; **at a ~** mit einem Schlag

stroll [strəul] n Spaziergang m **♦** vi schlendern; **~er** *(US)* n *(pushchair)* Sportwagen m

strong [strɒŋ] adj stark; *(firm)* fest; **they are 50 ~** sie sind 50 Mann stark; **~box** n Kassette f; **~hold** n Hochburg f; **~ly** adv stark; **~room** n Tresor m

strove [strəuv] pt of **strive**

struck [strʌk] pt, pp of **strike**

structure ['strʌktʃə*r*] n Struktur f, Aufbau m; *(building)* Bau m

struggle ['strʌgl] n Kampf m **♦** vi *(fight)* kämpfen

strum [strʌm] vt *(guitar)* klimpern auf +dat

strung [strʌŋ] pt, pp of **string**

strut [strʌt] n Strebe f, Stütze f **♦** vi stolzieren

stub [stʌb] n Stummel m; *(of cigarette)* Kippe f **♦** vt: **to ~ one's toe** sich dat den Zeh anstoßen; **~ out** vt ausdrücken

stubble ['stʌbl] n Stoppel f

stubborn ['stʌbən] adj hartnäckig

stuck [stʌk] pt, pp of **stick** **♦** adj *(jammed)* klemmend; **~-up** adj hochnäsig

stud [stʌd] n *(button)* Kragenknopf m; *(place)* Gestüt nt **♦** vt *(fig)*: **~ded with** übersät mit

student ['stjuːdənt] n Student(in) m(f); *(US)* Student(in) m(f), Schüler(in) m(f) **♦** adj Studenten-; **~ driver** *(US)* n Fahrschüler(in) m(f)

studio ['stjuːdɪəu] n Studio nt; *(for art-*

ist) Atelier *nt;* **~ apartment** *(US) n* Appartement *nt;* **~ flat** *n* Appartement *nt*

studious ['stju:dɪəs] *adj* lernbegierig

study ['stʌdɪ] *n* Studium *nt;* (*investigation*) Studium *nt,* Untersuchung *f;* (*room*) Arbeitszimmer *nt;* (*essay etc*) Studie *f* ♦ *vt* studieren; (*face*) erforschen; (*evidence*) prüfen ♦ *vi* studieren

stuff [stʌf] *n* Stoff *m;* (*inf*) Zeug *nt* ♦ *vt* stopfen, füllen; (*animal*) ausstopfen; **~ing** *n* Füllung *f;* **~y** *adj* (*room*) schwül; (*person*) spießig

stumble ['stʌmbl] *vi* stolpern; **to ~ across** (*fig*) zufällig stoßen auf *+acc*

stumbling block ['stʌmblɪŋ-] *n* Hindernis *nt*

stump [stʌmp] *n* Stumpf *m*

stun [stʌn] *vt* betäuben; (*shock*) niederschmettern

stung [stʌŋ] *pt, pp of* **sting**

stunk [stʌŋk] *pp of* **stink**

stunned *adj* benommen, fassungslos

stunning ['stʌnɪŋ] *adj* betäubend; (*news*) überwältigend, umwerfend

stunt [stʌnt] *n* Kunststück *nt,* Trick *m*

stunted ['stʌntɪd] *adj* verkümmert

stuntman ['stʌntmæn] (*irreg*) *n* Stuntman *m*

stupefy ['stju:pɪfaɪ] *vt* betäuben; (*by news*) bestürzen

stupendous [stju:'pendəs] *adj* erstaunlich, enorm

stupid ['stju:pɪd] *adj* dumm; **~ity** [stju:'pɪdɪtɪ] *n* Dummheit *f*

stupor ['stju:pə*] *n* Betäubung *f*

sturdy ['stɜ:dɪ] *adj* kräftig, robust

stutter ['stʌtə*] *n* Stottern *nt* ♦ *vi* stottern

sty [staɪ] *n* Schweinestall *m*

stye [staɪ] *n* Gerstenkorn *nt*

style [staɪl] *n* Stil *m;* (*fashion*) Mode *f;* **stylish** *adj* modisch; **stylist** ['staɪlɪst] *n* (*hair stylist*) Friseur *m,* Friseuse *f*

stylus ['staɪləs] *n* (Grammofon)nadel *f*

suave [swɑ:v] *adj* zuvorkommend

sub... [sʌb] *prefix* Unter...; **~conscious** *adj* unterbewusst ♦ *n:* **the ~conscious** das Unterbewusste; **~contract** *vt* (*vertraglich*) untervermitteln; **~divide** *vt* unterteilen; **~dued** *adj* (*lighting*) gedämpft; (*person*) still

subject [*n, adj* 'sʌbdʒɪkt, *vb* səb'dʒɛkt] *n* (*of kingdom*) Untertan *m;* (*citizen*) Staatsangehörige(r) *mf;* (*topic*) Thema *nt;* (*SCH*) Fach *nt;* (*GRAM*) Subjekt *nt* ♦ *adj:* **to be ~ to** unterworfen sein *+dat;* (*exposed*) ausgesetzt sein *+dat* ♦ *vt* (*subdue*) unterwerfen; (*expose*) aussetzen; **~ive** [səb'dʒɛktɪv] *adj* subjektiv; **~ matter** *n* Thema *nt*

sublet [sʌb'lɛt] (*irreg: like* let) *vt* untervermieten

sublime [sə'blaɪm] *adj* erhaben

submachine gun ['sʌbmə'ʃi:n-] *n* Maschinenpistole *f*

submarine [sʌbmə'ri:n] *n* Unterseeboot *nt,* U-Boot *nt*

submerge [səb'mɜ:dʒ] *vt* untertauchen; (*flood*) überschwemmen ♦ *vi* untertauchen

submission [səb'mɪʃən] *n* (*obedience*) Gehorsam *m;* (*claim*) Behauptung *f;* (*of plan*) Unterbreitung *f;* **submissive** [səb'mɪsɪv] *adj* demütig, unterwürfig (*pej*)

submit [səb'mɪt] *vt* behaupten; (*plan*) unterbreiten ♦ *vi* sich ergeben

subnormal [sʌb'nɔ:ml] *adj* minderbegabt

subordinate [sə'bɔ:dɪnət] *adj* untergeordnet ♦ *n* Untergebene(r) *mf*

subpoena [səb'pi:nə] *n* Vorladung *f* ♦ *vt* vorladen

subscribe [səb'skraɪb] *vi:* **to ~ to** (*view etc*) unterstützen; (*newspaper*) abonnieren; **~r** *n* (*to periodical*) Abonnent *m;* (*TEL*) Telefonteilnehmer *m*

subscription [səb'skrɪpʃən] *n* Abonnement *nt;* (*money subscribed*) (Mitglieds)beitrag *m*

subsequent ['sʌbsɪkwənt] *adj* folgend, später; **~ly** *adv* später

subside [səb'saɪd] *vi* sich senken; **~nce** [səb'saɪdns] *n* Senkung *f*

subsidiarity [səbsɪdɪˈærɪtɪ] n (POL) Subsidiarität f

subsidiary [səbˈsɪdɪərɪ] adj Neben- ♦ n Tochtergesellschaft f

subsidize [ˈsʌbsɪdaɪz] vt subventionieren

subsidy [ˈsʌbsɪdɪ] n Subvention f

subsistence [səbˈsɪstəns] n Unterhalt m

substance [ˈsʌbstəns] n Substanz f

substantial [səbˈstænʃl] adj (strong) fest, kräftig; (important) wesentlich; **~ly** adv erheblich

substantiate [səbˈstænʃieɪt] vt begründen, belegen

substitute [ˈsʌbstɪtju:t] n Ersatz m ♦ vt ersetzen; **substitution** [sʌbstɪˈtjuːʃən] n Ersetzung f

subterfuge [ˈsʌbtəfjuːdʒ] n Vorwand m; (trick) Trick m

subterranean [sʌbtəˈreɪnɪən] adj unterirdisch

subtitle [ˈsʌbtaɪtl] n Untertitel m; **~d** adj untertitelt, mit Untertiteln versehen

subtle [ˈsʌtl] adj fein; **~ty** n Feinheit f

subtotal [ˈsʌbtəʊtl] n Zwischensumme f

subtract [səbˈtrækt] vt abziehen; **~ion** [səbˈtrækʃən] n Abziehen nt, Subtraktion f

suburb [ˈsʌbɜːb] n Vorort m; **the ~s** die Außenbezirke pl; **~an** [səˈbɜːbən] adj Vorort(s)-, Stadtrand-; **~ia** [səˈbɜːbɪə] n Vorstadt f

subversive [sʌbˈvɜːsɪv] adj subversiv

subway [ˈsʌbweɪ] n (US) U-Bahn f, (BRIT) Unterführung f

succeed [səkˈsiːd] vi (person) erfolgreich sein, Erfolg haben; (plan etc also) gelingen ♦ vt (nach)folgen +dat; **to ~ed in doing it** es gelang ihm, es zu tun; **~ing** adj (nach)folgend

success [səkˈses] n Erfolg m; **~ful** adj erfolgreich; **to be ~ful (in doing sth)** Erfolg haben (bei etw); **~fully** adv erfolgreich

succession [səkˈseʃən] n (Aufeinan-

der)folge f; (to throne) Nachfolge f

successive [səkˈsesɪv] adj aufeinander folgend

successor [səkˈsesər] n Nachfolger(in) m(f)

succinct [səkˈsɪŋkt] adj knapp

succulent [ˈsʌkjulənt] adj saftig

succumb [səˈkʌm] vi: **to ~ (to)** erliegen (+dat); (yield) nachgeben (+dat)

such [sʌtʃ] adj solche(r, s); **~ a book** ein Buch; **~ books** solche Bücher; **~ courage** so ein Mut; **~ a long trip** so eine lange Reise; **~ a lot of** so viel(e); **~ as** wie; **a noise ~ as to** ein derartiger Lärm, dass; **as ~** an sich; **~-and-~ a time** die und die Zeit

suck [sʌk] vt saugen; (lollipop etc) lutschen

sucker [ˈsʌkər] (inf) n Idiot m

suction [ˈsʌkʃən] n Saugkraft f

sudden [ˈsʌdn] adj plötzlich; **all of a ~** auf einmal; **~ly** adv plötzlich

suds [sʌdz] npl Seifenlauge f; (lather) Seifenschaum m

sue [suː] vt verklagen

suede [sweɪd] n Wildleder nt

suet [ˈsuːɪt] n Nierenfett nt

Suez [ˈsuːɪz] n: **the ~ Canal** der Suezkanal

suffer [ˈsʌfər] vt (er)leiden ♦ vi leiden; **~er** n Leidende(r) mf; **~ing** n Leiden nt

suffice [səˈfaɪs] vi genügen

sufficient [səˈfɪʃənt] adj ausreichend; **~ly** adv ausreichend

suffix [ˈsʌfɪks] n Nachsilbe f

suffocate [ˈsʌfəkeɪt] vt, vi ersticken

suffrage [ˈsʌfrɪdʒ] n Wahlrecht nt

sugar [ˈʃugər] n Zucker m ♦ vt zuckern; **~ beet** n Zuckerrübe f; **~ cane** n Zuckerrohr nt; **~y** adj süß

suggest [səˈdʒest] vt vorschlagen; (show) schließen lassen auf +acc; **~ion** [səˈdʒestʃən] n Vorschlag m; **~ive** adj anregend; (indecent) zweideutig

suicide [ˈsuːɪsaɪd] n Selbstmord m; **to commit ~** Selbstmord begehen

suit [suːt] n Anzug m; (CARDS) Farbe f

♦ *vt* passen +*dat; (clothes)* stehen +*dat;* **well ~ed** *(well matched)* **~able** *adj* geeignet, passend; **~ably** *adv* passend, angemessen

suitcase ['su:tkeɪs] *n* (Hand)koffer *m*

suite [swi:t] *n (of rooms)* Zimmerflucht *f; (of furniture)* Einrichtung *f;* (MUS) Suite *f*

suitor ['su:tər] *n* (JUR) Kläger(in) *m(f)*

sulfur ['sʌlfər] (US) *n* = **sulphur**

sulk [sʌlk] *vi* schmollen; **~y** *adj* schmollend

sullen ['sʌlən] *adj* mürrisch

sulphur ['sʌlfər] (US **sulfur**) *n* Schwefel *m*

sultana [sʌl'tɑ:nə] *n (fruit)* Sultanine *f*

sultry ['sʌltrɪ] *adj* schwül

sum [sʌm] *n* Summe *f; (money)* Betrag *m,* Summe *f; (arithmetic)* Rechenaufgabe *f;* **~ up** *vt, vi* zusammenfassen

summarize ['sʌməraɪz] *vt* kurz zusammenfassen

summary ['sʌmərɪ] *n* Zusammenfassung *f* ♦ *adj (justice)* kurzerhand erteilt

summer ['sʌmər] *n* Sommer *m* ♦ *adj* Sommer-; **~house** *n (in garden)* Gartenhaus *nt;* **~time** *n* Sommerzeit *f*

summit ['sʌmɪt] *n* Gipfel *m;* **~ (conference)** *n* Gipfelkonferenz *f*

summon ['sʌmən] *vt* herbeirufen; (JUR) vorladen; *(gather up)* aufbringen; **~s** (JUR) *n* Vorladung *f* ♦ *vt* vorladen

sump [sʌmp] (BRIT) *n* (AUT) Ölwanne *f*

sumptuous ['sʌmptjuəs] *adj* prächtig

sun [sʌn] *n* Sonne *f;* **~bathe** *vi* sich sonnen; **~block** *n* Sonnenschutzcreme *f;* **~burn** *n* Sonnenbrand *m;* **~burnt** *adj* sonnenverbrannt, sonnengebräunt; **to be ~burnt** *(painfully)* einen Sonnenbrand haben

Sunday ['sʌndɪ] *n* Sonntag *m;* **~ school** *n* Sonntagsschule *f*

sundial ['sʌndaɪəl] *n* Sonnenuhr *f*

sundown ['sʌndaʊn] *n* Sonnenuntergang *m*

sundries ['sʌndrɪz] *npl (miscellaneous items)* Verschiedene(s) *nt*

sundry ['sʌndrɪ] *adj* verschieden; **all and ~** alle

sunflower ['sʌnflaʊər] *n* Sonnenblume *f*

sung [sʌŋ] *pp of* **sing**

sunglasses ['sʌnglɑ:sɪz] *npl* Sonnenbrille *f*

sunk [sʌŋk] *pp of* **sink**

sun: **~light** ['sʌnlaɪt] *n* Sonnenlicht *nt;* **~lit** ['sʌnlɪt] *adj* sonnenbeschienen; **~ny** ['sʌnɪ] *adj* sonnig; **~rise** *n* Sonnenaufgang *m;* **~ roof** *n* (AUT) Schiebedach *nt;* **~screen** ['sʌnskriːn] *n* Sonnenschutzcreme *f;* **~set** ['sʌnset] *n* Sonnenuntergang *m;* **~shade** ['sʌnʃeɪd] *n* Sonnenschirm *m;* **~shine** ['sʌnʃaɪn] *n* Sonnenschein *m;* **~stroke** ['sʌnstrəʊk] *n* Hitzschlag *m;* **~tan** ['sʌntæn] *n* (Sonnen)bräune *f;* **~tan oil** *n* Sonnenöl *nt*

super ['su:pər] *(inf)* adj prima, klasse

superannuation [su:pərænju'eɪʃən] *n* Pension *f*

superb [su:'pəːb] *adj* ausgezeichnet, hervorragend

supercilious [su:pə'sɪlɪəs] *adj* herablassend

superficial [su:pə'fɪʃəl] *adj* oberflächlich

superfluous [su'pəːfluəs] *adj* überflüssig

superhuman [su:pə'hju:mən] *adj (effort)* übermenschlich

superimpose ['su:pərɪm'pəʊz] *vt* übereinander legen

superintendent [su:pərɪn'tendənt] *n* Polizeichef *m*

superior [su'pɪərɪər] *adj* überlegen; *(better)* besser ♦ *n* Vorgesetzte(r) *m(f);* **~ity** [supɪərɪ'ɒrɪtɪ] *n* Überlegenheit *f*

superlative [su'pəːlətɪv] *adj* überragend

super: **~man** ['su:pəmæn] *(irreg) n* Übermensch *m;* **~market** ['su:pəmɑ:kt] *n* Supermarkt *m;* **~natural** [su:pə'nætʃərəl] *adj* übernatürlich; **~power** ['su:pəpaʊər] *n* Weltmacht

f

supersede [su:pə'si:d] *vt* ersetzen
supersonic ['su:pə'sɔnɪk] *adj* Überschall-
superstition [su:pə'stɪʃən] *n* Aberglaube *m*; **superstitious** [su:pə'stɪʃəs] *adj* abergläubisch
supervise ['su:pəvaɪz] *vt* beaufsichtigen, kontrollieren; **supervision** [su:pə'vɪʒən] *n* Aufsicht *f*; **supervisor** ['su:pəvaɪzə'] *n* Aufsichtsperson *f*; **supervisory** ['su:pəvaɪzərɪ] *adj* Aufsichts-
supper ['sʌpə'] *n* Abendessen *nt*
supplant [sə'plɑ:nt] *vt* (person, thing) ersetzen
supple ['sʌpl] *adj* geschmeidig
supplement [*n* 'sʌplɪmənt, *vb* sʌplɪ'ment] *n* Ergänzung *f*; (in book) Nachtrag *m* ♦ *vt* ergänzen; **~ary** [sʌplɪ'mentərɪ] *adj* ergänzend; **~ary benefit** (BRIT: old) *n* ≈ Sozialhilfe *f*
supplier [sə'plaɪə'] *n* Lieferant *m*
supplies [sə'plaɪz] *npl* (food) Vorräte *pl*; (MIL) Nachschub *m*
supply [sə'plaɪ] *vt* liefern ♦ *n* Vorrat *m*; (~ing) Lieferung *f*; see also **supplies**; **~ teacher** (BRIT) *n* Vertretung *f*
support [sə'pɔ:t] *n* Unterstützung *f*; (TECH) Stütze *f* ♦ *vt* (hold up) stützen, tragen; (provide for) ernähren; (be in favour of) unterstützen; **~er** *n* Anhänger(in) *m(f)*
suppose [sə'pəuz] *vt, vi* annehmen; **to be ~d to do sth** etw tun sollen; **~dly** [sə'pəuzɪdlɪ] *adv* angeblich; **supposing** *conj* angenommen; **supposition** [sʌpə'zɪʃən] *n* Voraussetzung *f*
suppress [sə'pres] *vt* unterdrücken
supremacy [su'preməsɪ] *n* Vorherrschaft *f*, Oberhoheit *f*
supreme [su'pri:m] *adj* oberste(r, s), höchste(r, s)
surcharge ['sə:tʃɑ:dʒ] *n* Zuschlag *m*
sure [ʃuə'] *adj* sicher, gewiss; **~!** (of course) klar!; **to make ~ of sth/that** sich einer Sache *gen* vergewissern/

vergewissern, dass; **~ enough** (with past) tatsächlich; (with future) ganz bestimmt; **~-footed** *adj* sicher (auf den Füßen); **~ly** *adv* (certainly) sicherlich, gewiss; **~ly it's wrong** das ist doch wohl falsch
surety ['ʃuərətɪ] *n* Sicherheit *f*
surf [sə:f] *n* Brandung *f*
surface ['sə:fɪs] *n* Oberfläche *f* ♦ *vt* (roadway) teeren ♦ *vi* auftauchen; **~ mail** *n* gewöhnliche Post *f*
surfboard ['sə:fbɔ:d] *n* Surfbrett *nt*
surfeit ['sə:fɪt] *n* Übermaß *nt*
surfing ['sə:fɪŋ] *n* Surfen *nt*
surge [sə:dʒ] *n* Woge *f* ♦ *vi* wogen
surgeon ['sə:dʒən] *n* Chirurg(in) *m(f)*
surgery ['sə:dʒərɪ] *n* (BRIT: place) Praxis *f*; (: time) Sprechstunde *f*; (treatment) Operation *f*; **to undergo ~** operiert werden; **~ hours** (BRIT) *npl* Sprechstunden *pl*
surgical ['sə:dʒɪkl] *adj* chirurgisch; **~ spirit** (BRIT) *n* Wundbenzin *nt*
surly ['sə:lɪ] *adj* verdrießlich, grob
surmount [sə:'maunt] *vt* überwinden
surname ['sə:neɪm] *n* Zuname *m*
surpass [sə:'pɑ:s] *vt* übertreffen
surplus ['sə:pləs] *n* Überschuss *m* ♦ *adj* überschüssig, Über(schuss)-
surprise [sə'praɪz] *n* Überraschung *f* ♦ *vt* überraschen; **~d** *adj* überrascht; **surprising** *adj* überraschend; **surprisingly** *adv* überraschend(erweise)
surrender [sə'rendə'] *n* Kapitulation *f* ♦ *vi* sich ergeben
surreptitious [sʌrəp'tɪʃəs] *adj* heimlich; (look also) verstohlen
surrogate ['sʌrəgɪt] *n* Ersatz *m*; **~ mother** *n* Leihmutter *f*
surround [sə'raund] *vt* umgeben; **~ing** *adj* (countryside) umliegend; **~ings** *npl* Umgebung *f*; (environment) Umwelt *f*
surveillance [sə:'veɪləns] *n* Überwachung *f*
survey [*n* 'sə:veɪ, *vb* sə:'veɪ] *n* Übersicht *f* ♦ *vt* überblicken; (land) vermessen;

~or [sə'vaɪəʳ] n Land(ver)messer(in) m(f)

survival [sə'vaɪvl] n Überleben nt

survive [sə'vaɪv] vt, vi überleben; **survivor** [sə'vaɪvəʳ] n Überlebende(r) mf

susceptible [sə'sɛptəbl] adj: **~ (to)** empfindlich (gegen); (charms etc) empfänglich (für)

suspect [n 'sʌspɛkt, vb səs'pɛkt] n Verdächtige(r) mf ♦ adj verdächtig ♦ vt verdächtigen; (think) vermuten

suspend [səs'pɛnd] vt verschieben; (from work) suspendieren; (hang up) aufhängen; (SPORT) sperren; **~ed sentence** n (JUR) zur Bewährung ausgesetzte Strafe; **~er belt** n Strumpf(halter)gürtel m; **~ers** npl (BRIT) Strumpfhalter m; (US) Hosenträger pl

suspense [səs'pɛns] n Spannung f

suspension [səs'pɛnʃən] n (from work) Suspendierung f; (SPORT) Sperrung f; (AUT) Federung f; **~ bridge** n Hängebrücke f

suspicion [səs'pɪʃən] n Misstrauen nt; Verdacht m; **suspicious** [səs'pɪʃəs] adj misstrauisch; (causing ~) verdächtig

sustain [səs'teɪn] vt (maintain) aufrechterhalten; (confirm) bestätigen; (injury) davontragen; **~able** adj (development, growth etc) aufrechtzuerhalten; **~ed** adj (effort) anhaltend

sustenance ['sʌstɪnəns] n Nahrung f

swab [swɔb] n (MED) Tupfer m

swagger ['swægəʳ] vi stolzieren

swallow ['swɔləʊ] n (bird) Schwalbe f; (of food etc) Schluck m ♦ vt (ver)schlucken; **~ up** vt verschlingen

swam [swæm] pt of **swim**

swamp [swɔmp] n Sumpf m ♦ vt überschwemmen

swan [swɔn] n Schwan m

swap [swɔp] n Tausch m ♦ vt: **to ~ sth (for sth)** etw (gegen etw) tauschen or eintauschen

swarm [swɔːm] n Schwarm m ♦ vi: to **~ or be ~ing with** wimmeln von

swarthy ['swɔːðɪ] adj dunkel, braun

swastika ['swɔstɪkə] n Hakenkreuz nt

swat [swɔt] vt totschlagen

sway [sweɪ] vi schwanken; (branches) schaukeln, sich wiegen ♦ vt schwenken; (influence) beeinflussen

swear [sweəʳ] (pt swore, pp sworn) vi (promise) schwören; (curse) fluchen; to **~ to sth** schwören auf etw acc; **~word** n Fluch m

sweat [swɛt] n Schweiß m ♦ vi schwitzen

sweater ['swɛtəʳ] n Pullover m

sweatshirt ['swɛtʃəːt] n Sweatshirt nt

sweaty ['swɛtɪ] adj verschwitzt

Swede [swiːd] n Schwede m, Schwedin f

swede [swiːd] (BRIT) n Steckrübe f

Sweden ['swiːdn] n Schweden nt

Swedish ['swiːdɪʃ] adj schwedisch ♦ n (LING) Schwedisch nt

sweep [swiːp] (pt, pp swept) n (chimney ~) Schornsteinfeger m ♦ vt fegen, kehren; **~ away** vt wegfegen; **~ past** vi vorbeisausen; **~ up** vi zusammenkehren; **~ing** adj (gesture) schwungvoll; (statement) verallgemeinernd

sweet [swiːt] n (course) Nachtisch m; (candy) Bonbon nt ♦ adj süß; **~corn** n Zuckermais m; **~en** vt süßen; (fig) versüßen; **~heart** n Liebste(r) mf; **~ness** n Süße f; **~ pea** n Gartenwicke f

swell [swɛl] (pt swelled, pp swollen or swelled) n Seegang m ♦ adj (inf) todschick ♦ vt (numbers) vermehren ♦ vi (also: **~ up**) (an)schwellen; **~ing** n Schwellung f

sweltering ['swɛltərɪŋ] adj drückend

swept [swɛpt] pt, pp of **sweep**

swerve [swɜːv] vt, vi ausscheren

swift [swɪft] n Mauersegler m ♦ adj geschwind, schnell, rasch; **~ly** adv geschwind, schnell, rasch

swig [swɪg] n Zug m

swill [swɪl] n (for pigs) Schweinefutter nt ♦ vt spülen

swim [swɪm] (pt swam, pp swum) n: to **go for a ~** schwimmen gehen ♦ vi

schwimmen ♦ vt (cross) (durch-)schwimmen; **~mer** n Schwimmer(in) m(f); **~ming** n Schwimmen nt; **~ming cap** n Badehaube f, Badekappe f; **~ming costume** (BRIT) n Badeanzug m; **~ming pool** n Schwimmbecken nt; (private) Swimmingpool m; **~ming trunks** npl Badehose f; **~suit** n Badeanzug m

swindle ['swindl] n Schwindel m, Betrug m ♦ vt betrügen

swine [swain] n (also fig) Schwein nt

swing [swiŋ] (pt, pp **swung**) n (child's) Schaukel f; (movement) Schwung m ♦ vt schwingen ♦ vi schwingen, schaukeln; (turn quickly) schwenken; **in full ~** in vollem Gange; **~ bridge** n Drehbrücke f; **~ door** (BRIT) n Schwingtür f

swingeing ['swindʒiŋ] (BRIT) adj hart; (taxation, cuts) extrem

swinging door ['swiŋiŋ-] (US) n Schwingtür f

swipe [swaip] n Hieb m ♦ vt (inf: hit) hart schlagen; (: steal) klauen

swirl [swə:l] vi wirbeln

swish [swiʃ] adj (inf: smart) schick ♦ vi zischen; (grass, skirts) rascheln

Swiss [swis] adj Schweizer, schweizerisch ♦ n Schweizer(in) m(f); **the ~** npl (people) die Schweizer pl

switch [switʃ] n (ELEC) Schalter m; (change) Wechsel m ♦ vt (ELEC) schalten; (change) wechseln ♦ vi wechseln; **~ off** vt ab- or ausschalten; **~ on** vt an- or einschalten; **~board** n Zentrale f; (board) Schaltbrett nt

Switzerland ['switsələnd] n die Schweiz

swivel ['swivl] vt (also: ~ round) drehen ♦ vi (also: ~ round) sich drehen

swollen ['swəulən] pp of **swell**

swoon [swu:n] vi (old) in Ohnmacht fallen

swoop [swu:p] n Sturzflug m; (esp by police) Razzia f ♦ vi (also: ~ down) stürzen

swop [swɔp] = **swap**

sword [sɔ:d] n Schwert nt; **~fish** n Schwertfisch m

swore [swɔ:r] pt of **swear**

sworn [swɔ:n] pp of **swear**

swot [swɔt] vt, vi pauken

swum [swʌm] pp of **swim**

swung [swʌŋ] pt, pp of **swing**

sycamore ['sikəmɔ:r] n (US) Platane f; (BRIT) Bergahorn m

syllable ['siləbl] n Silbe f

syllabus ['siləbəs] n Lehrplan m

symbol ['simbl] n Symbol nt; **~ic(al)** [sim'bɔlik(l)] adj symbolisch

symmetry ['simitri] n Symmetrie f

sympathetic [simpə'θetik] adj mitfühlend

sympathize ['simpəθaiz] vi mitfühlen; **~r** n (POL) Sympathisant(in) m(f)

sympathy ['simpəθi] n Mitleid nt, Mitgefühl nt; (condolence) Beileid nt; **with our deepest ~** mit tief empfundenem Beileid

symphony ['simfəni] n Sinfonie f

symptom ['simptəm] n Symptom nt; **~atic** [simptə'mætik] adj (fig): **~atic of** bezeichnend für

synagogue ['sinəgɔg] n Synagoge f

synchronize ['siŋkrənaiz] vt synchronisieren

syndicate ['sindikit] n Konsortium nt

synonym ['sinənim] n Synonym nt; **~ous** [si'nɔniməs] adj gleichbedeutend

synopsis [si'nɔpsis] n Zusammenfassung f

synthetic [sin'θetik] adj synthetisch; **~s** npl (man-made fabrics) Synthetik f

syphon ['saifən] n = **siphon**

Syria ['siriə] n Syrien nt

syringe [si'rindʒ] n Spritze f

syrup ['sirəp] n Sirup m; (of sugar) Melasse f

system ['sistəm] n System nt; **~atic** [sistə'mætik] adj systematisch; **~ disk** n (COMPUT) Systemdiskette f; **~s analyst** n Systemanalytiker(in) m(f)

T, t

ta [tɑː] (BRIT: inf) excl danke!

tab [tæb] n Aufhänger m; (name ~) Schild nt; **to keep ~s on** (fig) genau im Auge behalten

tabby ['tæbɪ] n (also: ~ cat) getigerte Katze f

table ['teɪbl] n Tisch m; (list) Tabelle f ♦ vt (PARL: propose) vorlegen, einbringen; **to lay** or **set the ~** den Tisch decken; **~cloth** n Tischtuch nt; **~ d'hôte** [tɑːblˈdəʊt] n Tagesmenü nt; **~ lamp** n Tischlampe f; **~mat** n Untersatz m; **~ of contents** n Inhaltsverzeichnis nt; **~spoon** n Esslöffel m; **~spoonful** n Esslöffel m (voll)

tablet ['tæblɪt] n (MED) Tablette f

table tennis n Tischtennis nt

table wine n Tafelwein m

tabloid ['tæblɔɪd] n Zeitung f in kleinem Format; (pej) Boulevardzeitung f

tabulate ['tæbjʊleɪt] vt tabellarisch ordnen

tacit ['tæsɪt] adj stillschweigend

taciturn ['tæsɪtɜːn] adj wortkarg

tack [tæk] n (small nail) Stift m; (US: thumbtack) Reißzwecke f; (stitch) Heftstich m; (NAUT) Lavieren nt; (course) Kurs m ♦ vt (nail) nageln; (stitch) heften ♦ vi aufkreuzen

tackle ['tækl] n (for lifting) Flaschenzug

m; (NAUT) Takelage f; (SPORT) Tackling nt ♦ vt (deal with) anpacken, in Angriff nehmen; (person) festhalten; (player) angehen

tacky ['tækɪ] adj klebrig

tact [tækt] n Takt m; **~ful** adj taktvoll

tactical ['tæktɪkl] adj taktisch

tactics ['tæktɪks] npl Taktik f

tactless ['tæktlɪs] adj taktlos

tadpole ['tædpəʊl] n Kaulquappe f

taffy ['tæfɪ] (US) n Sahnebonbon nt

tag [tæg] n (label) Schild nt, Anhänger m; (maker's name) Etikett nt; **~ along** vi mitkommen

tail [teɪl] n Schwanz m; (of list) Ende nt ♦ vt folgen +dat; **~ away** or **off** vi abfallen, schwinden; **~back** (BRIT) n (AUT) (Rück)stau m; **~ coat** n Frack m; **~ end** n Schluss m, Ende nt; **~gate** n (AUT) Heckklappe f

tailor ['teɪlə'] n Schneider m; **~ing** n Schneidern nt; **~made** adj maßgeschneidert; (fig): **~made for sb** jdm wie auf den Leib geschnitten

tailwind ['teɪlwɪnd] n Rückenwind m

tainted ['teɪntɪd] adj verdorben

take [teɪk] (pt **took**, pp **taken**) vt nehmen; (trip, exam, PHOT) machen; (capture: person) fassen; (: town: also COMM, FIN) einnehmen; (carry to a place) bringen; (get for o.s.) sich dat nehmen; (gain, obtain) bekommen; (put up with) hinnehmen; (respond to) aufnehmen; (interpret) auffassen; (assume) annehmen; (contain) Platz haben für; (GRAM) stehen mit; **to ~ sth from sb** jdm etw wegnehmen; **to ~ sth from sth** (MATH: subtract) etw von etw abziehen; (extract, quotation) etw einer Sache dat entnehmen; **~ after** vt fus ähnlich sein +dat; **~ apart** vt auseinander nehmen; **~ away** vt (remove) wegnehmen; (carry off) wegbringen; **~ back** vt (return) zurückbringen; (retract) zurücknehmen; **~ down** vt (pull down) abreißen; (write down) aufschreiben; **~ in** vt (deceive) hereinlegen; (under-

talc [tælk] n (also: **~um powder**) Talkumpuder m

tale [teɪl] n Geschichte f, Erzählung f; **to tell ~s** (fig: lie) Geschichten erfinden

talent ['tælnt] n Talent nt; **~ed** adj begabt

talk [tɔːk] n (conversation) Gespräch nt; (rumour) Gerede nt; (speech) Vortrag m ♦ vi sprechen, reden; **~s** npl (POL etc) Gespräche pl; **to ~ about** sprechen von +dat or über +acc; **to ~ sb into doing sth** jdn überreden, etw zu tun; **to ~ sb out of doing sth** jdm ausreden, etw zu tun; **to ~ shop** fachsimpeln; **~ over** vt besprechen; **~ative** adj gesprächig

tall [tɔːl] adj groß; (building) hoch; **to be 1 m 80 ~** 1,80 m groß sein; **~boy** (BRIT) n Kommode f; **~ story** n übertriebene Geschichte f

tally ['tælɪ] n Abrechnung f ♦ vi

übereinstimmen

talon ['tælən] n Kralle f

tame [teɪm] adj zahm; (fig) fade

tamper ['tæmpə*] vi: **to ~ with** herumpfuschen an +dat

tampon ['tæmpɔn] n Tampon m

tan [tæn] n (Sonnen)bräune f; (colour) Gelbbraun nt ♦ adj (colour) (gelb)braun ♦ vt bräunen ♦ vi braun werden

tang [tæŋ] n Schärfe f

tangent ['tændʒənt] n Tangente f; **to go off at a ~** (fig) vom Thema abkommen

tangerine [tændʒə'riːn] n Mandarine f

tangible ['tændʒəbl] adj greifbar

tangle ['tæŋgl] n Durcheinander nt; (trouble) Schwierigkeiten pl; **to get in(to) a ~** sich verheddern

tank [tæŋk] n (container) Tank m, Behälter m; (MIL) Panzer m; **~er** ['tæŋkə*] n (ship) Tanker m; (vehicle) Tankwagen m

tanned [tænd] adj gebräunt

tantalizing ['tæntəlaɪzɪŋ] adj verlockend; (annoying) quälend

tantamount ['tæntəmaunt] adj: **~ to** gleichbedeutend mit

tantrum ['tæntrəm] n Wutanfall m

tap [tæp] n Hahn m; (gentle blow) Klopfen nt ♦ vt (strike) klopfen; (supply) anzapfen; (telephone) abhören; **on ~** (fig: resources) zur Hand; **~-dancing** n Steppen nt

tape [teɪp] n Band nt; (magnetic) (Ton)band nt; (adhesive) Klebstreifen m ♦ vt (record) aufnehmen; **~ deck** n Tapedeck nt; **~ measure** n Maßband nt

taper ['teɪpə*] vi spitz zulaufen

tape recorder n Tonbandgerät nt

tapestry ['tæpɪstrɪ] n Wandteppich m

tar [tɑː] n Teer m

target ['tɑːgɪt] n Ziel nt; (board) Zielscheibe f

tariff ['tærɪf] n (duty paid) Zoll m; (list) Tarif m

tarmac ['tɑːmæk] n (AVIAT) Rollfeld nt

tarnish ['tɑːnɪʃ] vt matt machen; (fig)

---

stand) begreifen; (include) einschließen; **~ off** vi (plane) starten ♦ vt (remove) wegnehmen; (clothing) ausziehen; (imitate) nachmachen; **~ on** vt (undertake) übernehmen; (engage) einstellen; (opponent) antreten gegen; **~ out** vt (girl, dog) ausführen; (extract) herausnehmen; (insurance) abschließen; (licence) sich dat geben lassen; (book) ausleihen; (remove) entfernen; **to ~ sth out of sth** (drawer, pocket etc) etw aus etw herausnehmen; **~ over** vt übernehmen ♦ vi: **to ~ over from sb** jdn ablösen; **~ to** vt fus (like) mögen; (adopt as practice) sich dat angewöhnen; **~ up** vt (raise) aufnehmen; (dress etc) kürzer machen; (occupy) in Anspruch nehmen; (engage in) sich befassen mit; (take up with sb) mit jdm anfangen; **~home pay** n Nettolohn m; **~n** pp of take; **~off** n (AVIAT) Start m; (imitation) Nachahmung f; **~out** (US) adj =

takeaway n, **~over** n (COMM) Übernahme f ♦ n takings ['teɪkɪŋz] npl (COMM) Einnahmen pl

beflecken

tarpaulin [tɑːˈpɔːlɪn] n Plane f

tarragon [ˈtærəgən] n Estragon m

tart [tɑːt] n (Obst)torte f; (inf) Nutte f
♦ adj scharf; **~ up** (inf) vt aufmachen;
(person) auftakeln

tartan [ˈtɑːtn] n Schottenkaro f ♦ adj
mit Schottenkaro

tartar [ˈtɑːtəʳ] n Zahnstein m

tartar(e) sauce [ˈtɑːtə-] n Remoula-
densoße f

task [tɑːsk] n Aufgabe f; **to take sb to
~** sich dat jdn vornehmen; **~ force** n
Sondertrupp m

tassel [ˈtæsl] n Quaste f

taste [teɪst] n Geschmack m; (sense)
Geschmackssinn m; (small quantity)
Kostprobe f; (liking) Vorliebe f ♦ vt
schmecken; (try) probieren ♦ vi
schmecken; **can I have a ~ of this
wine?** kann ich diesen Wein probieren?; **to have a ~ for** sth etw mögen;
in good/bad ~ geschmackvoll/
geschmacklos; **you can ~ the garlic
(in it)** man kann den Knoblauch he-
rausschmecken; **to ~ of** sth nach einer
Sache schmecken; **~ful** adj ge-
schmackvoll; **~less** adj (insipid) fade;
(in bad ~) geschmacklos; **tasty** [ˈteɪstɪ]
adj schmackhaft

tattered [ˈtætəd] adj = **in tatters**

tatters [ˈtætəz] npl: **in ~** in Fetzen

tattoo [təˈtuː] n Zapfenstreich m;
(on skin) Tätowierung f ♦ vt tätowieren

tatty [ˈtætɪ] (BRIT: inf) adj schäbig

taught [tɔːt] pt, pp of **teach**

taunt [tɔːnt] n höhnische Bemerkung f
♦ vt verhöhnen

Taurus [ˈtɔːrəs] n Stier m

taut [tɔːt] adj straff

tawdry [ˈtɔːdrɪ] adj (bunt und) billig

tax [tæks] n Steuer f ♦ vt besteuern;
(strain) strapazieren; (strength) angreifen; **~able** adj (income) steuerpflichtig;
~ation [tækˈseɪʃən] n Besteuerung f; **~
avoidance** n Steuerumgehung f; **~
disc** (BRIT) n (AUT) Kraftfahrzeugsteuer-

plakette f; **~ evasion** n Steuerhinter-
ziehung f; **~-free** adj steuerfrei

taxi [ˈtæksɪ] n Taxi nt ♦ vi (plane) rollen;
~ driver n Taxifahrer m; **~ rank** (BRIT)
♦ n Taxistand m; **~ stand** n Taxistand m

tax: ~payer n Steuerzahler m; **~ relief**
n Steuerermäßigung f; **~ return** n
Steuererklärung f

TB n abbr (= tuberculosis) Tb f, Tbc f

tea [tiː] n Tee m; (meal) (frühes) A-
bendessen nt; **high ~** (BRIT) Abendessen nt; **~ bag** n Teebeutel m; **~ break**
(BRIT) n Teepause f

teach [tiːtʃ] (pt, pp **taught**) vt lehren,
(SCH) lehren, unterrichten; (show): **to ~
sb** sth jdm etw beibringen ♦ vi lehren,
unterrichten; **~er** n Lehrer(in) m(f);
~er's pet n Lehrer's Liebling m; **~ing**
n (~er's work) Unterricht m; (doctrine)
Lehre f

tea: ~ cloth n Geschirrtuch nt; **~ cosy**
n Teewärmer m; **~cup** n Teetasse f; **~
leaves** npl Teeblätter pl

team [tiːm] n (workers) Team nt; (SPORT)
Mannschaft f; (animals) Gespann nt;
~work n Gemeinschaftsarbeit f,
Teamarbeit f

teapot [ˈtiːpɔt] n Teekanne f

tear¹ [tɛəʳ] (pt **tore**, pp **torn**) n Riss m
♦ vt zerreißen; (muscle) zerren ♦ vi
(zer)reißen; (rush) rasen; **~ along** n
(rush) entlangrasen; **~ up** vt (sheet of
paper etc) zerreißen

tear² [tɪəʳ] n Träne f; **~ful** [ˈtɪəful] adj
weinend; (voice) weinerlich; **~ gas**
[ˈtɪəgæs] n Tränengas nt

tearoom [ˈtiːruːm] n Teestube f

tease [tiːz] n Hänsler m ♦ vt necken

tea set n Teeservice nt

teaspoon [ˈtiːspuːn] n Teelöffel m

teat [tiːt] n Brustwarze f; (of animal)
Zitze f; (of bottle) Sauger m

tea time n (in the afternoon) Teestunde
f; (mealtime) Abendessen nt

tea towel n Geschirrtuch nt

technical [ˈteknɪkl] adj technisch;
(knowledge, terms) Fach~; **~ity**

technician [tɛkˈnɪʃən] n technische Einzelheit f; (JUR) Formsache f; **~ly** adv technisch; (speak) spezialisiert; (fig) genau genommen

technician [tɛkˈnɪʃən] n Techniker m

technique [tɛkˈniːk] n Technik f

techno [ˈtɛknəʊ] n Techno m

technological [tɛknəˈlɒdʒɪkl] adj technologisch

technology [tɛkˈnɒlədʒɪ] n Technologie f

teddy (bear) [ˈtɛdɪ-] n Teddybär m

tedious [ˈtiːdɪəs] adj langweilig, ermüdend

tee [tiː] n (GOLF: object) Tee nt

teem [tiːm] vi (swarm): **to ~ (with)** wimmeln (von); **it is ~ing (with rain)** es gießt in Strömen

teenage [ˈtiːneɪdʒ] adj (fashions etc) Teenager-, jugendlich; **~r** n Teenager m, Jugendliche(r) mf

teens [tiːnz] npl Teenageralter nt

tee-shirt [ˈtiːʃəːt] n T-Shirt nt

teeter [ˈtiːtə*] vi schwanken

teeth [tiːθ] npl of **tooth**

teethe [tiːð] vi zahnen; **teething ring** n Beißring m; **teething troubles** npl (fig) Kinderkrankheiten pl

teetotal [ˈtiːˈtəʊtl] adj abstinent

tele: **~communications** npl Fernmeldewesen nt; **~conferencing** n Telefon- or Videokonferenz; **~gram** n Telegramm nt; **~graph** n Telegraf m; **~graph pole** n Telegrafenmast m

telephone [ˈtɛlɪfəʊn] n Telefon nt, Fernsprecher m ♦ vt anrufen; (message) telefonisch mitteilen; **to be on the ~** (talking) telefonieren; (possessing phone) Telefon haben; **~ booth** n Telefonzelle f; **~ box** n (BRIT) Telefonzelle f; **~ call** n Telefongespräch nt, Anruf m; **~ directory** n Telefonbuch nt; **~ number** n Telefonnummer f; **telephonist** [təˈlɛfənɪst] n (BRIT) Telefonist(in) m(f)

telephoto lens [ˈtɛlɪˈfəʊtəʊ-] n Teleobjektiv nt

telesales [ˈtɛlɪseɪlz] n Telefonverkauf m

telescope [ˈtɛlɪskəʊp] n Teleskop nt, Fernrohr nt ♦ vt ineinander schieben

televise [ˈtɛlɪvaɪz] vt durch das Fernsehen übertragen

television [ˈtɛlɪvɪʒən] n Fernsehen nt; **on ~** im Fernsehen; **~ (set)** n Fernsehapparat m, Fernseher m

teleworking [ˈtɛlɪwɜːkɪŋ] n Telearbeit f

telex [ˈtɛlɛks] n Telex nt ♦ vt per Telex schicken

tell [tɛl] (pt, pp told) vt (story) erzählen; (secret) ausplaudern; (say, make known) sagen; (distinguish) erkennen; (be sure) wissen ♦ vi (talk) sprechen; (be sure) wissen; (divulge) es verraten; (have effect) sich auswirken; **to ~ sb to do sth** jdm sagen, dass er etw tun soll; **to ~ sb sth** or **sth to sb** jdm etw sagen; **to ~ sb by sth** jdn an etw dat erkennen; **to ~ sth from** etw unterscheiden von; **to ~ of sth** von etw sprechen; **~ off** vt: **to ~ sb off** jdn ausschimpfen

teller [ˈtɛlə*] n Kassenbeamte(r) mf

telling [ˈtɛlɪŋ] adj verräterisch; (blow) hart

telltale [ˈtɛlteɪl] adj verräterisch

telly [ˈtɛlɪ] (BRIT: inf) n abbr (= television) TV nt

temp [tɛmp] n abbr (= temporary) Aushilfssekretärin f

temper [ˈtɛmpə*] n (disposition) Temperament m; (anger) Zorn m ♦ vt (tone down) mildern; (metal) härten; **to be in a (bad) ~** wütend sein; **to lose one's ~** die Beherrschung verlieren

temperament [ˈtɛmprəmənt] n Temperament nt; **~al** [tɛmprəˈmɛntl] adj (moody) launisch

temperate [ˈtɛmprət] adj gemäßigt

temperature [ˈtɛmprətʃə*] n Temperatur f; (MED: high ~) Fieber nt; **to have** or **run a ~** Fieber haben

template [ˈtɛmplɪt] n Schablone f

temple [ˈtɛmpl] n Tempel m; (ANAT) Schläfe f

temporal [ˈtɛmpərl] adj (of time) zeitlich; (worldly) irdisch, weltlich

temporarily ['tempərəlɪ] adv zeitweilig, vorübergehend

temporary ['tempərərɪ] adj vorläufig; (road, building) provisorisch

tempt [tempt] vt (persuade) verleiten; (attract) reizen, (ver)locken; **to ~ sb into doing sth** jdn dazu verleiten, etw zu tun; **~ation** [temp'teɪʃən] n Versuchung f; **~ing** adj (person) verführerisch; (object, situation) verlockend

ten [ten] num zehn

tenable ['tenəbl] adj haltbar

tenacious [tə'neɪʃəs] adj zäh, hartnäckig

tenacity [tə'næsɪtɪ] n Zähigkeit f, Hartnäckigkeit f

tenancy ['tenənsɪ] n Mietverhältnis nt

tenant ['tenənt] n Mieter m; (of larger property) Pächter m

tend [tend] vt (look after) sich kümmern um ♦ vi: **to ~ to do sth** etw gewöhnlich tun

tendency ['tendənsɪ] n Tendenz f; (of person) Tendenz f, Neigung f

tender ['tendə'] adj zart; (loving) zärtlich ♦ n (COMM: offer) Kostenanschlag m ♦ vt (an)bieten; (resignation) einreichen; **~ness** n Zartheit f; (being loving) Zärtlichkeit f

tendon ['tendən] n Sehne f

tenement ['tenəmənt] n Mietshaus nt

tennis ['tenɪs] n Tennis nt; **~ ball** n Tennisball m; **~ court** n Tennisplatz m; **~ player** n Tennisspieler(in) m(f); **~ racket** n Tennisschläger m; **~ shoes** npl Tennisschuhe pl

tenor ['tenə'] n Tenor m

tenpin bowling ['tenpɪn-] n Bowling nt

tense [tens] adj angespannt ♦ n Zeitform f

tension ['tenʃən] n Spannung f

tent [tent] n Zelt nt

tentacle ['tentəkl] n Fühler m; (of sea animals) Fangarm m

tentative ['tentətɪv] adj (movement)

unsicher; (offer) Probe-; (arrangement) vorläufig; (suggestion) unverbindlich; **~ly** adv versuchsweise; (try, move) vorsichtig

tenterhooks ['tentəhʊks] npl: **to be on ~** auf die Folter gespannt sein

tenth [tenθ] adj zehnte(r, s)

tent peg n Hering m

tent pole n Zeltstange f

tenuous ['tenjuəs] adj schwach

tenure ['tenjuə'] n (of land) Besitz m; (of office) Amtszeit f

tepid ['tepɪd] adj lauwarm

term [tɜːm] n (period of time) Zeit(raum m) f; (limit) Frist f; (SCH) Quartal nt; (UNIV) Trimester nt; (expression) Ausdruck m ♦ vt (be)nennen; **~s** npl (conditions) Bedingungen pl; **in the short/long ~** auf kurze/lange Sicht; **to be on good ~s with sb** gut mit jdm auskommen; **to come to ~s with** (person) sich einigen mit; (problem) sich abfinden mit

terminal ['tɜːmɪnl] n (BRIT: also: **coach ~**) Endstation f; (AVIAT) Terminal m; (COMPUT) Terminal nt or m ♦ adj Schluss-; (MED) unheilbar; **~ly** adj (MED): **~ly ill** unheilbar krank

terminate ['tɜːmɪneɪt] vt beenden ♦ vi enden, aufhören

termini ['tɜːmɪnaɪ] npl of **terminus**

terminus ['tɜːmɪnəs] (pl **termini**) n Endstation f

terrace ['terəs] n (BRIT: row of houses) Häuserreihe f; (in garden etc) Terrasse f; **the ~s** npl (BRIT: SPORT) die Ränge; **~d** adj (garden) terrassenförmig angelegt; (house) Reihen-

terrain [te'reɪn] n Gelände nt

terrible ['terɪbl] adj schrecklich, entsetzlich, fürchterlich; **terribly** adv fürchterlich

terrier ['terɪə'] n Terrier m

terrific [tə'rɪfɪk] adj unwahrscheinlich; **~! klasse!**

terrified adj: **to be ~ of sth** vor etw schreckliche Angst haben

terrify ['terɪfaɪ] vt erschrecken

territorial [terɪ'tɔːrɪəl] adj Gebiets-, territorial

territory ['terɪtərɪ] n Gebiet nt

terror ['terəʳ] n Schrecken m

terrorism ['terərɪzəm] n Terrorismus m; **~ist** n Terrorist(in) m(f); **~ize** vt terrorisieren

terse [tɜːs] adj knapp, kurz, bündig

test [test] n Probe f; (examination) Prüfung f; (PSYCH, TECH) Test m ♦ vt prüfen; (PSYCH) testen

testicle ['testɪkl] n (ANAT) Hoden m

testify ['testɪfaɪ] vi aussagen; **to ~ to** sth etw bezeugen

testimony ['testɪmənɪ] n (JUR) Zeugenaussage f; (fig) Zeugnis nt

test match n (SPORT) Länderkampf m

test tube n Reagenzglas nt

tetanus ['tetənəs] n Wundstarrkrampf m, Tetanus m

tether ['teðəʳ] vt anbinden ♦ n: **at the end of one's ~** völlig am Ende

text [tekst] n Text m; (of document) Wortlaut m; **~book** n Lehrbuch nt

textiles ['tekstaɪlz] npl Textilien pl

texture ['tekstʃəʳ] n Beschaffenheit f

Thai [taɪ] adj thailändisch ♦ n Thailänder(in) m(f); **~land** n Thailand nt

Thames [temz] n: **the ~** die Themse

than [ðæn, ðən] prep (in comparisons) als

thank [θæŋk] vt danken +dat; **you've him to ~ for your success** Sie haben Ihren Erfolg ihm zu verdanken; **~ you (very much)** danke (vielmals), danke schön; **~ful** adj dankbar; **~less** adj undankbar; **~s** npl Dank m ♦ excl danke!; **~s to** zu danken +gen; **T~sgiving (Day)** (US) n Thanksgiving Day m

---

Thanksgiving Day

Thanksgiving (Day) ist ein Feiertag in den USA, der auf den vierten Donnerstag im November fällt. Er soll daran erinnern, wie die Pilgerväter die gute Ernte im Jahre 1621 feierten. In Kanada gibt es einen ähnlichen Erntedanktag (der aber nichts mit den Pilgervätern zu tun hat) am zweiten Montag im Oktober.

KEYWORD

that [ðæt, ðət] adj (demonstrative: pl those) der/die/das; jene(r, s); **that one** das da

♦ pron 1 (demonstrative: pl those) das; **who's/what's that?** wer ist da/was ist das?; **is that you?** bist du das?; **that's what he said** genau das hat er gesagt; **what happened after that?** was passierte danach?; **that is** das heißt

2 (relative: subject) der/die/das, die; (: direct obj) den/die/das, die; (: indirect obj) dem/der/dem, denen; **all (that) I have** alles, was ich habe

3 (relative: of time): **the day (that)** an dem Tag, als; **the winter (that) he came** in dem Winter, in dem er kam

♦ conj dass; **he thought that I was ill** er dachte, dass ich krank sei, er dachte, ich sei krank

♦ adv (demonstrative) so; **I can't work that much** ich kann nicht so viel arbeiten

thatched [θætʃt] adj strohgedeckt; (cottage) mit Strohdach

thaw [θɔː] n Tauwetter nt ♦ vi tauen; (frozen foods, fig: people) auftauen ♦ vt (auf)tauen lassen

---

KEYWORD

the [ðiː, ðə] def art 1 der/die/das; **to play the piano/violin** Klavier/Geige spielen; **I'm going to the butcher's/ the cinema** ich gehe zum Fleischer/ ins Kino; **Elizabeth the First** Elisabeth die Erste

2 (+adj to form noun) das, die; **the rich and the poor** die Reichen und die Armen

3 (in comparisons): **the more he**

works the more he earns je mehr er arbeitet, desto mehr verdient er

---

theatre ['θɪətə*] (US **theater**) n Theater nt; (for lectures etc) Saal m; (MED) Operationssaal m; **~goer** n Theaterbesucher(in) m(f); **theatrical** [θɪ'ætrɪkl] adj Theater-; (career) Schauspieler-; (showy) theatralisch

theft [θeft] n Diebstahl m

their [ðeə*] adj ihr; see also **my**; **~s** pron ihre(r, s); see also **mine**²

them [ðem, ðəm] pron (acc) sie; (dat) ihnen; see also **me**

theme [θiːm] n Thema nt; (MUS) Motiv nt; **~ park** n (thematisch gestalteter) Freizeitpark m; **~ song** n Titelmusik f

themselves [ðəm'selvz] pl pron (reflexive) sich (selbst); (emphatic) selbst; see also **oneself**

then [ðen] adv (at that time) damals; (next) dann ♦ conj also, folglich; (furthermore) ferner ♦ adj damalig; **from ~** on von da an; **by ~** bis dahin; **the ~ president** der damalige Präsident

theology [θɪ'ɒlədʒɪ] n Theologie f

theoretical [θɪə'retɪkl] adj theoretisch; **~ly** adv theoretisch

theory ['θɪərɪ] n Theorie f

therapist ['θerəpɪst] n Therapeut(in) m(f)

therapy ['θerəpɪ] n Therapie f

KEYWORD

there [ðeə*] adv **1**: **there is, there are** es or da ist/sind; (there exists/exist also) es gibt; **there are 3 of them** (people, things) es gibt 3 davon; **there has been an accident** da war ein Unfall
2 (place) da, dort; (direction) dahin, dorthin; **put it in/on there** leg es dahinein/dorthinauf
3: **there, there** (esp to child) na, na

there: **~abouts** ['ðeərə'bauts] adv (place) dort in der Nähe, dort irgendwo; (amount): **20 or ~abouts** unge-

---

fähr 20; **~after** [ðeər'ɑːftə*] adv danach; **~by** ['ðeəbaɪ] adv dadurch, damit

therefore ['ðeəfɔː*] adv deshalb, daher

there's ['ðeəz] = **there is; there has**

thermometer [θə'mɒmɪtə*] n Thermometer nt

Thermos ['θɜːməs] ® n Thermosflasche f

thesaurus [θɪ'sɔːrəs] n Synonymwörterbuch nt

these [ðiːz] pron, adj (pl) diese

theses ['θiːsiːz] npl of **thesis**

thesis ['θiːsɪs] (pl **theses**) n (for discussion) These f; (UNIV) Dissertation f, Doktorarbeit f

they [ðeɪ] pl pron sie; (people in general) man; **~ say that ...** (it is said that) es wird gesagt, dass ...; **~'d** = **they had; they would; ~'ll** = **they shall; they will; ~'re** = **they are; they've** = **they have**

thick [θɪk] adj dick; (forest) dicht; (liquid) dickflüssig; (slow, stupid) dumm, schwer von Begriff ♦ n: **in the ~ of** mitten in +dat; **it's 20 cm ~** es ist 20 cm dick or stark; **~en** vi (fog) dichter werden ♦ vt (sauce etc) verdicken; **~ness** n Dicke f; Dichte f; Dickflüssigkeit f, **~set** adj untersetzt; **~skinned** adj dickhäutig

thief [θiːf] (pl **thieves**) n Dieb(in) m(f)

thieves [θiːvz] npl of **thief**

thieving ['θiːvɪŋ] n Stehlen nt ♦ adj diebisch

thigh [θaɪ] n Oberschenkel m

thimble ['θɪmbl] n Fingerhut m

thin [θɪn] adj dünn; (person) dünn, mager; (excuse) schwach ♦ vt: **to ~ (down)** (sauce, paint) verdünnen

thing [θɪŋ] n Ding nt; (affair) Sache f; **my ~s** meine Sachen pl; **the best ~ would be to ...** das Beste wäre, ...; **how are ~s?** wie gehts?

think [θɪŋk] (pt, pp **thought**) vi, vt kennen; **what did you ~ of them?** was halten Sie von ihnen?; **to ~ about sth/sb** nachdenken über etw/jdn; **I'll**

~ **about it** ich überlege es mir; **to ~ of doing sth** vorhaben or beabsichtigen, etw zu tun; **I ~ so/not** ich glaube (schon)/glaube nicht; **to ~ well of** sb viel von jdm halten; ~ **over** vt überdenken; ~ **up** vt sich dat ausdenken; ~ **tank** n Expertengruppe f

thinly ['θɪnlɪ] adv dünn; (disguised) kaum

third [θɜːd] adj dritte(r, s) ♦ n (person) Dritte(r) mf; (part) Drittel nt; ~**ly** adv drittens; ~ **party insurance** (BRIT) n Haftpflichtversicherung f; ~**-rate** adj minderwertig; **T~ World** n: **the T~ World** die Dritte Welt f

thirst [θɜːst] n (also fig) Durst m; ~**y** adj (person) durstig; (work) durstig machend; **to be ~y** Durst haben

thirteen [θɜː'tiːn] num dreizehn

thirty ['θɜːtɪ] num dreißig

KEYWORD

---

this [ðɪs] adj (demonstrative: pl these) diese(r, s); **this evening** heute Abend; **this one** diese(r, s)
♦ pron (demonstrative: pl these) dies, das; **who/what is this?** wer/was ist das?; **this is where I live** hier wohne ich; **this is what he said** das hat er gesagt; **this is Mr Brown** dies ist Mr Brown; (on telephone) hier ist Mr Brown
♦ adv (demonstrative): **this high/long** etc so groß/lang etc

---

thistle ['θɪsl] n Distel f

thorn [θɔːn] n Dorn m; ~**y** adj dornig; (problem) schwierig

thorough ['θʌrə] adj gründlich; ~**bred** n Vollblut nt ♦ adj reinrassig, Vollblut-; ~**fare** n Straße f; **"no ~fare"** "Durchfahrt verboten"; ~**ly** adv gründlich; (extremely) äußerst

those [ðəʊz] pl pron die (da), jene ♦ adj die, jene

though [ðəʊ] conj obwohl ♦ adv trotzdem

thought [θɔːt] pt, pp of **think** ♦ n (idea) Gedanke m; (thinking) Denken nt, Denkvermögen nt; ~**ful** adj (thinking) gedankenvoll, nachdenklich; (kind) rücksichtsvoll, aufmerksam; ~**less** adj gedankenlos, unbesonnen; (unkind) rücksichtslos

thousand ['θaʊzənd] num tausend; **two ~** zweitausend; ~**s of** tausende or Tausende (von); ~**th** adj tausendste(r, s)

thrash [θræʃ] vt verdreschen; (fig) (vernichtend) schlagen; ~ **about** vi um sich schlagen; ~ **out** vt ausdiskutieren

thread [θred] n Faden m, Garn nt; (TECH) Gewinde nt; (in story) Faden m ♦ vt (needle) einfädeln; ~**bare** adj fadenscheinig

threat [θret] n Drohung f; (danger) Gefahr f; ~**en** vi bedrohen ♦ vi drohen; **to ~en sb with sth** jdm etw androhen

three [θriː] num drei; ~**-dimensional** adj dreidimensional; ~**-piece suite** n dreiteilige Polstergarnitur f; ~**-wheeler** n Dreiradwagen m

thresh [θreʃ] vt, vi dreschen

threshold ['θreʃhəʊld] n Schwelle f

threw [θruː] pt of **throw**

thrift [θrɪft] n Sparsamkeit f; ~**y** adj sparsam

thrill [θrɪl] n Reiz m, Erregung f ♦ vt begeistern, packen; **to be ~ed with** (gift etc) sich unheimlich freuen über +acc; ~**er** n Krimi m; ~**ing** adj spannend; (news) aufregend

thrive [θraɪv] (pt thrived, pp thrived) vi: ~ **(on)** gedeihen (bei); **thriving** ['θraɪvɪŋ] adj blühend

throat [θrəʊt] n Hals m, Kehle f; **to have a sore ~** Halsschmerzen haben

throb [θrɒb] vi klopfen, pochen

throes [θrəʊz] npl: **in the ~ of** mitten in +dat

throne [θrəʊn] n Thron m; **on the ~** auf dem Thron

throng ['θrɒŋ] n (Menschen)schar f ♦ vt sich drängen in +dat

throttle ['θrɒtl] n Gashebel m ♦ vt erdrosseln

through [θru:] prep durch; (time) während +gen; (because of) aus, durch ♦ adv durch ♦ adj (ticket, train) durchgehend; (finished) fertig; **to put sb ~ (to)** jdn verbinden (mit); **to be ~** (TEL) eine Verbindung haben; (finished) fertig sein; **no ~ way** (BRIT) Sackgasse f; **~out** [θru:'aut] prep (place) überall in +dat; (time) während +gen ♦ adv überall; die ganze Zeit

throw [θrəu] (pt threw, pp thrown) n Wurf m ♦ vt werfen; **to ~ a party** eine Party geben; **~ away** vt wegwerfen; (waste) verschwenden; (money) verschwenden; **~ off** vt abwerfen; (pursuer) abschütteln; **~ out** vt hinauswerfen; (rubbish) wegwerfen; (plan) verwerfen; **~ up** vt, vi (vomit) speien; **~away** adj Wegwerf-; **~in** n Einwurf m; **~n** pp of **throw**

thru [θru:] (US) = **through**

thrush [θrʌʃ] n Drossel f

thrust [θrʌst] (pt, pp thrust) vt, vi (push) stoßen

thud [θʌd] n dumpfe(r) (Auf)schlag m

thug [θʌg] n Schlägertyp m

thumb [θʌm] n Daumen m ♦ vt (book) durchblättern; **to ~ a lift** per Anhalter fahren (wollen); **~tack** (US) n Reißzwecke f

thump [θʌmp] n (blow) Schlag m; (noise) Bums m ♦ vi hämmern, pochen ♦ vt schlagen auf +acc

thunder ['θʌndə*] n Donner m ♦ vi donnern; (train etc): **to ~ past** vorbeidonnern ♦ vt brüllen; **~bolt** n Blitz m; **~clap** n Donnerschlag m; **~storm** n Gewitter nt, Unwetter nt; **~y** adj gewitterschwül

Thursday ['θə:zdɪ] n Donnerstag m

thus [ðʌs] adv (in this way) so; (therefore) somit, also, folglich

thwart [θwɔ:t] vt vereiteln, durchkreuzen; (person) hindern

thyme [taɪm] n Thymian m

thyroid ['θaɪrɔɪd] n Schilddrüse f

tiara [tɪ'ɑ:rə] n Diadem nt

tic [tɪk] n Tick m

tick [tɪk] n (sound) Ticken nt; (mark) Häkchen n ♦ vi ticken ♦ vt abhaken; **in a ~** (BRIT: inf) sofort; **~ off** vt abhaken; (person) ausschimpfen; **~ over** vi (engine) im Leerlauf laufen; (fig) auf Sparflamme laufen

ticket ['tɪkɪt] n (for travel) Fahrkarte f; (for entrance) (Eintritts)karte f; (price ~) Preisschild nt; (luggage ~) (Gepäck)schein m; (raffle ~) Los nt; (parking ~) Strafzettel m; (in car park) Parkschein m; **~ collector** n Fahrkartenkontrolleur m; **~ inspector** n Fahrkartenkontrolleur m; **~ office** n (THEAT etc) Kasse f; (RAIL etc) Fahrkartenschalter m

tickle ['tɪkl] n Kitzeln nt ♦ vt kitzeln; (amuse) amüsieren; **ticklish** ['tɪklɪʃ] adj (also fig) kitzlig

tidal ['taɪdl] adj Flut-, Tide-; **~ wave** n Flutwelle f

tidbit ['tɪdbɪt] (US) n Leckerbissen m

tiddlywinks ['tɪdlɪwɪŋks] n Floh(hüpf)spiel nt

tide [taɪd] n Gezeiten pl; **high/low ~** Flut f/Ebbe f

tidy ['taɪdɪ] adj ordentlich ♦ vt aufräumen, in Ordnung bringen

tie [taɪ] n (BRIT: neck) Krawatte f, Schlips m; (sth connecting) Band nt; (SPORT) Unentschieden nt ♦ vt (fasten, restrict) binden ♦ vi (SPORT) unentschieden spielen; (in competition) punktgleich sein; **to ~ in a bow** zur Schleife binden; **to ~ a knot in sth** einen Knoten in etw acc machen; **~ down** vt festbinden; **to ~ sb down to** jdn binden an +acc; **~ up** vt (dog) anbinden; (parcel) festmachen; (boat) festmachen; (person) fesseln; **to be ~d up** (busy) beschäftigt sein

tier [tɪə*] n Rang m; (of cake) Etage f

tiff [tɪf] n Krach m

tiger ['taɪgə*] n Tiger m

tight [taɪt] adj (close) eng, knapp;

tile

(*schedule*) gedrängt; (*firm*) fest; (*control*) streng; (*stretched*) stramm, (an)gespannt; (*inf*: drunk) blau, stramm ♦ *adv* (*squeeze*) fest; **~en** *vt* anziehen, anspannen; (*restrictions*) verschärfen ♦ *vi* sich spannen; **~-fisted** *adj* knauserig; **~ly** *adv* eng; fest; (*stretched*) straff; **~-rope** *n* Seil *nt*; **~s** *npl* (*esp BRIT*) Strumpfhose *f*

tile [taɪl] *n* (on roof) Dachziegel *m*; (on wall or floor) Fliese *f*; **~d** (roof) gedeckt, Ziegel-; (floor, wall) mit Fliesen belegt

till [tɪl] *n* Kasse *f* ♦ *vt* bestellen ♦ *prep, conj* = **until**

tiller ['tɪlə*r*] *n* Ruderpinne *f*

tilt [tɪlt] *vt* kippen, neigen ♦ *vi* sich neigen

timber ['tɪmbə*r*] *n* (wood) Holz *nt*

time [taɪm] *n* Zeit *f*; (*occasion*) Mal *nt*; (*rhythm*) Takt *m* ♦ *vt* zur rechten Zeit tun, zeitlich einrichten; (*SPORT*) stoppen; **in 2 weeks' ~** in 2 Wochen; **a long ~** lange; **for the ~ being** vorläufig; **4 at a ~** zu jeweils 4; **from ~ to ~** gelegentlich; **to have a good ~** sich amüsieren; **in ~** (*soon enough*) rechtzeitig; (*after some* ~) mit der Zeit; (*MUS*) im Takt; **in no ~** im Handumdrehen; **any ~** jederzeit; **on ~** pünktlich, rechtzeitig; **five ~s 5** fünfmal 5; **what ~ is it?** wie viel Uhr ist es?, wie spät ist es?; **at ~** manchmal; **~ bomb** *n* Zeitbombe *f*; **~less** *adj* (*beauty*) zeitlos; **~ limit** *n* Frist *f*; **~ly** *adj* rechtzeitig; günstig; **~ off** *n* freie Zeit *f*; **~r** *n* (~ switch: in kitchen) Schaltuhr *f*; **~ scale** *n* Zeitspanne *f*; **~-share** *adj* Timesharing-; **~ switch** (*BRIT*) *n* Zeitschalter *m*; **~table** *n* (*RAIL*) Fahrplan *m*; (*SCH*) Stundenplan *m*; **~ zone** *n* Zeitzone *f*

timid ['tɪmɪd] *adj* ängstlich, schüchtern

timing ['taɪmɪŋ] *n* Wahl *f* des richtigen Zeitpunkts, Timing *nt*

timpani ['tɪmpənɪ] *npl* Kesselpauken *pl*

tin [tɪn] *n* (metal) Blech *nt*; (*BRIT*: can)

Büchse *f*, Dose *f*; **~foil** *n* Stanniolpapier *nt*

tinge [tɪndʒ] *n* (colour) Färbung *f*, (fig) Anflug *m* ♦ *vt* färben; **~d with** mit einer Spur von

tingle ['tɪŋgl] *n* Prickeln *nt* ♦ *vi* prickeln

tinker ['tɪŋkə*r*] *n* Kesselflicker *m*; **~ with** *vt fus* herumpfuschen an +*dat*

tinkle ['tɪŋkl] *vi* klingeln

tinned [tɪnd] (*BRIT*) *adj* (food) Dosen-, Büchsen-

tin opener [-əupnə*r*] (*BRIT*) *n* Dosen- or Büchsenöffner *m*

tinsel ['tɪnsl] *n* Rauschgold *nt*

tint [tɪnt] *n* Farbton *m*; (slight colour) Anflug *m*; (hair) Tönung *f*; **~ed** *adj* getönt

tiny ['taɪnɪ] *adj* winzig

tip [tɪp] *n* (pointed end) Spitze *f*; (money) Trinkgeld *nt*; (hint) Wink *m*, Tipp *m* ♦ *vt* (slant) kippen; (hat) antippen; (~ over) umkippen; (waiter) ein Trinkgeld geben +*dat*; **~-off** *n* Hinweis *m*, Tipp *m*; **~ped** (*BRIT*) *adj* (cigarette) Filter-

tipsy ['tɪpsɪ] *adj* beschwipst

tiptoe ['tɪptəu] *n*: **on ~** auf Zehenspitzen

tiptop [tɪp'tɔp] *adj*: **in ~ condition** tipptopp, erstklassig

tire ['taɪə*r*] *n* (*US*) = **tyre** ♦ *vt, vi* ermüden, müde machen/werden; **~d** *adj* müde; **to be ~d of** *etw* satt haben; **~less** *adj* unermüdlich; **~some** *adj* lästig

tiring ['taɪərɪŋ] *adj* ermüdend

tissue ['tɪʃuː] *n* Gewebe *nt*; (paper handkerchief) Papiertaschentuch *nt*; **~ paper** *n* Seidenpapier *nt*

tit [tɪt] *n* (bird) Meise *f*; **~ for tat** wie du mir, so ich dir

titbit ['tɪtbɪt] (*US* **tidbit**) *n* Leckerbissen *m*

titillate ['tɪtɪleɪt] *vt* kitzeln

title ['taɪtl] *n* Titel *m*; **~ deed** *n* Eigentumsurkunde *f*; **~ role** *n* Hauptrolle *f*

titter ['tɪtə*r*] *vi* kichern

titular ['tɪtjʊlər] adj (in name only) nominell

TM abbr (= trademark) Wz

KEYWORD

to [tuː, tə] prep **1** (direction) zu; nach; **I go to France/school** ich gehe nach Frankreich/zur Schule; **to the left** nach links

2 (as far as) bis

3 (with expressions of time) vor; **a quarter to 5** Viertel vor 5

4 (for, of) für; **secretary to the director** Sekretärin des Direcktors

5 (expressing indirect object): **to give sth to sb** jdm etw geben; **to talk to sb** mit jdm sprechen; **I sold it to a friend** ich habe es einem Freund verkauft

6 (in relation to) zu; **30 miles to the gallon** 30 Meilen pro Gallone

7 (purpose, result) zu; **my surprise** zu meiner Überraschung

♦ with vb **1** (infin): **to go/eat gehen/** essen; **to want to do sth** etw tun wollen; **to try/start to do sth** versuchen/anfangen, etw zu tun; **he has a lot to lose** er hat viel zu verlieren

2 (with vb omitted): **I don't want to** ich will (es) nicht

3 (purpose, result) um; **I did it to help you** ich tat es, um dir zu helfen

4 (after adj etc): **ready to use** gebrauchsfertig; **too old/young to ...** zu alt/jung, um ... zu ...

♦ adv: **push/pull the door to** die Tür zuschieben/zuziehen

toad [təʊd] n Kröte f; **~stool** n Giftpilz m

toast [təʊst] n (bread) Toast m; (drinking) Trinkspruch m ♦ vt trinken auf +acc; (bread) toasten; (warm) wärmen; **~er** n Toaster m

tobacco [tə'bækəʊ] n Tabak m; **~nist** [tə'bækənɪst] n Tabakhändler m;

~nist's (shop) n Tabakladen m

toboggan [tə'bɒgən] n (Rodel)schlitten m; **~ing** n Rodeln nt

today [tə'deɪ] adv heute; (at the present time) heutzutage

toddler ['tɒdlər] n Kleinkind nt

toddy ['tɒdɪ] n (Whisky)grog m

to-do [tə'duː] n Theater nt

toe [təʊ] n Zehe f; (of sock, shoe) Spitze f; **to ~ the line** (fig) sich einfügen; **~nail** n Zehennagel m

toffee ['tɒfɪ] n Sahnebonbon nt; **~ apple** (BRIT) n kandierte(r) Apfel m

together [tə'geðər] adv zusammen; (at the same time) gleichzeitig; **~ with** zusammen mit; gleichzeitig mit

toil [tɔɪl] n harte Arbeit f, Plackerei f ♦ vi sich abmühen, sich plagen

toilet ['tɔɪlət] n Toilette f ♦ cpd Toiletten-; **~ bag** n Waschbeutel m; **~ paper** n Toilettenpapier nt; **~ries** ['tɔɪlətrɪz] npl Toilettenartikel pl; **~ roll** n Rolle f Toilettenpapier; **~ water** n Toilettenwasser nt

token ['təʊkən] n Zeichen nt; (gift ~) Gutschein m; **book/record ~** (BRIT) Bücher-/Plattengutschein m

Tokyo ['təʊkjəʊ] n Tokio nt

told [təʊld] pt, pp of **tell**

tolerable ['tɒlərəbl] adj (bearable) erträglich; (fairly good) leidlich

tolerant ['tɒlərnt] adj: **be ~ (of)** vertragen +acc

tolerate ['tɒləreɪt] vt dulden; (noise) ertragen

toll [təʊl] n Gebühr f ♦ vi (bell) läuten

tomato [tə'mɑːtəʊ] (pl **~es**) n Tomate f

tomb [tuːm] n Grab(mal) nt

tomboy ['tɒmbɔɪ] n Wildfang m

tombstone ['tuːmstəʊn] n Grabstein m

tomcat ['tɒmkæt] n Kater m

tomorrow [tə'mɒrəʊ] n Morgen m ♦ adv morgen; **the day after ~** übermorgen; **~ morning** morgen früh; **a week ~** morgen in einer Woche

ton [tʌn] n Tonne f (BRIT = 1016kg; US = 907kg); **~s of** (inf) eine Unmenge von

tone [təun] n Ton m; **~ down** vt (criticism, demands) mäßigen; (colours) abtonen; **~ up** vt in Form bringen; **~deaf** adj ohne musikalisches Gehör

tongs [tɒŋz] npl Zange f; (curling ~) Lockenstab m

tongue [tʌŋ] n Zunge f; (language) Sprache f; **with ~ in cheek** scherzhaft; **~tied** adj stumm, sprachlos; **~twister** n Zungenbrecher m

tonic ['tɒnɪk] n (drink) Tonic m; (MED) Stärkungsmittel nt

tonight [tə'naɪt] adv heute Abend

tonsil ['tɒnsl] n Mandel f; **~litis** [tɒnsɪ'laɪtɪs] n Mandelentzündung f

too [tu:] adv zu; (also) auch; **~ bad!** Pech!; **~ many** zu viele

took [tuk] pt of **take**

tool [tu:l] n (also fig) Werkzeug nt; **~box** n Werkzeugkasten m

toot [tu:t] n Hupen nt ♦ vi tuten; (AUT) hupen

tooth [tu:θ] (pl **teeth**) n Zahn m; **~ache** n Zahnschmerzen pl, Zahnweh nt; **~brush** n Zahnbürste f; **~paste** n Zahnpasta f; **~pick** n Zahnstocher m

top [tɒp] n Spitze f; (of mountain) Gipfel m; (of tree) Wipfel m; (toy) Kreisel m; (~ gear) vierte(r)/fünfte(r) Gang m ♦ adj oberste(r, s) ♦ vt (list) an erster Stelle stehen auf +dat; **on ~ of** oben auf +dat; **from ~ to bottom** von oben bis unten; **~ off** (US) vt auffüllen; **~ up** vt auffüllen; **~ floor** n oberste(s) Stockwerk nt; **~ hat** n Zylinder m; **~heavy** adj kopflastig

topic ['tɒpɪk] n Thema nt, Gesprächsgegenstand m; **~al** adj aktuell

top: **~less** ['tɒplɪs] adj (bather etc) oben ohne; **~level** ['tɒplevl] adj auf höchster Ebene; **~most** ['tɒpməust] adj oberste(r, s)

topple ['tɒpl] vt, vi stürzen, kippen

top-secret ['tɒp'si:krɪt] adj streng geheim

topsy-turvy ['tɒpsɪ'tɜ:vɪ] adj durcheinander ♦ adj auf den Kopf gestellt

torch [tɔ:tʃ] n (BRIT: ELEC) Taschenlampe f; (with flame) Fackel f

tore [tɔ:*] pt of **tear¹**

torment [n 'tɔ:ment, vb tɔ:'ment] n Qual f ♦ vt (distress) quälen

torn [tɔ:n] pp of **tear¹** ♦ adj hin- und hergerissen

torrent ['tɒrnt] n Sturzbach m; **~ial** [tə'renʃl] adj wolkenbruchartig

torrid ['tɒrɪd] adj heiß

tortoise ['tɔ:təs] n Schildkröte f; **~shell** ['tɔ:təʃel] n Schildpatt m

torture ['tɔ:tʃə*] n Folter f ♦ vt foltern

Tory ['tɔ:rɪ] (BRIT) n (POL) Tory m ♦ adj Tory-, konservativ

toss [tɒs] vt schleudern; **to ~ a coin** or **to ~ up for sth** etw mit einer Münze entscheiden; **to ~ and turn** (in bed) sich hin und her werfen

tot [tɒt] n (small quantity) bisschen m; (small child) Knirps m

total ['təutl] n Gesamtheit f; (money) Endsumme f ♦ adj Gesamt-, total ♦ vt (add up) zusammenzählen; (amount to) sich belaufen auf

totalitarian [təutælɪ'teərɪən] adj totalitär

totally ['təutəlɪ] adv total

totter ['tɒtə*] vi wanken, schwanken

touch [tʌtʃ] n Berührung f; (sense of feeling) Tastsinn m ♦ vt (feel) berühren; (come against) leicht anstoßen; (emotionally) rühren; **a ~ of** (fig) eine Spur von; **to get in ~ with sb** sich mit jdm in Verbindung setzen; **to lose ~** (friends) Kontakt verlieren; **~ on** vt fus (topic) berühren, erwähnen; **~ up** vt (paint) auffrischen; **~-and-go** adj riskant, knapp; **~down** n Landen nt, Niedergehen nt; **~ed** adj (moved) gerührt; **~ing** adj rührend; **~line** n Seitenlinie f; **~-sensitive screen** n (COMPUT) berührungsempfindlicher Bildschirm m; **~y** adj empfindlich, reizbar

tough [tʌf] adj zäh; (difficult) schwierig

◆ n Schläger(typ) m; **~en** vt zäh machen; (make strong) abhärten

toupee ['tu:peɪ] n Toupet nt

tour ['tuə'] n Tour f ◆ vi umherreisen; (THEAT) auf Tour sein; auf Tour gehen; **~ guide** n Reiseleiter(in) m(f)

tourism ['tuərɪzm] n Fremdenverkehr m, Tourismus m

tourist ['tuərɪst] n Tourist(in) m(f) ◆ cpd (class) Touristen-; **~ office** n Verkehrsamt nt

tournament ['tuənəmənt] n Turnier nt

tousled ['tauzld] adj zerzaust

tout [taut] vi: **to ~ for** auf Kundenfang gehen für ◆ n: **~ ticket** ~ Kundenschlepper(in) m(f)

tow [təu] vt (ab)schleppen; **on** (BRIT) or **in** (US) ~ (AUT) im Schlepp

toward(s) [tə'wɔ:d(z)] prep (with time) gegen; (in direction of) nach

towel ['tauəl] n Handtuch nt; **~ling** n (fabric) Frottee nt or m; **~ rack** (US) n Handtuchstange f; **~ rail** n Handtuchstange f

tower ['tauə'] n Turm m; **~ block** (BRIT) n Hochhaus nt; **~ing** adj hochragend

town [taun] n Stadt f; **to go to ~** (fig) sich ins Zeug legen; **~ centre** n Stadtzentrum nt; **~ clerk** n Stadtdirektor m; **~ council** n Stadtrat m; **~ hall** n Rathaus nt; **~ plan** n Stadtplan m; **~ planning** n Stadtplanung f

towrope ['təurəup] n Abschlepptau nt

tow truck (US) n Abschleppwagen m

toxic ['tɒksɪk] adj giftig, Gift-

toy [tɔɪ] n Spielzeug nt; **~ with** vt fus spielen mit; **~shop** n Spielwarengeschäft nt

trace [treɪs] n Spur f ◆ vt (follow a course) nachspüren +dat; (find out) aufspüren; (copy) durchpausen; **tracing paper** n Pauspapier nt

track [træk] n (mark) Spur f; (path) Weg m; (racetrack) Rennbahn f; (RAIL) Gleis nt ◆ vt verfolgen; **to keep ~ of sb** jdn im Auge behalten; **~ down** vt aufspüren; **~suit** n Trainingsanzug m

tract [trækt] n (of land) Gebiet nt

traction ['trækʃən] n (power) Zugkraft f; (AUT: grip) Bodenhaftung f; (MED): **in ~** im Streckverband

tractor ['træktə'] n Traktor m

trade [treɪd] n (commerce) Handel m; (business) Geschäft nt, Gewerbe f; (people) Geschäftsleute pl; (skilled manual work) Handwerk n ◆ vi: **to ~ (in)** handeln (mit) ◆ vt tauschen; **~ in** vt in Zahlung geben; **~ fair** n Messe f; **~-in price** n Preis, zu dem etw in Zahlung genommen wird; **~mark** n Warenzeichen nt; **~ name** n Handelsbezeichnung f; **~r** n Händler m; **~sman** (irreg) n (shopkeeper) Geschäftsmann m; (workman) Handwerker m; (delivery man) Lieferant m; **~ union** n Gewerkschaft f; **~ unionist** n Gewerkschaftler(in) f

trading ['treɪdɪŋ] n Handel m; **~ estate** (BRIT) n Industriegelände nt

tradition [trə'dɪʃən] n Tradition f; **~al** adj traditionell, herkömmlich

traffic ['træfɪk] n Verkehr m; (esp in drugs): **~ (in)** Handel m (mit) ◆ vi: **to ~ in** (esp drugs) handeln mit; **~ calming** n Verkehrsberuhigung f; **~ circle** (US) n Kreisverkehr m; **~ jam** n Verkehrsstauung f; **~ lights** npl Verkehrsampel f; **~ warden** n ~ Verkehrspolizist m (ohne amtliche Befugnisse), Politesse f (ohne amtliche Befugnisse)

tragedy ['trædʒədɪ] n Tragödie f

tragic ['trædʒɪk] adj tragisch

trail [treɪl] n (track) Spur f; (of smoke) Rauchfahne f; (of dust) Staubwolke f; (road) Pfad m, Weg m ◆ vt (animal) verfolgen; (person) folgen +dat; (drag) schleppen ◆ vi (hang loosely) schleifen; (plants) sich ranken; (be behind) hinterherhinken; (SPORT) weit zurückliegen; (walk) zuckeln; **~ behind** vi zurückbleiben; **~er** n Anhänger m; (US: caravan) Wohnwagen m; (for film) Vorschau f; **~er truck** (US) n Sattelschlepper m

train [treɪn] n Zug m; (of dress) Schleppe f; (series) Folge f ♦ vt (teach: person) ausbilden; (: animal) abrichten; (: mind) schulen; (SPORT) trainieren; (aim) richten ♦ vi (exercise) trainieren; (study) ausgebildet werden; **~ of thought** Gedankengang m; **to ~ sth on** (aim) etw richten auf +acc; **~ed** adj (eye) geschult; (person, voice) ausgebildet; **~ee** n Lehrling m; Praktikant(in) m(f); **~er** n Ausbilder m; (SPORT) Trainer m; **~ers** npl Turnschuhe pl; **~ing** n (for occupation) Ausbildung f; (SPORT) Training nt; **in ~ing** im Training; **~ing college** n pädagogische Hochschule f, Lehrerseminar nt; **~ing shoes** npl Turnschuhe pl

traipse [treɪps] vi latschen

trait [treɪt] n Zug m, Merkmal nt

traitor ['treɪtə*] n Verräter m

trajectory [trə'dʒɛktərɪ] n Flugbahn f

tram [træm] (BRIT) n (also: **~car**) Straßenbahn f

tramp [træmp] n Landstreicher m ♦ vi (trudge) stampfen, stapfen

trample ['træmpl] vt (nieder)trampeln ♦ vi (herum)trampeln; **to ~ (underfoot)** herumtrampeln auf +dat

trampoline ['træmpəlɪn] n Trampolin m

tranquil ['træŋkwɪl] adj ruhig, friedlich; **~lity** [træŋ'kwɪlɪtɪ] (US **tranquility**) n Ruhe f; **~lizer** (US **tranquilizer**) n Beruhigungsmittel nt

transact [træn'zækt] vt abwickeln; **~ion** [træn'zækʃən] n Abwicklung f; (piece of business) Geschäft nt, Transaktion f

transcend [træn'sɛnd] vt übersteigen

transcription [træn'skrɪpʃən] n Transkription f; (product) Abschrift f

transfer [n 'trænsfə*, vb træns'fə:*] n (~ring) Übertragung f; (of business) Umzug m; (being ~red) Versetzung f; (design) Abziehbild nt; (SPORT) Transfer m ♦ vt (business) verlegen; (person) versetzen; (prisoner) überführen; (drawing)

übertragen; (money) überweisen; **to ~ the charges** (BRIT: TEL) ein R-Gespräch führen; **~ desk** n (AVIAT) Transitschalter m

transform [træns'fɔːm] vt umwandeln; **~ation** [trænsfə'meɪʃən] n Umwandlung f, Verwandlung f

transfusion [træns'fjuːʒən] n Blutübertragung f, Transfusion f

transient ['trænzɪənt] adj kurz(lebig)

transistor [træn'zɪstə*] n (ELEC) Transistor m; (RAD) Transistorradio nt

transit ['trænzɪt] n: **in ~** unterwegs

transition [træn'zɪʃən] n Übergang m; **~al** adj Übergangs-

transit lounge n Warteraum m

translate [trænz'leɪt] vt, vi übersetzen; **translation** [trænz'leɪʃən] n Übersetzung f; **translator** [trænz'leɪtə*] n Übersetzer(in) m(f)

transmission [trænz'mɪʃən] n (of information) Übermittlung f; (ELEC, MED, TV) Übertragung f; (AUT) Getriebe nt

transmit [trænz'mɪt] vt (message) übermitteln; (ELEC, MED, TV) übertragen; **~ter** n Sender m

transparency [træns'pɛərnsɪ] n Durchsichtigkeit f; (BRIT: PHOT) Dia(positiv) nt

transparent [træns'pærnt] adj durchsichtig; (fig) offenkundig

transpire [træns'paɪə*] vi (turn out) sich herausstellen; (happen) passieren

transplant [vb træns'plɑːnt, n 'trænsplɑːnt] vt umpflanzen; (MED, also fig: person) verpflanzen ♦ n (MED) Transplantation f; (organ) Transplantat nt

transport [n 'trænspɔːt, vb træns'pɔːt] n Transport m, Beförderung f ♦ vt befördern; transportieren; **means of ~** Transportmittel nt; **~ation** ['trænspɔː'teɪʃən] n Transport m, Beförderung f; (means) Beförderungsmittel nt; (cost) Transportkosten pl; **~ café** (BRIT) n Fernfahrerlokal nt

trap [træp] n Falle f; (carriage) zweirädrige(r) Einspänner *m*; (*inf: mouth*) Klappe *f* ♦ *vt* fangen; (*person*) in eine Falle locken; **~door** *n* Falltür *f*

trappings ['træpıŋz] *npl* Aufmachung *f*

trash [træʃ] *n* (*rubbish*) Plunder *m*; (*non-sense*) Mist *m*; **~ can** (*US*) *n* Mülleimer *m*; **~y** (*inf*) *adj* minderwertig, wertlos; (*novel*) Schund-

traumatic [trɔː'mætık] *adj* traumatisch

travel ['trævl] *n* Reisen *nt* ♦ *vi* reisen ♦ *vt* (*distance*) zurücklegen; (*country*) bereisen; **~s** *npl* (*journeys*) Reisen *pl*; **~ agency** *n* Reisebüro *nt*; **~ agent** *n* Reisebürokaufmann(-frau) *m(f)*; **~ler** (*US* **traveler**) *n* Reisende(r) *mf*; (*sales-man*) Handlungsreisende(r) *m*; **~ler's cheque** (*US* **traveler's check**) *n* Reise-scheck *m*; **~ling** (*US* **traveling**) *n* Rei-sen *nt*; **~sick** *adj* reisekrank; **~ sick-ness** *n* Reisekrankheit *f*

trawler ['trɔːlə*r*] *n* (*NAUT, FISHING*) Fisch-dampfer *m*, Trawler *m*

tray [treı] *n* (*tea ~*) Tablett *nt*; (*for mail*) Ablage *f*

treacherous ['tretʃərəs] *adj* ver-räterisch; (*road*) tückisch

treachery ['tretʃərı] *n* Verrat *m*

treacle ['triːkl] *n* Sirup *m*, Melasse *f*

tread [tred] (*pt* **trod**, *pp* **trodden**) *n* Schritt *m*, Tritt *m*; (*of stair*) Stufe *f*; (*on tyre*) Profil *nt* ♦ *vi* treten; **~ on** *vt fus* treten auf *+acc*

treason ['triːzn] *n* Verrat *m*

treasure ['treʒə*r*] *n* Schatz *m* ♦ *vt* schätzen

treasurer ['treʒərə*r*] *n* Kassenverwalter *m*, Schatzmeister *m*

treasury ['treʒərı] *n* (*POL*) Finanzminis-terium *nt*

treat [triːt] *n* besondere Freude *f* ♦ *vt* (*deal with*) behandeln; **to ~ sb to sth** jdm etw spendieren

treatise ['triːtız] *n* Abhandlung *f*

treatment ['triːtmənt] *n* Behandlung *f*

treaty ['triːtı] *n* Vertrag *m*

treble ['trebl] *adj* dreifach ♦ *vt* verdrei-fachen; **~ clef** *n* Violinschlüssel *m*

tree [triː] *n* Baum *m*; **~ trunk** *n* Baum-stamm *m*

trek [trek] *n* Treck *m*, Zug *m*; (*inf*) an-strengende(r) Weg *m* ♦ *vi* trecken

trellis ['trelıs] *n* Gitter *nt*; (*for gardening*) Spalier *nt*

tremble ['trembl] *vi* zittern; (*ground*) beben

tremendous [trı'mendəs] *adj* gewal-tig, kolossal; (*inf: good*) prima

tremor ['tremə*r*] *n* Zittern *nt*; (*of earth*) Beben *nt*

trench [trentʃ] *n* Graben *m*; (*MIL*) Schützengraben *m*

trend [trend] *n* Tendenz *f*; **~y** (*inf*) *adj* modisch

trepidation [trepı'deıʃən] *n* Beklom-menheit *f*

trespass ['trespas] *vi*: **to ~ on** wider-rechtlich betreten; **"no ~ing"** „Betre-ten verboten"

trestle ['tresl] *n* Bock *m*; **~ table** *n* Klapptisch *m*

trial ['traıəl] *n* (*JUR*) Prozess *m*; (*test*) Versuch *m*, Probe *f*; (*hardship*) Prüfung *f*; **by ~ and error** durch Ausprobieren; **~ period** *n* Probezeit *f*

triangle ['traıæŋgl] *n* (*MUS*) Dreieck *nt*; (*MUS*) Triangel *f*; **triangular** [traı'æŋgjulə*r*] *adj* dreieckig

tribal ['traıbl] *adj* Stammes-

tribe [traıb] *n* Stamm *m*; **~sman** (*irreg*) *n* Stammesangehörige(r) *m*

tribulation [trıbju'leıʃən] *n* Not *f*, Mühsal *f*

tribunal [traı'bjuːnl] *n* Gericht *nt*; (*in-quiry*) Untersuchungsausschuss *m*

tributary ['trıbjutərı] *n* Nebenfluss *m*

tribute ['trıbjuːt] *n* (*admiration*) Zei-chen *nt* der Hochachtung; **to pay ~ to sb/sth** jdm/einer Sache Tribut zollen

trick [trık] *n* Trick *m*; (*CARDS*) Stich *m* ♦ *vt* überlisten, beschwindeln; **to play a ~ on sb** jdm einen Streich spielen; **that should do the ~** dass müsste ei-gentlich klappen; **~ery** *n* Tricks *pl*

trickle ['trıkl] *n* Tröpfeln *n*; (*small river*)

Rinnsal nt ♦ vi tröpfeln; (seep) sickern

tricky ['trɪkɪ] adj (problem) schwierig; (situation) kitzlig

tricycle ['traɪsɪkl] n Dreirad nt

trifle ['traɪfl] n Kleinigkeit f; (COOK) Trifle m ♦ adv: **a ~** ... ein bisschen ...;

trifling adj geringfügig

trigger ['trɪgər] n Drücker m; **~ off** vt auslösen

trim [trɪm] adj gepflegt; (figure) schlank ♦ n (gute) Verfassung f; (embellishment, on car) Verzierung f ♦ vt (clip) schneiden; (trees) stutzen; (decorate) besetzen; (sails) trimmen; **~mings** npl (decorations) Verzierung f, Verzierungen pl; (extras) Zubehör nt

Trinity ['trɪnɪtɪ] n: **the ~** die Dreieinigkeit f

trinket ['trɪŋkɪt] n kleine(s) Schmuckstück nt

trip [trɪp] n (kurze) Reise f; (outing) Ausflug m; (stumble) Stolpern nt ♦ vi (stumble) stolpern; **on a ~** auf Reisen; **~ up** vi stolpern, einen Fehler machen ♦ vt zu Fall bringen; (fig) hereinlegen

tripe [traɪp] n (food) Kutteln pl; (rubbish) Mist m

triple ['trɪpl] adj dreifach

triplets ['trɪplɪts] npl Drillinge pl

triplicate ['trɪplɪkət] n: **in ~** in dreifacher Ausfertigung

tripod ['traɪpɒd] n (PHOT) Stativ nt

trite [traɪt] adj banal

triumph ['traɪʌmf] n Triumph m ♦ vi: **to ~ (over)** triumphieren (über +acc);

~ant [traɪˈʌmfənt] adj triumphierend

trivia ['trɪvɪə] npl Trivialitäten pl

trivial ['trɪvɪəl] adj gering(fügig), trivial

trod [trɒd] pt of **tread**; **~den** pp of **tread**

trolley ['trɒlɪ] n Handwagen m; (in shop) Einkaufswagen m; (for luggage) Kofferkuli m; (table) Teewagen m; **~ bus** n Oberleitungsbus m, Obus m

trombone [trɒmˈbəʊn] n Posaune f

troop [truːp] n Schar f; (MIL) Trupp m;

~s npl (MIL) Truppen pl; **~ in/out** vi hinein-/hinausströmen; **~ing the colour** n (ceremony) Fahnenparade f

trophy ['trəʊfɪ] n Trophäe f

tropic ['trɒpɪk] n Wendekreis m; **~al** adj tropisch

trot [trɒt] n Trott m ♦ vi trotten; **on the ~** (BRIT: fig: inf) in einer Tour

trouble ['trʌbl] n (problems) Ärger m; (worry) Sorge f; (in industry) Unruhen pl; (effort) Mühe f; (MED): **stomach ~** Magenbeschwerden pl ♦ vt (disturb) stören ♦ vi: **~s** npl (POL etc) Unruhen pl; **to ~ to do sth** sich bemühen, etw zu tun; **to be in ~** Probleme or Ärger haben; **to go to the ~ of doing sth** sich die Mühe machen, etw zu tun; **what's the ~?** was ist los?; (to sick person) wo fehlts?; **~d** adj (person) beunruhigt; (country) geplagt; **~-free** adj sorglos; **~maker** n Unruhestifter m; **~shooter** n Vermittler m; **~some** adj lästig, unangenehm; (child) schwierig

trough [trɒf] n Trog m; (channel) Rinne f, Kanal m; (MET) Tief nt

trousers ['traʊzəz] npl Hose f

trout [traʊt] n Forelle f

trowel ['traʊəl] n Kelle f

truant ['truːənt] n: **to play ~** (BRIT) (die Schule) schwänzen

truce [truːs] n Waffenstillstand m

truck [trʌk] n Lastwagen m; (RAIL) offene(r) Güterwagen m; **~ driver** n Lastwagenfahrer m; **~ farm** n (US) n Gemüsegärtnerei f

trudge [trʌdʒ] vi sich (mühselig) dahinschleppen

true [truː] adj (exact) wahr; (genuine) echt; (friend) treu

truffle ['trʌfl] n Trüffel f or m

truly ['truːlɪ] adv wirklich; **yours ~** Ihr sehr ergebener

trump [trʌmp] n (CARDS) Trumpf m

trumpet ['trʌmpɪt] n Trompete f

truncheon ['trʌntʃən] n Gummiknüppel m

trundle ['trʌndl] vt schieben ♦ vi: **to ~**

along entlangrollen

trunk [trʌŋk] n (of tree) (Baum)stamm m; (ANAT) Rumpf m; (box) Truhe f, Überseekoffer m; (of elephant) Rüssel m; (US: AUT) Kofferraum m; ~s npl (also: swimming ~s) Badehose f

truss [trʌs] vt (also: ~ up) fesseln

trust [trʌst] n (confidence) Vertrauen nt; (for land etc) Treuhandvermögen nt ♦ vt (rely on) vertrauen +dat, sich verlassen auf +acc; (hope) hoffen; (entrust): **to ~ sth to sb** jdm etw anvertrauen; ~**ed** adj treu; ~**ee** [trʌsˈtiː] n Vermögensverwalter m; ~**ful** adj vertrauensvoll; ~**ing** adj vertrauensvoll; ~**worthy** adj vertrauenswürdig; (account) glaubwürdig

truth [truːθ] n Wahrheit f; ~**ful** adj ehrlich

try [traɪ] n Versuch m ♦ vt (attempt) versuchen; (test) (aus)probieren; (JUR: person) unter Anklage stellen; (: case) verhandeln; (courage, patience) auf die Probe stellen ♦ vi (make effort) versuchen, sich bemühen; **to have a ~** es versuchen; **to ~ to do sth** versuchen, etw zu tun; ~ **on** vt (dress) anprobieren; (hat) aufprobieren; ~ **out** vt ausprobieren; ~**ing** adj schwierig

T-shirt [ˈtiːʃəːt] n T-Shirt nt

T-square [ˈtiːskwɛə*] n Reißschiene f

tub [tʌb] n Wanne f, Kübel m; (for margarine etc) Becher m

tubby [ˈtʌbɪ] adj rundlich

tube [tjuːb] n Röhre f, Rohr nt; (for toothpaste etc) Tube f; (underground) U-Bahn f; (AUT) Schlauch m

tuberculosis [tjubəːkjuˈləusɪs] n Tuberkulose f

tube station n (in London) U-Bahnstation f; **tubing** [ˈtjuːbɪŋ] n Schlauch m; **tubular** [ˈtjuːbjulə*] adj röhrenförmig

TUC (BRIT) n abbr = **Trades Union Congress**

tuck [tʌk] n (fold) Falte f, Einschlag m ♦ vt (put) stecken; (gather) fälteln, ein-

schlagen; ~ **away** vt wegstecken; ~ **in** vt hineinstecken; (blanket etc) feststecken; (person) zudecken ♦ vi (eat) hineinhauen, zulangen; ~ **up** vt (child) warm zudecken; ~ **shop** n Süßwarenladen m

Tuesday [ˈtjuːzdɪ] n Dienstag m

tuft [tʌft] n Büschel m

tug [tʌg] n (jerk) Zerren nt, Ruck m; (NAUT) Schleppdampfer m ♦ vt, vi zerren, ziehen; (boat) schleppen; ~ **of war** n Tauziehen nt

tuition [tjuːˈɪʃən] n (BRIT) Unterricht m; (: private ~) Privatunterricht m; (US: school fees) Schulgeld nt

tulip [ˈtjuːlɪp] n Tulpe f

tumble [ˈtʌmbl] n (fall) Sturz m ♦ vi fallen, stürzen; ~ **to** vt fus kapieren; ~**down** adj baufällig; ~ **dryer** (BRIT) n Trockner m; ~**r** [ˈtʌmblə*] n (glass) Trinkglas nt

tummy [ˈtʌmɪ] (inf) n Bauch m; ~ **upset** n Magenverstimmung f

tumour [ˈtjuːmə*] (US **tumor**) n Geschwulst f, Tumor m

tumultuous [tjuːˈmʌltjuəs] adj (welcome, applause etc) stürmisch

tuna [ˈtjuːnə] n T(h)unfisch m

tune [tjuːn] n Melodie f ♦ vt (MUS) stimmen; (AUT) richtig einstellen; **to sing in ~/out of ~** richtig/falsch singen; **to be out of ~ with** nicht harmonieren mit; ~ **in** vi einstellen; ~ **up** vi (MUS) stimmen; ~**ful** adj melodisch; ~**r** n (RAD) Tuner m; (person) (Instrumenten)stimmer m; **piano ~r** Klavierstimmer(in) m(f)

tunic [ˈtjuːnɪk] n Waffenrock m; (loose garment) lange Bluse f

tuning [ˈtjuːnɪŋ] n (RAD, AUT) Einstellen nt; (MUS) Stimmen nt; ~ **fork** n Stimmgabel f

Tunisia [tjuːˈnɪzɪə] n Tunesien nt

tunnel [ˈtʌnl] n einen Tunnel m, Unterführung f ♦ vi einen Tunnel anlegen

turbulent [ˈtəːbjulənt] adj stürmisch

tureen [təˈriːn] n Terrine f

turf [təːf] n Rasen m; (piece) Sode f ♦ vt mit Grassoden belegen; ~ **out** (inf) vt rauswerfen

turgid ['təːdʒɪd] adj geschwollen

Turk [təːk] n Türke m, Türkin f

Turkey ['təːkɪ] n Türkei f

turkey ['təːkɪ] n Puter m, Truthahn m

Turkish ['təːkɪʃ] adj türkisch ♦ n (LING) Türkisch nt

turmoil ['təːmɔɪl] n Aufruhr m, Tumult m

turn [təːn] n (rotation) (Um)drehung f; (performance) (Programm)nummer f; (MED) Schock m ♦ vt (rotate) drehen; (change position of) umdrehen, wenden; (page) umblättern; (transform): **to ~ sth into sth** etw in etw acc verwandeln; (direct) zuwenden ♦ vi (rotate) sich drehen; (change direction: in car) abbiegen; (: wind) drehen; (~ round) umdrehen, wenden; (become) werden; (leaves) sich verfärben; (milk) sauer werden; (weather) umschlagen; **to do sb a good ~** jdm etwas Gutes tun; **it's your ~** du bist dran or an der Reihe; **in ~**, **by ~s** abwechselnd; **to take ~s** sich abwechseln; **it gave me quite a ~** das hat mich schön erschreckt; **"no left ~"** (AUT) "Linksabbiegen verboten"; **~ away** vi sich abwenden; **~ back** vt umdrehen; (person) zurückschicken; (clock) zurückstellen ♦ vi umkehren; **~ down** vt (refuse) ablehnen; (fold down) umschlagen; **~ in** vi (go to bed) ins Bett gehen ♦ vt (fold inwards) einwärts biegen; **~ off** vi abbiegen ♦ vt ausschalten; (tap) zudrehen; (machine, electricity) abstellen; **~ on** vt (light) anschalten, einschalten; (tap) aufdrehen; (machine) anstellen; **~ out** vt (prove to be) sich erweisen; (people) sich entwickeln ♦ vt (light) ausschalten; (gas) abstellen; (produce) produzieren; **how did the cake ~ out?** wie ist der Kuchen geworden?; **~ over** vi (person) sich umdrehen ♦ vt (object) umdrehen, wenden; (page) umblättern; **~ round**

vi (person, vehicle) sich herumdrehen; (rotate) sich drehen; **~ up** vi auftauchen ♦ vt (collar) hochklappen, hochstellen; (nose) rümpfen; (increase: radio) lauter stellen; (: heat) höher drehen; **~ing** n (in road) Abzweigung f; **~ing point** n Wendepunkt m

turnip ['təːnɪp] n Steckrübe f

turnout ['təːnaut] n (Besucher)zahl f

turnover ['təːnəuvə*] n Umsatz m; (of staff) Wechsel m

turnpike ['təːnpaɪk] (US) n gebührenpflichtige Straße f

turn: **~stile** ['təːnstaɪl] n Drehkreuz nt; **~table** [-teɪbl] n (of record player) Plattenteller m; (RAIL) Drehscheibe f; **~up** (BRIT) n (on trousers) Aufschlag m

turpentine ['təːpəntaɪn] n Terpentin nt

turquoise ['təːkwɔɪz] n (gem) Türkis m; (colour) Türkis nt ♦ adj türkisfarben

turret ['tʌrɪt] n Turm m

turtle ['təːtl] n Schildkröte f; **~ neck (sweater)** n Pullover m mit Schildkrötkragen

tusk [tʌsk] n Stoßzahn m

tussle ['tʌsl] n Balgerei f

tutor ['tjuːtə*] n (teacher) Privatlehrer m; (college instructor) Tutor m; **~ial** [tjuː'təːrɪəl] n (UNIV) Kolloquium nt, Seminarübung f

tuxedo [tʌk'siːdəu] (US) n Smoking m

TV [tiː'viː] n abbr (= television) TV nt

twang [twæŋ] n scharfe(r) Ton m; (of voice) Näseln nt

tweezers ['twiːzəz] npl Pinzette f

twelfth [twelfθ] adj zwölfte(r, s)

twelve [twelv] num zwölf; **at ~ o'clock** (midday) um 12 Uhr; (midnight) um null Uhr

twentieth ['twentɪɪθ] adj zwanzigste(r, s)

twenty ['twentɪ] num zwanzig

twice [twaɪs] adv zweimal; **~ as much** doppelt so viel

twiddle ['twɪdl] vt, vi: **to ~ (with) sth** an etw dat herumdrehen; **to ~ one's**

thumbs (fig) Däumchen drehen

twig [twɪg] n dünne(r) Zweig m ♦ vt (inf) kapieren, merken

twilight ['twaɪlaɪt] n Zwielicht nt

twin [twɪn] n Zwilling m ♦ adj Zwillings-; (very similar) Doppel- ♦ vt (towns) zu Partnerstädten machen; **~bedded room** n Zimmer nt mit zwei Einzelbetten; **~ beds** npl zwei (gleiche) Einzelbetten pl

twine [twaɪn] n Bindfaden m ♦ vi (plants) sich ranken

twinge [twɪndʒ] n stechende(r) Schmerz m, Stechen nt

twinkle ['twɪŋkl] n Funkeln nt, Blitzen nt ♦ vi funkeln

twinned adj: to be ~ with die Partnerstadt von ... sein

twirl [twɜːl] n Wirbel m ♦ vt, vi (herum)wirbeln

twist [twɪst] n (~ing) Drehung f; (bend) Kurve f ♦ vt (turn) drehen; (make crooked) verbiegen; (distort) verdrehen ♦ vi (wind) sich drehen; (curve) sich winden

twit [twɪt] (inf) n Idiot m

twitch [twɪtʃ] n Zucken nt ♦ vi zucken

two [tuː] num zwei; **to put ~ and ~ together** seine Schlüsse ziehen; **~-door** adj zweitürig; **~-faced** adj falsch; **~-fold** adj, adv zweifach, doppelt; **to increase ~-fold** verdoppeln; **~-piece** adj zweiteilig; **~-piece (suit)** n Zweiteiler m; **~-piece (swimsuit)** n zweiteilige(r) Badeanzug m; **~-seater** n (plane, car) Zweisitzer m; **~some** n Paar nt; **~-way** adj (traffic) Gegen-

tycoon [taɪˈkuːn] n: **(business) ~** (Industrie)magnat m

type [taɪp] n Typ m, Art f; (PRINT) Type f ♦ vt, vi Maschine schreiben, tippen; **~-cast** adj (THEAT, TV) auf eine Rolle festgelegt; **~face** n Schrift f; **~script** n maschinegeschriebene(r) Text m; **~writer** n Schreibmaschine f; **~written** adj maschinegeschrieben

typhoid ['taɪfɔɪd] n Typhus m

typical ['tɪpɪkl] adj: ~ (of) typisch (für)

typify ['tɪpɪfaɪ] vt typisch sein für

typing ['taɪpɪŋ] n Maschineschreiben nt

typist ['taɪpɪst] n Maschinenschreiber(in) m(f), Tippse f (inf)

tyrant ['taɪərənt] n Tyrann m

tyre ['taɪə'] (US tire) n Reifen m; **~ pressure** n Reifendruck m

U, u

U-bend ['juːbend] n (in pipe) U-Bogen m

udder ['ʌdə'] n Euter nt

UFO ['juːfəʊ] n abbr (= unidentified flying object) UFO nt

ugh [əːh] excl hu

ugliness ['ʌglɪnɪs] n Hässlichkeit f

ugly ['ʌglɪ] adj hässlich; (bad) böse, schlimm

UHT abbr (= ultra heat treated): **UHT milk** H-Milch f

UK n abbr = **United Kingdom**

ulcer ['ʌlsə'] n Geschwür nt

Ulster ['ʌlstə'] n Ulster nt

ulterior [ʌlˈtɪərɪə'] adj: ~ **motive** Hintergedanke m

ultimate ['ʌltɪmət] adj äußerste(r, s), allerletzte(r, s); **~ly** adv schließlich, letzten Endes

ultrasound ['ʌltrəsaʊnd] n (MED) Ultraschall m

umbilical cord [ʌmˈbɪlɪkl-] n Nabelschnur f

umbrella [ʌmˈbrelə] n Schirm m

umpire ['ʌmpaɪə'] n Schiedsrichter m ♦ vt, vi schiedsrichtern

umpteenth [ʌmpˈtiːnθ] (inf) adj zig; **for the ~ time** zum x-ten Mal

UN n abbr = **United Nations**

unable [ʌnˈeɪbl] adj: **to be ~ to do sth** etw nicht tun können

unacceptable [ʌnəkˈseptəbl] adj unannehmbar, nicht akzeptabel

unaccompanied [ʌnəˈkʌmpənɪd] adj ohne Begleitung

unaccountably [ʌnə'kauntəblɪ] *adv* unerklärlich

unaccustomed [ʌnə'kʌstəmd] *adj* nicht gewöhnt; (*unusual*) ungewohnt; ~ **to** nicht gewöhnt an +*acc*

unanimous [ju:'nænɪməs] *adj* einmütig; (*vote*) einstimmig; **~ly** *adv* einmütig; einstimmig

unarmed [ʌn'ɑ:md] *adj* unbewaffnet

unashamed [ʌnə'ʃeɪmd] *adj* schamlos

unassuming [ʌnə'sju:mɪŋ] *adj* bescheiden

unattached [ʌnə'tætʃt] *adj* ungebunden

unattended [ʌnə'tendɪd] *adj* (*person*) unbeaufsichtigt; (*thing*) unbewacht

unauthorized [ʌn'ɔ:θəraɪzd] *adj* unbefugt

unavoidable [ʌnə'vɔɪdəbl] *adj* unvermeidlich

unaware [ʌnə'weə'] *adj*: **to be ~ of sth** sich *dat* einer Sache *gen* nicht bewusst sein; **~s** *adv* unversehens

unbalanced [ʌn'bælənst] *adj* unausgeglichen; (*mentally*) gestört

unbearable [ʌn'bɛərəbl] *adj* unerträglich

unbeatable [ʌn'bi:təbl] *adj* unschlagbar

unbeknown(st) [ʌnbɪ'nəun(st)] *adv*: **~ to me** ohne mein Wissen

unbelievable [ʌnbɪ'li:vəbl] *adj* unglaublich

unbend [ʌn'bend] (*irreg: like* bend) *vt* gerade biegen ♦ *vi* aus sich herausgehen

unbias(s)ed [ʌn'baɪəst] *adj* unparteiisch

unborn [ʌn'bɔ:n] *adj* ungeboren

unbreakable [ʌn'breɪkəbl] *adj* unzerbrechlich

unbridled [ʌn'braɪdld] *adj* ungezügelt

unbroken [ʌn'brəukən] *adj* (*period*) ununterbrochen; (*spirit*) ungebrochen; (*record*) unübertroffen

unburden [ʌn'bɜ:dn] *vt*: **to ~ o.s.** (jdm) sein Herz ausschütten

unbutton [ʌn'bʌtn] *vt* aufknöpfen

uncalled-for [ʌn'kɔ:ldfɔ:'] *adj* unnötig

uncanny [ʌn'kænɪ] *adj* unheimlich

unceasing [ʌn'si:sɪŋ] *adj* unaufhörlich

unceremonious [ʌnsɛrɪ'məunɪəs] *adj* (*abrupt, rude*) brüsk; (*exit, departure*) überstürzt

uncertain [ʌn'sɜ:tn] *adj* unsicher; (*doubtful*) ungewiss; (*unreliable*) unbeständig; (*vague*) undeutlich, vag(e); **~ty** *n* Ungewissheit *f*

unchanged [ʌn'tʃeɪndʒd] *adj* unverändert

unchecked [ʌn'tʃekt] *adj* ungeprüft; (*not stopped: advance*) ungehindert

uncivilized [ʌn'sɪvɪlaɪzd] *adj* unzivilisiert

uncle ['ʌŋkl] *n* Onkel *m*

uncomfortable [ʌn'kʌmfətəbl] *adj* unbequem, ungemütlich

uncommon [ʌn'kɒmən] *adj* ungewöhnlich; (*outstanding*) außergewöhnlich

uncompromising [ʌn'kɒmprəmaɪzɪŋ] *adj* kompromisslos, unnachgiebig

unconcerned [ʌnkən'sɜ:nd] *adj* unbekümmert; (*indifferent*) gleichgültig

unconditional [ʌnkən'dɪʃənl] *adj* bedingungslos

unconscious [ʌn'kɒnʃəs] *adj* (MED) bewusstlos; (*not meant*) unbeabsichtigt ♦ *n*: **the ~** das Unbewusste; **~ly** *adv* unbewusst

uncontrollable [ʌnkən'trəuləbl] *adj* unkontrollierbar, unbändig

unconventional [ʌnkən'venʃənl] *adj* unkonventionell

uncouth [ʌn'ku:θ] *adj* grob

uncover [ʌn'kʌvə'] *vt* aufdecken

undecided [ʌndɪ'saɪdɪd] *adj* unschlüssig

undeniable [ʌndɪ'naɪəbl] *adj* unleugbar

under ['ʌndə'] *prep* unter ♦ *adv* darunter; **~ there** da drunter; **~ repair** in Reparatur

underage [ʌndər'eɪdʒ] *adj* minderjährig

undercarriage ['ʌndəkærɪdʒ] (BRIT) n (AVIAT) Fahrgestell nt

undercharge [ʌndə'tʃɑːdʒ] vt: **to ~ sb** jdm zu wenig berechnen

undercoat ['ʌndəkəʊt] n (paint) Grundierung f

undercover [ʌndə'kʌvər] adj Geheim-

undercurrent ['ʌndəkʌrnt] n Unterströmung f

undercut [ʌndə'kʌt] (irreg: like cut) vt unterbieten

underdeveloped ['ʌndədɪ'veləpt] adj Entwicklungs-, unterentwickelt

underdog ['ʌndədɒg] n Unterlegene(r) mf

underdone [ʌndə'dʌn] adj (COOK) nicht gar, nicht durchgebraten

underestimate ['ʌndər'estɪmeɪt] vt unterschätzen

underexposed ['ʌndərɪks'pəʊzd] adj unterbelichtet

underfoot [ʌndə'fʊt] adv am Boden

undergo [ʌndə'gəʊ] (irreg: like go) vt (experience) durchmachen; (test, operation) sich unterziehen +dat

undergraduate [ʌndə'grædjuət] n Student(in) m(f)

underground ['ʌndəgraʊnd] n U-Bahn f ♦ adj Untergrund-

undergrowth ['ʌndəgrəʊθ] n Gestrüpp nt, Unterholz nt

underhand(ed) [ʌndə'hænd(ɪd)] adj hinterhältig

underlie [ʌndə'laɪ] (irreg: like lie) vt zugrunde or zu Grunde liegen +dat

underline [ʌndə'laɪn] vt unterstreichen; (emphasize) betonen

underling ['ʌndəlɪŋ] n Handlanger m

undermine [ʌndə'maɪn] vt untergraben

underneath [ʌndə'niːθ] adv darunter ♦ prep unter

underpaid [ʌndə'peɪd] adj unterbezahlt

underpants ['ʌndəpænts] npl Unterhose f

underpass ['ʌndəpɑːs] (BRIT) n Unterführung f

underprivileged [ʌndə'prɪvɪlɪdʒd] adj benachteiligt, unterprivilegiert

underrate [ʌndə'reɪt] vt unterschätzen

undershirt ['ʌndəʃɜːt] (US) n Unterhemd nt

undershorts ['ʌndəʃɔːts] (US) npl Unterhose f

underside ['ʌndəsaɪd] n Unterseite f

underskirt ['ʌndəskɜːt] (BRIT) n Unterrock m

understand [ʌndə'stænd] (irreg: like stand) vt, vi verstehen; **I ~ that ...** ich habe gehört, dass ...; **am I to ~ that ...?** soll das (etwa) heißen, dass ...?; **what do you ~ by that?** was verstehen Sie darunter?; **it is understood that ...** es wurde vereinbart, dass ...; **to make o.s. understood** sich verständlich machen; **is that understood?** ist das klar?; **~able** adj verständlich; **~ing** n Verständnis nt ♦ adj verständnisvoll

understatement ['ʌndəsteɪtmənt] n (quality) Untertreibung f; **that's an ~!** das ist untertrieben!

understood [ʌndə'stʊd] pt, pp of understand ♦ adj klar; (implied) angenommen

understudy ['ʌndəstʌdɪ] n Ersatz(schau)spieler(in) m(f)

undertake [ʌndə'teɪk] (irreg: like take) vt unternehmen ♦ vi: **to ~ to do sth** sich verpflichten, etw zu tun

undertaker ['ʌndəteɪkər] n Leichenbestatter m

undertaking ['ʌndəteɪkɪŋ] n (enterprise) Unternehmen nt; (promise) Verpflichtung f

undertone ['ʌndətəʊn] n: **in an ~** mit gedämpfter Stimme

underwater ['ʌndə'wɔːtər] adv unter Wasser ♦ adj Unterwasser-

underwear ['ʌndəweər] n Unterwäsche f

underworld ['ʌndəwɜːld] n (of crime)

Unterwelt f

underwriter ['ʌndəraɪtəʳ] n Assekurant m

undesirable [ʌndɪ'zaɪərəbl] adj unerwünscht

undies ['ʌndɪz] (inf) npl (Damen)unterwäsche f

undisputed ['ʌndɪs'pju:tɪd] adj unbestritten

undo [ʌn'du:] (irreg: like do) vt (unfasten) öffnen, aufmachen; (work) zunichte machen; **~ing** n Verderben nt

undoubted [ʌn'dautɪd] adj unbezweifelt; **~ly** adv zweifellos, ohne Zweifel

undress [ʌn'dres] vt ausziehen ♦ vi sich ausziehen

undue [ʌn'dju:] adj übermäßig

undulating ['ʌndjuleɪtɪŋ] adj wellenförmig; (country) wellig

unduly [ʌn'dju:lɪ] adv übermäßig

unearth [ʌn'ə:θ] vt (dig up) ausgraben; (discover) ans Licht bringen

unearthly [ʌn'ə:θlɪ] adj (hour) nachtschlafen

uneasy [ʌn'i:zɪ] adj (worried) unruhig; (feeling) ungut

uneconomic(al) ['ʌni:kə'nɔmɪk(l)] adj unwirtschaftlich

uneducated [ʌn'edjukeɪtɪd] adj ungebildet

unemployed [ʌnɪm'plɔɪd] adj arbeitslos ♦ npl: **the ~** die Arbeitslosen pl

unemployment [ʌnɪm'plɔɪmənt] n Arbeitslosigkeit f

unending [ʌn'endɪŋ] adj endlos

unerring [ʌn'ə:rɪŋ] adj unfehlbar

uneven [ʌn'i:vn] adj (surface) uneben; (quality) ungleichmäßig

unexpected [ʌnɪks'pektɪd] adj unerwartet; **~ly** adv unerwartet

unfailing [ʌn'feɪlɪŋ] adj nie versagend

unfair [ʌn'feəʳ] adj ungerecht, unfair

unfaithful [ʌn'feɪθful] adj untreu

unfamiliar [ʌnfə'mɪlɪəʳ] adj ungewohnt; (person, subject) unbekannt; **to be ~ with** nicht kennen +acc, nicht vertraut sein mit

unfashionable [ʌn'fæʃnəbl] adj unmodern; (area etc) nicht in Mode

unfasten [ʌn'fɑ:sn] vt öffnen, aufmachen

unfavourable [ʌn'feɪvrəbl] (US **unfavorable**) adj ungünstig

unfeeling [ʌn'fi:lɪŋ] adj gefühllos, kalt

unfinished [ʌn'fɪnɪʃt] adj unvollendet

unfit [ʌn'fɪt] adj ungeeignet; (in bad health) nicht fit; **~ for sth** zu or für etw ungeeignet

unfold [ʌn'fəuld] vt (cloth, paper) auseinander falten ♦ vi (develop) sich entfalten

unforeseen ['ʌnfɔ:'si:n] adj unvorhergesehen

unforgettable [ʌnfə'getəbl] adj unvergesslich

unforgivable [ʌnfə'gɪvəbl] adj unverzeihlich

unfortunate [ʌn'fɔ:tʃənət] adj unglücklich, bedauerlich; **~ly** adv leider

unfounded [ʌn'faundɪd] adj unbegründet

unfriendly [ʌn'frendlɪ] adj unfreundlich

ungainly [ʌn'geɪnlɪ] adj linkisch

ungodly [ʌn'gɔdlɪ] adj (hour) nachtschlafen; (row) heillos

ungrateful [ʌn'greɪtful] adj undankbar

unhappiness [ʌn'hæpɪnɪs] n Unglück nt, Unglückseligkeit f

unhappy [ʌn'hæpɪ] adj unglücklich; **~ with** (arrangements etc) unzufrieden mit

unharmed [ʌn'hɑ:md] adj wohlbehalten, unversehrt

UNHCR n abbr (= United Nations High Commission for Refugees) Flüchtlingshochkommissariat der Vereinten Nationen

unhealthy [ʌn'helθɪ] adj ungesund

unheard-of [ʌn'hə:dɔv] adj unerhört

unhurt [ʌn'hə:t] adj unverletzt

unidentified [ʌnaɪ'dentɪfaɪd] adj unbekannt, nicht identifiziert

uniform ['ju:nɪfɔ:m] n Uniform f ♦

einheitlich; **~ity** [juːnɪˈfɔːmɪtɪ] n Einheitlichkeit f

unify [ˈjuːnɪfaɪ] vt vereinigen

unilateral [juːnɪˈlætərəl] adj einseitig

uninhabited [ʌnɪnˈhæbɪtɪd] adj unbewohnt

unintentional [ʌnɪnˈtenʃənəl] adj unabsichtlich

union [ˈjuːnjən] n (uniting) Vereinigung f; (alliance) Bund m, Union f; (trade ~) Gewerkschaft f; **U~ Jack** n Union Jack m

unique [juːˈniːk] adj einzig(artig)

UNISON [ˈjuːnɪsn] n Gewerkschaft der Angestellten im öffentlichen Dienst

unison [ˈjuːnɪsn] n Einstimmigkeit f; **in ~** einstimmig

unit [ˈjuːnɪt] n Einheit f; **kitchen ~** Küchenelement nt

unite [juːˈnaɪt] vt vereinigen ♦ vi sich vereinigen; **~d** adj vereinigt; (together) vereint; **U~d Kingdom** n Vereinigte(s) Königreich nt; **U~d Nations (Organization)** n Vereinte Nationen pl; **U~d States (of America)** n Vereinigte Staaten pl (von Amerika)

unit trust (BRIT) n Treuhandgesellschaft f

unity [ˈjuːnɪtɪ] n Einheit f; (agreement) Einigkeit f

universal [juːnɪˈvɜːsl] adj allgemein

universe [ˈjuːnɪvɜːs] n (Welt)all nt

university [juːnɪˈvɜːsɪtɪ] n Universität f

unjust [ʌnˈdʒʌst] adj ungerecht

unkempt [ʌnˈkempt] adj ungepflegt

unkind [ʌnˈkaɪnd] adj unfreundlich

unknown [ʌnˈnəʊn] adj: **~ (to sb)** (jdm) unbekannt

unlawful [ʌnˈlɔːful] adj illegal

unleaded [ʌnˈledɪd] adj bleifrei, unverbleit; **I use ~** ich fahre bleifrei

unleash [ʌnˈliːʃ] vt entfesseln

unless [ʌnˈles] conj wenn nicht, es sei denn; **~ he comes** es sei denn, er kommt; **~ otherwise stated** sofern nicht anders angegeben

unlike [ʌnˈlaɪk] adj unähnlich ♦ prep im Gegensatz zu

unlikely [ʌnˈlaɪklɪ] adj (not likely) unwahrscheinlich; (unexpected: combination etc) merkwürdig

unlimited [ʌnˈlɪmɪtɪd] adj unbegrenzt

unlisted [ʌnˈlɪstɪd] (US) adj nicht im Telefonbuch stehend

unload [ʌnˈləʊd] vt entladen

unlock [ʌnˈlɒk] vt aufschließen

unlucky [ʌnˈlʌkɪ] adj unglücklich; (person) unglückselig; **to be ~** Pech haben

unmarried [ʌnˈmærɪd] adj unverheiratet, ledig

unmask [ʌnˈmɑːsk] vt entlarven

unmistakable [ʌnmɪsˈteɪkəbl] adj unverkennbar

unmitigated [ʌnˈmɪtɪɡeɪtɪd] adj ungemildert, ganz

unnatural [ʌnˈnætʃrəl] adj unnatürlich

unnecessary [ʌnˈnesəsərɪ] adj unnötig

unnoticed [ʌnˈnəʊtɪst] adj: **to go ~** unbemerkt bleiben

UNO [ˈjuːnəʊ] n abbr = **United Nations Organization**

unobtainable [ʌnəbˈteɪnəbl] adj: **this number is ~** kein Anschluss unter dieser Nummer

unobtrusive [ʌnəbˈtruːsɪv] adj unauffällig

unofficial [ʌnəˈfɪʃl] adj inoffiziell

unpack [ʌnˈpæk] vt, vi auspacken

unparalleled [ʌnˈpærəleld] adj beispiellos

unpleasant [ʌnˈpleznt] adj unangenehm

unplug [ʌnˈplʌɡ] vt den Stecker herausziehen von

unpopular [ʌnˈpɒpjʊləʳ] adj (person) unbeliebt; (decision etc) unpopulär

unprecedented [ʌnˈpresɪdəntɪd] adj beispiellos

unpredictable [ʌnprɪˈdɪktəbl] adj unvorhersehbar; (weather, person) unberechenbar

unprofessional [ʌnprəˈfeʃənl] adj unprofessionell

UNPROFOR n abbr (= United Nations Protection Force) UNPROFOR f

unqualified [ʌn'kwɔlɪfaɪd] adj (success) uneingeschränkt, voll; (person) unqualifiziert

unquestionably [ʌn'kwestʃənəblɪ] adv fraglos

unravel [ʌn'rævl] vt (disentangle) ausfasern, entwirren; (solve) lösen

unreal [ʌn'rɪəl] adj unwirklich

unrealistic ['ʌnrɪə'lɪstɪk] adj unrealistisch

unreasonable [ʌn'riːznəbl] adj unvernünftig; (demand) übertrieben

unrelated [ʌnrɪ'leɪtɪd] adj ohne Beziehung; (family) nicht verwandt

unrelenting [ʌnrɪ'lentɪŋ] adj unerbittlich

unreliable [ʌnrɪ'laɪəbl] adj unzuverlässig

unremitting [ʌnrɪ'mɪtɪŋ] adj (efforts, attempts) unermüdlich

unreservedly [ʌnrɪ'zɜːvɪdlɪ] adv offen; (believe, trust) uneingeschränkt; (cry) rückhaltlos

unrest [ʌn'rest] n (discontent) Unruhe f; (fighting) Unruhen pl

unroll [ʌn'rəʊl] vt aufrollen

unruly [ʌn'ruːlɪ] adj (child) undiszipliniert; schwer lenkbar

unsafe [ʌn'seɪf] adj nicht sicher

unsaid [ʌn'sed] adj: to leave sth ~ etw ungesagt lassen

unsatisfactory ['ʌnsætɪs'fæktərɪ] adj unbefriedigend; unzulänglich

unsavoury [ʌn'seɪvərɪ] (US unsavory) adj (fig) widerwärtig

unscathed [ʌn'skeɪðd] adj unversehrt

unscrew [ʌn'skruː] vt aufschrauben

unscrupulous [ʌn'skruːpjʊləs] adj skrupellos

unsettled [ʌn'setld] adj (person) rastlos; (weather) wechselhaft

unshaven [ʌn'ʃeɪvn] adj unrasiert

unsightly [ʌn'saɪtlɪ] adj unansehnlich

unskilled [ʌn'skɪld] adj ungelernt

unspeakable [ʌn'spiːkəbl] adj (joy)

unsagbar; (crime) scheußlich

unstable [ʌn'steɪbl] adj instabil; (mentally) labil

unsteady [ʌn'stedɪ] adj unsicher

unstuck [ʌn'stʌk] adj: to come ~ sich lösen; (fig) ins Wasser fallen

unsuccessful [ʌnsək'sesful] adj erfolglos

unsuitable [ʌn'suːtəbl] adj unpassend

unsure [ʌn'ʃʊəʳ] adj unsicher; to be ~ of o.s. unsicher sein

unsuspecting [ʌnsəs'pektɪŋ] adj nichts ahnend

unsympathetic ['ʌnsɪmpə'θetɪk] adj gefühllos; (response) abweisend; (unlikeable) unsympathisch

untapped [ʌn'tæpt] adj (resources) ungenützt

unthinkable [ʌn'θɪŋkəbl] adj unvorstellbar

untidy [ʌn'taɪdɪ] adj unordentlich

untie [ʌn'taɪ] vt aufschnüren

until [ən'tɪl] prep, conj bis; ~ he comes bis er kommt; ~ then bis dann; ~ now bis jetzt

untimely [ʌn'taɪmlɪ] adj (death) vorzeitig

untold [ʌn'təʊld] adj unermesslich

untoward [ʌntə'wɔːd] adj widrig

untranslatable [ʌntrænz'leɪtəbl] adj unübersetzbar

unused [ʌn'juːzd] adj unbenutzt

unusual [ʌn'juːʒuəl] adj ungewöhnlich

unveil [ʌn'veɪl] vt enthüllen

unwanted [ʌn'wɒntɪd] adj unerwünscht

unwavering [ʌn'weɪvərɪŋ] adj standhaft, unerschütterlich

unwelcome [ʌn'welkəm] adj (at a bad time) unwillkommen; (unpleasant) unerfreulich

unwell [ʌn'wel] adj: to feel or be ~ sich nicht wohl fühlen

unwieldy [ʌn'wiːldɪ] adj sperrig

unwilling [ʌn'wɪlɪŋ] adj: to be ~ to do sth nicht bereit sein, etw zu tun; ~ly adv widerwillig

unwind [ʌn'waɪnd] (*irreg: like wind²*) *vt* abwickeln ♦ *vi* (*relax*) sich entspannen

unwise [ʌn'waɪz] *adj* unklug

unwitting [ʌn'wɪtɪŋ] *adj* unwissentlich

unworkable [ʌn'wɜːkəbl] *adj* (*plan*) undurchführbar

unworthy [ʌn'wɜːðɪ] *adj* (*person*): ~ (of sth) (einer Sache *gen*) nicht wert

unwrap [ʌn'ræp] *vt* auspacken

unwritten [ʌn'rɪtn] *adj* ungeschrieben

KEYWORD

up [ʌp] *prep*: **to be up sth** oben auf etw *dat* sein; **to go up sth** (auf) etw *acc* hinaufgehen; **up that road ge-hen Sie die Straße hinauf**
♦ *adv* **1** (*upwards, higher*) oben, auf; **put it up a bit higher** stell es etwas weiter nach oben; **up there** da oben, dort oben; **up above** hoch oben

2: **to be up** (*out of bed*) auf sein; (*prices, level*) gestiegen sein; (*building, tent*) stehen

3: **up to** (*as far as*) bis; **up to now** bis jetzt

4: **up to** (*depending on*): **it's up to you** das hängt von dir ab; (*equal to*): **he's not up to it** (*job, task etc*) er ist dem nicht gewachsen; (*inf: be doing: showing disapproval, suspicion*): **what is he up to?** was führt er im Schilde?; **it's not up to me to decide** die Entscheidung liegt nicht bei mir; **his work is not up to the required standard** seine Arbeit entspricht nicht dem geforderten Niveau
♦ *n*: **ups and downs** (*in life, career*) Höhen und Tiefen *pl*

---

up-and-coming [ʌpənd'kʌmɪŋ] *adj* aufstrebend

upbringing ['ʌpbrɪŋɪŋ] *n* Erziehung *f*

update [ʌp'deɪt] *vt* auf den neuesten Stand bringen

upgrade [ʌp'greɪd] *vt* höher einstufen

upheaval [ʌp'hiːvl] *n* Umbruch *m*

uphill ['ʌp'hɪl] *adj* ansteigend; (*fig*) mühsam ♦ *adv*: **to go ~** bergauf gehen/fahren

uphold [ʌp'həʊld] (*irreg: like hold*) *vt* unterstützen

upholstery [ʌp'həʊlstərɪ] *n* Polster *nt*; Polsterung *f*

upkeep ['ʌpkiːp] *n* Instandhaltung *f*

upon [ə'pɒn] *prep* auf

upper ['ʌpə*] *n* (*on shoe*) Oberleder *nt* ♦ *adj* obere(r, s), höhere(r, s); **to have the ~ hand** die Oberhand haben; **~class** *adj* vornehm; **~most** *adj* oberste(r, s), höchste(r, s); **what was ~most in my mind** was mich in erster Linie beschäftigte; **~ sixth** (*BRIT: SCOL*) *n* Abschlussklasse *f*

upright ['ʌpraɪt] *adj* aufrecht

uprising ['ʌpraɪzɪŋ] *n* Aufstand *m*

uproar ['ʌprɔː*] *n* Aufruhr *m*

uproot [ʌp'ruːt] *vt* ausreißen

upset [*n* 'ʌpsɛt, *vb, adj* ʌp'sɛt] (*irreg: like set*) *n* Aufregung *f* ♦ *vt* (*overturn*) um-werfen; (*disturb*) aufregen, bestürzen; (*plans*) durcheinander bringen ♦ *adj* (*person*) aufgeregt; (*stomach*) verdor-ben

upshot ['ʌpʃɒt] *n* (End)ergebnis *nt*

upside-down ['ʌpsaɪd-] *adv* verkehrt herum

upstairs [ʌp'stɛəz] *adv* oben; (*go*) nach oben ♦ *adj* (*room*) obere(r, s), Ober- ♦ *n* obere(s) Stockwerk *nt*

upstart ['ʌpstɑːt] *n* Emporkömmling *m*

upstream [ʌp'striːm] *adv* stromauf-wärts

uptake ['ʌpteɪk] *n*: **to be quick on the ~** schnell begreifen; **to be slow on the ~** schwer von Begriff sein

uptight [ʌp'taɪt] (*inf*) *adj* (*nervous*) ner-vös; (*inhibited*) verklemmt

up-to-date ['ʌptə'deɪt] *adj* (*clothes*) modisch, modern; (*information*) neu-este(r, s)

upturn ['ʌptɜːn] *n* Aufschwung *m*

upward ['ʌpwəd] *adj* nach oben ge-richtet; **~(s)** *adv* aufwärts

uranium [jʊə'reɪnɪəm] *n* Uran *nt*

urban ['ə:bən] *adj* städtisch, Stadt-; ~ **clearway** *n* Stadtautobahn *f*

urchin ['ə:tʃɪn] *n (boy)* Schlingel *m; (sea ~)* Seeigel *m*

urge [ə:dʒ] *n* Drang *m* ♦ *vt:* **to ~ sb to do sth** jdn (dazu) drängen, etw zu tun

urgency ['ə:dʒənsɪ] *n* Dringlichkeit *f*

urgent ['ə:dʒənt] *adj* dringend

urinal ['juərɪnl] *n (public)* Pissoir *nt*

urinate ['juərɪneɪt] *vi* urinieren

urine ['juərɪn] *n* Urin *m*, Harn *m*

urn [ə:n] *n* Urne *f; (tea ~)* Teemaschine *f*

US *n abbr* = **United States**

us [ʌs] *pron uns; see also* **me**

USA *n abbr* = **United States of America**

usage ['ju:zɪdʒ] *n* Gebrauch *m; (esp LING)* Sprachgebrauch *m*

use [*n* ju:s, *vb* ju:z] *n (employment)* Gebrauch *m; (point)* Zweck *m* ♦ *vt* gebrauchen; **in ~** in Gebrauch; **out of ~** außer Gebrauch; **to be of ~** nützlich sein; **it's no ~** es hat keinen Zweck; **what's the ~?** was solls?; **~d to** *(accustomed to)* gewöhnt an +*acc;* **she ~d to live here** *(formerly)* sie hat früher mal hier gewohnt; **~ up** *vt* aufbrauchen, verbrauchen; **~d** *adj (car)* Gebraucht-; **~ful** *adj* nützlich; **~fulness** *n* Nützlichkeit *f;* **~less** *adj* nutzlos, unnütz; **~r** *n* Benutzer *m;* **~r-friendly** *adj (computer)* benutzerfreundlich

usher ['ʌʃə*r*] *n* Platzanweiser *m;* **~ette** [ʌʃə'ret] *n* Platzanweiserin *f*

usual ['ju:ʒuəl] *adj* gewöhnlich, üblich; **as ~** wie üblich; **~ly** *adv* gewöhnlich

usurp [ju:'zə:p] *vt* an sich reißen

utensil [ju:'tensl] *n* Gerät *nt;* **kitchen ~s** Küchengeräte *pl*

uterus ['ju:tərəs] *n* Gebärmutter *f*

utilitarian [ju:tɪlɪ'teərɪən] *adj* Nützlichkeits-

utility [ju:'tɪlɪtɪ] *n (usefulness)* Nützlichkeit *f; (also:* **public ~)** öffentliche(r) Versorgungsbetrieb *m;* ~

room *n* Hauswirtschaftsraum *m*

utilize ['ju:tɪlaɪz] *vt* benützen

utmost ['ʌtməust] *adj* äußerste(r, s) ♦ *n:* **to do one's ~** sein Möglichstes tun

utter ['ʌtə*r*] *adj* äußerste(r, s), höchste(r, s), völlig *♦ vt* äußern, aussprechen; **~ance** *n* Äußerung *f;* **~ly** *adv* äußerst, absolut, völlig

U-turn ['ju:'tə:n] *n (AUT)* Kehrtwendung *f*

V, v

v. *abbr* = **verse; versus; volt;** (= *vide*) see

vacancy ['veɪkənsɪ] *n (BRIT: job)* offene Stelle *f; (room)* freie(s) Zimmer *nt;* **"no vacancies** "belegt"

vacant ['veɪkənt] *adj* leer; *(unoccupied)* frei; *(house)* leer stehend, unbewohnt; *(stupid)* (gedanken)leer; **~ lot** *(US) n* unbebaute(s) Grundstück *nt*

vacate [və'keɪt] *vt (seat)* frei machen; *(room)* räumen

vacation [və'keɪʃən] *n* Ferien *pl,* Urlaub *m;* **~ist** *(US)* *n* Ferienreisende(r) *f(m)*

vaccinate ['væksɪneɪt] *vt* impfen

vaccine ['væksi:n] *n* Impfstoff *m*

vacuum ['vækjum] *n* Vakuum *nt;* ~ **bottle** *n* (US) Thermosflasche *f;* ~ **cleaner** *n* Staubsauger *m;* ~ **flask** (BRIT) *n* Thermosflasche *f;* **~-packed** *adj* vakuumversiegelt

vagina [və'dʒaɪnə] *n* Scheide *f*

vague [veɪg] *adj* vag(e); *(absent-minded)* geistesabwesend; **~ly** *adv* unbestimmt, vag (e)

vain [veɪn] *adj* eitel; *(attempt)* vergeblich; **in ~** vergebens, umsonst

valentine ['væləntaɪn] *n (also:* ~ **card)** Valentinsgruß *m;* **V~'s Day** *n* Valentinstag *m*

valet ['vælɪt] *n* Kammerdiener *m*

valiant ['vælɪənt] *adj* tapfer

valid ['vælɪd] *adj* gültig; *(argument)* stichhaltig; *(objection)* berechtigt; **~ity**

valley [ˈvælɪtɪ] n Gültigkeit f

valley [ˈvælɪ] n Tal nt

valour [ˈvælə°] (US **valor**) n Tapferkeit f

valuable [ˈvæljuəbl] adj wertvoll; (time) kostbar; **~s** npl Wertsachen pl

valuation [væljuˈeɪʃən] n (FIN) Schätzung f; Beurteilung f

value [ˈvæljuː] n Wert m; (usefulness) Nutzen m ♦ vt (prize) (hoch) schätzen, werthalten; (estimate) schätzen; **~ added tax** (BRIT) n Mehrwertsteuer f; **~d** adj (hoch) geschätzt

valve [vælv] n Ventil n; (BIOL) Klappe f; (RAD) Röhre f

van [væn] n Lieferwagen m; (BRIT: RAIL) Waggon m

vandal [ˈvændl] n Rowdy m; **~ism** n mutwillige Beschädigung f; **~ize** vt mutwillig beschädigen

vanguard [ˈvænɡɑːd] n (fig) Spitze f

vanilla [vəˈnɪlə] n Vanille f; **~ ice cream** n Vanilleeis nt

vanish [ˈvænɪʃ] vi verschwinden

vanity [ˈvænɪtɪ] n Eitelkeit f; **~ case** n Schminkkoffer m

vantage [ˈvɑːntɪdʒ] n: **~ point** gute(r) Aussichtspunkt m

vapour [ˈveɪpə°] (US **vapor**) n (mist) Dunst m; (gas) Dampf m

variable [ˈvɛərɪəbl] adj wechselhaft, veränderlich; (speed, height) regulierbar

variance [ˈvɛərɪəns] n: **to be at ~ (with)** nicht übereinstimmen (mit)

variation [vɛərɪˈeɪʃən] n Variation f; (in prices etc) Schwankung f

varicose [ˈværɪkəus] adj: **~ veins** Krampfadern pl

varied [ˈvɛərɪd] adj unterschiedlich; (life) abwechslungsreich

variety [vəˈraɪətɪ] n (difference) Abwechslung f; (varied collection) Vielfalt f; (COMM) Auswahl f; (sort) Sorte f, Art f; **~ show** n Varietee nt, Varieté nt

various [ˈvɛərɪəs] adj verschieden; (several) mehrere

varnish [ˈvɑːnɪʃ] n Lack m; (on pottery)

Glasur f ♦ vt lackieren

vary [ˈvɛərɪ] vt (alter) verändern; (give variety to) abwechslungsreicher gestalten ♦ vi sich (ver)ändern; (prices) schwanken; (weather) unterschiedlich sein

vase [vɑːz] n Vase f

Vaseline [ˈvæsɪliːn] ® n Vaseline f

vast [vɑːst] adj weit, groß, riesig

VAT [væt] n abbr (= value added tax) MwSt f

vat [væt] n große(s) Fass nt

vault [vɔːlt] n (of roof) Gewölbe nt; (tomb) Gruft f; (in bank) Tresorraum m; (leap) Sprung m ♦ vt (also: **~ over**) überspringen

vaunted [ˈvɔːntɪd] adj: **much-~** viel gerühmt

VCR n abbr = video cassette recorder

VD n abbr = venereal disease

VDU n abbr = visual display unit

veal [viːl] n Kalbfleisch nt

veer [vɪə°] vi sich drehen; (of car) ausscheren

vegan [ˈviːɡən] n Vegan m, radikale(r) Vegetarier(in) f

vegeburger [ˈvedʒɪbɜːɡə°] n vegetarische Frikadelle f

vegetable [ˈvedʒtəbl] n Gemüse nt ♦ adj Gemüse-; **~s** npl (CULIN) Gemüse nt

vegetarian [vedʒɪˈtɛərɪən] n Vegetarier(in) m(f) ♦ adj vegetarisch

vegetate [ˈvedʒɪteɪt] vi (dahin)vegetieren

veggieburger [ˈvedʒɪbɜːɡə°] n = **vegeburger**

vehement [ˈviːɪmənt] adj heftig

vehicle [ˈviːɪkl] n Fahrzeug nt; (fig) Mittel nt

veil [veɪl] n (also fig) Schleier m ♦ vt verschleiern

vein [veɪn] n Ader f; (mood) Stimmung f

velocity [vɪˈlɒsɪtɪ] n Geschwindigkeit f

velvet [ˈvelvɪt] n Samt m ♦ adj Samt-

vendetta [venˈdetə] n Fehde f; (in family) Blutrache f

vending machine [ˈvendɪŋ-] n Automat m

vendor [ˈvendə*] n Verkäufer m

veneer [vəˈnɪə*] n Furnier(holz) nt; (fig) äußere(r) Anstrich m

venereal disease [vɪˈnɪərɪəl-] n Geschlechtskrankheit f

Venetian blind [vɪˈniːʃən-] n Jalousie f

vengeance [ˈvendʒəns] n Rache f; **with a ~** gewaltig

venison [ˈvenɪsn] n Reh(fleisch) nt

venom [ˈvenəm] n Gift nt

vent [vent] n Öffnung f; (in coat) Schlitz m; (fig) Ventil nt ♦ vt (emotion) abreagieren

ventilate [ˈventɪleɪt] vt belüften; **ventilator** [ˈventɪleɪtə*] n Ventilator m

ventriloquist [venˈtrɪləkwɪst] n Bauchredner m

venture [ˈventʃə*] n Unternehmung f, Projekt nt ♦ vt wagen; (life) aufs Spiel setzen ♦ vi sich wagen

venue [ˈvenjuː] n Schauplatz m

verb [vɜːb] n (GRAM) Zeitwort nt, Verb nt; **~al** adj (spoken) mündlich; (translation) wörtlich; (GRAM) verbal; **~ally** adv mündlich

verbatim [vɜːˈbeɪtɪm] adv Wort für Wort ♦ adj wortwörtlich

verbose [vɜːˈbəus] adj wortreich

verdict [ˈvɜːdɪkt] n Urteil nt

verge [vɜːdʒ] n (BRIT) Rand m ♦ vi: **to ~ on** grenzen an +acc; **"soft ~s"** (BRIT: AUT) "Seitenstreifen nicht befahrbar"; **on the ~ of doing sth** im Begriff, etw zu tun

verify [ˈverɪfaɪ] vt (über)prüfen; (confirm) bestätigen; (theory) beweisen

veritable [ˈverɪtəbl] adj wirklich, echt

vermin [ˈvɜːmɪn] npl Ungeziefer nt

vermouth [ˈvɜːməθ] n Wermut m

versatile [ˈvɜːsətaɪl] adj vielseitig

verse [vɜːs] n (poetry) Poesie f; (stanza) Strophe f; (of Bible) Vers m; **in ~** in Versform

version [ˈvɜːʃən] n Version f; (of car) Modell nt

versus [ˈvɜːsəs] prep gegen

vertebrate [ˈvɜːtɪbrɪt] adj Wirbel-

vertical [ˈvɜːtɪkl] adj senkrecht

vertigo [ˈvɜːtɪgəu] n Schwindel m

very [ˈverɪ] adv sehr ♦ adj (extreme) äußerste(r, s); **the ~ book which** genau das Buch, welches; **the ~ last** ... der/die/das allerletzte ...; **at the ~ least** allerwenigstens; **~ much** sehr

vessel [ˈvesl] n (ship) Schiff nt; (container) Gefäß nt

vest [vest] n (BRIT) Unterhemd nt; (US: waistcoat) Weste f

vested interests [ˈvestɪd-] npl finanzielle Beteiligung f; (people) finanziell Beteiligte pl; (fig) persönliche(s) Interesse nt

vestige [ˈvestɪdʒ] n Spur f

vestry [ˈvestrɪ] n Sakristei f

vet [vet] n abbr (= veterinary surgeon) Tierarzt/-ärztin m(f)

veteran [ˈvetərn] n Veteran(in) m(f)

veterinarian [vetrɪˈnɛərɪən] n (US) n Tierarzt m/-ärztin f

veterinary [ˈvetrɪnərɪ] adj Veterinär-; **~ surgeon** (BRIT) n Tierarzt m/-ärztin f

veto [ˈviːtəu] (pl **~es**) n Veto nt ♦ vt sein Veto einlegen gegen

vex [veks] vt ärgern; **~ed** adj verärgert; **~ed question** umstrittene Frage f

VHF abbr (= very high frequency) UKW f

via [ˈvaɪə] prep über +acc

viable [ˈvaɪəbl] adj (plan) durchführbar; (company) rentabel

vibrant [ˈvaɪbrnt] adj (lively) lebhaft; (bright) leuchtend; (full of emotion: voice) bebend

vibrate [vaɪˈbreɪt] vi zittern, beben; (machine, string) vibrieren; **vibration** [vaɪˈbreɪʃən] n Schwingung f; (of machine) Vibrieren nt

vicar [ˈvɪkə*] n Pfarrer m; **~age** n Pfarrhaus nt

vice [vaɪs] n (evil) Laster nt; (TECH) Schraubstock m

vice-chairman [vaɪsˈtʃɛəmən] n stellvertretende(r) Vorsitzende(r) m

vice-president [vaɪsˈprezɪdənt] n Vizepräsident m

vice squad n ≈ Sittenpolizei f

vice versa ['vaɪsɪ'vɜːsə] adv umgekehrt

vicinity [vɪ'sɪnɪtɪ] n Umgebung f; (closeness) Nähe f

vicious ['vɪʃəs] adj gemein, böse; ~ **circle** n Teufelskreis m

victim ['vɪktɪm] n Opfer nt

victor ['vɪktə*] n Sieger m

Victorian [vɪk'tɔːrɪən] adj viktorianisch; (fig) (sitten)streng

victorious [vɪk'tɔːrɪəs] adj siegreich

victory ['vɪktərɪ] n Sieg m

video ['vɪdɪəu] adj Fernseh-, Bild- ♦ n (~ film) Video nt; (~ cassette) Videokassette f; (also: ~ cassette recorder) Videorekorder m; ~ **tape** n Videoband nt; ~ **wall** n Videowand m

vie [vaɪ] vi wetteifern

Vienna [vɪ'enə] n Wien nt

Vietnam ['vjet'næm] n Vietnam nt; ~**ese** adj vietnamesisch ♦ n inv (person) Vietnamese m, Vietnamesin f

view [vjuː] n (sight) Sicht f; (scene) Aussicht f; (opinion) Ansicht f; (intention) Absicht f ♦ vt (situation) betrachten; (house) besichtigen; **to have sth in** ~ etw beabsichtigen; **on** ~ ausgestellt; **in** ~ **of** wegen +gen, angesichts +gen; ~**er** n (PHOT: small projector) Gucki m; (TV) Fernsehzuschauer(in) m(f); ~**finder** n Sucher m; ~**point** n Standpunkt m

vigil ['vɪdʒɪl] n (Nacht)wache f; ~**ant** adj wachsam

vigorous ['vɪgərəs] adj kräftig; (protest) energisch, heftig

vile [vaɪl] adj (mean) gemein; (foul) abscheulich

villa ['vɪlə] n Villa f

village ['vɪlɪdʒ] n Dorf nt; ~**r** n Dorfbewohner(in) m(f)

villain ['vɪlən] n Schurke m

vindicate ['vɪndɪkeɪt] vt rechtfertigen

vindictive [vɪn'dɪktɪv] adj nachtragend, rachsüchtig

vine [vaɪn] n Rebstock m, Rebe f

vinegar ['vɪnɪgə*] n Essig m

vineyard ['vɪnjɑːd] n Weinberg m

vintage ['vɪntɪdʒ] n (of wine) Jahrgang m; ~ **car** n Oldtimer m (zwischen 1919 und 1930 gebaut); ~ **wine** n edle(r) Wein m

viola [vɪ'əulə] n Bratsche f

violate ['vaɪəleɪt] vt (law) übertreten; (rights, rule, neutrality) verletzen; (sanctity, woman) schänden; **violation** [vaɪə'leɪʃən] n Übertretung f; Verletzung f

violence ['vaɪələns] n (force) Heftigkeit f; (brutality) Gewalttätigkeit f

violent ['vaɪələnt] adj (strong) heftig; (brutal) gewalttätig, brutal; (contrast) krass; (death) gewaltsam

violet ['vaɪələt] n Veilchen nt ♦ adj veilchenblau, violett

violin [vaɪə'lɪn] n Geige f, Violine f; ~**ist** n Geiger(in) m(f)

VIP n abbr (= very important person) VIP m

virgin ['vɜːdʒɪn] n Jungfrau f ♦ adj jungfräulich, unberührt; ~**ity** [vɜː'dʒɪnɪtɪ] n Unschuld f

Virgo ['vɜːgəu] n Jungfrau f

virile ['vɪraɪl] adj männlich; **virility** [vɪ'rɪlɪtɪ] n Männlichkeit f

virtually ['vɜːtjuəlɪ] adv praktisch, fast

virtual reality ['vɜːtjuəl-] n (COMPUT) virtuelle Realität f

virtue ['vɜːtjuː] n (moral goodness) Tugend f; (good quality) Vorteil m, Vorzug m; **by** ~ **of** aufgrund or auf Grund +gen

virtuous ['vɜːtjuəs] adj tugendhaft

virulent ['vɪrulənt] adj (poisonous) bösartig; (bitter) scharf, geharnischt

virus ['vaɪərəs] n (also COMPUT) Virus m

visa ['viːzə] n Visum nt

vis-à-vis [viːzə'viː] prep gegenüber

viscous ['vɪskəs] adj zähflüssig

visibility [vɪzɪ'bɪlɪtɪ] n (MET) Sicht(weite) f

visible ['vɪzəbl] adj sichtbar; **visibly** adv sichtlich

vision ['vɪʒən] n (ability) Sehvermögen nt; (foresight) Weitblick m; (in dream, image) Vision f

visit ['vɪzɪt] n Besuch m ♦ vt besuchen; (town, country) fahren nach; **~ing hours** npl (in hospital etc) Besuchszeiten pl; **~or** n (in house) Besucher(in) m(f); (in hotel) Gast m; **~or centre** n Touristeninformation f

visor ['vaɪzə'] n Visier nt; (on cap) Schirm m; (AUT) Blende f

vista ['vɪstə] n Aussicht f

visual ['vɪzjuəl] adj Seh-, visuell; **~ aid** n Anschauungsmaterial nt; **~ display unit** n Bildschirm(gerät nt) m; **~ize** vt sich +dat vorstellen; **~ly-impaired** adj sehbehindert

vital ['vaɪtl] adj (important) unerlässlich; (necessary for life) Lebens-, lebenswichtig; (lively) vital; **~ity** [vaɪ'tælɪtɪ] n Vitalität f; **~ly** adv: **~ly important** äußerst wichtig; **~ statistics** npl (fig) Maße pl

vitamin ['vɪtəmɪn] n Vitamin nt

vivacious [vɪ'veɪʃəs] adj lebhaft

vivid ['vɪvɪd] adj (graphic) lebendig; (memory) lebhaft; (bright) leuchtend; **~ly** adv lebendig; lebhaft; leuchtend

V-neck ['viːnɛk] n V-Ausschnitt m

vocabulary [vəu'kæbjuləri] n Wortschatz m, Vokabular nt

vocal ['vəukl] adj Vokal-, Gesang-; (fig) lautstark; **~ cords** npl Stimmbänder pl

vocation [vəu'keɪʃən] n (calling) Berufung f; **~al** adj Berufs-

vociferous [vəu'sɪfərəs] adj lautstark

vodka ['vɔdkə] n Wodka m

vogue [vəug] n Mode f

voice [vɔɪs] n Stimme f; (fig) Mitspracherecht n ♦ vt äußern; **~ mail** n (COMPUT) Voice-Mail f

void [vɔɪd] n Leere f ♦ adj (invalid) nichtig, ungültig; (empty): **~ of** ohne, bar +gen; see **null**

volatile ['vɔlətaɪl] adj (gas) flüchtig; (person) impulsiv; (situation) brisant

volcano [vɔl'keɪnəu] n Vulkan m

volition [və'lɪʃən] n Wille m; **of one's**

own ~ aus freiem Willen

volley ['vɔlɪ] n (of guns) Salve f; (of stones) Hagel m; (tennis) Flugball m; **~ball** n Volleyball m

volt [vəult] n Volt nt; **~age** n (Volt)spannung f

volume ['vɔljuːm] n (book) Band m; (size) Umfang m; (space) Rauminhalt m; (of sound) Lautstärke f

voluntarily ['vɔləntrɪlɪ] adv freiwillig

voluntary ['vɔləntəri] adj freiwillig

volunteer [vɔlən'tɪə'] n Freiwillige(r) mf ♦ vi sich freiwillig melden; **to ~ to do sth** sich anbieten, etw zu tun

vomit ['vɔmɪt] n Erbrochene(s) nt ♦ vt spucken ♦ vi sich übergeben

vote [vəut] n Stimme f; (ballot) Abstimmung f; (result) Abstimmungsergebnis nt; (franchise) Wahlrecht nt ♦ vt u wählen; **~r** n Wähler(in) m(f); **voting** ['vəutɪŋ] n Wahl f

voucher ['vautʃə'] n Gutschein m

vouch for [vautʃ-] n bürgen für

vow [vau] n Versprechen n; (REL) Gelübde nt ♦ vt geloben

vowel ['vauəl] n Vokal m

voyage ['vɔɪdʒ] n Reise f

vulgar ['vʌlgə'] adj (rude) vulgär; **~ity** [vʌl'gærɪtɪ] n Vulgarität f

vulnerable ['vʌlnərəbl] adj (easily injured) verwundbar; (sensitive) verletzlich

vulture ['vʌltʃə'] n Geier m

W, w

wad [wɔd] n (bundle) Bündel nt; (of paper) Stoß m; (of money) Packen m

waddle ['wɔdl] vi watscheln

wade [weɪd] vi: **to ~ through** waten durch

wafer ['weɪfə'] n Waffel f; (REL) Hostie f; (COMPUT) Wafer f

waffle ['wɔfl] n Waffel f; (inf: empty talk) Geschwafel nt ♦ vi schwafeln

waft [wɔft] vt, vi wehen

wag [wæg] vt (tail) wedeln mit ♦ vi wedeln

wage [weɪdʒ] n (also: ~s) (Arbeits)lohn m ♦ vt: **to ~ war** Krieg führen; **~ earner** n Lohnempfänger m(f); **~ packet** n Lohntüte f

wager ['weɪdʒə'] n Wette f ♦ vt, vi wetten

waggle ['wægl] vi wackeln

wag(g)on ['wægən] n (horse-drawn) Fuhrwerk nt; (US: AUT) Wagen m; (BRIT: RAIL) Wag(g)on m

wail [weɪl] n Wehgeschrei nt ♦ vi wehklagen, jammern

waist [weɪst] n Taille f; **~coat** (BRIT) n Weste f; **~line** n Taille f

wait [weɪt] n Wartezeit f ♦ vi warten; **to lie in ~ for sb** jdm auflauern; **I can't ~ to see him** ich kanns kaum erwarten ihn zu sehen; **"no ~ing"** (BRIT: AUT) „Halteverbot"; **~ behind** vi zurückbleiben; **~ for** vt fus warten auf +acc; **~ on** vt fus bedienen; **~er** n Kellner m; **~ing list** n Warteliste f; **~ing room** n (MED) Wartezimmer nt; (RAIL) Wartesaal m; **~ress** n Kellnerin f

waive [weɪv] vt verzichten auf +acc

wake [weɪk] (pt woke, waked, pp woken) vt wecken ♦ vi (also: ~ up) aufwachen ♦ n (NAUT) Kielwasser nt; (for dead) Totenwache f; **to ~ up to** (fig) sich bewusst werden +gen

waken ['weɪkn] vt aufwecken

Wales [weɪlz] n Wales nt

walk [wɔːk] n Spaziergang m; (gait) Gang m; (route) Weg m ♦ vi (stroll) spazieren gehen; (longer) wandern; **~s of life** Sphären pl; **a 10-minute ~** 10 Minuten zu Fuß; **to ~ out on sb** (inf) jdn sitzen lassen; **~er** n Spaziergänger m; (hiker) Wanderer m; **~ie-talkie** ['wɔːkɪ'tɔːkɪ] n tragbare(s) Sprechfunkgerät nt; **~ing** n Gehen nt; (hiking) Wandern nt ♦ adj Wander-; **~ing shoes** npl Wanderschuhe pl; **~ing stick** n Spazierstock m; **W~man** ['wɔːkmən] ® n Walkman m ®; **~out** n Streik m; **~over** (inf) n leichte(r) Sieg

m; **~way** n Fußweg m

wall [wɔːl] n (inside) Wand f; (outside) Mauer f; **~ed** adj von Mauern umgeben

wallet ['wɒlɪt] n Brieftasche f

wallflower ['wɔːlflauə'] n Goldlack m; **to be a ~** (fig) ein Mauerblümchen sein

wallop ['wɒləp] (inf) vt schlagen, verprügeln

wallow ['wɒləu] vi sich wälzen

wallpaper ['wɔːlpeɪpə'] n Tapete f

walnut ['wɔːlnʌt] n Walnuss f

walrus ['wɔːlrəs] n Walross nt

waltz [wɔːlts] n Walzer m ♦ vi Walzer tanzen

wan [wɒn] adj bleich

wand [wɒnd] n (also: magic ~) Zauberstab m

wander ['wɒndə'] vi (roam) (herum)wandern; (fig) abschweifen

wane [weɪn] vi (moon) abnehmen; (fig) schwinden

wangle ['wæŋgl] (inf) vt: **to ~ sth** etw richtig hindrehen

want [wɒnt] n (lack) Mangel m ♦ vt (need) brauchen; (desire) wollen; (lack) nicht haben; **~s** npl (needs) Bedürfnisse pl; **for ~ of** aus Mangel an +dat; mangels +gen; **to ~ to do sth** etw tun wollen; **to ~ sb to do sth** wollen, dass jd etw tut; **~ed** adj (criminal etc) gesucht; **"cook ~ed"** (in adverts) „Koch/Köchin gesucht"; **~ing** adj: **to be found ~ing** sich als unzulänglich erweisen

wanton ['wɒntn] adj mutwillig, zügellos

war [wɔː'] n Krieg m; **to make ~** Krieg führen

ward [wɔːd] n (in hospital) Station f; (of city) Bezirk m; (child) Mündel nt; **~ off** vt abwenden, abwehren

warden ['wɔːdn] n (guard) Wächter m, Aufseher m; (BRIT: in youth hostel) Herbergsvater m; (UNIV) Heimleiter m; (BRIT: also: traffic ~) ≈ Verkehrspolizist m, ≈ Politesse f

warder ['wɔːdə*] (BRIT) n Gefängniswärter m

wardrobe ['wɔːdrəub] n Kleiderschrank m; (clothes) Garderobe f

warehouse ['wɛəhaus] n Lagerhaus nt

wares [wɛəz] npl Ware f

warfare ['wɔːfɛə*] n Krieg m; Kriegsführung f

warhead ['wɔːhɛd] n Sprengkopf m

warily ['wɛərɪlɪ] adv vorsichtig

warlike ['wɔːlaɪk] adj kriegerisch

warm [wɔːm] adj warm; (welcome) herzlich ♦ vt, vi wärmen; **I'm** ~ mir ist warm; **it's** ~ es ist warm; ~ **up** vi aufwärmen ♦ vt warm werden; ~-**hearted** adj warmherzig; ~**ly** adv warm; herzlich; ~**th** n Wärme f; Herzlichkeit f

warn [wɔːn] vt: to ~ (of or against) warnen (vor +dat); ~**ing** n Warnung f; **without** ~**ing** unerwartet; ~**ing light** n Warnlicht nt; ~**ing triangle** n (AUT) Warndreieck nt

warp [wɔːp] vt verziehen; ~**ed** adj wellig; (fig) pervers

warrant ['wɔrnt] n (for arrest) Haftbefehl m

warranty ['wɔrəntɪ] n Garantie f

warren ['wɔrən] n Labyrinth nt

Warsaw ['wɔːsɔː] n Warschau nt

warship ['wɔːʃɪp] n Kriegsschiff nt

wart [wɔːt] n Warze f

wartime ['wɔːtaɪm] n Krieg m

wary ['wɛərɪ] adj misstrauisch

was [wɔz] pt of **be**

wash [wɔʃ] n Wäsche f ♦ vt waschen; (dishes) abwaschen ♦ vi sich waschen; (do ~ing) waschen; **to have a** ~ sich waschen; ~ **away** vt abwaschen, wegspülen; ~ **off** vt abwaschen; ~ **up** vi (BRIT) spülen; (US) sich waschen; ~**able** adj waschbar; ~**basin** n Waschbecken nt; ~ **bowl** (US) n Waschbecken nt; ~ **cloth** (US) n (face cloth) Waschlappen m; ~**er** n (TECH) Dichtungsring m; (machine) Waschmaschine f; ~**ing** n Wäsche f; ~**ing machine**

n Waschmaschine f; ~**ing powder** (BRIT) n Waschpulver nt; ~**ing-up** n Abwasch m; ~**ing-up liquid** n Spülmittel nt; ~-**out** (inf) n (event) Reinfall m; (person) Niete f; ~**room** n Waschraum m

wasn't ['wɔznt] = **was not**

wasp [wɔsp] n Wespe f

wastage ['weɪstɪdʒ] n Verlust m; **natural** ~ Verschleiß m

waste [weɪst] n (wasting) Verschwendung f; (what is ~d) Abfall m ♦ adj (useless) überschüssig, Abfall-; ~ (of object) verschwenden; (time, life) vergeuden ♦ vi: to ~ **away** verkommen, verkümmern; ~**s** npl (land) Einöde f; ~ **disposal unit** (BRIT) n Müllschlucker m; ~**ful** adj verschwenderisch; (process) aufwändig, aufwendig; ~ **ground** (BRIT) n unbebaute(s) Grundstück nt; ~**land** n Ödland nt; ~**paper basket** n Papierkorb m; ~ **pipe** n Abflussrohr nt

watch [wɔtʃ] n Wache f; (for time) Uhr f ♦ vt ansehen; (observe) beobachten; (be careful of) aufpassen auf +acc; (guard) bewachen ♦ vi zusehen; **to be on the** ~ (for sth) Ausschau halten (nach); **to** ~ **TV** fernsehen; **to** ~ **sb doing sth** jdm bei etw zuschauen; ~ **out** vi Ausschau halten; (be careful) aufpassen; ~ **out!** pass auf!; ~**dog** n Wachhund m; (fig) Wächter m; ~**ful** adj wachsam; ~**maker** n Uhrmacher m; ~**man** (irreg) n (also: **night** ~**man**) (Nacht)wächter m; ~ **strap** n Uhrarmband nt

water ['wɔːtə*] n Wasser nt ♦ vt (be)gießen; (river) bewässern; (horses) tränken ♦ vi (eye) tränen; ~**s** npl (of sea, river etc) Gewässer nt; ~ **down** vt verwässern; ~ **closet** (BRIT) n (Wasser)klosett nt; ~**colour** (US **watercolor**) n (painting) Aquarell nt; (paint) Wasserfarbe f; ~**cress** n (Brunnen)kresse f; ~**fall** n Wasserfall m; ~ **heater** n Heißwassergerät nt; ~**ing can** n Gießkanne f; ~ **level** n Wasserstand m; ~**lily** n Seerose f; ~**line** n Wasserlinie f

~logged adj (ground) voll Wasser; **~main** n Haupt(wasser)leitung f; **~mark** n Wasserzeichen nt; (on wall) Wasserstandsmarke f; **~melon** n Wassermelone f; **~ polo** n Wasserball(spiel) nt; **~proof** adj wasserdicht; **~shed** n Wasserscheide f; **~skiing** n Wasserskilaufen nt; **~ tank** n Wassertank m; **~tight** adj wasserdicht; **~way** n Wasserweg m; **~works** npl Wasserwerk nt; **~y** adj wäss(e)rig

watt [wɔt] n Watt nt

wave [weɪv] n Welle f; (with hand) Winken nt ♦ vt (move to and fro) schwenken; (hand, flag) winken mit ♦ vi (person) winken; (flag) wehen; **~length** n (also fig) Wellenlänge f

waver ['weɪvəʳ] vi schwanken

wavy ['weɪvɪ] adj wellig

wax [wæks] n Wachs nt; (sealing ~) Siegellack m; (in ear) Ohrenschmalz nt ♦ vt (floor) (ein)wachsen ♦ vi (moon) zunehmen; **~works** npl Wachsfigurenkabinett nt

way [weɪ] n Weg m; (method) Art und Weise f; (direction) Richtung f; (habit) Gewohnheit f; (distance) Entfernung f; (condition) Zustand m; **which ~? -this ~** welche Richtung - hier entlang; **on the ~** (en route) unterwegs; **to be in the ~** im Weg sein; **to go out of one's ~ to do sth** sich besonders anstrengen, um etw zu tun; **to lose one's ~** sich verirren; **"give ~"** (BRIT: AUT) „Vorfahrt achten!"; **in a ~** in gewisser Weise; **by the ~** übrigens; **in some ~s** in gewisser Hinsicht; **"~ in"** (BRIT) „Eingang"; **"~ out"** (BRIT) „Ausgang"

waylay [weɪ'leɪ] (irreg: like **lay**) vt auflauern +dat

wayward ['weɪwəd] adj eigensinnig

W.C. (BRIT) n WC nt

we [wiː] pl pron wir

weak [wiːk] adj schwach; **~en** vt schwächen ♦ vi schwächer werden; **~ling** n Schwächling m; **~ness** n Schwäche f

wealth [welθ] n Reichtum m; (abundance) Fülle f; **~y** adj reich

wean [wiːn] vt entwöhnen

weapon ['wepən] n Waffe f

wear [weəʳ] (pt **wore**, pp **worn**) n (clothing): **sports/baby ~** Sport-/Babykleidung f ♦ (use) Verschleiß m ♦ vt (have on) tragen; (smile etc) haben; (use) abnutzen ♦ vi (last) halten; (become old) sich verschleißen; **evening ~** Abendkleidung f; **~ and tear** Verschleiß m; **~ away** vt verbrauchen ♦ vi schwinden; **~ down** vt (people) zermürben; **~ off** vi sich verlieren; **~ out** vt verschleißen; (person) erschöpfen

weary ['wɪərɪ] adj müde ♦ vt ermüden ♦ vi überdrüssig werden

weasel ['wiːzl] n Wiesel nt

weather ['weðəʳ] n Wetter nt ♦ vt (resist) überstehen; **under the ~** (fig: ill) angeschlagen (inf); **~-beaten** adj verwittert; **~cock** n Wetterhahn m; **~ forecast** n Wettervorhersage f; **~ vane** n Wetterfahne f

weave [wiːv] (pt **wove**, pp **woven**) vt weben; **~r** n Weber(in) m(f); **weaving** n (craft) Webkunst f

web [web] n Netz nt; (membrane) Schwimmhaut f; **the (World-Wide) W~** das Web

website [websaɪt] n (COMPUT) Website f, Webseite f

wed [wed] (pt, pp **wedded**) vt heiraten ♦ n: **the newly-~s** npl die Frischvermählten pl

we'd [wiːd] = **we had; we would**

wedding ['wedɪŋ] n Hochzeit f; **silver/golden ~ anniversary** Silberhochzeit f/goldene Hochzeit f; **~ day** n Hochzeitstag m; **~ dress** n Hochzeitskleid nt; **~ present** n Hochzeitsgeschenk nt; **~ ring** n Trauring m, Ehering m

wedge [wedʒ] n Keil m; (of cheese etc) Stück nt ♦ vt (fasten) festklemmen; (pack tightly) einkeilen

Wednesday ['wednzdɪ] n Mittwoch m

wee [wiː] (SCOTTISH) adj klein, winzig

weed [wiːd] n Unkraut nt ♦ vt jäten; **~killer** n Unkrautvertilgungsmittel nt

weedy ['wiːdɪ] adj (person) schmächtig

week [wiːk] n Woche f; **a ~ today/on Friday** heute/Freitag in einer Woche; **~day** n Wochentag m; **~end** n Wochenende nt; **~ly** adj wöchentlich; (wages, magazine) Wochen- ♦ adv wöchentlich

weep [wiːp] (pt, pp **wept**) vi weinen; **~ing willow** n Trauerweide f

weigh [weɪ] vt, vi wiegen; **to ~ anchor** den Anker lichten; **~ down** vt niederdrücken; **~ up** vt abschätzen

weight [weɪt] n Gewicht nt; **to lose/put on ~** abnehmen/zunehmen; **~ing** n (allowance) Zulage f; **~lifter** n Gewichtheber m; **~lifting** n Gewichtheben nt; **~y** adj (heavy) gewichtig; (important) schwerwiegend, schwer wiegend

weir [wɪəʳ] n (Stau)wehr nt

weird [wɪəd] adj seltsam

welcome ['wɛlkəm] n Willkommen nt, Empfang m ♦ vt begrüßen; **thank you - you're ~!** danke - nichts zu danken

welder ['wɛldəʳ] n (person) Schweißer(in) m(f)

welding ['wɛldɪŋ] n Schweißen nt

welfare ['wɛlfɛəʳ] n Wohl nt; (social) Fürsorge f; **~ state** n Wohlfahrtsstaat m; **~ work** n Fürsorge f

well [wɛl] n Brunnen m; (oil ~) Quelle f ♦ adj (in good health) gesund ♦ adv gut ♦ excl nun!, na schön!; **I'm ~** es geht mir gut; **get ~ soon!** gute Besserung!; **as ~** auch; **as ~ as** sowohl als auch; **~ done!** gut gemacht!; **to do ~** (person) gut zurechtkommen; (business) gut gehen; **~ up** vi emporsteigen; (fig) aufsteigen

we'll [wiːl] = **we will; we shall**

well: ~-behaved ['wɛlbɪ'heɪvd] adj wohlerzogen; **~-being** ['wɛl'biːɪŋ] n Wohl nt; **~-built** ['wɛl'bɪlt] adj kräftig gebaut; **~-deserved** ['wɛldɪ'zɜːvd] adj wohlverdient; **~-dressed** ['wɛl'drɛst]

adj gut gekleidet; **~-heeled** ['wɛl'hiːld] (inf) (wealthy) gut gepolstert

wellingtons ['wɛlɪŋtənz] npl (also: **wellington boots**) Gummistiefel pl

well: ~-known ['wɛl'nəun] adj bekannt; **~-mannered** ['wɛl'mænəd] adj wohlerzogen; **~-meaning** ['wɛl'miːnɪŋ] adj (person) wohlmeinend; (action) gut gemeint; **~-off** ['wɛl'ɔf] adj gut situiert; **~-read** ['wɛl'rɛd] adj (sehr) belesen; **~-to-do** ['wɛltə'duː] adj wohlhabend; **~-wisher** ['wɛlwɪʃəʳ] n Gönner m

Welsh [wɛlʃ] adj walisisch ♦ n (LING) Walisisch nt; **the ~** npl (people) die Waliser pl; **~ Assembly** n walisische Versammlung f; **~man/woman** (irreg) n Waliser(in) m(f)

went [wɛnt] pt of **go**

wept [wɛpt] pt, pp of **weep**

were [wɜːʳ] pt pl of **be**

we're [wɪəʳ] = **we are**

weren't [wɜːnt] = **were not**

west [wɛst] n Westen m ♦ adj West-, westlich ♦ adv westwärts, nach Westen; **the W~** der Westen; **~ Country** (BRIT) n: **the W~ Country** der Südwesten Englands; **~erly** adj westlich, West- ♦ n (CINE) Western m; **W~ Indian** adj westindisch ♦ n Westindier(in) m(f); **W~ Indies** npl Westindische Inseln pl; **~ward(s)** adv westwärts

wet [wɛt] adj nass; **to get ~** nass werden; **"~ paint"** "frisch gestrichen"; **~ blanket** n (fig) Triefel m; **~ suit** n Taucheranzug m

we've [wiːv] = **we have**

whack [wæk] n Schlag m ♦ vt schlagen

whale [weɪl] n Wal m

wharf [wɔːf] n Kai m

wharves [wɔːvz] npl of **wharf**

what [wɔt] adj **1** (in questions) welche(r, s), was für ein(e); **what size is it?** welche Größe ist das?

2 (*in exclamations*) was für ein(e); **what a mess!** was für ein Durcheinander!
♦ *pron* (*interrogative/relative*) was; **what are you doing?** was machst du gerade?; **what are you talking about?** wovon reden Sie?; **what is it called?** wie heißt das?; **what about ...?** wie wär's mit ...?; **I saw what you did** ich habe gesehen, was du gemacht hast
♦ *excl* (*disbelieving*) wie, was; **what, no coffee!** wie, kein Kaffee?; **I've crashed the car - what!** ich hatte einen Autounfall - was!

whatever [wɔt'evər] *adj:* ~ **book** welches Buch auch immer ♦ *pron:* **do ~ is necessary** tu, was (immer auch) nötig ist; ~ **happens** egal, was passiert; **nothing** ~ überhaupt *or* absolut gar nichts; **do ~ you want** tu, was (immer) du (auch) möchtest; **no reason** ~ *or* **whatsoever** überhaupt *or* absolut kein Grund
whatsoever [wɔtsəu'evər] *adj see* **whatever**
wheat [wi:t] *n* Weizen *m*
wheedle ['wi:dl] *vt:* **to ~ sb into doing sth** jdn dazu überreden, etw zu tun; **to ~ sth out of sb** jdm etw abluchsen
wheel [wi:l] *n* Rad *nt*; (*steering ~*) Lenkrad *nt*; (*disc*) Scheibe *f* ♦ *vt* schieben; ~**barrow** *n* Schubkarren *m*; ~**chair** *n* Rollstuhl *m*; ~ **clamp** *n* (*AUT*) Parkkralle *f*
wheeze [wi:z] *vi* keuchen

KEYWORD

when [wɛn] *adv* wann
♦ *conj* **1** (*at, during, after the time that*) wenn; (*in past*) als; **she was reading when I came in** sie las, als ich hereinkam; **be careful when you cross the road** seien Sie vorsichtig, wenn Sie über die Straße gehen
2 (*on, at which*) als; **on the day when**

I met him an dem Tag, an dem ich ihn traf
3 (*whereas*) wo ... doch

whenever [wɛn'evər] *adv* wann (auch) immer; (*every time that*) jedes Mal wenn ♦ *conj* (*any time*) wenn
where [wɛər] *adv* (*direction*) wohin; ~ **from** woher; **this is** ~ ... hier ...; ~**abouts** ['wɛərəbauts] *adv* wo ♦ *n* Aufenthaltsort *m*; **nobody knows his** ~**abouts** niemand weiß, wo er ist; ~**as** [wɛər'æz] *conj* während, wo ... doch; ~**by** *pron* woran, wodurch, womit, wovon; ~**upon** *conj* worauf, wonach; (*at beginning of sentence*) daraufhin; ~**ver** [wɛər'evər] *conj* wo auch immer
wherewithal ['wɛəwiðɔ:l] *n* nötige (Geld)mittel *pl*
whet [wɛt] *vt* (*appetite*) anregen
whether ['wɛðər] *conj* ob; **I don't know** ~ **to accept or not** ich weiß nicht, ob ich es annehmen soll oder nicht; ~ **you go or not** ob du gehst oder nicht; **it's doubtful/unclear** ~ ... es ist zweifelhaft/nicht klar, ob ...

KEYWORD

which [wɪtʃ] *adj* **1** (*interrogative: direct, indirect*) welche(r, s); **which one?** welche(r, s)?
2: in which case in diesem Fall; **by which time** zu dieser Zeit
♦ *pron* **1** (*interrogative*) welche(r, s); (*of people also*) wer
2 (*relative*) der/die/das; (*referring to people*) was; **the apple which you ate/which is on the table** der Apfel, den du gegessen hast/der auf dem Tisch liegt; **he said he saw her, which is true** er sagte, er habe sie gesehen, was auch stimmt

whichever [wɪtʃ'evər] *adj* welche(r, s) auch immer; (*no matter which*) ganz gleich welche(r, s); ~ **book you take** welches Buch du auch nimmst; ~ **car**

you prefer egal welches Auto du vorziehst

whiff [wɪf] n Hauch m

while [waɪl] n Weile f ♦ conj während; **for a ~** eine Zeit lang; **~ away** vt (time) sich dat vertreiben

whim [wɪm] n Laune f

whimper ['wɪmpə'] n Wimmern nt ♦ vi wimmern

whimsical ['wɪmzɪkəl] adj launisch

whine [waɪn] n Gewinsel nt, Gejammer nt ♦ vi heulen, winseln

whip [wɪp] n Peitsche f; (POL) Fraktionsführer m ♦ vt (beat) peitschen; (snatch) reißen; **~ped cream** n Schlagsahne f

whip-round ['wɪpraund] (BRIT: inf) n Geldsammlung f

whirl [wɜːl] n Wirbel m ♦ vt, vi (herum)wirbeln; **~pool** n Wirbel m; **~wind** n Wirbelwind m

whirr [wɜː'] vi schwirren, surren

whisk [wɪsk] n Schneebesen m ♦ vt (cream etc) schlagen; **to ~ sb away** or **off** mit jdm davon sausen

whisker ['wɪskə'] n: **~s** (of animal) Barthaare pl; (of man) Backenbart m

whisky ['wɪskɪ] (US, IRISH **whiskey**) n Whisky m

whisper ['wɪspə'] n Flüstern nt ♦ vt, vi flüstern

whistle ['wɪsl] n Pfiff m; (instrument) Pfeife f ♦ vt, vi pfeifen

white [waɪt] n Weiß nt; (of egg) Eiweiß nt ♦ adj weiß; **~ coffee** (BRIT) n Kaffee m mit Milch; **~-collar worker** n Angestellte(r) m; **~ elephant** n (fig) Fehlinvestition f; **~ lie** n Notlüge f; **~ paper** n (POL) Weißbuch nt; **~wash** n (paint) Tünche f; (fig) Ehrenrettung f ♦ vt (paint) tünchen; (fig) rein waschen

whiting ['waɪtɪŋ] n Weißfisch m

Whitsun ['wɪtsn] n Pfingsten nt

whittle ['wɪtl] vt: **to ~ away** or **down** stutzen, verringern

whizz [wɪz] vi: **to ~ past** or **by** vorbeizischen, vorbeischwirren; **~ kid** (inf) n Kanone f

who [huː] pron **1** (interrogative) wer; (acc) wen; (dat) wem; **who is it?**, **who's there?** wer ist da?

2 (relative) der/die/das; **the woman/ man who spoke to me** die Frau/der Mann, die/der mit mir sprach

whodu(n)nit [huː'dʌnɪt] (inf) n Krimi m

whoever [huː'evə'] pron wer/wen/wem auch immer; (no matter who) ganz gleich wer/wen/wem

whole [həʊl] adj ganz ♦ n Ganze(s) nt; **the ~ of the town** die ganze Stadt; **on the ~**, **as a ~** im Großen und Ganzen; **~food(s)** n(pl) Vollwertkost f; **~hearted** [həʊl'hɑːtɪd] adj rückhaltlos; **~heartedly** adv von ganzem Herzen; **~meal** adj (bread, flour) Vollkorn-; **~sale** n Großhandel m ♦ adj (trade) Großhandels-; (destruction) Massen-; **~saler** n Großhändler m; **~some** adj bekömmlich, gesund; **~wheat** adj **= wholemeal**

wholly ['həʊlɪ] adv ganz, völlig

whom [huːm] pron **1** (interrogative: acc) wen; (: dat) wem; **whom did you see?** wen haben Sie gesehen?; **to whom did you give it?** wem haben Sie es gegeben?

2 (relative: acc) den/die/das; (: dat) dem/der/dem; **the man whom I saw/to whom I spoke** der Mann, den ich sah/mit dem ich sprach

whooping cough ['huːpɪŋ-] n Keuchhusten m

whore [hɔː'] n Hure f

whose [huːz] adj (possessive: interrogative) wessen; (: relative) dessen; (after f and pl) deren ♦ pron wessen; **~ book is this?**, **~ is this book?** wessen Buch ist dies?; **~ is this?** wem gehört das?

why [waɪ] adv warum, weshalb
♦ conj warum, weshalb; **that's not why I'm here** ich bin nicht deswegen hier; **that's the reason why** deshalb
♦ excl (expressing surprise, shock) na so was; (explaining) also dann; **why, it's you!** na so was, du bist es!

wick [wɪk] n Docht m
wicked ['wɪkɪd] adj böse
wicker ['wɪkəʳ] n (also: ~**work**) Korbgeflecht nt
wicket ['wɪkɪt] n Tor nt, Dreistab m
wide [waɪd] adj breit; (plain) weit; (in firing) daneben ♦ adv: **to open ~** weit öffnen; **to shoot ~** danebenschießen; **~-angle lens** n Weitwinkelobjektiv nt; **~-awake** adj hellwach; **~ly** adv weit; (known) allgemein; **~n** vt erweitern; **~ open** adj weit geöffnet; **~spread** adj weitverbreitet, weit verbreitet
widow ['wɪdəu] n Witwe f; **~ed** adj verwitwet; **~er** n Witwer m
width [wɪdθ] n Breite f, Weite f
wield [wiːld] vt schwingen, handhaben
wife [waɪf] (pl **wives**) n (Ehe)frau f, Gattin f
wig [wɪg] n Perücke f
wiggle ['wɪgl] n Wackeln nt ♦ vt wackeln mit ♦ vi wackeln
wild [waɪld] adj wild; (violent) heftig; (plan, idea) verrückt; **~erness** ['wɪldənɪs] n Wildnis f, Wüste f; **~-goose chase** n (fig) fruchtlose(s) Unternehmen nt; **~life** n Tierwelt f; **~ly** adv wild, ungestüm; (exaggerated) irrsinnig; **~s** npl: **the ~s** die Wildnis f
wilful ['wɪlful] (US **willful**) adj (intended) vorsätzlich; (obstinate) eigensinnig

will [wɪl] aux vb **1** (forms future tense) werden; **I will finish it tomorrow** ich mache es morgen zu Ende

2 (in conjectures, predictions): **he will** or **he'll be there by now** er dürfte jetzt da sein; **that will be the postman** das wird der Postbote sein

3 (in commands, requests, offers): **will you be quiet!** sei endlich still!; **will you help me?** hilfst du mir?; **will you have a cup of tea?** trinken Sie eine Tasse Tee?; **I won't put up with it!** das lasse ich mir nicht gefallen!
♦ vt wollen
♦ n Wille m; (JUR) Testament nt

willing ['wɪlɪŋ] adj gewillt, bereit; **~ly** adv bereitwillig, gern; **~ness** n (Bereit)willigkeit f
willow ['wɪləu] n Weide f
willpower ['wɪl'pauəʳ] n Willenskraft f
willy-nilly ['wɪlɪ'nɪlɪ] adv einfach so
wilt [wɪlt] vi (ver)welken
wily ['waɪlɪ] adj gerissen
win [wɪn] (pt, pp **won**) n Sieg m ♦ vt, vi gewinnen; **to ~ sb over** or **round** jdn gewinnen, jdn dazu bringen
wince [wɪns] vi zusammenzucken
winch [wɪntʃ] n Winde f
wind¹ [wɪnd] n Wind m; (MED) Blähungen pl
wind² [waɪnd] (pt, pp **wound**) vt (rope) winden; (bandage) wickeln ♦ vi (turn) sich winden; **to ~ up** vt (clock) aufziehen; (debate) (ab)schließen
windfall ['wɪndfɔːl] n unverhoffte(r) Glücksfall m
winding ['waɪndɪŋ] adj (road) gewunden
wind instrument ['wɪnd-] n Blasinstrument nt
windmill ['wɪndmɪl] n Windmühle f
window ['wɪndəu] n Fenster nt; **~ box** n Blumenkasten m; **~ cleaner** n Fensterputzer m; **~ envelope** n Fensterbriefumschlag m; **~ ledge** n Fenstersims m; **~ pane** n Fensterscheibe f; **~ shopping** n Schaufensterbummel m; **to go ~-shopping** einen Schaufensterbummel machen; **~sill** n Fensterbank f

wind: **~pipe** n Luftröhre f; **~ power** n Windenergie f; **~screen** (BRIT) n Windschutzscheibe f; **~screen washer** n Scheibenwaschanlage f; **~screen wiper** n Scheibenwischer m; **~shield** (US) n = windscreen; **~swept** adj vom Wind gepeitscht; (person) zerzaust; **~y** adj windig

wine [waɪn] n Wein m; **~ bar** n Weinlokal nt; **~ cellar** n Weinkeller m; **~glass** n Weinglas nt; **~ list** n Weinkarte f; **~ merchant** n Weinhändler m; **~ tasting** n Weinprobe f; **~ waiter** n Weinkellner m

wing [wɪŋ] n Flügel m; (MIL) Gruppe f; **~s** npl (THEAT) Seitenkulisse f; **~er** n (SPORT) Flügelstürmer m

wink [wɪŋk] n Zwinkern nt ♦ vi zwinkern, blinzeln

winner ['wɪnə*] n Gewinner m; (SPORT) Sieger m

winning ['wɪnɪŋ] adj (team) siegreich, Sieger-; (goal) entscheidend; **~ post** n Ziel nt; **~s** npl Gewinn m

winter ['wɪntə*] n Winter m ♦ adj (clothes) Winter- ♦ vi überwintern; **~ sports** npl Wintersport m; **wintry** ['wɪntrɪ] adj Winter-, winterlich

wipe [waɪp] n: **to give sth a ~** etw (ab)wischen ♦ vt wischen; **~ off** vt abwischen; **~ out** vt (debt) tilgen; (destroy) auslöschen; **~ up** vt aufwischen

wire [waɪə*] n Draht m; (ELEC) Telegramm nt ♦ vt telegrafieren; **to ~ sb** jdm telegrafieren; **~less** ['waɪəlɪs] (BRIT) n Radio(apparat nt) nt

wiring ['waɪərɪŋ] n elektrische Leitungen pl

wiry ['waɪərɪ] adj drahtig

wisdom ['wɪzdəm] n Weisheit f; (of decision) Klugheit f; **~ tooth** n Weisheitszahn m

wise [waɪz] adj klug, weise ♦ suffix: **~wise** adv timewise zeitlich gesehen

wisecrack ['waɪzkræk] n Witzelei f

wish [wɪʃ] n Wunsch m ♦ vt wünschen; **best ~es** (on birthday etc) alles Gute;

with best **~es** herzliche Grüße; **to ~ sb goodbye** jdn verabschieden; **he ~ed me well** er wünschte mir Glück; **to ~ to do sth** etw tun wollen; **~ for** vt fus sich dat wünschen; **~ful thinking** n Wunschdenken nt

wishy-washy ['wɪʃɪwɒʃɪ] (inf) adj (ideas, argument) verschwommen

wisp [wɪsp] n (Haar)strähne f; (of smoke) Wölkchen nt

wistful ['wɪstful] adj sehnsüchtig

wit [wɪt] n (also: **~s**) Verstand m no pl; (amusing ideas) Witz m; (person) Witzbold m

witch [wɪtʃ] n Hexe f; **~craft** n Hexerei f

with [wɪð, wɪθ] prep **1** (accompanying, in the company of) mit; **we stayed with friends** wir übernachteten bei Freunden; **I'll be with you in a minute** einen Augenblick, ich bin sofort da; **I'm not with you** (I don't understand) das verstehe ich nicht; **to be with it** (inf: up-to-date) auf dem Laufenden sein; (: alert) (voll) da sein (inf)

2 (descriptive, indicating manner etc) mit; **the man with the grey hat** der Mann mit dem grauen Hut; **red with anger** rot vor Wut

withdraw [wɪθ'drɔː] (irreg: like draw) vt zurückziehen; (money) abheben; (remark) zurücknehmen ♦ vi sich zurückziehen; **~al** n Zurückziehung f; Abheben nt; Zurücknahme f; **~n** adj (person) verschlossen

wither ['wɪðə*] vi (ver)welken

withhold [wɪθ'həʊld] (irreg: like hold) vt: **to ~ sth (from sb)** (jdm) etw vorenthalten

within [wɪð'ɪn] prep innerhalb +gen ♦ adv innen; **~ sight of** in Sichtweite von; **~ the week** innerhalb dieser Woche; **~ a mile of** weniger als eine Meile von

without [wɪð'aut] *prep* ohne; ~ **sleeping** etc ohne zu schlafen *etc*

withstand [wɪθ'stænd] (*irreg: like* **stand**) *vt* widerstehen +*dat*

witness ['wɪtnɪs] *n* Zeuge *m*, Zeugin *f* ♦ *vt* (*see*) sehen, miterleben; (*document*) beglaubigen; ~ **box** *n* Zeugenstand *m*; ~ **stand** (*US*) *n* Zeugenstand *m*

witticism ['wɪtɪsɪzəm] *n* witzige Bemerkung *f*

witty ['wɪtɪ] *adj* witzig, geistreich

wives [waɪvz] *pl of* **wife**

wk *abbr* = **week**

wobble ['wɒbl] *vi* wackeln

woe [wəu] *n* Kummer *m*

woke [wəuk] *pt of* **wake**

woken ['wəukn] *pp of* **wake**

wolf [wulf] (*pl* **wolves**) *n* Wolf *m*

woman ['wumən] (*pl* **women**) *n* Frau *f*; ~ **doctor** *n* Ärztin *f*; ~**ly** *adj* weiblich

womb [wu:m] *n* Gebärmutter *f*

women ['wɪmɪn] *pl of* **woman**; ~'s **lib** *n* Frauenrechtsbewegung *f*

won [wʌn] *pt, pp of* **win**

wonder ['wʌndə^r] *n* (*marvel*) Wunder *nt*; (*surprise*) Staunen *nt*, Verwunderung *f* ♦ *vi* sich wundern ♦ *vt*: **I** ~ **whether** ... ich frage mich, ob ...; **it's no** ~ **that** es ist kein Wunder, dass; **to** ~ **at** sich wundern über +*acc*; **to** ~ **about** sich Gedanken machen über +*acc*; ~**ful** *adj* wunderbar, herrlich

won't [wəunt] = **will not**

woo [wu:] *vt* (*audience etc*) umwerben

wood [wud] *n* Holz *nt*; (*forest*) Wald *m*; ~ **carving** *n* Holzschnitzerei *f*; ~**ed** *adj* bewaldet; ~**en** *adj* (*also fig*) hölzern; ~**pecker** *n* Specht *m*; ~**wind** *n* Blasinstrumente *pl*; ~**work** *n* Holzwerk *nt*; (*craft*) Holzarbeiten *pl*; ~**worm** *n* Holzwurm *m*

wool [wul] *n* Wolle *f*; **to pull the** ~ **over sb's eyes** (*fig*) jdm Sand in die Augen streuen; ~**len** (*US* **woolen**) *adj* Woll-; ~**lens** *npl* Wollsachen *pl*; ~**ly** (*US* **wooly**) *adj* wollig; (*fig*) schwammig

word [wɜːd] *n* Wort *nt*; (*news*) Bescheid *m* ♦ *vt* formulieren; **in other** ~**s** anders gesagt; **to break/keep one's** ~ sein Wort brechen/halten; ~ **processing** *n* Textverarbeitung *f*; ~ **processor** *n* Textverarbeitung *f*

wore [wɔː^r] *pt of* **wear**

work [wɜːk] *n* Arbeit *f*; (*ART, LITER*) Werk *nt* ♦ *vi* arbeiten; (*machine*) funktionieren; (*medicine*) wirken; (*succeed*) klappen; ~**s** *n sg* (*BRIT: factory*) Fabrik *f*, Werk *nt* ♦ *npl* (*of watch*) Werk *nt*; **to be out of** ~ arbeitslos sein; **in** ~**ing order** in betriebsfähigem Zustand; ~ **loose** *vi* sich lockern; ~ **on** *vi* weiterarbeiten ♦ *vt* fus arbeiten an +*dat*; (*influence*) bearbeiten; ~ **out** *vi* (*sum*) aufgehen ♦ *vt* (*problem*) lösen; (*plan*) klappen ♦ *vt* (*problem*) lösen; (*plan*) ausarbeiten; **it** ~**s out at £100** das gibt *or* macht £100; ~ **up** *vt*: **to get** ~**ed up** sich aufregen; ~**able** *adj* (*soil*) bearbeitbar; (*plan*) ausführbar; ~**aholic** [wɜːkə'hɔlɪk] *n* Arbeitssüchtige(r) *f*(*m*); ~**er** *n* Arbeiter(in) *m*(*f*); ~ **experience** *n* Praktikum *nt*; ~**force** *n* Arbeiterschaft *f*; ~**ing class** *n* Arbeiterklasse *f*; ~**ing-class** *adj* Arbeiter-; ~**man** (*irreg*) *n* Arbeiter *m*; ~**manship** *n* Arbeit *f*, Ausführung *f*; ~**sheet** *n* Arbeitsblatt *nt*; ~**shop** *n* Werkstatt *f*; ~ **station** *n* Arbeitsplatz *m*; ~**-to-rule** (*BRIT*) *n* Dienst *m* nach Vorschrift

world [wɜːld] *n* Welt *f*; **to think the** ~ **of sb** große Stücke auf jdn halten; ~**ly** *adj* weltlich, irdisch; ~**-wide** *adj* weltweit

World-Wide Web ['wɜːldwaɪd] *n* World Wide Web *nt*

worm [wɜːm] *n* Wurm *m*

worn [wɔːn] *pp of* **wear** ♦ *adj* (*clothes*) abgetragen; ~**-out** *adj* (*object*) abgenutzt; (*person*) völlig erschöpft

worried ['wʌrɪd] *adj* besorgt, beunruhigt

worry ['wʌrɪ] *n* Sorge *f* ♦ *vt* beunruhigen ♦ *vi* (*feel uneasy*) sich sorgen, sich dat Gedanken machen; **~ing** adj beunruhigend

worse [wɜːs] adj schlechter, schlimmer ♦ adv schlimmer, ärger ♦ n Schlimmere(s) nt, Schlechtere(s) nt; **a change for the ~** eine Verschlechterung; **~n** vt verschlimmern ♦ vi sich verschlechtern; **~ off** adj (fig) schlechter dran

worship ['wɜːʃɪp] n Verehrung f ♦ vt anbeten; **Your W~** (BRIT: to mayor) Herr/Frau Bürgermeister; (: to judge) Euer Ehren

worst [wɜːst] adj schlimmste(r, s), schlechteste(r, s) ♦ adv am schlimmsten, am ärgsten ♦ n Schlimmste(s) nt, Ärgste(s) nt; **at ~** schlimmstenfalls

worth [wɜːθ] n Wert m ♦ adj wert; **it's ~ it** es lohnt sich; **to be ~ one's while (to do sth)** die Mühe wert sein(, etw zu tun); **~less** adj wertlos; (person) nichtsnutzig; **~while** adj lohnend, der Mühe wert; **~y** adj wert, würdig

KEYWORD

would [wʊd] aux vb 1 (conditional tense): **if you asked him he would do it** wenn du ihn fragtest, würde er es tun; **if you had asked him he would have done it** wenn du ihn gefragt hättest, hätte er es getan

2 (in offers, invitations, requests): **would you like a biscuit?** möchten Sie ein Plätzchen?; **would you ask him to come in?** würden Sie ihn bitte hineinbitten?

3 (in indirect speech): **I said I would do it** ich sagte, ich würde es tun

4 (emphatic): **it WOULD have to snow today!** es musste ja ausgerechnet heute schneien!

5 (insistence): **she wouldn't behave** sie wollte sich partout nicht anständig benehmen

6 (conjecture): **it would have been midnight** es mag ungefähr Mitternacht gewesen sein; **it would seem so** es sieht wohl so aus

7 (indicating habit): **he would go there on Mondays** er ging jeden Montag dorthin

would-be ['wʊdbiː] (pej) adj Möchtegern-

wouldn't ['wʊdnt] = **would not**

wound¹ [wuːnd] n (also fig) Wunde f ♦ vt verwunden, verletzen (also fig)

wound² [waʊnd] pt, pp of **wind²**

wove [wəʊv] pt of **weave**; **~n** pp of **weave**

wrangle ['ræŋgl] n Streit m ♦ vi sich zanken

wrap [ræp] vt einwickeln; **~ up** einwickeln; (deal) abschließen; **~per** n Umschlag m, Schutzhülle f; **~ping paper** n Einwickelpapier nt

wrath [rɔθ] n Zorn m

wreak [riːk] vt (havoc) anrichten; (vengeance) üben

wreath [riːθ] n Kranz m

wreck [rek] n (ship) Wrack nt; (sth ruined) Ruine f ♦ vt zerstören; **~age** n Trümmer pl

wren [ren] n Zaunkönig m

wrench [rentʃ] n (spanner) Schraubenschlüssel m; (twist) Ruck m ♦ vt reißen, zerren; **to ~ sth from sb** jdm etw entreißen or entwinden

wrestle ['resl] vi: **to ~ (with sb)** (mit jdm) ringen; **~r** n Ringer(in) m(f); **wrestling** n Ringen nt

wretched ['retʃɪd] adj (inf) verflixt

wriggle ['rɪgl] n Schlängeln nt ♦ vi sich winden

wring [rɪŋ] (pt, pp **wrung**) vt wringen

wrinkle ['rɪŋkl] n Falte f, Runzel f ♦ vt runzeln ♦ vi sich runzeln; (material) knittern; **~d** adj faltig, schrumpelig

wrist [rɪst] n Handgelenk nt; **~watch** n Armbanduhr f

writ [rɪt] n gerichtliche(r) Befehl m

write [raɪt] (pt **wrote**, pp **written**) vt, vi schreiben; **~ down** vt aufschreiben; **~ off** vt (dismiss) abschreiben; **~ out** vt (essay) abschreiben; (cheque) ausstellen; **~ up** vt schreiben; **~-off** n: **it is a ~-off** das kann man abschreiben; **~r** n Schriftsteller m

writhe [raɪð] vi sich winden

writing ['raɪtɪŋ] n (act) Schreiben nt; (handwriting) (Hand)schrift f; **in ~** schriftlich; **~ paper** n Schreibpapier nt

written ['rɪtn] pp of **write**

wrong [rɒŋ] adj (incorrect) falsch; (morally) unrecht ♦ n Unrecht nt ♦ vt Unrecht tun +dat; **he was ~ in doing that** es war nicht recht von ihm, das zu tun; **you are ~ about that, you've got it ~** da hast du Unrecht; **to be in the ~** im Unrecht sein; **what's ~ with your leg?** was ist mit deinem Bein los?; **to go ~** (plan) schief gehen; (person) einen Fehler machen; **~ful** adj unrechtmäßig; **~ly** adv falsch; (accuse) zu Unrecht

wrong number n (TEL): **you've got the ~** Sie sind falsch verbunden

wrote [rəʊt] pt of **write**

wrought [rɔːt] adj: **~ iron** Schmiedeeisen nt

wrung [rʌŋ] pt, pp of **wring**

wry [raɪ] adj ironisch

wt. abbr = **weight**

WWW n abbr (= World Wide Web): **the ~** das WWW

X, x

Xmas ['eksməs] n abbr = **Christmas**

X-ray ['eksreɪ] n Röntgenaufnahme f ♦ vt röntgen; **~-s** npl Röntgenstrahlen pl

xylophone ['zaɪləfəʊn] n Xylofon nt, Xylophon nt

Y, y

yacht [jɒt] n Jacht f; **~ing** n (Sport)segeln nt; **~sman** (irreg) n Sportsegler m

Yank [jæŋk] (inf) n Ami m

yap [jæp] vi (dog) kläffen

yard [jɑːd] n Hof m; (measure) (englische) Elle f, Yard nt (0,91 m); **~stick** n (fig) Maßstab m

yarn [jɑːn] n (thread) Garn nt; (story) (Seemanns)garn nt

yawn [jɔːn] n Gähnen nt ♦ vi gähnen; **~ing** adj (gap) gähnend

yd. abbr = **yard(s)**

yeah [jeə] (inf) adv ja

year [jɪəʳ] n Jahr nt; **to be 8 ~s old** acht Jahre alt sein; **an eight-year-old child** ein achtjähriges Kind; **~ly** adj, adv jährlich

yearn [jɜːn] vi: **to ~ (for)** sich sehnen (nach); **~ing** n Verlangen nt, Sehnsucht f

yeast [jiːst] n Hefe f

yell [jel] n gellende(r) Schrei m ♦ vi laut schreien

yellow ['jeləʊ] adj gelb ♦ n Gelb nt

yelp [jelp] n Gekläff nt ♦ vi kläffen

yes [jes] adv ja ♦ n Ja nt, Jawort nt; **to say ~** Ja or ja sagen; **to answer ~** mit Ja antworten

yesterday ['jestədɪ] adv gestern ♦ n Gestern nt; **~ morning/evening** gestern Morgen/Abend; **all day ~** gestern den ganzen Tag; **the day before ~** vorgestern

yet [jet] adv noch; (in question) schon; (up to now) bis jetzt ♦ conj doch, dennoch; **it is not finished ~** es ist noch nicht fertig; **the best ~** das bisher Beste; **as ~** bis jetzt; (in past) bis dahin

yew [juː] n Eibe f

yield [jiːld] n Ertrag m ♦ vt (result, crop) hervorbringen; (interest, profit) abwerfen; (concede) abtreten ♦ vi nachgeben; (MIL) sich ergeben; **"~"** (US: AUT) „Vorfahrt gewähren"

YMCA n abbr (= Young Men's Christian Association) CVJM m

yob [jɒb] (BRIT: inf) n Halbstarke(r) f(m), Rowdy m

yoga ['jəʊgə] n Joga m

yoghurt ['jɒgət] n Jog(h)urt m

yog(h)urt ['jɒgət] n = **yoghourt**

yoke [jəʊk] n (also fig) Joch nt

yolk   617   zucchini

yolk [jəuk] n Eidotter m, Eigelb nt

you [ju:] pron **1** (subj, in comparisons: familiar form: sg) du; (: pl) ihr; (in letters also) du, ihr; (: polite form) Sie; **you Germans** ihr Deutschen; **she's younger than you** sie ist jünger als du/Sie

2 (direct object, after prep +acc: familiar form: sg) dich; (: pl) euch; (in letters also) dich, euch; (: polite form) Sie; **I know you** ich kenne dich/euch/Sie

3 (indirect object, after prep +dat: familiar form: sg) dir; (: pl) euch; (in letters also) dir, euch; (: polite form) Ihnen; **I gave it to you** ich gab es dir/euch/Ihnen

4 (impers: one: subj) man; (: direct object) einen; (: indirect object) einem; **fresh air does you good** frische Luft tut gut

you'd [ju:d] = you had; you would

you'll [ju:l] = you will; you shall

young [jʌŋ] adj jung ♦ npl: **the ~ die** Jungen pl; **~ster** n Junge m, junge(r) Bursche m, junge(s) Mädchen nt

your [jɔ:ʳ] adj (familiar: sg) dein; (: pl) euer, eure pl; (polite) Ihr; see also **my**

you're [juəʳ] = you are

yours [jɔ:z] pron (familiar: sg) deine(r, s); (: pl) eure(r, s); (polite) Ihre(r, s); see also **mine²**

yourself [jɔ:'sɛlf] pron (emphatic) selbst; (familiar: sg: acc) dich (selbst); (: dat) dir (selbst); (: pl) euch (selbst); (polite) sich (selbst); see also **oneself**; **yourselves** pl pron (reflexive: familiar) euch; (: polite) sich; (emphatic) selbst; see also **oneself**

youth [ju:θ] n Jugend f; (young man) junge(r) Mann m; **~s** npl (young people) Jugendliche m; **~ club** n Jugendzentrum nt; **~ful** adj jugendlich; **~ hostel**

---

n Jugendherberge f

you've [ju:v] = you have

Yugoslav ['ju:gəuslɑ:v] adj jugoslawisch ♦ n Jugoslawe m, Jugoslawin f; **~ia** [ju:gəu'slɑ:viə] n Jugoslawien nt

yuppie ['jʌpɪ] (inf) n Yuppie m ♦ adj yuppiehaft, Yuppie-

YWCA n abbr (= Young Women's Christian Association) CVJF m

Z, z

zany ['zeɪnɪ] adj (ideas, sense of humour) verrückt

zap [zæp] vt (COMPUT) löschen

zeal [zi:l] n Eifer m; **~ous** ['zɛləs] adj eifrig

zebra ['zi:brə] n Zebra nt; **~ crossing** (BRIT) n Zebrastreifen m

zero ['zɪərəu] n Null f; (on scale) Nullpunkt m

zest [zɛst] n Begeisterung f

zigzag ['zɪgzæg] n Zickzack m

Zimbabwe [zɪm'bɑ:bwɪ] n Zimbabwe nt

Zimmer frame ['zɪmə-] n Laufgestell nt

zip [zɪp] n Reißverschluss m ♦ vt (also: ~ up) den Reißverschluss zumachen +gen

zip code (US) n Postleitzahl f

zipper ['zɪpəʳ] (US) n Reißverschluss m

zit [zɪt] (inf) n Pickel m

zodiac ['zəudɪæk] n Tierkreis m

zombie ['zɒmbɪ] n: **like a ~** (fig) wie im Tran

zone [zəun] n (also MIL) Zone f, Gebiet nt; (in town) Bezirk m

zoo [zu:] n Zoo m

zoology [zu:'ɔlədʒɪ] n Zoologie f

zoom [zu:m] vi: **to ~ past** vorbeisausen; **~ lens** n Zoomobjektiv nt

zucchini [zu:'ki:nɪ] (US) npl Zucchini pl

GERMAN IRREGULAR VERBS
*with 'sein'

infinitive	present indicative (2nd, 3rd sg.)	imperfect	past participle
aufschrecken*	schrickst auf, schrickt auf	schrak *or* schreckte auf	aufgeschreckt
ausbedingen	bedingst aus, bedingte aus	bedang *or* bedingte aus	ausbedungen
backen	bäckst, bäckt	backte *or* buk	gebacken
befehlen	befiehlst, befiehlt	befahl	befohlen
beginnen	beginnst, beginnt	begann	begonnen
beißen	beißt, beißt	biss	gebissen
bergen	birgst, birgt	barg	geborgen
bersten*	birst, birst	barst	geborsten
bescheißen*	bescheißt, bescheißt	beschiss	beschissen
bewegen	bewegst, bewegt	bewog	bewogen
biegen	biegst, biegt	bog	gebogen
bieten	bietest, bietet	bot	geboten
binden	bindest, bindet	band	gebunden
bitten	bittest, bittet	bat	gebeten
blasen	bläst, bläst	blies	geblasen
bleiben*	bleibst, bleibt	blieb	geblieben
braten	brätst, brät	briet	gebraten
brechen*	brichst, bricht	brach	gebrochen
brennen	brennst, brennt	brannte	gebrannt
bringen	bringst, bringt	brachte	gebracht
denken	denkst, denkt	dachte	gedacht
dreschen	drisch(e)st, drischt	drasch	gedroschen
dringen*	dringst, dringt	drang	gedrungen
dürfen	darfst, darf	durfte	gedurft
empfehlen	empfiehlst, empfiehlt	empfahl	empfohlen
erbleichen*	erbleichst, erbleicht	erbleichte	erblichen
erlöschen*	erlischt, erlischt	erlosch	erloschen
erschrecken*	erschrickst, erschrickt	erschrak	erschrocken
essen	isst, isst	aß	gegessen
fahren*	fährst, fährt	fuhr	gefahren

infinitive	present indicative (2nd, 3rd sg.)	imperfect	past participle
fallen*	fällst, fällt	fiel	gefallen
fangen	fängst, fängt	fing	gefangen
fechten	fichtst, ficht	focht	gefochten
finden	findest, findet	fand	gefunden
flechten	flichtst, flicht	flocht	geflochten
fliegen*	fliegst, fliegt	flog	geflogen
fliehen*	fliehst, flieht	floh	geflohen
fließen*	fließt, fließt	floß	geflossen
fressen	frisst, frisst	fraß	gefressen
frieren	frierst, friert	fror	gefroren
gären*	gärst, gärt	gor	gegoren
gebären*	gebierst, gebiert	gebar	geboren
geben	gibst, gibt	gab	gegeben
gedeihen*	gedeihst, gedeiht	gedieh	gediehen
gehen*	gehst, geht	ging	gegangen
gelingen*	——, gelingt	gelang	gelungen
gelten	giltst, gilt	galt	gegolten
genesen*	gene(se)st, genest	genas	genesen
genießen	genießt, genießt	genoss	genossen
geraten*	gerätst, gerät	geriet	geraten
geschehen*	——, geschieht	geschah	geschehen
gewinnen	gewinnst, gewinnt	gewann	gewonnen
gießen	gießt, gießt	goss	gegossen
gleichen	gleichst, gleicht	glich	geglichen
gleiten*	gleitest, gleitet	glitt	geglitten
glimmen	glimmst, glimmt	glomm	geglommen
graben	gräbst, gräbt	grub	gegraben
greifen	greifst, greift	griff	gegriffen
haben	hast, hat	hatte	gehabt
halten	hältst, hält	hielt	gehalten
hängen	hängst, hängt	hing	gehangen
hauen	haust, haut	haute	gehauen
heben	hebst, hebt	hob	gehoben
heißen	heißt, heißt	hieß	geheißen
helfen	hilfst, hilft	half	geholfen
kennen	kennst, kennt	kannte	gekannt
klimmen*	klimmst, klimmt	klomm	geklommen
klingen	klingst, klingt	klang	geklungen
kneifen	kneifst, kneift	kniff	gekniffen

620

infinitive	present indicative (2nd, 3rd sg.)	imperfect	past participle
kommen*	kommst, kommt	kam	gekommen
können	kannst, kann	konnte	gekonnt
kriechen*	kriechst, kriecht	kroch	gekrochen
laden	lädst, lädt	lud	geladen
lassen	lässt, lässt	ließ	gelassen
laufen*	läufst, läuft	lief	gelaufen
leiden	leidest, leidet	litt	gelitten
leihen	leihst, leiht	lieh	geliehen
lesen	liest, liest	las	gelesen
liegen*	liegst, liegt	lag	gelegen
lügen	lügst, lügt	log	gelogen
mahlen	mahlst, mahlt	mahlte	gemahlen
meiden	meidest, meidet	mied	gemieden
melken	melkst, melkt	melkte	gemolken
messen	misst, misst	maß	gemessen
misslingen*	——, misslingt	misslang	misslungen
mögen	magst, mag	mochte	gemocht
müssen	musst, muss	musste	gemusst
nehmen	nimmst, nimmt	nahm	genommen
nennen	nennst, nennt	nannte	genannt
pfeifen	pfeifst, pfeift	pfiff	gepfiffen
preisen	preist, preist	pries	gepriesen
quellen*	quillst, quillt	quoll	gequollen
raten	rätst, rät	riet	geraten
reiben	reibst, reibt	rieb	gerieben
reißen*	reißt, reißt	riss	gerissen
reiten*	reitest, reitet	ritt	geritten
rennen*	rennst, rennt	rannte	gerannt
riechen	riechst, riecht	roch	gerochen
ringen	ringst, ringt	rang	gerungen
rinnen*	rinnst, rinnt	rann	geronnen
rufen	rufst, ruft	rief	gerufen
salzen	salzt, salzt	salzte	gesalzen
saufen	säufst, säuft	soff	gesoffen
saugen	saugst, saugt	sog	gesogen
schaffen	schaffst, schafft	schuf	geschaffen
scheiden	scheidest, scheidet	schied	geschieden
scheinen	scheinst, scheint	schien	geschienen
schelten	schiltst, schilt	schalt	gescholten
scheren	scherst, schert	schor	geschoren

infinitive	present indicative (2nd, 3rd sg.)	imperfect	past participle
schieben	schiebst, schiebt	schob	geschoben
schießen	schießt, schießt	schoss	geschossen
schinden	schindest, schindet	schindete	geschunden
schlafen	schläfst, schläft	schlief	geschlafen
schlagen	schlägst, schlägt	schlug	geschlagen
schleichen*	schleichst, schleicht	schlich	geschlichen
schleifen	schleifst, schleift	schliff	geschliffen
schließen	schließt, schließt	schloss	geschlossen
schlingen	schlingst, schlingt	schlang	geschlungen
schmeißen	schmeißt, schmeißt	schmiss	geschmissen
schmelzen*	schmilzt, schmilzt	schmolz	geschmolzen
schneiden	schneidest, schneidet	schnitt	geschnitten
schreiben	schreibst, schreibt	schrieb	geschrieben
schreien	schreist, schreit	schrie	geschrie(e)n
schreiten	schreitest, schreitet	schritt	geschritten
schweigen	schweigst, schweigt	schwieg	geschwiegen
schwellen*	schwillst, schwillt	schwoll	geschwollen
schwimmen*	schwimmst, schwimmt	schwamm	geschwommen
schwinden*	schwindest, schwindet	schwand	geschwunden
schwingen	schwingst, schwingt	schwang	geschwungen
schwören	schwörst, schwört	schwor	geschworen
sehen	siehst, sieht	sah	gesehen
sein*	bist, ist	war	gewesen
senden	sendest, sendet	sandte	gesandt
singen	singst, singt	sang	gesungen
sinken*	sinkst, sinkt	sank	gesunken
sinnen	sinnst, sinnt	sann	gesonnen

infinitive	present indicative (2nd, 3rd sg.)	imperfect	past participle
sitzen*	sitzt, sitzt	saß	gesessen
sollen	sollst, soll	sollte	gesollt
speien	speist, speit	spie	gespie(e)n
spinnen	spinnst, spinnt	spann	gesponnen
sprechen	sprichst, spricht	sprach	gesprochen
sprießen*	sprießt, sprießt	sproß	gesprossen
springen*	springst, springt	sprang	gesprungen
stechen	stichst, sticht	stach	gestochen
stecken	steckst, steckt	steckte or stak	gesteckt
stehen	stehst, steht	stand	gestanden
stehlen	stiehlst, stiehlt	stahl	gestohlen
steigen*	steigst, steigt	stieg	gestiegen
sterben*	stirbst, stirbt	starb	gestorben
stinken	stinkst, stinkt	stank	gestunken
stoßen	stößt, stößt	stieß	gestoßen
streichen	streichst, streicht	strich	gestrichen
streiten*	streitest, streitet	stritt	gestritten
tragen	trägst, trägt	trug	getragen
treffen	triffst, trifft	traf	getroffen
treiben*	treibst, treibt	trieb	getrieben
treten*	trittst, tritt	trat	getreten
trinken	trinkst, trinkt	trank	getrunken
trügen	trügst, trügt	trog	getrogen
tun	tust, tut	tat	getan
verderben	verdirbst, verdirbt	verdarb	verdorben
verdrießen	verdrießt, verdrießt	verdross	verdrossen
vergessen	vergisst, vergisst	vergaß	vergessen
verlieren	verlierst, verliert	verlor	verloren
verschleißen	verschleißt, verschleißt	verschliss	verschlissen
wachsen*	wächst, wächst	wuchs	gewachsen
wägen	wägst, wägt	wog	gewogen
waschen	wäschst, wäscht	wusch	gewaschen
weben	webst, webt	webte or wob	gewoben
weichen*	weichst, weicht	wich	gewichen
weisen	weist, weist	wies	gewiesen
wenden	wendest, wendet	wandte	gewandt
werben	wirbst, wirbt	warb	geworben
werden*	wirst, wird	wurde	geworden

infinitive	present indicative (2nd, 3rd sg.)	imperfect	past participle
werfen	wirfst, wirft	warf	geworfen
wiegen	wiegst, wiegt	wog	gewogen
winden	windest, windet	wand	gewunden
wissen	weißt, weiß	wusste	gewusst
wollen	willst, will	wollte	gewollt
wringen	wringst, wringt	wrang	gewrungen
zeihen	zeihst, zeiht	zieh	geziehen
ziehen*	ziehst, zieht	zog	gezogen
zwingen	zwingst, zwingt	zwang	gezwungen